CONTRACTUAL RIGHTS AND LIABILITIES IN CIRCULAR BUSINESS MODELS

CONTRACTUAL RIGHTS AND LIABILITIES IN CIRCULAR BUSINESS MODELS

A Study of Consumer Protection in Product-as-a-Service Contracts

Harry SLACHMUYLDERS

INTERSENTIA

Intersentia
Lefebvre Belgium SA
Avenue Jean Monnet 4
1348 Louvain-la-Neuve
Belgium
contact@larcier-intersentia.com

Distribution for the UK and
Rest of the World (incl. Eastern Europe)
Ingram Publisher Services UK
1 Deltic Avenue, Rooksley
Milton Keynes MK13 8LD
United Kingdom
Tel: +44 1752 202 301 | Fax: +44 1752 202 331
Email: orders@nbninternational.com

Distribution for France and other countries
Interforum Editis
92 avenue de France
75013 Paris
France

Distribution for the USA and Canada
Independent Publishers Group
Order Department
814 North Franklin Street
Chicago, IL 60610
USA
Tel: +1 800 888 4741 (toll free) | Fax: +1 312 337 5985
Email: orders@ipgbook.com

Distribution for Belgium and Luxembourg
Larcier-Intersentia
Avenue Jean Monnet 4
1348 Louvain-la-Neuve
Belgium

Contractual Rights and Liabilities in Circular Business Models. A Study of Consumer Protection in Product-as-a-Service Contracts

Cover design by Danny Juchtmans / www.dsigngraphics.be

ISBN 978-1-83970-491-8
D/2025/06040/0274
NUR 827

British Library Cataloguing in Publication Data. A catalogue record for this book is available from the British Library.

SUMMARY

The "servitisation" of the economy – a shift from buying products to using "products-as-service" – is a potential enabler of the shift from the linear to the circular economy. Although such "product-service systems" ("PSS") have a huge potential, also in economic terms, consumers often feel uncertain and hesitant to engage in new circular business models and PSS contracts given the lack of a clear regulatory framework.

This book first sets out a conceptual framework of three main types of product-as-a-service contracts (product-oriented, use-oriented, result-oriented PSS) based on real-life examples. Second, it identifies and analyses the relevant EU regulations as well as the national (BE, NL) contract laws applicable to these contracts. Third, it evaluates the current regulatory framework of product-as-a-service contracts in order to identify its strengths and weaknesses. Fourth, legal solutions are proposed to tackle the identified weaknesses and to promote balanced, truly sustainable product-as-a-service contracts. These include, amongst others, (i) detailed proposals for the modernisation of Belgian contract law, (ii) broader policy recommendations, such as to adopt an EU directive on the quality and conformity of (bundles of) services, and (iii) a detailed proposal of a set of balanced model clauses for product-as-a-service contracts that can serve as a source of inspiration for legal professionals and businesses.

PREFACE

In linear business models, producers and commercial intermediaries transfer ownership over products to final consumers, who buy and own these products for some time, and then discard them (turn them into "waste"). The consumer sales contract represents the final link in global value chains which consist of multiple cross-border commercial contracts. Existing consumer laws in EU Member States provide for extensive protection of consumers in the context of such "ownership-based" consumption of products, and even, to some extent, encourage unsustainable consumption choices. EU waste law has attempted to mitigate the worst environmental impacts of the linear economy and throw-away society, by establishing a waste hierarchy and, for certain products such as electronic devices and batteries, imposing extended producer responsibility (EPR) schemes.

In contrast, circular business models (CBMs) break away from this traditional approach. Here, manufacturers or retailers no longer sell their products down the chain but become service providers who retain ownership of the product and its material resources. The final user does not "consume" the product but rather enjoys "access-based" consumption, based on a rental contract, a lease contract, a contract of works, a service contract, or another contract directly concluded with the service provider – typically online.

Two major types of "product-service systems" (PSS) can be distinguished. "Use-oriented" PSSs grant an exclusive right of use of a particular product (e.g. a gravel e-bike) to a single user during a specific period of time against a one-off or periodical fee. By contrast, in "result-oriented" PSSs, a service provider undertakes to guarantee a particular functional result (e.g. two-wheel e-mobility) over a particular period of time through access to a whole range of products (e.g. various e-bike types) on a "pay-per-use" or subscription basis.

This ongoing servitisation of the economy – including the shift from selling products to selling "products-as-a-service" and similar service models – is often presented as an enabler of the shift from a linear to a more circular economy. CBMs and PSSs certainly have a large economic potential and are now also on the rise in consumer markets. Whether such models are truly more sustainable and really incentivise more sustainable production and consumption patterns and levels, depends on various factors, including the contract design and the (not always so rational, let alone eco-friendly) behaviour of both the service provider and the consumer involved in such models.

Empirical research shows that consumers may feel uncertain and reluctant to engage in CBMs and PSSs. Service readiness varies depending on the type of consumers or products involved. More generally, various issues related to using rather than buying products (such as health and safety concerns) may also inhibit consumers to shift to access-based consumption. Also, various *legal barriers*, whether real or perceived, play a role, for instance with regard to quality and safety requirements, conformity with the contract, contract duration, insolvency, over-indebtedness, etc.

The book you have in front of you meticulously navigates the contract life cycle and identifies, analyses and compares all relevant Belgian and Dutch contract law rules applicable to the various stages of both use-oriented and result-oriented PSS, from formation over performance to end-of-life. The book highlights that the legal framework for PSS contracts is less developed, often ambiguous, and less protective of consumer interests than the framework for "classic" sales contracts. The book identifies, within the existing legal framework, the main legal barriers that hinder consumers from transitioning to product-as-a-service contracts.

Another of the book's strengths is its interdisciplinary approach, connecting the economic, technological, legal and environmental aspects of PSS contracts. Servitisation makes contract drafting increasingly demanding; it can be a complex exercise to build a balanced "service ladder". This book critically discusses and analyses more than twenty real-life T&Cs of PSS providers and proposes a set of balanced model clauses for PSS contracts. These model clauses were developed over the past years in a co-creation process with Dr. Christopher Borucki, integrating also the input by Prof. dr. Vincent Sagaert, Prof. dr. Dorothy Gruyaert, Dr. Benjamin Verheye, Dr. Elias Van Gool and Drs. Kato Deschepper.

In our view, this book is a wonderful and exceptional piece of academic research, for several compelling reasons. First, because of the true originality and broad scope of the topic. Second, because of the quality of the in-depth comparative analysis of use- and result-oriented PSS under Belgian, Dutch and EU law. Third, because of the balanced recommendations it sets out in order to make Belgian contract law and EU consumer law more fit for circular business models. Fourth, because of its critical discussion of the latest EU initiatives to make the EU market and the consumer more fit for the transition to the circular economy. Finally, because of its timely and impactful contribution to the ongoing reform of the Belgian Civil Code, more specifically as regards the proposed Book 7 on

"Specific Contracts" (under the direction of Prof. dr. Bernard Tilleman and Prof. dr. Paul-Alain Foriers).

The research done by Harry Slachmuylders would not have been possible without the support by KU Leuven Internal Funds (C24M/19/003) and the intense cooperation with our colleagues from the Faculty of Economics and Business (Prof. dr. Johan Eyckmans and Prof. dr. Sandra Rousseau), to whom we are deeply grateful.

We are convinced that this book will inspire your thinking, challenge your long-held assumptions, and offer fresh ideas and solutions for shaping a more circular future. Enjoy the read!

Prof. dr. Bert Keirsbilck and Prof. dr. Evelyne Terryn
Supervisors of the PhD thesis by Harry Slachmuylders

CONTENTS

ACKNOWLEDGEMENTS

"Do it the hard way, and it's easy sailing
Do it the hard way, and it's hard to lose
Only the soft way has a chance of failing
You have to choose"
– Chet Baker[1]

This book is the commercial version of my PhD thesis, which I defended on 18 November 2024. Since the very beginning of my PhD journey, the first thing I always did when consulting a legal book or a doctoral dissertation was reading the acknowledgements section. While doing this, I often imagined and eagerly anticipated the day when I would write my own acknowledgements. Now it is finally my turn to reminisce and look back on five wonderful years at KU Leuven. These paragraphs are dedicated to those without whom this project would not have been possible, and to whom I am eternally grateful.

First and foremost, my sincerest gratitude goes out to my supervisor, Prof. Dr. Bert Keirsbilck. People often say that a great supervisor is crucial to completing a PhD and I could not have been more fortunate in this regard. His ideas, insights and guidance have not only elevated the quality of this book, but he has also played a pivotal role in further shaping me into the lawyer and person I am today. Over the years, he evolved from a supervisor to a real *compagnon de route* and a mentor, both professionally and personally. He consistently took the time to read my texts and review my ideas, often with remarkable speed and an exceptional level of depth and attention to detail. He never ceased to believe in me, was always there for encouraging words or a push in the right direction, and I have always appreciated our open and sincere dialogue. Especially commendable was the importance he attached to a positive working environment and strong team spirit, making the Brussels campus really feel like a second home.

My co-supervisor, Prof. Dr. Evelyne Terryn, was an invaluable support throughout my doctoral journey. From the very beginning, she took an active role, involving me in projects, reviewing my work, and providing detailed feedback. She always found the right words to encourage me, especially during

[1] Chet Baker, "Do it the hard way", track from the album Chet Bakers Sings: It Could Happen To You (1958).

the challenging final months. I am deeply grateful for the time she devoted to reading numerous chapters in those last months, despite her very busy agenda.

I am thankful that Prof. Dr. Bernard Tilleman has played such an important part in my formation as a lawyer. From the first class of Introduction to Law, to our meetings and interactions when I was the Peer Assisted Learning coordinator of VRG,[2] and now as a valued member of my supervisory committee, he was never far away. His encyclopaedic knowledge of Belgian contract law and expertise following the drafting of Book 7 of the Belgian Civil Code have significantly pushed this book to a higher level.

I had the pleasure of meeting Prof. Dr. Vanessa Mak during the early months of my PhD journey at a conference in Bruges. After our engaging conversations, I was very glad when she agreed to be part of my supervisory committee. I greatly appreciate her constructive feedback on the Dutch law sections of my dissertation, as well as her sincere kindness.

I am utmost grateful to Prof. Dr. Janja Hojnik, for accepting to be part of my examination committee. Her seminal articles on servitisation have shaped the topic I was so honoured to write my PhD on. I really enjoyed her lectures on Regulatory Aspects of Servitisation during the Global Law Programme in the winter semester of 2023/24 and genuinely appreciate her warm personality.

When considering whom to invite to preside over my PhD defense, one name came immediately to mind. Prof. Dr. Vincent Sagaert was one of my most memorable professors during my studies at KU Leuven. Throughout the five years of my PhD, I was fortunate to cross paths with him multiple times and collaborate on various projects related to servitisation. I am deeply grateful that he graciously agreed to take on this role.

Beyond my examination committee, I am also deeply grateful for all the enriching encounters and enjoyable conversations I had over the years with other professors and legal scholars, whether at conferences, during the PEPP programme, or just when navigating the Leuven or Brussels campuses of KU Leuven. A special mention goes out to Prof. Dr. Joeri Vananroye, who took the time to meet with me when I first expressed my interest in pursuing a PhD and connected me with Prof. Keirsbilck. I would also like to sincerely thank the colleagues of CEDON (Prof. Dr. Sandra Rousseau, Prof. Dr. Johan Eyckmans and Dr. Carolien Lavigne) for our very fruitful and enriching cooperation as part of the C2 project.

Writing this book would not have been the same without the colleagues with whom I had the pleasure to share this experience. I cannot thank the administrative and library staff – Johan, Karin, Line, Mieke, Carla, Leyla and all the colleagues of the Rbib – enough for all their help with the practical aspects and administrative hurdles that came up over the years. A special thanks to

[2] VRG, the Royal Flemish Law Society ("*Koninklijk Vlaams Rechtsgenootschap*") is the faculty student association for KU Leuven law students.

Johan for never growing tired of me when I was advocating for a better coffee machine, a standing desk or whatever else I set my mind on that week, and for the ever-friendly banter and chit chat. A heartfelt thank you to my colleagues at the Brussels campus – Eveline, Anaïs, Charline, Dorien, Ward, Erika, Elisa, Zeno, Joren, Maxim, Lieselotte, Emma, Line, Andi and Lies – for immediately making me feel at home, for your helpful advice and support, engaging conversations, enjoyable coffee breaks and an overall portion of good vibes. My sincerest appreciation goes to all the former and new colleagues of Consumer Competition Market (CCM), with special mention to Lennard, Richard, Joris, Liesbet, Christof, Elias, Jozefien, Tom, Friso, Justine, Estelle, Bruno, Sofia and Arnaud. The memories of our writer's retreat in Watou, sharing tapas and churros in Sevilla, the coffee and ice-cream breaks ending up at a terrace on the Oude Markt, and our retreat to the gardens of Annevoie will certainly last a lifetime. There is a special place in my heart for my CCM Brussels colleagues. Elisa, if I had to thank you for all you have contributed to my PhD journey over the last years, I would get to write another book. Thank you for sharing laughs, stories, and tears with me in room 04.A04-06, for your kind and encouraging words and for all your help with my dissertation and the practical aspects of the defence. Not only did you volunteer to proofread more than 200 (!) pages, but you also tirelessly answered all my questions and were always there for emotional support. Zeno and Joren, thank you for always cheering me up, distracting me with interesting conversations that had nothing to do with my PhD, sharing a pizza and a beer with me in Scott's bar or Mort Subite, and – during the clutch moments – helping me with my bibliography and proofreading my conclusion.

Starting my career as a lawyer while completing the final stages of my PhD was undoubtedly a challenge, but there is no firm where I would rather have done it than at Linklaters LLP. I extend my heartfelt gratitude to the partners of the Litigation, Arbitration & Investigations practice – Stefaan Loosveld, Xavier Taton and Florence Danis – for all their support and understanding, as well as their genuine interest in my research. I am grateful to all my incredible Linklaters LAI colleagues – Bo, Jasper, Gert-Jan, Zoë, Nicolas, Matthias, Pierre-Noé, Ina, Sara, Bruno, Céline, Sacha, Lucy, Kevin, Laura, Guillaume, Léonard and Wannes – for welcoming me so warmly. Your encouraging words, the way you cheered me up after long days (and nights), and your readiness to step in and take stuff of my plate (even unasked) have made all the difference the last six months.

To the immensely diverse group of people that I am so lucky to call my friends, I cannot express how grateful I am for having you in my life, whether we met at school, in Leuven, in Stellenbosch, during the PEPP programme, or elsewhere. Thank you to all the friends I made through VRG and/or HdR – with special mention to Sirine, Esther, Charlotte R., Lorenz, Younes, Geert, Diana, Emma, Isabelle and Marie. The things I learnt from you go far beyond "law in the books" and I will always cherish the wonderful moments we shared in Leuven and beyond. An extra special mention goes out to two persons. Charlotte R., I'll never forget the moment our friendship began. Dancing behind the bar at the Rector during a cocktail-party shift, we just instantly "clicked". Eight and a half years later, I couldn't be happier that our "tandem project" is still going strong and producing such amazing memories. Lorenz, from the moment we became "*collega's*" for the PAL project, our friendship just worked. Thank you for always understanding me completely, for sharing my sense of humour and for always providing exactly the advice and distraction I need. The musical distractions by my friends of the Leuvense Studentenfanfare (with special mention to the self-proclaimed "(g)old generation": Perreke, Fille, Lowie, Boeje, Armada, Erik, Bats, Bock, Dobby, Roizee and Turbo[3]) were instrumental in completing this project. Thank you for all the unforgettable concerts we played and activities we spent together. Tom and Richard, thank you so much for all our moments of escapism, ranging from our writer's retreat at the seaside to our Bond evenings and memorable dinners at Basils. To my dearest friends from high school (also known as the "Slav Squat" – Jaak (Jakob), Cédric, Kobe, Jente, Ymke, Bart and Iris), thank you for filling my life with joy, for spending the important moments together, and for reminding me what life looks like outside of the "legal bubble". Jaak, thank you for being my housemate for three years and counting, for sharing highs and lows, Sunday-morning Bialetti coffees, late-night vinyl sessions, and all the moments in between. Please know that your patience when writing my PhD took priority over doing the dishes will never be forgotten.

Above all, I am profoundly grateful to my family. Words will never fully capture my appreciation for all you've done for me. To my parents, thank you for your constant support and encouragement, for making it possible for me to study law – both in Leuven and Stellenbosch – and for giving me the freedom to do it my way. Your trust and belief in my potential have been the foundation of everything I have achieved. To my siblings, Wout en Antje, I am so incredibly proud of you both. While we are each unique in our own way, we stand by each other through every high and low, no matter what. Please know that I will always be there whenever you need me. *Opa*, thank you for all the unforgettable memories from our ski trips with the grandchildren and for your pride when sharing my achievements with others. *Oma en Pépé*, thank you for being my safe haven, a place I could always retreat to with love and comfort. Together with my parents, you have literally raised me (up) in every way.

---

3 Their real names are known by the author.

1. INTRODUCTION

1.1. PROBLEM SETTING

"With the price of resources and energy becoming increasingly volatile, can today's linear economy work in the long term? What if we didn't buy the goods we use, but instead favoured access and performance over ownership?"
– Ellen Macarthur Foundation[4]

1.1.1. TOWARDS A MORE CIRCULAR ECONOMY

1. Circular economy – Since the industrial revolution, our economy has predominately been characterised by a linear approach of growth and resource consumption following a "take – make – use – dispose" pattern.[5] Producers extract resources, use them to manufacture a product, and sell this product to a customer who in turn discards it as waste when it no longer serves its purpose.[6] Mankind however became aware that this linear approach upon which traditional business models are built exhausts global resources and causes environmental concerns.[7] The "circular economy" – with key elements such as resource-efficiency and life-cycle thinking ("closing the loop")[8] – provides an alternative framework and is one of the most promising ways of making our (linear) economy more sustainable.[9] This is achieved by making more sustainable purchasing decisions and keeping materials and products in the value chain for as long as possible instead of replacing them.[10]

---

4 Ellen Macarthur Foundation, "What if we don't buy Products and We Buy Service? Circular Economy Explained", https://ellenmacarthurfoundation.org/videos/what-if-we-dont-buy-products-and-we-buy-service?

5 EC, *Towards a circular economy: A zero waste programme for Europe*, 2.7.2014, COM (2014) 398 final, 2.

6 Ellen Macarthur Foundation, *Towards the Circular Economy vol. 1. Economic and business rationale for an accelerated transition*, EMF, 2013, 14–20.

7 EC, *Roadmap to a Resource Efficient Europe*, 20.9.2011, COM(2011) 571 final, 1–2.

8 A. Murray, K. Skene and K. Haynes, "The Circular Economy: An Interdisciplinary Exploration of the Concept and Application in a Global Context", *J.Bus.Ethics* 2017, (369) 369–380.

9 N.M. Bocken, I. De Pauw, C. Bakker and B. Van Der Grinten, "Product design and business model strategies for a circular economy", *JIPE* 2016, (308) 308.

10 N. Kobza and A. Schuster, "Building a responsible Europe – the value of circular economy", *IFAC-PapersOnLine* 2013, (111) 111–116.

2. Circular economy strategies and circular business models – In a circular economy, various strategies and business models across many sectors are used to keep materials and products in the economy for as long as possible.[11] These strategies include long-lasting design, sharing access or ownership, maintenance and repair, reuse, refurbishing, remanufacturing and recycling, etc.[12] This book focuses on the "servitisation" of the economy – a shift from buying products to using "products-as-a-service" – which is said to have a huge potential to contribute to the shift towards a more circular economy in the movable consumer products and services sector.[13]

3. Circular economy as policy priority of the European Union – The circular economy is high on the international and supranational agenda. Not only is the development of the circular economy closely linked to the UN Sustainable Development Goals ("SDGs"), especially SDG 12 on sustainable consumption and production, but it is also a policy priority of the European Union.[14] Four years after the introduction of the first Circular Economy Action Plan[15] in 2015, the European Commission continued this course by announcing its ambitious European Green Deal.[16] This is the Commission's response to climate and environmental-related challenges, which aims to transform the EU economy into a more resource-efficient and competitive economy where economic growth is not dependent on resource use and net emissions of greenhouse gasses are abolished by 2050.[17] One of the main building blocks of the European Green Deal was the adoption of a New Circular Economy Action Plan for a cleaner and more competitive Europe ("New Circular Economy Action Plan") on 11 March 2020.[18] It announces various legislative and non-legislative

---

11 See for an overview of 5 categories of circular business models: Accenture Strategy, *Circular Advantage – Innovative business models and technologies to create value in a world without limits to growth*, 2014, 12–14.

12 M. Geissdoerfer, P. Savaget, N.M.P. Bocken and E.J. Hultink, "The Circular Economy – A new sustainability paradigm?", *J.Clean.Prod.* 2017, (757) 759. For use-cases and good practices see the following databases: https://circulareconomy.europa.eu/platform/good-practices; www.ellenmacarthurfoundation.org/case-studies; www.circulareconomyclub.com/solutions/; www.rebus.eu.com/rapporten-en-case-studies/.

13 See e.g. EC, *Closing the loop – An EU action plan for the Circular Economy*, 2.12.2015, COM(2015) 614 final, 7: "*innovative forms of consumption can also support the development of the circular economy, e.g. [...] consuming services rather than products [...]*"; EMF, *Towards the Circular Economy Vol.2: Opportunities for the consumer goods sector*, 2013, 26.

14 See also the explicit reference to sustainable development in Art. 3(3) TEU.

15 EC, *Closing the loop – An EU action plan for the Circular Economy*, 2.12.2015, COM(2015) 614 final. This action plan was mainly implemented through legislative action concerning eco-design, resource-efficiency, waste management and energy efficiency. See: EC, *Report on the implementation of the Circular Economy Action Plan*, 4.3.2019, COM(2019) 190 final.

16 EC, *The European Green Deal*, 11.12.2019, COM(2019) 640 final.

17 EC, *The European Green Deal*, 11.12.2019, COM(2019) 640 final, 2.

18 EC, *A new Circular Economy Action Plan For a cleaner and more competitive Europe*, 11.3.2020, COM(2020) 98 final.

initiatives[19] along the entire life cycle of products, services and business models, targeting for example their design, encouraging circular economy processes, stimulating sustainable consumption, and aiming to guarantee that used resources stay in the EU economy for a maximum amount of time.[20]

4. Circular economy and green transition as priority of EU consumer law – Specific to EU consumer law, the circular economy and the green transition are also key priorities in the EU Commission's New Consumer Agenda 2020.[21] In the wake of the European Green Deal and the New Consumer Agenda, four initiatives relevant to consumer law can be highlighted.[22] First, the "**Sustainable products initiative**"[23] resulted in a proposal for a regulation aiming to extend the scope of the Ecodesign Directive to a broader range of products (not only energy-related products) and virtually all economic operators involved in a product's value chain.[24] The Ecodesign for Sustainable Products Regulation[25] ("ESPR") was published on 28 June 2024 in the Official Journal and entered into force on 18 July 2024. Second, the "**Strengthening the role of consumers in the green transition initiative**"[26] led to a proposal for a directive proposing various legislative changes to the Unfair Commercial Practices Directive and the Consumer Rights Directive, mainly regarding combating unfair commercial practices that prevent consumers to make informed choices for greener products and pre-contractual consumer information on sustainability.[27] The Empowering

19 EC, *A new Circular Economy Action Plan For a cleaner and more competitive Europe*, 11.3.2020, COM(2020) 98 final, Annex.

20 EC, *A new Circular Economy Action Plan For a cleaner and more competitive Europe*, 11.3.2020, COM(2020) 98 final.

21 EC, *New Consumer Agenda. Strenghtening consumer resilience for sustainable recovery*, 13.11.2020, COM(2020) 696 final.

22 See for a more in-depth discussion of these initiatives: B. Keirsbilck and E. Terryn, "Duurzaamheid en consumentenrecht" in A. Van Hoe and G. Croisant (eds.), *Droit et durabilité / Recht en duurzaamheid*, Antwerp, Intersentia, 2022, (433) 433–494. See also: A. De Franceschi, "The Sustainability of Consumer and Market Law: Green Claims, Greenwashing and the Right to Repair", *EuCML* 2023, (45) 45–48.

23 See: https://ec.europa.eu/info/law/better-regulation/have-your-say/initiatives/12567-Sustainable-products-initiative_en.

24 EC, *Proposal for a Regulation of the European Parliament and of the Council establishing a framework for setting ecodesign requirements for sustainable products and repealing Directive 2009/125/EC*, 30.3.2022, COM(2022) 142 final.

25 Regulation (EU) 2024/1781 of the European Parliament and of the Council of 13 June 2024 establishing a framework for the setting of ecodesign requirements for sustainable products, amending Directive (EU) 2020/1828 and Regulation (EU) 2023/1542 and repealing Directive 2009/125/EC, *OJ L*, 2024/1781, 28.6.2024.

26 See: https://ec.europa.eu/info/law/better-regulation/have-your-say/initiatives/12467-Consumer-policy-strengthening-the-role-of-consumers-in-the-green-transition_en.

27 EC, *Proposal for a Directive of the European Parliament and of the Council amending Directives 2005/29/EC and 2011/83/EU as regards empowering consumers for the green*

Consumers for the Green Transition Directive[28] ("ECGTD") was published on 6 March 2024 in the Official Journal. It must be implemented by the Member States by 27 March 2026 and the implementing provisions will have to be applied from 27 September 2026 onwards. Third, from the "**Environmental performance of products & businesses – substantiating claims initiative**"[29] came a proposal for the Green Claims Directive, which aims to require businesses to substantiate claims about the carbon footprint of their products/ services with standard methods.[30] As regards this directive, the European Parliament adopted its first reading position on 12 March 2024 and the Council adopted its "general approach" on 17 June 2024, which means that trilogues can now start. Finally, the "**Sustainable consumption of goods – promoting repair and reuse initiative**"[31] resulted in a proposal for a Directive on commons rules promoting the repair of goods.[32] The Right to Repair Directive was adopted on 13 June 2024 and entered into force on 30 July 2024. It will require manufacturers and, under certain conditions, other market players to repair in-scope products outside the legal guarantee and to inform consumers of this obligation; amend the rules on the legal guarantee of the Sale of Goods Directive ("SGD")[33] to make the remedy of repair more attractive than the remedy of replacement; and introduce other measures to promote repair. Member States have to transpose it into national rules and apply it from 31 July 2026.

5. THE NETHERLANDS AND BELGIUM AS CIRCULAR ECONOMY PIONEERS – The circular economy and servitisation are also on the agenda of the EU Member States. For example, the Netherlands was one of the pioneers among the EU Member States to present a Circular Economy Program in 2014, quickly followed by an extensive plan called "A Circular Economy in the

transition through better protection against unfair practices and better information, 30.3.2022, COM(2022) 143 final.

28 Directive (EU) 2024/825 of the European Parliament and of the Council of 28 February 2024 amending Directives 2005/29/EC and 2011/83/EU as regards empowering consumers for the green transition through better protection against unfair practices and through better information, *OJ L*, 2024/825, 6.3.2024.

29 See: https://ec.europa.eu/info/law/better-regulation/have-your-say/initiatives/12511-Environmental-performance-of-products-businesses-substantiating-claims_en.

30 EC, *Proposal for a Directive of the European Parliament and of the Council on substantiation and communication of explicit environmental claims (Green Claims Directive)*, 22.3.2023, COM(2023) 166 final.

31 See: https://ec.europa.eu/info/law/better-regulation/have-your-say/initiatives/13150-Sustainable-consumption-of-goods-promoting-repair-and-reuse_en.

32 EC, *Proposal for a Directive of the European Parliament and of the Council on common rules promoting the repair of goods and amending Regulation (EU) 2017/2394, Directives (EU) 2019/771 and (EU) 2020/1828*, 22.3.2023, COM(2023) 155 final.

33 Art. 13(2) of Directive (EU) 2019/771 of the European Parliament and the Council of 20 May 2019 on certain aspects concerning contracts for the sale of goods, amending Regulation (EU) 2017/2394 and Directive 2009/22/EC, and repealing Directive 1999/44/EC, OJ L 319, 22.5.2019, 28–50.

Netherlands by 2050" in September 2016.[34] This plan recognises the potential of the sharing economy and product-as-a-service models, while at the same time acknowledging the existence of challenges regarding laws, regulations and incentive schemes.[35] These efforts were further continued in 2019 with the "Circular Economy Implementation Programme 2019–2023",[36] which was updated in 2021.[37] In this implementation programmes there is attention for as-a-service models, for example through support for pilot projects.[38] Recently, the Dutch Government presented a new "National Program Circular Economy 2023–2030" to build on all these policy initiatives.[39] This program outlines a strategy for transitioning to a circular economy and includes measures to reduce waste, increase recycling and reuse of materials, and promote sustainable production and consumption. Additionally, it includes targets for reducing greenhouse gas emissions and creating new jobs. The program emphasises the need for collaboration between government, businesses, and civil society, and sets out a roadmap for implementation over the next 8 years. Business models based on servitisation are mentioned as a key approach to achieving a circular economy.[40]

Belgium is working on the transition towards a more circular economy as well. In 2016, the Belgian Federal ministries for economy and public health and environment jointly drew up a roadmap to support the transition towards a more circular economy.[41] In doing so, they wanted to work together with all stakeholders to make Belgium an example of the circular economy. To achieve this, the document listed 21 measures to be completed by 2019 aimed

---

34 Government of the Netherlands, "A circular economy in the Netherlands by 2050", 2016, available at www.rijksoverheid.nl/onderwerpen/circulaire-economie/nederland-circulair-in-2050.

35 Government of the Netherlands, "A circular economy in the Netherlands by 2050", 2016, 26.

36 Government of the Netherlands, "Uitvoeringsprogramma Circulaire Economie 2019–2023", 2019, available at www.rijksoverheid.nl/onderwerpen/circulaire-economie/documenten/rapporten/2019/02/08/uitvoeringsprogramma-2019–2023.

37 Government of the Netherlands, "Uitvoeringsprogramma Circulaire Economie 2021–2023", 2021, available at www.rijksoverheid.nl/onderwerpen/circulaire-economie/documenten/rapporten/2021/10/18/uitvoeringsprogramma-circulaire-economie.

38 Government of the Netherlands, "Uitvoeringsprogramma Circulaire Economie 2021–2023", 2021, 39–40; Government of the Netherlands, "Uitvoeringsprogramma Circulaire Economie 2019–2023", 2019, 48.

39 Government of the Netherlands, "Nationaal Programma Circulaire Economie 2023–2030", 2023, available at www.rijksoverheid.nl/documenten/beleidsnotas/2023/02/03/nationaal-programma-circulaire-economie-2023–2030.

40 Government of the Netherlands, "Nationaal Programma Circulaire Economie 2023–2030", 2023, available at www.rijksoverheid.nl/documenten/beleidsnotas/2023/02/03/nationaal-programma-circulaire-economie-2023–2030, 28–29.

41 K. Peeters and M.C. Marghem, "Samen de Economie doen draaien dankzij de circulaire economie in ons land", 2016, available at www.health.belgium.be/nl/samen-de-economie-doen-draaien-dankzij-de-circulaire-economie-ons-land.

at supporting innovation, boosting the competitiveness of Belgian companies, better protecting consumers and upgrading environmental capital. On 9 December 2021, the federal government announced a new federal circular economy action plan that aims to significantly reduce the use of raw materials and the materials footprint in production and consumption.[42] The plan sets out 25 measures to move away from the linear economy to a circular economy. For example, measure 7 seeks to explore the possibility of creating a legal framework for "designing" certain new services and measure 8 aims to develop and distribute a methodology for companies wishing to establish a product-as-a-service business model.[43] The federal action plan is intended to complement the circular economy actions of the Belgian regions, which also have ambitious strategies for the transition from a linear to a circular economy.[44, 45]

1.1.2. CIRCULAR BUSINESS MODELS

1.1.2.1. Servitisation and product-service systems

6. Servitisation – Our economy is increasingly shifting from a manufacturing economy to a service economy.[46] Part of this evolution is the so-called trend of "servitisation". The term servitisation was first used by Vandermerwe and Rada in 1988 and is traditionally defined as "*the process of*

---

42 Belgian Federal Government, "Federaal actieplan circulaire economie", 9 December 2021, available at www.health.belgium.be/sites/default/files/uploads/fields/fpshealth_theme_file/paf_16_dec_2021_nl_clean.pdf.

43 Belgian Federal Government, "Federaal actieplan circulaire economie", 9 December 2021, 18–19.

44 **Flanders:** Flemish Government, "Regeerakkoord van de Vlaamse Regering 2019–2023", 2019, available at www.vlaanderen.be/publicaties/regeerakkoord-van-de-vlaamse-regering-2019–2024, 146–147. See also the circular economy strategy of Flanders at: http://vlaanderen-circulair.be. **Wallonia:** Walloon Government, "Déclaration de politique régionale Wallonie. Avoir le courage de changer pour que l'avenir s'éclare", 2024–2029, available at www.wallonie.be/sites/default/files/2024–07/DPR2024–2029.pdf, 19–20. The circular economy strategy of Wallonia is available at https://economiecirculaire.wallonie.be/fr. **Brussels:** Brussels government, "Be Circular – Gewestelijk programma voor circulaire economie 2016–2020", 2016, available at https://leefmilieu.brussels/themas/economie-transitie/be-circular-gewestelijk-programma-voor-circulaire-economie and its update in February 2019: www.circulareconomy.brussels/actualisering-van-het-gewestelijk-programma-voor-circulaire-economie-na-de-tussentijdse-evaluatie/?lang=nl. See also www.circulareconomy.brussels for more information on the circular economy strategy of Brussels.

45 See also EC, *The EU Environmental Implementation Review 2019 Country Report – Belgium*, 4.4.2019, SWD(2019) 112 final, 4–8 for a discussion of policy initiatives in Belgium.

46 M. Boehm and O. Thomas, "Looking beyond the rim of one's teacup: a multidisciplinary literature review of Product-Service Systems in Information Systems, Business Management, and Engineering & Design", *J.Clean.Prod.* 2013, (245) 245.

creating value by adding services to products."[47] These two management scholars saw an "*increased offering of fuller market packages or 'bundles' of customer-focused combinations of goods, services, support, self-service and knowledge*" in order to add value to corporate offerings.[48] The main idea of these "servitised" business models is that rather than a specific product, the user needs a specific functionality: "*They don't want quarter-inch drill bits, they want quarter-inch holes.*"[49] As a result, these new models entail a shift from selling products to offering "products-as-a-service" ("PaaS")[50] or – from a consumer perspective – from buying products to using products ("access-based consumption").[51]

7. PRODUCT-SERVICE SYSTEMS – Research on the phenomenon of servitisation really developed at the end of the 1990's when the term product-service system ("PSS") was introduced by GOEDKOOP et al. being a "*marketable set of products and services, capable of jointly fulfilling a user's need.*"[52] Since then, several academics have picked up the term and the underlying concept and developed it further.[53] Both the concepts of servitisation and PSS emphasise the shift

---

47 S. VANDERMERWE and J. RADA, "Servitization of Business: Adding Value by Adding Services", *Eur.Man.J.* 1988, vol. 6, (314) 314–324. See also H. LIGHTFOOT, T.S. BAINES and P. SMART, "The servitisation of manufacturing: A systematic literature review of interdependent trends", *IJOPM* 2013, vol. 33, (1408) 1408–1434.

48 S. VANDERMERWE and J. RADA, "Servitization of Business: Adding Value by Adding Services", *Eur.Man.J.* 1988, vol. 6, (314) 314. See also P. WEINGERL and J. HOJNIK, "'Servitization' and Movables. Legal Initiatives and Challenges in Slovenia" in B. KEIRSBILCK and E. TERRYN (eds.), *Consumer Protection in a Circular Economy*, Antwerp, Intersentia, 2019, (225) 226.

49 E.T. FREEMAN, "Buying quarter inch holes: public support through results", *Archival Issues* 2000, (91) 91–100; T. LEVITT, *The Marketing Imagination*, New York, Free Press, 1983, Ch. 7, 1.

50 R. OLIVA and R. KALLENBERG, "Managing the transition from products to services", *IJSIM* 2003, vol. 14, (160) 160–172.

51 E.g. S.J. LAWSON, M.R. GLEIM, R. PERREN and J. HWANG, "Freedom from ownership: An exploration of access-based consumption", *J.Bus.Res.* 2016, (2615) 2615–2623 and F. BARDHI and G.M. ECKHARDT, "Access-Based Consumption: The Case of Car Sharing", *J.Consu.Res.* 2012, vol. 39, (881) 881–898.

52 M.J. GOEDKOOP, C.J.G. VAN HALEN, H.R.M. TE RIELE and P.J.M. ROMMENS, *Product service systems: Ecological and economic basics*, Report for Dutch Ministries of Environment (VROM) and Economic Affairs (EZ), 1999, 18; A. ANNARELLI, C. BATTISTELLA and F. NONINO, *The Road to Servitization, How Product Service Systems Can Disrupt Companies' Business Models*, Cham, Springer, 2019, 1. See also A. TUKKER and U. TISCHNER, "Product-services as a research field: past, present and future. Reflections from a decade of research", *J.Clean.Prod.* 2006, vol. 14, (1552) 1552.

53 See e.g. O.K. MONT, *Product-Service Systems*, Final Report. Stockholm, The International Institute of Industrial environmental Economics, 2000, 34. R.G. MEIJKAMP, *Changing consumer behavior through Eco-efficient services. An empirical study of car sharing in the Netherlands*, Doctoral thesis Delft University of Technology, 2000,, 35; E. MANZINI and C. VEZZOLI, *Product-service systems and sustainability. Opportunities for sustainable solutions*, United Nations Environment Programme, Division of Technology Industry and Economics, Production and Consumption Branch, Milan, 2002, 4; A. TUKKER, C. BERG and U. TISCHNER, "Product-services: a specific value proposition" in A. TUKKER and U. TISCHNER (eds.), *New Business for Old Europe. Product-Service Development, Competitiveness and Sustainability*,

from products to services and the changed property rights to meet customer demands on a new level.[54] However, the research on PSS is strongly based on the reduced environmental impact, while research on servitisation (value-adding services) focuses more on how businesses can change their value proposition to meet customer needs in a more service-oriented way.[55] As a result, environmental impacts in the context of servitisation are rather subordinate but not completely absent. Indeed, service orientation can create incentives for the producer that indirectly affect the environmental performance of production and consumption.[56] Despite the differences between servitisation and PSS, the terms are often used interchangeably to indicate the same concept.[57] Therefore, in the context of this book, both the term "PSS contracts" and "servitised business models" will be used to refer to circular business models that involve a shift from products to services.

8. Types of PSS – PSS can be categorised in many ways. The most widely accepted and reported categorisation of PSS is based on the object of the contract and shift in ownership.[58] This way, three main types of PSS are distinguished: product-oriented, use-oriented, and result-oriented PSS.[59]

(i) In **product-oriented PSS**, services (maintenance, repair ...) are added to the traditional sale of a product (after-sales services). These business models therefore still entail a transfer of ownership (as opposed to use- and result-oriented PSS).

London, Routledge, 2006, (22) 31; and T.S. Baines, H.W. Lightfoot, S. Evans, A. Neely, R. Greenough, J. Peppard, R. Roy, E. Shehab, A. Braganza, A. Tiwari, J.R. Alcock, J.P. Angus, M. Bastl, A. Cousens, P. Irving, M. Johnson, J. Kingston, H. Lockett, V. Martinez, P. Michele, D. Tranfield, I.M. Walton and H. Wilson, "State-of-the-art in product-service systems", *Proceedings of the Institution of Mechanical Engineers, Part B: Journal of Engineering Manufacture* 2007, (1543) 1543.

54 S. Fischer, S. Steger, N.D. Jordan, M. O'Brien and P. Schepelmann, *Leasing Society. Report requested by the European Parliament's Committee on Environment, Public Health and Food Safety*, 2012, 12.

55 C. Kühl, B. Tjahjono, M. Bourlakis and E. Aktas, "Implementation of Circular Economy principles in PSS operations", *Procedia CIRP* 2018, vol. 73, (124) 125.

56 S. Fischer, S. Steger, N.D. Jordan, M. O'Brien and P. Schepelmann, *Leasing Society. Report requested by the European Parliament's Committee on Environment, Public Health and Food Safety*, 2012, 10–12.

57 A. Annarelli, C. Battistella and F. Nonino, *The Road to Servitization, How Product Service Systems Can Disrupt Companies' Business Models*, Cham, Springer, 2019, 9.

58 A. Tukker, "Eight Types of Product-Service System: Eight Ways to Sustainability? Experiences from Suspronet", *Bus.Strat.Env.* 2004, vol. 13, (246) 248.

59 W. Reim, V. Parida and D. Örtqvist, "Product-Service Systems (PSS) business models and tactics – a systematic literature review", *J.Clean.Prod.* 2015, vol. 97, (61) 61–75; A. Tukker, "Eight Types of Product-Service System: Eight Ways to Sustainability? Experiences from Suspronet", *Bus.Strat.Env.* 2004, vol. 13, (246) 248.

(ii) **Use-oriented PSS** (also called "product-as-a-service" contracts) entail a right of use for the customer of a specific product against the payment of a one-off or periodical fee.[60] These contracts are characterised by the fact that producers retain ownership and responsibility for the product during its entire life cycle.[61] Some use-oriented PSS are limited to a mere right of use against payment, but others are also combined with additional services. Examples include contracts whereby household appliances (e.g. "*Bundles*", "*Blue Movement*"), bicycles (e.g. "*Swapfiets*") or furniture (e.g."*Live Light*", Ikea) are rented out to consumers.

(iii) **Result-oriented PSS** do not relate to one or more specific products but a specific functional result. To fulfil this specific need, the producer is given the freedom to achieve this result in the most efficient way. In return, the customer pays a service fee for a certain quality or continuity that is guaranteed by a performance contract. The price for this service can be calculated both on a "pay-per-use" basis or a subscription basis.[62] A good example of a result-oriented PSS is Philips' "*light-as-a-service*" model.[63]

9. Focus of this book – This book focuses mainly on business models that do not entail a transfer of ownership (use-oriented PSS and result-oriented PSS). After all, PSS where ownership is retained and customers pay for access or performance are considered the most suitable business models for the circular economy.[64] Additionally, the characteristics of these business models (e.g. no transfer of ownership, different allocation of responsibility, etc.) present more challenges to consumers than product-oriented PSS. However, this does not mean that product-oriented PSS will be entirely neglected. Where relevant, reference will also be made to these types of PSS to make useful comparisons.

---

60 A. Azarenko, R. Roy, E. Shehab and A. TIiwari, "Technical Product-Service systems: some implications for the machine tool industry", *JMTM* 2009, vol. 20, (700) 703.

61 B. Keirsbilck and S. Rousseau, "The Marketing Stage: Fostering Sustainable Consumption Choices" in B. Keirsbilck and E. Terryn (eds.), *Consumer Protection in a Circular Economy*, Antwerp, Intersentia, 2019, (93) 112.

62 B. Keirsbilck, E. Terryn and E. Van Gool, "Consumentenbescherming bij servitisation en product-dienst-systemen (PDS)" in *Preadviezen VVSR-BN 2019*, Den Haag, Boom juridische uitgevers, 2019, (11) 13.

63 Philips – who retains the ownership – manufactures, installs, maintains, upgrades, and recycles the lighting equipment for the customer in exchange for a subscription fee. See: www.lighting.philips.nl/systemen/aanbod-van-pakketten/winkels-en-horeca/light-as-a-service-retail.

64 C. Kühl, B. Tjahjono, M. Bourlakis and E. Aktas, "Implementation of Circular Economy principles in PSS operations", *Procedia CIRP* 2018, vol. 73, (124) 125.

Figure 1. Categorisation of PSS[65]

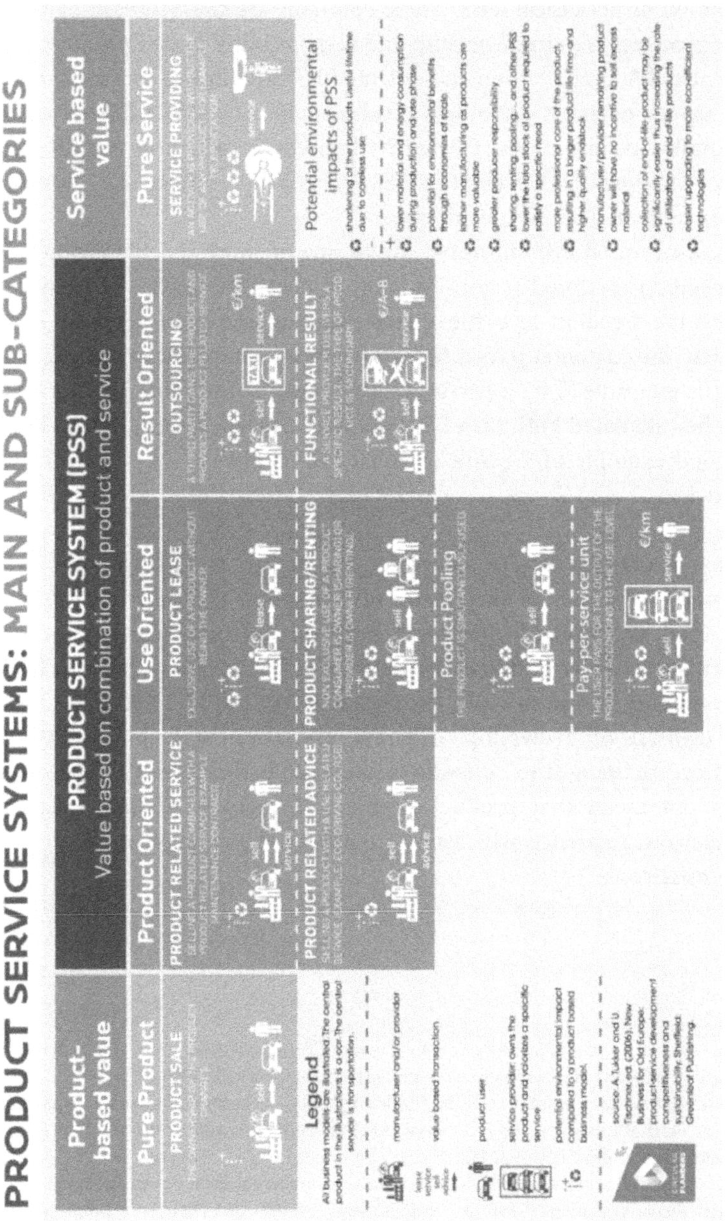

---

65 See: https://vlaanderen-circulair.be/en/knowledge/what-is-it/product-service-systems with reference to A. Tukker, C. Berg and U. Tischner, "Product-services: a specific value proposition" in A. Tukker and U. Tischner (eds.), *New Business for Old Europe. Product-Service Development, Competitiveness and Sustainability*, London, Routledge, 2006, (22) 33.

10. Different types, yet distinction is not always clear cut – The distinction between these three types of PSS is used throughout this book to analyse different servitised business models. Yet, the importance of this distinction should not be exaggerated. In practice, real-life PSS offers often exhibit characteristics of both use- and result-oriented PSS and there is often no clear-cut borderline. This will also become clear in the section on the contractual qualification of these business models.[66] Regardless, this typology allows for structure in the wide range of these often complex business models and therefore serves as a useful anchoring tool.

1.1.2.2. Characteristics of servitisation and PSS

11. More complex relationship between the consumer and the supplier – From a legal point of view, PSS contracts (especially use-oriented and result-oriented PSS) differ significantly from traditional linear sales contracts. Indeed, in the case of use-oriented and result-oriented PSS, consumers do not buy a product against payment of the total price and no transfer of ownership takes place. Instead, they subscribe to an often rather complex service contract[67] and become recipients of a bundle of services against the payment of a periodical fee or "pay-per-use" fee.[68] This shift from sales to services results in a more complex relationship between the consumer and the supplier.

12. Shift from one-off transaction to an ongoing service – The relationship between the consumer and the supplier is characterised by a shift from a one-off transaction to an ongoing service. In contrast to traditional sales contracts, where the contractual relationship ends in most cases with the delivery of the purchased good,[69] PSS contracts are characterised by the fact that a long-term relationship is established between the user and the service provider. This makes it even more important that both parties, the PSS supplier and the consumer, have a clear idea of their mutual obligations and what remedies they have in case the other party does not fulfil its contractual obligations.

---

66 See Chapter 3.

67 Service contracts are often seen as the mirror image of a sales contract. See for example the negative definition of the term "service contract" in the CRD: *"any contract other than a sales contract under which the trader supplies or undertakes to supply a service to the consumer and the consumer pays or undertakes to pay the price thereof"* (Art. 21(6) CRD). A.C. van Schaick, "Digitalisering en vermogensrecht" in J.H. Gerards and A.C. van Schaick (eds.), *Preadviezen Vereniging voor Burgerlijk Recht: Digitalisering, vermogensrecht, de platformeconomie en grondrechten*, Zutphen, Paris, 2019, (7) no. 23.

68 See *supra* no. 8.

69 However, also in the case of the sales contract, delivery is no longer a purely final matter. After all, the new sales law makes the concept of conformity dependent on periodic software updates. See Art. 6(d) SGD and Art. 7(3)-(4) SGD.

13. SHIFT FROM OWNERSHIP TO ACCESS/ACCESSIBILITY – Servitisation and PSS contracts entail a shift from ownership to access/accessibility. This has interesting consequences. First, the fact that the service supplier retains the ownership of the product means that he will stay responsible for repair and maintenance throughout the duration of the contract.[70] Second, through PSS, individuals can gain access to luxury goods, which they otherwise might not be able to afford. For example, through PSS, a student who likes to drink high-end coffee but does not have the opportunity to invest in an expensive professional espresso machine can gain access to this machine by paying a monthly fee.[71] Third, PSS also provide opportunities for people (often students or young professionals) who only live in a certain place or city for a short time. For example, a student can use a bicycle or washing machine "as a service" for a limited amount of time, without the need to buy these products.

14. SHIFT FROM OFFLINE TO ONLINE AND DISINTERMEDIATION – PSS contracts are very often offered exclusively or predominantly online and there is often a direct link between the producer and the consumer which excludes intermediaries from the distribution chain ("*cutting out the middleman*"). However, this need not always be the case. It is certainly possible for manufacturers to offer PSS to another business, which in turn will offer these services to the end-user.[72]

15. LINK WITH THE PLATFORM ECONOMY AND COLLABORATIVE/SHARING ECONOMY – The rise of servitisation and PSS business models (sometimes also described with the concept of the "functional (service) economy"[73]) is closely

---

70 Compare this with a sales contract where there is only an obligation to repair during the legal guarantee period.

71 However, this also entails a risk of consumer over-indebtedness. In addition, consumer organisations warn that leasing products is often more expensive than buying them. See for example: www.afm.nl/nl-nl/consumenten/themas/lenen/private-lease. See for an overview of the underlying reasons for this: R. KOOLHOVEN, "Bescherming tegen overkreditering bij huur en lease van producten als diensten (PaaS)", *WPNR* 2021, vol. 7345, (835) 839–840.

72 E. MANZINI and C. VEZZOLI, "A strategic design approach to develop sustainable product service systems: examples taken from the 'environmentally friendly innovation' Italian prize", *J.Clean.Prod.* 2003, (851) 854.

73 See: W.R. STAHEL, "The Functional Economy: Cultural and Organizational Change", *International Journal of Performability Engineering* 2005, vol. 1 issue 2, (121) 121–130, which defines the 'functional economy' as *"one that optimises the use (or function) of goods and services and thus the management of existing wealth (goods, knowledge, and nature). The economic objective of the functional economy is to create the highest possible use value for the longest possible time while consuming as few material resources and energy as possible. This functional economy is therefore considerably more sustainable, or dematerialized, than the present economy, which is focused on production and related material flows as its principal means to create wealth."* According to STAHEL, this can be achieved through a shift from a production (and therefore ownership) oriented economy to a functional or service-oriented economy.

linked and sometimes overlaps with the concepts of the "platform economy" and the "collaborative" or "sharing" economy.[74, 75] The concept of the platform economy refers to economic activities facilitated by online platforms such as Amazon, Etsy, Google or Uber.[76] These platforms act as intermediaries by connecting two or more groups of users at different sides of a multi-sided market and enabling interactions between them.[77] This allows businesses to offer services to consumers without the need to buy certain goods themselves or avoid the need to produce more new goods.[78] The collaborative or sharing economy refers to economic and/or social activities involving peer-to-peer transactions, which are generally facilitated by online platforms.[79, 80] An interesting example of this convergence of servitisation, the platform economy and the collaborative economy within the movable consumer goods sector is "*Peerby*".[81] "*Peerby*" is an online platform for sharing goods with your neighbours.[82] The platform makes it possible for consumers to borrow and lend (free of charge) or to rent and hire (for a fee) goods that are not often used, such as a drill, a barbecue, an (electric) (cargo) bicycle, etc. Registration with "*Peerby*" is free. Once registered, consumers can offer their things for loan or rent. For rentals "*Peerby*" charges 15% service and warranty costs, loans remain free of charge. Consumers who want to borrow or hire must take out a (yearly or monthly) paid membership.[83]

---

74 The term "peer-to-peer economy" is also sometimes used, involving mutual transactions between individuals not operating in the context of a professional activity.

75 See on the interplay of servitisation, the platform economy, and the sharing/peer-to-peer ("P2P") economy: E. Van Gool, "De nieuwe Richtlijn Consumentenkoop en duurzame consumptie" in E. Terryn and I. Claeys (eds.), *Nieuw recht inzake koop & digitale inhoud en diensten*, Mortsel, Intersentia, 2020, (303) 323–324.

76 M. Kenney and J. Zysman, "The Rise of the Platform Economy", *Issues in Science and Technology* 2016, (61) 61–69.

77 See for an extensive analysis of the concept of online platforms: F. Bostoen, *Abuse of Platform Power – Leveraging Conduct in Digital Markets under EU Competition Law and Beyond*, Paris, Concurrences, 2023, 9–21. See also EC, *Online Platforms and the Digital Single Market Opportunities and Challenges for Europe*, 25.5.2016, COM(2016) 288 final, 2–3 for a description of the characteristics of online platforms.

78 "*Blablacar*" can be cited as an example in the transport sector (www.blablacar.com). Examples in the accommodation sector are "Airbnb" (www.airbnb.com/), "*Couchsurfing*" (www.couchsurfing.com) or "*Huizenruil*" (www.huizenruil.com/nl/). In addition, reference can also be made to so-called repair cafes. See: www.repaircafe.org.

79 See: EC, *A European agenda for the collaborative economy*, 2.6.2016, COM(2016) 356 final. See for an analysis of the legal consequences and challenges of the collaborative economy V. Hatzopoulos, *The Collaborative Economy and EU Law*, London, Bloomsbury Publishing Plc, 2018, 270 p.

80 Examples of online services include online marketplaces, social networks, app stores, content sharing websites, etc. See also EC, *Online Platforms and the Digital Single Market Opportunities and Challenges for Europe*, 25.5.2016, COM(2016) 288 final, 2–3 for a description of the characteristics of online platforms.

81 www.peerby.com/nl-be.

82 In this sense, Peerby is part of the P2P economy, a term that refers to the growing number of transactions between individuals who do not operate as part of a professional activity.

83 See: www.peerby.com/beta/faq/hoe-werkt-het-peerby-lidmaatschap.

This business models thus combines elements of servitisation (use of the product rather than ownership) with elements from the collaborative economy (sharing products with your neighbours) and the platform economy (users on both sides of the market are connected through an online platform).

16. Importance of data – PSS are also very often characterised by the importance of usage data for guaranteeing the optimal performance of the service. After all, the increasing digitalisation of our society[84] opens technical possibilities for businesses to increasingly monitor products and services, which can lead to valuable insights for the business on consumer behaviour and enable an increasing personalisation of the service for the consumer.

17. Often standard contract on a "take it or leave it" basis – PSS providers almost always use standard contracts on a "take it or leave it" basis. Upon acceptance of the PSS offer by the consumer, these general terms and conditions will apply to the contractual relationship with the PSS supplier. However, drafting PSS contracts often proves more difficult than drafting sales contracts. Offering increasingly complex PSS requires companies to further develop their contractual and relational capabilities. This results in much creativity and innovation in contract design, yet also much legal uncertainty for the contracting parties, especially the consumer.

1.1.2.3. Examples and use-cases of servitisation and PSS

18. Circular business models have existed for some time in B2B markets ... – The idea of integrating products and services is not entirely new. Examples of servitisation and PSS have existed for decades in business-to-business ("B2B") markets. For instance, Rolls-Royce is often mentioned as a manufacturing company leading the way in offering not only services but also integrated solutions. Rather than engine maintenance provided based on a "time and materials" contract, Rolls-Royce distinguished itself from its competitors by offering its clients an "integrated solution" in the form of a fixed price maintenance per flying hour basis.[85] This novel type of performance-based service contract was originally marketed as "*Power-by-the-hour*" and is now offered under the name "*TotalCare*".[86, 87] Other examples in B2B markets include Xerox's "PagePack"[88] model for their photocopying machines, Philips' "*Light as*

[84] See *infra* no. 22.

[85] R. Wise and P. Baumgartner, "Go downstream: The new profit imperative in manufacturing", *Harvard Business Review* 1999, (133) 138.

[86] www.rolls-royce.com/media/our-stories/discover/2017/totalcare.aspx.

[87] D.J. Smith, "Power-by-the-hour: the role of technology in reshaping business strategy at Rolls-Royce", *Technology Analysis & Strategic Management* 2013, (987) 999; J. Hojnik, "The Servitization of Industry: EU Law Implications and Challenges", *CML Rev.* 2016, vol. 53, (1575) 1580.

[88] www.office.xerox.com/latest/MPSBR-04E.pdf.

a Service",[89] Kaer's "*Airconditioning-as-a-service*",[90] Q-lite, which offers displays as a service,[91] leasing programs for plants in the workspace,[92] French train manufacturer Alstrom's "*Train life services*"[93] offering parts and maintenance supply services to transport companies, and many others.[94]

19. ... AND ARE NOW INCREASINGLY ON THE RISE IN B2C MARKETS – Recently, servitisation and PSS contracts are also expanding to business-to-consumer ("B2C") markets. In the clothing sector, the Dutch company Mudjeans offers a "*Lease a Jeans*" formula where consumers can lease a pair of jeans for a monthly fee.[95] When the jeans are worn out, or after 12 months, the consumer can send in the jeans to receive a new pair while Mudjeans recycles the old pair. Another example in the fashion industry is the "*Rent the Runway*" subscription, which allows women to rent up to four designer pieces at a time and swap these out for others when they no longer feel like wearing them.[96] Similar examples of such a "fashion library" exist in Belgium and the Netherlands. In Belgium there is "*Dressr*",[97] where women can also rent up to four items at a time. Members get discounts to purchase rented items. The Dutch fashion library "*Lena*"[98] works slightly differently: renting a garment costs an X amount of credits per day; one credit costs 25 cents. Consumers can rent the garment for as long as they want and get a discount on the purchase price if they buy the rented garment.

In the home printer industry, the information technology company HP introduced the "*HP Instant Ink*" plan where the monthly subscription fee is based on the number of printed pages and not on the amount of ink used.[99] Subscription formulas are also available in the household appliances sector. Subscriptions for Miele washing machines, tumble dryers and dishwashers are made available by "*Bundles*"[100] while "*Blue Movement*"[101] offers subscription plans for BSH (Bosch) machines. In Flanders, there is the "*Papillon*" project of

---

89 www.lighting.philips.nl/systemen/aanbod-van-pakketten/winkels-en-horeca/light-as-a-service-retail. Philips is not the only company to have implemented this business model. Similarly, the Belgian company ETAP Lighting International offers "*Light as a Service*" contracts. See www.etaplighting.com/nl/c-laas.

90 www.kaer.com/. See also www.ellenmacarthurfoundation.org/circular-examples/cooling-as-a-service-kaer.

91 www.q-lite.com/nl/.

92 See e.g. www.anygreen.be/en/.

93 www.alstom.com/; T.S. BAINES, "Exploring Service Innovation and the Servitization of the Manufacturing Firm", *Research-Technology Management* 2015, vol. 58, (9) 9.

94 J. HOJNIK, "The Servitization of Industry: EU Law Implications and Challenges", *CML Rev.* 2016, vol. 53, (1575) 1580.

95 https://mudjeans.com/pages/lease-a-jeans-mud-jeans.

96 http://renttherunway.com.

97 https://dressr.be.

98 https://lena-library.com.

99 https://instantink.hpconnected.com/uk/en/l/?jumpid=ps_ymsnq52e6k.

100 http://bundles.nl/en/.

101 http://bluemovement.nl.

Samenlevingopbouw West-Vlaanderen[102] and BSH Home Appliances, which is specifically aimed at people with energy debts and old energy-consuming appliances in the home.[103] In the furniture sector, "*Live Light*"[104] makes it possible to rent your interior at a monthly price, "*Still Kitchens*"[105] offers kitchens as-a-service and Ikea announced pilot projects in which it will rent out its products to consumers.[106] Another example in the heating, air ventilation and cooling ("HAVC") sector is the Dutch company "*Saman*",[107] which offers the opportunity to rent a hybrid or all-electric heat pump for the consumer's house.[108]

Servitisation and PSS contracts have many applications for urban mobility as well. First, there are well-known shared e-scooters from providers such as "*Lime*",[109] "*Bird*",[110] and "*Dott*"[111] that operate based on a pay-per-use model. The ride-sharing company "*Uber*"[112] has a similar offer for bikes and scooters. Different cities in Belgium also offer their own bike sharing solutions. Examples are "*Villo!*"[113] in Brussels, "*Velo*"[114] in Antwerp and "*Blue Bike*"[115] which has locations near numerous train stations. Examples in the Netherlands include "*Cargoroo*"[116] and "*Urbee*"[117] which are both offered in multiple cities such as Amsterdam, Rotterdam, Utrecht, The Hague, etc. Second, there is "*Swapfiets*",[118] a service where you can rent a bike for a monthly fee. In return, the company guarantees that you will always have a working bicycle while your subscription is active. The abovementioned supplier "*Bird*" announced a similar subscription for a personal e-scooter.[119] Finally, there are car-sharing services such as "*Cambio*",[120] "*Poppy*",[121] "*Miles*"[122] and "*Sixt Share*".[123]

---

102 www.samenlevingsopbouwwvl.be/.
103 https://vlaanderen-circulair.be/nl/doeners-in-vlaanderen/detail/papillon.
104 https://live-light.com/.
105 www.wearestill.com/subscription.
106 www.theguardian.com/business/2019/feb/04/kitchen-for-rent-ikea-to-trial-leasing-of-furniture.
107 www.samangroep.nl/.
108 www.samangroep.nl/huren/warmtepompen-huur/.
109 www.li.me/en-us/home.
110 www.bird.co/.
111 Ridedott.com/nl.
112 www.uber.com/be/nl/ride/how-it-works/scooters-and-bikes/.
113 www.villo.be/nl/home.
114 www.velo-antwerpen.be/.
115 www.blue-bike.be/nl.
116 https://cargoroo.nl/.
117 https://urbee.nl/en.
118 http://swapfiets.be/en/.
119 https://rent.bird.co/.
120 www.cambio.be/en-vla.
121 https://poppy.be/en.
122 https://miles-mobility.com/en-be.
123 www.sixt.nl/share/#/.

Examples in the consumer electronics sector include "*Fairphone Easy*",[124] "*Swapphone*"[125] and "*Grover*".[126] With "*Fairphone Easy*", you rent a sustainable smartphone[127] including protective accessories (screen protector, protective case) for a fixed price per month. It also includes all-in repair and a swap service. "*Swapphone*" offers Samsung smartphones and iPhones for rent, including additional services such as repair and replacement in case of defects. Consumers pay a monthly or annual fee, depending on the model. "*Grover*" offers a wide range of consumer electronics for rent, including smartphones, headphones, game consoles, and even drones.[128] In case of damage to the product, they cover 90% of the repair costs. In addition to these already existing business models, Apple is rumoured to be working on a hardware subscription service for iPhones.[129] Yet another supplier operating in this sector is "*Gerrard Street*"[130] (recently renamed "*Repeat*"[131]), a subscription service for modular headphones.

There are also servitised solutions for sports, leisure, and family life. The French sporting goods company Decathlon released its test project "*We Play Circular*" in 2021 focusing on sports equipment.[132] For a monthly fee, you got access to a library of Decathlon products where you could borrow equipment for a certain budget.[133] When you returned the products, your budget reopened and you could borrow other sports equipment, even for different sports. Although this pilot project was eventually cancelled, Decathlon still offers rental services for sports equipment such as ski equipment, bicycles, football clothing,

---

124 https://shop.fairphone.com/nl/fairphone-easy. Fairphone, in collaboration with Circle Economy, has also done a pilot project for B2B contracts called "*Fairphone-as-a-Service*", see: Circle Economy, "The Circular Phone, Legal, operational and financial solutions to unlock the potential of the 'Fairphone-as-a-service' model", 31 December 2017, available at www.circle-economy.com/resources/the-circular-phone. See for a discussion on the contract terms of this business model also: A. Fischer, S. Pascucci and W. Dolfsma, "Designing a circular contract Template: Insights from the fairphone-as-a-Service project", *J.Clean.Prod.* 2022, vol. 364, (132487) 132487.

125 https://swapphone.be.

126 www.grover.com/nl-en.

127 *Fairphone Easy* offers a subscription plan for the Fairphone 4. This smartphone aims to be as sustainable as possible by using recycled, responsibly sourced, and conflict-free materials as much as possible, offering 5 years of warranty, and allowing maximal repairability by offering affordable spare parts and making sure no parts are glued shut. See https://shop.fairphone.com/en/.

128 For an overview of the available products, see: www.grover.com/nl-en/trending.

129 See M. Gurman, "Apple is working on a Hardware Subscription Service for iPhones", Bloomberg, 24 March 2022, available at www.bloomberg.com/news/articles/2022-03-24/apple-is-working-on-a-hardware-subscription-service-for-iphones. On iPhone "as-a-service", see also: H. Slachmuylders, "iPhone as a Service? Some thoughts on Apple's rumoured hardware subscription service", *CCM Blog* 4 April 2022, https://law.kuleuven.be/ccm/blog/?p=321.

130 https://gerrardstreet.nl/hoehetwerkt/.

131 https://repeat.audio/.

132 www.gondola.be/nl/news/decathlon-gaat-producten-verhuren-vanaf-2021.

133 For example, if your monthly fee amounted to € 15, you could borrow sports equipment for a budget of € 150.

etc.[134] "*Op Wielekes*"[135] offers a library of children's bicycles. Members pay an annual membership fee and in return always have access to a good and quality children's bicycle which they can exchange for a larger one if needed. Finally, "*de Babytheek*"[136] is a lending service for baby equipment.

20. Several terms and conditions of these examples serve as use-cases – The contracts used by these examples of servitised business models in B2C markets vary widely. As a result, they give a good idea of the various rights and obligations consumers may have under such business models. Therefore, several terms and conditions of the business models described above will be analysed in this book.[137]

1.1.3. THE RISE OF SERVITISATION AND PSS

21. Explaining the rise of servitisation and PSS – This rise in servitisation and PSS contracts in B2C markets can be explained by technological, economic, social, and environmental factors.

1.1.3.1. Digitalisation and IoT

22. Digitalisation as enabler of access-based consumption – First, the technological evolution and increasing digitalisation of society that characterise the twenty-first century have been key ingredients for the transition from products to services.[138] Recent advances in digital technologies such as the

134 www.decathlon.be/nl/Rent_lp-RCGASH.

135 www.opwielekes.be.

136 https://babytheek.wordpress.com.

137 See *infra* no. 57.

138 See e.g. J. Hojnik, "Servitization, IoT and Circular Economy. Need for Regulatory Intervention at EU Level? " in B. Keirsbilck, E. Terryn, J. Eyckmans, S. Rousseau and D. Voinot (eds.), *Servitization and circular economy: economic and legal challenges*, Antwerp, Intersentia, 2023, (33) 33–42; M. Ardolino, M. Rapaccini, N. Saccani, P. Gaiardelli, G. Crespi and C. Ruggeri, "The role of digital technologies for the service transformation of industrial companies", *International Journal of Production Research* 2018, (2116) 2116–2132; C. Lerch and M. Gotsch, "Digitalized Product-Service Systems in Manufacturing Firms: A Case Study Analysis", *Research-Technology Management* 2015, (45) 45–52; N. Kryvinska, S. Kaczor, C. Strauss and M. Greguš, "Servitization – Its Raise through Information and Communication Technologies" in M. Snene and M. Leonard (eds.), *Exploring Services Science*, Cham, Springer, 2014, (72) 72–81; D.J. Smith, "Power-by-the-hour: the role of technology in reshaping business strategy at Rolls-Royce", *Technology Analysis & Strategic Management* 2013, (987) 988; C. Kowalkowski, D. Kindström and H. Gebauer, "ICT as a catalyst for service business orientation", *Journal of Business & Industrial Marketing* 2013, (506) 506–511; H.W. Lightfoot, T.S. Baines and P. Smart, "Emerging Technology and the Service Delivery Supply Chain" in H.K. Chan, F. Lettice and O.A. Durowoju (eds.), *Decision-Making for Supply Chain Integration*, London, Springer, 2012, (211) 211–226; P. Weingerl and J. Hojnik, "'Servitization' and Movables. Legal Initiatives and Challenges in

Internet of Things ("IoT"), Cloud Computing ("CC"), Big Data Analytics ("BDA"), robotics and 5G networks enable manufacturers to link products with intelligent digital systems allowing them to operate autonomously or be remote-controlled by their user and communicate with other devices (where interoperability permits) and/or the manufacturer.[139]

These digitised solutions are a huge enabler of access-based consumption since they create technical possibilities for the manufacturer to monitor the use (e.g. pages printed, cups of coffee made, number of washes, hours the light was on, etc.) of his products by the user. This way, the manufacturer knows exactly how much he should charge the user, and the user only pays for his actual use. In addition to monitoring the use of the product, these digitised products also allow creating deeper relationships with customers by adding additional services such as information services, maintenance and repair, other after-sales services, and even deliveries.

23. Examples: "smart kitchen" and "smart ventilation" – An example that appeals to the imagination is that of a "smart kitchen". This is a kitchen that contains a fully integrated set of interconnected and internet-connected household appliances equipped with sensors, control services via a smartphone or laptop and other automatic functions.[140] These sensors and automatic functions can be used to inform the supplier when a specific device needs repair or replacement, to automate and optimise functions relating to energy management, to monitor and gain insight on consumer behaviour and presumably in the future even to facilitate deliveries of products such as food for a smart-fridge, coffee for a connected coffee maker or detergent for a (dish) washing machine.[141] The consumer can gain access to this smart kitchen in exchange for a monthly fee and the supplier can use the digital ecosystem to offer additional services and products.

"Smart ventilation" builds on the same idea. Sensors and connected devices ensure continuous monitoring of air quality. This enables tailoring ventilation to the needs of the specific place and the consumer (for example "silent hours" at night) and allows to react to sudden increases in moisture and odour. At the same time, an app on the consumer's smartphone or laptop can be used to customise and monitor the activity of the ventilation systems.

Slovenia" in B. Keirsbilck and E. Terryn (eds.), *Consumer Protection in a Circular Economy*, Antwerp, Intersentia, 2019, (225) 229.

139 OECD, *Consumer policy and the smart home*, OECD publishing, 2018, No. 268, 4–6; C. Lerch and M. Gotsch, "Digitalized Product-Service Systems in Manufacturing Firms: A Case Study Analysis", *Research-Technology Management* 2015, (45) 45.

140 B. Keirsbilck, E. Terryn and E. Van Gool, "Consumentenbescherming bij servitisation en product-dienst systemen (PDS)", *TPR* 2019, (817) 822–823.

141 M.B.M. Loos, "Consumentenbescherming bij slimme koelkasten en zelfrijdende auto's", *Tijdschrift voor Consumentenrecht & Handelspraktijken* 2018, (174) 174–176.

1.1.3.2. Societal reasons: emergence of alternatives for ownership and private property

24. ALTERNATIVES TO INDIVIDUAL OWNERSHIP AND PRIVATE PROPERTY GAIN IMPORTANCE – Second, the rise of servitisation and PSS can be explained by a societal development that has gained momentum in recent years: the emergence of alternatives to individual ownership.[142] Many of these alternatives have been developed in the wake of the increased digitalisation described above: Spotify and Netflix are subscription-based options for people who do not longer wish to buy and own CDs and DVDs. Pictures and files are backed up in cloud services such as iCloud and Google Drive instead of on a physical carrier such as a USB disk or an external hard drive. We no longer buy a version of Microsoft Office as a one-time purchase but subscribe to Office 365, an example of Software as a Service ("SaaS").

Yet, ownership alternatives are not limited to the digital sphere. The emergence of the sharing economy and platform economy makes it possible to share cars, bicycles, electric scooters and even guest rooms or holiday homes via online platforms.[143] Additionally, leasing of cars has become ever more popular. In addition to a financial lease ("*business lease*") which has been around for much longer in B2B relations, companies now also increasingly offer private lease ("*operational lease*") contracts to consumers.[144] This allows the consumer to use the car for a long-term period at a fixed fee while the leasing company retains the ownership. When the contract expires, the car is returned to the leasing company.[145] Especially for millennials, often young professionals and students who value flexibility so they can move housing quickly,[146] renting instead of owning things such as furniture, bikes or household appliances is becoming the new normal.[147]

---

142 The special issue of 2018 of the Dutch journal Ars Aequi ("De eigendom voorbij") is dedicated to these alternatives to ownership.

143 A. DE BOECK, "The 'Circular Economy' – National Legal Initiatives and Challenges Concerning Movables – Belgium" in B. KEIRSBILCK and E. TERRYN (eds.), *Consumer Protection in a Circular Economy*, Antwerp, Intersentia, 2019, (185) 190–191. See for an in-depth analysis of the sharing economy and EU law also: V. HATZOPOULOS, *The Collaborative Economy and EU Law*, London, Bloomsbury Publishing Plc, 2018, 270 p. See for a legal analysis of the platform economy: B. DEVOLDER (ed.), *The Platform Economy. Unravelling the Legal Status of Online Intermediaries*, Antwerp, Intersentia, 2019, 398 p.

144 J. DE VOGEL, "Private Lease: Consumer Credit in Disguise? ", *EuCML* 2020, vol. 9, (51) 52.

145 J. DE VOGEL, "Private Lease: Consumer Credit in Disguise? ", *EuCML* 2020, vol. 9, (51) 52.

146 P. LAGERWAARD refers to this as "Swap residents" (*Swapbewoners*). These are residents who settle but do not commit themselves and can be gone in a moment. It typifies residents who engage in long-term dependencies as little as possible and whose possessions, such as a bicycle, are exchangeable. See: See: P. LAGERWAARD, "Swap-bewoners", De Groene Amsterdammer, 1 August 2019, available at www.groene.nl/artikel/swap-bewoners.

147 See for example: www.thetimes.co.uk/article/why-more-millennials-are-renting-furniture-art-and-even-dining-rooms-3wm0x2m6n; and www.theguardian.com/business/2020/aug/15/never-knowingly-under-leased-john-lewis-moves-to-rent-out-its-furniture.

25. Enjoyment instead of private property – The emergence of alternatives to ownership has coincided with the rise of an alleged "New Consumerism".[148] According to this view, consumers increasingly reassess their priorities and focus on the things they really value. Advertisements take advantage of this. Some marketing teams even go as far as saying "*by not owning things you are not owned by things*".[149] Indeed, nowadays, some consumers nowadays attach less value to ownership or wealth but rather to their "*lifestyle*" (a marketing term).[150] This means that identity, prestige and social position are mainly determined by living a life according to a certain style that is often (but certainly not always[151]) characterised by a generous use of expensive, luxurious and fashionable goods and/or extravagant and high-priced vacations.[152] This way of life requires the rapid replacement or renewal of the goods that surround the consumer, where it is irrelevant that the consumer does not own the goods that express this *lifestyle*. On the contrary, ownership is impractical.[153]

26. Risks associated with the movement away from ownership – Yet the movement away from ownership and private property also comes with considerable risks. Private property rights are critical for the development of the individual, giving him a very strong position in relation to goods (e.g. the possibility of revindication, selling a good on the second-hand market, lending the good to a close friend, etc.). Also, private property rights have an important economic and social order function since they allow for the efficient allocation of resources in society (e.g. avoidance of moral hazard and tragedy of the commons).[154] Since this research aims to promote circular business models,

---

148 See Euromonitor, *Report, The New Consumerism: Redefining Ownership, Values and Priorities*, 2016, as described by A. De Boeck, "The 'Circular Economy' – National Legal Initiatives and Challenges Concerning Movables – Belgium" in B. Keirsbilck and E. Terryn (eds.), *Consumer Protection in a Circular Economy*, Antwerp, Intersentia, 2019, (185) 186.

149 Quote used in an advertisement for the Volvo XC40 with Care by Volvo: "*the car you subscribe to*", see www.youtube.com/watch?v=cDy8U_xyGNo.

150 A.C. van Schaick, "Digitalisering en vermogensrecht" in J.H. Gerards and A.C. van Schaick (eds.), *Preadviezen Vereniging voor Burgerlijk Recht: Digitalisering, vermogensrecht, de platformeconomie en grondrechten*, Zutphen, Paris, 2019, (7) no. 14.

151 Another example of this focus on enjoyment instead of private property can be illustrated by the trend of *minimalism*: the idea of owning fewer possessions and decluttering your home.

152 A.C. van Schaick, "Digitalisering en vermogensrecht" in J.H. Gerards and A.C. van Schaick (eds.), *Preadviezen Vereniging voor Burgerlijk Recht: Digitalisering, vermogensrecht, de platformeconomie en grondrechten*, Zutphen, Paris, 2019, (7) no. 14.

153 A.C. van Schaick, "Digitalisering en vermogensrecht" in J.H. Gerards and A.C. van Schaick (eds.), *Preadviezen Vereniging voor Burgerlijk Recht: Digitalisering, vermogensrecht, de platformeconomie en grondrechten*, Zutphen, Paris, 2019, (7) no. 14, with reference to S. Fischer, S. Steger, N.D. Jordan, M. O'Brien and P. Schepelmann, *Leasing Society. Report requested by the European Parliament's Committee on Environment, Public Health and Food Safety*, 2012, 58 p.

154 V. Mak, "Van ownership naar access. Is toegang de nieuwe eigendom?", *Ars Aequi* 2018, (664) 664; Y. Al Salman and R. Claassen, "From Ownership to Access. A Philosophical

these issues should at least be kept in mind when moving further and further away from the traditional idea of ownership and private property.

1.1.3.3. Economic opportunities for businesses and consumers

27. Economic opportunities of PSS – Third, the rise of servitisation and PSS contracts offer significant advantages and economic opportunities for both businesses and consumers.

28. Advantages of PSS for businesses – In addition to benefitting the business's reputation by engaging in more circular business models,[155] producers can use servitisation and PSS contracts to pursue further growth and profit.[156] Indeed, combining or replacing sales with services allows businesses to differentiate their output and create competitive and marketing advantages (e.g. by using customised "all-in" offers). This results in new market opportunities and the possibility to attract new customers. Another advantage is that these servitised business models are not as easy to copy as their traditional counterparts.[157] Third, servitisation also makes it possible to obtain more information about customer satisfaction and the use of products and services.[158] This allows companies to form stronger relationships with their customers strengthening customer loyalty[159] and interaction.[160] Fourth, the use of long-term contracts, periodical payments and the fact that the residual value of the product stays with the firm can increase the firm's stability of revenues.[161] Finally, PSS allow producers to reduce costs (e.g. by disintermediation[162] or by

---

Perspective on the Rise of Access-Based Consumption", *Ars Aequi* 2018, (566) 567. See also V. Mak, "Consumentenbescherming bij servitisation", *TPR* 2019, (779) 786–787.

155 A. De Boeck, "The 'Circular Economy' – National Legal Initiatives and Challenges Concerning Movables – Belgium" in B. Keirsbilck and E. Terryn (eds.), *Consumer Protection in a Circular Economy*, Antwerp, Intersentia, 2019, (185) 185.

156 A. Annarelli, C. Battistella and F. Nonino, *The Road to Servitization, How Product Service Systems Can Disrupt Companies' Business Models*, Cham, Springer, 2019, 22–23.

157 R. Oliva and R. Kallenberg, "Managing the transition from products to services", *IJSIM* 2003, vol. 14, (160) 160.

158 W. Reim, V. Parida and D. Örtqvist, "Product-Service Systems (PSS) business models and tactics – a systematic literature review", *J.Clean.Prod.* 2015, vol. 97, (61) 69.

159 J. Hojnik, "The Servitization of Industry: EU Law Implications and Challenges", *CML Rev.* 2016, vol. 53, (1575) 1590; A. Tukker, "Eight Types of Product-Service System: Eight Ways to Sustainability? Experiences from Suspronet", *Bus.Strat.Env.* 2004, vol. 13, (246) 247.

160 W. Reim, V. Parida and D. Örtqvist, "Product-Service Systems (PSS) business models and tactics – a systematic literature review", *J.Clean.Prod.* 2015, vol. 97, (61) 68–69.

161 M.E. Kreye and D.P. van Donk, "Servitization for consumer products: an empirical exploration of challenges and benefits for supply chain partners", *IJOPM* 2021, vol. 41 issue 5, (494) 496; R. Oliva and R. Kallenberg, "Managing the transition from products to services", *IJSIM* 2003, vol. 14, (160) 160.

162 F. Bostoen and W. Devroe, "From sales to subscriptions in the car sector: Competition law implications of servitisation and the refusal to sell to consumers", *European Competition Law Review* 2018, vol. 39, (411) 411–419.

reusing and remanufacturing components and products) and thus generate increased profit margins.[163]

29. Advantages of PSS for consumers – Customers can also reap the advantages of PSS.[164] First and foremost, the availability of new PSS means that the variety of products, services and combinations thereof is growing. This can result in more service flexibility, higher quality, more personalisation, higher delivered value, and improved satisfaction of needs for consumers.[165] In addition, the increased competition and disintermediation can result in lower prices. Third, PSS often entail lower entry costs and allow access to high-end and luxury products that the customer might otherwise not be able to afford. Fourth, since customers are no longer responsible for maintenance and repair – either because they do not own the product or because maintenance and repair is covered by an after-sales service – they do not have to fear unexpected costs nor concerns linked to monitoring products status or end-of-life disposal.[166] This is especially true for use-oriented and result-oriented PSS because the supplier remains responsible for the continuous availability of a specific product or specific functionality. Finally, PSS allow greater business responsiveness to consumer preferences and needs because producers are in constant contact with their customers.[167]

30. Challenges of implementing PSS business models – PSS and circular business models are certainly on the rise. Yet, various economic, behavioural, and legal barriers still exist to the transition from products to services on both sides of the market.

31. Challenges of implementing PSS business models for businesses – Businesses face various challenges when implementing a PSS business model.[168] As a first challenge, businesses can be confronted with increased up-front

---

163 R. Oliva and R. Kallenberg, "Managing the transition from products to services", *IJSIM* 2003, vol. 14, (160) 160; A. Annarelli, C. Battistella and F. Nonino, *The Road to Servitization, How Product Service Systems Can Disrupt Companies' Business Models*, Cham, Springer, 2019, 22–23.

164 O.K. Mont, "Clarifying the concept of product-service systems", *J.Clean.Prod.* 2002, vol. 10, (237) 240.

165 A. Annarelli, C. Battistella and F. Nonino, *The Road to Servitization, How Product Service Systems Can Disrupt Companies' Business Models*, Cham, Springer, 2019, 22–23.

166 A. Annarelli, C. Battistella and F. Nonino, *The Road to Servitization, How Product Service Systems Can Disrupt Companies' Business Models*, Cham, Springer, 2019, 22–23.

167 B. Keirsbilck, E. Terryn and E. Van Gool, "Consumentenbescherming bij servitisation en product-dienst-systemen (PDS)" in *Preadviezen VVSR-BN 2019*, Den Haag, Boom juridische uitgevers, 2019, (11) 15.

168 See for an overview e.g. European Environment Agency, *EAA Report 2017/6 Circular by Design – Products in the Circular Economy*, Luxembourg, EU Publications Office, 2017, 26; A. Richter and M. Steven, "On the Relation Between Industrial Product-Service Systems and Business Models", *Oper.Res.Proc.* 2008, (97) 97–98; H. Gebauer, E. Fleisch and T. Friedli,

investment requirements.[169] After all, offering PSS requires substantial initial investments in a large "pool" of products that can be offered as-a-service, with no immediate return on investment for the PSS supplier.

This is linked with the second challenge, namely that PSS may initially result in a lower rate of revenue generation. Indeed, compared to traditional product sales, the revenue is spread over an extended period (namely the product's lifecycle) instead of the short-term revenue generated by selling products. However, as already explained above, the revenue may become more stable and sustainable in the long term.

Problems and costs associated with disintermediation form a third challenge. While eliminating intermediaries in the value chain and directly interacting with customers can reduce costs, improve customer relationships and create additional revenue, it also requires the PSS supplier to assume additional responsibilities, risks and costs that were previously handled by intermediaries.

Fourth, PSS suppliers need a logistics system for delivery, installation and collection of products. This of course brings additional costs and may involve complex coordination, transportation and inventory management processes to ensure smooth service delivery. Offering products as-a-service also entails the risk of cannibalising the business's existing traditional sales of products. This may lead to a decline in standalone product sales and potential conflicts within the business's product portfolio.

Furthermore, offering PSS business models generally leads to higher transaction costs due to the need for more complex contracts, as these contracts encompass both product and service elements. Drafting, negotiating and managing such contracts can result in increased legal expenses and administrative efforts. Other challenges relate to the potential difficulty in determining the "service-life" of the products (how long the product should "serve" before being replaced or refurbished) and determining what the residual value should be at the end of the contract (as this is important for financial planning and risk assessment).[170]

Finally, the adoption of PSS introduces the risk of moral hazard,[171] which is the risk that PSS users may behave less carefully than in a situation where

---

"Overcoming the Service Paradox in Manufacturing Companies", *European Management Journal* 2005, vol. 23, (14) 14–26.

169 H. Janssens and C. Levie, *Financiering van de circulaire economie. Uitdagingen en aanbevelingen*, Econocom, 2019, 47.

170 See for example European Environment Agency, *EAA Report 2017/6 Circular by Design - Products in the Circular Economy*, Luxembourg, EU Publications Office, 2017, 26; A. Richter and M. Steven, "On the Relation Between Industrial Product-Service Systems and Business Models", *Oper.Res.Proc.* 2008, (97) 97–98; H. Gebauer, E. Fleisch and T. Friedli, "Overcoming the Service Paradox in Manufacturing Companies", *European Management Journal* 2005, vol. 23, (14) 14–26.

171 H. Gebauer, C. Saul and S. Joncourt, "Use-oriented product service systems in the early industry life cycle", *Ekonomiaz* 2016, vol. 89, (194) 212 and 218.

they own the product outright.[172] This can result in increased wear and tear, decreased product lifespan and potential conflicts between the business and the customer regarding liability for damages.

32. Challenges of implementing PSS business models on the consumer side – On the consumer side, behavioural literature has illustrated that customers often appear to be reluctant to embrace these new business models.[173] Different behavioural barriers were identified: some depending on consumer characteristics (optimism, innovativeness, risk perceptions, perceived lack of control), others depending on the type of product (e.g. respondents were more favourable about renting or leasing home appliances than smartphones,[174] home textiles or beds).[175] Other barriers resulted from various consumer concerns related to using rather than owning products.[176]

1.1.3.4. Environmental factors

33. PSS as enabler of the circular economy – Last but certainly not least, the rise of servitisation and PSS can be explained by environmental factors. Businesses often promote PSS as an eco-friendly and more circular alternative to the traditional sale of consumer products ("green claims").[177] Many academics also argue that the ongoing process of servitisation could contribute to the shift towards a more circular economy. The underlying idea is that servitisation can encourage manufacturers (i.e. service providers who retain ownership of the product) to extend the lifespan of products by using better materials and improving repairability, durability, and recyclability.[178] It is also claimed

---

172 See on customer misbehaviour in service contracts and renting contracts: T. Schaefers, K. Wittkowski, S. Benoit and R. Ferraro, "Contagious Effects of Customer Misbehavior in Access-Based Services", *Journal of Service Research* 2015, vol. 19 issue 1, (3) 3–21 and J.F. Durgee and G.C. O'Connor, "An exploration into renting as consumption behavior", *Psychology & Marketing* 1995, vol. 12 issue 2, (89) 89–104.

173 E. Vaittinen, M. Martinsuo and R. Ortt, "Business customers' readiness to adopt manufacturer's new services", *Journal of Service Theory and Practice* 2018, vol. 28, (52) 52–78.

174 S. Rousseau, "Millennials' acceptance of product-service systems: Leasing smartphones in Flanders (Belgium)", *J.Clean.Prod.* 2020, vol. 246, 118992.

175 For a more in-depth analysis, see B. Keirsbilck and S. Rousseau, "The Marketing Stage: Fostering Sustainable Consumption Choices" in B. Keirsbilck and E. Terryn (eds.), *Consumer Protection in a Circular Economy*, Antwerp, Intersentia, 2019, (93) 115–119.

176 F. Bardhi and G.M. Eckhardt, "Access-Based Consumption: The Case of Car Sharing", *J.Consu.Res.* 2012, vol. 39, (881) 881–898.

177 B. Keirsbilck and S. Rousseau, "The Marketing Stage: Fostering Sustainable Consumption Choices" in B. Keirsbilck and E. Terryn (eds.), *Consumer Protection in a Circular Economy*, Antwerp, Intersentia, 2019, (93) 113.

178 For a good example, see the case of Swapfiets: Swapfiets pushes its suppliers to provide more durable parts for their bikes (such as flexible mudguards that do not break when something strikes them instead of the traditional hard plastic mudguards). As a sidenote, Swapfiets itself is partnering with a PSS supplier for some parts of the bike, such as the tyres. As Swapfiets gets a fee per flat tyre, this provides an incentive for this supplier to also supply sustainable

that servitisation can lead to a more sustainable design of products, reducing their ecological footprint.[179] Additionally, PSS offer the possibility to decouple economic growth from the number of products sold, thereby reducing the need to produce new products from raw materials.[180] Finally, some academics argue that PSS can encourage consumers to use products (and materials) more efficiently.[181]

34. Criticism regarding sustainability of PSS – Yet the ecological nature of servitisation and PSS is by no means a given. Indeed, as was already illustrated in empirical studies, servitisation does not necessarily contribute to the transition to a circular economy. For example, a study of eight types of PSS found that most of these business models only marginally reduce the environmental impact.[182] Research has also shown that ownership is not necessarily detrimental to the circular economy; the responsibility for using the product in a sustainable way then simply lies with the consumer-owner.[183] The sustainability of these business models depends on more factors than just the fact that the PSS supplier retains ownership of the product.

35. Sustainability depends on the design and implementation of PSS – The sustainability of a PSS business model depends a lot on how it is designed and implemented. For example, the economic incentive to design products

---

products. See: P. Lalkens, "De zoektocht naar de volledig recycleerbare fiets", *FD* 26 February 2023, https://fd.nl/bedrijfsleven/1468479/de-zoektocht-naar-de-volledig-recyclebare-fiets.

179 See for an overview: J. Hojnik, "Ecological modernization through servitisation: EU regulatory support for sustainable product-service systems", *RECIEL* 2018, vol. 27, (162) 164–165. See also e.g. A. Plepys, E. Heiskranen and O. Mont, "European Policy Approaches to Promote Servicizing", *J.Clean.prod.* 2015, vol. 97, (117) 118; T.T. Sousa and P.A.C. Miguel, "Product-service Systems as a Promising Approach to Sustainability: Exploring the Sustainable Aspects of a PSS in Brazil", *Procedia CIRP* 2015, vol. 30, (138) 138; E. Manzini and C. Vezzoli, *Product-service systems and sustainability. Opportunities for sustainable solutions*, United Nations Environment Programme, Division of Technology Industry and Economics, Production and Consumption Branch, Milan, 2002, 14.

180 D. Borg, O. Mont and H. Schoonover, "Consumer Acceptance and Value in Use-Oriented Product-Service Systems: Lessons from Swedish Consumer Goods Companies", *Sustainability* 2020, 12, 8079, (1) 2; A. Tukker, "Product services for a resource-efficient and circular economy – a review", *J.Clean.Prod.* 2015, vol. 97, (76) 76.

181 J. Hojnik, "Ecological modernization through servitisation: EU regulatory support for sustainable product-service systems", *RECIEL* 2018, vol. 27, (162) 164.

182 A. Tukker, "Eight Types of Product-Service System: Eight Ways to Sustainability? Experiences from Suspronet", *Bus.Strat.Env.* 2004, vol. 13, (246) 246–260. Another study showed that in the case of shared e-scooters, the environmental impact depends on the lifespan of the e-scooters and the chosen materials, the process of collection and recharging, and the transport alternatives that they replace. See: J. Hollingsworth, B. Copeland and J. Johnson, "Are e-scooters polluters? The environmental impacts of shared dockless electric scooters", *Environ. Res. Lett.* 2019, vol. 14 issue 8, (https://iopscience.iop.org/article/10.1088/1748-9326/ab2da8/pdf).

183 J. Hojnik, "Ecological modernization through servitisation: EU regulatory support for sustainable product-service systems", *RECIEL* 2018, vol. 27, (162) 165–166; K. Demyttenaere, I. Dewit and A. Jacoby, "The influence of ownership on the sustainable use of product-service systems – a literature review", *Procedia CIRP* 2016, vol. 47, (180) 182.

for durability, repair and upgrading does not apply if products are not offered by their manufacturers but by a separate PSS supplier. This is even more true when these products are not specifically designed for offering PSS.[184] Also, according to TUKKER and TISCHNER, some products are more suitable to be offered as PSS than others. Products that are expensive, technically advanced, require maintenance and repair, are easy to transport, are infrequently used by customers, and are not strongly influenced by brand names, fashion, etc. typically work better for a PSS business model.[185] This explains why as-a-service models are currently more common in B2B relationships than in B2C relationships. The market situation and consumer preferences also play a role regarding the sustainability of PSS. For example, the PSS supplier may for commercial reasons be tempted to prematurely (i.e. before the end of their useful life) retire the products used for the PSS and replace them with new models.[186] Thus, businesses that want to offer truly sustainable PSS must take these concerns into account when designing PSS; merely offering services instead of selling products is not enough to achieve sustainable solutions.[187]

36. SUSTAINABILITY OF PSS ALSO DEPENDS ON THE MINDSET OF SUPPLIERS AND USERS – The sustainability of PSS depends not only on its design and operation, but also on the mindset of the suppliers who offer them and the PSS users who engage in them. PSS suppliers often base their choice for PSS on economic rather than ecological reasons. As a result, not all PSS are necessarily more sustainable than traditional business models based on the sale of products (risk of "greenwashing").[188] How consumers interact with the service also has an impact on the sustainability of PSS. Studies showed that in some cases PSS even have a negative effect on sustainability due to careless use of a product by customers who are not the owner or to an increase in "unnecessary"

---

184 E. HEISKANEN and M. JALAS, "Can services lead to radical eco-efficient improvements? – A review of the debate and evidence", *Corp. Soc. Responsib. Environ. Mgmt* 2003, vol. 10, (186) 192.

185 A. TUKKER, "Product services for a resource-efficient and circular economy – a review", *J.Clean.Prod.* 2015, vol. 97, (76) 86 with reference to A. TUKKER and U. TISCHNER, "Product-services as a research field: past, present and future. Reflections from a decade of research", *J.Clean.Prod.* 2006, vol. 14, (1552) 1552–1555.

186 C.M.D.S. PAVILLON, "Herijking van consumentencontractenrecht: duurzaamheid als nieuw ijkpunt?" in C.M.D.S. PAVILLON and W.H. VAN BOOM (eds.), *Preadviezen Vereniging voor Burgerlijk Recht: Privaatrechtelijke bescherming herijkt*, Zutphen, Paris, 2021, (11) 86 with reference to V.V. AGRAWAL, M. FERGUSON, L.B. TOKTAY and V.M. THOMAS, "Is Leasing Greener Than Selling?", *Management Science* 2012, vol. 58 issue 3, (523) 524.

187 A.P. BARQUET, J. SEIDEL, G. SELIGER and H. KOHL, "Sustainability Factors for PSS Business Models", *Procedia CIRP* 2016, vol. 47, (436) 436.

188 J. HOJNIK, "Ecological modernization through servitisation: EU regulatory support for sustainable product-service systems", *RECIEL* 2018, vol. 27, (162) 165–166; A. TUKKER, "Product services for a resource-efficient and circular economy – a review", *J.Clean.Prod.* 2015, vol. 97, (76) 85–87.

consumption of PSS that are cheaper than purchasing the product (so-called "rebound effects").[189]

37. European Commission acknowledges potential "rebound effects" of servitisation but wishes to promote servitised business models – Thus, although new "servitised" business models have the potential to facilitate the transition to a more circular economy, they can involve "rebound effects" as well. This was also acknowledged by the European Commission in The European Green Deal: "*New business models based on renting and sharing goods and services will play a role as long as they are truly sustainable and affordable.*"[190] Despite the possible rebound effects, the European Commission wishes to promote these business models. For example, the EC's New Circular Economy Action plan puts forward "*incentivising product-as-a-service or other models where producers keep the ownership of the product or the responsibility for its performance throughout its lifecycle*"[191] and the New Consumer Agenda claims that "*promoting new consumption concepts and behaviours, such as [...], new business models allowing consumers to buy a service rather than a good, [...]*"[192] can make an important contribution to the "*green transition.*"

38. Sustainability should be a key focus when promoting PSS – Given the questions often raised about the contribution of servitisation to the circular economy, claims about the ecological character of PSS should always be carefully assessed.[193] Accordingly, when promoting these business models sustainability should also always be considered. Servitisation should not be a goal in itself.

---

189 European Environment Agency, *EAA Report 2017/6 Circular by Design – Products in the Circular Economy*, Luxembourg, EU Publications Office, 2017, 18–19; European Environment Agency, *EAA Report 2016/2 Circular by design – Products in the circular economy*, Luxembourg, EU Publications Office, 2016, 15–16. H. Herring and R. Roy, "Technological innovation, energy efficient design, and the rebound effect", *Technovation* 2007, vol. 27 issue 4, (194) 194; E.G. Hertwich, "Consumption and the rebound effect: An industrial ecology perspective", *J. Ind. Ecol.* 2005, vol. 9 issue 1–2, (85) 85; B. Jansen, M. Van Lieshout, M. Scheppers and R. Servaes, *Producten worden diensten: een duurzame waardepropositie voor Vlaanderen*, Mechelen, OVAM, 2010, 108. See for a study of the 'rebound effects' of car-sharing in Flanders also: D.A. Chapman, J. Eyckmans and K. Van Acker, "Does Car-Sharing Reduce Car-Use? An Impact Evaluation of Car-Sharing in Flanders, Belgium", *Sustainability* 2020, vol. 12 issue 19, 8155.

190 EC, *The European Green Deal*, 11.12.2019, COM(2019) 640 final.

191 EC, *A new Circular Economy Action Plan For a cleaner and more competitive Europe*, 11.3.2020, COM(2020) 98 final 4.

192 EC, *New Consumer Agenda. Strenghtening consumer resilience for sustainable recovery*, 13.11.2020, COM(2020) 696 final 8.

193 B. Keirsbilck, E. Terryn and E. Van Gool, "Consumentenbescherming bij servitisation en product-dienst systemen (PDS)", *TPR* 2019, (817) 826–828; B. Keirsbilck and S. Rousseau, "The Marketing Stage: Fostering Sustainable Consumption Choices" in B. Keirsbilck and E. Terryn (eds.), *Consumer Protection in a Circular Economy*, Antwerp, Intersentia, 2019, (93) 113–115; V. Mak and E. Terryn, "Circular Economy and Consumer Protection: The Consumer as a Citizen and the Limits of Empowerment Through Consumer Law", *Journal of Consumer Policy* 2020, vol. 43, (227) 227 and 239.

There must be guarantees that PSS are indeed more sustainable than traditional sales contracts. The legal and contractual framework can and should also play a role here. Therefore, this book also aims to examine the extent to which contract terms and legal rules facilitate the sustainability of PSS and propose legal solutions on how their potential for sustainability could possibly be improved.

1.1.4. LIMITED REGULATORY FRAMEWORK FOR PSS CONTRACTS

39. Legal framework does not (yet) reflect shift from sales to services – The trend of servitisation and emergence of PSS contracts mean that many traditional consumer sales contracts are increasingly being complemented by services (product-oriented PSS) or even replaced by services (use-oriented and result-oriented PSS). However, businesses and consumers that make or want to make the shift from sales to services are confronted with legal challenges or uncertainties, in particular given the absence of an extensive and clear regulatory framework at both the EU and national level.[194]

1.1.4.1. Limited regulatory framework at the EU level

40. Limited rules on services at the EU level – The emergence of PSS contracts in the context of the circular and functional economy and the growing importance of the service sector in the EU can hardly be denied. Yet, legal literature and EU consumer and contract law remain predominantly focused on the classic linear model of selling products and transferring ownership.[195] Indeed, consumer sales legislation is largely harmonised and provides mandatory rules protecting consumers.[196] In contrast, there is only limited EU harmonisation in the area of service contracts and PSS contracts.[197]

---

194 J. Hojnik, "The Servitization of Industry: EU Law Implications and Challenges", *CML Rev.* 2016, vol. 53, (1575) 1575–1624.

195 T. Hartlief, "Koop als gids voor het contractenrecht?", *NJB* 2019/2493, (3007) 3007; E. Tjong Tjin Tai, "Services as product: commodification of contracts in European Private Law", Tisco Working Paper Series on Banking, Finance and Services, No. 07/2010, available at www.ssrn.com/link/tilburg-tisco-banking-financing.html, 3. See for the same observation in Germany: M. Schmidt-Kessel, "Verbracherschutz am Ende des Kaufrechtsparadigmas", *Verbraucher und Recht* 2023, (121) 121–123.

196 See: Directive 2019/771 of the European Parliament and of the Council of 20 May 2019 on certain aspects concerning contracts for the sale of goods, amending Regulation (EU) 2017/2394 and Directive 2009/22/EC, and repealing Directive 1999/44/EC, *OJ L* 136, 22.5.2019, 28–50 and its predecessor: Directive 1999/44 of the European Parliament and of the Council of 25 May 1999 on certain aspects on the sale of consumer goods and associated guarantees, *OJ L* 171, 7.7.1999, 12–16.

197 A. De Franceschi, "Ensuring Circularity in Service Contracts" in B. Keirsbilck, E. Terryn, J. Eyckmans, S. Rousseau and D. Voinot (eds.), *Servitization and circular economy: economic and legal challenges*, Antwerp, Intersentia, 2023, (167) 168.

First, there is the E-commerce Directive[198] but this directive only applies to information society services.[199] The Digital Services Act[200] ("DSA") builds on the E-commerce Directive by addressing new challenges online, particularly in relation to online intermediaries. Second, the Consumer Rights Directive[201] ("CRD"), the Unfair Contract Terms Directive[202] ("UCTD") and the Unfair Commercial Practices Directive[203] ("UCPD") provide relevant rules for service contracts but do not contain a general set of rules for service contracts.

In the early 1990s, an attempt was made to create uniform rules on liability for service providers,[204] but the proposal was ultimately shut down by the Commission due to fierce opposition.[205] In 2006, from a completely different angle, a legal framework for services in the internal market was created and the Services Directive[206] ("SD") saw the light of day. Nevertheless, Article 2 SD excludes important services from the scope of this Directive and, according to the preamble, it does in principle not affect the contractual relations between the service provider and the client.[207] Instead, it mainly focuses on prohibiting national measures restricting the provision of services and does not

---

198 Directive 2000/31 of the European Parliament and the Council of 8 June 2000 on certain legal aspects of information society services, in particular electronic commerce, in the Internal Market, *OJ L* 178, 17.7.2000, 1–16.

199 Art. 1 E-commerce Directive 2000/31.

200 Regulation (EU) 2022/2065 of the European Parliament and of the Council of 19 October 2022 on a Single Market For Digital Services and amending Directive 2000/31/EC (Digital Services Act), *OJ L* 277, 27.10.2022, 1–102.

201 Directive 2011/83 of the European Parliament and of the Council of 25 October 2011 on consumer rights, amending Council Directive 93/13/EEC and Directive 1999/44/EC of the European Parliament and of the Council and repealing Council Directive 85/577/EEC and Directive 97/7/EC of the European Parliament and of the Council, *OJ L* 304, 22.11.2011, 64–88.

202 Directive 93/13/EEC of 5 April 1993 on unfair terms in consumer contracts, *OJ L* 95, 21.4.1993, 29–34.

203 Directive 2005/29 of the European Parliament and the Council of 11 May 2005 concerning unfair business-to-consumer commercial practices in the internal market and amending Council Directive 84/450/EEC, Directives 97/7/EC, 98/27/EC and 2002/65/EC of the European Parliament and of the Council and Regulation (EC) No 2006/2004 of the European Parliament and of the Council, *OJ L* 149, 11.6.2005, 22–39.

204 EC, *Proposal for a Council Directive on the liability of suppliers of services*, 18.1.1991, COM(90) 482 final. See for a discussion of this proposal e.g. A. De Boeck, "Het Voorstel van E.G.-Richtlijn inzake de Aansprakelijkheid voor Gebrekkige Diensten", *RW* 1993–94, (585) 585–624.

205 M.B.M. Loos, "Service Contracts" in A.S. Hartkamp, M.W. Hesselink and E.H. Hondius (eds.), *Towards a European Civil Code*, Alphen aan den Rijn, Kluwer law international, 2011, (757) 758.

206 Directive 2006/123/EC of the European Parliament and of the Council of 12 December 2006 on services in the internal market, *OJ L* 376, 27.12.2006, 36–68. See generally on the Services Directive e.g. P. Delimatsis, "From Sachi to Uber: 60 Years of Services Liberalisation, Ten Years of the Services Directive in the EU", *YEL* 2018, (188) 188–250; V. Hatzopoulos, "Assessing the Services Directive", *CYELS* 2018, (215) 215–261.

207 Recital 90 SD.

provide substantive harmonisation.[208] As a result, except for the information requirements of Article 22 SD, it has only little impact on the contractual relationship between a service provider and a client.[209]

Finally, there is the Digital Content and Digital Services Directive[210] ("DCD"). This Directive is highly relevant to use-oriented and – to an even greater extent – result-oriented PSS.[211] After all, these business models are increasingly characterised by the fact that the delivered products are connected to the internet to achieve and optimise the promised result by transmitting data on usage, need for repair, etc.[212] Many additional services of PSS contract may therefore be qualified as a digital service within the meaning of this Directive[213] and as a result fall within its scope.[214] Nevertheless, it is important to point out that this Directive only applies to those parts of the contract that concern the digital content or the digital service.[215] Other services remain subject to national law on service contracts or (sector) specific Union law, where relevant.[216]

---

208 T. Heremans, *Professional services in the EU internal market: Quality regulation and self-regulation*, Oxford, Hart Publishing, 2012, 233–234.

209 M.B.M. Loos, "Service Contracts" in A.S. Hartkamp, M.W. Hesselink and E.H. Hondius (eds.), *Towards a European Civil Code*, Alphen aan den Rijn, Kluwer law international, 2011, (757) 758–759. See for a discussion of the impact of the Services Directive 2006/123 on contractual relations: M. Schauer, "Contract Law of the Services Directive", *ECLR* 2008, vol. 4, (1) 323–394.

210 Directive 2019/770 of the European Parliament and of the Council of 20 May 2019 on certain aspects concerning contracts for the supply of digital content and digital services, *OJ L* 136, 22.5.2019, 1–27. See for a more in-depth analysis of this Directive: I. Claeys and E. Terryn (eds.), *Nieuw recht inzake koop en digitale inhoud en diensten*, Antwerp, Intersentia, 2020, 426 p.

211 See regarding the implementation of this Directive in Belgium and the relevance for PSS contracts: H. Slachmuylders, "Belgian draft law for digital content and digital services – relevance for Product as a Service contracts", *CCM Blog* 10 January 2022, https://law.kuleuven.be/ccm/blog/?p=286.

212 H. Slachmuylders, B. Keirsbilck, E. Terryn and E. Van Gool, "Duurzaam ondernemen en het recht: circulaire bedrijfsmodellen – juridische knelpunten" in *De rol van de bedrijfsjurist in de duurzame ontwikkeling van de onderneming / Le rôle du juriste d'entreprise dans le développement durable: Jaarboek Dag van de bedrijfsjurist 2020/Annuaire Journée du juriste d'entreprise 2020*, Brussels, Larcier, 2021, (7) 28–29; B. Keirsbilck, E. Terryn and E. Van Gool, "Consumentenbescherming bij servitisation en product-dienst systemen (PDS)", *TPR* 2019, (817) 830, 838 and 839.

213 According to Art. 2(2) DCD, a "digital service" is defined as "*(a) a service that allows the consumer to create, process, store or access data in digital form; or (b) a service that allows the sharing of or any other interaction with data in digital form uploaded or created by the consumer or other users of that service*".

214 Art. 3(6) DCD. See also: R. Steennot, "Het toepassingsgebied van de nieuwe garantieregelingen voor goederen, digitale inhoud en digitale diensten", *DCCR* 2022, issue 135–136, (3) 20–21.

215 Art. 3(6) DCD.

216 Recital 33 DCD.

Figure 2. European legal framework of PSS

Consumer Rights Directive 2011/83 ("CRD")	**Unfair Commercial Practices Directive 2005/29 ("UCPD")**	**Unfair Contract Terms Directive 93/13 ("UCTD")**	**Services Directive 2006/123 ("SD")**	**Digital Services and Digital Content Directive 2019/770 ("DCD")**
Precontractual information requirements	Prohibition of unfair commercial practices	Prohibition of unfair terms	Limited scope: important services excluded	Conformity of digital services
Distance (service) contracts: right of withdrawal	E.g. misleading actions or omissions; aggressive commercial practices	Relevant for combating unbalanced terms in PSS contracts	Little impact on contractual relations between service provider and client	Liabilities and remedies for non-conformity
	Relevant for combating "greenwashing"		Pre-contractual information requirements	Rights and obligations in the event of termination of the contract
				! scope: only "digital services"!

In conclusion, although several EU directives apply to and have an impact on PSS contracts, there is not a general set of contract law rules for services at the EU level. Indeed, apart from these Directives, there is no detailed EU regulation on the quality,[217] liability[218] and safety[219] of services, on the formation of (product-) service contracts, on the legal guarantee for services that are not in conformity with the contract,[220] etc. The fact that no EU harmonisation in this area was ever achieved is mainly attributed to *"the complexity and diversity of services."*[221]

1.1.4.2. Limited regulatory framework at the national level

41. Also limited regulatory framework at the national level – Given the lack of comprehensive EU harmonisation, service contracts – also B2C – thus remain mainly subject to national default law and contractual freedom. However, also at the national level, and certainly in Belgium,

---

217 Only since 2012 does Regulation 1025/2012 of the European Parliament and of the Council of 25 October 2012 on European standardisation, amending Council Directives 89/686/EEC and 93/15/EEC and Directives 94/9/EC, 94/25/EC, 95/16/EC, 97/23/EC, 98/34/EC, 2004/22/EC, 2007/23/EC, 2009/23/EC and 2009/105/EC of the European Parliament and of the Council and repealing Council Decision 87/95/EEC and Decision No 1673/2006/EC of the European Parliament and of the Council, *OJ L* 316, 14.11.2012, 12–33 ("European Standardization Regulation") apply to goods as well as services. See also Art. 26 of the Services Directive 2006/123 containing several "soft" provisions on the policy on the "quality" of services. See also: EC, *European Standards for the 21st Century*, 1.6.2016, COM(2016) 358 final, which explicitly states that *"ICT and service standards should be key priorities of the European Standardisation System so that Europe can fully grasp the benefits of the digitisation and servicification of the economy"* (own emphasis).

218 It should be noted that damage caused by a defective product used in the provision of a service will be recoverable under Directive 85/374 of 25 July 1985 on the approximation of the laws, regulations and administrative provisions of the Member States concerning liability for defective products, *OJ L* 210, 7.8.1985, 29–33 ("Product Liability Directive"). However, the Product Liability Directive does not cover intangible goods, inadequate services, careless advice, etc.

219 Although Art. 2 of Directive 2001/95 of 3 December 2001 on general product safety, *OJ L* 11, 15.1.2002, 4–17 ("General Product Safety Directive") defines the reach of the product safety regime to include any product intended for consumer use or likely use "including in the context of providing a service", there is no counterpart to this Directive in the area of safety of services.

220 The 2-year legal guarantee for consumer goods and the remedies for non-conformity established by the SGD are not applicable to services.

221 See EC, *Explanatory Memorandum to the Commission Proposal for a European Parliament and Council Directive on the sale of consumer goods and associated guarantees*, 18.06.1996, COM(95) 520 final, 11: *"the complexity and diversity of services do not lend themselves to a simple extension to services of rules governing the sale of goods"*. See also EC, *Green Paper on Guarantees for Consumer Goods and After-Sales Services*, 15.11.1993, COM(93) 509 final, 7: *"in the context of this project and bearing in mind the subsidiarity principle, the Commission decided to concentrate on the questions raised by the sale of products, although it is aware that similar problems may arise in the domain of services. But because services are so heterogeneous, they may be difficult to treat in a global matter."*

there is only a patchwork of limited and often only default rules for service contracts.[222]

42. Regulatory framework for service contracts in Belgium – The old Belgian Civil Code 1804 (*oud Burgerlijk Wetboek, ancien Code Civil*, "old BCC") distinguishes between three service contracts. First, there is the contract for services (*aanneming, contrat d'entreprise*), which in the old BCC is called the hire of work (*huur van werk, louage d'ouvrage*).[223] Second, there is the deposit contract (*bewaargeving, dépôt*),[224] and finally there is the mandate contract[225] (*lastgeving, mandat*).[226] Under current Belgian law, the determining criterion to distinguish between these three types of contracts is the object (*voorwerp, l'objet*), i.e. the subject matter of the service contract in question. If the object is a juridical act, it will be a mandate contract. If, on the other hand, the object constitutes a material act, the contract will qualify as a contract for services or a deposit contract. Here, the deposit contract can be seen as a *lex specialis* of the contract for services that deals with the temporary deposit and preservation of another's movable tangible property. Besides these three named service contracts regulated in the old Civil Code, many other (unnamed) service contracts exist. As will be illustrated throughout this book, the rules of the contract for services (*aanneming, contrat d'entreprise*) are the most relevant in the context of PSS contracts. However, the contract for services is only briefly regulated and most of these provisions do not apply to non-construction contracts.[227]

43. Regulatory framework for rental contracts for movables in Belgium – In many cases, PSS contracts will (at least partly) be qualified as a rental contract for movables. The Belgian Civil Code does not provide any specific provisions for the rental contract for movables. To fill the gap, settled case law applies the general provisions applicable to rental contracts for immovables[228] by analogy, unless they are incompatible with the nature of the rental contract for movables.[229] While these provisions contain useful default

---

222 H. Slachmuylders, B. Keirsbilck, E. Terryn and E. Van Gool, "Duurzaam ondernemen en het recht: circulaire bedrijfsmodellen – juridische knelpunten" in *De rol van de bedrijfsjurist in de duurzame ontwikkeling van de onderneming / Le rôle du juriste d'entreprise dans le développement durable: Jaarboek Dag van de bedrijfsjurist 2020/Annuaire Journée du juriste d'entreprise 2020*, Brussels, Larcier, 2021, (7) 27–29.

223 Art. 1787–1799 old BCC.

224 Art. 1915–1954*quater* old BCC.

225 Art. 1984–2010 old BCC.

226 A. Verbeke and B. Tilleman, "(Re-)codificatie van het contractenrecht? Illustraties aan de hand van kooprecht, aanneming en onbenoemde contracten" in *Tweehonderd jaar Burgerlijk Wetboek. Bicentenaire du Code Civil*, Brussels, Belgisch Federaal Parlement/Parlement Fédéral de Belgique, 2004, (64) 76.

227 See *infra* no. 377 and the references cited there.

228 Art. 1714–1762*bis* old BCC.

229 See *infra* no. 387 and the references cited there.

rules on the basic obligations of both parties, they are non-mandatory and will only apply in case the parties did not include a specific contractual arrangement in the PSS contract.[230]

44. Reform of the Belgian Civil Code – In the future, a new legal framework for service contracts and rental contracts will apply in Belgium. The "new" Belgian Civil Code (*Burgerlijk Wetboek, Code Civil,* hereinafter "BCC") was introduced by the Law of 13 April 2019 and entered into force on 1 November 2020. This new BCC will consist of 10 books, which are adopted in different stages.[231] Specifically for contract law, the Law of 28 April 2022 containing Book 5 "Obligations" of the Civil Code was published in the Belgian Official Gazette (*Belgisch Staatsblad, Moniteur belge*) on 1 July 2022 and entered into force on 1 January 2023. This Book contains the general law of obligations. On 16 April 2024, a draft law inserting Book 7 "special contracts" into the Civil Code[232] was published. This draft law seeks to introduce a new modernised legal framework, aiming to simplify and restructure the legal rules applicable to special contracts as well as improving the coherence and consistency between the various special contracts.

45. Regulatory framework for service contracts in the Netherlands – In the Netherlands, Title 7.7 of the New Dutch Civil Code 1992 (*Nieuw Burgerlijk Wetboek,* "DCC") provides a general chapter[233] on service contracts.[234] According to Tjong Tjin Tai, this makes it quite unique as it is the only Civil Code in the EU that has such a general chapter.[235] Most of the rules in the general section of Title 7.7 are default law.[236] Exceptions are the client's right to terminate the contract,[237] which cannot be deviated from if the client is a consumer, and the fact that a consumer does not have to pay a compensation if he terminates the contract.[238, 239]

230 *Ibid.*

231 See: https://justitie.belgium.be/nl/bwcc.

232 Explanatory Memorandum, Parliamentary Papers Chamber of Representatives 2023–24, no. 55–3973/001.

233 I.e. not limited to a specific type of service contracts.

234 Art. 7:400–7:413 DCC.

235 T.F.E. Tjong Tjin Tai, "Service Contracts in the Dutch Civil Code" in R. Zimmerman (ed.), *Service Contracts*, Tübingen, Mohr Siebeck, 2010, (167) 167.

236 These rules include *i.a.* a general duty of care (Art. 7:401 DCC), specific information and warning duties (Art. 7:402–403 DCC), a duty to follow/refuse instructions (Art. 7:402 DCC), a duty to provide account (7:403(2) DCC), rules on payment of salary and costs (Art. 7:405–7:406 DCC), rules on termination (Art. 7:408–7:410 DCC), and calculation of the price in case of early termination (Art. 7:411 DCC).

237 Art. 7:408(1) DCC. According to Art. 7:408(3) DCC, the consumer does not have to pay a compensation if he terminates the contract.

238 Art. 7:408(3) DCC. In this case, Art. 7:411 DCC provides a special rule for the calculation of the service provider's salary, which is also mandatory law.

239 Art. 7:413 DCC.

In addition to the general rules applicable to all service contracts, Title 7.7 also contains rules for some specific contracts, namely mandate,[240] brokerage,[241] commercial agency[242] and medical treatment.[243] Some contracts are excluded from the scope of Title 7.7 and (with one exception) regulated elsewhere,[244] namely the labour contract,[245] the contract for works,[246] the storage contract,[247] the publishing contract and the transportation contract. This approach is criticised, as some authors argue that these exclusions are mostly dogmatically incorrect. According to this view, the contract for works and storage contract would particularly benefit from being qualified as a *species* of the contract for services.[248]

46. Regulatory framework for rental contracts for movables in the Netherlands – Under Dutch law, the general provisions applicable to all rental contracts apply to the rental of for movables.[249] The remaining provisions of title 7.4 of the Dutch Civil Code only apply to rental contracts for residential spaces and rental contracts for retail spaces. The general provisions of the rental contract provide a useful framework for the basic obligations of the parties. However, just like under Belgian law, they are mostly non-mandatory, so the contracting parties can deviate from them and flesh out their own contractual regime.

1.1.4.3. Legal challenges arising from the limited regulatory framework of PSS

47. Legal challenges of shift from sales to services – The limited regulatory framework at both the EU and national level gives rise to legal uncertainty and legal challenges for businesses and consumers wishing to engage in new circular business models and PSS.

---

240 Art. 7:414–7:424 DCC.
241 Art. 7:425–427 DCC.
242 Art. 7:428–7:445 DCC.
243 Art. 7:446–7:468 DCC.
244 See: Art. 7:400(1) DCC. The exception is the publishing contract, which is not regulated at all in the DCC.
245 See Title 7.10 DCC (Art. 7:610-Art. 7:686a DCC).
246 Art. 7:550–7:569 DCC.
247 Art. 7:600–7:609 DCC.
248 See e.g. T.F.E. Tjong Tjin Tai, *Asser 7-IV Bijzondere Overeenkomsten - Opdracht, incl. de geneeskundige behandelingsovereenkomst en de reisovereenkomst*, Deventer, Wolters Kluwer, 2022, no. 35; M.A.M.C. Van den Berg and S. van Gulijk, *Mr. C. Assers Handleiding tot de beoefening van het Nederlands Burgerlijk Recht. 7. Bijzondere overeenkomsten. Deel VI. Aanneming van werk*, Deventer, Wolters Kluwer, 2022, no. 26; M.B.M. Loos, "Consumentenbescherming bij de koop van onroerende zaken en aanneming van werk: een nog altijd onevenwichtig en onvoldoende doordacht wetsvoorstel ", *NTBR* 2002/8, (356) 364; S.C.J.J. Kortmann, "De overeenkomst van opdracht, de lastgeving en de geneeskundige behandelingsovereenkomst", *WPNR* 1990, vol. 5982, (740) 742–743; C.J.H. Brunner, "De opdracht (Ontwerp boek 7, titel 7)", *WPNR* 1974, vol. 5285, (783), 784–785.
249 Art. 7:201–7:230 DCC.

A first challenge arises from the necessity for businesses and consumers to navigate a **dual framework of both EU and national law.** While several EU (consumer law) directives apply to and have an impact on PSS contracts (e.g. by providing a control of unfair terms, granting a right of withdrawal, etc.), there is not a general set of rules applicable to PSS contracts at the EU level. This means that PSS contracts are for the most part regulated by national contract laws, which can vary significantly between Member States.

Another challenge is situated at the national level, namely the **question of contractual qualification**. Indeed, to determine which default rules apply to PSS contracts, a contractual qualification exercise is necessary. Since PSS contracts are often complex and contain elements of several named contracts (most often the rental contract for movables and/or the contract for services), this will not always prove to be an easy task. Nevertheless, the contractual qualification of a PSS contract can make a big difference, for instance in terms of the possibility to (unilaterally) terminate the contract.

Consumers are also confronted with the **lack of a mandatory legal framework** for contracts for services and rental contracts for movables, especially regarding non-conformity of the products/services and the corresponding remedies. This means that many contractual rights and obligations are left to the contractual freedom of the parties, which may result in an unfavourable situation for the consumer.

Finally, due to the unclear and dispersed regulatory framework for services and rental contracts for movables, as well as the often complex nature of PSS contracts, businesses face **difficulties to draft balanced contracts** that are compliant with all relevant legal rules while at the same time providing an adequate and sufficiently comprehensive framework for these new business models.

1.2. METHODOLOGY

"The pessimist sees difficulty in every opportunity.
The optimist sees the opportunity in every difficulty"
– Winston Churchill

1.2.1 SCIENTIFIC OBJECTIVES AND RESEARCH QUESTIONS

48. Research objectives and main research question – As mentioned, in absence of a clear regulatory framework, users feel uncertain and hesitant to engage in new, circular PSS contracts. The starting point of this research is that the acceptability of PSS for users and their willingness to engage in new, circular

PSS contracts can be increased if the contractual challenges are identified and addressed adequately. As a result, this research aims at (i) defining and classifying different types of PSS contracts (ii) describing and (iii) evaluating the relevant contractual rules addressing PSS contracts, and if necessary, (iv) proposing legal solutions. These objectives lead to the main research question: "*How are PSS contracts currently regulated under EU and national consumer contract law and, if necessary, how could the current regulatory framework be improved?*"

49. Sub-research objectives and sub-research questions – The central research question is examined based on four building blocks: (methodology see *infra* 1.2.3.2).

(i) First, it is necessary to develop a conceptual framework that offers grip throughout the rest of the research. The first sub-research objective is to describe and explain what PSS contracts are, to identify the various types of PSS contracts and explain how different business models fit in these categories. To fulfil this first research objective, the research answers the following sub-research question: "*What are PSS contracts, which types of PSS contracts exist, and which business models fit within these concepts?*" **(SRQ1: descriptive + classifying)**

(ii) Second, this research aims to bring together and describe the relevant EU rules as well as the national contract laws applicable to PSS contracts. More specifically, a selection of general terms and conditions is examined to identify the main contractual rights and obligations of the users and suppliers of PSS contracts. This analysis is the starting point for an in-depth analysis of the existing regulatory framework in the EU and selected Member States. This second sub-research objective translates into the second sub-research question: "*To what extent and how are PSS contracts currently regulated under EU law and the national consumer contract laws of selected Member States?*" **(SRQ2: descriptive + comparative)**.

(iii) The outputs of SRQ2 serve as the basis for an evaluative study of the current regulatory framework of PSS contracts using the evaluation criteria of legal certainty; consistency and coherence; fairness of balance of contractual rights and obligations of suppliers and users; and sustainability. Based on this evaluation, the research identifies the strengths and weaknesses of the current regulatory framework. As such, the evaluation answers the third sub-research question: "*What are the strengths and weaknesses of the current regulatory framework of PSS contracts in the EU and selected Member States?*" **(SRQ3: evaluative)**

(iv) The fourth research objective is to tackle the weaknesses identified in the evaluation conducted by SRQ3 and propose possible legal solutions to facilitate a more circular and servitised economy. A wide range of possible solutions such as voluntary schemes, standard contracts, insurance, standardisation of services, the involvement of a platform, mandatory legislation, etc. are considered against the normative criteria set out in RQ3. This answers the final sub-research question: "*How could the current regulatory framework of PSS contracts be improved?*" **(SRQ4: normative)**

1.2.2. RELEVANCE

1.2.2.1. Academic and theoretical relevance

50. ACADEMIC AND THEORETICAL RELEVANCE – First and foremost, providing an answer to these research questions provides value from an academic and theoretical perspective by contributing to the scientific knowledge on the legal framework of circular business models. A detailed analysis and identification of all legal issues in general terms and conditions of PSS contracts was lacking in legal literature and there was an urgent need for a precise identification and analysis of the relevant legal rules applicable to PSS contracts in the EU and selected Member States. This was especially true for an analysis of the applicability of the existing contractual liability regimes to PSS contracts. Second, this research is also relevant because it also contributes to the scientific knowledge of the legal framework applicable to (consumer) (service) contracts in general. Finally, the relevance of this book lies in the fact that it researches the challenges of circular PSS contracts in the field of law against the background of (business-)economics through interaction and collaboration with researchers from CEDON (*Centrum voor Economie en Duurzaam Ondernemen*[250]). This answers the call by several influential legal scholars to integrate insights from behavioural economics to support the transition towards more sustainable consumption patterns.[251]

1.2.2.2. Societal and economic relevance

51. SOCIETAL AND ECONOMIC RELEVANCE – Second, this research also entails a great societal and economic relevance because it aims to provide specific, measurable, and practical results that will benefit (i) policy makers, (ii) consumers, (iii) businesses, and (iv) the society at large.

---

250 Research Centre for Economics and Corporate Sustainability. See: https://feb.kuleuven.be/research/sustainability.

251 See e.g. J. HOJNIK, M. RUZZIER and M. KONEČNIK RUZZIER, "Transition towards Sustainability: Adoption of Eco-Products among Consumers", *Sustainability* 2019, vol. 11 issue 16, (4308) who state: "*transition to sustainability is a long-term challenge which should also actively engage consumers, as consumption causes environmental stress*"; See also: H.-W. MICKLITZ, "Squaring the Circle? Reconciling Consumer Law and the Circular Economy", *EuCML* 2019, vol. 6, (229) 228. See also: J.J.A. BRASPENNING and P. VERBRUGGEN, "Gedragswetenschappelijke inzichten in het consumentenrecht", *TvC* 2017–6, (242).

(i) For several years, the concept of the circular economy is high on the agenda of **policymakers** at the regional, national and EU level. This has resulted in a wide variety of policy papers, guidelines, and policy packages. Still, policymakers are searching for additional input on how to overcome legal and economic barriers for the private sector to deploy more circular business models.
(ii) **Consumers** are the stakeholders that are most directly affected by the topic of this research that precisely focuses on consumer protection of consumers engaging in PSS and circular business models.
(iii) **Businesses** are also key actors as they decide on the business models and PSS they offer to consumers. The results of this research will be of great interest to businesses to better understand the motives of consumers and the legal barriers for viable and sustainable PSS.
(iv) Finally, the benefit for **the society at large** is illustrated by the fact that this research aims to contribute to tackling some of the greatest contemporary societal challenges. Indeed, the subject of the research and its objectives link directly to several of the United Nations' Sustainable Development Goals (SDGs), most notably SDG 12 on responsible consumption and production.[252]

1.2.3. RESEARCH METHODS

1.2.3.1. General methodology

52. Doctrinal legal research, including comparative law – The research methodology consisted of doctrinal legal research, including comparative law. First, the choice for doctrinal legal research reflects the academic training of the author and fits the nature of the subject matter and the goals of the research. Second, comparative legal research was essential to achieve useful insights because of the lack of a clear EU legal framework on PSS and the importance of national law. Additionally, as existing studies on PSS were mainly conducted from the field of (behavioural) economics, insights from this field necessarily had an impact on this research ("limited interdisciplinary" research). Since this book is the result of a C2 project[253] in collaboration with the KU Leuven Center for Economics and Corporate Sustainability (CEDON), there has been interaction and collaboration with researchers from CEDON.

---

252 See www.un.org/sustainabledevelopment/sustainable-development-goals/.

253 C2 Project C24M/19/003: Contractual rights and liabilities in circular business models. This has also led to the publication of a book on servitisation and circular economy. See: B. Keirsbilck, E. Terryn, J. Eyckmans, S. Rousseau, D. Voinot (eds.), "Servitization and circular economy: economic and legal challenges", Antwerp, Intersentia, 2023, 217 p.

53. Comparative method – The comparative research was performed using the "functional method".[254] A few reasons underpin this choice: (i) the functional method is designed for micro-comparisons across different legal systems,[255] which this research pursues; (ii) this method allows to take into account non-legal societal factors such as political, social, and economic insights.[256] Given the interdisciplinary nature of this research, this is an important advantage; and (iii) it allows for a deep analysis of the chosen system based on extensive source materials,[257] which is necessary given the complexity of the rules governing services.

54. Selected legal systems – The following criteria were used for the selection of the legal systems:

(i) The chosen legal systems must have legislative or practical experience with the circular economy and/or servitisation.
(ii) The available source material must be diverse, sufficiently scientific, and accessible.
(iii) The chosen legal systems must have a sufficient connection with each other but should not be too similar.

Based on these criteria, **Belgium** and **the Netherlands** were selected for the comparative analysis. First, many Dutch firms are pioneering in PSS and the country is very focused on the circular economy in terms of policy and academic focus.[258] Also in Belgium there has been a great deal of attention for the transition to a more circular economy[259] and Belgian businesses are also increasingly offering new, circular PSS.[260] Second, there is a myriad of available source material. Finally, both legal systems are sufficiently linked but still contain significant differences. For example, while the Belgian law on

---

254 See in general on the functional method: R. Michaels, "The Functional Method of Comparative Law" in M. Reimann and R. Zimmermann (eds.), *The Oxford handbook of Comparative Law*, Oxford, Oxford University Press, 2019, (346) 346–389.

255 W. Pintens, *Inleiding tot de rechtsvergelijking*, Leuven, Universitaire Pers Leuven, 1998, 64.

256 G. Danneman, "Comparative Law: Study of Similarities or Differences?" in M. Reimann and R. Zimmerman (eds.), *The Oxford Handbook of Comparative Law*, Oxford, Oxford University Press, 2006, (383) 404; W. Devroe, *Rechtsvergelijking in een context van Europeanisering en globalisering*, Leuven, Acco, 2010, 50.

257 K. Zweigert and H. Kötz, *An Introduction to Comparative Law*, Oxford, Oxford University Press, 1998, 40.

258 Government of the Netherlands, "A circular economy in the Netherlands by 2050", 2016, available at www.rijksoverheid.nl/onderwerpen/circulaire-economie/nederland-circulair-in-2050.

259 See https://vlaanderen-circulair.be/nl/doeners-in-vlaanderen for an overview of local initiatives implementing the ideas of a more circular economy.

260 See: K. Peeters and M.C. Marghem, "Samen de Economie doen draaien dankzij de circulaire economie in ons land", 2016, available at www.health.belgium.be/nl/samen-de-economie-doen-draaien-dankzij-de-circulaire-economie-ons-land.

the contract for services is only briefly regulated (see the rules on *aanneming, contract d'entreprise*), the Dutch rules on the contract for services (*opdracht*) are regulated somewhat more extensively. Also, contrary to Belgian law, similar sales rules apply to both B2B and B2C contracts in the Netherlands.

55. European Principles – To combat the potential risk that the selection of two legal systems (BE, NL) was too narrow to find adequate European answers to the challenges of PSS, and to make policy recommendations for the EU legislator, this book has also considered earlier comparative work, namely the Principles of European Law on Service Contracts[261] ("**PEL SC**") and the Draft Common Frame of Reference[262] ("**DCFR**") when proposing legal solutions. Both instruments have their origins in efforts of European legal Scholars who have worked on principles common to the national legal orders of the European Union to supplement the rules at the European and national level.[263] The (non-binding) PEL SC were drafted between 1999 and 2006 by the Tilburg Team of the Study Group on a European Civil Code (SGECC). The DCFR sets out principles of European contract law drawn up by a study group composed of leading academics dealing with contract law within the EU, led by the German professor C. von Bar. In Book IV. C. of the DCFR, a slightly modified version of the PEL SC was implemented. Although the PEL SC and the DCFR will not become a European Civil Code, their academic value can hardly be underestimated as hundreds of legal scholars from all over the EU have worked on it. There is no doubt that these (non-binding) European Principles can have a great influence. National legislatures in several European countries have already started to modernise their national contract laws and many of these national codifications or reforms are inspired by the PECL ("Principles of European Contract Law") and the DCFR.[264]

1.2.3.2. Methodology per research question

A. First research question: conceptual framework (descriptive + classifying)

56. Literature review – The first step of this research was to carry out a literature review to describe the concept of PSS contracts, identify the various types of PSS contracts and explain how different business models and practices

261 M. Barendrecht, C. Jansen, M. Loos, A. Pinna, R. Cascão and S. Van Gulijk (eds.), *Principles of European Law: Service Contracts (PEL SC)*, Munich, Sellier, 2006, 1034 p.

262 C. Von Bar, E. Clive, H. Schulte-Nölke, H. Beale, J. Herre, J. Huet, M. Storme, S. Swann, P. Varul, A. Veneziano and F. Zoll (eds.), *Principles, Definitions and Model Rules of European Private Law. Draft Common Frame of Reference (DCFR) (Outline edition)*, Munich, Sellier European Law Publishers, 2009, 643 p.

263 I. Claeys and T. Tanghe, *Nieuw Algemeen Contractenrecht*, Antwerp, Intersentia, 2023, 22. For an interesting working tool, see J. Basedow, K.J. Hopt and R. Zimmermann (eds.), *The Max Planck Encyclopedia of European Private Law*, Oxford, Oxford University Press, 2012, 1949 p.

264 I. Claeys and T. Tanghe, *Nieuw Algemeen Contractenrecht*, Antwerp, Intersentia, 2023, 24–25.

fit in these categories. The literature review consisted of an in-depth analysis of national and international documents, scientific journals, legislation, case law and legal doctrine to select the most relevant information for a comprehensive but concise summary of the concept. The final purpose of this research question was to formulate a selection of "working definitions" and "use-cases" that will offer a grip throughout the rest of this research.

B. Second research question: current regulatory framework of PSS (descriptive + comparative)

57. Analysis of terms and conditions – For answering the second research question, the research selected 20 general terms and conditions of PSS suppliers established in Belgium and the Netherlands that are offering contracts to consumers (see Annex A. Analysed terms and conditions). The business models of these PSS suppliers were discussed above.[265] The collection of these general terms and conditions, contracts and other relevant legal documents was done through contacts with the network of stakeholders of the C2 project[266] and available general terms and conditions on the internet. Economic literature on the product/sector dimension of PSS and the inputs and requests of the network of stakeholders were also considered while making this selection. The following terms and conditions were selected:

(i) In the **household appliances** sector: Blue Movement, Bundles and Papillon.
(ii) In the **consumer electronics** sector: Fairphone Easy, Swapphone, Grover and Gerrard Street (Repeat).
(iii) In the **clothing** sector: Mudjeans, Dressr and Lena.
(iv) In the **furniture** sector: Live Light.
(v) In the **heat, air ventilation and cooling** ("HAVC") sector: Saman heat pumps.
(vi) In the **home printer** sector: HP Instant Ink.
(vii) In the **(urban) mobility** sector: Swapfiets, Villo, Cambio, Lime and Dott.
(viii) Additionally, insights from the analysis of two B2B model contracts will also be discussed were relevant, namely Agoria's[267] **"Efficiency-as-a-Service" model contract**[268] and Circle Economy's[269] **Circular service**

---

265 See *supra* no. 19.
266 See Annex B for a list of the stakeholders involved in the C2 project.
267 Agoria unites nearly 2,000 technology companies from the manufacturing, digital and telecoms sectors, 70 per cent of which are SMEs. This makes it the largest party within the Federation of Belgian Enterprises (FEB). See: www.agoria.be/nl/over-ons.
268 www.agoria.be/en/climate-environment-energy/circular-economy/new-business-models/a-standardized-contract-to-help-you-develop-your-efficiency-as-a-service-offering.
269 Circle Economy is a think tank with an international team of experts based in Amsterdam. They aim to empower businesses, cities and nations with practical and scalable solutions to put the circular economy into action. See: www.circle-economy.com/about.

contract template[270] drafted within the framework of the "circular phone" project.

This research used these 20 general terms and conditions as a starting point to assess the main contractual rights and obligations of the contracting parties against the background of the applicable EU and national contract laws.

58. Analysis of existing regulatory framework – Using the legal analysis of these 20 general terms and conditions as a starting point, this research described the existing regulatory framework of PSS contracts in the EU and selected Member States. Thus, the relevant EU rules (*i.a.* the SD, the UCTD, the CRD, the SGD, the DCD), including their case law and implementation in the selected Member States, as well as the relevant Belgian and Dutch contract law rules (*i.a.* on the contract for services and the rental contract for movables), including their case law and doctrine, were analysed. Instead of opting for an instrument-by-instrument analysis and description, a practical approach was chosen in which the different legal rules at EU and national level (and their interplay) were discussed in an integrated manner.

59. Reality check through interactions with researchers from CEDON – During the course of the C2 project underlying this research, there were multiple interactions with researchers from CEDON through informal meetings, workshops, seminars, and (international) conferences. The aim of these interactions was to achieve a degree of "cross-fertilisation" between the two disciplines of law and economics, and not to fall into the trap of disregarding important interconnected issues by focussing only on the legal piece of the puzzle. Thus, input and suggestions from a legal point of view were provided for the drafting of the consumer surveys that identified the behavioural and economic barriers to the acceptability of PSS. At the same time, the results of these consumer surveys were considered and used in the legal analysis, for example for evaluating the (perceived) fairness of certain contractual terms and for developing balanced default rules.

C. Third research question: evaluation of current regulatory framework of PSS (evaluative)

60. Evaluation based on four criteria – The purpose of the third research question was to evaluate whether PSS contracts are adequately addressed by the current regulatory framework. This evaluation was done based on four

270 Circle Economy, "The Circular Phone, Legal, operational and financial solutions to unlock the potential of the 'Fairphone-as-a-service' model", 31 December 2017, available at www.circle-economy.com/resources/the-circular-phone.

evaluative criteria: legal certainty; consistency and coherence; fairness of balance of contractual rights and obligations of consumers and PSS suppliers; and sustainability.

61. Legal certainty – According to the Court of Justice of the European Union ("CJEU"), the concept of legal certainty is a "fundamental principle" of EU law and means that "*rules should be clear and precise, so that individuals may be able to ascertain unequivocally what their rights and obligations are and may take steps accordingly.*"[271] In addition to this definition by the CJEU, there is a myriad of different definitions available in academic and policy-oriented literature.[272] For example, the report accompanying the Legal Certainty Index states that "*legal certainty implies that laws should be at least accessible, intelligible and stable and have predictable effects.*"[273] So, to meet the requirements of legal certainty, this research assumed that consumers must be able to predict what rules will be applicable and what their rights and obligations will be when engaging in PSS contracts. Therefore, possible proposed legal solutions were developed to provide more certainty concerning the rights and remedies for consumers who opt to subscribe to a PSS instead of buying a product.

62. Consistency and coherence – The second evaluative criterion used in this research was that of consistency and coherence of the law. Consistency simply means non-contradiction, whereas coherence refers to "*a set of propositions which, taken together, 'makes sense' in its entirety.*"[274] These criteria were used to evaluate the consistency and coherence between different EU legal instruments, between EU and national rules, and between national rules themselves. Similarly, the proposed legal solutions were designed to logically fit together without any contradictions. Additionally, in view of consistency and coherence, this research avoided any further fragmentation of private law in general and (consumer) contract law in particular as much as possible. Therefore, when drafting new rules for service contracts, the current regulatory framework was adhered to as much as possible, so the different (consumer) (service) contracts fit well together.

---

271 CJEU, Judgment of 14 April 2005, C-110/03, *Belgium v Commission*, ECLI:EU:C:2005:223, §30.

272 See for an overview: M. Fenwick, M. Siems and S. Wrbka, "The State of the Art and Shifting Meaning of Legal Certainty" in M. Fenwick, M. Siems and S. Wrbka (eds.), *The Shifting Meaning of Legal Certainty in Comparative and Transnational Law*, Oxford, Hart, 2017, (1) 1–27.

273 B. Deffains and C. Kessidijan, *Index of Legal Certainty, Report for the Civil Law Initiative*, Civil Law Initiative, 2015, 9, www.fondation-droitcontinental.org/en/index-legal-certainty/.

274 N. MacCormick, *Rhetoric and The Rule of Law*, Oxford, Oxford University Press, 2005, 189, 190 and 206; N. MacCormick, *Legal Reasoning*, Oxford, Clarendon, 1978, 152 and 195.

63. Fair balance of contractual rights and obligations of consumers and PSS suppliers – Whether business models based on servitisation and PSS will be successful in contributing to the green transition depends not only on how they are designed and how accessible they are to consumers.[275] The applicable regulatory framework is also of fundamental importance.[276] In (consumer) contract law, the right balance must be found between the rights and obligations of PSS suppliers and PSS users and between mandatory and default law.[277] Indeed, although consumers should be actively engaged in the progress of developing a more circular economy, this development requires actions taken on both sides of the market. Therefore, there must be a fair balance between consumer protection and consumer interests on the one hand and the interests of suppliers and the possibility to come to easy business transactions on the other hand. In most cases the consumer is still the weaker party in comparison to the supplier, who determines the price, quality and availability of goods, services, and business models. As a result, to strike a fair balance, the proposed solutions for an adequate legal framework aimed to reduce this asymmetry between suppliers and consumers as much as possible. At the same time, many PSS business models are still in their infant stages. Consequently, overly strict consumer law rules should not stifle innovation in these new sectors and the willingness of PSS suppliers to offer these business models.

64. Sustainability – Finally, the nature of the circular economy, servitisation and PSS contracts rendered it necessary to pay specific attention to sustainability. Indeed, the goal of this research was to develop a legal framework that promotes circular PSS business models that are truly sustainable.[278] Sustainable development is commonly defined as "*development that meets the needs of the present without compromising the ability of future generations to meet their own needs*"[279] and plays an important role in the EU treaties[280] and the legal systems

---

[275] C.M.D.S. Pavillon, "Dwingend consumentenrecht en de overgang naar een circulaire economie: het mes snijdt aan twee kanten", *Ars Aequi* 2022, (576) 579.

[276] T. Hartlief, "De boer en de consument als helden in nieuw privaatrecht", *NJB* 2022/91.

[277] A.M. Schmidt, "Diensten in de circulaire economie en enkele mogelijke privaatrechtelijke belemmeringen", *M en R* 2017, (812) 817.

[278] See also: Y. Al Salman and R. Claassen, "From Ownership to Access. A Philosophical Perspective on the Rise of Access-Based Consumption", *Ars Aequi* 2018, (566) 567, where sustainability as a normative criterion to evaluate what is at stake in the choice between ownership and access.

[279] UN, *Report of the World Commission on Environment and Development: Our Common Future*, 1987, 16; M. Geissdoerfer, P. Savaget, N.M.P. Bocken and E.J. Hultink, "The Circular Economy – A new sustainability paradigm?", *J.Clean.Prod.* 2017, (757) 758.

[280] See Art. 3(3) TEU, Art. 11 TFEU and Art. 191 TFEU.

of Member States.[281, 282] The concept of sustainability has various aspects that are often described by the 3 P's that should be balanced with each other in a harmonious way: People, Planet and Profit.[283] However, balancing all three aspects in one business model is unfortunately not always possible. This research has focused mainly on the circular potential of PSS business models and therefore on their potential for *environmental* sustainability. Nevertheless, this does not mean that the other aspects of sustainability were not considered. The interests of consumers (People) and businesses (Profit) were also taken into account.[284]

Indeed, several actors can and should be involved in furthering (environmental) sustainability objectives. Businesses have an important responsibility to take sustainability into account when carrying out their economic activities.[285] This does not necessarily have to go against their bottom line. Indeed, pursuing societal value and sustainability does not stand in the way of creating economic value and *vice versa*. On the contrary, in a good business model, both components reinforce each other.[286] Businesses can benefit from consumer's increasing "willingness to pay" for environmentally friendly products or services. Jean Tirole gives a great example in this regard: a coffee shop chain does not sacrifice profit by offering fair trade coffee if it responds to a demand from its customers who are prepared to pay a little bit more for a fair and qualitative cup of coffee.[287] Circular PSS business models should therefore

281 See for Belgium e.g. the general interest in sustainability expressed in various places in the new Book 3 "Goods" of the Belgian Civil Code (Art. 3.39, 3.50, 3.67, 3.133–3.134, and Art. 3.43(1) BCC). See for a discussion of these provisions and the sustainability interest in Book 3 BCC: D. Gruyaert, "Privaat en publiek goederenrecht en duurzaamheid" in A. Van Hoe and G. Croisant (eds.), *Droit et durabilité / Recht en duurzaamheid*, Antwerp, Intersentia, 2022, (495) 497 *et seq.*; V. Sagaert, *Goederenrecht*, Mechelen, Wolters Kluwer, 2021, 145 *et seq.*

282 See for a convincing argument why the United Nations *Brundtland* definition is very suited as a starting point for legal research on private law and sustainability: B. Akkermans, B. Hoops, E. van der Sijde and B. Verheye, "Duurzaam privaatrecht voor de 21ste eeuw: het leven van een rechtswetenschappelijke subdiscipline", *TPR* 2023, (199) 206, no. 7.

283 Also called the triple bottom line, see: J. Elkington, *Cannibals with Forks.The Triple Bottom Line of 21st Century Business*, Oxford, Capstone Publishing Ltd, 1997, 402 p. and The Economist, "Triple Bottom Line", 17 November 2009, available at www.economist.com/news/2009/11/17/triple-bottom-line.

284 C.M.D.S. Pavillon, "Herijking van consumentencontractenrecht: duurzaamheid als nieuw ijkpunt?" in C.M.D.S. Pavillon and W.H. van Boom (eds.), *Preadviezen Vereniging voor Burgerlijk Recht: Privaatrechtelijke bescherming herijkt*, Zutphen, Paris, 2021, (11) 45.

285 Compare also with: United Nations Human Rights, "Guiding Principles on Business and Human Rights: Implementing the United Nations 'Protect, Respect and Remedy' Framework", 2011, available at www.ohchr.org/sites/default/files/Documents/Publications/GuidingPrinciplesBusinessHR_EN.pdf. ("Ruggie Principles") where the responsibility of businesses to respect human rights is one of the three pillars.

286 R. Houben, "Maatschappelijk verantwoord ondernemen", *RW* 2023, (803) 811.

287 J. Tirole, *Economics for the common good*, Princeton and Oxford, Princeton University Press, 2017, 188–189.

be designed to both support sustainability and meet consumer wants and needs, while also generating profits for the PSS supplier. This requires a legal framework that enables and encourages businesses to offer sustainable business models while also protecting their bottom line. For example, this may include the availability of adequate remedies for when consumers do not fulfil their obligations under the PSS contract.

Consumers can also play a role in furthering the sustainability agenda.[288] Indeed, by changing their consumption patterns, including the use and consumption of more sustainable goods which at the same time require more sustainable production processes, consumers can have a significant impact on environmental sustainability.[289] However, although consumers often consider the ecological nature of goods or services to be important, it must be noted that consumer protection and sustainability often conflict.[290] Although arguably one of the most telling examples of this tension concerns the impact of the right of withdrawal and free returns,[291] a few examples specific to PSS contracts can also be mentioned. Indeed, while these new business models can give rise to environmental gains, there is the risk that a multitude of subscriptions cause new forms of consumer over-indebtedness. Additionally, there are possible risks and disadvantages for consumers if they no longer own the products they use. As a result, the legal framework for PSS contracts and proposed legal solutions aim to not only strike a balance between consumer protection and business

---

288 P. McDonagh, S. Dobscha and A. Prothero, "Sustainable Consumption and Production: Challenges for Transformative Consumer Research" in D.G. Mick, S. Pettigrew, C. Pechmann and J.L. Ozanne (eds.), *Transformative Consumer Research for Personal and Collective Well-Being*, London, Routledge, 2012, (267) 272. See however critical regarding the idea that consumers *alone* can solve the environmental and climate crisis: E. Terryn, "Circulaire economie" in E.H. Hondius and V. Mak (eds.), *Handboek Consumentenrecht*, Vijfde druk, Zutphen, Paris, 2020, (53) 54.

289 P. McDonagh, S. Dobscha and A. Prothero, "Sustainable Consumption and Production: Challenges for Transformative Consumer Research" in D.G. Mick, S. Pettigrew, C. Pechmann and J.L. Ozanne (eds.), *Transformative Consumer Research for Personal and Collective Well-Being*, London, Routledge, 2012, (267) 272. See also: D. Ivanova, J. Barrett, D. Wiedenhofer, B. Macura, M. Callaghan and F. Creutzig, "Quantifying the potential for climate change mitigation of consumption options", *Environ. Res. Lett.* 2020, vol. 15 issue 9, (1) 1. This article points out that household consumption amounts to around two-thirds of global GHG emissions and that changes in consumption patterns to low-carbon alternatives therefore present a great and urgently required potential for emission reductions. See in the same sense also the sixth Intergovernmental Panel on Climate Change ("IPCC") assessment report of 2022: IPCC, *Climate Change 2022: Mitigation of Climate Change*, www.ipcc.ch/report/ar6/wg3/downloads/report/IPCC_AR6_WGIII_FullReport.pdf, 2022, 17–39.

290 C.M.D.S. Pavillon, "Herijking van consumentencontractenrecht: duurzaamheid als nieuw ijkpunt?" in C.M.D.S. Pavillon and W.H. van Boom (eds.), *Preadviezen Vereniging voor Burgerlijk Recht: Privaatrechtelijke bescherming herijkt*, Zutphen, Paris, 2021, (11) 27–30; K. Tonner, "Consumer Protection and Environmental Protection: Contradictions and Suggested Steps Towards Integration", *Journal of Consumer Policy* 2000, (63) 63; T. Wilhelmsson, "Consumer Law and the Environment: From Consumer to Citizen", *Journal of Consumer Policy* 1998, (45) 45.

291 See *infra* no. 192.

interests and between business interests and environmental sustainability, but also between consumer protection and environmental sustainability.[292]

Still, it is necessary to highlight that consumer law (and by extension private law) alone cannot solve all issues regarding the transition towards a more sustainable society.[293] Market based solutions and self-regulation are also needed, as well as additional public law initiatives such as tax law measures, subsidies and additional instruments of environmental law and waste law.[294]

D. Fourth research question: proposing solutions (normative)

65. Proposing legal solutions – The purpose of the fourth research question was to propose legal solutions to resolve the legal challenges to facilitating a more circular and servitised economy described above.[295] The normative criteria that were used for developing these solutions are the same as the evaluative criteria used in research question 3 (i.e. legal certainty, consistency and coherence, fair balance, and sustainability).[296] Additionally, the following elements were considered when developing these legal solutions:

(i) First, the diversity of business models for PSS and other service contracts makes it more difficult to work out a set of rights, obligations and remedies that guarantees a high level of consumer protection for all types of PSS. This means that it is perfectly possible that multiple solutions (e.g. default rules on conformity at the national level, standardisation of services, model clauses) should be adopted together to achieve the desired results.

(ii) Second, when opting for the adoption of a minimum set of mandatory rules, it is important to keep in mind that this could risk stifling

292 See in this regard for example: V. Mak and E. Lujinovic, "Towards a Circular Economy in EU Consumer Markets – Legal Possibilities and Legal Challenges and the Dutch Example", *EuCML* 2019, (4) 5; E. Terryn, "A Right to Repair? Towards Sustainable Remedies in Consumer Law", *ERPL* 2019, (851) 851.

293 B. Keirsbilck and E. Terryn, "Duurzaamheid en consumentenrecht" in A. Van Hoe and G. Croisant (eds.), *Droit et durabilité / Recht en duurzaamheid*, Antwerp, Intersentia, 2022, (433) 439–440; E. Terryn and E. Van Gool, "Kunnen we e-commerce vergroenen door het consumentencontractenrecht te herzien?", *Tijdschrift voor Consumentenrecht en handelspraktijken* 2021, vol. 1, (15) 16 and 27; E. Van Gool and A. Michel, "The New Consumer Sales Directive 2019/771 and Sustainable Consumption", *EuCML* 2021, vol. 10 issue 4, (136) 139; E. Terryn, "Circulaire economie" in E.H. Hondius and V. Mak (eds.), *Handboek Consumentenrecht*, Vijfde druk, Zutphen, Paris, 2020, (53) 54; V. Mak and E. Terryn, "Circular Economy and Consumer Protection: The Consumer as a Citizen and the Limits of Empowerment Through Consumer Law", *Journal of Consumer Policy* 2020, vol. 43, (227) 229.

294 Compare also with critical voices on the role of private law in achieving public objectives: I.S.J. Houben, "Autonomie in het contractenrecht: de bescherming van de ondernemer", *Ars Aequi* 2017, vol. 7–8, (600) 604–605; T. Hartlief, "Autonomie en solidariteit. Beweging in het verbintenissenrecht", *WPNR* 2004, vol. 6564, (106) 107.

295 See *supra* no. 47.

296 See *supra* no. 61–64.

innovation. After all, the (B2C) market for (sustainable) PSS is still developing. Default rules are more flexible in this sense, while at the same time still offering some consumer protection as they can be taken into account when assessing the (un)legality of deviating contractual clauses.[297] Thus, mandatory rules should only be adopted when absolutely necessary and lawmakers must leave enough room for dynamism of the PSS market.

(iii) Finally, when drafting and adopting legal rules or model clauses for PSS contracts, a balance must not only be found between the rights and obligations of businesses and consumers, but the sustainability aspect should always be very explicitly included in the consideration and choice for a particular solution.[298, 299] Thus, the problematic mismatch between the "green" marketing of PSS and the sometimes minimal or even negative impact on the environment of PSS business models[300] can be mitigated as much as possible.[301]

Based on these normative criteria and elements to be taken into account, the solutions proposed in this research are situated at three levels: (i) proposing an improved legislative framework at the national level; (ii) proposing legislative changes and policy recommendations at the EU level; and (iii) drafting model clauses for PSS contracts that provide a solid framework for the rights and obligations of consumers and businesses that pass the unfairness test, while also taking into account sustainability interests.

66. Legislative changes at the national level – Building on the descriptive and evaluative conclusions following from the first three research questions,[302] this book proposes **a new regulatory framework at the national level (Belgium).** This regulatory framework was developed to balance the interests of service suppliers and consumers, while also considering (environmental) sustainability interests. The main principles of this new regulatory framework

---

297 CJEU, Judgment of 14 March 2013, C-415/11, *Mohamed Aziz*, ECLI:EU:C:2013:164.

298 In this sense, it is interesting to note that sustainability requirements are increasingly entering private law. See e.g. Art. 1833 of the French Civil Code: "*Toute société doit avoir un objet licite et être constituée dans l'intérêt commun des associés. La société est gérée dans son intérêt social, en prenant en considération les enjeux sociaux et environnementaux de son activité*" (own emphasis). Art. 509 of the new Chinese Civil Code is also interesting in this sense: "*Each party shall fully perform its own obligations as agreed. The parties shall abide by the principle of good faith, and perform obligations of notification, assistance, confidentiality, etc. in accordance with the nature and purpose of the contract and the usage of trade. In performing a contract, the parties shall avoid wasting resources, polluting the environment, and compromising ecology*" (own emphasis).

299 B. Keirsbilck, E. Terryn and E. Van Gool, "Consumentenbescherming bij servitisation en product-dienst systemen (PDS)", *TPR* 2019, (817) 885–886.

300 See *supra* no. 34–37.

301 As already indicated *supra* no. 38.

302 S. Taekema, "Theoretical and Normative Frameworks for Legal Research: Putting Theory into Practice", *Law and Method* 2018, (1) 12–13 and 15.

can be summarised as follows. First, it aims to minimise qualification problems as much as possible through internal homogenisation, for example by adopting a uniform notion of (non-)conformity for all (consumer) contracts, inspired by the provisions of EU sales law and the DCFR. Second, it aims to boost legal certainty and consumer protection by proposing more appropriate and modern default rules on the main obligation of the service provider/PSS supplier (i.e. performing the service and making the product available), as well as remedies for breach of contract. Also here, inspiration is drawn from EU sales law and the DCFR. Third, the potential role of standardisation of services (both at the national level[303] and at EU level) is highlighted as a tool to operationalise the default rules containing the abstract notions of (non-)conformity and (non-)performance. The proposed national legal framework was developed throughout the five years of the PhD research underlying this book. Upon publication of the Draft Law of 16 April 2024 inserting Book 7 "special contracts" into the Civil Code[304] during the end-phase of this research, these proposals were further finetuned and cross-checked with the published Draft Law.

67. Legislative changes at the EU level – The book also proposes **policy recommendations and proposals for legislative changes at the EU level**. Policy recommendations include, among others, (i) adopting measures encouraging European standardisation organisations to develop service standards for PSS contracts, as well as providing incentives for PSS suppliers to adopt these service standards; (ii) setting up labelling schemes (e.g. similar to energy labelling schemes) with harmonised quality criteria (e.g. in terms of fairness, sustainability, etc.) for PSS standard contracts; and (iii) taking measures to facilitate the development and adoption of standard contracts for PSS. Proposals for legislative changes include, amongst others, (i) addressing ambiguities regarding the distinction between the notions "contracts for services", "contracts in respect of goods" and "sales contracts" in the context of the consequences of exercising the right of withdrawal; (ii) considering to adopt a harmonised legal framework at the EU level for services and/or PSS, either by means of a general directive on conformity of services (where inspiration can be drawn from the SGD and DCD), or a specific directive for "package services" or "bundles of services" (where inspiration can be drawn from the Package Travel Directive); and (iii) streamlining the existing EU consumer acquis with the other proposed changes, for example including a prohibition in the UCPD blacklist for practices such as displaying a quality label or stamp of approval for their terms and conditions that they have not actually received.

303 At the national level, the first steps for circular economy standards have already been taken. See the British Standard 8001; http://ecostandard.org/first-standard-on-circular-economy.

304 Explanatory Memorandum, *Parliamentary Papers* Chamber of Representatives 2023–24, no. 55-3973/001.

68. Model clauses for PSS contracts – Finally, **model clauses for PSS contracts** were drafted with the aim of promoting the adoption of (truly sustainable) PSS business models.[305] These model clauses contribute to the adoption of PSS business models on three fronts. On the business side, as mentioned above, businesses often face increased transaction costs if they wish to offer product-as-a-service contracts due to need to draft more complex contracts. By using these model clauses, businesses can save time, effort and resources compared to if they would create customised clauses from scratch. On the consumer side, these model clauses were drafted with the aim of protecting the interests of consumers, which are often the weaker parties to these contracts. Thus, these model clauses are compliant with mandatory rules regarding business-to-consumer relationships, both under EU, Belgian and Dutch law. This does not only benefit consumers, as non-compliance with these mandatory rules can have far-reaching consequences for businesses, such as partial nullity of the unfair clause in question without the possibility to rely on national default rules. On the sustainability side, these model clauses also take into account the sustainability and circularity challenges and opportunities for PSS, for example by including clauses that combat the risk of moral hazard, clauses and recitals dealing with contractual interpretation and environmental sustainability, and clauses containing explicit circular guarantees. These model clauses can act as the low-hanging fruit to create an adequate legal regime for PSS contracts. A potential next step for the (EU or national) legislator could be to endorse similar model clauses or standard contracts in order to create a "presumption of fairness" if PSS suppliers use these terms and conditions for their PSS contracts.

1.2.4. SCOPE

69. Focus on consumer law and contract law – As the topic of servitisation and PSS touches on various legal branches and covers a myriad of different topics, it is necessary to carve out the scope of the research. This book mainly focuses on consumer law and contract law, as these legal branches must be analysed together to determine the rights and obligations of the parties under a PSS contract. In these areas, the relevant EU rules, and their implementation in selected Member States (BE, NL) are analysed as well as the national default law of these selected Member States. Moreover, to get the full picture of the rights and obligations of the parties, insights from other complementary and interdependent legal branches are also incorporated. For example, a limited

[305] See also the research report for the *Steunpunt Circulaire Economie* which translates the findings of this doctoral research into model clauses that can be freely used by businesses: C. Borucki, H. Slachmuylders, B. Keirsbilck, D. Gruyaert and E. Terryn, *Model clauses for Product-as-a-Service (PaaS) contracts*, CE Center. Circular Economy Policy Research Center, 2022–23, 95 p.

analysis of property law and insolvency law is needed for clauses that allow the PSS supplier to retain the ownership of the product (for example in insolvency proceedings), such as retention of title clauses or a building right.

70. Excluded legal branches – Several legal branches are excluded from the scope of this book. First, questions of product liability law, product safety law and tort law will not be addressed. This is because these issues mainly position themselves within the extracontractual sphere and thus would deviate from the central theme of the book. Additionally, a research project covering these legal branches already exists at KU Leuven.[306] Second, questions of competition law, data protection law, and intellectual property law will also not be examined.[307] After all, these are all distinct legal fields which are complex and extensive. Given the depth of research and analysis required for each of these areas, incorporating them would distract from the main focus of this book. At the same time, some of these questions are also already being addressed by other authorsat KU Leuven.[308] Finally, although greenwashing of servitisation and PSS is certainly an important issue, this book will not delve into Unfair Commercial Practices law. This is justified because the problem of greenwashing is not limited to servitisation or PSS and there is already plenty of research available on this topic.[309]

---

306 See the PhD thesis of dr. Elias Van Gool on "Product Liability in a More Circular Economy: A Study of Liability for Alternative Methods of Distributing and Producing Consumer Goods", defended at KU Leuven on 9 September 2024.

307 See for an overview of competition law issues (including tying and bundling, and vertical and horizontal integration) and the data dimension of servitisation: J. Hojnik, "The Servitization of Industry: EU Law Implications and Challenges", *CML Rev.* 2016, vol. 53, (1575) 1590–1600. See also for an intellectual property law perspective of the movement away from ownership and servitisation (for example due to the use of licenses instead of a transfer of ownership for digital goods, digital content and IoT products): A. Perzanowski and J. Schultz, *The End of Ownership: Personal Property in the Digital Economy*, Cambridge, MIT Press, 2016, 249 p.

308 See for competition law: L. Van Acker, F. Bostoen and W. Devroe, "Servitization and competition law" in B. Keirsbilck, E. Terryn, J. Eyckmans, S. Rousseau and D. Voinot (eds.), *Servitization and circular economy: economic and legal challenges*, Antwerp, Intersentia, 2023, (69) 69–90; F. Bostoen and W. Devroe, "From sales to subscriptions in the car sector: Competition law implications of servitisation and the refusal to sell to consumers", *European Competition Law Review* 2018, vol. 39, (411) 411–419. See also the PhD thesis of dr. Liesbet Van Acker on *Vertical Sustainability Agreements: An Assessment of the Limits and Possibilities for Sustainable Supply Chains under EU Competition Law.* See for competition law and data protection law, the PhD thesis of dr. Christof Koolen: C. Koolen, *Innovation and consumer protection in internet of things ecosystems. Protecting end users at the crossroads between consumer, competition, and data*, PhD thesis KU Leuven, 2023, 637 p.

309 See for example: A. Michel, *Premature Obsolescence: In Search of an Improved Legal Framework*, Cambridge, Intersentia, 2023, 240–321. See also on this topic: A. De Franceschi, "The Sustainability of Consumer and Market Law: Green Claims, Greenwashing and the Right to Repair", *EuCML* 2023, (45) 45–48; E. Van Gool, "'Climate-washing': B2C communicatie in de klimaatcrisis beoordeeld in het licht van oneerlijke handelspraktijken", *DCCR* 2023, vol. 138, (3) 3–60; J.E.S. Hamster, "Vijftig tinten groen – de vele civiele kleuren van greenwashing", *NTBR* 2022/49, C.M.D.S. Pavillon and R. Koolhoven, "'Verhuurder

71. Main focus on use-oriented and result-oriented PSS in B2C markets – The book thus mainly focuses on consumer law and contract law. However, feasibility constraints make it necessary to further define its scope. First, although most circular business models are first applied in a B2B context, this book focuses on the legal barriers of PSS offered to consumers, precisely because PSS are now also on the rise in a B2C context. Second, although reference is made to product-oriented PSS when interesting comparisons can be made, this book mainly focuses on developing legal solutions for use-oriented and result-oriented PSS. This is because the new characteristics of these business models, including the lack of transfer of ownership and a different allocation of responsibility, present more challenges to consumers than product-oriented PSS, which still qualify as sales contracts. Additionally, use-oriented and result-oriented PSS are deemed more suitable for the circular economy than product-oriented PSS.[310]

72. Focus on movable goods – Finally, this book will only analyse questions regarding PSS for movable (non-food) goods. Questions relating to circular business models in the real estate sector[311] and the transition to a circular economy in the food sector[312] are therefore not addressed. This choice is

doucht elders ook' Over misleidende milieuclaims door deelplatformen en individuele remedies in driehoeksverhoudingen", *SEW* 2022, (120) 120–133; E. Terryn, "Consumenten correct informeren over ecologische duurzaamheid: een uitdaging en een must?", *Tijdschrift voor Consumentenrecht en Handelspraktijken* 2021, vol. 5, (256) 256–259; C. Borucki, "Als de vos de passie preekt… Corporate greenwashing als misleidende handelspraktijk", *DCCR* 2018, (31) 31–55.

310 C. Kühl, B. Tjahjono, M. Bourlakis and E. Aktas, "Implementation of Circular Economy principles in PSS operations", *Procedia CIRP* 2018, vol. 73, (124) 125.

311 See on circular business models in the real estate sector the research project by Kato De Schepper on "The unitary principle in property law: an enemy to the circular economy?" (*"Het eenheidsbeginsel in het goederenrecht: een vijand voor de circulaire economie?"*). See also for **Belgium** e.g. V. Sagaert and K. De Schepper, "Property Law and Circular Economy" in B. Keirsbilck, E. Terryn, J. Eyckmans, S. Rousseau and D. Voinot (eds.), *Servitization and circular economy: economic and legal challenges*, Antwerp, Intersentia, 2023, (181) 181–209; V. Sagaert, "De zakenrechtelijke motoren van een circulaire vastgoedeconomie: een SWOT-analyse", *TPR* 2021, (1543) 1543–1558; B. Verheye, "Toekomst van de circulaire vastgoedeconomie", *TPR* 2019, (107) 107–196. For **the Netherlands**, see the research project by Ellen Maathuis at the Radboud University Nijmegen (www.ru.nl/personen/maathuis-e). See also e.g. E.C.A. Vermeulen, *Circulair bouwen: knelpunten en oplossingen in het goederenrecht: van eigendom naar product-as-a-service*, Nijmegen, Ars Aequi Libri, 2020, 110 p.; R. Koolhoven, "Gebouwen en hun bestanddelen in een meer circulair goederenrecht" in C.W. Backes, M.N. Boeve, R. Koolhoven and D.J. Versteeg (eds.), *Circulair bouwen. Preadviezen voor de vereniging van bouwrecht 46*, Den Haag, Stichting Instituut voor Bouwrecht, 2018, (6) 6–54; M.A.B. Chao-Duivis, "Privaatrechtelijke aspecten van de circulaire economie in het bijzonder circulair bouwen (Deel I)", *TBR* 2017/139, (915) 915–921.

312 See e.g. M. Hamam, G. Chinnici, G. Di Vita, G. Pappalardo, B. Pecorino, G. Maesano and M. D'Amico, "Circular Economy Models in Agro-Food Systems: A Review", *Sustainability* 2021, vol. 13, 3453. https://doi.org/10.3390/su13063453. See also: V. Vermeyen, L. Alaerts, S. Van Schoubroeck, S. Van Passel and K. Van Acker, *Circular economy*

mainly inspired by the fact that property law plays a very large role in circular business models in the real estate sector, which would lead the book too far away from consumer law and contract law. Additionally, different rules apply to the contracts of sale and rental of movables compared to the sale and rental of immovable property, as the SGD does not apply to sales contracts for immovable goods. The exclusion of food law from the scope, in turn, is justified because this area of law is characterised by highly technical rules, which would distract too much attention from the contract law narrative.

1.3. STRUCTURE

"In our rich consumers' civilization we spin cocoons around ourselves and get possessed by our possessions."
– Max Lerner[313]

73. PSS UNDER GENERAL CONTRACT LAW – After this introduction of the topic and the description of the research design, **Chapter 2** starts by setting out some basic principles of general contract law and applying them to PSS contracts. This provides the necessary context, concepts and legal building blocks that allow the following chapters to delve deeper in the contractual rights and liabilities of the PSS user and the PSS supplier.

First, the formation of the PSS contract is discussed (section 2.2). This section analyses the requirements for the validity of the PSS contract, such as consent, capacity, object and cause, tailored to PSS contracts. It also discusses the process of formation of the PSS contract, such as offer and acceptance, pre-contractual information, and the conclusion of the contract through representation, in the specific content of PSS contracts.

Second, this chapter looks at the widespread use of standard contracts and general terms and conditions for PSS (section 2.3). This section explores the role, function and risks of using standard contracts for PSS contracts. It also discusses the requirements for incorporation/enforceability of the terms and conditions into the PSS contract. Furthermore, it deals with the (un)fairness of the terms and conditions, mainly through an analysis of the Unfair Contract Terms Directive ("UCTD") and its national implementation in Belgian and the Netherlands.

indicators for the food system, CE Center publication NO. 20, CE Center Circular Economy. Policy Research Center, October 2021, 67 p.

313 Quote from the column "What shall I save" in the New York Post (10 September 1952), reprinted in M. LERNER, *The Unfinished Country*, New York, Simon and Schuster, 1959, 35.

Third, the possibility and conditions of the PSS user-consumer's right of withdrawal is examined (section 2.4). Here, there is a particular focus on the difference between the right of withdrawal for product-oriented PSS (which qualify as sales contracts for the purposes of the CRD) and use-oriented and result-oriented PSS (which qualify as service contracts for the purposes of the CRD).

The fourth section deals with interpretation of the PSS contract (section 2.5). This section examines the principles of contractual interpretation, such as the basic premise that the court must seek out the common intent of the parties rather than the literal meaning of the words, and other interpretation rules. It also considers the impact of sustainability on the interpretation of the contract, for example through an explicit mention of circular economy objectives in the preambles of the PSS contract.

Fifth, this chapter introduces the concept of liability for breach of the PSS contract (section 2.6). This section defines the notion of breach of contract and identifies the different natures of obligations (obligation of means, result, guarantee) and the impact of these classifications on contractual liability. Furthermore, it introduces the concepts and application of *force majeure* and hardship/changed circumstances in relation to PSS contracts. Finally, it sets out a general overview of the remedies available to the contracting parties in case one of the parties is in breach of the PSS contract.

Finally, this chapter contains an analysis of the rules on the duration of the PSS contract (section 2.7). This section compares fixed term and open-ended PSS contracts in terms of their consequences. It also examines the possibility for the PSS user to terminate the contract early for both duration types, as well as the possibility of concluding fixed term contracts with an automatic extension/renewal.

74. Contractual qualification of three main types of PSS – The book continues in **Chapter 3** with the contractual qualification of the three main types of PSS.

The first section of this chapter considers some general aspects of contractual qualification (section 3.2). These include the conventional qualification of the PSS contract by the parties, the issue of mixed contracts, and it explores the concept of unnamed contracts.

Second, it discusses the legal nature and applicable rules of product-oriented PSS contracts (section 3.3). The fact that the ownership of a product is transferred leads to a qualification as a sales contract. Additionally, it discusses the legal qualification of additional services, product-oriented PSS as mixed contracts and considers the specific applicable rules if product-oriented PSS contracts (partly) relate to goods with digital elements, such as software of smart products.

Third, the qualification of use-oriented PSS is examined (section 3.4). Here, different situations are conceivable, such as a PSS contract where the PSS supplier grants the PSS user a mere right of use over a product against payment of a price, a short-term and occasional service, or use-oriented PSS grafted onto a leasing model. It also explores the consequences of mixed use-oriented PSS contracts and addresses the specific issues of digital services that are part of use-oriented PSS contracts, such as usage monitoring. Depending on the business model, use-oriented PSS will generally be qualified as a rental contract and/or a contract for services.

Fourth, the legal nature and consequences of result-oriented PSS contracts are investigated (section 3.5). The fact that the PSS supplier promises to deliver a specific functional result to the PSS user leads to a qualification as a service contract. Also here, the legal implications and consequences of digital services that are part of the result-oriented PSS are considered.

75. OBLIGATION OF THE PSS SUPPLIER TO ENSURE THE AVAILABILITY OF THE PRODUCT/SERVICE – **Chapter 4** deals with the main obligation of the PSS supplier, namely the obligation to ensure the availability of the product and/or service. Building on the insights of Chapter 3 (qualification), this is done through an analysis of the legal framework applicable to the three main types of PSS. Moreover, as the content of this obligation will also depend on what is stipulated in the PSS contract, this chapter also takes into account the 20 selected general terms and conditions of PSS suppliers in Belgium and the Netherlands against the background of these applicable legal rules. Finally, where the control regime of unfair contract terms poses limits to the contractual freedom of the PSS supplier, this is also highlighted and discussed.

The obligation to ensure the availability of the product/service breaks down into two sub aspects.

First, the PSS supplier must make the product and/or the service available to the PSS user (section 4.2). Here, the rules and modalities for delivering the product (e.g, in terms of time and place) or supplying the service are discussed. Additionally, the legal implications of transferring or not transferring the ownership of the product, as well as the differences regarding the transfer of the risk are examined.

Second, the product/service must be in conformity with the PSS contract (section 4.3). This section examines the legal standards and requirements for ensuring that the product/service conforms to the PSS contract in terms of quality, quantity, description, and performance. It also discusses the liability of the PSS supplier for non-conformity, including the remedies available to the PSS user.

Finally, the chapter evaluates the legal framework on the obligation to make the product/service available and conformity and proposes legal solutions, including modernising national contract law, standardisation of services and EU harmonisation (section 4.4), as well as the use of balanced standard contracts and model clauses (section 4.5).

76. Obligation of the PSS user to pay the price of the PSS – The main obligation of the PSS user is discussed in **Chapter 5**, namely paying the price of the PSS.

First, the chapter examines the obligation to pay the price and the different forms this can take (e.g. monthly fees, pay-per-use fee, mandatory insurance, etc.) (section 5.2). This is done through an analysis of the legal framework applicable to the three types of PSS contracts and the various general terms and conditions of the selected PSS contracts. Additionally, this section deals with the transparency requirement of pricing clauses and the remedies available to the PSS supplier if the PSS user does not pay the price.

Second, this chapter deals with the practice and validity and limits of price change clauses (section 5.3). Thus, this section describes the concept of price change clauses in long-term PSS contracts and sets out the limits to the freedom of the parties to include such clauses in their contract. Additionally, real-life examples of price change clauses in the selected PSS contracts are analysed, and model clauses compliant with both Belgian, Dutch and EU law are proposed.

The third section of this chapter deals with set off clauses (i.e. clauses dealing with the mode of extinguishment where reciprocal obligations are extinguished to the extent of the smaller amount or quantity) (section 5.4). Here, the concept of set off and set off clauses, as well as the limits to these clauses is discussed. Also here, the book proposes some model clauses PSS suppliers can use in their contracts.

77. Additional services – **Chapter 6** deals with the additional services often offered by the PSS supplier in addition to its obligation to make the product/service available.

First, the installation obligation of the PSS supplier is discussed (section 6.2). Thus, the legal basis of the installation obligation for the three main types of PSS and the consequences of a defective installation are discussed and evaluated. Moreover, this section also examines the content of real-life contract terms on the installation of the product. This section concludes by proposing legal solutions, including legislative changes and model clauses for the installation obligation of the PSS supplier.

Second, the chapter deals with the PSS supplier's obligation to maintain and repair/replace the product (section 6.3). This section starts with a discussion of the legal basis of the maintenance and repair/replacement obligation for the three main types of PSS. As the legal provisions are mostly default law, these are complemented by an analysis of clauses in real-life PSS contracts. As such, the question as to whether the PSS user can perform repairs and/or maintenance is also discussed. Finally, this section evaluates the current legal framework of the PSS supplier's maintenance, repair and replacement obligations and proposes legal solutions (including model clauses).

The third section of this chapter deals with updates (section 6.4). This includes the obligation of the PSS supplier to supply the updates (including the role of updates in terms of conformity) and the obligation of the PSS user to install the supplied updates.

Finally, this chapter addresses the possibility to include innovation obligations for the PSS supplier in the PSS contract (section 6.5).

78. Ownership, moral hazard and end of contract/end-of-life of the product – The consequences arising from the fact that consumers do not longer own the products they use within the framework of use-oriented or result-oriented PSS contracts are discussed in **Chapter 7**.

The first section deals with the question of how the PSS supplier can protect its right of ownership of the product (section 7.2). Thus, the problem of accession and how this can be (contractually) combated (e.g. by means of retention of title clauses or by establishing a right of *superficies*) is discussed. Other risks of loss of ownership (and possible solutions to these risks) are also analysed, such as the risk of acquisitive prescription of the movable product.

The second section deals with the risk of moral hazard and how this risk can be combated in the PSS contract (section 7.3). The main solution for combating the risk of moral hazard is the PSS user's obligation to take care of the product. This obligation is analysed under the rules applicable to use-oriented and result-oriented PSS and compared with product-oriented PSS where such an obligation is absent. Then, the section discusses contractual limits to moving the product. This can either be a prohibition to move the product without express consent of the PSS supplier, or a prohibition to cross borders with the product. Finally, this section explores the incentives for proper use of the product for PSS, such as rewards if no maintenance, repair or replacement of the product is needed within a certain period of time.

The third section of this chapter examines the legal issues related to the end of the PSS contract and end-of-life stage of the product (section 7.4). Thus, the obligation of the PSS user to return the product is discussed under the different types of PSS. It compares the absence of such an obligation in product-oriented PSS contracts with the restitution obligation present in use-oriented and result-oriented PSS contracts. Then, the mirror obligation, namely the PSS supplier's obligation to take back the product is addressed. After that, this section analyses the concept and implications of circular guarantees for PSS. Finally, this section sets out model clauses for these obligations and circular guarantees and proposes some possible legislative changes for use-oriented and result-oriented PSS.

79. General conclusion and policy recommendations – **Chapter 8**, the final chapter of this book, concludes and gives an overview of the various proposed policy recommendations.from this book.

2. PSS UNDER GENERAL CONTRACT LAW

2.1. INTRODUCTION

80. PSS UNDER GENERAL CONTRACT LAW – This chapter sets out some basic principles of general contract law and applies them to PSS contracts. This provides the necessary context, concepts and legal building blocks that allow the following chapters to delve deeper in the contractual rights and liabilities of the PSS user and the PSS supplier.

First, the formation of the PSS contract is discussed. Section 2.2 analyses the requirements for the validity of the PSS contract, such as consent, capacity, object and cause. It also discusses the process of formation of the PSS contract, such as offer and acceptance, pre-contractual information, and the conclusion of the contract through representation.

Second, this chapter looks at the widespread use of standard contracts and general terms and conditions for PSS. Section 2.3 explores the role, function, and risks of using standard contracts for PSS contracts, as well as the requirements for incorporation/enforceability of the terms and conditions into the PSS contract. Furthermore, it deals with the (un)fairness of the terms and conditions, mainly through an analysis of the Unfair Contract Terms Directive ("UCTD") and its national implementation in Belgian and the Netherlands.

The PSS user-consumer's right of withdrawal is examined in section 2.4. Here, there is a particular focus on the difference between the right of withdrawal for product-oriented PSS (which qualify as sales contracts for the purposes of the CRD) and use-oriented and result-oriented PSS (which qualify as service contracts for the purposes of the CRD).

The fourth section deals with interpretation of the PSS contract. Section 2.5 examines the principles of contractual interpretation, such as the basic premise that the court must seek out the common intent of the parties rather than the literal meaning of the words, and other interpretation rules. It also considers the impact of sustainability on the interpretation of the contract, for example through an explicit mention of circular economy objectives in the preambles of the PSS contract.

Fifth, this chapter introduces the concept of liability for breach of the PSS contract. Section 2.6 defines the notion of breach of contract and identifies the different natures of obligations (obligation of means, result, guarantee) and the impact of these classifications on contractual liability. Furthermore, it introduces the concepts and application of *force majeure* and hardship/changed circumstances in relation to PSS contracts. Finally, it sets out a general overview of the remedies available to the contracting parties in case one of the parties is in breach of the PSS contract.

Finally, this chapter contains an analysis of the rules on the duration of the PSS contract Section 2.7 compares fixed term and open-ended PSS contracts in terms of their consequences. It also examines the possibility for the PSS user to terminate the contract early for both duration types, as well as the possibility of concluding fixed term contracts with an automatic extension/renewal.

2.2. FORMATION OF THE PSS CONTRACT

"It is not philanthropy but self-interested behavior to create economic value by creating societal value."
– Michael E. Porter & Mark R. Kramer[314]

2.2.1. FORMATION OF THE PSS CONTRACT

81. Formation of the PSS contract – Before the parties are bound by the provisions in the PSS contract, the contract must be validly concluded. This section therefore deals with the formation of the PSS contract. First, the requirements for the validity of the PSS contract are discussed (section 2.2.1.1.). Then, this section looks at the pre-contractual information requirements containing the information the PSS supplier must disclose to the PSS user (section 2.2.1.2.). Third, the contract formation process, which is based on the concepts of offer and acceptance, is described (section 2.2.1.3.). Fourth, this section briefly looks at situations where the PSS supplier is represented by a third party, such as a retailer (section 2.2.1.4.). Finally, the consequences of a validly concluded PSS contract, i.e. the binding force of the contract, are highlighted (section 2.2.1.5.).

2.2.1.1. Requirements for the validity of the PSS contract

82. Four requirements for the validity of the PSS contract – The Belgian Civil Code sets out four requirements for the validity of a contract. Thus, the following must be present at the time of conclusion of the PSS contract: (i) the free and enlightened consent of each contracting party; (ii) the capacity of each party to be able to enter into contracts; (iii) a determinable and lawful object; (iv)

[314] M.E. Porter and M.R. Kramer, "Creating Shared Value", *Harvard Business Review* 2011, (1) 17.

a lawful cause.[315] The old Dutch Civil Code contained a similar provision that listed these same four validity requirements.[316] However, as a result of intense discussions in Dutch legal doctrine, this provision did not make its return to the "new" DCC.[317] Still, also in the new DCC the PSS contracts are subjected both to requirements regarding their valid formation[318] (e.g. consent and capacity) and their lawful content[319] (e.g. determinable object and lawful cause).[320]

83. Determinable and lawful object and sustainability/circularity guarantees – Regarding the free and enlightened consent of the parties (including the issues regarding vices of consent[321]), the capacity of the parties, and the requirement of a lawful cause, PSS contracts are not different from other contracts. Therefore, these validity requirements will not be discussed in depth.[322] However, the third criterion of a determinable and lawful object[323] does require some special consideration, particularly in the case where the parties want to include sustainability or circularity guarantees in the PSS contract.[324]

315 Art. 5.27 BCC.

316 See Art. 1356 old DCC.

317 C.H. Sieburgh, *Mr. C. Assers Handleiding tot de beoefening van het Nederlands Burgerlijk Recht. 6. Verbintenissenrecht. Deel III. Algemeen overeenkomstenrecht*, Deventer, Wolters Kluwer, 2022, no. 95.

318 See for an overview: C.H. Sieburgh, *Mr. C. Assers Handleiding tot de beoefening van het Nederlands Burgerlijk Recht. 6. Verbintenissenrecht. Deel III. Algemeen overeenkomstenrecht*, Deventer, Wolters Kluwer, 2022, no. 106.

319 See for an overview: C.H. Sieburgh, *Mr. C. Assers Handleiding tot de beoefening van het Nederlands Burgerlijk Recht. 6. Verbintenissenrecht. Deel III. Algemeen overeenkomstenrecht*, Deventer, Wolters Kluwer, 2022, no. 282.

320 C.H. Sieburgh, *Mr. C. Assers Handleiding tot de beoefening van het Nederlands Burgerlijk Recht. 6. Verbintenissenrecht. Deel III. Algemeen overeenkomstenrecht*, Deventer, Wolters Kluwer, 2022, no. 95.

321 These are error, fraud, violence, abuse of circumstances. **Belgium**: See Art. 5.33 BCC (vices of consent in general) and Art. 5.34–5.37 BCC (error, fraud, violence, abuse of circumstances). **The Netherlands**: Art. 6:228 DCC (error) and Art. 3:44 DCC (violence, fraud and abuse of circumstances).

322 See for a discussion of these validity requirements for **Belgium**: e.g. I. Claeys and T. Tanghe, *Nieuw Algemeen Contractenrecht*, Antwerp, Intersentia, 2023, 235–334; P. Wéry, *Droit des obligations. Volume 1. Theorie générale du contrat*, Brussels, Larcier, 2021, 229–335. For **the Netherlands**, see: C.H. Sieburgh, *Mr. C. Assers Handleiding tot de beoefening van het Nederlands Burgerlijk Recht. 6. Verbintenissenrecht. Deel III. Algemeen overeenkomstenrecht*, Deventer, Wolters Kluwer, 2022, no. 106–161 and no. 283–347.

323 **Belgium**: Art. 5.46–5.51 BCC. See for a discussion: V. Sagaert, *Beginselen van verbintenissenrecht. De contractuele en quasi-contractuele verbintenissen*, Leuven, LeA Uitgevers, 2023, 76–81. **The Netherlands**: See Art. 6:227 DCC (determinability of the obligation) and Art. 3:40 DCC (lawfulness of the obligation, i.e. not contrary to the law, public policy or morality). See for a discussion: C.H. Sieburgh, *Mr. C. Assers Handleiding tot de beoefening van het Nederlands Burgerlijk Recht. 6. Verbintenissenrecht. Deel I. De verbintenis in het algemeen, eerste gedeelte*, Deventer, Wolters Kluwer, 2020, no. 20 *et seq.*

324 Compare also with C. Borucki, S. Declercq and K. Dewaele, "Maatschappelijk verantwoord ondernemen en MVO-clausules: struikelblokken en perspectieven" in A. Van Hoe and G. Croisant (eds.), *Droit et durabilité / Recht en duurzaamheid*, Antwerp,

First, under Belgian law, the requirement of a determinable and lawful object prescribes that the performance (*prestatie, prestation*) must be possible.[325] One could interpret this requirement to mean that a performance that is impossible at the time the PSS contract is concluded, such as overly ambitious sustainability or circularity guarantees (e.g. "*this PSS offer is 100% sustainable*"), cannot be part of the PSS contract.[326] The DCC, on the other hand, does not contain a requirement that the performance must be possible. According to SIEBURGH, it follows that the traditional doctrine that it is not possible to commit to an impossible performance is incorrect.[327] She argues that if the creditor did not know that the performance which the debtor promised was impossible, there is no ground for the invalidity of the obligation.[328] In this case, it must be assessed whether the non-performance of the impossible obligation is imputable to the debtor, in which case he will be contractually liable.[329, 330]

Second, the performance must be determined or at least determinable without requiring a new exchange of consent among the parties.[331] This means that the PSS contract must contain sufficiently concrete criteria on how the promises contained in the sustainability or circularity guarantees are materialised.[332] Conversely, overly vague and general (sustainability) guarantees will also be problematic.[333]

Looking at these two requirements together, it is clear that the PSS supplier must pay close attention to how sustainability and circular guarantees are included in the PSS contract. These guarantees must be sufficiently concrete,

Intersentia, 2021, (251) 264–266, no. 17–18 regarding the requirement of a determinable and lawful object in the context of corporate social responsibility ("CSR") clauses.

325 See Art. 5.47 BCC.

326 See in this sense: C. BORUCKI, H. SLACHMUYLDERS, B. KEIRSBILCK, D. GRUYAERT and E. TERRYN, *Model clauses for Product-as-a-Service (PaaS) contracts*, CE Center. Circular Economy Policy Research Center, 2022–23, 15.

327 C.H. SIEBURGH, *Mr. C. Assers Handleiding tot de beoefening van het Nederlands Burgerlijk Recht. 6. Verbintenissenrecht. Deel I. De verbintenis in het algemeen, eerste gedeelte*, Deventer, Wolters Kluwer, 2020, no. 25–26.

328 By contrast, if the creditor knew at the time of conclusion of the contract that performance was impossible, he cannot reasonably expect performance.

329 Art. 6:74 *et seq.* DCC and Art. 6:265 *et seq.* DCC.

330 C.H. SIEBURGH, *Mr. C. Assers Handleiding tot de beoefening van het Nederlands Burgerlijk Recht. 6. Verbintenissenrecht. Deel I. De verbintenis in het algemeen, eerste gedeelte*, Deventer, Wolters Kluwer, 2020, no. 25–26.

331 **Belgium**: Art. 5.49(1) BCC. **The Netherlands**: Art. 6:227 DCC.

332 **Belgium**: V. SAGAERT, *Beginselen van verbintenissenrecht. De contractuele en quasi-contractuele verbintenissen*, Leuven, LeA Uitgevers, 2023, 78. **The Netherlands**: P.S. BAKKER, "Art. 227 – Burgerlijk Wetboek Boek 6. Bepaalbaarheid bij totstandkoming overeenkomst" in *Sdu Commentaar Vermogensrecht*, 10 June 2022, 1; C.H. SIEBURGH, *Mr. C. Assers Handleiding tot de beoefening van het Nederlands Burgerlijk Recht. 6. Verbintenissenrecht. Deel I. De verbintenis in het algemeen, eerste gedeelte*, Deventer, Wolters Kluwer, 2020, no. 23.

333 Compare with C. BORUCKI, H. SLACHMUYLDERS, B. KEIRSBILCK, D. GRUYAERT and E. TERRYN, *Model clauses for Product-as-a-Service (PaaS) contracts*, CE Center. Circular Economy Policy Research Center, 2022–23, 15.

while also remaining attainable. Further in this book, some guidelines as well as practical examples will be given on how to include sustainability and circularity in the PSS contract.[334]

84. Nullity as sanction if one (or more) of these requirements are not met – If the PSS contract fails to meet one or more of these validity requirements, the sanction is nullity.[335] Nullity should be distinguished from the termination of the contract, as nullity is a sanction for defects in the formation stage, while the termination is a sanction for defects during the performance stage.[336] A distinction is made between absolute and relative nullity.[337] Nullity is absolute when the rule violated is of public policy and thus aims to protect the public interest. In this case, any interested party can invoke it. Nullity is relative when the rule violated is of mandatory law, and thus aims to protect a private interest.[338] In this case, only the protected party can invoke it.[339] However, the strict distinction between absolute and relative nullity has lost much of its importance, especially in the light of the doctrine of *ex officio* review by the court with regard to unfair terms in B2C contracts.[340] Under Belgian law, nullity never takes effect by operation of law but must be established.[341] This means that a PSS contract for which the validity requirements are not met is actually

---

334 See *infra* section 7.4.3.

335 **Belgium**: Art. 5.57(1) BCC. **The Netherlands**: See Art. 3:32 DCC (lack of capacity), Art. 3:34 and Art. 3:34 *juncto* Art. 6:228 DCC (mental illness and vices of consent), Art. 3:39 DCC (form defects), Art. 3:40 DCC (lawfulness of the obligation, i.e. not contrary to the law, public policy or morality). See also: C.H. Sieburgh, *Mr. C. Assers Handleiding tot de beoefening van het Nederlands Burgerlijk Recht. 6. Verbintenissenrecht. Deel III. Algemeen overeenkomstenrecht*, Deventer, Wolters Kluwer, 2022, no. 95.

336 V. Sagaert, *Beginselen van verbintenissenrecht. De contractuele en quasi-contractuele verbintenissen*, Leuven, LeA Uitgevers, 2023, 87; I. Claeys and T. Tanghe, *Nieuw Algemeen Contractenrecht*, Antwerp, Intersentia, 2023, 335 and 338; S. Stijns, *Verbintenissenrecht*, Boek 1, Bruges, Die Keure, 2022, 162.

337 **Belgium**: Art. 5.58 BCC. See on the distinction e.g. S. Stijns, *Verbintenissenrecht*, Boek 1, Bruges, Die Keure, 2022, 165–167; P. Wéry, *Droit des obligations. Volume 1. Theorie générale du contrat*, Brussels, Larcier, 2021, 344–353, no. 326–330; M. Dupont, "Nullité absolue et nullité relative" in P. Wéry (ed.), *La nullité des contrats*, Brussels, Larcier, 2006, (33) 33–82. **The Netherlands**: C.H. Sieburgh, *Mr. C. Assers Handleiding tot de beoefening van het Nederlands Burgerlijk Recht. 6. Verbintenissenrecht. Deel III. Algemeen overeenkomstenrecht*, Deventer, Wolters Kluwer, 2022, no. 612.

338 The main examples include vices of consent (error, fraud, violence, abuse of circumstances). See Art. 5.33 *et seq.* BCC.

339 This also means that the protected party can waive the nullity, which is called confirmation of the nullity. This is not possible for absolute nullity. **Belgium**: See Art. 5.61 BCC. **The Netherlands**: Art. 3:55 DCC; C.H. Sieburgh, *Mr. C. Assers Handleiding tot de beoefening van het Nederlands Burgerlijk Recht. 6. Verbintenissenrecht. Deel III. Algemeen overeenkomstenrecht*, Deventer, Wolters Kluwer, 2022, no. 625.

340 See on this *ex officio* review *infra* no. 150–151.

341 I. Claeys and T. Tanghe, *Nieuw Algemeen Contractenrecht*, Antwerp, Intersentia, 2023, 335–336, no. 388; V. Sagaert, *Beginselen van verbintenissenrecht. De contractuele en quasi-contractuele verbintenissen*, Leuven, LeA Uitgevers, 2023, 94, no. 177.

not null and void, but voidable, and as such will continue to have effects until it is voided.[342] The establishment of nullity can be done both through amicable agreement, judicial nullity and – introduced by the new BCC – extrajudicial nullity.[343] Under Dutch law, on the other hand, a distinction is made between juridical acts that are null and void by operation of law[344] and juridical acts that are voidable.[345, 346] In the first case, the court will determine the nullity *ex officio*, without the need for an action by a party or a third party.[347] In the latter, a voidable juridical act is set aside either by an extrajudicial declaration or through judicial nullity following an action by the protected person.[348]

85. Consequences of nullity – The nullity deprives the PSS contract of its effect from the day it was entered into, and all its effects must therefore be erased.[349] This means that both parties can no longer claim performance of the PSS contract, and what has already been performed must be undone or restituted.[350, 351] Needless to say, this is a very drastic sanction. This is why there is a tendency under Belgian law to apply the sanction of nullity with flexibility so the consequences of this sanction are not disproportionate to the objective of the violated norm: nullity should be tailor-made (*nietigheid is "maatwerk"*[352]).[353]

---

342 Art. 5.59(1) BCC.

343 Art. 5.59(2) and 5.59(3) BCC.

344 See e.g. Art. 3:40(1) DCC ("*A juridical act that is contrary to morality or public order by virtue of its content or purport is null and void*").

345 See e.g. Art. 3:40(2) DCC ("*Violation of a mandatory statutory provision shall lead to nullity of the juridical act, but, if the provision only serves to protect one of the parties to a multi-sided juridical act, only to its voidability, insofar as the purport of the provision does not indicate otherwise.*" [own emphasis]). See also Art. 6:233 DCC (unreasonably onerous contract terms), discussed *infra* no. 176.

346 R.W.E. van Leuken, M.M.C. van de Moosdijk and V. Tweehuysen, *Hartkamps Compendium van het vermogensrecht*, Deventer, Wolters Kluwer, 2017, 63–64, no. 85; C.H. Sieburgh, *Mr. C. Assers Handleiding tot de beoefening van het Nederlands Burgerlijk Recht. 6. Verbintenissenrecht. Deel III. Algemeen overeenkomstenrecht*, Deventer, Wolters Kluwer, 2022, 607–609.

347 See e.g. HR (NL) 15 November 1985, ECLI:NL:PHR:1985:AD3292, *NJ* 1986, 227, case note W.C.L. van der Grinten.

348 Art. 3:49 DCC.

349 **Belgium**: Art. 5.62(1) BCC. **The Netherlands**: Art. 3:53(1) DCC.

350 **Belgium**: See for the restitution of what has already been performed: Art. 5.115–5.124 BCC. **The Netherlands**: Art. 3:53 DCC.

351 **Belgium**: S. Stijns, *Verbintenissenrecht*, Boek 1, Bruges, Die Keure, 2022, 166–167. **The Netherlands**: C.H. Sieburgh, *Mr. C. Assers Handleiding tot de beoefening van het Nederlands Burgerlijk Recht. 6. Verbintenissenrecht. Deel III. Algemeen overeenkomstenrecht*, Deventer, Wolters Kluwer, 2022, no. 637.

352 As first argued by W. Van Gerven, see: W. Van Gerven, *Algemeen deel in Beginselen van Belgisch Privaatrecht*, I, Antwerp, Standaard, 1973, 443, no. 138.

353 See for an in-depth analysis: F. Peeraer, *Nietigheid van een overeenkomst en derden, in het bijzonder de schuldeisers te goeder trouw*, Antwerp, Intersentia, 2019, 852 p.; T. Tanghe, *Gedeeltelijke ontbinding en vernietiging van overeenkomsten*, Antwerp, Intersentia, 2015, 348 p.

Different techniques are used in this regard, including partial nullity and reduction, mitigation and conversion as alternative for nullity, the limitation of restitution obligations, and compensation for damages as complementary or substitute sanction.[354]

2.2.1.2. Pre-contractual information for PSS contracts

86. Importance of information requirements in the PSS contract formation process – In the formation process of the PSS contract, information and transparency obligations play a crucial role to protect the PSS user-consumer from an information asymmetry. After all, consumers looking to enter into a PSS contract are often faced with a wide range of different PSS offers, which can make it difficult to compare. For example, the total cost of long-term and complex PSS contracts may consist of (a combination of) different components such as periodic fees, pay-per-use components, as well as a deposit or deductible.[355] In addition, consumers may have to pay for joined offers, ancillary products, product modifications or updates. Moreover, the price of a possible purchase option at the end of the contract may also be relevant in the comparison. The main characteristics of the service can also differ between multiple PSS offers. For example, not all PSS offers contain the same additional services or have the same duration. Additionally, the products offered "as a service" may also differ from other PSS offers on the market in other ways (e.g. energy consumption of the product, durability of the product, etc.). Besides information on the cost and main characteristics of the PSS, consumers are also not always aware of their legal rights, such as the applicability of a legal or commercial guarantee, a right of withdrawal, an option to terminate the contract early, etc.

Below, we provide a general overview of the main information and transparency requirements that apply to PSS suppliers. Here, it is important to note from the outset that many of these different sets of information obligations must be complied with cumulatively, which often gives rise to overlap and the risk of an "information overload".[356]

354 See for a discussion of these techniques under **Belgian law**: S. Stijns, *Verbintenissenrecht*, Boek 1, Bruges, Die Keure, 2022, 169–176. Compare with **Dutch law**, where partial nullity and conversion are also used, see Art. 3:41 and 3:42 DCC; C.H. Sieburgh, *Mr. C. Assers Handleiding tot de beoefening van het Nederlands Burgerlijk Recht. 6. Verbintenissenrecht. Deel III. Algemeen overeenkomstenrecht*, Deventer, Wolters Kluwer, 2022, no. 645–658; R.W.E. van Leuken, M.M.C. van de Moosdijk and V. Tweehuysen, *Hartkamps Compendium van het vermogensrecht*, Deventer, Wolters Kluwer, 2017, 72–75 no. 97–99.

355 Also called the "own risk" (*eigen risico, franchise*), which is a strategy used by some PSS suppliers to deal with the "moral hazard" problem. See e.g. the terms and conditions of *Swapfiets*, which stipulate that in case the rented bicycle is stolen, the renter is obliged to notify *Swapfiets*, file a police report and pay a deductible of € 60.

356 E. Terryn and B. Keirsbilck, "Informatieverplichtingen in het consumenten- en ondernemingsrecht" in E.S. Van Aggelen (ed.), *Informatie en recht*, Antwerp, Intersentia, 2021, (117) 125 and 146.

87. General information requirements from the Services Directive – A first set of information requirements has its origin in the Services Directive.[357] Article 22 SD sets out general information requirements, including detailed information on the identity of the PSS supplier, its general terms and conditions, the main features of the service, and the price of the service if a price is pre-determined by the provider for a given type of service.[358] These information requirements apply irrespective of whether an agreement is entered into with the PSS supplier. In Belgium, these information requirements were implemented in Article III.74-III.78 BCEL.[359] In the Netherlands, they can be found in Article 6:230a-6:230f of the DCC.[360]

The information mentioned above must be made available to recipients[361] of the service in any case.[362] The PSS supplier has the choice between making it available on its own initiative, easily accessible electronically or at the place where the service is provided or the contract is concluded, or in information documents supplied to the recipient.[363] In addition, the Services Directive and its national implementing provisions also require certain additional information to be made available if requested by a recipient. This mainly concerns the method of calculating the price if no pre-determined price has been set for a given type of service, any codes of conduct to which the supplier is subject, and – under Belgian law[364] – previous versions of the general terms and conditions.[365] The information must be made available or communicated in a clear and unambiguous manner.[366] In terms of timing, this should be done in good time before the conclusion of the contract or, where there is no written contract, before the service is provided.[367] Under Belgian law, the burden of proof that these information requirements have been met and that the information provided is accurate lies with the PSS supplier.[368] This is not the case under the Directive and under Dutch law.[369]

---

357 See on the Services Directive also *supra* no. 40.

358 See Art. 22 SD.

359 See for an elaborate analysis of the Belgian provisions: L. Ballon, "Boek III. Vrijheid van vestiging, dienstverlening en algemene verplichtingen van de ondernemingen" in B. Keirsbilck and E. Terryn (eds.), *Het Wetboek van economisch recht: van nu en straks?*, Antwerp, Intersentia, 2014, (65) 98–104.

360 See for an analysis of the Dutch provisions: M.Y. Schaub, "De informatieplichten van de Dienstenrichtlijn (art. 6:230a-f BW)", *TvC* 2014, (21) 21–30.

361 This is a very broad concept, covering all possible recipients of a service, regardless of whether they act for professional or non-professional purposes. **EU**: See Art. 4(4) SD. **Belgium**: See Art. I.2, 7° BCEL. **The Netherlands**: See Art. 6:230a DCC.

362 **EU**: Art. 22(1) SD. **Belgium**: Art. III.74 BCEL. **The Netherlands**: Art. 6:230b DCC.

363 **EU**: Art. 22(2) SD. **Belgium**: Art. III.75 BCEL. **The Netherlands**: Art. 6:230c DCC.

364 See Art. III.76, 5° BCEL.

365 **EU**: Art. 22(3) SD. **Belgium**: Art. III.76 BCEL. **The Netherlands**: Art. 6:230d DCC.

366 **EU**: Art. 22(4) SD. **Belgium**: Art. III.77 BCEL. **The Netherlands**: Art. 6:230e DCC.

367 *Ibid.*

368 **Belgium**: Art. III.78 BCEL.

369 See for **the Netherlands**: T.J. De Graaf, "Naar een coherente(re) implementatie van de informatieplichten met betrekking tot (algemene) voorwaarden voortvloeiend uit de

88. Precontractual information requirements from the Consumer Rights Directive – Besides the general information obligations from the Services Directive, the PSS supplier must also comply with several pre-contractual information obligations arising from the consumer law acquis. The first instrument that can be mentioned here is the Consumer Rights Directive. This Directive contains two long and very detailed sets of information requirements. On the one hand, Article 5 CRD provides general precontractual information requirements for contracts other than distance or off-premises contracts.[370] On the other, Article 6 CRD contains specific information requirements for distance[371] and off-premises[372] contracts.[373] These provisions require PSS suppliers to provide information to consumers in a clear and comprehensive manner before the consumer is bound by the (distance or off-premises) contract, for example on the main characteristics of the services, the identity of the PSS supplier, the total price of the services, the duration of the contract, etc.[374] Specifically for distance or off-premises contracts, the CRD also includes information requirements regarding the right of withdrawal, such as the conditions, time limit and procedures for exercising it, as well as the model withdrawal form set out in Annex I(B) to the CRD.[375, 376] This already extensive

---

e-commerce-richtlijn en dienstenrichtlijn", *NTBR* 2018/24, para 2.4; M.Y. Schaub, "De informatieplichten van de Dienstenrichtlijn (art. 6:230a-f BW)", *TvC* 2014, (21) 27.

370 **Belgium**: implemented in Art. VI.2 BCEL. **The Netherlands**: implemented in Art. 6:230*l* DCC.

371 Art. 2(7) CRD defines "distance contract" as "*any contract concluded between the trader and the consumer under an organised distance sales or service-provision scheme without the simultaneous physical presence of the trader and the consumer, with the exclusive use of one or more means of distance communication up to and including the time at which the contract is concluded.*" **Belgium**: Art. I.8, 15° BCEL. **The Netherlands**: Art. 230g, *sub* e. DCC.

372 According to Art. 2(8) CRD, an "off-premises contract" means "*any contract between the trader and the consumer: (a) concluded in the simultaneous physical presence of the trader and the consumer, in a place which is not the business premises of the trader; (b) for which an offer was made by the consumer in the same circumstances as referred to in point (a); (c) concluded on the business premises of the trader or through any means of distance communication immediately after the consumer was personally and individually addressed in a place which is not the business premises of the trader in the simultaneous physical presence of the trader and the consumer; or (d) concluded during an excursion organised by the trader with the aim or effect of promoting and selling goods or services to the consumer.*" **Belgium**: Art. I.8, 31° BCEL. **The Netherlands**: Art. 230g, *sub* f. DCC.

373 **Belgium**: implemented in Art. VI.45 BCEL (distance contracts) and Art. VI.64 BCEL (off-premises contracts). **The Netherlands**: implemented in Art. 6:230m DCC (for both distance and off-premises contracts).

374 According to the CJEU, this information can be brought to the consumer's attention, prior to the conclusion of the contract, in the general terms and conditions on a website, which the consumer accepts by ticking the box provided for that purpose. See: CJEU, Judgment of 24 February 2022, C-536/20, *Tiketa*, ECLI:EU:C:2022:112, para. 46.

375 **EU**: Art. 6(1), (h) CRD. See also Art. 6(1), (i)-(k) CRD for other information requirements linked to the right of withdrawal. **Belgium**: Art. VI.45, §1, 8° BCEL and Art. VI.45, §1, 9°-11° BCEL (distance contracts) and VI.64, §1, 7° BCEL and Art. VI.64, §1, 8°-10° BCEL (off-premises contracts). **The Netherlands**: Art. 6:230m, *sub* h. and Art. 6:230m, *sub* i.-k. DCC (for both distance and off-premises contracts).

376 For the sanction for not complying with these information obligations, see *infra* no. 198.

list of information requirements was recently extended by the Directive to empower consumers for the green transition,[377] which amended Articles 5 and 6 of the CRD to also provide consumers with pre-contractual information on the legal guarantee, commercial guarantees of durability, availability of software updates and repairability of goods.[378] For distance and off-premises PSS contracts, the burden of proof that these information requirements have been met and that the information provided is accurate is explicitly placed on the PSS supplier-trader.[379] For the general information requirements of the CRD, on the other hand, the burden of proof is not explicitly reversed.[380]

89. Other pre-contractual information requirements arising from the EU consumer acquis – The EU consumer acquis contains several other pre-contractual information requirements for specific types of consumer contracts. For example, if the PSS contract is concluded by electronic means, the information requirements of the E-commerce Directive will apply.[381] If a consumer credit agreement is added to a product-oriented PSS, the PSS supplier will have to comply with the specific information requirements of the Consumer Credit Directive,[382] Finally, for some types of PSS such as use-oriented PSS for

---

377 Directive (EU) 2024/825 of the European Parliament and of the Council of 28 February 2024 amending Directives 2005/29/EC and 2011/83/EU as regards empowering consumers for the green transition through better protection against unfair practices and through better information, *OJ L*, 2024/825, 6.3.2024.

378 Art. 2(2) and 2(3) Empowering Consumers for the Green Transition Directive. See for a discussion: M. Zarro, "Environmental sustainability and consumer relations between administrative and judicial remedies", *REDC* 2023, (175) 179–181.

379 EU: Art. 6(9) CRD. **Belgium**: Art. VI.62 BCEL. **The Netherlands**: Art. 6:230n(4) DCC.

380 See G. Straetmans and R. Steennot, *Handboek consumentenbescherming en marktpraktijken*, Antwerp, Intersentia, 2023, 96–97, where it is argued that although the majority of **Belgian** case law and legal doctrine (see citations there) assumes that, in the absence of special regulation, it is up to the consumer to prove that information obligations have not been fulfilled (*actori incumbit probatio*), the principle of effectiveness would nevertheless imply that the consumer cannot be expected to prove that he did not receive certain information. They support their argument on the cases CJEU, Judgment of 18 December 2014, C-449/13, *Consumer Finance*, ECLI:EU:C:2014:2464 and CJEU, Judgment of 10 June 2021, Joined cases C-776/19-C-1982/19, *BNP Paribas Personal Finance*, ECLI:EU:C:2021:470. Also under **Dutch** law, the general law of obligations applies, so the burden of proof in principle lies with the consumer. See: C.M.D.S. Pavillon, "De Richtlijn consumentenrechten" in E.H. Hondius and V. Mak (eds.), *Handboek Consumentenrecht*, Vijfde druk, Zutphen, Paris, 2020, (99) 117.

381 EU: Art. 10 E-commerce Directive. **Belgium**: Art. XII.7 BCEL. See also: E. Terryn and J. Goddaer, "Boek XII. Recht van de elektronische economie" in B. Keirsbilck and E. Terryn (eds.), *Het Wetboek van economisch recht: van nu en straks?*, Antwerp, Intersentia, 2014, (303) 317–320. **The Netherlands**: Art. 6:227b DCC. See also A.S. Hartkamp, *Mr. C. Assers Handleiding tot de beoefening van het Nederlands Burgerlijk Recht. 3. Vermogensrecht algemeen. Deel I. Europees recht en Nederlands vermogensrecht*, Deventer, Wolters Kluwer, 2023, no. 271.

382 Art. 5 and 6 Directive 2008/48/EC of the European Parliament and of the Council of 23 April 2008 on credit agreements for consumers and repealing Council Directive 87/102/EEC, *OJ L* 133, 22.5.2008, p. 66–92. See also Art. 9 and 10 of the New Consumer Credit Directive as

washing machines, the well-known energy labelling obligations will also be relevant.[383]

90. Formal requirements ensuring access to information after conclusion of the PSS contract – Information obligations also come into play after the PSS contract is concluded. This mainly concerns formal requirements that allow the PSS user to effectively access the provided (pre-contractual) information at a later time, i.e. the requirement of a durable medium.[384] Particular reference can be made here to the Consumer Rights Directive, which requires for distance PSS contracts for the PSS supplier to provide the PSS user with the confirmation of the contract concluded, on a durable medium within a reasonable time after conclusion of the distance PSS contract, and at the latest at the time of the delivery of the goods or before the performance of the service begins.[385] Additionally, for product-oriented PSS, the SGD also contains an obligation to provide a commercial guarantee statement on a durable medium at the latest at the time of delivery of the goods.[386]

91. Transparency requirement arising from the Unfair Contract Terms Directive – Not only specific information duties play a role, but open standards are also relevant for assessing the pre-contractual information duties of the PSS supplier. Thus, it follows from the transparency requirement of the Unfair Contract Terms Directive that the PSS supplier must inform the PSS user of the general terms and conditions applicable to the contract.[387] If the PSS user did not have the reasonable opportunity to examine the terms of the PSS contract, the UCTD allows to render the terms non-binding.[388]

92. Remedies and enforcement of information requirements – The question arises as to what remedies are open to the PSS user if these

outlined in the Political agreement on the New Consumer Credit Directive: https://data.consilium.europa.eu/doc/document/ST-7758-2023-INIT/en/pdf.

383 See for the Energy labelling framework: Regulation (EU) 2017/1369 of the European Parliament and of the Council of 4 July 2017 setting a framework for energy labelling and repealing Directive 2010/30/EU, *OJ L* 198, 28.7.2017, p. 1–23. See for an overview of all rules and requirements for energy labelling and eco-design: https://commission.europa.eu/energy-climate-change-environment/standards-tools-and-labels/products-labelling-rules-and-requirements/energy-label-and-ecodesign/rules-and-requirements_en.

384 E. Terryn and B. Keirsbilck, "Informatieverplichtingen in het consumenten- en ondernemingsrecht" in E.S. Van Aggelen (ed.), *Informatie en recht*, Antwerp, Intersentia, 2021, (117) 149.

385 EU: Art. 8(7) CRD. Implemented in **Belgium** in Art. VI.46, §7 BCEL and in **the Netherlands** in Art. 6:230v(7) DCC.

386 EU: Art. 17(2) SGD. Implemented in **Belgium** in Art. 1649*septies*, §2 old BCC and in **the Netherlands** in Art. 6a(3) DCC.

387 EU: See Recital 20 and Art. 5 UCTD. Implemented in **Belgium** in Art. VI.35, §1 BCEL and in **the Netherlands**: in Art. 6:238(2) DCC.

388 This is discussed more in-depth *infra* no. 155–158.

information requirements are not met by the PSS supplier. First and foremost, the PSS user can invoke the sanctions under general contract law, such as the possibility of claiming (extra)contractual liability, or the nullity of the contract if the conditions of one of the vices of consent are met.[389] Second, under Belgian law, there are examples of case law in which courts have ruled that (certain) general terms and conditions are unenforceable if they were not or insufficiently brought to the consumer's knowledge.[390] Third, the different instruments of the EU consumer acquis also provide for some specific sanctions and remedies. For example, the Consumer Rights Directive provides for the extension of the withdrawal period if certain information on the right or withdrawal[391] was not provided,[392] the prohibition of charging certain fees if certain information was not provided,[393] and the consumer not being bound by the contract or order if certain information was not provided.[394] Additionally, the Unfair Contract Terms Directive also provides in the possibility of declaring an unclear and therefore unfair clause null and void.[395] Finally, a failure to provide information may constitute a misleading omission (provided the information is essential) and providing false or misleading information may constitute a misleading action within the meaning of the

---

389 **Belgium**: E. Terryn and B. Keirsbilck, "Informatieverplichtingen in het consumenten- en ondernemingsrecht" in E.S. Van Aggelen (ed.), *Informatie en recht*, Antwerp, Intersentia, 2021, (117) 158; I. Claeys and T. Tanghe, *Nieuw Algemeen Contractenrecht*, Antwerp, Intersentia, 2023, 163–165. **The Netherlands**: C.M.D.S. Pavillon, "De Richtlijn consumentenrechten" in E.H. Hondius and V. Mak (eds.), *Handboek Consumentenrecht*, Vijfde druk, Zutphen, Paris, 2020, (99) 117.

390 See e.g. Antwerp (BE) 12 February 2018, *RW* 2018–19, 1110, *TBO* 2018, 231 (According to Art. 4 WMPC (now Art. VI.2, 7° BCEL), a seller must inform the consumer about his terms and conditions and explicitly draw the consumer's attention to a heavy-handed cancellation clause whereby the consumer can only cancel the contract – barring *force majeure* – on payment of 30% of the price. A mere reference to the terms and conditions printed on the back of the order form is not sufficient in such circumstances. The cancellation clause is not enforceable). Compare also with: Antwerp (BE) 5 March 2018, *RABG* 2019, 902 (regarding an exemption clause). In **the Netherlands**, it may be possible to obtain the same result based on the rules on general terms and conditions of Art 6:231 *et seq.* DCC.

391 See for a discussion of the right of withdrawal *infra* section 2.4.

392 **EU**: Art. 10 CRD. **Belgium**: Art. VI.48 BCEL. **The Netherlands**: Art. 6:230o(2) DCC.

393 **EU**: see e.g. Art. 6(6) CRD (If the trader has not complied with the information requirements on additional charges or other costs, the consumer shall not bear those charges or costs) and Art. 14(1), second para. CRD (prohibition in distance contracts to charge the costs of returning the goods if the trader did not inform the consumer that these costs were for his account). Implemented in **Belgium** in Art. VI.45, §5 BCEL and Art. VI.51(3) BCEL respectively and in **the Netherlands** in Art. 6:230n(3) DCC and Art. 6:230s(2) DCC respectively.

394 **EU**: Art. 8(2) CRD (in case of non-compliance with the specific obligation in distance contracts to be concluded by electronic means to make the consumer aware that the order implies an obligation to pay and obtain the consumer's consent to this). **Belgium**: Art. VI.46, §2(2) BCEL. **The Netherlands**: Art. 6:230v(3) DCC.

395 **EU**: Art. 3 and 5 UCTD (the UCTD speaks of "not be binding" as sanction for unfairness, leaving the consequences of unfair terms to the Member States, see *infra* no. 174). **Belgium**: Art. VI.82 *juncto* Art. VI.84 BCEL. **The Netherlands**: Art. 6:233 DCC.

Unfair Commercial Practices Directive.[396] This means that if the conditions are met, the sanctions and remedies for unfair commercial practices can also be invoked by the PSS user.[397]

93. Limitations of information requirements and possible solutions – The overview outlined above shows that if PSS suppliers want to offer their PSS to consumers, they must comply with various information requirements, both in the pre-contractual stage and after concluding the PSS contract. Unfortunately, however, this does not mean that consumers are optimally informed and protected when engaging in a PSS contract. Indeed, insights from behavioural sciences have shown that information requirements as a protection tool for consumers have considerable limitations[398] and different biases.[399] In addition, consumers may also be overwhelmed by the amount and complexity of information they receive (the so-called "information overload").[400] Furthermore, the timing at which the information should be provided to the consumer is also not always optimal.[401] For example, most information requirements require the information to be provided "*before the consumer is bound by the contract.*"[402] Nevertheless, some information may be better provided at a different time. For example, providing information on the available means of payment and shipping options makes the most sense before the consumer starts the ordering process,

---

396 EU: Art. 6 UCPD (misleading actions) and Art. 7 UCPD (misleading omissions). **Belgium:** Art. VI.97 BCEL (misleading actions) and Art. VI.99 BCEL (misleading omissions). **The Netherlands:** See Art. 6:193c DCC (misleading actions) and Art. 6:193d DCC (misleading omissions). See also Art. 6:193f, *sub* b. DCC, which identifies the information referred to in Art. 6:230m(1), *sub* a.-c., e.-h., o. and p. (information requirements for distance and off-premises contracts) and Art. 6:230v(1)-(3), (5), the first sentence of (6), and (7) as essential. Dutch law thus goes beyond what is required by the Directive. See: C.M.D.S. Pavillon, "De Richtlijn consumentenrechten" in E.H. Hondius and V. Mak (eds.), *Handboek Consumentenrecht*, Vijfde druk, Zutphen, Paris, 2020, (99) 117.

397 EU: Art. 11–13 UCPD. **Belgium:** See Art. VI.97 and Art. VI.38 BCEL. See for an application: J.P. Charleroi (BE) 1 February 2017, *T.Vred.* 2017, 510, case note H. Jacquemin. **The Netherlands:** See Art. 6:193j(3) DCC.

398 See e.g. C. Schneider and O. Ben-Shahar, *More than you wanted to know: the failure of mandated disclosure*, Princeton, Princeton University Press, 2014, and Y. Bakos, F. Marotta-Wurgler and D.R. Trossen, "Does Anyone Read the Fine Print? Consumer Attention to Standard-Form Contracts", *The Journal of Legal Studies* 2014, afl. 43, vol. 43, (1) 1–35.

399 Examples include the *confirmation bias* (searching for information that confirms the truth of a certain (pre)proposition), *overoptimism* (causing us to underestimate the chance that a negative scenario such as theft or damage to the rented property will affect us), and so on. In addition, the fact that many contracts are non-negotiable, which makes it rational not to read general terms and conditions or pre-contractual information, also plays a role. See: B. Keirsbilck, E. Terryn and E. Van Gool, "Consumentenbescherming bij servitisation en product-dienst systemen (PDS)", *TPR* 2019, (817) 843, footnote 129 and the references there.

400 See A. Michel, *Premature Obsolescence: In Search of an Improved Legal Framework*, Cambridge, Intersentia, 2023, 239, no. 339 and the references there.

401 G. Helleringer and A.-L. Sibony, "European consumer protection through the behavioral lens", *Columbia Journal of European Law* 2017, (607) 627–628.

402 See e.g. Art. 6(1) CRD.

while providing information on how to return the product is best suited when the product is delivered to the consumer.[403] Regarding consumers who wish to make informed sustainable consumption choices by entering into a PSS contract, the recent Directive on Empowering Consumers for the Green Transition is certainly to be welcomed, as the proposed rules can enhance consumers' rights and enable them to make informed and sustainable choices. However, the same concern also applies here. These proposed rules add to the already extensive list of information obligations that PSS suppliers must comply with.

From the perspective of the PSS supplier, the current regime on information obligations is also sub-optimal. As mentioned, many of these (very extensive and detailed) information obligations must be complied with cumulatively, which is not always obvious for the PSS supplier to do this correctly.[404] Thus, these obligations can create administrative and financial burdens, especially for start-ups or SMEs lacking the necessary resources or expertise, which will in turn translate to the risk for consumers that products and services may become more expensive. Various authors have therefore already called, rightly in my view, for further integration and streamlining of these information requirements, together with an improved methodology and timing of information provision.[405] Another solution, which has its origin from insights from behavioural sciences, is to pay more attention to how information is provided. For example, the use of pictograms and labels similar to the aforementioned energy labels[406] could provide a solution to inform consumers in a quick, clear, recognisable, and accessible way.[407]

2.2.1.3. Formation of the PSS contract through offer and acceptance

94. Offer and acceptance – The formation of a PSS contract takes place in two consecutive steps: an offer and an acceptance.[408] The PSS contract is thus

---

403 G. Helleringer and A.-L. Sibony, "European consumer protection through the behavioral lens", *Columbia Journal of European Law* 2017, (607) 628.

404 E. Terryn and B. Keirsbilck, "Informatieverplichtingen in het consumenten- en ondernemingsrecht" in E.S. Van Aggelen (ed.), *Informatie en recht*, Antwerp, Intersentia, 2021, (117) 146.

405 See e.g. B. Keirsbilck, E. Terryn, A. Michel and I. Alogna, *Sustainable Consumption and Consumer Protection Legislation, In-Depth Analysis for the Committee on Internal Market and Consumer Protection (IMCO), Policy Department for Economic, Scientific and Quality of Life Policies*, Luxembourg, European Parliament, 2020, 14–16; B. Keirsbilck and S. Rousseau, "The Marketing Stage: Fostering Sustainable Consumption Choices" in B. Keirsbilck and E. Terryn (eds.), *Consumer Protection in a Circular Economy*, Antwerp, Intersentia, 2019, (93) 124; European Commission Directorate-General for Justice and Consumers, *Study for the Fitness Check of EU consumer and marketing law – Final report. Part 1, main report*, Luxemburg, EU Publications Office, 262–263, 268 and 457.

406 See *supra* no. 89.

407 E. Terryn and B. Keirsbilck, "Informatieverplichtingen in het consumenten- en ondernemingsrecht" in E.S. Van Aggelen (ed.), *Informatie en recht*, Antwerp, Intersentia, 2021, (117) 147.

408 **Belgium**: Art. 5.18 BCC. **The Netherlands**: Art. 6:217 DCC.

concluded when the acceptance of the PSS user follows an earlier offer by the PSS supplier.

95. Offer: concept – An offer is a proposal to contract which contains all the essential and substantial elements of the envisaged PSS contract and the intention of the PSS supplier[409] to be bound by that contract, so that the PSS user's acceptance is sufficient to conclude the contract.[410]

96. Binding force of the offer – The offer is binding on the person from whom it emanates (i.e. the PSS supplier). This follows from its nature as a unilateral juridical act.[411] For an offer addressed to one or more specific persons, this binding force starts from the moment it reaches the PSS user.[412] This situation is mostly conceivable in the case of highly personalised PSS offers, which will often (but not always) be the case with result-oriented PSS. In most cases, however, the PSS supplier will make an offer to the public, for example through (online) advertisements, a website or an in-store display.[413] In the case of offers to the public, the offer will be binding as soon as it is externalised.[414] However, this needs to be nuanced, as some proposals to contract do not (yet)

---

409 Usually, the offer goes out from the PSS supplier. Therefore, we will start from the premise that the PSS supplier makes the offer. However, as we will see further (*infra* no. 101), sometimes the offer can also emanate from the PSS user, particularly if the PSS supplier has made an invitation to make an offer.

410 **Belgium**: Art. 5.19(1) BCC. V. Sagaert, *Beginselen van verbintenissenrecht. De contractuele en quasi-contractuele verbintenissen*, Leuven, LeA Uitgevers, 2023, 52; I. Claeys and T. Tanghe, *Nieuw Algemeen Contractenrecht*, Antwerp, Intersentia, 2023, 195–196; S. Stijns, *Verbintenissenrecht*, Boek 1, Bruges, Die Keure, 2022, 153; C. Delforge, "L'offre de contracter et la formation du contrat (1ère partie)", *TBBR* 2004, (550) 550 and 552 *et seq.* **The Netherlands**: The DCC does not define the term "offer", but a definition can be found in other provisions such as Art. 14 CISG. See: C.H. Sieburgh, *Mr. C. Assers Handleiding tot de beoefening van het Nederlands Burgerlijk Recht. 6. Verbintenissenrecht. Deel III. Algemeen overeenkomstenrecht*, Deventer, Wolters Kluwer, 2022, no. 163–164 and C. Spierings, *De eenzijdige rechtshandeling (diss. Nijmegen)*, Deventer, Wolters Kluwer, 2016, 190.

411 **Belgium**:: S. Stijns, *Verbintenissenrecht*, Boek 1, Bruges, Die Keure, 2022, 153, with reference to Cass. (BE) 9 May 1980, *Arr.Cass.* 1979–80, 1132 and 1139, *Pas.* 1980, 1120 and 1127, *RW* 1982–83, 319, *JT* 1981, 206. **The Netherlands**: C. Spierings, *De eenzijdige rechtshandeling (diss. Nijmegen)*, Deventer, Wolters Kluwer, 2016, 190–191; C.J. Van Zeben, J.W. Du Pon and M.M. Olthof, *Parlementaire geschiedenis van het Nieuwe burgerlijk wetboek. Boek 6: Algemeen gedeelte van het verbintenissenrecht*, Deventer, Kluwer, 1981, 878.

412 **Belgium**: Art. 5.19(2) *juncto* Art. 1.5 BCC; V. Sagaert, *Beginselen van verbintenissenrecht. De contractuele en quasi-contractuele verbintenissen*, Leuven, LeA Uitgevers, 2023, 53; I. Claeys and T. Tanghe, *Nieuw Algemeen Contractenrecht*, Antwerp, Intersentia, 2023, 201. **The Netherlands**: C.H. Sieburgh, *Mr. C. Assers Handleiding tot de beoefening van het Nederlands Burgerlijk Recht. 6. Verbintenissenrecht. Deel III. Algemeen overeenkomstenrecht*, Deventer, Wolters Kluwer, 2022, no. 172.

413 Most PSS suppliers offer their services on their website. Other PSS suppliers, most notably Swapfiets, (also) have their own physical shops where potential PSS users can receive information and conclude a PSS contract.

414 **Belgium**: Art. 5.19(2) BCC. **The Netherlands**: C.H. Sieburgh, *Mr. C. Assers Handleiding tot de beoefening van het Nederlands Burgerlijk Recht. 6. Verbintenissenrecht. Deel III. Algemeen*

constitute an offer, but merely an invitation to the recipient to make an offer. Traditional examples of such invitations to make an offer constitute proposals for contracts *intuitu personae* such as a job advertisement or offering a house for sale or rent on a real estate website.[415] However, this practice is also used sometimes in the context of PSS contracts, as will be discussed below.[416]

97. (IR)REVOCABILITY AND DURATION OF THE OFFER – Under Belgian law, the binding force of the offer means that the PSS supplier cannot change or revoke its offer once it has reached the prospective PSS user, or, in case of a public offer, once it has been externalised.[417] The offer remains irrevocable for the time specified in the offer, or, in the absence thereof, for a reasonable time.[418] However, the binding force of the offer may expire earlier if the offer is rejected or if the recipient makes a counter-offer or proposes changes to the offer.[419] Under Dutch law, the situation is slightly different. Here, the basic rule is that the offer is revocable, in the sense that the PSS supplier can withdraw the offer before it has been accepted by the recipient and before a communication containing the acceptance has been sent.[420] On the other hand, the offer is irrevocable if it includes a deadline for acceptance or if the irrevocability otherwise follows from the offer (e.g. if the offer expressly states that it is irrevocable).[421] If the offer does not contain a deadline, it expires if it is not accepted within a reasonable time, or if it is rejected by the recipient.[422]

98. ACCEPTANCE: CONCEPT – The acceptance is the unilateral juridical act expressing the full and unconditional agreement of the recipient (which is most of the time the PSS user) to an offer.[423] The recipient of the offer remains

---

overeenkomstenrecht, Deventer, Wolters Kluwer, 2022, no. 169; C. SPIERINGS, *De eenzijdige rechtshandeling (diss. Nijmegen)*, Deventer, Wolters Kluwer, 2016, 191–192.

415 **Belgium**: See I. CLAEYS and T. TANGHE, *Nieuw Algemeen Contractenrecht*, Antwerp, Intersentia, 2023, 200–201 and the examples of case law relating to the sale of an immovable good cited there. See also S. STIJNS, *Verbintenissenrecht*, Boek 1, Bruges, Die Keure, 2022, 153; **The Netherlands**: J. DEN HOED and Y.G. BLEI WEISSMAN, *Groene Serie Verbintenissenrecht, Art. 6:217 BW*, 2022, para. 3.110 *et seq.* C.H. SIEBURGH, *Mr. C. Assers Handleiding tot de beoefening van het Nederlands Burgerlijk Recht. 6. Verbintenissenrecht. Deel III. Algemeen overeenkomstenrecht*, Deventer, Wolters Kluwer, 2022, no. 170.

416 See *infra* no. 101.

417 Art. 5.19(2) BCC.

418 Art. 5.19(3) BCC.

419 Art. 5.19(4) BCC.

420 Art. 6:219(1)-(2) DCC.

421 Art. 6:219(1) DCC; C.H. SIEBURGH, *Mr. C. Assers Handleiding tot de beoefening van het Nederlands Burgerlijk Recht. 6. Verbintenissenrecht. Deel III. Algemeen overeenkomstenrecht*, Deventer, Wolters Kluwer, 2022, no. 175.

422 Art. 6:221 DCC.

423 **Belgium**: Art. 5.20 BCC. V. SAGAERT, *Beginselen van verbintenissenrecht. De contractuele en quasi-contractuele verbintenissen*, Leuven, LeA Uitgevers, 2023, 53; A. DE BOECK, "Aanbod en aanvaarding" in *Comm.Bijz.Ov.*, Antwerp, Kluwer, 2008, (173)194. **The Netherlands**:

free to accept it or not, and without having to give any motive.[424] By accepting the offer, the PSS contract comes into existence according to the elements and conditions included in the offer.[425] There are no special formal requirements for the acceptance of an offer.[426]

99. Place and time of conclusion of PSS contract – The contract is formed at the time and place where the acceptance reaches the offeror.[427] Belgian law explicitly confirms that in the case of a contract concluded by electronic means, unless the parties have agreed otherwise, this place shall be presumed to be the place of residence of the offeror.[428] This also seems to be the logical interpretation under Dutch law.[429]

100. Offer and acceptance in PSS contracts concluded by electronic means – If the PSS contract is concluded by electronic means, the question arises which acts are considered offer and acceptance, and when and where a contract concluded by electronic means is concluded. The E-commerce Directive does not provide special rules on offer and acceptance of contracts concluded by electronic means, which is due to the diversity of the legal rules on formation of contract in the different EU Member States.[430] However, this Directive does contain two principles that must be complied with when a PSS user places an order using technological means. Thus, the PSS supplier must acknowledge the receipt of the PSS user's order without undue delay and by electronic means, and the order and the acknowledgement of receipt are deemed to be received when

J. Hijma, C.C. van Dam, W.A.M. Van Schendel and W.L. Valk (eds.), *Rechtshandeling en Overeenkomst*, Deventer, Wolters Kluwer, 2022, 61.

424 See for **Belgium**: e.g. Cass. (BE) 13 September 1991, *Arr.Cass.* 1991–92, 38, *Pas.* 1992, I, 33, *RW* 1991–92, 882, case note K. Broeckx, *TRV* 1993, case note D. Van Gerven.

425 **Belgium**: I. Claeys and T. Tanghe, *Nieuw Algemeen Contractenrecht*, Antwerp, Intersentia, 2023, 206. **The Netherlands**: C.H. Sieburgh, *Mr. C. Assers Handleiding tot de beoefening van het Nederlands Burgerlijk Recht. 6. Verbintenissenrecht. Deel III. Algemeen overeenkomstenrecht*, Deventer, Wolters Kluwer, 2022, no. 164.

426 **Belgium**: V. Sagaert, *Beginselen van verbintenissenrecht. De contractuele en quasi-contractuele verbintenissen*, Leuven, LeA Uitgevers, 2023, 54. **The Netherlands**: J. Hijma, C.C. van Dam, W.A.M. Van Schendel and W.L. Valk (eds.), *Rechtshandeling en Overeenkomst*, Deventer, Wolters Kluwer, 2022, 61–62; C.H. Sieburgh, *Mr. C. Assers Handleiding tot de beoefening van het Nederlands Burgerlijk Recht. 6. Verbintenissenrecht. Deel III. Algemeen overeenkomstenrecht*, Deventer, Wolters Kluwer, 2022, no. 165 and 165b.

427 **Belgium**: Art. 5.21 *juncto* Art. 1.5 BCC. **The Netherlands**: Art. 3:37(3) DCC. C.H. Sieburgh, *Mr. C. Assers Handleiding tot de beoefening van het Nederlands Burgerlijk Recht. 6. Verbintenissenrecht. Deel III. Algemeen overeenkomstenrecht*, Deventer, Wolters Kluwer, 2022, no. 181–183 and no. 185.

428 Art. 5.21 BCC.

429 C.H. Sieburgh, *Mr. C. Assers Handleiding tot de beoefening van het Nederlands Burgerlijk Recht. 6. Verbintenissenrecht. Deel III. Algemeen overeenkomstenrecht*, Deventer, Wolters Kluwer, 2022, no. 185.

430 I. Claeys and T. Tanghe, *Nieuw Algemeen Contractenrecht*, Antwerp, Intersentia, 2023, 208.

the parties to whom they are addressed are able to access them.[431] Both under Belgian and Dutch law, these principles are mandatory law in contracts with consumers.[432] Under Dutch law, until receipt of the acceptance is confirmed, the PSS user can terminate the contract.[433] The Belgian implementing provisions, on the other hand, do not provide a specific termination possibility if a receipt of the acceptance is not sent. Apart from these principles, under both Belgian and Dutch law, a PSS contract concluded by electronic means is concluded according to the general rules of offer and acceptance as outlined above.[434]

101. Clauses on offer and acceptance: invitation to make an offer – In some cases, there will not be an offer by the PSS supplier in the strict legal sense, but merely an invitation to make an offer directed towards the (prospective) PSS user.[435] This will be the case if the terms and conditions of the PSS supplier provide that by placing an order, the (prospective) PSS user makes an offer for the conclusion of the PSS contract, or by stating that all offers are subject to change (*onder voorbehoud, sous réserve de modifications*). The general terms and conditions of *Grover* provide a good example of such a clause.[436] According to these terms, the PSS user makes a binding offer for the conclusion of the PSS contract after placing an item in the shopping basket, reviewing the rental price and clicking on the "confirm" button on the summary page. At this point, the PSS user cannot longer correct or cancel his offer, and he will receive a confirmation of his order. However, this confirmation is subject to change: *Grover* will check the order, and only after this check and the accompanying confirmation email will the PSS contract become effective.

> Terms and conditions Grover – Art. 4.2.1 "You can place a Rental Item in the rental basket in the Grover app and on the Website by clicking on the relevant button on the offer page. The amount of the payable rent will be displayed to You

---

431 EU: Art. 11(1) E-commerce Directive. **Belgium**: Art.XII.9 BCEL. **The Netherlands**: Art. 6:227c DCC.

432 **Belgium**: Art. XII.10 BCEL. **The Netherlands**: Art. 6:277b(6) DCC.

433 Art. 6:227b(2), second-to-last sentence DCC.

434 **Belgium**: see e.g. F. Debusseré, "Enkele verbintenisrechtelijke beginselen bekeken door de bril van de elektronische handel" in P. Van Eecke and J. Dumortier (eds.), *Elektronische handel. Commentaar bij de wetten van 11 maart 2003*, Bruges, Die Keure, 2003, (131) 151 *et seq*. **The Netherlands**: S. Gellaerts and C.M. Jobse, *Inleiding ICT en recht*, Deventer, Wolters Kluwer, 2022, 123–124. See also: E.D.C. Neppelenbroek, *Elektronisch contractenrecht*, The Hague, Boom Juridisch, 2019, 75 *et seq*.

435 **Belgium**: C. Delforge, "L'offre de contracter et la formation du contrat (1ère partie)", *TBBR* 2004, (550) 554–557. **The Netherlands**: J. den Hoed and Y.G. Blei Weissman, *Groene Serie Verbintenissenrecht, Art. 6:217 BW*, 2022, para. 3.67 and 3.68; F.J. de Vries, *De overeenkomst in het algemeen*, Deventer, Wolters Kluwer, 2016, no. 37. **EU**: See for a comparative law perspective: H. Beale, B. Fauvarque-Cosson, J. Rutgers and S. Vogenauer, *Ius Commune Casebooks for the Common Law of Europe. Cases, Materials and Text on Contract Law*, Third edition, Oxford, Hart, 2019, 210–211.

436 Art. 4.2.1 Terms and Conditions Grover (for orders via the Grover app or the website).

on the offer page. You will make a binding offer for the conclusion of the contract only when You click on the respective button on the summary page. Up until this point in time, You can check Your information in the order mask at any time and correct it if necessary. Upon this order, You will receive a conformation of Your order subject to change. After a successful check of the order, You will receive an email from us confirming the rental of the selected Merchandise, hereinafter referred to as 'Contract Conformation'. The Rental Agreement becomes effective on receipt of the Contract Conformation."

102. (Un)fairness of clauses on invitation to make an offer? – The question arises whether these terms are not unfair. After all, the Belgian blacklist of unfair terms bans clauses that aim to make the PSS contract binding on the PSS user, whereas the provision of the services by the PSS supplier is subject to a condition whose realisation depends on the PSS suppliers own will alone (also called potestative clauses).[437] These terms are also included in a similar way in the UCTD Annex.[438] Under Dutch law, these terms will generally fall under the blacklisted category of terms which completely deprive the counterparty (i.e. the PSS user) of the right to demand the performance promised by the user of general terms and conditions (i.e. the PSS supplier).[439] In addition, the reflex effect of the more broadly worded provision of the UCTD Annex can also be considered in order to make a case that these terms are unreasonably onerous.[440]

While some authors in Belgian legal doctrine claim that this blacklist provision prevents consumers from being the first to sign a contract,[441] the clause as quoted above does not fall within the scope of these blacklisted

437 Art. VI.83, 1° BCEL. See for examples: Antwerp (BE) 17 December 2007, *NjW* 2008, 448, case note R. Steennot (clause concerning a purchase promise whereby the prospective buyer definitively undertakes to buy the good as soon as the prospective seller demands it, while the seller accepts the purchase promise without an obligation to sell); Commissie Onrechtmatige Bedingen, *Advies nr. 19 over de algemene voorwaarden van de exploitanten van vaste telefoondiensten*, Brussels, 29 March 2006, (clause in which a telecom operator stipulates that the contract takes effect on the day of the operator's acceptance of the registered application); Ct. Hasselt (BE) 6 March 2000, *Limb.Rechtsl.* 2000, 429 (clause stating that orders are subject to approval by the management). R. Steennot, "Commentaar bij art. VI.83, 1° WER" in *Handels- en economisch recht. Commentaar met overzicht van rechtspraak en rechtsleer*, Mechelen, Kluwer, loose-leaf, 2017, (381) 383; P. Cambie, *Onrechtmatige bedingen*, Ghent, Larcier, 2009, 221–222.

438 Paragraph 1, point (c) UCTD Annex.

439 Art. 6:236, *sub* a. DCC. See M.B.M. Loos, *Algemene voorwaarden*, The Hague, Boom juridisch, 2018, 307, no. 348.

440 Paragraph 1, point (c) UCTD Annex; M.B.M. Loos, *Algemene voorwaarden*, The Hague, Boom juridisch, 2018, no. 348 and (on the reflex effect) no. 415–420.

441 C. Biquet-Mathieu and A. Vervoir, "Aperçu de la loi relative au crédit à la consommation après la réforme du 24 mars 2003" in *Chronique de droit à l'usage des juges de paix et de police*, Cahier no. 42, 2004, (1) 64, no. 84: "*Il ne faudrait pas négliger qu'en vertu de l'article [VI.83, 1° BCEL], il est interdit au prêteur de soumettre la signature du consommateur un document contractuel engageant irrévocablement le consommateur alors que le prêteur conservait lui la liberté d'être engagé ou de ne pas être engagé par ce même document.*"

provisions. Indeed, as rightly argued by STEENNOT, it only prohibits the inclusion of a clause stipulating that the business, which signed[442] the agreement, is only bound if a condition is realised whose fulfilment depends solely on its will.[443] This does not include the practice of getting the consumer to sign first, i.e. be the first to make an offer.[444] Moreover, since the (prospective) PSS user's offer constitutes only a unilateral juridical act, there is no contract (yet) and thus no voidable contractual term.[445, 446] The same argument can also be applied to Dutch law. Since *Grover* has only issued an invitation to make an offer, it has not yet promised any performance, so the conditions of Article 6:236, *sub* a. DCC are not met. Contrary to Belgian law, however, the Explanatory Memorandum of the DCC states that, if necessary, the provisions on unfair terms can also be applied accordingly to unilateral juridical acts using general terms and conditions.[447] The example that is given is an offer or acceptance by the user of the general terms and conditions, of which the validity is subject to formal requirements contained in general terms and conditions, which would be contrary to Article 6:236, *sub* l. DCC or Article 6:237, *sub* m. DCC.[448]

---

442 Or, alternatively, if the contract was concluded through a verbal agreement. Compare with: COMMISSIE ONRECHTMATIGE BEDINGEN, *Advies nr. 19 over de algemene voorwaarden van de exploitanten van vaste telefoondiensten*, Brussels, 29 March 2006, 7–8. (In the "general" section of a telecom contract, before the actual contract provisions, it was stated that the contract is concluded verbally. A provision in the actual general terms and conditions then stated that the contract takes effect from the moment the telecom operator accepts the registered application. According to the Commission on Unfair Terms, in this way, a distinction is made between the formation of the contract, which is in principle verbal, and the entry into force of the contract due to the written confirmation. It considered this to be contrary to Art. 32.1 WHPC (now Art. VI.83, 1° BCEL)).

443 R. STEENNOT, "Commentaar bij art. VI.83, 1° WER" in *Handels- en economisch recht. Commentaar met overzicht van rechtspraak en rechtsleer*, Mechelen, Kluwer, loose-leaf, 2017, (381) 384–385. Compare also with I. CLAEYS and T. TANGHE, *Nieuw Algemeen Contractenrecht*, Antwerp, Intersentia, 2023, 199–200 and G. STRAETMANS and R. STEENNOT, *Handboek consumentenbescherming en marktpraktijken*, Antwerp, Intersentia, 2023, 368–369.

444 *Ibid.*

445 See the opening sentence of Art. VI.83 BCEL and Art. I.8, 22° BCEL, which both speak of every "term or condition in a contract between a business and a consumer." See on the material scope of the Belgian rules on unfair terms also *infra* no. 148.

446 J. BAEL, "De impact van de wetgeving inzake marktpraktijken en bescherming van de consument op de verkoop van onroerende goederen: het nieuwe Boek VI van het wetboek van economisch recht.", *Rechtskroniek voor het Notariaat* 2014, (137) 163; R. STEENNOT, "Commentaar bij art. VI.83, 1° WER" in *Handels- en economisch recht. Commentaar met overzicht van rechtspraak en rechtsleer*, Mechelen, Kluwer, loose-leaf, 2017, (381) 385.

447 C.J. VAN ZEBEN, J.W. DU PON, W.H.M. REEHUIS and E.E. SLOB, *Parlementaire Geschiedenis van het Nieuwe Burgerlijk Wetboek. Invoering Boeken 3, 5 en 6: Boek 6: Algemeen gedeelte van het verbintenissenrecht*, Deventer, Kluwer, 1990, 1713 with reference to 1521, sub 7.

448 J. DEN HOED and Y.G. BLEI WEISSMAN, *Groene Serie Verbintenissenrecht, Art. 6:217 BW*, 2022, para. 3.7.5.2.

103. ALTHOUGH FAIR, CLAUSES ON INVITATION TO MAKE AN OFFER ARE NOT CONSUMER FRIENDLY – Although clauses containing an invitation to offer such as those used by *Grover* are thus strictly speaking not unfair *de lege lata*, the practice employed by *Grover* can, in my view, be considered unclear at best and misleading at worst. After all, throughout the entire order process, the consumer is under the impression that if he completes the ordering process, he will have concluded a subscription contract. This follows from the use of the button "Subscribe" (*Abonneren*) in the Dutch version of the website and "Add to cart" in the English version of the website (see Figure 3). After the product is added to the consumer's cart, the next button states "Continue to checkout", where the consumer must provide his personal data and shipping information and choose a payment method (credit card or PayPal). Nowhere does the ordering process indicate that making an order actually constitutes making an offer, nor that the order is subject to acceptance by *Grover*. This is merely "buried" in the general terms and conditions.

Figure 3. Screenshot of *Grover's* ordering process

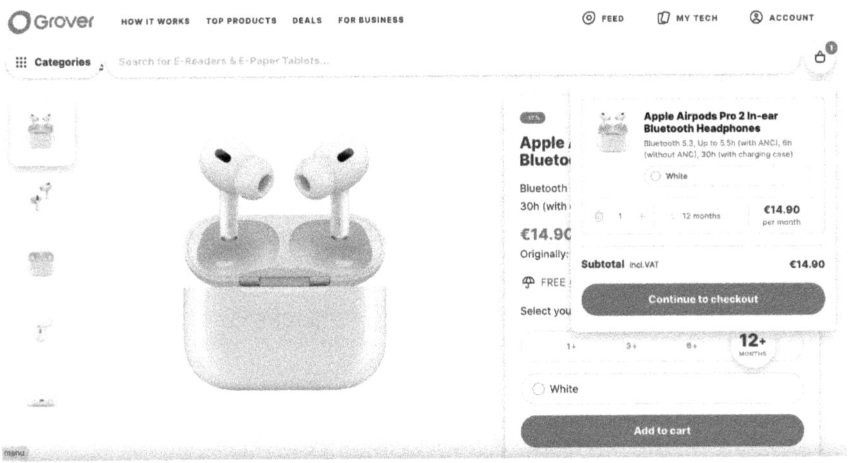

The question even arises whether, in this situation, the theory of legitimate reliance (*vertrouwensleer, théorie de l'apparance/théorie de la confiance légitime*) could correct the will theory (*wilsleer, consensualisme*) if it turns out that the consumer, taking into account all the concrete circumstances,[449] could have legitimately assumed that the PSS supplier did have a will to be bound by the proposal displayed on the web shop.[450] This would then result in the PSS contract

449 E.g. the substantive precision and clarity of the proposal, which are arguably present in this case, and the fact that no reservations were made during the order process.

450 **Belgium**: See on the trust theory as correction on the will theory e.g. S. STIJNS, *Verbintenissenrecht*, Boek 1, Bruges, Die Keure, 2022, 67–69; I. CLAEYS and T. TANGHE, *Nieuw Algemeen Contractenrecht*, Antwerp, Intersentia, 2023, 216–221; S. STIJNS and I. SAMOY, "La confiance légitime en droit des obligations" in S. STIJNS and P. WÉRY (eds.),

being concluded regardless of the PSS supplier's conformation. After all, it may generally be presumed that a person who formulates a proposal in the economic sphere that includes all the essential and substantial elements will actually want to make a legal commitment.[451] In my view, this is especially true when the ordering process is designed to resemble an online shop (similar to Amazon or bol.com), where by placing an item in their basket, clicking order, and paying, consumers generally enter into a contract immediately.

104. *De lege ferenda:* extending the scope of Article VI.83, 1° BCEL? – As established above, Article VI.83, 1° BCEL does *de lege lata* not apply to unilateral juridical acts, such as an offer by the consumer following an invitation to make an offer by the PSS supplier. Some authors in Belgian legal doctrine already advocated for extending the scope of this blacklisted term to unilateral juridical acts as well.[452] Their argument relies on the *ratio legis* of Article VI.83, 1° BCEL, which is to avoid consumers undertaking obligations while the business does not also commit itself.[453] In other words, the aim of Article VI.83, 1° BCEL is that the business must commit itself at least to the same extent as the consumer, as otherwise there is a significant imbalance in the parties' rights and obligations.[454] In my view, a total ban on making an offer subject to change or issuing an invitation to offer would go too far. After all, the freedom of contract and freedom of enterprise of the PSS supplier must not be disproportionately restricted. In some cases, the person of the prospective PSS user (especially his financial situation) or the capabilities and capacity of his home will be relevant for the PSS supplier to decide whether to enter into a

---

De bronnen van niet-contractuele verbintenissen, Bruges, Die Keure, 2007, (47) 47–98; I. Verougstraete, "Wil en vertrouwen bij het totstandkomen van overeenkomsten", *TPR* 1990, (1163) 1178, no. 20 *et seq.* **The Netherlands**: C.H. Sieburgh, *Mr. C. Assers Handleiding tot de beoefening van het Nederlands Burgerlijk Recht. 6. Verbintenissenrecht. Deel III. Algemeen overeenkomstenrecht*, Deventer, Wolters Kluwer, 2022, no. 122 *et seq.* See also: F.J. de Vries, *De overeenkomst in het algemeen*, Deventer, Wolters Kluwer, 2016, no. 51.

451 **Belgium**: A. De Boeck, "Aanbod en aanvaarding" in *Comm.Bijz.Ov.*, Antwerp, Kluwer, 2008, (173) 184, no. 21. **The Netherlands**: See in a similar sense: F.J. de Vries, *De overeenkomst in het algemeen*, Deventer, Wolters Kluwer, 2016, no. 37: "Many agreements are concluded by filling in an application form. […] If the form does not require more than filling in name and address details (e.g. in a web shop), this is an indication that providing/displaying the form is an offer, which is accepted by filling in and sending." [own translation].

452 J. Bael, "De impact van de wetgeving inzake marktpraktijken en bescherming van de consument op de verkoop van onroerende goederen: het nieuwe Boek VI van het wetboek van economisch recht.", *Rechtskroniek voor het Notariaat* 2014, (137) 163–164.

453 J. Bael, "De impact van de wetgeving inzake marktpraktijken en bescherming van de consument op de verkoop van onroerende goederen: het nieuwe Boek VI van het wetboek van economisch recht.", *Rechtskroniek voor het Notariaat* 2014, (137) 163.

454 Compare also with P.-Y. Erneux, "La protection des consommateurs dans les ventes immobilières: questions d'actualité" in B. Kohl (ed.), *La vente immobilière. Aspects civils, administratifs et fiscaux*, Liège, Anthemis, 2010, (275) 308, no. 58: "*le législateur combat toujours les situations dans lesquelles l'engagement de l'entreprise ne se situe pas au niveau de celui du consommateur.*"

contract with the prospective PSS user. However, an instance like the one above, where it is not clear that there is no offer but only an offer subject to change, is problematic in my opinion. After all, the clause discussed above allows *Grover* to get out of the contract (or, more accurately, not conclude a contract), while the PSS user is already definitively bound. A possible solution could therefore be to allow the prospective PSS user-consumer who has responded to an invitation to make an offer to revoke that offer as long as it has not been accepted by the PSS supplier.[455, 456] If it is a distance or off-premises contract, the PSS user can of course also exercise his right of withdrawal.[457]

105. ALTERNATIVE CLAUSES ON OFFER AND ACCEPTANCE – Notwithstanding that clauses on invitation to make an offer are thus valid, they are not the most consumer-friendly option. In my view, a better alternative for an offer and acceptance clause can be found in the general terms and conditions of *Blue Movement*.[458] According to these terms and conditions, the contract is concluded at the time of acceptance by the PSS user of the offer of BSH (the PSS supplier) regarding the subscription, by placing an order through the website.

> TERMS AND CONDITIONS BLUE MOVEMENT – Art. 2.1 "User can enter into a Subscription Contract via the Website. The Contract is concluded at the moment of acceptance by User of BSH's offer regarding the Subscription by placing an order via the Website."

The terms and conditions of *Swapphone* have a similar clause. The contract enters into force at the time of acceptance by the PSS user.[459] Swapphone then confirms the receipt of the acceptance; the PSS user can still cancel the contract until he has received the confirmation of Swapphone.[460]

> TERMS AND CONDITIONS SWAPPHONE – Art. 4.1 "A Rental Contract, [...], comes into effect at the time of the User's acceptance of the offer and fulfilment of the conditions set out therein." Art. 4.2 "If the User has accepted the offer electronically, Swapphone shall immediately confirm the receipt of the acceptance of the offer electronically. Until the receipt of this acceptance is confirmed by Swapphone, the User may terminate the Rental Contract."

---

455 Compare with H. BEALE, B. FAUVARQUE-COSSON, J. RUTGERS and S. VOGENAUER, *Ius Commune Casebooks for the Common Law of Europe. Cases, Materials and Text on Contract Law*, Third edition, Oxford, Hart, 2019, 211–212, referring to the fact that the French *Commission des clauses abusives* (Commission for Unfair Terms) has recommended that clauses stipulating that the client will be bound definitively in order to prevent a prospective client from withdrawing between his signing of the order form and the confirmation of the trader should be prohibited in contracts between businesses and consumers.

456 See for an example: Art. 4.2 Terms and Conditions Swapphone, discussed in no. 105.

457 See *infra* section 2.3.

458 Art. 2.1 Terms and Conditions Blue Movement.

459 Art. 4.1 Terms and Conditions Swapphone.

460 Art. 4.2 Terms and Conditions Swapphone.

2.2.1.4. Contracting through representation

106. The PSS supplier may use a representative to conclude the PSS contract – In some cases, the contract will not be concluded by the PSS supplier itself. This is particularly the case if the PSS supplier relies on a representative, such as a distribution or retail partner, to market and "sell" the PSS. This is an application of the concept of representation (*vertegenwoordiging, représentation*), allowing the juridical act performed by a representative (the distribution partner) to be imputed to the represented party (the PSS supplier).[461] Both offer and acceptance can be made by a representative.[462]

107. Representation requires power of representation – For the juridical acts performed by the representative to be imputed to the PSS supplier, the representative must have power of representation.[463] The legal basis of this power of representation will in the context of PSS contracts generally be a juridical act,[464] for instance a mandate contract between the PSS supplier and the representative.[465] The starting point is that the represented PSS supplier can only be bound if the representative has remained within the limits of his power of representation.[466] However, there are exceptions to this general principle, namely if the PSS supplier ratifies[467] (*bekrachtiging, ratification*) the *ultra vires*

---

461 **Belgium**: Art. 1.8, §1 BCC. See e.g. I. Claeys and T. Tanghe, *Nieuw Algemeen Contractenrecht*, Antwerp, Intersentia, 2023, 413–414; P. Wéry, *Droit des obligations. Volume 1. Theorie générale du contrat*, Brussels, Larcier, 2021, 188, no. 161–162. **The Netherlands**: J. Hijma, C.C. van Dam, W.A.M. Van Schendel and W.L. Valk (eds.), *Rechtshandeling en Overeenkomst*, Deventer, Wolters Kluwer, 2022, no. 81–82.

462 S. Stijns, *Verbintenissenrecht*, Boek 1, Bruges, Die Keure, 2022, 157.

463 **Belgium**: I. Claeys and T. Tanghe, *Nieuw Algemeen Contractenrecht*, Antwerp, Intersentia, 2023, 416. **The Netherlands**: S.C.J.J. Kortmann, *Mr. C. Assers Handleiding tot de beoefening van het Nederlands Burgerlijk Recht. 3. Deel III. Vermogensrecht algemeen. Volmacht en vertegenwoordiging*, Deventer, Wolters Kluwer, 2017, no. 5.

464 Apart from this, the power of representation can also derive from the law (e.g. parents of a minor) or a court decision (appointment of bankruptcy trustee). Under Belgian law, this is explicitly confirmed in Art. 1.8, §2 BCC.

465 **Belgium**: Art. 1984 old BCC; V. Sagaert, *Beginselen van verbintenissenrecht. De contractuele en quasi-contractuele verbintenissen*, Leuven, LeA Uitgevers, 2023, 70. **The Netherlands**: See Art. 3:60 DCC (power of representation: refers to the competence to perform juridical acts on behalf of another person) and Art. 7:414 DCC (mandate contract, which is the legal relationship from which the power of representation is derived); J. Hijma, C.C. van Dam, W.A.M. Van Schendel and W.L. Valk (eds.), *Rechtshandeling en Overeenkomst*, Deventer, Wolters Kluwer, 2022, no. 92; T.F.E. Tjong Tjin Tai, *Asser 7-IV Bijzondere Overeenkomsten – Opdracht, incl. de geneeskundige behandelingsovereenkomst en de reisovereenkomst*, Deventer, Wolters Kluwer, 2022, no. 220–224 and 228; S.C.J.J. Kortmann, *Mr. C. Assers Handleiding tot de beoefening van het Nederlands Burgerlijk Recht. 3. Deel III. Vermogensrecht algemeen. Volmacht en vertegenwoordiging*, Deventer, Wolters Kluwer, 2017, no. 8.

466 **Belgium**: Art. 1.8, §4 BCC and (specifically for the mandate contract) Art. 1998(2) old BCC. **The Netherlands**: J. Hijma, C.C. van Dam, W.A.M. Van Schendel and W.L. Valk (eds.), *Rechtshandeling en Overeenkomst*, Deventer, Wolters Kluwer, 2022, no. 98.

467 **Belgium**: Art. 1.8, §4 BCC. See on the ratification: R. Jafferali and P.A. Foriers, *Confirmation, ratification et condition suspensive: la rétroactivité des droits contractuels*

juridical act of the representative, or if the conditions of the theory of the apparent mandate[468] (*schijnvertegenwoordiging, le mandat apparent*) are met.

108. Direct and indirect representation – A distinction is made between direct representation (*onmiddellijke/rechtstreekse vertegenwoordiging, représentation parfait/immédiate*) and indirect representation (*middellijke/onrechtstreekse vertegenwoordiging, représentation imparfaite/médiate*).[469] In the case of direct representation, the representative acts *in the name* and *on behalf* of the represented party.[470] The representative, after the PSS contract is concluded, disappears from the legal relationship. On the other hand, the representation is indirect if the representative acts *on behalf* of the represented party but *in his own name*.[471] In this case, the representative does not disappear from the legal relationship after the conclusion of the PSS contract. Either the representative discloses to the prospective PSS user that he is contracting on someone else's behalf but does not disclose the identity of the PSS supplier (i.e. a commission agreement), or does not disclose at all that he is working on someone else's behalf (i.e. a name lending agreement).[472] If a PSS contract is concluded through representation, this will generally be done through direct representation where

inachevés, Brussels, Larcier, 2011, 112 *et seq.* **The Netherlands**: Art. 3:69 DCC; J. Hijma, C.C. van Dam, W.A.M. Van Schendel and W.L. Valk (eds.), *Rechtshandeling en Overeenkomst*, Deventer, Wolters Kluwer, 2022, no. 108; S.C.J.J. Kortmann, *Mr. C. Assers Handleiding tot de beoefening van het Nederlands Burgerlijk Recht. 3. Deel III. Vermogensrecht algemeen. Volmacht en vertegenwoordiging*, Deventer, Wolters Kluwer, 2017, no. 83.

468 **Belgium**: Art. 1.8, §5 BCC; P. Wéry, *Le mandat*, Brussels, Larcier, 2019, no. 209-211-1; A. Van Oevelen, *Overeenkomsten. 2: Bijzondere overeenkomsten: E. Aanneming van werk, lastgeving, in Beginselen van Belgisch Privaatrecht*, Mechelen, Wolters Kluwer, 2017, 623, no. 510 *et seq.*; B. Tilleman, *Lastgeving*, Deurne, Story-Scientia en Kluwer Rechtswetenschappen België, 1997, 223–224, no. 434. **The Netherlands**: Art. 3:61(2) DCC; J. Hijma, C.C. van Dam, W.A.M. Van Schendel and W.L. Valk (eds.), *Rechtshandeling en Overeenkomst*, Deventer, Wolters Kluwer, 2022, no. 101.

469 **Belgium**: I. Claeys and T. Tanghe, *Nieuw Algemeen Contractenrecht*, Antwerp, Intersentia, 2023, 415–416; S. Stijns, *Verbintenissenrecht*, Boek 1, Bruges, Die Keure, 2022, 158–159; P. Wéry, *Droit des obligations. Volume 1. Theorie générale du contrat*, Brussels, Larcier, 2021, 190–191, no. 165. **The Netherlands**: S.C.J.J. Kortmann, *Mr. C. Assers Handleiding tot de beoefening van het Nederlands Burgerlijk Recht. 3. Deel III. Vermogensrecht algemeen. Volmacht en vertegenwoordiging*, Deventer, Wolters Kluwer, 2017, no. 6.

470 **Belgium**: Art. 1.8, §1(2) BCC; **The Netherlands**: J. Hijma, C.C. van Dam, W.A.M. Van Schendel and W.L. Valk (eds.), *Rechtshandeling en Overeenkomst*, Deventer, Wolters Kluwer, 2022, no. 81.

471 **Belgium**: Art. 1.8, §1(3) BCC; I. Samoy, *Middellijke vertegenwoordiging*, Antwerp, Intersentia, 2005, 762 p. **The Netherlands**: Art. 7:419, 7:420, 7:421 and 7:424 DCC; S.C.J.J. Kortmann, *Mr. C. Assers Handleiding tot de beoefening van het Nederlands Burgerlijk Recht. 3. Deel III. Vermogensrecht algemeen. Volmacht en vertegenwoordiging*, Deventer, Wolters Kluwer, 2017, no. 102.

472 **Belgium**: I. Claeys and T. Tanghe, *Nieuw Algemeen Contractenrecht*, Antwerp, Intersentia, 2023, 415–416; S. Stijns, *Verbintenissenrecht*, Boek 1, Bruges, Die Keure, 2022, 159. **The Netherlands**: S.C.J.J. Kortmann, *Mr. C. Assers Handleiding tot de beoefening van het Nederlands Burgerlijk Recht. 3. Deel III. Vermogensrecht algemeen. Volmacht en vertegenwoordiging*, Deventer, Wolters Kluwer, 2017, no. 102.

the representative discloses the capacity and identity of the PSS supplier to the (prospective) PSS user.

109. Contracting through representation: example – *Grover* can serve as an example of a PSS supplier that, in addition to making its PSS available through its own website, uses representatives (distribution partners) to conclude PSS contracts.[473] The prospective PSS user can conclude a PSS contract with *Grover* at the location of the distribution partner and with the distribution partner's assistance. An online sales portal is used for this purpose. Just like the situation where the contract is concluded directly with *Grover*, the terms and conditions outline that the prospective PSS user makes a binding offer, which *Grover* will then accept after checking the order. After the PSS contract is concluded, the distribution partner makes the product available to the PSS user.

> Terms and conditions Grover – Art. 4.2.2. "*You can also get a rental through the agency of a stationary dealer, who is involved as a distribution partner of Grover,* hereinafter referred to as 'Distribution Partner'. *An online portal (hereinafter referred to as 'Sales Portal') will be used for this purpose at the location of the Distribution Partner.* The operator of the Sales Portal is Grover Nederland B.V. You can place an order via the Sales Portal. If You are not registered yet, You can register in the same process. You select the Rental items available at the Distribution Partner and place a request for a rental on the Sales Portal. The amount of the payable rent will be displayed to You. *You will make a binding offer for the conclusion of the contract only when You click on the button 'Rent subject to payment' on the summary page.* Up until this point in time, You can check Your information in the order mask at any time and correct it if necessary by means of the change button. Regarding the details of the respective offer, it is referred to the description of the offer on the Sales Portal, hereinafter referred to as 'Offer Description'. You will receive an email in which We conform the receipt of your order and in which We ask You to verify Your email address. After You have verified Your email address, We will Check Your order. *After a successful check of the order, You will receive a 'Contract Confirmation'. The Rental Agreement becomes effective on receipt of this Contract Confirmation. The Distribution Partner helps You with the registration and orders.* On receipt of the Contract Confirmation, the Distribution of the Distribution Partner will transfer the Rental Item to You." (own emphasis).

110. Contractual clauses limiting the PSS supplier's obligation to respect commitments made by representatives are unfair – The PSS supplier will be bound by the obligations entered into by the representative in its name and on its behalf. Should the PSS supplier limit its obligations in general terms and conditions, i.e. stipulate that it is committed to less than the

---

[473] See Art. 4.2.2 Terms and Conditions Grover.

commitments undertaken by the representative, these can be challenged using the unfair terms rules.[474]

Under Belgian law, Article VI.83, 29° BCEL bans clauses with the object or effect of "*limiting the trader's obligations to respect commitments undertaken by his agents or making his commitments subject to compliance with a particular formality.*"[475] The wording of this provision is similar to point (n) of the UCTD Annex.[476] This provision prohibits not only the complete restriction of the agreed obligation, but also any limitation that disadvantages the consumer compared to what was agreed with the representative.[477] In addition, this provision aims to prohibit clauses where the PSS supplier stipulates that it is bound only after a special formality has been fulfilled (i.e. clauses making the formation or performance of the obligation dependent on a formality not imposed by law).[478] This could include, for example, a clause stating that the PSS supplier is bound only after the order accepted by the representative has been confirmed in writing by the PSS supplier.[479]

Under Dutch law, these representation clauses can be challenged based on Article 6:238(1), *sub* b. DCC. According to this provision, the PSS supplier cannot rely on limitations in the general terms and conditions regarding the representative's power of representation that the PSS user-consumer did not know and did not have to expect.[480] In addition, this provision is closely connected to Article 6:236, *sub* l. DCC, which blacklists clauses that, to the detriment of the consumer, impose formal requirements that deviate from the legal rules on the form and effect of declarations of will (Art. 3:37 DCC).[481]

111. Application to terms and conditions *Grover* – If we analyse the representation clause in the terms and conditions of *Grover* cited

474 P. Cambie, *Onrechtmatige bedingen*, Ghent, Larcier, 2009, 222.

475 R. Steennot, "Commentaar bij art. VI.83, 29° WER" in *Handels- en economisch recht. Commentaar met overzicht van rechtspraak en rechtsleer*, Mechelen, Kluwer, loose-leaf, 2017, (587) 587.

476 Paragraph 1, point (n) UCTD Annex.

477 I. Demuynck, *De inhoudelijke controle van onrechtmatige bedingen*, Thesis submitted to obtain the degree of Doctor of Laws, University of Ghent, 2000, 404. Compare also with: F. Bogaert and B. Van Baeveghem, "Contractuele aspecten van de Wet Marktpraktijken" in I. Claeys, R. Steennot and M. Tison (eds.), *Economisch Recht: Ondernemingen, concurrenten en consumenten. Postuniversitaire Cyclus Willy Delva 2010–2011*, Mechelen, Kluwer, 2011, (1) 50, where it is argued that this provision does not provide a lot of additional consumer protection compared to the general law of obligations. Relying on the theory of the legitimate reliance and apparent mandate will generally yield the same results. See also: P. Cambie, *Onrechtmatige bedingen*, Ghent, Larcier, 2009, 223.

478 I. Demuynck, *De inhoudelijke controle van onrechtmatige bedingen*, Thesis submitted to obtain the degree of Doctor of Laws, University of Ghent, 2000, 404.

479 Compare with: S. Stijns, "De leer der onrechtmatige bedingen in de WHPC na de Wet van 7 december 1998", *TBH* 2000, (148) 162.

480 M.B.M. Loos, *Algemene voorwaarden*, The Hague, Boom juridisch, 2018, no. 396–398.

481 J. den Hoed and Y.G. Blei Weissman, *Groene Serie Verbintenissenrecht, Art. 6:217 BW*, 2022, no. 3.68.

above[482] against the provisions described in the previous paragraph, it will not be unfair under Belgian and Dutch law. First, this clause does not limit *Grover's* obligation to respect the commitments made by the distribution partner but rather describes the process of renting through a distribution partner, who acts as an agent of *Grover*. Since an online sales platform operated by *Grover* itself is also used for the conclusion of the contract, *Grover* also retains active control over the formation process of the PSS contract. Second, the clause does also not impose any specific formal requirements that deviate from the general contract law rules but only specifies the steps and conditions for placing an order via the sales portal and, by doing so, receiving a contract formation. Still, the same caveat applies regarding the fact that the *Grover's* contract proposal through the online sales platform is only an invitation to make an offer.[483] It would, in my view, be more appropriate that it is made clear to consumers in an explicit manner and during the order process (i.e. not just in the terms and conditions) that the order placed through the online sales platform is subject to change and must still be checked and approved by *Grover*.

2.2.1.5. Consequences of validly concluded PSS contract: binding force

112. Binding force of validly concluded PSS contract – If the PSS contract is validly concluded, its content is binding upon the parties who entered into it.[484] Or, as the well-known adage goes, *pacta sunt servanda*.

113. Consequences of the binding force of the PSS contract – The binding force of the contract is a fundamental principle of contract law and entails several consequences.[485] However, there also exist various nuances and exceptions to this fundamental principle.

First, the binding force of the PSS contract means that each party can legally enforce the performance and application of the contents of the PSS contract.[486]

---

482 Art. 4.2.2 Terms and Conditions Grover discussed *supra* no. 109.

483 Compare with *supra* no. 103–104.

484 **Belgium**: See Art. 5.69 BCC: "A contract formed validly is law to those who entered into it" (formerly Art. 1134(1) old BCC). **The Netherlands**: Art. 6:248(1) DCC: "A contract not only has legal effects agreed by the parties, but also those which, according to the nature of the contract, arise from law, custom or the requirements of reasonableness and fairness."

485 **Belgium**: See e.g. I. Claeys and T. Tanghe, *Nieuw Algemeen Contractenrecht*, Antwerp, Intersentia, 2023, 434–436; V. Sagaert, *Beginselen van verbintenissenrecht. De contractuele en quasi-contractuele verbintenissen*, Leuven, LeA Uitgevers, 2023, 33–34; P. Wéry, *Droit des obligations. Volume 1. Theorie générale du contrat*, Brussels, Larcier, 2021, 400–407. **The Netherlands**: See e.g. J. Hijma, C.C. van Dam, W.A.M. Van Schendel and W.L. Valk (eds.), *Rechtshandeling en Overeenkomst*, Deventer, Wolters Kluwer, 2022, 15; C.H. Sieburgh, *Mr. C. Assers Handleiding tot de beoefening van het Nederlands Burgerlijk Recht. 6. Verbintenissenrecht. Deel III. Algemeen overeenkomstenrecht*, Deventer, Wolters Kluwer, 2022, no. 41 *et seq.*

486 J.H. Nieuwenhuis, *Drie beginselen van contractenrecht*, Deventer, Kluwer, 1979, 62.

The parties have access to the courts for this purpose. Nevertheless, in some cases, the PSS user or PSS supplier will be confronted with limits to enforcing the obligations under the PSS contract, for example in case of *force majeure* or insolvency of the other party.

Second, the court is also bound by the PSS contract and may, in principle, not modify the PSS contract unless the parties agree to do so. However, this should also be nuanced, as the law on multiple occasions gives the court an option to mitigate or set aside certain content in the contract. This is for example the case with unreasonably high indemnity clauses (in a non-B2C context),[487] the option of granting a judicial grace period under Belgian law,[488] or, also under Belgian law, if one of the parties has committed an abuse of circumstances.[489] In addition, the requirements of good faith and the prohibition of abuse of rights (Belgium) and the requirements of reasonableness and fairness (the Netherlands) may also impose restrictions or corrections to the (agreed-upon) rules of the PSS contract.[490] In the case of changed circumstances or hardship, the court also has the power to modify (and even terminate) the contract if the conditions to do so are met.[491]

Third, the binding force of the contract also means that one of the parties in principle cannot terminate the PSS contract unilaterally.[492] However, there are also exceptions to this principle, for example in case of an open-ended PSS contract,[493] if a contractual termination clause is included in the PSS contract,[494]

---

487 **Belgium**: Art. 5.88, §2 BCC. **The Netherlands**: Art. 6:94 DCC.

488 See Art. 5.201 BCC.

489 **Belgium**: See Art. 5.37 BCC, which states that the weaker party can claim an amendment of its obligations by the court and, if the abuse is decisive, relative nullity. Compare, however, with **the Netherlands**, where Art. 3:44(1) and (4) DCC sanctions abuse of circumstances "only" with the voidability of the juridical act.

490 **Belgium**: Art. 5.73. and Art. 1.10 BCC. See: I. Claeys and T. Tanghe, *Nieuw Algemeen Contractenrecht*, Antwerp, Intersentia, 2023, no. 599 and no. 95 *et seq*. **The Netherlands**: Art. 6:2 DCC and Art. 6:248(2) DCC. See for an analysis of the requirements of reasonableness and fairness: H.N. Schelhaas, *Redelijkheid en billijkheid, Mon.BW nr. A5*, Deventer, Wolters Kluwer, 2017, 164 p.

491 **Belgium**: Art. 5.74 BCC. **The Netherlands**: Art. 6:258 DCC.

492 See explicitly under Belgian law: Art. 5.70(1) BCC.

493 **Belgium**: Art. 5.75(2) BCC. **The Netherlands**: HR (NL) 28 October 2011, ECLI:NL:HR:2011:BQ9854, (*Gemeente De Ronde Venen/Stedin*), *NJ* 2012/685, case note T.F.E. Tjong Tjin Tai, para. 3.5.1. (If the law and the contract do not provide for a regulation of the termination of an open-ended duration contract, it can in principle be terminated. The requirements of reasonableness and fairness may imply, in connection with the nature and content of the contract and the circumstances of the case, that termination is only possible if a sufficiently serious ground for termination exists, that a certain notice period must be observed or that termination must be accompanied by the offer to pay compensation (for damages).). This was also confirmed in: HR (NL) 14 June 2013, ECLI:NL:HR:2013:BZ4163, (*Auping/Beverslaap*), *NJ* 2013/341, para. 3.6; HR (NL) 10 June 2016, ECLI:NL:HR:2016:1134, (*Pensioenfonds/Alcatel-Lucent*), *NJ* 2016/450, case note T.F.E. Tjong Tjin Tai, para. 4.4.2 and HR (NL) 2 February 2018, ECLI:NL:HR:2018:141, (*Goglio/SMQ*), *NJ* 2018/98, para. 3.6.2. See: e.g. J. Hijma, C.C. van Dam, W.A.M. Van Schendel and W.L. Valk (eds.), *Rechtshandeling en Overeenkomst*, Deventer, Wolters Kluwer, 2022, 328–331.

494 See *infra* sections 2.7.1.2. and 2.7.2.2.

or if a specific legal rule provides in a unilateral termination option, such as is the case with the contract for services.[495] Moreover, contracting parties who are presumed to be in a weaker position *vis a vis* the other party are sometimes granted a right of withdrawal.[496] This is most notably the case for distance PSS contracts.[497] Finally, the parties cannot unilaterally amend the PSS contract either, unless the PSS contract contains a (valid) unilateral amendment clause in favour of the amending party (or a third party).[498]

114. Parties can terminate or amend PSS contract by mutual consent – The principle of the binding force of the PSS contract does of course not prevent that the parties to a PSS contract can always terminate or amend their agreement by mutual consent.

2.3. USE OF GENERAL TERMS AND CONDITIONS

"You know I don't read this crap!
I am a dyslexic, talented actress with questionable English –
that's why I overpay you to protect me!"
– Salma Hayek[499]

2.3.1. CONTRACTS OF ADHESION AND GENERAL TERMS AND CONDITIONS FOR PSS

115. PSS suppliers often make use of contracts of adhesion and general terms and conditions – As mentioned, PSS are often offered in the form of a contract of adhesion[500] (*toetredingscontract, contrat d'adhésion*) on a "take it or leave it" basis.[501] This allows PSS suppliers to offer rather standardised PSS offers to a large number of users.[502] Contracts of adhesion have the advantage that a multitude of PSS contracts can be concluded in a very short

495 **Belgium**: Art. 1794 old BCC. **The Netherlands**: See Art. 7:408 DCC for the contract for services. Compare also with Art. 7:764 DCC for the contract for works.
496 See for a general provision on the right of withdrawal under Belgian law: Art. 5.22 BCC.
497 See *infra* section 2.4.
498 See explicitly under Belgian law: Art. 5.70(2) BCC.
499 Quote from the episode "Joan Is Awful" of Netflix series Black Mirror (S06E01) which paints a dystopian picture of what can happen to people who do not read long user agreements.
500 See Art. 5.10 BCC: "A contract is a contract of adhesion if it is drawn up in advance and unilaterally by one party and is non-negotiable." Compare also with Art. 6:231, *sub* a. DCC.
501 See *supra* no. 17.
502 The fact that some terms of the PSS contract are negotiable does not necessarily preclude that there is no contract of adhesion, e.g. if the overall assessment leads to the conclusion that the contract is in fact a contract of adhesion, see Art. 5.10(2) BCC.

time, without the need to negotiate the terms of each contract.[503] However, there are also risks associated with this ubiquitous use of contracts of adhesion and general terms and conditions.

116. Contracts of adhesion give PSS supplier far-reaching freedom to shape the contractual relationship – The use of contracts of adhesion gives the PSS supplier far-reaching power to shape the contractual relationship between himself and the PSS user. Indeed, the use of a contract of adhesion precludes the opportunity of the PSS user to enter into negotiations, so his contractual freedom is limited to whether or not he enters into the contract.[504] On top of this, consumers often do not read the general terms and conditions of standard contracts, either because they do not have the time, motivation or legal knowledge to do this.[505] This is compounded by the fact that PSS contracts are often offered online, where it is common for consumers to declare their agreement to the standard terms by clicking "*I agree*".

117. Contracts of adhesion can create an asymmetric relationship – Since PSS users cannot negotiate the terms of their contract and often do not read the terms and conditions, PSS contracts of adhesion can lead to an asymmetric relationship between the PSS supplier and the PSS user. This creates the risk that the PSS supplier may impose unilateral (and unreasonable) terms that the consumer could not reasonably expect.[506] In this case, the freedom of contract

---

503 **Belgium**: A. De Boeck, "De tegenstelbaarheid van algemene voorwaarden", *TBBR* 2019, (63) 63; A. Geldhof and M. Hoebeeck, "Toetredingscontracten en algemene contractvoorwaarden" in *Comm.Bijz.Ov.*, Mechelen, Kluwer, loose-leaf, 2010, 190. **The Netherlands:** C.H. Sieburgh, *Mr. C. Assers Handleiding tot de beoefening van het Nederlands Burgerlijk Recht. 6. Verbintenissenrecht. Deel III. Algemeen overeenkomstenrecht*, Deventer, Wolters Kluwer, 2018, no. 459.

504 R. Dekkers, A.L. Verbeke, N. Carette and K. Vanhove, *Handboek burgerlijk recht, Deel III, Verbintenissen, bewijsleer en gebruikelijke contracten*, Antwerp, Intersentia, 2007, 61; K. De Vulder and D. Rombouts, "De elektronische algemene voorwaarden en hun tegenstelbaarheid" in S. Ongena (ed.), *Algemene voorwaarden*, Mechelen, Kluwer, 2006, (31) 33. However, see W. van Gerven and A. Van Oevelen, *Verbintenissenrecht*, Leuven, Acco, 2021, 64–65 where it is stated that this freedom is rather limited when the standard contract concerns essential goods and/or services.

505 See e.g. E. Terryn and B. Keirsbilck, "Informatieverplichtingen in het consumenten- en ondernemingsrecht" in E.S. Van Aggelen (ed.), *Informatie en recht*, Antwerp, Intersentia, 2021, (117) 125–132; M. Gisgand, "'I agree to the Terms and Conditions': de evidentie voorbij" in *Juridische Meesterwerken VUB 2017–2018*, Ghent, Larcier, 2020, (199) 200; O. Ben-Shahar, "The Myth of the 'Opportunity to Read' in Contract Law", *European Review of Contract Law* 2009, vol. 5 issue 1, (1) 2–3.

506 **Belgium**: K. Vanderschot, "Instemming met algemene voorwaarden: kennisname en aanvaardingsclausules" in S. Stijns and K. Vanderschot (eds.), *Contractuele clausules rond de (niet-)uitvoering en de beëindiging van contracten*, Antwerp, Intersentia, 2006, (1) 3. **The Netherlands**: C.H. Sieburgh, *Mr. C. Assers Handleiding tot de beoefening van het Nederlands Burgerlijk Recht. 6. Verbintenissenrecht. Deel III. Algemeen overeenkomstenrecht*, Deventer, Wolters Kluwer, 2018, no. 459.

is not sufficient to guarantee consumers' economic rights and self-determination on the market.[507] Therefore, consumer law provides corrective mechanisms.

118. Protection against abuse of PSS contracts of adhesion – There are two mechanisms to protect PSS users from the abuse of contracts of adhesion in an asymmetric relationship. A first corrective mechanism concerns the enforceability (BE: *tegenstelbaarheid, opposabilité*; NL: *gebondenheid*) of general terms and conditions against the PSS user.[508] This is closely related to the formation of the contract, and more specifically to whether the general terms and conditions are part of the PSS contract (incorporation). Essentially, the issue is whether both parties (and the protected party – i.e. the PSS user – in particular) have given their effective consent to the general terms and conditions. If the effective consent of the PSS user is lacking, the general terms and conditions of the PSS supplier will not be enforceable. This requirement of effective consent is generally linked to a transparency and information obligation for the PSS supplier that uses general terms and conditions – i.e. the terms and conditions must be brought to the attention of consumers.[509]

A second corrective mechanism relates to the content of the contract by imposing limits on the permissible terms. Indeed, in a B2C context, significantly imbalanced contractual clauses can be challenged based on the control mechanism of unfair terms of UCTD and its national implementation (BE: *onrechtmatige bedingen, clauses abusives*; NL: *onredelijk bezwarende bedingen*).[510]

2.3.2. INCORPORATION AND ENFORCEABILITY OF GENERAL TERMS AND CONDITIONS

119. Incorporation of standard terms into the PSS contract – The UCTD does not (explicitly[511]) deal with the incorporation of general terms

---

507 E. Terryn, "Consumentenrecht anno 2022: van silo- naar systeemdenken?", *Tijdschrift voor Consumentenrecht & Handelspraktijken* 2022, vol. 5, (214) 214; E. Terryn, *Bedenktijden in het consumentenrecht*, Antwerp, Intersentia, 2008, 27 *et seq.*; G. Straetmans, *Consument en markt: onderzoek naar de rechtspositie van de consument op de Europese interne markt. Met de financiële sector als toetssteen*, Antwerp, Kluwer, 1988, 68 *et seq.* See also: J. Drexl, *Die wirtschaftliche Selbstbestimmung des Verbrauchers*, Munich, Mohr Siebeck, 1998, 681 p.

508 **Belgium**: I. Claeys and T. Tanghe, *Nieuw Algemeen Contractenrecht*, Antwerp, Intersentia, 2023, 222–223. **The Netherlands**: C.H. Sieburgh, *Mr. C. Assers Handleiding tot de beoefening van het Nederlands Burgerlijk Recht. 6. Verbintenissenrecht. Deel III. Algemeen overeenkomstenrecht*, Deventer, Wolters Kluwer, 2018, no. 460.

509 P. Rott, "Standard Terms" in H.-W. Micklitz, J. Stuyck and E. Terryn (eds.), *Cases, Materials and Text on Consumer Law*, Oxford, Hart, 2010, (279) 282.

510 See Directive 93/13/EEG of 5 April 1993 on unfair terms in consumer contracts, *OJ L* 95, 21.4.1993, p. 29–34. **Belgium**: implemented in Art. VI. 82–84 BCEL. **The Netherlands**: implemented in Art. 6:233, a) DCC.

511 See, however, EC, *Guidance on the interpretation of Council Directive 93/13/EEC on unfair terms in consumer contracts*, 27.9.2019, 2019/C 323/04, 22: the transparency requirement

and conditions into the PSS contract.[512] This is because Member States were afraid that the EU could interfere with the national rules on conclusion and formation of contracts.[513] As a result, the question regarding incorporation and enforceability of general terms and conditions is governed by the rules of national law.

120. Reading guide – This section deals with the incorporation of standard terms into the PSS contract under Belgian and Dutch law. Section 2.3.2.1 sets out the general requirements for incorporation of general terms and conditions. As PSS contracts are often concluded online, section 2.3.2.2 discusses how these requirements are applied in an online context, especially with regard to *clickwrap*, *browsewrap* and *scrollwrap* terms and conditions. Finally, section 2.3.2.3 looks at (the validity and effects of) clauses relating to knowledge and acceptance of general terms and conditions.

2.3.2.1. Requirements for incorporation and enforceability

121. Belgian law: general terms and conditions must be known and accepted – According to the Belgian general law of obligations, standard terms and conditions are only part of the contract if (i) the PSS user has taken knowledge of them or was reasonably able to take knowledge of them (*kennisname, connaissance*) (ii) at the latest at the time of conclusion of the contract and (iii) has also accepted them expressly or tacitly (*aanvaarding, acceptation*).[514]

---

of the UCTD (Art. 4(2) and Art. 5 UCTD) means that consumers must be given the real opportunity to become acquainted with the contract terms before the conclusion of the contract. See also Point 1(i) of the Annex and Recital 20 UCTD.

512 E. Terryn, "Transparantie en algemene voorwaarden – Nood aan hervorming?", *TPR* 2017, (13) 35.

513 P. Rott, "Standard Terms" in H.-W. Micklitz, J. Stuyck and E. Terryn (eds.), *Cases, Materials and Text on Consumer Law*, Oxford, Hart, 2010, (279) 282. See also: E. Terryn, "Transparantie en algemene voorwaarden – Nood aan hervorming?", *TPR* 2017, (13) 21, fn 34.

514 See Art. 5.23 BCC: "*De opname van algemene voorwaarden van een partij in het contract vereist hun effectieve kennis door de andere partij of ten minste de mogelijkheid voor deze om er effectief kennis van te nemen, alsook hun aanvaarding.*" See also: I. Claeys and T. Tanghe, *Nieuw Algemeen Contractenrecht*, Antwerp, Intersentia, 2023, 223; W. van Gerven and A. Van Oevelen, *Verbintenissenrecht*, Leuven, Acco, 2021, 111; A. De Boeck, "De tegenstelbaarheid van algemene voorwaarden", *TBBR* 2019, (63) 63–64; J. Schraeyen, E. Enkels, S. Van den Broeke and T. De Clerck, *Algemene voorwaarden*, 2012, Ghent, Larcier, 2012, 11–21; A. Geldhof and M. Hoebeeck, "Toetredingscontracten en algemene contractvoorwaarden" in *Comm.Bijz.Ov.*, Mechelen, Kluwer, loose-leaf, 2010, 190–191; C.A. Dumont De Chassart, "De tegenstelbaarheid van algemene voorwaarden 'offline'" in S. Ongena (ed.), *Algemene voorwaarden*, Mechelen, Kluwer, 2006, (1) 4; R. Kruithof, H. Bocken, F. De Ly and B. De Temmerman, "Verbintenissenrecht (1981–1992). Overzicht van rechtspraak", *TPR* 1994, (171) 268–277; E. Dirix and A. Van oevelen, "Kroniek van het verbintenissenrecht (1985–1992) (eerste deel)", *RW* 1992–93, (1209) 1213–1215.

122. Reasonable possibility of taking knowledge of the terms and conditions – Without the reasonable possibility of taking knowledge of the general terms and conditions, there can be no consent of the PSS user.[515] Yet, a reasonable possibility suffices.[516] It is therefore not required that the PSS user has actually read the general terms and conditions.[517] This is logical because the PSS supplier is not in a position to force the PSS user to actually read the terms and conditions, unless they would be discussed individually, which would in turn negate the very advantage of standard terms.[518] In practice, this requirement is most often met by providing the PSS user with a physical copy of the general terms and conditions. Where the PSS contract is offered online, the terms and conditions will generally be available on the PSS supplier's website.

123. Before the conclusion of the PSS contract – The second condition relates to *when* the PSS user must have the reasonable possibility of taken knowledge of the general terms and conditions. This must be before (or at the latest at the time of) the conclusion of the PSS contract.[519] This is also logical, since the knowledge of the general terms and conditions is linked to the requirement of consent (*toestemming, consentement*) as a validity requirement of the contract.[520] General terms and conditions that are only later disclosed to the PSS user (e.g. in an order confirmation, invoice, etc.) are therefore not enforceable, unless they are accepted by the PSS user.[521]

---

515 See: Cass. (BE) 20 April 2017, AR C.16.0341.F, *NjW* 2017, 540, case note P. Brulez, *DAOR* 2017, 54, case note; Cass. (BE) 16 September 2016, AR C.14.0424.N, *TBBR* 2018, 154, case note C. Helas, *RW* 2017–18, 822 (summary); Cass. (BE) 19 December 2011, AR C.10.0587.F, *Arr. Cass.* 2011, 2664, *Pas.* 2011, 2813, *RW* 2013–14, 337 (summary), *T.Gez.* 2012, 381, case note T. Vansweevelt.

516 A. De Boeck, "De tegenstelbaarheid van algemene voorwaarden", *TBBR* 2019, (63) 14–15; D. Bruloot and R. Steennot, "Clausules i.v.m. de tegenwerpelijkheid van algemene voorwaarden" in G.-L. Ballon, H. De Decker, V. Sagaert, E. Terryn, B. Tilleman and A.-L. Verbeke (eds.), *Contractuele clausules. Gemeenrechtelijke clausules. Volume I*, Antwerp, Intersentia, 2013, (359) 370.

517 Ghent (BE) 6 January 2022, *T. Verz.* 2022, 179; M. Gisgand, "'I agree to the Terms and Conditions': de evidentie voorbij" in *Juridische Meesterwerken VUB 2017–2018*, Ghent, Larcier, 2020, (199) 210.

518 D. Bruloot and R. Steennot, "Clausules i.v.m. de tegenwerpelijkheid van algemene voorwaarden" in G.-L. Ballon, H. De Decker, V. Sagaert, E. Terryn, B. Tilleman and A.-L. Verbeke (eds.), *Contractuele clausules. Gemeenrechtelijke clausules. Volume I*, Antwerp, Intersentia, 2013, (359) 370; K. Vanderschot, "Instemming met algemene voorwaarden: kennisname en aanvaardingsclausules" in S. Stijns and K. Vanderschot (eds.), *Contractuele clausules rond de (niet-)uitvoering en de beëindiging van contracten*, Antwerp, Intersentia, 2006, (1) 4, no. 8.

519 Cass. (BE) 19 December 2011, AR C.10.0587.F, *Arr.Cass.* 2011, 2664, *Pas.* 2011, 2813, *RW* 2013–14, 337 (summary), *T.Gez.* 2012, 381, case note T. Vansweevelt; A. De Boeck, "De tegenstelbaarheid van algemene voorwaarden", *TBBR* 2019, (63) 68, no. 25; K. Vanderschot, "Instemming met algemene voorwaarden: kennisname en aanvaardingsclausules" in S. Stijns and K. Vanderschot (eds.), *Contractuele clausules rond de (niet-)uitvoering en de beëindiging van contracten*, Antwerp, Intersentia, 2006, (1) 17.

520 Art. 1108 old BCC.

521 Brussels (BE) 23 November 2001, *DAOR* 2002, 244; A. De Boeck, "De tegenstelbaarheid van algemene voorwaarden", *TBBR* 2019, (63) 68, no. 25.

124. Acceptance of general terms and conditions – Third, the PSS user must also have accepted the general terms and conditions.[522] However, this acceptance does not necessarily have to be explicit. The Belgian Court of Cassation has confirmed that the acceptance of general terms and conditions can also be tacit or implicit.[523] However, a mere silence is not enough; there must be a circumstantial silence (*omstandig stilzwijgen*, *silence circonstancié*).[524] This means silence that cannot be interpreted other than in the sense of consent (e.g. if the PSS user took note or could reasonable have taken note of the terms and made no objection).[525] For B2C contracts, Bruloot and Steennot argue that this reasonable knowledge on the part of the consumer requires, in principle, the handing over of the terms and conditions.[526]

125. Consequences if these requirements are lacking – If these requirements (knowledge and acceptance) are not fulfilled, the general terms and conditions drafted by the PSS supplier will not be part of the PSS contract and therefore will not apply.[527] In this case, the PSS contract will be governed by the applicable default rules.

126. Dutch law: acceptance of general terms and conditions sufficient – Under Dutch law, the question of whether the general terms and conditions as a whole form part of the content of the contract is answered based on the rules for the formation of contracts.[528] This means that the enforceability

---

522 See e.g. Cass. (BE) 17 October 1975, *Arr.Cass.* 1976, 224; Liège (BE) 19 March 2018, *T.Verz.* 2019, 339. See also: L.A. Nyssen and D. Philippe, "L'opposabilité des conditions générales" in *Contrat et protection des consommateurs*, Limal, Anthemis, 2016, (109) 148 and the references there; R. Kruithof, H. Bocken, F. De Ly and B. De Temmerman, "Verbintenissenrecht (1981–1992). Overzicht van rechtspraak", *TPR* 1994, (171) 171, no. 72 and the references there.

523 See: Cass. (BE) 20 May 1988, *Arr.Cass.* 1987–88, 1237 and Cass. (BE) 11 December 1970, *Arr. Cass.* 1971, 369; P. Van Ommeslaghe, *Traité de droit civil belge, Tome II. Les Obligations*, Volume 1, Brussels, Bruylant, 2013, 506.

524 See: Brussels (BE) 9 June 1992, *JMLB* 1994, 201; Comm. Antwerp (BE) 12 June 1995, *TBH* 1995, 908; D. Bruloot and R. Steennot, "Clausules i.v.m. de tegenwerpelijkheid van algemene voorwaarden" in G.-L. Ballon, H. De Decker, V. Sagaert, E. Terryn, B. Tilleman and A.-L. Verbeke (eds.), *Contractuele clausules. Gemeenrechtelijke clausules. Volume I*, Antwerp, Intersentia, 2013, (359) 372; P. Van Ommeslaghe, *Traité de droit civil belge, Tome II. Les Obligations*, Volume 1, Brussels, Bruylant, 2013, 505.

525 E. Dirix and A. Van Oevelen, "Verbintenissenrecht (Gerechtelijke jaren 1978–1979 en 1979–1980)", *RW* 1980–81, (2368) 2384; R. Kruithof, H. Bocken, F. De Ly and B. De Temmerman, "Verbintenissenrecht (1981–1992). Overzicht van rechtspraak", *TPR* 1994, (171) 537–538 and 543.

526 D. Bruloot and R. Steennot, "Clausules i.v.m. de tegenwerpelijkheid van algemene voorwaarden" in G.-L. Ballon, H. De Decker, V. Sagaert, E. Terryn, B. Tilleman and A.-L. Verbeke (eds.), *Contractuele clausules. Gemeenrechtelijke clausules. Volume I*, Antwerp, Intersentia, 2013, (359) 373.

527 I. Claeys and T. Tanghe, *Nieuw Algemeen Contractenrecht*, Antwerp, Intersentia, 2023, 223.

528 C.J. Van Zeben, J.W. Du Pon, W.H.M. Reehuis and E.E. Slob, *Parlementaire Geschiedenis van het Nieuwe Burgerlijk Wetboek. Invoering Boeken 3, 5 en 6: Boek 6: Algemeen gedeelte van het verbintenissenrecht*, Deventer, Kluwer, 1990, 1573.

of general terms and conditions is governed by the system of offer and acceptance.[529] Consequently, under Dutch law, it is sufficient that the PSS user has accepted the validity of the terms and conditions for their incorporation into the contract and thus their enforceability. Whether the consumer has accepted the offer and the general terms and conditions must be determined based on Article 3:33 and 3:35 DCC.[530] Acceptance requires that the PSS user expressly or tacitly expresses its will to include the proposed general terms and conditions in the contract.[531] This can take the form of signing a written agreement or by other means.[532, 533] There are no specific form requirements.[534] The acceptance covers the terms and conditions in general, as a complex, and not with respect to (the contents of) each individual term.[535] Moreover, according to Article 6:232 DCC, the PSS user who has accepted the validity of general terms and conditions shall also be bound if, at the time of concluding the contract, he was unaware of the contents of the general terms and conditions, regardless of whether the PSS supplier knew or should have known this.[536]

529 Art. 6:217 *et seq.* DCC. See: J. Hijma, *Algemene voorwaarden, Monografieën BW nr. B55*, Deventer, Wolters Kluwer, 2016, no. 19; R.A.F. Willems, "Het hanteren van algemene voorwaarden: werk aan de webwinkel", *Contracteren* 2013, (59), 60; M.W. Scheltema and T.F.E. Tjong Tjin Tai, "Overeenkomsten sluiten door openen en klikken?", *Computerrecht* 2003, (244), 244.

530 According to Art. 3:33 DCC, "*a juridical act requires the will of the acting person to establish a specific legal effect, which will must be expressed through a statement of the acting person.*" However, it is possible that the legal effect which the acting party desires and what the counterparty draws from the acting party's statement differs. In this situation, Art. 3:35 DCC protects legitimate expectations the counterparty might have: "*Towards him who has interpreted another person's statement or behavior, in accordance with the meaning that he reasonably could give to it in the circumstances, as a statement with a certain content of this other person addressed to him, cannot be appealed to the absence of a with that statement corresponding will.*" This means that the acting person must consider the expectations that he creates in the counterparty by his statement.

531 Art. 3:33 DCC.

532 Examples in an offline environment include: a declaration of applicability in writing or orally, the handing over of a paper (e.g. a quotation or invoice) on which the conditions are printed, reference to the place where the conditions have been deposited, an (eye-catching) sign in a shop, etc. Examples in an online environment include: the inclusion of general terms and conditions in the ordering process, in a separate window, via a hyperlink, or with the text "general terms and conditions apply." See e.g. C.H. Sieburgh, *Mr. C. Assers Handleiding tot de beoefening van het Nederlands Burgerlijk Recht. 6. Verbintenissenrecht. Deel III. Algemeen overeenkomstenrecht*, Deventer, Wolters Kluwer, 2018, no. 474; J. Hijma, *Algemene voorwaarden, Monografieën BW nr. B55*, Deventer, Wolters Kluwer, 2016, no. 19; R.A.F. Willems, "Het hanteren van algemene voorwaarden: werk aan de webwinkel", *Contracteren* 2013, (59) 60.

533 Art. 6:231, c) DCC.

534 Art. 3:37 DCC.

535 J. Hijma, *Algemene voorwaarden, Monografieën BW nr. B55*, Deventer, Wolters Kluwer, 2016, no. 20; R.A.F. Willems, "Het hanteren van algemene voorwaarden: werk aan de webwinkel", *Contracteren* 2013, (59) 60.

536 Art. 2:232 DCC; C.H. Sieburgh, *Mr. C. Assers Handleiding tot de beoefening van het Nederlands Burgerlijk Recht. 6. Verbintenissenrecht. Deel III. Algemeen overeenkomstenrecht*,

127. Dutch law: information duty as counterbalance to "quick incorporation" – All this means that under Dutch law, the PSS user will be bound by the general terms and conditions relatively quickly.[537] It is sufficient that he has accepted the validity of the general terms and conditions, regardless of whether he knew their content. This is also the case even if the PSS supplier knew that the PSS user did not know its contents. However, the question regarding the consumer's knowledge of the general terms and conditions is not entirely irrelevant under Dutch law. Indeed, as a counterbalance to the "quick incorporation" ("*snelle gebondenheid*") of general terms and conditions,[538] the DCC contains a ground for annulment if the PSS supplier did not comply with an information duty.[539] According to this provision, a term in the general terms and conditions is voidable if the PSS supplier has not given the PSS user a reasonable opportunity to take knowledge of the general terms and conditions before or at the time of concluding the contract.[540] The PSS user is free to choose between the voidability of one or more specific clauses, or the voidability of the general terms and conditions as a whole.[541] He does not have to prove that he was harmed by the annulled term; the breach of the information duty is sufficient.[542] Moreover, the burden of proof that the PSS user has been given a reasonable opportunity to take knowledge of the terms and conditions lies with the PSS supplier.[543]

128. Reasonable opportunity to take knowledge of the general terms and conditions – The DCC further contains rules specifying when the PSS supplier has provided the PSS user with a reasonable opportunity to take knowledge of the general terms and conditions. Here, a distinction is made depending on whether the service offered by the PSS supplier falls within the scope of the Services Directive. If the Services Directive applies – which will

---

Deventer, Wolters Kluwer, 2018, no. 474; R.H.C. Jongeneel, "Gebondenheid" in B. Wessels and R.H.C. Jongeneel (eds.), *Algemene voorwaarden*, Deventer, Wolters Kluwer, 2017, (123) no. 6.1.

537 M.B.M. Loos, "Algemene voorwaarden bij consumentenovereenkomsten" in E.H. Hondius and V. Mak (eds.), *Handboek Consumentenrecht*, Zutphen, Paris, 2020, (121) 131–132.

538 Art. 6:231, *sub* c DCC *juncto* Art. 6:323 DCC.

539 M.B.M. Loos, "Algemene voorwaarden bij consumentenovereenkomsten" in E.H. Hondius and V. Mak (eds.), *Handboek Consumentenrecht*, Zutphen, Paris, 2020, (121) 132.

540 Art. 6:233, *sub* b DCC and Art. 6:234 of the DCC. R.H.C. Jongeneel, "Gebondenheid" in B. Wessels and R.H.C. Jongeneel (eds.), *Algemene voorwaarden*, Deventer, Wolters Kluwer, 2017, (123) no. 6.1.

541 HR (NL) 17 December 1999, ECLI:NL:HR:1999:AA3876, (*Breg/Makelaardij Asper*), *NJ* 2000/140, para. 3.5; C.J. Van Zeben, J.W. Du Pon, W.H.M. Reehuis and E.E. Slob, *Parlementaire Geschiedenis van het Nieuwe Burgerlijk Wetboek. Invoering Boeken 3, 5 en 6: Boek 6: Algemeen gedeelte van het verbintenissenrecht*, Deventer, Kluwer, 1990, 1584–1585.

542 E.H. Hondius, "Groene Serie Verbintenissenrecht, art. 6:233 BW" loose-leaf, para. 64.

543 HR (NL) 11 July 2008, ECLI:NL:HR:2008:BD1394, (*BV Lommerse-Uitendaal/Atria Watermanagement*), *NJ* 2008/416, para. 5.2.1.

be the case for almost all services offered in a PSS contract[544] – a more lenient information requirement applies, which means that the PSS supplier will have fulfilled this information requirement more easily than in the case where the Services Directive does not apply.[545] Indeed, PSS suppliers subject to the special regime may fulfil the information requirement by: (i) providing (*verstrekken*) the general terms and conditions; (ii) making them easily accessible to the PSS user at the place where the service is provided or the contract is concluded; (iii) making them easily accessible to the PSS user electronically at an address communicated by the PSS supplier; and (iv) including them in contractual documents provided by the PSS supplier.[546] Especially the second and the third option make this regime more lenient than if the Services Directive would not apply.[547]

129. Handing over or sending terms and conditions – Alternatively, in the – rather exceptional – case that the service provided by the PSS supplier does not fall within the scope of the Services Directive (e.g. an additional insurance contract[548]) the reasonable opportunity to take knowledge must be assessed based on Article 6:234 DCC. According to this provision, the PSS supplier gave the reasonable opportunity to examine the terms if he handed over (*ter hand heeft gesteld*) the general terms and conditions before or at the time of conclusion of the contract.[549] If such handing over is "not reasonably possible",[550] the PSS supplier may also inform that these general terms and conditions are available for examination at its offices, at a Chamber of Commerce, or at the registry of a court, and that they will be sent free of charge upon request.[551] If the PSS

544 See Art. 2 SD. Recital 33 SD further makes clear that the concept of "service" within the meaning of the SD must be interpreted very broadly.

545 M.Y. Schaub, "De combinatie van publiekrecht en privaatrecht in de Dienstenrichtlijn en de gevolgen daarvan voor het contractenrecht", *NTBR* 2023/22, para. 4.1; M.B.M. Loos, "Algemene voorwaarden bij consumentenovereenkomsten" in E.H. Hondius and V. Mak (eds.), *Handboek Consumentenrecht*, Zutphen, Paris, 2020, (121) 136; J. Hijma, *Algemene voorwaarden, Monografieën BW nr. B55*, Deventer, Wolters Kluwer, 2016, no. 41b. See in this regard also Schaub who states that the implementation of the Services Directive lowered the level of consumer protection: M.Y. Schaub, "De informatieplichten van de Dienstenrichtlijn (art. 6:230a-f BW)", *TvC* 2014, (21) 26.

546 Art. 6:234(1) *juncto* Art. 6:230c DCC.

547 C.M.D.S. Pavillon, "De invloed van Europese richtlijnen op de Nederlandse regeling van algemene voorwaarden (afdeling 6.5.3 BW)" in A.S. Hartkamp (ed.), *De invloed van het Europese recht op het Nederlands privaatrecht*, Deventer, Kluwer, 2013, (233) no. 37.

548 See Art. 2(2) (b) SD.

549 Art. 6:234(1) DCC.

550 This should be understood as *factually not possible* (e.g. contracts concluded by phone or vending machine) or factually possible but *impractical* (e.g. mass contracts, such as passenger rail, tram, or bus contracts). See: C.J. Van Zeben, J.W. Du Pon, W.H.M. Reehuis and E.E. Slob, *Parlementaire Geschiedenis van het Nieuwe Burgerlijk Wetboek. Invoering Boeken 3, 5 en 6: Boek 6: Algemeen gedeelte van het verbintenissenrecht*, Deventer, Kluwer, 1990,1581 and 1585.

551 Art. 6:234(1) DCC.

supplier does not hand over or send the terms upon request of the PSS user, they are voidable.

130. Handing over or sending terms and conditions by electronic means – As PSS contracts are mainly concluded online, physically handing over or sending the terms and conditions will be rather rare. More often, the terms and conditions will be sent by electronic means. The DCC accommodates this by also accepting that the PSS supplier has provided the reasonable possibility to examine the terms and conditions if he has made them available to the PSS user electronically before or at the time of the conclusion of the contract, provided they can be stored by the PSS user and are accessible to him for later reference.[552] If such electronic availability is not reasonably possible, the PSS supplier must make it known, before the conclusion of the contract, where these conditions may be accessed electronically and that they will be sent electronically or by other means on request.[553] If the PSS contract is not concluded online, then the PSS supplier can only send the terms of the contract by electronic means if the PSS user has given his/her *explicit* consent.[554] Consequently, the mere statement that the terms and conditions can be accessed online is not sufficient if the PSS contract is not concluded by electronic means.[555]

131. Conclusion on requirements incorporation of general terms and conditions – Thus, both Belgian and Dutch law require in a certain sense the acceptance and (reasonable possibility of) examination of the general terms and conditions. The difference is that under Belgian law, both requirements must be fulfilled for the conditions to be part of the contract content. Under Dutch law, on the other hand, the terms and conditions form part of the contract content as of their acceptance by the PSS user but can be nullified if the PSS supplier has not provided the PSS user with a reasonable possibility to examine them. Although acceptance and examination can thus be distinguished dogmatically, in practice they show a certain coherence since they are (in most cases) two conditions which must be met at the time of conclusion of the contract if the PSS supplier wants to invoke his terms and conditions successfully.[556]

---

552 Art. 6:234(2) DCC.

553 *Ibid.*

554 Art. 6:234(3) DCC.

555 HR (NL) 11 February 2011, ECLI:NL:HR:2011:BO7108, (*First Data B.V./KPN Hotspots Schiphol B.V.*), *NJ* 2011/571, case note J. Hijma; Ct. Rotterdam (NL) 23 March 2005, ECLI:NL:RBROT:2005:AT8336, (*H./Advocatenkantoor B. B.V.*), *NJF* 2005/225; J.H.M. Spanjaard, "Artikel 6:234 BW of de moeizame relatie van de Nederlandse wetgever met Europese regelgeving", *Contracteren* 2012, (27) 30.

556 R.H.C. Jongeneel, "Gebondenheid" in B. Wessels and R.H.C. Jongeneel (eds.), *Algemene voorwaarden*, Deventer, Wolters Kluwer, 2017, (123) no 6.1.

2.3.2.2. *Incorporation of terms and conditions in PSS contracts concluded online*

132. "I AGREE". ENFORCEABILITY OF *CLICKWRAP, SCROLLWRAP* AND *BROWSEWRAP* TERMS AND CONDITIONS – As mentioned above, many PSS users give their consent to be bound by the PSS contract by clicking "*I agree*" on the PSS supplier's website. This can take various forms. *Clickwrap* terms and conditions require consumers to click on a box that they agree with the general terms and conditions. *Scrollwrap* terms go a step further: they require consumers to scroll through all the terms and conditions before they can click the box. Websites using *Browsewrap* terms on the other hand, refer to their terms and conditions using a hyperlink, and state that the consumer agrees to the terms solely by using the website or placing the order.[557] Are these general terms and conditions enforceable?

133. *CLICKWRAP* TERMS AND CONDITIONS ARE ENFORCEABLE – It is generally accepted that if the website of a PSS supplier makes the conclusion of the PSS contract dependent on clicking on a box implying acceptance of the general terms and conditions (*clickwrap*), these are enforceable against the PSS user.[558] After all, the PSS user cannot continue the process of online contracting without explicitly stating that he has taken note of and accepted the general terms and conditions of the PSS supplier.[559] In this sense, it is not sufficient that

---

557 **Belgium**: See e.g. G. HERMANS, "De toepasselijkheid van algemene voorwaarden bij online contracteren", *DAOR* 2018, vol. 4 issue 128, (73) 78–80; C. HELAS, "L'opposabilité des conditions générales contractuelles en ligne. 'Error 404: this page cannot be found'", *TBBR* 2018, vol. 2018 issue 3, (155) 161, nr. 26.1 and 26.2; L.A. NYSSEN and D. PHILIPPE, "L'opposabilité des conditions générales" in *Contrat et protection des consommateurs*, Limal, Anthemis, 2016, (109) 146–147; Q. VAN ENIS, "L'opposabilité des conditions générales off-line et on-line: de la suite dans les idées?" in M. BERLINGIN, D. GRISARD, B. KOHL, D. MOUGENOT and Q. VAN ENIS (eds.), *Les conditions générales*, Limal, Anthemis, 2009, (9) 27–28; K. DE VULDER and D. ROMBOUTS, "De elektronische algemene voorwaarden en hun tegenstelbaarheid" in S. ONGENA (ed.), *Algemene voorwaarden*, Mechelen, Kluwer, 2006, (31) 45–46, no. 64 and 53, no. 78. **The Netherlands**: See e.g. E. NEPPELENBROEK, "De verstrekking van juridische voorwaarden in het voorportaal van de cloud", *Contracteren* 2020, (132) 136–137.

558 **Belgium**: B. DEVOLDER, *Gebruikersbescherming in de deeleconomie*, Bruges, die Keure, 2022, 313, no. 420 and the references cited there; **The Netherlands**: E. NEPPELENBROEK, "De verstrekking van juridische voorwaarden in het voorportaal van de cloud", *Contracteren* 2020, (132) 136; R.A.F. WILLEMS, "Het hanteren van algemene voorwaarden: werk aan de webwinkel", *Contracteren* 2013, (59) 60; M.W. SCHELTEMA and T.F.E. TJONG TJIN TAI, "Overeenkomsten sluiten door openen en klikken?", *Computerrecht* 2003, (244) 244.

559 C. HELAS, "L'opposabilité des conditions générales contractuelles en ligne. 'Error 404: this page cannot be found'", *TBBR* 2018, vol. 2018, afl. 3, (155) 161; G. HERMANS, "De toepasselijkheid van algemene voorwaarden bij online contracteren", *DAOR* 2018, vol. 4, afl. 128, (73) 80; Q. VAN ENIS, "L'opposabilité des conditions générales off-line et on-line: de la suite dans les idées?" in M. BERLINGIN, D. GRISARD, B. KOHL, D. MOUGENOT and Q. VAN ENIS (eds.), *Les conditions générales*, Limal, Anthemis, 2009, (9) 28–29.

the acceptance of the general terms and conditions is ticked by default on the website.[560]

134. Scrolling through terms and conditions (*scrollwrap*) is not required for enforceability – It is not required that PSS users must actually scroll through the terms and conditions (*scrollwrap*).[561] It is sufficient that the terms and conditions are available by clicking on a hyperlink.[562]

135. Enforceability of *browsewrap* terms and conditions depends on factual circumstances – If the PSS supplier's website does not provide an explicit acceptance mechanism, e.g. by only referring to the general terms and conditions available behind a hyperlink (*browsewrap*), enforceability of these terms and conditions becomes more difficult.[563] Whether the terms and conditions were accessible and whether the PSS user was able to take note of them prior to concluding the contract will depend on the concrete factual circumstances. The burden of proof lies on the PSS supplier.[564]

136. Terms and conditions only made available through hyperlink without any reference during ordering process are not enforceable – A final possibility is that the general terms and conditions are made available through a hyperlink at the bottom of the webpage, without being referred to at all during the online ordering process. Here it is clear that this is not sufficient

---

560 Q. Van Enis, "L'opposabilité des conditions générales off-line et on-line: de la suite dans les idées?" in M. Berlingin, D. Grisard, B. Kohl, D. Mougenot and Q. Van Enis (eds.), *Les conditions générales*, Limal, Anthemis, 2009, (9) 28–29.

561 B. Devolder, *Gebruikersbescherming in de deeleconomie*, Bruges, die Keure, 2022, 313, no. 420.

562 **Belgium**: B. Devolder, *Gebruikersbescherming in de deeleconomie*, Bruges, die Keure, 2022, 313, no. 420; T. Declerck and M. Debacker, "Hoe algemene voorwaarden online te gebruiken?" in T. Fransen and G. Ristiaensen (eds.), *E-commerce. Uw webshop fiscaal en juridisch doorgelicht*, Mechelen, Wolters Kluwer, 2016, (43) 47. **The Netherlands**: E. Neppelenbroek, "De verstrekking van juridische voorwaarden in het voorportaal van de cloud", *Contracteren* 2020, (132) 136–137.

563 **Belgium**: see B. Devolder, *Gebruikersbescherming in de deeleconomie*, Bruges, die Keure, 2022, 314, no. 421 and the references cited there. **The Netherlands**: E. Neppelenbroek, "De verstrekking van juridische voorwaarden in het voorportaal van de cloud", *Contracteren* 2020, (132) 136; R.A.F. Willems, "Het hanteren van algemene voorwaarden: werk aan de webwinkel", *Contracteren* 2013, (59) 61.

564 C. Helas, "L'opposabilité des conditions générales contractuelles en ligne. 'Error 404: this page cannot be found'", *TBBR* 2018, vol. 2018, afl. 3, (155) 161–162; F. Dechamps and L. Vancaelemont, "Les obligations contractuelles et internet" in A. Cruquenaire, D. De Sart, F. Dechamps, B. Dessart, M. Dupont, P.A. Foriers, J.-F. Germain, F. Glansdorff, J.-S. Lenaerts, E. Van Den Haute, L. Vancaelement and C. Verdure (eds.), *Les obligations contractuelles en pratique: Questions choisies*, Limal, Anthemis, 2013, (75) 86; Q. Van Enis, "L'opposabilité des conditions générales off-line et on-line: de la suite dans les idées?" in M. Berlingin, D. Grisard, B. Kohl, D. Mougenot and Q. Van Enis (eds.), *Les conditions générales*, Limal, Anthemis, 2009, (9) 29.

to fulfil the double condition that the PSS user took note of and accepted the general terms and conditions.[565]

2.3.2.3. Knowledge and acceptance clauses

137. Knowledge and acceptance clauses – In some cases, PSS contracts contain clauses stipulating that a contracting party has actually read all the clauses of the contract (i.e. has taken knowledge of its content) and has accepted them as part of the contract. The value of these clauses is rather limited. Indeed, the Belgian unfair terms blacklist[566] prohibits terms in consumer contracts which have the object or effect of irrefutably binding the consumer to terms with which he had no real opportunity of becoming acquainted before the conclusion of the contract.[567] This provision is based on point (i) of the indicative list of the UCTD[568] and was implemented *verbatim* in the Belgium blacklist. The Dutch blacklist and grey list contain no such prohibition, but in practice these terms are combated with the transparency requirement of Article 6:233, *sub* b. DCC.[569]

Thus, even if such knowledge and acceptance clauses are included in the PSS contract, it remains to be assessed whether the requirements for incorporation of terms and conditions[570] (i.e. knowledge and acceptance) are indeed met. In other words, the PSS user can still prove that there was no possibility to consent. If the clause merely refers to the other clauses of the contract, the knowledge and acceptance can be inferred from the general signature on the contract (which makes the clause somewhat redundant). If the clause refers to a separate set of terms and conditions, the clause in and of itself does not demonstrate that there was at least a reasonable possibility for the PSS user to gain knowledge of those terms and conditions and accept them (which is the intended purpose of the clause).

138. Acceptance clauses: examples – The terms and conditions of *Dressr* contain a clause that may likely come into conflict with these provisions.

---

565 K. De Vulder and D. Rombouts, "De elektronische algemene voorwaarden en hun tegenstelbaarheid" in S. Ongena (ed.), *Algemene voorwaarden*, Mechelen, Kluwer, 2006, (31) 53.

566 See *infra* section 2.3.3.

567 Art. VI.83, 26° BCEL; P. Cambie, *Onrechtmatige bedingen*, Ghent, Larcier, 2009, 217; D. Bruloot and R. Steennot, "Clausules i.v.m. de tegenwerpelijkheid van algemene voorwaarden" in G.-L. Ballon, H. De Decker, V. Sagaert, E. Terryn, B. Tilleman and A.-L. Verbeke (eds.), *Contractuele clausules. Gemeenrechtelijke clausules. Volume I*, Antwerp, Intersentia, 2013, (359) 379.

568 See also *supra* no. 119.

569 M.B.M. Loos, *Algemene voorwaarden*, The Hague, Boom juridisch, 2018, no. 358. See for examples: HR (NL) 11 July 2008, ECLI:NL:HR:2008:BD1394, (*BV Lommerse-Uitendaal/Atria Watermanagement*), *NJ* 2008/416; HR (NL) 21 September 2007, ECLI:NL:HR:2007:BA9610, (*Kwekerij de Engel/Enthoven Electra*), *NJ* 2009/50, case note J. Hijma.

570 See *supra* no. 131.

According to these terms, the PSS supplier of *Dressr* reserves the right to amend the terms at any time without prior notice.[571] Notice of any change will be posted on the website where the terms are made available, and the PSS user is asked to check this webpage periodically for changes.[572] The clause then continues by stating that the PSS user's continued use of the website after any changes or revisions to the terms shall indicate his agreement with the terms.[573] It is highly questionable that in this case there is a real opportunity of becoming acquainted with the terms of the PSS contract. Apart from this, the practice of acceptance clauses for PSS contracts does not really seem problematic, as none of the other analysed contracts included such an acceptance clause.

2.3.3. (UN)FAIRNESS OF GENERAL TERMS AND CONDITIONS

139. Legality of general terms and conditions: unfair contract terms – The second corrective mechanism on abuse of standard contracts consists in a control of the legality of general terms and conditions – i.e. whether they do not contain unfair terms. Both the EU and national legislators have been active in regulating standard contracts.[574] At the EU level, standard contracts and general terms and conditions have been regulated by the UCTD. To this end, it prohibits significantly imbalanced contractual terms that are not individually negotiated in B2C contracts.[575] At the national level, many Member States – including Belgium and the Netherlands[576] – provide for increased consumer protection in the area of unfair contract terms.[577] This increased consumer protection is compatible with the UCTD since it constitutes minimum harmonisation and allows Member States to adopt or retain more stringent provisions to ensure a maximum degree of consumer protection.[578] Further attempts to fully harmonise control of unfair contract terms have failed,

---

571 Art. 25 (Changes to our terms) Terms and Conditions Dressr.

572 *Ibid.*

573 *Ibid.*

574 P. Rott, "Standard Terms" in H.-W. Micklitz, J. Stuyck and E. Terryn (eds.), *Cases, Materials and Text on Consumer Law*, Oxford, Hart, 2010, (279) 279; M. Ebers, "Unfair Contract Terms Directive (93/13)" in M. Ebers, H. Schulte-Nölke and C. Twigg-Flesner (eds.), *EC consumer law compendium: the consumer acquis and its transposition in the member states*, Munich, Sellier, 2008, (197) 205.

575 Art. 3 UCTD.

576 **Belgium**: Art. I.8, 22° BCEL and Art. VI.82–84 BCEL. **The Netherlands**: Art. 6:233, a), Art. 6:236 and Art. 6:237 DCC.

577 For an overview of the legal framework on unfair contract terms in the Member States of the EU, see: M. Ebers, "Unfair Contract Terms Directive (93/13)" in M. Ebers, H. Schulte-Nölke and C. Twigg-Flesner (eds.), *EC consumer law compendium: the consumer acquis and its transposition in the member states*, Munich, Sellier, 2008, (197) 206–220.

578 Art. 8 UCPD.

notably the European Commission's 2008 Proposal for a Directive on Consumer Rights[579] and Chapter 8[580] of the Proposed Common European Sales Law[581] ("CESL"), which was withdrawn by the European Commission.[582] The DCFR also contains rules on unfair terms, including a grey list of terms which are presumed to be unfair in contracts between a business and a consumer.[583]

As a result, the PSS provider does not have absolute freedom when drafting PSS contracts and the consumer can use the control mechanism of the UCTD and its national implementation to challenge significantly imbalanced contractual clauses of, *i.a.*, rights of use, distribution of risk, unreasonable limits to maintenance and repair, suspension rights, etc.[584] This section outlines the scope of application of the UCTD and its national implementation, discusses the unfairness test and the consequences of unfairness, and briefly looks at the enforcement of unfair contract terms law. The application of these rules to specific terms found in PSS contracts is done in the other chapters of this book.

140. The UCTD's enforcement mechanism – Two provisions of the UCTD deal with the way consumers should be protected against unfair contract terms. First, consumers must have recourse to individual enforcement.[585] To this end, Member States must implement procedural rules allowing unfair terms to be rendered non-binding in individual litigation between traders and consumers.[586] While the Member States have a certain procedural autonomy in ensuring this, a few procedural requirements follow from the principle of *effectiveness*,[587] which is explicitly confirmed in the UCTD,[588] and the principle

579 EC, *Proposal for a Directive of the European Parliament and of the Council on consumer rights*, 8.10.2008, COM(2008) 614, final.

580 Chapter 8 of the CESL included *i.a.* a blacklist of contract terms which are always unfair (Art. 84) and a grey list of contract terms which are presumed to be unfair (Art. 85).

581 EC, *Proposal for a Regulation of the European Parliament and of the Council on a Common European Sales Law*, 11.10.2011, COM(2011) 635 final See Art. 79–85 CESL.

582 P. Rott, "Unfair contract terms" in C. Twigg-Flesner (ed.), *Research Handbook on EU Consumer and Contract Law*, Cheltenham, Edward Elgar, 2016, (287) 287.

583 See Art. II. - 9:401-Art. II. - 9:410 DCFR. The grey list of terms which are presumed to be unfair in contracts between a business and a consumer is found in Art. II. - 9:410 DCFR.

584 H. Slachmuylders, "iPhone as a Service? Some thoughts on Apple's rumoured hardware subscription service", *CCM Blog* 4 April 2022, https://law.kuleuven.be/ccm/blog/?p=321; B. Keirsbilck, E. Terryn and E. Van Gool, "Consumentenbescherming bij servitisation en product-dienst systemen (PDS)", *TPR* 2019, (817) 840; V. Mak, "Consumentenbescherming bij servitisation", *TPR* 2019, (779) 789.

585 Art. 6(1) UCTD.

586 See *infra* no. 174 *et seq.*

587 This principle implies that the implementing national rules may not make it in practice impossible or excessively difficult to exercise the rights conferred on consumers by EU law. See: CJEU, Judgment of 18 February 2016, C-49/14, *Finanmadrid*, ECLI:EU:C:2016:98, para. 40; CJEU, Judgment of 17 July 2014, C-169/14, *Sánchez Morcillo*, ECLI:EU:C:2014:2099, para. 31 and the case law cited.

588 See Art. 7(1) UCTD: "*Member States shall ensure that, in the interests of consumers and of competitors, adequate and effective means exist to prevent the continued use of unfair terms in contracts with consumers by sellers or suppliers.*"

of *equivalence*.[589] These include, amongst others, the obligation for national courts to assess unfair contract terms *ex officio*[590] and the fact that the non-binding character of unfair terms cannot be subject to a limitation period.[591,592] In Belgium, unfair terms are prohibited and null and void.[593] In the Netherlands, unfair terms are voidable.[594]

Second, Member States must also organize effective public or collective enforcement. Accordingly, the UCTD requires Member States to adopt rules "*whereby persons or organisations that have a legitimate interest under national law in protecting consumers may take action according to the national law concerned before the courts or before competent administrative bodies for a decision as to whether contractual terms drawn up for general use are unfair, so that they can apply appropriate and effective means to prevent the continued use of such terms.*"[595] These actions may be directed separately or jointly against a number of sellers or suppliers from the same economic sector or their associations which use or recommend the use of the same general contract terms or similar terms.[596] In Belgium, this collective enforcement is fleshed out by the possibility for consumer organisations[597] of suing for an injunction (*vordering tot staking, action en cessation*) with the president of the commercial court to prohibit the continued use of the allegedly unfair term.[598] In the Netherlands, consumer and industry organisations can take action against unreasonably onerous terms by means of a collective action procedure.[599] The main claim within this collective action procedure is the declaration by the Hague Court of Appeal that a particular term is unreasonably onerous.[600] In addition, three ancillary actions may be brought. These include (i) an injunction against using or promoting the terms affected by the judgment; (ii) in proceedings against an industry organisation, an injunction to revoke a recommendation to use those terms; and (iii) an order to make the judgment public or have it made public.[601]

---

589 This principle implies that the procedural rules for actions safeguarding an individual's rights under EU law must be no less favourable than those governing similar domestic actions. See: CJEU, Judgment of 21 April 2016, C-377/14, *Radlinger and Radlingerová*, ECLI:EU:C:2016:283, para. 48; CJEU, Judgment of 18 February 2016, C-49/14, *Finanmadrid*, ECLI:EU:C:2016:98, para. 40; CJEU, Judgment of 17 July 2014, C-169/14, *Sánchez Morcillo*, ECLI:EU:C:2014:2099, para. 31 and the case law cited.

590 See *infra* no. 150 and 151.

591 CJEU, Judgment of 21 November 2002, C-473/00, *Cofidis*, ECLI:EU:C:2002:705, para. 38.

592 See for an in-depth discussion of the implications of the principles of effectiveness and equivalence for the UCTD: EC, *Guidance on the interpretation of Council Directive 93/13/EEC on unfair terms in consumer contracts*, 27.9.2019, 2019/C 323/04, 44–62.

593 Art. VI.84 BCEL. See *infra* no. 175.

594 Art. 6:233 DCC. See *infra* no. 176.

595 Art. 7(2) UCTD.

596 Art. 7(3) UCTD.

597 However, other actors can also sue for an injunction, see: Art. XVII.7 BCEL.

598 See, Art. XVII.1 BCEL, Art. XVII.2 BCEL and Art. XVII.12 BCEL.

599 Art. 6:240–6:242 DCC.

600 Art. 6:240(1) *juncto* Art. 6:241(1) DCC.

601 Art. 6:241(3), *sub* a-c DCC.

2.3.3.1. *Scope of application*

141. Personal scope of the UCTD: contracts between traders and a consumer – Most PSS contracts in B2C markets fall within the personal scope of the UCTD as implemented in Belgium and the Netherlands. The UCTD applies to contracts between a seller or a supplier and a consumer (B2C).[602] The notion of "seller or supplier" must be interpreted quite broadly, as it refers to any natural or legal person who is acting for his trade, business or profession, regardless of its public or private nature.[603] In fact, it must be interpreted in the same way as the notion of "trader" in other consumer law directives.[604] Clearly, PSS suppliers fall under this definition of "seller or supplier". A "consumer" for the purposes of the Directive is any natural person who is acting for purposes outside his trade, business, or profession.[605] PSS users who thus enter into a PSS contract outside any economic activity will fall under the scope of the UCTD. According to the CJEU, the system of consumer protection of the UCTD is based on "the idea that the consumer is in a weak position vis-à-vis the seller or supplier, as regards both his bargaining power and his level of knowledge." This leads to the consumer agreeing to terms drawn up in advance by the seller or supplier without being able to influence the content of the terms."[606] Given the minimum harmonisation nature of the Directive, the Member States can of course extend the personal scope of the national rules implementing the UCTD, for example by also applying them to contracts concluded between two sellers or suppliers or between two consumers.

---

602 Art. 1(1) UCTD.

603 Art. 2(c) UCTD. See also CJEU, Judgment of 30 May 2013, C-488/11, *Asbeek Brusse*, ECLI:EU:C:2013:341, para. 25–31 (even though the term "seller or supplier" of Art. 2(c) UCTD differs between certain language versions, this notion must be interpreted uniformly and in light of the Directive's objectives. Consequently, a more restrictive terminology used in certain language versions of the UCTD and its national transposition cannot restrict the types of contracts covered by the UCTD and, therefore, its scope of application). See also Recital 10 UCTD ("*all* contracts concluded between sellers or suppliers and consumers").

604 See e.g. CJEU, Judgment of 17 May 2018, C-147/16, *Karel de Grote Hogeschool*, ECLI:EU:C:2018:320 para. 51. Here, the CJEU refers to CJEU, Judgment of 3 October 2013, C-59/12, *Zentrale zur Bekämpfung unlauteren Wettbewerbs*, ECLI:EU:C:2013:634, para. 32 which concerns the term "trader" of Art. 2(b) of the UCPD.

605 Art. 2(b) UCTD. See also CJEU, Judgment of 3 September 2015, C-110/14, *Costea*, ECLI:EU:C:2015:538 (a natural person who practices as a lawyer and concludes a credit agreement with a bank, in which the purpose of the credit is not specified, may be regarded as a "consumer", where that agreement is not linked to that lawyer's profession).

606 CJEU, Judgment of 27 June 2000, Joined Cases C-240/98-C-244/98, *Océano Grupo*, ECLI:EU:C:2000:346, para. 25. This statement is part of settled case law of the Court, see also e.g. CJEU, Judgment of 17 May 2018, C-147/16, *Karel de Grote Hogeschool*, ECLI:EU:C:2018:320, para. 54; CJEU, Judgment of 3 September 2015, C-110/14, *Costea*, ECLI:EU:C:2015:538, para. 18; CJEU, Judgment of 17 July 2014, C-169/14, *Sánchez Morcillo*, ECLI:EU:C:2014:2099, para. 22; CJEU, Judgment of 30 May 2013, C-488/11, *Asbeek Brusse*, ECLI:EU:C:2013:341, para. 31; CJEU, Judgment of 26 April 2012, C-472/10, *Invitel*, ECLI:EU:C:2012:242, para. 33.

142. Personal scope Belgian rules: different regimes B2C, B2B and C2C – The chapter of Book VI of the BCEL on unfair contract terms applies to contracts concluded between a business and a consumer.[607] A "business" is defined as "*any natural or legal person pursuing an economic objective on a lasting basis, as well as its associations.*"[608] A "consumer" is "*any natural person acting for purposes outside his trade, business, craft or profession.*"[609] This chapter therefore does not apply to PSS contracts between two or more businesses (B2B) or contracts between two or more consumers (C2C). However, since 1 December 2020, B2B contracts are subject to a similar regime inspired by the rules on unfair terms in B2C contracts.[610] In addition, the BCC also contains a general rule on unfair contract terms in standard contracts.[611] This provision is mainly relevant for C2C contracts, as the regimes of Book VI BCEL (unfair terms in contracts with consumers and unfair terms in contracts concluded between businesses) take precedence.[612] Given its scope, this book only focuses on the Belgian rules on unfair terms in B2C contracts.

143. Personal scope Dutch rules: "user" who uses general terms and conditions towards a "counterparty", with specific rules for consumer protection – The Dutch rules on unfair terms have a very broad personal scope of application. In principle, these rules apply to any contract in which "general terms and conditions"[613] are used by a "user"[614] towards a "counterparty",[615] albeit that certain categories of counterparties (notably legal persons that exceed a certain size) cannot invoke the grounds for annulment.[616] The notion "user" should not be confused with the PSS user, as it refers to the person who uses general terms and conditions in a contract (i.e. the PSS supplier). The

607 See Art. VI.82-VI.87 BCEL.

608 See Art. I.8., 39° BCEL. Dutch: "*iedere natuurlijke persoon of rechtspersoon die op duurzame wijze een economisch doel nastreeft, alsmede zijn verenigingen.*" French: "*toute personne physique ou personne morale poursuivant de manière durable un but économique, y compris ses associations.*"

609 Art. I.1, 2° BCEL. Dutch: "*iedere natuurlijke persoon die handelt voor doeleinden die buiten zijn handels-, bedrijfs-, ambachts- of beroepsactiviteit vallen.*" French: "*toute personne physique qui agit à des fins qui n'entendent pas dans le cadre de son activité commerciale, industrielle, artisanale ou libérale.*"

610 See Art. VI.91/1-VI.91/10 BCEL. See also: E. Terryn, "Onrechtmatige bedingen tussen ondernemingen" in W. Devroe, E. Terryn and B. Keirsbilck (eds.), *Nieuw economisch recht in b2b-relaties*, Antwerp, Intersentia, 2020, (95) 95–147.

611 Art. 5.52 BCC.

612 A. De Boeck and T. Hick, "Totstandkoming van contracten: het komend recht in de rechtspraak" in A. De Boeck and S. Stijns (eds.), *Themis Verbintenissenrecht nr. 120*, Antwerp, Intersentia, 2022, (1) 35, no. 48.

613 See Art. 6:231 *sub* a. DCC. See *infra* no. 149.

614 See Art. 6:231 *sub* b. DCC.

615 Art. 6:231 *sub* c. DCC. This is the party that, by written signature or otherwise, has accepted the validity of general terms and conditions.

616 Art. 6:235(1) DCC.

"counterparty" is the party that, by written signature or otherwise, has accepted the validity of general terms and conditions (i.e. the PSS user). Thus, under Dutch law, it is irrelevant for the review of unfair terms whether the contract is between two or more companies (B2B), between a business and a consumer (B2C) or between consumers (C2C).[617] However, there is additional protection for PSS users that are "consumers", which are defined as "*natural persons not acting in the exercise of a profession or business.*" Indeed, certain terms are always considered unreasonably onerous (blacklist) and other terms are presumed to be unreasonably onerous (grey list) if they appear in general terms and conditions used in contracts with consumers.[618]

144. Material scope of the UCTD: not individually negotiated contract terms – The UCTD's unfairness control mechanism is limited to the terms of the PSS contract that have not been individually negotiated.[619] Since most PSS contracts use standard general term and conditions, this requirement will in most cases be met. The form in which the terms are set out (e.g. printed, online, offline, handwritten, in multiple documents or even oral) makes no difference.[620] Whether terms have been subject to individual negotiations is a question of fact to be assessed by the national courts.[621] Yet the Directive does contain some presumptions and provisions on the burden of proof regarding this question. According to the Directive, a term is always regarded as "not individually negotiated" where it has been drafted in advance, and the consumer therefore has not been able to influence the wording or substance of the term.[622] This will typically, but not exclusively, be the case with standard, standardised, or pre-formulated contract terms – as is most often the case with PSS contracts.[623]

---

617 M.B.M. Loos, "Algemene voorwaarden bij consumentenovereenkomsten" in E.H. Hondius and V. Mak (eds.), *Handboek Consumentenrecht*, Zutphen, Paris, 2020, (121) 122.

618 Art. 6:236 DCC (blacklist) and Art. 6:237 DCC (grey list).

619 Art. 3(1) UCTD: "*A contractual term which has not been individually negotiated shall be regarded as unfair if, contrary to the requirement of good faith, it causes a significant imbalance in the parties' rights and obligations arising under the contract, to the detriment of the consumer*" (own emphasis).

620 Recital 11 UCTD.

621 EC, *Guidance on the interpretation of Council Directive 93/13/EEC on unfair terms in consumer contracts*, 27.9.2019, 2019/C 323/04 13.

622 Art. 3(2) UCTD.

623 Art. 3(2), first subpara. *in fine* UCTD: "*particularly in the context of a pre-formulated standard contract*"; Recital 9 UCTD: "*in particular against one-sided standard contracts and the unfair exclusion of essential rights in contracts*" (own emphasis). See also: CJEU, Judgment of 28 July 2016, C-191/15, *Verein für Konsumenteninformation v Amazon*, ECLI:EU:C:2016:612, para. 63: "*Article 3(2) of Directive 93/13 specifies that a term must always be regarded as not individually negotiated where it has been drafted in advance by the seller or supplier and the consumer has therefore not been able to influence the substance of the term, particularly in the context of a pre-formulated standard contract. As the Advocate General observes in point 84 of his Opinion, general terms and conditions such as those at issue in the main proceedings correspond to that description*" (own emphasis).

The fact that a certain specific term or certain aspects of a term are negotiated individually does not preclude the UCTD from applying to the other terms of the PSS contract if an overall assessment indicates that it is nevertheless a pre-formulated standard contract.[624] The burden of proof that a term has been individually negotiated lies with the trader.[625]

145. UCTD: EXCLUSION OF CONTRACT TERMS REFLECTING MANDATORY STATUTORY OR REGULATORY PROVISIONS – The UCTD also excludes contractual terms that reflect mandatory statutory or regulatory provisions or provisions stemming from international agreements to which the Member States or the Union are a party.[626] The rationale behind this exclusion is that fairness control is not needed if certain contracts are governed by legislation, as legislation is supposed to strike a fair balance between the rights and obligations of the parties.[627] A provision has to be considered *mandatory* within the meaning of the UCTD if (i) it applies to the parties of the contract independently of their choice and (ii) it applies by default in the absence of other arrangements established by the parties (default law).[628] As a result, if certain terms of the PSS contract reflect national (default) law, the UCTD does not apply. Both Belgium and the Netherlands did not explicitly implement this provision.[629] However, it seems rather unlikely that clauses reflecting national (default) law can be successfully challenged before Belgian and Dutch courts. Indeed, when adopting national default law, the legislator has already sought a balance between the rights and obligations of the parties. Therefore, it seems that it is not for the courts to question this balance – also pursuant to the principle of separation of powers.

146. UCTD: "CORE TERMS" EXCLUDED FROM UNFAIRNESS TEST, IN SO FAR AS THEY ARE IN PLAIN INTELLIGIBLE LANGUAGE – Contract terms relating to the main subject matter of the contract or the price and remuneration ("core terms") fall within the scope of the UCTD.[630] However, the particularity of these core

---

624 Art. 3(2), second subpara. UCTD.

625 Art. 3(2), third subpara. UCTD.

626 Art. 1(2) UCTD.

627 CJEU, Judgment of 20 September 2018, C-51/17, *OTP Bank v Ilyés and Kiss*, ECLI:EU:C:2018:750, para. 53; CJEU, Judgment of 21 March 2013, C-92/11, *RWE Vertrieb AG*, ECLI:EU:C:2013:180, para. 28. See also Recital 13 UCTD.

628 CJEU, Judgment of 3 April 2019, C-266/18, *Aqua Med*, ECLI:EU:C:2019:282, para. 33; CJEU, Order of 7 December 2017, C-446/17, *Woonhaven Antwerpen*, ECLI:EU:C:2017:954, para. 25; CJEU, Judgment of 20 September 2017, C-186/17, *Andriciuc*, ECLI:EU:C:2017:703, para. 29; CJEU, Judgment of 30 April 2014, C-280/13, *Barclays Bank*, ECLI:EU:C:2014:279, para. 31 and 42; CJEU, Judgment of 10 September 2014, C-34/13, *Kušionová*, ECLI:EU:C:2014:2189, para. 77; CJEU, Judgment of 21 March 2013, C-92/11, *RWE Vertrieb AG*, ECLI:EU:C:2013:180, para. 26.

629 See *infra* respectively no. 148 and no. 149.

630 CJEU, Judgment of 9 July 2015, C-348/14, *Bucura*, ECLI:EU:C:2015:447, para. 50; CJEU, Order of 16 November 2010, C-76/10, *Pohotovost'*, ECLI:EU:C:2010:685, para. 72; CJEU, Judgment

terms is that they are in principle excluded from the unfairness test.[631] Indeed, according to the Directive, assessment of the unfair nature of the terms shall relate "*neither to the definition of the main subject matter of the contract nor to the adequacy of the price and remuneration, on the one hand, as against the services or goods supplie[d] in exchange, on the other.*"[632] Consequently, clauses of the PSS contract that lay down the essential obligations of the PSS contract (e.g. the product that is made available, its quantity or quality, the additional services that are provided, etc.) as well as the pricing structure (e.g. monthly fee, pay-per-use component, etc.) are not subjected to the unfairness test. Since this exclusion is an exception to the substantive test of unfair terms, it must, according to the Court of Justice, be interpreted strictly. Terms that are ancillary to these core terms, such as terms that merely specify the modalities of the performances,[633] do not fall within the concept of core term.[634]

Yet the non-application of the unfairness test to core terms is subject to an exception. Indeed, the inapplicability of the unfairness test only applies "*in so far as these terms are in plain intelligible language*" (the so-called transparency requirement).[635] Moreover, the CJEU confirmed in *Caja de Ahorros y Monte de Piedad de Madrid* that the minimum harmonisation level of the UCTD allows Member States to submit core terms to the unfairness control mechanism.[636] However, both Belgium and the Netherlands have implemented this exclusion of core terms from the unfairness test in their national legislation.[637]

147. UCTD: EXCLUDED TYPES OF CONTRACTS – Finally, certain contracts are also excluded from the scope of the UCTD. This includes contracts relating to employment, contracts relating to succession rights, contracts relating to rights under family law and contracts relating to the incorporation and organisation of companies or partnership agreements.[638] MICKLITZ points out that this is not a formal exclusion, but rather a consequence of the fact that the contracting parties will not normally meet as "seller or supplier" and

---

of 3 June 2010, C-484/08, *Caja de Ahorros y Monte de Piedad de Madrid v Asociación de Usuarios de Servicios Bancarios (Ausbanc)*, ECLI:EU:C:2010:309, para 32.

631 H.-W. MICKLITZ, "Unfair terms in consumer contracts" in N. REICH, H.-W. MICKLITZ, P. ROTT and K. TONNER (eds.), *European Consumer Law*, Antwerp, Intersentia, 2014, (125) 138.

632 Art. 4(2) UCTD.

633 E.g. clauses on price increases and price adjustments, terms on the modalities of payment and delivery or terms regarding the liability of the parties.

634 CJEU, Judgment of 23 April 2015, C-96/14, *Van Hove*, ECLI:EU:C:2015:262, para. 33; CJEU, Judgment of 26 February 2015, C-143/13, *Matei and Matei*, ECLI:EU:C:2015:127, para. 54; CJEU, Judgment of 30 April 2014, C-26/13, *Kásler*, ECLI:EU:C:2014:282, para. 50.

635 Art. 4(2) *in fine* UCTD. See *infra* no. 155.

636 CJEU, Judgment of 3 June 2010, C-484/08, *Caja de Ahorros y Monte de Piedad de Madrid v Asociación de Usuarios de Servicios Bancarios (Ausbanc)*, ECLI:EU:C:2010:309, para. 28–29.

637 **Belgium**: Art. VI.82(3) BCEL. **The Netherlands**: Art. 6:231 *sub* a. DCC.

638 Recital 10 UCTD. See also Recital 19 UCTD.

"consumer" in these areas of law.[639] Of course, PSS contracts do not fall under this exclusion.

148. Material scope Belgian rules: all terms in B2C contracts – Unlike the UCTD, which scope is limited in various ways,[640] the Belgian rules on unfair terms have a very broad material scope of application.[641] Indeed, the ban on unfair terms applies in principle to all terms in B2C contracts,[642] regardless of whether the terms are individually negotiated (i.e. not limited to standard contracts).[643] In line with the UCTD, the BCEL contains an exclusion for core terms from the unfairness test, in so far as they are in plain and intelligible language.[644] In addition, Belgium has also not transposed the provision excluding contract terms reflecting mandatory statutory or regulatory provisions from the scope of the UCTD,[645] which is justified given the minimum harmonisation nature of the Directive.[646]

149. Material scope Dutch rules: contracts using general terms and conditions – The Dutch rules on unfair terms apply to all contracts using "general terms and conditions". These are one or more terms drafted to be included in a number of contracts, with the exception of terms indicating

639 H.-W. Micklitz, "Unfair terms in consumer contracts" in N. Reich, H.-W. Micklitz, P. Rott and K. Tonner (eds.), *European Consumer Law*, Antwerp, Intersentia, 2014, (125) 138–139.

640 See *supra* no. 144–147.

641 J. Stuyck and B. Keirsbilck, *Handels- en economisch recht. 2: Mededingingsrecht. A: Handelspraktijken en contracten met consumenten in Beginselen van Belgisch Privaatrecht*, Mechelen, Kluwer, 2024, 797, no. 827 *et seq.*; S. Stijns, "Onrechtmatige bedingen" in J. Stuyck, G. Straetmans and P. Wytinck (eds.), *Recente wetswijzigingen inzake handelspraktijken*, Antwerp, Kluwer, 2000, (187) 200–203.

642 See Art. I.8, 22° BCEL.

643 The Belgian rules on unfair terms in B2B contracts have a similar scope, see Art. VI.91/3, §1 BCEL. Compare with the general regime of Art. 5.52 BCC (which mainly applies to C2C contracts) which only prohibits manifestly imbalanced terms that are "non-negotiable" (*beding waarover niet kan worden onderhandeld, clause non négociable*).

644 Art. VI.82(3) BCEL. In Dutch: "*de beoordeling van het onrechtmatige karakter van bedingen heeft geen betrekking op de bepaling van het eigenlijke voorwerp van de overeenkomst, noch op de gelijkwaardigheid van enerzijds de prijs of vergoeding en anderzijds de als tegenprestatie te leveren producten of te verrichten diensten, voor zover die bedingen duidelijk en begrijpelijk zijn geformuleerd.*"; in French: "*L'appréciation du caractère abusif des clauses ne porte ni sur la définition de l'objet principal du contrat, ni sur l'adéquation entre le prix et la rémunération d'une part, et les biens ou services à fournir en contrepartie, d'autre part, pour autant que ces clauses soient rédigées de manière claire et compréhensible.*"

645 Art. 1(2) UCTD.

646 J. Stuyck, "Le caractère abusif d'une disposition d'un règlement d'un transporteur public" (case note J.P. Thuin 24 October 2011), *DCCR* 2012, (190) 193; R. Steennot, G. Straetmans, E. Terryn, B. Keirsbilck and B. Wyseur, "Overzicht van rechtspraak. Consumentenbescherming (2008-2014) – Marktpraktijken (2011-2014)", *TPR* 2015, (1311) 1526–1527.

essential performances ("core terms").[647] Consequently, standard PSS contracts containing general terms and conditions can be assessed under the Dutch rules. However, core terms of a PSS contract fall outside of the material scope of the Dutch rules, as the exclusion of core terms from the unfairness test was implemented in the definition of the notion "general terms and conditions".[648]

As a rule of thumb, core terms are considered clauses that contain the essentials of the contract, as well as how the price is determined.[649] As mentioned above, for PSS contracts, this includes *i.a.* clauses on which product is made available (including its quality or quantity), clauses on which additional services are provided, as well as clauses on the monthly fee and pay-per-use pricing structure.[650] According to case law of the Dutch Supreme Court, the objective nature of the notion core term implies that the parties, in practice the PSS supplier ("user" of the general terms and conditions), cannot define a term as a core term to evade review under the open standard.[651] Clauses that meet the description of a term on the grey list or the blacklist are not core clauses in any case.[652] Just like under the UCTD, the so-called transparency requirement provides for an exception on the exclusion of core terms: if a core term is not formulated in clear and intelligible language, it can still be tested against the open standard.[653]

Comparable to Belgium, the Netherlands did not implement the provision excluding contract terms reflecting mandatory statutory or regulatory provisions

---

647 Art. 6:231 *sub* a. DCC. The Dutch DCC also explicitly confirms that contracts relating to employment and collective bargaining agreements are not covered by the regime on unfair terms, see Art. 6:245 DCC.

648 Art. 6:231 *sub* a. DCC.

649 HR (NL) 19 September 1997, ECLI:NL:HR:1997:ZC2435, (*Assoud/Nationale Sporttotalisator*), *NJ* 1998, 6, para. 3.4.2, fourth subpara.: "*het begrip 'bedingen die de kern van de prestaties aangeven' [moet] zo beperkt mogelijk worden opgevat, waarbij als vuistregel kan worden gesteld dat 'kernbedingen' veelal zullen samenvallen met de essentialia zonder welke een overeenkomst, bij gebreke van voldoende bepaalbaarheid van de verbintenissen, niet tot stand komt.*" See also: R.H.C. Jongeneel, "Gebondenheid" in B. Wessels and R.H.C. Jongeneel (eds.), *Algemene voorwaarden*, Deventer, Wolters Kluwer, 2017, (123)106; J. Hijma, *Algemene voorwaarden, Monografieën BW nr. B55*, Deventer, Wolters Kluwer, 2016, no. 14.

650 The extent of cover in an insurance contract and the duration of travel in a travel contract are also referred to as being core terms.

651 HR (NL) 21 February 2003, ECLI:NL:HR:2003:AF1563, (*Stous/Parkwoningen Hoge Heide*), *NJ* 2004/567, para. 3.4.2: "*Waar in de wetsgeschiedenis wordt opgemerkt dat bepalend is of een beding van zo wezenlijke betekenis is dat zonder dat beding de overeenkomst niet tot stand zou zijn gekomen of zonder dit beding niet van wilsovereenstemming omtrent het wezen van de overeenkomst sprake zou zijn, moet zulks dan ook in de zojuist bedoelde objectieve zin worden begrepen, en kan daaraan niet worden ontleend dat de subjectieve inzichten van de partijen of een van hen van belang zouden zijn. De vraag of partijen zelf bedingen tot kernbedingen kunnen bestempelen, moet ontkennend worden beantwoord.*"

652 C.H. Sieburgh, *Mr. C. Assers Handleiding tot de beoefening van het Nederlands Burgerlijk Recht. 6. Verbintenissenrecht. Deel III. Algemeen overeenkomstenrecht*, Deventer, Wolters Kluwer, 2018, no. 468. Compare with the case law on the UCTD: CJEU, Judgment of 26 February 2015, C-143/13, *Matei and Matei*, ECLI:EU:C:2015:127, para. 59–60.

653 See *infra* no. 160.

from the scope of the UCTD.[654] As a result, a contractual clause in the PSS contract that reflects the content of a statutory provision can be reviewed under the Dutch rules on unfair terms. Yet, Loos rightly points out that these clauses will hardly ever be considered unfair, precisely because they reflect a statutory provision.[655]

150. Obligation for the national courts to check *ex officio* whether case falls within scope of the UCTD – According to the Court of Justice, national courts must determine of its own motion (*ex officio*) whether a particular term falls within the scope of the UCTD.[656] The rationale behind this *ex officio* control is that consumers are generally are in a weaker position than the businesses with whom they contract.[657] Indeed, there is a structural risk that consumers are unaware of their rights and as a result do not raise an argument based on the unfair terms regime. Thus, national courts play an important and active role in assessing the fairness of terms in PSS contracts with consumers.

151. Obligation for the national courts to assess unfairness of terms *ex officio* – The national courts' obligation to consider the UCTD *ex officio* is not limited to examining its scope of application. Indeed, according to the Court's case law, the national court is also obliged to examine *ex officio* the unfairness of a term within the scope of the UCTD, provided it has the legal and factual elements necessary to do so.[658] The rationale behind this *ex officio* review is twofold: it prevents an individual consumer from being bound by an unfair term, and it can deter sellers and suppliers from using unfair terms in

654 Art. 1(2) UCTD.

655 M.B.M. Loos, "Algemene voorwaarden bij consumentenovereenkomsten" in E.H. Hondius and V. Mak (eds.), *Handboek Consumentenrecht*, Zutphen, Paris, 2020, (121) 124; Compare with R.H.C. Jongeneel, "Gebondenheid" in B. Wessels and R.H.C. Jongeneel (eds.), *Algemene voorwaarden*, Deventer, Wolters Kluwer, 2017, (123) 101 who refers to HR (NL) 23 February 2001, ECLI:NL:HR:2001:AB0220, (*Montoya en Cloudstorm/ABN Amro*), *NJ* 2001/277, para. 3.8.2: "*Met [art. 6:140 lid 2 BW] stemt het bepaalde in art. 13 overeen. Daaruit vloeit voort dat het in art. 13 vervatte beding in beginsel niet als onredelijk bezwarend kan worden aangemerkt.*"

656 This was first held by the CJEU (Grand Chamber) in CJEU, Judgment of 9 November 2010, C-137/08, *VB Pénzügyi Lízing*, ECLI:EU:C:2010:659, para. 56 and later confirmed in CJEU, Judgment of 17 May 2018, C-147/16, *Karel de Grote Hogeschool*, ECLI:EU:C:2018:320, para. 30. See for an in-depth analysis of the *ex officio* doctrine: J. Werbrouck, *Doorwerking van het Europees consumentenrecht in het nationaal procesrecht*, Antwerp, Intersentia, 2023, 315–527.

657 EC, *Guidance on the interpretation of Council Directive 93/13/EEC on unfair terms in consumer contracts*, 27.9.2019, 2019/C 323/04, 48.

658 CJEU, Judgment of 4 June 2009, C-243/08, *Pannon*, ECLI:EU:C:2009:350, para. 32. See also earlier case law of the CJEU in which it recognised that national courts have the *power* to examine unfair terms on their own motion: CJEU, Judgment of 27 June 2000, Joined Cases C-240/98-C-244/98, *Océano Grupo*, ECLI:EU:C:2000:346, para. 26, 28 and 29; CJEU, Judgment of 21 November 2002, C-473/00, *Cofidis*, ECLI:EU:C:2002:705, para. 32–33; CJEU, Judgment of 26 October 2006, C-168/05, *Mostaza Claro*, ECLI:EU:C:2006:675, para. 27–28.

their contracts with consumers.[659] Thus the national court must assess of its own motion whether a contractual term is potentially unfair if the consumer fails to argue this.[660] This is also the case even if the consumer does not appear in court, and even if he is represented by a lawyer who fails to invoke the unfairness of the term.[661] This obligation of *ex officio* review applies even more if the consumer challenges the validity or fairness of the contract without explicitly invoking the legal provisions on unfair contract terms.[662] However, the consumer may decide to oppose the non-application of a term after being informed of its (possibly) unfair nature by the national court.[663] In addition, the trader should also be given the opportunity when he was informed by the court of the (potentially) unfair nature of a term set out his view on the unfairness of the term.[664]

2.3.3.2. Overview of the unfairness test

152. THE UNFAIRNESS TEST OF THE UCTD: COMBINATION OF TRANSPARENCY REQUIREMENTS, *INTERPRETATIO CONTRA PROFERENTEM* RULE, GENERAL TEST

---

659 *Ex officio* control thus aims to achieve both the objective pursued by Art. 6(1) UCTD and Art. 7 UCTD.

660 See also: CJEU, Judgment of 14 March 2013, C-415/11, *Mohamed Aziz*, ECLI:EU:C:2013:164, para. 46; CJEU, Judgment of 21 February 2013, C-472/11, *Banif Plus Bank*, ECLI:EU:C:2013:88, para. CJEU, Order of 16 November 2010, C-76/10, *Pohotovosť*, ECLI:EU:C:2010:685, para. 23. See for an application in **Belgium**: Ghent (BE) 26 October 2012, *Jaarboek Marktpraktijken* 2012, 286, case note. P. CAMBIE, *TGR* 2014, 46; Ghent (BE) 4 January 2012, *NjW* 2012, 73, case note R. STEENNOT; J.P. Charleroi (BE) 4 July 2008, *JLMB* 2008, 1658. See also the case law mentioned in R. STEENNOT, G. STRAETMANS, E. TERRYN, B. KEIRSBILCK and B. WYSEUR, "Overzicht van rechtspraak. Consumentenbescherming (2008-2014) – Marktpraktijken (2011-2014)", *TPR* 2015, (1311) 1530, fn. 969. For an application in **the Netherlands**, see: HR (NL) 13 September 2013, *NJ* 2014/274, case note H.B. KRANS, *TvC* 2013, issue 6, 262, case note M.B.M. Loos and R.R.M. DE MOOR; Ct. Rotterdam (NL) 18 June 2010, ECLI:NL:RBROT:2010:BN5171, *NJF* 2010/395.

661 A. ANCERY and M. WISSINK, "ECJ 4 June 2009, Pannon GSM Zrt. v. Erzsébet Sustikné Győrfi", *ERPL* 2010, vol. 18 issue 2, (307) 316. See also: J. STUYCK and B. KEIRSBILCK, *Handels- en economisch recht. 2: Mededingingsrecht. A: Handelspraktijken en contracten met consumenten in Beginselen van Belgisch Privaatrecht*, Mechelen, Kluwer, 2024, 801, no. 831; R. STEENNOT, G. STRAETMANS, E. TERRYN, B. KEIRSBILCK and B. WYSEUR, "Overzicht van rechtspraak. Consumentenbescherming (2008-2014) – Marktpraktijken (2011-2014)", *TPR* 2015, (1311) 1529.

662 CJEU, Judgment of 30 May 2013, C-397/11, *Jőrös*, ECLI:EU:C:2013:340, para. 30, 35 and 36.

663 CJEU, Judgment of 4 June 2009, C-243/08, *Pannon*, ECLI:EU:C:2009:350, para. 35. This waiver of the sanctioning of an unfair term by the consumer will be rather rare but cannot be entirely ruled out. E.g. the case of an unfair jurisdiction clause whereby the consumer has already made the trip to court and wants to reach a judgment. See: A. VAN OEVELEN, S. RUTTEN and F. DUPON, "Ambtshalve inroepbaarheid van Europees consumentenrecht, materieelrechtelijk en procesrechtelijk beschouwd" in G. STRAETMANS and M. ROZIE (eds.), *Doorwerking van het Europese recht in de nationale rechterlijke praktijk*, Antwerp, Intersentia, 2012, (95) 106; M.J.M. VERHOEVEN, "Bespreking van HvJ 4 juni 2009, C-243/08 inzake Pannon GSM Zrt. t/ Ersébet Sustikné Gyorfi", *SEW* 2009, (453) 455.

664 CJEU, Judgment of 30 May 2013, C-488/11, *Asbeek Brusse*, ECLI:EU:C:2013:341, para. 52; CJEU, Judgment of 21 February 2013, C-472/11, *Banif Plus Bank*, ECLI:EU:C:2013:88 para. 31 and 36.

AND "GREY LIST" – The unfairness test of the UCTD can be summarised as follows. First, **transparency** plays a key role in unfair contract terms law.[665] This is reflected in the fact that terms that are offered to the consumer in writing are required to be drafted in plain intelligible language.[666] Second, where there is doubt about the meaning of a term, the **interpretation** most favourable to the consumer shall prevail (*interpretatio contra proferentem*).[667] Third, **the general test** provides that a contractual term which has not been individually negotiated shall be regarded as unfair if, contrary to the requirement of good faith, it causes a significant imbalance in the parties' rights and obligations arising under the contract, to the detriment of the consumer.[668] Fourth, in addition to the general test, the **Annex** to the Directive contains an indicative and non-exhaustive list of the terms which may be regarded as unfair ("grey list"[669]).[670]

153. BELGIAN IMPLEMENTATION OF THE UCTD UNFAIRNESS TEST: FOUR SETS OF RULES, INCLUDING BLACKLIST OF PROHIBITED TERMS – The unfairness test of the UCTD was implemented in Belgium by including four sets of rules for consumer contracts in Book VI of the BCEL. (i) The **transparency rule** requires that all written terms must be drafted in plain and intelligible language.[671] This rule also comes into play when assessing whether a term is unfair or not.[672] (ii) An **interpretation provision** provides that, in case of doubt about the meaning of a term, the interpretation most favourable to the consumer prevails (*interpretatio contra proferentem*).[673] In addition, a contract between a business and a consumer can be interpreted, *inter alia*, by the commercial practices directly related to it.[674] (iii) The general unfairness test is found in a **"catch all" rule.**[675] According to the definition of an "unfair term" (*onrechtmatig beding, clause abusive*), a term that by itself or in conjunction with the other term creates a significant imbalance between the parties' rights and obligations to the detriment of the consumer is prohibited and null and void.[676] (iv) A term

665 P. ROTT, "Unfair contract terms" in C. TWIGG-FLESNER (ed.), *Research Handbook on EU Consumer and Contract Law*, Cheltenham, Edward Elgar, 2016, (287) 301; H.-W. MICKLITZ, "Unfair terms in consumer contracts" in N. REICH, H.-W. MICKLITZ, P. ROTT and K. TONNER (eds.), *European Consumer Law*, Antwerp, Intersentia, 2014, (125) 142.

666 Art. 5, first sentence UCTD.

667 Art. 5, second sentence UCTD.

668 Art. 3(1) UCTD.

669 See CJEU, Judgment of 26 February 2015, C-143/13, *Matei and Matei*, ECLI:EU:C:2015:127, para. 60 where the Court refers to the Annex as a "grey list". However, this notion should not be confused with the "grey list" in the Netherlands of terms that are presumed to be unfair.

670 Art. 3(3) UCTD.

671 Art. VI.37, §1 BCEL.

672 See Art. VI.82(2) BCEL.

673 Art. VI.37, §2 (1) BCEL.

674 Art. VI.37, §2 (2) BCEL.

675 Art. I.8, 22° BCEL.

676 See for an application: Cass. (BE) 21 December 2009, AR C.08.0499.F, *Arr.Cass.* 2009, 3120, concl. J. GENICOT, *JT* 2010, 391, case note P. ERNEUX, *Pas.* 2009, 3129, concl. J. GENICOT, *Jaarboek Handelspraktijken & Mededinging* 2009, 217.

included in the (extensive) **blacklist** of prohibited terms is in any case unfair, prohibited and void.[677] In practice, a contract term will be tested first against the transparency and interpretation rules, then against the blacklist and finally assessed against the general ("catch all") rule.[678]

154. Dutch implementation of the UCTD unfairness test: transparency, *interpretatio contra proferentem*, general test, and various lists of terms – In the Netherlands, the UCTD is implemented in Title 6.5.3 of the DCC ("general terms and conditions"). This title therefore does not only contain provisions on the incorporation and enforceability of general terms and conditions,[679] but also their legality. The **transparency requirement** and **interpretation rule** are incorporated almost verbatim in the DCC.[680] The **general test** provides that a term in general terms and conditions is voidable if it is unreasonably onerous (*onredelijk bezwarend*) for the counterparty, taking into account the nature and other terms of the contract, all the circumstances attending the conclusion of the contract, the mutually recognisable interests of the parties and the other circumstances of the case.[681] This general test is complemented by several lists of terms. First, there is a **blacklist** of terms that are always considered unreasonably onerous if used against consumers.[682] Second, a **grey list** sets out terms that are presumed to be unreasonably onerous if used against consumers.[683] In addition, there are two lists that are not incorporated in Title 6.5.3 DCC. The third list is referred to as the **blue list** (or European list)[684] and consists of the indicative and non-exhaustive list of terms annexed to the UCTD.[685] It contains 17 terms that *may* be regarded as unfair partially overlapping with the above-mentioned blacklist and grey list.[686] The court must consider the fact that a term is on the blue list when assessing its potentially unreasonable onerous nature.[687]

677 Art. VI.83 BCEL.

678 I. Claeys and T. Tanghe, *Nieuw Algemeen Contractenrecht*, Antwerp, Intersentia, 2023, 313.

679 See *supra* no. 119 *et seq.*

680 Art. 6:238(2) DCC.

681 Art. 6:233 *sub* a. DCC.

682 Art. 6:236 DCC.

683 Art. 6:237 DCC.

684 The CJEU refers to this list as the "grey list", see CJEU, Judgment of 26 February 2015, C-143/13, *Matei and Matei*, ECLI:EU:C:2015:127, para. 60.

685 M.B.M. Loos, "Algemene voorwaarden bij consumentenovereenkomsten" in E.H. Hondius and V. Mak (eds.), *Handboek Consumentenrecht*, Zutphen, Paris, 2020, (121) 158.

686 C.M.D.S. Pavillon, "De invloed van Europese richtlijnen op de Nederlandse regeling van algemene voorwaarden (afdeling 6.5.3 BW)" in A.S. Hartkamp (ed.), *De invloed van het Europese recht op het Nederlands privaatrecht*, Deventer, Kluwer, 2013, (233) 245, no. 18.

687 M.B.M. Loos, "Algemene voorwaarden bij consumentenovereenkomsten" in E.H. Hondius and V. Mak (eds.), *Handboek Consumentenrecht*, Zutphen, Paris, 2020, (121) 158. See also: CJEU, Judgment of 26 April 2012, C-472/10, *Invitel*, ECLI:EU:C:2012:242, para. 26: "*If the content of the annex does not suffice in itself to establish automatically the unfair nature of a contested term, it is nevertheless an essential element on which the competent court may base its assessment as to the unfair nature of that term.*"

The last list concerns the **Hague list** (*Haagse lijst*),[688] which contains clauses that have been declared unreasonably onerous in collective action proceedings[689] at the request of industry and consumer associations.[690]

2.3.3.3. *Transparency requirements and interpretation rule*

155. Transparency requirements: overview – The transparency requirements of the UCTD and its national implementation apply to *all* (not individually negotiated[691]) contract terms of the PSS contract. These transparency requirements therefore also apply to core terms that otherwise escape the unfairness test.[692] First, there is a "procedural" component to these transparency requirements: consumers must be given an opportunity to examine the terms of the PSS contract. Second, the "material" component relates to the intelligibility of the terms. If the PSS user has access to the general terms and conditions, he must also be able to understand them. Finally, to support this procedural and material component, there is also an interpretation rule to ensure that ambiguous terms are interpreted in favour of the PSS user.

156. Consumer must be given an opportunity to examine the terms of the PSS contract – The first aspect of the transparency requirements is the actual opportunity to examine all terms of the PSS contract before its conclusion, which follows from the recitals of the UCTD.[693] In many legal systems, such as Belgium,[694] this is first and foremost a problem of incorporation, which is governed by national contract law. If the consumer did not have the reasonable opportunity to take knowledge of the contract terms, they are not part of the contract.[695] However, the UCTD also provides for a sanction mechanism if the reasonable

---

688 L.J.H. Mölenberg, *Het collectief actierecht voor consumentenorganisaties op het terrein van algemene voorwaarden*, Arnhem, Gouda Quint, 1995, 224.

689 See Art. 6:240 *juncto* Art. 6:241(3) DCC.

690 Art. 6:243 DCC.

691 Under **Belgian** law, this also applies to individually negotiated contract terms in the PSS contract. See *supra* no. 148.

692 See Art 5 and Art. 4(2) UCTD that uses the same wording "*plain intelligible language*". According to the Court of Justice, both requirements have the same scope. See: CJEU, Judgment of 30 April 2014, C-26/13, *Kásler*, ECLI:EU:C:2014:282, para. 69.

693 Recital 20 UCTD. This requirement was originally included in the European Commission's proposal but was dropped in the final text. Nevertheless, according to the Commission – and confirmed by the Court of Justice – it is still part of the Directive. EC, *Report from the Commission on the implementation of Council Directive 93/13/EEC of 5 April 1993 on unfair terms in consumer contracts*, 27.04.2000, COM(2000) 248 final, 17–18; CJEU, Judgment of 21 March 2013, C-92/11, *RWE Vertrieb AG*, ECLI:EU:C:2013:180, para. 43–44. See also CJEU, Judgment of 10 May 2001, C-144/99, *Commission / The Netherlands*, ECLI:EU:C:2001:257 where the CJEU ordered the Netherlands to include this requirement in its national legislation.

694 See *supra* no. 122 and 123.

695 Dutch law follows a different approach: if the PSS user accepted the general terms and conditions, they are part of the contract. However, they are voidable if he did not have the

opportunity to examine the terms and conditions is lacking.[696] Indeed, the Court of Justice links the lack of pre-contractual information about the general terms and conditions to the unfairness of the terms.[697] In *Naranjo*, it held that the unfairness of a contractual clause could be assessed and that the term could be declared non-binding if the consumer did not have the necessary information on the contractual conditions and the consequences of entering into that contract before its conclusion.[698] Consequently, the UCTD also allows to render the terms non-binding if the PSS user did not have the reasonable opportunity to examine the terms of the PSS contract. The difference with the national rules on incorporation is that this assessment is done through the unfairness test.[699]

157. Contract terms of the PSS contract must be in plain intelligible language –The material component of transparency under the UCTD requires that the terms of the PSS contract are drafted in plain intelligible language.[700] This is a relatively vague and open standard, which was given further substance by the CJEU. First, the content of the general terms and conditions must be formally and grammatically intelligible.[701] In addition, it is also required that the average consumer[702] – on the basis of clear and intelligible criteria – must

---

reasonable opportunity to take knowledge of the terms. See Art. 6:233, *sub* b. DCC and the discussion *supra* no. 127.

696 E. Terryn, "Transparantie en algemene voorwaarden – Nood aan hervorming?", *TPR* 2017, (13) 21–22.

697 CJEU, Judgment of 21 December 2016, Joined Cases C-154/15, C-307/15 and C-308/15, *Naranjo*, ECLI:EU:C:2016:980, para. 50–51.

698 CJEU, Judgment of 21 December 2016, Joined Cases C-154/15, C-307/15 and C-308/15, *Naranjo*, ECLI:EU:C:2016:980, para. 51: "*Therefore, the assessment of the unfairness, in accordance with Article 3(1) of Directive 93/13, of a contractual clause relating to the definition of the main subject-matter of a contract, where the consumer did not have, before the conclusion of that contract, the necessary information on the contractual conditions and the consequences of entering into that contract, falls within the scope of that directive in general and of Article 6(1) of that directive, in particular.*"

699 E. Terryn, "Transparantie en algemene voorwaarden – Nood aan hervorming?", *TPR* 2017, (13) 22.

700 Art. 5 UCTD. **Belgium**: Art. VI.37, §1 WER. **The Netherlands**: Art. 6:238(2) DCC.

701 CJEU, Judgment of 30 April 2014, C-26/13, *Kásler*, ECLI:EU:C:2014:282, para. 71.

702 This is a consumer "*who is reasonably well informed and reasonably observant and circumspect.*" See: CJEU, Judgment of 30 April 2014, C-26/13, *Kásler*, ECLI:EU:C:2014:282, para. 74 and confirmed in, amongst others, CJEU, Judgment of 18 November 2021, C-212/20, *A. S.A.*, ECLI:EU:C:2021:934, para. 42–43; CJEU, Judgment of 5 June 2019, C-38/17, *GT*, ECLI:EU:C:2019:461, para. 34; CJEU, Judgment of 20 September 2018, C-51/17, *OTP Bank v Ilyés and Kiss*, ECLI:EU:C:2018:750, para. 27; CJEU, Judgment of 26 February 2015, C-143/13, *Matei and Matei*, ECLI:EU:C:2015:127, para. 75 and CJEU, Judgment of 9 July 2015, C-348/14, *Bucura*, ECLI:EU:C:2015:447, para. 56. It is therefore not the concrete consumer who entered into the contract who is considered, but a reference consumer who is assessed *in abstracto*. See e.g. J. Waelkens, "De interpretatieregel in het voordeel van de consument", *TPR* 2014, (989) 1003–1005. This benchmark of the average consumer was recently criticised in legal doctrine, see: F. Esposito and M. Grochowski, "The Consumer Benchmark, Vulnerability, and the Contract Terms Transparency: A Plea for Reconsideration", *ERCL* 2022, vol. 18 issue

be able to evaluate the economic consequences of a contract term or contract.[703] That question must be examined in light of all the relevant facts, including the promotional material and information provided by the PSS supplier in the negotiation of the PSS contract.[704] This rather broad understanding of transparency implies that before the conclusion of the PSS contract, the PSS supplier must provide clear information on the contract terms and their implications so that the PSS user can understand the extent of its rights and obligations before being bound by it.[705]

158. Plain and intelligible language: practical factors – The UCTD guidance document further sets out factors that, in the European Commission's view, can be relevant for assessing whether a term in the PSS contract is drafted in plain intelligible language.[706] A first factor is the comprehensibility of the individual terms, for example in terms of the wording and the terminology used, but also the position and perspective the consumer to whom the terms are addressed,[707] as well as whether he/she is familiar with the language in which the terms are drafted. Second, the way in which the terms are presented is also relevant. For example, the visual presentation of the terms to the PSS contract (e.g. font size, colour, contrast of the words with the background), the structure of the PSS contract (structured in a logical manner?), whether important terms are given the prominence they deserve (i.e. not hidden in the fine print), or

---

1, (1) 1–31. Here, it is argued that in some circumstances, the transparency should be assessed using the yardstick of the vulnerable consumer, rather than the average consumer.

703 CJEU, Judgment of 30 April 2014, C-26/13, *Kásler*, ECLI:EU:C:2014:282, para. 75. See also: CJEU, Judgment of 20 September 2017, C-186/17, *Andriciuc*, ECLI:EU:C:2017:703, para. 44 and 45; CJEU, Judgment of 28 July 2016, C-191/15, *Verein für Konsumenteninformation v Amazon*, ECLI:EU:C:2016:612, para. 68; CJEU, Judgment of 23 April 2015, C-96/14, *Van Hove*, ECLI:EU:C:2015:262, para. 40. See also CJEU, Judgment of 26 February 2015, C-143/13, *Matei and Matei*, ECLI:EU:C:2015:127, para. 77 where the CJEU added that one of the elements to assess transparency is whether the reason for including a term in a contract was explained to the consumer. This has – rightly – been criticised in legal doctrine, see e.g. J. Stuyck and B. Keirsbilck, *Handels- en economisch recht. 2: Mededingingsrecht. A: Handelspraktijken en contracten met consumenten in Beginselen van Belgisch Privaatrecht*, Mechelen, Kluwer, 2024, 803, fn. 294; E. Terryn, "Transparantie en algemene voorwaarden – Nood aan hervorming?", *TPR* 2017, (13) 25–26; R. Steennot, G. Straetmans, E. Terryn, B. Keirsbilck and B. Wyseur, "Overzicht van rechtspraak. Consumentenbescherming (2008-2014) – Marktpraktijken (2011-2014)", *TPR* 2015, (1311) 1514.

704 CJEU, Judgment of 20 September 2017, C-186/17, *Andriciuc*, ECLI:EU:C:2017:703, para. 46; CJEU, Judgment of 26 February 2015, C-143/13, *Matei and Matei*, ECLI:EU:C:2015:127, para. 75; CJEU, Judgment of 30 April 2014, C-26/13, *Kásler*, ECLI:EU:C:2014:282, para. 74.

705 CJEU, Judgment of 20 September 2017, C-186/17, *Andriciuc*, ECLI:EU:C:2017:703, para. 48; CJEU, Judgment of 21 December 2016, Joined Cases C-154/15, C-307/15 and C-308/15, *Naranjo*, ECLI:EU:C:2016:980, para. 50; CJEU, Judgment of 21 March 2013, C-92/11, *RWE Vertrieb AG*, ECLI:EU:C:2013:180, para. 44.

706 EC, *Guidance on the interpretation of Council Directive 93/13/EEC on unfair terms in consumer contracts*, 27.9.2019, 2019/C 323/04, 25–26.

707 See also CJEU, Judgment of 23 April 2015, C-96/14, *Van Hove*, ECLI:EU:C:2015:262, para. 48.

whether the terms can be reasonably expected in a PSS contract are all aspects to be considered.[708] Moreover, the requirement that contract terms must be drafted in plain intelligible language may also imply that contract terms whose effect can only be understood by reading them together cannot be placed in different parts of the PSS contract.[709]

159. Interpretation of unclear clauses in favour of PSS user – Linked with the transparency requirements of the UCTD is the interpretation rule in favour of the consumer. According to this rule, where there is doubt about the meaning of a term in the PSS contract, the interpretation most favourable to the PSS user shall prevail.[710, 711] It does not apply in collective proceedings[712] and, as the *lex specialis*, it takes precedence over the general national interpretation rules.[713] Consequently, provided that there is indeed doubt about the term in the PSS contract, the interpretation most favourable to the PSS user should be applied and it is not necessary to ascertain beforehand what the common intention of the parties was.

According to the CJEU in *Van Hove,* unclear terms of the PSS contract that are not exempt from the unfairness test (i.e. that are not core terms within the meaning of the UCTD) can also be interpreted in favour of the PSS user.[714] As a result, the national court can in this case either annul an unclear term in the PSS contract (for example, if it creates a significant imbalance between the rights and obligations of the parties), or it can interpret the clause in favour of the PSS user.

---

708 EC, *Guidance on the interpretation of Council Directive 93/13/EEC on unfair terms in consumer contracts*, 27.9.2019, 2019/C 323/04 25.

709 EC, *Guidance on the interpretation of Council Directive 93/13/EEC on unfair terms in consumer contracts*, 27.9.2019, 2019/C 323/04 26, with reference to the Opinion of Advocate General Hogan of 15 May 2019 in Case C-621/17, *Kiss and CIB Bank*, ECLI:EU:C:2019:411, para. 41.

710 Art. 5, second sentence UCTD. **Belgium**: Art. VI.37, §2 BCEL. **The Netherlands**: Art. 6:248(2), second sentence DCC.

711 See also *infra* no. 253, 255 and 265.

712 CJEU, Judgment of 9 September 2004, C-70/03, *Commission v Spain*, ECLI:EU:C:2004:505. The rationale behind this exclusion is to avoid the business defending itself against the action for cessation by saying that the clause is not unfair when interpreted in favour of the consumer. For collective injunction proceedings, see: Art. 7(2) UCTD; in **Belgium**: Art. XVII.2 and Art. XVII.12 BCEL; and in **the Netherlands**: Art. 6:240–6:242 DCC.

713 J. Waelkens, "De interpretatieregel in het voordeel van de consument", *TPR* 2014, (989) 1012. For the general rules on interpretation in **Belgium**, see Art. 5.64–5.66 BCC (formerly Art. 1156–1164 old BCC) and Art. 1602 old BCC. In **the Netherlands**, the DCC does, contrary to the old DCC, not have any rules on the interpretation of contracts. The interpretation of contracts is left to case law and legal scholarship, which can draw inspiration from some general provisions such as Art 6:248 and Art 3:35 DCC. See: C.H. Sieburgh, *Mr. C. Assers Handleiding tot de beoefening van het Nederlands Burgerlijk Recht. 6. Verbintenissenrecht. Deel III. Algemeen overeenkomstenrecht*, Deventer, Wolters Kluwer, 2022, no. 354.

714 CJEU, Judgment of 23 April 2015, C-96/14, *Van Hove*, ECLI:EU:C:2015:262, para. 49.

However, if the interpretation in favour of the consumer does not bring relief, the court has no choice but to annul the unclear clause.[715]

2.3.3.4. *The general test*

160. The general test of the UCTD: "catch all" for terms "contrary to the requirement of good faith" and "causing a significant imbalance" – The UCTD's general test provides a "catch all" rule for unfair terms in PSS contracts concluded with consumers. According to the general test, contract terms are to be regarded as unfair if (i) contrary to the requirement of good faith, (ii) they cause a significant imbalance in the parties' rights and obligations arising under the contract, to the detriment of the consumer.[716] This is of course a very open-worded test. The question thus arises how national courts must apply these two concepts to PSS contracts. The case law of the CJEU provides several indications in this regard.

161. "Contrary to the requirement of good faith" – Regarding the yardstick of "good faith", the CJEU has held that it is particularly relevant whether the PSS supplier could reasonably assume that the PSS user would have agreed to a specific term in the PSS contract had there been individual negotiations.[717] It does so by referencing the Recitals of the UCTD, which refer to the bargaining power of the parties and explain that the requirement of good faith entails that the PSS supplier must deal fairly and equitably with the PSS user, and take his legitimate interest into account.[718] This clarification is not really relevant for Belgian law, as the Belgian implementation of the general test does not include the requirement that the contract term is contrary to the requirement of good faith, which is allowed given the minimum harmonisation nature of the UCTD.[719, 720] The Dutch implementation does not explicitly refer to

715 J. Stuyck and B. Keirsbilck, *Handels- en economisch recht. 2: Mededingingsrecht. A: Handelspraktijken en contracten met consumenten in Beginselen van Belgisch Privaatrecht*, Mechelen, Kluwer, 2024, 806; R. Steennot, G. Straetmans, E. Terryn, B. Keirsbilck and B. Wyseur, "Overzicht van rechtspraak. Consumentenbescherming (2008-2014) – Marktpraktijken (2011-2014)", *TPR* 2015, (1311) 1518; J. Waelkens, "De interpretatieregel in het voordeel van de consument", *TPR* 2014, (989) 1039–1041.

716 Art. 3(1) UCTD.

717 CJEU, Judgment of 26 January 2017, C-421/14, *Banco Primus*, ECLI:EU:C:2017:60, para. 60; CJEU, Judgment of 14 March 2013, C-415/11, *Mohamed Aziz*, ECLI:EU:C:2013:164, para. 69. See also CJEU, Judgment of 20 September 2017, C-186/17, *Andriciuc*, ECLI:EU:C:2017:703, para. 57.

718 Recital 16 UCTD.

719 EC, *Guidance on the interpretation of Council Directive 93/13/EEC on unfair terms in consumer contracts*, 27.9.2019, 2019/C 323/04, 30.

720 Art. I.8, 22° BCEL. According to some authors, this ensures more legal certainty and consumer protection, as the consumer's burden of proof would be heavier if he must prove separately that there is a breach of the requirement of good faith. See: S. Stijns, "De leer der onrechtmatige bedingen in de WHPC na de Wet van 7 december 1998", *TBH* 2000,

the requirement of good faith, but mentions the "mutual interests of the parties" (*wederzijds kenbare belangen van de partijen*).[721]

162. "Causing a significant imbalance": relevance of default rules – The analysis of whether a term in the PSS contract causes a "significant imbalance" requires examining how this term influences the rights and obligations of the parties to the PSS contract.[722] In *Aziz*, the CJEU clarified that this must be done primarily by comparing the contract term with the rules of national default law that would apply in the absence of the contract term.[723] This comparative analysis allows the national court to evaluate whether the contract term places the PSS user in a less favourable legal position than he would be under national default law.[724] This may be the case, for instance, if the contract term restricts the rights that the PSS user would otherwise have, if it impairs the exercise of these rights, or if it saddles the PSS user with additional obligations that he would not have under national default law.[725] However, the mere fact that the contract term places the PSS user in a less favourable legal position than he would be under national default law does not suffice; the imbalance must be "significant". This is the case, according to the CJEU, if there is a "*sufficiently serious impairment of the legal situation in which the consumer [...] is placed by reason of the relevant national provisions.*"[726]

163. Other relevant criteria in absence of default rules – If there are no relevant default rules, the criterion of a significant imbalance must

(148) 200–201; I. Demuynck, "De Wet van 3 april 1997 betreffende oneerlijke bedingen in overeenkomsten gesloten tussen beoefenaren van vrije beroepen en hun cliënten: much ado about nothing? ", *RW* 1997–1998, (1313) 1330–1331. Stuyck and Keirsbilck also rightly state that the interpretation of this "good faith" requirement would not really make sense, as the Belgian rules on unfair terms also apply to individually negotiated contract terms. See: J. Stuyck and B. Keirsbilck, *Handels- en economisch recht. 2: Mededingingsrecht. A: Handelspraktijken en contracten met consumenten in Beginselen van Belgisch Privaatrecht*, Mechelen, Kluwer, 2024, 808.

721 Art. 6:233, *sub* a. DCC.

722 EC, *Guidance on the interpretation of Council Directive 93/13/EEC on unfair terms in consumer contracts*, 27.9.2019, 2019/C 323/04, 30.

723 CJEU, Judgment of 14 March 2013, C-415/11, *Mohamed Aziz*, ECLI:EU:C:2013:164, para. 68. This was later confirmed in e.g. CJEU, Judgment of 16 January 2014, C-226/12, *Constructora Principado*, ECLI:EU:C:2014:10, para. 21; CJEU, Judgment of 26 January 2017, C-421/14, *Banco Primus*, ECLI:EU:C:2017:60, para. 59 and CJEU, Judgment of 20 September 2017, C-186/17, *Andriciuc*, ECLI:EU:C:2017:703, para. 59.

724 EC, *Guidance on the interpretation of Council Directive 93/13/EEC on unfair terms in consumer contracts*, 27.9.2019, 2019/C 323/04 30–31.

725 CJEU, Judgment of 16 January 2014, C-226/12, *Constructora Principado*, ECLI:EU:C:2014:10, para. 23.

726 CJEU, Judgment of 16 January 2014, C-226/12, *Constructora Principado*, ECLI:EU:C:2014:10, para. 23.

be assessed in light of other criteria.[727] The UCTD itself gives a few examples, namely the nature of the goods or services to which the contract relates, all the other terms of the contract or another contract on which it is dependent, and all the circumstances attending the conclusion of the contract.[728] The UCTD guidance mentions a few more, such as fair and equitable market practices or a comparison of the rights and obligations of the parties, taking into account the nature of the contract and other related terms.[729]

164. Indicative list as an essential element for determining unfairness of a term – The CJEU has also repeatedly stated that the indicative list of contract terms in the Annex of the UCTD is an essential element on which the assessment may be based as to whether a given term is unfair.[730] Of course, as both Belgian and Dutch law have a blacklist of unfair terms,[731] the terms of the PSS contract that fit the description of a term on any of these lists do not need to be assessed against the criteria of the general test. A similar logic applies to the terms on the Dutch grey list, as these terms are presumed to be unfair.[732]

165. Case-by-case analysis with wide margin of discretion for national courts – Within this framework created by the CJEU, national courts have a very wide margin of discretion to assess clauses in a PSS contract.[733] Indeed, while the CJEU's role consists of giving guidance on the interpretation of the UCTD's concepts of transparency and unfairness, national courts are tasked with the assessment of transparency and unfairness of the terms used in a specific contract in light of the specific circumstances of each case.[734] This is

---

727 C.H. Sieburgh, *Mr. C. Assers Handleiding tot de beoefening van het Nederlands Burgerlijk Recht. 6. Verbintenissenrecht. Deel III. Algemeen overeenkomstenrecht*, Deventer, Wolters Kluwer, 2022, no. 484.

728 Art. 4(1) UCTD. For the implementation in **Belgium**, see Art. VI.82 BCEL:"*alle omstandigheden rond de sluiting van de overeenkomst, alsmede alle andere bedingen van de overeenkomst of van een andere overeenkomst waarvan deze afhankelijk is, op het ogenblik waarop de overeenkomst is gesloten in aanmerking genomen, rekening houdend met de aard van de producten waarop de overeenkomst betrekking heeft.*" In the **The Netherlands**, see Art. 6:233, *sub* a. DCC: "*de aard en de overage inhoud van de overeenkomst, de wijze waarop de voorwaarden zijn tot stand gekomen, […] en de overige omstandigheden van het geval.*"

729 EC, *Guidance on the interpretation of Council Directive 93/13/EEC on unfair terms in consumer contracts*, 27.9.2019, 2019/C 323/04, 30.

730 See e.g. CJEU, Judgment of 26 April 2012, C-472/10, *Invitel*, ECLI:EU:C:2012:242, para. 25–26; CJEU, Order of 16 November 2010, C-76/10, *Pohotovosť*, ECLI:EU:C:2010:685, para. 56 and 58; CJEU, Judgment of 4 June 2009, C-243/08, *Pannon*, ECLI:EU:C:2009:350, para. 37–38.

731 **Belgium**: Art. VI.83 BCEL. **The Netherlands**: Art. 6:236 DCC.

732 Art. 6:237 DCC.

733 **Belgium**: J. Stuyck and B. Keirsbilck, *Handels- en economisch recht. 2: Mededingingsrecht. A: Handelspraktijken en contracten met consumenten in Beginselen van Belgisch Privaatrecht*, Mechelen, Kluwer, 2024, 807.

734 CJEU, Judgment of 1 April 2004, C-237/02, *Freiburger Kommunalbauten*, ECLI:EU:C:2004:209, para. 23–25. See also e.g. CJEU, Judgment of 26 January 2017, C-421/14,

why the CJEU generally does not provide a final answer on the assessment of the unfairness of a specific term, leaving this to the referring national court.[735] Consequently, it is for the national court to determine whether a term in the PSS contract meets the requirements of good faith, balance and transparency on a case-by-case basis.[736] If it decides that a particular term in the PSS contract is unfair or not transparent, the Belgian Court of Cassation and the Dutch Supreme can only assess whether this decision is justified in law (i.e. not in fact).[737]

166. Considering sustainability when applying the general test? – The question arises what role sustainability can and should play in applying the open norm of the general test to terms in a PSS contract. Pavillon argues in this sense that there is some room for (diffuse) sustainability interests to put limits on the freedom of contract through contract law open norms such as public policy and morality[738] (*openbare orde en goede zeden, ordre public et bonnes mœurs*) and reasonableness and fairness,[739] but also the general test of the UCTD.[740] Her argument for the impact of sustainability on contract law open norms is based on the underlying idea that sustainability (care for people and the environment) can be traced back to fundamental rights, and that the recent *Shell* judgment[741]

Banco Primus, ECLI:EU:C:2017:60, para. 57; CJEU, Judgment of 16 January 2014, C-226/12, *Constructora Principado*, ECLI:EU:C:2014:10, para. 20; CJEU, Judgment of 14 March 2013, C-415/11, *Mohamed Aziz*, ECLI:EU:C:2013:164, para. 66; CJEU, Judgment of 26 April 2012, C-472/10, *Invitel*, ECLI:EU:C:2012:242, para. 22; CJEU, Judgment of 4 June 2009, C-243/08, *Pannon*, ECLI:EU:C:2009:350, para. 42–43.

735 However, in certain cases the CJEU did provide fairly clear indications as to the unfairness of a term. See e.g. CJEU, Judgment of 28 July 2016, C-191/15, *Verein für Konsumenteninformation v Amazon*, ECLI:EU:C:2016:612, para. 71; CJEU, Judgment of 27 June 2000, Joined Cases C-240/98-C-244/98, *Océano Grupo*, ECLI:EU:C:2000:346, para. 21–24.

736 EC, *Guidance on the interpretation of Council Directive 93/13/EEC on unfair terms in consumer contracts*, 27.9.2019, 2019/C 323/04, 22.

737 **Belgium**: Cass. (BE) 21 December 2009, AR C.08.0499.F, *Arr.Cass.* 2009, 3120, concl. J. Genicot, *JT* 2010, 391, case note P. Erneux, *Pas.* 2009, 3129, concl. J. Genicot, *Jaarboek Handelspraktijken & Mededinging* 2009, 217. See for an application in **the Netherlands**: HR (NL) 21 September 2012, ECLI:NL:HR:2012:BW6135, *NJ* 2013/431, case note H.J. Snijders, *TvA* 2014/14, case note G.J. Meijer, *JIN* 2012/184, case note N. de Boer, *NJB* 2012/2038, para. 3.4 and 3.5.

738 **Belgium**: Art. 1.3(3) and Art. 1.3(4) BCC. **The Netherlands**: Art. 3:40 DCC.

739 **Belgium**: Art. 5.71 BCC. **The Netherlands**: Art. 6:248(2) DCC.

740 C.M.D.S. Pavillon, "Herijking van consumentencontractenrecht: duurzaamheid als nieuw ijkpunt?" in C.M.D.S. Pavillon and W.H. van Boom (eds.), *Preadviezen Vereniging voor Burgerlijk Recht: Privaatrechtelijke bescherming herijkt*, Zutphen, Paris, 2021, (11) 58 and 62.

741 Ct. The Hague (NL) 26 May 2021, ECLI:NL:RBDHA:2021:5337, (*Milieudefensie et al. v. Royal Dutch Shell*), *JM* 2021/95, case note W.T. Douma, *JA* 2021/93, case note B.A. Kuiper-Slendebroek, *JOR* 2021/208, case note S.J.M. Biesmans, *M en R* 2021/86, case note G.A. van der Veen. In this case, the Court of The Hague relies on fundamental rights (in particular, the right to life of Art. 2 of the European Convention on Human Rights ("ECHR") and the right to respect for private and family life of Art. 8 ECHR) and soft law (*i.a.* the UN Guiding Principles on Business and Human Rights ("Ruggie Principles") and the UN SDG's), among others, to give substance to the unwritten duty of care of Art. 6:162 DCC. Much ink has already been spilled in legal doctrine on this important and far-reaching judgment.

in The Netherlands established that these fundamental rights must also be observed by private parties.[742] Similarly, KRYLA-CUDNA argues that in some cases, the principle of good faith may limit the exercise of a remedy for breach of contract where both repair and replacement may ensure an adequate protection of the (consumer) buyer of a good who claims performance.[743] The principle of good faith is an open norm that consists in a duty for the parties to take each other interests into account.[744] It requires concretisation, which provides for an possibility to bring moral values, such as honesty and proper conduct, into the contract.[745] Given this, several arguments can be given for observing sustainability goals in applying the principle of good faith. For instance, it can be argued that proper conduct in our current society (in which there is an increasing focus on environmental issues such as dangerous climate change) requires some form of awareness of and contribution to environmental and sustainability objectives.[746] Moreover, ensuring that our planet remains liveable concerns all people on earth, so taking sustainability into account in the contract is also in the interest of the contracting parties (exactly what the principle of good faith aims to achieve). Therefore, sustainability could in some cases have an impact on contractual relationships through open norms in private law such as good faith, reasonableness and fairness and the general test of the UCTD.[747]

See critically on the role of open ECHR provisions in interpreting private law open norms e.g, J. BOUCKAERT and S. FRANÇOIS, "Actieve rol voor de rechter bij het bepalen van het (ondernemings)beleid? Noot onder het Shell-vonnis van 26 mei 2021" in A. VAN HOE and G. CROISANT (eds.), *Droit et durabilité / Recht en duurzaamheid*, Antwerp, Intersentia, 2022, (3) 25–26; H. DE WULF and L. VAN MARCKE, "Duurzaamheid en Vennootschapsrecht" in A. VAN HOE and G. CROISANT (eds.), *Droit et durabilité / Recht en duurzaamheid*, Antwerp, Intersentia, 2022, (349) 390; C. ZOETHOUT, "Rechter of politiek? Over het klimaatarrest en het debat over rechterlijk activisme in Nederland", *TBP* 2020, (242) 242–249; R. HOUBEN, "Maatschappelijk verantwoord ondernemen", *RW* 2023, (803) 814. See for another view: R. FELTKAMP, A. FRANÇOIS and L. CORNELIS, "Le droit privé au service d'une société durable: rêve ou réalité démocratique?" in A. VAN HOE and G. CROISANT (eds.), *Droit et durabilité / Recht en duurzaamheid*, Antwerp, Intersentia, 2022, (105) 126–127, no. 22.

742 C.M.D.S. PAVILLON, "Herijking van consumentencontractenrecht: duurzaamheid als nieuw ijkpunt?" in C.M.D.S. PAVILLON and W.H. VAN BOOM (eds.), *Preadviezen Vereniging voor Burgerlijk Recht: Privaatrechtelijke bescherming herijkt*, Zutphen, Paris, 2021, (11) 58.

743 K. KRYLA-CUDNA, "Sales contracts and the circular economy", *ERPL* 2020, vol. 28 issue 6, (1207) 1214.

744 See e.g. M.W. HESSELINK, "The Concept of Good Faith" in A.S. HARTKAMP, M.W. HESSELINK, E.H. HONDIUS, C. MAK and C.E. DU PERRON (eds.), *Towards a European Civil Code. Fourth Revised and Expanded Edition*, Alphen aan den Rijn, Kluwer Law International, 2011, (619) 621 and the references cited there.

745 *Ibid.*

746 Compare with K. KRYLA-CUDNA, "Sales contracts and the circular economy", *ERPL* 2020, vol. 28, afl. 6, (1207) 1215.

747 See also D. HUG, "Contractual Interpretation and Environmental Sustainability", *CCM Blog* 20 October 2022, https://law.kuleuven.be/ccm/blog/?p=420 for an interesting view on the role of environmental sustainability for the interpretation of contractual terms.

167. Limits to considering sustainability when applying the general test – The possibility of placing limits on consumer's freedom of contract seems, however, rather limited so far, especially in the case of the general test of the UCTD. After all, the rationale behind the UCTD is to promote the internal market and to protect the *economic* interests of consumers.[748] Moreover, the criterion of the general test is that clauses are unfair if they create a significant imbalance in the parties' rights and obligations "*to the detriment of the consumer*" (and not "*to the detriment of the environment*").[749] Furthermore, one could argue that clauses neglecting sustainability interests could be "*contrary to the requirement of good faith*",[750] but this wording was not implemented as such in the Belgian and Dutch version of the general test. A possible solution could be to argue that unsustainable contract terms are in the long run to the detriment of the consumer, as all of humankind will bear the consequences of climate change and environmental problems. This way, (environmental) sustainability can be used to shape and interpret the consumer notion. Admittedly, this interpretation is rather far-fetched, especially given the traditionally very individual nature of private law.[751]

The case law of the CJEU also demonstrates the limits to considering sustainability when applying the general test. Indeed, when interpreting consumer law, the CJEU has so far relied heavily on balancing the interests of consumers and businesses, without taking into account other objectives of EU law such as (environmental) sustainability.[752] Nevertheless, sustainable development, a high level of environmental protection and improving the quality of the environment are clear objectives of the EU, as outlined in Article 3(3) TEU and Article 11 TFEU.[753] Additionally, Article 37 of the Charter also requires that a high level of environmental protection and the improvement of the quality of the environment be integrated into the policies of the Union and ensured in accordance with the principle of sustainable development.[754] Both primary and secondary EU law must be interpreted in the light of the Charter.[755]

[748] Recital 1 and 9 UCTD.

[749] See Art. 3(1) UCTD.

[750] *Ibid.*

[751] Compare with critical voices on the role of private law in achieving public objectives: I.S.J. Houben, "Autonomie in het contractenrecht: de bescherming van de ondernemer", *Ars Aequi* 2017, vol. 7–8, (600) 604–605; T. Hartlief, "Autonomie en solidariteit. Beweging in het verbintenissenrecht", *WPNR* 2004, vol. 6564, (106) 107.

[752] See e.g. CJEU, Judgment of 5 May 2022, C-179/21, *Victorinox*, ECLI:EU:C:2022:353; CJEU, Judgment of 27 March 2019, C-681/17, *slewo*, ECLI:EU:C:2019:255.

[753] E. Terryn, "Informatie over commerciële garanties: pleidooi voor een duurzame interpretatie van het consumentenrecht", *DCCR* 2023, (133) 138.

[754] Art. 37 Charter of Fundamental Rights of the European Union, *OJ C* 326, 26.10.2012, 391–407.

[755] K. Lenaerts and J.A. Guttiérez-Fons, "The place of the Charter in the EU Constitutional Edifice" in S. Peers, T. Hervey, J. Kenner and A. Ward (eds.), *The EU Charter of Fundamental Rights: A commentary*, Oxford, Hart, 2014, (1559) 1572.

Moreover, Article 11 TFEU, which calls for the integration of "*environmental protection requirements*" into Union policies and actions "*in particular with a view to promoting sustainable development*", also has a greater role to play than currently is the case.[756] This is why TERRYN argues – convincingly in my view – that objectives of (environmental) sustainability and environmental protection should also be taken into account when interpreting (EU) consumer law.[757] This is not to say that (environmental) sustainability interests should always prevail, just that they should be taken into consideration.[758]

168. POTENTIAL SOLUTION: "INTEGRATING" ENVIRONMENTAL PROTECTION AS OBJECTIVE OF REVISED UCTD – Thus, while there are already arguments to consider sustainability interest when applying the general test of the UCTD, it is clear that *de lege lata* this possibility is rather limited and underutilised in practice. A potential solution could be to revise the UCTD and to add environmental protection as an explicit objective. Here, inspiration could be drawn from Empowering Consumers for the Green Transition Directive, which in amending the UCPD and CRD aims "*to contribute to the proper functioning of the internal market, based on a high level of consumer protection and environmental protection, and to make progress in the green transition.*"[759] A proposed recital acknowledging this objective is set out below.

If environmental protection were to be "integrated" as an explicit objective, this purpose will have to be taken into account in the interpretation and enforcement of the unfair terms rules. Examples of clauses where such an environmental protection objective could play a role in the assessment of (un) fairness are clauses that only offer unsustainable remedies to the consumer in case the product breaks down (e.g. clauses that only allow replacement of the product and exclude the remedy of repair); clauses that oblige the consumer to use proprietary (non- eco-friendly) products for the use or maintenance of a certain product, on penalty of invalidating the (commercial) guarantee (e.g. obligation to only use proprietary laundry detergent or cleaning products that are harmful to the environment); clauses that prohibit certain products or accessories from being used for more than a set amount of times, even though their lifespan or capacity is greater (e.g. ink cartridges that only allow printing a limited amount of pages, even if they are not empty); etc.

---

756 B. SJAFJELL and J. WAELKENS (eds.), *The Greening of European Business under EU Law: Taking Article 11 TFEU Seriously*, London, Routledge, 2015, 206 p.

757 E. TERRYN, "Informatie over commerciële garanties: pleidooi voor een duurzame interpretatie van het consumentenrecht", *DCCR* 2023, (133) 141–142.

758 E. TERRYN, "Informatie over commerciële garanties: pleidooi voor een duurzame interpretatie van het consumentenrecht", *DCCR* 2023, (133) 142.

759 Recital 1 Empowering Consumers for the Green Transition Directive.

Proposed Recital #1

In order to contribute to the proper functioning of the internal market, based on a high level of consumer protection and environmental protection, and to make progress in the green transition, consumers should be protected against the abuse of power by the seller or supplier in one-sided standard contracts, in particular against unfair contract terms causing a significant imbalance to the detriment of the consumer, with due consideration to their sustainability impact.

2.3.3.5. The lists of (potentially) unfair terms

169. Four different lists – As already mentioned above, both the UCTD and Belgian and Dutch law contain a system of lists of unfair terms. The Annex of the UCTD features a "grey list" (in the Netherlands also often called the "blue list") which is an indicative and non-exhaustive list of 17 terms which may be regarded as unfair.[760] The Belgian Code of Economic Law contains an extensive blacklist of 33 contractual terms that, once they appear in a PSS contract concluded between a business and a consumer, are always prohibited and null and void.[761] The Dutch Civil Code has two lists, namely a "blacklist"[762] of 20 terms that are deemed unfair in contracts between businesses and consumers and a "grey list"[763] of 15 terms that are presumed to be unfair in contracts between businesses and consumers.

170. "Terms with the object or effect of" – Rather than formally or literally enumerating the terms that are black or grey listed, the three legal systems take another approach. The first sentence of the respective provisions indicates that the terms referred to include all clauses that "have the object or effect" of achieving what is listed.[764]

171. Four different lists overlap but contain significant differences – As these lists and certain terms on them partially overlap, they sometimes complement each other but also contain important differences.[765] Moreover, these lists are quite long and do not have a textual nor visual

760 Annex to the UCTD *juncto* Art. 3(3) UCTD.
761 Art. VI.83 *juncto* Art. VI.84 BCEL.
762 Art. 6:236 DCC.
763 Art. 6:237 DCC.
764 See Paragraph 1, first sentence Annex to the UCTD; Art. VI.83, first sentence BCEL, Art. 6:236, first sentence and Art. 6:237, first sentence DCC respectively.
765 M.B.M. Loos, "Algemene voorwaarden bij consumentenovereenkomsten" in E.H. Hondius and V. Mak (eds.), *Handboek Consumentenrecht*, Zutphen, Paris, 2020, (121), 158; C.M.D.S. Pavillon, "De invloed van Europese richtlijnen op de Nederlandse regeling van algemene voorwaarden (afdeling 6.5.3 BW)" in A.S. Hartkamp (ed.), *De invloed van het Europese recht op het Nederlands privaatrecht*, Deventer, Kluwer, 2013, (233) no. 18.

structure, making it often difficult to find out whether a certain term is black or grey listed. Therefore, a pain point from the perspective of legal certainty and coherence is the lack of logical overview and structure, both when analysing the lists in isolation and when comparing the national lists and the list of the UCTD Annex.[766]

172. Terms of PSS contracts analysed will be tested against the different lists throughout this book – As a result of this overlap and these differences, the terms of the PSS contracts analysed must be substantively tested against the different lists of black and grey listed clauses.[767] This is why throughout this book, the terms found in the real-life PSS contracts analysed are contrasted with the different terms listed in these four different but overlapping lists.

173. Proposed solution: streamlining lists of unfair terms at EU level – The fact that these lists contain significant differences and do not have a textual or visual structure is detrimental in terms of legal certainty, both for the PSS supplier and the PSS user. These differences are especially problematic for PSS suppliers wishing to offer their services in multiple Member States. After all, this increases transaction costs, as it becomes more challenging to draft PSS contracts that comply with all the different lists in the different Member States where the PSS supplier offers or wishes to offer its services. At the same time, for consumers, this pluralism of lists makes it less clear whether a certain term in their (PSS) contract is (presumed) unfair.

In my view, it would therefore be better to streamline these lists at the EU level, making use of a "corrected" maximum harmonisation technique. The content of the unfair terms lists can then be determined by a comparative law analysis of the different lists at the national level, while also taking the lists in the DCFR and/or CESL as a starting point.[768] The EU Member States would then at least have to implement these terms into their national unfair terms provisions. To combat the risk that the use of maximum harmonisation is too politically sensitive for the Member States, the revised UCTD list(s) could leave room for (limited) national additions to the unfair terms list(s), allowing to take into account local legal developments and contractual practices.

---

766 See in this view also P. Cambie, *Onrechtmatige bedingen*, Ghent, Larcier, 2009, 340, no. 408.

767 S. Geiregat, *Een rechtsvergelijkende studie over oneerlijke bedingen. Richtlijn 93/13/EEG van de Raad van 5 april 1993 betreffende oneerlijke bedingen in consumentenovereenkomsten: omzetting in de Belgische en Italiaanse rechtsorde en actueel overzicht van de communautaire rechtspraak*, Thesis for obtaining the degree of Master of Laws, Ghent University, 2014–2015, 120.

768 See Art. II. – 9:410 DCFR and Art. 84 and 85 CESL.

Policy Recommendation #1

- **Consider streamlining the unfair terms lists by replacing the indicative and non-exhaustive list of the Annex to the UCTD with a uniform blacklist and/or grey list at the EU level by making use of a (corrected) maximum harmonisation technique. The content of this blacklist and/or grey list can be determined by a comparative law analysis at the national level, as well as using the DCFR and/or CESL as a starting point.**
- **Consider leaving some room to the Member States to include additional unfair terms to the blacklist and/or grey list taking into account local legal developments and contractual practices.**

2.3.3.6. Consequences of unfairness

174. UCTD: UNFAIR TERM IS NON-BINDING ON THE CONSUMER – Once it has been established that a term is unfair, the question arises as to the consequences of this unfairness. In this regard, the UCTD provides that unfair terms used by a seller or supplier in a contract concluded with a consumer shall, as provided for under their national law, not be binding on the consumer.[769] The expression "not binding" was chosen to functionally reflect the differences between Member States in terms of sanctioning in a broad and neutral way.[770] Consequently, it is up to Member States to determine the legal consequences of the unfairness of a certain contract term in a PSS contract.[771] Where the national court finds that a term is unfair, it must establish all the consequences arising under national law to ensure that the consumer is not bound by that term.[772]

175. BELGIUM: UNFAIR TERM IS PROHIBITED AND NULL AND VOID – Under Belgian law, unfair terms are prohibited and null and void (*verboden en nietig, nules et interdites*).[773] The contract remains binding on the parties if it is capable of

769 Art. 6(1) UCTD.

770 M. FARINA, "Unfair Terms and Supplementation of the Contract", *ERPL* 2021, (441) 445; C. LEONE, "Case note Abanca Corporación Bancaria, S.A. v Alberto García Salamanca Santos", *REDC* 2020, (317) 317; F. CAFAGGI and P. IAMICELI, "The Principles of Effectiveness, Proportionality and Dissuasiveness in the Enforcement of EU Consumer Law: The Impact of a Triad on the Choice of Civil Remedies and Administrative Sanctions", *ERPL* 2017, (575) 584; H.-W. MICKLITZ and N. REICH, "The Court and Sleeping Beauty: The Revival of the Unfair Contract Terms Directive (UCTD)", *CML Rev.* 2014, (771) 792.

771 P. ROTT, "Unfair contract terms" in C. TWIGG-FLESNER (ed.), *Research Handbook on EU Consumer and Contract Law*, Cheltenham, Edward Elgar, 2016, (287) 302; M. TRENREIRO, "The Community Directive on Unfair Terms and National Legal Systems. The Principle of Good Faith and Remedies for Unfair Terms", *ERPL* 1995, vol. 3 issue 2, (273) 281.

772 CJEU, Judgment of 30 May 2013, C-397/11, *Jőrös*, ECLI:EU:C:2013:340, para. 41. See also: M. TRENREIRO, "The Community Directive on Unfair Terms and Nationfal Legal Systems. The Principle of Good Faith and Remedies for Unfair Terms", *ERPL* 1995, vol. 3, afl. 2, (273) 282.

773 Art. VI.84, §1 BCEL.

continuing in existence without the unfair terms.[774] Consequently, a Belgian court that finds (*ex officio* if necessary[775]) that a term in a PSS contract is unfair must declare this term null and void. The nullity of this term does not automatically lead to the nullity of the PSS contract, except in the (exceptional) case where the PSS contract cannot continue to exist without the term.[776] Since the provisions on unfair terms are concerned with the protection of private interests, it involves relative nullity.[777] This does not affect the obligation of *ex officio* review by the national court: public order and *ex officio* review are not synonyms.[778]

176. The Netherlands: unreasonably onerous terms are voidable – The Dutch rules on unfair terms in general terms and conditions stipulate that the sanction for the unreasonably onerous nature of a term is its voidability (*vernietigbaarheid*).[779] This means that the term is valid up to the moment of nullification and has the legal consequences intended with it until it is nullified. The counterparty is required to invoke the voidability, i.e. to take action to free itself from this unreasonably onerous term.[780] In light of the entry into force of the UCTD, however, the question has been raised whether this sanction – voidability – goes far enough in contracts with consumers.[781] Therefore, having regard to the principle of conforming interpretation of EU law, this sanction should be interpreted that it does not interfere with the obligation for national courts to check *ex officio* whether a term falls within the scope of the UCTD and the obligation to assess *ex officio* whether a term is unfair.[782] Consequently, the national court can either annul the term[783] or not apply the term.[784, 785]

---

774 *Ibid.*

775 See *supra* no. 151.

776 R. Steennot, G. Straetmans, E. Terryn, B. Keirsbilck and B. Wyseur, "Overzicht van rechtspraak. Consumentenbescherming (2008-2014) – Marktpraktijken (2011-2014)", *TPR* 2015, (1311) 1595–1596, no. 240 and 241.

777 This means that nullity can only be invoked by the person protected by the rule (i.e. the consumer), who can also waive this nullity. See: J. Stuyck and B. Keirsbilck, *Handels- en economisch recht. 2: Mededingingsrecht. A: Handelspraktijken en contracten met consumenten in Beginselen van Belgisch Privaatrecht*, Mechelen, Kluwer, 2024, 843, no. 845. This was acknowledged by the Court of Cassation, see: Cass. (BE) 26 May 2005, *JT* 2005, 679 (on the Liberal Professions Act: the provisions on unfair terms are not of public order).

778 R. Steennot, *Onrechtmatige bedingen in de wet van 6 april 2010 betreffende marktpraktijken en consumentenbescherming*, Mechelen, Kluwer, 2012, 243; J. Stuyck, "Case Note Case C-243/08, Pannon GSM Zrt. and Case C-40/08, Asturcom Telecominicaciones SL", *CML Rev.* 2010, (879) 892.

779 Art. 6:233 DCC.

780 M.B.M. Loos, *Algemene voorwaarden*, The Hague, Boom juridisch, 2018, 190, no. 195.

781 M.B.M. Loos, "Algemene voorwaarden bij consumentenovereenkomsten" in E.H. Hondius and V. Mak (eds.), *Handboek Consumentenrecht*, Zutphen, Paris, 2020, (121) 122.

782 C.H. Sieburgh, *Mr. C. Assers Handleiding tot de beoefening van het Nederlands Burgerlijk Recht. 6. Verbintenissenrecht. Deel III. Algemeen overeenkomstenrecht*, Deventer, Wolters Kluwer, 2018, no. 479.

783 Art. 3:40(2) DCC.

784 Art. 6:248(2) DCC.

785 Loos prefers the first option. See: M.B.M. Loos, *Algemene voorwaarden*, The Hague, Boom juridisch, 2018, 345, no. 422.

177. Contract remains binding on the parties if it can exist without unfair terms – If one or more terms of the PSS contract are unfair, the PSS contract shall continue to bind the parties upon those terms if it is capable of continuing in existence without these unfair terms.[786] The consequence of unfairness is therefore the partial nullity of the PSS contract.[787] As regards the criteria for assessing whether a contract can indeed continue to exist without the unfair terms, the Court of Justice stated that the advantage that one of the parties (i.e. the consumer) gains from the annulment of the contract cannot be considered the decisive criterion.[788] Only when the term is essential to the PSS contract can the national court annul the entire contract.[789] An example of terms that do not affect the nullity of the contract are indemnity clauses, these are not essential to the contract.[790]

178. No reduction of the term to lawful or reasonable content – According to the CJEU, the nullity of the term implies that it cannot be reduced by the national court to what can be considered lawful or reasonable.[791] Consequently, manifestly excessive indemnity clauses or clauses on the interest rate on late payments cannot be mitigated to achieve a new balance of interests

786 EU: Art. 6(1) UCTD. **Belgium**: Art. VI.84, §1, (2) BCEL. **The Netherlands**: Art. 6:233 DCC (This provision only refers to "the term" as being voidable, not the entire contract). See also Art. 3:41 DCC on partial nullity.

787 **Belgium**: J. Reniers and F. Van den Abeele, "Beperkte aanvullingsmogelijkheid bij vernietiging onrechtmatig beding", *DCCR* 2021, (3) 4; J. Stuyck and B. Keirsbilck, *Handels- en economisch recht. 2: Mededingingsrecht. A: Handelspraktijken en contracten met consumenten in Beginselen van Belgisch Privaatrecht*, Mechelen, Kluwer, 2024, 844, no. 846; S. Stijns, "Onrechtmatige bedingen" in J. Stuyck, G. Straetmans and P. Wytinck (eds.), *Recente wetswijzigingen inzake handelspraktijken*, Antwerp, Kluwer, 2000, (187) 238. **The Netherlands**: M.B.M. Loos, "Rechtsgevolgen van onredelijk bezwarende bedingen in algemene voorwaarden", *WPNR* 2012/6940, (561) 561; M.B.M. Loos, "Partiële nietigheid van onredelijk bezwarende bedingen in algemene voorwaarden", *WPNR* 1997/6260, (155) 155.

788 CJEU, Judgment of 15 March 2012, C-453/10, *Pereničová*, ECLI:EU:C:2012:144, para. 32.

789 See for an application in **Belgium**: Antwerp (BE) 17 December 2007, *NjW* 2008, 448, case note R. Steennot (nullity of a clause concerning a purchase promise whereby the prospective buyer definitively undertakes to buy the good as soon as the prospective seller demands it, while the seller accepts the purchase promise without an obligation to sell. The nullity of the clause leads to the nullity of the contract as the contract cannot continue to exist without the clause). In **the Netherlands**, according to Art. 3:41 DCC, the entire contract is null and void if there is an "indissoluble link" (*onverbrekelijk verband*) between the annulled term and the rest of the contract.

790 E.g. Liège (BE) 21 February 2005, *JLMB* 526.

791 This was first confirmed by the Court of Justice in CJEU, Judgment of 14 June 2012, C-618/10, *Banco Español de Crédito*, ECLI:EU:C:2012:349, para. 65. See also: R. Steennot, "De bescherming van de consument door het Hof van Justitie: een brug te ver?", *TPR* 2017, (81) 156–157; S. Geiregat, "Nietigheid en 'meest gunstige interpretatie': de remedies bij onrechtmatige bedingen in consumentenovereenkomsten in het licht van de rechtspraak van het Hof van Justitie", *TPR* 2016, vol. 2016, (97) 133; H.-W. Micklitz and N. Reich, "The Court and Sleeping Beauty: The Revival of the Unfair Contract Terms Directive (UCTD)", *CML Rev.* 2014, (771) 792.

and must be annulled.[792] Similarly, national courts are also not allowed to opt for a conversion[793] of the term according to the hypothetical will of the parties, i.e. a replacement of the term by one that the parties would have chosen in the knowledge that the original term was unfair.[794] The reasoning of the Court of Justice is that the reduction of unfair terms would result in traders bearing little risk from using them, and even benefitting from them to some extent, as they would remain partially binding.[795]

179. In principle no application of default law after annulment of an unfair term – From this case law also follows that national courts are also in principle not allowed to fill the gap created by the annulment of an unfair term by a provision of national default law.[796] The practical implications of this are quite far-reaching. Namely, it means that if a clause in the PSS contract is annulled, the PSS supplier cannot invoke the national default law applicable to the situation regulated by that contractual clause.[797] For example, if an indemnity clause in the PSS contract is unfair (e.g. because it is excessive[798] or not reciprocal[799]), the PSS supplier cannot claim damages under general contract law.[800] Similarly, in the case of a clause stipulating an excessive negligence

792 CJEU, Judgment of 30 May 2013, C-488/11, *Asbeek Brusse*, ECLI:EU:C:2013:341, para. 59 and 60 (reduction of an indemnity clause); CJEU, Judgment of 14 June 2012, C-618/10, *Banco Español de Crédito*, ECLI:EU:C:2012:349, para. 65 (reduction of a late interest rate clause of 29% to 19%). See for more examples: J. Reniers and F. Van den Abeele, "Beperkte aanvullingsmogelijkheid bij vernietiging onrechtmatig beding", *DCCR* 2021, (3) 4, fn. 6.

793 Art. 3:42 DCC. Contrary to the Netherlands, Belgium has no general legal regime on conversion. See: F. Peeraer, "Nietigverklaring vs. gerechtelijke conversie van een contract of van een contractueel beding" in S. Stijns and P. Wéry (eds.), *De rol van de rechter in het contract*, Bruges, Die Keure, 2014, (321) 324, no. 5.

794 M.B.M. Loos, "Algemene voorwaarden bij consumentenovereenkomsten" in E.H. Hondius and V. Mak (eds.), *Handboek Consumentenrecht*, Zutphen, Paris, 2020, (121) 164–165; A.S. Hartkamp, "Oneerlijke contractsbedingen en de gevolgen van hun niet-verbindendheid", *Ars Aequi* 2017, (218) 221.

795 CJEU, Judgment of 14 June 2012, C-618/10, *Banco Español de Crédito*, ECLI:EU:C:2012:349, para. 69; CJEU, Judgment of 30 May 2013, C-488/11, *Asbeek Brusse*, ECLI:EU:C:2013:341, para. 59.

796 CJEU, Judgment of 27 January 2021, Joined cases C-229/19 and C-289/19, *Dexia Nederland*, ECLI:EU:C:2021:68, para. 66–67. See also: C. Pavillon and J. Spanjaard, "Civielrechtelijke sancties op oneerlijke bedingen. De 'alles of niets'-benadering bevestigd", *NJB* 2021, (1562) 1562–1563.

797 P. Cambie, "Specifieke wettelijke regelingen van verwijlinteresten bij hypothecair krediet en de autonome toetsing van oneerlijke bedingen: het arrest Unibanco", *DCCR* 2015, (93) 99.

798 **Belgium**: Art. VI.83, 24° BCEL. **The Netherlands**: indemnity clauses are not on the grey- or blacklist, but they can be challenged when they are unreasonably onerous within the meaning of Art. 6:233, *sub* a. DCC.

799 **Belgium**: Art. VI.83, 17° BCEL. See for an application: J.P. Genk (BE) 17 November 2020, *T.Vred.* 2021, 567, case note R. Steennot. **The Netherlands**: contrary to Belgium, the Dutch grey list and blacklist do not contain a provision on non-reciprocal indemnity clauses. Yet, they can still be challenged based on Art. 6:233, *sub* a. DCC.

800 J. Reniers and F. Van den Abeele, "Beperkte aanvullingsmogelijkheid bij vernietiging onrechtmatig beding", *DCCR* 2021, (3) 6; M.E. Storme, "On the Usefulness of Default Rules

interest rate, the national court cannot apply the statutory rate.[801] The Belgian Court of Cassation follows the CJEU's strict view. In a case concerning a B2C rental contract that contained a non-reciprocal indemnity clause stipulating a relocation fee, it overturned a judgment in which the court awarded damages based on general contract law.[802] Since the indemnity clause was not an essential element of the rental contract,[803] it would not lead to the annulment of the entire contract, leaving no room for the court to apply national default law.

180. Exception: application of default law to avoid the annulment of the contract to the detriment of the consumer – However, the strict application of these principles laid down by the CJEU would in some cases lead to a solution which is disadvantageous to the PSS user. As this would be contrary to the aim of the UCTD, the CJEU has allowed, under strict conditions, the application of national default law instead of an unfair term.[804]

In *Kásler*, the Court of Justice ruled that the UCTD does not preclude a rule of national law that enables national courts to cure the invalidity of an unfair term by substituting it for a provision of national default law, provided that the contract cannot continue to exist after deleting the unfair term.[805] In this particular case, the annulment of a term in a credit agreement would have led to the annulment of the entire contract, as it could not continue to exist without the annulled term (i.e. it was an essential term). This would be very disadvantageous for the consumer, as he would have to repay the outstanding balance of the loan all at once.[806] Substituting the (essential) unfair term with national default law therefore is consistent with the objective of the UCTD, being to replace the formal balance between the rights and obligations of the contract parties laid down in the contract with a real balance that restores equality between these

and Disproportionate Sanctions in Consumer Law", *ERPL* 2021, (399) 399; L. Midrez, "L'éviction du droit supplétif en cas d'annulation d'une clause abusive: un malentendu?", *Rev.Dr.ULiège* 2021, (243) R. Steennot, "Nietigheid van schadevergoedingsbedingen verhindert reductie en toekenning van schadevergoeding op grond van gemeen recht (case note J.P. Genk 17 November 2020)", *T.Vred.* 2021, (568) 569; R. Steennot, "De bescherming van de consument door het Hof van Justitie: een brug te ver?", *TPR* 2017, (81) 161; C.M.D.S. Pavillon, "Het Europees verbod op de herziening van oncerlijke bedingen: welke ruimte is er nog voor dwingend en aanvullend nationaal recht?", *Tijdschrift voor de Procespraktijk* 2015, vol. 3, (76) 74; R. Steennot, G. Straetmans, E. Terryn, B. Keirsbilck and B. Wyseur, "Overzicht van rechtspraak. Consumentenbescherming (2008-2014) – Marktpraktijken (2011-2014)", *TPR* 2015, (1311) 1598.

801 **Belgium:** Art. 5.240 BCC. **The Netherlands:** Art. 6:119 DCC.

802 Cass. (BE) 9 October 2020, AR C.19.0631.N, *Jaarboek Marktpraktijken* 2020, 147. This judgment deviates from earlier case law (in a B2B context) by the Belgian Court of Cassation where it allowed the mitigation/reduction of excessive non-compete clauses: Cass. (BE) 25 June 2015, *TBBR* 2016, 187.

803 See *infra* no. 180.

804 L. Midrez, "L'éviction du droit supplétif en cas d'annulation d'une clause abusive: un malentendu?", *Rev.Dr.ULiège* 2021, (243) 250.

805 CJEU, Judgment of 30 April 2014, C-26/13, *Kásler*, ECLI:EU:C:2014:282, para. 85.

806 CJEU, Judgment of 30 April 2014, C-26/13, *Kásler*, ECLI:EU:C:2014:282, para. 83–84.

parties.[807] This was further clarified in *Banco Español* and *Unicaja Banco* where the Court of Justice explicitly stated that the possibility for a national court of substituting a national default rule for an unfair term is limited to cases in which the invalidity of the unfair term would require the court to annul the contract in its entirety, thereby exposing the consumer to disadvantageous consequences.[808] Therefore, default law should only be applied if it is to the consumer's advantage and cannot be applied if this would be to the detriment of the consumer.[809] In *Dziubak*, the CJEU added that the national court can only fill the gap with rules of national default law. This means that the court cannot supplement the PSS contract on the basis of national provisions not of supplementary law but of a general nature, which refer to the principles of equity (rules of social conduct) and established customs.[810, 811]

In summary, if a term of the PSS contract is unfair, and provided that the PSS contract cannot not continue to exist without this annulled term and this would be to the detriment of the consumer (i.e. it is an essential term), the gaps in the PSS contract can only be filled by specific provisions of national default law and not by applying national open standards such as reasonableness and fairness. By contrast, if the unfair term is non-essential, the national court cannot apply national default law to fill the gap created by the annulled unfair term.

181. Nullity as a deterrent, did the CJEU go too far? – The deterrent effect attached by the CJEU to the sanction for the use of unfair terms (i.e. no application of default rules in case of the annulment of a non-essential unfair term) is criticised by quite some authors in legal doctrine.[812] The main idea is

807 CJEU, Judgment of 30 April 2014, C-26/13, *Kásler*, ECLI:EU:C:2014:282, para. 82.

808 CJEU, Judgment of 21 January 2015, C-482/13, *Unicaja Banco*, ECLI:EU:C:2015:21, para. 32; CJEU, Judgment of 14 June 2012, C-618/10, *Banco Español de Crédito*, ECLI:EU:C:2012:349, para. 73.

809 R. Steennot, "De bescherming van de consument door het Hof van Justitie: een brug te ver?", *TPR* 2017, (81) 160–161; P. Cambie, "Specifieke wettelijke regelingen van verwijlinteresten bij hypothecair krediet en de autonome toetsing van oneerlijke bedingen: het arrest Unibanco", *DCCR* 2015, (93) 98–99; J.T. Nowak, "De bevoegdheid van EU-lidstaten voor de aanname van regels van nationaal procesrecht: grenzen in de rechtspraak van het Hof van Justitie" in N. Cariat and J.T. Nowak (eds.), *Le droit de l'Union européenne et le juge belge / Het recht van de Europese Unie en de Belgische rechter*, Brussels, Bruylant, 2015, (23) 50–51; F. Peeraer, "De inhoud van het transparantiegebod en de mogelijkheid tot aanvulling van intransparante kernbedingen in richtlijn nr. 93/13", *TBH* 2015, (693) 698–699.

810 See for **Belgium**: Art. 5.71 BCC (formerly Art. 1135 old BCC). For **the Netherlands**, see: Art. 6:248 DCC.

811 CJEU, Judgment of 3 October 2019, C-260/18, *Dziubak*, ECLI:EU:C:2019:819, para. 28 and 62. This decision was heavily criticised by some legal scholars, see: F. Esposito, "Dziubak Is a Fundamentally Wrong Decision: Superficial Reasoning, Disrespectful of National Courts, Lowers the Level of Consumer Protection", *ERCL* 2020, vol. 16 issue 4, (538) 538–551; F. Esposito and L. de Almeida, "European Union Litigation", *ERCL* 2021, vol. 17 issue 1, (106) 95–97.

812 Geiregat e.g. accuses the Court of Justice of having created a private penalty. See: S. Geiregat, "Verfijning van de transparantievereiste en duiding van de rol van aanvullend

that the CJEU is overshooting the purpose of the Directive and that there are other, less far-reaching means of achieving the goal of Article 7(1) UCTD, for example through public enforcement (i.e. criminal or administrative sanctions). Other authors, such as STEENNOT and HONDIUS, argue that the CJEU's approach may yet lead to achieving effective protection against unfair terms.[813] They state that this strict private law sanction may well be necessary to achieve consumer protection against unfair terms and that it is not necessarily unjustified to place the risk of using an unfair term on a business who is not satisfied with the default law.[814] Indeed, the case law of the CJEU provides an incentive for PSS suppliers to think twice before including unfair terms in their PSS contract, as the consequences can be very serious. However, while this has indeed the potential to ensure a higher level of consumer protection, which may benefit the adoption of PSS, this sanction is, in my view, disproportionate. After all, national default rules contain sufficient safeguards for consumers so that they do have a right to an effective remedy.[815] At the same time, their aim is to strike a fair balance between the rights and obligations of the PSS supplier and the PSS user. This is even reflected in the UCTD itself, namely by stating that contractual terms which reflect mandatory statutory or regulatory provisions shall not be subject to the Directive.[816] Yet so far, the CJEU has not changed its course on this issue.

---

nationaal recht in het EU-recht inzake oneerlijke bedingen", *TBBR* 2015, (153) 157 and 162. PEERAER argues from a law and economics analysis that even a full annulment of an unfair term does not always have a deterrent effect if the likelihood of enforcement of this sanction is relatively low. After all, many businesses realize that the number of cases in which a consumer will actually invoke the nullity sanction is relatively limited. See: F. PEERAER, "Het volledige verbod op herziening van onrechtmatige bedingen: de botte bijl van het Hof van Justitie?", *TBBR* 2013, (320) 328–329. See also: M.E. STORME, "On the Usefulness of Default Rules and Disproportionate Sanctions in Consumer Law", *ERPL* 2021, (399) 400; L. MIDREZ, "L'éviction du droit supplétif en cas d'annulation d'une clause abusive: un malentendu?", *Rev.Dr.ULiège* 2021, (243) 249; J. RENIERS and F. VAN DEN ABEELE, "Beperkte aanvullingsmogelijkheid bij vernietiging onrechtmatig beding", *DCCR* 2021, (3) 13–14; C. PAVILLON and J. SPANJAARD, "Civielrechtelijke sancties op oneerlijke bedingen. De 'alles of niets'-benadering bevestigd", *NJB* 2021, (1562) 1564 and 1569.

813 R. STEENNOT, "De bescherming van de consument door het Hof van Justitie: een brug te ver?", *TPR* 2017, (81) 164. See in this sense also HONDIUS who refers to this as a "macro sanction for a macro phenomenon" (the macro phenomenon being the use of unfair terms). E.H. HONDIUS, "Terug naar Banesto: de afwijzing van geltungserhaltende Reduktion", *WPNR* 2013/6967, (203) 203–204.

814 R. STEENNOT, "De bescherming van de consument door het Hof van Justitie: een brug te ver?", *TPR* 2017, (81) 164. See also M.B.M. LOOS, "Algemene voorwaarden bij consumentenovereenkomsten" in E.H. HONDIUS and V. MAK (eds.), *Handboek Consumentenrecht*, Zutphen, Paris, 2020, (121) 164.

815 M.E. STORME, "On the Usefulness of Default Rules and Disproportionate Sanctions in Consumer Law", *ERPL* 2021, (399) 400.

816 Art. 1(2) UCTD. See also CJEU, Judgment of 3 October 2019, C-260/18, *Dziubak*, ECLI:EU:C:2019:819, para. 59–60: "*Those provisions are meant to reflect the balance that the legislature intended to establish between all the rights and obligations of the parties to certain contracts in cases where the parties have not departed from a standard rule provided for by the*

182. Restitution obligation for all unduly paid amounts based on unfair terms – Setting aside an unfair term has the effect that the term is deemed never to have existed, so it cannot affect the consumer. This means that the consumer must be restored to the situation he would have been without the unfair term. Consequently, any amounts unduly paid on the basis of an unfair term – for example under an unfair indemnity clause – must be refunded.[817]

2.3.4. FAIR MODEL CLAUSES AS SOLUTION FOR LACK OF EXTENSIVE LEGAL FRAMEWORK

183. Fair model clauses as low-hanging fruit – When considering solutions for the lack of an extensive legal framework for PSS contracts, it is first necessary to pick the low-hanging fruit. Here, drafting standard contracts with balanced and fair model clauses where sustainability is also taken in mind forms an excellent starting point.

184. Improving legal certainty: filling the gap of the current regulatory framework with standard contracts – First, standard contracts and model clauses allow to set out the rights and obligations of the parties in a detailed way, and with a specific focus on as-a-service business models. This overcomes the current lack of an extensive legal framework for services and the difficulty of drafting general rules for services caused by their heterogenic and diverse nature. Indeed, standard contracts allow subjecting use-oriented and result-oriented PSS to a tailormade legal framework, including conformity requirements, which in turn promotes legal certainty.

185. Standard contracts can help improve consumer confidence in PSS and lead to a fair balance between rights and obligations of the parties – A second argument in favour of standard contracts is that the use of balanced standard contracts by PSS suppliers can help improve consumer confidence in servitised business models. This is especially the case for standard contracts that have been approved by regulators or endorsed by stakeholder organisations (e.g. business or consumer associations). This could prevent the inclusion of clauses in the general terms and conditions that do not pass the

national legislature in relation to the contracts concerned, or indeed have expressly opted for a rule introduced by the national legislature to that end to be applicable."

817 F. Cafaggi and P. Iamiceli, "The Principles of Effectiveness, Proportionality and Dissuasiveness in the Enforcement of EU Consumer Law: The Impact of a Triad on the Choice of Civil Remedies and Administrative Sanctions", *ERPL* 2017, (575) 583 and 591; A.S. Hartkamp, "Oneerlijke contractsbedingen en de gevolgen van hun niet-verbindendheid", *Ars Aequi* 2017, (218) 221; H.-W. Micklitz and N. Reich, "The Court and Sleeping Beauty: The Revival of the Unfair Contract Terms Directive (UCTD)", *CML Rev.* 2014, (771) 796.

unfair terms test, which helps to achieve a fair balance between the rights and obligations of the parties. Using stakeholder-endorsed standard contracts is not only to the advantage of the consumer, as this may also create marketing advantages for PSS suppliers using such model contracts for their PSS offers.

186. Risk of unbalanced standard contracts? – While standard contracts can thus improve consumer confidence and help achieve a fair balance, there is a risk that standard terms and conditions drawn up by a business association will not take consumers' interests sufficiently into account.[818] Here the Belgian Special Advisory Committee on Unfair Terms[819] (*Bijzondere Raadgevende Commissie "Onrechtmatige Bedingen", Commission Consultative Spéciale "Clauses Abusives"*) in which consumer organisations are also represented, could potentially play a role in subjecting standard contracts to a critical analysis.[820] Alternatively, a stamp of approval from a national or European consumer organisation (e.g. "*these terms and conditions are fair*" accompanied by a label), or even an EU labelling scheme (potentially even with a presumption of fairness or presumption of compliance with the UCTD) for endorsed standard contracts could also lead to a fair balance between the rights and obligations of the parties while simultaneously having an positive effect on consumer trust in the terms and conditions and their uptake of circular business models.[821] In this case, it is of course important to prohibit the display of a label or stamp of approval that the terms and conditions have not in fact been awarded.[822] This prohibition can either be added to the UCTD or – even better – to the UCPD (where similar prohibitions regarding non-compliance with codes of conduct already exist,[823] and where the proposal on empowering consumers for the green transition aims to ban displaying a sustainability label which is not based on a certification scheme or not established by public authorities[824]).

---

818 Compare with C.M.D.S. Pavillon, "Herijking van consumentencontractenrecht: duurzaamheid als nieuw ijkpunt?" in C.M.D.S. Pavillon and W.H. van Boom (eds.), *Preadviezen Vereniging voor Burgerlijk Recht: Privaatrechtelijke bescherming herijkt*, Zutphen, Paris, 2021, (11) 80 arguing that self-regulation can play a role, but the courts must always look critically at general terms and conditions in consumer PSS contracts that have been created in this way.

819 See: Royal Decree of 13 December 2017 on establishing the special advisory commission 'unfair terms' within the Central Business Council, *BS* 28 December 2017.

820 B. Keirsbilck, E. Terryn and E. Van Gool, "Consumentenbescherming bij servitisation en product-dienst systemen (PDS)", *TPR* 2019, (817) 884–885.

821 M. Elshout, M. Elsen, J. Leenheer, M.B.M. Loos and J. Luzak, A., *Study on Consumers' attitudes towards Terms and Conditions (T&Cs). Final Report*, Luxemburg, Publications Office of the European Union, 2016, Executive Summary, 6.

822 A.-L. Sibony, "Data and Arguments: Empirical Research in Consumer Law" in H.-W. Micklitz, A.-L. Sibony and F. Esposito (eds.), *Research Methods in Law and Consumer Law*, Cheltenham, Edward Elgar, 2018, (165) 202.

823 Art. 6(2), (b) UCPD.

824 EC, *Proposal for a Directive of the European Parliament and of the Council amending Directives 2005/29/EC and 2011/83/EU as regards empowering consumers for the green*

187. Standard contracts can (and must) take sustainability into account – A third argument, which is at the same time also a prerequisite for the desirability of this solution, is that standard contracts can explicitly take sustainability into account when establishing and determining the rights and obligations of the parties to a (use-oriented or result-oriented) PSS contract. This can either be the case in the preamble of the contract, which allows to interpret the contract in a sustainable way, by giving preference to sustainable remedies in case of a lack of conformity of the product (most notably repair) or by explicitly including circular guarantees, for example on what happens with the product(s) after the PSS supplier has taken them back (e.g. reuse, remanufacturing, refurbishing, recycling).

188. Policy recommendation #2: developing standard contracts – The above-mentioned arguments translate into policy recommendation #2. A first step is developing standard contracts for (use-oriented and result-oriented) PSS. These standard contracts can either be developed by academia, business associations, or policy institutes.[825] They should incorporate best practices and allow for enough flexibility and customisation, depending on the specific market or business model. At the same time, they should maintain a core set of essential clauses to promote consistency and coherence. To aid in the fulfilment of this policy recommendation, examples of balanced model clauses that comply with the EU, Belgian and Dutch unfair terms rules will be included throughout this book.

The second step is setting up (EU or national) labelling schemes for standard contracts so consumers can more easily assess the fairness of terms and conditions. The quality criteria for these labels can be identified by a task force where representatives from academia, business associations, and consumer organisations work jointly together with policy makers. This allows for coordinating efforts, sharing expertise and ensuring that these standard contracts meet the needs of all stakeholders. The third step is monitoring

---

transition through better protection against unfair practices and better information, 30.3.2022, COM(2022) 143 final, Annex, point (1), proposing to amend the Annex of the UCPD to insert a point 2a: "Displaying a sustainability label which is not based on a certification scheme or not established by public authorities."

825 See for an example of standard terms and conditions developed by academia: C. Borucki, H. Slachmuylders, B. Keirsbilck, D. Gruyaert and E. Terryn, *Model clauses for Product-as-a-Service (PaaS) contracts*, CE Center. Circular Economy Policy Research Center, 2022–23, 87 p. Other examples of standard terms and conditions are Agoria's "Efficiency-as-a-Service" model contract (www.agoria.be/en/services/expertise/green-transition/circular-economy/new-business-models/a-standardized-contract-to-help-you-develop-your-efficiency-as-a-service-offering) and Circle Economy's Circular service contract template drafted within the framework of the "circular phone" project. See: Circle Economy, "The Circular Phone, Legal, operational and financial solutions to unlock the potential of the 'Fairphone-as-a-service' model", 31 December 2017, available at www.circle-economy.com/resources/the-circular-phone.

compliance with these standard contracts. Finally, establishing a "presumption of fairness" or a "presumption of compliance" can be considered.

Policy Recommendation #2

- Consider taking measures to facilitate the development and adoption of standardised contracts for (use-oriented and result-oriented) PSS.
- Consider setting up (EU or national) labelling schemes (e.g. similar to energy labelling schemes) with harmonised quality criteria for PSS standard contracts. The criteria that can be considered are the fairness of the contract (i.e. whether the rights and obligations of the business and consumer are balanced) and whether sustainability is considered in determining the rights and obligations of the parties.
- Consider establishing a monitoring and compliance mechanism to ensure that service providers/PSS suppliers stating that their terms and conditions were awarded a quality label or stamp of approval were effectively awarded this label or stamp of approval.
- Consider establishing a "presumption of fairness" or "presumption of compliance with the UCTD" if PSS suppliers use endorsed standard contracts or model clauses in their PSS contracts.

189. PROPOSAL FOR AMENDING ANNEX I OF THE UCPD TO BAN FALSELY DISPLAYING QUALITY LABELS OR STAMPS OF APPROVAL FOR T&Cs – In order to avoid that PSS suppliers display a quality label or stamp of approval for their terms and conditions that they have not actually received, proposed amendment #1 aims to add a new point to Annex I of the UCPD banning these practices.

Proposed Amendment #1

Annex I to Directive 2005/29/EC is amended as follows:

(1) the following point 2b is inserted:

"2b. Displaying a quality label or stamp of approval by consumer organisations or public authorities for terms and conditions if such label or stamp of approval has not been awarded in reality".

2.4. WITHDRAWAL FROM DISTANCE OR OFF-PREMISES PSS CONTRACTS

"The stark reality is that throwing away is the least bad thing economically for businesses."
- Carl Dalhammar[826]

190. RIGHT OF WITHDRAWAL AS NUANCE TO BINDING FORCE OF THE PSS CONTRACT – As mentioned above, the consequence of a validly concluded PSS contract is that its content will be binding on the parties. However, even if the PSS contract is validly concluded, there are situations where the PSS user can still get out of the contract. This is because a (mandatory) legal provision and/or the PSS contract itself (by virtue of the freedom of contract) may grant a right of withdrawal to the PSS user.[827] A right of withdrawal entitles a party during a period of time after the conclusion of the contract to unilaterally inform the other party that it is withdrawing from the contract, without statement of reasons.[828] As such, the right of withdrawal limits and nuances the principle of the binding force of the contract.[829] Several European Directives grant mandatory withdrawal rights to consumers in specific situations where they are deemed to deserve additional protection because they are in a weaker position during the conclusion of the contract.[830] For what follows, we focus on the right of withdrawal in the CRD for distance and off-premises PSS contracts. In addition, the practice of commercial or voluntary withdrawal rights (i.e. where the PSS supplier goes beyond the mandatory legal protection) is also discussed.

191. LEGAL RIGHT OF WITHDRAWAL IN B2C DISTANCE OR OFF-PREMISES PSS CONTRACTS – As mentioned above, PSS contracts are often concluded online. If concluded online, such contacts constitute distance contracts. "Distance

826 Researcher at Lund University. See: L. WALKER, "Free online returns are costing the Earth, study confirms", 27 January 2023, available at www.brusselstimes.com/360092/free-online-returns-are-costing-the-earth-study-confirms

827 V. SAGAERT, *Beginselen van verbintenissenrecht. De contractuele en quasi-contractuele verbintenissen*, Leuven, LeA Uitgevers, 2023, 33. See for an extensive study on the right of withdrawal: E. TERRYN, *Bedenktijden in het consumentenrecht*, Antwerp, Intersentia, 2008, 686 p.

828 EU: Art. 9 CRD. **Belgium**: Art. 5.22 BCC (general contract law) and Art. VI.45-VI.53 BCEL (for distance contracts). **The Netherlands**: Art. 6:230o DCC.

829 R. SCHULZE, F. ZOLL and J. WATSON, *European Contract Law*, Baden-Baden, Nomos München, Oxford, Hart Publishing, 2021, 157; G. HOWELLS, C. TWIGG-FLESNER and T. WILHELMSSON, *Rethinking EU Consumer Law*, Abingdon, Routledge, 2018, 113; M. LOOS, "Rights of Withdrawal" in G. HOWELLS and R. SCHULZE (eds.), *Modernising and Harmonising Consumer Contract Law*, Munich, Sellier European Law Publishers, 2009, (237) 241.

830 See e.g. Art. 9 CRD; Art. 14 Consumer Credit Directive 2008 and Art. 26 of Consumer Credit Directive 2023; Art. 6 Distance Marketing of Financial Services Directive 2002/65/EC; Art. 6 Timeshare Directive 2008/122/EC, etc.

contracts" are defined as "*any contract concluded between the trader and the consumer under an organised distance sales or service-provision scheme without the simultaneous physical presence of the trader and the consumer, with the exclusive use of one or more means of distance communication up to and including the time at which the contract is concluded.*"[831] Not only PSS contracts concluded online are thus covered, but also, for example, PSS contracts that are concluded over the phone.[832] Exceptionally, a PSS contract can also constitute an off-premises contract,[833] for example, if it is concluded in the consumer's home following an invitation from the PSS supplier for a home visit. PSS contracts concluded at a trade fair for circular business models may also be classified as off-premises contracts, unless they were concluded at a trade fair stand which may be regarded as a "business premises" within the meaning of the CRD.[834, 835] For B2C distance and off-premises PSS contracts, the CRD provides for a mandatory right of withdrawal for the consumer within a period of 14 days without giving any reason.[836] The rules on the right of withdrawal are fully harmonised and implemented in Belgium in Articles VI.47-VI.53 and VI.62–63 BCEL (for distance contracts) and in Articles VI.67-VI.73 BCEL (for off-premises contracts). In the Netherlands, they can be found in Articles 6:230o-6:230s DCC (for both distance and off-premises contracts).

192. Environmental impact of right of withdrawal – The consumer's right of withdrawal without justification in distance contracts and the free return policies that often accompany this right is a telling example of the tension between sustainability and consumer protection.[837] From a consumer protection point of view, the right of withdrawal provides a considerably strong position

---

831 Art. 2(7) CRD.

832 So far, however, the author has no knowledge of PSS suppliers that offer their PSS over the phone.

833 See Art. 2(8) CRD: "'*off-premises contract' means any contract between the trader and the consumer: (a) concluded in the simultaneous physical presence of the trader and the consumer, in a place which is not the business premises of the trader; (b) for which an offer was made by the consumer in the same circumstances as referred to in point (a); (c) concluded on the business premises of the trader or through any means of distance communication immediately after the consumer was personally and individually addressed in a place which is not the business premises of the trader in the simultaneous physical presence of the trader and the consumer; or (d) concluded during an excursion organised by the trader with the aim or effect of promoting and selling goods or services to the consumer.*"

834 See CJEU, Judgment of 7 August 2018, C-485/17, *Verbraucherzentrale Berlin*, ECLI:EU:C:2018:642, para. 43–46. This depends on all the factual circumstances, in particular on whether, given the appearance of the stand and the information relayed on the premises of the fair itself, an average consumer could reasonably assume that the trader is carrying out his activities there and will solicit him in order to conclude a contract, which is for the national court to ascertain.

835 CJEU, Judgment of 21 October 2020, Case C-529/19, *Möbel Kraft*, ECLI:EU:C:2020:846, para. 16.

836 Art. 9–16 CRD.

837 See *supra* no. 64.

to consumers. However, the rebound effects of this right of withdrawal have severe environmental consequences (both in terms of destroyed products and double transport for returning the goods), as well as a negative impact on the profit margins of businesses.[838] In response to these rebound effects, convincing voices have been raised in legal doctrine to revisit the modalities of the right to withdrawal.[839] These proposals include rethinking the duration of the withdrawal period, recalibrating the rights and obligations of the parties during the withdrawal period, extending the exceptions to the right of withdrawal, but also more drastic changes limiting the (exercise of the) right of withdrawal.[840] While we agree that (the modalities of) the right of withdrawal should be thoroughly re-examined in the light of (environmental) sustainability, this book limits itself to an analysis (and accompanying recommendations) specifically tailored to PSS contracts, in particular regarding the distinction between the consequences of exercising the right of withdrawal in service contracts compared to sales contracts.

2.4.1. WITHDRAWAL PERIOD

193. 14-DAY WITHDRAWAL PERIOD – The withdrawal period for distance and off-premises PSS contracts is 14 (calendar[841]) days.[842] However, the start of this withdrawal period differs between service contracts (i.e. use-oriented and result-oriented PSS) and sales contracts (i.e. product-oriented PSS).[843] For (digital) service contracts, the withdrawal period is calculated from the day after the PSS contract was concluded, for sales contracts (also sales contracts with additional services[844]) the day after the delivery of the product.[845] For most PSS contracts, the start of the withdrawal period will therefore be *the day after* the contract was concluded. Here, it is noteworthy that some PSS suppliers have misunderstood

---

838 E. Terryn and E. Van Gool, "The Role of European Consumer Regulation in Shaping the Environmental Impact of E-Commerce", *EuCML* 2021, vol. 10 issue 3, (89) 94–95.

839 See: E. Terryn and E. Van Gool, "The Role of European Consumer Regulation in Shaping the Environmental Impact of E-Commerce", *EuCML* 2021, vol. 10, afl. 3, (89) 95–100.

840 *Ibid.*

841 See Recital 41 CRD: "*[...] all periods contained in this Directive should be understood to be expressed in calendar days. Where a period expressed in days is to be calculated from the moment at which an event occurs or an action takes place, the day during which that event occurs or that action takes place should not be considered as falling within the period in question.*" (Own emphasis).

842 EU: Art. 9(1) CRD. **Belgium**: Art. VI.47, §1 BCEL. **The Netherlands**: Art. 6:230o(1) DCC.

843 See for the qualification of the three types of PSS business models under the CRD *infra* no. 353.

844 This follows from the CRD's definition of the notion "sales contract". See Art. 2(5) CRD. **Belgium**: Art. I.8, 33° BCEL. **The Netherlands**: Art. 6:230g(2) DCC.

845 EU: Art. 9(2) CRD. Additionally, for sales contracts involving instalment deliveries and other modes of delivery other criteria define the start of the withdrawal period. See Art. 9(2), (i)-(iii) CRD. **Belgium**: Art. VI.47, §2 BCEL. **The Netherlands**: Art. 6:230o(1) DCC.

the legal text, stating in the PSS contract that the withdrawal period starts the day of the conclusion of the contract.

> Terms and conditions Swapphone – Art. 4.3 "The Lessee may cancel the Rental Contract *within a period of fourteen (14) days* without stating reasons, *starting on the day the rental contract is concluded*." (Own emphasis).

> Terms and conditions HP Instant Ink – Art. 9(d) "Mandatory right of withdrawal. If you are a consumer, the above termination options do not limit your legal right of withdrawal. You have the right to withdraw from this contract without giving reasons *within fourteen (14) days from the day of entering into this contract.* You have the right to notify HP via the procedure described in paragraph 9.a or via the cancellation form below. [...]" (Own emphasis).

194. Difference between start of withdrawal period for sales contracts and service contracts not always convincing in context of PSS contracts – The reason why the withdrawal period for sales contracts only starts after the delivery of the product is that only then the information asymmetry regarding the delivered product is removed.[846] However, with the rise of PSS business models, this difference is not always convincing.[847] After all, for some services, in particular use-oriented PSS where the product is shipped to the consumer, the information asymmetry also disappears only after the delivery of the product. If the product is not delivered within the 14-day period following the conclusion of the PSS contract, the PSS user will not be able to inspect the product before deciding whether to exercise his right of withdrawal. Some PSS suppliers even use (one could in some circumstances even say abuse) this difference between sales and service contracts by stating in the PSS contract that the product will only be delivered after the 14-day withdrawal period. For example, the terms and conditions of *Saman Group* state that if the PSS user exercises his right of withdrawal, the heat pump will not be installed.

> Terms and conditions Saman Group – Art. 4.1 "It is possible for the Lessee to cancel the Rental Contract without statement of reasons within the legal withdrawal period of fourteen (14) days. The withdrawal period starts on the day the Rental Agreement is concluded between the Lessee and Saman Group." Art. 4.2 "*Exercising the right of withdrawal and thus terminating the Rental Contract will result in the Heat Pump System not being installed by Saman Group and not being rented to the Lessee.*" (Own emphasis).

[846] G. Straetmans and R. Steennot, *Handboek consumentenbescherming en marktpraktijken*, Antwerp, Intersentia, 2023, 444, no. 509.

[847] See in the same sense: H. Jacquemin and L.-A. Denis, "La protection des utilisateurs de 'produits en tant que service'", *JT* 2023, (425) 436, no. 44.

To a certain extent, this is understandable in this specific situation. After all, installing (and removing) a heat pump on the PSS user's premises is substantial, costly and may involve wasting precious resources. As a result, removing the heat pump after exercising the right of withdrawal would have very negative consequences regarding the interests of the PSS supplier and sustainability interests that arguably outweigh the interests of the consumer. However, other situations are conceivable where such clauses are used to (non-justifiably) circumvent the legal right of withdrawal and as such create a significant imbalance between the rights of the PSS user and the PSS supplier. This could include, for example, use-oriented PSS contracts for smaller products such as consumer electronics or products requiring limited installation such as furniture or household appliances. From a consumer protection point of view, one might argue that it would be better to align the start of the withdrawal period for sales contracts and service contracts where the delivery of a good is essential for the start of the service. However, from a sustainability point of view and taking into account the interests of businesses, there may in specific circumstances also be good reasons to make the withdrawal period start when the contract is signed, as the example of Saman Heat Pumps illustrates well. A potential solution where these different interests can be balanced could be to challenge these clauses delaying the delivery of the product until after the expiry of the withdrawal period using the general test of the UCTD.[848] If there is no reason why the PSS user should deserve less consumer protection if he only wants the right to use the product instead of the ownership of the same product, such as with smaller products that the consumer could also buy, the clause could then be declared null and void. If, on the other hand, there are good reasons why the product should not be delivered or installed before the expiry of the withdrawal period, such as where this would with certainty entail a disproportionate waste of precious resources, the clause could be upheld.

195. PSS USER-CONSUMER CANNOT WAIVE RIGHT OF WITHDRAWAL – A separate but related issue are clauses regarding the right of withdrawal stating that the PSS user waives his right of withdrawal from the moment the product is made available if he opts to have the product delivered within the 14-day withdrawal period. The terms and conditions of *Live Light* provide an example of this. These terms first confirm the fact that the PSS user-consumer can exercise his right of withdrawal within 14 days of signing the contract, which is in line with the legal provisions of the right of withdrawal. However, the clause then continues by stipulating that if the consumer opts to have the product delivered within the withdrawal period, he waives his right of withdrawal. Since the rules on the right of withdrawal are mandatory law, such clauses where the consumer waives his

848 See *supra* no. 160 *et seq.* **EU**: Art. 3(1) UCTD. **Belgium**: Art. I.8, 22° BCEL. **The Netherlands**: Art. 6:233, *sub* a. DCC.

right of withdrawal are invalid.[849] As we will see further, this situation also does not fall under the exceptions to the right of withdrawal (e.g. the exception for fully performed service contracts[850]).[851]

> TERMS AND CONDITIONS LIVE LIGHT – Art. 3.4 "Right of withdrawal: only users-consumers (hereinafter referred to as the 'Consumer') within the meaning of article I.1, 2° of the Belgian Code of Economic Law are granted the right of withdrawal. This right allows the Consumer to withdraw its order within 14 days of signing. *If the Consumer opts to have the Goods delivered within the period of 14 days after the conclusion of the Rental agreement, it expressly waives any right of withdrawal from the moment the Goods are made available.*" (Own emphasis).

196. SOME PSS CONTRACTS PROVIDE THAT WITHDRAWAL PERIOD STARTS WHEN PSS USER TAKES PHYSICAL POSSESSION OF THE GOOD – Some PSS suppliers go further than what is legally required and offer additional consumer protection. Similar to what the situation would be if a sales contract was concluded, they include a clause in the use-oriented PSS contract that stipulates that the withdrawal period starts when the PSS user (or a third party designated by him) has received the good. This is the case, for example, with the terms and conditions of *Blue Movement* and *Grover*. In my view, this makes sense, as the consumer can only inspect the rented product after it is delivered.

> TERMS AND CONDITIONS BLUE MOVEMENT – Art. 2.3 "User may cancel a Contract with BSH during a withdrawal period of 14 days without statement of reasons. *The withdrawal period starts on the day after User, or a third party designated in advance by User, who is not the carrier, has received the Product.* [...]." (Own emphasis).

> TERMS AND CONDITIONS GROVER – Art. 7.2.1 "Insofar as You have a right to withdraw (in Dutch: herroepingsrecht), You have the right to withdraw this contract within fourteen days without a statement of reasons. *The withdrawal period is fourteen days from the day of receipt of the Rental item.*" (Own emphasis).

197. CONTRACTUAL EXTENSION OF WITHDRAWAL PERIOD – PSS suppliers can grant a longer withdrawal period to the PSS user-consumer based on the principle of the freedom of contract. For example, *Repeat/Gerrard Street* allows the PSS user to exercise his right of withdrawal within 30 days of receipt. Additionally, the terms and conditions of *Bundles* provide that the PSS user can cancel the contract during a withdrawal period of 15 days.

---

849 **Belgium**: Art. VI.63(2) BCEL. **The Netherlands**: Art. 6:230i(1) DCC.

850 **EU**: Art. 16(a) CRD. **Belgium**: Art. VI.53, 1° BCEL. **The Netherlands**: Art. 6:230p, *sub* d. DCC.

851 See *infra* section 2.4.4.

Terms and conditions Repeat/Gerrard Street – Art. 4.1 "You may return the headphones at any time *within 30 days of receipt*. You can do this by sending the headphones in the received packaging to Gerrard Street, Blaak 6 (3rd floor), 3011TA in Rotterdam." 4.2 "If we have received the product and it is undamaged, we will refund the full purchase price within 14 days." (Own emphasis).

Terms and conditions Bundles – Art. 6.5 "Customer may cancel a Contract with Bundles free of charge during a *withdrawal period of 15 days* without stating reasons, unless the Product has already been installed at the Customer's premises, in which case the Relocation Fee will be charged for returning the Product." (Own emphasis).

198. 12-month extension as sanction for non-compliance with information requirements regarding right of withdrawal – As already briefly mentioned higher,[852] the PSS supplier offering distance or off-promises PSS contracts must, where a right of withdrawal exists, inform the PSS user-consumer of the conditions, time limit and procedures for exercising that right, as well as the model withdrawal form set out in Annex I(B) of the CRD.[853] The burden of proof that these information requirements are complied with, lies with the PSS supplier.[854] If the PSS supplier has not supplied the PSS user with that information, the withdrawal period is extended by 12 months from the end of the initial withdrawal period.[855] If the PSS supplier still provides the information within the extended withdrawal period (e.g. six months after concluding the PSS contract), the withdrawal period is again shortened to a period of 14 days after receiving the information.[856]

199. New withdrawal period after expiry of free trial period? – During the third stakeholder workshop of the C2 project,[857] offering a free trial was proposed by the audience as one of the possible ways to convince consumers to engage in PSS business models.[858] The question then arises as to the relationship between a free trial period and the right of withdrawal: after the expiry of the free trial period and thus at the start of a paying subscription, is the PSS user-consumer (again) entitled to a right of withdrawal?

---

852 See *supra* no. 88.

853 EU: Art. 6(1), (h) CRD. **Belgium**: Art. VI.45, §1, 8° BCEL (distance contracts) and Art. VI.64, §1, 7° BCEL (off-premises contracts). **The Netherlands**: Art. 6:230m, *sub* h. DCC (for both distance and off-premises contracts).

854 EU: Art. 6(9) CRD. **Belgium**: Art. VI.62 BCEL. **The Netherlands**: Art. 6:230n(4) DCC.

855 EU: Art. 10(1) CRD. **Belgium**: Art. VI.48(1) BCEL (distance contracts) and Art. VI.68(1) BCEL (off-premises contracts). **The Netherlands**: Art. 6:230o(2) DCC.

856 EU: Art. 10(2) CRD **Belgium**: Art. VI.48(2) BCEL (distance contracts) and Art. VI.68(2) BCEL (off-premises contracts). **The Netherlands**: Art. 6:230o(2) DCC.

857 Third stakeholder workshop contractual rights and liabilities in circular business models, Brussels, 8 March 2023.

858 So far, however, PSS suppliers do not really offer free trial periods, apart from the free rides often offered by e-scooter companies such as Dott and Lime.

This question was addressed in a recent CJEU judgment regarding *Sofatutor*,[859] an online learning platform for primary and secondary school students, which granted a free trial period of 30 days from the conclusion of the contract after which the subscription is automatically renewed (this time paid) for a fixed period of time. In this case, the Austrian Consumer Information Association argued that the consumer is entitled to a right of withdrawal not only when a free trial period is concluded, but also when the contract is renewed. The CJEU ruled that the consumer's right to withdraw from a distance contract is guaranteed only once for a services contract which provides for an initially free trial period after which (unless the consumer terminates or withdraws from the contract during that period) payment is required for an automatically renewed (unless that contract is terminated) fixed term contract.[860] However, it added the requirement that the consumer must be informed in a clear, comprehensive and explicit manner by that trader that, after that initial free period, payment will be required for that performance of services.[861] If this is not the case, the consumer does have a new right of withdrawal after the free trial period.

Therefore, from this case law follows that if a PSS supplier were to offer a free trial period, the PSS user-consumer does not have a (new) right of withdrawal after the expiry of that free period, as long as he is properly informed about the fact that after that free trial period, the service will become payable.

2.4.2. EXERCISE OF THE RIGHT OF WITHDRAWAL

200. Model withdrawal form or any other unequivocal statement – The PSS user-consumer that wants to exercise his right of withdrawal has several options. First, he can use the model withdrawal form made available and provided by the PSS supplier. However, this is not an obligation. The PSS user-consumer can also make any other unequivocal statement setting out his decision to withdraw from the contract (e.g. by calling, sending an email, a letter, etc.).[862] In contrast, merely returning the product (without statement) is in principle not sufficient for exercising the right of withdrawal, as products can also be returned for other reasons (such as a lack of conformity).[863] However, some PSS suppliers also allow returning the product without other communication of exercising the right of withdrawal.[864]

---

859 See: www.sofatutor.com.

860 CJEU, Judgment of 5 October 2023, C-565/22, *Sofatutor*, ECLI:EU:C:2023:735.

861 *Ibid.*

862 **EU**: Art. 11(1) CRD. **Belgium**: Art. VI.49, §1 BCEL and Art. VI.69, §1 BCEL. **The Netherlands**: Art. 6:230o(3) DCC.

863 G. Straetmans and R. Steennot, *Handboek consumentenbescherming en marktpraktijken*, Antwerp, Intersentia, 2023, 445.

864 See e.g. Art. 4.1 Terms and Conditions Repeat/Gerrard Street: "*You may return the headphones at any time within 30 days of receipt. You can do this by sending the headphones*

201. Sending communication within withdrawal period is sufficient – The withdrawal is timely if the communication concerning the exercise of the right of withdrawal is sent by the PSS user-consumer within the withdrawal period.[865] This means that the PSS supplier may still be faced with a timely withdrawal up to a few days after the withdrawal period has expired, for example if the notification is sent by post.

202. Exercising right of withdrawal through website of PSS supplier – The PSS supplier may additionally offer the PSS user-consumer the option of giving notice of exercising the right of withdrawal electronically via its website or app.[866] Not surprisingly, in these times of digitalisation, most PSS suppliers do indeed offer this possibility. If the right of withdrawal is exercised through the website or app, the PSS supplier must communicate to the PSS user-consumer an acknowledgement of receipt of the withdrawal on a durable medium without delay so that the consumer can prove that he has indeed exercised his right of withdrawal.[867]

203. Burden of proof lies on the PSS user-consumer – The burden of proof that the right of withdrawal was (timely) exercised lies with the PSS user-consumer.[868] Consequently, it is advisable that this is done in a way that allows subsequent proof that the right of withdrawal has indeed been exercised (in a timely manner).[869]

2.4.3. CONSEQUENCES OF EXERCISING THE RIGHT OF WITHDRAWAL

204. Exercising right of withdrawal terminates the obligations of the parties – If the PSS user-consumer decides to exercise his right of withdrawal, this terminates the obligations of the parties under the PSS contract. More specifically, the parties are no longer required to perform the distance or off-premises PSS contract or, where the consumer responded to

<u>in the received packaging to Gerrard Street</u>, Blaak 6 (3rd floor), 3011TA in Rotterdam" (own emphasis).

865 EU: Art. 11(2) CRD. **Belgium**: Art. VI.49, §2 BCEL (distance contracts) and Art. VI.69, §2 BCEL (off-premises contracts). **The Netherlands**: Art. 6:230o(3) DCC.

866 EU: Art. 11(3) CRD. **Belgium**: Art. VI.49, §3 BCEL (distance contracts) and Art. VI.69, §3 BCEL (off-premises contracts). **The Netherlands**: Art. 6:230o(4) DCC.

867 *Ibid.*

868 EU: Art. 11(4) CRD. **Belgium**: Art. VI.49, §4 BCEL (distance contracts) and Art. VI.69, §4 BCEL (off-premises contracts). **The Netherlands**: Art. 6:230o(5) DCC.

869 Compare with Recital 44 CRD. See also: G. Straetmans and R. Steennot, *Handboek consumentenbescherming en marktpraktijken*, Antwerp, Intersentia, 2023, 445.

an invitation to make an offer,[870] to conclude the distance or off-premises PSS contract.[871]

205. Duty of restitution – Often, the parties to the PSS contract will have already performed some of their obligations (at least in part) during the withdrawal period, such as delivering the product, performing the additional services, or paying the price. The benefits both parties received under the PSS contract withdrawn from must then be reciprocally restituted. For this, the CRD contains rules on the consequences of the right of withdrawal in respect of goods (i.e. return of the goods and reimbursement) and a special regime for the right of withdrawal in respect of service contracts, where the consumer essentially pays a compensation for the services already received.[872]

When discussing these rules regarding the parties' duty of restitution, legal textbooks generally distinguish between sales contracts (as being contracts in respect of goods) and contracts for services.[873] However, for use-oriented and result-oriented PSS there will often be a combination of these two aspects. Indeed, use-oriented and result-oriented PSS qualify as service contracts within the meaning of the CRD,[874] but at the same time goods are also made available to the consumer (as part of a rental contract or as accessory to the service). The question therefore arises whether the rules "in respect of goods" (e.g. obligation to return the goods, liability for diminished value of the goods, etc.) must also be applied to the use-oriented or result-oriented PSS contract in addition to the compensation mechanism for services performed during the withdrawal period.

Recital 50 of the CRD seems to provide part of the solution. It states that "*for contracts having as their object both goods and services, the rules provided for in this directive on the return of goods should apply to the goods aspects and the compensation regime for services should apply to the services aspects.*"[875] This would mean that in the case of a use-oriented PSS, the rules on returning the product and compensation for diminished value caused by mishandling the product should be applied, as should the compensation rules for the use that the

870 See *supra* no. 101.

871 EU: Art. 12 CRD. **Belgium**: Art. VI.52 §1 BCEL (distance contracts) and Art. VI.72, §1 BCEL (off-premises contracts). **The Netherlands**: Art. 6:230q(1) DCC.

872 See: EC, *Guidance on the interpretation and application of Directive 2011/83/EU of the European Parliament and of the Council on consumer rights*, 29.12.2021, 2021/C 525/01, 54–60.

873 See for **Belgium** e.g. G. Straetmans and R. Steennot, *Handboek consumentenbescherming en marktpraktijken*, Antwerp, Intersentia, 2023, 445–446 and 449–454. See for **the Netherlands** e.g. E.D.C. Neppelenbroek, *Elektronisch contractenrecht*, The Hague, Boom Juridisch, 2019, 232–239.

874 See: EC, *Guidance on the interpretation and application of Directive 2011/83/EU of the European Parliament and of the Council on consumer rights*, 29.12.2021, 2021/C 525/01, 10: "*If a contract for the rental of goods only includes an option to transfer ownership, not an obligation, it should be classified as a service contract for the purpose of the Directive.*"

875 Recital 50 CRD.

PSS user-consumer has already enjoyed during the withdrawal period. However, the applications of this recital in the CRD Guidance Document and in legal doctrine always relate to combinations of sales contracts and service contracts. Examples include sales contracts with additional services (e.g. buying a household appliance with delivery and installation)[876] or service contracts where the consumer also buys goods (e.g. a language course where the consumer also buys coursebooks).[877] In contrast, the situation where there is (only) a service contract where goods are made available to the consumer as part of the service remains unaddressed in the CRD Guidance Document and legal doctrine.

Nevertheless, in my view, it is appropriate in this case to also apply the rules "in respect of goods" and the rules on withdrawal from contracts for services cumulatively. After all, Articles 13 and 14 CRD do not explicitly refer to sales contracts, and only applying the rules for service contracts would result in a lacuna as to what should happen to the goods used for the performance of the service after the PSS user-consumer has exercised his right of withdrawal. This would be unacceptable from a legal certainty perspective and go against the interests of the PSS suppliers, since they would not be able to invoke the rules of the right of withdrawal to get their products back (in a timely manner) or receive compensation for improper use of their products by the PSS user-consumer during the withdrawal period. This leads to proposed amendment #2, which aims to amend recital 50 of the CRD by adding the phrase "*or service contracts where goods are delivered to the consumer.*"[878]

Proposed Amendment #2

(50) […] For contracts having as their object both goods and services, **or for service contracts where goods are delivered to the consumer**, the rules provided for in this Directive on the return of goods should apply to the goods aspects and the compensation regime for services should apply to the services aspects.

206. Specific consequences of right of withdrawal for personal data, digital content and digital services – The Omnibus Directive (EU) 2019/216[879] also introduced specific rules on the consequences of the right of withdrawal with regard to the personal data of the consumer and the use of

876 EC, *Guidance on the interpretation and application of Directive 2011/83/EU of the European Parliament and of the Council on consumer rights*, 29.12.2021, 2021/C 525/01, 61.

877 EC, *Guidance on the interpretation and application of Directive 2011/83/EU of the European Parliament and of the Council on consumer rights*, 29.12.2021, 2021/C 525/01, 9; E.D.C. Neppelenbroek, *Elektronisch contractenrecht*, The Hague, Boom Juridisch, 2019, 197 and 237.

878 Compare also with proposed amendment #3, *infra* p. 159.

879 Directive (EU) 2019/2161 of the European Parliament and of the Council of 27 November 2019 amending Council Directive 93/13/EEC and Directives 98/6/EC, 2005/29/EC and

digital content and digital services. Both the PSS supplier and the PSS user-consumer have certain obligations in this case.[880]

2.4.3.1. Consequences of the right of withdrawal for contracts in respect of goods

207. Consequences of right of withdrawal in respect of goods – If the PSS user-consumer withdraws from a PSS contract where goods are delivered to the PSS user-consumer, the obligations already performed must be reversed. More concretely, the PSS user-consumer will have to send the product back (unless the PSS supplier offered to collect it) and the PSS supplier must pay back the price. In addition, exercising the right of withdrawal will also result in the termination of any ancillary contracts regarding the product (e.g. maintenance contract or insurance).

208. PSS user must send back the product – If the PSS user-consumer withdraws from a PSS contract where a product was made available to him, he must send back the product or hand it over to the PSS supplier or to a person authorised by the PSS supplier to receive the good(s), unless the PSS supplier has offered to collect the product itself.[881] Especially for larger products (e.g. household appliances such as washing machines or smart fridges), the PSS supplier will in practice most likely arrange the return of these products. The PSS user-consumer must return the product without undue delay and in any case not later than 14 days from the day on which he communicated his decision to withdraw from the PSS contract. This deadline shall be met if the consumer sends back the goods before the period of 14 days has expired.[882] As a result, it is possible that the product may not reach the PSS supplier until after the withdrawal period has expired.

> Terms and conditions Swapphone – Art. 7.5 "The Lessee shall return the Smartphone to Swapphone as soon as possible, but within fourteen (14) days from the day the decision to exercise the right of withdrawal is communicated by the Lessee. This is not required if Swapphone has offered to collect the Smartphone itself. The Lessee has complied with the return period in any case if he returns the Smartphone before the withdrawal period has expired."

209. Costs of returning the product in principle borne by PSS user – The direct costs of returning the product are in principle borne by the PSS user-consumer, unless the PSS supplier has failed to inform the consumer of this

---

2011/83/EU of the European Parliament and of the Council as regards the better enforcement and modernisation of Union consumer protection rules, *OJ L* 328, 18.12.2019, 7–28.

880 These will be discussed *infra* no. 228 *et seq.*

881 EU: Art. 14(1) CRD. **Belgium**: Art. VI.51, §1 BCEL (distance contracts) and Art. VI.71, §1 BCEL (off-premises contracts). **The Netherlands**: Art 6:230s(1) DCC.

882 *Ibid.*

requirement.[883] In addition, it is also possible that the PSS supplier has agreed to pay these costs for commercial reasons, for example to lower the threshold to enter into a contract. Various PSS suppliers, including *Swapphone*, *Repeat/Gerrard Street* and *Lena Library*, do indeed stipulate in their terms and conditions that the PSS user-consumer will bear the cost of returning the product.

> Terms and conditions Swapphone – Art. 7.9 "The lessee bears the costs of returning the Smartphone."

> Terms and conditions Repeat/Gerrard Street – Art. 4.3 "You are responsible for the costs of the return shipment."

> Terms and conditions Grover – Art. 7.2.2 "You shall bear the direct costs for the return shipment of the Rental Item. Returning the rental item to the wrong adress may result in delay of repayment."

> Terms and conditions Lena Library – Art. 11.2 "The total amount (purchase amount + shipping costs outwards) of the order will, after the process of article 11.1 is properly completed, refunded to the buyer's account. *Shipping costs for returns are therefore for the customer.*" (Own emphasis)[884]

210. PSS user will be liable for diminished value caused by mishandling the product – The PSS user-consumer can withdraw from the PSS contract regardless of how the product has been handled during the withdrawal period.[885] However, the consumer will be liable for any diminished value of the product resulting from the handling of the product other than what is necessary to establish its nature, characteristics and functioning.[886, 887]

---

883 EU: Art. 14(1), para. 2 CRD *juncto* Art. 6(1)(i) CRD. **Belgium**: Art. VI.51, §1(2) BCEL *juncto* Art. VI.45, §1, 9° BCEL (distance contracts) and Art. VI.71, §1(2) *juncto* Art. VI.64, §1, 8° BCEL (off-premises contracts). **The Netherlands**: Art. 6:230s(2) DCC *juncto* Art. 6:230m(1), *sub* i. DCC.

884 It should, however, be noted that this clause relates to purchase orders, i.e. items from the fashion library where the PSS user has exercised the purchase option after having tried them as part of the subscription service. It does therefore not relate to the (rented) items that are part of the subscription service.

885 See Recital 47 CRD: "*Some consumers exercise their right of withdrawal after having used the goods to an extent more than necessary to establish the nature, characteristics and the functioning of the goods. In this case the consumer should not lose the right to withdraw but should be liable for any diminished value of the goods. [...]*" (own emphasis).

886 EU: Art. 14(2) CRD. **Belgium**: Art. VI.51, §2 BCEL (distance contracts) and Art. VI.71, §2 BCEL (off-premises contracts). **The Netherlands**: Art. 6:230s(3) DCC.

887 The Proposal for the Omnibus Directive (EU) 2019/216 aimed to add an exception to Art. 16 CRD (exceptions to the right of withdrawal) for the supply of goods that the consumer has handled, during the right of withdrawal period, other than what is necessary to establish the nature, characteristics and functioning of the goods. However, this exception did not make it to the final version of the text. From a sustainability perspective, this is of course regrettable. See also *infra* no. 212.

According to the recitals of the CRD, this is assessed by making a comparison with the extent to which the consumer would be able to handle and inspect the product in a brick-and-mortar shop.[888] Still, the distinction between testing the product and using the product will not always be easy to make. For example, does establishing the nature, characteristics and functioning of a washing machine mean connecting the washing machine to the water and drainage system or also doing a load of laundry? Based on a literal interpretation of the legal provisions, it could be argued that doing a load of laundry is indeed necessary to establish the functioning of the washing machine. From a teleological interpretation, on the other hand, one could argue that doing a load of laundry constitutes a use that goes further than necessary because generally a consumer will not be able to do laundry in a brick-and-mortar electronics store.[889] In practice, various PSS suppliers, including *Swapphone* and *Repeat/Gerrard Street* deal with this in a rather flexible way, namely by stating that the PSS user-consumer must handle the product and its packaging with care during the withdrawal period. Blue Movement, on the other hand, refers to the use a consumer can make of the product in a physical shop.

> TERMS AND CONDITIONS SWAPPHONE – Art. 7.6 "*During the withdrawal period, the Lessee must use the Smartphone* in accordance with Article 5.1 of the general terms and conditions." Art. 5.1 "The Lessee is obliged to use the Smartphone *carefully, competently, with due diligence and in accordance with the applicable legal provisions and instructions* of Swapphone and the manufacturer for the purpose for which it is intended and not in violation of the aforementioned." (Own emphasis).

> TERMS AND CONDITIONS REPEAT/GERRARD STREET – Art. 4.3 "During the time you have to consider whether you want to keep the headphones, *you must handle the product and its packaging with care*." (Own emphasis).

> TERMS AND CONDITIONS BLUE MOVEMENT – Art. 2.3 "[...] The Lessee shall handle the Product and its packaging with care. The Lessee shall unpack or use the Product only to the extent necessary to establish the nature, characteristics and functioning of the Product. *The basic principle here is that the Lessee may only handle and inspect the Product as he would be allowed to do in a shop*." (Own emphasis).

In any case, the burden of proof that the PSS user-consumer mishandled the product during the withdrawal period lies on the PSS supplier (*actori incumbit*

---

888 See Recital 47 CRD: "*In order to establish the nature, characteristics and functioning of the goods, the consumer should only handle and inspect them in the same manner as he would be allowed to do in a shop. For example, the consumer should only try on a garment and should not be allowed to wear it. Consequently, the consumer should handle and inspect the goods with due care during the withdrawal period.*" (Own emphasis).

889 EC, *Guidance on the interpretation and application of Directive 2011/83/EU of the European Parliament and of the Council on consumer rights*, 29.12.2021, 2021/C 525/01, 57.

probatio[890]), which will not always be an easy task.[891] For this proof that the PSS user-consumer's use of the product exceeded that of merely testing it, PSS suppliers could potentially rely on usage data from smart products or products with a built-in digital clock. For non-connected products, on the other hand, this will be harder. A possible strategy in this case could be to attach a large visible tag or protective seal to the product which cannot be removed.[892]

211. DETERMINING THE AMOUNT OF THE DIMINISHED VALUE OF THE PRODUCT – If the PSS user-consumer mishandled the product during the withdrawal period, he will thus be liable for the diminished value of the product.[893] This can consist in the cleaning or repair costs, but also the objectively justified loss of the PSS supplier if the goods cannot be sold as new (in case of product-oriented PSS) or cannot be used anymore for future (use-oriented or result-oriented) PSS contracts.[894] This assessment is not limited to the product itself, but also extends to its packaging, as a product without the original packaging or abnormal damage to the packaging can be considered depreciated.

212. IN PRACTICE, CONSUMER LIABILITY FOR DIMINISHED VALUE CAUSED BY MISHANDLING THE GOODS IS RARELY USED – Besides the difficulty of proving that the PSS user-consumer mishandled the product during the withdrawal period,[895] there are additional barriers that result in this liability rarely being invoked in practice.[896] For instance, many businesses report that it is difficult to determine the diminished value correctly or to reach an agreement on this diminished value with the consumer.[897] Moreover, it is generally assumed that the business

---

890 **Belgium**: Art. 8.4(1) BCC and Art. 870 Belgian Judicial Code. **The Netherlands**: Art. 150 Dutch Code of Civil Procedure.

891 The fact that the burden of proof cannot be placed on the consumer was also recognised by the CJEU, see: CJEU, Judgment of 3 September 2009, C-489/07, *Messner*, ECLI:EU:C:2009:502, para. 27.

892 Compare with the practice of Zalando to attach a large tag to expensive luxury clothes. If the tag is detached, Zalando assumes the garment has been worn (used). After all, trying on (testing) does not require removing the tag. P. NEERMAN, "Zalando tackles returns with annoyingly oversized tag", 18 January 2019, available at www.retaildetail.eu/news/fashion/zalando-tackles-returns-annoyingly-oversized-tag/.

893 EU: Art. 14(2) CRD. **Belgium**: Art. VI.51, §2 BCEL (distance contracts) and Art. VI.71, §2 BCEL (off-premises contracts). **The Netherlands**: Art. 6:230s(3) DCC.

894 EC, *Guidance on the interpretation and application of Directive 2011/83/EU of the European Parliament and of the Council on consumer rights*, 29.12.2021, 2021/C 525/01, 56.

895 See *supra* no. 210.

896 C. MARKOU, "Directive 2011/83/EU on Consumer Rights" in A.R. LODDER and A.D. MURRAY (eds.), *EU Regulation of E-commerce. A Commentary*, Cheltenham, Edward Elgar publishing, 2017, (177) 217–218; E. TERRYN, "Overeenkomsten op afstand en buiten de verkoopruimten na de omzetting van de Omnibusrichtlijn", *DCCR* 2022, vol. no. 135–136, (133) 150.

897 RPA, CSES and EPRD, *Study on the application of the Consumer Rights Directive 2011/83/EU*, https://ec.europa.eu/newsroom/document.cfm?doc_id=44637, European Commission, 2017, 115.

is not allowed to immediately deduct the compensation for depreciation from the amount to be refunded to the consumer (set-off[898]) if there is any discussion about this.[899] This often leads to the full amount being reimbursed anyway, both because this is more efficient and to avoid negative consumer reviews.[900] In this sense, it is regrettable, both from a business as from a sustainability perspective, that the proposed exception to be added to Article 16 CRD in the Proposal for the Omnibus Directive (EU) 2019/216 did not make it to the final text. This Proposal aimed to add an exception to the right of withdrawal for "*the supply of goods that the consumer has handled, during the right of withdrawal period, other than what is necessary to establish the nature, characteristics or functioning of the goods.*"[901] In other words, the consumer would lose his right of withdrawal if he mishandled the goods during the withdrawal period causing them to lose (part of) their value. Since this proposed amendment did not pass, the consumer remains (in practice) unsanctioned if he reduces the value of the product during the withdrawal period, which is obviously detrimental to both sustainability interests and business interests.[902]

213. PSS SUPPLIER MUST REIMBURSE PAYMENTS RECEIVED FROM THE PSS USER – The PSS supplier must reimburse all payments received from the PSS user-consumer, including the standard delivery costs.[903] Only if the PSS user-consumer expressly opted for a type of delivery other than the least expensive type of standard delivery, the PSS supplier must not reimburse the supplementary costs (e.g. for priority shipping) and must only partially reimburse the delivery costs.[904] The reimbursement must be done using the same means of payment as the PSS user-consumer used for the initial

898 See on set-off also *infra* section 5.4.

899 G. STRAETMANS and R. STEENNOT, *Handboek consumentenbescherming en marktpraktijken*, Antwerp, Intersentia, 2023, 451 with reference to the standpoint of the Belgian Economic Inspection.

900 RPA, CSES and EPRD, *Study on the application of the Consumer Rights Directive 2011/83/EU*, https://ec.europa.eu/newsroom/document.cfm?doc_id=44637, European Commission, 2017, 115; EXPERTGROEP GET RID OF RETURNS, *Blue Paper Get Rid of Returns. Analyse van retouren van online fashionaankopen en een verkenning van oplossingsrichtingen*, https://shoppingtomorrow.nl/nl/themas/logistics/delivery-distribution/get-rid-of-returns, 2019–2020, 6.

901 See Art. 2, points 14 and 15 of EC, *Proposal for a Directive of the European Parliament and of the Council amending Council Directive 93/13/EEC of 5 April 1993, Directive 98/6/EC of the European Parliament and of the Council, Directive 2005/29/EC of the European Parliament and of the Council and Directive 2011/83/EU of the European Parliament and of the Council as regards better enforcement and modernisation of EU consumer protection rules*, 11.4.2018, COM/2018/0185 final.

902 See in the same sense: E. TERRYN, "Overeenkomsten op afstand en buiten de verkoopruimten na de omzetting van de Omnibusrichtlijn", *DCCR* 2022, vol. no. 135–136, (133) 150.

903 EU: Art. 13(1) CRD. **Belgium**: Art. VI.50, §1 BCEL (distance contracts) and Art. VI.70, §1 BCEL (distance contracts). **The Netherlands**: Art. 6:230r(1) DCC.

904 EU: Art. 13(2) CRD. **Belgium**: Art. VI.50, §2 BCEL (distance contracts) and Art. VI.70, §2 BCEL (off-premises contracts). **The Netherlands**: Art. 6:230r(3) DCC.

transaction, unless he has *expressly* (i.e. not in general terms and conditions) agreed otherwise and provided that no fees are incurred as a result of such reimbursement.[905] In other words, if the payment was made with a credit card, reimbursement with vouchers will not be allowed unless the consumer expressly agrees.[906] This is to avoid forcing the consumer, who has paid in cash, to spend the reimbursed amount with the same business, which would undermine the effectiveness of the right of withdrawal.[907]

> Terms and conditions Grover – Art. 7.2.2. "If You withdraw from this contract, we shall refund all payments to You that we have received from you, including the delivery costs (except from the additional costs incurred because You have chosen a different delivery type than the one offered by Us, which is the most efficient standard delivery), […]. We will use the same payment instrument for this refund, as the one that you used in the original transaction, unless explicitly agreed otherwise with You. You will never be charged any fees for the repayment."

214. Timing of the reimbursement – The PSS supplier must carry out the reimbursement without undue delay and in any case not later than 14 days from the day on which he is informed on the consumer's decision to withdraw from the PSS contract. However, for sales contracts, the PSS supplier can withhold the reimbursement beyond this deadline until he has received the product or at least evidence has been supplied by the consumer that the goods have been sent back.[908]

This provision is, however, not as PSS supplier friendly as may appear at first sight.[909] If the PSS supplier receives the product after the 14-day period has expired, he must reimburse the PSS user-consumer without undue delay (under normal circumstances a few working days) and thus the PSS supplier has no fresh 14-day period.[910] Moreover, the "evidence that the goods have been sent back" should be understood as being a written statement from the transport of postal service specifying the sender and recipient and does not involve a guarantee that the goods in question have been inspected and

905 EU: Art. 13(1), para. 2 CRD. **Belgium**: Art. VI.50, §1(2) BCEL (distance contracts) and Art. VI.70, §1(2) BCEL (distance contracts). **The Netherlands**: Art. 6:230r(2) DCC.

906 See Recital 46 CRD: "*The reimbursement should not be made by voucher unles the consumer has used vouchers for the initial transaction or has expressly accepted them.*"

907 G. Straetmans and R. Steennot, *Handboek consumentenbescherming en marktpraktijken*, Antwerp, Intersentia, 2023, 447.

908 EU: Art. 13(3) CRD. **Belgium**: Art. VI.50, §3 BCEL (distance contracts) and Art. VI.70, §3 BCEL (off-premises contracts). **The Netherlands**: Art. 6:230r(4) DCC.

909 C. Markou, "Directive 2011/83/EU on Consumer Rights" in A.R. Lodder and A.D. Murray (eds.), *EU Regulation of E-commerce. A Commentary*, Cheltenham, Edward Elgar publishing, 2017, (177) 217.

910 EC, *Guidance on the interpretation and application of Directive 2011/83/EU of the European Parliament and of the Council on consumer rights*, 29.12.2021, 2021/C 525/01, 55.

verified.[911] As a result, this does not necessarily mean that the goods have not been mishandled or their value diminished. Consequently, even if the PSS supplier were entitled to compensation under Article 14(2) CRD (liability of the consumer for diminished value of the goods caused by mishandling),[912] he will have to reimburse the PSS user-consumer upon receiving the evidence that the product has been sent back.[913] Finally, it is hard to see why the CRD reserves this possibility for the PSS supplier to withhold reimbursement only for sales contracts (i.e. product-oriented PSS) and not for rental contracts (i.e. use-oriented PSS). After all, also in the case of rental contracts for movables, the goods are in the physical possession of the consumer. Being able to withhold the reimbursement will also then provide useful (or even necessary) leverage to get the consumer to return the goods. In practice, also PSS suppliers offering use-oriented PSS (which are qualified as rental contracts) reserve the right to withhold the reimbursement of the PSS user-consumer's payments until the products have been returned or proof of return has been provided in their terms and conditions. An example can be found in the terms and conditions of *Grover:*

> Terms and conditions Grover – Art. 7.2.2. "If You withdraw from this contract, We shall refund all payments to You that We have Received from you, […] without delay and at the latest within fourteen days from the day on which the notification of Your withdrawal from this contract was received by Us. […] *We can refuse to refund the payment until we have received the return of the products or until You have provided proof that You have returned the products, whichever is the earlier date.*" (Own emphasis).

As pointed out above,[914] the drafting of the CRD probably did not consider that, in addition to sales contracts and "pure" service contracts, there is also a third category consisting of service contracts under which movable goods are made available to consumers (i.e. rental contracts). Proposed amendment #3 therefore proposes to delete the reference to "*sales contracts*" in Article 13(3) CRD and replace this with "*contracts where goods are delivered to the consumer*", to also include rental contracts for movables and other service contracts where the goods are physically placed in the possession of the consumer.

---

911 EC, *Guidance on the interpretation and application of Directive 2011/83/EU of the European Parliament and of the Council on consumer rights*, 29.12.2021, 2021/C 525/01, 55.

912 See *supra* no. 210.

913 C. Markou, "Directive 2011/83/EU on Consumer Rights" in A.R. Lodder and A.D. Murray (eds.), *EU Regulation of E-commerce. A Commentary*, Cheltenham, Edward Elgar publishing, 2017, (177) 218.

914 See *supra* no. 205.

Proposed Amendment #3

Article 13

Obligations of the trader in the event of withdrawal

3. Unless the trader has offered to collect the goods himself, with regard to ~~sales contracts~~ **contracts where goods are delivered to the consumer**, the trader may withhold the reimbursement until he has received the goods back, or until the consumer has supplied evidence of having sent back the goods, whichever is the earliest.

215. Termination of ancillary contracts – If the PSS user-consumer exercises his right of withdrawal, this also automatically (i.e. without the consumer having to take additional actions) terminates any ancillary contract without any costs for the consumer.[915] "Ancillary contracts" within the meaning of the CRD are *"contract[s] by which the consumer acquires goods or services related to a distance contract or an off-premises contract and where those goods are supplier or those services are provided by the trader or by a third party on the basis of an arrangement between that third party and the trader."*[916] Examples of such ancillary contracts may include product-oriented PSS where the PSS user enters into an additional maintenance contract with the PSS supplier in addition to purchasing the (smart) product, or a PSS contract where the PSS user enters into an additional insurance contract with an insurance company that works with the PSS supplier.

2.4.3.2. Consequences of the right of withdrawal in respect of contracts for services

216. Compensation obligation for services already performed – As long as a contract for services (i.e. use-oriented and result-oriented PSS) is not fully performed, the PSS user can in principle exercise his right of withdrawal.[917] However, the PSS user will in some circumstances have a compensation obligation for the (part of the) services already performed by the PSS supplier. Four situations can be discerned here.

217. First situation: PSS contract takes effect after expiry of withdrawal period – A first situation is that the PSS contract takes effect only

[915] EU: Art. 15(1) CRD. **Belgium**: Art. VI.52, §2 BCEL (distance contracts) and Art. VI.72, §2 BCEL (off-premises contracts). **The Netherlands**: Art. 6:230q(2) DCC.

[916] EU: Art. 2(15) CRD. **Belgium**: Art. I.8, 38° BCEL. **The Netherlands**: Art. 6:230g, *sub* 1 DCC.

[917] See *infra* no. 231.

after the expiry of the withdrawal period. The clause of *Saman Group* discussed above provides a good example of this situation.[918] In this case, the PSS user-consumer has 14 days starting from the day after the conclusion of the contract to change his mind. Since the service has not yet commenced, there is nothing for the PSS supplier to be compensated for. Any amounts paid in advance by the PSS user-consumer must be refunded by the PSS supplier.[919]

218. Second situation: PSS contract takes effect within withdrawal period; not expressly requested by PSS user – In the second situation, the PSS contract takes effect within the 14-day withdrawal period. The CRD lays down formal requirements for when consumers wish to start the performance of distance or off-premises PSS contracts before the expiry of the withdrawal period. If the PSS user-consumer wants the performance of services to begin during the withdrawal period, and the PSS contract includes an obligation to pay (which will generally be the case), the PSS supplier must require that the PSS user-consumer makes an *express request* and must request the PSS user-consumer to *acknowledge* that, once the contract has been fully performed, he will no longer have the right of withdrawal.[920] If the PSS user-consumer withdraws from the PSS contract and the PSS supplier did not comply with this requirement to obtain the PSS user-consumer's express request for immediate performance, the PSS user-consumer cannot be charged for the services performed in whole or in part during the withdrawal period.[921] What the PSS user-consumer has already paid must be refunded.[922]

219. "Express request" implies positive action by PSS user-consumer – The term "express request" relates to a positive action by the PSS user-consumer, such as ticking a box during the order process on the website of the PSS supplier.[923] The use of a pre-ticked box or a clause in the general terms of

918 See *supra* no. 194.

919 E.D.C. Neppelenbroek, *Elektronisch contractenrecht*, The Hague, Boom Juridisch, 2019, 236.

920 EU: Art 8(8) CRD (for distance contracts) and Art. 7(3) CRD (for off-premises contracts). Both provisions are presented identically, except that Art. 7(3) requires the PSS supplier to obtain the consumer's request for immediate performance on a durable medium. **Belgium**: Art. VI.46, §8 BCEL (for distance contracts) and Art. VI.65, §2(2) BCEL (for off-premises contracts). **The Netherlands**: Art. 6:230v(8) DCC (for distance contracts) and Art. 6:230t(3) DCC (for off-premises contracts).

921 EU: Art. 14(4) CRD. **Belgium**: Art. VI.51, §4, 1°, b) BCEL (for distance contracts) and Art. VI.71, §4, 1°, b) BCEL (for off-premises contracts). **The Netherlands**: Art; 6:230s(5), *sub* a., 2° DCC (for both distance and off-premises contracts).

922 E.D.C. Neppelenbroek, *Elektronisch contractenrecht*, The Hague, Boom Juridisch, 2019, 236.

923 EC, *Guidance on the interpretation and application of Directive 2011/83/EU of the European Parliament and of the Council on consumer rights*, 29.12.2021, 2021/C 525/01, 59.

conditions for this purpose is in principle not sufficient.[924] The consent and acknowledgement can be acquired before, during, or after the PSS contract is concluded, as long as it happens before the performance of the PSS contract commences. According to the CRD Guidance Document, the following wording could for example be used[925]:

- ❒ "*I hereby request immediate performance of the service contract and acknowledge that I will lose my right of withdrawal from the service contract once the service is fully performed*"; or:
- ❒ "*I hereby request performance of the service contract on/as from [specific date during the withdrawal period] and acknowledge that I will lose my right of withdrawal from the service contract once the service is fully performed.*"

220. In practice, various PSS suppliers do not require express request during ordering process to start immediate performance of PSS contract – The question arises whether this requirement is met in practice by the PSS suppliers of the analysed contracts. A quick sample of some ordering processes of PSS contracts, where all steps were completed until the last step where payment information had to be provided, showed that various PSS suppliers do not meet this requirement to require the express request to start immediate performance of the PSS contract during the withdrawal period.[926] Of course, this is not the whole picture, as the PSS supplier may also require the express request to start immediate performance of the PSS contract by having the PSS user sign a form before installing the product (e.g. a washing machine) or upon collection of the product by the PSS user in a physical shop (e.g. a Swapfiets bicycle).

221. Third situation: PSS contract takes effect within withdrawal period as expressly requested by PSS user – In a third situation, the PSS contract takes effect within the withdrawal period, and this was explicitly requested by the PSS user-consumer. Also in this case, the PSS user-consumer can still withdraw from the PSS contract even after making this express

924 See CJEU, Judgment of 1 October 2019, C-673/17, *Planet49*, ECLI:EU:C:2019:801, para. 65, as cited by EC, *Guidance on the interpretation and application of Directive 2011/83/EU of the European Parliament and of the Council on consumer rights*, 29.12.2021, 2021/C 525/01, 59.

925 EC, *Guidance on the interpretation and application of Directive 2011/83/EU of the European Parliament and of the Council on consumer rights*, 29.12.2021, 2021/C 525/01, 59.

926 E.g. *Bundles, Blue Movement, Swapfiets, Fairphone Easy* and *Grover* are examples of PSS suppliers who do not require the prospective PSS user-consumer to tick a box during the online ordering process. *Swapphone* does have such a box and *Dressr* has a provision in its general terms and conditions regarding this express request (see *infra* no. 222).

request.[927] Therefore, the clause included in the terms and conditions of *Live Light* cited above, where the PSS user-consumer waives his right of withdrawal from the moment the product is made available if he opts to have the product delivered within the withdrawal period, is not legally valid.[928] In this situation, the PSS user-consumer will have a compensation obligation for the (part of the) services already performed by the PSS supplier.

222. Proportionate amount of compensation – If the PSS user-consumer decides to withdraw from the PSS contract during the withdrawal period after requesting its immediate performance, he will be required to pay an amount to the PSS supplier which is in proportion to what has been provided at the time of exercising the right of withdrawal compared with the total price of the PSS contract.[929] To give a concrete example: if a PSS user expressly requested the start of the services within the withdrawal period, used the product/service for ten days and then decided to withdraw from the PSS contract, he will have to pay a compensation to the PSS supplier of 1/3rd of the monthly fee.[930] A real-life example can be found in the general terms and conditions of *Dressr.* These terms stipulate that the PSS user acknowledges and requests that the provision of the subscription services starts immediately and that if he withdraws from the contract, he will owe a charge proportionate to the number of days in the month through which the services have been provided. However, during the order process there is no explicit box the PSS user-consumer must tick to request the immediate performance, only a click-wrap box for the general terms and conditions that include this request.[931] Thus, if the interpretation of the requirement of the "express request" in the CRD Guidance Document is strictly followed, this will in principle not be sufficient.[932]

> Terms and Conditions Dressr – Art. 5 (Consumer cancellation rights for subscriptions) "You normally have the right to cancel a subscription within 14 days after the date we send you the confirmation of our acceptance of your subscription request. *However, you acknowledge that we start provision of the subscription services*

---

927 See Recital 50 UCTD: "*The consumer should benefit from his right of withdrawal even in case he has asked for the provision of services before the end of the withdrawal period.*"

928 Art. 3.4 Terms and Conditions Live Light. See *supra* no. 196.

929 EU: Art. 14(3) CRD. **Belgium**: Art. VI.51, §3 BCEL (distance contracts) and Art. VI.71, §3 BCEL (off-premises contracts). **The Netherlands**: Art. 6:230s(4) DCC.

930 Compare with Art. 3(2)(d) of Regulation (EEC, Euratom) No 1182/71 of the Council of 3 June 1971 determining the rules applicable to periods, dates and time limits, *OJ L* 124, 8.6.1971, 1–2: "*If a period includes parts of months, the month shall, for the purpose of calculating such parts, be considered as having thirty days*" (own emphasis).

931 On click-wrap general terms and conditions, see *infra* no. 132 and 133.

932 See *supra* no. 219. EC, *Guidance on the interpretation and application of Directive 2011/83/EU of the European Parliament and of the Council on consumer rights*, 29.12.2021, 2021/C 525/01, 59.

> *immediately following this confirmation (which, by registering for a subscription, you request us to do)* and that if you cancel within the 14-day period then *the charge you pay us* (and which we will deduct from any refund otherwise due to you) *will be proportionate to the number of days in the month through which the services have been provided.*" (Own emphasis)

Another real-life example can be found in the terms and conditions of *Swapphone*. This clause stipulates that by signing, the prospective PSS user authorises *Swapphone* to start the provision of services before the withdrawal period has expired. Contrary to the examples we have seen above, *Swapphone's* order process does explicitly require the PSS user-consumer to tick a box in which he requests the direct delivery of the subscription within the withdrawal period (see Figure 4.). As a result, *Swapphone* indeed meets the requirement of the "express request" of the PSS user-consumer to start the service within the withdrawal period, which is needed for claiming the proportional compensation for services performed within the withdrawal period. However, the amount stipulated in *Swapphone's* terms and conditions is too high, as it states that this amount will be equal to the fee for one full month's rental instead of an amount which is in proportion to what has been provided at the time of exercising the right of withdrawal compared with the total price of the PSS contract. As a result, this clause will not be valid. The question then arises whether the PSS supplier can fall back on the proportionate compensation provision of the CRD itself instead of the contractual clause. Given the CJEU's case law in the field of unfair contract terms, where it prohibits the reduction of unfair terms to their lawful or reasonable content or the application of default rules,[933] it seems that this question must be answered in the negative.

> Terms and conditions Swapphone – Art. 7.10 "If the Lessee exercises the right of withdrawal, Swapphone shall be entitled to charge Lessee a reasonable amount, as Lessee has already used Swapphone's services from the effective date of the Rental Contract. *This amount is equal to the fee for one (1) full month's rental* as mentioned in the Rental Contract. *The Lessee, by signing the Rental Contract, authorises Swapphone to start the provision of services already before the withdrawal period has expired* and the Lessee, by signing, also agrees that it shall owe Swapphone the fee as mentioned in this article in case of exercising the right of withdrawal." (Own emphasis).

933 See *infra* no. 178 *et seq.*

Figure 4. Screenshot from *Swapphone's* ordering process for an iPhone 15.[934] (Own marking added).

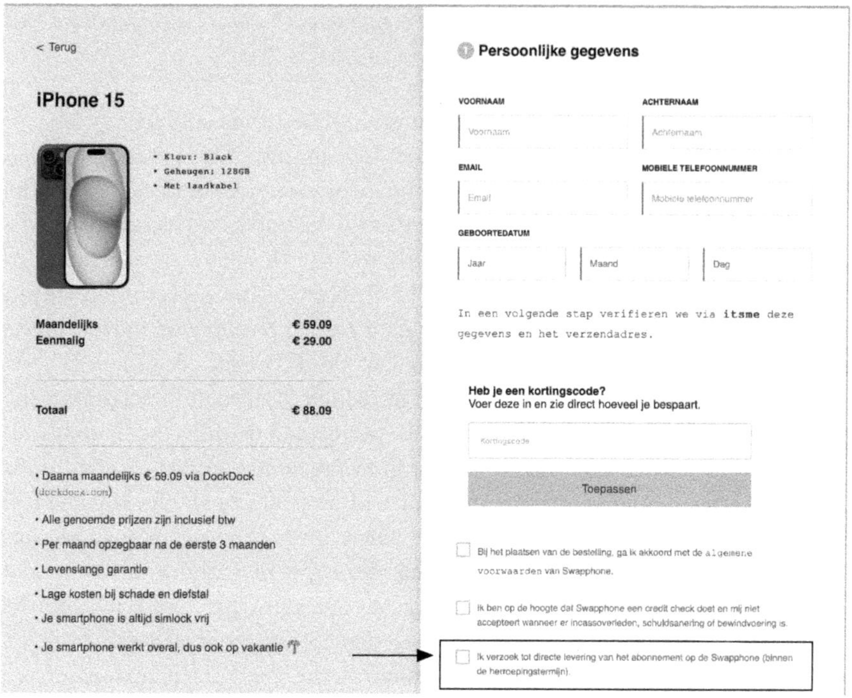

223. One-off costs (such as installation costs) may be included in the calculation of the compensation – This method *pro rata temporis* to calculate the compensation owed by the PSS user-consumer may however be deviated from, as was also confirmed by the CJEU.[935] If one or more of the PSS supplier's services involving one-off costs are to be provided in full immediately from the beginning of the performance of the PSS contract (e.g. the installation of the product), the PSS supplier may include them in the calculation of the compensation.[936] This does, however, require that the price of those separate services (which will be higher than the proportionate compensation calculated on the basis of the total price) is clearly defined in the PSS contract. After all, the PSS user-consumer should be able to make an informed decision on whether

934 Screenshot taken from https://shop.swapphone.be/products/checkout#cartTop.

935 CJEU, Judgment of 8 October 2020, C-641/19, *PE Digital*, ECLI:EU:C:2020:808; R. Steennot, "Herroeping van een gedeeltelijk uitgevoerde digitale dienstenovereenkomst en de daarbij door de consument verschuldigde vergoeding", *TvC* 2021, (109) 109–117.

936 CJEU, Judgment of 8 October 2020, C-641/19, *PE Digital*, ECLI:EU:C:2020:808, para. 29 and 32.

he should agree to start performance of the PSS contract within the withdrawal period.[937]

An application of this different calculation method can be found in the terms and conditions of both *Bundles* and *Blue Movement*, which state that the PSS user may be charged a "Relocation Fee" or "costs for installation, de-installation and returning". In both cases, these costs are not defined in the general terms and conditions but can be found in the special terms and conditions of the PSS contract (*Bundles*),[938] or on the website of the PSS supplier (*Blue Movement*).[939] However, also here, the question remains whether the requirement of an "express request" has been met.[940] Both *Bundles* and *Blue Movement* do not include a box to be ticked in their online order process regarding this express request. So, it depends on whether the PSS user-consumer made this express request in some other way, such as in the documents signed before/at delivery of the product. If not, we are in the second situation[941] and the PSS supplier will not be able to claim compensation for the services provided in the withdrawal period.

> Terms and conditions Bundles – Art. 6.5 "Customer may cancel a Contract with Bundles free of charge during a withdrawal period of 15 days without stating reasons, *unless the Product has already been installed at the Customer's premises, in which case the Relocation Fee will be charged for returning the Product.*" (Own emphasis).

> Terms and conditions Blue Movement – Art. 2.4 "If the Lessee cancels the Contract within the withdrawal period, the Product must be returned to BSH. *Any costs that BSH charges for installation and de-installation, and costs for returning, are stated on the Website.*" (Own emphasis).

224. Reduction to market value if total price is excessive – The CRD contains a safeguard to protect consumers from abuse regarding the compensation owed if they withdraw from a service contract whose performance began during the withdrawal period. If the total price is excessive, the compensation should be based on and reduced to the market value of the service provided.[942] According to the CJEU, in order to assess the market value

937 G. Straetmans and R. Steennot, *Handboek consumentenbescherming en marktpraktijken*, Antwerp, Intersentia, 2023, 453.

938 See Art. 1, l) Terms and Conditions Bundles, which defines the "Relocation Fee" as "*the fee as specified in the Contract payable by the Customer to Bundles for carrying out a relocation of the Device as described in clause 6.6 or for returning the Device as a result of the termination of the Subscription as described in clause 12 of these terms and conditions.*" (Own emphasis).

939 See Art. 2(4) Terms and Conditions Blue Movement.

940 See *supra* no. 219–220.

941 See *supra* no. 218.

942 EU: Art. 14(3) CRD. See also Recital 50: "*[…] The calculation of the proportionate amount should be based on the price agreed in the contract unless the consumer demonstrates that the total price is itself disproportionate, in which case the amount to be paid shall be calculated*

and thus whether the total price is excessive, account should be taken of the price of the service offered by the trader concerned to other consumers under the same conditions and that of the equivalent service supplied by other traders at the time of the conclusion of the contract.[943]

As an example, consider a use-oriented PSS contract where a consumer gets access to a product (e.g. a washing machine or e-bicycle) for € 75 a month. During the withdrawal period but after starting the service, the consumer discovers that other PSS suppliers offer an identical service for € 15 a month (5 times as much). The consumer can then prove the excessive nature of the price to pay only a proportionate amount of compensation based on the market price of € 15/month instead of the contractually agreed price of € 75/month. Although this example is very clear because the services are identical, in practice different PSS offers will differ from each other in several ways. For example, is it the same (or a comparable) product? Is all repair and maintenance included? How fast and responsive are the assistance services? Is there insurance? How much does the consumer have to pay if the product is lost or damaged? The PSS user-consumer will therefore not always have an easy task proving the excessive price, especially if the price difference is relatively low, or the difference in (additional) services is greater. There is also, as always, the consideration that for small amounts, for reasons of procedural economy, it does not always make sense to go to court to challenge the excessive price.

This provision is remarkable as it is an (indirect) application of the doctrine of *iustum pretium* (right price) not accepted in Belgium and the Netherlands.[944] However, its scope of application is limited, as price control only takes place if the PSS user-consumer exercises his right of withdrawal after the performance of the PSS contract has started during the withdrawal period. Thus, PSS users-consumers who do not exercise their right of withdrawal are not protected (under that provision) against excessive pricing of the PSS.

225. No compensation if PSS supplier has failed to provide information on right of withdrawal – Even if the PSS user-consumer has expressly requested the immediate performance of the PSS contract during the withdrawal period, there is an exception to the compensation obligation. The PSS user-consumer shall not bear any costs for withdrawing from the PSS contract during the withdrawal period if the PSS supplier has failed to provide

---

on the basis of the market value of the service provided. The market value should be defined by comparing the price of an equivalent service performed by other traders at the time of conclusion of the contract […]." **Belgium**: Art. VI.51, §3 BCEL (for distance contracts) Art. VI.71, §3 BCEL (for off-premises contracts). **The Netherlands**: Art. 6:230s(4) DCC.

943 CJEU, Judgment of 8 October 2020, C-641/19, *PE Digital*, ECLI:EU:C:2020:808, para. 37.

944 **Belgium**: G. Straetmans and R. Steennot, *Handboek consumentenbescherming en marktpraktijken*, Antwerp, Intersentia, 2023, 453. **The Netherlands**: E.D.C. Neppelenbroek, *Elektronisch contractenrecht*, The Hague, Boom Juridisch, 2019, 236.

information on the conditions, time limit and procedures for exercising the right of withdrawal as well as the model withdrawal form set out in Annex I(B) of the CRD[945] or on the fact that the PSS user-consumer will be liable to pay reasonable costs if he withdraws after an express request to start the PSS contract during the withdrawal period.[946, 947] As already mentioned, the burden of proof that these information requirements are complied with lies with the PSS supplier.[948]

226. Fourth situation: PSS contract took effect within withdrawal period as expressly requested by PSS user and PSS contract has been fully performed – The final possible situation is that the PSS user-consumer expressly requested the immediate performance of the PSS contract, acknowledged the fact that once the contract has been fully performed, he will no longer have the right of withdrawal, and the service is fully performed within the withdrawal period. In this case, the PSS user-consumer will no longer have a right of withdrawal.[949, 950] However, since most PSS contracts are long-term contracts (i.e. longer than 14 days and often automatically renewed), this situation will not arise very often and will in practice be limited to short-term pay-per-use PSS contracts.

227. No compensation if PSS supplier has failed to provide information on right of withdrawal, even if service is fully performed – Also here, the PSS user-consumer will be exempt from any obligation to pay if the PSS supplier did not provide him with the information regarding the right of withdrawal,[951] even if the PSS-user consumer exercised his right of withdrawal after the full performance of the PSS contract.[952] This shows that non-compliance with the information obligations and other obligations regarding the express consent of the PSS user can have very far-reaching consequences for the PSS supplier and its ability to claim any compensation if the PSS user withdraws from the PSS contract.

---

945 EU: Art. 6(1)(h) CRD. **Belgium**: Art. VI.45, §1, 8° BCEL (distance contracts) and Art. VI.64, §1, 7° BCEL (off-premises contracts). **The Netherlands**: Art. 6:230m(1), *sub* h. DCC.

946 EU: Art. 6(1) (j) CRD. **Belgium**: Art. VI.45, §1, 10° BCEL (distance contracts) and Art. VI.64, §1, 9° BCEL (off-premises contracts). **The Netherlands**: Art. 6:230m(1), *sub* j. DCC.

947 EU: Art. 14(4)(a)(i) CRD. **Belgium**: Art. VI.51, §4, 1°, a) BCEL (distance contracts) and Art. VI.71, §4, 1°, a) BCEL (off-premises contracts). **The Netherlands**: Art. 6:230s(5), *sub* a., 1° DCC.

948 EU: Art. 6(9) CRD. **Belgium**: Art. VI.62 BCEL. **The Netherlands**: Art. 6:230n(4) DCC.

949 EU: Art. 16(a) CRD. **Belgium**: Art. VI.53, 1° BCEL (distance contracts) and Art. VI.73, 1° BCEL (off-premises contracts). **The Netherlands**: Art; 6:230p, *sub* d. DCC.

950 See also *infra* no. 231.

951 EU: Art. 14(4)(a)(i) CRD. **Belgium**: Art. VI.51, §4, 1°, a) BCEL (distance contracts) and Art. VI.71, §4, 1°, a) BCEL (off-premises contracts). **The Netherlands**: Art. 6:230s(5), *sub* a., 1° DCC.

952 As was recently confirmed by the CJEU. See: CJEU, Judgment of 17 May 2023, C-97/22, *DC v HJ*, ECLI:EU:C:2023:413.

2.4.3.3. Consequences of right of withdrawal for personal data and digital content

228. Obligations of the PSS supplier regarding personal data and digital content – Besides the consequences of the right of withdrawal in respect of goods and the specific regime for compensation for services provided in the withdrawal period, the CRD also contains, since the Omnibus Directive (EU) 2019/216, some obligations for the PSS supplier in respect of consumers' personal data and digital content.

First, the CRD explicitly confirms that the PSS supplier must comply with the obligations of the General Data Protection Regulation 2016/679[953] ("GDPR") in respect of the personal data of the PSS user-consumer.[954] Second, the PSS supplier must also refrain from using any content other than personal data, which was provided or created by the PSS user-consumer when using the digital content or digital service supplied by the PSS supplier.[955] According to the European legislator, examples of this content could include digital images, video and audio files and content created on mobile devices.[956] The rationale behind this is that consumers should not be discouraged from exercising their right of withdrawal because they would no longer have access to this content.[957] However, there are exceptions to this obligation, namely when this content (i) has no utility outside the context of the digital content or digital service supplied by the PSS supplier; (ii) only relates to the consumer's activity when using the digital content or digital service supplied by the PSS supplier; (iii) has been aggregated with other data by the PSS supplier and cannot be disaggregated or only with disproportionate efforts; or (iv) has been generated jointly by the consumer and others, and other consumers are able to continue to make use of the content.[958] The PSS user-consumer has the right to retrieve this digital content free of charge, within a reasonable time and in a commonly used and machine-readable format and without hindrance of the PSS supplier, except if the requirements of exceptions (i)-(iii) are met.[959]

---

953 Regulation (EU) 2016/679 of the European Parliament and of the Council of 27 April 2016 on the protection of natural persons with regard to the processing of personal data and on the free movement of such data, and repealing Directive 95/46/EC (General Data Protection Regulation), *OJ L* 119, 4.5.2016, 1–88.

954 EU: Art. 13(4) CRD. **Belgium**: Art. VI.50, §4 BCEL (distance contracts) and Art. VI.70, §4 BCEL (off-premises contracts). **The Netherlands**: This provision was not explicitly implemented into Dutch law, probably because of its didactic function.

955 EU: Art. 13(5) CRD. **Belgium**: Art. VI.50, §5 BCEL (distance contracts) and Art. VI.70, §5 BCEL (off-premises contracts). **The Netherlands**: Art. 6:230r(5) DCC.

956 Compare with Recital 69 DCD.

957 E. Terryn, "Overeenkomsten op afstand en buiten de verkoopruimten na de omzetting van de Omnibusrichtlijn", *DCCR* 2022, vol. no. 135–136, (133) 154, no. 37.

958 EU: Art. 13(5) CRD. **Belgium**: Art. VI.50, §5 BCEL (distance contracts) and Art. VI.70, §5 BCEL (off-premises contracts). **The Netherlands**: Art. 6:230r(5) DCC.

959 EU: Art. 13(6)-(7) CRD. **Belgium**: Art. VI.50, §6-§7 BCEL (distance contracts) and Art. VI.70, §6-§7 BCEL (off-premises contracts). **The Netherlands**: Art. 6:230r(6) DCC.

229. Obligations of the PSS user regarding digital content – If the PSS user-consumer withdraws from a PSS contract where additional digital content or digital services are added to the contract, the PSS user-consumer must refrain from using this digital content or digital services and from making it available to third parties.[960] The PSS supplier may prevent any further use of the digital content or digital service by the consumer, for example by making it inaccessible or by disabling the user account of the PSS user-consumer.[961]

2.4.4. EXCEPTIONS TO THE RIGHT OF WITHDRAWAL

230. Limitative list of exceptions to the right of withdrawal – The CRD contains a *limitative*[962] list of 13 exceptions in which the PSS user-consumer will not have a right of withdrawal or will lose his right of withdrawal, unless the PSS contract explicitly grants such a right.[963] Other exceptions to the right of withdrawal cannot be included in the PSS contract.[964] According to the case law of the CJEU, these exceptions must be interpreted strictly to achieve a high level of consumer protection.[965] However, no additional conditions (i.e. not present in the legal text) may be imposed for relying on the exceptions.[966]

This section does not discuss all exceptions to the right of withdrawal, but the focus is on those relevant to PSS. Similarly to what we have seen above in the context of the consequences of the right of withdrawal,[967] exceptions to the right of withdrawal are often categorised in two main categories, namely exceptions with regard to service contracts and exceptions with regard to contracts in respect of goods. However, as we will see below, this classification is not as clear-cut anymore with use-oriented and result-oriented PSS, as these PSS are considered service contracts, but goods are also made available as part of the contract.

960 EU: Art. 14(2a) CRD. **Belgium**: Art. VI.51, §6 BCEL (distance contracts) and Art. VI.71, §6 BCEL (off-premises contracts). **The Netherlands**: Art. 6:230s(7) DCC.

961 EU: Art. 13(8) CRD. **Belgium**: Art. VI.50, §8 BCEL (distance contracts) and Art. VI.70, §8 BCEL (off-premises contracts). **The Netherlands**: Art. 6:230r(7) DCC.

962 As the CRD constitutes maximum harmonisation, the Member States cannot introduce additional exceptions in their national legislation.

963 EU: Art. 16 CRD. **Belgium**: Art. VI.53 BCEL (distance contracts) and Art. VI.73 BCEL (off-premises contracts). **The Netherlands**: Art. 6:230p DCC.

964 Compare also with Art. 3.4 Terms and Conditions Live Light, discussed *supra* no. 195, which does not fall under any of the exceptions to the right of withdrawal and is therefore not legally valid.

965 See e.g. CJEU, Judgment of 14 May 2020, C-208/19, *NK*, ECLI:EU:C:2020:382, para. 40; CJEU, Judgment of 27 March 2019, C-681/17, *slewo*, ECLI:EU:C:2019:255, para 21.

966 See CJEU, Judgment of 21 October 2020, Case C-529/19, *Möbel Kraft*, ECLI:EU:C:2020:846, where the CJEU ruled that the fact that the trader had not begun to produce the goods was irrelevant for the application of Art. 16(c) CRD (exception for the supply of goods made to the consumer's specifications or clearly personalised).

967 See *supra* no. 205.

2.4.4.1. Exceptions with regard to service contracts

231. No right of withdrawal after full performance of service contracts – As already briefly mentioned,[968] the PSS user-consumer cannot exercise his right of withdrawal for PSS contracts that qualify as service contracts (i.e. use-oriented and result-oriented PSS) after the service has been fully performed, provided that the performance has begun with the PSS user-consumer's prior express consent and acknowledgement that he will lose his right of withdrawal once the contract has been fully performed by the PSS supplier.[969] This exception only applies if the service is *fully* performed. Partial performance, as mentioned above, will not result in the loss of the right of withdrawal (although the PSS user-consumer will have to pay a compensation for the partial performance if the requirements are met).[970] In most cases, however, this exception will not apply, as most PSS contracts are long-term contracts that are renewed monthly. Therefore, the service will usually not be fully performed during the 14-day withdrawal period. A real-life example of a clause where this exception does not apply can be found in the terms and conditions of *Villo*. According to these terms, the withdrawal period ends automatically with the first use of the service (i.e. using a shared bicycle). However, although the first ride will be fully completed, the full service (i.e. a subscription for access to short-term shared bicycle rentals) will not be fully performed, making this clause invalid.

> Terms and conditions Villo – Art. 3.3(5) "The Customer has a withdrawal period of fifteen (15) days from the day of subscription on the Internet. *This period ends automatically with the first use of the service.* […]" (Own emphasis).

In addition, the loss of the right of withdrawal is subject to a double condition, at least if the PSS contract places the consumer under an obligation to pay (which will generally be the case). Thus, the performance of the service must have begun with the *express consent* of the PSS user-consumer, and he must have *acknowledged* that he will lose the right of withdrawal once the service has been fully performed. These conditions run parallel to the rules for compensation for partial performance of the service and must be interpreted accordingly.[971] The burden of proof that these conditions are met lies on the PSS supplier. As with the rules on compensation for partial performance, a provision in the general

---

968 See *supra* no. 226.

969 **EU**: Art. 16(a) CRD. **Belgium**: Art. VI.53, 1° BCEL (distance contracts) and Art. VI.73, 1° BCEL (off-premises contracts). **The Netherlands**: Art. 6:230p, *sub* d. DCC.

970 See *supra* no. 226–227.

971 EC, *Guidance on the interpretation and application of Directive 2011/83/EU of the European Parliament and of the Council on consumer rights*, 29.12.2021, 2021/C 525/01 58–59.

terms and conditions of the PSS contract does not suffice; a ticked box, on the other hand, does.[972]

232. No right of withdrawal for contracts with a specific date or period of performance – A second exception from the right of withdrawal are contracts for the provision of accommodation other than for residential purpose, transport (of goods),[973] car rental services, catering or services related to leisure activities if the contract provides for a specific date or period of performance.[974] This exception is thus subject to two cumulative requirements. First, the PSS contract must relate to one of the services listed in this provision. Although this exception covers a wide range of service contracts (e.g. booking a hotel room, a rental car, catering at a wedding party, or purchasing tickets to a museum, concert, cinema, or sports match), few PSS contracts actually offer these listed services. *Cambio* is perhaps the best example, as are other pay-per-use shared car services such as *Poppy*[975] or *Miles*.[976] Second, the PSS contract should stipulate "a specific date or period of performance". The rationale behind this requirement is that granting a right of withdrawal to the consumer would be inappropriate if the conclusion of the contract implies the setting aside of capacity.[977] In a recent judgment, the CJEU further clarified that it is irrelevant whether the trader could still find an alternative use for the capacity freed up by the exercise of the right of withdrawal.[978] Thus, given the requirement of a specific date or period of performance, the exception will not apply to *Cambio's* framework agreement (i.e. the subscription that provides the framework for concluding short-term car rental agreements), but only the individual rental agreements where a specific period or timeframe is stipulated.

233. "Car rental services [...] for specific date or period of performance": not limited to short term car rental services, car leasing contracts also covered – Although most car leasing contracts are not PSS contracts in the strict sense of the word, PSS contracts and leasing

---

972 Compare with *supra* no. 219.

973 The Belgian text refers to "transport" (*vervoer, transport*), instead of the narrower "transport of goods" in the CRD and the Dutch text. However, the Belgian law does not conflict with the directive, as the CRD (unlike book VI BCEL) does not apply to contracts on passenger transport services (see Art. 3(3)(k) CRD) and therefore does not provide a right of withdrawal for distance passenger transport contracts either. See: R. Steennot, "Commentaar bij art. VI.53 WER" in *Handels- en economisch recht. Commentaar met overzicht van rechtspraak en rechtsleer*, Mechelen, Wolters Kluwer, loose-leaf, 2022, (209) 219, no. 12.

974 **EU**: Art. 16(l) CRD. **Belgium**: Art. VI.53, 12° BCEL (distance contracts) and Art. VI.73, 12° BCEL (off-premises contracts). **The Netherlands**: Art. 6:230p, *sub* e. DCC.

975 https://poppy.be/en.

976 https://miles-mobility.com/en-be.

977 See Recital 49 CRD.

978 CJEU, Judgment of 31 March 2022, C-96/21, *Eventim*, ECLI:EU:C:2022:238.

contracts are often mentioned in the same breath.[979] In a recent case, the CJEU had to consider whether the exception for "car rental services" with a "specific date or period of performance" also applies to a distance or off-premises car leasing contract concluded for a period of 24 months.[980]

First, the CJEU assessed whether leasing contracts constitute "car rental services".[981] Here, it held that the main purpose of such contracts is indeed to allow the consumer to use the vehicle for a specific period of performance, in return for the monthly payment of a sum of money throughout that period. According to the Court, the fact that leasing contracts also contain a credit element does not detract from the application of this exception. Second, the CJEU held that this exception is not limited to short-term rental contracts, but that the term "specific" is also capable of covering rental contracts of a longer duration (*in casu* 24 months), provided that that duration is set out in sufficient detail in the contract.[982] Third, the CJEU also decided that including car leasing contracts for a period of 24 months into the scope of the exception laid down in Article 16(l) CRD is in line with its objective, namely protecting traders against the risk associated with setting aside some capacity which the trader may find difficult to fill if a right of withdrawal was exercised. According to the Court, since the trader acquires the relevant vehicle at the request of the consumer and in accordance with his specifications, it may find it difficult to put that vehicle to a different use without suffering disproportionate difficulties.[983] The CJEU also added that this interpretation is consistent with the interpretation laid down in Article 16(c) CRD (goods made to the consumer's specifications or clearly personalised[984]).[985] Given these arguments, the CJEU decided that car leasing contracts indeed fall within the exception of Article 16(l) CRD, so consumers engaging in distance or off-premises financial or operational car leasing contracts will not have a right of withdrawal.[986]

2.4.4.2. Exceptions with regard to contracts in respect of goods

234. Goods made to the consumer's specifications or clearly personalised – A first specific exception to the right of withdrawal for contracts relating to goods is the exception for the supply of goods made to the consumer's

979 See for the similarities and differences between (use-oriented) PSS contracts and leasing contracts *infra* section 3.4.3.
980 CJEU, Judgment of 21 December 2023, Joined Cases C-38/21, C-47/21 and C-232/21, *VK and Others v BMW Bank GmbH and Others*, ECLI:EU:C:2023:1014.
981 *Ibid.*, para. 190–191.
982 *Ibid.*, para. 192–193.
983 *Ibid.*, para. 194–199.
984 Discussed *infra* no. 234.
985 CJEU, Judgment of 21 December 2023, Joined Cases C-38/21, C-47/21 and C-232/21, *VK and Others v BMW Bank GmbH and Others*, ECLI:EU:C:2023:1014, para. 200.
986 *Ibid.*, para. 201–202.

specifications or clearly personalised.[987] For this exception to apply, the CJEU held that it is irrelevant whether the trader has already started production of the good.[988] "Goods made to the consumer's specifications" are defined as "*non-fabricated goods made on the basis of an individual choice or decision of the consumer.*"[989] This could include, for example, custom-made furniture, kitchens, etc. An important distinguishing factor is whether the PSS user-consumer has provided specifications such as specific measurements, or specific personalised features, such as a particular design or particular components of the product(s) that are not part of the PSS supplier's general offer to the public.[990] If, on the other hand, the PSS user-consumer configures goods by choosing from predetermined standard options offered by the PSS supplier, such as the colour of a smartphone or couch, or the assembly of a piece of furniture or kitchen based on standard elements, then these goods should not be considered to be made to the consumer's specifications.[991]

Given these conditions, use-oriented and result-oriented PSS contracts will only rarely relate to "goods made to the consumer's specifications". Indeed, personalisation in these PSS offers is often achieved by using "modules", which are regarded as pre-determined standard options offered by the PSS supplier instead of real made-to-measure products. *STILL Circular Kitchens*[992] can serve as an example of this, as this circular business model offers "custom-built" kitchens as-a-service, by using different modules that are listed in the PSS supplier's catalogue.[993] As such, the PSS user-consumer will still have a right of withdrawal in this case. This exception is therefore more likely to be relevant in product-oriented PSS where a custom-made product is sold to the consumer to which additional services are added. Moreover, the question remains whether this exception even applies to use-oriented and result-oriented PSS. After all, this exception only applies to contracts in respect of goods, not to contracts in respect of services.[994] Again, the question therefore arises whether these types

---

987 EU: Art. 16(c) CRD. See also Recital 49 CRD, which refers to tailor-made curtains as examples of such goods. **Belgium**: Art. VI.51, 3° BCEL (distance contracts) and Art. VI.71, 3° BCEL (off-premises contracts). **The Netherlands**: Art. 6:230p, *sub* f., 1° DCC.

988 CJEU, Judgment of 21 October 2020, Case C-529/19, *Möbel Kraft*, ECLI:EU:C:2020:846. See for an extensive analysis: R. Steennot, "Sale of goods made to the consumer's specifications at a trade fair: ab initio no right of withdrawal", *Maastricht Journal of European and Comparative Law* 2021, (406) 410 *et seq.*

989 EU: Art. 2(4) CRD. **Belgium**: Art. I.8, 30° BCEL. **The Netherlands**: This definition is included in the exception itself, see Art. 6:230p, *sub* f., 1° DCC.

990 EC, *Guidance on the interpretation and application of Directive 2011/83/EU of the European Parliament and of the Council on consumer rights*, 29.12.2021, 2021/C 525/01 66.

991 EC, *Guidance on the interpretation and application of Directive 2011/83/EU of the European Parliament and of the Council on consumer rights*, 29.12.2021, 2021/C 525/01 66.

992 www.wearestill.com.

993 See the different modules at: www.wearestill.com/kitchens.

994 G. Straetmans and R. Steennot, *Handboek consumentenbescherming en marktpraktijken*, Antwerp, Intersentia, 2023, with reference to CJEU, Judgment of 14 May 2020, C-208/19, *NK*, ECLI:EU:C:2020:382 (Contract with an architect to design a house. Even if the plans are

of PSS contracts should be classified only as service contracts, or also considered as contracts in respect of goods.[995] From the traditional perspective of a linear economy, one could argue that there is no reason to treat custom-made products differently depending on whether they are sold or rented.[996] Thus, in this interpretation, it would be logical to also apply this exception to use-oriented and result-oriented PSS. From the perspective of a circular economy, on the other hand, one might question whether this exception is necessary for the PSS supplier. After all, the aim of these business models is to be able to reuse products after the contract with a particular PSS user has ended. In any case, this problem will not arise very often, as many circular use-oriented and result-oriented PSS use modules, resulting in this exception not being applicable anyway.

235. Goods sealed for health protection or hygiene reasons – Consumers also have no right of withdrawal in contract for the supply of sealed goods which are not suitable for return due to health protection or hygiene reasons and were unsealed after delivery.[997] However, the CJEU recently gave a narrow interpretation to this exception.[998] It ruled that this exception does not apply to a mattress whose protective cover was removed by the consumer after delivery. Only if a good can definitively no longer be sold after breaking the seal due to reasons of health protection or hygiene, because the very nature of that good makes it impossible or excessively difficult for the company to take the necessary measures allowing for resale without affecting either of those requirements, the exception applies.[999] According the CJEU, a mattress, even though it may have been used, does not become definitively unfit for being used by a third party or for being sold again.[1000] It recalled that one and the same

made available on paper and the contract therefore results in the handing over of a tangible movable good, that handover is ancillary to the main object of the contract which consists in an intellectual performance.).

995 Compare with *supra* no. 205.

996 Compare also with CJEU, Judgment of 21 December 2023, Joined Cases C-38/21, C-47/21 and C-232/21, *VK and Others v BMW Bank GmbH and Others*, ECLI:EU:C:2023:1014, para. 200: "*That interpretation is consistent with the exception of the right of withdrawal provided for in Article 16(c) of Directive 2011/83, concerning 'the supply of goods made to the consumer's specifications or clearly personalised'. It is true that a leasing agreement such as that at issue in the main proceedings in Case C-38/21 concerns not the supply of goods, but the provision of a service. However, the fact remains that that other exception demonstrates the EU legislature's intention to exclude the right of withdrawal in cases where goods have been manufactured or made to the consumer's precise specifications, which is the case where a new vehicle is ordered based on the consumer's precise specifications with a view to use in the context of a leasing agreement*" (own emphasis).

997 **EU**: Art. 16(e) CRD. **Belgium**: Art. VI.53, 5° BCEL (distance contracts) and Art. VI.73, 5° BCEL (off-premises contracts). **The Netherlands**: Art. 6:230p, *sub* f., 3° BCEL.

998 CJEU, Judgment of 27 March 2019, C-681/17, *slewo*, ECLI:EU:C:2019:255. See for an in-depth analysis: A. Michel, "Matelas et vêtements dans le même sac?", *DCCR* 2020, (34) 34–46.

999 CJEU, Judgment of 27 March 2019, C-681/17, *slewo*, ECLI:EU:C:2019:255, para. 40.

1000 CJEU, Judgment of 27 March 2019, C-681/17, *slewo*, ECLI:EU:C:2019:255, para. 42.

mattress is used by successive guests at a hotel, that there is a market for second-hand mattresses and that used mattresses can be deep cleaned.[1001] Given this case law, it seems that this exception will practically never apply to PSS contracts. Even PSS contracts for furniture that is used very intensively (think sofas or a bed) are therefore not covered by this exception.

2.4.5. MODEL CLAUSES REGARDING THE RIGHT OF WITHDRAWAL

236. Model clause on right of withdrawal – If the PSS contract constitutes a distance or off-premises contract, the following model clause can be used to comply with the requirements of the CRD in relation to the right of withdrawal. As discussed above, the starting point of the withdrawal period will differ depending on whether the PSS contract qualifies as a sales contract (physical possession of the product) or as a service contract (conclusion of the contract).

Model clause #1 – Right of withdrawal

- **If the contract has been concluded from a distance or off-premises, [the PSS user] has the right to withdraw with immediate effect from this contract without giving any reason within fourteen days of [the conclusion of the contract/the day on which the consumer or a third party appointed by the PSS user, who is not the carrier, acquires physical possession of the product]. [The PSS user] is to make an unequivocal statement setting out the decision to withdraw. To this end, the consumer may use the following model withdrawal form. It is not mandatory to use this form.**

Model withdrawal form:

To: [name PSS supplier, geographical address PSS supplier and, where applicable fax number and e-mail address of PSS supplier]

I/We (*) hereby give notice that I/We (*) withdraw from my/our (*) contract of sale of the following goods (*)/for the provision of the following service (*),

Ordered on (*)/received on (*)

Name of consumer(s):

[1001] *Ibid.*

Address of consumer(s):

Signature of consumer(s):

Date:

(*) Delete as appropriate

[This withdrawal form can be filled out electronically on [the website/app of the PSS supplier]. If [the PSS user] makes use of this option, [the PSS supplier] immediately sends a written confirmation of receipt.].

237. Model clauses on return of the product after exercising right of withdrawal – The following model clauses concern the consequences of the exercise of the right of withdrawal by the PSS user, more specifically regarding the return of the product. The first model clause is most suited for smaller products that are easy to move. Thus, the model clause stipulates that the PSS user can return the product using parcel shipping (e.g. for small consumer electronics such as a smartphone or a coffee maker), or by dropping it off at a specified location (e.g. for a bicycle). The second model clause deals with the question who bears the costs of returning the product. The contracting parties are allowed to stipulate that the PSS user must pay the costs for returning the good. However, in many cases the PSS supplier will agree to bear these costs for commercial reasons, for example to lower the threshold to enter into a PSS contract.

Alternatively, the contracting parties may agree that the PSS supplier collects the product at a specified location, often the PSS user's premises. The third, fourth and fifth clauses as stipulated below deal with this option. It is most fitting for larger products, such as household appliances or large furniture items. At the same time, this can also serve the interests of the PSS supplier, as it can control the process of returning the product and can ensure its safety. Also here, the contracting parties are free to provide that the PSS user must bear the costs of picking up the product. However, in practice, most PSS suppliers agree to bear these costs, unless a moving lift, crane or similar moving equipment is required.

Model clause #2 – Return of the product after exercising right of withdrawal

- **If [the PSS user] withdraws from the contract, [the PSS user] is responsible for returning the product to [the PSS supplier] [by parcel shipping/at specified location], within fourteen days of the withdrawal.**

- [The PSS user/the PSS supplier] bears the costs of returning the product. These costs are [fixed at reasonable amount/estimated to be maximally [specified amount]]. [[The PSS user] may, at their discretion, choose to return the product using a postal carrier of their own choice. In this case, [the PSS user] bears the costs of the return and the return is at [the PSS user's] own risk.].

- If [the PSS user] withdraws from the contract, [the PSS supplier] shall be solely responsible for arranging [and bearing the costs of] pick-up of the product at [specified location (e.g. the PSS user's premises)]. [The pick-up must be conducted at a time mutually agreed upon between the PSS user and the PSS supplier and must occur within fourteen days of the withdrawal.]

- [The PSS user] bears the costs of picking-up the product. These costs are [fixed at reasonable amount/estimated to be maximally [specified amount]].

- [The PSS supplier] bears the costs of picking-up the product, unless a moving lift, crane or similar moving equipment is required, in which case [the PSS user] is to pay the rental fee of this equipment/is to pay [a reasonable amount].

238. Model clauses on condition of the product upon return – The following model clauses deal with the condition the product must be in upon its return to the PSS supplier. The first model clause provides that the product must be in a reusable condition, including its accessories and original packaging. It confirms that the PSS user may only use and test the product to the extent necessary to establish the nature, characteristics, and functioning of the product. In this sense, the PSS contract may specify what the reasonable use for testing is. For example, it may stipulate that certain testing conditions are to be met (e.g. only testing the product using accompanying samples, only testing the product indoors, etc.).

The second model clause deals with the situation where the product is returned in a non-reusable condition because the PSS user has used the product to a larger extent than necessary to establish the nature, characteristics, and functioning of the product. Where this is the case, this model clause allows the PSS supplier to charge a reasonable amount to compensate for the decrease in value of the product. It is advisable that it is made clear in the PSS contract how this reasonable amount is calculated. In product-oriented PSS, this can be assessed in view of the fitness for resale of the product. In use-oriented and result-oriented PSS, this can be assessed in light of the costs to repair and clean the product so it can be reused by another PSS user. Including such a clause in the PSS contract may have an additional advantage in terms of sustainability. Indeed, an explicit provision informing the PSS user that this reasonable amount may be charged may reduce the risk of moral hazard and result in the PSS user being more cautious in testing the product.

Model clause #3 – Condition of the product upon return

- [The PSS user] is to return the product in a reusable condition, including all accessories[, such as instruction manuals, batteries, keys, etc.] and packaging materials. The opening of the packaging and testing of the product is only permitted to the extent necessary to establish the nature, characteristics, and functioning of the product. [Specifically, the product may only be tested in a specified manner (e.g. the washing machine may only be used with the included laundry detergent sample, the micro-mobility product may only be tested on a clean, paved road, etc.)].
- If the product is returned in a non-reusable condition because [the PSS user] has used the product to a larger extent than necessary to establish the nature, characteristics, and functioning of the product, [the PSS supplier] may charge [a reasonable amount (e.g. a percentage of the total price of the product, the costs of cleaning and repairing the product)] to [the PSS user], to compensate for the decrease in value of the product.

239. Model clauses on refund of payments received by the PSS supplier – If the PSS user decides to withdraw from the contract, the PSS supplier must refund all payments received, including the costs of delivery, without undue delay and in any event not later than fourteen days. The first model clause may be used to comply with the requirements of the CRD and its implementing national legislation in respect with this refund obligations.

If the PSS contract qualifies as a contract for services (i.e. in the case of use-oriented and result-oriented PSS), and the PSS user agrees that the performance of the service (immediately) starts during the withdrawal period, the PSS supplier has the right to retain a proportionate amount of the payments made by the PSS user for services that have already been provided up to the date of withdrawal.[1002] The second model clause provides an example of a clause allowing the PSS supplier to retain such proportionate amount, as well as a checkbox that can be used during the process of concluding the contract so the PSS user-consumer is informed of this right.

Model clause #4 – Refund of the price after exercising right of withdrawal

- Upon receipt of the returned product in its original condition, or upon receiving evidence from [the PSS user] that the product has been sent back, whichever occurs first, [the PSS supplier] shall refund all payments received, including the costs of delivery, without undue delay and in any event not later than fourteen

1002 See *supra* no. 221 *et seq.*

days from the day on which [the PSS supplier] is informed of [the PSS user's] decision to withdraw from the contract. The refund will be made using the same means of payment as used by [the PSS user] for the initial transaction, unless expressly agreed otherwise by [the PSS user]. In any case, [the PSS user] will not incur any fees as a result of such refund.

- If [the PSS user] withdraws from the contract, [the PSS supplier] refunds any payments made by [the PSS supplier] for services that have not yet been provided. [The PSS supplier] is entitled to retain a proportionate amount of the payments made by the consumer for services that have already been provided up to the date of withdrawal. The calculation of this proportionate amount is as follows: [specified calculation based on the total price agreed in the contract].

Before signing the contract, [the PSS user] is to indicate agreement with this right to proportionate payment by checking a checkmark in the designated checkbox:

❒ I hereby request performance of the service contract on/as from [specific date during the withdrawal period] and acknowledge that I will be held to partial payment in case of partial performance.

2.5. INTERPRETATION OF THE PSS CONTRACT

"Wie leest, die interpreteert: het hoeft geen betoog dat van eenzelfde tekst of uitdrukking vaak meerdere lezingen mogelijk zijn. Het is in de wereld van de kunst een bron van vermaak en van betovering; in het rechtsverkeer wordt het een bron van meningsverschillen tussen rechtssubjecten"
– Ludo Cornelis[1003]

2.5.1. CONCEPT OF CONTRACTUAL INTERPRETATION

240. Concept and need of contractual interpretation – If the validity requirements are met and the PSS contract is validly concluded, the next step is interpreting the PSS contract.[1004] Contractual interpretation is the technique

1003 *"Who reads, interprets: needless to say, several readings are often possible of the same text or expression. In the world of art, it is a source of entertainment and of enchantment; in the world of law, it becomes a source of disagreement between legal subjects"* (own translation). See: L. Cornelis, *Algemene theorie van de verbintenis*, Antwerp, Intersentia, 2000, 262.

1004 **Belgium**: I. Claeys and T. Tanghe, *Nieuw Algemeen Contractenrecht*, Antwerp, Intersentia, 2023, 439. **The Netherlands**: C.H. Sieburgh, *Mr. C. Assers Handleiding tot de beoefening van het Nederlands Burgerlijk Recht. 6. Verbintenissenrecht. Deel III. Algemeen overeenkomstenrecht*, Deventer, Wolters Kluwer, 2022, no. 354 and 362.

that allows the reader (e.g. the parties, a court, a lawyer, etc.) to determine the exact meaning and scope of the PSS contract.[1005] The question of interpretation will mainly arise in the event of ambiguity, when the parties have a dispute regarding the interpretation of a particular contractual clause in the PSS contract or the general terms and conditions.

241. INTERPRETATION MEANS ESTABLISHING THE MEANING OF THE DECLARATION OF WILL OF THE PARTIES – Interpretation means determining exactly what the parties agreed in their joint declaration of will and the resulting legal consequences thereof.[1006] In other words, interpretation allows to establish the meaning, content, and scope of the clauses and obligations expressed by the PSS supplier and the PSS user in their contractual declaration of will.

242. READING GUIDE – This section first discusses the principles and rules of contractual interpretation (section 2.5.2). It then examines what role sustainability considerations can play in the interpretation of circular PSS contracts (section 2.5.3). Finally, the possibilities and limits for the parties to include interpretation clauses in the PSS contract are discussed, which are also illustrated with some examples from real-life PSS contracts (section 2.5.4).

2.5.2. PRINCIPLES OF CONTRACTUAL INTERPRETATION

243. CONTRACTUAL INTERPRETATION PRINCIPLES – In Belgium, the contractual interpretation rules are found in Articles 5.64–5.66 of the BCC. These relate to the basic rule that the court must determine the common intent of the parties, including interpretation guidelines to guide the court on how to determine this. In addition to these provisions, the Belgian Court of Cassation had, under the old BCC, also recognised the interpretative effect of the principle of good faith.[1007] However, this principle was not (explicitly) (re)codified in

---

1005 See for a doctoral thesis on contractual interpretation in **Belgium**: J. WAELKENS, *Interpretatie van overeenkomsten en eenzijdige rechtshandelingen*, Antwerp, Intersentia, 2016, 914 p. (Part I) and 270 p. (Part II). For **the Netherlands**, see: A.M.M. HENDRIKX, *Methoden van contractsuitleg: een model voor de uitleg van een overeenkomst (R&P nr. CA26)*, Deventer, Wolters Kluwer, 2023, 480 p.

1006 **Belgium**: W. DE BONDT, "Uitlegging van overeenkomsten naar de geest: mogelijkheden, grenzen en alternatieven", *RW* 1996–97, (1001) 1001–1002. **The Netherlands**: C.H. SIEBURGH, *Mr. C. Assers Handleiding tot de beoefening van het Nederlands Burgerlijk Recht. 6. Verbintenissenrecht. Deel III. Algemeen overeenkomstenrecht*, Deventer, Wolters Kluwer, 2022, no. 362.

1007 Cass. (BE) 23 March 2006, AR C.03.0626.N, *Arr.Cass.* 2006, 688, concl. D. Thijs, *Pas.* 2006, 671, *RW* 2006–07, 874, case note A. VAN OEVELEN. See also Cass. (BE) 5 June 2014, AR C.13.0549.N, *Arr.Cass.* 2014, 1418, concl. A. Van Ingelgem, *RW* 2014–15, 1543, case note, *TBBR* 2016, 281.

the "new" BCC.[1008] Nonetheless, there are good reasons to believe that the interpretative function of the good faith principle will continue to play a role also under the "new" BCC.[1009]

In the Netherlands, the old DCC contained some provisions on the interpretation of contracts in Article 1378 *et seq.* old DCC. However, these have not made their return in the (current) DCC. The reason was that they were considered partly redundant, partly incorrect.[1010] With the sole exception of the *contra proferentem rule* in the Dutch rules on general terms and conditions and unfair terms,[1011] the issue of contractual interpretation is therefore left entirely to case law and legal scholarship.[1012] Also under Dutch law, the basic rule is that the common intent of the parties must be identified. In this regard, inspiration is often drawn from general legal provisions, notably Articles 3:33 and 3:35 DCC (the so-called *wilsvertrouwensleer*[1013]) and Article 6:248 DCC (reasonableness and fairness).[1014]

2.5.2.1. Basic rule: common intent of the parties

244. Belgian law: common intent of the parties – Under Belgian law, the basic rule for interpretation is laid down in Article 5.64 BCC. This provision states that the court must seek out the common intent of the parties to the contract, rather than to adhere to the literal meaning of the words.[1015] This interpretation rule takes precedence over the other interpretation rules of general contract law.[1016] What matters here is the *actual* common will or intent of the parties, which will in principle take precedence over the expressed will if these do not correspond.[1017] In seeking out the actual will of the parties to

---

1008 Compare also with the Explanatory Memorandum of Art. 5.73 BCC (performance in good faith and prohibition of abuse of rights), where reference is only made to the supplementary and mitigating effect of the principle of good faith. Explanatory Memorandum, *Parliamentary Papers* Chamber of Representatives 2020–21, no. 55–1806/1, 83.

1009 See in this sense: I. Claeys and T. Tanghe, *Nieuw Algemeen Contractenrecht*, Antwerp, Intersentia, 2023, 452–453, no. 547.

1010 C.J. Van Zeben, J.W. Du Pon and M.M. Olthof, *Parlementaire geschiedenis van het Nieuwe burgerlijk wetboek. Boek 6: Algemeen gedeelte van het verbintenissenrecht*, Deventer, Kluwer, 1981, 916.

1011 Art. 6:238(2) DCC. See *supra* no. 154 and 159.

1012 A.M.M. Hendrikx, *Methoden van contractsuitleg: een model voor de uitleg van een overeenkomst (R&P nr. CA26)*, Deventer, Wolters Kluwer, 2023, 2.

1013 See: J. Hijma, C.C. van Dam, W.A.M. Van Schendel and W.L. Valk (eds.), *Rechtshandeling en Overeenkomst*, Deventer, Wolters Kluwer, 2022, no. 31 *et seq.*

1014 C.H. Sieburgh, *Mr. C. Assers Handleiding tot de beoefening van het Nederlands Burgerlijk Recht. 6. Verbintenissenrecht. Deel III. Algemeen overeenkomstenrecht*, Deventer, Wolters Kluwer, 2022, no. 354.

1015 Art. 5.64(1) BCC.

1016 I. Claeys and T. Tanghe, *Nieuw Algemeen Contractenrecht*, Antwerp, Intersentia, 2023, 446, no. 539.

1017 A. De Boeck, "Het nieuwe verbintenissenrecht", *NjW* 2022, (610) 617; I. Claeys and T. Tanghe, *Nieuw Algemeen Contractenrecht*, Antwerp, Intersentia, 2023, 446, no. 539.

the PSS contract, the court must place itself *at the time of concluding* the PSS contract,[1018] regardless of what the parties later (when a dispute arises) try to make of their original will.[1019] Moreover, it is the *common* will of the parties that is decisive for interpreting the PSS contract, and not the will of a single (stronger or weaker) party.[1020]

245. Both PSS contract and context used to determine common intent of the parties – In principle, the court is free to use both internal (i.e. the PSS contract itself) and external elements (i.e. the contractual context, such as precontractual drafts, correspondence, advertisements, the PSS supplier's website, etc.) to determine the common intent of the parties to the PSS contract.[1021] However, there is an important limit here. If the PSS contract is set out in writing, the court may not give the contract an interpretation that is manifestly[1022] irreconcilable with the purport of that writing, taking into account its intrinsic elements and the circumstances in which it was established and executed.[1023] In other words, the court must not make the written document "lie".[1024] This means that the court must start from the reading of the PSS contract without making abstraction from it, but it can use external elements from the context of the PSS contract to uncover the common intent of the parties, as long as it does not disregard the legal probative value of the signed written document.[1025]

246. Belgian law: (non-binding) guidelines for finding the common intent of the parties – Article 5.65 of the BCC contains guidelines that can help the court to establish the common intent of the parties to the PSS contract.[1026] According to the Explanatory Memorandum, these are merely guidelines, with no binding nature.[1027] They are subsidiary to the basic rule of

---

1018 See in this sense Art. 5.64(1) BCC, which refers to the common intent the parties "*have had*" (*hebben gehad, a été*).

1019 A. De Boeck and J. Waelkens, "Interpretatie" in *Comm.Bijz.Ov.*, Mechelen, Kluwer, 2016, (181) 203, no. 16.

1020 Cass. (BE) 24 November 1966, *Arr.Cass.* 1967, 399, *Pas.* 1967, I, 386.

1021 C. Borucki, H. Slachmuylders, B. Keirsbilck, D. Gruyaert and E. Terryn, *Model clauses for Product-as-a-Service (PaaS) contracts*, CE Center. Circular Economy Policy Research Center, 2022–23, 29.

1022 Thus, this pertains to a marginal review competence for the court. See Explanatory Memorandum, *Parliamentary Papers* Chamber of Representatives 2020–21, no. 55–1806/1, 76.

1023 Art. 5.64(2) DCC.

1024 Imagery derived from F. Dumon, "De motivering van de vonnissen en arresten en de bewijskracht van de akten", *RW* 1978–79, (258) 276, no. 13, 298, no. 28, 310, no. 37 and 311, no. 39. Also used by the Belgian Court of Cassation in Cass. (BE) 2 March 2021, AR P.20.1234.N, *NC* 2021, 345.

1025 I. Claeys and T. Tanghe, *Nieuw Algemeen Contractenrecht*, Antwerp, Intersentia, 2023, 449.

1026 Explanatory Memorandum, *Parliamentary Papers* Chamber of Representatives, 2020–21, no. 55–1806/1, 77.

1027 *Ibid.*

the common intent of the parties, so they can only be applied if Article 5.64 BCC does not provide a solution.

These guidelines include: (i) if a clause is susceptible of two meanings, it is to be understood it in a meaning that gives it some effect rather than one that gives it no effect; (ii) words that are susceptible of two meanings are to be understood in the meaning that best conforms to the subject matter of the contract; (iii) that what is ambiguous is interpreted in accordance with the usages in the region and industry concerned and in accordance with the usual relations among the parties; (iv) all clauses of a contract are interpreted in light of the others so that each is given the meaning derived from the contract as a whole; (v) however general the terms used, the contract only covers those subject matters in regard of which it appears that the parties intended to enter into a contract; (vi) if the parties have mentioned a case as a way of explaining the obligation, they are not deemed to have intended to limit its extent as regards the unmentioned cases that legally fall under the scope of the obligation; vii) the performance of the contract before a dispute arises is taken into account for the interpretation of the contract.[1028]

247. Dutch law: *Haviltex* standard of interpretation – As mentioned above, the DCC does not contain specific rules on contractual interpretation. Instead, when considering how to interpret a contract, the standard established in the Dutch Supreme Court's *Haviltex* judgment is still the starting point.[1029] The *Haviltex* standard of interpretation provides that the question of how a (*in casu* written[1030]) contract regulates the relationship of the parties cannot be answered solely on the basis of a linguistic interpretation of the provisions of that contract. Instead, the answer to this question is based on the meaning that the parties could reasonably attribute to these provisions in the given circumstances and to what they could reasonably expect from each other in this respect.[1031]

1028 Art. 5.65 BCC. (Translation taken from the work of dr. Christopher Borucki who translated the Belgian Civil Code into English as part of a post-doctoral research project at KU Leuven).

1029 H.N. Schelhaas, *Redelijkheid en billijkheid, Mon.BW nr. A5*, Deventer, Wolters Kluwer, 2017, 31.

1030 However, the Dutch Supreme Court has also recognised the applicability of the *Haviltex* standard of interpretation in contracts concluded orally, see: HR (NL) 4 September 2009, ECLI:NL:HR:2009:BI6319, (*Van Regteren/VGK*), *NJ* 2009/397.

1031 HR (NL) 13 March 1981, ECLI:NL:HR:1981:AG4158, (*Haviltex*), *NJ* 1981/635, case note C.J.H. Brunner, *RvdW* 1981, 43: ("*De vraag hoe in een schriftelijk contract de verhouding van partijen is geregeld en of dit contract een leemte laat die moet worden aangevuld, kan niet worden beantwoord op grond van alleen maar een taalkundige uitleg van de bepalingen van dat contract. Voor de beantwoording van die vraag komt het immers aan op de zin die pp. in de gegeven omstandigheden over en weer redelijkerwijs aan deze bepalingen mochten toekennen en op hetgeen zij te dien aanzien redelijkerwijs van elkaar mochten verwachten. Daarbij kan mede van belang zijn tot welke maatschappelijke kringen partijen behoren en welke rechtskennis van zodanige partijen kan worden verwacht.*").

This is essentially an application of the so-called *wilsvertrouwensleer* laid down in Articles 3:33 and 3:35 DCC.[1032]

248. Dutch law: wording of the PSS contract is not decisive for determining common intent of the parties – It follows from the *Haviltex* standard of interpretation that the court must primarily determine the common (subjective) intent of the parties to the PSS contract. Here, the wording of the PSS contract is never decisive in itself. What matters is what the parties to the PSS contract could reasonably infer about each other's intent and will from each other's statements and conduct in the specific circumstances (i.e. legitimate reliance).[1033] If the parties understood each other well and meant the same thing, incorrect or unclear wording of the PSS contract plays no role.[1034] If, on the other hand, one of the parties claims that it could justifiably construe the PSS contract differently than would seem obvious based on the literal meaning of the words, the court adjudicating the dispute may not only rely on the written contract but most also take into account the specific circumstances (i.e. the contractual context), and the consequences that this party was entitled to draw from them.[1035]

249. Dutch law: relevant circumstances that can be taken into account – The question arises then what these relevant specific circumstances for interpreting a (PSS) contract are. The answer to this question is simple: *all* concrete circumstances can be relevant.[1036] Some (non-exhaustive) examples of such circumstances are: the wording of a contract (term), the structure of the contract, its relationship to previous contracts, the preamble, the nature of the contract, the commercial purpose of the contract, the (circumstances of) the formation of the contract, the performance of the contract, the capacity of the parties (e.g. consumer vs professional, whether or not a lawyer or legal counsel

---

1032 W.L. Valk, "De maatstaf voor uitleg" in H.N. Schelhaas and W.L. Valk (eds.), *Preadviezen Vereniging voor Burgerlijk Recht: Uitleg van rechtshandelingen*, Zutphen, Paris, 2016, (13) 16; J. Hijma, C.C. van Dam, W.A.M. Van Schendel and W.L. Valk (eds.), *Rechtshandeling en Overeenkomst*, Deventer, Wolters Kluwer, 2022, 294, no. 264.

1033 J. Hijma, C.C. van Dam, W.A.M. Van Schendel and W.L. Valk (eds.), *Rechtshandeling en Overeenkomst*, Deventer, Wolters Kluwer, 2022, 294, no. 265.

1034 W.L. Valk, "De maatstaf voor uitleg" in H.N. Schelhaas and W.L. Valk (eds.), *Preadviezen Vereniging voor Burgerlijk Recht: Uitleg van rechtshandelingen*, Zutphen, Paris, 2016, (13) 19.

1035 J. Hijma, C.C. van Dam, W.A.M. Van Schendel and W.L. Valk (eds.), *Rechtshandeling en Overeenkomst*, Deventer, Wolters Kluwer, 2022, 294, no. 265.

1036 Compare with HR (NL) 20 February 2004, ECLI:NL:HR:2004:AO1427, (*DSM/Fox*), *NJ* 2005/493, case note C.E. du Perron, para. 4.5: "*De hiervoor […] weergegeven rechtspraak heeft als gemeenschappelijke grondslag dat bij de uitleg van een schriftelijk contract telkens van beslissende betekenis zijn alle omstandigheden van het concrete geval, gewaardeerd naar hetgeen de maatstaven van redelijkheid en billijkheid meebrengen.*" (Own emphasis).

provided expert assistance during the formation), etc.[1037] Here, it is important to highlight that although the wording and text of the PSS contract are not decisive, they will obviously play an important role.[1038]

250. Dutch law: guidelines for interpretation? – Contrary to Belgian law, the Dutch DCC contains no guidelines for finding the common intent of the parties. However, this does not mean that no interpretation principles are used in legal practice. Indeed, even without an explicit legal basis, interpretation guidelines similar to the Belgian guidelines and partly inspired by the provisions of the old DCC[1039] are sometimes used.[1040] The most notable examples are the principle of interpretation *contra proferentem* and the priority of individually negotiated clauses over clauses in general terms and conditions.[1041] Still, the case law of the Dutch Supreme Court is rather cautious, avoiding to formulate and recognise general interpretation rules, but rather speaking of points of view (*gezichtspunten*) that can be taken into account when applying the *Haviltex* standard of interpretation.[1042]

2.5.2.2. Interpretation in light of principle of good faith/reasonableness and fairness?

251. Belgian law: interpretative function of principle of good faith – It will often prove difficult for the court to find the common intent of the parties at the time of concluding the contract if the parties themselves do not agree on it after a dispute has arisen. In that case, the court will in practice often consider what reasonable parties would have wanted in the same context.[1043] Under

---

1037 See e.g. R.P.J.L. Tjittes, *Uitleg van schriftelijke contracten*, Nijmegen, Ars Aequi, 2009, 32; H.N. Schelhaas, *Redelijkheid en billijkheid, Mon.BW nr. A5*, Deventer, Wolters Kluwer, 2017, 34–35.

1038 See in this sense e.g. HR (NL) 29 October 1999, ECLI:NL:HR:1999:AA1484, (*Ekkersrijt/De Rooy*), *NJ* 1999/823; HR (NL) 5 April 2013, ECLI:NL:HR:2013:BY8101, (*Lundiform/Mexx*), *NJ* 2013/2014. See also: W.L. Valk, "De maatstaf voor uitleg" in H.N. Schelhaas and W.L. Valk (eds.), *Preadviezen Vereniging voor Burgerlijk Recht: Uitleg van rechtshandelingen*, Zutphen, Paris, 2016, (13) 23–24.

1039 Art. 1379 *et seq.* old DCC.

1040 See for an overview e.g. C.H. Sieburgh, *Mr. C. Assers Handleiding tot de beoefening van het Nederlands Burgerlijk Recht. 6. Verbintenissenrecht. Deel III. Algemeen overeenkomstenrecht*, Deventer, Wolters Kluwer, 2022, no. 376 and W.L. Valk, "De maatstaf voor uitleg" in H.N. Schelhaas and W.L. Valk (eds.), *Preadviezen Vereniging voor Burgerlijk Recht: Uitleg van rechtshandelingen*, Zutphen, Paris, 2016, (13) 21–23.

1041 W.L. Valk, "De maatstaf voor uitleg" in H.N. Schelhaas and W.L. Valk (eds.), *Preadviezen Vereniging voor Burgerlijk Recht: Uitleg van rechtshandelingen*, Zutphen, Paris, 2016, (13) 22.

1042 See e.g. HR (NL) 24 September 1993, ECLI:NL:HR:1.993:ZC1069, (*Brackel/UNAT*), *NJ* 1993/760, para. 4.5 (on interpretation *contra proferentem*) and HR (NL) 13 June 2003, ECLI:NL:HR:2003:AF5538, (*Jonker/Heipro c.s.*), *NJ* 2003/506, para. 3.6 (on priority of individually negotiated clauses over clauses in general terms and conditions).

1043 On this subject, see e.g. M.E. Storme, *De invloed van de goede trouw op de kontraktuele schuldvorderingen*, Brussels, Story-Scientia, 1990, 116–126.

the old BCC, the Belgian Court of Cassation recognised this "interpretative function" of the principle of good faith.[1044] It did add, however, that pursuant to such an interpretation, the court may not impose additional obligations that are incompatible with the "nature and scope of the contract"[1045] or the "common intent of the parties."[1046] Consequently, the Court of Cassation maintained the common intent of the parties as the basic principle for interpretation but recognised that if that intent is not clearly expressed, there is room for a good faith interpretation, or, put differently, a reasonable interpretation.[1047] As already mentioned above, the "new" BCC does not contain a provision on the interpretative function of the principle of good faith but sticks to the common intent of the parties (Art. 5.64 and 5.65).[1048] Nevertheless, it is conceivable that courts will in practice continue to resort to reasonable interpretation as a fallback option (either expressly or implicitly).[1049]

252. Dutch law: interpretation in light of reasonableness and fairness – The question of the role of reasonableness and fairness in interpreting a PSS contract also arises under Dutch law. Indeed, like the current BCC, there is no (direct) provision in the DCC confirming the interpretative function of the principle of reasonableness and fairness. Instead, the interpretative function of reasonableness and fairness is based on the *wilsvertrouwensleer* of Articles 3:33 and 3:35 DCC and has been further developed in case law.[1050] As such, there is no consensus in legal doctrine on whether the interpretation of legal acts should be seen as a third function of reasonableness and fairness.[1051]

1044 Cass. (BE) 23 March 2006, AR C.03.0626.N, *Arr.Cass.* 2006, 688, concl. D. Thijs, *Pas.* 2006, 671, *RW* 2006–07, 874, case note A. Van Oevelen: "*The court may interpret the contract between the parties and determine its effects in the light of the obligation to perform in good faith*" (own translation).

1045 Cass. (BE) 23 March 2006, AR C.03.0626.N, *Arr.Cass.* 2006, 688, concl. D. Thijs, *Pas.* 2006, 671, *RW* 2006–07, 874, case note A. Van Oevelen (regarding a mortgage mandate: no additional requirement of prior notification to the client of the intention to establish the mortgage).

1046 Cass. (BE) 5 June 2014, AR C.13.0549.N, *Arr.Cass.* 2014, 1418, concl. A. Van Ingelgem, *RW* 2014–15, 1543, case note, *TBBR* 2016, 281 (no additional obligations regarding the application of an express termination clause).

1047 I. Claeys and T. Tanghe, *Nieuw Algemeen Contractenrecht*, Antwerp, Intersentia, 2023, 450–451.

1048 See also the Explanatory Memorandum of Art. 5.73 BCC (performance in good faith and prohibition of abuse of rights), where reference is only made to the supplementary and mitigating effect of the principle of good faith. Explanatory Memorandum, *Parliamentary Papers* Chamber of Representatives 2020–21, no. 55–1806/1, 83. See critically: I. Claeys and T. Tanghe, *Nieuw Algemeen Contractenrecht*, Antwerp, Intersentia, 2023, 451.

1049 I. Claeys and T. Tanghe, *Nieuw Algemeen Contractenrecht*, Antwerp, Intersentia, 2023, 452.

1050 H.N. Schelhaas, *Redelijkheid en billijkheid, Mon.BW nr. A5*, Deventer, Wolters Kluwer, 2017, 11–12.

1051 Pro: C.H. Sieburgh, *Mr. C. Assers Handleiding tot de beoefening van het Nederlands Burgerlijk Recht. 6. Verbintenissenrecht. Deel I. De verbintenis in het algemeen, eerste gedeelte*, Deventer, Wolters Kluwer, 2020, no. 56; M.W. Hesselink, *De redelijkheid en billijkheid in het*

However, theoretical discussions aside, the Dutch Supreme Court confirmed the role of reasonableness and fairness in its *DSM/Fox* judgment, ruling that: "*[...] in interpreting a written contract, all the circumstances of the concrete case, valued according to what the standards of reasonableness and fairness entail, are of decisive importance in each case*" (own emphasis).[1052] It is therefore rather undisputed[1053] that in determining the statements of the parties and the circumstances of the case, reasonableness and fairness will indeed also play a role.[1054]

2.5.2.3. Specific interpretation rules

253. Belgian law: specific subsidiary (binding) interpretation rules – If, despite the principle of common intent of the parties, the guidelines to find this common intent, and the principle of reasonable interpretation, the court remains uncertain as to what the parties to the PSS contract really intended when entering into the PSS contract, the BCC provides for three subsidiary interpretation rules in Article 5.66 BCC. These rules are to be applied only if doubt concerning the common intent of the parties persists, but are, according to the explanatory memorandum, not mere guidelines but binding interpretation rules.[1055] First, a contract of adhesion is interpreted against the party who has drawn it up.[1056] In most cases, the PSS contract and its general terms and conditions will be drawn up by the PSS supplier, which means that in case of persisting doubt, unclear clauses will be interpreted in favour of the PSS user. Second, exemption clauses are interpreted against the debtor of the obligation.[1057] A third, more general, interpretation rule states that clauses are

---

Europese privaatrecht, Deventer, Wolters Kluwer, 1999, 58 and 131. **Contra**: J. Hijma, C.C. van Dam, W.A.M. Van Schendel and W.L. Valk (eds.), *Rechtshandeling en Overeenkomst*, Deventer, Wolters Kluwer, 2022, 308, no. 277; W.L. Valk, "Verder denken over uitleg van rechtshandelingen: kan het eenvoudiger?", *NJB* 2018/1360 (internet version), (1) 3–4.

1052 HR (NL) 20 February 2004, ECLI:NL:HR:2004:AO1427, (*DSM/Fox*), *NJ* 2005/493, case note C.E. du Perron, para. 4.5: "*[...] bij de uitleg van een schriftelijk contract telkens van beslissende betekenis zijn alle omstandigheden van het concrete geval, gewaardeerd naar hetgeen de maatstaven van redelijkheid en billijkheid meebrengen.*" (Own emphasis).

1053 See W.L. Valk, "Verder denken over uitleg van rechtshandelingen: kan het eenvoudiger?", *NJB* 2018/1360 (internet version), (1) 4, who agrees that adding the statement "reasonableness and fairness may also play a role" to the *Haviltex* standard of interpretation is correct as the principle of reasonableness and fairness plays an important role in the entirety of the general law of obligations and private law. However, he does question the added value of this addition if it does not set out what this role consists of concretely.

1054 C.H. Sieburgh, *Mr. C. Assers Handleiding tot de beoefening van het Nederlands Burgerlijk Recht. 6. Verbintenissenrecht. Deel III. Algemeen overeenkomstenrecht*, Deventer, Wolters Kluwer, 2022, no. 362 and 364.

1055 Explanatory Memorandum, *Parliamentary Papers* Chamber of Representatives 2020–21, no. 55–1806/1, 78.

1056 Art. 5.66(1), 1° BCC.

1057 Art. 5.66(1), 2° BCC.

interpreted against its beneficiary.[1058] Both interpretation rules are applied clause by clause. In most cases (but certainly not always), this means that the clause in the PSS contract will be interpreted in favour of the PSS user. Finally, the second paragraph of this provision makes a "pedagogical" cross-reference[1059] to Article VI.37 BCEL, which states that where there is doubt about the meaning of a clause the interpretation most favourable to the consumer shall prevail.[1060]

254. Belgian law: complex interplay between different interpretation rules – The myriad of different interpretation rules may render it difficult for the court to know whether to apply the basic rule of common intent of the parties, the subsidiary interpretation rules, or to apply a reasonable interpretation.[1061] In practice, however, the court will have a rather wide margin of discretion in interpreting the PSS contract, combining these different interpretation rules, to ultimately fall back on the principle of a reasonable interpretation.

255. Dutch law: no specific interpretation rules besides *interpretatio contra proferentem* in B2C contracts using general terms and conditions – In the absence of general statutory interpretation rules and guidelines, the DCC also has no specific subsidiary interpretation rules.[1062] An exception, however, is Article 6:238(2) DCC, which implements Article 5 UCTD. This provision provides for a specific interpretation rule in B2C contracts using general terms and conditions. As explained above, clauses must be drafted clearly and comprehensibly, and where there is doubt about the meaning of a clause, the interpretation most favourable to the consumer prevails.[1063]

2.5.3. INTERPRETATION OF THE PSS CONTRACT AND SUSTAINABILITY

256. Sustainability considerations and interpretation of the PSS contract – Given the possible role servitisation and PSS can play in the transition towards a more circular and sustainable economy, the question

1058 Art. 5.66(1), 3° BCC.
1059 Explanatory Memorandum, *Parliamentary Papers* Chamber of Representatives 2020–21, no. 55–1806/1, 78.
1060 Art. 5.66(2) BCC. See for a discussion of Art. VI.37 BCEL also *supra* no. 159.
1061 See I. Claeys and T. Tanghe, *Nieuw Algemeen Contractenrecht*, Antwerp, Intersentia, 2023, 458–460 and the examples on indemnification clauses and clauses for the benefit of a third party mentioned there.
1062 C.H. Sieburgh, *Mr. C. Assers Handleiding tot de beoefening van het Nederlands Burgerlijk Recht. 6. Verbintenissenrecht. Deel III. Algemeen overeenkomstenrecht*, Deventer, Wolters Kluwer, 2022, no. 376.
1063 Art. 6:248(2), second sentence DCC. See also *supra* no. 159.

arises what role sustainability considerations can play in the interpretation of circular PSS contracts.[1064] There are roughly three options here. First, the parties may have explicitly acknowledged in the PSS contract or its preambles that they want circular economy and sustainability objectives as part of their contractual relationship. Second, the parties may not have explicitly included that sustainability considerations should be included in their contractual relationship, but this is clear from the contractual context. Third, the question arises what role sustainability considerations can play in a (PSS) contract if their integration is not covered by the will or common intent of the parties.

257. First option: parties explicitly acknowledge to include sustainability considerations in the PSS contract – The first option, which is advisable from a circular economy point of view, is to explicitly acknowledge and include sustainability and circular economy objectives in the PSS contract. This will make it clear to the court that in case of ambiguity of a particular term in the PSS contract or in the general terms and conditions, sustainability objectives were indeed part of the common intent of the parties and the term may be interpreted accordingly. There are several methods to do so.

258. Explicitly recognising circularity and sustainability in recitals – A first method is to include "recitals" in the preambles of the PSS contract (also sometimes called the "whereas clause").[1065] The preambles are the part of the contractual document that precedes the binding provisions. Generally, the language in these preambles is broader and more open than is the case with the actual obligations of the parties (e.g. parties will "acknowledge" or "recognise" certain principles instead of "committing" to something). Their purpose is to set the stage for the main content of the PSS contract by providing a short and concise introduction to the contract, for example on its formation process, its underlying values, the identity, and motives of (one of) the parties, etc. These statements as such do not bind the parties, but they can contribute to the interpretation of the PSS contract.[1066]

In the context of circular PSS business models, it is advisable for the parties to the PSS contract to indicate that sustainability and circularity are integral

---

1064 See on this topic e.g. D. Hug, "Contractual Interpretation and Environmental Sustainability", *CCM Blog* 20 October 2022, https://law.kuleuven.be/ccm/blog/?p=420. This blogpost is a summary of a broader draft working paper which was presented by Dario Hug at a post-doctoral seminar at KU Leuven on 29 June 2022.

1065 See also on this subject: C. Borucki, H. Slachmuylders, B. Keirsbilck, D. Gruyaert and E. Terryn, *Model clauses for Product-as-a-Service (PaaS) contracts*, CE Center. Circular Economy Policy Research Center, 2022–23, 30.

1066 M. Fontaine and F. De Ly, *Drafting International Contracts: An Analysis of Contract Clauses*, Transnational Publishers, Inc., Ardsley, New York, 2006, 59; L. Moris, "Preambules" in E. Terryn, A.-L. Verbeke, H. De Decker, G.-L. Ballon, B. Tilleman and V. Sagaert (eds.), *Gemeenrechtelijke clausules (contractuele clausules)*, Antwerp, Intersentia, 2013, (311) 314.

considerations of their contractual relationship. Circle Economy's Circular service contract template (which was developed for *Fairphone as a Service* in the B2B sector) gives a few useful examples in this regard.[1067] According to this template, the recitals can include, among other things, the background of the circular PSS contract (from a linear to a circular service model), the background of the parties and their interest in the circular economy, and the circular objectives that are being pursued with the circular PSS contract. Examples of such circular objectives could be ensuring the repair, re-use and/or recycling of the product at the end of its technical or economic life or that of any of its components; placing the responsibility for repair, re-use and recycling with the PSS supplier and not passing it on to the PSS user; the fact that the PSS supplier is better suited to know what to do with the product in case of defects or at the end of the technical or economic life of the product; the ambition to reduce the energy consumption of the product over its lifecycle; etc.).[1068] Whenever a clause is ambiguous or unclear, the court can then interpret it in the way that it is most sustainable (in its meaning given to it by the parties).[1069]

259. Definitions of "circularity" and "sustainability" – A second (complementary) method to explicitly include circularity and sustainability into the PSS contract is by defining these terms at the start of the contract, so it is clear what is meant by these concepts.[1070] This can, in turn, give additional guidance to the court when interpreting the PSS contract in a sustainable way. The parties need not limit themselves to just defining sustainability and circularity. These concepts can be further operationalised by also specifying what is meant by the instruments to achieve sustainability and circularity. Think of concepts such as reuse, refurbishing, remanufacturing, repurposing, energy efficiency, carbon footprint, etc.[1071] The parties can either include their

---

1067 Circle Economy, "The Circular Phone, Legal, operational and financial solutions to unlock the potential of the 'Fairphone-as-a-service' model", 31 December 2017, available at www.circle-economy.com/resources/the-circular-phone, 22.

1068 Circle Economy, "The Circular Phone, Legal, operational and financial solutions to unlock the potential of the 'Fairphone-as-a-service' model", 31 December 2017, available at www.circle-economy.com/resources/the-circular-phone, 22.

1069 See also on this subject: C. Borucki, H. Slachmuylders, B. Keirsbilck, D. Gruyaert and E. Terryn, *Model clauses for Product-as-a-Service (PaaS) contracts*, CE Center. Circular Economy Policy Research Center, 2022–23, 30.

1070 See on definition clauses for **Belgian law** e.g. J. Waelkens, "Prioriteitsclausules" in G.-L. Ballon, H. De Decker, V. Sagaert, E. Terryn, B. Tilleman and A.-L. Verbeke (eds.), *Contractuele clausules. Gemeenrechtelijke clausules. Volume I*, Antwerp, Intersentia, 2013, (115) 130–133 and for **Dutch law** e.g. H.N. Schelhaas, "Uitleg en contractvorming" in H.N. Schelhaas and W.L. Valk (eds.), *Preadviezen Vereniging voor Burgerlijk Recht: Uitleg van rechtshandelingen*, Zutphen, Paris, 2016, (171) 183–184.

1071 See for examples of model definitions: C. Borucki, H. Slachmuylders, B. Keirsbilck, D. Gruyaert and E. Terryn, *Model clauses for Product-as-a-Service (PaaS) contracts*, CE Center. Circular Economy Policy Research Center, 2022–23, 36–37.

own definitions or they can refer to external definitions, explicitly giving the external element interpretative force.[1072] These definitions can, for example, be taken from EU legislation or policy documents,[1073] reports by NGOs such as the Ellen MacArthur Foundation, or they can be taken from technical (service) standards, such as those developed by the International Organization for Standardization ("ISO")[1074] or the European Committee for Standardization ("CEN").[1075, 1076]

260. (Binding) circularity guarantees or sustainability clauses – Finally, the parties can also include (binding) circularity guarantees or sustainability clauses in the PSS contract.[1077] This will be discussed more in depth elsewhere (see *infra* section 7.4.3).

261. Analysed PSS contracts do not contain explicit references to circular economy and sustainability – The analysed PSS contracts do not contain any references to sustainability or circular economy in their preambles, nor do they generally contain definitions of concepts related to sustainability or circular economy at the start of the contract. In my view, this is a missed opportunity, as many of these PSS business models are being marketed as being "green", "blue" or "sustainable".

262. Second option: circularity and sustainability not explicitly acknowledged in the PSS contract but referenced in marketing or advertising – The second option is that circularity and sustainability are not explicitly acknowledged or mentioned in the PSS contract or its preambles but are referenced in marketing of advertising of the PSS supplier. In this case, it can be argued that environmental sustainability and circular economy principles can be seen as "implied" or "inferred" contractual terms, i.e. terms that are not expressly formulated by the parties in the contract but nevertheless

1072 C. Borucki, H. Slachmuylders, B. Keirsbilck, D. Gruyaert and E. Terryn, *Model clauses for Product-as-a-Service (PaaS) contracts*, CE Center. Circular Economy Policy Research Center, 2022–23, 30.

1073 See e.g. the definition of "circular economy" in Art. 2(9) Regulation (EU) 2020/852 of the European Parliament and of the Council of 18 June 2020 on the establishment of a framework to facilitate sustainable investment, and amending Regulation (EU) 2019/2088.

1074 See e.g. ISO 14001 on environmental management. Additionally, ISO is also working on a circular economy standard, see: www.iso.org/committee/7203984.html.

1075 See for the work of CEN and CENELEC on standardisation with regard to environment and sustainability: www.cencenelec.eu/areas-of-work/cen-cenelec-topics/environment-and-sustainability/.

1076 See more in-depth on technical standards and standardisation for services *infra* no. 575.

1077 See also more general on sustainability clauses (mainly in the context of B2B global value chains): V. Ulfbeck and O. Hansen, "Sustainability Clauses in an unsustainable Contract Law?", *ERCL* 2020, vol. 16 issue 1, (186) 186–205.

have a guiding influence on their contractual relationship.[1078] We see that the PSS suppliers of the analysed PSS contracts in almost all cases highlight the "sustainable", "circular", "green" or "blue" nature of their products and services, for example on their website and/or in their sustainability policies. In this case, there is no doubt that these statements from marketing and advertisements belong to the contractual context. Additionally, the court can use these statements to determine the tacitly declared common intent of the parties.[1079] Therefore, both under the Belgian interpretation rules and under the Dutch *Haviltex* standard, the court can (and should) take sustainability and circular economy statements into account when interpreting the PSS contract and seeking out the common intent of the parties.

Figure 5. Examples of marketing used by *Bundles* and *Grover* highlighting the sustainable nature of their services[1080]

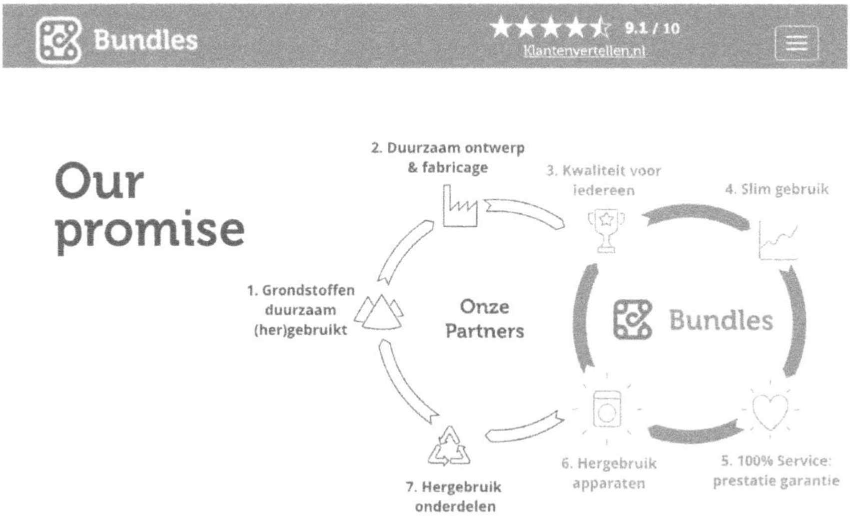

[1078] See D. Hug, "Contractual Interpretation and Environmental Sustainability", *CCM Blog* 20 October 2022, https://law.kuleuven.be/ccm/blog/?p=420; V. Ulfbeck and O. Hansen, "Sustainability Clauses in an unsustainable Contract Law?", *ERCL* 2020, vol. 16, afl. 1, (186) 194; C. Poncibò, "The Contractualisation of Environmental Sustainability", *ERCL* 2016, vol. 12 issue 4, (335) 338.

[1079] D. Hug, "Contractual Interpretation and Environmental Sustainability", *CCM Blog* 20 October 2022, https://law.kuleuven.be/ccm/blog/?p=420; V. Ulfbeck and O. Hansen, "Sustainability Clauses in an unsustainable Contract Law?", *ERCL* 2020, vol. 16, afl. 1, (186) 195.

[1080] Screenshots taken from https://bundles.nl/en/ and www.grover.com/nl-en/g-about/sustainability.

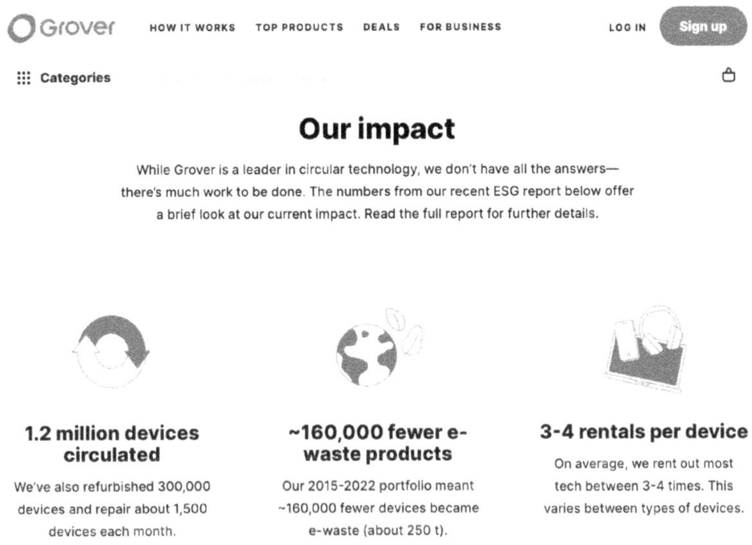

263. Third option: sustainable interpretation even if no mention of sustainability and circularity? – The third possible situation is that the parties to a PSS contract have not acknowledged sustainability in their contract, nor do they make reference to sustainability or circularity in their marketing and advertising. Can the PSS contract then be interpreted in a sustainable way? Or, more fundamentally, what if the parties do not want to consider sustainability in their contractual relationship? Are there cases where the court can engage in sustainable interpretation even against the will of the parties?

Regarding this question, Hug suggests various ways in which environmental sustainability could enter private law through contractual interpretation, even against the will of the parties.[1081] A first option is to insert an "ecological principle" into private law. The new Chinese Civil Code ("CCC") provides a prime example of this. Article 9 of the General Provisions sets out this ecological principle as follows: "*When conducting a civil activity, a person of the civil law shall act in a manner that facilitates conservation of resources and protection of the ecological environment.*"[1082] This general ecological principle is further implemented in various more concrete "green provisions".[1083] In the field of

[1081] See D. Hug, "Contractual Interpretation and Environmental Sustainability", *CCM Blog* 20 October 2022, https://law.kuleuven.be/ccm/blog/?p=420. This blogpost is a summary of a broader draft working paper entitled "Contractual Interpretation and Environmental Sustainability: Towards Sustainable Means and Rules of Interpretation", which was presented by Dario Hug at a post-doctoral seminar at KU Leuven on 29 June 2022.

[1082] M. Zhu, "The ecologization of the Chinese Civil Code", *Pravovedenie* 2020, vol. 64 issue 4, (511) 512.

[1083] J. Ouyang, "Unleashing the Green Principle in the Chinese Civil Code. Embedding Private Law into the Green Transition", *EuCML* 2023, (203) 204.

contract law, Article 509(3) CCC provides that: "*The parties shall avoid wasting the resources, polluting the environment, or damaging the ecology in the course of the contract.*"[1084] OUYANG outlines that, in practice, the ecological principle serves four distinct functions in civil case law. These include a symbolic function (i.e. where it does not impact the interpretation of legal provisions or the outcome of the case but is mentioned to operationalise the concept of just conduct of private persons), an interpretative function (i.e. where it is used to choose the interpretation that is best aligned with sustainability values), a corrective function (i.e. where it is used to correct an outcome or limit the exercise of rights that would be detrimental to the environment) and a gap-filling function (i.e. to fill legislative lacunae).[1085] The introduction of an "ecological principle" could thus impose a legal and primary obligation on each contracting party (similar to the requirement of good faith) to take into account environmental sustainability in the performance of the contract. This could then be taken into account by the courts by means of interpreting or correcting the (content of the) PSS contract.

A second option involves an "eco-literate" understanding of the requirement of a lawful cause as validity requirement of the (PSS) contract.[1086] The cause consists of the determining motives that led each party to enter into the contract insofar as they were or should have been known by the other party.[1087] The cause is unlawful if it is contrary to public order.[1088] The question then arises whether the concept of the lawful cause could permit a social control of contracts, where a distinction is made between contracts "*that are socially worth legal enforcement and those that should not receive legal protection*"?[1089] Or, put differently, could the contract be considered unlawful/contrary to public order if it (or the motives behind it) goes against interests of (environmental) sustainability (e.g. because it does not sufficiently take into account externalities by exploiting the environment or the workers)?[1090]

1084 M. ZHU, "The ecologization of the Chinese Civil Code", *Pravovedenie* 2020, vol. 64, afl. 4, (511) 518–520.

1085 J. OUYANG, "Unleashing the Green Principle in the Chinese Civil Code. Embedding Private Law into the Green Transition", *EuCML* 2023, (203) 205.

1086 See D. HUG, "Contractual Interpretation and Environmental Sustainability", *CCM Blog* 20 October 2022, https://law.kuleuven.be/ccm/blog/?p=420 and D. HUG, "Towards a Sustainable Interpretation of Standard Contract Terms?" in M. SANTOS SILVA, M. CLÉMENT, A. NICOLUSSI, P.S. CODERCH, C. WENDEHORST and F. ZOLL (eds.), *Private Law and Sustainability*, Antwerp, Intersentia, 2024, (28), para. 3.2.2.

1087 Art. 5.53 BCC. See also *supra* no. 82.

1088 Art. 5.56 *juncto* Art. 1.3 BCC.

1089 See in this sense: U. MATTEI and A. QUARTA, *The Turning Point in Private Law – Ecology, Technology and the Commons*, Cheltenham and Northhampton, Edward Edgar Publishing, 2018, 93, 110 and 119 and R. FELTKAMP, A. FRANÇOIS and L. CORNELIS, "Le droit privé au service d'une société durable: rêve ou réalité démocratique?" in A. VAN HOE and G. CROISANT (eds.), *Droit et durabilité / Recht en duurzaamheid*, Antwerp, Intersentia, 2022, (105) 141)-142.

1090 R. FELTKAMP, A. FRANÇOIS and L. CORNELIS, "Le droit privé au service d'une société durable: rêve ou réalité démocratique?" in A. VAN HOE and G. CROISANT (eds.), *Droit et durabilité / Recht en duurzaamheid*, Antwerp, Intersentia, 2022, (105) 126 *et seq.*

A third option how sustainability considerations could, according to Hug, potentially influence the process of contractual interpretation relates to the horizontal effect of human rights and constitutional fundamental rights.[1091] The consequences of dangerous global warming and other environmental issues can clearly compromise a whole range of fundamental rights, such as the right to life, the right to protection of property, and the right to respect for private and family life.[1092, 1093] These fundamental rights are not only relevant in the vertical relationship with the State under whose public authority the holder falls, but can also be observed in the horizontal relationship with other holders of such rights.[1094] As these fundamental rights constitute subjective rights of the contractual parties but also third parties, public authorities (including the courts) should ensure that they are respected, also in a contractual private law dispute between two or more holders.[1095] As a result of this reasoning, the court should then also take into account the extent to which an unsustainable contract may harm human rights, and interfere where appropriate.[1096] Related to this issue, one could also argue that future generations also have a legal right to a clean and healthy environment (intergenerational justice).[1097] Mattei and Quarta argue that this could be conceptualised in the field of contract law by applying the principle of good faith in a way that each individual living today also has an enforceable duty to act for future generations in the same way a trustee would.[1098] The new Belgian property law contains an application of this idea. With regard to common objects (i.e. wild animals, the sea, rivers, the air, etc.), the "new" BCC states that they do not belong to anyone and must be used in the general interest, including the interest of future generations.[1099] On the

---

1091 D. Hug, "Contractual Interpretation and Environmental Sustainability", *CCM Blog* 20 October 2022, https://law.kuleuven.be/ccm/blog/?p=420.

1092 See Art. 2 of the European Convention for Human Rights ("ECHR") (right to life); Art. 1 of Protocol No. 1 ECHR (right to protection of property); Art. 8 ECHR (right to respect for private and family life).

1093 See in this sense HR (NL) 20 December 2019, ECLI:NL:HR:2019:2006, (*Urgenda*), para. 5.2.2 and 5.2.3; R. Feltkamp, A. François and L. Cornelis, "Le droit privé au service d'une société durable: rêve ou réalité démocratique?" in A. Van Hoe and G. Croisant (eds.), *Droit et durabilité / Recht en duurzaamheid*, Antwerp, Intersentia, 2022, (105) 160.

1094 See N. Van Leuven, *Contracteren en mensenrechten, een mensenrechtelijke lezing van het contract*, Antwerp, Intersentia, 2009, 39 *et seq.* and 54 *et seq.*

1095 R. Feltkamp, A. François and L. Cornelis, "Le droit privé au service d'une société durable: rêve ou réalité démocratique?" in A. Van Hoe and G. Croisant (eds.), *Droit et durabilité / Recht en duurzaamheid*, Antwerp, Intersentia, 2022, (105) 155–156.

1096 Compare also with Art. I. – 1:102(2) DCFR, which states that the rules in the DCFR (so, including the rules on contractual interpretation (Book II, Chapter 8, Section 1 DCFR).

1097 C. Poncibò, "The Contractualisation of Environmental Sustainability", *ERCL* 2016, vol. 12, afl. 4, (335) 339 *et seq.* and B.H. Weston, "The Theoretical Foundations of Intergenerational Ecological Justice: An Overview", *Human Rights Quarterly* 2012, (251) 251–266.

1098 U. Mattei and A. Quarta, *The Turning Point in Private Law – Ecology, Technology and the Commons*, Cheltenham and Northhampton, Edward Edgar Publishing, 2018, 150.

1099 Art. 3.43(1) BCC.

other hand, in a recent judgment on the scope of the prohibition on abuse of rights, the Belgian Court of Cassation ruled that when an individual invokes a right against another individual (in this case a claim for cutting a tree, albeit under the old property law[1100]), the court may not assess the proportionality of the exercise of that right in the light of collective interest distinct from their interests.[1101] The question therefore remains to what extent this (criticised)[1102] case law leaves room for an application of the principle of good faith with regard to future generations.[1103]

Finally, HUG also raises the question whether climate policies or circular action plans at the international, supranational or national level can be regarded as context for the interpretation of the contractual relationship, even if this goes against the common intent of the parties.[1104] For example, consider an ambiguous term in a PSS contract where it is unclear which party has to assume the dismantling, take-back or return costs of a still-functioning product at the end of the PSS contract. In this case, if climate policy documents are considered as context, the court could rely on the New Circular Action Plan[1105] to interpret the PSS contract in a way that these costs are borne by the PSS supplier as he will be able to repurpose and remarket the product.[1106]

264. EVALUATION: SUSTAINABLE INTERPRETATION AGAINST WILL OF THE PARTIES REMAINS CONTROVERSIAL AND FUNDAMENTAL QUESTIONS REMAIN – Most of these hypotheses are rather controversial or would require rather paradigmatic changes to our legal system, either by the legislator or by the courts. In many cases, they risk being at odds with the autonomy and freedom of the individual, require a difficult balancing act on which behaviours, business models and contracts may be "sacrificed" on the altar of (environmental) sustainability,[1107] and may in some cases compromise the principle of legal

1100 Art. 37 Rural Code (*Veldwetboek, Code rural*), now Art. 3.134 BCC.

1101 Cass. (BE) 22 October 2021, AR C.20.0265.F, *RW* 2021–22, 1105, case note D. GRUYAERT, *TBH* 2022, 407, case note J. VAN DE VOORDE, *JT* 2022, 76, case note F. GLANSDORFF.

1102 See: D. GRUYAERT, "Het Hof van Cassatie aanvaardt geen duurzaamheidsargumenten bij de beoordeling van rechtsmisbruik" (case note Cass. 22 October 2021), *RW* 2021–22, (1105) 1105–1108.

1103 See for an explorative analysis of the question what effect the general interest can have on the exercise of rights, linked to the prohibition on the *actio popularis*: J. VAN DE VOORDE, "Kan het openbaar belang in rekening worden genomen bij rechtsmisbruik?" (case note Cass. 22 October 2021), *TBH* 2022, (408) 408–426.

1104 D. HUG, "Contractual Interpretation and Environmental Sustainability", *CCM Blog* 20 October 2022, https://law.kuleuven.be/ccm/blog/?p=420.

1105 EC, *A new Circular Economy Action Plan For a cleaner and more competitive Europe*, 11.3.2020, COM(2020) 98 final.

1106 D. HUG, "Contractual Interpretation and Environmental Sustainability: Towards Sustainable Means and Rules of Interpretation", working paper presented at a post-doctoral seminar at KU Leuven on 29 June 2022, 18.

1107 Compare with: H.-W. MICKLITZ, "Squaring the Circle? Reconciling Consumer Law and the Circular Economy", *EuCML* 2019, vol. 6, (229) 235.

certainty for the contracting parties. On the other hand, there is no denying that – at least in legal doctrine and civil society – more and more attention is being paid to the externalities generated by human actions, not only in the field of public law but also in private law.[1108] In this regard, it is unavoidable that we are moving towards a contract law in which environmental interests (at least in part) must be taken into account alongside the interests of the contractual parties. So far, however, the legislator seems rather hesitant or even unwilling to include express obligations integrating collective interests such as environmental sustainability into contract law.[1109] At the same time, courts have also been reluctant so far to accept the greening of consumer law through interpretation.[1110]

Given the controversial nature of these hypotheses and the fundamental questions that remain still unsolved, it seems (for now) better to focus on what is

1108 Compare also with A. Van Hoe, "De (strikt?) privaatrechtelijke dimensie van rechtsmisbruik", *Corporate Finance Lab* 13 November 2021, https://corporatefinancelab.org/2021/11/13/de-strikt-privaatrechtelijke-dimensie-van-rechtsmisbruik/: "*Hiermee wordt ingegaan tegen de onmiskenbare maatschappelijke en juridische tendens om bij de concrete rechtsuitoefening met zoveel mogelijk belangen rekening te houden.*"

1109 See in this sense the critical analysis of Books 1 and 5 of the "new" Belgian Civil Code by Régine Feltkamp and Ludo Cornelis, criticising that the legal text and explanatory memorandum of Books 1 and 5 make no mention of and do not deal with the environmental sustainability challenges that our society faces and will ever increasingly face. L. Cornelis and R. Feltkamp, "Geen duurzame toekomst met verouderde juridische concepten", 16 April 2021, available at www.tijd.be/opinie/algemeen/geen-duurzame-toekomst-met-verouderde-juridische-recepten/10298914.html; L. Cornelis and R. Feltkamp, "Vrijheid, blijheid en na ons de zondvloed. Kunnen we echt niet beter?", *Juristenkrant* 2021, (16) 16–17; L. Cornelis and R. Feltkamp, "Editoriaal: Boeken 1 en 5 van het nieuwe BW: meer van hetzelfde voor rechtspersonen en vennootschappen?", *TRV* 2021, (535) 535–536; L. Cornelis and R. Feltkamp, "Boek 1 Nieuw Burgerlijk Wetboek (algemeen deel): zoektocht naar oplossingen voor een privaatrecht op maat van de hedendaagse maatschappelijke uitdagingen", 2021, available at https://corporatefinancelab.org/2021/05/17/van-geen-kwaad-bewust/ also published on www.lawbackontrack.org/publications/boek-1-nieuw-burgerlijk-wetboek-algemeen-deel-zoektocht-naar-oplossingen-voor-een-privaatrecht-op-maat-van-de-hedenda agse-maatschappelijke-uitdagingen; R. Feltkamp, "Code rood voor het privaatrecht" in E. Alofs, E. Goossens, J. Van Doninck and K. Byttebier (eds.), *Redelijk eigenzinnig: liber amicorum Eric Brewaeys, Philippe Colle, Erna Guldix en Bruno Maes*, Herentals, Knops publishing, 2022, (395) 395–408. See also the discussion in Parliamentary Justice Committee in June 2021 for Books 1 and 5 of the new Belgian Civil Code: www.dekamer.be/media/index.html?language=nl&sid=55U1904#video (from 1h15').

1110 H.-W. Micklitz, "Squaring the Circle? Reconciling Consumer Law and the Circular Economy", *EuCML* 2019, vol. 6, (229) 237. See e.g. CJEU, Judgment of 27 March 2019, C-681/17, *slewo*, ECLI:EU:C:2019:255 (consumer can still exercise its right of withdrawal in a distance contract even if the protective seal of a mattress was removed after delivery) and CJEU, Judgment of 5 May 2022, C-179/21, *Victorinox*, ECLI:EU:C:2022:353 (on the information requirement in the CRD for commercial guarantees: seller must provide information about commercial guarantee only if consumer has a legitimate interest in information about that guarantee to decide whether to enter into a contract with the seller), where only a balancing exercise between the interests of consumers and businesses was done, without considering environmental sustainability. Compare also with the national case law mentioned *infra* in fn. 1114 and 2499.

in front of us. After all, in the context of PSS contracts, the tools for sustainable interpretation of the contract are already there, as was illustrated above.[1111] The low-hanging fruit, therefore, is to provide PSS suppliers (and by extension consumers) with the tools to effectively include sustainability and circularity considerations in their contract, which can then be taken into account by the courts when interpreting the contract.

265. CONFLICT BETWEEN SUSTAINABLE INTERPRETATION AND OTHER INTERPRETATION RULES? – Consider an ambiguously worded clause in the PSS contract regarding the replacement or "swapping" of the product in case of a defect where it is not entirely clear whether this replacement obligation relates to the whole product or only the broken part of the product.[1112] In this case, there is a risk that a sustainable interpretation of this contract term conflicts with other interpretation rules, in particular the interpretation *contra proferentem* rule arising from the UCTD.[1113] After all, for the PSS user, getting a completely new product is usually seen as the most favourable interpretation.[1114] For example, if the camera module of a *Fairphone Easy* smartphone is broken and the screen has some minor scratches, most people will agree that the consumer is better off with a completely new smartphone (with unscratched screen) than with a smartphone with only the replaced camera module. For the environment, on the other hand, the most desirable option is obviously to only replace the camera module as this extends the lifetime of the smartphone.

Is there then still a possibility of interpreting the PSS contract in the most sustainable way? *In dubio pro natura*? A first possible argument is that, from a sustainability perspective, the option that maximises the product's lifetime and protects (at least indirectly) the PSS user's right to a clean and healthy environment does benefit the consumer's interests.[1115] This is especially the

---

1111 See *supra* no. 257–262.

1112 Example inspired by C.M.D.S. Pavillon, "Herijking van consumentencontractenrecht: duurzaamheid als nieuw ijkpunt?" in C.M.D.S. Pavillon and W.H. van Boom (eds.), *Preadviezen Vereniging voor Burgerlijk Recht: Privaatrechtelijke bescherming herijkt*, Zutphen, Paris, 2021, (11) 77.

1113 EU: Art. 5(2) UCTD. **Belgium**: Art. 5.66(2) BCC *juncto* Art. VI.37, §2 BCEL. Compare also with Art. 5.66(1), 1° BCC. **The Netherlands**: Art. 6:238(2) DCC. See also *supra* no. 159.

1114 Ct. Amsterdam (NL) 18 April 2017, ECLI:NL:RBAMS:2017:2519, (*Apple Retail Netherlands*), *AR* 2017/2104; Ct. Amsterdam (NL) 8 July 2016, ECLI:NL:RBAMS:2016:4197, (*Apple Retail Netherlands*), *TvC* 2017, 183, case note V. Mak; Ct. Glostrup (DK) 9 December 2016, Case number BS 10E-3689/2014 (all three deciding that Apple must provide the consumer with a new product and not a refurbished one to replace a defective product). See: V. Mak and E. Terryn, "Circular Economy and Consumer Protection: The Consumer as a Citizen and the Limits of Empowerment Through Consumer Law", *Journal of Consumer Policy* 2020, vol. 43, (227) 236.

1115 See in this sense: C.M.D.S. Pavillon, "Herijking van consumentencontractenrecht: duurzaamheid als nieuw ijkpunt?" in C.M.D.S. Pavillon and W.H. van Boom (eds.), *Preadviezen Vereniging voor Burgerlijk Recht: Privaatrechtelijke bescherming herijkt*, Zutphen, Paris, 2021, (11) 77.

case if sufficient guarantees are given that the PSS user's right of use is not unnecessarily interrupted (e.g. by providing a replacement smartphone during the repair process or by circular design where the consumer can quickly and easily replace the camera module himself). Alternatively, one could argue that the *contra proferentem* rule does not even apply, either because each meaning of the clause has approximately equal advantages and disadvantages for each party (namely, the burden on the environment), or because in view of the mutual sustainability interest, there is no doubt about the (sustainable) meaning of the term.[1116]

2.5.4. INTERPRETATION CLAUSES

266. Interpretation clauses – The Belgian general contract law rules on contractual interpretation are not mandatory law.[1117] As a result, the PSS contract may contain different interpretation rules, for example by choosing or excluding a certain interpretation or certain interpretation methods.[1118] Also under Dutch law, interpretation clauses are in principle valid.[1119] This was recognised in a recent judgment of the Dutch Supreme Court, in which it ruled that a clause according to which the literal text prevailed (in deviation from the *Haviltex* standard) and the contract therefore had to be interpreted "exclusively grammatically" was valid.[1120] However, the possibility to contractually influence the contractual interpretation rules is not unlimited. Both under Belgian and Dutch law, the parties may not completely exclude interpretation in the light of the principle of good faith/reasonableness and fairness.[1121]

1116 See D. Hug, "Towards a Sustainable Interpretation of Standard Contract Terms?" in M. Santos Silva, M. Clément, A. Nicolussi, P.S. Coderch, C. Wendehorst and F. Zoll (eds.), *Private Law and Sustainability*, Antwerp, Intersentia, 2024, (28), para. 2.2 and C.M.D.S. Pavillon, "Herijking van consumentencontractenrecht: duurzaamheid als nieuw ijkpunt?" in C.M.D.S. Pavillon and W.H. van Boom (eds.), *Preadviezen Vereniging voor Burgerlijk Recht: Privaatrechtelijke bescherming herijkt*, Zutphen, Paris, 2021, (11) 77.

1117 See Art. 5.3(2) BCC.

1118 W. Buelens, "Interpretatie en kwalificatie van het contract" in T. Vansweevelt and B. Weyts (eds.), *Handboek Verbintenissenrecht (tweede editie)*, Antwerp, Intersentia, 2023, (295) 333.

1119 H.N. Schelhaas, "Uitleg en contractvorming" in H.N. Schelhaas and W.L. Valk (eds.), *Preadviezen Vereniging voor Burgerlijk Recht: Uitleg van rechtshandelingen*, Zutphen, Paris, 2016, (171) 174.

1120 HR (NL) 25 August 2023, ECLI:NL:HR:2023:1131, *NJB* 2023/1051, *RvdW* 2023/857.

1121 **Belgium**: W. Buelens, "Interpretatie en kwalificatie van het contract" in T. Vansweevelt and B. Weyts (eds.), *Handboek Verbintenissenrecht (tweede editie)*, Antwerp, Intersentia, 2023, (295) 333. **The Netherlands**: H.N. Schelhaas, "Uitleg en contractvorming" in H.N. Schelhaas and W.L. Valk (eds.), *Preadviezen Vereniging voor Burgerlijk Recht: Uitleg van rechtshandelingen*, Zutphen, Paris, 2016, (171) 173, with reference to C.H. Sieburgh, *Mr. C. Assers Handleiding tot de beoefening van het Nederlands Burgerlijk Recht. 6.*

267. Content of and limits to interpretation clauses – Interpretation clauses can take various forms.[1122] For example, the parties may stipulate that the PSS contract should be interpreted according to the actual will of the parties, according to the objective or reasonable will of the parties, or that the literal meaning of the text will prevail. The parties may also stipulate a hierarchy between the internal elements (e.g. the relationship between the actual provisions and the annexes of the PSS contract, between the framework agreement and the implementing contracts,[1123] or between the general and special terms and conditions) or the external elements that can play a role in the interpretation process.[1124] In addition, the parties to the PSS contract may also include an interpretation clause stating that the "most sustainable interpretation" will prevail.

Interestingly, most of the analysed PSS contracts do not contain any interpretation clauses. The terms and conditions of *HP Instant Ink* form the exception. These terms and conditions contain an example of a clause stating that, in case of doubt, the contract should not be interpreted strictly in favour of the PSS user or against the PSS supplier.

> Terms and conditions HP Instant Ink – Art. 11(h.) Miscellaneous: "[...] This Agreement will be interpreted without application of any strict construction in favour of You or against HP."

Is this clause valid or are there limits to the contractual freedom for drafting interpretation clauses? First, the Belgian blacklist and the UCTD Annex both list terms that (i) give the right to the PSS supplier to unilaterally decide whether the service is in conformity with the contract and (ii) that give the PSS supplier the exclusive right to interpret a clause in the PSS contract.[1125] Under Dutch law, clauses regarding the self-assessment of non-performance are also blacklisted.[1126] Regarding the exclusive right to interpret a clause, Jongeneel argues that this is contrary to the Dutch interpretation rules and should therefore be disregarded.[1127] In any case, the inclusion of this term in the UCTD Annex

---

Verbintenissenrecht. Deel III. Algemeen overeenkomstenrecht, Deventer, Wolters Kluwer, 2022, no. 380.

1122 See e.g. M. Fontaine and F. De Ly, *Drafting International Contracts: An Analysis of Contract Clauses*, Transnational Publishers, Inc., Ardsley, New York, 2006, 105 *et seq.* and F. Walschot, "Interpretatieclausules" in CBR (ed.), *Nuttige tips voor goede contracten*, Mechelen, Kluwer, 2004, (22) 22–25.

1123 Dott e.g. makes use of a framework agreement ("App Agreement"). According to Dott's general terms and conditions, every time the user makes use of an e-scooter, a separate "Individual Rental Agreement" is concluded.

1124 I. Claeys and T. Tanghe, *Nieuw Algemeen Contractenrecht*, Antwerp, Intersentia, 2023, 462.

1125 EU: Art. 1, *sub* m. UCTD Annex. **Belgium**: Art. VI.83, 6° BCEL.

1126 Art. 6:236, *sub* d. DCC.

1127 R.H.C. Jongeneel, "De blauwe lijst" in B. Wessels and R.H.C. Jongeneel (eds.), *Algemene voorwaarden*, Deventer, Wolters Kluwer, 2017, (355) 382, para. 13.7.

means that it should also be taken into account when assessing unfairness under the Dutch general test.[1128] If we apply this to the clause of *HP Instant Ink*, it is clear that it does not fall under the description of the (under Belgian law black) listed term, as it does not give a unilateral or exclusive right to the PSS supplier to interpret the contract. However, such clause does in B2C contracts conflict with the *interpretatio contra proferentem* rule, which is mandatory law and thus cannot be deviated from.[1129, 1130]

268. Contractual interpretation and entire agreement clauses – In practice, PSS suppliers also often include an entire agreement clause (*vierhoekenbeding, clause d'intégralité de l'accord*) into their general terms and conditions.[1131] Entire agreement clauses typically provide that the document contains the entire contract and that the parties are not bound by external elements such as pre-contractual documents or correspondence, pre- or post-contractual statements and behaviours, etc. In other words, only the provisions of the document itself (in Dutch: "between the four corners") bind the parties to the PSS contract and no obligations can be claimed from external documents.[1132] Examples can be found in the general terms and conditions of *Dressr, HP Instant Ink* and *Dott*. Additionally, the two B2B model contracts (by Agoria and Circle Economy) also contain a model clause for an entire agreement clause.[1133]

> Terms and Conditions Dressr – Art. 25 (Changes to our terms): "[…] The terms of Service constitute the entire agreement between you and Dressr regarding the use of the Website and any provision of Services by Dressr."
>
> Terms and conditions HP Instant Ink – Art. 11(g.) Entire Agreement; Order of Precedence: "The terms of this Agreement, together with the Service Description Terms and other HP terms expressly referenced in this Agreement or applicable to the Service or Service Plan that You have agreed to, constitute the entire understanding between You and HP relating to the service and will supersede any previous communication, representation or agreement whether oral or written. […]"
>
> Terms and conditions Dott – Art 13(6) "These Terms are the entire agreement relating to its subject matter and supersede all prior or contemporaneous oral or

1128 Art. 6:233, *sub* a. DCC.
1129 EU: Art. 5(2) UCTD. **Belgium**: Art. VI.37, §2 BCEL. **The Netherlands**: Art. 6:238(2) DCC.
1130 J. Waelkens, "De interpretatieregel in het voordeel van de consument", *TPR* 2014, (989) 1012.
1131 See on entire agreement clauses e.g. W. Vaassen, "Entire Agreement Clauses" in G.-L. Ballon, H. De Decker, V. Sagaert, E. Terryn, B. Tilleman and A.-L. Verbeke (eds.), *Contractuele clausules. Gemeenrechtelijke clausules. Volume I*, Antwerp, Intersentia, 2013, (71) 71–113; F. Walschot, "Vierhoekenclausule" in CBR (ed.), *Nuttige tips voor goede contracten*, Mechelen, Kluwer, 2004, (151) 151–154.
1132 I. Claeys and T. Tanghe, *Nieuw Algemeen Contractenrecht*, Antwerp, Intersentia, 2023, 462.
1133 See Art. 17 Agoria Efficiency-as-a-Service model contract and Art. 15.3 Circle Economy Circular service contract template.

written communications, understandings, and proposals of you and us relating to the subject matter of these Terms."

An entire agreement clause thus has as its effect that no obligations can arise out of any documents or statements external to (the general conditions of) the PSS contract. However, this does not necessarily mean that these external elements cannot be relevant for the interpretation of the PSS contract. Unless the PSS contract also explicitly provides that external elements (e.g. statements on sustainability in communications, company policies, marketing, advertisements, etc.) cannot be used for the interpretation of the PSS contract,[1134] the court can still rely on them for determining the scope of the obligations of the parties.[1135] In the example clauses cited above, the PSS suppliers of the analysed contracts did not include such an explicit provision in the contract. Even if the PSS supplier were to explicitly exclude the interpretative value of the elements external to the contractual document or general terms and conditions, this could – depending on the specific circumstances – potentially be challenged based on the prohibition on abuse of rights[1136] (i.e. contrary to good faith/reasonableness and fairness) or the general test of the UCTD and its implementing provisions.[1137]

1134 E.g. by adding the following words to the clause: "*previous agreements, oral statements and other documents may not be used to interpret this contract.*"

1135 **Belgium**: W. Buelens, "Interpretatie en kwalificatie van het contract" in T. Vansweevelt and B. Weyts (eds.), *Handboek Verbintenissenrecht (tweede editie)*, Antwerp, Intersentia, 2023, (295) 333; W. Vaassen, "Entire Agreement Clauses" in G.-L. Ballon, H. De Decker, V. Sagaert, E. Terryn, B. Tilleman and A.-L. Verbeke (eds.), *Contractuele clausules. Gemeenrechtelijke clausules. Volume I*, Antwerp, Intersentia, 2013, (71) 77. **The Netherlands**: H.N. Schelhaas, "Uitleg en contractvorming" in H.N. Schelhaas and W.L. Valk (eds.), *Preadviezen Vereniging voor Burgerlijk Recht: Uitleg van rechtshandelingen*, Zutphen, Paris, 2016, (171) 176–179. Compare also with Art. II. – 2:105 DCFR *("(1) If a contract document contains an individually negotiated clause stating that the document embodies all the terms of the contract (a merger clause), any prior statements, undertakings or agreements which are not embodied in the document do not form part of the contract. (2) If the merger clause is not individually negotiated it establishes only a presumption that the parties intended that their prior statements, undertakings, or agreements were not to form part of the contract. This rule may not be excluded or restricted. (3) The parties' prior statements may be used to interpret the contract. This rule may not be excluded or restricted except by an individually negotiated clause. (4) […]"*) and Art. 2.1.17 Unidroit Principles 2016 ("*A contract in writing which contains a clause indicating that the writing completely embodies the terms on which the parties agreed cannot be contradicted or supplemented by evidence of prior statements or agreements. However, such statements or agreements may be used to interpret the writing*") [both with own emphasis].

1136 See in this sense: I. Claeys and T. Tanghe, *Nieuw Algemeen Contractenrecht*, Antwerp, Intersentia, 2023, 463.

1137 EU: Art. 3 UCTD. **Belgium**: Art. I.8, 22° BCEL. **The Netherlands**: Art. 6:233, *sub* a. DCC.

2.6. LIABILITY FOR BREACH OF THE PSS CONTRACT

"Ubi jus ibi remedium"
- Latin maxim[1138]

2.6.1. BREACH OF CONTRACT

269. CONTRACTUAL LIABILITY PRESUPPOSES BREACH OF CONTRACT – When a PSS contract has been validly concluded, the obligations arising from it must be fulfilled. The question of contractual liability arises if one of the parties to the PSS contract fails to fulfil its contractual obligations. For example, the PSS user does not pay the price, the PSS supplier takes too long to repair or replace the product in case of defects, the additional digital services are not available, a faulty washing machine "as a service" causes damage to the PSS user's home, etc.

The party that fails to fulfil its contractual obligations will be contractually liable if this non-performance is qualified as a breach of contract (*wanprestatie,*[1139] *inexécution fautive*). For this, it is required that the non-performance (*niet-nakoming, inexécution*) is due to the fault of the debtor or of a person for whom he is responsible or of an object which he uses in the performance of his contractual obligations.[1140] In other words, a breach of contract is an imputable non-performance of a due and payable contractual obligation.[1141] If, on the other hand, the non-performance of the contractual obligation is not imputable to the debtor but is due to *force majeure*, there is no breach of contract and the creditor cannot invoke the remedies for contractual liability.[1142, 1143]

1138 Latin for *"where there is a right there is a legal remedy."* This legal maxim articulates the principle that where someone's (subjective) legal right is frustrated, denied or destroyed, the law provides a remedy to protect it, demand performance or award damages in compensation. See: J. Law and E.A. Martin, "Ubi jus ibi remedium" in *Oxford Reference: A Dictonary of Law (7 ed.)*, Oxford, Oxford University Press, 2014, available online at: www.oxfordreference.com/display/10.1093/oi/authority.20110803110448446#.

1139 In Belgium, the Dutch term *contractbreuk* is also used to describe a breach of contract.

1140 **Belgium**: S. Stijns, *Verbintenissenrecht*, Boek 1, Bruges, Die Keure, 2022, 185.

1141 **Belgium**: I. Claeys and T. Tanghe, *Nieuw Algemeen Contractenrecht*, Antwerp, Intersentia, 2023, 633. **The Netherlands**: Art. 6:74 (1) DCC; C.H. Sieburgh, *Mr. C. Assers Handleiding tot de beoefening van het Nederlands Burgerlijk Recht. 6. Verbintenissenrecht. Deel I. De verbintenis in het algemeen, eerste gedeelte*, Deventer, Wolters Kluwer, 2020, no. 332; G.T. de Jong, H.B. Krans and M.H. Wissink, *Verbintenissenrecht algemeen (Studiereeks Burgerlijk Recht, deel 4)*, Deventer, Wolters Kluwer, 2018, 109–111 and 154.

1142 See *infra* section 2.6.4.

1143 **Belgium**: I. Claeys and T. Tanghe, *Nieuw Algemeen Contractenrecht*, Antwerp, Intersentia, 2023, 863. **The Netherlands**: Art. 6:75 DCC; G.T. de Jong, H.B. Krans and M.H. Wissink, *Verbintenissenrecht algemeen (Studiereeks Burgerlijk Recht, deel 4)*, Deventer, Wolters Kluwer, 2018, 154. **DCFR**: Art. III. – 3:104 DCFR.

2.6.2. NATURE OF THE OBLIGATIONS

270. Non-performance depends on content of the contract and nature of the obligation – The non-performance is determined in relation to the obligations stipulated in a valid PSS contract. Therefore, the content and scope of the contractual obligations must first be determined before it can be concluded that there is a breach of the PSS contract.[1144] In the event of a dispute, the judge will determine the actual scope of the obligation, taking into account what the parties have explicitly or implicitly agreed. If necessary, the gaps in the contractual arrangements will be filled by law, custom, fairness and/or good faith.[1145] Here, the nature of the obligation – whether it is an obligation of means or an obligation of result or guarantee – plays a major role in determining whether there is a breach of contract.[1146]

271. Distinction between obligation of means, obligation of result and obligation of guarantee – In general, three types of obligations are distinguished when determining a breach of contract: an obligation of means (*middelenverbintenis/inspanningsverbintenis, obligation de moyens*), an obligation of result (*resultaatsverbintenis, obligation de résultat*) and an obligation of guarantee (*garantieverbintenis, obligation de garantie*).[1147]

272. Obligation of means – In the case of an **obligation of means**, there is a breach of contract only if the PSS supplier or PSS user has not made the necessary

1144 **Belgium**: P. Brulez, "Over de draagwijdte van contractuele verbintenissen: garantie-, resultaats-, middelenverbintenissen" in K. Swinnen and M. Mathieu (eds.), *De contractuele fout*, Bruges, Die Keure, 2019, (1) 1; S. Stijns, *Verbintenissenrecht*, Boek 1, Bruges, Die Keure, 2022, 185.

1145 **Belgium**: Art. 5.71(1) BCC (Formerly Art. 1135 and Art. 1160 old BCC). I. Claeys and T. Tanghe, *Nieuw Algemeen Contractenrecht*, Antwerp, Intersentia, 2023, 481–492. **The Netherlands**: See Art. 6:248 (1) DCC; C.H. Sieburgh, *Mr. C. Assers Handleiding tot de beoefening van het Nederlands Burgerlijk Recht. 6. Verbintenissenrecht. Deel I. De verbintenis in het algemeen, eerste gedeelte*, Deventer, Wolters Kluwer, 2020, no. 55–59.

1146 **Belgium**: P. Wéry, *Droit des obligations. Volume 1. Theorie générale du contrat*, Brussels, Larcier, 2021, 557, no. 546.

1147 **Belgium**: I. Claeys and T. Tanghe, *Nieuw Algemeen Contractenrecht*, Antwerp, Intersentia, 2023, 637; P. Brulez, "Over de draagwijdte van contractuele verbintenissen: garantie-, resultaats-, middelenverbintenissen" in K. Swinnen and M. Mathieu (eds.), *De contractuele fout*, Bruges, Die Keure, 2019, (1) 1–2. **The Netherlands**: C.H. Sieburgh, *Mr. C. Assers Handleiding tot de beoefening van het Nederlands Burgerlijk Recht. 6. Verbintenissenrecht. Deel I. De verbintenis in het algemeen, eerste gedeelte*, Deventer, Wolters Kluwer, 2020, no. 192; G.T. de Jong, *Niet-nakoming van verbintenissen (Mon. BW B22)*, Deventer, Wolters Kluwer, 2006, 7; T.F.E. Tjong Tjin Tai, "Toerekenbare niet-nakoming en de zorg van een goed schuldenaar", *WPNR* 2004, vol. 6574, (285) 286–287; J.D.A. Den Tonkelaar, *Resultaatsverbintenissen en inspanningsverbintenissen*, Zwolle, Tjeenk Willink, 1982, 64 *et seq.*; A. Pitlo and M.F.H.J. Bolweg, *Het Nederlands Burgerlijk Wetboek, deel 3. Algemeen deel van het verbintenissenrecht*, Arnhem, Gouda Quint, 1979, 83 *et seq.*; L.C. Hofmann and S.N. Van Opstall, *Het Nederlands Verbintenissenrecht. Deel 1, eerste gedeelte*, Groningen, H.D. Tjeenk Willink, 1976, 70 *et seq.*

efforts or has not used the necessary means to achieve the desired result. The result itself is not promised.[1148] This means that the creditor will have to prove that the debtor did not act as a prudent and reasonable person would have acted in the same circumstances when fulfilling this contractual obligation.[1149] In other words, the creditor must prove a contractual fault of his counterparty by using the objective and abstract *bonus pater familias* criterion.[1150]

273. Obligation of result – If an obligation of the PSS supplier or PSS user is considered an **obligation of result**, there is a breach of contract if the promised result was not achieved.[1151] If this result is not achieved, he will be liable, even if he has acted carefully and made efforts to achieve the promised result.[1152] Thus, the creditor does not have to prove any negligence on the part of the debtor but only that the promised result has not been achieved.[1153] The debtor can only

1148 **Belgium**: A. Van Oevelen, "Kwaliteitsstandaarden bij de verkoop van goederen en de levering van diensten" in I. Claeys, W. Delva and R. Steennot (eds.), *Aansprakelijkheid, veiligheid en kwaliteit*, Ghent, Kluwer, 2015, (1) 3.

1149 **Belgium**: Art. 5:72 (1) BCC. This criterion used to be derived from Art. 1137 old BCC. P. Wéry, *Droit des obligations. Volume 1. Theorie générale du contrat*, Brussels, Larcier, 2021, 548, no. 548; L. Cornelis, *Algemene theorie van de verbintenis*, Antwerp, Intersentia, 2000, 179; R. Kruithof, H. Bocken, F. De Ly and B. De Temmerman, "Verbintenissenrecht (1981–1992). Overzicht van rechtspraak", *TPR* 1994, (171) 496; R. Kruithof, "Overzicht van rechtspraak (1974–1980). Verbintenissen", *TPR* 1983, (495) 616, no. 110. **The Netherlands**: C.H. Sieburgh, *Mr. C. Assers Handleiding tot de beoefening van het Nederlands Burgerlijk Recht. 6. Verbintenissenrecht. Deel I. De verbintenis in het algemeen, eerste gedeelte*, Deventer, Wolters Kluwer, 2020, no. 192.

1150 **Belgium**: I. Claeys and T. Tanghe, *Nieuw Algemeen Contractenrecht*, Antwerp, Intersentia, 2023, 639; P. Brulez, "Over de draagwijdte van contractuele verbintenissen: garantie-, resultaats-, middelenverbintenissen" in K. Swinnen and M. Mathieu (eds.), *De contractuele fout*, Bruges, Die Keure, 2019, (1) 3–4; S. Stijns, *Verbintenissenrecht*, Boek 1, Bruges, Die Keure, 2022, 186–187.

1151 **Belgium**: W. van Gerven and A. Van Oevelen, *Verbintenissenrecht*, Leuven, Acco, 2021, 34 and 171; S. Stijns, *Verbintenissenrecht*, Boek 1, Bruges, Die Keure, 2022, 10. **The Netherlands**: T.F.E. Tjong Tjin Tai, "Toerekenbare niet-nakoming en de zorg van een goed schuldenaar", *WPNR* 2004, vol. 6574, (285) 286.

1152 **Belgium**: Art. 5.72(2) BCC (formerly Art. 1147 old BCC). I. Claeys and T. Tanghe, *Nieuw Algemeen Contractenrecht*, Antwerp, Intersentia, 2023, 640; P. Brulez, "Over de draagwijdte van contractuele verbintenissen: garantie-, resultaats-, middelenverbintenissen" in K. Swinnen and M. Mathieu (eds.), *De contractuele fout*, Bruges, Die Keure, 2019, (1) 3. See also Art. 5.72 (2) BCC: "*De resultaatsverbintenis is een verbintenis die de schuldenaar ervan verplicht om een bepaald resultaat te bereiken. Indien het resultaat niet wordt bereikt, wordt de fout van de schuldenaar vermoed, tenzij overmacht wordt aangetoond.*" **The Netherlands**: C.H. Sieburgh, *Mr. C. Assers Handleiding tot de beoefening van het Nederlands Burgerlijk Recht. 6. Verbintenissenrecht. Deel I. De verbintenis in het algemeen, eerste gedeelte*, Deventer, Wolters Kluwer, 2020, no. 192; T.F.E. Tjong Tjin Tai, "Toerekenbare niet-nakoming en de zorg van een goed schuldenaar", *WPNR* 2004, vol. 6574, (285) 286.

1153 **Belgium**: Cass. (BE) 14 November 2012, AR P.11.1611.F, www.cass.be; Cass. (BE) 10 December 1953, *Arr.Cass.* 1954, 244. P. Wéry, *Droit des obligations. Volume 1. Theorie générale du contrat*, Brussels, Larcier, 2021, 559, no. 548.

release himself from being contractually liable when he can prove that his non-performance is due to force majeure.[1154]

274. Obligation of guarantee – If the PSS supplier or PSS user has committed itself to an **obligation of guarantee**, then there is also a breach of contract if the promised result has not been achieved, but the debtor will also be liable if its non-performance is due to force majeure.[1155]

275. How to distinguish between these types of obligations? – Which obligations in the PSS contract qualify as obligations of means or obligations of result or guarantee depends on the specific circumstances. It is, in fact, perfectly possible that some parts of the PSS contract qualify as an obligation of result and others as an obligation of means.[1156] Different criteria exist to distinguish between these different types of obligations.[1157]

276. Common intention of the parties: PSS contract explicitly or implicitly qualifies the obligation – First, this qualification often depends on the common intention of the parties.[1158] This may be inferred from the fact

1154 **Belgium**: See Art. 5.226 BCC. See for an application e.g. Cass. (BE) 30 October 2015, AR C.14.0296.F, www.cass.be and Cass. (BE) 14 September 2015, AR. S.13.0030.N, www.cass.be. I. Claeys and T. Tanghe, *Nieuw Algemeen Contractenrecht*, Antwerp, Intersentia, 2023, 640.

1155 **Belgium**: P. Wéry, *Droit des obligations. Volume 1. Theorie générale du contrat*, Brussels, Larcier, 2021, 564, no. 551; J.-L. Fagnart, "Les obligations de garantie" in H. Bekaert, R.E. Bell and J. Carpizo (eds.), *Mélanges en hommage au professeur Jean Baugniet*, Brussels, Services auxiliaires des revues notariales, 1976, (233) 223–262; P. Brulez, "Over de draagwijdte van contractuele verbintenissen: garantie-, resultaats-, middelenverbintenissen" in K. Swinnen and M. Mathieu (eds.), *De contractuele fout*, Bruges, Die Keure, 2019, (1) 4–5. The obligation of guarantee is not mentioned in Art. 5.72 BCC. According to Claeys and Tanghe, this is most likely because the obligation to guarantee only receives limited attention in legal doctrine. The Explanatory Memorandum of the Proposal Law of Obligations, on the other hand, does mention the obligation of guarantee, namely as a variant of the obligation of result (*Parl. St.* Chamber of Representatives 2019, nr. 55–0174/1, 77). See: I. Claeys and T. Tanghe, *Nieuw Algemeen Contractenrecht*, Antwerp, Intersentia, 2023, 641. **NL**: G.T. de Jong, H.B. Krans and M.H. Wissink, *Verbintenissenrecht algemeen (Studiereeks Burgerlijk Recht, deel 4)*, Deventer, Wolters Kluwer, 2018, 165–168.

1156 **Belgium**: S. Stijns, *Verbintenissenrecht*, Boek 1, Bruges, Die Keure, 2022, 11. **The Netherlands**: T.F.E. Tjong Tjin Tai, *Asser 7-IV Bijzondere Overeenkomsten – Opdracht, incl. de geneeskundige behandelingsovereenkomst en de reisovereenkomst*, Deventer, Wolters Kluwer, 2018, no. 85; J.D.A. Den Tonkelaar, *Resultaatsverbintenissen en inspanningsverbintenissen*, Zwolle, Tjeenk Willink, 1982, 74.

1157 **Belgium**: For an extensive overview, see: P. Brulez, "Over de draagwijdte van contractuele verbintenissen: garantie-, resultaats-, middelenverbintenissen" in K. Swinnen and M. Mathieu (eds.), *De contractuele fout*, Bruges, Die Keure, 2019, (1) 9–27. **The Netherlands**: Whether and to what extent the obligations constitute an obligation of means or an obligation of result is to be determined by interpretation of the law or of the contract. See: C.H. Sieburgh, *Mr. C. Assers Handleiding tot de beoefening van het Nederlands Burgerlijk Recht. 6. Verbintenissenrecht. Deel I. De verbintenis in het algemeen, eerste gedeelte*, Deventer, Wolters Kluwer, 2020, no. 370 and the references there.

1158 **Belgium**: Cass. (BE) 3 May 1984, *Arr.Cass.* 1983–84, 1147, concl. E. Krings; Cass. (BE) 18 May 1990, *Arr.Cass.* 1989–90, 1195. **The Netherlands**: HR (NL) 14 April 2006,

that the parties explicitly refer to their obligations in the contract as obligations of result or obligations of means. However, even if these terms are not used in the contract, the contractual wording can make it very clear whether the parties intended an obligation of result or means.[1159]

If, for example, the PSS contract stipulates that the PSS user shall have a working product again within 48 hours in the event of a defect, this obligation will most likely be qualified as an obligation of result. On the other hand, a clause stating that in the event of a defect, the PSS supplier will make reasonable efforts to provide the PSS user with a working product again as soon as possible will most likely be qualified as an obligation of means. Additionally, the qualification of the PSS supplier's obligation to provide the service will also depend on how the output specifications are described and what continuity of service is guaranteed. Indeed, the PSS supplier may qualify his obligation as an obligation of means, for example by providing that there is only an event of default if the interruption exceeds a certain period or that it is sufficient for the provider to make reasonable efforts to ensure continuity of service.[1160]

277. Common intention of the parties: examples – The terms and conditions of *Swapphone* provide a good example of an obligation that is expressly qualified as an obligation of means. According to the contract, the PSS user has the right to "swap" his smartphone (i.e. get a repair or replacement of the smartphone) in case of defects.[1161] In the terms and conditions, it is stipulated that Swapphone *strives* to swap the smartphone within one working day after the PSS user contacted Swapphone via phone, email or WhatsApp.[1162] Subsequently, the contract explicitly states that this deadline is only a target deadline and not a strict one; exceeding it does not give any right to damages or compensation, nor to termination of the contract.[1163]

278. Other distinction criteria – If the common intent of the parties is not apparent or expressed in the contract, other criteria should be considered. The most commonly used criterion relates to the question whether the intended

---

ECLI:NL:HR:2006:AU6521, *NJ* 2006/259; T.F.E. Tjong Tjin Tai, *Asser 7-IV Bijzondere Overeenkomsten – Opdracht, incl. de geneeskundige behandelingsovereenkomst en de reisovereenkomst*, Deventer, Wolters Kluwer, 2018, no. 85.

1159 **Belgium**: P. Brulez, "Over de draagwijdte van contractuele verbintenissen: garantie-, resultaats-, middelenverbintenissen" in K. Swinnen and M. Mathieu (eds.), *De contractuele fout*, Bruges, Die Keure, 2019, (1) 11–12. See for an example: Cass. (BE) 15 January 2010, *Arr. Cass.* 2010, 186 (Contract of sterilisation normally constitutes an obligation of means on the part of the doctor, but was in this case nevertheless considered an obligation of result due to the declarations of the doctor at the time of contract conclusion).

1160 B. Keirsbilck, E. Terryn and E. Van Gool, "Consumentenbescherming bij servitisation en product-dienst systemen (PDS)", *TPR* 2019, (817) 870–871.

1161 Art. 6.1 Terms and Conditions Swapphone.

1162 Art. 6.3 Terms and Conditions Swapphone.

1163 Art. 6.4 Terms and Conditions Swapphone.

result of the obligation is subject to chance.[1164] If there is a high degree of certainty that the result will be achieved, there is generally an obligation of result. The reverse also applies: if the proper performance of an obligation also depends on all sorts of factors and risks over which the debtor has no control, then the obligations will generally be qualified as an obligation of means.[1165] In addition, the fact that the debtor is not dependent on an action of the other party, and therefore has complete control over his promised performance, may also be an indication of an obligation of result.[1166] Yet another approach links the type of obligation to the object of the obligation. Thus, obligations to give (*dare*) and to not do something (*non facere*) would be obligations of result, whereas obligations to do (*facere*) would in principle be obligations of means (unless expressly stipulated otherwise).[1167] However, Claeys and Tanghe rightly point out in this regard that one should not generalise too quickly and that it is better to examine the type of obligation one obligation at a time, considering the concrete circumstances of the case.[1168]

279. Courts ultimately decide on the qualification of the obligation – The question of whether an obligation from the PSS contract constitutes an obligation of means, obligation of result or an obligation of guarantee is ultimately assessed by the courts. It is generally accepted that this is a factual assessment/a question of interpretation of the contract and that the Belgian Court of Cassation and the Dutch Supreme Court can only check that the court does not draw any unrelated or unjustifiable conclusions from the facts it establishes.[1169]

1164 **Belgium**: I. Claeys and T. Tanghe, *Nieuw Algemeen Contractenrecht*, Antwerp, Intersentia, 2023, 641–643; B. Kohl, *Contrat d'entreprise*, Brussels, Bruylant, 2016, 140. **The Netherlands**: T.F.E. Tjong Tjin Tai, "Toerekenbare niet-nakoming en de zorg van een goed schuldenaar", *WPNR* 2004, vol. 6574, (285) 286–287; J.D.A. Den Tonkelaar, *Resultaatsverbintenissen en inspanningsverbintenissen*, Zwolle, Tjeenk Willink, 1982, 64 *et seq.*

1165 **Belgium**: P. Brulez, "Over de draagwijdte van contractuele verbintenissen: garantie-, resultaats-, middelenverbintenissen" in K. Swinnen and M. Mathieu (eds.), *De contractuele fout*, Bruges, Die Keure, 2019, (1) 15–16; L. Van Valckenborgh, "De kwalificatie van een verbintenis als resultaats- of middelenverbintenis", *TBBR* 2011, (222) 224.

1166 **Belgium**: A. Van Oevelen, "Kwaliteitsstandaarden bij de verkoop van goederen en de levering van diensten" in I. Claeys, W. Delva and R. Steennot (eds.), *Aansprakelijkheid, veiligheid en kwaliteit*, Ghent, Kluwer, 2015, (1) 4; B. Dubuisson, "Questions choisies en droit de la responsabilité contractuelle" in P. Wéry (ed.), *La théorie générale des obligations*, Brussels, CUP, 1998, (93) 111.

1167 **Belgium**: P. Brulez, "Over de draagwijdte van contractuele verbintenissen: garantie-, resultaats-, middelenverbintenissen" in K. Swinnen and M. Mathieu (eds.), *De contractuele fout*, Bruges, Die Keure, 2019, (1) 21–22. **The Netherlands**: G.T. de Jong, H.B. Krans and M.H. Wissink, *Verbintenissenrecht algemeen (Studiereeks Burgerlijk Recht, deel 4)*, Deventer, Wolters Kluwer, 2018, 45; D. Haas, *De grenzen van het recht op nakoming (R&P nr. 167)*, Deventer, Kluwer, 2009, 70.

1168 **Belgium**: I. Claeys and T. Tanghe, *Nieuw Algemeen Contractenrecht*, Antwerp, Intersentia, 2023, 643.

1169 **Belgium**: Cass. (BE) 5 September 2019, AR C.18.0302.N, *TBBR* 2020, 520, case note M. Schouteden, *NjW* 2020, 78, case note F. Auvray and K. Ronsijn, *JLMB* 2020, 1068, case

2.6.3. CONTRACTUAL LIABILITY FOR THIRD PARTIES OR OBJECTS

280. Contractual liability not only for personal fault but also faults of auxiliaries – In some cases, the PSS supplier will not fulfil the obligations of the PSS contract itself, but will rely on auxiliaries (agents, employees, other auxiliaries) to do so. For example, it is conceivable that a subcontractor is used for the installation and transport of a smart washing machine or for the maintenance and repair of a bicycle. In this case, the PSS supplier will be liable not only for his own personal fault but also the faults by these agents, employees, or auxiliaries.[1170] The fault of an auxiliary does not qualify as *force majeure*.[1171]

281. Contractual liability for objects used in the performance of the contract – In addition, the PSS supplier (or his auxiliaries) may use objects (machines, tools, products, raw materials, etc.) in the performance of its contractual obligations. Think, for example, of the PSS supplier providing a washing machine or a bicycle or repairing these products using the wrong tools. Except in cases of *force majeure*, the PSS supplier will also be contractually liable for these objects both when the breach of contract is due to a personal fault of the PSS supplier or its auxiliaries in using this object (such as misuse or using the wrong object) and when it is due to a defective object used in the performance of the PSS contract.[1172]

---

note G. Genicot, *RABG* 2020, 554; Cass. (BE) 7 February 1992, *Arr.Cass.* 1991–92, 529, *Pas.* 1992, I, 503; I. Claeys and T. Tanghe, *Nieuw Algemeen Contractenrecht*, Antwerp, Intersentia, 2023, 643; A. Van Oevelen, "Kwaliteitsstandaarden bij de verkoop van goederen en de levering van diensten" in I. Claeys, W. Delva and R. Steennot (eds.), *Aansprakelijkheid, veiligheid en kwaliteit*, Ghent, Kluwer, 2015, (1) 4; P. Van Ommeslaghe, *Droit des obligations, I*, Brussels, Bruylant, 2010, 41, no. 16. **The Netherlands**: HR (NL) 14 April 2006, ECLI:NL:HR:2006:AU6521, *NJ* 2006/259, para 3.3.2. According to the Dutch Supreme Court, the question whether there is an obligation of means or an obligation of result is a matter of interpretation of the contract. Consequently, it can only examine legal complaints (*rechtsklachten*) or complaints regarding the reasons (*motiveringsklachten*) for the court's decision on the nature of the obligation.

1170 **Belgium**: See Art. 5.229 BCC (formerly Art. 1245 old BCC), Art. 1735, Art. 1797, and Art. 1994 old BCC. See also: Cass. (BE) 25 May 2012, *Arr.Cass.* 2012, 1427, *JLMB* 2012, 1364, *RW* 2013–14, 338, case note B. Van Den Bergh; Cass. (BE) 27 February 2003, *Arr.Cass.* 2003, 513, *Pas.* 2003, 422, *TBBR* 2004, 410. B. Weyts and T. Vansweevelt, *Handboek Verbintenissenrecht*, Antwerp, Intersentia, 2019, 353. **The Netherlands**: Art. 6:76 DCC. G.T. de Jong, H.B. Krans and M.H. Wissink, *Verbintenissenrecht algemeen (Studiereeks Burgerlijk Recht, deel 4)*, Deventer, Wolters Kluwer, 2018, 157. **DCFR**: Art. III. – 2:106 DCFR.

1171 **Belgium**: S. Stijns, *Verbintenissenrecht*, Boek 1, Bruges, Die Keure, 2022, 189.

1172 **Belgium**: See Art. 5.230 BCC. S. Stijns, *Verbintenissenrecht*, Boek 1, Bruges, Die Keure, 2022,190; L. Cornelis, *Algemene theorie van de verbintenis*, Antwerp, Intersentia, 2000, 589. **The Netherlands**: Art. 6:77 DCC; G.T. de Jong, H.B. Krans and M.H. Wissink, *Verbintenissenrecht algemeen (Studiereeks Burgerlijk Recht, deel 4)*, Deventer, Wolters Kluwer, 2018, 160–161. See also with regard to the Dutch contract for services: T.F.E.

2.6.4. *FORCE MAJEURE*

282. Circumstances not imputable to the debtor may make the performance of the contractual obligations impossible – In the performance of the PSS contract, the parties may be faced with circumstances that make it impossible to fulfil the contractual obligations. Typical examples are fire, disease, epidemic, natural disaster, government action, strike, a terrorist- or cyber-attack, etc., but in the context of PSS contracts, one can also think of power failures or the loss of internet connection of connected products that are not the fault of the consumer. Additionally, one may think of a legal prohibition for offering the service, such as the recent ban of shared e-scooters in Paris.[1173]

283. Concept of *force majeure* – The concept of *force majeure* refers to any event that is not imputable to the debtor or a third party for whom the debtor is responsible, and which makes the performance of the contractual obligation reasonably impossible. As already explained above, if the non-performance of the contractual obligation is due to *force majeure*, there is no breach of contract and therefore no contractual liability.[1174] *Force majeure* plays a role in both obligations of means and obligations of result, but in practice it is mainly invoked in connection with obligations of result, as it allows the debtor to escape contractual liability if he does not achieve the promised result.[1175]

284. Requirements of *force majeure* – Under Belgian law, a debtor may invoke *force majeure* if the performance of his obligation became reasonably[1176] impossible due to an impediment that occurred after the conclusion of the contract, and which is not imputable to the debtor.[1177] Non-imputability means

---

Tjong Tjin Tai, *Asser 7-IV Bijzondere Overeenkomsten – Opdracht, incl. de geneeskundige behandelingsovereenkomst en de reisovereenkomst*, Deventer, Wolters Kluwer, 2022, no. 207.

1173 See: D. Berretta, "After the Paris ban, what's next for e-scooters?", 6 April 2023, available at https://eurocities.eu/latest/after-the-paris-ban-whats-next-for-e-scooters/. The free-floating e-bikes of Tier, Dott and Lime, however, remain available in Paris, also after the ban.

1174 **Belgium**: Art. 5.99 and Art. 5.266 (1) BCC. (Formerly Art. 1147 and 1148 old BCC). S. Stijns, *Verbintenissenrecht*, Boek 1, Bruges, Die Keure, 2022, 196. **The Netherlands**: Art. 6:74 (1) and Art. 6:75 DCC. **DCFR**: Art. III. – 3:104 DCFR.

1175 P. Wéry, *Droit des obligations. Volume 1. Theorie générale du contrat*, Brussels, Larcier, 2021, 578 no. 562.

1176 Under the old law, there was discussion whether this impossibility must be reasonable or absolute. An extensive case law analysis showed that the first option was the most commonly used criterion: M. De Potter De Ten Broeck, *Gewijzigde omstandigheden in het contractenrecht*, Antwerp, Intersentia, 2017, 69. This also seems to be the approach in the "new" BCC, although this was not explicitly confirmed in the legal text. See: Explanatory Memorandum, *Parliamentary Papers* Chamber of Representatives 2020–21, no. 55–1806/1, 261: "*The impossibility must be assessed in a reasonable and humane manner.*"

1177 Art. 5.226, §1 BCC. V. Sagaert, *Beginselen van verbintenissenrecht. De contractuele en quasi-contractuele verbintenissen*, Leuven, LeA Uitgevers, 2023, 102; I. Claeys and T. Tanghe, *Nieuw Algemeen Contractenrecht*, Antwerp, Intersentia, 2023, 863.

that the impediment is not due to a fault of the debtor or he is not responsible for it under the law or a juridical act.[1178] Whether the performance of the obligation is indeed impossible is assessed taking into account the unforeseeable and unavoidable nature of the impediment to performance.[1179] Dutch law has similar requirements for *force majeure*. According to the DCC, for a debtor to invoke *force majeure* there must be an impediment to the performance of the obligation which does not result from his fault and is not at his risk, i.e. not for his account under the law,[1180] a juridical act,[1181] or generally accepted principles.[1182, 1183]

285. No *force majeure* if debtor is in default – If the debtor is in default at the time the impossibility to perform the obligation occurs – i.e. the debtor had been given notice of default[1184] for the imputable non-performance of the obligation – he cannot rely on *force majeure*.[1185] He will then have to bear the risk of *force majeure* himself.

286. Consequences of *force majeure* – If the conditions for *force majeure* are met, the debtor cannot invoke the remedies for breach of contract (unless the PSS contract contains an obligation of guarantee). As regards the consequences of *force majeure*, a distinction is made between temporary impossibility and permanent impossibility.

287. Performance of the obligation is temporarily impossible – If the impediment is only temporary, the debtor's obligation shall be suspended until performance becomes possible again (if still useful)[1186] or becomes permanently impossible.[1187] At the same time, the obligation of the other party to the PSS

1178 Art. 5.225 BCC.

1179 Art. 5.226, §1 BCC. The unforeseeability and unavoidability are assessed taking into account the ability of a reasonable and prudent person to foresee these circumstances at the time of contract conclusion, respectively his ability to avoid these circumstances. See: V. Sagaert, *Beginselen van verbintenissenrecht. De contractuele en quasi-contractuele verbintenissen*, Leuven, LeA Uitgevers, 2023, 102.

1180 E.g. the above-mentioned Art. 6:76 (liability for auxiliaries) and 6:77 DCC (liabilities for objects used in the performance of contractual obligations).

1181 E.g. contractual derogations of the provisions on liability for non-performance.

1182 E.g. generally accepted: illness of the debtor, danger to life, health, freedom (provided this was not foreseeable at time of conclusion of the contract), government measures. Generally not accepted: financial incapacity; inexperience.

1183 Art. 6:75 DCC. See for an in-depth discussion: C.H. Sieburgh, *Mr. C. Assers Handleiding tot de beoefening van het Nederlands Burgerlijk Recht. 6. Verbintenissenrecht. Deel I. De verbintenis in het algemeen, eerste gedeelte*, Deventer, Wolters Kluwer, 2020, no. 340–361 and G.T. de Jong, H.B. Krans and M.H. Wissink, *Verbintenissenrecht algemeen (Studiereeks Burgerlijk Recht, deel 4)*, Deventer, Wolters Kluwer, 2018, 154–164.

1184 **Belgium**: Art. 5.231–5.233 BCC. **The Netherlands**:

1185 **Belgium**: Art. 5.227 BCC. **The Netherlands**: Art. 6:84 DCC.

1186 **Belgium**: Cass. (BE) 13 January 1956, *Arr.Cass.* 1956, 367.

1187 **Belgium**: Art. 5.102 and Art. 5.226, §1, third sentence BCC. I. Claeys and T. Tanghe, *Nieuw Algemeen Contractenrecht*, Antwerp, Intersentia, 2023, 863–864 and 878. See in detail about

contract will also be suspended in view of the principle of reciprocity.[1188] When the impediment is lifted, the obligations generally resume their effect. A concrete example: if the PSS supplier does not fulfil its repair obligation in time due to a cause that can be qualified as *force majeure* (e.g. fire or flooding in the workshop, global shortage of spare parts or microchips due to supply chain problems, etc.) the obligation of the PSS user to pay the monthly fee will also be suspended. If this impediment is removed and the performance of the repair obligation becomes possible again (e.g. the spare parts are available again, a new workshop is opened, etc.), the PSS user's payment obligation also resumes.

288. PERFORMANCE OF THE OBLIGATION IS PERMANENTLY IMPOSSIBLE – Under Belgian law, permanent *force majeure* results in the extinguishment of the obligation that has become impossible.[1189] If this *force majeure* situation relates to a principal obligation of the PSS contract that become fully and permanently impossible, the PSS contract will be terminated in its entirety by operation of law.[1190] This termination has no retroactive effect. If, on the other hand, the *force majeure* situation is permanent but partial, termination of the PSS is limited to that part of the PSS contract that is affected, provided the contract is divisible according to the intention of the parties, taking into account its nature and purport.[1191] Under Dutch law, on the other hand, *force majeure* does not lead to the extinguishment of the impossible obligation but only precludes a claim for performance as long as it prevents the debtor from performing.[1192] This distinction is mainly relevant if the debtor performs despite the *force majeure* (e.g. delivery of a product or service despite a legal

---

the distinction between temporary and permanent *force majeure*: M. DE POTTER DE TEN BROECK, "Tijdelijke versus definitieve overmacht", *NjW* 2017, (378) 378–383 and L. CORNELIS, "De schorsing van verbintenissen", *TPR* 2008, (467) 495–499. **The Netherlands**: C.H. SIEBURGH, *Mr. C. Assers Handleiding tot de beoefening van het Nederlands Burgerlijk Recht. 6. Verbintenissenrecht. Deel I. De verbintenis in het algemeen, eerste gedeelte*, Deventer, Wolters Kluwer, 2020, no. 378.

1188 **Belgium**: Art. 5.102, first sentence BCC. **The Netherlands**: C.H. SIEBURGH, *Mr. C. Assers Handleiding tot de beoefening van het Nederlands Burgerlijk Recht. 6. Verbintenissenrecht. Deel I. De verbintenis in het algemeen, eerste gedeelte*, Deventer, Wolters Kluwer, 2020, no. 378.

1189 Art. 5.99 BCC *juncto* Art. 5.266, §1, (2) BCC.

1190 Art. 5.100(1) BCC *juncto* Art. 5.265 BCC.

1191 Art. 5.100(2) BCC.

1192 C.J. VAN ZEBEN, J.W. DU PON and M.M. OLTHOF, *Parlementaire geschiedenis van het Nieuwe burgerlijk wetboek. Boek 6: Algemeen gedeelte van het verbintenissenrecht*, Deventer, Kluwer, 1981, 486 and 488. Under the old DCC, however, the situation was the same as under Belgian law. See: C.H. SIEBURGH, *Mr. C. Assers Handleiding tot de beoefening van het Nederlands Burgerlijk Recht. 6. Verbintenissenrecht. Deel I. De verbintenis in het algemeen, eerste gedeelte*, Deventer, Wolters Kluwer, 2020, no. 373 with reference to L.E.H. RUTTEN, *Mr. C. Asser's Handleiding tot de beoefening van het Nederlands Burgerlijk Recht. 4. Verbintenissenrecht. Deel I. De verbintenis in het algemeen*, Zwolle, W.E.J. Tjeenk Willink, 1981, 273 *et seq.*

prohibition[1193]).[1194] Irrespective of this, the consequences remain the same as under Belgian law: if the *force majeure* is permanent, the operation of the obligation is, in principle, permanently cancelled. If the permanent *force majeure* relates to only a part of the performance, the creditor retains the right to the other part.[1195]

289. Who bears the risk of *force majeure*? (theory of risk) – The question arises who bears the risk if the performance has become reasonably impossible due to *force majeure*. This question is answered using the so-called theory of risk (*risicoleer, théorie des risques*).[1196] First, *force majeure* has as a result that the debtor is released from the performance that has become reasonably impossible. In principle, this would mean that the creditor bears the risk of *force majeure* (*res perit creditore*). However, as PSS contracts are reciprocal contracts, the fact that the impossible obligation of the debtor extinguishes also leads to the extinguishment of the creditor's obligation. The basis for this lies in the reciprocity (i.e. legal connection) of the obligations of the PSS contract.[1197] As a result, the debtor of the impossible obligation bears the risk of *force majeure* in the end (*res perit debitori*). As an example: due to a legal prohibition for free-floating e-scooters in the city Brussels, the PSS supplier can no longer offer its services. Due to *force majeure*, its obligation to provide access to the e-scooters extinguishes. However, as this contract is a reciprocal contract, the PSS user is also released from his obligation to pay the price. Therefore, in the end, the PSS supplier bears the risk.[1198] Under Belgian law, an additional rule applies to product-oriented PSS. Here, unless the parties contractually agree to the contrary, the risk of *force majeure* transfers together with the transfer of ownership (*res perit domino*).[1199] This means that the PSS user bears the risk of

---

1193 For an example of such a prohibition in the context of PSS, see the Paris ban on e-scooter rentals: D. Berretta, "After the Paris ban, what's next for e-scooters?", 6 April 2023, available at https://eurocities.eu/latest/after-the-paris-ban-whats-next-for-e-scooters/.

1194 G.J.P. de Vries, *Recht op nakoming en op schadevergoeding en ontbinding wegens tekortkoming*, Zwolle, W.E.J. Tjeenk Willink, 1997, §1.4.

1195 C.H. Sieburgh, *Mr. C. Assers Handleiding tot de beoefening van het Nederlands Burgerlijk Recht. 6. Verbintenissenrecht. Deel I. De verbintenis in het algemeen, eerste gedeelte*, Deventer, Wolters Kluwer, 2020, no. 372.

1196 **Belgium**: V. Sagaert, *Beginselen van verbintenissenrecht. De contractuele en quasi-contractuele verbintenissen*, Leuven, LeA Uitgevers, 2023, 105. **The Netherlands**: C.H. Sieburgh, *Mr. C. Assers Handleiding tot de beoefening van het Nederlands Burgerlijk Recht. 6. Verbintenissenrecht. Deel I. De verbintenis in het algemeen, eerste gedeelte*, Deventer, Wolters Kluwer, 2020, no. 374 and 377.

1197 **Belgium**: Cass. (BE) 4 February 2005, *Arr.Cass.* 2005, 281, *RW* 2005–06, 587. **The Netherlands**: C.H. Sieburgh, *Mr. C. Assers Handleiding tot de beoefening van het Nederlands Burgerlijk Recht. 6. Verbintenissenrecht. Deel I. De verbintenis in het algemeen, eerste gedeelte*, Deventer, Wolters Kluwer, 2020, no. 377.

1198 See for an application in the framework of the rental contract for movables (Art. 1722 old BCC) *infra* no. 439.

1199 Art. 5.80 BCC.

loss or damages to the product from the moment he becomes the owner of the product, which can be before he is actually in possession of the product.[1200]

290. Rules on *force majeure* are not mandatory: *force majeure* clauses – The rules on *force majeure* in the Belgian and Dutch Civil Codes are not mandatory law. As a result, the parties to a PSS contract are in principle free to derogate from the legal provisions for *force majeure* and flesh out their own contractual regime.[1201] *Force majeure* clauses (*overmachtsclausule, force majeure clause*) can take various forms. For example, they can explicitly list the circumstances qualifying as *force* majeure,[1202] they can restrict or extend the facts which must be regarded as facts of *force majeure* in their contractual relationship, and they may even exclude *force majeure* altogether.[1203] Moreover, they can also stipulate a notification obligation and damage limitation measures and modulate the effects of force majeure.[1204]

291. Limits to the validity of *force majeure* clauses – However, there are also limitations to the validity of a *force majeure* clause. First, a *force*

1200 Under Belgian law, the transfer of ownership of a *species* good occurs by consent (*solo consensu*) and therefore not by material transfer (delivery) or with the drawing up of a separate deed or agreement to transfer ownership. For *genus* goods, see Art. 3.44(3) BCC, this occurs at the time of individualisation of the goods. However, see for consumer sales where the seller ships the goods to the consumer: Art. VI.44 BCEL which provides that the risk is only transferred if the consumer or a person he designated has received the good. Under Dutch law, a different regime applies where the starting point is that the transfer of risk occurs with the delivery of the product. See Art. 7:10 DCC and 7:11 DCC (the latter being the special regime for consumer sales). See for a discussion: P. Klik, *Koop en Consumentenkoop*, Deventer, Wolters Kluwer, 2022, 102–106.

1201 **Belgium**: I. Claeys and T. Tanghe, *Nieuw Algemeen Contractenrecht*, Antwerp, Intersentia, 2023, 891. **The Netherlands**: C. Cauffman and P. Croes, *Groene Serie Verbintenissenrecht, Art. 6:75 BW*, Deventer, Deventer, 2021, no. 7.1; C.H. Sieburgh, *Mr. C. Assers Handleiding tot de beoefening van het Nederlands Burgerlijk Recht. 6. Verbintenissenrecht. Deel I. De verbintenis in het algemeen, eerste gedeelte*, Deventer, Wolters Kluwer, 2020, no. 362; G.T. de Jong, *Niet-nakoming van verbintenissen (Mon. BW B22)*, Deventer, Wolters Kluwer, 2006, 18.

1202 Here it is important to indicate whether this list is exhaustive or not.

1203 This is tantamount to stipulating an obligation of guarantee.

1204 See more extensively on *force majeure* clauses: **Belgium**: A. Draulans and J. Rasquin, "Overmachts-, imprevisie- en hardshipclausules" in G.-L. Ballon, H. De Decker, V. Sagaert, E. Terryn, B. Tilleman and A.-L. Verbeke (eds.), *Contractuele clausules. Gemeenrechtelijke clausules. Volume II*, Antwerp, Intersentia, 2013, (1191) 1191–1253; D. Philippe, "Les clauses de force majeure, d'imprévision et de transfert de risques" in *Les clauses applicables en cas d'inexécution des obligations contractuelles*, Brussels, La Charte, 2001, (2) 2–31. **The Netherlands**: C.H. Sieburgh, *Mr. C. Assers Handleiding tot de beoefening van het Nederlands Burgerlijk Recht. 6. Verbintenissenrecht. Deel I. De verbintenis in het algemeen, eerste gedeelte*, Deventer, Wolters Kluwer, 2020, 363; C. Cauffman and P. Croes, *Groene Serie Verbintenissenrecht, Art. 6:75 BW*, Deventer, Deventer, 2021, no. 7.1 and 7.7; C.R. Christiaans, "Exoneratie- en overmachtclausules" in B. Wessels (ed.), *Praktijkhandleiding algemene voorwaarden*, Deventer, Kluwer, 2015, (79) 79–106.

majeure clause may amount to a disguised exemption clause.[1205] In that case, the clause must be tested against the conditions of validity which apply to exemption clauses.[1206] Second, *force majeure* clauses can also be tested against the control regime of unfair terms.[1207] For example, under Belgian law, the blacklist of unfair terms prohibits clauses that "do not allow the consumer to terminate the contract in the event of force majeure, except against payment of compensation."[1208] Some case law interprets this provision broadly, by stating that it also prohibits clauses that prohibit the consumer from invoking force majeure as a defence against a claim from the business seeking damages.[1209] This may be the case, for example, if a clause states that in the event of internet failure (even if due to *force majeure*, for example a fault by the Internet Service Provider) of a smart washing machine, a fixed number of wash cycles will be charged.[1210] The result of this clause would be that the risk of *force majeure* would be borne by the consumer, which is not permitted under Belgian law.[1211]

292. *FORCE MAJEURE* CLAUSES IN PSS CONTRACTS – Several of the analysed PSS contracts contain clauses that explicitly or implicitly regulate the consequences of *force majeure*. For example, several PSS suppliers place the risk of damage or loss due to an external cause (including water and fire damage, but not limited to this) on the PSS user, who is obliged to bear the costs incurred by the PSS supplier to repair or replace the device.[1212] As will be discussed more in-depth further, the validity of these clauses – at least under Belgian law but possibly also under Dutch law – is questionable.[1213]

1205 **Belgium**: I. Claeys and T. Tanghe, *Nieuw Algemeen Contractenrecht*, Antwerp, Intersentia, 2023, 893–894. **The Netherlands**: C. Cauffman and P. Croes, *Groene Serie Verbintenissenrecht, Art. 6:75 BW*, Deventer, Deventer, 2021, no. 7.1 and 7.7.

1206 See *infra* no. 312.

1207 **Belgium**: An overly broad *force majeure* clause may also in certain cases unduly restrict the consumer's legal rights in the event of non-performance (Art. VI.83, 30° BCEL) or violate the general standard of unfair terms (Art. I.8, 22° and VI.84 BCEL). See also: R. Steennot, "Commentaar bij art. VI.83, 30° WER" in *Handels- en economisch recht. Commentaar met overzicht van rechtspraak en rechtsleer*, Mechelen, Kluwer, loose-leaf, 2017, (591) 596. **The Netherlands**: C. Cauffman and P. Croes, *Groene Serie Verbintenissenrecht, Art. 6:75 BW*, Deventer, Deventer, 2021, no. 7.7 and 7.8.

1208 Art. VI.83, 12° BCEL.

1209 See: R. Steennot, "Commentaar bij art. VI.83, 12° WER" in *Handels- en economisch recht. Commentaar met overzicht van rechtspraak en rechtsleer*, Mechelen, Kluwer, loose-leaf, 2017, (453) 455–456. See for an application regarding a rental contract for movables: Ct. Antwerp (BE) 30 June 2011, *RW* 2013–14, 269.

1210 See e.g. Art. 4(4) Terms and Conditions Bundles; B. Keirsbilck, E. Terryn and E. Van Gool, "Consumentenbescherming bij servitisation en product-dienst systemen (PDS)", *TPR* 2019, (817) 873–874.

1211 Compare also with M.B.M. Loos, *Algemene voorwaarden*, The Hague, Boom juridisch, 2018, 313, no. 345a who argues that these terms can fall within the scope of paragraph 1, point (e) of the indicative list of the UCTD Annex (which, in turn, also affect Dutch law).

1212 Art. 10.9 Terms and Conditions Bundles.

1213 See *infra* no. 440.

2.6.5. HARDSHIP/CHANGE OF CIRCUMSTANCES

293. CONCEPT OF HARDSHIP/CHANGE OF CIRCUMSTANCES – The concept of hardship or change of circumstances refers to provisions (either statutory or contractual) that allow for the renegotiation or termination of the PSS contract when unexpected events fundamentally alter the contractual balance.[1214] The concept of hardship differs from that of *force majeure*. Unlike *force majeure* where the changed circumstances make performance of the obligation impossible, in case of hardship the changed circumstances only make performance significantly more difficult, burdensome or costly.[1215] In the Netherlands, the doctrine of hardship/unforeseen circumstances (*onvoorziene omstandigheden*) exists already for quite some time.[1216] Under Belgian law, the doctrine of hardship (*verandering van omstandigheden, changement de circonstances*[1217]) was only recently introduced in the BCC with the adoption of Book 5 BCC.[1218]

294. THE NETHERLANDS: HARDSHIP/UNFORESEEN CIRCUMSTANCES DOCTRINE IN ARTICLE 6:258 DCC – Under Dutch law, the doctrine of hardship/unforeseen circumstances is found in Article 6:258 DCC. According to this provision, the court may, at the request of one of the parties, modify the consequences of a contract or terminate it partially or entirely on account of unforeseen circumstances of such nature that, according to standards of reasonableness and fairness, the other party may not expect the contract to be maintained unchanged.[1219] The contract cannot be modified or terminated based on hardship/unforeseen circumstances if, by virtue of the nature of the contract or generally accepted practice, the circumstances are for the account of the party invoking them.[1220] Thus, "unforeseen circumstances" are to be understood as circumstances, entered into after the conclusion of the PSS contract, which the parties did not include (expressly or tacitly) in their contract, and which they did not foresee.[1221]

1214 **Belgium**: S. STIJNS, *Verbintenissenrecht*, Boek 1, Bruges, Die Keure, 2022, 200, no. 217. **The Netherlands:** C.H. SIEBURGH, *Mr. C. Assers Handleiding tot de beoefening van het Nederlands Burgerlijk Recht. 6. Verbintenissenrecht. Deel III. Algemeen overeenkomstenrecht*, Deventer, Wolters Kluwer, 2022, no. 436–457.

1215 I. CLAEYS and T. TANGHE, *Nieuw Algemeen Contractenrecht*, Antwerp, Intersentia, 2023, 895.

1216 Art. 6:258(1) DCC.

1217 The terminology *imprevisie, imprévision* is also used in Belgium. However, the Belgian legislator opted to use the term *verandering van omstandigheden, changement de circonstances* in the BCC. See Art. 5.74 BCC.

1218 Art. 5.74 BCC.

1219 Art. 6:258 DCC. C.H. SIEBURGH, *Mr. C. Assers Handleiding tot de beoefening van het Nederlands Burgerlijk Recht. 6. Verbintenissenrecht. Deel III. Algemeen overeenkomstenrecht*, Deventer, Wolters Kluwer, 2022, no. 439.

1220 Art. 6:258(2) DCC.

1221 C.H. SIEBURGH, *Mr. C. Assers Handleiding tot de beoefening van het Nederlands Burgerlijk Recht. 6. Verbintenissenrecht. Deel III. Algemeen overeenkomstenrecht*, Deventer, Wolters Kluwer, 2022, no. 441.

295. Belgium: introduction of the hardship/change of circumstances doctrine in Book 5 BCC – The introduction of Article 5.74 BCC ("change of circumstances") as part of the new Belgian law of obligations marked the debut of the hardship doctrine in Belgian contract law for all contracts concluded from 1 January 2023. If the conditions for change of circumstances are met, the parties to the PSS contract are under the obligation to renegotiate their contractual relationship with a view to its adaptation or even termination. In case one of the contracting parties refuses to renegotiate or if the negotiations fail within a reasonable time limit, the court may, at the request of one of the parties, either adapt the contract to align it with what the parties would reasonably have agreed at the time of the conclusion of the PSS contract had they taken the change of circumstances into account, or terminate the PSS contract in whole or in part.

The conditions for invoking change of circumstances under Belgian law are rather strict. Indeed, this requires that (i) a change of circumstances makes performance of the contract excessively onerous; (ii) this change of circumstances was unforeseeable at the time of contracting; (iii) the change is not imputable to the debtor[1222]; (iv) the debtor did not assume this risk; and (v) invoking change of circumstances is neither excluded by the law nor the contract.[1223]

296. Hardship clauses – Before the introduction of Book 5 BCC, contractual clauses were used to deal with the lack of a hardship regime in Belgian law. Only where such a clause was provided for in the contract could the parties invoke the figure of hardship when changing circumstances did not constitute *force majeure*. Now, the hardship/change of circumstances regime applies to all contracts concluded after 1 January 2023. However, even after the introduction of change of circumstances in the BCC, hardship clauses remain useful. Indeed, hardship clauses will often list certain circumstances as *a priori* "unforeseeable at the time of contracting" and "making performance of the contract excessively onerous". This fosters legal certainty and can avoid unnecessary discussions. Of course, as Article 5.74 BCC is not mandatory law, the PSS contract can also exclude hardship/change of circumstances altogether. Excluding hardship/change of circumstances could be preferable for some PSS suppliers as finding a new agreement through negotiations will not always prove easy, and resort to the courts in case of failed negotiations can be rather unpredictable.

Under Dutch law, the legal framework of hardship/unforeseen circumstances is mandatory law.[1224] This means that the contracting parties cannot exclude the application of the regime of hardship/unforeseen circumstances to their PSS

1222 Art. 5.225 BCC.

1223 Art. 5.74(2) BCC.

1224 See Art. 6:250 DCC. C.H. Sieburgh, *Mr. C. Assers Handleiding tot de beoefening van het Nederlands Burgerlijk Recht. 6. Verbintenissenrecht. Deel III. Algemeen overeenkomstenrecht*, Deventer, Wolters Kluwer, 2022, no. 448.

contract. However, this does not mean that the parties cannot contractually modulate the hardship rules or make their scope narrower by explicitly defining certain circumstances which cannot be considered "unforeseen".[1225]

297. Model clauses on hardship/change of circumstances – The following model clauses deal with hardship/change of circumstances. The first model clause provides an example that can be used for the PSS supplier's obligation to reach the specified output/make the product-service available. Indeed, in case of result-oriented PSS where the PSS supplier provides "heating", "cooling" or "light" to the PSS user, potentially in combination with guarantees regarding energy usage, a change in the location of the PSS user's premises where the service is provided (e.g. an extension to the building), can significantly affect the obligations of the PSS supplier. This model clause can be used to mitigate such a situation. The second model clause deals with the obligations of the PSS user, more specifically the obligation to pay the price of the (additional) service(s). For example, a significant surge (or decrease) in energy prices, for example due to geopolitical issues, may impact the contractual relationship to the extent that the principles of reasonableness and fairness require the PSS contract to be renegotiated. The third model clause provides an example of a clause excluding the possibility of hardship/change of circumstances in the contractual relationship. This last clause cannot be used under Dutch law, as the Dutch regime of unforeseen circumstances is mandatory law.[1226] As an alternative, the last model clause can be used to explicitly exclude certain circumstances from the scope of application of the hardship/unforeseen circumstances rules.

Model clause #5 – Hardship/change of circumstances

- **The obligations of [the PSS supplier] to [reach the specified output/to make the product-service available] are based on the current state of [the PSS user's home/business premises] where the service is to be provided. If alterations are made to this location that render the fulfilment of this obligation more onerous, the contracting parties are to renegotiate the contract in good faith. If the negotiations between the parties fail to result in an agreement within [specified period of time] from the date of the [the initial meeting to renegotiate/the request for renegotiating based on change of circumstances], [the parties may submit this issue before the courts/the contract is deemed to be terminated].**[1227]

[1225] C.H. Sieburgh, *Mr. C. Assers Handleiding tot de beoefening van het Nederlands Burgerlijk Recht. 6. Verbintenissenrecht. Deel III. Algemeen overeenkomstenrecht*, Deventer, Wolters Kluwer, 2022, no. 448.

[1226] See *supra* no. 297.

[1227] Model clause based on C. Borucki, H. Slachmuylders, B. Keirsbilck, D. Gruyaert and E. Terryn, *Model clauses for Product-as-a-Service (PaaS) contracts*, CE Center. Circular Economy Policy Research Center, 2022–23, 87.

- The obligations of [the PSS user] to [pay the price of the (additional) service(s)] are based on the current state of [the electricity prices]. In the event of [a significant surge/a significant decrease in electricity prices (e.g. defined as an increase/decrease exceeding 30% over the average price calculated for the previous six months)], the contracting parties are to renegotiate the contract in good faith. If the negotiations between the parties fail to result in an agreement within [specified period of time] from the date of the [the initial meeting to renegotiate/the request for renegotiating based on change of circumstances], [the parties may submit this issue before the courts/the contract is deemed to be terminated].

- The contracting parties agree that no party shall be excused from performing its obligations under this contract on the basis of hardship/change of circumstances.

- The contracting parties agree that the following circumstances do not give rise to the application of hardship/unforeseen circumstances: [specified examples (e.g. increase/decrease in energy prices, etc.)].

2.6.6. REMEDIES FOR BREACH OF THE PSS CONTRACT

298. Remedies for breach of the PSS contract – If one of the parties is in breach of the PSS contract (either through an imputable complete non-performance or an imputable late or defective performance),[1228] the creditor of this obligation has access to various remedies. Under Belgian law, these remedies are listed in Article 5.224 BCC (general remedies in case of non-performance) and Article 5.83 BCC (remedies for non-performance in contractual relationships). Under Dutch law, these remedies are found in title 6.1.9 of the DCC (entitled "the consequences of non-performance of an obligation") and title 6.5.5 (which contains rules for reciprocal contracts, more specifically on termination (*ontbinding*, *résolution*) and suspension (*exception non adimpleti contractus*, "enac")).

299. Overview of available remedies for breach of the PSS contract – The remedies for breach of the PSS contract can be summarised as follows.

First, the creditor can claim **specific performance** of the obligation, possibly with additional compensation for the late performance of the obligation.[1229] In Belgium this remedy is referred to as performance in kind[1230] (*uitvoering in*

1228 E.g. the PSS user does not pay the monthly fee (on time), the PSS supplier does not deliver the product, the PSS user has no access to the service, maintenance and repair do not take place within the agreed timeframe, etc.

1229 **Belgium**: See Art. 5.84 and 5.234–5.236 BCC. **The Netherlands**: Art. 3:296 (1) DCC.

1230 Art. 5.84 and 5.234 BCC.

natura, exécution en nature) and in the Netherlands it is referred to as the right of performance[1231] (*recht op nakoming*). The remedy of specific performance allows the creditor to enforce in court what the debtor of the non-performing obligation would have done if he had performed his obligation spontaneously.[1232] In other words, the debtor is induced by a court order to fulfil his obligation. For example, the PSS user may demand performance from the PSS supplier if he is unable to access the service, or if the product is defective and is not repaired or is repaired late. The basic principle is that such performance is carried out by the debtor himself, but the creditor may also ask the court to authorise him to perform the obligation himself or to have it performed by a third party at the debtor's expense.[1233] Under Belgian law, in exceptional circumstances such as urgency, it is even possible under certain conditions to opt for extrajudicial replacement of the debtor (yet this remains subject to a potential *a posteriori* judicial review).[1234]

Second, the creditor can claim **compensation for damages** (*schadeherstel, réparation du dommage*) instead of specific performance or in addition to specific performance.[1235] To claim compensation for damages, the creditor must prove (i) a fault (i.e. a breach of contract); (ii) its damage; and (iii) the causal link between the breach of contract and the damage.[1236] According to the "compensatory principle", the creditor of the non-performed obligation can in principle demand full damage restoration (*integrale vergoeding van de schade,*

1231 Art. 3:296 DCC.

1232 **Belgium**: I. Claeys and T. Tanghe, *Nieuw Algemeen Contractenrecht*, Antwerp, Intersentia, 2023, 682. **The Netherlands**: D. Haas, *De grenzen van het recht op nakoming (R&P nr. 167)*, Deventer, Kluwer, 2009, para. 1.1.

1233 **Belgium**: Art. 5.85 and Art. 5.235 BCC. See also Art. 1144 and Art. 1143 old BCC. **The Netherlands**: Art. 3:299 DCC.

1234 Art. 5.85(3) BCC.

1235 **Belgium**: Art. 5.86 and Art. 5.237–5.238 BCC. Formerly Art. 1146–1155 old BCC. In Belgium, a creditor can only invoke a claim for damages in subsidiary order (if performance is impossible or would constitute an abuse of rights), see e.g. P. Wéry, *Droit des obligations. Volume 1. Theorie générale du contrat*, Brussels, Larcier, 2021, no. 504; S. De Rey, "Uitvoering in natura en uitvoering bij equivalent" in *Comm.Bijz.Ov.*, 2021, (59) no. 4; W. van Gerven and A. Van Oevelen, *Verbintenissenrecht*, Leuven, Acco, 2021, no. 184. **The Netherlands**: Art. 6:74(1) DCC.

1236 **Belgium**: See e.g. I. Claeys and T. Tanghe, *Nieuw Algemeen Contractenrecht*, Antwerp, Intersentia, 2023, 702–703; S. De Rey and S. Stijns, "Sancties wegens wanprestatie: kroniek van de recenste evoluties", *TBBR* 2022, (2) no. 23; P. Wéry, *Droit des obligations. Volume 1. Theorie générale du contrat*, Brussels, Larcier, 2021, no. 536; S. De Rey, *Herstel in natura*, Bruges, Die Keure, 2019, no. 189; J.-F. Germain, "Responsabilité contractuelle et remèdes à l'inexécution du contrat" in J.-F. Romain (ed.), *Droit des obligations. Notions et mécanismes en matière de responsabilité*, Brussels, Bruylant, 2014, (107) 110–111; P. Van Ommeslaghe, *Traité de droit civil belge, Tome II. Les Obligations*, Volume 1, Brussels, Bruylant, 2013, no. 799; S. Stijns, D. Van Gerven and P. Wéry, "Chronique de jurisprudence (1985–1995). Les obligations: les sources", *JT* 1996, (689) no. 102 *et seq.* **The Netherlands**: J. Smits, "De verkrijging van schadevergoeding bij niet-nakoming" in J. Smits and S. Stijns (eds.), *Remedies in het Belgisch en Nederlands contractenrecht*, Antwerp, Intersentia, 2000, (115) 121–136.

réparation intégrale du dommage) by the debtor.[1237] This means that the remedy of compensation for damages aims to place the creditor of the non-performed obligation in the position he would have been in if the debtor had fulfilled this obligation.[1238] However, under Belgian law, in principle, only foreseeable damage is eligible for compensation (except in cases of an intentional non-performance).[1239] Strictly speaking, Dutch law has no such limitation, although also there the foreseeability of the damage will be taken into account when assessing the presence of a causal link.[1240] Unlike Anglo-Saxon legal systems, punitive damages are not allowed under Belgian and Dutch law.[1241]

Third, in reciprocal contracts, which is the case with PSS contracts, the creditor may also choose the remedy of **termination** (*ontbinding, résolution*) of the contract, possibly with additional compensation for damages.[1242] Under Belgian law, termination has in principle retroactive effect to the time of contract conclusion.[1243] This means that the situation must be restored to where the parties would have been if they had never concluded the contract. The obligations already performed give rise to a restitution obligation.[1244] Under Dutch law, on the other hand, the DCC explicitly provides that the termination has no retroactive effect.[1245] The termination releases the parties from any obligations affected thereby that have not yet

---

1237 **Belgium**: I. Claeys and T. Tanghe, *Nieuw Algemeen Contractenrecht*, Antwerp, Intersentia, 2023, 699–700, no. 917; S. De Rey and S. Stijns, "Sancties wegens wanprestatie: kroniek van de recenste evoluties", *TBBR* 2022, (2) 23, no. 30 *et seq.*; B. Verkempinck, *Schadevergoeding wegens wanprestatie in Europees perspectief*, Bruges, Die Keure, 2017, 1147 p.; P.-A. Foriers and E. De Duve, "Aspects du dommage réparable et des dommages et intérêts" in M. Dupont (ed.), *Les obligations contractuelles*, Brussels, Larcier, 2016, (322) 345; I. Durant, "La réparation dite intégrale du dommage. Rapport belge" in B. Dubuisson and P. Jourdain (eds.), *Le dommage et sa réparation dans la responsabilité contractuelle et extracontractuelle*, Brussels, Bruylant, 2015, (441) 441 *et seq.* **The Netherlands**: J. Smits, "De verkrijging van schadevergoeding bij niet-nakoming" in J. Smits and S. Stijns (eds.), *Remedies in het Belgisch en Nederlands contractenrecht*, Antwerp, Intersentia, 2000, (115) 131.

1238 **Belgium**: V. Sagaert, *Beginselen van verbintenissenrecht. De contractuele en quasi-contractuele verbintenissen*, Leuven, LeA Uitgevers, 2023, 121, no. 226. **The Netherlands**: J. Smits, "De verkrijging van schadevergoeding bij niet-nakoming" in J. Smits and S. Stijns (eds.), *Remedies in het Belgisch en Nederlands contractenrecht*, Antwerp, Intersentia, 2000, (115) 131.

1239 Art. 5.87 BCC.

1240 Art. 6:98 DCC; J. Smits, "De verkrijging van schadevergoeding bij niet-nakoming" in J. Smits and S. Stijns (eds.), *Remedies in het Belgisch en Nederlands contractenrecht*, Antwerp, Intersentia, 2000, (115) 135–136.

1241 I. Vrancken, "Punitive damages in het buitencontractueel aansprakelijkheidsrecht", *TBBR* 2014, (426) 426; C. Cauffman, "Naar een punitief Europees verbintenissenrecht? Een rechtsvergelijkende studie naar de draagwijdte, de grondwettigheid en de wenselijkheid van het bestraffend karakter van het verbintenissenrecht", *TPR* 2007, (799) 799–865.

1242 **Belgium**: Art. 5.90–5.96 BCC. Formerly Art. 1184(2) old BCC. **The Netherlands**: Art. 6:265–6:277 DCC.

1243 Art. 5.95(1) BCC.

1244 Art. 5.95(2) BCC. These restitution obligations are governed by Art. 5.115–5.122 BCC.

1245 Art. 6:269 DCC. However, this is subject to an exception, namely that an offer of performance made after termination has been claimed has no effect if the termination is declared.

been performed.[1246] To the extent that they have already been performed, the legal basis for such performance remains intact, but an obligation arises for the parties to undo what they have already received.[1247] Since the remedy of termination has such far-reaching consequences, it requires a fundamental non-performance,[1248] i.e. a non-performance that is sufficiently serious to warrant the termination of the PSS contract.[1249] Under both Belgian and Dutch law, termination can be either judicial or extrajudicial.[1250] If the creditor opts for an extrajudicial termination, this may be subjected to an *a posteriori* judicial review.

Fourth, the creditor has the right to a **price reduction** (*prijsvermindering, réduction du prix*) in case of a non-performance that is not sufficiently serious to justify the termination of the PSS contract.[1251] Under Belgian law, this remedy for non-performance has been extended to the general law of obligations with the introduction of Book 5 BCC (before this, it already existed as a remedy for non-performance of some special contracts, such as the sales contract[1252] and the rental contract[1253]). Under Dutch law, the remedy of price reduction is a form of partial termination (*partiële ontbinding*).[1254] The amount of the price reduction is established in function of the difference between the value of the performance received and the value of the agreed performance at the time of the conclusion of the contract.[1255]

Finally, the creditor may also **suspend his obligations** in the event of non-performance by relying on the *exceptio non adimpleti contractus* ("enac").[1256] For

1246 Art. 6:271 DCC. See regarding these restitution obligations also Art. 6:272–6:276 DCC.

1247 Art. 6:271 DCC.

1248 Here it is important to note that under Dutch law, a breach of contract (i.e. an *imputable* non-performance) is not necessary for the remedy of termination. Every sufficiently serious non-performance (imputable or not imputable, and therefore also in the case of *force majeure*) allows the creditor to terminate the contract. See: C.H. Sieburgh, *Mr. C. Assers Handleiding tot de beoefening van het Nederlands Burgerlijk Recht. 6. Verbintenissenrecht. Deel III. Algemeen overeenkomstenrecht*, Deventer, Wolters Kluwer, 2022, no. 681.

1249 **Belgium**: 5.90 BCC. **The Netherlands**: Art. 6:265 (1) DCC; C.H. Sieburgh, *Mr. C. Assers Handleiding tot de beoefening van het Nederlands Burgerlijk Recht. 6. Verbintenissenrecht. Deel III. Algemeen overeenkomstenrecht*, Deventer, Wolters Kluwer, 2022, no. 684.

1250 **Belgium**: see Art. 5.91 BCC (judicial termination) and Art. 5.93 BCC (extrajudicial termination). **The Netherlands**: see Art. 6:267(2) DCC (judicial termination) and Art. 6:267(1) DCC (extrajudicial termination).

1251 **Belgium**: Art. 5.97 BCC. **The Netherlands**: Art. 6:265 and 6:270 DCC.

1252 Art. 1644 old BCC and Art. 1649*quinquies* old BCC.

1253 Art. 1722 old BCC and Art. 1724 old BCC.

1254 Art. 6:265 *juncto* Art. 6:270 DCC. C.H. Sieburgh, *Mr. C. Assers Handleiding tot de beoefening van het Nederlands Burgerlijk Recht. 6. Verbintenissenrecht. Deel III. Algemeen overeenkomstenrecht*, Deventer, Wolters Kluwer, 2022, no. 672.

1255 **Belgium**: V. Sagaert, *Beginselen van verbintenissenrecht. De contractuele en quasi-contractuele verbintenissen*, Leuven, LeA Uitgevers, 2023, 120, no. 224. **The Netherlands**: C.H. Sieburgh, *Mr. C. Assers Handleiding tot de beoefening van het Nederlands Burgerlijk Recht. 6. Verbintenissenrecht. Deel III. Algemeen overeenkomstenrecht*, Deventer, Wolters Kluwer, 2022, no. 695–697.

1256 **Belgium**: Art. 5.98 and 5.239 BCC. The enac has also been recognised by the Court of Cassation as a general principle of law. See e.g. Cass. (BE) 24 September 2009, *Arr.Cass.* 2009, example, the PSS user can stop paying the monthly fee if the PSS supplier does not fulfil its obligations under the contract, or the PSS supplier can suspend the service if the PSS user does not pay its fees. In the case of "smart" products that are made available as part of a PSS, the software often allows the PSS supplier to suspend the performance of the service remotely if the PSS user does not fulfil its contractual obligations. In the case of "smart" machines or printers, this can often even be done remotely. For example, HP's instant ink subscription disables the ink cartridge of the printer when the subscription is terminated, resulting in a non-functional printer. Similarly, both the terms and conditions of *Fairphone Easy* and *Swapphone* allow the PSS supplier to lock the smartphone through a "lost mode" if the PSS user does not pay the monthly fee.[1257]

Often, a **prior notice of default** (*ingebrekestelling, mise en demeure*) is required before these remedies can be invoked. In Belgium, it is a general principle of law that a notice of default is in principle required for the application of a remedy for non-performance.[1258] However, there are certain exceptions to this principle, in particular where the notice of default would no longer serve any purpose[1259] or in case of contractual exceptions to the requirement of a notice of default. Under Dutch law, a prior notice of default giving the debtor a last chance to fulfil his obligation is also in many cases a requirement for claiming compensation for damages or for terminating the contract.[1260]

300. Rules on remedies for breach of contract are not mandatory law – The rules on the remedies for breach of contract are not mandatory law. As a result, the PSS contract may specify, modify, or even (partially)

2097, *Pas.* 2009, 1979, *RW* 2010–11, 1346 and Cass. (BE) 21 November 2003, *Arr.Cass.* 2003, 2175, *Pas.* 2003, 1864, *TBBR* 2006, 39, case note P. Wéry. **The Netherlands**: See Art. 6:52–6:57 DCC for the general rules on the right to suspend performance and Art. 6:262–264 DCC on the enac specifically.

1257 See Art. 9.3 Terms and Conditions Fairphone Easy and Art. 9.1 Terms and Conditions Swapphone.

1258 Art. 5.231(2) and Art. 5.83, *in fine* BCC. See also Cass. (BE) 9 April 1976, *Arr.Cass.* 1976, 921 where this was first recognised by the Belgian Court of Cassation. S. De Rey and S. Stijns, "Algemene sancties wegens toerekenbare niet-nakoming: actuele ontwikkelingen" in A. De Boeck and S. Stijns (eds.), *Themis 2021–2022 nr. 120: Verbintenissenrecht*, Antwerp, Intersentia, 2022, (79) 80; P. Wéry, *Droit des obligations. Volume 1. Theorie générale du contrat*, Brussels, Larcier, 2021, no. 442; B. Weyts and T. Vansweevelt, *Handboek Verbintenissenrecht*, Antwerp, Intersentia, 2019, no. 1085 and 1091; R. Dekkers, A.L. Verbeke, N. Carette and K. Vanhove, *Handboek burgerlijk recht, Deel III, Verbintenissen, bewijsleer en gebruikelijke contracten*, Antwerp, Intersentia, 2007, 213.

1259 Art. 5.233 BCC. This is e.g. the case: 1) when an obligation not to do something (*non facere*) has been breached; 2) when the performance of an obligation has become impossible; 3) when the performance of the obligation is no longer in the creditor's interest; 4) when the debtor gives notice that he will not perform his obligation; 5) when the law or the contract states that the debtor will be in default merely by the lapse of time; or 6) in the case of non-contractual liability.

1260 G.T. de Jong, H.B. Krans and M.H. Wissink, *Verbintenissenrecht algemeen (Studiereeks Burgerlijk Recht, deel 4)*, Deventer, Wolters Kluwer, 2022, 108, no. 128.

exclude these remedies. In addition, under certain conditions, the PSS supplier can also exclude all or part of its liability in a so-called exemption clause (*exoneratieclausule* or *bevrijdingsbeding, clause exonératoire*). The freedom to contractually specify or exclude remedies for contractual liability, as well as the stipulation of an exemption clause, may be subject to some limitations, notably due to the control regime of the UCTD and its national implementation. For example, under Belgian law, terms that may "*unduly exclude or restrict the consumer's legal rights against the business in the event of a complete or partial breach of contract or of defective performance by the business of one of its contractual obligations*" are unfair.[1261]

Additionally, the general unfairness test can also be used to combat terms on remedies for breach of contract that create a significant imbalance between the rights of the PSS user and the PSS supplier.[1262]

301. Replacement clauses – As the rules on specific performance and (extra) judicial replacement are default law, this allows the parties to specify, amend or even (partially) exclude these remedies.[1263] For example, a prior judicial authorisation for replacement may be expressly required or excluded (although such a clause was not stipulated in any of the PSS contracts analysed). In addition, the PSS supplier may also include a replacement clause in the PSS contract that specifies for which defaults a replacement is possible (and not possible). This may also include a provision regarding the costs of the replacement. The PSS contract may also limit or expressly exclude judicial or extrajudicial replacement, for example in an *exclusive remedies clause* which does not include replacement.[1264]

However, there are limits to the freedom to contractually regulate performance in kind and (extra)judicial replacement in B2C contracts. As mentioned above, according to Article VI.83, 30° BCEL are unfair: "terms that unduly exclude or restrict the consumer's legal rights against the business in the event of a complete or partial breach of contract or of defective performance by the business of one of its contractual obligations." The question of whether a replacement clause *unduly* excludes or restricts the legal rights of the consumer must be assessed by the court, which has a wide margin of appreciation.[1265]

1261 See Art. VI.83, 30° BCEL.

1262 **Belgium**: Art. I.8, 22° BCEL. **The Netherlands**: Art. 6:233, *sub* a. DCC.

1263 P. Van Ommeslaghe, *Traité de droit civil belge, Tome II. Les Obligations*, Volume 1, Brussels, Bruylant, 2013, 861; P. Wéry, "Les clauses relatives au remplacement du débiteur défaillant" in P. Wéry (ed.), *Les clauses applicables en cas d'inexécution des obligations contractuelles*, Brussels, La Charte, 2001, (229) 230–248.

1264 I. Claeys and T. Tanghe, *Nieuw Algemeen Contractenrecht*, Antwerp, Intersentia, 2023, 698–699.

1265 J. Stuyck and B. Keirsbilck, *Handels- en economisch recht. 2: Mededingingsrecht. A: Handelspraktijken en contracten met consumenten in Beginselen van Belgisch Privaatrecht*, Mechelen, Kluwer, 2024, 807; R. Steennot, "Commentaar bij art. VI.83, 30° WER" in *Handels- en economisch recht. Commentaar met overzicht van rechtspraak en rechtsleer,*

Here, the court must consider whether an exclusion or restriction is not reasonably justifiable, for example because the consumer is disproportionately disadvantaged compared to the PSS supplier.[1266] Moreover, replacement and exclusive remedy clauses can be tested against the general standard of review for unfair terms[1267] and invoking them may not constitute an abuse of rights/go against the principles of reasonableness and fairness.[1268]

302. Replacement clauses in analysed PSS contracts – Most analysed PSS contracts do not contain a replacement clause. A possible explanation for this is that servitisation contracts for movables are less likely to involve exceptional circumstances that justify replacement. In addition, (extra)judicial replacement may be less useful for these "small" contracts than for "larger" contracts such as a contract for works for an immovable property. It will often be more useful to opt for the (extrajudicial) termination of the PSS contract and/or damages. Finally, there is a significant risk that these clauses may fail the unfair contract terms test.

The general terms and conditions of *Blue Movement* do contain a replacement clause (albeit a relatively implicit one). They state that the PSS user is not permitted to have repairs made to the product by parties other than BSH, unless BSH remains in default of making the repairs even after a notice of default.[1269] The PSS user may not reduce the periodical fee in this situation.[1270] The question arises whether this last sentence is legally valid in a B2C context. Indeed, Article VI. 83, 9° BCEL states that in a consumer contract are unfair: "clauses obliging the consumer to fulfil his obligations, while the business has not fulfilled or is in default of fulfilling its own obligations."[1271] The objective of this provision is to ensure that consumers can invoke the enac if the business fails to perform its obligations.[1272] In the case of *Blue Movement*, this clause prohibiting the PSS user from withholding the periodical fee in case of a replacement would be tantamount to preventing the consumer from invoking the enac.[1273]

Mechelen, Kluwer, loose-leaf, 2017, (591) 595; S. Stijns, "De leer der onrechtmatige bedingen in de WHPC na de Wet van 7 december 1998", *TBH* 2000, (148) 162.

1266 P. Cambie, *Onrechtmatige bedingen*, Ghent, Larcier, 2009, 278–279.

1267 **Belgium**: Art. I.8, 22° BCEL. **The Netherlands**: Art. 6:233, *sub* a. DCC.

1268 **Belgium**: See Art. 5.73(2), 2° BCC. **The Netherlands**: Art. 6:248 DCC.

1269 Art. 9.2, third sentence Terms and Conditions Blue Movement.

1270 Art. 9.2, fourth sentence Terms and Conditions Blue Movement.

1271 See also *infra* no. 308.

1272 R. Steennot, "Commentaar bij art. VI.83, 9° WER" in *Handels- en economisch recht. Commentaar met overzicht van rechtspraak en rechtsleer*, Mechelen, Kluwer, loose-leaf, 2017, (439) 440; J. Stuyck and B. Keirsbilck, *Handels- en economisch recht. 2: Mededingingsrecht. A: Handelspraktijken en contracten met consumenten in Beginselen van Belgisch Privaatrecht*, Mechelen, Kluwer, 2024, 824–825; P. Cambie, *Onrechtmatige bedingen*, Ghent, Larcier, 2009, 254.

1273 Compare with Pres. Leuven (sum. proc.) (BE) 1 September 1992, *Jaarboek Handelspraktijken* 1992, 193 (is unlawful: clause stating that the buyer undertakes to pay on the due date in any

303. Model replacement clauses – The contracting parties may include replacement clauses in the PSS contract dealing with the issue of repair by the PSS user or a third party. For example, they may include a clause prohibiting the PSS user to attempt to repair the product himself, as well as having a third party attempt to repair the product. As such, these clauses exclude the extrajudicial replacement of the debtor (i.e. the PSS supplier) as a contractual remedy for the obligation to remedy defects. These model clauses will be set out and discussed *infra* under the obligation for the PSS supplier to maintain and repair the product.[1274]

304. Indemnity clauses – An indemnity clause (BE: *schadebeding, clause indemnitaire*; NL: *boetebeding*) is a clause that determines in advance the compensation for damages in case of breach of contract. This compensation can either be the payment of a monetary amount, or the performance of a determinate prestation.[1275] Under Belgian law, indemnity clauses have a purely "compensatory" function. This means that "punitive" indemnity clauses are not allowed.[1276] By contrast, under Dutch law, indemnity clauses may have a dual function, namely a compensatory function for the damages caused by the breach of contract and an incentive function to provide an incentive to fulfil the obligations under the contract.[1277] If the contracting parties have included an indemnity clause in the PSS contract, the creditor of the non-fulfilled obligation will not have to prove the existence and the extent of the damages.[1278] He will not receive less than the amount fixed in the indemnity clause, just as conversely the debtor will not owe more.[1279]

---

case, even in case of dispute) and Commissie Onrechtmatige Bedingen, *Advies nr. 9 over de algemene voorwaarden van abonnementen voor mobiele telefonie*, Brussels, 11 June 2002, 21 (are unfair: clauses stipulating that disputing an invoice does not release the consumer from his payment obligation).

1274 See *infra* no. 755.

1275 **Belgium**: Art. 5.88 BCC. V. Sagaert, *Beginselen van verbintenissenrecht. De contractuele en quasi-contractuele verbintenissen*, Leuven, LeA Uitgevers, 2023, 122–123, no. 228. **The Netherlands**: Art. 6:91 DCC. C.H. Sieburgh, *Mr. C. Assers Handleiding tot de beoefening van het Nederlands Burgerlijk Recht. 6. Verbintenissenrecht. Deel III. Algemeen overeenkomstenrecht*, Deventer, Wolters Kluwer, 2022, no. 414 and 416.

1276 I. Claeys and T. Tanghe, *Nieuw Algemeen Contractenrecht*, Antwerp, Intersentia, 2023, 738, no. 975; S. Stijns, *Verbintenissenrecht*, Boek 1, Bruges, Die Keure, 2022, 239.

1277 C.H. Sieburgh, *Mr. C. Assers Handleiding tot de beoefening van het Nederlands Burgerlijk Recht. 6. Verbintenissenrecht. Deel III. Algemeen overeenkomstenrecht*, Deventer, Wolters Kluwer, 2022, no. 414.

1278 **Belgium**: Cass. (BE) 3 February 1995, *Arr.Cass.* 1995, 130; I. Claeys and T. Tanghe, *Nieuw Algemeen Contractenrecht*, Antwerp, Intersentia, 2023, 737, no. 974. **The Netherlands**: C.H. Sieburgh, *Mr. C. Assers Handleiding tot de beoefening van het Nederlands Burgerlijk Recht. 6. Verbintenissenrecht. Deel III. Algemeen overeenkomstenrecht*, Deventer, Wolters Kluwer, 2022, no. 414.

1279 **Belgium**: Art. 5.88, §1 BCC. V. Sagaert, *Beginselen van verbintenissenrecht. De contractuele en quasi-contractuele verbintenissen*, Leuven, LeA Uitgevers, 2023, 123. **The Netherlands**: C.H. Sieburgh, *Mr. C. Assers Handleiding tot de beoefening van het Nederlands Burgerlijk*

Indemnity clauses are valid in principle under both Belgian and Dutch law, although they are subject to certain validity requirements and/or limits. The Belgian blacklist contains two limits on indemnity clauses in B2C contracts. First, indemnity clauses may not be excessive, which means that the compensation amount may not be clearly disproportionate to the damage that may be suffered by the PSS supplier.[1280] To avoid the indemnity clause being deemed excessive, the amount of the indemnity can be linked to the actual loss (e.g. in case of a late return of a product, a *pro rata* amount equal to the fee that the PSS supplier would otherwise be able to charge to another PSS user) and/or limit it to a maximum amount (e.g. in case the PSS user does not return the product or returns the product too late, the indemnity could be the price needed to pay for a replacement product, as well as the administrative costs of ordering and processing the replacement product).[1281] Second, indemnity clauses must be reciprocal.[1282] This means that if the PSS contract contains an indemnity clause targeting the PSS user-consumer, the PSS contract must also contain a similar or equivalent indemnity clause targeting the PSS supplier.[1283] For assessing the reciprocity of an indemnity clause, the entire PSS contract must be considered. For example, the obligation to return the product at the end of the PSS contract will generally rest solely on the PSS user (besides, of course, the PSS supplier's obligation to receive the product). Thus, an indemnity clause containing a late return fee if the PSS user does not return the product on time cannot be made reciprocal in and of itself. However, an equivalent indemnity clause can be included elsewhere in the PSS contract, for example in case the PSS supplier fails to make the product available at the agreed start date of the PSS contract.[1284] Under Dutch law, indemnity clauses are not on the grey- or blacklist,[1285] but they can be challenged when they are unreasonably onerous within the meaning of article 6:233, *sub* a. DCC.[1286] For indemnity clauses not included in general terms and conditions (and therefore not subject to the Dutch unfair terms regime), the court may mitigate the indemnity clause upon the debtor's

Recht. 6. Verbintenissenrecht. Deel III. Algemeen overeenkomstenrecht, Deventer, Wolters Kluwer, 2022, no. 414.

1280 Art. VI.83, 24° WER. In non-B2C contracts, Art. 5.88, §2 old BCC allows for mitigation of such clauses. However, according to the case law of the CJEU, the sanction for unfair indemnity clauses is their nullity without mitigation being allowed. See *supra* no. 178.

1281 C. Borucki, H. Slachmuylders, B. Keirsbilck, D. Gruyaert and E. Terryn, *Model clauses for Product-as-a-Service (PaaS) contracts*, CE Center. Circular Economy Policy Research Center, 2022–23, 22.

1282 Art. VI.83, 17° BCEL. Belgian law is therefore stricter than the indicative list of the UCTD.

1283 By contrast, an indemnity clause solely targeting the PSS supplier must not necessarily be reciprocal.

1284 C. Borucki, H. Slachmuylders, B. Keirsbilck, D. Gruyaert and E. Terryn, *Model clauses for Product-as-a-Service (PaaS) contracts*, CE Center. Circular Economy Policy Research Center, 2022–23, 22.

1285 Art. 6:236 and 6:237 DCC.

1286 C.H. Sieburgh, *Mr. C. Assers Handleiding tot de beoefening van het Nederlands Burgerlijk Recht. 6. Verbintenissenrecht. Deel III. Algemeen overeenkomstenrecht*, Deventer, Wolters Kluwer, 2022, no. 426.

request if this is required by standards of reasonableness and fairness, on the understanding that it cannot grant the creditor less compensation for damages than would have been due by virtue of the statutory provisions.[1287] The court's mitigation power cannot be excluded in the PSS contract.[1288]

305. Model clauses on compensation for damages – The following model indemnity clauses can be used for situations where the PSS user returns the product too late. They stipulate a reasonable amount of damages, calculated either pro rata based on the monthly fee, or corresponding to the price of a replacement product. To ensure fairness, a reciprocal indemnity clause was also drafted for the PSS supplier in case the product is not delivered on time. Including other indemnity clauses in the PSS contract (for other breaches of contract) in line with these principles is of course also possible.

Model clause #6 – compensation for damages

- **If [the PSS user] does not return the product within the stipulated time, [the PSS user] shall pay a compensation for damages of [reasonable amount] per day of delay, calculated on a pro-rata basis equal to the monthly fee. In any case, this compensation for damages shall not exceed [reasonable maximum amount], corresponding to the price needed for a replacement product plus the administrative costs associated with ordering and processing the replacement.**
- **If [the PSS supplier] fails to make the product available to [the PSS user] at [the agreed start date of the contract/the agreed date of delivery], [the PSS supplier] shall pay a compensation for damages of [reasonable amount], which represents the cost that [the PSS user] incurs due to the unavailability of the product. In any case, this compensation for damages shall not exceed [reasonable amount].**

306. Termination clauses – As the rules on the remedy of termination are not mandatory law, the PSS contract may include a wide variety of termination clauses relating to the conditions for (judicial or extrajudicial) termination, as well as the consequences or extent of the termination. For example, the contracting parties may exclude the possibility of an extrajudicial termination by requiring a judicial authorisation to terminate the PSS contract.[1289]

[1287] Art. 6:94(1) DCC. H.N. Schelhaas, *Groene Serie Verbintenissenrecht, commentaar op art. 6:94 BW*, 2017, no. 12. Additionally, these clauses may not be unacceptable in the light of reasonableness and fairness (Art. 6:248 DCC). See: HR (NL) 17 December 2004, *NJ* 2005/271.

[1288] Art. 6:94(3) DCC. C.H. Sieburgh, *Mr. C. Assers Handleiding tot de beoefening van het Nederlands Burgerlijk Recht. 6. Verbintenissenrecht. Deel III. Algemeen overeenkomstenrecht*, Deventer, Wolters Kluwer, 2022, no. 425.

[1289] **Belgium**: I. Claeys and T. Tanghe, *Nieuw Algemeen Contractenrecht*, Antwerp, Intersentia, 2023, 833. **The Netherlands**: C.H. Sieburgh, *Mr. C. Assers Handleiding tot de beoefening van het Nederlands Burgerlijk Recht. 6. Verbintenissenrecht. Deel III. Algemeen overeenkomstenrecht*, Deventer, Wolters Kluwer, 2022, no. 689.

Alternatively, they may include an express termination clause. This is a clause that gives a contracting party or all contracting parties the right to unilaterally terminate the contract without judicial intervention in the event of a series of enumerated breaches of contract.[1290] The contracting parties may also agree in advance whether a certain non-performance is sufficiently serious to warrant the termination of the contract.[1291] The PSS contract may also set out procedural requirements and time limits, as well as provide a final grace period during which the party in default can still fulfil its obligations. Yet another category of clauses relates to termination clauses that allow the PSS contract to be partially terminated.[1292] This can be particularly useful in very complex PSS contracts where several (severable) accessory services are included. Finally, the PSS contract may also contain an arrangement regarding the restitution of the product after termination of the contract.[1293]

As with the other remedies for breach of contract, there are some limits to the parties' contractual freedom to include termination clauses in the PSS contract. Both the Belgian and Dutch unfair terms blacklists prohibit clauses that prohibit the PSS user-consumer from claiming the termination of the contract in case the PSS supplier fails to comply with its obligations.[1294] Under Belgian law, it should also again be taken into account that terms that unduly exclude or restrict the consumer's legal rights against the business in the event of a breach of contract are unfair.[1295] Finally, both under Belgian and Dutch law, termination clauses may be violating the general unfairness test if they create a significant imbalance between the rights and obligations to the detriment of the consumer.[1296] For use-oriented PSS contracts, which will often (at least partly) qualify as a rental contract, it is important to note that Article 1762*bis* of the old BCC, which prohibits express termination clauses in rental contracts for immovables, does not apply to rental contracts for movables.[1297] Nevertheless, express termination clauses in use-oriented PSS contracts qualifying as a rental

1290 **Belgium**: I. Claeys and T. Tanghe, *Nieuw Algemeen Contractenrecht*, Antwerp, Intersentia, 2023, 630. **The Netherlands**: C.H. Sieburgh, *Mr. C. Assers Handleiding tot de beoefening van het Nederlands Burgerlijk Recht. 6. Verbintenissenrecht. Deel III. Algemeen overeenkomstenrecht*, Deventer, Wolters Kluwer, 2022, no. 689.

1291 **Belgium**: I. Claeys and T. Tanghe, *Nieuw Algemeen Contractenrecht*, Antwerp, Intersentia, 2023, 831. **The Netherlands**: C.H. Sieburgh, *Mr. C. Assers Handleiding tot de beoefening van het Nederlands Burgerlijk Recht. 6. Verbintenissenrecht. Deel III. Algemeen overeenkomstenrecht*, Deventer, Wolters Kluwer, 2022, no. 684.

1292 I. Claeys and T. Tanghe, *Nieuw Algemeen Contractenrecht*, Antwerp, Intersentia, 2023, 833.

1293 See on the obligation of the PSS user to return the product also *infra* section 7.4.1.

1294 **Belgium**: Art. VI.83, 7° BCEL. **The Netherlands**: Art. 6:236, *sub* b. DCC.

1295 Art. VI.83, 30° BCEL.

1296 **Belgium**: Art. I.8, 22° BCEL. **The Netherlands**: Art. 6:233, *sub* a. DCC.

1297 See: Ct. Hoei (BE) 11 March 1947, *Pas.* 1947, III, 27. See also: S. Stijns, S. Jansen and F. Peeraer, "Schorsing en beëindiging van de huurovereenkomst naar gemeen recht" in M. Dambre, B. Hubeau and S. Stijns (eds.), *Handboek algemeen huurrecht*, Bruges, die Keure, 2015, (685) 745, no. 68; C. Marr, "Le contrat de location mobilière: quelle réglementation appliquer face au mutisme du Code Civil?", *TBBR* 2008, (217) 217.

contract for movables may in certain circumstances be unfair under the general test if, alone or in conjunction with other clauses in the PSS contract, they create a significant imbalance between the parties' rights and obligations.[1298]

307. Model clauses on termination of the PSS contract – The following model clauses can be used to regulate the remedy of termination in the PSS contract. The first model clause explicitly excludes the possibility of extrajudicial termination by requiring a judicial authorisation for the termination of the PSS contract. The second model contract serves as an express termination clause. It states that a party (in this case the PSS supplier, but it can also be adapted to serve as an express termination clause for the benefit of the PSS user) has the right to unilaterally terminate the PSS contract without judicial authorisation being required if the other party does not comply with one of the listed obligations. The third model clause provides that each party has the right to terminate the PSS contract in case of a repeated failure to fulfil the obligations under the terms and conditions of the PSS contract. The fourth model clause provides an example of a clause defining in advance which breaches of contract are sufficiently serious to warrant a termination of the PSS contract. The fifth model clause requires a final grace period to be granted before a party can terminate the contract. The sixth model clause may serve as an example to enable the parties to partially terminate the PSS contract. Finally, the last model clause on termination deals with the restitution obligation of the PSS user after termination of the contract.

Model clause #7 – termination of the contract

- **The parties agree that any termination of this contract must be authorised by a competent judicial authority. Extrajudicial termination is hereby explicitly excluded.**

- **[The PSS supplier] has the right to unilaterally terminate the contract without judicial authorisation being required in the event of the following breaches of contract:**

  (i) [the PSS user] is in default of the payment obligations [for two successive billing periods];

  (ii) [the PSS user] has failed to comply with the terms of the contract and/or uses the product or service in a manner which is contrary to its intended use or contrary to these terms;

  (iii) [other breaches of contract allowing for an extrajudicial termination].

1298 I. Claeys and T. Tanghe, *Nieuw Algemeen Contractenrecht*, Antwerp, Intersentia, 2023, 835.

- **Either party has the right to terminate the contract if the other party has repeatedly failed to fulfil its obligations under these terms.**
- **The parties agree in advance that the following non-performances are considered sufficiently serious to warrant termination of this contract:**

  (i) failure to deliver the product within [reasonable timeframe (e.g. two weeks)] of the agreed delivery date;

  (ii) intentional damage to the product or damage due to gross negligence;

  (iii) [other breaches of contract deemed sufficiently serious by the contracting parties].
- **Before the contract can be terminated, the defaulting party must be given a written notice of default specifying the breach and providing a final grace period of [reasonable period] to fulfil its obligations.**
- **In cases of non-performance regarding [specific accessory service (e.g. monthly deliveries of laundry detergent)], any affected party can opt for partial termination of those services, leaving the rest of the contract intact.**
- **Upon termination of the contract, [the PSS user] must return the product to [the PSS supplier] within [reasonable amount of time (e.g. 7 days)]. The returned product must be in its original condition, excluding normal wear and tear.**

308. ENAC CLAUSES – Under both Belgian and Dutch law, the legal provisions on the enac are not mandatory law nor of public order.[1299] This means that, in principle, the contracting parties can extend, limit or exclude the possibility to suspend the obligations under the PSS contract in case of non-performance.[1300]

Regarding the validity of clauses governing, limiting or excluding the enac and the right to suspend performance under the contract, there are again a number of limits on the parties' freedom of contract. Under Belgian law, clauses obliging the PSS user-consumer to fulfil his obligations, while the PSS user-business has not fulfilled or is in default of fulfilling its own obligations are unfair *per se*.[1301] As such, the enac may not be excluded in PSS contracts with consumers. Additionally, an undue exclusion or limitation of a legal right

1299 **Belgium**: D. DECLOEDT, "ENAC-clausules of opschortingsclausules" in E. TERRYN, A.-L. VERBEKE, H. DE DECKER, G.-L. BALLON, B. TILLEMAN and V. SAGAERT (eds.), *Contractuele clausules. Gemeenrechtelijke clausules. Volume II*, Antwerp, Intersentia, 2013, (1035) 1035–1142; J. HERBOTS, "De exceptie van niet-nakoming", *TPR* 1991, (380) 386. **The Netherlands**: P.T.J. WOLTERS, *Opschortingsrechten (Mon. BW B32b)*, Deventer, Wolters Kluwer, 2022, 6–7.

1300 *Ibid.*

1301 Art. VI.83, 9° BCEL.

in cases of default, such as the enac, is unfair in a B2C relationship.[1302] Under Dutch law, clauses excluding or limiting the legal right of the PSS user-consumer to suspend performance, as well as clauses granting the PSS supplier-business a more far-reaching right to suspend performance than it is entitled to under the law, are blacklisted and therefore unfair *per se*.[1303] Finally, as always, enac clauses can be combated using the general unfairness test[1304] if they create a significant imbalance to the detriment of the consumer, or be contrary to the prohibition of abuse of law/the principles of reasonableness and fairness.

309. Model enac clauses – As both Belgian and Dutch law prohibit clauses that exclude the right of consumers to suspend their obligations in case of a breach of contract by the PSS supplier, the following model clauses deal with how the right to suspend the obligations under the contract can be made concrete in the PSS contract.

The first model clause deals with the situation where the PSS supplier fails to perform the obligations under the PSS contract, for example when the product is unavailable, or the additional services are not performed. The second model clause is the mirror provision. It provides that the PSS supplier may suspend its obligations, such as maintenance, repair or replacement of the product, if the PSS user does not comply with obligations (e.g. the obligation to pay the price[1305] or the obligation to take care of the product as a reasonable and careful person[1306]). Finally, the last model clause specifically deals with the situation where the PSS user does not pay the monthly fee for a PSS where "smart" products are offered as-a-service. It provides that the PSS supplier will send a notice of default granting a final grace period. If the PSS user still does not pay the monthly fee, the product may be disabled from a distance. For example, the cartridges of a "smart" printer can be disabled, a smartphone can be put in "lost mode" or a "smart" washing machine can be remotely switched off.

Model clause #8 – right to suspend the obligations under the contract

- **If [the PSS supplier] fails to perform the obligations under this contract, this will result in the loss of the right to payment by [the PSS user], until [the PSS supplier] has performed the obligations.**

1302 Art. VI.83, 30° BCEL.
1303 Art. 6:236, *sub* c. DCC.
1304 **Belgium:** Art. I.8, 22° BCEL. **The Netherlands:** Art. 6:233, *sub* a. DCC.
1305 See on this obligation *infra* section 5.2.
1306 See on this obligation *infra* section 7.3.1.

- **If [the PSS user] fails to perform the obligations under this contract, this will result in the loss of [specified right (e.g. the right to maintenance and repair, and, where applicable, to a replacement product)] by [the PSS supplier] until [the PSS user] has performed the obligations.**
- **If [the PSS user] fails to pay the monthly fee as stipulated in this contract, [the PSS supplier] will sent a notice of default, granting a final grace period of [reasonable amount of time (e.g. 14 days)] to rectify the default. If the payment is not received within this grace period, [the PSS supplier] reserves the right to suspend its obligations under this contract by remotely disabling access to the product and additional services until full payment is received. [Additionally, the PSS supplier may seek other remedies for breach of contract, including but not limited to termination of the contract and compensation for damages].**

310. NOTICE OF DEFAULT CLAUSES – The contracting parties may include clauses on the requirement of a prior notice of default clauses in the PSS contract. The content of these clauses will usually be that no notice of default is required in case of breach of contract.[1307] Since notice of default clauses deviate from the general law of obligations, they are usually interpreted restrictively or strictly, and thus must be drafted precisely and unambiguously.[1308] For example, a judgment of the Antwerp Court of Appeal held that a clause stating that "*interest will be due by operation of law*" is not sufficient to conclude that no notice of default is required.[1309] On the other hand, a clause that stated that "*this agreement shall be terminated by operation of law and without any formality if* …", was considered a valid contractual exception to the requirement of a prior notice of default.[1310]

311. NOTICE OF DEFAULT CLAUSES IN ANALYSED PSS CONTRACTS – The PSS contracts analysed make frequent use of notice of default clauses. For instance, several PSS contracts stipulate that in case of non-payment of the periodical fee,

---

1307 **Belgium**: I. CLAEYS and T. TANGHE, *Nieuw Algemeen Contractenrecht*, Antwerp, Intersentia, 2023, 667. **The Netherlands**: C.H. SIEBURGH, *Mr. C. Assers Handleiding tot de beoefening van het Nederlands Burgerlijk Recht. 6. Verbintenissenrecht. Deel III. Algemeen overeenkomstenrecht*, Deventer, Wolters Kluwer, 2022, no. 388.

1308 I. CLAEYS and T. TANGHE, *Nieuw Algemeen Contractenrecht*, Antwerp, Intersentia, 2023, 667; R. VAN RANSBEECK, "Sancties bij niet nakoming – Ingebrekestelling" in *Comm.Bijz. Ov.*, Mechelen, Kluwer, 2015, (147) 157; R. KRUITHOF, H. BOCKEN, F. DE LY and B. DE TEMMERMAN, "Verbintenissenrecht (1981–1992). Overzicht van rechtspraak", *TPR* 1994, (171) 628.

1309 Antwerp (BE) 17 November 2008, *Limb.Rechtsl.* 2009, 109, case note I. SAMOY (regarding a termination clause in a sales contract for an immovable property).

1310 Antwerp (BE) 1 December 2008, *Limb.Rechtsl.* 2009, 294, case note E. MONARD. See also Brussels (BE) 22 January 2013, *Res Jur.Imm.* 2014, 236 (clause that stated that "*the contractor will be liable by operation of law to pay a delay penalty of […]*" is a valid notice of default clause).

the PSS user will be in default by operation of law (*van rechtswege, de plein droit*) without a notice of default being required. This is for example the case with *Live Light* and *Mudjeans*.[1311] Other contracts, such as those of *Swapfiets* and *Blue Movement* stipulate that in case of non-payment, the PSS user is in default by operation of law, but that before additional charges or negligence interest are charged, the PSS user is given another reminder to pay within a certain time.[1312] It is also possible that the PSS contract gives the PSS user an "informal" grace period in case of non-payment of the periodic fee before sending a formal notice of default. For example, the terms and conditions of *Bundles* provide that a digital reminder is sent first, and if it is not complied with, a formal notice of default will follow.[1313] The PSS contract may also confirm the principle that a prior notice of default is always required for certain remedies, such as the termination of the contract. For example, the terms and conditions of *Bundles* set out an explicit requirement for a notice of default before termination of the contract is possible.[1314] Finally, several PSS offers provide for immediate termination of the PSS contract without notice of default in exhaustively listed situations (e.g. death of the PSS user, the PSS user is no longer in possession of the product, PSS user is placed under guardianship, incorrect information provided by the PSS user, third parties wish to seize the product, etc.).[1315]

312. Exemption clauses – The PSS supplier may also attempt to exempt itself or limit its liability through a variety of exemption clauses (*exoneratieclausule, clause exonératoire*). Although exemption clauses are recognised in principle under Belgian law and Dutch law because of the parties' freedom of contract, they are subject to very strict conditions.[1316]

For example, under Belgian law these clauses must (i) not be contrary to mandatory law or public order; (ii) not free the service provider from personal fraud or intent; and (iii) not devoid the contract of its purpose.[1317] In addition, Article VI. 83, 13° of the BCEL in a B2C context also prohibits exemption for personal gross negligence and exemption for intent of auxiliaries.[1318] However, this provision only concerns clauses intended to completely *exclude* the liability

---

1311 Art. 8.3 Terms and Conditions Live Light and Art. 4.5 Terms and Conditions Mudjeans.

1312 Art. 10.3 Terms and Conditions Swapfiets and Art. 5.7 Terms and Conditions Blue Movement.

1313 Art. 5 Terms and Conditions Bundles.

1314 Art. 12.5 Terms and Conditions Bundles.

1315 Art. 12.2 Terms and Conditions Bundles and Art. 12.2 Terms and Conditions Blue Movement.

1316 **Belgium**: See: A. Van Oevelen, "Exoneratiebedingen en vrijwaringsbedingen" in V. Sagaert and D. Lambrecht (eds.), *Actuele ontwikkelingen inzake verbintenissenrecht*, Antwerp, Intersentia, 2009, (1) 1–36. **The Netherlands**: C. Cauffman and P. Croes, *Groene Serie Verbintenissenrecht, Art. 6:75 BW*, Deventer, Deventer, 2021, no. 7.7.

1317 S. Stijns, *Verbintenissenrecht*, Boek 1, Bruges, Die Keure, 2022, 211–215. See also Art. 5.89 BCC.

1318 See also Art. VI.83, 25° BCEL, which prohibits exemption clauses for death or personal injury to the consumer.

of the PSS supplier and not to *limit* the liability of the PSS supplier. Yet, clauses unduly limiting the liability of the PSS supplier can still be combated using other provisions of unfair clauses, including the general standard.[1319]

Also under Dutch law, the PSS supplier can, in principle, exempt itself from liability.[1320] These exemption clauses may not be contrary to mandatory law or public order[1321] and may also be invalid if they are unacceptable in the light of reasonableness and fairness (Art. 6:248 DCC).[1322] Furthermore, in the case of an exemption clause included in general terms and conditions, the exemption can be annulled if it is unreasonably onerous (Art. 6:233 *sub* a. DCC).[1323] In particular for B2C contracts, Article 6:237, *sub* f. DCC should also be mentioned. According to this grey list provision, a clause in general terms and conditions "*which fully or partially releases the user*[1324] *or a third party from a statutory obligation to pay damages*" is presumed to be unreasonably onerous.[1325]

313. Model exemption clause – The following model clause can serve as an example of a valid exemption clause, at least under Belgian law. It limits (instead of totally excluding) the PSS supplier's liability to direct damages arising out of or relating to the performance of the PSS contract. Additionally, the amount of liability can be limited to a percentage of the contract value (e.g. the total amounts paid or payable by the PSS user during the 12 months prior to the incident giving rise to liability) or the amount covered by the professional liability insurance taken out by the PSS supplier. Finally, it also acknowledges the limits Belgian law places on exemption clauses, namely by confirming that the clause does not exclude the PSS supplier's (or its auxiliaries') liability for fraud, intentional fault, gross negligence, death or personal injury to the consumer, as well as any other forms of liability that cannot be limited or excluded due to mandatory legal provisions. This provision can also be used under Dutch law, although it will be (rebuttably) presumed unreasonably onerous by virtue of Article 6:237, *sub* f. DCC if used in general terms and conditions. The PSS

1319 Art. I.8, 22° BEC. See also: Art. VI.83, 25° BCEL and VI.83, 30° BCEL.

1320 T.F.E. Tjong Tjin Tai, *Asser 7-IV Bijzondere Overeenkomsten – Opdracht, incl. de geneeskundige behandelingsovereenkomst en de reisovereenkomst*, Deventer, Wolters Kluwer, 2018, no. 211. See, however, for a comprehensive overview of the limits to exemption clauses: C.H. Sieburgh, *Mr. C. Assers Handleiding tot de beoefening van het Nederlands Burgerlijk Recht. 6. Verbintenissenrecht. Deel I. De verbintenis in het algemeen, eerste gedeelte*, Deventer, Wolters Kluwer, 2020, no. 364–369.

1321 See Art. 3:40 DCC. This is e.g. the case with exemption clauses regarding fraud or intent.

1322 G.T. de Jong, H.B. Krans and M.H. Wissink, *Verbintenissenrecht algemeen (Studiereeks Burgerlijk Recht, deel 4)*, Deventer, Wolters Kluwer, 2018, 171–172.

1323 See also: T.H.M. Wechem, "Leren exonereren: een aantal gezichtspunten ten aanzien van het contractueel reguleren van aansprakelijkheid", *Contracteren* 2019, vol. 3, (89) 89–99.

1324 This is the user of the general terms and conditions (the PSS supplier) and not the PSS user.

1325 See also: J. Hijma, *Algemene voorwaarden, Monografieën BW nr. B55*, Deventer, Wolters Kluwer, 2016, chapter 6.

supplier will therefore have to prove that in those situations, a limitation of liability is not unreasonably onerous in that specific case.

Model clause #9 – Liability under this contract

- **To the fullest extent permitted by [Belgian] law, [the PSS supplier] shall not be liable for any indirect, incidental or consequential damage, including but not limited to loss of profits, revenue or data. [The PSS supplier's] liability for any claim arising out of or relating to the performance of this contract shall be limited to direct damages only, and such liability shall not exceed [specific amount or percentage of the contract value/the amount covered by the professional liability insurance taken out by the PSS supplier]. Nothing in this contract shall exclude or limit [the PSS supplier's or its auxiliaries'] liability for fraud, intentional fault, gross negligence, death or personal injury to the consumer, or any breach of obligations imposed by mandatory [Belgian] law that cannot be contractually excluded or limited.**

2.7. DURATION OF THE PSS CONTRACT

314. Duration, (early) termination and extension/renewal of the PSS contract – This section addresses the duration of the PSS contract. This includes the question of (early) termination of the PSS contract and extension or renewal of the PSS contract. In the first subsection, the concept of and rules applicable to fixed-term PSS contracts – i.e. PSS contracts containing an extinctive term – are discussed (section 2.7.1). The second subsection then continues with an analysis of the rules applicable to open-ended PSS contracts – i.e. PSS contracts entered into for an indeterminate term (section 2.7.2). Finally, the third subsection sets out some model clauses regarding the duration of the contract for both fixed-term and open-ended PSS contracts (section 2.7.3).

2.7.1. FIXED-TERM PSS CONTRACTS

2.7.1.1. Concept

315. Fixed-term PSS contracts: extinctive term – The PSS contract is entered into for a fixed term if it contains an extinctive term.[1326] An extinctive term is a certain and future event that leads to the extinction of the obligation or contract.[1327] The extinctive term may have an exact date (e.g. 1 March) or

1326 Art. 5.76(1) BCC; I. Claeys and T. Tanghe, *Nieuw Algemeen Contractenrecht*, Antwerp, Intersentia, 2023, 522, no. 645.

1327 See for a definition: Art. 5.149 BCC.

duration (e.g. one month, one year). However, the exact date or duration of the term does not necessarily have to be known already at the conclusion of the contract. Indeed, a PSS contract may also be a fixed-term contract if it specifies a future event that is certain, but with uncertain timing. For example, the parties to the PSS contract can make the extinctive term dependent on the date when it is no longer (reasonably) possible to repair the product. It is certain that the product will one day break down, but the exact date on which this will happen is unknown.[1328] Alternatively, the extinctive term may also be determinable (rather than determined), for example in case of a contract for the completion of a specific work or service.[1329]

316. EXAMPLES – The majority of the PSS contracts analysed provide an extinctive term and therefore constitute fixed-term PSS contracts. Examples include *Blue Movement*, *Papillon*, and *Fairphone Easy*.

> TERMS AND CONDITIONS BLUE MOVEMENT – Art. 11.1 "The Contract is entered into for the specific duration agreed between BSH and Lessee at the time of entering into the Contract (Minimum Contract Period), in accordance with the terms of the relevant Subscription."

> TERMS AND CONDITIONS PAPILLON – Art. 2.1 "This Rental Contract is entered into for a term of ten years, commencing on the date of delivery of the Appliance in accordance with what is set out below."

> TERMS AND CONDITIONS FAIRPHONE *EASY* – Art. 7.1 "The As-a-Service Agreement and Subscription are concluded for a definite period of time. [...]" Art. 7.3 "The As-a-Service and Subscription time period are agreed upon in the order process. [...]"

317. CONSEQUENCE OF EXTINCTIVE TERM: PSS CONTRACT AUTOMATICALLY EXTINGUISHES FOR THE FUTURE – When the extinctive term has expired, the PSS contract automatically extinguishes for the future (*ex nunc*).[1330] This means that, in principle, no notice or other notification is needed to trigger the extinctive term and terminate the fixed-term PSS contract.[1331] However, these rules may be deviated from by the parties or by a statutory provision. For example, the parties may derogate from the automatic end of the fixed-term PSS contract by including a tacit extension or renewal clause in the PSS contract.[1332] Additionally, both

1328 C. BORUCKI, H. SLACHMUYLDERS, B. KEIRSBILCK, D. GRUYAERT and E. TERRYN, *Model clauses for Product-as-a-Service (PaaS) contracts*, CE Center. Circular Economy Policy Research Center, 2022–23, 73.

1329 I. CLAEYS and L. PHANG, "Van bepaalde duur naar onbepaalde duur en terug", *TPR* 2008, (375) 430.

1330 Art. 5.151 BCC.

1331 I. CLAEYS and T. TANGHE, *Nieuw Algemeen Contractenrecht*, Antwerp, Intersentia, 2023, 523, no. 647.

1332 See on tacit extension or renewal *infra* no. 325 *et seq.*

the Belgian and Dutch rental contract rules provide that if the lessee keeps paying the rental price and the lessor does not object to the continued use of the product, the rental contract will be tacitly renewed.[1333, 1334]

318. In principle no subjective right to extend or renew fixed-term PSS contract – Fixed-term PSS contracts thus end automatically or by operation of law upon expiry of the contractually agreed duration. However, they can be extended or renewed (tacitly or expressly) if provided for by contract or law. Without such contractual or statutory grounds, the parties cannot claim a subjective right to extend or renew the PSS contract. In other words, the parties to the PSS contract resume their freedom of contract (including the freedom not to contract) after the expiry of the contract term.[1335]

2.7.1.2. Early termination of fixed-term PSS contracts?

319. In principle no early termination – A fixed-term PSS contract must in principle be performed until its end.[1336] Given the principle of the binding force of the contract, the contracting parties may not unilaterally terminate a fixed-term PSS contract early.[1337] If one of the contracting parties does so anyway, this will generally constitute a breach of the PSS contract. Of course, this does not affect the ability of contracting parties to terminate the contract by mutual consent.

320. Statutory provision, the contract or usages may grant right to unilaterally terminate fixed-term contracts – A contracting party can unilaterally terminate a fixed-term PSS contract only if a statutory provision, the PSS contract or usages[1338] provide for that right to unilaterally terminate the PSS contract.[1339] An application of this rule can be found in the terms and conditions of *Blue Movement*.[1340]

1333 **Belgium**: Art. 1738–1740 old BCC. **The Netherlands**: Art. 7:230 DCC.

1334 See more in-depth *infra* no. 881.

1335 I. Claeys and T. Tanghe, *Nieuw Algemeen Contractenrecht*, Antwerp, Intersentia, 2023, 524, no. 649.

1336 Explanatory Memorandum, *Parliamentary Papers* Chamber 2020–21, no. 55–1806/1, 88–89.

1337 **Belgium**: Art. 5.70 BCC; I. Claeys and T. Tanghe, *Nieuw Algemeen Contractenrecht*, Antwerp, Intersentia, 2023, 435, no. 525. **The Netherlands**: C.H. Sieburgh, *Mr. C. Assers Handleiding tot de beoefening van het Nederlands Burgerlijk Recht. 6. Verbintenissenrecht. Deel III. Algemeen overeenkomstenrecht*, Deventer, Wolters Kluwer, 2022, no. 408.

1338 In the context of PSS contracts, usages as a source of a unilateral termination right will be less relevant. The contract between a client and a lawyer and between a patient and a doctor are typical examples, where both parties have the right to terminate the contract at any time given the relationship of trust underlying the contract. See: I. Claeys and T. Tanghe, *Nieuw Algemeen Contractenrecht*, Antwerp, Intersentia, 2023, 537–538.

1339 Art. 5.76(3) BCC.

1340 Art. 11.2 Terms and Conditions Blue Movement.

TERMS AND CONDITIONS BLUE MOVEMENT – Art. 11.2 "The Contract cannot be terminated by the Lessee during the Minimum Contract Period (as indicated in the ordering process) unless specifically agreed otherwise in writing in the Conditions or by separate agreement between BSH and Lessee."

321. STATUTORY PROVISIONS ALLOWING TO UNILATERALLY TERMINATE THE CONTRACT – In the first place, a contracting party may derive the right to unilaterally terminate the fixed-term PSS contract from a statutory provision. In the context of PSS contracts, the rules of the contract for services stand out.

Under Belgian law, if the fixed-term PSS contract is qualified as a contract for services (which will generally be the case with result-oriented PSS and some types of use-oriented PSS),[1341] the PSS user-client (and not the PSS supplier-service provider) has the right to unilaterally terminate the fixed-term contract.[1342] However, that termination comes with the obligation to compensate the PSS supplier-service provider for all his expenses, all his work and loss of profit.[1343] This rule is only default law, so the PSS contract may deviate from this. Additionally, it also does not apply to open-ended PSS contracts that qualify as contracts for services.[1344] Also under Dutch law, if the PSS contract is qualified as a contract for services, the PSS user-client has a unilateral termination right "at all times".[1345] This provision applies to both fixed-term and open-ended contracts for services. In contracts where the PSS user is a non-professional client (which will be the case if he is a consumer), this rule is even mandatory law.[1346] As a result, this unilateral termination right cannot be deviated from in B2C PSS contracts that qualify as a contract for services. Even more, this also implies that this right cannot be modulated by imposing a contractual notice period.[1347] Additionally, the Dutch rules of the contract for services provide that non-professional clients who use their unilateral termination right cannot be liable for damages in respect of that termination.[1348] However, they must still reimburse expenses incurred by the service provider[1349] and may also be owned

1341 See *infra* section 3.5 and section 3.4.2.

1342 Art. 1794 old BCC.

1343 *Ibid.*

1344 F. VERMANDER, *De opzegging van overeenkomsten*, Antwerp, Intersentia, 2014, 156.

1345 Art. 7:408(1) DCC; T.F.E. TJONG TJIN TAI, *Asser 7-IV Bijzondere Overeenkomsten – Opdracht, incl. de geneeskundige behandelingsovereenkomst en de reisovereenkomst*, Deventer, Wolters Kluwer, 2022, no. 160.

1346 Art. 7:413(2) DCC; T.F.E. TJONG TJIN TAI, *Asser 7-IV Bijzondere Overeenkomsten – Opdracht, incl. de geneeskundige behandelingsovereenkomst en de reisovereenkomst*, Deventer, Wolters Kluwer, 2022, no. 164.

1347 T.F.E. TJONG TJIN TAI, *Asser 7-IV Bijzondere Overeenkomsten – Opdracht, incl. de geneeskundige behandelingsovereenkomst en de reisovereenkomst*, Deventer, Wolters Kluwer, 2022, no. 164.

1348 Art. 7:408(3) DCC. This provision is mandatory law (Art. 7:413(1) DCC).

1349 Art. 7:406 DCC.

fees for the already performed services.[1350, 1351] Thus, in this case, a potential early termination fee may only cover these expenses and fees and should not include damages.[1352]

If the PSS contract is qualified as a rental contract for movables,[1353] the Belgian and Dutch statutory provisions do not regulate the termination option and its modalities in a mandatory way (contrary to, for example, the rules applicable to residential or commercial rental contracts).[1354] As a result, the contractual parties can deviate from these provisions and fletch out their own contractual regime.

322. Contract clauses allowing to unilaterally terminate the contract (early termination clauses) – A second possible basis for a contracting party to terminate a fixed-term PSS contract early is if the PSS contract contains a clause allowing unilateral termination of the contract, i.e. an early termination clause.[1355] Such a clause gives one or more parties the right to terminate the contract unilaterally and specifies the modalities to do so. For example, the clause may state that a written notification is needed for exercising the unilateral termination right and may also stipulate a notice period that must be taken into account before the contract is terminated. The Belgian and Dutch unfair terms rules do not contain any specific mandatory rules on this type of clause (except for the Belgian blacklist which prohibits clauses allowing the PSS supplier to unilaterally terminate the contract without compensation for the consumer[1356]). However, it is advisable that the clause grants the right to terminate to each party (and not merely to the PSS supplier). Indeed, as convincingly argued by Bruloot, non-reciprocal unilateral termination clauses (i.e. clauses where the PSS user does not have the option to terminate the PSS

1350 Art. 7:411 DCC.

1351 T.F.E. Tjong Tjin Tai, *Asser 7-IV Bijzondere Overeenkomsten – Opdracht, incl. de geneeskundige behandelingsovereenkomst en de reisovereenkomst*, Deventer, Wolters Kluwer, 2022, no. 164.

1352 See *infra* no. 340.

1353 See *infra* section 3.4.1.

1354 **Belgium**: see Art. 1737 old BCC. **The Netherlands**: see Art. 7:228 DCC.

1355 **Belgium**: see e.g. F. Vermander, "Eenzijdige opzeggingsclausules" in E. Terryn, A.-L. Verbeke, H. De Decker, G.-L. Ballon, B. Tilleman and V. Sagaert (eds.), *Contractuele clausules. Gemeenrechtelijke clausules. Volume II*, Antwerp, Intersentia, 2013, (1529) 1546 (general law of obligations); T. Soete, "Opzeggingsclausules" in E. Terryn, A.-L. Verbeke, H. De Decker, G.-L. Ballon, B. Tilleman and V. Sagaert (eds.), *Huur (contractuele clausules)*, Antwerp, Intersentia, 2017, (579) 588 (rental contract); and F. Bruloot, "Opzegclausules" in E. Terryn, A.-L. Verbeke, H. De Decker, G.-L. Ballon, B. Tilleman and V. Sagaert (eds.), *Aanneming. Bouwwerken (contractuele clausules)*, Antwerp, Intersentia, 2016, (237) 250 (contract for services). **The Netherlands**: C.H. Sieburgh, *Mr. C. Assers Handleiding tot de beoefening van het Nederlands Burgerlijk Recht. 6. Verbintenissenrecht. Deel III. Algemeen overeenkomstenrecht*, Deventer, Wolters Kluwer, 2022, no. 408.

1356 See *infra* no. 324.

contract while the PSS supplier does) run the risk of being declared null and void under the general unfair terms test.[1357, 1358]

323. Early termination fee – Early termination clauses in fixed-term PSS contracts may stipulate an early termination fee.[1359] This early termination fee acts as a form of compensation for the right to unilaterally terminate the contract. For example, the terms and conditions of *Blue Movement* provide that if the PSS user terminates the contract during the so-called "Minimum Contract Period" (which is the term agreed to in the order process), he owes an amount of 50% of the remaining monthly fees.

> Terms and Conditions Blue Movement – Art. 11.3 "In case the Lessee has agreed a Minimum Contract Period of more than 24 months, and the Lessee terminates the Contract during the Minimum Contract Period, the Lessee shall owe an amount equal to 50% of the remaining Monthly Amounts."

In the context of PSS contracts, the early termination fee may enable the PSS supplier to recover certain investment costs. The difference between early termination clauses stipulating an early termination fee and indemnity clauses is that the former is unrelated to a breach of contract.[1360] As such, termination clauses are not subject to the strict requirements of and limits to indemnity clauses.[1361] However, they can still be tested against the general unfairness test[1362] or (mostly in a non-B2C context) deemed to violate the prohibition of abuse of rights (BE) or the principle of reasonableness and fairness (NL).[1363]

1357 **Belgium**: Art. I.8, 22° BCEL. **The Netherlands**: Art. 6:233, *sub* a. DCC.

1358 F. Bruloot, "Opzegclausules" in E. Terryn, A.-L. Verbeke, H. De Decker, G.-L. Ballon, B. Tilleman and V. Sagaert (eds.), *Aanneming. Bouwwerken (contractuele clausules)*, Antwerp, Intersentia, 2016, (237) 250.

1359 Under Dutch law, as regards PSS contracts that qualify as a contract for services, Art. 7:408(3) *juncto* Art. 7:413(1) DCC contain an exception to this principle. Indeed, as mentioned *supra* no. 321, non-professional clients making use of their unilateral termination right may not be liable for damages in respect of their termination, except for the compensation of expenses made by the PSS supplier (Art. 7:406 DCC) or payment of fees for the already performed services (Art. 7:411 DCC).

1360 I. Claeys and T. Tanghe, *Nieuw Algemeen Contractenrecht*, Antwerp, Intersentia, 2023, 535, no. 665.

1361 See *supra* no. 304. Under Belgian law, this includes the prohibition of non-reciprocal and excessive indemnity clauses, see Art. VI.83, 17° and 24° BCEL.

1362 Art. I.8, 22° BCEL.

1363 **Belgium**: F. Vermander, "Eenzijdige opzeggingsclausules" in E. Terryn, A.-L. Verbeke, H. De Decker, G.-L. Ballon, B. Tilleman and V. Sagaert (eds.), *Contractuele clausules. Gemeenrechtelijke clausules. Volume II*, Antwerp, Intersentia, 2013, (1529) 1545. **The Netherlands**: Art. 6:248(1) DCC; C.H. Sieburgh, *Mr. C. Assers Handleiding tot de beoefening van het Nederlands Burgerlijk Recht. 6. Verbintenissenrecht. Deel III. Algemeen overeenkomstenrecht*, Deventer, Wolters Kluwer, 2022, no. 408.

324. Belgian law: early termination fee required if PSS supplier terminates fixed-term contract early – Under Belgian law, the PSS supplier is obliged to pay an early termination fee if the PSS contract allows unilateral termination of the fixed-term PSS contract (except for cases of *force majeure*).[1364] This is also linked with the Belgian prohibition of clauses allowing the PSS supplier to retain advances paid by the PSS user if the former terminates the PSS contract.[1365]

2.7.1.3. Extension or renewal of fixed-term PSS contracts

325. Explicit or tacit extension or renewal of the PSS contract – Both the law and the PSS contract may provide for an explicit or tacit extension or renewal of the fixed-term PSS contract.[1366] In the first case, the PSS contract is extended or renewed because the parties have explicitly expressed their intention or agreement to do so. In the second case, the extension or renewal takes place implicitly, i.e. without the parties having to do anything at the end of the initial term to trigger the extension or renewal.[1367] Extension of renewal can take place once but can also be agreed more than once. The tacit extension or renewal can be prevented by objecting to it in time (within the time limit and in accordance with the modalities stipulated by law or the PSS contract).

326. Examples of tacit extension or renewal clauses in PSS contracts – Various fixed-term PSS contracts analysed include tacit extension or renewal clauses. Often, automatic extensions after the initial contract term take place monthly. An example of such a clause can be found in the terms and conditions of *Live Light*.

> Terms and conditions Live Light – Art. 6.2 “The Tenant can opt to extend the Rental agreement during and after the Initial Duration. Unless indicated otherwise by the Tenant at the end of the Initial Duration, the Rental contract will be automatically extended from month to month under the same conditions.” *(Own emphasis).*

1364 Art. VI.83, 10° BCEL.

1365 Art. VI.83, 28° BCEL. See also *infra* no. 338.

1366 See Art. 5.77 and 5.78 BCC. An **extension** has the effect of continuing the original contract and extending its duration. All contractual provisions normally remain the same, only the extinctive term is postponed. If the extension does not specify a term, the contract is now an open-ended contract. A **renewal** has the effect that the “old” contract is definitively extinguished by the expiry of the stipulated term. Therefore, a new contract is entered into with same content as the original contract. The renewed contract can both be a fixed-term contract or an open-ended contract.

1367 I. Claeys and T. Tanghe, *Nieuw Algemeen Contractenrecht*, Antwerp, Intersentia, 2023, 527–528, no. 655.

Alternatively, the PSS contract may also stipulate that upon expiry of the initial period, the contract is extended for an indefinite period. The terms and conditions of *Gerrard Street/Repeat* provide an example of such an extension for an indefinite period.

Terms and conditions Gerrard Street/Repeat – Art. 9.1 "The subscription is entered into for an initial period as stated in the subscription contract. Upon expiry of the period, the contract shall continue for an indefinite period."

Automatic renewals usually take place on the same conditions, including the term of the renewed contract (although this is not required). The terms and conditions of *Fairphone Easy* contain an example of an automatic tacit renewal clause. These terms provide that after the expiry of the extinctive term, the contract is renewed automatically on the same conditions unless the PSS user notifies *Fairphone* of the fact that he does not wish to renew the contract.

Terms and conditions Fairphone Easy – Art. 7.1 "The As-a-Service Agreement and Subscription are concluded for a definite period of time. After the expiry of the term, the As-a-Service Agreement and Subscription are renewed automatically on the same conditions or may be renewed for a new adapted Agreement unless You notify Us no later than thirty (30) days prior to the end of the term that You do not wish to renew. Upon the commencement of a new term, You will be able to cancel Your As-a-Service Agreement at any time in line with the thirty (30) day notice period."

327. Tacit extension may be explicitly excluded – Other PSS contracts, such as Papillon, explicitly exclude tacit extension of the PSS contract. In this case, the PSS contract automatically terminates upon expiry of the extinctive term. If the parties want to continue the contractual relationship, they will have to conclude a new PSS contract.

Terms and conditions Papillon – Art. 2.2 and 2.3 "Current Rental Contract is not subject to tacit extension. The Rental Contract shall terminate by operation of law on the expiry of the aforementioned term."

328. Belgian law: limits to tacit renewal or extension clauses – The Belgian mandatory (consumer) legislation places several limits on tacit renewal or extension clauses in B2C contracts.

First, there is Article VI.91 BCEL, which applies to service contracts or sales contracts having as their object both sales as services containing a tacit extension clause. As a result, this provision applies to all three main types of PSS contracts. It contains the following principles: (i) a formality requirement: the tacit renewal clause must appear in bold type and in a box separate from the text on the front of the first page of the contract; (ii) a minimum content requirement: the clause must contain the consequences of the tacit renewal, including the fact that he has the right to terminate the contract in accordance with Article VI.91, §2 BCEL and the deadline and modalities of notification to oppose a tacit renewal; and (iii) a maximum notice period: after the renewal, the consumer may terminate the contract at any time without compensation subject to compliance with a contractually defined notice period (which may not exceed two months).[1368]

In practice, however, most PSS contracts analysed do not comply with this provision (especially the formality requirement). Article VI.91 WER contains no civil sanction in this case. Of course, the PSS user will simply be able to terminate the contract in accordance with this provision, but the disregard of the formal requirements does not *in itself* allow for the nullity of the PSS contract or the tacit renewal clause in question.[1369] Of course, clauses not complying with this provision may be challenged under the transparency requirement and the general test of the unfair terms rules, for example if it is not sufficiently clear or intelligible to the average consumer, or if it creates a significant imbalance between the rights and obligations of the PSS supplier and the PSS user.[1370]

Second, several provisions of the blacklist of unfair terms limit contractual freedom regarding tacit renewal or extension clauses in B2C PSS contracts. Indeed, Article VI.83, 20° BCEL blacklists clauses that automatically extend a fixed-term contract in the absence of a contrary notification by the consumer, where an overly distant date from the end of the contract has been set as the deadline for notification of the consumer's desire not to extend the contract. This general provision of the Belgian blacklist thus also applies to all three main types of PSS contracts. The more specific Article VI.83, 19° BCEL, which applies to fixed-term contracts in which there are subsequent deliveries of products, prohibits clauses with the object or effect of extending the contract for an unreasonable period of time if the consumer does not terminate in time. This blacklisted provision thus applies to product-oriented PSS where there are periodical deliveries of products, such as laundry detergent for a washing machine or groceries for a smart fridge.

329. Dutch law: limits to tacit renewal or extension clauses – Also under Dutch law, there are limits to tacit extension or renewal clauses. Article 6:236, *sub* j. DCC and Article 6:237, *sub* k. and l. DCC contain rules aimed at preventing consumers from being locked into contracts for too long.

1368 For an extensive discussion of this provision, see: R. Steennot and E. Terryn, "Commentaar bij artikel VI.91 WER" in *Handels- en economisch recht. Commentaar met overzicht van rechtspraak en rechtsleer*, Mechelen, Kluwer, Loose-leaf, 2022, (29) 29–40.

1369 Ct. Limburg (BE) 15 January 2014, *DCCR* 2015, issue 106, 104, case note S. Geiregat.

1370 Art. I.8, 22° and Art. VI.82 BCEL.

Article 6:236, *sub* j. DCC applies to tacit extension or renewal clauses in contracts for regular delivery of goods or regular provision of services.[1371] It prohibits these tacit renewals/extensions, unless the consumer can at all times terminate the extended or renewed contract with a notice period of one month.[1372] According to JONGENEEL, this blacklisted provision does not apply to rental contracts, as the extension or renewal of these contracts is extensively regulated in the DCC.[1373] This is certainly the case for residential or immovable rental contracts, but, in my view, this argument is less convincing for the rental contract for movables.[1374] Moreover, these rules are only default law so parties can deviate from them. This can still lead to situations where the consumer is left with an unwanted tacit renewal. Therefore, as use-oriented PSS contracts qualifying as a rental contract for movables closely resemble contracts for services, there is, in my view, an argument to be made to also apply this blacklisted provision to these types of contracts. At least, it could serve as a source of inspiration for assessing tacit extension or renewal clauses in these PSS contracts against the general unfairness test.

The issues of termination and renewal/extension are also addressed in the Dutch grey list. According to Article 6:237, *sub* k. DCC, are presumed unreasonably onerous: contracts for regular delivery of goods or regular provision of services for longer than one year, unless the consumer has the right to terminate the contract after each year.[1375] Like Article 6:236, *sub* j. DCC, this grey listed provisions do in principle not apply to PSS contracts qualifying as rental contracts, but there are good arguments to apply this rule by analogy.[1376] Additionally, Article 6:237, *sub* l. DCC provides that terms with the object or effect of binding the consumer to a longer notice period than the notice period the trader must respect are presumed unreasonably onerous.[1377] Contrary to Article 6:237, *sub* k. DCC, this grey listed provision applies to *all* contracts containing a termination right (so also rental contracts).[1378]

1371 In the sense of Art. 7:400 DCC.

1372 Art. 6:236, *sub* j. DCC.

1373 R.H.C. JONGENEEL, "De zwarte lijst" in B. WESSELS and R.H.C. JONGENEEL (eds.), *Algemene voorwaarden*, Deventer, Wolters Kluwer, 2017, (253) 283.

1374 See Art. 7:228(1) DCC: "*A rental contract entered into for a fixed term shall terminate, without notice being required, when that term has expired.*" and 7:230 DCC: "*If, after the expiration of a rental contract, the lessee, with the consent of the lessor, retains the use of the rented good, the contract shall, unless a different intention becomes apparent, be extended for an indeterminate period, regardless of the term for which it was entered into.*" These provisions do indeed deal with the duration of the contract and tacit renewal, but do not provide any protection against an "unwanted" tacit renewal if the PSS user did not terminate the contract in time.

1375 Art. 6:237, *sub* k. DCC.

1376 See for an example (regarding internet subscription with a minimum duration of 2 years): Ct. Zwolle (NL) 4 October 2006, *LJN* AY9541.

1377 Art. 6:237, *sub* l. DCC.

1378 R.H.C. JONGENEEL, "De grijze lijst" in B. WESSELS and R.H.C. JONGENEEL (eds.), *Algemene voorwaarden*, Deventer, Wolters Kluwer, 2017, (311) 348–349.

2.7.2. OPEN-ENDED PSS CONTRACTS

2.7.2.1. Concept

330. Open-ended PSS contracts: no extinctive term – If the PSS contract does not contain an extinctive term, it is an open-ended PSS contract.[1379] In other words, if the parties to the PSS contract did not contractually define the duration of the PSS contract, it is entered into for an indeterminate term.

331. Examples – While the majority of the PSS contracts analysed are fixed-term PSS contracts (often with tacit renewal or extension clauses),[1380] there are also PSS contracts that stipulate that they are concluded for an indefinite period of time and thus constitute open-ended PSS contracts. The terms and conditions of *Bundles* provided an example of such a clause defining the PSS contract as open-ended:

> Terms and Conditions Bundles – Art. 12.1 "Use of the Product commences upon delivery of the Product to User for an indefinite period of time."

2.7.2.2. Early termination of open-ended PSS contracts?

332. Unilateral termination of open-ended PSS contracts? – Under Belgian law, a contracting party to an open-ended PSS contract can in principle unilaterally terminate the contract at any time, subject to a reasonable notice period.[1381] This is a general principle of law, which was codified in the new BCC.[1382] This rule is of public policy (*openbare orde, ordre public*), so the contracting parties cannot contractually exclude or limit the unilateral termination option. They are, on the other hand, allowed to contractually modulate this termination option.[1383]

Under Dutch law, on the other hand, the situation is different. Contrary to Belgian law, the unilateral termination right in open-ended contracts is not a general principle of law and the contractual parties may in principle exclude the possibility to unilaterally terminate an open-ended contract.[1384] However, a clause of non-terminability may conflict with the principle of reasonableness and

---

1379 Art. 5.75(1) BCC.

1380 See *supra* no. 316.

1381 Art. 5.75(2) BCC.

1382 See e.g. Cass. (BE) 9 October 2020, AR C.20.0117.N, *https://juportal.be* 15 October 2020; Cass. (BE) 28 June 2019, AR C.18.0410.N, *https://juportal.be* 24 juli 2019, concl. A. Van Ingelgem, *NjW* 2020, 122, case note A. Coppens; Cass. (BE) 29 May 2015, *Arr.Cass.* 2015, 1421, *Pas.* 2015, 1393.

1383 See Cass. (BE) 16 October 1969, *Arr.Cass.* 1970, 167, *Pas.* 1970, I, 147.

1384 I. Claeys and L. Phang, "Van bepaalde duur naar onbepaalde duur en terug", *TPR* 2008, (375) 386.

fairness (Art. 6:248(2) DCC) or the rule of Article 6:258 DCC, which allows to change or terminate the contract in view of certain changed circumstances.[1385] If the contract or a statutory provision do not regulate the termination of an open-ended contract, it can in principle be terminated.[1386] However, the requirements of reasonableness and fairness may imply, in connection with the nature and content of the contract and the circumstances of the case, that termination is only possible if a sufficiently serious ground for termination exists, that a certain notice period must be observed or that termination must be accompanied by the offer to pay compensation (for damages).[1387]

333. Reasonable notice period – Under Belgian law, the unilateral termination option must be exercised in accordance with the principle of good faith. This means that the contracting party that unilaterally terminates the open-ended PSS contract must observe a reasonable notice period, the length of which must be assessed on a case-by-case basis.[1388] Where reasonable notice is not given or complied with, the terminating party must compensate the damage suffered by its co-contractor for failure to comply with this obligation.[1389] In addition, the Belgian blacklist of unfair terms in B2C contracts prohibits clauses with the object or effect of "*binding the consumer for an indeterminate period of time, without clearly stating a reasonable notice period.*"[1390] This means that open-ended PSS contracts where the PSS user is a consumer must aways contain an explicit (and clear) clause stating a reasonable notice period.[1391]

Also under Dutch law, the principle of reasonableness and fairness will generally require the terminating party to observe a reasonable notice period.[1392] This is the case both where the contract or a statutory provision does not provide for a right of termination,[1393] and where such a right is provided

---

1385 C.H. Sieburgh, *Mr. C. Assers Handleiding tot de beoefening van het Nederlands Burgerlijk Recht. 6. Verbintenissenrecht. Deel III. Algemeen overeenkomstenrecht*, Deventer, Wolters Kluwer, 2022, no. 408.

1386 HR (NL) 28 October 2011, ECLI:NL:HR:2011:BQ9854, (*Gemeente De Ronde Venen/Stedin*), *NJ* 2012/685, case note T.F.E. Tjong Tjin Tai.

1387 *Ibid.* See for examples: HR (NL) 14 June 2013, ECLI:NL:HR:2013:BZ4163, (*Auping/Beverslaap*), *NJ* 2013/341; HR (NL) 10 June 2016, ECLI:NL:HR:2016:1134, (*Pensioenfonds/Alcatel-Lucent*), *NJ* 2016/450, case note T.F.E. Tjong Tjin Tai.

1388 Cass. (BE) 13 January 2022, AR C.21.0357.N, *RW* 2021–22, 1433, case note T. Tanghe; Cass. (BE) 7 June 2012, AR C.11.0449.N, *Arr.Cass.* 2012, 1567, *Pas.* 2012, 1317.

1389 Cass. (BE) 28 June 2019, AR C.18.0410.N, *https://juportal.be* 24 juli 2019, concl. A. Van Ingelgem, *NjW* 2020, 122, case note A. Coppens.

1390 Art. VI.38, 18° BCEL.

1391 R. Steennot, "Commentaar bij art. VI.83, 18° WER" in *Handels- en economisch recht. Commentaar met overzicht van rechtspraak en rechtsleer*, Mechelen, Wolters Kluwer, loose-leaf, 2017, (509) 511.

1392 C.H. Sieburgh, *Mr. C. Assers Handleiding tot de beoefening van het Nederlands Burgerlijk Recht. 6. Verbintenissenrecht. Deel III. Algemeen overeenkomstenrecht*, Deventer, Wolters Kluwer, 2022, no. 409.

1393 Compare with *supra* no. 332.

for, but the principle of reasonableness and fairness imposes additional requirements.[1394]

334. Belgian law: prohibition of clauses allowing the PSS supplier to unilaterally terminate open-ended PSS contract without reasonable notice period – In a B2C context, the Belgian blacklist explicitly prohibits clauses in open-ended PSS contracts allowing the PSS supplier to terminate the contract without a reasonable notice period, except in the case of *force majeure*.[1395] The Dutch blacklist and grey list do not contain a similar provision, although such clauses may also be combated using the general unfairness test and/or the principle of reasonableness and fairness.[1396]

335. Contractually modulating unilateral termination option – As mentioned above, the rule that any party must be able to unilaterally terminate an open-ended contract at any time is – at least under Belgian law – of public policy.[1397] However, this does not prevent the PSS contract from modulating the unilateral termination right, although the exercise of this right should not be made impossible.[1398] This means that it is not allowed to exclude this right in the PSS contract or grant it to only one contracting party. On the other hand, the PSS contract may stipulate a certain notice period, a compensation clause, a motivation obligation, or a formality.[1399] However, those modalities should not erode the right of unilateral termination so that exercise becomes reasonably impossible. Thus, a notice period of multiple years, an extremely high compensation clause or excessively strict formalities will not be permissible.[1400]

Also under Dutch law, it is possible to freely modulate the unilaterally termination option, provided this does not conflict with the requirements of reasonableness and fairness.[1401] However, Dutch law contains an exception to the possibility to contractually modulate the unilateral termination option. Indeed, in PSS contracts that qualify as contracts for services under Dutch law, the non-professional client who makes use of its right to unilaterally terminate the contract "at all times" may not be subjected to a notice period, nor be held

---

1394 C.H. Sieburgh, *Mr. C. Assers Handleiding tot de beoefening van het Nederlands Burgerlijk Recht. 6. Verbintenissenrecht. Deel III. Algemeen overeenkomstenrecht*, Deventer, Wolters Kluwer, 2022, no. 408.

1395 Art. VI.83, 11° BCEL.

1396 Art. 6:233, *sub* a. DCC and Art. 6:248(1) DCC.

1397 See *supra* no. 332.

1398 Cass. (BE) 16 October 1969, *Arr.Cass.* 1970, 167, *Pas.* 1970, I, 147.

1399 I. Claeys and L. Phang, "Van bepaalde duur naar onbepaalde duur en terug", *TPR* 2008, (375) 452.

1400 I. Claeys and T. Tanghe, *Nieuw Algemeen Contractenrecht*, Antwerp, Intersentia, 2023, 554, no. 695.

1401 C.H. Sieburgh, *Mr. C. Assers Handleiding tot de beoefening van het Nederlands Burgerlijk Recht. 6. Verbintenissenrecht. Deel III. Algemeen overeenkomstenrecht*, Deventer, Wolters Kluwer, 2022, no. 408.

liable for damages in respect of this termination (except for expenses incurred and payment of fees for already performed services).[1402]

336. Minimum period in which the contract is non-terminable – The fact that parties can modulate the termination option also implies that the PSS contract can specify a minimum period in which the parties cannot unilaterally terminate the contract. In essence, this amounts to a PSS contract that is a fixed-term contract for the first part which then (tacitly) becomes an open-ended contract.[1403] Once the PSS contract of mixed duration has become open-ended, it must of course be possible to unilaterally terminate it.[1404]

337. Early termination fee – Just like in fixed-term PSS contracts,[1405] an early termination fee is also a possible way to contractually modulate the unilateral termination right in open-ended PSS contracts.[1406] This may enable the PSS supplier to recover investment costs if the open-ended PSS contract is terminated (too) early in its term. However, also here, an unreasonably high early termination fee may run counter to the freedom to unilaterally terminate the open-ended contract. As already mentioned above,[1407] while termination clauses are not subject to the strict requirements of and limits to indemnity clauses,[1408] they can still be tested against the general unfairness test[1409] or (mostly in a non-B2C context) violate the prohibition of abuse of rights (BE) or reasonableness and fairness (NL).[1410]

338. Belgian law: prohibition of clauses allowing the PSS supplier to retain advances paid by the PSS user if the PSS supplier itself terminates the contract – The Belgian unfair terms blacklist prohibits

1402 See *supra* no. 321.

1403 See Brussels (BE) 9 February 2010, AR 2007/AR/2834 unpublished, as cited by I. Claeys and T. Tanghe, *Nieuw Algemeen Contractenrecht*, Antwerp, Intersentia, 2023, 555: "*Geen enkel wettelijk beding verzet zich ertegen dat een overeenkomst gemengd zou zijn wat betreft duurtijd, dit wil zeggen dat zij tot een bepaalde datum van vaste duur zou zijn, en ná die datum voor onbepaalde tijd zou gesloten worden.*"

1404 I. Claeys and T. Tanghe, *Nieuw Algemeen Contractenrecht*, Antwerp, Intersentia, 2023, 555. See also: F. Vermander, "Eenzijdige opzeggingsclausules" in E. Terryn, A.-L. Verbeke, H. De Decker, G.-L. Ballon, B. Tilleman and V. Sagaert (eds.), *Contractuele clausules. Gemeenrechtelijke clausules. Volume II*, Antwerp, Intersentia, 2013, (1529) 1545.

1405 See *supra* no. 323.

1406 Cass. (BE) 16 October 1969, *Arr.Cass.* 1970, 167, *Pas.* 1970, I, 147.

1407 See *supra* no. 323.

1408 See *supra* no. 304.

1409 Art. I.8, 22° BCEL.

1410 **Belgium**: F. Vermander, "Eenzijdige opzeggingsclausules" in E. Terryn, A.-L. Verbeke, H. De Decker, G.-L. Ballon, B. Tilleman and V. Sagaert (eds.), *Contractuele clausules. Gemeenrechtelijke clausules. Volume II*, Antwerp, Intersentia, 2013, (1529) 1545. **The Netherlands**: Art. 6:248(1) DCC; C.H. Sieburgh, *Mr. C. Assers Handleiding tot de beoefening van het Nederlands Burgerlijk Recht. 6. Verbintenissenrecht. Deel III. Algemeen overeenkomstenrecht*, Deventer, Wolters Kluwer, 2022, no. 408.

clauses that stipulate that the PSS supplier has the right to retain any advance payments done by the PSS user-consumer if the PSS supplier terminates the contract.[1411] This means that the PSS supplier cannot at the same time be the terminating party and claim an early termination fee in the form of the retained advance payments. This rule also applies to fixed-term PSS contracts. The Dutch blacklist and grey list do not contain a similar provision, although it will of course be possible to combat these clauses using the general unfairness test.[1412]

2.7.3. MODEL CLAUSES REGARDING THE DURATION OF THE PSS CONTRACT

2.7.3.1. Model clauses for fixed-term PSS contracts

339. Model clauses on fixed-term – As mentioned above, most of the PSS contracts analysed contain an extinctive term. The following model clauses provide an example of how PSS suppliers may define their contracts as fixed term contracts. The first model clause sets out the extinctive term, which may either be the term agreed between the PSS supplier and the PSS user or specific amount of time, namely x months or x years. The second model clause deals with the start date of the fixed-term contract. This can either be or upon conclusion of the contract. This model clause can also be used to define the end date of the fixed-term PSS contract. This can be a fixed date but may also be linked to the average expected useful lifespan of the product. Optionally, the PSS contract may provide that the PSS contract is not terminated on this specified end date if the contract is explicitly or implicitly extended or renewed under the terms of the contract.[1413]

Model clause #10 – Fixed-term contract

- **The contract is entered into for [the specific duration agreed between the PSS supplier and the PSS user/a term of (x months/x years)].**
- **The contract commences [on effective start date/upon delivery of the product/ upon conclusion of the contract] and remains in force until [end date (e.g. fixed date or the average expected useful lifespan of the product)][, unless the contract is explicitly or implicitly extended or renewed under the terms of this contract].**

340. Model clauses on (early) termination of the fixed-term PSS contract – The following model clauses deal with the (early) termination of

[1411] Art. VI.83, 28° BCEL.
[1412] Art. 6:233, *sub* a. DCC.
[1413] See for model clauses on contract extension/renewal *infra* no. 341.

the fixed-term PSS contract. The first model clause repeats the general principle that fixed-term contracts shall be terminated by operation of law on the expiry of the extinctive term. It also confirms that early termination of the fixed-term PSS contract is not possible.

Alternatively, the PSS contract may allow for early termination under the terms stipulated in the contract. The second to sixth model clause set out the terms for such early termination. As mentioned above, it is advisable that the PSS contract grants the right to terminate the PSS contract early to each party (and not merely the PSS supplier or the PSS user).[1414] Under Belgian law, an early termination fee is possible in a fixed-term PSS contract. The fourth model clause is an example of a clause stipulating such fee. This fee can either be modelled to Article 1794 old BCC (thus holding the PSS user liable for the actual costs and expenses and lost profits) or consist of a reasonable lump sum (e.g. the monthly fees for x months). As mentioned above,[1415] such a clause is not allowed under Dutch law for PSS contracts that qualify as a contract for services, as the non-professional client's unilateral termination right for these contracts is mandatory law.[1416] However, it is still possible to include a clause regarding the reimbursement of expenses incurred by the service provider and the payment of fees for the already performed services.[1417] For PSS contracts qualifying as a rental contract under Dutch law, on the other hand, this clause can be used without any problem. The fifth model clause stipulates that early termination is only possible after a certain minimum period. Also this clause is not allowed for PSS contracts that qualify as a contract for services under Dutch law, as the unilateral termination right of the non-professional client can be exercised "at all time". Again, it can be used for PSS contract that qualify as a rental contract under Dutch law. Finally, the sixth model clause provides that the terminating party can cancel its termination before the effective end date of the contract if it changes its mind.

Model clause #11 – (Early) termination of the (fixed-term) contract

- **The contract shall be terminated by operation of law on the expiry of the aforementioned term. Early termination of the contract is not possible.**
- **Early termination is only possible under the terms of this contract.**
- **Either party can terminate the contract by [written] notification to the other party. The contract ends after [specified reasonable period of time] after this notification.**

[1414] See *supra* no. 322.
[1415] See *supra* no. 321.
[1416] Art. 7:408(1) *juncto* Art. 7:413 DCC.
[1417] See Art. 7:406 and 7:411 DCC.

- **The terminating party is to pay an early termination fee to the other party. This early termination fee consists of [the actual costs and expenses and lost profits/a reasonable lump sum (e.g. x months of recurrent monthly fees in a subscription-based model)].**

- **Early termination is only possible after [specified period of time] from the start date of the contract.**

- **The terminating party may cancel the termination at any time before the effective end date of the contract by [written] notification of this decision.**

341. Model clauses on extension/renewal of the fixed-term PSS contract – The following model clauses deal with the extension or renewal of the fixed-term PSS contract. Two options are possible here: either the PSS contract does not allow tacit extension/renewal, or the PSS contract contains a tacit extension/renewal clause. The first model clause can be used to exclude the possibility of tacit extension and renewal. In this case, the contract shall be terminated by operation of law upon the expiry of the extinctive term. The second model clause can be used as a tacit extension/renewal clause. It is modelled to comply with the requirements of Article VI.91 BCEL, which is mandatory law in Belgium.[1418] The automatic extension/renewal clause must be placed in bold letters and in a frame separate from the text, on the front of the first page of the PSS contract.

Model clause #12 – Extension/renewal

- **The contract is not subject to tacit extension/renewal. The contract shall be terminated by operation of law upon the expiry of the aforementioned term.**

- **The contract is automatically extended/renewed by an additional term of [specified reasonable duration (e.g. one month)] at the expiration of the initial term and every subsequent term thereafter if either party does not give a [written] notification of the desire not to extend/renew. This notification is to be given at least [a reasonable amount of time (e.g. five business days)] prior to the expiration of the initial term or any subsequent extended term. [[The PSS user]] may, after the automatic extension/renewal of the contract, terminate the contract at any time without compensation subject to a notice period of [specified period which may not exceed 2 months (BE)/one month (NL)]].**[1419]

[1418] See *supra* no. 328.

[1419] **Belgium**: This sentence reflects the minimum content requirement of Art. VI.91, §2 BCEL, which is a mandatory provision under Belgian law applicable to service contracts and sales contracts having as their object both sales and services. **The Netherlands**: See Art. 6:236, *sub* j. DCC.

2.7.3.2. Model clauses for open-ended PSS contracts

342. Model clause on indeterminate term – The following clause provides an example of a clause on the duration of an open-ended contract. It is characterised by the fact that there is no extinctive term, but the contract is concluded for an indefinite period of time.

> **Model clause #13 – Open-ended contract/indeterminate term**
>
> - **The contract commences [on effective start date/upon delivery of the product/ upon conclusion of the contract] and remains in force for an indefinite period of time until it is terminated under the terms of this contract.**

343. Model clauses on termination of the open-ended contract – Open-ended contracts are in principle terminable at all times,[1420] provided the terminating party respects a reasonable notice period.[1421] The first model clause confirms this principle by stating that each party can terminate the contract by written notification. It also sets out the reasonable notice period for doing so. The second model clause grants each party the right to terminate the PSS contract and requires a written confirmation of this decision.

> **Model clause #14 – Termination of the (open-ended) contract**
>
> - **Each party can terminate the contract at any time by [written] notification to the other party with a notice period of [specified reasonable period of time].**
> - **The terminating party may cancel the termination at any time before the effective end date of the contract by [written] notification of this decision.**

344. Model clauses on early termination of open-ended contract with minimum term – The following model clauses can be used to impose a minimum contract term in an open-ended PSS contract.[1422] The first model clause states that early termination is only possible after a certain minimum period. The second model clause does allow early termination during the minimum period but imposes an early termination fee. Note that these model clauses cannot be used for PSS contracts that qualify as a contract for services

[1420] Under Dutch law, this is not the case if the unilateral termination possibility has been contractually excluded. Nevertheless, such a clause may be contrary to the principles of reasonableness and fairness (Art. 6:248(2) DCC) or the rule of Art. 6:258 DCC. See *supra* no. 332.

[1421] See *supra* no. 333.

[1422] Compare with *supra* no. 336.

under Dutch law, as the unilateral termination right of the non-professional client "at all times" is mandatory law.[1423]

Model clause #15 – Early termination of the (open-ended) contract with a minimum term

- **Termination is only possible after [specified reasonable period of time]. [This provision does not affect the consumer's right of withdrawal in accordance with [Art. xxx] of this contract.].**
- **If the contract is terminated within [specified minimum period], the terminating party is to pay an early termination fee of [reasonable amount (e.g. x months of recurrent monthly fees in a subscription-based model)] to the other party.**

2.8. CONCLUSION

345. PSS UNDER GENERAL CONTRACT LAW: CONCLUSION – The aim of this chapter was to set out some basic principles of general contract law and apply them to PSS contracts. Thus, this chapter discussed the (i) the formation of the PSS contract; (ii) the use of general terms and conditions; (iii) the right of withdrawal; (iv) the interpretation of the PSS contract; (v) general aspects of liability for breach of the PSS contract; and (vi) the duration of the PSS contract.

346. FORMATION OF THE PSS CONTRACT AND RIGHT OF WITHDRAWAL – The first section of this chapter dealt with the **formation of the PSS contract.**[1424]

There are four requirements for the validity of the PSS contract, namely consent, capacity, object and cause. If one of these validity requirements is lacking, the sanction will be the nullity of the PSS contract.[1425] Before the PSS contract is concluded, the PSS supplier must comply with different (pre-contractual) information requirements.[1426] These information requirements are found in a number of legal instruments, such as the SD, the CRD, and the E-commerce Directive. The recent Directive on Empowering Consumers for the Green Transition also added new information requirements regarding durability and sustainability. Although these information requirements may help consumers take informed and sustainable choices, for example by allowing them to compare different PSS offers, information requirements are still subject to important limitations. For example, for PSS users-consumers, the amount

[1423] Art. 7:408(1) *juncto* Art. 7:413 DCC. See *supra* no. 321.
[1424] See *supra* section 2.2.
[1425] See *supra* section 2.2.1.1.
[1426] See *supra* section 2.2.1.2.

and complexity of information may lead to an "information overload", while for PSS suppliers, complying with a myriad of information requirements (scattered across different legal instruments) may impose significant administrative and financial burdens. Further integration and streamlining of these information requirements, together with an improved methodology and timing of information provision might remedy some of these limitations.[1427]

The contract formation process itself is characterised by the fact that an offer of the PSS supplier meets the acceptance of the PSS user.[1428] Here, there was a particular focus on PSS contracts concluded via electronic means, and PSS contracts offered online that involved only an "invitation for the PSS user to make an offer". While the latter is – *de lege lata* – not unfair under the rules on unfair terms, it was advocated that the PSS user should be allowed to withdraw his offer as long as the PSS user has not accepted it.

Finally, it was highlighted that in some cases, the PSS supplier may use a representative to conclude the PSS contract.[1429] In this case, the PSS supplier will be bound by the commitments made by its representative.

If all these conditions are met and proceses are followed, the PSS contract will be validly concluded. Consequently, its content will be binding on the contracting parties (with certain nuances and exceptions such as the possibility of unilateral termination and the exercise of the consumer's right of withdrawal).[1430]

347. Use of general terms and conditions – The second section of this chapter discussed the frequent **use of contracts of adhesion and general terms and conditions** for PSS contracts on a "take it or leave it" basis.[1431] Contracts of adhesion and general terms and conditions have the advantage that a multitude of PSS contracts can be concluded in a short time without the need to negotiate the terms of each individual contract. However, at the same time, this leads to the risk that the PSS supplier may impose unilateral and unreasonable terms that the PSS user could not reasonably expect. There are two mechanisms to protect PSS users from abuse regarding general terms and conditions.

The first corrective mechanism concerns the **enforceability of general terms and conditions** against the PSS user.[1432] This issue is closely related to the formation of the PSS contract, and more specifically whether the general terms and conditions are part of the PSS contract (incorporation). Under Belgian law, the enforceability of general terms and conditions requires the knowledge (or at least the reasonable possibility of knowledge) and acceptance by the PSS

1427 See *supra* no. 94.
1428 See *supra* section 2.2.1.3.
1429 See *supra* section 2.2.1.4.
1430 See *supra* section 2.2.1.5.
1431 See *supra* section 2.3.
1432 See *supra* section 2.3.2.

user before or at the time of concluding the PSS contract. Under Dutch law, the acceptance of the terms and conditions is in principle sufficient, but the general terms and conditions are voidable if the PSS supplier has not given the PSS user a reasonable possibility to take knowledge of the general terms and conditions before or at the time of concluding the PSS contract. As a result, the same requirements roughly apply under both legal systems. The enforceability of terms and conditions in PSS contracts concluded online was also considered. It is generally accepted that *clickwrap* terms and conditions (i.e. terms and conditions where the PSS user's acceptance is recorded by clicking on a box) are enforceable. It is not required that PSS users scroll through the terms and conditions (*scrollwrap*). The enforceability of *browsewrap* terms and conditions (i.e. when the website only refers to the terms and conditions without explicit acceptance mechanism) depends on the concrete factual circumstances. Finally, terms and conditions that are merely made available through a hyperlink without any reference during the ordering process will generally not be enforceable. PSS suppliers may include knowledge and acceptance clauses in their general terms and conditions. The value of this clauses is rather limited in practice, as they can be combated using the unfair terms test. This means that the PSS supplier will still have to prove the (reasonable possibility of) knowledge and acceptance of the terms and conditions by the PSS user.

The second corrective mechanism concerns the **control of the legality of general terms and conditions**, i.e. whether they do not contain unfair terms.[1433] At the EU level, PSS users-consumers are protected against unfair standard contracts by the UCTD, which prohibits significantly imbalanced contractual terms that are not individually negotiated. At the national level, both Belgian and Dutch law provide for increased consumer protection in the area of unfair contract terms (e.g. by broadening the scope of the unfair terms control and/or by adopting blacklists or grey lists), which is compatible with the UCTD given its minimum harmonisation nature. The unfairness test of the UCTD and its Belgian and Dutch implementation can be summarised as follows: (i) a transparency test requires terms to be written in plain intelligible language; (ii) where there is doubt about the meaning of a term, the interpretation most favourable to the PSS user-consumer shall prevail; (iii) the general test provides that a term shall be regarded as unfair if it causes a significant imbalance in the parties' rights and obligations; (vi) in addition to the general test, there is a system of lists that help the PSS user-consumer prove that certain terms are unfair. Under the UCTD, there is an indicative and non-exhaustive list of terms that may be regarded unfair. Belgian law and Dutch law both go further, namely by means of a blacklist of terms that are unfair *per se*, and, only in the case of the Netherlands, a grey list of terms that are (rebuttably) *presumed* to be unfair.

1433 See *supra* section 2.3.

The UCTD is a very strong tool for ensuring consumer protection in PSS contracts. Indeed, although the UCTD only provides a negative protection mechanism, namely by only allowing for the annulment of unbalanced clauses instead of guaranteeing a minimum of rights and remedies, it largely has stood the test of time. Especially the open norm of the general unfairness test, the transparency requirement and the *contra proferentem* interpretation rule are sufficiently flexible to deal with all types of unfair terms in B2C PSS contracts.[1434] Nevertheless, this research has advocated for a few tweaks *de lege ferenda*. First, sustainability interests should also be considered when applying the general unfairness test.[1435] This already follows *de lege lata* from Article 11 TFEU, but largely remains dead letter so far. Adding sustainability interests to the purposes of the UCTD (e.g. in a recital) – as was also done for the UCPD and the CRD in the Empowering Consumers for the Green Transition Directive – could further pave the way towards more sustainable PSS contracts. This does not necessarily mean that sustainability interests should always prevail over consumer protection interests, but they should at least be considered. Second, the different lists of unfair terms at EU level and at national level partially overlap, complement each other, but also contain important differences. Moreover, these lists are quite long and do not have a textual nor visual structure, making it often difficult to find out whether a certain term is black or grey listed. This is why this research has proposed to streamline the lists of unfair terms at the EU level, making use of a "corrected" maximum harmonisation technique.[1436] This would mean that the content of a European blacklist and/or grey list, determined by a comparative law analysis of the different lists at the national level while also taking the lists in the DCFR and/or CESL as a starting point, should be adopted *verbatim* by the EU Member States. However, the revised UCTD list(s) could leave room for (limited) national additions to the unfair terms list(s), allowing to take into account local legal developments and contractual practices. Finally, as to the consequences of unfairness, this research argued that the deterrent effect attached by the CJEU to the sanction for unfair terms is disproportionate (i.e. no application of default rules in case of the annulment of a non-essential unfair term).[1437] After all, national default rules sufficiently take into account the balance between the rights and obligations of businesses and consumers.

1434 However, the lack of an extensive legal framework for service contracts may still make the application of the general test for PSS contracts more difficult than for sales contracts (where there is a clear, mostly mandatory, legal framework that can be used as a "baseline"). Alternatively, (balanced) standard contracts – potentially developed in collaboration with consumer organisations and/or endorsed by legislators – may also provide a useful "baseline" to test potentially unfair clauses against.

1435 See *supra* no. 166–168.

1436 See *supra* no. 173.

1437 See *supra* no. 181.

Besides the changes to the UCTD, this section highlighted the role **balanced standard contracts and model clauses** can play as a solution for promoting (truly sustainable) PSS contracts. Therefore, it was recommended to take measures to facilitate the development of standardised contracts for use-oriented and result-oriented PSS. This could even be supplemented with an (EU or national) labelling scheme with harmonised quality criteria for (standard) contracts used in PSS. To promote the uptake of these standard contracts and/or model clauses, they could be granted a "presumption of fairness" or "presumption of compliance with the UCTD" if they are taken up by PSS suppliers in their PSS contracts. This way, legal certainty for the PSS supplier is ensured, while the PSS user is protected by balanced and fair terms and conditions.

348. Right of withdrawal – The conditions, consequences and exceptions of the PSS user's **right of withdrawal**, i.e. the right to get out of a validly concluded PSS contract during a 14-day withdrawal period, was discussed in the third section of this chapter.[1438] Here, there was a particular focus on the difference between the right of withdrawal for sales contracts and service contracts. For instance, the withdrawal period for service contracts already starts the day after the contract is concluded, whereas for sales contracts this withdrawal period only starts the day after the delivery of the product. Additionally, for service contracts, if the PSS user-consumer decides to withdraw from the PSS contract during the withdrawal period after requesting its immediate performance, he will have to pay a proportionate amount of compensation. Such a compensation obligation does not exist for sales contracts. Regarding the duty of restitution after exercising the right of withdrawal, a lacuna in the CRD was identified. Indeed, a distinction is often made between sales contracts (as contracts "in respect of goods") and contracts for services. However, in case of use-oriented and result-oriented PSS, there will often be a combination of these two aspects. Therefore, it was proposed to also apply the rules "in respect of goods" and the rules on withdrawal from contracts for services cumulatively.[1439] In the same vein, it was also proposed to amend Article 13 CRD (which currently only applies to sales contracts), so that the PSS supplier may withhold – also for use-oriented and result-oriented PSS – reimbursement of the price until he has received the goods back.[1440] Finally, balanced model clauses on the right of withdrawal were drafted that can be used in real-life PSS contracts.

349. Interpretation of the PSS contract – The fourth section of this chapter analysed the issue of **interpretation of the PSS contract.**[1441] The question of interpretation will mainly arise in the event of ambiguity, when the

1438 See *supra* section 2.4.
1439 See *supra* no. 205.
1440 See *supra* no. 214.
1441 See *supra* section 2.5.

parties have a dispute regarding the scope or meaning of a particular clause in the PSS contract or the general terms and conditions.

Both under Belgian and Dutch law, the basic rule is that the common intent of the parties must be identified, rather than to adhere to the literal meaning of the words. In Belgium, this principle is found in legal provisions on contractual interpretation of the BCC,[1442] whereas in the Netherlands this follows from the famous *Haviltex* judgment[1443] of the Dutch Supreme Court. If the common intent of the parties cannot be identified, both Belgian and Dutch law leave room for interpretation in light of the principle of good faith/the principles of reasonableness and fairness. This basically means that the court will consider what reasonable parties would have wanted in the same context. Furthermore, Belgian law also contains subsidiary interpretation rules if doubt concerning the common intent of the parties persists, including the *contra proferentem* rule arising from the UCTD.[1444] Dutch law, on the other hand, contains no such subsidiary interpretation rules, except for the *contra proferentem* rule arising from the rules on unfair terms.[1445]

This section has also assessed which role (environmental) sustainability considerations can play in the interpretation of (circular) PSS contracts.[1446] There are roughly three options here. First, the PSS contract may explicitly acknowledge and include sustainability and circular economy objectives in the contract (or its preambles). Then, it is clear that in case of ambiguity of a particular term in the terms and conditions, sustainability interests were indeed part of the common intent of the parties and the term may be interpreted accordingly. The second option is that circularity and sustainability are not explicitly acknowledged or mentioned in the PSS contract or its preambles but are referenced in marketing or advertising of the PSS supplier. In this case, it can be argued that (environmental) sustainability and circular economy principles can be seen as "implied" or "inferred contractual terms", i.e. terms that are not expressly formulated by the parties but nevertheless have a guiding influence on their contractual relationship. Third, it was considered whether the PSS contract can be interpreted in a sustainable way, even if the contracting parties have not mentioned or acknowledged sustainability interests whatsoever. Even more, are there cases where the court can engage in sustainable interpretation against the will of the parties? Although there are some arguments to do so, this remains very controversial or would require rather paradigmatic changes to our legal system. This is why this research has argued to focus on the low-hanging fruit, namely to provide PSS suppliers and consumers with the tools to effectively

1442 Art. 5.64–5.66 BCC.
1443 HR (NL) 13 March 1981, ECLI:NL:HR:1981:AG4158, (*Haviltex*), *NJ* 1981/635, case note C.J.H. Brunner, *RvdW* 1981, 43.
1444 Art. 5.66 BCC *juncto* Art. VI.37 BCEL.
1445 Art. 6:238(2) DCC.
1446 See *supra* section 2.5.3.

include sustainability and circularity considerations in their contract, which can then be taken into account by the courts when interpreting the contract.

350. Liability for breach of the PSS contract – The fifth section of this chapter dealt with **liability for breach of the PSS contract.**[1447] If one of the contracting parties does not fulfil one or more of its contractual obligations, they shall be contractually liable if this non-performance constitutes a breach of contract. For this, it is required that the non-performance is due to a fault of the debtor or his agents, employees or auxiliaries, or caused by an object which he uses in the performance of his contractual obligations. In other words, a breach of contract is an imputable non-performance of the contractual obligations in the PSS contract.

The existence of a breach of contract is determined in relation to the **content and scope of the contractual obligations** in the PSS contract, and whether they qualify as an obligation of means, an obligation of result, or an obligation of guarantee.[1448] In the case of an obligation of means, there is a breach of contract only if the debtor has not made the necessary efforts or has not used the necessary means to achieve the desired result, without promising the result. This means that the creditor will have to prove that the debtor did not act as a prudent and reasonable person would have acted in the same circumstances when fulfilling this contractual obligation. If the obligation is considered an obligation of result, there is a breach of contract if the promised result is not achieved by the debtor (even if he has acted as a prudent and reasonable person), unless he can prove that the non-performance is due to *force majeure*. In the case of an obligation of guarantee, the debtor will be liable if the promised result has not been achieved, even in the case of *force majeure*. It depends on the specific circumstances whether obligations in the PSS contract qualify as an obligation of means, result, or guarantee. The main criterion is the common intent of the parties (e.g. the parties may explicitly qualify their obligation as an obligation of result or this may follow from the contractual wording), but other criteria are also used, such as whether the result of the obligation is subject to chance.

In the performance of the PSS contract, the contracting parties may be faced with unexpected circumstances that make it impossible to fulfil the contractual obligations. In this case, there will be ***force majeure***.[1449] Typical examples of *force majeure* are fire, disease, epidemic, natural disaster, government action, strike, etc. In the context of PSS contracts, one can also think of power failures or the loss of internet connection of "smart" products. If the non-performance of the contractual obligation is not imputable to the debtor but due to *force majeure*, there will be no breach of contract and therefore no contractual liability. In

1447 See *supra* section 2.6.
1448 See *supra* section 2.6.2.
1449 See *supra* section 2.6.4.

case of permanent *force majeure*, the debtor whose performance has become impossible is released from his obligations. If the impossibility is only temporary, the debtor's obligation shall be suspended until performance becomes possible again (if still useful) or becomes permanently impossible.

If instead of making performance of the obligation impossible, the unexpected circumstances only make performance of the obligation significantly more difficult, burdensome or costly, there is no *force majeure*, but **hardship or change of circumstances.**[1450] The concept of hardship or change of circumstances refers to provisions (either statutory or contractual) that allow for the renegotiation or termination of the PSS contract when unexpected events fundamentally alter the contractual balance. Both Belgian law and Dutch law contain such statutory provisions that allow for the renegotiation or termination of the PSS contract in case of changed circumstances.

The creditor facing breach of contract by his debtor has access to various **remedies for breach of contract.**[1451] First, he can claim specific performance of the obligation, possibly with additional compensation for late performance. The basic principle is that such performance is carried out by the debtor himself, but the creditor may also ask the court to authorise him to perform the obligation himself or have it performed by a third party at the debtor's expense. In certain exceptional circumstances, there is no need for a judicial intervention and the creditor may resort to extrajudicial replacement (subject to an *a posteriori* review by the court). Second, the creditor may claim damages instead of performance. Third, in reciprocal contracts, which is the case with PSS contracts, the creditor may choose to terminate the contract, possibly with additional damages. However, termination requires a fundamental (i.e. sufficiently serious) non-performance. Fourth, the creditor may claim a price reduction in case of a non-performance that does not warrant the termination of the PSS contract. Finally, the creditor may suspend his obligations in the event of non-performance by relying on the *exceptio non adimpleti contractus* ("enac").

The rules on contractual liability, *force majeure*, hardship, and the remedies for breach of contract are not mandatory law. As a result, the parties are free to derogate from the default legal framework and flesh out their own contractual regime. However, their freedom is not unlimited, as the unfair terms control regime of the UCTD and its national implementation places restrictions on what the contracting parties can validly agree in the PSS contract. This is why, as a solution to promote truly circular PSS business models, this research has set out **balanced model clauses** throughout this section on contractual liability that stand the test of both the EU, Belgian and Dutch rules on unfair terms.

1450 See *supra* section 2.6.5.

1451 See *supra* section 2.6.6.

351. Duration of the PSS contract – The sixth and final section of this chapter addressed the **duration of the PSS contract.**[1452] This included the question of (early) termination of the PSS contract and extension and renewal of the PSS contract.

A distinction is made between fixed-term and open-ended PSS contracts. **Fixed-term PSS contracts** contain an extinctive term (i.e. a certain and future event that leads to the extinction of an obligation or contract).[1453] A fixed-term PSS contract must in principle be performed until its end and may generally not be unilaterally terminated by one of the contracting parties. However, there are exceptions to this principle, namely if a statutory provision,[1454] the PSS contract itself, or usages provide for that right to unilaterally terminate the contract. In principle, when the extinctive term has expired, the fixed-term PSS contract automatically extinguishes for the future. However, both the law and the PSS contract may provide for an explicit or tacit extension or renewal of the PSS contract.

If the PSS contract does not contain an extinctive term, it is an **open-ended PSS contract.**[1455] Under Belgian law, it is a general principle of law that open-ended PSS contracts can in principle be unilaterally terminated at any time, subject to a reasonable notice period. Under Dutch law, on the other hand, the unilateral termination right in open-ended contracts is not a general principle of law and the contractual parties may in principle exclude the possibility to unilaterally terminate an open-ended contract. However, a clause of non-terminability may conflict with the principle of reasonableness and fairness or the rule of Article 6:258 DCC, which allows to change or terminate the contract in view of certain changed circumstances.

The rules on duration of the contract are generally not mandatory law (except for the Belgian general principle of law that open-ended contracts are always terminable). This is why, as a solution to promote truly circular PSS business models, **balanced model clauses** have been drafted on the duration of the PSS contract.[1456]

1452 See *supra* section 2.7.

1453 See *supra* section 2.7.1.

1454 E.g. if the fixed-term PSS contract is qualified as a contract for services, the client has the right to unilaterally terminate the contract both under Belgian and Dutch law. See: Art. 1794 old BCC and Art. 7:408(1) DCC.

1455 See *supra* section 2.7.2.

1456 See *supra* section 2.7.3.

3. CONTRACTUAL QUALIFICATION OF THREE MAIN TYPES OF PSS

"If it looks like a duck, swims like a duck, and quacks like a duck, then it probably is a duck!"
– The "duck test"[1457]

3.1. INTRODUCTION

352. Importance of contractual qualification – PSS contracts are usually concluded between two parties: a) the PSS supplier and b) the PSS user. Yet more complex constructions are also possible. For example, PSS contracts can be offered through a platform, or a third party can be involved in the financing of the product. The parties to a PSS contract derive rights and obligations from both EU law and national law. To determine which rules apply to PSS contracts, it is therefore important to consider their contractual qualification.

353. Qualification under EU law – When considering the qualification of the PSS contract under EU law, the CRD is the first legal instrument that comes to mind. This directive makes a distinction between a "sales contract" and a "services contract". According to the CRD, a "sales contract" means "*any contract under which the trader transfers or undertakes to transfer the ownership of goods to the consumer and the consumer pays or undertakes to pay the price thereof, including any contract having as its object both goods and services.*"[1458]

1457 The duck test involves a type of abductive reasoning, which implies that an unknown subject can be classified by observing that subject's usual characteristics. The phrase was popularised during the Cold War in 1950 by Richard Cunningham Patterson Jr., the United States ambassador to Guatemala. Patterson used it to accuse Guatemala's Jacobo Arbenz Guzmán government of being Communist by arguing: "*Suppose you see a bird walking around in a farm yard. This bird has no label that says 'duck'. But the bird certainly looks like a duck. Also, he goes to the pond and you notice that he swims like a duck. Then he opens his beak and quacks like a duck. Well, by this time you have probably reached the conclusion that the bird is a duck, whether he's wearing a label or not.*"

1458 Art. 2(5) CRD. Since product-oriented PSS still entail a transfer of ownership and the traditional sale of product is just complemented by after-sales services, the latter part of the definition of the CRD implies that product-oriented PSS constitute sales contracts, at least for the purposes of this Directive. See in the same sense: J. Hojnik, "The Servitization of Industry: EU Law Implications and Challenges", *CML Rev.* 2016, vol. 53, (1575) 1606.

Consequently, if a PSS contract has as its main purpose the transfer of ownership of a good, it is to be qualified as a sales contract, even if it also covers additional services such as installation, maintenance, repair, etc.[1459] As a result, product-oriented PSS will generally qualify as a sales contract for the purposes of the CRD, unless separate contracts are concluded for the services part of the product-oriented PSS. The SGD has a similar definition of "sales contract". According to this Directive, "sales contract" means "*any contract under which the seller transfers or undertakes to transfer ownership of goods to a consumer, and the consumer pays or undertakes to pay the price thereof.*"[1460] Additionally, it states that "*contracts between a consumer and a seller for the supply of goods to be manufactured or produced shall also be deemed sales contracts for the purpose of this Directive.*"[1461]

On the other hand, a "service contract" within the meaning of the CRD means "*any contract other than a sales contract under which the trader supplies or undertakes to supply a service, including a digital service, to the consumer.*"[1462] As use-oriented and result-oriented PSS do not entail a transfer of ownership, they are considered "service contracts" under EU law. However, the negative and broad definition of service contracts is a great illustration of the fact that despite the EU's important legislative initiatives in the field of contract law and consumer protection law, service contracts are being rather disregarded. The service contract has been reduced to the counterpart of the sales contract and, unlike the sales contract, is only fragmentarily regulated throughout various directives.[1463] While the SGD provides an extensive legal framework for sales contracts, there is no such thing as a "Service Provision Directive" (except for the DCD and the Package Travel Directive). Consequently, substantive rules regulating the contract between the PSS provider and the PSS users are left to national contract law.

354. Qualification under national law – Given the lack of a clear and elaborate legal framework for service contracts at the EU level, PSS contracts – especially use-oriented and result-oriented PSS – are mostly governed by national contract law. Most national legal rules applicable to service contracts are not mandatory law so the contracting parties can flesh out their own contractual regime. However, in the absence of contractual regulations, the contractual relationship will be governed by the default rules on the corresponding named contract(s). Under the current legal framework, there are some important differences here, for example regarding conformity with the contract and the

---

1459 J. Hojnik, "The Servitization of Industry: EU Law Implications and Challenges", *CML Rev.* 2016, vol. 53, (1575) 1606.

1460 Art. 1(1) SGD.

1461 Art. 3(2) SGD.

1462 Art. 2(6) CRD.

1463 E.g. the CRD, the UCPD, the UCTD, and the DCD.

possibility to terminate the contract. This is why an important first step in determining the rights and obligations of the parties to a PSS contract is the legal qualification of this contract under national law. In the future, the issue of contractual qualification will hopefully become less important, at least under Belgian law. Indeed, further in this book, there is a plea for more internal homogenisation, for example by adopting a uniform notion of (non-)conformity for all (consumer) contracts, inspired by EU sales law and the DCFR, which can be applied across the board. It is therefore to be welcomed that the draft law of 16 April 2024 inserting Book 7 "special contracts" into the Civil Code also aims to provide more consistency between the various named contracts, particularly regarding the obligation to deliver in conformity with the contract.[1464]

355. Contractual qualification of three main types of PSS – Since PSS contracts are often complex and often contain features of different (named or unnamed) contracts such as the rental contract, the contract for services, the (operational) leasing contract, etc., their qualification under Belgian or Dutch law currently often gives rise to difficulties. The issue of contractual qualification of the three main types of PSS is dealt with in four sections.

The first section of this chapter discusses some general aspects of contractual qualification (section 3.2).

Even though the focus of this book is mainly on use-oriented and result-oriented PSS, the second section of this chapter looks at the contractual qualification of product-oriented PSS to show that these contracts pose fewer problems in terms of consumer protection (section 3.3). In most cases, a trade-off will have to be made between the rules on sales contracts and contracts for services.

The third section tackles the contractual qualification of use-oriented PSS (section 3.4). First, we look at use-oriented PSS that are limited to the provision of a good against the payment of a periodic fee. Second, we consider short term and occasional services, as is the case with most "pay-per-use" agreements. Third, we compare use-oriented PSS contracts to (operational) leasing contracts. Fourth, we look at use-oriented PSS contracts where the provision of a good is complemented by additional services. Finally, use-oriented PSS supplemented by digital services are discussed. In general, the rules on the rental contract for movables and/or a services contract (contract for works, contract for services) will apply to use-oriented PSS contracts.

The fourth section looks at the contractual qualification of result-oriented PSS (section 3.5). We will see that these contracts will generally be governed by the rules on the contracts for services. The last section concludes and gives a schematic overview (section 3.6).

[1464] Explanatory Memorandum, *Parliamentary Papers* Chamber of Representatives 2023–24, no. 55-3973/001, 6.

3.2. GENERAL ASPECTS OF CONTRACTUAL QUALIFICATION

"The distinguishing property of man is to search for and to follow after truth."
– Marcus Tullius Cicero[1465]

356. General aspects of contractual qualification – In this section, some general aspects of contractual qualification are discussed. First, the possibility and limitations for the parties to qualify their PSS contract themselves (conventional qualification) are addressed, including the cases in which the court may deviate from this conventional qualification (judicial qualification, often a *re*-qualification). Second, the situation where the PSS contract contains features of two or more named contracts is examined. In this case, the PSS contract is a mixed contract to which one of the three qualification theories (absorption, cumulation, "*sui generis*") must be applied to find the applicable legal rules. Third, this section examines in which cases a PSS contract can be regarded as an unnamed contract and which rules apply if this is the case.

3.2.1. CONVENTIONAL QUALIFICATION OF PSS CONTRACTS

357. Principle of freedom of contract – The principle of freedom of contract (*contractsvrijheid, la liberté contractuelle*), often regarded as an aspect of the principle of party autonomy (*principe van de wilsautonomie,*[1466] *principe de l'autonomie de la volonté*),[1467] is at the heart of the old

1465 Marcus Tullius Cicero, *De Officiis [On Duties, On Moral Duty; The Offices]*, Book 1, chapter 4 (1.4), section 13, 44 BC (Translation by C.R. Edmonds, 1874).

1466 In the Netherlands (and recently also gaining importance in Belgium), the term "*partijautonomie*" is used more often.

1467 **Belgium**: See e.g. I. Claeys and T. Tanghe, *Nieuw Algemeen Contractenrecht*, Antwerp, Intersentia, 2023, 69; P. Wéry, *Droit des obligations. Volume 1. Theorie générale du contrat*, Brussels, Larcier, 2021, 127–130; B. Weyts and T. Vansweevelt, *Handboek Verbintenissenrecht*, Antwerp, Intersentia, 2019, 129; S. Stijns, *Verbintenissenrecht*, Boek 1, Bruges, die Keure, 2022, 52; P. Van Ommeslaghe, *Traité de droit civil belge, Tome II. Les Obligations*, Volume 1, Brussels, Bruylant, 2013, 168 *et seq.*; P. Van Ommeslaghe, "L'autonomie de la volonté: du Code Civil à nos jours" in R. Feltkamp and F. Vanbossele (eds.), *Wilsautonomie, contractvrijheid en ondernemingscontracten: welke toekomst beschoren?*, Antwerp, Intersentia, 2012, (1) 6; B. Tilleman and A.L. Verbeke, "(Re-) codification du droit des contrats? Illustrations à l'aide du droit de la vente, de l'entreprise et des contrats innommés" in H. Cousy, S. Stijns, B. Tilleman and A.L. Verbeke (eds.), *Droit des contrats. France, Belgique*, Brussels, Larcier, 2005, (21) 22–23; R. Kruithof, "Leven en dood van het contract", *RW* 1985–86, (2731) 2737–2740. **The Netherlands**: See e.g.: B.W.M. Nieskens-Isphording, *Het fait accompli in het vermogensrecht: een (rechtsvergelijkend) onderzoek naar een aanvullende wijze van ontstaan en tenietgaan van verbintenissen*, Deventer, Kluwer, 1991, 28–29; J.B.M. Vranken, "Over partijautonomie,

BCC,[1468] the "new" BCC[1469] and the DCC.[1470] This principle traditionally entails that each individual is free to decide whether or not to enter into a contract and that the contracting parties are free to determine the content of their contract.[1471]

The principle of freedom of contract has some important implications. First, parties can in principle freely choose their co-contractor and even refuse to conclude a contract with a certain person.[1472] Second, the freedom to regulate the content of their contract means that parties can deviate from the legal

contractsvrijheid en de grondslag van gebondenheid in het verbintenissenrecht" in M.A.B. Chao-Duivis and H.A.W. Vermeulen (eds.), *Beginselen van het contractenrecht*, Deventer, W.E.J. Tjeenk Willink, 2000, (145) 146–147. However, see J.H. Nieuwenhuis, *Drie beginselen van contractenrecht*, Deventer, Kluwer, 1979, 6 claiming that party autonomy presupposes freedom of contract: there is no point in wondering whether the parties gave their consent if they are not free to enter into contracts in the first place. This point of view was also adopted by C.E. du Perron, *Overeenkomst en derden: een analyse van de relativiteit van de contractswerking*, Deventer, Kluwer, 1999, 14–23.

1468 Strangely enough, the principle of freedom of contract was not explicitly anchored in the old BCC. Nevertheless, this principle is traditionally identified with the principle of party autonomy, which the Belgian Court of Cassation sees enshrined in Art. 1134, §1 of the old BCC (the binding force of the contract). See e.g. Cass. (BE) 26 June 2017, *www.cass.be* 13 July 2017, *TBBR* 2018, 362, case note V. Withofs; Cass. (BE) 23 November 2009, *Arr.Cass.* 2009, 2756, concl. J. Genicot, *Pas.* 2009, 2721, concl. J. Genicot, *RW* 2010–11, 1434, case note A. Van Oevelen; Cass. (BE) 27 November 2008, *Arr.Cass.* 2008, 2738, *Pas.* 2008, 2685.

1469 In the "new" BCC, the principle of freedom of contract is explicitly included in Art. 5.14 BCC.

1470 **Belgium**: I. Claeys and T. Tanghe, *Nieuw Algemeen Contractenrecht*, Antwerp, Intersentia, 2023, 67; W. van Gerven and A. Van Oevelen, *Verbintenissenrecht*, Leuven, Acco, 2021, 71–72; S. Stijns and S. Jansen, "De basisbeginselen van het contractenrecht: kroniek van de recentste evoluties", *TBBR* 2013, (2) 3; S. Stijns and E. Swaenepoel, "De evolutie van de basisbeginselen in het contractenrecht, geïllustreerd aan de hand van het contractueel evenwicht" in I. Samoy (ed.), *Evolutie van de basisbeginselen van het contractenrecht*, Antwerp, Intersentia, 2010, (1) 2–3; R. Kruithof, "Leven en dood van het contract", *RW* 1985–86, (2731) 2734–2735. **The Netherlands**: C.H. Sieburgh, *Mr. C. Assers Handleiding tot de beoefening van het Nederlands Burgerlijk Recht. 6. Verbintenissenrecht. Deel III. Algemeen overeenkomstenrecht*, Deventer, Wolters Kluwer, 2018, no. 41; F.J. de Vries, *De overeenkomst in het algemeen*, Deventer, Wolters Kluwer, 2016, 3–4. The principle of freedom of contract is not expressly stated in any legal provision but is implied in Art. 6:248 DCC.

1471 **Belgium**: H. De Page, *Traité élémentaire de droit civil belge*, II, Brussels, Bruylant, 1964, 336–339; S. Stijns, *Verbintenissenrecht*, Boek 1, Bruges, die Keure, 2022, 53; A. Van Oevelen, "Algemene rechtsbeginselen in het verbintenissen- en contractenrecht" in M. Van Hoecke (ed.), *Algemene rechtsbeginselen*, Mechelen, Kluwer, 1991, (95) 98–99; P. Wéry, *Droit des obligations. Volume 1. Theorie générale du contrat*, Brussels, Larcier, 2021, 127–131. **The Netherlands**: C.H. Sieburgh, *Mr. C. Assers Handleiding tot de beoefening van het Nederlands Burgerlijk Recht. 6. Verbintenissenrecht. Deel III. Algemeen overeenkomstenrecht*, Deventer, Wolters Kluwer, 2018, no. 41.

1472 See e.g. Cass. (BE) 13 September 1991, *Arr.Cass.* 1991–92, 38, *Pas.* 1992, I, 33, *RW* 1991–92, 882, case note K. Broeckx, *TRV* 1993, case note D. Van Gerven; J. De Coninck, "Grondbeginselen van het contractenrecht" in *Comm. Bijz.Ov.*, IV, Mechelen, Kluwer, looseleaf, 2010, (119) 154. However, according to the Belgian Court of Cassation, refusal of contract may in some cases constitute abuse of rights (*rechtsmisbruik*, *l'abus de droit*). This was first acknowledged in Cass. (BE) 7 October 2011, *Arr.Cass.* 2011, 2032, *Pas.* 2011, 2148, concl. A. Henkens, *RW* 2012–13, 1181, case note S. Jansen and S. Stijns, *TBBR* 2012, 489, case note A. De Boeck and recently confirmed in Cass. (BE) 27 April 2020, *RW* 2020–2021, 1500, case note regime of their contract since, in general, these legal rules are only default law. Third, instead of opting for a named contract (a contract with a specific legal regime laid down in the civil code or other national legislation), parties may also conclude an unnamed contract. Finally, parties can always modify or terminate their contract by means of consensus.[1473] However, this does not mean that the freedom of contract is absolute. Parties are not allowed to deviate from public policy rules and mandatory rules.[1474] The principles of party autonomy and freedom of contract are also recognised by the DCFR. According to Article II. – 1:102 (1) DCFR, parties are free to make a contract or other juridical act and to determine its contents, albeit subject to any applicable mandatory rules.[1475]

358. Freedom of contract and conventional qualification clauses – As parties are free to determine the content of their contract, in practice they often try to put their stamp on the qualification of the contract by including a qualification clause or by naming the contract themselves. The question arises what the implications are for the qualification of a PSS contract if the parties decide to give their agreement a conventional qualification.

359. Belgian law: conventional qualification as starting point – Under Belgian law, parties are in principle free to qualify their PSS contract themselves and this conventional qualification will serve as a starting point.[1476] The courts may however overrule a conventional qualification on the basis of the parties' common intention or if the conventional qualification is contrary to rules

T. Hick and F. Van Den Abeele, *TBBR* 2021, 155, case note S. Jansen and S. Stijns, *T.Not.* 2021, 368, case note M. Meirlaen.

1473 **Belgium**: S. Stijns, *Verbintenissenrecht*, Boek 1, Bruges, die Keure, 2022, 53; A. Van Oevelen, "Algemene rechtsbeginselen in het verbintenissen- en contractenrecht" in M. Van Hoecke (ed.), *Algemene rechtsbeginselen*, Mechelen, Kluwer, 1991, (95) 104; P. Wéry, *Droit des obligations. Volume 1. Theorie générale du contrat*, Brussels, Larcier, 2021, 130; J. De Coninck, "Grondbeginselen van het contractenrecht" in *Comm. Bijz.Ov.*, IV, Mechelen, Kluwer, loose-leaf, 2010, (119) 143 and 154. **The Netherlands**: I.S.J. Houben, *Mr. C. Assers Handleiding tot de beoefening van het Nederlands Burgerlijk Recht. 7. Bijzondere overeenkomsten. Deel X. Onbenoemde overeenkomsten*, Deventer, Wolters Kluwer, 2019, no. 1–3.

1474 **Belgium**: Art. 1.3(3) BCC. See also e.g. P. Van Ommeslaghe, *Traité de droit civil belge, Tome II. Les Obligations*, Volume 1, Brussels, Bruylant, 2013, 173; P. Wéry, *Droit des obligations. Volume 1. Theorie générale du contrat*, Brussels, Larcier, 2021, 134–135. **The Netherlands**: Art. 3:40(1) and 3:40(2) DCC. See also e.g. F.J. de Vries, *De overeenkomst in het algemeen*, Deventer, Wolters Kluwer, 2016, 2.

1475 See II. – 1:102 (1) DCFR, see also Art. 1:102 PECL.

1476 B. Van Den Bergh, "'What's in a name': over de kwalificatie van overeenkomsten en het onderscheid tussen huur en aanneming" (case note Cass. 3 September 2010), *RW* 2011–12, (566) 566–567; A.L. Verbeke and T. Gladinez, "Vijf tendensen in tien jaar Cassatie over aanneming" in B. Tilleman and A.L. Verbeke (eds.), *Bijzondere Overeenkomsten*, Bruges, die Keure, 2017, (139) 139–40; B. Kohl, *Contrat d'entreprise*, Brussels, Bruylant, 2016, 140; B. Keirsbilck, E. Terryn and E. Van Gool, "Consumentenbescherming bij servitisation en product-dienst systemen (PDS)", *TPR* 2019, (817) 830–831.

of mandatory law or public policy.[1477] This is also reflected in Article 5.68 of the BCC.[1478] Nevertheless, if neither party disputes the conventional qualification, the courts will very often follow it and apply the rules of the contract to which the parties have indicated that they want to subject their legal relationship.[1479] This extensive priority of the conventional qualification was recognised by the Belgian Court of Cassation in several "qualification judgments".[1480]

According to the Belgian Court of Cassation, when the specific factual elements do not allow the exclusion of the qualification given by the parties, the court cannot give a different qualification to the contract.[1481] As a result, the court *can* only depart from the conventional qualification if the specific factual elements are incompatible with that qualification.[1482] Moreover, if there is more than one possible qualification in view of the specific factual elements, the court cannot substitute the conventional qualification.[1483] However, it

1477 I. Claeys and T. Tanghe, *Nieuw Algemeen Contractenrecht*, Antwerp, Intersentia, 2023, 477–478; W. Van Eeckhoutte, "'Gezag' in de cassatierechtspraak. Een kwestie van bewijs, interpretatie en kwalificatie", *NjW* 2005, (2) 9–11.

1478 "*Van de kwalificatie die door de partijen aan het contract is gegeven, kan enkel worden afgeweken indien zij onverenigbaar is met de bedingen ervan of met dwingendrechtelijke regels of regels van openbare orde.*"

1479 C. Marr, "Le contrat d'entreprise hors construction et la protection des consommateurs" in P. De Page, B. Sindic and C. Marr (eds.), *Récyclage en droit: Droit des contrats*, Liège, Anthemis, 2007, (145) 158.

1480 Cass. (BE) 23 December 2002, *JTT* 2003, 271, *Pas.* 2002, I, 2469, *RW* 2005–06, 24; Cass. (BE) 28 April 2003, *Arr.Cass* 2003, 1050, *NjW* 2003, 886, *RABG* 2003, 1093, case note M. Demedts, *JTT* 2003, 261; Cass. (BE) 8 December 2003, *JTT* 2004, 122, case note; Cass. (BE) 3 May 2004, *TBBR* 2005, 271, case note F. Van Remoortel, *NjW* 2005, 18, case note W. Van Eeckhoutte, *Arr.Cass.* 2004, 771, *Pas.* 2004, 755; Cass. (BE) 6 December 2004, *NjW* 2005, 21, *Arr.Cass.* 2004, 1955; Cass. (BE) 9 June 2008, *Arr.Cass.* 2008, 1489, *TBBR* 2010, 196; A.L. Verbeke and T. Gladinez, "Vijf tendensen in tien jaar Cassatie over aanneming" in B. Tilleman and A.L. Verbeke (eds.), *Bijzondere Overeenkomsten*, Bruges, die Keure, 2017, (139) 140; J. Waelkens, *Interpretatie van overeenkomsten en eenzijdige rechtshandelingen*, Antwerp, Intersentia, 2016, 421, no. 309; B. Kohl, *Contrat d'entreprise*, Brussels, Bruylant, 2016, 141. See also J.F. Van Drooghenbroeck, "Le juge et le contrat", *TBBR* 2007, (595) 595–620.

1481 Cass. (BE) 23 December 2002, *JTT* 2003, 271, *Pas.* 2002, I, 2469, *RW* 2005–06, 24; Cass. (BE) 28 April 2003, *Arr.Cass* 2003, 1050, *NjW* 2003, 886, *RABG* 2003, 1093, case note M. Demedts, *JTT* 2003, 261; Cass. (BE) 6 December 2004, *NjW* 2005, 21, *Arr.Cass.* 2004, 1955: "*lorsque les éléments soumis à son appréciation ne permettent pas d'exclure la qualification donnée par les parties à la convention qu'elles ont conclue, le juge du fond ne peut y substituer une qualification différente.*" See also: Cass. (BE) 23 May 2011, *JTT* 2011, 392; Cass. (BE) 10 June 2013, *JTT* 2013, 320.

1482 Cass. (BE) 23 December 2002, *JTT* 2003, 271, *Pas.* 2002, I, 2469, *RW* 2005–06, 24; Cass. (BE) 28 April 2003, *Arr.Cass* 2003, 1050, *NjW* 2003, 886, *RABG* 2003, 1093, case note M. Demedts, *JTT* 2003, 261; Cass. (BE) 8 December 2003, *JTT* 2004, 122, case note; Cass. (BE) 3 May 2004, *TBBR* 2005, 271, case note F. Van Remoortel, *NjW* 2005, 18, case note W. Van Eeckhoutte, *Arr.Cass.* 2004, 771, *Pas.* 2004, 755; Cass. (BE) 6 December 2004, *NjW* 2005, 21, *Arr.Cass.* 2004, 1955; Cass. (BE) 25 May 2009, *Arr.Cass.* 2009, 1370, *JT* 2009, 28, case note, *JTT* 2009, 389, *Pas.* 2009, 1263; Cass. (BE) 10 October 2011, *Arr.Cass.* 2011, 2059, concl. J. Genicot, *JTT* 2012, 21, concl. J. Genicot, case note, *RABG* 2012, 947, case note V. Dooms, *T.Aann.* 2014, 76, concl. J. Genicot, case note V. Renard.

1483 J. Waelkens, *Interpretatie van overeenkomsten en eenzijdige rechtshandelingen*, Antwerp, Intersentia, 2016, 421, no. 309; B. Kohl, *Contrat d'entreprise*, Brussels, Bruylant, 2016, 141.

should be noted that, according to the Court of Cassation, this does not mean that the conventional qualification has the probative value of a (rebuttable) presumption.[1484] The situation is different if one of the parties contests this conventional qualification or if this qualification appears inappropriate given the factual elements specifically brought to the attention of the judge ("*des faits spécialement invoqués*"). In this case, the judge *must* depart from this conventional qualification.[1485]

As a result, when parties give a conventional qualification to their PSS contract (for example a use-oriented PSS regarding household appliances as a rental contract for movables) the courts must, under Belgian law, respect this conventional qualification unless it is contrary to rules of mandatory law or public policy, or the specific factual elements clearly contradict this qualification. In this case, the judge has the *power* to undo the conventional qualification and, when one of the parties disputes the qualification or "specially invokes" factual elements incompatible with the conventional qualification, the judge even has the *duty* to do so.

360. Dutch law: conventional qualification not decisive – Under Dutch law, neither the name given to the contract by the parties nor conventional qualification clauses are decisive for the qualification of a contract.[1486] Instead, the actual performance and content of a contract prevail over the subjective intent of the parties.[1487] This prevents parties from circumventing certain

---

1484 See: Cass. (BE) 20 March 2006, *RW* 2006–07, 131, case note, *Arr.Cass.* 2006, 649 and Cass. (BE) 7 February 2007, *RW* 2007–08, 781, case note K. Nevens; B. Van Den Bergh, "'What's in a name': over de kwalificatie van overeenkomsten en het onderscheid tussen huur en aanneming" (case note Cass. 3 September 2010), *RW* 2011–12, (566) 567; K. Nevens, "Kwalificatie, bewijslast en bewijsrisico" (case note Cass. 3 May 2004), *RW* 2004–05, (1220) 1222; A.L. Verbeke and T. Gladinez, "Vijf tendensen in tien jaar Cassatie over aanneming" in B. Tilleman and A.L. Verbeke (eds.), *Bijzondere Overeenkomsten*, Bruges, die Keure, 2017, (139) 140. See also earlier judgments: Cass. (BE) 3 May 2004, *TBBR* 2005, 271, case note F. Van Remoortel, *NjW* 2005, 18, case note W. Van Eeckhoutte, *Arr.Cass.* 2004, 771, *Pas.* 2004, 755 and Cass. (BE) 6 December 2004, *NjW* 2005, 21, *Arr.Cass.* 2004, 1955. Cass. (BE) 23 May 2011, *JTT* 2011, 392; Cass. (BE) 10 June 2013, *JTT* 2013, 320.

1485 Cass. (BE) 14 April 2005, *Arr.Cass.* 2005, 868, concl. P. De Koster, *JT* 2005, 659, case note J. Van Compernolle, *JLMB* 2005, 856, case note G. Deval, *Pas.* 2005, 862, concl. P. De Koster. See also: J.F. Van Drooghenbroeck, "Le juge et le contrat", *TBBR* 2007, (595) 601–604, no. 14–20 and B. Kohl, *Contrat d'entreprise*, Brussels, Bruylant, 2016, 140–141, no. 63.

1486 HR (NL) 19 December 2008, ECLI:NL:HR:2008:BG7294, *BNB* 2009/56, case note R.J. Koopman: ("*de juridische kwalificatie van een overeenkomst wordt bepaald door de inhoud van die overeenkomst en niet door de naam die partijen aan de overeenkomst hebben gegeven*"). See for example: HR (NL) 16 January 2004, ECLI:NL:PHR:2004:AM2315 (*Badawy/ Atlanta*), *NJ* 2004, 164, case note H.J. Snijders where parties named their contract as an agency agreement, while in fact parties agreed to an exclusive distribution agreement; G.K.L. de Wijkerslooth, "'Ceci n'est pas une pipe?' Over uitleg en kwalificatie van de (huur)overeenkomst", *HIP* 2020/35, (11) 12; F.J. de Vries, *De overeenkomst in het algemeen*, Deventer, Wolters Kluwer, 2016, 31.

1487 P.J. Tanja and G.J. Standhardt, "Uitleg en kwalificatie van een overeenkomst", *BB* 2020/31, (155) 156.

mandatory rules.[1488] Yet, this does not mean that the wording and name of a contract are completely irrelevant: some courts do occasionally attach value to these elements.[1489]

The relevance of conventional qualifications was clarified by the Dutch Supreme Court in its *Inscharing* judgment. This judgment is in line with and in some respects clarifies previous jurisprudence[1490] on qualification by distinguishing between the interpretation and qualification of the contract.[1491] According to the Dutch Supreme Court, the court must first determine the *content* of the contract, i.e. the rights and obligations agreed upon by the parties, by using the *Haviltex* standard (interpretation).[1492, 1493] The *Haviltex* standard of interpretation provides that the question of how a written contract regulates the relationship of the parties cannot be answered solely on the basis of a linguistic interpretation of the provisions of that contract. Instead the answer to this question is based on the meaning that the parties could reasonably attribute to these provisions in the given circumstances and to what they could reasonably expect from each other in this respect.[1494] Then, in a second stage, the court must determine whether the actual content of the contract falls within the legal

1488 G.K.L. de Wijkerslooth, "'Ceci n'est pas une pipe?' Over uitleg en kwalificatie van de (huur)overeenkomst", *HIP* 2020/35, (11) 12.

1489 HR (NL) 13 April 2001, ECLI:NL:HR:2001:AB1064, *NJ* 2001, 336, *JOL* 2001, 262, *RvdW* 2001, 85, *JWB* 2001/118: ("*Weliswaar behoeft de benaming die de partijen zelf aan de overeenkomst geven niet beslissend te zijn voor de kwalificatie ervan doch dat neemt niet weg dat deze wel een rol bij de kwalificatie kan spelen*"); See also Hof 's-Hertogenbosch (NL) 26 October 2004, ECLI:NL:GHSHE:2004:AR7508, *NJF* 2005, 345; I.S.J. Houben, *Mr. C. Assers Handleiding tot de beoefening van het Nederlands Burgerlijk Recht. 7. Bijzondere overeenkomsten. Deel X. Onbenoemde overeenkomsten*, Deventer, Wolters Kluwer, 2019, no. 20; L. van den Berg (case note HR (NL) 25 March 2011), *RSV* 2011/166).

1490 See e.g. HR (NL) 10 July 2015, ECLI:NL:HR:2015:1830, (*Searocco/Altena*), *JWB* 2015/269, *NJ* 2015/321, *NJB* 2015/1408, *RCR* 2015/71; HR (NL) 14 November 1997, ECLI:NL:HR:1997:ZC2495, (*Groen/Schoevers*), *JAR* 1997/263; HR (NL) 10 December 2004, ECLI:NL:PHR:2004:AP2651, (*Diosynth/Groot-van-Veen*), *NJ* 2005/239; HR (NL) 25 March 2011, ECLI:NL:HR:2011:BP3887, (*De Gouden Kooi*), *NJ* 2011/594.

1491 HR (NL) 20 December 2019, ECLI:NL:HR:2019:2034, (*Inscharing*), *NJB* 2020/17, *NJ* 2020/43, *RvdW* 2020/136, *RCR* 2020/24.

1492 See also HR (NL) 10 July 2015, ECLI:NL:HR:2015:1830, (*Searocco/Altena*), *JWB* 2015/269, *NJ* 2015/321, *NJB* 2015/1408, *RCR* 2015/71.

1493 See on the interpretation of the PSS contract and the *Haviltex* standard of interpretation also *infra* section 2.5, in particular no. 247.

1494 HR (NL) 13 March 1981, ECLI:NL:HR:1981:AG4158, (*Haviltex*), *NJ* 1981/635, case note C.J.H. Brunner, *RvdW* 1981, 43: ("*De vraag hoe in een schriftelijk contract de verhouding van partijen is geregeld en of dit contract een leemte laat die moet worden aangevuld, kan niet worden beantwoord op grond van alleen maar een taalkundige uitleg van de bepalingen van dat contract. Voor de beantwoording van die vraag komt het immers aan op de zin die pp. in de gegeven omstandigheden over en weer redelijkerwijs aan deze bepalingen mochten toekennen en op hetgeen zij te dien aanzien redelijkerwijs van elkaar mochten verwachten. Daarbij kan mede van belang zijn tot welke maatschappelijke kringen partijen behoren en welke rechtskennis van zodanige partijen kan worden verwacht.*"). See also F.J. de Vries, *De overeenkomst in het algemeen*, Deventer, Wolters Kluwer, 2016, 31 and 27.

definition of a named contract (qualification).[1495] It is irrelevant whether the parties actually intended to make the contract subject to that legal regime, what matters is whether the content (i.e. the agreed rights and obligations) have the characteristics of that named contract.[1496]

However, in practice it will often be difficult to clearly distinguish between these two stages: when interpreting the contract, the court will already consider the law and whether the parties have tried to circumvent a certain legal regime.[1497]

Thus, under Dutch law, the conventional qualification and name of a PSS contract is in principle irrelevant. The court must first determine the rights and obligations of the parties using the *Haviltex* standard (interpretation) and then check whether the content of the contract falls within the legal definition of a named contract (qualification).

361. Conventional qualification must not conflict with public policy and mandatory rules – As mentioned higher, the freedom of contract is limited by mandatory and public policy rules. As a result, the conventional qualification must in no case conflict with these mandatory and public policy rules.[1498] For product-oriented PSS contract, the mandatory rules on consumer sales[1499] are specifically relevant. Additionally, for all types of PSS contracts, the rules on the supply of digital content and digital services[1500] will also play a very important role.

362. Conventional qualification in analysed PSS contracts – Several analysed PSS contracts give a conventional qualification to their contract, at

1495 HR (NL) 20 December 2019, ECLI:NL:HR:2019:2034, (*Inscharing*), *NJB* 2020/17, *NJ* 2020/43, *RvdW* 2020/136, *RCR* 2020/24.

1496 HR (NL) 20 December 2019, ECLI:NL:HR:2019:2034, (*Inscharing*), *NJB* 2020/17, *NJ* 2020/43, *RvdW* 2020/136, *RCR* 2020/24. See also the judgment of the Dutch Supreme Court on the qualification of an employment contract where the Dutch Supreme Court came to a similar conclusion: HR (NL) 6 November 2020, ECLI:NL:HR:2020:1746, (*X/Gemeente Amsterdam*), *JAR* 2020/287, case note S. Said, *NJB* 2020/2735 (no. 3.2.2 and 3.2.3).

1497 P.J. Tanja and G.J. Standhardt, "Uitleg en kwalificatie van een overeenkomst", *BB* 2020/31, (155) 157.

1498 **Belgium**: R. Dekkers, A.L. Verbeke, N. Carette and K. Vanhove, *Handboek burgerlijk recht, Deel III, Verbintenissen, bewijsleer en gebruikelijke contracten*, Antwerp, Intersentia, 2007, 15. **The Netherlands**: I.S.J. Houben, *Mr. C. Assers Handleiding tot de beoefening van het Nederlands Burgerlijk Recht. 7. Bijzondere overeenkomsten. Deel X. Onbenoemde overeenkomsten*, Deventer, Wolters Kluwer, 2019, no. 20.

1499 EU: Directive (EU) 2019/771 of the European Parliament and the Council of 20 May 2019 on certain aspects concerning contracts for the sale of goods, amending Regulation (EU) 2017/2394 and Directive 2009/22/EC, and repealing Directive 1999/44/EC, OJ L 319, 22.5.2019, 28–50. **Belgium**: Art. 1649*bis* – 1649*octies* old BCC. **The Netherlands**: see Art. 7:1 – 7:50 DCC.

1500 EU: Directive (EU) 2019/770 of the European Parliament and of the Council of 20 May 2019 on certain aspects concerning contracts for the supply of digital content and digital services, OJ L 136, 22.5.2019, 1–27.

least implicitly. For example, in the household appliances sector, the contracts used by the *Papillon* project are explicitly named rental contract for movables ("*huurovereenkomst roerend goed*"). Similarly, *Blue Movement* also uses the wording general terms and conditions for the rental of domestic appliances ("*Algemene Voorwaarden Bluemovement voor verhuur van huishoudelijke apparaten*"). Interestingly, this does not apply to *Bundles* although it offers a similar service. Its terms and conditions refer only to "the contract" and "the subscription".[1501] In other sectors too, some PSS suppliers explicitly name their contract as a rental contract. Examples include *Grover* ("*Rental Agreement*"), *Dressr* ("*online rental subscription service*"), *Lena* ("*huurovereenkomsten*"), Still other PSS use an intermediate solution. They name their contract as a "subscription" but use the term "Renter" and other derivatives of the verb "to rent" throughout the contract. Examples of this approach are *Swapfiets* and *Repeat/Gerrard Street*. The odd one out in the selection is *Mudjeans*. This is the only example in the analysed PSS contracts that uses the terms "Buyer" and "Seller". However, this makes sense since the *Lease a Jeans* formula allows the PSS user to acquire the ownership of the jeans at the end of the 12-month period if he decides to keep the jeans instead of exchanging them for a new pair. Finally, some PSS completely steer clear of the term "rental contract". For example, *Fairphone easy* explicitly uses the term "As-A-Service Agreement", *HP Instant Ink* utilises "subscription ink or toner cartridge supply service", "service plan" and "subscription", and *Live Light* refers to "the Agreement" and "the User".

3.2.2. MIXED CONTRACTS

363. Mixed contract or two or more separate contracts? – When qualifying PSS contracts, it should also be considered whether the contract consists of two or more separate contracts which remain subject to their own legal rules, or one mixed contract. Mixed contracts are contracts that have essential characteristics of two or more named contracts.[1502] This distinction depends on the contractual arrangements and, unless it is unambiguously demonstrated by the individual design of the separate contracts (for example by the fact that both contracts have separate prices, different times of conclusion, different objects and/or different parties), the former view is only rarely accepted.[1503]

1501 See Art. 1, i) and Art. 3 Terms and Conditions Bundles.

1502 **Belgium**: R. Dekkers, A.L. Verbeke, N. Carette and K. Vanhove, *Handboek burgerlijk recht, Deel III, Verbintenissen, bewijsleer en gebruikelijke contracten*, Antwerp, Intersentia, 2007, 16. **The Netherlands**: C.H. Sieburgh, *Mr. C. Assers Handleiding tot de beoefening van het Nederlands Burgerlijk Recht. 6. Verbintenissenrecht. Deel III. Algemeen overeenkomstenrecht*, Deventer, Wolters Kluwer, 2018, no. 67.

1503 **Belgium**: See for example Liège (BE) 15 December 2005, *JT* 2006, 308 where the contract where the seller of a car agreed to equip the car to run on LPG fuel was qualified as a separate contract. See also P. Brulez, *Koop en aanneming: faux amis?*, Antwerp, Intersentia, 2015,

364. Mixed contracts: three theories – If a PSS contract is a mixed contract, three theories can be used to determine which rules apply: the **absorption theory**, which applies the rules for the main component to the whole contract; the **cumulation theory** or combination theory which applies the rules applicable to every component in parallel; and – as a last resort – a **"*sui generis*" qualification**. The latter considers the mixed contract as an unnamed contract, which is in principle only subjected to general contract law, whereas the legal provisions applicable to named contracts may be applicable by analogy.[1504]

365. Three theories: advantages and disadvantages – Each of these theories has advantages and disadvantages. The absorption theory is preferable when it is clear which is the main component of the contract, but in practice this is often rather difficult to determine. The cumulation theory is useful when the different components are clearly distinguishable and has the advantage that mandatory rules are applied to the largest extent possible.[1505] However, this parallel application of the rules applicable to both named contracts can sometimes lead to incompatible legal consequences. The "*sui generis*" theory avoids these objections but does not provide a criterion for deciding which rules can and cannot be applied by analogy.[1506]

121–122 and B. Keirsbilck, E. Terryn and E. Van Gool, "Consumentenbescherming bij servitisation en product-dienst systemen (PDS)", *TPR* 2019, (817) 831. **The Netherlands**: C.H. Sieburgh, *Mr. C. Assers Handleiding tot de beoefening van het Nederlands Burgerlijk Recht. 6. Verbintenissenrecht. Deel III. Algemeen overeenkomstenrecht*, Deventer, Wolters Kluwer, 2018, no 67; M.E. Hinskens-van Neck and L.A.R. Siemerink, "Gemengde overeenkomsten. De betekenis van art. 6:215 BW in de praktijk: kwalificatie van overeenkomsten", *MvV* 2012, (1) 3; F.C. Borst, A.S. Rueb and M.F.A. Evers, "Gemengde overeenkomsten met een huurelement en gemengde huurovereenkomsten", *WR* 2004, 20, Section 2.3; H.J. Rossel, *Huurrecht algemeen*, Deventer, Kluwer, 2007, 18–19; A.G. Castermans and H.B. Krans, "Gemengde overeenkomsten", *NbBW* 2003, (104) 104–105. For an example see HR (NL) 26 February 1993, ECLI:NL:HR:1993:ZC0889, (*Kasteel Hoensbroek*), *NJ* 1993, 581, case note P.A. Stein where one "rental contract" was split into two separate agreements.

1504 **Belgium**: e.g. P. Brulez, *Koop en aanneming: faux amis?*, Antwerp, Intersentia, 2015, 83–91; V. Sagaert, B. Tilleman and A.L. Verbeke, *Vermogensrecht in kort bestek*, Antwerp, Intersentia, 2019, 15–16; R. Dekkers, A.L. Verbeke, N. Carette and K. Vanhove, *Handboek burgerlijk recht, Deel III, Verbintenissen, bewijsleer en gebruikelijke contracten*, Antwerp, Intersentia, 2007, 15–16. **The Netherlands**: e.g. C.H. Sieburgh, *Mr. C. Assers Handleiding tot de beoefening van het Nederlands Burgerlijk Recht. 6. Verbintenissenrecht. Deel III. Algemeen overeenkomstenrecht*, Deventer, Wolters Kluwer, 2018, no. 67–68; S. Verbeek-Meinhardt, *Groene Serie Verbintenissenrecht, artikel 215 Boek 6 BW*, Deventer, Wolters Kluwer, loose-leaf, no. 4; I.S.J. Houben, *Mr. C. Assers Handleiding tot de beoefening van het Nederlands Burgerlijk Recht. 7. Bijzondere overeenkomsten. Deel X. Onbenoemde overeenkomsten*, Deventer, Wolters Kluwer, 2019, no. 8; J. Hijma, *Mr. C. Assers Handleiding tot de beoefening van het Nederlands Burgerlijk Recht. 7. Bijzondere overeenkomsten. Deel I. Koop en ruil*, Deventer, Kluwer, 2019, no. 19.

1505 **Belgium**: I. Claeys and T. Tanghe, *Nieuw Algemeen Contractenrecht*, Antwerp, Intersentia, 2023, 479–470. **The Netherlands**: I.S.J. Houben, *Mr. C. Assers Handleiding tot de beoefening van het Nederlands Burgerlijk Recht. 7. Bijzondere overeenkomsten. Deel X. Onbenoemde overeenkomsten*, Deventer, Wolters Kluwer, 2019, nr. 10.

1506 **Belgium**: I. Claeys and T. Tanghe, *Nieuw Algemeen Contractenrecht*, Antwerp, Intersentia, 2023, 480–481. **The Netherlands**: C.H. Sieburgh, *Mr. C. Assers Handleiding tot de*

366. Preference under Belgian law – The old Belgian Civil Code did not specify which theory is preferable. This changed with the "new" Belgian Civil Code where Article 5.67 BCC does provide some guidance when to apply each of the three qualification theories.[1507] Nevertheless, no theory is explicitly put forward by the BCC as the basic rule and the choice between the three qualification theories therefore often remains a matter to be decided on a case-by-case basis. Most Belgian case law and legal doctrine on mixed contracts deal with the distinction between a sales contract (*koop, vente*) and a contract for services (*aanneming, contrat d'entreprise*). More specifically, they mostly deal with contracts which are concerned with the transfer of a good still to be manufactured. Although it is necessary to determine the most appropriate legal qualification on a case-by-case basis and considering the specific circumstances,[1508] the majority of legal doctrine prefers the absorption theory (the specificity criterion in particular) to settle these qualification issues.[1509] However, where this would lead to an artificial unification of a complex contract, there is also a possibility to apply these rules cumulatively.[1510]

367. Preference under Dutch law – Dutch law on the other hand does give a clear rule of thumb: the Dutch legislator took the cumulation theory as a starting point, which does not detract from the fact that they also use different theories depending on the concrete situation. This is reflected in the caveat of Article 6:215 of the Dutch Civil Code "*unless the provisions are incompatible, or their scope is incompatible with the nature of the contract.*"[1511] This reflects the

beoefening van het Nederlands Burgerlijk Recht. 6. Verbintenissenrecht. Deel III. Algemeen overeenkomstenrecht, Deventer, Wolters Kluwer, 2018, no 68.

1507 See also: Explanatory Memorandum, *Parliamentary Papers* Kamer 2021, no. 55-1805-001, 78–80.

1508 P. Brulez, *Koop en aanneming: faux amis?*, Antwerp, Intersentia, 2015, 83; C. Marr, "Le contrat d'entreprise hors construction et la protection des consommateurs" in P. De Page, B. Sindic and C. Marr (eds.), *Récyclage en droit: Droit des contrats*, Liège, Anthemis, 2007, (145) 159; W. Goossens, *Aanneming van werk: het gemeenrechtelijk dienstencontract*, Bruges, die Keure, 2003, 56; B. Tilleman, *Overeenkomsten. 2: Bijzondere overeenkomsten. A: Verkoop. 1: Tostandkoming en kwalificatie van de koop, in Beginselen van Belgisch Privaatrecht*, Antwerp, Story-Scientia, 2001, 313; G. Van Hecke, "De la nature du contrat d'entreprise dans lequel l'entrepreneur fournit la matière" (case note Liège (BE) 13 December 1949), *RCJB* 1951, (100) 104.

1509 See e.g. V. Sagaert, B. Tilleman and A.L. Verbeke, *Vermogensrecht in kort bestek*, Antwerp, Intersentia, 2019, 15–16; F. Burssens, *Handboek Aannemingsrecht*, Antwerp, Intersentia, 2019, 5; B. Kohl, *Contrat d'entreprise*, Brussels, Bruylant, 2016, 77–80; M. Schoups and M. Somers, "Raakvlakken tussen koop en aanneming: recente tendensen op het vlak van de aansprakelijkheid voor gebreken in het geleverde goed", *TBO* 2012, (233) 233–234; S. Stijns, B. Tilleman, W. Goossens, B. Kohl and E. Swaenepoel, "Aanneming: Begrip. Totstandkoming. Bewijs", *TPR* 2008, (1665) 1666.

1510 W. Goossens, *Aanneming van werk: het gemeenrechtelijk dienstencontract*, Bruges, die Keure, 2003, 110.

1511 Art. 6:215 Dutch BW. See for an example: HR (NL) 10 March 2017, ECLI:NL:HR:2017:405, (*Kasteelcatering*), *WR* 2017/97, *RCR* 2017/54, *NJB* 2017/675, *RvdW* 2017/342. See also: P.S.

legal doctrine that argues that there is no absolute theory that can apply to all mixed contracts.[1512] The application of these theories to PSS contracts will be further explained below.

3.2.3. UNNAMED (SERVICE) CONTRACTS

368. PSS CONTRACT AS AN UNNAMED CONTRACT – The (service) contracts laid down in the Belgian and Dutch Civil Codes do not cover the entire spectrum.[1513] In addition to the so-called named contracts (or "nominate contracts") laid down in the respective civil codes, there are also unnamed contracts (or "innominate contracts") that cannot be classified under any of the known contract forms.[1514] This follows from the principles of party autonomy and freedom of contract which allow parties to determine the content of their contract without having to respect the existing limits of a named contract.[1515] As a result, it is not inconceivable that in some cases a PSS contract cannot be fitted into the straitjacket of named contracts and therefore constitutes an unnamed contract.

Various authors have attempted to divide the unnamed contracts into different categories according to their degree of "unnamedness".[1516]

BAKKER, "Samenloop bij gemengde overeenkomsten: Enige gedachten over de toepassing van art. 6:215 BW naar aanleiding van HR 10 maart 2017, ECLI:NL:HR:2017:405, RvdW 2017/342", *MvV* 2017, (136) 136–142.

1512 See e.g. I.S.J. HOUBEN, *Mr. C. Assers Handleiding tot de beoefening van het Nederlands Burgerlijk Recht. 7. Bijzondere overeenkomsten. Deel X. Onbenoemde overeenkomsten*, Deventer, Wolters Kluwer, 2019, no. 9; T.F.E. TJONG TJIN TAI, *Asser 7-IV Bijzondere Overeenkomsten – Opdracht, incl. de geneeskundige behandelingsovereenkomst en de reisovereenkomst*, Deventer, Wolters Kluwer, 2018, no. 47.

1513 **Belgium**: See e.g. W. GOOSSENS, *Aanneming van werk: het gemeenrechtelijk dienstencontract*, Bruges, die Keure, 2003, 245; P. WÉRY, *Droit des obligations. Volume 1. Theorie générale du contrat*, Brussels, Larcier, 2021, 97–102; R. KRUITHOF, H. BOCKEN, F. DE LY and B. DE TEMMERMAN, "Verbintenissenrecht (1981–1992). Overzicht van rechtspraak", *TPR* 1994, (171) 238–239. **The Netherlands**: See e.g. C.H. SIEBURGH, *Mr. C. Assers Handleiding tot de beoefening van het Nederlands Burgerlijk Recht. 6. Verbintenissenrecht. Deel III. Algemeen overeenkomstenrecht*, Deventer, Wolters Kluwer, 2018, no. 66.

1514 It is sometimes noted that these terms are inaccurate as the criterion is not whether the contract has been given a name, but whether it has been separately regulated by law. Therefore, named contracts are also referred to as "special contracts" (*bijzondere overeenkomsten, contrats spéciaux*). See: C.H. SIEBURGH, *Mr. C. Assers Handleiding tot de beoefening van het Nederlands Burgerlijk Recht. 6. Verbintenissenrecht. Deel III. Algemeen overeenkomstenrecht*, Deventer, Wolters Kluwer, 2018, no. 66.

1515 **Belgium**: H. DE PAGE, *Traité élémentaire de droit civil belge*, IV, Brussels, Bruylant, 1972, n0. 1. **The Netherlands**: I.S.J. HOUBEN, *Mr. C. Assers Handleiding tot de beoefening van het Nederlands Burgerlijk Recht. 7. Bijzondere overeenkomsten. Deel X. Onbenoemde overeenkomsten*, Deventer, Wolters Kluwer, 2019, no. 1.

1516 **Belgium**: H. DE PAGE, *Traité élémentaire de droit civil belge*, IV, Brussels, Bruylant, 1972; R. VANDEPUTTE, *De overeenkomst. Haar ontstaan, haar uitvoering en verdwijning, haar bewijs*, Brussels, Larcier, 1977, 20–21; R. KRUITHOF, H. BOCKEN, F. DE LY and B. DE TEMMERMAN,

(i) The first category are not truly unnamed contracts, but contracts which on closer inspection do fall within the definition of a named contract. There is *no impossibility* to qualify the contracts in this category as a named contract, but in fact there are some *qualification difficulties* (also called pseudo-unnamed contracts).[1517] One should therefore be careful not to jump to the conclusion that a PSS contract concerns an unnamed contract. In many cases, after thorough qualification, a connection can be found with a named contract, in many cases a contract for services.[1518]

(ii) The second category concerns *complex contracts* that consist of a combination of several named agreements.[1519] These are, in fact, mixed contracts which have characteristics that make them transcend their components (none of the components is predominant) and should therefore be regarded as unnamed contracts.[1520] In order to determine the applicable rules to these contracts, it is often appropriate to use the cumulation theory.[1521] Given the nature of PSS contracts, this category will be quite common. After all, PSS contracts often consist of various components that will need to be weighed against each other.

"Verbintenissenrecht (1981–1992). Overzicht van rechtspraak", *TPR* 1994, (171) 239–240; no. 4. W. Goossens, *Aanneming van werk: het gemeenrechtelijk dienstencontract*, Bruges, die Keure, 2003, 245–246. **The Netherlands**: I.S.J. Houben, *Mr. C. Assers Handleiding tot de beoefening van het Nederlands Burgerlijk Recht. 7. Bijzondere overeenkomsten. Deel X. Onbenoemde overeenkomsten*, Deventer, Wolters Kluwer, 2019, no. 4. However, HOUBEN notes in no. 5 that unnamed contracts regularly fall into more than one of these categories. One should therefore be wary of a too strict classification of unnamed contracts.

1517 **Belgium**: R. Kruithof, H. Bocken, F. De Ly and B. De Temmerman, "Verbintenissenrecht (1981–1992). Overzicht van rechtspraak", *TPR* 1994, (171) 239, no. 45; H. De Page, *Traité élémentaire de droit civil belge*, IV, Brussels, Bruylant, 1972, 13–15, no. 4. A. **The Netherlands**: I.S.J. Houben, *Mr. C. Assers Handleiding tot de beoefening van het Nederlands Burgerlijk Recht. 7. Bijzondere overeenkomsten. Deel X. Onbenoemde overeenkomsten*, Deventer, Wolters Kluwer, 2019, no. 4.

1518 **Belgium**: According to some authors, the Belgian contract for services (*aanneming, contrat d'entreprise*) functions as a kind of residual contract or ultimate remedy against the qualification of a contract as an unnamed contract. See P. Brulez, *Koop en aanneming: faux amis?*, Antwerp, Intersentia, 2015, 43 and the references there. **The Netherlands**: Also in the Netherlands, the contract for services (*opdracht*) functions as a residual category for service contracts. See: I.S.J. Houben, *Mr. C. Assers Handleiding tot de beoefening van het Nederlands Burgerlijk Recht. 7. Bijzondere overeenkomsten. Deel X. Onbenoemde overeenkomsten*, Deventer, Wolters Kluwer, 2019, no. 2 (also described by P. Brulez, *Koop en aanneming: faux amis?*, Antwerp, Intersentia, 2015, 45); F.J. de Vries, *De overeenkomst in het algemeen*, Deventer, Wolters Kluwer, 2016, no. 20.

1519 **Belgium**: L. De Keyser, "Onbenoemde overeenkomsten en roerende leasing" in J.H. Herbots (ed.), *Actuele problemen van bijzondere overeenkomsten*, Antwerp, Kluwer, 1980, (439) 441.

1520 **Belgium**: W. Goossens, *Aanneming van werk: het gemeenrechtelijk dienstencontract*, Bruges, die Keure, 2003, 250.

1521 **Belgium**: R. Kruithof, H. Bocken, F. De Ly and B. De Temmerman, "Verbintenissenrecht (1981–1992). Overzicht van rechtspraak", *TPR* 1994, (171) 239–240.

(iii) A third category is that of contracts which are ancillary to or derive from one or more named contracts but contain (or do not contain) a particular element which distinguishes this contract from the relevant named contract(s) and places it in the category of *genuine unnamed contracts*. Specifically, one can think of PSS contracts that have the essential characteristics of a particular type of contract (for example a rental contract or a contract for services), but which have other characteristics or features that make them not an application of this named contract, but an unnamed contract.[1522] An example under Belgian law that is often mentioned is when a service is provided by gratuitous title (*om niet, à titre gratuit*).[1523] In this case, it is not a contract for services but an unnamed service contract.[1524] However, it is clear that these *genuine unnamed contracts* will be rather rare, especially in the case of PSS contracts, as these are generally contracts by onerous title (*onder bezwarende titel, à titre onéreux*).

(iv) The fourth category builds on the previous three and concerns the *autonomous contracts*. In economic life, as a result of societal phenomena, there is a constant need for "new" forms of contract, which are often based on self-regulation and (legal) practice.[1525] Gradually, these new contracts become more and more widespread and evolve in such a way that they take on a more or less standardised form (e.g. by the frequent recurrence of certain clauses of model contracts) and well-known name (often inspired by Anglo-American evolutions), so that they in fact constitute a *quasi-named contract*. Examples include leasing, franchising, factoring, internet access (ISP-agreement), service level agreement (SLA), catering, engineering, and sponsoring, etc.[1526] A possible next step would then be

---

1522 **Belgium**: I. Claeys and T. Tanghe, *Nieuw Algemeen Contractenrecht*, Antwerp, Intersentia, 2023, 17. **The Netherlands**: I.S.J. Houben, *Mr. C. Assers Handleiding tot de beoefening van het Nederlands Burgerlijk Recht. 7. Bijzondere overeenkomsten. Deel X. Onbenoemde overeenkomsten*, Deventer, Wolters Kluwer, 2019, no 4.

1523 **Belgium**: W. Goossens, *Aanneming van werk: het gemeenrechtelijk dienstencontract*, Bruges, die Keure, 2003, 227 and 251. For an application see: Brussels (BE) 18 December 1937, *Pas.* 1938, II, 102, second column, third whereas.

1524 **Belgium**: P. Brulez, *Koop en aanneming: faux amis?*, Antwerp, Intersentia, 2015, 215; W. Goossens, *Aanneming van werk: het gemeenrechtelijk dienstencontract*, Bruges, die Keure, 2003, 227.

1525 **The Netherlands**: M.E. Hinskens-van Neck and L.A.R. Siemerink, "Gemengde overeenkomsten. De betekenis van art. 6:215 BW in de praktijk: kwalificatie van overeenkomsten", *MvV* 2012, (1) 2, no. 3; W. Snijders, "De openheid van het vermogensrecht. Van syndicaatszekerheden, domeinnamen en nieuwe contractsvormen" in S.C.J.J. Kortmann and e.a. (eds.), *Onderneming en 10 jaar nieuw burgerlijk recht*, Deventer, Kluwer, 2002, (27) 50.

1526 **The Netherlands**: M.E. Hinskens-van Neck and L.A.R. Siemerink, "Gemengde overeenkomsten. De betekenis van art. 6:215 BW in de praktijk: kwalificatie van overeenkomsten", *MvV* 2012, (1) 2, no. 3; F.J. de Vries, *De overeenkomst in het algemeen*, Deventer, Wolters Kluwer, 2016, no. 20.

for this development to attract the attention of the legislator and for these contracts to be regulated by law and thus upgraded to a genuine named contract. However, with autonomous contracts it should always be borne in mind that it is possible that a thorough qualification can still lead to a qualification as a named contract or combination thereof.[1527] The question is then how far the autonomous character really goes or how the autonomy that has developed in practice should be legally translated.

The development of PSS contracts is in full swing. It could be argued that some categories of PSS contracts are already so well established that they already qualify as autonomous contracts (for example "*Light as a Service*" contracts). At least in the long term, by analogy with leasing contracts, it is possible that a standardised form of contract will be available for (some categories of) PSS contracts due to the influence of model contracts by professional or consumer organisations. Nevertheless, as we will see in the next sections, the autonomous character of PSS contracts cannot be overestimated, as in many cases these contracts can indeed be subsumed under (a combination of) named contracts.

369. RULES APPLICABLE TO UNNAMED CONTRACTS – When a PSS contract is considered an unnamed contract, it is governed by the contractual terms and conditions, the rules of general contract law[1528] and customs (*het gebruik, la coutume*). In addition, the rules of similar named contracts (in most cases the contract for services) may be applied by analogy, if this is in line with the intention of the parties and the general economy of the PSS contract in question.[1529] As a result, the importance of qualifying a PSS contract as an unnamed contract should not be overestimated. After all, in many cases, the rules of the rental contract for movables and the contract for services will be applied by analogy, supplemented by the rules of general contract law.

3.3. QUALIFICATION OF PRODUCT-ORIENTED PSS

370. CONTRACTUAL QUALIFICATION OF PRODUCT-ORIENTED PSS – This section will describe the legal qualification of product-oriented PSS contracts under both

---

1527 **Belgium**: W. GOOSSENS, *Aanneming van werk: het gemeenrechtelijk dienstencontract*, Bruges, die Keure, 2003, 253.

1528 **Belgium**: Art. 1101–1369 BCC. **The Netherlands**: Book 3 and 6 DCC.

1529 **Belgium**: S. STIJNS, *Verbintenissenrecht*, Boek 1, Bruges, die Keure, 2022, 35; R. DEKKERS, A.L. VERBEKE, N. CARETTE and K. VANHOVE, *Handboek burgerlijk recht, Deel III, Verbintenissen, bewijsleer en gebruikelijke contracten*, Antwerp, Intersentia, 2007, 15; W. GOOSSENS, *Aanneming van werk: het gemeenrechtelijk dienstencontract*, Bruges, die Keure, 2003, 254–255. **The Netherlands**: I.S.J. HOUBEN, *Mr. C. Assers Handleiding tot de beoefening van het Nederlands Burgerlijk Recht. 7. Bijzondere overeenkomsten. Deel X. Onbenoemde overeenkomsten*, Deventer, Wolters Kluwer, 2019, no. 21.

Belgian and Dutch law. First, the consequences of the fact that product-oriented PSS still involve a transfer of ownership are discussed (section 3.3.1). Second, the qualification of additional services added to the contract is considered (section 3.3.2). Third, this section covers the situation where product-oriented PSS consist of two or more named contracts and thus constitute a mixed contract (section 3.3.3). Finally, this section looks at product-oriented PSS regarding so-called "goods with digital elements" (section 3.3.4).

3.3.1. TRANSFER OF OWNERSHIP IMPLIES QUALIFICATION AS SALES CONTRACT

371. Transfer of ownership as essential characteristic – As indicated above and in contrast to use-oriented and result-oriented PSS, the PSS user still becomes the owner of the product that is central to the product-oriented PSS contract. Under both Belgian and Dutch law, the transfer of ownership is an essential feature of the sales contract (*koopovereenkomst, contrat de vente*).

372. Belgium: Product-oriented PSS as sales contract – Under Belgian law, a sales contract is a reciprocal contract in which one party (the seller) undertakes to transfer the ownership of an object to the other party (the buyer) for a price.[1530] As product-oriented PSS still involve a transfer of ownership, these PSS contracts (or at least a part of them) will generally be qualified as a sales contract. In this scenario, the PSS user is in a strong position, as he has extensive legal remedies in case the good is not in conformity with the contract.

The seller must deliver a good that "*is in conformity with the contract.*"[1531] If the contract is subjected to general sales law,[1532] there is a distinction between, on the one hand, the regime for the non-conforming delivery[1533] where the buyer has the choice to terminate the sale or opt for forced execution and, on the other hand, the regime for hidden defects[1534] which provides for a right of choice for the buyer to terminate the sales contract ("*actio redhibitoria*") or to keep the property with a reduction in price ("*actio quanti minoris*").[1535] The

1530 B. Tilleman, M. Herbosch and F. Van den Abeele, *Bijzondere overeenkomsten – A. Koop – Deel 1. Totstandkoming en kwalificatie van de koop*, Mechelen, Wolters Kluwer, 2024, 3–5; E. Van den Haute, *Traité des contrats spéciaux*, Brussels, Larcier, 2024, 75; M. Dambre, *Bijzondere overeenkomsten: de essentie*, Bruges, die Keure, 2022, 3; P.-A. Foriers and F. Glansdorff, *Contrats spéciaux*, I, Brussels, PUB, 1998–99, 9. See also the (incomplete) definition in Art. 1582 old BCC that defines a sales contract as "*a contract whereby one party undertakes to deliver a good and the other party undertakes to pay a price for it.*"

1531 Art. 1604 old BCC.

1532 Art. 1582–1701 old BCC.

1533 Art. 1610 old BCC.

1534 Art. 1644 old BCC.

1535 M. Dambre, *Bijzondere overeenkomsten: de essentie*, Bruges, die Keure, 2022, 93–94. The draft law of 16 April 2024 inserting Book 7 "special contracts" into the Civil Code aims to

regime of hidden defects requires the PSS user to file his claim within a "short time".[1536] In general, the general sales law rules are default law, which allows for deviations and contractual specifications (for example of the duration of the "short time") in the terms and conditions of the PSS supplier. However, the seller is not allowed to exempt himself for defects of which he is aware.[1537] In the case of a specialised seller, it is even (rebuttably) presumed that the seller is aware of the defects.[1538]

If the PSS user is a consumer and, within the framework of the product-oriented PSS contract, purchases a movable tangible good from a professional seller, he will benefit from the protection of the mandatory regime of consumer sales law[1539] in the old BCC.[1540] These provisions constitute a *lex specialis* with respect to general sales law and were introduced by the Consumer Sales Act[1541] to transpose the Consumer Sales Directive 1999.[1542, 1543] Later, these rules were modernised with the Sale of Goods Directive 2019 ("SGD"),[1544] implemented in Belgium in 2022.[1545] Of particular importance are Article 1649*ter* old BCC, which includes both the obligation to deliver in conformity and the obligation to indemnify for hidden defects (the so-called "monistic" regime of consumer

abolish this distinction. See: Explanatory Memorandum, Parliamentary Papers Chamber of Representatives 2023–24, no. 55-3973/001, 22–23.

1536 Art. 1648 old BCC.

1537 Art. 1643 old BCC.

1538 Cass. (BE) 18 October 2001, *Arr.Cass.* 2001, 1721, *Pas.* 2001, I, 1659; Cass. (BE) 7 December 1990, *Pas.* 1990, I, 346; Mons (BE) 12 March 2001, *TBBR* 2002, 245; Liège (BE) 7 November 2005, *TBBR* 2006, 620. This presumption was not retained in the draft law of 16 April 2024 inserting Book 7 "special contracts" into the Civil Code. See: Explanatory Memorandum, Parliamentary Papers Chamber of Representatives 2023–24, no. 55-3973/001, 19–20.

1539 Art. 1649*bis* – 1649*octies* old BCC.

1540 For the scope of application see Art. 1649*bis*, §1 of the old BCC, which states that the consumer sales rules apply to "*sales of consumer goods by a seller to a consumer.*" See R. Steennot, G. Straetmans, E. Terryn, B. Keirsbilck and B. Wyseur, "Overzicht van rechtspraak. Consumentenbescherming (2008-2014) – Marktpraktijken (2011-2014)", *TPR* 2015, (1311) 1803; H. Slachmuylders, "Herstelling door een derde en de hiërarchie van de remedies in de consumentenkoop", *DCCR* 2020, (135) 136.

1541 Act 1 September 2004 on the protection of consumers in respect of the sale of consumer goods, *BS* 21 September 2004.

1542 Directive 1999/44/EC of the European Parliament and of the Council of 25 May 1999 on certain aspects of the sale of consumer goods and associated guarantees, *OJ* L 171, 7.7.1999, 12–16.

1543 C. Cauffman, "Vijf jaar Wet Consumentenkoop – overzicht van rechtspraak" in K. Wauters (ed.), *Feestbundel Monard-D'Hulst 20 jaar*, Ghent, Larcier, 2010, (155) 155–156.

1544 Directive (EU) 2019/771 of the European Parliament and the Council of 20 May 2019 on certain aspects concerning contracts for the sale of goods, amending Regulation (EU) 2017/2394 and Directive 2009/22/EC, and repealing Directive 1999/44/EC, OJ L 319, 22.5.2019, 28–50.

1545 Act 20 March amending the provisions of the old Civil Code relating to consumer sales, inserting a new Title VIbis into Book III of the old Civil Code and amending the Code of Economic Law, *BS* 31 March 2022.

sales),[1546] and Article 1649*quater* old BCC, which contains rules regarding the reversal of the burden of proof and the guarantee period.[1547]

373. Dutch law: product-oriented PSS as sales contract – Under Dutch law, sale is the agreement under which one party (the seller) engages itself to give a good and the other party (the buyer) to pay a price in money in return.[1548] The obligation to give a good implies two obligations, namely the obligation to provide the ownership and the obligation to deliver (provide possession).[1549] Just like under Belgian law, the sales contract is thus aimed at transferring the ownership of a certain (movable or immovable) good against the payment of a sum of money.[1550] In view of the fact that product-oriented PSS contracts have the transfer of ownership as an essential characteristic, the rules of the sales contract will, also under Dutch law, generally (at least in part) apply to product-oriented PSS.

The legal regime for the sale of a product is quite extensive. The special provisions for the sales contract are included in the first title of Book 7 DCC.[1551] In sales contracts with a buyer other than a consumer, most rules are default law, which means that they can be deviated from by the PSS supplier.[1552] For consumer sales contracts,[1553] however, there are a number of special provisions.[1554] Additionally, a large number of the default provisions from title 7.1 have been upgraded to mandatory law for consumer sales.[1555] In view of the

1546 R. Steennot, "Artikel 1649*ter* BW" in *Artikelsgewijze Commentaar Bijzondere Overeenkomsten*, Mechelen, Kluwer, 2015, (37) 40; Y. Ninane, "Le défaut de la chose vendue selon le régime de la garantie des biens de consommation" in C. Delforge and J. Van Zuylen (eds.), *Les défauts de la chose, Responsabilités contractuelle et extracontractuelle*, Limal, Anthemis, 2015, (35) 59.

1547 B. Keirsbilck, E. Terryn and E. Van Gool, "Consumentenbescherming bij servitisation en product-dienst systemen (PDS)", *TPR* 2019, (817) 832.

1548 Art. 7:1 DCC.

1549 Art. 7:9 DCC. J. Hijma, *Mr. C. Assers Handleiding tot de beoefening van het Nederlands Burgerlijk Recht. 7. Bijzondere overeenkomsten. Deel I. Koop en ruil*, Deventer, Kluwer, 2019, no. 10.

1550 H.N. Schelhaas, "Koopovereenkomst" in H.N. Schelhaas and A.J. Verheij (eds.), *Bijzondere overeenkomsten in Studiereeks Burgerlijk Recht*, Deventer, Wolters Kluwer, 2023, (15) 16, no. 17.

1551 Art. 7:1 – 7:50 DCC.

1552 H.N. Schelhaas, "Koopovereenkomst" in H.N. Schelhaas and A.J. Verheij (eds.), *Bijzondere overeenkomsten in Studiereeks Burgerlijk Recht*, Deventer, Wolters Kluwer, 2023, (15) 16, no. 16.

1553 Consumer sale is defined in Art. 7:5 DCC as "*a sale of movable property concluded between a seller acting in the course of his trade, business, craft or profession and a buyer, a natural person, acting for purposes not related to his trade, business, craft or profession.*"

1554 Art. 7:6a, 7:8, 7:11, 7:13, 7:18, 7:21(4), (5) and (6), Art. 7:22, 7:23 (1), 7:24, 7:25, 7:26(4), 7:28 and 7:35 DCC.

1555 Art. 7:6 DCC; J. Hijma, *Mr. C. Assers Handleiding tot de beoefening van het Nederlands Burgerlijk Recht. 7. Bijzondere overeenkomsten. Deel I. Koop en ruil*, Deventer, Kluwer, 2019, 95.

layered structure of the DCC, Books 3, 5 and 6 are also important to get a full picture of the rights and obligations of the parties.[1556]

The delivered good must be in conformity with the contract.[1557] This is not the case, if, also in view of the nature of the good and the seller's statements about it, it does not possess the properties which the buyer could expect on the basis of the agreement.[1558] In addition, the delivered good is also not in conformity with the agreement if a different good is delivered than agreed or if the quantity differs from what was agreed.[1559, 1560] Consequently, the buyer can reasonably expect a minimum limit to the quality of the product when entering into a sales contract.[1561] In the case of a consumer sales contract, the DCC provides for three special provisions regarding conformity.[1562] In particular, it is important to note that the burden of proof is reversed in consumer sales contracts.[1563] If a defect in the good reveals itself within six months of delivery, it is assumed that the good already failed to comply with the agreement at the time of delivery, unless the nature of the good or the nature of the deviation dictates otherwise.[1564]

Like Belgian law, the DCC provides for extensive remedies for the buyer in case the seller fails to fulfil his obligations. First and foremost, he may temporarily suspend his own performance (payment of the purchase price) until the seller fulfils his performance.[1565] If this has no effect, he can choose between three remedies: performance[1566] (*nakoming*), termination[1567] (*ontbinding*) and (supplementary or substitute) damages[1568] (*schadevergoeding*).[1569]

1556 H.N. Schelhaas, "Koopovereenkomst" in H.N. Schelhaas and A.J. Verheij (eds.), *Bijzondere overeenkomsten in Studiereeks Burgerlijk Recht*, Deventer, Wolters Kluwer, 2023, (15) 15, no. 13.

1557 Art. 7:17 DCC. See in detail about conformity in sales: P. Klik, *Conformiteit bij koop*, Diss. doct. Erasmus universiteit Rotterdam, 2008, 418 p.

1558 Art. 7:17(2) DCC.

1559 Art. 7:17(3) DCC.

1560 H.N. Schelhaas, "Koopovereenkomst" in H.N. Schelhaas and A.J. Verheij (eds.), *Bijzondere overeenkomsten in Studiereeks Burgerlijk Recht*, Deventer, Wolters Kluwer, 2023, (15) 30, no. 31.

1561 V. Mak, "Consumentenbescherming bij servitisation", *TPR* 2019, (779) 787.

1562 See Art. 7:18 DCC; H.N. Schelhaas, "Koopovereenkomst" in H.N. Schelhaas and A.J. Verheij (eds.), *Bijzondere overeenkomsten in Studiereeks Burgerlijk Recht*, Deventer, Wolters Kluwer, 2023, (15) 33, no. 32.

1563 Art. 7:18(2) DCC.

1564 V. Mak, "Consumentenbescherming bij servitisation", *TPR* 2019, (779) 787.

1565 Art. 6:52 and 6:262 DCC.

1566 Art. 7:20–7:21 DCC.

1567 Art. 7:22 DCC.

1568 Art. 7:24, 7:36 and 7:37 DCC.

1569 For each of these remedies a special provision for the sales contract is included in Book 7 DCC, but in most cases they do not deviate but merely build on the general rules of Book 6 of the DCC (Art. 7:22(4) DCC). See also H.N. Schelhaas, "Koopovereenkomst" in H.N. Schelhaas and A.J. Verheij (eds.), *Bijzondere overeenkomsten in Studiereeks Burgerlijk Recht*, Deventer, Wolters Kluwer, 2023, (15) 35, no. 34.

If the buyer opts for performance, he can choose between three options to remedy the non-conforming purchase: delivery of the missing good, repair and replacement.[1570] In the case of an common sales contract, the buyer is entitled to repair if the seller can "reasonably satisfy" this.[1571] Furthermore, no replacement can be demanded if the non-conformity is too small or if the good was destroyed or deteriorated after the time that the buyer should reasonably have taken into account that it would be destroyed.[1572] Compared to general sales law, it is easier to opt for performance under the regime of consumer sales law. Indeed, repair and replacement are the primary remedies and will only be rejected if it turns out that repair or replacement is impossible or cannot be demanded of the seller.[1573] For instance, this is the case when the costs of repair or replacement are disproportionate to the costs of exercising another remedy.[1574]

3.3.2. QUALIFICATION OF ADDITIONAL SERVICES

374. Additional services are added to the sales contract – The second essential characteristic of product-oriented PSS is the fact that additional after-sales services are added to the classic sale of a product. Examples include maintenance, repair, a take-back obligation for recycling, information exchange, management services and so on. The applications and possibilities of these additional services are numerous. Think of the purchase of a car with maintenance, a conventional extended warranty, and a subscription to increasingly important on-board services, ranging from multimedia to (semi-)autonomous driving. Other examples are the purchase of a boiler with installation, maintenance and repair for a specified period and including remote monitoring and control options, or the purchase of a smart ventilation system[1575] with "predictive maintenance"[1576] as an additional service.[1577]

1570 Art. 7:21 DCC.

1571 See Art. 7:21(1) *sub* b. DCC: "*mits de verkoper hieraan redelijkerwijs kan voldoen.*"

1572 See Art. 7:21(1) *sub* c. DCC: "*tenzij de afwijking van het overeengekomene te gering is om dit te rechtvaardigen, dan wel de zaak na het tijdstip dat de koper redelijkerwijze met ongedaanmaking rekening moet houden, teniet of achteruit is gegaan doordat hij niet als een zorgvuldig schuldenaar voor het behoud ervan heeft gezorgd.*"

1573 Art. 7:21(4) DCC.

1574 H.N. Schelhaas, "Koopovereenkomst" in H.N. Schelhaas and A.J. Verheij (eds.), *Bijzondere overeenkomsten in Studiereeks Burgerlijk Recht*, Deventer, Wolters Kluwer, 2023, (15) 37–38, no. 39.

1575 The Renson Healthbox 3.0 is an example of a smart ventilation systems in a B2C context. See: -www.renson.eu/nl-be/producten-zoeken/ventilatie/mechanische-ventilatie/units/healthbox-3-0.

1576 *Predictive maintenance* means optimising the maintenance of a product by intervening when certain monitored thresholds are exceeded.

1577 B. Keirsbilck, E. Terryn and E. Van Gool, "Consumentenbescherming bij servitisation en product-dienst systemen (PDS)", *TPR* 2019, (817) 821.

375. Belgian law: additional services as "*aanneming*" / "*contrat d'entreprise*" – Under Belgian law, most of these service components will qualify as a contract for services (*aanneming, contrat d'entreprise*). Although these rules were originally drawn up with the construction contract (*aanneming van bouwwerken, l'entreprise de construction*) in mind, it is assumed that these rules also apply to other service contracts, insofar as the specific nature of the construction contract does not preclude this.[1578] As a result, the contract for services – together with mandate[1579] (*lastgeving, mandat*) and the deposit contract (*bewaargeving, dépôt*) – serves as the legal basis of all service contracts in Belgium.[1580] Occasionally, however, it is possible that the service component of a product-oriented PSS contract also covers other named service contracts, such as the loan[1581] (*bruikleen, prêt à usage*) of a replacement device during a repair.[1582]

Contrary to other named contracts, the contract for services is not defined in the old BCC.[1583] In absence of a legal definition, legal doctrine and case law fill the gap.[1584] Core elements of the contract for services are (i) the absence of

---

1578 H. De Page, *Traité élémentaire de droit civil belge*, IV, Brussels, Bruylant, 1972, 984–985, no. 859; B. Kohl, *Contrat d'entreprise*, Brussels, Bruylant, 2016, 22; G. Baert, *Aanneming van werk*, Antwerp, Story-Scientica, 2001, 6, no. 6; A. Van Oevelen, *Overeenkomsten. 2: Bijzondere overeenkomsten: E. Aanneming van werk, lastgeving, in Beginselen van Belgisch Privaatrecht*, Mechelen, Wolters Kluwer, 2017, 22.

1579 A mandate contract is characterised by the fact that the agent is entrusted with the task of carrying out a juridical act in the name and on behalf of a third party (power of representation), whereas the contract for services only entails material or intellectual acts for the benefit of the client, without representation. See e.g. P. Wéry, *Le mandat*, Brussels, Larcier, 2019, 63–64 and B. Tilleman, *Lastgeving*, Deurne, Story-Scientia en Kluwer Rechtswetenschappen België, 1997, no. 4 and no. 12. See also: B. Kohl, *Contrat d'entreprise*, Brussels, Bruylant, 2016, 98. However, in the "new" Belgian Civil Code, the new rules on representation are to be found in Book I (General Provisions). As a result, we are moving towards a single regime for service contracts. See: Art. 1.8 BCC.

1580 A. Van Oevelen, *Overeenkomsten. 2: Bijzondere overeenkomsten: E. Aanneming van werk, lastgeving, in Beginselen van Belgisch Privaatrecht*, Mechelen, Wolters Kluwer, 2017, 22; W. Goossens, *Aanneming van werk: het gemeenrechtelijk dienstencontract*, Bruges, die Keure, 2003, 137; M. Dambre, "Dienstenprestaties: laveren tussen aanneming, bewaargeving en lastgeving" in *Chronique de droit à l'usage des juges de paix et de police 2010 / Rechtskroniek voor de vrede- en politierechters 2010*, Bruges, die Keure / la Charte, 2010, (147) 149.

1581 See Art. 1875–1891 old BCC.

1582 See for example: Ct. Leuven (BE) 29 April 1988, *TBBR* 1990, 428, case note D. Deli (the transfer of a replacement television under a contract for services for the repair of a television).

1583 B. Kohl, *Contrat d'entreprise*, Brussels, Bruylant, 2016, 21–22; G. Baert, *Aanneming van werk*, Antwerp, Story-Scientica, 2001, 5–6.

1584 For definitions in case law see e.g. Cass. (BE) 3 September 2010, *Arr.Cass.* 2010, 2091, *Pas.* 2010, 2187, *RW* 2011–12, 565, case note B. Van Den Bergh: "*Aanneming is de overeenkomst waarbij een persoon zich ertoe verbindt tegen betaling van een prijs een bepaald intellectueel of stoffelijk werk te verrichten voor een ander door het stellen van materiële handelingen; de overeenkomst van aanneming die veronderstelt dat de aannemer of zijn werkkracht onafhankelijk is bij de uitoefening van zijn werk, is niet onverenigbaar met samenwerking, algemene instructies of een controle door de opdrachtgever op het werk van de aannemer.*" and Brussels (BE) 19 December 2002, *Res Jur.Imm.* 2003, 138: "*une convention par laquelle*

a relationship of subordination between the contractor and the principal, (ii) carrying out material or intellectual acts without power of representation, and (iii) against a counter performance.[1585] Since it can include both material and intellectual performances and may relate to movable or immovable goods, the contract for services covers a myriad of human activities, all very different from one another. According to legal literature, the following activities are examples of the service contract: maintenance, repair, cleaning, preservation, creation, realisation or construction, entertainment, care, advice, etc.[1586] As established above, many of these services are indeed offered as additional services to PSS contracts.

376. Consumer protection under "*aanneming*" / "*contrat d'entreprise*" – Most additional services in product-oriented PSS will thus meet the abovementioned definition of the contract for services. Yet, this qualification as a contract for services does not mean that it is clear what rights and obligations the parties to a PSS contract have towards each other. After all, the contract for services is only briefly regulated in Articles 1789–1799 of the old BCC and most of these provisions only apply to contracts concerning manufacturing or producing tangible objects[1587] or building contracts[1588] (construction contract for services).[1589] Thus, the non-construction contract for services suffers from insufficient and outdated regulation.[1590]

The few provisions applicable to non-construction contracts for services are clearly incomplete, dealing mainly with the regime applicable in the event of the occurrence of a risk.[1591] An exception is Article 1794 old BCC, which establishes

---

une personne, l'entrepreneur, s'engage envers une autre, le maître de l'ouvrage, à exécuter contre rémunération et de manière indépendante, un travail déterminé, qu'il soit manuel ou intellectuel (à l'exclusion d'un acte juridique)." For definitions in legal doctrine see e.g. H. De Page, *Traité élémentaire de droit civil belge*, IV, Brussels, Bruylant, 1972, no. 844; W. Goossens, *Aanneming van werk: het gemeenrechtelijk dienstencontract*, Bruges, die Keure, 2003, 3; B. Kohl, *Contrat d'entreprise*, Brussels, Bruylant, 2016, 22–23.

1585 A. Van Oevelen, *Overeenkomsten. 2: Bijzondere overeenkomsten: E. Aanneming van werk, lastgeving, in Beginselen van Belgisch Privaatrecht*, Mechelen, Wolters Kluwer, 2017, 17–18.

1586 C. Marr, "Le contrat d'entreprise hors construction et la protection des consommateurs" in P. De Page, B. Sindic and C. Marr (eds.), *Récyclage en droit: Droit des contrats*, Liège, Anthemis, 2007, (145) 151–152. See also for examples in case law of the contract for services: S. Stijns, B. Tilleman, W. Goossens, B. Kohl and E. Swaenepoel, "Aanneming: Begrip. Totstandkoming. Bewijs", *TPR* 2008, (1665) 1665.

1587 E.g. Art. 1789–1791 old BCC.

1588 E.g. Art. 1792–1793 old BCC.

1589 A. Van Oevelen, *Overeenkomsten. 2: Bijzondere overeenkomsten: E. Aanneming van werk, lastgeving, in Beginselen van Belgisch Privaatrecht*, Mechelen, Wolters Kluwer, 2017, 20.

1590 F. Glansdorff, "Les contrats de service: notion et qualifications" in F. Glansdorff and P.-A. Foriers (eds.), *Les contrats de service*, Brussels, Jeune barreau de Bruxelles, 1994, (1) 9.

1591 C. Marr, "Le contrat d'entreprise hors construction et la protection des consommateurs" in P. De Page, B. Sindic and C. Marr (eds.), *Récyclage en droit: Droit des contrats*, Liège, Anthemis, 2007, (145) 171.

a right of unilateral termination for the client specific to the contract for services, and which applies to both construction and non-construction contracts.[1592] The client who makes use of this unilateral right to terminate the contract does not have to prove any fault by the service provider or even invoke any reason. However, he is obliged to compensate the service provider for all expenses, services already rendered and loss of profit.[1593] For this reason, this option is rarely used in the context of non-construction contracts for services.[1594] The limited level of consumer protection due to the rudimentary legal framework for the contract for services is further exacerbated by the fact that most of the provisions of the contract for services are not mandatory law. This gives the PSS supplier a far-reaching power to deviate from them in the general terms and conditions of the PSS contract.[1595]

377. DUTCH LAW: MOST ADDITIONAL SERVICES QUALIFY AS "*OPDRACHT*", REPAIR AS "*AANNEMING VAN WERK*" – Unlike Belgian law, the DCC has different sections for the contract for works[1596] (*aanneming van werk*) and the contract for services[1597] (*opdracht*). While the contract for works aims at "*the construction and delivery of a tangible good*",[1598] the contract for services is a more general category that applies to "*activities other than the construction of a tangible good.*"[1599, 1600] This is quite unique among the legal systems of the EU Member States, as most civil codes do not have a general chapter on service contracts.[1601]

Numerous agreements – examples include advice, analysis, guidance, control, implementation, monitoring, support, research, etc. – under which one party provides a service fall under the regime of the contract for services.[1602]

1592 Cass. (BE) 4 September 1980, *Pas.* 1981, I, 7; Cass. (BE) 13 October 1910, *JCB* 1911, 26.

1593 Art. 1794 old BCC.

1594 C. MARR, "Le contrat d'entreprise hors construction et la protection des consommateurs" in P. DE PAGE, B. SINDIC and C. MARR (eds.), *Récyclage en droit: Droit des contrats*, Liège, Anthemis, 2007, (145) 172.

1595 W. GOOSSENS, *Aanneming van werk: het gemeenrechtelijk dienstencontract*, Bruges, die Keure, 2003, 3 and 137; A. VAN OEVELEN, *Overeenkomsten. 2: Bijzondere overeenkomsten: E. Aanneming van werk, lastgeving, in Beginselen van Belgisch Privaatrecht*, Mechelen, Wolters Kluwer, 2017, 22.

1596 Art. 7:750–7:769 DCC.

1597 Art. 7:400–7:414 DCC.

1598 Art. 7:750(1) DCC: "*Een werk van stoffelijke aard tot stand te brengen en op te leveren.*"

1599 Art. 7:400(1) DCC: "*Werkzaamheden te verrichten die in iets anders bestaan dan het tot stand brengen van een werk van stoffelijke aard.*"

1600 HR 6 March 1991, *NJ* 1991, 415; J.J. DAMMINGH, "Dienstverlening: de overeenkomst van opdracht" in E.H. HONDIUS and V. MAK (eds.), *Handboek Consumentenrecht*, Vijfde druk, Zutphen, Paris, 2020, (267) 269; T.F.E. TJONG TJIN TAI, *Asser 7-IV Bijzondere Overeenkomsten – Opdracht, incl. de geneeskundige behandelingsovereenkomst en de reisovereenkomst*, Deventer, Wolters Kluwer, 2018, nr. 37.

1601 T.F.E. TJONG TJIN TAI, "Service Contracts in the Dutch Civil Code" in R. ZIMMERMAN (ed.), *Service Contracts*, Tübingen, Mohr Siebeck, 2010, (167) 167.

1602 In this sense, Tjong Tjin Tai formulated a fourfold typology of services: (i) person-oriented services by a professional (e.g. a lawyer); (ii) services focused on the person of the client by a

This is due to the large definition of the contract for services in Article 7:400(1) DCC. This definition provides that the contract for services is "*the contract by which one party, the service provider (opdrachtnemer), agrees to the other party, the client (opdrachtgever), otherwise than on the basis of an employment contract, to perform activities other than construction of a tangible good, storage of goods, the publishing of works, or the transportation of persons or goods.*"[1603] The contract for services is in fact a residual category: if the other special contracts (employment contract, contract for works and transport contract) do not apply, the contract is qualified as a contract for services.[1604] Consequently, in the Netherlands, additional services will very often be governed by the rules on the contract for services set out in title 7.7 of the Dutch BW.[1605]

Despite the wide scope of the contract for services, it is not unlimited.[1606] Especially important for PSS contracts is the distinction of the contract for services from the contract for works. The notion that the contract for works aims at "*the construction of a tangible good*" must be interpreted broadly. It does not only concern the creation of new goods (such as e.g. a building or a truck),[1607] but also the work on these goods, such as processing them, converting them, extending them, repairing them and demolishing them.[1608] Moreover, the contract for works also covers the processing of moveable goods, such as the repair of a car, shoes and cleaning of clothes.[1609] Consequently, installation,

"servant" (e.g. a maid); the (common) ready-made service (e.g. a piano player's home concert) and the collective ready-made service (e.g. a subscription to a telecom company or a film screening in a cinema). See T.F.E. Tjong Tjin Tai, *Asser 7-IV Bijzondere Overeenkomsten – Opdracht, incl. de geneeskundige behandelingsovereenkomst en de reisovereenkomst*, Deventer, Wolters Kluwer, 2018, no. 21.

1603 "*De overeenkomst van opdracht is de overeenkomst waarbij de ene partij, de opdrachtnemer, zich jegens de andere partij, de opdrachtgever, verbindt anders dan op grond van een arbeidsovereenkomst werkzaamheden te verrichten die in iets anders bestaan dan het tot stand brengen van een werk van stoffelijke aard, het bewaren van zaken, het uitgeven van werken of het vervoeren of doen vervoeren van personen of zaken.*" See also: S.C.J.J. Kortmann, "De overeenkomst van opdracht, de lastgeving en de geneeskundige behandelingsovereenkomst", *WPNR* 1990, vol. 5982, (740) 741.

1604 W. Goossens, *Aanneming van werk: het gemeenrechtelijk dienstencontract*, Bruges, ddie Keure, 2003, 33.

1605 V. Mak, "Consumentenbescherming bij servitisation", *TPR* 2019, (779) 793.

1606 M.A.M.C. van den Berg, *Mr. C. Assers Handleiding tot de beoefening van het Nederlands Burgerlijk Recht. 7. Bijzondere overeenkomsten. Deel VI. Aanneming van werk*, Deventer, Wolters Kluwer, 2017, no. 20.

1607 For example, see: Ct. Rotterdam (NL) 21 April 2004, *NJF* 2004/385.

1608 See Explanatory Memorandum, *Parliamentary Papers I* 1992/93, 23 095, no. 38a, 9–10. See also: M.A.B. Chao-Duivis, "Aanneming van werk" in H.N. Schelhaas and A.J. Verheij (eds.), *Bijzondere overeenkomsten in Studiereeks Burgerlijk Recht*, Deventer, Kluwer, 2021, (445) 446.

1609 Explanatory Memorandum, *Parliamentary Papers II* 1992/93, 23095, no. 3, 12. See also: M.A.B. Chao-Duivis, "Aanneming van werk" in H.N. Schelhaas and A.J. Verheij (eds.), *Bijzondere overeenkomsten in Studiereeks Burgerlijk Recht*, Deventer, Kluwer, 2021, (445) 446; M.A.M.C. van den Berg, *Mr. C. Assers Handleiding tot de beoefening van het Nederlands Burgerlijk Recht. 7. Bijzondere overeenkomsten. Deel VI. Aanneming van werk*, Deventer,

repairs and maintenance of products of a product-oriented PSS contract will be covered by the rules of the contract for works and not of the contract for services. Yet the distinction is not always clear.[1610] A criterion that is sometimes put forward is whether the emphasis is on the tangible good that is processed or on the intellectual or creative character of the work.[1611] In the latter case, such as, for example, the production of a painting, there is no longer a contract for works but a contract for services.[1612]

378. Consumer protection under contract for services – The question arises as to the consequences for the consumer of the qualification of a service component as a contract for services. The rules of the contract for services are complemented by general contract law, in particular the general provision that the consumer is entitled to performance of the agreed obligations.[1613] This is further specified for the contract for services by stating that the service provider must observe the care of a good service provider in its activities.[1614] This is a relatively open standard that leads to the question of what the parties have agreed

---

Wolters Kluwer, 2017, 25–27; J.J. Dammingh, "Dienstverlening: de overeenkomst van opdracht" in E.H. Hondius and V. Mak (eds.), *Handboek Consumentenrecht*, Vijfde druk, Zutphen, Paris, 2020, (267) 269; T.F.E. Tjong Tjin Tai, *Asser 7-IV Bijzondere Overeenkomsten – Opdracht, incl. de geneeskundige behandelingsovereenkomst en de reisovereenkomst*, Deventer, Wolters Kluwer, 2018, 37. However, see the criticism by M.B.M. LOOS, who argues that a qualification as a contract for services would be more suited: M.B.M. Loos, "Consumentenbescherming bij de koop van onroerende zaken en aanneming van werk: een nog altijd onevenwichtig en onvoldoende doordacht wetsvoorstel ", *NTBR* 2002/8, (356) 363.

1610 F.J.A. van der Ven, "Eden versus Whistler", *GROM* 2013, (103) 144–146. In Dutch legal literature, it is sometimes claimed that it would be better to regulate the contract for works as a *species* of the contract for services. See e.g.: T.F.E. Tjong Tjin Tai, *Asser 7-IV Bijzondere Overeenkomsten – Opdracht, incl. de geneeskundige behandelingsovereenkomst en de reisovereenkomst*, Deventer, Wolters Kluwer, 2018, 35; M.A.M.C. van den Berg, *Mr. C. Assers Handleiding tot de beoefening van het Nederlands Burgerlijk Recht. 7. Bijzondere overeenkomsten. Deel VI. Aanneming van werk*, Deventer, Wolters Kluwer, 2017, no. 27; C.E.C. Jansen, *Aanneming van werk, Monografieën BW nr. 84*, Deventer, Kluwer, 2013, no. 6; M.B.M. Loos, "Consumentenbescherming bij de koop van onroerende zaken en aanneming van werk: een nog altijd onevenwichtig en onvoldoende doordacht wetsvoorstel ", *NTBR* 2002/8, (356); S.C.J.J. Kortmann, "De overeenkomst van opdracht, de lastgeving en de geneeskundige behandelingsovereenkomst", *WPNR* 1990, vol. 5982, (740) 742–743.

1611 T.F.E. Tjong Tjin Tai, *Asser 7-IV Bijzondere Overeenkomsten – Opdracht, incl. de geneeskundige behandelingsovereenkomst en de reisovereenkomst*, Deventer, Wolters Kluwer, 2018, no. 37.

1612 C.E. Du Perron, "Opdracht" in A.L. Croes, N. Frenk, C.E. du Perron and A.F. Salomons (eds.), *Pitlo. Het Nederlands burgerlijk recht. Deel 6. Bijzondere overeenkomsten*, Arnhem, Gouda Quint, 1995, (220) 223; S.C.J.J. Kortmann, "De overeenkomst van opdracht, de lastgeving en de geneeskundige behandelingsovereenkomst", *WPNR* 1990, vol. 5982, (740) 743.

1613 Art. 3:296 DCC. C.H. Sieburgh, *Mr. C. Assers Handleiding tot de beoefening van het Nederlands Burgerlijk Recht. 6. Verbintenissenrecht. Deel I. De verbintenis in het algemeen, eerste gedeelte*, Deventer, Wolters Kluwer, 2020, no. 190.

1614 Art. 7:401 DCC: "*De opdrachtnemer moet bij zijn werkzaamheden de zorg van een goed opdrachtnemer in acht nemen.*"

on in each specific case and whether this constitutes an obligation of means or obligation of result.[1615] In addition, the service provider must comply with timely and responsible instructions regarding the execution of the service;[1616] he must keep the client informed of his activities regarding the execution of the order[1617] and has an accountability obligation regarding the manner in which he has performed the service.[1618, 1619]

Additionally, in addition to the termination provisions of general contract law,[1620] special rules apply regarding the termination (*opzegging*) of the contract for services.[1621] For example, the client may terminate the contract at any time, irrespective of whether it is a fixed-term or open-ended contract.[1622] For contracts for services where the client is a consumer, this termination option is even mandatory law.[1623] The client's right to terminate the contract for services does not alter the fact that he will still have to (partly) pay the price of the service.[1624] However, if the client is a consumer, he will not owe any compensation in respect of a termination.[1625] This provision is also mandatory law and therefore cannot be derogated from to the detriment of the consumer.[1626]

The DCC thus provides for a specific chapter on service contracts, which is more extensive than the Belgian rules on the contract for services. Most provisions are default law, but some rules of the contract for services offer mandatory protection to consumers (mostly with regard to the termination

---

1615 C.H. Sieburgh, *Mr. C. Assers Handleiding tot de beoefening van het Nederlands Burgerlijk Recht. 6. Verbintenissenrecht. Deel I. De verbintenis in het algemeen, eerste gedeelte*, Deventer, Wolters Kluwer, 2020, 192. See more specific for the contract for services: J.J. Dammingh, "Dienstverlening: de overeenkomst van opdracht" in E.H. Hondius and V. Mak (eds.), *Handboek Consumentenrecht*, Vijfde druk, Zutphen, Paris, 2020, (267) 275; S.Y.T. Meijer, "Opdracht" in H.N. Schelhaas and A.J. Verheij (eds.), *Bijzondere overeenkomsten in Studiereeks Burgerlijk Recht*, Deventer, Wolters Kluwer, 2023, (231) 233, no. 236.

1616 Art. 7:402 DCC.

1617 Art. 7:403(1) DCC.

1618 Art. 7:403(2) DCC.

1619 J.J. Dammingh, "Dienstverlening: de overeenkomst van opdracht" in E.H. Hondius and V. Mak (eds.), *Handboek Consumentenrecht*, Vijfde druk, Zutphen, Paris, 2020, (267) 273.

1620 For an overview, see: C.H. Sieburgh, *Mr. C. Assers Handleiding tot de beoefening van het Nederlands Burgerlijk Recht. 6. Verbintenissenrecht. Deel III. Algemeen overeenkomstenrecht*, Deventer, Wolters Kluwer, 2018, no. 601–603.

1621 S.Y.T. Meijer, "Opdracht" in H.N. Schelhaas and A.J. Verheij (eds.), *Bijzondere overeenkomsten in Studiereeks Burgerlijk Recht*, Deventer, Wolters Kluwer, 2023, (231) 244, no. 248.

1622 Art. 7:408 DCC. J.J. Dammingh, "Dienstverlening: de overeenkomst van opdracht" in E.H. Hondius and V. Mak (eds.), *Handboek Consumentenrecht*, Vijfde druk, Zutphen, Paris, 2020, (267) 291–292.

1623 Art. 7:413(2) *juncto* Art. 7:408(1) and 7:408(3) DCC.

1624 See Art. 7:411 DCC.

1625 Art. 7:408(3) DCC.

1626 See Art. 7:413(1) DCC. However, requirements of reasonableness and fairness (*redelijkheid en billijkheid*) may derogate from a mandatory provision. See: HR (NL) 30 March 2001, ECLI:NL:PHR:2001:AB0808, (*Phoenix*), *JOL* 2001, 213, *JWB* 2001/98.

option of the consumer).[1627] Nevertheless, the rules in the DCC do not solve all contractual problems that may arise during a PSS contract, and, in many cases, the rights and obligations of the parties will depend on the general terms and conditions of the PSS supplier.

379. Consumer protection under the contract for works – As established above, maintenance and repair will, under Dutch law, be qualified as a contract for works and not as a contract for services. The question arises as to what kind of protection for the consumer this will provide.

The legal framework of the contract for works is regulated fairly concisely in Title 7.12 of the DCC.[1628] The reason for this is that in construction practice there is a highly developed system of general terms and conditions of the contract for works.[1629] The main obligations of the contractor (*aannemer*) are the construction of a tangible good and the delivery[1630] (*oplevering*) thereof.[1631] The main obligation of the client (*opdrachtgever*) is to pay a price in money in return.[1632] In addition, the contractor must warn the client about inaccuracies in the construction or work that is assigned to him[1633] and is allowed to let subcontractors perform the work under his guidance and directions.[1634] The DCC also provides in rules on price increases due to additional work.[1635] Title 7.12 DCC also contains several liability provisions, in particular on liability after delivery,[1636] on repair of defects[1637] and on liability for materials and resources.[1638, 1639] Finally, Title 7.12 DCC also contains provisions for the

1627 B. Wessels, "Algemene bepalingen inzake de overeenkomst van opdracht" in C. Van Dam and B. Wessels (eds.), *Opdracht en dienstverlening*, Zwolle, Tjeenk Willink, 1994, (1) 8.

1628 M.A.B. Chao-Duivis, "Aanneming van werk" in H.N. Schelhaas and A.J. Verheij (eds.), *Bijzondere overeenkomsten in Studiereeks Burgerlijk Recht*, Deventer, Kluwer, 2021, (445) 447; M.A.M.C. van den Berg, *Mr. C. Assers Handleiding tot de beoefening van het Nederlands Burgerlijk Recht. 7. Bijzondere overeenkomsten. Deel VI. Aanneming van werk*, Deventer, Wolters Kluwer, 2017, no. 7.

1629 This concerns in particular the Uniform Administrative Terms for the Execution of Works and Technical Installations 2012 (*Uniforme administratieve voorwaarden voor de uitvoering van werken en van technische installatiewerken 2012*, "UAV 2012/1989") and the Uniform Administrative Terms (*Uniforme Administratieve Voorwaarden*, "UAV-GC 2005"). The latter are subjected to review and will soon be updated. ("UAV-GC 2020"). See: www.crow.nl/thema-s/contracteren/uav-en-uav-gc/tervisielegging-uav-gc-2020.

1630 See Art. 7:758 DCC.

1631 Art. 7:750 DCC.

1632 Art. 7:750 DCC.

1633 Art. 7:754 DCC.

1634 Art. 7:751 DCC. However, liability for the performance of the contract remains with the contractor and is governed by Art. 6:76 DCC.

1635 Art. 7:755 DCC.

1636 Art. 7:758(2) and (3) DCC.

1637 Art. 7:759 DCC.

1638 Art. 7:760 DCC.

1639 M.A.B. Chao-Duivis, "Aanneming van werk" in H.N. Schelhaas and A.J. Verheij (eds.), *Bijzondere overeenkomsten in Studiereeks Burgerlijk Recht*, Deventer, Kluwer, 2021, (445) 449.

termination of the contract for works, and the consequences of such termination. The client has a unilateral right to terminate the contract at any time.[1640] In the event of such termination, he will have to pay the price or the entire work, less any savings for the contractor resulting from the termination, against delivery by the contractor of the work already completed.[1641] In case of a breach of contract, both parties can terminate the contract.[1642] In the unfortunate case the contractor dies or becomes unable to work, either party may terminate the contract, insofar as, in view of the nature of the contract, it can derive a reasonable interest in termination from the death or permanent disability.[1643]

Most of the provisions of Title 7.12 DCC are default law. However, the legal regime of the contract for works also contains mandatory rules. For instance, the rules on additional work[1644] and liability for concealed hidden defects[1645] are mandatory law in the first section (general provisions), while the second section (construction of a house on behalf of a consumer) is mandatory in its entirety. Apart from the rules on the contractor's liability for concealed hidden defects,[1646] however, it is possible to deviate from these provisions by means of a standard regulation.[1647, 1648] Nevertheless, for the repair of movable goods that are part of product-oriented PSS, a consumer remains largely at the mercy of the general conditions of the PSS supplier.

3.3.3. PRODUCT-ORIENTED PSS AS MIXED CONTRACT

380. BELGIUM: ABSORPTION THEORY TO DISTINGUISH SALES CONTRACT AND CONTRACT FOR SERVICES – Unless the PSS consists of two or more independent and separate agreements, a product-oriented PSS will be regarded as one mixed contract where a trade-off should be made between the rules governing sales contracts and contracts for services.

In Belgium, the majority of case law and legal doctrine applies the absorption theory and, in particular, the specificity criterion[1649] to identify the determining

1640 Art. 7:764(1) DCC.

1641 Art. 7:764(2) DCC.

1642 Art. 7:756 DCC.

1643 Art. 7:763 DCC.

1644 Art. 7:755 DCC.

1645 Art. 7:762 DCC.

1646 Art. 7:762 DCC.

1647 In the sense of Art. 6:214 DCC.

1648 M.A.M.C. VAN DEN BERG, *Mr. C. Assers Handleiding tot de beoefening van het Nederlands Burgerlijk Recht. 7. Bijzondere overeenkomsten. Deel VI. Aanneming van werk*, Deventer, Wolters Kluwer, 2017, no. 14. See in more detail about standard regulation: C.H. SIEBURGH, *Mr. C. Assers Handleiding tot de beoefening van het Nederlands Burgerlijk Recht. 6. Verbintenissenrecht. Deel III. Algemeen overeenkomstenrecht*, Deventer, Wolters Kluwer, 2018, no. 512.

1649 The *specificity criterion* stipulates that when the characteristic performance does not assume a standard form but must meet specific and context-specific requirements, there is a contract for

factor of the contract when distinguishing between a sales contract or a contract for services.[1650] However, this mostly concerns contracts for the supply of goods to be manufactured or produced (*overeenkomsten tot levering van te vervaardigen of voort te brengen goederen, contrats de fourniture de biens à fabriquer ou à produire*), which in the case of movable tangible goods in a B2C context always fall under the regime of consumer sales.[1651]

A type of product-oriented PSS for which there are applications in published case law are those where the characteristic performance, in addition to the supply of a good, consists of an installation, for example kitchen, electrical or indoor air-conditioning appliances. Here too, the absorption doctrine is mostly applied, whereby both the economic criterion[1652] and subjective criteria[1653] are used.[1654] In a B2C context, these contracts also qualify as a sales contract under the consumer sales rules.[1655] An exception to this rule is if the sale and installation of the goods are part of a broader services contract, such as a renovation of a pool where the sold goods (e.g. filtration system featuring a pump) are ancillary to the renovation services.[1656] In this case, the consumer sales rules do not apply.[1657]

When the absorption theory is used, the entire product-oriented PSS contract will thus be qualified as a sales contract or contract for services, depending on the specific situation. Nevertheless, as explained below, in some cases it seems better to apply the cumulation theory to qualify product-oriented PSS contracts.

381. Belgium: cumulation theory better suited for complex product-oriented PSS contracts – For complex product-oriented PSS with more diversified services such as maintenance, repair and/or digital services that are less integrated with the delivery, the cumulation theory appears to be the best qualification method, provided that the sale and service components are

services and no sales contract (and *vice versa*). See *i.a.* Cass. (BE) 25 February 1985, *Pas.* 1985, I, 613; Cass. (BE) 19 June 1980, *JT* 1980, 616; Antwerp (BE) 6 March 2017, *TBO* 2018, 38, case note M. Schoups and D. Verhoeven; Liège (BE) 26 January 2009, *T. Aann.* 2009, 366; Mons (BE) 9 October 2000, *AJT* 2001–02, 87; Comm. Brussels (BE) 13 January 1988, *JT* 1988, 587.

1650 A. Van Oevelen, *Overeenkomsten. 2: Bijzondere overeenkomsten: E. Aanneming van werk, lastgeving, in Beginselen van Belgisch Privaatrecht*, Mechelen, Wolters Kluwer, 2017, 22; P. Brulez, *Koop en aanneming: faux amis?*, Antwerp, Intersentia, 2015, 76.

1651 **Belgium**: Art. 1649*bis*, §3 old BCC. **EU**: See Art. 3(2) and Recital 17 of the SGD.

1652 This criterion entails that there is a contract for services if the economic value of the services exceeds the value of the goods supplied (and vice versa). See e.g. Brussels (BE) 9 November 2004, *RW* 2007–08, 152; Ghent (BE) 1 March 2007, *T. Aann.* 2010, 202.

1653 See e.g. Ghent (Jaarboek Handelspraktijken en Mededinging) 4 December 2006, *2006* 253; Liège (BE) 29 January 1999, *TBBR* 2000, 313; JP. Brussels (BE) 15 January 1988, *T.Aann.* 1989, 208.

1654 B. Keirsbilck, E. Terryn and E. Van Gool, "Consumentenbescherming bij servitisation en product-dienst systemen (PDS)", *TPR* 2019, (817) 833.

1655 **Belgium**: Art. 1649*ter*, §8 old BCC. **EU**: see Art. 3(2) and Recital 17 of the SGD 2019. B. Keirsbilck, E. Terryn and E. Van Gool, "Consumentenbescherming bij servitisation en product-dienst systemen (PDS)", *TPR* 2019, (817) 833.

1656 CJEU, 7 September 2017, C-247/16, *Schottelius*, ECLI:EU:C:2017:638, para. 44.

1657 CJEU, 7 September 2017, C-247/16, *Schottelius*, ECLI:EU:C:2017:638, para. 46.

sufficiently distinct.[1658] Given the fact that the timing and object of the additional services in these types of product-oriented PSS differs from the delivery of the product, this will usually be the case. In addition, the risk of incompatibilities between the two legal regimes is low, considering the summary legal regime of the contract for services.[1659]

Another advantage of the cumulation theory is that it will result in more legal certainty for consumers when engaging in product-oriented PSS, since the distinct legal regimes are applied to the distinct PSS components. Only if the sale and service components are indivisible and incompatibilities between the rules of the sales contract and the contract for services would arise, is it better to apply the absorption theory.[1660] Again, in a B2C context, the absorption theory can only be applied so that the entire contract falls under the rules of consumer sales.[1661]

382. The Netherlands: cumulation theory as starting point to qualify mixed contracts, other theories also used – Also under Dutch law, a product-oriented PSS contract will generally be considered one mixed contract where a trade-off should be made between the rules on the sales contract, the contract for services and/or the contract for works. As mentioned above,[1662] Dutch law uses the cumulation theory as a starting point to resolve qualification discussions of mixed contracts.[1663] Yet, depending on the specific circumstances, the other qualification theories are also used.[1664]

1658 B. Kohl, *Contrat d'entreprise*, Brussels, Bruylant, 2016, 74; W. Goossens, *Aanneming van werk: het gemeenrechtelijk dienstencontract*, Bruges, die Keure, 2003, 77–78; B. Tilleman, *Overeenkomsten. 2: Bijzondere overeenkomsten. A: Verkoop. 1: Tostandkoming en kwalificatie van de koop, in Beginselen van Belgisch Privaatrecht*, Antwerp, Story-Scientia, 2001, 314. However, see also P. Brulez, *Koop en aanneming: faux amis?*, Antwerp, Intersentia, 2015, 85 and 122–124 who points out that here, too, the absorption theory is often used.

1659 See *supra* no. 376.

1660 E.g. the rules on termination and transfer of risk of either the contract for services or the sales contract apply to a contract in its entirety and cannot simply be split up. See: P. Brulez, "Het privaatrechtelijk onderscheid tussen goederen en diensten" in B. Tilleman and A.L. Verbeke (eds.), *Knelpunten verkoop roerende goederen*, Antwerp, Intersentia, 2009, (1) 17.

1661 Art. 1649*bis*, §3 old BCC and Art. 1649*ter*, §4 old BCC; C. Cauffman, "De nieuwe wet op de consumentenkoop", *TPR* 2005, (787) 796–797; J. Stuyck, "Historiek en toepassingsgebied van de richtlijn consumentenkoop en van de omzettingswet" in J. Stuyck and S. Stijns (eds.), *Het nieuwe kooprecht. De wet van 1 september 2004 betreffende de bescherming van de consumenten bij de verkoop van consumptiegoederen*, Antwerp, Intersentia, 2005, (1) 27; Y. Van Couter, B. Vanbrabant and E. Kairis, "De Consumentenkoop. De wet van 1 september 2004 betreffende de bescherming van de consumenten bij verkoop van consumptiegoederen", *CABG* 2005, (1) 7; B. Keirsbilck, E. Terryn and E. Van Gool, "Consumentenbescherming bij servitisation en product-dienst systemen (PDS)", *TPR* 2019, (817) 833–834.

1662 See *supra* no. 367.

1663 Art. 6:215 DCC; See also: A.G. Castermans and H.B. Krans, "Gemengde overeenkomsten", *NbBW* 2003, (104) 104–108.

1664 P. Brulez, *Koop en aanneming: faux amis?*, Antwerp, Intersentia, 2015, 85.

In the context of product-oriented PSS, the PSS supplier will often have to both supply and install a product (e.g. devices for a "smart kitchen", a "smart heating system" or a "smart ventilation system"). This is where the primacy of the cumulation theory under Dutch law comes into play: there will be both a sales contract (concerning the sale of the product) and a contract for works (concerning the installation).[1665] Consequently, the rules of both special contracts should be applied in parallel, unless the rules are incompatible or the nature of the agreement prevents the application of both rules.[1666] If the PSS user is a consumer, Article 7:18(3) DCC provides that if the seller has not only agreed to the delivery but also the installation of the good in a consumer sales contract, faulty installation is regarded as non-conformity.[1667] In practice, this means that if parties agree on the installation of the goods in addition to the delivery, as a rule there will be two contracts which are governed by their own rules: a consumer sales contract (concerning the goods) and a contract for works (concerning the installation).[1668] However, the DCC declares the regime on non-conformity of the consumer sales contract applicable across the board, even when it concerns a pure contract for works. Incidentally, Article 7:18(3) of the DCC does not prevent the rules regarding the contract for works from also applying to the installation.[1669]

In the situation described above, the sale and installation of products are still relatively distinct. The situation is more complex when the sales and construction components are more difficult to separate. Indeed, just like under Belgian law, most discussions are regarding contracts for the supply of goods to be manufactured or produced. In this case, the rules of the sales contract and the contract for works must be balanced. Case law and legal doctrine provide possible starting points for applying the absorption theory to choose between the sales contract and the contract for works.[1670] Yet, where there is still room

---

1665 J. Hijma, *Mr. C. Assers Handleiding tot de beoefening van het Nederlands Burgerlijk Recht. 7. Bijzondere overeenkomsten. Deel I. Koop en ruil*, Deventer, Kluwer, 2019, no. 19; M.A.M.C. Van den Berg and S. van Gulijk, *Mr. C. Assers Handleiding tot de beoefening van het Nederlands Burgerlijk Recht. 7. Bijzondere overeenkomsten. Deel VI. Aanneming van werk*, Deventer, Wolters Kluwer, 2022, no. 35.

1666 A.G. Castermans and H.B. Krans, "Gemengde overeenkomsten", *NbBW* 2003, (104) 104.

1667 The same applies if the buyer himself installs the item defectively and this is due to the instructions supplied (Art. 7:18(3), second sentence DCC). See for an in depth discussion M.B.M. Loos, *Consumentenkoop, Monografieën BW, nr. B65b*, Deventer, Wolters Kluwer, 2019, no. 32.

1668 Explanatory Memorandum, *Parliamentary Papers II* 2000/01, 27809, no. 3, 20.

1669 Explanatory Memorandum, *Parliamentary Papers II* 2000/01, 27809, no. 3, 20; J. Hijma, *Mr. C. Assers Handleiding tot de beoefening van het Nederlands Burgerlijk Recht. 7. Bijzondere overeenkomsten. Deel I. Koop en ruil*, Deventer, Kluwer, 2019, no. 514.

1670 For example: the question of whether the object is economically replaceable (if not, contract for works); the difference between movable and immovable goods (movable goods are more likely be subjected to a sales contract, immovable objects are more likely to be a contract for works); the method of manufacture (series production: purchase; custom-made: contract for works) and so on. See: J. Hijma, *Mr. C. Assers Handleiding tot de beoefening van het*

for doubt, the cumulation theory is indicated as the best option to avoid a choice between the sales contract and the contract for works.[1671] In this case, the two regimes are applied side by side. In the event of incompatible provisions, a choice may then be made between the competing sales and construction provision in the light of a concrete legal question.[1672]

However, an exception applies if the conditions for the application of the regime regarding consumer sales are met.[1673] If the movable good to be delivered has yet to be constructed and the contract also meets the description of the contract for works in Article 7:750 DCC, while the parties act in a B2C context,[1674] then the contract is regarded as a consumer sale pursuant to Article 7:5(4) DCC. The provisions of the sales contract and the contract for works then apply in parallel, and in the event of conflict the sales rules take precedence.[1675]

Finally, for product-oriented PSS contracts that include additional services other than installation, repair and maintenance (e.g. monitoring, support, control), a trade-off must be made between the sales contract and the contract for services.[1676] In principle, the absorption theory applies here: the rules for the type of contract that the PSS contract in question primarily covers, will generally apply.[1677] In the case of product-oriented PSS contracts, this will often be the sales contract. However, the law also allows application of the cumulation theory for additional services.[1678] When following this theory, the additional services

Nederlands Burgerlijk Recht. 7. Bijzondere overeenkomsten. Deel I. Koop en ruil, Deventer, Kluwer, 2019, no. 21; M.A.M.C. van den Berg, *Mr. C. Assers Handleiding tot de beoefening van het Nederlands Burgerlijk Recht. 7. Bijzondere overeenkomsten. Deel VI. Aanneming van werk*, Deventer, Wolters Kluwer, 2017, no. 33 and the references cited there.

1671 J. Hijma, *Mr. C. Assers Handleiding tot de beoefening van het Nederlands Burgerlijk Recht. 7. Bijzondere overeenkomsten. Deel I. Koop en ruil*, Deventer, Kluwer, 2019, no. 21.

1672 J. Hijma, *Mr. C. Assers Handleiding tot de beoefening van het Nederlands Burgerlijk Recht. 7. Bijzondere overeenkomsten. Deel I. Koop en ruil*, Deventer, Kluwer, 2019, no. 21.

1673 See Art. 7:5 DCC. See for an in depth discussion about the scope of application: M.B.M. Loos, *Consumentenkoop, Monografieën BW, nr. B65b*, Deventer, Wolters Kluwer, 2019, 15–26.

1674 See Art. 7:5(1) DCC.

1675 Art. 7:5(4) *in fine* DCC; M.A.M.C. Van den Berg and S. van Gulijk, *Mr. C. Assers Handleiding tot de beoefening van het Nederlands Burgerlijk Recht. 7. Bijzondere overeenkomsten. Deel VI. Aanneming van werk*, Deventer, Wolters Kluwer, 2022, no. 35; J. Hijma, *Mr. C. Assers Handleiding tot de beoefening van het Nederlands Burgerlijk Recht. 7. Bijzondere overeenkomsten. Deel I. Koop en ruil*, Deventer, Kluwer, 2019, no. 22 and no. 106; P. Klik, *Koop en Consumentenkoop*, Deventer, Wolters Kluwer, 2017, 29 and 100–101; See for an example: Hof Arnhem-Leeuwarden (NL) 6 October 2015, *RCR* 2016/4.

1676 See also: J. Hijma, *Mr. C. Assers Handleiding tot de beoefening van het Nederlands Burgerlijk Recht. 7. Bijzondere overeenkomsten. Deel I. Koop en ruil*, Deventer, Kluwer, 2019, no. 18.

1677 V. Mak, "Consumentenbescherming bij servitisation", *TPR* 2019, (779) 794, fn. 49, with reference to: T.F.E. Tjong Tjin Tai, *Asser 7-IV Bijzondere Overeenkomsten – Opdracht, incl. de geneeskundige behandelingsovereenkomst en de reisovereenkomst*, Deventer, Wolters Kluwer, 2018, no. 47.

1678 Art. 6:215 DCC; HR (NL) 10 July 2015, ECLI:NL:HR:2015:1830, (*Searocco/Altena*), *JWB* 2015/269, *NJ* 2015/321, *NJB* 2015/1408, *RCR* 2015/71.

that are part of the PSS contract can thus be subject to the relevant provisions of the contract for services.[1679] Where the provisions of both types of contract are incompatible, it will depend on the purpose and scope of the different rules and the relative importance of both contracts as well as the intention of the parties which rule prevails. Often, this will be the rule that belongs to the type of contract to which the product-oriented PSS contract primarily corresponds, usually a sales contract.[1680] In this sense, for product-oriented PSS contracts with consumers, reference should also be made to Article 7:5(6) DCC. Based on this provision, contracts between professional suppliers and consumers whereby both goods are delivered, and services are provided, are partly considered as consumer contracts. More specifically, this means that Articles 7:9 (transfer of ownership), 7:11 (transfer of risk) and 7:19a DCC (default on delivery) must be applied to the product-oriented PSS contract.[1681]

3.3.4. PRODUCT-ORIENTED PSS AND GOODS WITH DIGITAL ELEMENTS

383. New legal framework for contracts combining sale of goods and digital content or digital services – Above, the emergence of "smart" kitchens and "smart" ventilation systems was already discussed.[1682] Indeed, the increasing digitalisation of products and the shift towards a more circular economy will only increase the importance of complex product-oriented PSS that combine the sale of goods with "embedded" digital services or digital content.[1683]

For these product-oriented PSS contracts, the SGD introduced a new (mandatory) regulatory framework that devotes considerable importance to mixed contracts.

384. "Goods with digital elements" are also governed by the consumer sales rules – Product-oriented PSS that combine the sale of goods with "embedded" digital services or digital content are also governed by the consumer sales rules. Indeed, the SGD and its national implementing

1679 T.F.E. Tjong Tjin Tai, *Asser 7-IV Bijzondere Overeenkomsten – Opdracht, incl. de geneeskundige behandelingsovereenkomst en de reisovereenkomst*, Deventer, Wolters Kluwer, 2018, no. 47.

1680 T.F.E. Tjong Tjin Tai, *Asser 7-IV Bijzondere Overeenkomsten – Opdracht, incl. de geneeskundige behandelingsovereenkomst en de reisovereenkomst*, Deventer, Wolters Kluwer, 2018, no. 47.

1681 V. Mak, "Consumentenbescherming bij servitisation", *TPR* 2019, (779) 797; J. Hijma, *Mr. C. Assers Handleiding tot de beoefening van het Nederlands Burgerlijk Recht. 7. Bijzondere overeenkomsten. Deel I. Koop en ruil*, Deventer, Kluwer, 2019, no. 106.

1682 See *supra* no. 23.

1683 B. Keirsbilck, E. Terryn and E. Van Gool, "Consumentenbescherming bij servitisation en product-dienst systemen (PDS)", *TPR* 2019, (817) 834.

provisions fully apply to "goods with digital elements".[1684] This concept covers goods that incorporate or are inter-connected with digital content or a digital service in such a way that the absence of that digital content or digital service would prevent the goods from performing their functions.[1685] It is not relevant whether the digital content or digital services provided with the goods under the sales contract are supplied by the seller or by a third party.[1686] Whether the incorporated or inter-connected digital content or digital service is part of the sales contract depends on the content of the contract. For example, the digital elements are part of the sales contract when the contract explicitly requires them or when they are normal for goods of the same type and the consumer could reasonably expect them (e.g. given the nature of the goods or given public statements made by or on behalf of the seller).[1687] If it is not clear, there is a presumption that the rules of the SGD apply to avoid uncertainty for both sellers and consumers.[1688] If these conditions are met, the legal guarantee for digital content or digital services of the DCD does not apply to the incorporated or inter-connected digital content or digital services.[1689]

If we apply this to the examples of the sale of "smart" fridge advertised with a built-in recipe application accessed via a touch screen, or a "smart" ventilation system advertised with a certain remote access application, both these applications would be part of the sales contract. It does not matter whether the application is pre-installed on the good itself (such as with the "smart" fridge) or must be downloaded on another device and is only inter-connected to the good (such as with the smartphone remote access application for the "smart" ventilation system).[1690]

If the digital elements are not necessary for the performance of the good's functions, only the supply of the good is covered by the SGD and its implementing national provisions. The rules of the DCD and its national implementing provisions will apply to the digital content or the digital service, provided the conditions for their scope of application are met.[1691] This will be the case if the service provider supplies or undertakes to supply digital content

---

1684 J. Vanherpe, "White Smoke, but Smoke Nonetheless: Some (Burning) Questions Regarding the Directives on Sale of Goods and Supply of Digital Content", *ERPL* 2020, (251) 254; J. Morais Carvalho, "Sale of Goods and Supply of Digital Content and Digital Services – Overview of Directives 2019/770 and 2019/771", *EuCML* 2019, (194) 197.

1685 EU: Art. 2(5)(b) SGD. **Belgium**: Art. 1649*bis*, §1, 4°, b old BCC. **The Netherlands**: Art. 7:5(1), *sub* b. DCC.

1686 EU: Art. 3(3) SGD. **Belgium**: Art. 1649*bis*, §2, (2) old BCC. **The Netherlands**: Art. 7:5a(1), *sub* a. DCC.

1687 Recital 15 SGD.

1688 EU: Art. 3(3) and Recital 15 SGD. **Belgium**: Art. 1649*bis*, §2, (2) and Art. 1701/2, §5 old BCC. **The Netherlands**: Art. 7:5a(1), *sub* b. DCC.

1689 EU: Art. 3(4) DCD. **Belgium**: Art. 1701/2, §5 old BCC. **The Netherlands**: Art. 50ab(2) DCC.

1690 Compare with the examples given in Recital 15 of SGD (smart TV, smartphone, and smartwatch).

1691 Recital 16 SGD.

or a digital service and the consumer pays or undertakes the price, or provides or undertakes to provide personal data.[1692] When the PSS contract consists of additional services that are not covered by the DCD (e.g. maintenance and repair), national law determines which qualification theory should be used. Depending on which theory is used, it is possible that the whole PSS contract is covered by the rules on consumer sales (absorption theory), or that the rules of the sales contract and a services contract are applied cumulatively (e.g. contract for services (BE), contract for works (NL)).[1693]

3.4. QUALIFICATION OF USE-ORIENTED PSS

385. CONTRACTUAL QUALIFICATION OF USE-ORIENTED PSS – Rather than entailing a transfer of ownership, the supplier of a use-oriented PSS merely allows the use and enjoyment of a product for a certain amount of time, often complemented with additional services. As a result, the rules on the sales contract do no longer apply. This section will describe the different types of use-oriented PSS and their legal qualification under both Belgian and Dutch law.

First, we look at use-oriented PSS that are limited to the provision of a good against the payment of a periodic fee (section 3.4.1). Second, we consider short term and occasional services, as is the case with most "pay-per-use" agreements (section 3.4.2). Third, we compare use-oriented PSS contracts to (operational) leasing contracts (section 3.4.3). Fourth, we look at use-oriented PSS contracts that constitute a "complex contract", i.e. where the provision of a good is complemented by additional services (section 3.4.4). Finally, we discuss the qualification of digital services that often supplement use-oriented PSS (section 3.4.5).

3.4.1. MERE RIGHT OF USE AGAINST PAYMENT OF PRICE

386. USE-ORIENTED PSS AS A RENTAL CONTRACT FOR MOVABLES – A first category of use-oriented PSS consists of PSS **limited to making a product** (e.g. washing machine, coffee machine) **available against a fee**. These contracts will, both under Belgian and Dutch law, generally qualify as a rental contract for movables (*huur van roerende goederen, location de biens mobiliers*).

387. BELGIAN LAW: RENTAL CONTRACT FOR MOVABLES – According to the old BCC, rental of goods is a contract whereby one party (the lessor) undertakes to

---

1692 EU: Art. 3(1)-(3) DCD. **Belgium**: Art. 1701/2, §1-§2 old BCC. **The Netherlands**: Art. 50ab(1) DCC.

1693 Recital 17 SGD.

give the other (the lessee or renter) the enjoyment of a good for a certain period and at a certain price, which the latter undertakes to pay.[1694] The rental contract thus consists of two essential elements: a) the peaceful use and enjoyment of a good and this b) against payment of a price.[1695, 1696] If a PSS user subscribes to a use-oriented PSS contract, both of these essential elements will be present in the contract: he will be provided with a certain product "as a service" and pay a monthly price for it.

The old BCC further specifies that it is possible to rent all kinds of goods, both movable and immovable.[1697] However, since renting movable goods was rather rare at the time of creation of the French Code Civil 1804, the old BCC does not contain any specific provisions for rental contracts for movables.[1698] Nowadays, renting movable goods does occur frequently. One can think of renting clothes, construction or gardening tools, cars and other vehicles, pianos, etc.[1699] Therefore, to fill the gap, settled case law applies the general rules applicable to rental contracts for immovables[1700] by analogy, unless they are incompatible with the nature of the rental contract for movables.[1701]

Even when leaving the specific rules for occupancy and immovable property out of consideration, the rules on rental contract in the old Belgian Civil Code still contain provisions regulating the basic obligations of both parties and thus provide a useful framework for use-oriented PSS. For example, the PSS supplier

---

1694 Art. 1709 old BCC.

1695 Cass. (BE) 4 January 1979, *Arr.Cass.* 1978–79, 500, *Pas.* 1979, I, 501, *RW* 1978–79, 2591; Cass. (BE) 25 June 1954, *Arr.Cass.* 1954, 701, *Pas.* 1954, I, 928. See also R. Timmermans, "Huurprijs" in *OGP*, 2019, Afl. 324, XVII.J, (99) 99. See also Art. 1728, 2° old BCC.

1696 E. Van den Haute, *Traité des contrats spéciaux*, Brussels, Larcier, 2024, 577; M. Dambre, *Bijzondere overeenkomsten: de essentie*, Bruges, die Keure, 2022, 163–165. See specifically for the rental contract for movables: C. Marr, "Le contrat de location de biens meubles" in *Guide juridique de l'entreprise. Traité théorique et pratique*, Book 39, Waterloo, Kluwer, 2007, 11.

1697 Art. 1713 old BCC.

1698 M. Dambre, *Bijzondere overeenkomsten: de essentie*, Bruges, die Keure, 2022, 171; Y. Merchiers, *Le bail en général*, Brussels, Larcier, 2015, 355, no. 604.

1699 M. Dambre, *Bijzondere overeenkomsten: de essentie*, Bruges, die Keure, 2022, 171; C. Marr, "Le contrat de location mobilière: quelle réglementation appliquer face au mutisme du Code Civil?", *TBBR* 2008, (217) 217; C. Marr, "Le contrat de location de biens meubles" in *Guide juridique de l'entreprise. Traité théorique et pratique*, Book 39, Waterloo, Kluwer, 2007, 9.

1700 See Art. 1714-1762*bis* old BCC.

1701 Cass. (BE) 8 April 1943, *Arr.Cass.* 1943, 85; Brussels (BE) 9 October 2014, *T.Verz.* 2015, 334; Antwerp (BE) 6 September 2010, *NjW* 2011, 339, case note M. Dambre; Ghent (BE) 9 September 2004, *Huur* 2005, 52; Mons (BE) 12 March 2003, *TBBR* 2008, 216, case note C. Marr; Ct. Antwerp (BE) 30 June 2011, *RW* 2013–14, 269; Ct. Nivelles (BE) 30 October 2003, *Res Jur.Imm.* 2004, 7; JP. Wolvertem (BE) 19 October 1995, *AJT* 1995–96, 231, case note B. Cattoir. See also C. Marr, "Le contrat de location mobilière: quelle réglementation appliquer face au mutisme du Code Civil?", *TBBR* 2008, (217) 217–218; C. Marr, "Le contrat de location de biens meubles" in *Guide juridique de l'entreprise. Traité théorique et pratique*, Book 39, Waterloo, Kluwer, 2007, 16–17. Are generally considered incompatible with the rental contract for movables: Art. 1715, 1728*bis*, 1736, 1738, 1739, 1740, 1743, 1752, and 1762*bis* of the old BCC.

should provide the peaceful enjoyment of the rented good[1702] and is responsible for defects.[1703] In addition, maintenance and major repairs are the responsibility of the PSS supplier,[1704] while the PSS user remains responsible for minor repairs.[1705] It is important to note however, that most of these rules are only of a default nature and therefore will only apply in case the parties (in practice often the PSS supplier) did not include a specific contractual arrangement in the PSS contract.[1706]

388. DUTCH LAW: RENTAL CONTRACT FOR MOVABLES – Dutch law has a similar definition of rental of goods.[1707] According to the DCC, a rental contract is an agreement whereby one party, the lessor (*verhuurder*), undertakes to provide the other party, the lessee (*huurder*), with the use[1708] of a good or part thereof and the lessee undertakes to provide a counter performance (often a payment).[1709] Therefore, also under Dutch law, use-oriented PSS fall under the definition of a rental contract.

Since the definition of a rental contract in the DCC refers to the use of a "good", this also includes movable goods.[1710] As described above,[1711] neither the conventional qualification nor the fact that the contracting parties are not aware that the PSS contract falls under the definition of a rental contract in the DCC is relevant for the qualification as a rental contract.[1712] Therefore, when the purpose of the PSS contract is to provide the use of a good to another party against a counter performance (often the periodic payment of a fee[1713]),

1702 Art. 1719 old BCC.

1703 Art. 1721 old BCC.

1704 Art. 1720 old BCC.

1705 Art. 1754 old BCC.

1706 V. SAGAERT, B. TILLEMAN and A.L. VERBEKE, *Vermogensrecht in kort bestek*, Antwerp, Intersentia, 2019, 256; C. MARR, "Le contrat de location de biens meubles" in *Guide juridique de l'entreprise. Traité théorique et pratique*, Book 39, Waterloo, Kluwer, 2007, 9.

1707 H.J. ROSSEL and A.H.T. HEISTERKAMP, *Mr. C. Assers Handleiding tot de beoefening van het Nederlands Burgerlijk Recht. 7. Bijzondere overeenkomsten. Deel II. Huur*, Deventer, Wolters Kluwer, 2017, no. 10.

1708 Essential is the "use" ("*het gebruik*"), i.e. relinquishing the actual power over the good. Mere "enjoyment" ("*het genot*") of the rented good is not enough. See N. AMIEL and T. VAN TATENHOVE, *Groene Serie Huurrecht, art. 7:201 BW*, Deventer, Kluwer, loose-leaf, no. A.4 and no. 7.1.

1709 See Art. 7:201 DCC. According to Art. 7:201(2) DCC, a rental contract can also relate to property rights ("*vermogensrechten*"). On the other hand, a lease agreement for agricultural land ("*pacht*") is excluded from the scope of the rental contract since these agreements are governed by a separate section (Art. 7:311 *et seq*. DCC).

1710 A.R. DE JONGE, *Huurrecht*, Den Haag, Boom Juridisch, 2019, 42; N. AMIEL and T. VAN TATENHOVE, *Groene Serie Huurrecht, art. 7:201 BW*, Deventer, Kluwer, loose-leaf, no. 8.1.

1711 See *supra* no. 360.

1712 H.J. ROSSEL, *Huurrecht algemeen*, Deventer, Kluwer, 2007, 1.

1713 However, periodic payment is not essential for the qualification as a rental contract, the payment of a lump sum may also constitute the counter performance. See H.J. ROSSEL, *Huurrecht algemeen*, Deventer, Kluwer, 2007, 6.

the general provisions applicable to all rental contracts will apply.[1714] These general provisions are found in Articles 7:201–7:230 DCC and are mostly non-mandatory.[1715] The remaining provisions of title 7.4 DCC only apply to rental contracts for residential spaces and rental contracts for retail spaces and are therefore not relevant for PSS contracts concerning movable goods.

The general provisions of the rental contract set out the obligations that the lessor and lessee have towards each other. For example, the lessor is obliged to provide a good which is free of defects.[1716] On the other hand, the lessee is expected to behave like a good lessee.[1717] However, most of these provisions are only default law. This gives the parties to a PSS contract a far-reaching freedom to agree on their own rights and obligations.

3.4.2. SHORT-TERM AND OCCASIONAL SERVICE

389. Short-term and occasional service – It is also possible that use-oriented PSS entail a **short-term and occasional service** rather than a right of use over a product during a certain period. Examples include most "pay-per-use" agreements, such as a washing machine where the PSS user pays "per wash" or an E-scooter sharing system where the PSS user pays depending on the distance travelled or the length of the ride.

390. Belgian law: no longer rental contract but contract for services? – Under Belgian law, it could be argued that when use-oriented PSS concern a short-term and occasional service there is no longer a rental contract for movables, but the entire contract qualifies as a "rental of work"[1718] (*huur van werk, louage d'ouvrage*). In most cases this will be a contract for services (*aanneming, contrat d'entreprise*).[1719]

Indeed, many short-term and occasional services offered in the context of use-oriented PSS involve the performance of material or intellectual

---

[1714] Title 7.4.1–7.4.4 DCC (except Art. 7:230a DCC). See: H.J. Rossel and A.H.T. Heisterkamp, *Mr. C. Assers Handleiding tot de beoefening van het Nederlands Burgerlijk Recht. 7. Bijzondere overeenkomsten. Deel II. Huur*, Deventer, Wolters Kluwer, 2017, no. 8.

[1715] For a list of the provisions of Title 7.4 of the Dutch Civil Code that are semi-mandatory or mandatory, see: Z.H. Duijnstee-van Imhoff, *Huurrecht geschetst*, Nijmegen, Ars Aequi Libri, 2016, 151–153.

[1716] Art. 7:203 and Art. 7:206 DCC.

[1717] Art. 7:213 DCC. See also: V. Mak, "Consumentenbescherming bij servitisation", *TPR* 2019, (779) 794; A.W. Jongbloed, "Huur" in H.N. Schelhaas and A.J. Verheij (eds.), *Bijzondere overeenkomsten in Studiereeks Burgerlijk Recht*, Deventer, Wolters Kluwer, 2023, (159) 165–166, no. 172.

[1718] See Art. 1710 and 1711 old BCC. The "rental of work" is a generic concept that includes both the employment contract and the contract for services, as a special form of rental contract together with the rental of goods (Art. 1708 old BCC).

[1719] B. Keirsbilck, E. Terryn and E. Van Gool, "Consumentenbescherming bij servitisation en product-dienst systemen (PDS)", *TPR* 2019, (817) 835.

acts in return for a counter performance, and this without a relationship of subordination, nor power of representation (for the definition of the contract for services, see *supra* no. 375). Nevertheless, the distinction between a rental contract for movables and a contract for services is not easily made. After all, for a qualification as a rental contract, it is sufficient that the price is determinable based on objective data existing at the time of conclusion of the agreement.[1720] The question whether the good is permanently in the control of the PSS user, even when it is not being used, may be relevant for a qualification as a rental contract.[1721]

For example, based on this criterion of whether the good is permanently in the control of the PSS user, it could be argued that a smart washing machine located in the PSS user's home that operates on a pay-per-wash basis should be qualified as a rental contract (with or without additional services), whereas an electric scooter which is freely available on the streets of a city and which is made available on a pay-per-minute or pay-per-kilometre basis should rather be qualified as a contract for services or possibly[1722] – but in my view less likely – a transport contract[1723] (*vervoersovereenkomst, contrat de transport*). Yet, case law has already accepted the short-term use of washing machines against the

---

1720 Cass. 15 Februari 1985, *Arr.Cass.* 1984–85, 822, *Pas.* 1985, I, 737, *RW* 1986–87, 543; Cass. 20 May 1994, *Arr.Cass.* 1994, 507, *Pas.* 1994, I, 928, *RW* 1995–96, 600.

1721 B. Keirsbilck, E. Terryn and E. Van Gool, "Consumentenbescherming bij servitisation en product-dienst systemen (PDS)", *TPR* 2019, (817) 825.

1722 As argued by B. Keirsbilck, E. Terryn and E. Van Gool, "Consumentenbescherming bij servitisation en product-dienst systemen (PDS)", *TPR* 2019, (817) 835, fn. 86.

1723 See: Cass. (BE) 20 September 2019, *TBH* 2019, 11163, commentary S. Tytgat and O. Vanden Berghe, *IHT* 2020, 109, *JLMB* 2020, 967, case note C. Parmentier which defines the transport contract as "*the contract by which one of the parties undertakes to the other, in return for remuneration, to move persons or goods. The carriage of goods normally involves loading and unloading.*" Already before this judgment, the following constitutive elements of the transport contract were identified in legal doctrine: (i) the movement of a good or a person from one place to another; (ii) by a professional carrier; (iii) who has full mastery over the good or person to be transported. See: J.P. Kesteloot, "La notion de contrat de transport", *IHT* 2021, (3) 14–19 and W. Goossens, *Aanneming van werk: het gemeenrechtelijk dienstencontract*, Bruges, die Keure, 2003, 201. See for examples in case law: Comm. Brussels (BE) 24 December 1947, *J.C.Br* 1948, 293 294, first whereas; Comm. Liège (BE) 12 April 1963, *JL* 1962–63, 282 283, first column, third whereas. This definition makes it very unlikely that electronic scooters that are available on a free-floating basis qualify as a transport contract since the PSS supplier does not have full mastery over the person to be transported. After all, the PSS user still must operate (steering, braking, etc.) the electric scooter himself. See: W. Verheyen and B. Pavlovski-dikker, "Micromobiliteit, duurzaamheid en veiligheid. Welke weg voor passagiersrechten in de roaring twenties?", *DCCR* 2021, (41) 44, no. 8 and 11 and fn. 13. Compare also with Cass. (FR) 7 February 1949, *D.* 1949, *Jur.*, 377, F. Derrida, where a ski tow was not considered transport as the skier himself plays an active role. The contract of transport by land and water is considered by the old BCC as a category of rental of work and services (see Art. 1799 old BCC). Formally, the transport contract is a specific contract for services to which certain rules of the contract for services apply (e.g. Art. 1794 old DCC) unless a special law provides otherwise. See: W. Goossens, *Aanneming van werk: het gemeenrechtelijk dienstencontract*, Bruges, die Keure, 2003, 200–201; H. De Page, *Traité élémentaire de droit civil belge*, IV, Brussels, Bruylant, 1972, no. 847; R. Dekkers, *Handboek*

payment of a fee in an (automatic) laundry – i.e. outside the PSS user's control – as a rental contract.[1724] Possibly, a potential conventional qualification[1725] of the use-oriented PSS contract could also be of decisive importance here to choose between a qualification as a rental contract or a contract for services.[1726]

391. Dutch law: no longer rental contract when use-oriented PSS as a whole reflects another named contract – Also under Dutch law, it could be argued that the relationship between the provider and the consumer in a use-oriented PSS contract involving a short-term and occasional service should no longer be qualified as a rental contract, but another named (or unnamed) contract, often a contract for services.[1727]

This was recognised by the Dutch Supreme Court in its timeshare judgment.[1728] According to this case law, it is possible that a contract, viewed in isolation, contains all the elements on the basis of which the legal description of a rental contract is met, but that in view of special circumstances, it should not be qualified as a rental contract.[1729] An example is "renting" a seat in a theatre or cinema: although formally the essential legal elements are met – a seat is given in use against payment of a price – the intended purpose of the contract is the enjoyment of the performance (a service) and not the seat.[1730] The decisive factor is whether in the given circumstances, in view of what the parties had in mind at the time when the contract was concluded, the content and purpose of

Burgerlijk Recht, II, Verbintenissen – Bewijsleer – Contracten – Zekerheden, Brussels, Bruylant, 1971, 622, no. 1103.

1724 Ct. Brussels (BE) 7 October 1961, *J.T.* 1962, 604 where the short-term use of washing machines against the payment of a fee in an (automatic) laundry was qualified as a rental contract.

1725 See *supra* no. 359.

1726 See for example the user agreement for electric scooters from "*Lime*": available at www.li.me/user-agreement/be where the services are consistently named as "rental and use of products." See also the terms and conditions of their competitors "*Bird*" (available at: www.bird.co/agreement/) and "*Dott*" (available at: https://ridedott.com/terms-and-conditions/belgium) both explicitly naming their agreements as rental agreements.

1727 Compare (regarding operational lease contracts) with J.A.M.P. Keijser, *Civielrechtelijke aspecten van leasing in Nederland*, 's-Gravenhage, VUGA, 1972, 20–22.

1728 HR (NL) 11 February 2011, ECLI:NL:HR:2011:BO7108, (*First Data B.V./KPN Hotspots Schiphol B.V.*), *NJ* 2011/571, case note J. Hijma: The question whether timeshare contracts should be classified as rental contracts cannot be answered either in the affirmative or in the negative, either in general or in principle.

1729 H.J. Rossel and A.H.T. Heisterkamp, *Mr. C. Assers Handleiding tot de beoefening van het Nederlands Burgerlijk Recht. 7. Bijzondere overeenkomsten. Deel II. Huur*, Deventer, Wolters Kluwer, 2017, no. 14.

1730 A.W. Jongbloed, "Huur" in H.N. Schelhaas and A.J. Verheij (eds.), *Bijzondere overeenkomsten in Studiereeks Burgerlijk Recht*, Deventer, Wolters Kluwer, 2023, (159) 161, no. 168. Other examples are the enjoyment of a seat on a train or bus (not a rental contract but a transport contract (*vervoersovereenkomst*); see Art. 8:80 *et seq.* DCC) and an admission to a hospital (not a rental contract of a room or a bed but a medical treatment agreement (*geneeskundige behandelingsovereenkomst*); see Art. 7:446 *et seq.* DCC).

the contract can, viewed as a whole, be regarded as a rental contract or another named contract.[1731]

For the qualification of use-oriented PSS contracts involving a short-term and occasional service, it will therefore be important to determine whether, viewed as a whole – also considering their content and purpose and what the parties had in mind when concluding the contract – they should be regarded as a rental contract or a contract for services (or another named contract). A few factors that may be possibly relevant to determine this are the determinability of the PSS user' right of use (which product can he use and what use can he make of this product?);[1732] the extent to which the good is in the physical control of the PSS user (permanently or occasionally?); and whether the parties' agreement primarily envisioned the rental of a specific product or the enjoyment of an integrated service.

392. Consequences for consumer protection in case of qualification as a service contract instead of rental contract – The qualification of use-oriented PSS contracts involving a short-term and occasional services as a contract for services (BE: *aanneming, contrat d'entreprise*; NL: *opdracht*) rather than a rental contract does not enhance the position of the consumer. As already set out above,[1733] the legal framework of the contract for services, both in Belgium and the Netherlands, is rather limited and mostly non-mandatory. Consequently, the rights and obligations of the parties will again very often depend on the general terms and conditions of the PSS supplier.

3.4.3. USE-ORIENTED PSS AND LEASING CONTRACTS

393. Servitisation and leasing contracts – Servitised business models and product-as-a-service contracts are sometimes referred to in literature and in practice as leasing contracts instead of rental contracts.[1734] Although use-

1731 HR (NL) 11 February 2011, ECLI:NL:HR:2011:BO7108, (*First Data B.V./KPN Hotspots Schiphol B.V.*), *NJ* 2011/571, case note J. Hijma; A.R. De Jonge, *Huurrecht*, Den Haag, Boom Juridisch, 2019, 29–30; G.K.L. de Wijkerslooth, "'Ceci n'est pas une pipe?' Over uitleg en kwalificatie van de (huur)overeenkomst", *HIP* 2020/35, (11) 14–15; F.J. de Vries, *De overeenkomst in het algemeen*, Deventer, Wolters Kluwer, 2016, 32–33.

1732 See for example the illustration in H.J. Rossel, *Huurrecht algemeen*, Deventer, Kluwer, 2007, 2: if a contract provides that a user may use a certain garage box in a row of several boxes, this user is given a key of this specific box, and the box is only intended and used for storing the car of this user, then it constitutes a rental contract. See HR (NL) 6 March 1964, ECLI:NL:HR:1964:29 (*Dorvo/Herngreen*), *NJ* 1964/215. If, on the other hand, the user has the right to park his car in "a" garage box every day, and the decision as to which box to park in is made by the service provider each time, there is no longer a rental contract but a *sui generis* contract.

1733 See *supra* no. 376 and no. 378.

1734 See e.g. S. van Gulijk, "De juridische kwalificatie van verdienstelijking in de gebouwde omgeving", *WPNR* 2021, vol. 7326, (409) 410–412; A.M. Schmidt, "Diensten in de circulaire oriented PSS contracts share similarities with leasing contracts, there are often essential differences between the two concepts. This section explores the similarities and differences between both concepts by comparing the legal qualification of the different forms of leasing contracts with different forms of use-oriented PSS contracts. Here, it is important to note from the outset that the leasing contract (being an unnamed contract) is not regulated as such in the Belgian[1735] and Dutch Civil Codes.[1736] Accordingly, due to their *sui generis* nature, inspiration is drawn from other named contracts for determining the rules applicable to leasing contracts, most notably the rental contract.

Leasing contracts often have a financing finality, which can under certain conditions result in the EU or national consumer credit rules (or specific national rules similar to (consumer) credit rules) being applicable. This often depends on the question of whether the contract contains a purchase obligation or purchase option. This section therefore also analyses the potential applicability of the EU consumer credit rules and their national counterparts to leasing contracts and explores the circumstances under which these rules could also apply to use-oriented PSS.

394. TWO (MAIN) TYPES OF LEASING CONTRACTS: FINANCIAL AND OPERATIONAL LEASING – There are many possible variants to the leasing contract, but in general two main forms can be distinguished: financial leasing and operational leasing.[1737]

395. FINANCIAL LEASING: FINANCING FINALITY AS MAIN CHARACTERISTIC – In financial leasing, also known as financial renting, the leasing company purchases a good in accordance with specific instructions from the future lessee

economie en enkele mogelijke privaatrechtelijke belemmeringen", *M en R* 2017, (812) 813–814; S. FISCHER, S. STEGER, N.D. JORDAN, M. O'BRIEN and P. SCHEPELMANN, *Leasing Society. Report requested by the European Parliament's Committee on Environment, Public Health and Food Safety*, 2012, 58 p.

1735 The Belgian Royal Decree no. 55 of 10 November 1967 regulating the legal status of companies specialising in financing leases, *BS* 14 November 1967 ("Belgian Royal Decree no. 55") lists some characteristics of the leasing contract but does not regulate the legal framework of leasing contracts as such. See Art. 1 Belgian Royal Decree no. 55. See also Cass. (BE) 17 June 1993, *Arr.Cass.* 1993, 598, *Pas.* 1993, I., 582 in which the Belgian Court of Cassation recognised the leasing contract.

1736 **Belgium**: K. VANHOVE, "Leasing: een complexe bijzondere overeenkomst" in P. BESELAERE, O. LENAERTS, B. TILLEMAN and A. VERBEKE (eds.), *Handboek leasing*, Bruges, die Keure, 2007, (41) 43. **The Netherlands**: G.M. KERPESTEIN, "Operationele lease en huurcomplicaties daarvan", *Journaal Huur & Verhuur* 2004/126.

1737 **Belgium**: B. VAN ITTERBEEK, "Toepassingen – Structuur" in P. BESELAERE, O. LENAERTS, B. TILLEMAN and A.L. VERBEKE (eds.), *Handboek Leasing*, Bruges, die Keure, 2007, (179) 179. **The Netherlands**: D.F.H. STEIN, "Operational lease en financial lease" in *Groene Serie Vermogensrecht, art. 3.227 BW*, Deventer, Wolters Kluwer, loose-leaf, 2023, para. 2.7.5; H.J. ROSSEL, *Huurrecht algemeen*, Deventer, Kluwer, 2007, 15; M.F.A. EVERS, *Huurrecht bedrijfsruimten*, Deventer, Kluwer, 2003, 35.

and then rents it to the lessee for a specific period of time.[1738] This contractual relationship is mainly characterised by its financing finality: a leasing contract provides a credit that is economically and fiscally more favourable than the classic purchase through a loan.[1739] By means of the instalments during this contractually defined period (in which the contract cannot be terminated), the lessee will generally repay the full amount invested by the leasing company (including interest, depreciation and profits).[1740] During the leasing contract, the leasing company retains the ownership of the leased good as collateral. The risk of depreciation, loss, wear and tear and damages lies with the lessee.[1741] At the end of the leasing contract, the lessee may acquire ownership of the leased good by exercising a *purchase option*, at a purchase price that is generally significantly lower than the market value of the leased good, or may decide to return the leased good to the leasing company.[1742] It is also possible that the financial leasing contract stipulates an *obligation to purchase* the leased good at the end of the contract.[1743]

396. Use-oriented PSS contracts versus financial leasing contracts – The main difference between use-oriented PSS and financial leasing contracts lies in the lack of financing finality in use-oriented PSS contracts. Indeed, the idea of most use-oriented PSS is that at the end of the contract term, the product goes back to the PSS supplier, who can then sustainably reuse or repurpose it. In this sense, the use of the product is the key focus of the operation, and the parties even want to prevent the PSS user from acquiring the ownership of the product. This is clearly juxtaposed with the concept of financial leasing, where the financing finality and purchase option are both an essential part of the contract. However, there are roughly two types of use-oriented PSS contracts that more closely resemble financial leasing contracts: use-oriented PSS contracts containing a purchase option and use-oriented PSS that essentially constitute hire purchase agreements.

1738 J. Woestyn, P. Leroy, V. Buyl, K. Vanhove, S. Baert, A. Hanselaer, F. Burssens, H. Lamon and R. Steennot, *Bijzondere overeenkomsten*, Antwerp, Maklu, 2006, 61.

1739 K. Vanhove, "Leasing: een complexe bijzondere overeenkomst" in P. Beselaere, O. Lenaerts, B. Tilleman and A. Verbeke (eds.), *Handboek leasing*, Bruges, die Keure, 2007, (41) 43; A. Vervaet and P. Beselaere, "Onroerende leasing [Financiële aspecten]" in R. Derine, H. Cousy, J. Couturier, W. Delva, J. Herbots and R. Vekeman (eds.), *Het onroerend goed in de praktijk*, Antwerp, Wolters Kluwer, 2008, (123) 124.

1740 M. van der Weide, "Lease en huurkoop onder de nieuwe titel 7.2b (goederenkrediet) van het Burgerlijk Wetboek", *WPNR* 2017/7158, (534) 534.

1741 D.F.H. Stein, "Operational lease en financial lease" in *Groene Serie Vermogensrecht, art. 3.227 BW*, Deventer, Wolters Kluwer, loose-leaf, 2023, para. 2.7.5.

1742 K. Vanhove, "Leasing: een complexe bijzondere overeenkomst" in P. Beselaere, O. Lenaerts, B. Tilleman and A. Verbeke (eds.), *Handboek leasing*, Bruges, die Keure, 2007, (41) 43 and 56–58.

1743 M. van der Weide, "Lease en huurkoop onder de nieuwe titel 7.2b (goederenkrediet) van het Burgerlijk Wetboek", *WPNR* 2017/7158, (534) 535.

397. Use-oriented PSS including a purchase option – A first type of use-oriented PSS resembling (financial) leasing contracts includes use-oriented PSS contracts that contain a purchase option which the PSS user can exercise at the end of the contract or sometimes even during the contract. For example, the contract of *Saman Group* both offers the option to purchase the heat pump at the end of the contract at the price stipulated in the contract and the option to purchase the heat pump at any time during the contract at a market price. A similar clause regarding the option to purchase the product during the term of the PSS contract can also be found in the terms and conditions of *Bundles*. However, while the presence of a purchase option in the contract is an important distinguishing criterion for the contractual qualification as finance leasing, it is nevertheless not decisive. Indeed, "ordinary" rental contracts can also contain a purchase option. In that case, the lessee pays for the use of the rented good and has the option to buy the good at the end of the contract by paying a residual fee.[1744] Similarly, with use-oriented PSS contracts that incorporate a purchase option, the PSS user pays for the use of the good and has the option to acquire the ownership later; however, the financing finality is absent. As a result, use-oriented PSS contracts including a purchase option should be distinguished from financial leasing contracts.

> Terms and conditions Saman Group – Art. 12.2 "At the end of the Rental Contract, Saman Group will dismantle and remove the Heat Pump System. Should the Lessee wish to take over the Heat Pump System at the end of the Rental Contract, this is possible at the amount specified in the Rental Contract." Art. 12.3 "If desired by the Lessee, during the term of the Rental Contract, the Heat Pump System can be purchased at a market price. The Lessee can request the purchase price from Saman Group at that time. If the Lessee wishes to take over the Heat Pump System during the term of the Rental Contract and is willing to pay the aforementioned price, the Rental Contract will be terminated prematurely by mutual consent between the parties."

> Terms and conditions Bundles – Art. 11 "A Product that has always been used within the framework of a Subscription from its initial placement can be bought/sold under the conditions of Bundles Residual Value. The Customer can request a current Residual Value price from Bundles at any time."

The inclusion of a purchase option in a use-oriented PSS contract will generally not disqualify it from being qualified as a rental contract. However, if the PSS user decides to exercise this purchase option, this will affect the qualification of the contract for the future. Indeed, it will have the effect of terminating the

[1744] K. Vanhove, "Leasing: een complexe bijzondere overeenkomst" in P. Beselaere, O. Lenaerts, B. Tilleman and A. Verbeke (eds.), *Handboek leasing*, Bruges, die Keure, 2007, (41) 57.

rental contract and concluding a sales contract, either at the residual value price stipulated in the PSS contract, or at the market price as agreed by the parties.

398. Purchase option where monthly fees already paid are deducted from sales price of the product – Some use-oriented PSS contracts offering a purchase option for the product include a provision that the monthly fees already paid by the PSS user are deducted from the sales price of the product. Such clauses can be found, for example, in the terms and conditions of *Live Light* and *Grover*. In a way, this practice where consumers can buy a movable product that they have been renting for a while, and where the accrued rental fees are subtracted from the initial sales price, is very similar to the concept of "hamster renting" (*hamsterhuren, location écureuil*) that has recently emerged with regard to immovable property.[1745] Although deducting the accrued rental fees from the original sales price comes closer to a financing finality than if there is a purchase option in the PSS contract independent from the rental amounts paid, in my view, the use of the product is still central. As a result, also these use-oriented PSS contracts must be qualified as rental contracts (often with additional services) where the PSS user has a purchase option at the end of the contract, and not as financial leasing contracts.[1746]

> Terms and conditions Live Light – Art. 7.6 "The Lessee can decide to purchase the Goods at any time. In any case, the Rents already paid will be deducted from the Sales Price of the Goods."
>
> Terms and conditions Grover – Art. 6 "If the object of the offer is a purchase option and if this purchase option has become part of the content of the contract, the following provisions shall apply:" 6.1 "You can exercise Your purchase option at any time during the rental contract [...]" Art 6.2 "The purchase price results from the Offer Description. [...] If You exercise the purchase option, the rent paid by You up until You exercise the purchase option will be deducted from the purchase price as listed in the Offer Description."

399. Purchase option compatible with circular economy principles? – At first glance, including a purchase option in the use-oriented PSS contract goes against the principles of servitisation and the circular economy. After all, exercising the purchase option has the effect that the PSS supplier will no

---

1745 See www.hamsterhuren.be. Sometimes, the term *rent-to-own* is also used. See for a legal analysis of this concept e.g. R. Timmermans, "Hamsterhuren of een woning huren met aankoopoptie: hoe realistisch is de eigendomsverwachting?", *Huur* 2017, (51) 51–62.

1746 Compare with K. Vanhove, "Leasing: een complexe bijzondere overeenkomst" in P. Beselaere, O. Lenaerts, B. Tilleman and A. Verbeke (eds.), *Handboek leasing*, Bruges, die Keure, 2007, (41) 57, where it is pointed out that in case of a dispute regarding the qualification as a rental contract or (financial) leasing contract, the court must seek out the common intention of the parties and the economic reality of the contract.

longer own nor have responsibility for (reusing or repurposing) the product. Yet including a purchase option can also have advantages, both from a consumer protection perspective and from a circular economy perspective. After all, as is discussed more in depth further, ownership gives the PSS user-consumer a strong position and ensures that he can accumulate wealth and use these products as collateral for his debts.[1747] In addition, if the PSS user-consumer can acquire the ownership of the product at the end of the contract or during the contract, this may also provide an incentive to treat the product well, thus mitigating the moral hazard risk associated with PSS.[1748]

400. Use-oriented PSS where the sum of the periodical fees represents sales price of the product (hire purchase) – A second type of PSS contracts that resemble financial leasing contracts are fixed term contracts where the sum of the periodical fees together adds up to the sales price of the product. The main difference with financial leasing contracts is that these contracts do not contain a purchase option, but instead the ownership of the product automatically passes after the PSS user has paid the last periodical fee. The "*Lease a Jeans*" formula of *Mudjeans* provides a good example of this concept. The PSS user pays a monthly fee for 12 months while *Mudjeans* retains the ownership of the jeans. After 12 months, the PSS user becomes the owner of the product and has a choice: either he can keep the jeans (for free), swap them for a new pair while *Mudjeans* recycles the jeans (and thus conclude a new 12-month contract, but with a discount), or return them for recycling without concluding a new contract (for free).[1749] These contracts are qualified as hire purchase, which is essentially a instalment sales contract (*verkoop op afbetaling, vente à temperament*) but under the form of a rental contract.[1750] Here, the rental fees are charged on the "sales price", after which, upon full payment, the rental contract is converted into a sales contract.[1751] Under Belgian law, these contracts fall within the scope of the consumer credit rules, as these contracts constitute instalment sales contracts within the meaning of Article I.9, 46° BCEL.[1752] Under Dutch law, they qualify as a goods credit agreement

[1747] See *infra* no. 444.

[1748] See *supra* no. 26 and 31.

[1749] See https://mudjeans.eu/pages/lease-a-jeans-2023.

[1750] E. Brewaeys, *Leasing van roerende goederen*, Antwerp, Kluwer Rechtswetenschappen, 1985, 16, no. 15.

[1751] K. Vanhove, "Leasing: een complexe bijzondere overeenkomst" in P. Beselaere, O. Lenaerts, B. Tilleman and A. Verbeke (eds.), *Handboek leasing*, Bruges, die Keure, 2007, (41) 59, no. 27.

[1752] This provision defines the "instalment sales contract" as "*any credit agreement, whatever its name or form, which normally leads to the acquisition of goods or the provision of services, sold by the creditor or the credit intermediary referred to in the last sentence of 35°(c) and the price of which is paid by means of periodic payments.*"

(*goederenkrediet*)[1753, 1754] and are also governed by the consumer credit rules.[1755]

401. Purchase option/obligation and the applicability of the EU consumer credit rules – Whether or not a purchase option or purchase obligation is included in a use-oriented PSS contract is relevant to the applicability of European consumer credit rules. Under the Consumer Credit Directive 2008/48/EC ("CCD1"), rental or leasing contracts where an obligation to purchase the object of the contract is not laid down in the contract itself or by any separate contract are excluded from the scope of the European consumer credit rules.[1756] This means that under the current European consumer credit rules, use-oriented PSS contracts are not covered by the CCD1, as long as they do not include a purchase *obligation*. In other words, a purchase *option* can perfectly be included in the PSS contract without triggering the applicability of the CCD1. As none of the PSS contracts analysed contained a purchase obligation, the relevance of the CCD1 for PSS contracts is rather limited under current law.

The scope of the new Consumer Credit Directive (EU) 2023/2225 ("CCD2"), however, was extended in a way that is relevant for some of the analysed (use-oriented) PSS. This Directive will repeal and replace the CCD1 and must be transposed by the Member States by 20 November 2025, and they must apply these measures from 20 November 2026.[1757] The CCD2 states that it does not apply to rental or leasing contracts where an obligation *or an option* to purchase the object of the contract is not laid down either in the contract itself or in any separate contract.[1758] Thus, the future European consumer credit rules will also apply to use-oriented PSS contracts including a purchase option and not only to use-oriented PSS which include a purchase obligation.[1759] This means that in the future, if the use-oriented PSS contract contains a purchase obligation, additional obligations will be placed on the PSS supplier and PSS users will enjoy extra consumer protection. These include, for example, pre-contractual

---

1753 See Art. 7:84(1) *juncto* Art. 7:84(2) and (3), *sub* b. DCC.

1754 See *infra* no. 403.

1755 Art. 7:58(1) *juncto* Art. 7:57(1), *sub* c. DCC.

1756 EU: Art. 2(2)(d) CCD1. See for an application: CJEU, Judgment of 21 December 2023, Joined Cases C-38/21, C-47/21 and C-232/21, *VK and Others v BMW Bank GmbH and Others*, ECLI:EU:C:2023:1014, para. 126–156 (leasing contract relating to a motor vehicle without purchase obligation falls within the scope of the CRD as a "service contract" within the meaning of art. 2(6) CRD. *By contrast, such a contract does not fall within the scope of either the Distance Marketing of Financial Services Directive 2002/65/EC or the CCD1.*)

1757 See Art. 48(1) CCD2.

1758 See Art. 2(2)(g) Directive (EU) 2023/2225 of the European Parliament and of the Council of 18 October 2023 on credit agreements for consumers and repealing Directive 2008/48/EC, *OJ L*, 2023/2225, 30.10.2023 ("CCD2").

1759 See also Recital 15 CCD2.

and contractual information requirements,[1760] an obligation to assess the creditworthiness of the consumer,[1761] a right of withdrawal,[1762] a prohibition of certain practices and advertising (e.g. product tying, pre-ticked boxed, unsolicited credit sales),[1763] caps on charges,[1764] conduct and supervision of creditors and credit intermediaries,[1765] etc.

402. Purchase option/obligation and Belgian consumer credit rules – When considering the applicability of national consumer credit law to use-oriented PSS with a purchase option, the situation is somewhat different, at least under Belgian law. The Belgian implementation of the CCD1 deviates from the scope of application of the Directive. Indeed, Article VII.3(2), 2° BCEL stipulates that Book VII BCEL does not apply to "*hiring agreements where no obligation to purchase the object of the agreement is laid down either by the agreement itself or by any separate agreement […].*" Thus, contrary to the Directive, the Belgian legislator did not exclude leasing contracts from the scope of application of the consumer credit rules. As the CCD1 allows Member States to maintain or introduce national legislation corresponding to its provisions to credit agreements outside the scope of the CCD1, this does not conflict with the Directive.[1766] If a leasing contract includes a purchase *option* (and no obligation), it will therefore also be subjected to the Belgian consumer credit rules.

The BCEL stipulates rules specific to "financing lease" (*financieringshuur, crédit-bail*) that apply in addition to the consumer credit rules.[1767] "Finance lease" is defined in the BCEL as "*any credit agreement, irrespective of its nature or form, by which one party undertakes to provide the other with the use of a tangible movable good at a fixed price, which the latter undertakes to pay periodically, and which includes, expressly or tacitly, a purchase offer. For the purposes of this law, the lessor shall be considered as a creditor or credit intermediary referred to in 35°, c), last sentence.*"[1768] Due to its broad definition, the concept of financing lease covers any rental operation of a movable good which may lead to the purchase of that good, namely leasing contracts, renting contracts with a purchase option

1760 See Art. 5 CCD2 (information must be provided free of charge regardless of the media used to provide it), Art. 7–13 CCD2 (pre-contractual information requirements) and Art. 20–21 CCD2 (form and information to be included in the credit agreement).

1761 Art. 18–19 CCD2.

1762 Art. 26–27 CCD2.

1763 Art. 14–17 CCD2.

1764 Art. 30–31 CCD2.

1765 Art. 32–33 CCD2 and Art. 37–38 CCD2.

1766 See Recital 10 CCD1.

1767 Art. VII.80-VII.82 BCEL. See for a discussion of these rules e.g. E. Van Poucke (ed.), *Kredieten voor consumenten*, Antwerp, Intersentia, 2021, 41 *et seq.*; D. Blommaert and J. Vannerom, "Commentaar bij art. VII.80 WER" in *Comm.Bijz.Ov*, Mechelen, Wolters Kluwer, loose-leaf, 2018, (81) 81–84.

1768 Art. I.9, 47° BCEL.

and hire purchase contracts.[1769] However, this leads to an inconsistency that the Belgian legislator does not seem to have noticed.[1770] On the one hand, according to Article VII.3(2), 2° BCEL, a rental contract that only contains a purchase option is excluded from the scope of application of the Belgian consumer credit rules. On the other hand, a rental contract containing a purchase option could also be considered as a financing lease within the meaning of Article I.9, 47° BCEL, resulting in the consumer credit rules being applicable. It is therefore unclear whether a use-oriented PSS (which qualifies as a rental contract) without a financing finality but with a purchase option should be covered by the Belgian consumer credit rules. According to the Belgian FPS Economy, the economic reality should be considered and that in the current wording of the law, these ambiguous cases should lead to the application of the consumer credit rules, taking into account the very broad definition of Article I.9, 47° BCEL.[1771] Therefore, it seems that the Belgian consumer credit rules and the specific rules on finance lease will indeed apply to use-oriented PSS with a purchase option. In any case, the implementation of the CCD2 will provide the Belgian legislator with an excellent opportunity to remedy this inconsistency, as the CCD2 extends the scope of the consumer credit rules to rental or leasing contracts where a purchase option is included in the contract or a separate contract.[1772]

403. Purchase option/obligation and Dutch consumer credit rules – Under Dutch law, the consumer credit rules do not apply to rental and lease contracts unless they: (i) contain an obligation to purchase the object of the agreement or such an obligation is added by a separate agreement, or (ii) they qualify as a goods credit agreement (*goederenkrediet*).[1773] Contrary to Belgian law, the Dutch legislator has thus literally implemented the CCD1's exception from the scope of application for rental and leasing contracts without a purchase obligation.[1774] However, a (use-oriented) PSS contract will still be subject to the consumer credit rules if it qualifies as a "goods credit agreement". This is a "*credit agreement, including a combination of agreements forming a commercial unity within the meaning of Article 57(5), relating to the provision by the creditor to the lender of the enjoyment of a movable good, other than a register good, provided that the period within which the credit must be repaid exceeds three months after the credit is made available or the enjoyment of the good has commenced.*"[1775] The DCC

[1769] D. Blommaert, F. Nichels and F. Bonnarens, "Commentaar bij art. I.9, 47° WER" in *Comm.Bijz.Ov.*, Mechelen, Wolters Kluwer, loose-leaf, 2016, (69) 70.

[1770] See in the same sense also the commentary of the Belgian FPS Economy on Art. VII.3(2), 2° BCEL, available at https://credit2consumer.be/nl/article/uitsluitingen.

[1771] See the commentary of the Belgian FPS Economy on Art. VII.3(2), 2° BCEL, available at https://credit2consumer.be/nl/article/uitsluitingen.

[1772] Art. 2(2)(g) CCD2.

[1773] See Art. 7:58(2), *sub* c) DCC.

[1774] Compare with Art. 2(2)(d) CCD1.

[1775] Art. 7:84(1) DCC.

gives as explicit examples instalment sales agreements, hire purchase agreements and all agreements having the same purport as a goods credit agreement regardless of their form or name.[1776] In addition, rental contracts can also fall under the scope of the goods credit agreement, namely if they have the same purport as a goods credit agreement.[1777] This will be the case if the rental contract has a financing finality (i.e. as is the case with finance leasing contracts).[1778] According to the explanatory memorandum, a rental contract with financing finality exists if, for example, it contains an obligation to purchase at the end of the contract or an option to purchase at a symbolic price.[1779] In addition, this may also be the case if the lessee ends up in "a position comparable to ownership", for instance when he is no longer required to pay any rental fees after a certain period of time.[1780] *Mudjeans'* Lease a Jeans program provides a good example of this.[1781] On the other hand, if the use-oriented PSS contract is limited to making a product available against a fee (with additional services) and does not contain a purchase option (or if it contains a purchase option against a realistic market price[1782]), it will not have the same purport as a goods credit agreement. As a result, most use-oriented PSS will under Dutch law qualify as an "ordinary" rental contract instead of a goods credit agreement (given they do not have a financing finality) and the Dutch consumer credit rules will therefore also not apply.[1783]

404. Operational leasing: use of the leased good is central – Operational leasing contracts constitute the second main form of leasing.[1784]

1776 Art. 7:84(2) DCC.

1777 Art. 7:84(3), *sub* c. DCC. See on this in detail: M. van der Weide, "Lease en huurkoop onder de nieuwe titel 7.2b (goederenkrediet) van het Burgerlijk Wetboek", *WPNR* 2017/7158, (534) 537–538.

1778 J.W.A. Biemans and A.C. van Schaick, *Mr. C. Assers Handleiding tot de beoefening van het Nederlands Burgerlijk Recht. 7. Bijzondere overeenkomsten. Deel IA. Kredietovereenkomst*, Deventer, Wolters Kluwer, 2021, no. 145.

1779 Explanatory Memorandum, *Parliamentary Papers* II 2015/16, 34442, no. 3, 25–26.

1780 J.W.A. Biemans and A.C. van Schaick, *Mr. C. Assers Handleiding tot de beoefening van het Nederlands Burgerlijk Recht. 7. Bijzondere overeenkomsten. Deel IA. Kredietovereenkomst*, Deventer, Wolters Kluwer, 2021, no. 145. See for an application: HR (NL) 13 June 2014, ECLI:NL:HR:2014:1385, (*Lindorff/Statia*), *NJ* 2015/477, case note J. Hijma (the contract relating to a phone subscription including a smartphone must be qualified as an instalment sales contract within the meaning of (currently) Art. 7:84 DCC), criticised by A.C. van Schaick, "Digitalisering en vermogensrecht" in J.H. Gerards and A.C. van Schaick (eds.), *Preadviezen Vereniging voor Burgerlijk Recht: Digitalisering, vermogensrecht, de platformeconomie en grondrechten*, Zutphen, Paris, 2019, (7) no. 41.

1781 See *supra* no. 400.

1782 See in this sense: J.W.A. Biemans and A.C. van Schaick, *Mr. C. Assers Handleiding tot de beoefening van het Nederlands Burgerlijk Recht. 7. Bijzondere overeenkomsten. Deel IA. Kredietovereenkomst*, Deventer, Wolters Kluwer, 2021, no. 145.

1783 See in the same sense: E.E. Maathuis, "De (gevolgen van de) kwalificatie van circulaire 'product as a service' contracten", *NTBR* 2023/33, para. 3.1.

1784 **Belgium**: B. Van Itterbeek, "Toepassingen – Structuur" in P. Beselaere, O. Lenaerts, B. Tilleman and A.L. Verbeke (eds.), *Handboek Leasing*, Bruges, die Keure, 2007, (179) 179,

Unlike financial leasing contracts, which are characterised by their financing finality, operational leasing contracts focus on the use of the leased asset. This means that the periodical payments are a compensation for the use of the leased asset and are generally not intended to finance the leased good or acquire the ownership of this good at the end of the contract.[1785] The lack of a financing finality has a few consequences. First, operational leasing contracts are often open-ended contracts, with a certain minimum period during which the contract cannot be terminated. This differs from financial leasing contracts, where the duration of the contract is based on the economic lifetime of the leased good.[1786] This means that an operational leasing contract can be shorter than the economic lifetime of the leased good, in which case this good will be returned to the leasing company, which will have to find a different use for it. Second, the pricing strategy of operational leasing contracts differs from financial leasing: the sum of the periodical payments does not add up to the purchase price of the good. Instead, the price reflects a compensation for the use of the good and the additional services.[1787] Third, the leasing company retains the ownership of the leased good. Contrary to financial leasing contracts, the leasing company bears the economic risk for depreciation, damages and loss of the leased good.[1788] Fourth, operational leasing contracts often contain additional services, including maintenance, repair and insurance.[1789] This is partly motivated by the fact that the lessor bears the economic risk and thus wants to keep the residual value of the leased asset as high as possible. These additional services are often not present in financial leasing contracts, as the economic risk lies with the lessee. Finally, operational leasing contracts will, as a general rule, not contain a purchase option, which is an essential characteristic of financial leasing. However, exceptionally, operational leasing contracts do contain a purchase option, albeit against the market value of the product at the time of exercising the option instead of the residual value laid down in a financial leasing contract.[1790]

---

no. 1. **The Netherlands**: D.F.H. Stein, "Operational lease en financial lease" in *Groene Serie Vermogensrecht, art. 3.227 BW*, Deventer, Wolters Kluwer, loose-leaf, 2023, para. 2.7.5.

1785 I.S.J. Houben and Y.A. Rampersad, "Financial lease en de nieuwe regeling van de overeenkomst van goederenkrediet", *WPNR* 2014/7010, (238) 239; M. van der Weide, "Lease en huurkoop onder de nieuwe titel 7.2b (goederenkrediet) van het Burgerlijk Wetboek", *WPNR* 2017/7158, (534) 534; J.J. van Hees, *Leasing (Onderneming & Recht nr. 8)*, Deventer, W.E.J. Tjeenk Willink, 1997, 8 *et seq.*

1786 M. van der Weide, "Lease en huurkoop onder de nieuwe titel 7.2b (goederenkrediet) van het Burgerlijk Wetboek", *WPNR* 2017/7158, (534) 534.

1787 F. Bruyns and S. Claeys, "Het eigendomsrecht van de leasinggever", *DAOR* 2016, (6) 10.

1788 F. Bruyns and S. Claeys, "Het eigendomsrecht van de leasinggever", *DAOR* 2016, (6) 9–10.

1789 M. van der Weide, "Lease en huurkoop onder de nieuwe titel 7.2b (goederenkrediet) van het Burgerlijk Wetboek", *WPNR* 2017/7158, (534) 534.

1790 I.S.J. Houben, *Mr. C. Assers Handleiding tot de beoefening van het Nederlands Burgerlijk Recht. 7. Bijzondere overeenkomsten. Deel X. Onbenoemde overeenkomsten*, Deventer, Wolters Kluwer, 2019, no. 50; I.S.J. Houben and Y.A. Rampersad, "Financial lease en de nieuwe regeling van de overeenkomst van goederenkrediet", *WPNR* 2014/7010, (238) 239.

405. Use-oriented PSS and operational leasing contracts – The characteristics of operational lease contracts described above clearly show that use-oriented PSS and operational lease contracts have many similarities.[1791] It is therefore not surprising that some authors (and real-life contracts) refer to use-oriented PSS contracts as (operational) lease.[1792] However, the relevance of the distinction between use-oriented PSS and operational leasing for the question of contractual qualification is limited, as operational leasing contracts are unnamed contracts to which the rules of the rental contract are generally applied.[1793] Since use-oriented PSS also qualify (at least partly) as rental contracts in most cases,[1794] a qualification of the use-oriented PSS as an operational lease will not result in the applicability of different legal rules.[1795] The importance of the distinction is mainly relevant for tax and accountancy reasons, which falls outside the scope of this book. Therefore, the contractual qualification of use-oriented PSS as an (operational) leasing contract is not considered further and instead the rules of the rental contract will be analysed and applied to use-oriented PSS.

3.4.4. USE-ORIENTED PSS AS A MIXED CONTRACT

406. Use-oriented PSS as a "complex contract" – In most cases, use-oriented PSS are not limited to a right of use and **additional services** that complement the right of use of a product are added to the contract (e.g. monitoring, maintenance, repair, replacement, etc.). Where a PSS contract concerns both the use of a good and the provision of a service, it constitutes a so-called "complex contract" which may give rise to qualification problems.[1796]

1791 Compare also with: E.E. Maathuis, "De (gevolgen van de) kwalificatie van circulaire 'product as a service' contracten", *NTBR* 2023/33, para. 3.1.

1792 See e.g. S. van Gulijk, "De juridische kwalificatie van verdienstelijking in de gebouwde omgeving", *WPNR* 2021, vol. 7326, (409) 410–412; R. Koolhoven, "Bescherming tegen overkreditering bij huur en lease van producten als diensten (PaaS)", *WPNR* 2021, vol. 7345, (835) 840; A.M. Schmidt, "Diensten in de circulaire economie en enkele mogelijke privaatrechtelijke belemmeringen", *M en R* 2017, (812) 813–814; S. Fischer, S. Steger, N.D. Jordan, M. O'Brien and P. Schepelmann, *Leasing Society. Report requested by the European Parliament's Committee on Environment, Public Health and Food Safety*, 2012, 58 p.

1793 **Belgium**: B. Van Itterbeek, "Toepassingen – Structuur" in P. Beselaere, O. Lenaerts, B. Tilleman and A.L. Verbeke (eds.), *Handboek Leasing*, Bruges, die Keure, 2007, (179), no. 3. **The Netherlands**: I.S.J. Houben, *Mr. C. Assers Handleiding tot de beoefening van het Nederlands Burgerlijk Recht. 7. Bijzondere overeenkomsten. Deel X. Onbenoemde overeenkomsten*, Deventer, Wolters Kluwer, 2019, no. 50.

1794 See *supra* section 3.4.1–3.4.2.

1795 See in the same sense: E.E. Maathuis, "De (gevolgen van de) kwalificatie van circulaire 'product as a service' contracten", *NTBR* 2023/33, para. 3.1.

1796 **Belgium**: Y. Merchiers, *Le bail en général*, Brussels, Larcier, 2015, 102–103; W. Goossens, *Aanneming van werk: het gemeenrechtelijk dienstencontract*, Bruges, die Keure, 2003, 108.

As explained above, a first step is to determine whether the PSS contract can be split into two separate agreements.[1797] Where this is possible, the PSS contract will be split into a rental contract (to which the legal rules governing rental contracts apply) and another type of contract (a service contract). Where the PSS contract cannot be split and therefore constitutes a mixed contract, it is necessary to consider how the three qualification theories for mixed contracts should be applied to the concrete situation.

407. Belgium: absorption theory when one of the components is dominant – Under Belgian law, a balancing act between the rules of the rental contract and the contract for services will have to be made. According to Belgian legal doctrine, the absorption theory seems appropriate when, according to the will of the parties, one of the two components (providing a right of use/provision of a service) clearly dominates the other component.[1798] In this case, according to the principle of *accessorium sequitur principale*, the legal provisions relating to the principal component will apply to the whole contractual relationship.[1799] Two situations are possible: one the one hand, the enjoyment of a good can be ancillary to or within the framework of a specific service. In this case, the contract for services will dominate and absorb the rental contract for movables. On the other hand, the services may also be subordinate to the provision of the good which will result in the application of the rules of rental contract. There are several applications of this in case law, but they mainly concern more traditional combinations of a rental contract and a contract for services such as telecommunication agreements,[1800] advertising agreements,[1801] and the provision of goods with associated labour.[1802, 1803]

1797 See *supra* no. 363. See for an example in **The Netherlands**: HR (NL) 26 February 1993, ECLI:NL:HR:1993:ZC0889, (*Kasteel Hoensbroek*), *NJ* 1993, 581, case note P.A. Stein as described by H.J. Rossel, *Huurrecht algemeen*, Deventer, Kluwer, 2007, 18–19.

1798 J. Vankerckhove, P. Coeckelberghs, A. Devreux, J.-M. Letier, B. Louveaux, B. Vandeputte and M. Vlies, *Le louage de choses 1: Les baux en général*, Brussels, Larcier, 2000, 8, no. 16.

1799 W. Goossens, *Aanneming van werk: het gemeenrechtelijk dienstencontract*, Bruges, die Keure, 2003, 109; J. Vankerckhove, P. Coeckelberghs, A. Devreux, J.-M. Letier, B. Louveaux, B. Vandeputte and M. Vlies, *Le louage de choses 1: Les baux en général*, Brussels, Larcier, 2000, 8, no. 16; H. De Page, *Traité élémentaire de droit civil belge*, IV, Brussels, Bruylant, 1972, no. 488.

1800 See e.g. Brussels (BE) 5 November 1997, *AJT* 1998–99, 850.

1801 See e.g. Brussels (BE) 5 October 1988, *TBH* 1989, 883; Comm. Brussels (BE) 1 April 1954, *J.C.Br* 1954, 382.

1802 A.L. Verbeke and T. Gladinez, "Vijf tendensen in tien jaar Cassatie over aanneming" in B. Tilleman and A.L. Verbeke (eds.), *Bijzondere Overeenkomsten*, Bruges, die Keure, 2017, (139) 141–143; B. Kohl, *Contrat d'entreprise*, Brussels, Bruylant, 2016, 90–93.

1803 B. Keirsbilck, E. Terryn and E. Van Gool, "Consumentenbescherming bij servitisation en product-dienst systemen (PDS)", *TPR* 2019, (817) 836.

408. Belgium: cumulation theory when absorption would lead to artificial unification of the contract – In some cases however, it is conceivable that the application of the absorption theory and the *accessorium sequitur principale* principle to the use-oriented PSS contract could lead to an artificial unification of a complex contract.[1804] This will be the case when the use- and service components of a PSS contract are less integrated, for example when the provision of a good is accompanied by maintenance or repair services or by additional deliveries of consumables. Then, it is often better to follow the cumulation theory and apply – as far as possible – the legal rules concerning the rental contract for movables and the contract for services cumulatively. Again, this has the additional advantages that the cumulation theory provides more legal certainty for consumers[1805] and provisions of mandatory law will apply to the largest extent possible.[1806]

409. The Netherlands: use-oriented PSS as a mixed contract – In the case of a complex use-oriented PSS contract containing characteristics of a rental contract and a contract for works (for maintenance and repairs) and/or a contract for services (for other services),[1807] and the contract cannot be split,[1808] Dutch law puts forward the cumulation theory to determine which rules apply to this contract.[1809] As a result, if a use-oriented PSS contract meets the description of two or more named contracts, the provision for each of these named contracts shall apply to the PSS contract in parallel, unless these provisions are incompatible, or their scope would be incompatible with the nature of the contract.[1810]

This means that if a use-oriented PSS contract has not only the characteristics of a rental contract, but also the characteristics of the contract for services or the contract for works, it will, in principle, be governed by the provisions of the

1804 W. Goossens, *Aanneming van werk: het gemeenrechtelijk dienstencontract*, Bruges, die Keure, 2003, 110.

1805 See *supra* no. 381.

1806 B. Keirsbilck, E. Terryn and E. Van Gool, "Consumentenbescherming bij servitisation en product-dienst systemen (PDS)", *TPR* 2019, (817) 836.

1807 See for the qualification of additional services *supra* no. 377.

1808 See for instance HR (NL) 26 February 1993, ECLI:NL:HR:1993:ZC0889, (*Kasteel Hoensbroek*), *NJ* 1993, 581, case note P.A. Stein), in which the contract was split into a rental agreement with respect to certain parts of an immovable property and "leased buffet rights" (*gepachte buffetrechten*) with respect to other parts thereof. See also: E.H.H. Schelhaas, "Hoe om te gaan met gemengde overeenkomsten na Hoge Raad 10 maart 2017? Is alles Haviltex?", *ORP* 2017/7; H.J. Rossel, *Huurrecht algemeen*, Deventer, Kluwer, 2007, 18–19.

1809 Ar. 6:215 DCC.

1810 A.W. Jongbloed, "Huur" in H.N. Schelhaas and A.J. Verheij (eds.), *Bijzondere overeenkomsten in Studiereeks Burgerlijk Recht*, Deventer, Wolters Kluwer, 2023, (159) 162–163, no. 169; F.C. Borst, A.S. Rueb and M.F.A. Evers, "Gemengde overeenkomsten met een huurelement en gemengde huurovereenkomsten", *WR* 2004, 20, para. 2.1.

rental contract and, additionally, the provisions of this other named contract.[1811] Both regimes then exist side by side. Only if there is a conflict, it should be determined what provision prevails.[1812]

The DCC does not indicate on how to act in case of a conflict.[1813] The Dutch legislator has explicitly chosen not to prescribe how to act if the main rule of cumulation cannot be applied and as a result it will often be a question of interpreting the provisions of the law which are applicable and the contract in the context of which they are invoked.[1814] Problems of interpretation should ultimately be left to the courts.[1815] In practice, mandatory or semi-mandatory rental provisions will often take precedence in the event of conflict with the provisions of the other contract.[1816] Yet, this is certainly not always the case and thus sometimes mandatory rental law will have to give way to conflicting provisions in the other contract.[1817] In this sense, it should also be noted that as use-oriented PSS mostly concern movable goods, few mandatory rules apply to them anyway. Which rules prevail in the event of a conflict will therefore often be decided based on the terms and conditions of the contract and their interpretation by the court.

1811 H.J. Rossel and A.H.T. Heisterkamp, *Mr. C. Assers Handleiding tot de beoefening van het Nederlands Burgerlijk Recht. 7. Bijzondere overeenkomsten. Deel II. Huur*, Deventer, Wolters Kluwer, 2017, no. 15. See for example V. Mak, "Consumentenbescherming bij servitisation", *TPR* 2019, (779) 794, who argues that the contract of Swapfiets can best be qualified as a rental contract with additional services (*huurovereenkomst met bijkomende dienstverlening*).

1812 A.W. Jongbloed, "Huur" in H.N. Schelhaas and A.J. Verheij (eds.), *Bijzondere overeenkomsten in Studiereeks Burgerlijk Recht*, Deventer, Wolters Kluwer, 2023, (159) 162–163, no. 169.

1813 See Art. 6:215 DCC.

1814 F.C. Borst, A.S. Rueb and M.F.A. Evers, "Gemengde overeenkomsten met een huurelement en gemengde huurovereenkomsten", *WR* 2004, 20, para. 2.1. C.J. Van Zeben, J.W. Du Pon and M.M. Olthof, *Parlementaire geschiedenis van het Nieuwe burgerlijk wetboek. Boek 6: Algemeen gedeelte van het verbintenissenrecht*, Deventer, Kluwer, 1981, 872.

1815 F.C. Borst, A.S. Rueb and M.F.A. Evers, "Gemengde overeenkomsten met een huurelement en gemengde huurovereenkomsten", *WR* 2004, 20, para. 2.1. C.J. Van Zeben, J.W. Du Pon and M.M. Olthof, *Parlementaire geschiedenis van het Nieuwe burgerlijk wetboek. Boek 6: Algemeen gedeelte van het verbintenissenrecht*, Deventer, Kluwer, 1981, 872.

1816 H.J. Rossel and A.H.T. Heisterkamp, *Mr. C. Assers Handleiding tot de beoefening van het Nederlands Burgerlijk Recht. 7. Bijzondere overeenkomsten. Deel II. Huur*, Deventer, Wolters Kluwer, 2017, no. 15.

1817 See C.J. Van Zeben, J.W. Du Pon and M.M. Olthof, *Parlementaire geschiedenis van het Nieuwe burgerlijk wetboek. Boek 6: Algemeen gedeelte van het verbintenissenrecht*, Deventer, Kluwer, 1981, 872 and – specifically for rental law – Explanatory Memorandum, *Parliamentary Papers II* 1997/98, 26089, no. 3, 8. See for an example: HR (NL) 10 March 2017, ECLI:NL:HR:2017:405, (*Kasteel Groeneveld*), *NJ* 2017/336 where the court ruled that the contract for services (catering services) was so central and predominant that the rules for the termination of the contract for services and not those for the termination of the rental contract had to be applied. See also E.H.H. Schelhaas, "Hoe om te gaan met gemengde overeenkomsten na Hoge Raad 10 maart 2017? Is alles Haviltex?", *ORP* 2017/7.

3.4.5. DIGITAL SERVICES AS PART OF USE-ORIENTED PSS

410. USE-ORIENTED PSS ARE OFTEN COMPLEMENTED WITH DIGITAL SERVICES – As mentioned above, the increasing digitalisation of products is an important enabler of access-based consumption.[1818] Indeed, digitalisation allows suppliers of use-oriented PSS to use "smart" connected devices that enable monitoring the use of the product.[1819] This has interesting applications. For example, suppliers can use these connected products to provide additional information and management services, provide predictive maintenance and repair services and/or for additional deliveries of goods (e.g. deliveries of washing powder when the smart washing machine runs out of detergent).[1820]

411. "SMART" PRODUCTS AND THE DCD – The DCD and its national implementing provisions are of a particular relevance for use-oriented PSS making "smart" products available to the consumer.[1821] These rules apply to any B2C contract for the supply of digital content or digital services against payment of a "price" in money or personal data, unless these data are only used for technical or regulatory purposes.[1822, 1823] "Digital content" is broadly defined as "*data produced and supplied in digital form*" (e.g. music, online videos, e-books, and digital games).[1824] Two types of "digital services" are covered by the Digital Content and Digital Services Directive: a) services allowing the consumer to create, process or store or access data in digital form; and b) services allowing for the sharing of data or other interaction with data in digital form uploaded or created by the consumer or other users of that service.[1825]

1818 See *supra* no. 22.

1819 H. SLACHMUYLDERS, "Belgian draft law for digital content and digital services – relevance for Product as a Service contracts", *CCM Blog* 10 January 2022, https://law.kuleuven.be/ccm/blog/?p=286.

1820 H. SLACHMUYLDERS, B. KEIRSBILCK, E. TERRYN and E. VAN GOOL, "Duurzaam ondernemen en het recht: circulaire bedrijfsmodellen – juridische knelpunten" in *De rol van de bedrijfsjurist in de duurzame ontwikkeling van de onderneming / Le rôle du juriste d'entreprise dans le développement durable: Jaarboek Dag van de bedrijfsjurist 2020/Annuaire Journée du juriste d'entreprise 2020*, Brussels, Larcier, 2021, (7) 28–29; B. KEIRSBILCK, E. TERRYN and E. VAN GOOL, "Consumentenbescherming bij servitisation en product-dienst systemen (PDS)", *TPR* 2019, (817) 830, 838 and 839.

1821 H. SLACHMUYLDERS, "Belgian draft law for digital content and digital services – relevance for Product as a Service contracts", *CCM Blog* 10 January 2022, https://law.kuleuven.be/ccm/blog/?p=286.

1822 EU: Art. 3(1)-(3) DCD. **Belgium**: Art. 1701/2, §1-§2 old BCC. **The Netherlands**: Art. 50ab(1) DCC.

1823 J. VANHERPE, "White Smoke, but Smoke Nonetheless: Some (Burning) Questions Regarding the Directives on Sale of Goods and Supply of Digital Content", *ERPL* 2020, (251) 255; J. MORAIS CARVALHO, "Sale of Goods and Supply of Digital Content and Digital Services – Overview of Directives 2019/770 and 2019/771", *EuCML* 2019, (194) 197.

1824 EU: Art. 2(1) DCD. **Belgium**: Art. 1701/1, 1° old BCC. **The Netherlands**: Art. 50aa, *sub* a. DCC.

1825 EU: Art. 2(2) DCD. **Belgium**: Art. 1701/1, 2° old BCC. **The Netherlands**: Art. 50aa, *sub* b. DCC.

Many additional services of use-oriented PSS contracts qualify as a digital service (e.g. monitoring the use of the product, using sensors for predictive maintenance and repair, using data to facilitate additional deliveries, etc.). However, in case of a bundle of digital content or digital services and other services, the rules of the DCD and its national implementation only apply to the elements concerning the digital content or digital services.[1826] Other (non-digital) elements of the use-oriented PSS contract therefore remain subject to national service contract law (i.e. the rules of the rental contract, contract for services, contract for works) or (sector) specific Union law, where relevant.[1827] Thus, the European legislator has chosen the cumulation theory to deal with these examples of mixed contracts.[1828]

412. Consumer protection under the DCD and its national implementation – The DCD and its national implementation mainly include rules on what will happen when the digital service is not in accordance with a number of subjective and objective conformity requirements. It regulates the trader's liability and the remedies available to the consumer.

The DCD contains mandatory rules on the conformity of digital services with the contract.[1829] This concerns both subjective requirements for conformity[1830] and objective requirements for conformity.[1831] Additionally, incorrect integration of the digital content or digital service into the consumer's digital environment is also regarded as a lack of conformity.[1832] The provision of updates is seen as both a subjective and an objective requirement of conformity. First, the digital content or the digital services must be updated as provided for in the contract (subjective conformity).[1833] Second, in contracts providing for continuous supply, it should be updated during the period it is to be supplied under the contract[1834] or, in a contract with a single act of supply or a series

1826 EU: Art. 3(6) DCD. **Belgium**: Art. 1701/2, §6 old BCC. **The Netherlands**: Art. 50ab(4) DCC.

1827 Recital 33 DCD.

1828 R. Steennot, "Het toepassingsgebied van de nieuwe garantieregelingen voor goederen, digitale inhoud en digitale diensten", *DCCR* 2022, afl. 135–136, (3) 20–21.

1829 EU: Art. 6–9 DCD. **Belgium**: Art. 1701/4–1701/7 old BCC. **The Netherlands**: Art. 50ad-50af DCC.

1830 EU: Art. 7 DCD. For example, whether the digital content or digital service is of the description, quantity, and quality, and possess the functionality, compatibility, interoperability, and other features, as required by the contract (Art. 7(a) DCD). The digital content and digital service should also be fit for the purpose for which the consumer requires it, provided he has made this known to the trader at the time of conclusion of the contract. (Art. 7(b) DCD). **Belgium**: Art. 1701/5 old BCC. **The Netherlands**: Art. 50ae(1) DCC.

1831 EU: Art. 8 DCD. For example, the digital content and digital service should be fit for the for the purposes for which they would normally be used (Art. 8(1)(a) DCD). **Belgium**: Art. 1701/6 old BCC. **The Netherlands**: Art. 50ae(2) DCC.

1832 EU: Art. 9 DCD. **Belgium**: Art. 1701/7 old BCC. **The Netherlands**: Art. 50af DCC.

1833 EU: Art. 7, (d) DCD. **Belgium**: Art. 1701/5, 4° old BCC. **The Netherlands**: Art. 50ae(1), *sub* d. DCC.

1834 EU: Art. 8(2)(a) DCD. **Belgium**: Art. 1701/6, §2, 1° old BCC. **The Netherlands**: In the Netherlands, this distinction between contracts for continuous supply and a single act of supply

of individual acts of supply, during the period in which the consumer may reasonably expect updates[1835] (objective conformity).

The DCD also provides rules concerning liability of the trader in case of a failure to supply the digital content or digital service,[1836] including a provision that places the burden of proof on the trader.[1837] Finally, rules regarding the remedies for non-conformity or failure to supply, including the modalities for the exercise of those remedies, are found in Articles 13 to 14 DCD.[1838]

Additionally, the Directive discusses the rights and obligations of the parties in the event of termination of the contract;[1839] provides in rules on the modification of the digital content and digital services;[1840] and contains a right of redress of the trader against the producer.[1841]

3.5. QUALIFICATION OF RESULT-ORIENTED PSS

413. CONTRACTUAL QUALIFICATION OF RESULT-ORIENTED PSS – This section addresses the contractual qualification of result-oriented PSS. These PSS contracts go one step further than use-oriented PSS. Indeed, result-oriented PSS are characterised by the fact that the PSS user does not want to acquire the ownership or obtain a right of use for one or more specific products. Instead, the PSS user wants an integrated service that guarantees a **specific functional result.**[1842]

3.5.1. SPECIFIC FUNCTIONAL RESULT IMPLIES QUALIFICATION AS SERVICES CONTRACT

414. BELGIUM: RESULT-ORIENTED PSS AS CONTRACT FOR SERVICES (“*AANNEMING*”) – In contrast to product-oriented and use-oriented PSS, result-oriented PSS will generally not constitute a mixed contract. This is because the object (*het voorwerp, l'objet*) of result-oriented PSS contracts is an integrated

or a series of individual acts of supply was not implemented. Consequently, under Dutch law, it seems that Art. 50ae(4) DCC applies across the board. This does not necessarily have to be a problem, as it can be argued that the consumer may reasonably expect updates during the period digital content or digital services have to be continuously supplied under the contract.

1835 EU: Art. 8(2)(b) DCD. **Belgium**: Art. 1701/6, §2, 2° old BCC. **The Netherlands**: Art. 50ae(4) DCC.

1836 EU: Art. 11 DCD. **Belgium**: Art. 1701/8 old BCC. **The Netherlands**: Art. 50ag DCC.

1837 EU: Art. 12 DCD. **Belgium**: Art. 1701/8, §1 old BCC. **The Netherlands**: Art. 50af(3) DCC.

1838 **Belgium**: Art. 1701/9–1701/12 old BCC. **The Netherlands**: Art. 50ah-50ai DCC.

1839 EU: Art. 15–17 DCD. **Belgium**: Art. 1701/13–1701/15 old BCC. **The Netherlands**: Art. 50aj-50ak and Art. 50ao DCC.

1840 EU: Art. 18 DCD. **Belgium**: Art. 1701/17 old BCC. **The Netherlands**: Art. 50al DCC.

1841 EU: Art. 20 DCD. **Belgium**: Art. 1701/16 old BCC. **The Netherlands**: Art. 50am *juncto* Art. 7:24–7:25 DCC.

1842 See *supra* no. 8.

service, rather than a combination of two or more named contracts. Under Belgian law, the question of the qualification of result-oriented PSS contracts will as a result, in most cases, result in the application of the rules of the contract for services to the entire PSS contract.[1843] As we shall see, result-oriented PSS do indeed contain all the essential elements of the contract for services[1844] already discussed above.[1845]

First, there is no relationship of subordination between the PSS supplier and the PSS user. Second, the performance of material of intellectual acts consists in offering, designing, and realising certain services to the PSS user, varying from offering light or ventilation "as a service" to the provision of printing solutions, engine power, etc. Finally, result-oriented PSS are provided against a counter performance, usually for a certain fee that is not related to the full purchase or investment cost of the products used to achieve the functional result.[1846]

415. Differences from other named and unnamed contracts – In addition, the difference between result-oriented PSS and other named (and unnamed) contracts is also clear.

First, result-oriented PSS clearly differ from the rental of goods.[1847] After all, the object of a result-oriented PSS contract is not the enjoyment of a specific good, but rather a specific functional result, i.e. a service. Although, in practice, the provision of a service will usually involve the provision of a good, this is not the finality of the result-oriented PSS contract. An important consequence of this is that the PSS provider can use different goods for the provision of the service during the duration of the PSS agreement, as long as these different goods allow for the functional result to be achieved.

Second, a result-oriented PSS agreement also clearly differs from a loan agreement (*bruikleen, prêt à usage*). A loan agreement creates a temporary right of use to a good and is established by the delivery of the good.[1848] The same

---

1843 A. Van Vaerenbergh and F. Leyman, "'Product als dienst'-overeenkomsten, een stap in de richting van de circulaire economie", *MER* 2019, (20) 23; B. Keirsbilck, E. Terryn and E. Van Gool, "Consumentenbescherming bij servitisation en product-dienst systemen (PDS)", *TPR* 2019, (817) 838.

1844 See *supra* no. 380.

1845 Cass. (BE) 3 September 2010, *Arr.Cass.* 2010, 2091, *Pas.* 2010, 2187, *RW* 2011–12, 565, case note B. Van Den Bergh; A. Van Oevelen, *Overeenkomsten. 2: Bijzondere overeenkomsten: E. Aanneming van werk, lastgeving, in Beginselen van Belgisch Privaatrecht*, Mechelen, Wolters Kluwer, 2017, 17–18.

1846 A. Van Vaerenbergh and F. Leyman, "'Product als dienst'-overeenkomsten, een stap in de richting van de circulaire economie", *MER* 2019, (20) 23.

1847 Art. 1709 old BCC.

1848 See the definition in Art. 1875 old BCC: loan or commodate is a contract whereby one party gives an item to another to use, with an obligation on the party receiving the item to return it after using it. See also: S. Vanderheyde, "Bruikleen" in E. Dirix and A. Van Oevelen (eds.), *Bijzondere overeenkomsten. Artikelsgewijze commentaar met overzicht van rechtspraak en rechtsleer*, Mechelen, Wolters Kluwer, 2016, (25) 25–26.

reasoning applies here: with a result-oriented PSS contract, the PSS user does not want to obtain the enjoyment of a particular good, but rather a certain result, i.e. service. Incidentally, the service of a result-oriented PSS contract does not necessarily have to be accompanied by the physical delivery of the object. In addition, the loan agreement is also a contract free of charge (*om niet, à titre gratuit*).[1849] Although this does not prevent certain duties and/or costs being imposed on the borrower,[1850] the free-of-charge nature of this contract makes it difficult to use in commercial relations with consumers.[1851]

Finally, result-oriented PSS contracts also differ from leasing contracts. There are many possible variants to the leasing contract, but in general two main forms can be distinguished: financial leasing and operational leasing.[1852]

In financial leasing, also known as financial renting, the leasing company purchases a good in accordance with specific instructions from the future lessee and then rents it to the lessee for a specific period of time.[1853] This contractual relationship is mainly characterised by its financing finality: a leasing contract provides a credit that is economically and fiscally more favourable than the classic purchase through a loan.[1854] During the leasing contract, the leasing company retains the ownership of the leased good as collateral. At the end of the leasing contract, the lessee may acquire ownership of the leased good by exercising a purchase option.[1855]

Result-oriented PSS, on the other hand, have no financing finality. After all, the PSS user only wants the offered service and is not interested in acquiring the ownership of the goods used to fulfil the specific functional result. In addition, the obligations of the PSS supplier in a result-oriented PSS contract

---

1849 Art. 1876 old BCC; See also S. Vanderheyde, "Bruikleen" in E. Dirix and A. Van Oevelen (eds.), *Bijzondere overeenkomsten. Artikelsgewijze commentaar met overzicht van rechtspraak en rechtsleer*, Mechelen, Wolters Kluwer, 2016, (25) 31; B. Tilleman and A.L. Verbeke, *Bijzondere overeenkomsten in kort bestek*, Antwerp, Intersentia, 2020, 218–219.

1850 B. Tilleman and A.L. Verbeke, *Bijzondere overeenkomsten in kort bestek*, Antwerp, Intersentia, 2020, 219–221 and 224.

1851 A. Van Vaerenbergh and F. Leyman, "'Product als dienst'-overeenkomsten, een stap in de richting van de circulaire economie", *MER* 2019, (20) 25.

1852 **Belgium**: B. Van Itterbeek, "Toepassingen – Structuur" in P. Beselaere, O. Lenaerts, B. Tilleman and A.L. Verbeke (eds.), *Handboek Leasing*, Bruges, die Keure, 2007, (179) 179. **The Netherlands**: H.J. Rossel, *Huurrecht algemeen*, Deventer, Kluwer, 2007, 15; M.F.A. Evers, *Huurrecht bedrijfsruimten*, Deventer, Kluwer, 2003, 35.

1853 J. Woestyn, P. Leroy, V. Buyl, K. Vanhove, S. Baert, A. Hanselaer, F. Burssens, H. Lamon and R. Steennot, *Bijzondere overeenkomsten*, Antwerp, Maklu, 2006, 61.

1854 K. Vanhove, "Leasing: een complexe bijzondere overeenkomst" in P. Beselaere, O. Lenaerts, B. Tilleman and A. Verbeke (eds.), *Handboek leasing*, Bruges, die Keure, 2007, (41) 43; A. Vervaet and P. Beselaere, "Onroerende leasing [Financiële aspecten]" in R. Derine, H. Cousy, J. Couturier, W. Delva, J. Herbots and R. Vekeman (eds.), *Het onroerend goed in de praktijk*, Antwerp, Wolters Kluwer, 2008, (123) 124.

1855 K. Vanhove, "Leasing: een complexe bijzondere overeenkomst" in P. Beselaere, O. Lenaerts, B. Tilleman and A. Verbeke (eds.), *Handboek leasing*, Bruges, die Keure, 2007, (41) 43.

(e.g. maintenance and repair, risk allocation, etc.) go beyond those of a leasing company, which are usually limited to financing and providing the leased good. Finally, the duration also differs whereas the leasing agreement is linked to the economic lifetime of the leased good, a result-oriented PSS contract may exceed the lifetime of the products used. In that case, the PSS supplier will have to replace the goods. As explained above,[1856] this may encourage the PSS supplier to use sustainable and high-quality products to achieve the agreed upon result, facilitating the transition to a more circular economy.[1857]

Result-oriented PSS are somewhat closer to operational leasing agreements since these contracts have a shorter duration and the total of the payments usually does not add up to the invested capital.[1858] In addition, these leasing agreements generally do not contain a purchase option.[1859] However, the same principle applies here: unlike an operational leasing agreement, a result-oriented PSS contract does not relate to a specific good, but to a service. Consequently, a qualification as a contract for services is most appropriate.[1860]

416. Contract for services: limited consumer protection – Result-oriented PSS thus qualify as a contract for services. However, as already discussed above, a qualification as contract for services alone does not clearly identify the rights and obligations that the PSS supplier and the consumer have towards each other.[1861] The old BCC regulates the contract for services only very briefly and many rules are merely default law. Where specific rules do exist, they are often too general to be easily applied to result-oriented PSS contracts and the general terms and conditions of the contract often deviate from them. Additionally, the contract for services is based on the liberal tradition, which sees the service supplier and the client as equal contracting parties. All these elements mean that a qualification as a contract for services does not result in much protection for the consumer when engaging in a result-oriented PSS contract.[1862]

417. The Netherlands: result-oriented PSS as contract for services ("*opdracht*") – Also under Dutch law, result-oriented PSS will usually no longer

1856 See *supra* no. 33.

1857 A. Van Vaerenbergh and F. Leyman, "'Product als dienst'-overeenkomsten, een stap in de richting van de circulaire economie", *MER* 2019, (20) 24.

1858 A. Vervaet and P. Beselaere, "Onroerende leasing [Financiële aspecten]" in R. Derine, H. Cousy, J. Couturier, W. Delva, J. Herbots and R. Vekeman (eds.), *Het onroerend goed in de praktijk*, Antwerp, Wolters Kluwer, 2008, (123) 124–125.

1859 A. Vervaet and P. Beselaere, "Onroerende leasing [Financiële aspecten]" in R. Derine, H. Cousy, J. Couturier, W. Delva, J. Herbots and R. Vekeman (eds.), *Het onroerend goed in de praktijk*, Antwerp, Wolters Kluwer, 2008, (123) 125.

1860 A. Van Vaerenbergh and F. Leyman, "'Product als dienst'-overeenkomsten, een stap in de richting van de circulaire economie", *MER* 2019, (20) 25.

1861 See *supra* no. 376.

1862 B. Keirsbilck, E. Terryn and E. Van Gool, "Consumentenbescherming bij servitisation en product-dienst systemen (PDS)", *TPR* 2019, (817) 839.

be a mixed contract. In view of their complex and integrated nature, they will no longer consist of a combination of two or more named contracts, but of one integrated service contract to which the rules of the contract for services, general contract law and the general terms and conditions of the contract will apply.[1863]

Indeed, result-oriented PSS contracts generally involve the performance of activities other than the construction of a tangible good, storage of goods, the publishing of works or the transportation of persons or goods, while no employment contract is involved. As under Belgian law, result-oriented PSS contracts do not qualify as a rental contract,[1864] since the object of result-oriented PSS contracts is a specific functional result (a service) and not the enjoyment of a specific good. Finally, result-oriented PSS contracts will also not be qualified as a contract for works[1865] since these contracts generally do not aim at "*the construction of a tangible good*", but instead they relate to an integrated service.

As mentioned above, the Dutch rules on the contract for services, laid down in Articles 7:400–7:413 of the DCC are more extensively regulated than the Belgian rules on the contract for services.[1866] Yet, the same concerns apply here. Most of the Dutch provisions on the contract for services are non-mandatory. The most notable exception is the PSS user-client's right to unilaterally terminate the result-oriented PSS contract right "at all times", which is mandatory law in contracts with consumers.[1867] Therefore the general terms and conditions of the PSS supplier will largely determine the content of the result-oriented PSS contract (and therefore the rights and obligations of both parties).

3.5.2. DIGITAL SERVICES AS PART OF RESULT-ORIENTED PSS

418. Ever increasing importance of digital services for result-oriented PSS – The importance of the digital content and digital services directive for use-oriented PSS was already discussed above. This applies even more to result-oriented PSS. After all, these business models are increasingly characterised by the fact that the delivered products are connected to the internet to achieve and optimise the promised result by transmitting data on usage, need for repair, etc.[1868]

1863 V. Mak, "Consumentenbescherming bij servitisation", *TPR* 2019, (779) 793–794.

1864 Art. 7:201 DCC.

1865 Art. 7:750 DCC.

1866 See *supra* no. 377.

1867 Art. 7:408(1) *juncto* Art. 7:413(2) DCC; T.F.E. Tjong Tjin Tai, *Asser 7-IV Bijzondere Overeenkomsten – Opdracht, incl. de geneeskundige behandelingsovereenkomst en de reisovereenkomst*, Deventer, Wolters Kluwer, 2022, no. 160. See also *supra* no. 321 and no. 378.

1868 H. Slachmuylders, B. Keirsbilck, E. Terryn and E. Van Gool, "Duurzaam ondernemen en het recht: circulaire bedrijfsmodellen – juridische knelpunten" in *De rol van de*

419. Digital services subject to conformity rules of DCD – As already discussed above in the context of use-oriented PSS,[1869] where the result-oriented PSS includes a "bundle" of digital content and digital services and other services, the rules of the DCD and its national implementation apply to the elements concerning the digital content or digital services.[1870] Other (non-digital) elements of the result-oriented PSS contract remain subject to national service contract law,[1871] which will be the contract for services under both Belgian and Dutch law. Thus, such PSS contracts are considered a mixed contract where the cumulation theory is applied.

3.6. CONCLUSION

420. Contractual qualification of three main types of PSS: conclusion – The purpose of this chapter was to address the question of contractual qualification in order to determine which national (default) rules apply to the three main types of PSS contracts. This chapter thus discussed (i) some general aspects of contractual interpretation; (ii) the qualification of product-oriented PSS; (iii) the qualification of use-oriented PSS and (iv) the qualification of result-oriented PSS.

Nevertheless, it is important to keep in mind that it will not always be obvious to classify a given business model into one of these three types of PSS contracts (and the corresponding contractual qualification). In practice, real-life PSS offerings in many cases exhibit characteristics of both use- and result-oriented PSS and there is often no clear-cut borderline. Consequently, the issue of contractual qualification of PSS business models will often need to be considered on a case-by-case basis, applying the principles set out in this chapter.

421. Conclusion on general principles of contractual interpretation – The first section of this chapter dealt with the **general aspects of contractual qualification.**[1872] These principles apply to all types of PSS contracts.

The principle of freedom of contract, in particular the freedom for the contracting parties to determine the content of their contract, allows the contracting parties to put their stamp on the qualification of a PSS contract

bedrijfsjurist in de duurzame ontwikkeling van de onderneming / Le rôle du juriste d'entreprise dans le développement durable: Jaarboek Dag van de bedrijfsjurist 2020/Annuaire Journée du juriste d'entreprise 2020, Brussels, Larcier, 2021, (7) 28–29; B. Keirsbilck, E. Terryn and E. Van Gool, "Consumentenbescherming bij servitisation en product-dienst systemen (PDS)", *TPR* 2019, (817) 830, 838 and 839.

1869 See *supra* no. 411.

1870 EU: Art. 3(6) DCD. **Belgium**: Art. 1701/2, §6 old BCC. **The Netherlands**: Art. 50ab(4) DCC.

1871 Recital 33 DCD.

1872 See *supra* section 3.2.

by including a qualification clause or by naming the PSS contract themselves. Under Belgian law, this **conventional qualification** will serve as a starting point. Nevertheless, the courts may overrule a conventional qualification based on the parties' common intention or if the conventional qualification is contrary to rules of mandatory law or public policy. Still, if neither party disputes the conventional qualification, the court will very often follow it and apply the rules of the contract to which the parties have indicated that they want to subject their contractual relationship. Under Dutch law, neither the name given to the contract by the parties nor conventional qualification clauses are decisive for the qualification of a contract. Instead, the actual performance and content of a contract prevail over the subjective intent of the parties. This prevents contracting parties from circumventing certain mandatory rules. Still, the wording and name of a contract are not entirely irrelevant, as some courts do occasionally attach value to these elements.

Often, PSS contracts will be **mixed contracts**, i.e. contracts that have essential characteristics of two or more named contracts. There are three theories that can be used to determine which rules apply to mixed contracts, each of which has its advantages and disadvantages: (i) the absorption theory, which applies the rules for the main component to the whole contract; (ii) the cumulation theory, which applies the rules applicable to every component in parallel; and (iii) a "*sui generis*" qualification, which basically considers the mixed contract as an unnamed contract. Under Belgian law, the BCC provides some guidance when to apply each of the three qualification theories. Nevertheless, no theory is explicitly put forward as the basic rule and the choice therefore often remains a matter to be decided on a case-by-case basis. Dutch law, on the other hand, does contain a clear basic rule. Indeed, the Dutch legislator explicitly took the cumulation theory as a starting point. Nevertheless, also under Dutch law, the other two theories are often used depending on the concrete situation.

The named (service) contracts laid down in the Belgian and Dutch Civil Codes do not cover the entire spectrum. In addition to the named contracts, there are also **unnamed contracts** that cannot be classified under any of the known contract forms. When a PSS contract is considered an unnamed contract, it is governed by its general terms and conditions, the rules of general contract law and customs. In addition, the rules of similar named contracts (in most cases the contract for services) may be applied by analogy, if this is in line with the intention of the parties and the general economy of the PSS contract in question.

422. CONCLUSION ON THE QUALIFICATION OF PRODUCT-ORIENTED PSS – The second section of this chapter dealt with the **qualification of product-oriented PSS** in the absence of a contractual qualification.[1873] Like traditional sales contracts, product-oriented PSS are characterised by a transfer of ownership.

[1873] See *supra* section 3.3.

In addition, additional (digital) services are added to the contract. A schematic overview of these conclusions is provided in Figure 6.[1874]

In both Belgium and the Netherlands, a **transfer of ownership** implies that the contract qualifies as a sales contract. While the provisions of general sales law are mostly default law, consumer sales law is largely harmonised by EU law and provides a solid (mandatory) framework for the rights and obligations of the PSS supplier and PSS user. In particular, it provides mandatory rules regarding the conformity of the product and the liability and remedies for non-conformity.

Product-oriented PSS are characterised by the fact that additional after-sales services are added to the sale of the product. Most **additional services** will, under Belgian law, be qualified as a contract for services (*aanneming, contrat d'entreprise*). The rules for the contract for services were originally drawn up with the construction contract in mind but now serves as the legal basis for all service contracts in Belgium. However, the Belgian contract for services is only briefly regulated in the old BCC and most of these provisions only apply to contracts concerning manufacturing or producing tangible objects or building contracts. As a result, the PSS contract will largely be regulated by the provisions in the terms and conditions.

In the Netherlands, the additional services of a product-oriented PSS contract may fall under two legal regimes. Indeed, the DCC contains different sections for the contract for works (*aanneming van werk*) and the more general contract for services (*opdracht*). The contract for works aims at "*the construction and delivery of a tangible good*", while the contract for services applies to "*activities other than the construction of a tangible good.*" Maintenance and repair are covered by the contract for works; (most) other additional services are covered by the contract for services. The Dutch rules on service contracts are also mainly default law (except for the (mandatory) provision containing the right for the PSS user-client to unilaterally terminate the PSS contract at all times) and offer a lower level of consumer protection than the rules governing consumer sales contracts.

Unless the product-oriented PSS contract consists of two or more independent and separate agreements – i.e. a sales contract and (at least) a service contract – it will be considered a **mixed contract**. Consequently, a balancing act must be made between the rules of the sales contract and the rules for the applicable service contract(s).

B2C product-oriented PSS contracts where the sale of the product is complemented with an **installation** under Belgian law always qualify as sales contracts (i.e. an application of the absorption theory). Under Dutch law, the cumulation theory is used for these contracts. There will be both a sales contract and a contract for works, but the non-conformity regime of the consumer sales contract also applies to faulty installation.

[1874] See *infra* p. 333.

For **mixed product-oriented PSS contracts** supplemented by **other additional services** than installation, the cumulation theory is often the most suitable qualification theory. In the Netherlands, this theory is put forward as the starting point, but also in Belgium it is used to avoid an artificial unification of the contract. Since product-oriented PSS contracts are often supplemented by additional services that are less integrated with the delivery (e.g. maintenance, repair, information services, etc.), it is therefore appropriate to apply the rules of the different legal regimes cumulatively. In practice, this means that both under Belgian and Dutch law, the rules of the sales contract will apply to the transfer of ownership. In Belgium, the contract for services will apply to all non-digital services, while in the Netherlands the contract for works will apply to maintenance and repair and other services will be governed by the more general contract for services.

Finally, this section discussed complex product-oriented PSS that combine the sale of goods with digital services or digital content. If these incorporated or inter-connected digital services or digital content are necessary for fulfilling the product's functions, it is a so-called **good with digital elements**. Goods with digital elements fully covered by the consumer sales rules introduced by the SGD. If the digital elements are *not* necessary for the performance of the good's functions, only the supply of the good is covered by the SGD and its implementing national provisions. The rules of the DCD and its national implementing provisions will apply to the digital content or the digital service. At the same time, national law will determine the qualification of (non-digital) additional services (e.g. maintenance and repair) that are not covered by the SGD or the DCD. Thus, either the rules for the sales contract will apply to the whole PSS contract (absorption theory), or the rules for the sales contract and the service contract in question will be applied simultaneously (cumulation theory).

423. Conclusion on the qualification of use-oriented PSS – The third section of this chapter addressed the **contractual qualification of use-oriented PSS** when there is no explicit conventional qualification by the parties.[1875] PSS suppliers offering use-oriented PSS allow the PSS user to use a product for a certain amount of time, often supplemented by additional services ("product as a service"). A schematic overview of these conclusions is provided in Figure 7.[1876]

Use-oriented PSS that are limited to a **mere right of use** over a product (e.g. washing machine, coffee maker) against a fee – and therefore do not comprise additional services – will qualify as a rental contract for movables (*huur van roerende goederen, location de biens mobiliers*). The rules applicable to the rental contract for movables provide a useful starting point for the rights and obligations of the parties to the PSS contract. Yet, both under Belgian and

[1875] See *supra* section 3.4.

[1876] See *infra* p. 334.

Dutch law these rules are rather limited and often non-mandatory. This gives the parties, and in particular the PSS supplier, a far-reaching freedom to include terms in the PSS contract that are not always to the consumer's benefit.

Use-oriented PSS can also entail a **short-term and occasional service** rather than a right of use of a product over a certain period. Examples include a "pay-per-use" washing machine or "free floating" e-scooter. In this situation, it could be argued that a qualification as contract for services (BE: *aanneming, contrat d'entreprise*; NL: *opdracht*) is more appropriate. A possible criterion for deciding between a qualification as a rental contract or a contract for services is whether the product is permanently in the control of the PSS user.

Some use-oriented PSS share similarities with a **leasing model**. There are two main forms of leasing contracts, namely financial leasing and operational leasing. Financial leasing contracts are characterised by their financing finality, which generally translates in the fact that sum of the monthly payments adds up to the full amount invested by the leasing company. At the end of the contract, the lessee will have the option (or even the obligation) to purchase the leased good at the residual value included in the leasing contract. Use-oriented PSS, however, generally do not have a financing finality. As such, they resemble more operational leasing contracts, where the use of the leased good is central to the operation. These contracts will generally not contain a purchase option, and if they do, this purchase option will be at the market price of the leased good. Leasing contracts are unnamed contracts and therefore not regulated in the Belgian and Dutch Civil Codes. Due to their *sui generis* nature, inspiration is drawn from other named contracts for determining the rules applicable to them, most notably the rental contract.

Whether the use-oriented PSS contract contains a purchase option (or even a purchase obligation) is important for the applicability of the consumer credit rules. Under the CCD1, rental and leasing contracts are excluded from the scope if they do not contain a purchase *obligation*. However, this will change in the future as the CCD2 extends the scope to include rental and leasing contracts with a purchase *option*. Under national law, we see that in Belgium, use-oriented PSS with a purchase option will most likely fall within the scope of the concept of financing lease, and therefore the consumer credit rules will apply. However, there are some inconsistencies regarding the general scope of application of Book 7 BCEL and the concept of financial leasing that will hopefully be resolved by the Belgian legislator following the implementation of the CCD2. Under Dutch law, rental, and leasing contracts (and therefore also use-oriented PSS) are excluded from the scope of the consumer credit rules, unless they constitute a goods credit agreement. Examples of the latter include instalment sales agreements, hire purchase agreements and all agreements having the same purport as a goods credit agreement regardless of their form or name. However, as use-oriented PSS generally do not have a financing finality, the Dutch rules on goods credit and Dutch consumer credit rules will only rarely apply.

A type of PSS contracts that resemble leasing contracts are fixed term contracts where the sum of the periodical fees together adds up to the sales price of the product. These contracts are qualified as **hire purchase**, which is essentially an instalment sales contract but under the form of a rental contract. In these contracts, the ownership of the product automatically passes after the PSS user has paid the last periodical fee. The rental fees are charged on the "sales price", after which, upon full payment, the rental contract is converted into a sales contract.

In most cases, **user-oriented PSS** are **supplemented by additional services**. These are mixed contracts to which the known qualification theories must be applied. When one of the components (rental contract or service contract) is dominant, it is appropriate to use the absorption theory and apply the rules of the dominant component to the entire contract. However, often the rental- and service components of a use-oriented PSS are less integrated (e.g. right of use and maintenance). Then, it is better to use the cumulation theory to avoid an artificial unification of the agreement.

Finally, if **digital services** are added to the use-oriented PSS contract, the rules of the DCD apply to the elements concerning the digital service. Yet, other elements of the contract remain subject to national service contract law (e.g. rental contract, contract for services, contract for works).

424. Conclusion on qualification of result-oriented PSS – The fourth section of this chapter addressed the **contractual qualification of result-oriented PSS** in the absence of an explicit conventional qualification by the parties.[1877] Result-oriented PSS are characterised by the fact that the PSS user does not want to acquire the ownership of the product nor obtain a right of use for one or more specific products. Instead, the PSS user wants an integrated service that guarantees a specific functional result. A schematic overview of these conclusions is provided in Figure 8.[1878]

Under Belgian law, the fact that the object of result-oriented PSS contracts is an integrated service rather than a combination of two or more named contracts means that the rules of the **contract for services** will generally apply to the entire PSS contract. Under Dutch law, result-oriented PSS will also usually no longer be a mixed contract. Indeed, rather than a combination of two or more named contracts, result-oriented PSS are to be considered an integrated service contract to which the rules of the contract for services, general contract law and the general terms and conditions of the PSS contract will apply. Both under Belgian and Dutch law, most of the provisions of the contract for services are non-mandatory (except for the client's unilateral termination right under Dutch law) and only provide limited consumer protection. Therefore, the terms and conditions of the PSS supplier will largely determine the content of the contract.

1877 See *supra* section 3.5.

1878 See *infra* p. 334.

Where the result-oriented PSS also includes **digital services or digital content**, the rules of the DCD and its national implementation apply to the elements concerning the digital content or digital services. Other (non-digital) elements of the result-oriented PSS contract remain subject to the national rules of the contract for services.

Figure 6. Schematic overview of contractual qualification of product-oriented PSS[1879]

	Sales contract	**Contract for services** (*Aanneming/ contrat d'entreprise* (BE); *opdracht* (NL))	**Contract for works** (*Aanneming van werk* (NL))	**Contract for the supply of digital content and digital services**
Sale of a product with installation	BE: X NL: X (Transfer of ownership) (BE: B2C installation services absorbed by consumer sales contract)	BE: / NL: /	BE: n/a NL: X (NL: B2C installation services covered by the rules of the contract for works, but non-conformity rules consumer sales apply)	BE: / NL: /
Complex product-oriented PSS (e.g. additional maintenance and repair services)	BE: X NL: X (Transfer of ownership)	BE: X NL: X (Maintenance and repair services (BE)) (Other, non-digital, services (BE, NL))	BE: n/a NL: X (Maintenance and repair services (NL))	BE: X NL: X (Digital elements not necessary for performing the good's functions)
Complex product-oriented PSS for "good with digital elements"	BE: X NL: X (Transfer of ownership) (Digital services necessary for performing the good's functions)	BE: X NL: X (Maintenance and repair services (BE)) (Other, non-digital, services (BE, NL))	BE: n/a NL: X (Maintenance and repair services (NL))	BE: / NL: /

1879 See for a discussion of the content in this Figure *supra* no. 422.

Figure 7. Schematic overview of contractual qualification of use-oriented PSS[1880]

<table>
<tr><th></th><th>Rental contract</th><th>Contract for services

(Aanneming/ contrat d'entreprise (BE); opdracht (NL))</th><th>Contract for works

(Aanneming van werk (NL))</th><th>Contract for the supply of digital content and digital services</th></tr>
<tr><td>Mere right of use (e.g. washing machine without additional services)</td><td>BE: X

NL: X</td><td>BE: /

NL: /</td><td>BE: n/a

NL: /</td><td>/</td></tr>
<tr><td rowspan="2">Short-term and occasional service (e.g. "pay-per-use" washing machine, e-scooter)</td><td>X

(If good = permanently in control of user)</td><td>/

(If good ≠ permanently in control of user)</td><td rowspan="2">BE: n/a

NL: /</td><td rowspan="2">X

(If digital services are included, which will often be the case)</td></tr>
<tr><td>/

(If good = permanently in control of user)</td><td>X

(If good ≠ permanently in control of user)</td></tr>
<tr><td>Mixed contract (e.g. washing machine with additional services and/or digital services)</td><td>X

(Right of use)</td><td>X

(Maintenance and repair services (BE))

(Other, non-digital, services (BE, NL))</td><td>BE: n/a

NL: X

(Maintenance and repair services)</td><td>X

(Digital services)</td></tr>
</table>

Figure 8. Schematic overview of contractual qualification of use-oriented PSS[1881]

	Rental contract	**Contract for services** (*Aanneming/ contrat d'entreprise* (BE); *opdracht* (NL))	**Contract for works** (*Aanneming van werk* (NL))	**Contract for the supply of digital content and digital services**
Complex integrated service	BE: / NL: /	BE: X NL: X	BE: n/a NL: /	X (digital services)

[1880] See for a discussion of the content in this Figure *supra* no. 423.

[1881] See for a discussion of the content in this Figure *supra* no. 424.

4. ENSURING THE AVAILABILITY OF THE PRODUCT/SERVICE

"Always a working Swapfiets for a fixed monthly fee."
– Website Swapfiets[1882]

4.1. INTRODUCTION

425. Obligation to ensure the availability of the product/service as main obligation of the PSS supplier – The main obligation of the PSS supplier in a PSS contract is to ensure the availability of the product and/or the service to the PSS user. This obligation falls into two sub-obligations. First, the PSS supplier must make the product/service available to the PSS user, which generally implies a delivery obligation. Depending on the contractual qualification of this obligation, the risk regime, which essentially boils down to the question which party bears the risk of loss or damages to the product due to *force majeure*, will also differ. These questions are discussed for the main three types of PSS in section 4.2. Second, it does not suffice to make the product/service available to the PSS user, this delivered product/service must also be in conformity with the PSS contract. Therefore, section 4.3. analyses the conformity requirements, the rules on liability for non-conformity and the available remedies for non-conformity for the three main types of PSS contracts. Section 4.4 evaluates the legal framework for these two sub-obligations and proposes normative solutions. Finally, section 4.5 sets out model clauses on the obligation to ensure the availability of the product/service for both use-oriented and result-oriented PSS contracts.

4.2. DELIVERY OF THE PRODUCT/SERVICE AND TRANSFER OF RISK

426. Making the product/service available – The first step in ensuring the availability of the product/service to the PSS user is making the product/

1882 https://swapfiets.be/en-BE.

service available, which generally implies a delivery obligation. Depending on the type of PSS and the corresponding contractual qualification, this obligation will take a different legal form. This section deals with these different obligations and looks at contractual arrangements in real-life PSS contracts. Additionally, the risk regime (i.e. the rules dealing with the question who bears the risks for losses or damages to the product caused by *force majeure*) associated with the delivery is also explored. Furthermore, this section discusses the implications of the fact that with use-oriented and result-oriented PSS, there is no transfer of ownership.

4.2.1. PRODUCT-ORIENTED PSS

4.2.1.1. Transfer of ownership and delivery of the product

427. TRANSFER OF OWNERSHIP AND DELIVERY OF THE PRODUCT – In product-oriented PSS, the PSS user becomes the owner of the product that is the object of the PSS contract, i.e. there is a transfer of ownership. As established above, this means that the contract will be qualified as a sales contract. In this case, the obligation to make the product available takes the form of the delivery of the product. Under Belgian law, there is an essential difference between the transfer of ownership and delivery. The transfer of ownership is an essential component of the sales contract and is established by the parties' consent (*solo consensu*).[1883] Delivery, on the other hand, is a consequence of the sales contract and is one of the seller's two main obligations.[1884] The obligation to deliver means that the PSS supplier must transfer the sold product to the PSS user so that he can take control and possession over it.[1885] Dutch law takes a different approach: the PSS supplier's two main obligations under the sales contract are (i) transferring the ownership of the product and (ii) delivering the product.[1886] The transfer of ownership in the case of movable goods is done by placing the good in the PSS user's possession (*bezit*).[1887] In addition, the PSS supplier also has an obligation to deliver the good (*aflevering*). This also requires placing the good in the PSS user's possession.[1888]

The concrete modalities of delivery (e.g. how, where, when and who pays the costs) will generally be regulated by the PSS contract. In the absence of a

[1883] V. SAGAERT, B. TILLEMAN and A.L. VERBEKE, *Vermogensrecht in kort bestek*, Antwerp, Intersentia, 2020, 138; M. DAMBRE, *Bijzondere overeenkomsten: de essentie*, Bruges, Die Keure, 2022, 59.

[1884] Art. 1603 old BCC.

[1885] Art. 1604 old BCC.

[1886] Art. 7:9(1) DCC. P. KLIK, "Consumentenkoop van roerende zaken" in E.H. HONDIUS and V. MAK (eds.), *Handboek Consumentenrecht*, Zutphen, Paris, 2020, (175) 181.

[1887] Art. 3:90 DCC.

[1888] Art. 7:9(2) DCC.

contractual arrangement by the parties, both the Belgian and Dutch Civil Code provide some guidelines for the modalities of the delivery.[1889] Regarding the time of delivery for consumer sales contracts, it follows from the CRD that, unless the parties have agreed otherwise, the PSS supplier must deliver the goods without undue delay and in any case within 30 days from the conclusion of the contract.[1890] Where the PSS supplier has failed to fulfil his obligation to deliver the goods at the time agreed upon with the PSS user-consumer or within the time limit of 30 days, the PSS user-consumer shall call upon the PSS supplier to make the delivery within an additional period of time appropriate to the circumstances. Failure to deliver within this additional period entitles the PSS user to terminate the contract.[1891] In addition, Belgian law blacklists clauses that grant the PSS supplier the right to unilaterally determine or change the delivery period.[1892]

4.2.1.2. Transfer of risk

428. Transfer of risk – Under Belgian law, it follows from the essential components of the sales contract that the product-oriented PSS contract is concluded when the parties agree on the product and the price.[1893] With this agreement, the ownership over the product is immediately transferred. The effect of this transfer of ownership is that, unless otherwise agreed,[1894] the risk is also transferred from the PSS supplier (the seller) to the PSS user (the buyer) at the time of the conclusion of the contract. By contrast, under Dutch law, delivery determines the transfer of risk.[1895] From the moment of delivery, the good is at the buyer's risk.[1896] In case of a product-oriented PSS contract where the product is shipped to the consumer, the CRD provides for a (mandatory) risk regime which is in line with the Dutch approach but deviates from the Belgian one. In this case, the risk of loss or damage to the product is only transferred when

---

1889 **Belgium**: Art. 1606 old BCC (the delivery of movable goods is done by actual handover, by handover of the keys to the building in which they are located, or by the mere consent of the parties if the handover cannot be made at the time of the sale, or if the buyer already had the goods in his possession in another capacity); Art. 1608 old BCC (in absence of a different contractual arrangement, costs of the delivery are for the seller and costs for the collection are for the buyer) and Art. 1609 old BCC (Unless otherwise agreed, delivery shall be made at the place where the goods sold were located at the time of sale). **The Netherlands**: Art. 7:9(2) DCC (Delivery means placing the good in the possession of the buyer) and Art. 7:12 DCC (Costs of delivery, including weighing and counting, shall be borne by the seller. Costs of collection and costs of a deed of sale and of transfer shall be borne by the buyer).

1890 Art. 18(1) CRD. **Belgium**: Art. VI.43, §1 BCEL. **The Netherlands**: Art. 7:9(4) DCC.

1891 Art. 18(2) CRD. **Belgium**: Art. VI.43, §2 BCEL. **The Netherlands**: Art. 7:19a DCC.

1892 Art. VI.83, 5° BCEL.

1893 Art. 1583 old BCC.

1894 Cass. (BE) 14 March 1955, *Pas.* 1955, I, 782.

1895 P. Klik, "Consumentenkoop van roerende zaken" in E.H. Hondius and V. Mak (eds.), *Handboek Consumentenrecht*, Zutphen, Paris, 2020, (175) 182.

1896 Art. 7:10(1) DCC.

the PSS user (or someone he designates other than the carrier) takes physical possession of the product.[1897] Nevertheless, the risk shall pass to the PSS user upon delivery to the carrier if the carrier was commissioned by the PSS user to carry the goods and that choice was not offered by the PSS supplier.[1898]

4.2.1.3. Implications of transfer of ownership

429. Transfer of ownership implies strong position for consumer – The transfer of ownership associated with a product-oriented PSS puts consumers in a very strong position. After all, the right of ownership is the most comprehensive right in rem that gives its holder far-reaching powers, such as the right to possession, enjoyment, use, disposition, indemnity against expropriation, etc.[1899] In addition, the right of ownership also plays an important role in the accumulation of the consumer's assets.[1900] Indeed, the owner of an asset is liable for his debts with this asset.[1901] Moreover, from a philosophical perspective, it is often claimed that private property rights are critical for the development of individuals' autonomy and for the efficient allocation of resources in our society.[1902] This can be illustrated by the fact that consumers often derive a certain identity from the goods they own (e.g. an expensive smartphone, clothes from a certain (sustainable) fashion brand, driving a sportscar, etc.). Additionally, private property rights are seen in law and economics literature as a solution to the overexploitation of shared resources[1903] (e.g. the "tragedy of the commons"[1904]) and, in the case of consumer goods, as a way of regulating access to scarce resources by enabling people to exchange goods on a mutually

---

1897 Art. 20, first sentence CRD, implemented in **Belgium** in Art. VI.44 BCEL and in **the Netherlands** in Art. 7:11(1) DCC.

1898 Art. 20, second sentence CRD. **Belgium**: Art. VI.44 BCEL. **The Netherlands**: Art. 7:11(2) DCC.

1899 B. Verheye, "Toekomst van de circulaire vastgoedeconomie", *TPR* 2019, (107) 119, also referring to the legal philosophical representation of a right in rem as a '*bundle of rights*' or '*bundle of sticks*' by the English legal philosopher Honoré. See: A.M. Honoré, "Ownership" in A.M. Honoré (ed.), *Making Law Bind. Essays Legal and Philosophical*, Oxford, Clarendon Press, 1987, (161) 161–191. See also V. Mak, "Consumentenbescherming bij servitisation", *TPR* 2019, (779) 805, no. 825.

1900 See Art. 3.35 BCC: *"A person's assets are the legal generality comprising the whole of existing and future property and obligations."*

1901 **Belgium**: Art. 3.36(1) BCC. **The Netherlands**: Art. 3:276 DCC.

1902 Y. Al Salman and R. Claassen, "From Ownership to Access. A Philosophical Perspective on the Rise of Access-Based Consumption", *Ars Aequi* 2018, (566) 567; D.H. Cole, "The law and economics approach to property", *Prop L Rev* 2014, (212) 212 and the references there. See also V. Mak, "Van ownership naar access. Is toegang de nieuwe eigendom?", *Ars Aequi* 2018, (664) 664 and 668.

1903 E.g. natural resources and the means of production.

1904 G. Hardin, "The Tragedy of the Commons", *Science* 1968, vol. 162 issue 3859, (1243) 1243–1248.

beneficial basis.[1905] Finally, ownership can incentivise consumers to treat their products more carefully than they would if they did not own them (avoiding "moral hazard").[1906]

4.2.2. USE-ORIENTED PSS

4.2.2.1. Right of use and delivery of the product

430. Providing a right of use and delivery of the product – In use-oriented PSS, the PSS user no longer becomes the owner of the product but making the product available takes the form of granting a right of use over the product. As discussed above, this means that in most cases of use-oriented PSS, (part of) the PSS contract will qualify as a rental contract.[1907] Under Belgian law, one of the three main obligations[1908] for the PSS supplier (lessor) following from this legal qualification is to deliver the product that is the object of the PSS contract to the PSS user (lessee).[1909] In the case of a use-oriented PSS contract for movables, this delivery is done by handing over the product.[1910] Also under Dutch law, the PSS supplier is obliged to place (and leave) the product at the PSS user's disposal, which implies an obligation to deliver.[1911] This means that the PSS supplier must physically make the product available for the PSS user.[1912]

431. Place and time of delivery – The modalities of the delivery (e.g. regarding the place and time of the delivery) are generally set out in the PSS

1905 H. Demsetz, "Toward a Theory of Property Rights", *The American Economic Review* 1967, vol. 57 issue 2, (347) 347–359.

1906 E.g. T. Schaefers, K. Wittkowski, S. Benoit and R. Ferraro, "Contagious Effects of Customer Misbehavior in Access-Based Services", *Journal of Service Research* 2015, vol. 19, afl. 1, (3) 3–21 and J.F. Durgee and G.C. O'Connor, "An exploration into renting as consumption behavior", *Psychology & Marketing* 1995, vol. 12, afl. 2, (89) 89–104.

1907 Art. 1709 old BCC.

1908 According to Art 1719 old BCC, the PSS supplier must (i) deliver the rented product to the PSS user (lessee); (ii) maintain that product in such a condition that it can serve the use for which it was rented; and (iii) allow the PSS user (lessee) the quiet enjoyment of it for as long as the rental contract lasts.

1909 Art. 1719, 1° old BCC.

1910 S. Marysse, "Rechten en verbintenissen van de verhuurder" in M. Dambre, B. Hubeau and S. Stijns (eds.), *Handboek algemeen huurrecht*, Bruges, Die Keure, 2015, (415) 421, no. 15.

1911 Art. 7:203 DCC.

1912 HR (NL) 23 February 2018, ECLI:NL:HR:2018:283, *WR* 2018/121; A.M. Kloosterman, "Art. 203 – Burgerlijk Wetboek Boek 7. Terbeschikkingstelling van zaak aan huurder" in *Sdu Commentaar Huurrecht*, 8 August 2022, para. 5; A.M. Kloosterman, "De verplichtingen van de verhuurder" in A.M. Kloosterman, H.J. Rossel and M.H. Rozeboom (eds.), *Hoofdlijnen in het huurrecht. Met vragen en antwoorden*, Deventer, Wolters Kluwer, 2020, (39) 39.

contract.[1913] For smaller products, such as smartphones, other small consumer electronics and clothing, this delivery is usually done via parcel shipping to the PSS user's address or a pick up point.[1914] For larger products or products that require installation, such as washing machines or furniture, it is often included in the contract that the PSS supplier (or its logistics partner) contacts the PSS user to make an appointment for the delivery and installation of the product.[1915]

Terms and Conditions Grover – Art. 8 "The Rental Item shall be delivered to the shipping address you have given."

Terms and Conditions Dressr – Art. 9 (delivery) "Deliveries will be made through Dressr's shipping partners and the method of shipping will be at Dressr's discretion. For all deliveries, you will be provided an estimated delivery date through the Website and through email once your order is placed."

Terms and Conditions Repeat/Gerrard Street – Art. 3.2 "We will deliver the headphones to the address you provided when ordering. You cannot change the address once we have already dispatched the package."

Terms and conditions Blue Movement – Art. 6.1 "After concluding the Contract, BSH or BSH's logistics partner will contact the User to make an appointment for delivery and installation of the Product."

Terms and Conditions Papillon – Art. 4.1 "The Lessor undertakes to deliver (or have delivered) the Product to the Lessee in a good state of repair within twenty working days of signing this Rental Contract. The effective delivery date will be determined by mutual agreement between BSH and the Lessee."

Terms and Conditions Live Light – Art. 5.1 "Live Light is responsible for arranging the transport and installation of the Goods at the User at the specified address."

1913 **Belgium**: See S. Marysse, "Rechten en verbintenissen van de verhuurder" in M. Dambre, B. Hubeau and S. Stijns (eds.), *Handboek algemeen huurrecht*, Bruges, Die Keure, 2015, (415) 423–424, no. 18 and 19. In the (rare) absence of a contractual arrangement, local customs should be applied. If no local custom exists, the movable good shall be delivered at the place where the contract was concluded. **The Netherlands**: See Art. 6:41 DCC. This provision also contains rules for the rare situation where the place of delivery is not determined in the contract. For individually specified goods, this will be at the place where the good was located at the conclusion of the contract (Art. 6:41, *sub* a DCC). C.H. Sieburgh, *Mr. C. Assers Handleiding tot de beoefening van het Nederlands Burgerlijk Recht. 6. Verbintenissenrecht. Deel I. De verbintenis in het algemeen, eerste gedeelte*, Deventer, Wolters Kluwer, 2020, no. 255.

1914 See e.g. Art. 8 Terms and Conditions Grover; Art. 3.2 Terms and Conditions Repeat/Gerrard Street; Art. 3.1–3.4 Terms and Conditions Mudjeans; Art. 9 (Delivery) Terms and Conditions Dressr.

1915 See e.g. Art. 6.1 Terms and Conditions Blue Movement; Art. 6.1 Terms and Conditions Bundles; Art. 4.1 Terms and Conditions Papillon.

In any case, the Belgian blacklist of unfair terms prohibits the PSS supplier to unilaterally determine or change the delivery period.[1916] Similarly, the Dutch grey list contains a presumption that clauses giving the PSS supplier an unusually long or inadequately defined period for performance (i.e. delivery) are unreasonably onerous.[1917] Problematic are thus clauses that state that delivery times are only approximations and do not bind the PSS supplier or clauses allowing the PSS supplier to postpone the delivery *"due to circumstances."*[1918] Examples of such a potentially problematic clause can be found in the Terms and Conditions of *Live Light* and *Grover*:

> Terms and Conditions Live Light – Art. 5.2 "Although Live Light will comply with the stated delivery times as much as possible, *these are only approximations and do not bind Live Light.* Live Light shall make every effort to make sure the Goods can actually be used by the User on the agreed date. *If the Goods can only be delivered at a later date due to circumstances, Live Light will inform the User as soon as possible and agree a new delivery date with it.*" (Own emphasis).

> Terms and conditions Grover – Art. 8 "[...] *The delivery periods indicated in the context of the Offer Description are approximate indications.* They therefore apply only as approximate values. If the indicated delivery date is exceeded by more than four weeks, each of the Parties have the right to withdraw from the contract. [...]" (Own emphasis).

432. Costs of delivery – If there are costs associated with the delivery, these shall in principle be borne by the PSS supplier, unless the parties have agreed otherwise.[1919] In practice, PSS suppliers often charge delivery or shipping costs

---

1916 Art. VI.83, 5° BCEL. Since the concept of 'products' also includes services, it covers both the delivery period of (immovable) goods (not necessarily under a sales contract) and the performance period in service contracts. See: R. Steennot, "Commentaar bij art. VI.83, 5° WER" in *Handels- en economisch recht. Commentaar met overzicht van rechtspraak en rechtsleer*, Mechelen, Kluwer, loose-leaf, 2017, (419) 420.

1917 Art. 6:237, *sub* e. DCC.

1918 **Belgium**: R. Steennot, "Commentaar bij art. VI.83, 5° WER" in *Handels- en economisch recht. Commentaar met overzicht van rechtspraak en rechtsleer*, Mechelen, Kluwer, loose-leaf, 2017, (419) 421–422; F. Bogaert and B. Van Baeveghem, "Contractuele aspecten van de Wet Marktpraktijken" in I. Claeys, R. Steennot and M. Tison (eds.), *Economisch Recht: Ondernemingen, concurrenten en consumenten. Postuniversitaire Cyclus Willy Delva 2010–2011*, Mechelen, Kluwer, 2011, (1) 34–35; P. Cambie, *Onrechtmatige bedingen*, Ghent, Larcier, 2009, 240; I. Demuynck, *De inhoudelijke controle van onrechtmatige bedingen*, Thesis submitted to obtain the degree of Doctor of Laws, University of Ghent, 2000, 551. Contra: A. De Caluwe, "Clauses abusives, conditions générales de vente et de service, règlement general d'opérations bancaires et polices d'assurances" in *La promotion des intérêts des consommateurs au sein d'une économie de marches*, Brussels, Story-Scientia, 1993, (445) 472. **The Netherlands**: M.B.M. Loos, *Algemene voorwaarden*, The Hague, Boom juridisch, 2018, 284, no. 309.

1919 **Belgium**: Art. 5.204 BCC; M. Dambre, B. Hubeau and S. Stijns (eds.), *Handboek algemeen huurrecht*, Bruges, Die Keure, 2015, 424, no. 21. **The Netherlands**: Art. 6:47(1) DCC. C.H.

to the PSS user. Sometimes, the contract also includes reservations for additional delivery costs because it is not a "standard" delivery. Think of circumstances associated with the delivery that require additional equipment, such as the need to use a moving lift or crane, or if the product (such as a washing machine) is to be taken to a high floor (e.g. the fifth floor or higher) without the availability of an elevator.[1920]

> TERMS AND CONDITIONS GROVER – Art. 9 "[…] All rental prices are understood as end prices and include the statutory value added tax. *Besides the end prices, further costs depending on the shipment type will be incurred*, which will be shown before the order is shipped." (Own emphasis).

> TERMS AND CONDITIONS BUNDLES – Art 6.2 "*Delivery and installation is free of charge, unless a removal lift, crane, boat or all-terrain vehicle is required for delivery and/or installation.* User is obliged and undertakes vis-à-vis Bundles to communicate to Bundles in good time all (additional) information required for the Contract, including information relating to matters that affect the (costs of and) work on installation. *Additional costs for installation shall be determined in mutual agreement and shall be for User's expense.*" (Own emphasis).

433. DELIVERY OF THE PRODUCT AS DESCRIBED IN THE PSS CONTRACT – The PSS supplier must deliver a product as described in the contract. This requires that the PSS supplier properly identifies the product in the PSS contract (or in an addendum thereto).[1921] There are several possibilities: either one specific product is indicated (e.g. by referring to a serial number, or by giving an explicit description of the product made available to the PSS user[1922]) or reference is made to the type of product that the PSS user can always expect (e.g. a bicycle with 5 gears, a washing machine with at least energy label A, etc.).[1923]

434. DELIVERY INCLUDING ACCESSORIES – The PSS supplier's obligation to deliver the product is not limited to the product itself but also extends to the accessories to that product.[1924] After all, without these accessories, the PSS user cannot have the use and enjoyment of the product as stipulated in the PSS

SIEBURGH, *Mr. C. Assers Handleiding tot de beoefening van het Nederlands Burgerlijk Recht. 6. Verbintenissenrecht. Deel I. De verbintenis in het algemeen, eerste gedeelte*, Deventer, Wolters Kluwer, 2020, no. 264.

1920 See e.g. Art. 6.3 Terms and Conditions Blue Movement.

1921 M. DAMBRE, *Bijzondere overeenkomsten: de essentie*, Bruges, Die Keure, 2022, 199.

1922 Compare with Art. 3.2 Terms and Conditions Swapphone: "*The offer contains a complete and accurate description of the Smartphone on offer.*"

1923 H. SLACHMUYLDERS, "Économie de la fonctionnalité – Le contrat de service: défis juridiques et solutions contractuelles", *Revue Juridique de l'Environnement* 2022, vol. 47 issue 1, (111) 118.

1924 See also Art. 3.9 BCC.

contract.[1925] Examples of these accessories may include instruction manuals, batteries, keys, protection cases, (bike) locks, smart plugs for monitoring energy consumption and usage data, etc.

> Terms and conditions Swapphone – Art. 4.8 "To prevent damage(s) to the Smartphone, it comes with a protection case and Nano screen protector. [...]"

> Terms and conditions Fairphone easy – Art. 4.5 "Upon conclusion of the As-a-Service Agreement, You can expect to receive access to the following: i) Fairphone 4 5G device (256 GB, 8 GB RAM); ii) a back cover protector in the colour of your choice; iii) standard screen protector with blue light filter; iv) USB-C cable if You have chosen to opt-in to payment of the cash price."

> Terms and conditions Bundles – Art. 7.1 "Bundles will deliver and install the Product free of charge and professionally, and User will also receive guidelines, instructions and a manual for use." Art. 7.2 "Where applicable, Bundles shall install a "Bundles Buddy" at the Customer's premises in addition to the Product. [...]"

> Terms and conditions Swapfiets – Art. 3.2 "The Bicycle comes with a ring- and push-in chain lock with one key." Art. 9.1 "Renter may add-on an Accessory Subscription to the Bicycle Subscription, provided the relevant Accessory is available in the city where Renter subscribed for a Bicycle."

4.2.2.2. Replacing the product with a similar product?

435. Replacing the product with a similar product? – Some of the analysed PSS contracts stipulate that the PSS supplier may replace the rented product with a similar product if the PSS supplier deems it necessary.[1926] This may be the case, for example, when the original product has become too old or is no longer supported, or because the stock of a certain product or replacement parts is exhausted.

> Terms and Conditions Blue Movement – Art. 3.1 "The User agrees that BSH may replace the Product at any time free of charge with a similar Product (provided its functionalities do not differ substantially)." Art. 3.2 "The Renter agrees that BSH may at any time and unilaterally change the type, number, or range of Products offered in a Subscription. In the event of such a change, BSH will ensure that the amount of the monthly charge is brought in line with the adjusted Subscription. This may involve connecting to another type of Subscription offered. The monthly amount will not be increased by the adjustment of the Subscription."

[1925] L. Simont and J. De Gavre, "Examen de jurisprudence (1969–1975). Les contrats spéciaux", *RCJB* 1977, (273) 249, no. 118.

[1926] Art. 3.1 and 3.2 Terms and Conditions Blue Movement; Art. 3.4 Terms and Conditions Bundles.

TERMS AND CONDITIONS BUNDLES – Art. 3.4 "Customer agrees that Bundles may replace the Product with a similar product at any time and change the specifications at its discretion."

The validity of these clauses is questionable. The Belgian blacklist prohibits clauses allowing the PSS supplier to unilaterally change the characteristics[1927] of the product to be delivered, if those characteristics are essential to the PSS user, or to the use for which he intends the product, at least insofar as this use was communicated to the PSS supplier and accepted by him or insofar as, in the absence of such specification, this use was reasonably foreseeable.[1928] The key question here is whether the characteristics are *essential* for the PSS user. This is clear if the PSS user has informed the PSS supplier of a specific use for which the product (in this case, a washing machine) is intended.[1929] If not, the PSS supplier must assume a use that is reasonably foreseeable. In my view, a (sharp) degradation of the product's functionalities and specifications is contrary to a reasonably foreseeable use and thus violates this blacklisted provision. In a similar sense, Belgian case law has already ruled that a clause which allowed the business, in the event of stock exhaustion, to replace the item requested by the consumer with another item of equal or higher value is prohibited, as soon as it appears that the characteristics of the different items may differ substantially.[1930] According to the court, the question whether the change in characteristics is arbitrary in nature or justified by objective reasons (exhaustion of stock) was irrelevant.[1931]

These clauses are also potentially problematic under Dutch law, particularly in the light of the grey list. Indeed, are presumed unreasonably onerous: clauses that give the PSS supplier the ability to provide a performance that differs substantially from the promised performance, unless the PSS user is authorised to terminate the contract in that case.[1932] There is no doubt that the identity

1927 As characteristics of a product may be considered: its nature, composition, origin, availability, date of manufacture, possibilities of use, conditions under which the product or service can be obtained, etc. See: R. STEENNOT, "Commentaar bij art. VI.83, 4° WER" in *Handels- en economisch recht. Commentaar met overzicht van rechtspraak en rechtsleer*, Mechelen, Kluwer, loose-leaf, 2017, (409) 412. Compare with Art. VI.97 BCEL which concerns misleading commercial practices towards consumers. See on this also: J. BAEL, "De impact van de wetgeving inzake marktpraktijken en bescherming van de consument op de verkoop van onroerende goederen: het nieuwe Boek VI van het wetboek van economisch recht.", *Rechtskroniek voor het Notariaat* 2014, (137) 214–215.

1928 Art. VI.83, 4° BCEL.

1929 Think of a family where the children play rugby, which needs a strong washing machine for the heavily soiled rugby jerseys.

1930 Pres. Brussels (sum. proc.) (BE), *DAOR* 1999, 178, case note G. BALLON, *Jaarboek Handelspraktijken & Mededinging* 1999, 401.

1931 *Ibid.*; R. STEENNOT, "Commentaar bij art. VI.83, 4° WER" in *Handels- en economisch recht. Commentaar met overzicht van rechtspraak en rechtsleer*, Mechelen, Kluwer, loose-leaf, 2017, (409) 415.

1932 Art. 6:237, *sub* c. DCC.

of the product made available in a product-as-a-service contract is among the essential features of the promised performance. Therefore, to the extent that the new product (including its functions) is *substantially* different from the replaced product, these clauses should, in my view, be presumed unreasonably onerous. According to Loos, who argues that this grey listed provision would not have been out of place on the Dutch blacklist, clauses falling under this description will only be justifiable in very exceptional circumstances.[1933]

4.2.2.3. Transfer of risk?

436. Risk for damages or losses borne by the PSS user, unless they were caused not by his fault – Since use-oriented PSS and result-oriented PSS do not involve a transfer of ownership, the risk regime differs from product-oriented PSS. Again, this depends on the legal qualification of the PSS contract. Both under Belgian and Dutch law, a qualification as a rental contract implies that the PSS user has an obligation to return the product to the PSS supplier at the end of the PSS contract.[1934] This means that damages to the product or losses thereof incurred during the PSS contract shall be borne by the PSS user, unless he can prove that they were caused by no fault of his own.[1935] This obligation is, at least under Belgian law, considered an obligation of result.[1936, 1937] Consequently, if the PSS user cannot fulfil his obligation to return the product

---

1933 M.B.M. Loos, *Algemene voorwaarden*, The Hague, Boom juridisch, 2018, 279–280.

1934 **Belgium**: This follows from Art. 1709 old BCC and Art. 1731, §2 old BCC. See also: R. Timmermans, *Inleiding tot het Vlaams Woninghuurdecreet*, Mechelen, Wolters Kluwer, 2018, 198; T. Vandromme, "Commentaar bij art. 1731 oud BW" in *Bijzondere overeenkomsten. Artikelsgewijze commentaar met overzicht van rechtspraak en rechtsleer*, Mechelen, Wolters Kluwer, loose-leaf, 2021, (145) 148, no. 4. **The Netherlands**: Art. 7:224(1) DCC. J.K. Six-Hummel, *Groene Serie Huurrecht, art. 7:224 BW*, Deventer, Kluwer, loose-leaf, 2012, note 21; H.J. Rossel and A.H.T. Heisterkamp, *Mr. C. Assers Handleiding tot de beoefening van het Nederlands Burgerlijk Recht. 7. Bijzondere overeenkomsten. Deel II. Huur*, Deventer, Wolters Kluwer, 2021, 121, no. 129.

1935 **Belgium**: Art. 1732 old BCC. See also specifically for fire damage: Art. 1733 old BCC. **The Netherlands**: Art. 7:224(2) DCC.

1936 See *supra* no. 273. **Belgium**: See: Cass. (BE) 16 November 1944, *Pas.* 1945, I, 34; Cass. (BE) 20 June 1940, *Pas.* 1940, I, 170; M. Dambre, "Rechten en verbintenissen van de huurder" in M. Dambre, B. Hubeau and S. Stijns (eds.), *Handboek algemeen huurrecht*, Bruges, Die Keure, 2015, (513) 582–583; Y. Merchiers, *Le bail en général*, Brussels, Larcier, 2015, 219, no. 272. See also: T. Vandromme, "Artikel 1732 oud BW – Aansprakelijkheid huurder voor beschadigingen aan gehuurde goed" in *Focus op bijzondere overeenkomsten*, Mechelen, Wolters Kluwer, 2022, (183) 184. **The Netherlands**: It can be assumed that this is also the case under Dutch law. Consequently, the PSS user will be liable in the event of the impossibility of returning the product unless he can prove that this cannot be attributed to him, i.e. if this is not due to his fault, nor for his risk under the law, juridical act or generally accepted principles (Art. 6:75 DCC).

1937 Compare with Art. 5.3 Terms and Conditions Live Light: *"The Goods are deemed to have been delivered and the risk of the Goods is deemed to have been transferred to the User when the Goods are installed at the agreed location."*

(e.g. because of loss) or he cannot return the product without damages, he is contractually liable. He can, however, escape this contractual liability by proving *force majeure*[1938] or by proving that the damages were not caused by his fault, for example by showing that he used the product as a reasonable and careful person and/or that the damages are due to the age of the product.[1939]

437. PSS USER'S LIABILITY FOR DAMAGES OR LOSSES DETERMINED BY COMPARING CONDITION OF THE PRODUCT AT THE START AND END OF THE PSS CONTRACT – The fact that the risk for damages or losses of the product is borne by the PSS user, means that he must return the product in the condition in which he received it, except for wear and tear due to normal use.[1940] Therefore, a comparison must be made between the condition of the product at the start of the PSS contract and the condition of the product when it is returned.[1941] Under Belgian law, unless otherwise specified in the PSS contract, the rules for the rental contract for immovables on the condition of the rented property at the end of the contract[1942] also apply to rental contracts for movables.[1943] Under Dutch

---

1938 **Belgium**: Art. 5.226 BCC. **The Netherlands**: Art. 6:75 DCC. See for applications: HR (NL) 1 November 2013, ECLI:NL:HR:2013:1080, *RvdW* 2013/1315 (Theft of rented sound equipment, not imputable breach of contract); HR (NL) 24 October 1997, ECLI:NL:HR:1997:ZC2469, (*Spruijt/Tichelaar*), *NJ* 1998/69 (stolen rental car without fault of renter, not imputable breach of contract). Whether a defence based on *force majeure* will be successful depends on the specific circumstances. For more examples see the lower case law cited in J.K. SIX-HUMMEL, *Groene Serie Huurrecht, art. 7:224 BW*, Deventer, Kluwer, loose-leaf, 2012, note 21.

1939 **Belgium**: DAMBRE refers to the obligation of Art. 1732 old BCC as a 'weakened' obligation of result. See: M. DAMBRE, "Rechten en verbintenissen van de huurder" in M. DAMBRE, B. HUBEAU and S. STIJNS (eds.), *Handboek algemeen huurrecht*, Bruges, Die Keure, 2015, (513) 582, no. 201. **The Netherlands**: Art. 7:244(2) DCC. H.J. ROSSEL and A.H.T. HEISTERKAMP, *Mr. C. Assers Handleiding tot de beoefening van het Nederlands Burgerlijk Recht. 7. Bijzondere overeenkomsten. Deel II. Huur*, Deventer, Wolters Kluwer, 2021, 124, no. 133. See also: Opinion AG G.R.B. VAN PEURSEM, 28 October 2016, in HR 16 December 2016, ECLI:NL:PHR:2016:1074, para. 2.1–2.12.

1940 **Belgium**: M. DAMBRE, *Bijzondere overeenkomsten: de essentie*, Bruges, Die Keure, 2022, 232. **The Netherlands**: J.K. SIX-HUMMEL, *Groene Serie Huurrecht, art. 7:224 BW*, Deventer, Kluwer, loose-leaf, 2012, note 21.

1941 T. VANDROMME, "Commentaar bij art. 1731 oud BW" in *Bijzondere overeenkomsten. Artikelsgewijze commentaar met overzicht van rechtspraak en rechtsleer*, Mechelen, Wolters Kluwer, loose-leaf, 2021, (145) 154, no. 10.

1942 See Art. 1731 old BCC.

1943 Antwerp (BE) 6 September 2010, *NjW* 2011, 339, case note M. DAMBRE; M. DAMBRE, "Bewijs van huurschade bij verhuring van roerende goederen" (case note Antwerp 6 September 2010), *NjW* 2011, (341) 341; B. KEIRSBILCK, E. TERRYN and E. VAN GOOL, "Consumentenbescherming bij servitisation en product-dienst systemen (PDS)", *TPR* 2019, (817) 852–853. See also C. MARR, "Le contrat de location mobilière: quelle réglementation appliquer face au mutisme du Code Civil?", *TBBR* 2008, (217) 218, no. 3 where is stated that Art. 1730 old BCC (obligatory rental inventory) does not apply to movable goods, but no mention is made of Art. 1731, §1 and Art. 1732 old BCC. Contra: T. VANDROMME, "Commentaar bij art. 1731 oud BW" in *Bijzondere overeenkomsten. Artikelsgewijze commentaar met overzicht van rechtspraak en rechtsleer*, Mechelen, Wolters Kluwer, loose-leaf, 2021, (145) 148, no. 3.

law, the rules on the condition of the product upon return are under the title applicable to all rental contracts. Both legal systems provide that in the absence of a circumstantial[1944] rental inventory (*plaatsbeschrijving, état de lieux*), there is a rebuttable presumption that the PSS user received the product in the same condition as the condition of the product at the end of the PSS contract.[1945] This means that if such a circumstantial rental inventory is lacking, the PSS supplier must prove that the damage was caused during the PSS contract, and that it is not due to normal wear and tear.[1946]

438. Belgian law: use-oriented PSS where the product is dispatched to the consumer: risk borne by PSS supplier until PSS user takes physical possession of the product – Under Belgian law, use-oriented PSS (i.e. rental contracts) where the PSS supplier dispatches products to the PSS user-consumer are also subject to the special (mandatory) risk regime arising from Article 20 CRD.[1947] Indeed, unlike the Directive, the Belgian legislator has extended the scope to *all* contracts where a business sends goods to the consumer.[1948] This means that the risk for damages or losses of the product are borne by the PSS supplier until the PSS user (or the person he designated) takes physical possession of the product.[1949] Clauses in the PSS contract that place the risk of loss or damage during transport of the product on the consumer will be null and void.[1950] Similarly, a clause in the PSS contract stipulating that the PSS supplier will not assume responsibility for packages that have been delivered on the doorstep and left alone by the shipping partner are not allowed.

> Terms and conditions Dressr – Art. 9 (Delivery) "Deliveries will be made through Dressr's shipping partners and the method of shipping will be at Dressr's discretion. For all deliveries, you will be provided an estimated delivery date through the Website and through email once your order is placed. You must provide Dressr with

---

1944 This means that the rental inventory must be detailed. The different parts of the products must be thoroughly described, which may include the use of photographs. Mere style clauses such as *"the lessee declares to have received the product in good condition"* in principle do not count as a circumstantial rental inventory. See: V. Sagaert, B. Tilleman and A.-L. Verbeke, *Vermogensrecht in kort bestek*, Antwerp, Intersentia, 2022, 276, no. 735.

1945 **Belgium**: Art. 1731, §1 old BCC. **The Netherlands**: Art. 7:224(2), last sentence DCC and Art. 7:218(2) DCC.

1946 M.B.M. Loos, "Servitization, consumentenhuur en consumentenkoop", *WPNR* 2022/7396, (944) 945.

1947 See *supra* no. 428.

1948 See Explanatory Memorandum, *Parliamentary Papers* Kamer 2013, no. 53-3018/001, 32–33. Compare with Art. 17 CRD stating that Art. 20 CRD only applies to sales contracts.

1949 Art. VI.44 BCEL. See also B. Keirsbilck, E. Terryn and E. Van Gool, "Consumentenbescherming bij servitisation en product-dienst systemen (PDS)", *TPR* 2019, (817) 854, mentioning that this was probably not the intention of the legislator.

1950 R. Steennot, "Commentaar bij art. VI.44 WER" in *Handels en Economisch recht: Commentaar met overzicht van rechtspraak en rechtsleer*, Mechelen, Wolters Kluwer, loose-leaf, 2021, (55) 56–57.

a safe and secure delivery location. *Once the package's tracking information shows it has been delivered, it is your responsibility to retrieve or track down the package. Dressr will not assume responsibility for packages that have been delivered but left unattended*, or that have been tampered with after proof of delivery. We recommend being present at the time of delivery and/or providing the safest possible delivery location for your package. Dressr Members are liable for Items stolen or damaged after delivery, up to price of the Items on the Dressr Website." (Own emphasis).

Under Dutch law, on the other hand, Article 20 CRD was implemented under the title of the sales contract,[1951] and the scope of application was therefore not extended to rental contracts for movables with consumers. This means that for use-oriented PSS where the product is shipped to a PSS user, Dutch law does not provide additional consumer protection against the loss of the product during the shipping process.

439. Loss or destruction of the product due to *force majeure* – The question arises as to the consequences if the product is destroyed or lost during the term of the PSS contract due to unforeseen circumstances or *force majeure*. Under the Belgian rental contract rules, the PSS contract shall in this case be automatically terminated.[1952] In the event of partial destruction or loss of the product, the PSS user may claim either a price reduction or even the termination of the PSS contract.[1953] In neither case will the PSS user be obliged to pay damages. This reflects the theory of risk (*risicoleer*, *théorie des risques*) of the general law of obligations, according to which the debtor is released from the performance that has become impossible without having to pay damages.[1954] This means that if the product is destroyed due to *force majeure*, the PSS supplier is released from its obligation to supply the product. However, because a PSS contract is a reciprocal contract, the PSS user's obligation also extinguishes.[1955] In other words, the extinction of the PSS supplier's obligation to supply the product also triggers the extinction of the PSS user's obligation to pay the price. Thus, the PSS supplier ultimately bears the risk of *force majeure*, as he will not be able to claim the price.

Under Dutch law, the situation is slightly different. If the rented product has a defect[1956] that the lessor is not required to remedy (namely because this

1951 See Art. 7:11(1) DCC.

1952 Art. 1722 old BCC. See for an application: Ct. Nivelles (BE) 30 October 2003, *Res Jur.Imm.* 2004, 7 (destruction of rented sanding machines. According to Art. 1722 old BCC, the lessee is released from his obligation to pay the rental fee of the destroyed sanding machines as well as from his obligation to return the goods (Art. 1732 old BCC)).

1953 *Ibid.*

1954 **Belgium**: Art. 5.226 *juncto* Art. 5.100 BCC.

1955 See also *supra* no. 289.

1956 Within the meaning of Art. 7:204(2) DCC, see *infra* no. 483. The situation where the rental enjoyment is rendered completely impossible due to a fault of the PSS user is therefore not covered by Art. 7:210 DCC.

is impossible or would require unreasonable expenses from the lessor),[1957] and this defect makes the rental enjoyment completely impossible, both parties can terminate the contract.[1958] As situations of *force majeure* are not imputable to the PSS user, both the PSS user and the PSS supplier will therefore be able to terminate the contract if the product is lost or completely destroyed during the term of the PSS contract. This solution is different from the old DCC, where the consequence was – just like under Belgian law – the automatic termination of the rental contract.[1959] However, this was deemed undesirable in light of legal certainty and therefore changed in the (new) DCC.[1960] In my view, the Dutch solution is better, as situations are perfectly conceivable where the product is destroyed due to *force majeure* but both parties want to continue the PSS contract because the rented good can (easily) be replaced. For example, a Swapfiets bicycle can be stolen although the PSS user took every reasonable precaution, or a washing machine can be destroyed beyond repair by a short circuit or a lightning strike. In both situations, it does not seem necessary that the contract is terminated automatically.

440. Limits on clauses contractually imposing the risk on the PSS user – Since the risk regime of the rental contract outlined above is not mandatory law, parties can in principle contractually deviate from these rules. Several analysed PSS contracts accordingly contain clauses that provide a contractual arrangement for the occurrence of a risk, namely by imposing the risk for loss or damage to the product on the PSS user, even in the case of *force majeure*.

> Terms and conditions Blue Movement – Art. 9.5 "In the event that the Product is damaged or lost (including theft), for whatever reason, the Renter shall be liable for the costs incurred by BSH in repairing or replacing the Product, as well as all other losses incurred by BSH as a result, including the replacement value."

> Terms and conditions Bundles – Art. 10.8 "In case of theft, User shall report it to the police and Bundles shall provide a copy of the report immediately thereafter. User is liable for the replacement value of the Product." Art. 10.9 "In case the Product is damaged or lost due to an external cause (such as water or fire damage but not limited to this), User shall be liable for the costs incurred by Bundles to replace or repair the Product."

1957 See Art. 6:206 DCC.

1958 Art. 7:210 DCC *juncto* Art. 6:267 DCC. See on this provision: A.R. De Jonge, *Huurrecht*, Den Haag, Boom Juridisch, 2019, 182–186; H.J. Rossel, *Huurrecht algemeen*, Deventer, Kluwer, 2007, 188 *et seq*.

1959 See Art. 7A:1589 old DCC.

1960 A.R. De Jonge, *Huurrecht*, Den Haag, Boom Juridisch, 2019, 185.

TERMS AND CONDITIONS PAPILLON – Art. 7.1 "The User is liable for loss and damage to the Product, regardless of whether such loss or damage is due to an act or omission by the User, third parties or in the event of force majeure."

TERMS AND CONDITIONS SWAPPHONE – Art. 10.1 "User shall bear all risks of any kind regarding the Smartphone, including but not limited to the risks of loss (including theft and misappropriation), destruction of or damage to the Smartphone from any cause whatsoever. These risks are for User from the moment of delivery to User. If such a risk materialises or if the Smartphone is unusable, defective or (due to a Defect) unavailable to the User for any other reason, User shall nevertheless remain obligated to fully comply with the Rental Agreement and therefore to pay the rental fees to Swapphone without any right to discount or reduction. The risk of the Smartphone shall pass to Swapphone at the time the Smartphone is returned by the User and is actually brought under the control of Swapphone or a third party to be designated by Swapphone."

OTHER EXAMPLES – Other analysed PSS contracts contain similar clauses. These include *Fairphone Easy*, *Lena*, *Live Light*, and *Saman Group*.[1961]

The validity of these clauses is questionable. Under Belgian law, there are two limitations to these clauses. First, as mentioned above, damages to or losses of the product that occurred during the transport commissioned by the PSS supplier cannot be contractually placed at the risk of the PSS user.[1962, 1963] Clauses that do aim to do so are null and void. Second, the Belgian rules on unfair terms also place limits on the validity of these clauses. Indeed, the Belgian blacklist prohibits clauses that *"do not allow the consumer to terminate the contract in the event of force majeure, except against payment of compensation."*[1964] There is *force majeure* in case of an impossibility that is not imputable to the PSS user (*ontoerekenbare onmogelijkheid, impossibilité pas imputable*) to fulfil its obligation.[1965] This takes into account the unforeseeable and unavoidable character of the circumstances (e.g. has the PSS user taken all possible precautions?).[1966] Belgian case law has already ruled in a case about a stolen rental car that it also follows from this provision that the risk of *force majeure*, which under the default rule of the rental contract rests with the business-lessor, may not be contractually placed on the consumer-lessee.[1967] Consequently, the PSS supplier will not be able to claim

1961 Art. 10.1 Terms and Conditions Fairphone Easy; Art. 4.2 Terms and Conditions Lena; Art. 9.2 and 9.3 Terms and Conditions Live Light; Art. 14.5 and 14.6 Terms and Conditions Saman Group.

1962 Art. VI.44 BCEL. B. KEIRSBILCK, E. TERRYN and E. VAN GOOL, "Consumentenbescherming bij servitisation en product-dienst systemen (PDS)", *TPR* 2019, (817) 854, no. 39.

1963 See also *supra* no. 438.

1964 Art. VI.83, 12° BCEL.

1965 Art. 5.226, §1 BCC.

1966 See more in depth on the requirement of a not imputable event: I. CLAEYS and T. TANGHE, *Nieuw Algemeen Contractenrecht*, Antwerp, Intersentia, 2023, 874–875.

1967 Ct. Antwerp (BE) 30 June 2011, *RW* 2013–14, 269. See also: R. STEENNOT, "Commentaar bij art. VI.83, 12° WER" in *Handels- en economisch recht. Commentaar met overzicht van* damages from the PSS user if the loss of or damage to the product is caused by an event qualifying as *force majeure*. Additionally, depending on the circumstances of the case, clauses that contractually place the risk on the PSS user may create a significant imbalance between the rights and obligations of the parties to the detriment of the consumer and therefore be considered unfair under the general unfairness test.[1968]

Contrary to Belgian law, clauses regulating the risk of *force majeure* are not explicitly listed on the Dutch lists of unfair terms. However, according to Loos, clauses that limit or restrict the possibility of the consumer to invoke *force majeure* can still be combated under Dutch law. He argues – rightly in my view – that these terms can fall within the scope of paragraph 1, point (e) of the indicative list of the UCTD Annex.[1969] This point tackles terms "requiring any consumer who fails to fulfil his obligation to pay a disproportionately high sum in compensation". According to Loos, and referring to the abovementioned Belgian case law, the compensation the consumer (PSS user) would have to pay to the user of general terms and conditions (PSS supplier) for losses or damages caused by events that qualify as *force majeure* is almost always disproportionate.[1970]

441. Liability of PSS user for imputable circumstances causing damage to the product – A better alternative is to stipulate in the terms and conditions that the PSS user will be liable for damages to the product, provided these are caused by circumstances which may be imputable to him. An example can be found in the terms and conditions of *Grover*:

> Terms and conditions Grover – Art. 12.2 (Liability of the Customer/Grover Care) "If the Customer is liable, *pursuant to circumstances which may be attributed to the Customer*, on the merits to Grover for damages, its liability per damage event – unless agreed otherwise – shall be reduced in amount to 50% of occurred damage. In deviation from the previous paragraph, the Customer's liability shall be reduced to 10% (Grover Care) of the occurred damage in the damage events listed below: i) display broken; ii) water damages; iii) strong signs of wear and tear [...] The aforementioned reduction of the customer's liability (to 50% or 10%) shall not apply in the following damage events: i) cases in which the device is no longer present: robbery, burglary, simple theft, leaving behind, forgetting, misplacing, etc.; ii) intentional damages." (Own emphasis).

rechtspraak en rechtsleer, Mechelen, Kluwer, loose-leaf, 2017, (453) 455–456 and the other examples cited there.

1968 Art. I.8, 22° BCEL.

1969 M.B.M. Loos, *Algemene voorwaarden*, The Hague, Boom juridisch, 2018, 313, no. 345a.

1970 *Ibid.*

442. Deductible in case of theft or loss of the product? – Besides clauses explicitly imposing the risk of *force majeure* on the consumer, some PSS contracts contain a clause stipulating that the PSS user owes a deductible to the PSS supplier in case of loss or theft of the product. Take *Swapfiets*'s terms and conditions, for example:

> Terms and Conditions Swapfiets – Art. 7.1 "In the event of the loss or theft of the Bicycle and/or the battery, the Customer will be obliged to report this to Swapfiets within 24 hours, to hand over to Swapfiets the key and to report this loss or theft to the police together with an employee of Swapfiets. In that event, the Customer will owe a deductible, which is different for each type of subscription.[1971] [...] After the report has been completed, the customer will receive a replacement Bicycle from Swapfiets." Art. 7.2 "If the Customer does not, or not in good time, report a loss or theft of the Bicycle, or if the Customer cannot hand over the Bicycle key to Swapfiets, the Customer will owe Swapfiets the compensation established in Table 1."

It follows from this clause that PSS users owe this deductible in case of theft even if they took the necessary precautions, namely double locking the bike (being able to hand over the bicycle key counts as proof that the bicycle was indeed locked). Theft will be regarded as *force majeure* if the PSS user took all the necessary precautions and thus did not commit a fault in its safekeeping or security obligation.[1972] This depends on the concrete circumstances.[1973] Hence, this clause also has the effect of prohibiting the consumer to invoke *force majeure* without paying compensation to the PSS supplier.[1974] It will therefore be regarded unfair, especially under Belgian law but arguably also under Dutch law.[1975]

Still, there are good reasons why PSS suppliers would include such a clause into the PSS contract. First, the deductible presumably covers the amount *Swapfiets* cannot claim from its theft insurance. This clause therefore allows

1971 The deductible is € 40 for the 'Original Subscription', € 60 for the 'Deluxe Subscription', € 220 for the 'Power 7 Subscription', and € 500 for the battery of the 'Power 7'.

1972 B. Weyts, "Overmacht bij de aansprakelijkheid van de detentor voor diefstal van aan hem toevertrouwde goederen" (case note Brussels 18 September 1997), *AJT* 1998–99, (39) 39–41 and N. Van De Sype and P. Van De Sype, "Over garagisten en gestolen voertuigen" (case note Ghent 16 October 2007), *TBBR* 2009, (430) 432 and the references cited there (fn. 13).

1973 For an application of a stolen rental bicycle where the *force majeure* defence of the lessee was not accepted by the court, see: J.P. Bruges (BE) 3 June 1983, *T.Vred.* 1984, 26, *T.Vred.* 1984, 117. Compare with Liège (BE) 19 October 2010, *JLMB* 2011, 473 regarding hotel deposit (Art. 1952–1954*quater* old BCC): theft escapes the hotelier's liability if it constitutes a case of *force majeure*. This is not the case if the stolen bicycle was placed in a room outside the youth hostel, locked with a simple padlock and on which no specific surveillance was exercised.

1974 See for another application of Art. VI.83, 12° BCEL: J.P. Wavre (BE) 18 February 2014, *DCCR* 2014, 93, case note J. Laffineur, *T.Vred.* 2015, 384, case note H. Jacquemin.

1975 See *supra* no. 439.

Swapfiets to shift the theft risk (i.e. the amount of the deductible *Swapfiets* cannot claim from the insurance company) to the PSS user, who is often also better placed to take the necessary precautions against theft. If the PSS supplier must pay for this theft risk anyway, it can potentially make offering PSS business models less viable. Alternatively, this could lead to a situation where this theft risk is factored into the price of the PSS, making the collective of all PSS users pay for it.[1976] Second, if consumers take out theft insurance on a bicycle they own, they are also subject to such deductible if their bicycle were to be stolen.[1977] Third, this deductible acts as an additional incentive for the PSS user to treat the product with care. For example, it may encourage the PSS user to think twice before parking his bicycle in an unsafe area of the city at night. In this way, the PSS supplier can combat the moral hazard risk associated with PSS contracts.

Although there are some good reasons for the PSS supplier to include a deductible to be paid by the PSS user in the event of theft of the product, consumers do not necessarily find this acceptable. In a survey conducted by CEDON, 1000 Flemish and 1000 Dutch respondents were asked what they would consider a "reasonable consequence" if the product of a PSS gets stolen. They could choose between three options ("never reasonable", "reasonable from the first occurrence", "only reasonable after several occurrences") for each consequence. Here, the results showed that respondents were more likely to find rather mild consequences reasonable, at least for the first occurrence (see Figure 9).[1978] This is consistent with the idea that consumers should not have to bear the risk of *force majeure*. Consequently, the fact that these clauses are unfair does, in my view, not prevent a fair balance between the rights and obligations of the PSS user and the PSS supplier, even though there may be some valid arguments in favour of these clauses.

1976 Of course, to a certain extent, this also applies to maintenance and repair of the Swapfiets bicycles: PSS users who ride their bicycles less or take better care of them subsidising the PSS users who rack up more kilometres or take less care of their bicycles.

1977 See e.g. Art. 4.6 Terms and Conditions of the insurance product 'AG Top Bicycle' (*AG Top Fiets*), available at: https://www.aginsurance.be/Retail/nl/Product%20Documents/24730N.pdf. The amount of this deductible is defined in the special conditions of the insurance contract and will generally be around € 50 for an 'average' bicycle.

1978 Survey conducted by C. Lavigne, S. Rousseau and J. Eyckmans. The results were presented during C. Lavigne, S. Rousseau and J. Eyckmans, "Product Service Systems. Willingness to adopt and willingness to pay for contractual elements", presented at: Third stakeholder workshop contractual rights and liabilities in circular business models, Brussels, 8 March 2023.

Figure 9. Responses of 1000 Flemish and 1000 Dutch respondents on consequences if product of PSS gets stolen[1979]

Consequence if the product gets stolen	Never Reasonable	Reasonable from the first occurrence	Only reasonable after several occurrences
Pay back full value	**58%**	28%	14%
Pay back part of the value	**42%**	**39%**	19%
Temporary suspension	32%	**47%**	21%
Banishment	**49%**	27%	24%
No consequences	15%	75%	10%

443. Mitigating the risk of loss and damages with mandatory insurance – A solution used by various PSS suppliers to mitigate the risk of loss and damages to the product consists in contractually requiring that the PSS user takes out an insurance covering the product.[1980] For example, according to the terms and conditions of *Bundles* and *Papillon*, the PSS user is obliged to properly insure the product against damage or loss due to fire, water damage and theft.[1981] Moreover, *Villo* requires that the PSS user has a liability insurance when he uses a *Villo* bicycle.[1982]

> Terms and conditions Bundles – Art 7.4 "User is obliged to properly insure the Product and, where applicable, Bundles Buddy against fire, water damage and theft, by making, if necessary, an endorsement on the policy of User's household insurance."

> Terms and conditions Papillon – Art. 7.2 "The User has taken out an insurance policy to insure the Product against loss or damage due to fire, theft, water damage, etc. The User undertakes to produce a copy of the insurance policy and proof of payment of the insurance premiums at the Supplier's first request."

1979 Table based on the data of C. Lavigne, S. Rousseau and J. Eyckmans. The results were presented during C. Lavigne, S. Rousseau and J. Eyckmans, "Product Service Systems. Willingness to adopt and willingness to pay for contractual elements", presented at: Third stakeholder workshop contractual rights and liabilities in circular business models, Brussels, 8 March 2023.

1980 The general rules applicable to the rental contract for (im)movables do not require the lessee to take out insurance for fire. However, the lessee who does not do this, takes a great amount of risk. Most often, the rental contract explicitly requires the lessee to take out insurance. L. De Wilde and E. Lievens, "Huur en verzekeringen" in M. Dambre, B. Hubeau and S. Stijns (eds.), *Handboek Algemeen Huurrecht*, Bruges, Die Keure, 2015, (240) 259. See more in depth on the liability of the lessee for fire damages: M. Dambre, "De verbintenis van de huurder tot teruggave van het gehuurde goed en zijn aansprakelijkheid voor brand", *TBBR* 2003, (620) 620–626.

1981 Art. 7.4 Terms and Conditions Bundles; Art. 7.2 Terms and Conditions Papillon.

1982 Art. 9.10 Terms and Conditions Villo.

4.2.2.4. *Implications of no transfer of ownership*

444. "Beyond ownership": weaker position for the consumer? – Above, we discussed for product-oriented PSS that the owner of a product has a relatively strong position *vis-à-vis* this product.[1983] With use-oriented PSS, on the other hand, there is a risk that the PSS user is in a weaker position than he would be if he concluded a sales contract. Indeed, a potential drawback for consumers is that the increase of servitised business models and PSS may result in their assets becoming increasingly a collection of rental contracts rather than ownership.[1984] This may make it harder for consumers to accumulate wealth and makes it impossible for them to use their products as collateral for their debts.

The bankruptcy of a PSS supplier, or even the fact that the PSS supplier decides to stop offering (a certain type of) PSS can also have far-reaching consequences. Whereas a consumer who owns a product (e.g. a washing machine) can be sure that it will remain at his disposal until the end of its useful life, a consumer who has a right of use over a product may in these situations be left out in the cold, for example when faced with a sudden claim for revindication.[1985] In some cases, the PSS supplier itself will not even be the owner, but a third party such as a bank or a leasing company, which can also file a claim for revindication.[1986] A possible solution for this problem could be to provide the PSS user with a (statutory) right of first refusal in case of bankruptcy of the PSS supplier.[1987] Such a provision could give the PSS user the option to purchase the product (e.g. at the residual value) if the bankruptcy trustee or a third party (e.g. leasing company) tries to revindicate the product following the PSS supplier's bankruptcy. Similar to the risk of discontinuation is the risk that the PSS supplier unilaterally modifies the PSS offer. This can result in a dissatisfactory experience for the consumer, for example if he must pay more than initially envisaged to get the same features.[1988]

1983 See *supra* no. 429.

1984 R. Koolhoven, "Bescherming tegen overkreditering bij huur en lease van producten als diensten (PaaS)", *WPNR* 2021, vol. 7345, (835) 5.

1985 B. Keirsbilck, E. Terryn and E. Van Gool, "Consumentenbescherming bij servitisation en product-dienst systemen (PDS)", *TPR* 2019, (817) 857–858, no. 43. See also A. Perzanowski and J. Schultz, *The End of Ownership: Personal Property in the Digital Economy*, Cambridge, MIT Press, 2016, 2–8, comparing the ownership of physical books with licensed e-books and illustrating that this can give rise to situations where the consumer no longer has access to his purchased book.

1986 H. Janssens and C. Levie, *Financiering van de circulaire economie. Uitdagingen en aanbevelingen*, Econocom, 2019, 20–41. See also Art. 6.12 Terms and Conditions Swapfiets: "*The Rental Customer is aware that the Bicycle could be owned by a leasing company. If the Bicycle is owned by a leasing company, the Rental Customer will be obliged, on the leasing company's demand, to either hand in the Bicycle to the leasing company or to be discharged from their obligations by paying the leasing company the future rent.*"

1987 See in this sense also B. Verheye, "Toekomst van de circulaire vastgoedeconomie", *TPR* 2019, (107) 180, no. 46.

1988 C. Wendehorst, "Consumer Contracts and the Internet of Things" in R. Schulze and D. Staudenmayer (eds.), *Digital Revolution. Challenges for Contract Law in Practice*, Baden-Baden, Nomos, 2016, (189) 200–201.

The risk that the consumer will be left without access to his product is not limited to use-oriented PSS. Similar problems can also arise in more traditional contracts where the ability to make use of the product depends on an app.[1989] For example, some models of the Belgian e-bike manufacturer *Cowboy*[1990] can only be unlocked by a smartphone app. If *Cowboy*, which has already gone through some tough financial times, would not get a buyer to keep the app updated after a potential bankruptcy, there is a risk that the electric motors of these models will stop working at some point.[1991] This could saddle *Cowboy* e-bike owners with a clunky, heavy and therefore nearly useless bicycle. Another example shows that these issues need not to be insurmountable. The Amsterdam-based e-bike company *VanMoof*[1992] was recently granted a two-month moratorium on payments,[1993] which ultimately led to its bankruptcy because no solution was found.[1994] Here, the same company *Cowboy* stepped in by developing an app[1995] with a digital bike key, allowing *VanMoof* users to continue using their bikes even after the bankruptcy.[1996] Another example is *Mealhero*, a Belgian meal delivery company that delivered food boxes that could be prepared in a special smart steamer. After scanning a QR code on each ingredient with the *Mealhero* app, the smart steamer selected the right cooking time and temperature. Unfortunately, these steamers became unusable after *Mealhero*'s bankruptcy.[1997] Eventually, a solution was found under the name *Mealhero 2.0*, namely by providing reusable smart labels that set cooking times which allows consumers to use their own ingredients with these steamers.[1998] In my view, these solutions are to be welcomed, both from the point of view

---

[1989] The same applies for 'goods with digital elements' within the meaning of Art 2, point (5)(b) SGD.

[1990] https://cowboy.com.

[1991] P. Van Maele, "Fietsmerk Cowboy flirt met faillissement: in het slechtste geval rijdt dan zelfs uw fiets niet meer", 9 February 2023, available at https://www.standaard.be/cnt/dmf20230209_96645193.

[1992] www.vanmoof.com/nl-BE.

[1993] D. Bervoet and B. Kurstjens, "Fabrikant van elektrische hipsterfietsen VanMoof staat op omvallen", 13 July 2023, available at https://www.tijd.be/ondernemen/algemeen/fabrikant-van-elektrische-hipsterfietsen-vanmoof-staat-op-omvallen/10480537.html.

[1994] W. De Preter, "Nederlandse e-bikemaker VanMoof failliet verklaard", 18 July 2023, available at https://www.tijd.be/ondernemen/transport/nederlandse-e-bikemaker-vanmoof-failliet-verklaard/10481229.html.

[1995] https://bikey-app.cowboy.com.

[1996] J. De Koker, "Fietsenmerk Cowboy gooit reddingsboei naar VanMoof-klanten", 14 July 2023, available at https://www.bruzz.be/samenleving/fietsenmerk-cowboy-gooit-reddingsboei-naar-vanmoof-klanten-2023-07-14.

[1997] See: K. Dee, "Gentse foodboxleverancier Mealhero failliet, klanten weten van niets", 5 September 2022, available at https://www.hln.be/economie/gentse-foodboxleverancier-mealhero-failliet-klanten-weten-van-niets~a3139f52/ and K. Dee, "Stomers Gentse foodboxleverancier binnenkort waardeloos, geen overnemer gevonden", 19 September 2022, available at https://www.hln.be/binnenland/stomers-gentse-foodboxleverancier-mealhero-binnenkort-waardeloos-geen-overnemer-gevonden~aecd3f3d/.

[1998] https://www.mealhero.me.

of consumer protection (as consumers do not lose access to their products) and from the point of view of sustainability (as products do not become unnecessarily worthless or unusable).

The shift from ownership to use and access also feels uncomfortable to some consumers. This is illustrated by the debate and criticism on the desirability of servitisation, PSS and access-based consumption.[1999] This was also reflected in the surveys organised by CEDON, particularly in the "do you have other questions or comments?" section.[2000] One specific potential problem here is that servitisation can limit consumer choice. For example, if a PSS supplier decides to no longer sell their products and only offer access-based consumption, consumers may be left with no other choice than to accept this model.[2001] This can be especially problematic if the PSS supplier is a dominant player in the market, as consumers will then only have few alternatives.[2002] One practice that comes in for particular criticism is found in the automotive sector, namely the so-called "internal product upgrades". Carmakers such as Tesla,[2003] Mercedes[2004] and BMW[2005] increasingly sell vehicles with features that are internally built-in but restricted by design. Examples include extra battery power, deactivated adaptive headlights, seat and steering wheel heating, parking assistant, etc. For an additional (one-off or monthly) fee, consumers can activate these optional features throughout the course of their ownership of the car. The difference with traditional (external) add-ons is that internal product upgrades are already built-in to the car the consumer has purchased but can (only) be

1999 See e.g. I. McCall, "You Will Own Nothing And Be Happy Now (Great Reset)", 16 July 2022, available at https://medium.com/yardcouch-com/you-will-own-nothing-and-be-happy-now-great-reset-2cb6ec88c732 referring to and heavily criticising World Economic Forum and I. Auken, "Welcome To 2030: I Own Nothing, Have No Privacy And Life Has Never Been Better", 10 November 2016, available at https://www.forbes.com/sites/worldeconomicforum/2016/11/10/shopping-i-cant-really-remember-what-that-is-or-how-differently-well-live-in-2030/?sh=ba9ab2017350 and World Economic Forum, "8 predictions for the world in 2030", 12 November 2016, available at https://www.weforum.org/agenda/2016/11/8-predictions-for-the-world-in-2030/. Although the style and arguments of this article are at some points a bit exaggerated, the idea behind it cannot be completely ignored as it reflects how some consumers think about servitisation and access-based consumption.

2000 Survey conducted by C. Lavigne, S. Rousseau and J. Eyckmans.

2001 Compare this with the rise of Software as a Service ('SaaS') which almost completely replaced the traditional one-off sale of software packages.

2002 In this sense, see also: W.H. van Boom, "Wordt eigendom minder belangrijk? (nee)", *NTBR* 2022/11, (83) 85–86. See regarding the consequences of this refusal to sell to end customers: L. Van Acker, F. Bostoen and W. Devroe, "Servitization and competition law" in B. Keirsbilck, E. Terryn, J. Eyckmans, S. Rousseau and D. Voinot (eds.), *Servitization and circular economy: economic and legal challenges*, Antwerp, Intersentia, 2023, (69) 84–89 and 91.

2003 https://www.tesla.com/support/upgrades.

2004 https://www.mercedes-benz.be/nl_BE/passengercars/services/mercedes-me/digital-extras.html.

2005 https://www.bmw.be/nl/shop/ls/cp/connected-drive.

activated if the consumer pays an additional fee. Because the cars are connected to the Internet (Internet of Things), the features can also be disabled remotely if the consumer stops paying this monthly fee. Studies have shown that consumers respond less favourably to internal product upgrades than to traditional external product upgrades.[2006] According to these studies the location of the feature (i.e. whether it is already built-in or physically detached) has negative effects for the consumer's willingness to pay, their relationship to the business, and even related third-party businesses such as leasing companies.[2007]

Yet the absence of ownership need not always be a problem for consumers. For example, there is perfectly conceivable situations where the consumer is only interested in use, rather than ownership (and the accompanying responsibilities and burdens).[2008] Think of classic examples where the PSS user only wants the use of a drill or is only interested in light and not necessarily the ownership of the light bulbs. PSS also have the advantage that the monthly cost of the product is predictable, and consumers do not face unexpected costs.[2009] Moreover, for students and (young) people who do not (want to) settle for a permanent residence right away, it can be more convenient to subscribe to products as a service instead of having to move them or sell them on the second-hand market each time they change residences. Provided that the consumer acquires an adequate right of use in these cases, and if adequate consumer protection measures are provided for, the absence of ownership does not pose a problem in my view.[2010] Also, the role of ownership for wealth accumulation and as collateral for debts should not be overestimated for movable consumer goods. After all, the average bicycle, washing machine, furniture piece, etc. have a rather low second-hand resale value. Exceptions are "timeless" products (i.e. products that are not affected by the whims of fashion) and products of exceptional quality (also in terms of sustainability), which are also more expensive to acquire, and therefore not attainable for every consumer. These are exactly the products that are also offered in PSS, at least the PSS we should promote.

2006 J. Garbas, S. Schubach, M. Mende, M.L. Scott and J.H. Schumann, "You want to sell this to me twice!? How perceptions of betrayal may undermine internal product upgrades", *Journal of the Academy of Marketing Science* 2023, (286) 286–309.

2007 J. Garbas, S. Schubach, M. Mende, M.L. Scott and J.H. Schumann, "You want to sell this to me twice!? How perceptions of betrayal may undermine internal product upgrades", *Journal of the Academy of Marketing Science* 2023, (286) 304.

2008 V. Mak, "Consumentenbescherming bij servitisation", *TPR* 2019, (779) 805, no. 25.

2009 See rather critical on this point: W.H. van Boom, "Wordt eigendom minder belangrijk? (nee)", *NTBR* 2022/11, (83) 84, who states that consumers' 'mental accounting' sometimes makes their willingness to pay for convenience greater than might be good for them.

2010 In the same sense: B. Keirsbilck, E. Terryn and E. Van Gool, "Consumentenbescherming bij servitisation en product-dienst systemen (PDS)", *TPR* 2019, (817) 850, no. 34 and B. Verheye, "Toekomst van de circulaire vastgoedeconomie", *TPR* 2019, (107) 120, no. 7.

4.2.3. RESULT-ORIENTED PSS

4.2.3.1. *Product as accessory to the service*

445. Provision of the product as accessory to the service – Where the object of the PSS contract is a complex and integrated service, as will be the case with result-oriented PSS (and some use-oriented PSS on a pay-per-use basis), the contract no longer takes the form of a rental contract but a contract for services. In a contract for services, providing the service takes precedence and the product is made available to facilitate this provision of the service. In other words, the right of use over the product is an accessory to the service.[2011] For instance, a minimum number of "light hours" will be achieved by supplying a certain number of light bulbs, a minimum number of printed pages by supplying printer cartridges, and a "healthy indoor climate" by supplying a smart ventilation system. The fact that the provision of the product is an accessory to the service, implies that the product remains under the PSS supplier's responsibility (he retains mastery over the good) which includes being able to reclaim the product at free will (*ad nutum*).[2012] Since in many cases the product will be located with the PSS user, the contract for services may be accompanied by an accessory deposit contract (BE: *bewaargeving, dépôt*; NL: *bewaarneming*),[2013] including a contractual provision granting the PSS user a right of use over the product.[2014]

2011 This is an application of the principle *'accessorium sequitur principale'*. **Belgium**: see e.g. B. Keirsbilck, E. Terryn and E. Van Gool, "Consumentenbescherming bij servitisation en product-dienst systemen (PDS)", *TPR* 2019, (817) 851, no. 34; B. Kohl, *Contrat d'entreprise*, Brussels, Bruylant, 2016, 88, no. 37; W. Goossens, M. Dambre and B. Hubeau, "Definiëring" in M. Dambre, B. Hubeau and S. Stijns (eds.), *Handboek algemeen huurrecht*, Bruges, Die Keure, 2015, (1) 7, no. 15; W. Goossens, *Aanneming van werk: het gemeenrechtelijk dienstencontract*, Bruges, Die Keure, 2003, 109, no. 122. **The Netherlands**: T.F.E. Tjong Tjin Tai, *Asser 7-IV Bijzondere Overeenkomsten – Opdracht, incl. de geneeskundige behandelingsovereenkomst en de reisovereenkomst*, Deventer, Wolters Kluwer, 2022, no. 17 and no. 47.

2012 B. Keirsbilck, E. Terryn and E. Van Gool, "Consumentenbescherming bij servitisation en product-dienst systemen (PDS)", *TPR* 2019, (817) 851, no. 34; W. Goossens, *Aanneming van werk: het gemeenrechtelijk dienstencontract*, Bruges, Die Keure, 2003, 119–120, no. 136.

2013 **Belgium**: Art. 1915 old BCC. V. Sagaert, B. Tilleman and A.-L. Verbeke, *Vermogensrecht in kort bestek*, Antwerp, Intersentia, 2022, 483, no. 1212; B. Keirsbilck, E. Terryn and E. Van Gool, "Consumentenbescherming bij servitisation en product-dienst systemen (PDS)", *TPR* 2019, (817) 851; See on the accessory deposit contract: B. Tilleman, S. De Rey, N. Debruyne, T. Gladinez, N. Van Damme and F. Van den Abeele, "Overzicht van rechtspraak bijzondere overeenkomsten aanneming (2007–2021)", *TPR* 2022, (365) 392–393, no. 22. **The Netherlands**: Art. 7:600 DCC. See: B.A. Schuijling, "Art. 600 – Burgerlijk Wetboek Boek 7. Bewaarneming" in *Sdu Commentaar Vermogensrecht*, 18 July 2022, para. 2.1 states that many contracts involve an element of deposit. If this element is of minor importance, there is no deposit contract. If the deposit is one of the main obligations, it may constitute a mixed contract within the meaning of Art. 6:215 DCC.

2014 **Belgium**: See Art. 1930 old BCC (The depositary may not handle the deposited item without the depositor's express or implied consent); M. Dambre, *Bijzondere overeenkomsten: de essentie*, Bruges, Die Keure, 2022, 531. **The Netherlands**: Art. 7:603(1) DCC (The depositary

In practice, the way the product is provided to the consumer and his usage rights will often be fully contractually regulated.

4.2.3.2. Transfer of risk?

446. Risk of damage and loss of the product – Under the Belgian rules for the contract for services, the risk and ownership of a movable good to be manufactured where the service provider supplies the materials is transferred upon delivery and acceptance.[2015] In result-oriented PSS, however, the PSS supplier supplies the products to facilitate performing the service, but there is no intention to transfer the ownership of these products.[2016] This means that the PSS supplier (as owner) bears the risk for loss or theft of the products used for providing the service.[2017] The Dutch rules for the contract for services do not stipulate special rules regarding the transfer of risk of the product. This is somewhat logical, as contrary to the contract for works,[2018] the contract for services is not aimed at the construction and delivery of a tangible good to be manufactured.[2019] So, unlike Belgian law, which does include a special

---

may only use the item to the extent authorised by the depositor, or the use necessary to maintain or bring the item in good condition). In principle, the deposit takes place in the interest of the depositor. However, the fact that the item may also be used in the interest of the depositary does not exclude deposit. See: HR (NL) 10 July 2015, ECLI:NL:HR:2015:1830, (*Searocco/Altena*), *JWB* 2015/269, *NJ* 2015/321, *NJB* 2015/1408, *RCR* 2015/71, para. 3.3.2.

2015 Art. 1788 old BCC; Ct. Brussels (BE) 22 June 1993, *TBBR* 1994, 422, *RRD* 1995, 46; J.-W. Verbeke, "Artikel 1788 oud BW – risicoverdeling bij aanneming waarbij de aannemer de materialen verstrekt" in *Focus op bijzondere overeenkomsten*, Mechelen, Wolters Kluwer, 2022, (360) 360; A. Van Oevelen, *Overeenkomsten. 2: Bijzondere overeenkomsten: E. Aanneming van werk, lastgeving, in Beginselen van Belgisch Privaatrecht*, Mechelen, Wolters Kluwer, 2017, 223–225; B. Kohl, *Contrat d'entreprise*, Brussels, Bruylant, 2016, 362, no. 146; P. Brulez, *Koop en aanneming: faux amis?*, Antwerp, Intersentia, 2015, 643; V. Van Houtte-Van Poppel and B. Kohl, "Commentaar bij art. 1788 BW" in *Bijzondere overeenkomsten. Artikelsgewijze commentaar met overzicht van rechtspraak en rechtsleer*, Mechelen, Kluwer, loose-leaf, 2011, (113) 115–116, no. 3–4.

2016 As a result-oriented PSS essentially amounts to a reciprocal, non-ownership transferring contract, the answer to the question of who bears the risk for loss and damage to the product under Art. 1788 old BCC will be the same as under the theory of risk from the general law of obligations. See: Art. 5.100 BCC; V. Sagaert, *Beginselen van verbintenissenrecht. De contractuele en quasi-contractuele verbintenissen*, Leuven, LeA Uitgevers, 2023, 104–105. See also: A. Van Oevelen, *Overeenkomsten. 2: Bijzondere overeenkomsten: E. Aanneming van werk, lastgeving, in Beginselen van Belgisch Privaatrecht*, Mechelen, Wolters Kluwer, 2017, 223.

2017 B. Keirsbilck, E. Terryn and E. Van Gool, "Consumentenbescherming bij servitisation en product-dienst systemen (PDS)", *TPR* 2019, (817) 853, no. 38. See also W. Goossens, *Aanneming van werk: het gemeenrechtelijk dienstencontract*, Bruges, Die Keure, 2003, 119–120, no. 136.

2018 See: Art. 7:750(1) DCC. The Dutch contract for works does provide a risk transfer mechanism similar to the Belgian contract for services. See: Art. 7:758(2) DCC. M.A.M.C. Van den Berg and S. van Gulijk, *Mr. C. Assers Handleiding tot de beoefening van het Nederlands Burgerlijk Recht. 7. Bijzondere overeenkomsten. Deel VI. Aanneming van werk*, Deventer, Wolters Kluwer, 2022, no. 118.

2019 Art. 7:400(1) DCC.

arrangement for the transfer of risk for the contract for services as it covers both types of services (construction and non-construction services), a transfer of ownership of the product is never possible under the Dutch contract for services.[2020] Consequently, the PSS supplier – just like under Belgian law – bears the risk (as owner) for loss or theft of the products it uses in the course of the performance of the service.[2021]

Of course, the exception to the rule that the PSS supplier bears the risk of loss or theft is the situation where the product has been destroyed or lost due to a fault by the PSS user, in which case the PSS user will be contractually liable.[2022] If the contract for services is accompanied by an accessory deposit contract, the PSS user has a duty of care and an obligation to return the product.[2023] The duty of care is an obligation of means where, as the deposit component of the PSS contract is done in the interest of the PSS user, the conduct of the PSS user is tested against the benchmark of a prudent and reasonable person in the same case.[2024] This means that the PSS user must take the necessary precautions against loss or depreciation, either due to an act of a third party (e.g. theft) or external circumstances (e.g. fire or water damage). The obligation to return the product, on the other hand, is an obligation of result.[2025] This means that the

2020 However, see the obligation to hand over and deliver stemming from Art. 7:402(2) DCC, where the service supplier must either give back the goods he used for performance of the service, or give the results of the service to the client (e.g. electronic files, documents, photos taken by a photographer, etc.). See on this obligation: T.F.E. Tjong Tjin Tai, *Asser 7-IV Bijzondere Overeenkomsten – Opdracht, incl. de geneeskundige behandelingsovereenkomst en de reisovereenkomst*, Deventer, Wolters Kluwer, 2022, no. 115.

2021 Compare also with the theory of risk and *force majeure* of the general law of obligations. See: C.H. Sieburgh, *Mr. C. Assers Handleiding tot de beoefening van het Nederlands Burgerlijk Recht. 6. Verbintenissenrecht. Deel I. De verbintenis in het algemeen, eerste gedeelte*, Deventer, Wolters Kluwer, 2020, no. 46.

2022 V. Van Houtte-Van Poppel and B. Kohl, "Commentaar bij art. 1788 BW" in *Bijzondere overeenkomsten. Artikelsgewijze commentaar met overzicht van rechtspraak en rechtsleer*, Mechelen, Kluwer, loose-leaf, 2011, (113) 117, no. 10.

2023 **Belgium**: Art. 1915 old BCC; V. Sagaert, B. Tilleman and A.-L. Verbeke, *Vermogensrecht in kort bestek*, Antwerp, Intersentia, 2022, 488–489. **The Netherlands**: Art. 7:600 DCC; A.J. Verheij, "Bewaarneming" in H.N. Schelhaas and A.J. Verheij (eds.), *Bijzondere overeenkomsten in Studiereeks Burgerlijk Recht*, Deventer, Wolters Kluwer, 2023, (417) 422, no. 370; A.C. van Schaick, *Asser 7-VIII Bewaarneming, borgtocht, vaststellingsovereenkomst, bruikleen, altijddurende rente, spel en weddenschap*, Deventer, Wolters Kluwer, 2018, no. 1.

2024 **Belgium**: Art. 1928 old BCC (*culpa levis in abstracto*). Compare with the lower standard of Art. 1927 old BCC which requires the depositary to take care of the goods in the same way as he does for his own goods (*culpa levis in concreto*). **The Netherlands**: Art. 7:602 DCC. N.E. Groeneveld-Tijssens, *Bewaarneming, Mon. BW B73*, Deventer, Wolters Kluwer, 2020, 11, no. 10–11; A.C. van Schaick, *Asser 7-VIII Bewaarneming, borgtocht, vaststellingsovereenkomst, bruikleen, altijddurende rente, spel en weddenschap*, Deventer, Wolters Kluwer, 2018, no. 9–10.

2025 **Belgium**: E.g. Ghent (BE) 27 February 2004, *TWVR* 2004, 197 and Brussels (BE) 4 January 2000, *RGAR* 2001, 13.398. **The Netherlands**: A.J. Verheij, "Bewaarneming" in H.N. Schelhaas and A.J. Verheij (eds.), *Bijzondere overeenkomsten in Studiereeks Burgerlijk Recht*, Deventer, Wolters Kluwer, 2023, (417) 430, no. 376.

PSS user will be liable if he cannot return the product, unless he can prove *force majeure*.[2026] The existence of *force majeure* is assessed in the light of the PSS user's duty of care, in particular whether the PSS user has taken all necessary and reasonable care of the product.[2027]

447. Limits on clauses contractually imposing the risk on the PSS user – Just like under the rental contract,[2028] the Belgian rules of the contract for services regulating the transfer of risk are not mandatory law.[2029] Consequently, the PSS contract can in principle stipulate that the risk for loss or damages to the product is imposed on the PSS user. However, here too, the unfair contract terms regime puts limits on the contractual freedom of the PSS supplier. Indeed, clauses that "*do not allow the consumer to terminate the contract in case of force majeure, except against payment of compensation*" will also be null and void in result-oriented PSS contracts.[2030] As with use-oriented PSS, this provision should be understood to mean that the consumer should be able to invoke *force majeure* based on general contract law, without being required to pay damages. It therefore follows that in result-oriented PSS, the risk of *force majeure* resting on the PSS supplier cannot be imposed on the PSS user, regardless of whether this is done explicitly or implicitly.[2031]

4.2.3.3. Implications of no transfer of ownership

448. Concerns regarding "weaker position" for the consumer equally apply to result-oriented PSS – The concerns discussed above for use-oriented PSS regarding the potential weaker position of the consumer if he no longer has the ownership of the products he uses[2032] also apply to result-oriented PSS, possibly even to a greater extent. After all, these business models

---

2026 **Belgium**: Art. 1929 old BCC. **The Netherlands**: Art. 6:75 DCC. A.J. Verheij, "Bewaarneming" in H.N. Schelhaas and A.J. Verheij (eds.), *Bijzondere overeenkomsten in Studiereeks Burgerlijk Recht*, Deventer, Wolters Kluwer, 2023, (417) 430, no. 376; N.E. Groeneveld-Tijssens, *Bewaarneming, Mon. BW B73*, Deventer, Wolters Kluwer, 2020, 29–30, no. 25.

2027 Cass. (BE) 7 March 2008, *Arr.Cass.* 2008, 651, *Pas.* 2008, 627, *RW* 2011–12, 583.

2028 See *supra* no. 440.

2029 A. Van Oevelen, *Overeenkomsten. 2: Bijzondere overeenkomsten: E. Aanneming van werk, lastgeving, in Beginselen van Belgisch Privaatrecht*, Mechelen, Wolters Kluwer, 2017, 231, no. 194; B. Kohl, *Contrat d'entreprise*, Brussels, Bruylant, 2016, 373, no. 150; V. Van Houtte-Van Poppel and B. Kohl, "Commentaar bij art. 1788 BW" in *Bijzondere overeenkomsten. Artikelsgewijze commentaar met overzicht van rechtspraak en rechtsleer*, Mechelen, Kluwer, loose-leaf, 2011, (113) 121, no. 17.

2030 Art. VI.83, 12° BCEL. Of course, these terms can also be tested against the general standard of Art. I.8, 22° BCEL.

2031 A. Van Oevelen, *Overeenkomsten. 2: Bijzondere overeenkomsten: E. Aanneming van werk, lastgeving, in Beginselen van Belgisch Privaatrecht*, Mechelen, Wolters Kluwer, 2017, 232–233, no. 195; B. Keirsbilck, E. Terryn and E. Van Gool, "Consumentenbescherming bij servitisation en product-dienst systemen (PDS)", *TPR* 2019, (817) 853, no. 38.

2032 See *supra* no. 444.

often do not relate to a single product such as a washing machine, a bicycle, or pieces of furniture, but are often highly integrated into the house or life of the PSS user, where replacing the service is not just a matter of buying or renting a similar product. So here too, sufficient safeguards must be in place for the PSS user, such as the possibility of giving him a right of first refusal or ensuring that support for the service does not stop at some point without a valid alternative.

4.3. CONFORMITY OF THE PRODUCT/SERVICE WITH THE PSS CONTRACT

449. Conformity of the product with the PSS contract – Not only must the PSS supplier provide the product and/or service to the PSS user, but the product/service must also be in conformity with the contract. The way conformity is assessed also varies between the three different types of PSS and depends on the contractual qualification of (the components of) the PSS contract.

4.3.1. PRODUCT-ORIENTED PSS: EXTENSIVE CONFORMITY RULES

450. Consumer sales contract: conformity with objective and subjective conformity requirements – For product-oriented PSS, providing the product (including so-called "goods with digital elements"), takes the form of a (consumer) sales contract.[2033] The rules on consumer sales contracts are fully harmonised by the SGD,[2034] providing extensive conformity requirements.[2035] A distinction is made between subjective and objective conformity requirements.[2036] Subjective conformity requirements result directly from the contractual relationship between the consumer and the PSS supplier. They relate to what the parties have stipulated in their contract, including pre-contractual discussions. Objective conformity requirements, on the other hand, are indirectly part of the contract because the consumer can reasonably

---

2033 EU: Art. 3(1) *juncto* Art. 2 SGD. **Belgium**: Art. 1649*bis*, §2 *juncto* Art. 1649*bis*, §1 old BCC. **The Netherlands**: Art. 7:5(1), *sub* a. DCC.

2034 Art. 4 SGD. This means that Member States cannot not maintain or introduce, in their national law, provisions diverging from those laid down in the SGD, including more, or less, stringent provisions to ensure a different level of consumer protection, unless otherwise provided for in the SGD.

2035 EU: Art. 6–8 SGD. **Belgium**: Art. 1649*ter*, §2–8 old BCC. **The Netherlands**: Art. 7:18 and 7:18a DCC.

2036 J. Vanherpe, "White Smoke, but Smoke Nonetheless: Some (Burning) Questions Regarding the Directives on Sale of Goods and Supply of Digital Content", *ERPL* 2020, (251) 259; J. Morais Carvalho, "Sale of Goods and Supply of Digital Content and Digital Services – Overview of Directives 2019/770 and 2019/771", *EuCML* 2019, (194) 198.

expect them to be. They respond to a consumer's legitimate expectations of a particular product. Both sets of conformity criteria should be seen side by side and complement each other without any hierarchical distinction.[2037]

4.3.1.1. Subjective conformity requirements

451. Subjective conformity requirements – The first step is looking at what the parties have agreed in the PSS contract. To conform with the contract, the product must meet the subjective conformity requirements established in the PSS contract, where applicable.[2038] The SGD sets these out in four points.

452. First point: description, type, quantity and quality – The first point mentions general conformity criteria such as the description, type, quantity and quality of the product.[2039] This means that the product must therefore conform to the PSS contract, even if the non-conformity does not affect the usability or value of the product (e.g. if the supplied product has a different colour).[2040] Specific for products with digital elements, they must have the functionality, compatibility and, in some cases, interoperability, as set out in the PSS contract. This means that the product must perform its functions ("functionality"[2041]) either with the usual hardware and software ("compatibility"[2042]) or with

2037 See recital 25 SGD ("*In order to safeguard the legitimate interests of both parties to a sales contract, conformity should be assessed based on both subjective and objective requirements for conformity*"). See also Art. 1649*ter*, §2 old BCC ("*in addition to meeting subjective conformity requirements*"). B. Tilleman and F. Van den Abeele, *Bijzondere overeenkomsten – A. Koop – Deel 2 Gevolgen van de koop*, Mechelen, Kluwer, 2022, 786. In the Netherlands, this distinction is not explicitly made but it is also present, see: P. Klik, *Koop en Consumentenkoop*, Deventer, Wolters Kluwer, 2022, 158. See for criticism on this distinction between objective and subjective conformity requirements: E. Van den Haute, "La directive (UE) 2019/771 relative à certains aspects concernant les contrats de vente et le futur droit belge de la vente de biens de consommation" in R. Jafferali, E. Van den Haute and A. Foriers (eds.), *Entre tradition et pragmatisme. Liber amicorum Paul Alain Foriers*, Volume 1, Brussels, Larcier, 2021, (655) 667, no. 13; F. Van den Abeele and B. Tilleman, "Conformiteit in de Richtlijn Consumentenkoop 2019: heeft de berg een muis gebaard?" in I. Claeys and E. Terryn (eds.), *Nieuw recht inzake koop & digitale inhoud en diensten*, Antwerp, Intersentia, 2020, (91) 97–98, no. 7; I. Bach, "Neue Richtlinien zum Verbrachsgüterkauf und zu Verbracherverträgen über digitale Inhalte", *Neue Juristische Wochenschrift* 2019, (1705) 1707.

2038 EU: Art. 6 SGD. **Belgium**: Art. 1649*ter*, §2 old BCC. **The Netherlands**: Art. 7:18(1) DCC.

2039 EU: Art. 6(a) SGD. **Belgium**: Art. 1649*ter*, §2, 1° old BCC. **The Netherlands**: Art. 7:18(1), *sub* a. DCC.

2040 **Belgium**: B. Tilleman and F. Van den Abeele, *Bijzondere overeenkomsten – A. Koop – Deel 2 Gevolgen van de koop*, Mechelen, Kluwer, 2022, 789. **The Netherlands**: M.B.M. Loos, *Consumentenkoop, Monografieën BW, nr. B65b*, Deventer, Wolters Kluwer, 2019, 68, no. 30; P. Klik, *Conformiteit bij koop*, Diss. doct. Erasmus universiteit Rotterdam, 2008, 331.

2041 See Art. 2(9) SGD; Art. 1649*bis*, §1, 8° old BCC; Art. 5(1), *sub* f. DCC: "*the ability to perform their functions having regard to their purpose.*"

2042 See Art. 2(8) SGD; Art. 1649*bis*, §1, 7° old BCC; Art. 5(1), *sub* e. DCC: "*the ability to function with hardware or software with which goods of the same type are normally used, without the need to convert the goods, hardware or software.*"

alternative hardware and software ("interoperability"[2043]).[2044] According to some authors, the latter distinction is relevant as interoperability is only mentioned as a subjective conformity requirement, whereas compatibility is listed both as a subjective and objective conformity requirement.[2045] Others convincingly argue that the list of objective criteria is not exhaustive, and that for some products interoperability may be part of the consumer's reasonable expectations, even if it is not explicitly included in the contract.[2046] These new conformity criteria are very important for product-oriented PSS, as they could help prevent "technological obsolescence"[2047] of the offered products (which are often connected to the internet and therefore at risk of becoming prematurely obsolete).[2048]

453. SECOND POINT: PARTICULAR PURPOSE AGREED BY THE PARTIES – The second point refers to any particular purpose agreed between the PSS user and the PSS supplier at the latest of the time of conclusion of the PSS contract.[2049] For evidentiary reasons, it may be advisable to put this particular purpose in writing or expressly include it in (or as an annex to) the PSS contract.[2050] Still, as product-oriented PSS contracts are mostly offered through standard contracts on a take it or leave it basis, this conformity criterion will be less important in practice.

454. THIRD POINT: ACCESSORIES AND INSTRUCTIONS – The third point includes the presence of all accessories and instructions, including on installation, as contractually agreed in the PSS contract.[2051] Think of (charging) cables, protective accessories such as a smartphone case, ink cartridges, washing

2043 See Art. 2(10) SGD; Art. 1649*bis*, §1, 9° old BCC; Art. 5(1), *sub* g. DCC: "*the ability to function with hardware or software different from those with which goods of the same type are normally used.*"

2044 D. STAUDENMAYER, "The Directives on Digital Contracts: First Steps Towards the Private Law of the Digital Economy", *ERPL* 2020, vol. 28 issue 2, (219) 237.

2045 D. STAUDENMAYER, "The Directives on Digital Contracts: First Steps Towards the Private Law of the Digital Economy", *ERPL* 2020, vol. 28, afl. 2, (219) 237.

2046 E. VAN GOOL and A. MICHEL, "The New Consumer Sales Directive 2019/771 and Sustainable Consumption", *EuCML* 2021, vol. 10, afl. 4, (136) 138, with reference to the wording "and other features" and "including" in Art. 7(1)(d) SGD. See in the same sense: B. TILLEMAN and F. VAN DEN ABEELE, *Bijzondere overeenkomsten – A. Koop – Deel 2 Gevolgen van de koop*, Mechelen, Kluwer, 2022, 790.

2047 Compare with: E. VAN GOOL and A. MICHEL, "The New Consumer Sales Directive 2019/771 and Sustainable Consumption", *EuCML* 2021, vol. 10, afl. 4, (136) 139.

2048 See for an overview of different ways a product can be prematurely obsolete: A. MICHEL, *Premature Obsolescence: In Search of an Improved Legal Framework*, Cambridge, Intersentia, 2023, 71–86.

2049 EU: Art. 6(b) SGD. **Belgium**: Art. 1649*ter*, §2, 2° old BCC. **The Netherlands**: Art. 7:18(1), *sub* b. DCC.

2050 A. VAN OEVELEN, "Het nieuwe begrip conformiteit" in S. STIJNS and J. STUYCK (eds.), *Het nieuwe kooprecht*, Antwerp, Intersentia, 2005, (29) 39.

2051 EU: Art. 6(c) SGD. **Belgium**: Art. 1649*ter*, §2, 3° old BCC. **The Netherlands**: Art. 7:18(1), *sub* c. DCC.

powder, etc. This also includes customer service if it is so agreed in the PSS contract.[2052]

455. Fourth point: updates – Finally, according to the fourth point, the product must be supplied with updates as stipulated by the PSS contract.[2053] This will further be discussed *infra* under the section dealing with the PSS supplier's update obligation[2054] and the PSS user's obligation to install the supplied updates.[2055]

456. Subjective conformity and sustainability – In the context of sustainable product-oriented PSS offers, sustainability guarantees can also act as a subjective conformity requirement.[2056] Indeed, the concept of subjective conformity will also be interpreted by taking into account specific precontractual information regarding sustainability.[2057] Thus, if the PSS supplier includes certain expectations in the PSS contract concerning the sustainability of the product, they will be relevant in assessing the conformity of the product, regardless of whether these expectations correspond to certain standards.[2058] For example, the PSS contract may stipulate that the product has a certain durability or life expectancy (e.g. expressed in time, charge cycles or use cycles), or that the product is easily reparable. Other sustainability guarantees may relate to whether the product was produced in an environmentally responsible way, e.g. using only recycled and durable materials.[2059] Eco-labels, recycling standards or other forms of marketing and advertising are often used for this purpose. If sustainability guarantees are not explicitly addressed in the pre-contractual phase or in the PSS contract, these elements may in some cases still form part of the objective conformity requirements.[2060]

2052 J. Morais Carvalho, "Sale of Goods and Supply of Digital Content and Digital Services – Overview of Directives 2019/770 and 2019/771", *EuCML* 2019, (194) 198.

2053 EU: Art. 6(d) SGD. **Belgium**: Art. 1649*ter*, §2, 4° old BCC. **The Netherlands**: Art. 7:18(1), *sub* d. DCC.

2054 See *infra* section 6.4.1.

2055 See *infra* section 6.4.2.

2056 These sustainability guarantees are especially relevant for the subjective conformity requirements laid down in Art. 6(a) and Art. 6(b) SGD.

2057 See Recital 32 *in fine* SGD.

2058 E. Van Gool, "De nieuwe Richtlijn Consumentenkoop en duurzame consumptie" in E. Terryn and I. Claeys (eds.), *Nieuw recht inzake koop & digitale inhoud en diensten*, Mortsel, Intersentia, 2020, (303) 334, no. 40; K. Tonner, E. Gawel, S. Schlacke, M. Alt and W. Bretschneider, "Gewährleistung und Garantie als Instrumente zur Durchsetzung eines nachhaltigen Produktumgangs", *Verbraucher und Recht* 2017, (3) 4–5.

2059 See e.g. See for example Fairphone, which focuses on the use of sustainable and fair materials, as well as a high level of repairability. www.fairphone.com/en/story/?ref=header.

2060 See *infra* no. 462.

4.3.1.2 *Objective conformity requirements*

457. Objective conformity requirements – In addition to the subjective conformity requirements, the product must also meet objective conformity requirements.[2061] These are also set out in the SGD in four points.

458. First point: "normal use" – First, the delivered product must be fit for the purposes for which goods of the same type would normally be used.[2062] Where applicable, this may take into account existing Union and national law, technical standards or, in the absence of such technical standards, applicable sector-specific industry codes of conduct. Normal wear and tear, for example in the case of second-hand or refurbished products, do not render the good unfit for the purposes for which goods of the same type are normally used.[2063] In contrast, abnormal wear and tear may constitute a non-conformity of the product.[2064]

459. Second point: compliance with sample or model – Where applicable, the product must comply with the quality and description of a sample or model that the PSS supplier made available to the consumer before conclusion

---

2061 EU: Art. 7(1) SGD. **Belgium**: Art. Art. 1649*ter*, §3 old BCC. **The Netherlands**: Art. 7:18(2) DCC.

2062 EU: Art. 7(1)(a) SGD. **Belgium**: Art. 1649*ter*, §3, 1° old BCC. **The Netherlands**: Art. 7:18(2), *sub* a. DCC. Compare also with Art. 7:17(2) DCC.

2063 **Belgium**: R. Steennot, G. Straetmans, E. Terryn, B. Keirsbilck and B. Wyseur, "Overzicht van rechtspraak. Consumentenbescherming (2008-2014) – Marktpraktijken (2011-2014)", *TPR* 2015, (1311) 1810, no. 514. See for an example of a second-hand Porsche car: Comm. Ghent (Section Kortrijk) (BE) 24 October 2019, *DCCR* 2020, 133, case note H. Slachmuylders (The one-time refill of 1.7 litres of engine oil is not a defect that prevents the normal use of a second-hand Porsche. The buyer also complained about the condition of the tyres. Tyres are subject to wear and when they are worn out, they need to be replaced. This is not a defect either.). By contrast, a fridge catching fire is not fit for the purposes which constitute normal use of the product. See: Comm. Dendermonde (BE) 1 March 2012, *RABG* 2013, 648. For more case law examples, see: B. Tilleman and F. Van den Abeele, *Bijzondere overeenkomsten – A. Koop – Deel 2 Gevolgen van de koop*, Mechelen, Kluwer, 2022, 793–797. **The Netherlands**: M.B.M. Loos, *Consumentenkoop, Monografieën BW, nr. B65b*, Deventer, Wolters Kluwer, 2019, 69, no. 30; P. Klik, *Koop en Consumentenkoop*, Deventer, Wolters Kluwer, 2022, 160 and 142–144; J. Hijma, *Mr. C. Assers Handleiding tot de beoefening van het Nederlands Burgerlijk Recht. 7. Bijzondere overeenkomsten. Deel I. Koop en ruil*, Deventer, Kluwer, 2019, no. 499–500.

2064 See for two examples in Belgium case law: Ct. Brussels (BE) 7 May 2009, *JT* 2009, 737 (there is abnormal wear and tear if a second-hand car breaks down less than six weeks after delivery and proves permanently unusable after repair) and J.P. Landen-Zoutleeuw (BE) 13 September 2007, *T.Vred.* 2009, 341, case note C. Delforge (the fact that a vehicle is 17 years old does not necessarily mean that defects such as a broken engine, oil leak, loss of power, temperature fluctuations, etc. are normal if a relatively high price was charged and a valid inspection certificate has been delivered). H. Slachmuylders, "Herstelling door een derde en de hiërarchie van de remedies in de consumentenkoop", *DCCR* 2020, (135) 138.

of the contract.[2065] This also may be the case, for example, with a free test period, or a test ride.[2066]

460. THIRD POINT: ACCESSORIES AND INSTRUCTIONS – The third objective conformity requirement relates to the availability of accessories, including packaging, installation instructions or other instructions, as the PSS user may reasonably expect to receive.[2067] This builds on the subjective conformity requirement that the PSS user must receive the accessories and instructions contractually agreed.[2068]

461. FOURTH POINT: QUANTITY, QUALITIES, AND OTHER FEATURES WHICH ARE NORMAL FOR PRODUCTS OF THE SAME TYPE – Finally, the fourth objective conformity requirement states that the product must have the quantity and the qualities and other features which are normal for products of the same type and which the PSS user may reasonably expect given the nature of the products.[2069] The provision makes explicit some quality characteristics: durability,[2070] functionality, compatibility and security. The new Right to Repair Directive[2071] also adds "repairability" as an objective conformity criterion.[2072] For interpreting this objective conformity requirement, the expectations of an average consumer should be considered, i.e. a consumer who is reasonably well-informed, observant and circumspect.[2073] These expectations may be based on several factors. First, they can depend on the nature of the good. Here, a distinction is often made between second-hand goods versus new goods or brand products versus non-brand products.[2074] In my view, the sustainable character of PSS

2065 EU: Art. 7(1)(b) SGD. **Belgium**: Art. 1649*ter*, §3, 2° old BCC. **The Netherlands**: Art. 7:18(2), *sub* b. DCC.

2066 See for an example in Belgian case law concerning an electric bicycle: Ct. Antwerp (Section Turnhout) (BE), *RW* 2017–18, 1396 (If the seller of an electric bicycle promised before the conclusion of a contract at the request of the buyer that the bicycle would provide assistance up to 45 km/h, while this is not the case afterwards, the bicycle does not meet the conformity requirements).

2067 EU: Art. 7(1)(c) SGD. **Belgium**: Art. 1649*ter*, §3, 3° old BCC. **The Netherlands**: Art. 7:18(2), *sub* c. DCC.

2068 See *supra* no. 454.

2069 EU: Art. 7(1)(d) SGD. **Belgium**: Art. 1649*ter*, §3, 4° old BCC. **The Netherlands**: Art. 7:18(2), *sub* d. DCC.

2070 See *infra* no. 462.

2071 Directive (EU) 2024/1799 of the European Parliament and of the Council of 13 June 2024 on common rules promoting the repair of goods and amending Regulation (EU) 2017/2394 and Directives (EU) 2019/771 and (EU) 2020/1828, *OJ L* 2024/1799, 10.7.2024 ('Right to Repair Directive').

2072 See Art. 16(1) Right to Repair Directive.

2073 CJEU, Judgment of 16 July 1998, C-210/96, *Gut Springenheide GmbH/Overkreisdirektor des Kreises Steinfurt*, ECLI:EU:C:1998:369, para. 31. B. TILLEMAN and F. VAN DEN ABEELE, *Bijzondere overeenkomsten – A. Koop – Deel 2 Gevolgen van de koop*, Mechelen, Kluwer, 2022, 800; M.B.M. LOOS, *Consumentenkoop, Monografieën BW, nr. B65b*, Deventer, Wolters Kluwer, 2019, 69; V. MAK, "De gemiddelde consument", *Ars Aequi* 2017, (592) 594.

2074 M.B.M. LOOS, *Consumentenkoop, Monografieën BW, nr. B65b*, Deventer, Wolters Kluwer, 2019, 69.

must also be taken into account when assessing what the legitimate expectations of an average PSS user-consumer are regarding the products that are offered. Second, public state statements made by the PSS supplier, the producer or his representative can also shape the consumer's legitimate expectations of the product. This means that the marketing and advertising by the PSS supplier – and where applicable the manufacturer of the products – regarding the qualities of the product also enter the contractual sphere. Only in rare cases will the PSS supplier not be bound by these public statements, namely (i) if the PSS supplier was not, and could not reasonably have been, aware of the public statement in question; (ii) if by the time of conclusion of the contract, the public statement has been corrected; and (iii) if the decision to buy the product could not have been influenced by this public statement.[2075] Finally, other circumstances at the time of the conclusion of the contract can also be taken into account.[2076]

462. Objective conformity and sustainability – Sustainability can also play a role as objective conformity requirement. The first thing to note here is the mention of "durability" in Article 7(1)(d) SGD as one of the quality requirements that consumers can reasonably expect.[2077] The Dutch text of the Directive translates this as "*duurzaamheid*" (sustainability). This should not be confused with "*duurzame ontwikkeling*" (sustainable development) or "*duurzame consumptie*" (sustainable consumption). "Durability" within the meaning of the SGD means "*the ability of the goods to maintain their required functions and performance through normal use.*"[2078] Consequently, the term "durability" has a narrower meaning than sustainability, as it only focuses on the lifespan of the products. Other aspects of "sustainable development",[2079] such as ecological aspects (environmental externalities of production, recyclability, etc.) and other social, economic, humanitarian or cultural aspects are not taken into account.[2080] Nevertheless, these other aspects may fall under "other features which are normal for the same type". Additionally, they can of course also be covered by the subjective conformity requirements, namely if they appear in the PSS contract or in advertising or other marketing of the PSS supplier.[2081] The question arises whether "repairability" falls under this definition of durability.

2075 EU: Art. 7(2) SGD. **Belgium**: Art. 1649*ter*, §4 old BCC. **The Netherlands**: Art. 7:18(3) DCC.

2076 B. Tilleman and F. Van den Abeele, *Bijzondere overeenkomsten – A. Koop – Deel 2 Gevolgen van de koop*, Mechelen, Kluwer, 2022, 800; A. Van Oevelen, "Het nieuwe begrip conformiteit" in S. Stijns and J. Stuyck (eds.), *Het nieuwe kooprecht*, Antwerp, Intersentia, 2005, (29) 41.

2077 Implemented in **Belgium** in Art. 1649*ter*, §3, 4° old BCC and in **the Netherlands** in Art. 7:18(2), *sub* d. DCC.

2078 Art. 2(13) SGD. See also Recital 13 SGD.

2079 Compare with the 17 SDGs of the United Nations.

2080 E. Van Gool, "De nieuwe Richtlijn Consumentenkoop en duurzame consumptie" in E. Terryn and I. Claeys (eds.), *Nieuw recht inzake koop & digitale inhoud en diensten*, Mortsel, Intersentia, 2020, (303) 336.

2081 See *supra* no. 456.

According to VAN GOOL and MICHEL this should be answered affirmatively as repair increases the lifespan of the products.[2082] Although from a traditional linear perspective one could argue that repair does not fall under "normal use", they make a convincing argument that in line of the EU's circular economy policy, standard repair should be a part of this.[2083] In my view, this is even more true for products that are part of a product-oriented PSS where repair is often an important part of the additional services offered to consumers.

463. OBLIGATION TO SUPPLY UPDATES SO THE PRODUCT REMAINS IN CONFORMITY – Besides the updates expressly agreed in the PSS contract (i.e. updates as a subjective conformity criterion), the SGD also contains an objective update obligation. Indeed, the SGD requires sellers of goods with digital elements to ensure that the consumer is informed of and supplied with updates, including security updates, that are necessary to keep those goods in conformity.[2084] As product-oriented PSS generally involve a continuous supply of the digital content or digital service,[2085] this obligation applies during the legal guarantee period or an agreed longer period of continuous supply.[2086]

464. POSSIBILITY TO DEVIATE FROM OBJECTIVE CONFORMITY REQUIREMENTS IN THE PSS CONTRACT – These objective conformity requirements are not set in stone. Under certain circumstances, the parties to the PSS contract can deviate from them to allow more flexibility.[2087] This may be the case, for example, when selling second-hand products[2088] as part of the product-oriented PSS or innovative products that differ from what is customary.[2089] Indeed, there is no lack of conformity if at the time of conclusion of the product-oriented PSS contract, the consumer was *specifically informed* that a particular characteristic of the product was deviating from the objective conformity requirements and the consumer *expressly and separately accepted* that deviation.[2090] This means

[2082] E. VAN GOOL and A. MICHEL, "The New Consumer Sales Directive 2019/771 and Sustainable Consumption", *EuCML* 2021, vol. 10, afl. 4, (136) 138.

[2083] E. VAN GOOL and A. MICHEL, "The New Consumer Sales Directive 2019/771 and Sustainable Consumption", *EuCML* 2021, vol. 10, afl. 4, (136) 138.

[2084] EU: Art. 7(3) SGD. **Belgium**: Art. 1649*ter*, §5 old BCC. **The Netherlands**: Art. 7:18(4) DCC.

[2085] By contrast, where the PSS contract provides for a single act of supply of the digital content or digital service, the PSS supplier must supply these updates for the time period that the consumer may reasonably expect. See Art. 7.3, (a) SGD.

[2086] EU: Art. 7(3) and 10(2) SGD. See also recitals 28–31 SGD. **Belgium**: Art. 1649*ter*, §5 and Art. 1649*quater*, §1(2) old BCC. **The Netherlands**: Art. 7:18(4) DCC.

[2087] B. TILLEMAN and F. VAN DEN ABEELE, *Bijzondere overeenkomsten – A. Koop – Deel 2 Gevolgen van de koop*, Mechelen, Kluwer, 2022, 808; P. KLIK, *Koop en Consumentenkoop*, Deventer, Wolters Kluwer, 2022, 163.

[2088] See Recital 36 SGD.

[2089] I. VAN WIJK, "De richtlijn digitale inhoud en digitale diensten: zijn de gebreken van de conceptrichtlijn hersteld?", *Tijdschrift voor internetrecht* 2019, (165) 171.

[2090] EU: Art. 7(5) SGD. **Belgium**: Art. 1649*ter*, §7 old BCC. **The Netherlands**: Art. 7:18(6) DCC.

that deviation from objective conformity criteria requires specific transparency requirements (both information and acceptance) and mere acknowledgement of the general terms and conditions by the PSS user will therefore not be sufficient.[2091] This could take the form of a separate consent form[2092] or, in an online context, by requiring the PSS user to tick a box[2093] or press a button.[2094] Nevertheless, considering the insights from behavioural sciences illustrating that consumers rarely read the terms and conditions they sign or click on,[2095] it remains questionable whether consumers always fully understand, consider and accept with full knowledge the deviations from objective conformity criteria. Yet it is uncertain whether there really is a valid alternative.

4.3.1.3. Correct installation as conformity requirement

465. Installation also considered as a conformity requirement – Various products offered with product-oriented PSS need to be installed before the PSS user can make useful use of them.[2096] For example, household appliances such as washing machines must be installed on the water supply and drain and goods with digital elements (e.g. smart products measuring the usage data of the device) are often controlled by an app or other software which must be installed on the device.[2097] Installation should therefore be interpreted broadly, namely as

---

2091 E. Van Gool, "De nieuwe Richtlijn Consumentenkoop en duurzame consumptie" in E. Terryn and I. Claeys (eds.), *Nieuw recht inzake koop & digitale inhoud en diensten*, Mortsel, Intersentia, 2020, (303) 337–338; F. Graf von Westphalen, "Some Thoughts on the Proposed Directive on Certain Aspects Concerning Contracts for the Sales of Goods", *EuCML* 2018, (66) 69–70; S. Jansen and S. Stijns, "Proposal for a Directive on Certain Aspects Concerning Contracts for the Online and Other Distance Sales of Goods: Scope of Application, Definitions and Conformity" in E. Terryn and I. Claeys (eds.), *Digital Content & Distance Sales*, Cambridge, Intersentia, 2017, (55) 71; V. Mak, *The new proposal for harmonized rules on certain aspects concerning contracts for the supply of digital content*, Workshop for the Juri Committee, PE 536.494, 2016, 17.

2092 J.H.M. Spanjaard, "Herziening consumentenrechten: verkenning van Richtlijn 2019/771", *Contracteren* 2019, (115) 119.

2093 A pre-ticked box, to be un-ticked by the PSS user if they do not agree, will not suffice. An affirmative acceptance action is required.

2094 B. Tilleman and F. Van den Abeele, *Bijzondere overeenkomsten – A. Koop – Deel 2 Gevolgen van de koop*, Mechelen, Kluwer, 2022, 808; E. Van Gool, "De nieuwe Richtlijn Consumentenkoop en duurzame consumptie" in E. Terryn and I. Claeys (eds.), *Nieuw recht inzake koop & digitale inhoud en diensten*, Mortsel, Intersentia, 2020, (303) 338.

2095 See e.g. Y. Bakos, F. Marotta-Wurgler and D.R. Trossen, "Does Anyone Read the Fine Print? Consumer Attention to Standard-Form Contracts", *The Journal of Legal Studies* 2014, afl. 43, vol. 43, (1) 1–35; O. Bar-Gill and O. Ben-Shahar, "Regulatory techniques in consumer protection: a critique of European consumer law", *CML Rev.* 2013, (109) 117–119; O. Ben-Shahar, "The Myth of the 'Opportunity to Read' in Contract Law", *European Review of Contract Law* 2009, vol. 5, afl. 1, (1) 1–28.

2096 See also *infra* no. 698 *et seq.*

2097 B. Tilleman and F. Van den Abeele, *Bijzondere overeenkomsten – A. Koop – Deel 2 Gevolgen van de koop*, Mechelen, Kluwer, 2022, 809.

any circumstance in which the good is linked to a new environment.[2098] Since incorrect installation of the purchased product can also render it unusable for it intended purpose, this will lead to non-conformity in two cases, even if there is nothing wrong with the product *in se*.[2099] Thus, any non-conformity arising from the incorrect installation of the product shall be regarded as a non-conformity of the product if: i) the installation forms part of the PSS contract and was carried out by the PSS supplier or under its responsibility; or ii) the installation was done by the PSS user (as was intended) and this incorrect installation was due to shortcomings in the installation instructions provided by the PSS supplier.[2100]

4.3.1.4. Liability for non-conformity and remedies

466. Liability of the PSS supplier for non-conformity during guarantee period – The PSS supplier will be liable for any lack of conformity that exists at the time of delivery of the product. Under the Directive and Belgian law, this liability is subject to a time limit of two years within which this lack of conformity must become apparent (the legal guarantee period).[2101] For goods with digital elements that are continuously supplied as part of the product-oriented PSS, the PSS supplier will also be liable for any lack of conformity of the digital content or digital service that occurs or becomes apparent within two years from the delivery of the product. If the PSS contract provides for the continuous supply of the digital content or digital service for more than two years, this guarantee period spans the entire period of time during which the digital content or digital service is to be supplied.[2102] In contrast, Dutch law uses an "open system" based on the expected lifetime of the product rather than the two-year period.[2103] For goods with digital elements, the update obligation (including security updates) of the PSS supplier is also not subject to a fixed time limit, but concerns the time limit which the PSS user may reasonably expect.[2104]

467. Future law: extension of guarantee period if PSS user-buyer opts for remedy of repair – In the near future, the rules regarding the legal guarantee period will slightly change. Indeed, to promote repair as the more

2098 J. Hijma, *Mr. C. Assers Handleiding tot de beoefening van het Nederlands Burgerlijk Recht. 7. Bijzondere overeenkomsten. Deel I. Koop en ruil*, Deventer, Kluwer, 2019, no. 514. Compare also with: M.B.M. Loos, *Consumentenkoop, Monografieën BW, nr. B65b*, Deventer, Wolters Kluwer, 2019, no. 32.

2099 B. Tilleman and F. Van den Abeele, *Bijzondere overeenkomsten – A. Koop – Deel 2 Gevolgen van de koop*, Mechelen, Kluwer, 2022, 810.

2100 EU: Art. 8 SGD. **Belgium**: Art. 1649*ter*, §8 old BCC. **The Netherlands**: Art. 7:18a(1) DCC.

2101 EU: Art. 10(1) SGD. **Belgium**: Art. 1649*quater*, §1(1) old BCC.

2102 EU: Art. 10(2) SGD. **Belgium**: Art. 1649*quater*, §1(2) old BCC.

2103 P. Klik, *Koop en Consumentenkoop*, Deventer, Wolters Kluwer, 2022, 165. See also *infra* no. 468.

2104 Art. 7:18(4) DCC.

sustainable remedy for non-conformity, the new Right to Repair Directive amends Article 10 of the SGD by inserting a paragraph 2a. This paragraph 2a states that if the buyer opts for the remedy of repair to bring the goods into conformity, the liability period shall be extended once by twelve months.[2105] Additionally, the Member States are free to introduce or maintain rules further incentivising the choice for the remedy of repair, for example by providing for additional extensions of the seller's liability if repair takes place again or by introducing a longer extension than twelve months if the buyer opts for the remedy of repair.[2106] Member States where, as is the case under Dutch law, there are no fixed time limits for the liability of the seller or where only a limitation period for the remedies applies, may derogate from the extension of the liability period of paragraph 2a Right to Repair Directive, provided that the liability of the seller or the limitation period for remedies in the event of repair is at least equivalent to three years.[2107]

468. SGD ALLOWS MEMBER STATES TO MAINTAIN OR ADOPT A LONGER LEGAL GUARANTEE PERIOD – The SGD allows Member States to maintain or introduce a longer legal guarantee period.[2108] In Belgium, the legislator did not opt for this.[2109] In contrast, the Netherlands opted for an "open system" when implementing the directive, focusing on the expected lifetime of the product rather than a strict two year period (i.e. a "lifespan guarantee").[2110] The argument was made that a consumer should expect an expensive washing machine, a car or a smart TV to have a longer lifespan than a cheap sandwich iron, computer cable or app.[2111] Both approaches have advantages and disadvantages.[2112] The Belgian system has the advantage of providing legal certainty, both for sellers (who are fairly certain after two years that they cannot be held liable[2113]) and for consumers (for whom the guarantee period is the minimum period within

2105 See Art. 16(2)(a) Right to Repair Directive.

2106 See Recital 40 and Art. 16(2)(b) Right to Repair Directive.

2107 Art. 16(2)(c) Right to Repair Directive.

2108 See: Art. 10(3) SGD. As discussed *supra* no. 467, the new Right to Repair Directive amends this provision so that Member States can also include rules on a longer extension of the liability period than twelve months if the consumer opts for the remedy of repair.

2109 B. TILLEMAN and F. VAN DEN ABEELE, *Bijzondere overeenkomsten – A. Koop – Deel 2 Gevolgen van de koop*, Mechelen, Kluwer, 2022, 826.

2110 Explanatory Memorandum, *Parliamentary Papers II* 2020/21, 35734, no. 3, 6 and 20. See also Finland, which has a similar system since 1978.

2111 Explanatory Memorandum, *Parliamentary Papers II* 2020/21, 35734, no. 3, 6.

2112 See for a study on the advantages and disadvantages: ICF, *Study on the costs and benefits of extending certain rights under the Consumer Sales and Guarantees Directive 1999/94/EC*, Luxemburg, EU Publications Office, 2017, 23–31.

2113 This should be nuanced as the regime of hidden defects from general sales law revives after the expiry of this guarantee period. See Art. 1649*quater*, §5 old BCC. Nevertheless, this does not offer the same protection as the conditions of application of the regime of hidden defects are much stricter than those of non-conformity in consumer sales law.

which they cannot lose their rights).[2114] The drawback of this approach is that this is an arbitrary time limit, which has been criticised in legal doctrine for being too short for many sustainable products.[2115] The advantage of the Dutch system is that it works with a time limit adjusted to the average lifetime of the product in question. Consumers therefore have longer protection for sustainable and durable products, while sellers, in the absence of an arbitrary time limit, no longer bear the risk for defects that are due to the product's expected lifespan having already expired.[2116] The disadvantage of this system is that it is considered complex and non-transparent, which does not benefit the legal certainty of consumers and businesses when confronted with the non-conformity of a product.[2117, 2118]

469. Presumption period – To help consumers prove that a lack of conformity already existed at the time of delivery, the SGD provides for a (rebuttable) presumption period in which the anteriority of the lack of conformity is presumed.[2119] Whereas this presumption period was six months under the CSD,[2120] it is doubled to one year in the SGD.[2121] However, this provision is only minimum harmonisation, allowing Member States to maintain or introduce a two-year period instead of this one-year period. The Belgian legislator has made

---

2114 B. Tilleman and F. Van den Abeele, *Bijzondere overeenkomsten – A. Koop – Deel 2 Gevolgen van de koop*, Mechelen, Kluwer, 2022, 826.

2115 E.g. E. Van Gool, "De nieuwe Richtlijn Consumentenkoop en duurzame consumptie" in E. Terryn and I. Claeys (eds.), *Nieuw recht inzake koop & digitale inhoud en diensten*, Mortsel, Intersentia, 2020, (303) 347; A. Michel, "La directive 1999/44/CE sur la garantie des biens de consommation: un remède efficace contre l'obsolescence programmée?", *REDC* 2016, (207) 226; S. Stijns, "De consumentenkoop: actuele knelpunten" in B. Tilleman and A.-L. Verbeke (eds.), *Knelpunten verkoop roerende goederen*, Antwerp, Intersentia, 2009, (21) 46; A.-L. Verbeke, "De termijnen" in S. Stijns and J. Stuyck (eds.), *Het nieuwe kooprecht: De wet van 1 september 2004 betreffende de bescherming van de consument bij verkoop van consumptiegoederen*, Antwerp, Intersentia, 2005, (83) 91 and 93.

2116 E. Van Gool, "De nieuwe Richtlijn Consumentenkoop en duurzame consumptie" in E. Terryn and I. Claeys (eds.), *Nieuw recht inzake koop & digitale inhoud en diensten*, Mortsel, Intersentia, 2020, (303) 349.

2117 ICF, *Study on the costs and benefits of extending certain rights under the Consumer Sales and Guarantees Directive 1999/94/EC*, Luxemburg, EU Publications Office, 2017, 61.

2118 Here, indicative time limits such as time limits used by insurers (in household insurance contracts), test data, and time limits specified by manufacturers can play a clarifying role. See: P. Klik, *Koop en Consumentenkoop*, Deventer, Wolters Kluwer, 2022, 164. Ecodesign or other mandatory product specific (EU) legislation can also provide a useful framework. See: E. Terryn, "A Right to Repair? Towards Sustainable Remedies in Consumer Law", *ERPL* 2019, (851) 859–860.

2119 Art. 11(1) SGD.

2120 See Art. 5(3) CSD.

2121 In this regard, Van Gool and Michel rightly argue that this should be welcomed, as such longer presumption period is valuable in the fight against premature obsolescence. See: E. Van Gool and A. Michel, "The New Consumer Sales Directive 2019/771 and Sustainable Consumption", *EuCML* 2021, vol. 10, afl. 4, (136) 142.

use of this possibility.[2122] The presumption period is therefore better aligned with the duration of the two-year legal guarantee period.[2123] In the Netherlands, by contrast, the one-year presumption period of the Directive applies.[2124]

470. Remedies for non-conformity – If the product shows a lack of conformity, the PSS-user-buyer has access to a number of remedies, characterised by a certain hierarchy (the so-called hierarchy of remedies).[2125] Repair and replacement are the primary remedies, while price reduction and termination are secondary remedies.[2126]

471. Primary remedies for non-conformity – In the first place, the PSS user-buyer has the right to demand from the PSS supplier-seller to bring the product back into conformity, by means of repair or replacement free of charge.[2127] The term "free of charge" means that the supplier must cover the costs of bringing the product back into conformity, for instance shipping costs and costs related to labour and materials.[2128] In addition, it is required that repairs or replacements are carried out within a reasonable period of time and without any significant inconvenience for the consumer.[2129] In principle, the PSS user-buyer has a free choice between these two primary remedies unless the chosen remedy would be impossible or disproportionate with the other remedy.[2130] This would be the case, for example, if the consumer would ask replacement of the product because of a minor scratch that can be easily repaired.[2131] While the proposal for the Right to Repair Directive contained an amendment to limit consumer choice between the primary remedies by elevating repair as the sole primary remedy if the costs for replacement are equal to or greater than the costs for repair,[2132]

2122 Art. 1649*quater*, §4 old BCC.

2123 B. Tilleman and F. Van den Abeele, *Bijzondere overeenkomsten – A. Koop – Deel 2 Gevolgen van de koop*, Mechelen, Kluwer, 2022, 819.

2124 Art. 7:18a(2) DCC.

2125 EU: Art. 13 SGD. **Belgium**: Art. 1649*quinquies*, §1 old BCC. **The Netherlands**: Art. 7:21 and 7:22 DCC.

2126 See on the hierarchy of remedies e.g. S. Jansen, *Consumer Sales Remedies in US and EU Comparative Perspective*, Cambridge, Intersentia, 2018, 13–104.

2127 EU: Art. 13(2) SGD. **Belgium**: Art. 1649*quinquies*, §2 *juncto* Art. 1649*quinquies*, §3, 1° old BCC. **The Netherlands**: Art. 7:21(1), *sub* b. and c. *juncto* Art. 7:21(2) DCC.

2128 EU: Art. 2(14) SGD. This list is not exhaustive, see: CJEU, Judgment of 17 April 2008, C-404/06, *Quelle*, ECLI:EU:C:2008:231, para. 31 and CJEU, Judgment of 16 June 2011, Joined Cases C-65/09 and C-87/09, *Gebr. Weber and Putz*, ECLI:EU:C:2011:396, para. 50. **Belgium**: Art. 1649*bis*, §1, 13° old BCC. **The Netherlands**: Art. 7:21(2) and 7:21(7) DCC.

2129 EU: Art. 14(1)(b) and (c) SGD. **Belgium**: Art. 1649*quinquies*, §3, 2° and 3° old BCC. **The Netherlands**: 7:21(3) DCC.

2130 EU: Art. 13(2) SGD. **Belgium**: Art. 1649*quinquies*, §2 old BCC. **The Netherlands**: Art. 7:21(5) DCC.

2131 Recital 48 SGD.

2132 See Art. 12 EC, *Proposal for a Directive of the European Parliament and of the Council on common rules promoting the repair of goods and amending Regulation (EU) 2017/2394,* this did not make it into the new Right to Repair Directive. Instead, to promote the choice for the more sustainable remedy of repair, the new Right to Repair Directive places on the seller the obligation to inform the consumer about their right to choose between repair and replacement as well as the extension[2133] of the guarantee period if the consumer opts for repair.[2134] While it is to some extent regrettable that repair was not elevated to the sole primary remedy for non-conformity (provided repair is not more expensive than replacement), the question remains whether this would really have been effective. After all, replacement by products which are mass-produced abroad is still often cheaper than labour-intensive local repair.[2135] Therefore, it is important to focus on measures that change the mindset of consumers by making repair more attractive. The extension of the legal guarantee period discussed above, as well as providing a replacement good free of charge during the repair may be a step in the right direction.

472. Secondary remedies for non-conformity – Only in subsidiary order is the PSS user-buyer entitled to the secondary remedies of proportional price reduction[2136] and termination.[2137] Just like under general contract law, the PSS user-buyer will not be entitled to terminate the contract if the lack of conformity is only minor.[2138] This will first be the case if the PSS supplier-seller refuses to bring the product into conformity because repair and replacement are impossible or disproportionate.[2139] Additionally, the PSS user-buyer is also entitled to claim price reduction or termination if: a) the PSS supplier-seller did either not complete repair or replacement, or refused repair or replacement; b) the lack of conformity appears despite the attempts of the PSS supplier-seller to bring the goods in conformity; c) the lack of conformity is so serious it justifies an immediate price reduction or termination; and d) it is clear from the circumstances or declared by the PSS supplier-seller that the product will

Directives (EU) 2019/771 and (EU) 2020/1828, 22.3.2023, COM(2023) 155 final proposing to amend Art. 13(2) SGD.

2133 For the extension of the guarantee period, see *supra* no. 467.

2134 Art. 16(3) Right to Repair Directive.

2135 See e.g. E. Van Gool and A. Michel, "The New Consumer Sales Directive 2019/771 and Sustainable Consumption", *EuCML* 2021, vol. 10, afl. 4, (136) 144 and H.-W. Micklitz, "Squaring the Circle? Reconciling Consumer Law and the Circular Economy", *EuCML* 2019, vol. 6, (229) 236.

2136 EU: Art. 15 SGD. **Belgium**: Art. 1649*quinquies*, §6 old BCC. **The Netherlands**: Art. 7:22(1), *sub* b. DCC.

2137 EU: Art. 16 SGD. **Belgium**: Art. 1649*quinquies*, §7 old BCC. **The Netherlands**: Art. 7:22(1), *sub* a. DCC.

2138 EU: Art. 13(5) SGD. **Belgium**: Art. 1649*quinquies*, §5, (2) old BCC **The Netherlands**: Art. 7:22(1), *sub* a. DCC.

2139 EU: Art. 13(3) SGD and Art. 13(4)(a) SGD. **Belgium**: Art. 1649*quinquies*, §4 old BCC. **The Netherlands**: Art. 7:22(2) *juncto* Art. 7:21(3) DCC.

not be brought into conformity within a reasonable time or without significant inconvenience for the consumer.[2140]

4.3.2. USE-ORIENTED PSS: NO HARMONISED RULES

473. No harmonised rules on conformity of rental contracts – Unlike product-oriented PSS where conformity is governed by harmonised consumer sales contract rules, there are no harmonised rules regarding conformity for use-oriented PSS. It is therefore a matter of national law whether the delivered product "as-a-service" is in conformity with the PSS contract. Here, the rules of the rental contract on conformity of the rented good should mainly be considered.

474. Conformity of the rented product: applicable rules – Under Belgian law, conformity of the rented product is assessed both at the start of the contract and during the contract. At the start of the PSS contract, the rented product must be in a good state of repair.[2141] During the PSS contract, the PSS supplier must ensure the quiet rental enjoyment of the product.[2142] This means that the PSS supplier must indemnify the PSS user for its own acts, for certain acts of third parties and for defects.[2143, 2144]

Under Dutch law, conformity of the rented products in use-oriented PSS contracts is assessed in light of the obligation to place and leave the product at the disposal of the PSS user and the rules regarding defects.[2145] The PSS supplier (lessor) must place the product at the disposal of the PSS user (lessee) and leave it to his disposal "to the extent necessary for the agreed use".[2146] In the event of defects[2147] in the product, the PSS supplier has, in addition to the remedies of general contract law, access to certain specific remedies.[2148, 2149]

2140 EU: Art. 13(4) SGD. **Belgium**: Art. 1649*quinquies*, §5 old BCC. **The Netherlands**: Art. 7:22(5) DCC.

2141 See Art. 1720(1) old BCC: *"in alle opzichten in goede staat van onderhoud"/"en bon état de réparations de toute espèce."*

2142 Art. 1719, 3° old BCC.

2143 Art. 1719, 3° old BCC *juncto* Art. 1723–1724 old BCC (own acts), Art. 1725–1727 old BCC (acts of third parties) and Art. 1721 old BCC (defects).

2144 See *infra* no. 482–493.

2145 Art. 7:203 and 7:204(2) DCC. M.B.M. Loos, "Servitization, consumentenhuur en consumentenkoop", *WPNR* 2022/7396, (944) 945; H.J. Rossel and A.H.T. Heisterkamp, *Mr. C. Assers Handleiding tot de beoefening van het Nederlands Burgerlijk Recht. 7. Bijzondere overeenkomsten. Deel II. Huur*, Deventer, Wolters Kluwer, 2021, no. 27.

2146 Art. 7:203 DCC.

2147 See *infra* no. 476.

2148 See *infra* no. 503–510.

2149 Art. 7:204(1) DCC.

4.3.2.1. *Conformity at the start of the PSS contract*

475. Belgian law: delivery in good state of repair – For the product to be in conformity with the PSS contract, it must first be in a good state of repair at the time of entering into the contract. The Belgian rules of the rental contract state in this regard that the PSS supplier must deliver the good in all respects in a good state of repair so that the good can serve the use for which it was intended by the contract.[2150] Like the consumer sales contract, the Belgian rules of the rental contract thus also have to some extent an objective and a subjective component of conformity. On the one hand, the product must be objectively in a good state of repair, taking into account what an average lessee can expect (objective conformity requirement).[2151] A potential element to take into account here is the fact that the product offered may be refurbished and/or already previously used by another consumer.[2152] This can mean that some scratches or other signs of use must be tolerated by the PSS user. On the other hand, the product must be fit for the purpose agreed in the PSS contract (subjective conformity requirement). For example, the terms and conditions of *Fairphone Easy* state that the PSS user can expect to receive access to a Fairphone 4 5G device (256 GB, 8 GB RAM), a back cover protector in the choice of the PSS user, a standard screen protection and a USB-C cable if the PSS user opted in to pay extra for this.[2153] Similar contractual arrangements can relate to the amount of gears of a bicycle, the revolutions per minute ("RPM") or energy label of a washing machine, etc. If the delivered product does not meet the specified characteristics, for example because it is a different product, or some gears or washing programs are damaged or non-functioning, the PSS user will be able to file a claim for non-conformity.

476. Dutch law: delivery in good state of repair covered by concept of "defect" – Contrary to Belgian law, Dutch law has no separate provisions on the obligation to deliver the product in a good state of repair and the obligation to indemnify for defects (i.e. ensuring quiet rental enjoyment). The Dutch defects regime covers both conformity issues at the start of the PSS contract and conformity issues during the PSS contract.[2154] There is a defect if the product has a condition, characteristic or any other circumstance not imputable to the PSS user, as result of which the product cannot provide the PSS user with

---

2150 Art. 1720(1) old BCC. See for an example where this legal provision was included *verbatim* in the PSS contract: Art. 4.1 Terms and Conditions Papillon.

2151 The PSS supplier will, however, not be held to perform luxury repairs. See: Y. Merchiers, *Le bail en général*, Brussels, Larcier, 2015, 169, no. 155.

2152 Some PSS contracts also explicitly mention this. See e.g. Art. 5.4 Terms and Conditions Fairphone Easy.

2153 Art. 4.5 Terms and Conditions Fairphone Easy.

2154 Explanatory Memorandum, *Parliamentary Papers II* 1999/00, 26089, no. 6, 12 and 21; Explanatory Memorandum, *Parliamentary Papers II* 1997/98, 26089, no. 3, 14.

the enjoyment that a lessee may expect from a well-maintained product of the kind covered by the PSS contract at the time of entering into the contract.[2155] Consequently, two conformity requirements similar to Belgian law follow from the Dutch concept of defect.[2156] They are independent and equally important, but also often overlap. (i) First, the PSS user may expect the enjoyment resulting from the contractual arrangements in the PSS contract itself (subjective criterion).[2157] This can relate to potential specific uses that the PSS user communicated to the PSS supplier. (ii) In addition to the contractually agreed rental enjoyment, the PSS user is also entitled to the enjoyment he can expect based on the objective criterion arising from the legal description of defect. This objective criterion relates to the enjoyment that a lessee (i.e. an average PSS user) may expect of a well-maintained product of the kind covered by the contract. A potential element to take into account here is the fact that the product offered may be refurbished and/or already previously used by another consumer.[2158] This can mean that some scratches or other signs of use must be tolerated by the PSS user.

477. Delivery in good state of repair/defects regime requires PSS supplier to perform both major and minor repairs before the start of the contract – For the product to be delivered in all respects in a good state of repair, the PSS supplier may be obliged to carry out both major repairs and minor repairs (i.e. repairs for which, unless otherwise agreed, the PSS user is responsible during the contract) before the delivery. The rationale behind this is that if these repairs are required during the PSS contract, they are presumed to be required because of a fault on the part of the PSS user or a person for whom he was responsible.[2159] This presumption does not yet apply at the time of or before delivery, as the PSS user then does not have the use and enjoyment of the product. In practice, however, PSS contracts often waive the PSS user's responsibility to carry out minor repairs, so these are often born by the PSS supplier after all.[2160]

2155 Art. 7:204(2) DCC.

2156 A.M. Kloosterman, "Art. 204 – Burgerlijk Wetboek Boek 7. Gebrek zaak bij huur" in *Sdu Commentaar Huurrecht*, 9 August 2022, para. 1.

2157 What constitutes the contractually agreed rental enjoyment must be assessed using the *Haviltex* standard of interpretation. See: HR (NL) 13 March 1981, ECLI:NL:HR:1981:AG4158, (*Haviltex*), *NJ* 1981/635, case note C.J.H. Brunner, *RvdW* 1981, 43. This means that the answer to this question is based on the meaning that the parties could reasonably attribute to these provisions in the given circumstances and to what they could reasonably expect from each other in this respect (also discussed *supra* no. 360).

2158 Some PSS contracts also explicitly mention this. See e.g. Art. 5.4 Terms and Conditions Fairphone Easy.

2159 Art. 1732 and Art. 1735 old BCC; S. Marysse, "Rechten en verbintenissen van de verhuurder" in M. Dambre, B. Hubeau and S. Stijns (eds.), *Handboek algemeen huurrecht*, Bruges, Die Keure, 2015, (415) 425.

2160 See *infra* no. 485.

Also under Dutch law, the conformity requirements must be assessed at the time of entering into the PSS contract.[2161] This means that the PSS user may assume that the product has been properly maintained at the start of the PSS contract, both in view of the use agreed in the PSS contract and in view of the use an average PSS user can expect from such a product.[2162] This applies even if there are visible defects or visible overdue maintenance at the time of entering into the contract.[2163] The PSS user is therefore not bound by the obligation to carry out minor repairs (which is normally the lessee's responsibility[2164]) at the start of the PSS contract,[2165] although it must again be said that this is most often contractually deviated from in PSS contracts anyway.[2166]

478. Obligation to deliver the product in good state of repair/concept of defect is not mandatory law – As the Belgian provision requiring the PSS supplier to deliver the good in a good state of repair is not mandatory law, the PSS contract can deviate from this obligation.[2167] The same applies to the Dutch concept of defect.[2168] Consequently, the PSS contract may validly stipulate that the PSS user accepts the product "as is".[2169] This may be the case, for example, in a PSS contract regarding a refurbished product, which has obvious signs of use and is made available at a lower price. Also legally valid is the clause stating that the PSS user has inspected the product and found it in good condition or is satisfied with the condition of the product, provided that the PSS user has actually been able to check the delivered product.[2170] These

[2161] A.M. Kloosterman, "Art. 204 – Burgerlijk Wetboek Boek 7. Gebrek zaak bij huur" in *Sdu Commentaar Huurrecht*, 9 August 2022, para. 3.2.

[2162] H.J. Rossel and A.H.T. Heisterkamp, *Mr. C. Assers Handleiding tot de beoefening van het Nederlands Burgerlijk Recht. 7. Bijzondere overeenkomsten. Deel II. Huur*, Deventer, Wolters Kluwer, 2021, no. 28.

[2163] Explanatory Memorandum, *Parliamentary Papers II* 1999/00, 26089, no. 6, 12 and 21; Explanatory Memorandum, *Parliamentary Papers II* 1997/98, 26089, no. 3, 14.

[2164] Art. 7:217 DCC.

[2165] H.J. Rossel and A.H.T. Heisterkamp, *Mr. C. Assers Handleiding tot de beoefening van het Nederlands Burgerlijk Recht. 7. Bijzondere overeenkomsten. Deel II. Huur*, Deventer, Wolters Kluwer, 2021, no. 28 and 42; J.K. Six-Hummel, *Groene Serie Huurrecht, art. 7:217 BW*, Deventer, Kluwer, loose-leaf, 2012, para. 29. Contra: M.B.M. Loos, "Servitization, consumentenhuur en consumentenkoop", *WPNR* 2022/7396, (944) 946.

[2166] See *infra* no. 485.

[2167] S. Marysse, "Rechten en verbintenissen van de verhuurder" in M. Dambre, B. Hubeau and S. Stijns (eds.), *Handboek algemeen huurrecht*, Bruges, Die Keure, 2015, (415) 429.

[2168] H.J. Rossel and A.H.T. Heisterkamp, *Mr. C. Assers Handleiding tot de beoefening van het Nederlands Burgerlijk Recht. 7. Bijzondere overeenkomsten. Deel II. Huur*, Deventer, Wolters Kluwer, 2021, no. 29.

[2169] Compare with Art. 7 Terms and Conditions Dressr. See also: R. Timmermans, "Circulair bouwen, cascohuur, servitisatie, Madaster en afstand van bestanddeelvorming", *Huur* 2021, (106) 108.

[2170] E.g. J.P. Namur (BE) 4 May 1973, *Pas.* 1974, III, 4. Compare, however, with *supra* no. 479 on Art. VI.83, 15° BCEL blacklisting clauses that stipulate an unreasonably short period of time for reporting defects in the delivered product. Cambie argues in this regard that with visible

clauses have the effect of waiving the PSS user's right to demand delivery of the product in a good state of repair at the start of the contract.[2171] However, they only relate to the condition of the product at the time of delivery and covers only its visible defects.[2172] Regarding hidden defects of the product, the PSS user retains the option of bringing an action for indemnification for defects against the PSS supplier.[2173] An example of these clauses can be found in the Terms and Conditions of *Papillon*, where the PSS user is obliged to sign the delivery note to acknowledge that he received the product in a good state of repair:

> TERMS AND CONDITIONS PAPILLON – Art. 4.3 "The User undertakes to sign the delivery note and the certificate of use to acknowledge the receipt of the Product in a good state of repair, unless otherwise stated in writing on the delivery note."

479. REPORTING PROBLEMS REGARDING THE STATE OF REPAIR OF THE PRODUCT – If the PSS user is not satisfied with the state of repair of the product, either because it is not suitable for its normal use or because it is not suitable for the intended use of the PSS user, he must report this to the PSS supplier as soon as possible.[2174] The PSS supplier can include a clause in the PSS contract requiring the PSS user to report any defects within a certain time. Examples can be found, among others, in the terms and conditions of *Live Light* and *Blue Movement:*

> TERMS AND CONDITIONS LIVE LIGHT – Art. 5.7 "At the time of installation, the User shall inspect the Goods for visible defects and sign the delivery note indicating they have been well received. In doing so, the User shall state any defects in the Goods on the relevant document. The Goods are deemed to have been delivered in good condition and in accordance with the Rental agreement, if not stated otherwise on the aforementioned document."

---

defects, a distinction should be made between defects which the consumer can immediately and easily identify upon delivery and those which cannot be identified immediately upon a quick inspection. As regards the former, Art. VI.83, 15° BCEL would not oppose a clause stating that accepting delivery implies acceptance of the conformity of the product, obviously insofar as the consumer has actually been able to check the delivered goods. In the second case, the consumer should always be granted a minimum term. See: P. CAMBIE, *Onrechtmatige bedingen*, Ghent, Larcier, 2009, 265.

2171 J.P. Torhout (BE) 22 June 2004, *T.Vred.* 2006, 242. J.P. Merksem (BE) 22 May 1980, *RW* 1980–81, 2560.

2172 See e.g. Cass. (BE) 4 February 1960, *Arr.Cass.* 1960, 507; Ct. Brussels (BE) 26 February 1954, *JT* 1954, 399; Comm. Mons (BE) 13 October 1999, *T.Vred.* 2001, 115; R. TIMMERMANS, "Circulair bouwen, cascohuur, servitisatie, Madaster en afstand van bestanddeelvorming", *Huur* 2021, (106) 109; Y. MERCHIERS, *Le bail en général*, Brussels, Larcier, 2015, 171, no. 157; S. MARYSSE, "Rechten en verbintenissen van de verhuurder" in M. DAMBRE, B. HUBEAU and S. STIJNS (eds.), *Handboek algemeen huurrecht*, Bruges, Die Keure, 2015, (415) 431; R. DEKKERS, A.L. VERBEKE, N. CARETTE and K. VANHOVE, *Handboek burgerlijk recht, Deel III, Verbintenissen, bewijsleer en gebruikelijke contracten*, Antwerp, Intersentia, 2007, 577.

2173 See e.g. J.P. Bruges (BE) 10 October 1980, *RW* 1981–82, 2426.

2174 In **the Netherlands**, this is explicitly confirmed in Art. 7:222 DCC. Failing to do so, the PSS user will be obliged to compensate the PSS supplier for the damage caused by the negligence.

> Terms and conditions Blue Movement – Art. 9.1 "User reports a malfunction, defect, flaw, theft and/or damage to the Product if reasonably possible within 5 calendar days after he discovered or reasonably should have discovered it. User shall be liable for damage to the Product and other damages caused by late notification."

The regime on unfair terms must also be taken into account here. For example, the BCEL blacklists clauses that stipulate an unreasonably short period of time for reporting defects in the delivered product.[2175] Consequently, this term cannot be too short.[2176] This depends on a case-by-case basis and is assessed by the court.[2177] For most cases of visible defects regarding the state of repair of the product at the time of delivery, a minimum period of 24 or 48 hours seems reasonable. Similarly, the Dutch grey list contains a presumption that forfeiture clauses (i.e. clauses that provide for the forfeiture of one's rights or the ability to raise certain defences as a sanction for certain behaviour by the PSS user, in this case the failure to report the defect in time) are unreasonably onerous, except if such conduct justifies the forfeiture of those rights or defences.[2178] Forfeiture clauses are therefore allowed, provided that they are not unreasonable, for instance because the time limit is too short.[2179]

4.3.2.2 Conformity during the PSS contract

480. Belgian law: quiet rental enjoyment during the PSS contract – Besides the obligation to deliver the product in a good state of repair, Belgian law requires the PSS supplier to ensure the quiet rental enjoyment of the product during the PSS contract for the product to be in conformity.[2180] This obligation to ensure the quiet rental enjoyment presupposes three sub-obligations, namely the obligation to indemnify for one's own acts,[2181] the obligation to indemnify

---

2175 Art. VI.83, 15° BCEL. As this provision refers to "delivered products", it is not limited to sales contracts, but also applies to services contracts. See: R. Steennot, "Commentaar bij art. VI.83, 15° WER" in *Handels- en economisch recht. Commentaar met overzicht van rechtspraak en rechtsleer*, Mechelen, Kluwer, loose-leaf, 2017, (479) 480–481; F. Bogaert and B. Van Baeveghem, "Contractuele aspecten van de Wet Marktpraktijken" in I. Claeys, R. Steennot and M. Tison (eds.), *Economisch Recht: Ondernemingen, concurrenten en consumenten. Postuniversitaire Cyclus Willy Delva 2010–2011*, Mechelen, Kluwer, 2011, (1) 39.

2176 See e.g. Antwerp (BE) 13 October 2009, *NjW* 2010, 702, case note R. Steennot (a clause stipulating that the lessee (of a ladder lift) must report any defect at the latest at the time of taking delivery and that taking delivery implies irrevocable acceptance is contrary to Art. VI.83, 15° BCEL).

2177 I. Demuynck, *De inhoudelijke controle van onrechtmatige bedingen*, Thesis submitted to obtain the degree of Doctor of Laws, University of Ghent, 2000, 466.

2178 Art. 6:237, *sub* h. DCC; R.H.C. Jongeneel, "De grijze lijst" in B. Wessels and R.H.C. Jongeneel (eds.), *Algemene voorwaarden*, Deventer, Wolters Kluwer, 2017, (311) 326.

2179 R.H.C. Jongeneel, "De grijze lijst" in B. Wessels and R.H.C. Jongeneel (eds.), *Algemene voorwaarden*, Deventer, Wolters Kluwer, 2017, (311) 327.

2180 Art. 1719, 3° old BCC.

2181 Art. 1719, 3° old BCC *juncto* Art. 1723 and Art. 1724 old BCC.

for acts of third parties[2182] and the obligation to indemnify for defects.[2183] The PSS supplier's obligation to ensure the quiet rental enjoyment, including its sub-obligations, is not mandatory law.[2184] This means that the PSS contract may deviate from these rules, or set out its own contractual arrangement. However, this contractual regime must not completely devoid the PSS contract of its purpose. Contractual deviations from the default rules should be interpreted restrictively and, in case of doubt, to the detriment of the PSS supplier.[2185]

481. Dutch law: defects regime – As explained above, the Dutch defects regime does not only apply at the start of the PSS contract but continues to play a role during the PSS contract.[2186] It is not limited to defects in the material condition of the product, but also covers the PSS supplier's own acts and certain acts of third parties.[2187] Consequently, the scope of this concept runs parallel to the Belgian concept of quiet rental enjoyment. For conceptual clarity, we will therefore from here on differ between defects *sensu strictu*, which refers to material defects of the product, and to defects *sensu lato*, which also includes the obligation to indemnify for the PSS supplier's own acts and certain acts of third parties (and thus resembles the Belgian umbrella concept of quiet rental enjoyment). Also under Dutch law, the provision setting out the concept of "defect" (*sensu lato*) applicable to the rental contract for movables is only default law,[2188] so it can be deviated from both to the detriment and benefit of the PSS user.[2189]

482. Obligation to indemnify for defects (*sensu strictu*) – Under Belgian law, the conformity of the rented product during the PSS contract will be assessed mainly in the light of the PSS supplier's obligation to indemnify the PSS

2182 Art. 1719, 3° old BCC *juncto* Art. 1725, Art. 1726 and Art. 1727 old BCC.

2183 Art. 1719, 3° old BCC *juncto* Art. 1721 old BCC.

2184 S. Marysse, "Rechten en verbintenissen van de verhuurder" in M. Dambre, B. Hubeau and S. Stijns (eds.), *Handboek algemeen huurrecht*, Bruges, Die Keure, 2015, (415) 459, 464 and 473.

2185 Y. Merchiers, *Le bail en général*, Brussels, Larcier, 2015, no. 195, no. 204 and no. 213. See also S. Marysse, "Rechten en verbintenissen van de verhuurder" in M. Dambre, B. Hubeau and S. Stijns (eds.), *Handboek algemeen huurrecht*, Bruges, Die Keure, 2015, (415) 460, 465 and 474 and the references there.

2186 See *supra* no. 474.

2187 H.J. Rossel and A.H.T. Heisterkamp, *Mr. C. Assers Handleiding tot de beoefening van het Nederlands Burgerlijk Recht. 7. Bijzondere overeenkomsten. Deel II. Huur*, Deventer, Wolters Kluwer, 2021, no. 30.

2188 Compare with Art. 7:242(1) DCC, which states that for the rental of residential premises (*huur van woonruimte*), it is not possible to deviate from Art. 7:204 DCC to the detriment of the consumer, except by way of standard regulation within the meaning of Art. 6:214 DCC.

2189 A.M. Kloosterman, "Art. 204 – Burgerlijk Wetboek Boek 7. Gebrek zaak bij huur" in *Sdu Commentaar Huurrecht*, 9 August 2022, para. 4; H.J. Rossel and A.H.T. Heisterkamp, *Mr. C. Assers Handleiding tot de beoefening van het Nederlands Burgerlijk Recht. 7. Bijzondere overeenkomsten. Deel II. Huur*, Deventer, Wolters Kluwer, 2021, no. 29.

user for defects, which is a sub-obligation of the obligation to ensure the quiet rental enjoyment.[2190] According to this obligation, the PSS supplier is responsible for all defects of the rented product that prevent its use, even if the PSS supplier may not have known about them when entering into the PSS contract.[2191] This obligation is generally considered an obligation of result.[2192] Also under Dutch law, conformity will mainly be assessed in the light of the obligation to remedy material defects (i.e. defects *sensu strictu*) which is part of the broader defects regime.

483. Concept of "defect" – The old BCC gives no guidance on what is to be understood by the term "defect". Generally, a defect within the meaning of this obligation refers to any defect in the product which renders it unfit for its normal or contractually intended use.[2193] Thus, here again, the notion of conformity entails an objective and a subjective component. It is irrelevant whether the defect existed before the start of the PSS contract or only manifested itself during the PSS contract.[2194] The defect must be inherent to the rented product. Consequently, defects that do not arise from the product itself (e.g. a circumstance not imputable to the PSS supplier such as *force majeure*, accidental circumstances, or government measures impacting the use of the product) are not covered by this obligation.[2195, 2196] As already explained above,[2197] the DCC explicitly defines the concept of defect, namely as "*any condition, characteristic or any other circumstance not imputable to the PSS user, as result of which the product cannot provide the PSS user with the enjoyment that a lessee may expect from a well-maintained product of the kind covered by the PSS contract at the time of entering into the contract.*"[2198]

484. PSS supplier is not responsible for defects caused by a fault of the PSS user – The PSS supplier can in principle not be held responsible

2190 Art. 1721 old BCC.

2191 Art. 1721(1) old BCC. See also: Liège (BE) 21 October 1966, *Pas.* 1967, II, 151.

2192 E.g. Liège (BE) 15 March 1999, *TBBR* 2000, 356, case note B. Hubeau; Ct. Brussels (BE) 8 May 2006, *TBBR* 2008, 40; Ct. Tournai (BE) 25 May 2004, *JLMB* 2006, 366; J.P. Jumet (BE) 16 September 1997, *JT* 1998, 292; S. Marysse, "Rechten en verbintenissen van de verhuurder" in M. Dambre, B. Hubeau and S. Stijns (eds.), *Handboek algemeen huurrecht*, Bruges, Die Keure, 2015, (415) 468.

2193 Ct. Brussels (BE) 8 May 2006, *TBBR* 2008, 40; J.P. Jumet (BE) 16 September 1997, *JT* 1998, 292.

2194 L. Simont, J. De Gavre and P.-A. Foriers, "Examen de jurisprudence (1981–1991). Les contrats spéciaux", *RCJB* 1996, (263) 287.

2195 S. Marysse, "Rechten en verbintenissen van de verhuurder" in M. Dambre, B. Hubeau and S. Stijns (eds.), *Handboek algemeen huurrecht*, Bruges, Die Keure, 2015, (415) 470–471.

2196 Of course, in some cases it is possible that these defects fall within the other sub-obligations of Art. 1719, 3° old BCC or Art. 1722 old BCC.

2197 See *supra* no. 476.

2198 Art. 7:204(2) DCC.

for defects that are due to a fault on the part of the PSS user.[2199] Therefore, it is important that the PSS user informs the PSS supplier without delay of the occurrence of any defects, or if an existing defect worsens.[2200] Of course, the PSS contract can deviate from this, for example by allowing one or two free reparations of defects that are caused by the PSS supplier per year (e.g. a broken smartphone screen).

> Terms and Conditions Fairphone Easy – Art. 6.2 "You may swap Your device only in case the following applies: [...] Your screen is damaged. You will be able to replace Your screen once a year. Please note anything beyond this yearly allowance will be subject to additional charges."

From a consumer point of view, these clauses are a good thing, as they contribute to the goal of "unburdening" the PSS user, which is the exact goal of many use-oriented PSS. However, from a circular economy perspective, these clauses should be treated with caution, as they may give rise to imprudent behaviour (moral hazard) on the part of the consumer and thus lead to more damaged products and thus suboptimal use of resources.

485. Minor defects are borne by the PSS user, unless contractually agreed otherwise – Both under Belgian and Dutch law, the PSS supplier's obligation to indemnify for defects does not apply to minor defects.[2201, 2202] This is a reflection of the PSS user's obligation to carry out minor repairs at his own expense during the PSS contract.[2203] In Belgium, this obligation is however

2199 **Belgium**: M. La Haye and J. Vankerckhove, "Louage de choses. Chronique de jurisprudence", *JT* 1961, (273) 278, no. 42. **The Netherlands**: H.J. Rossel and A.H.T. Heisterkamp, *Mr. C. Assers Handleiding tot de beoefening van het Nederlands Burgerlijk Recht. 7. Bijzondere overeenkomsten. Deel II. Huur*, Deventer, Wolters Kluwer, 2021, no. 33; A.W. Jongbloed, "Huur" in H.N. Schelhaas and A.J. Verheij (eds.), *Bijzondere overeenkomsten in Studiereeks Burgerlijk Recht*, Deventer, Wolters Kluwer, 2023, (159) 168–169, no. 174; A.M. Kloosterman, "De verplichtingen van de verhuurder" in A.M. Kloosterman, H.J. Rossel and M.H. Rozeboom (eds.), *Hoofdlijnen in het huurrecht. Met vragen en antwoorden*, Deventer, Wolters Kluwer, 2020, (39) 48. This is the case, for example, if the PSS user fails carry out obliged minor repairs (Art. 7:217 DCC) or for damage to the product caused by himself or by persons for whom he is liable (Art. 7:219 DCC).

2200 Compare with *supra* no. 479 on the duty for the PSS user to report defects regarding the state of repair of the product at the start of the PSS contract.

2201 I.e. defects resulting from normal use of the rented product and involving relatively low costs.

2202 See also *infra* no. 533.

2203 **Belgium**: Art. 1754 old BCC. M. Dambre, "Rechten en verbintenissen van de huurder" in M. Dambre, B. Hubeau and S. Stijns (eds.), *Handboek algemeen huurrecht*, Bruges, Die Keure, 2015, (513) 562; Y. Merchiers, *Le bail en général*, Brussels, Larcier, 2015, 215–216, no. 263. **The Netherlands**: Art. 7:217 DCC *juncto* Art. 7:204(2) and 7:206(2) DCC. H.J. Rossel and A.H.T. Heisterkamp, *Mr. C. Assers Handleiding tot de beoefening van het Nederlands Burgerlijk Recht. 7. Bijzondere overeenkomsten. Deel II. Huur*, Deventer, Wolters Kluwer, 2021, no. 108; J.K. Six-Hummel, *Groene Serie Huurrecht, art. 7:217 BW*, Deventer, Kluwer, loose-leaf, 2012, para. 21.

limited to the extent that the PSS user will not have to take responsibility for minor repairs caused by aging or *force majeure*.[2204] Also in the Netherlands, the PSS user does not have to carry out minor repairs caused by aging or normal use,[2205] but he will have to take responsibility for minor repairs due to *force majeure*.[2206] As the obligation to carry out minor repairs is only default law, the PSS contract can deviate from this by stating that the PSS supplier will also be responsible for minor defects and repairs. Most use-oriented PSS contracts do indeed contain such a clause to truly "unburden" the PSS user.[2207, 2208]

486. Obligation to indemnify for defects is limited to hidden defects under Belgian law, visible defects covered under Dutch law – Under Belgian law, the indemnity obligation of the PSS supplier is limited to hidden defects.[2209] Defects that were visible at the time of conclusion of the PSS contract are not covered.[2210] A visible defect exists if, after a normal inspection of the product, the PSS user should have noticed it before concluding the PSS contract.[2211] In contrast, the Dutch defects regime also applies to visible defects, of course unless the parties agree otherwise in the PSS contract.[2212]

487. Non-mandatory nature of concept of defects allows for setting out examples in the PSS contract – The non-mandatory character of the Belgian and Dutch obligation to indemnify for defects means the PSS contract can stipulate and define what conditions and characteristics of the product should be understood as a defect.[2213] For example, the terms and conditions of *Swapfiets* explicitly provide examples of the defects that are covered by the subscription, namely "a flat tire, a broken (chain) guard, a torn saddle, and

---

2204 Art. 1755 old BCC. M. Dambre, "Rechten en verbintenissen van de huurder" in M. Dambre, B. Hubeau and S. Stijns (eds.), *Handboek algemeen huurrecht*, Bruges, Die Keure, 2015, (513) 563.

2205 Art. 7:224(2) DCC.

2206 Explanatory Memorandum, *Parliamentary Papers II* 1997/98, 26089, no. 3, 27; J.K. Six-Hummel, *Groene Serie Huurrecht, art. 7:217 BW*, Deventer, Kluwer, loose-leaf, 2012, para. 21.

2207 V. Mak, "Consumentenbescherming bij servitization" in *Preadviezen VVSR-BN 2019*, Den Haag, Boom juridische uitgevers, 2019, (98) 794–795.

2208 See also *infra* no. 735.

2209 D. Janssen, "Droits et obligations du bailleur – La garantie des vices de la chose" in G. Benoit, I. Durant, P.-A. Foriers, M. Vanwijck-Alexandre and P. Wéry (eds.), *Le droit commun du bail*, Bruges, Die Keure, 2006, (176) 179, no. 173.

2210 Comm. Leuven (BE) 7 October 2014, *RW* 2016–17, 953, *TBO* 2016, 366.

2211 M. La Haye and J. Vankerckhove, "Louage de choses. Chronique de jurisprudence", *JT* 1961, (273) 278, no. 38–39.

2212 A.W. Jongbloed, "Huur" in H.N. Schelhaas and A.J. Verheij (eds.), *Bijzondere overeenkomsten in Studiereeks Burgerlijk Recht*, Deventer, Wolters Kluwer, 2023, (159) 169, no. 174.

2213 **Belgium**: S. Marysse, "Rechten en verbintenissen van de verhuurder" in M. Dambre, B. Hubeau and S. Stijns (eds.), *Handboek algemeen huurrecht*, Bruges, Die Keure, 2015, (415) 473. **The Netherlands**: A.M. Kloosterman, "Art. 204 – Burgerlijk Wetboek Boek 7. Gebrek zaak bij huur" in *Sdu Commentaar Huurrecht*, 9 August 2022, para. 4.

broken lighting"[2214] Similarly, *Fairphone Easy* also lists the cases in which the PSS user can swap its smartphone, namely in case of a damaged device (this includes *"damages caused by manufacturing defects, improper or inferior workmanship, materials and/or design"*), a damaged screen or a damaged battery (both limited to one free swap per year) and hardware issues.[2215]

488. Failure to ensure continuous availability of the product constitutes defect – The obligation to ensure the quiet rental enjoyment of the product (i.e. obligation to indemnify for defects *sensu lato*), in particular the obligation to indemnify for defects (*sensu strictu*), entails that the PSS supplier must in principle ensure the continuous availability of the product.[2216] This means that any interruptions in the enjoyment of the product, for example due to a defect, will give rise to an obligation for the PSS supplier to remedy the defect and/or trigger its contractual liability.

489. Clauses on ensuring (near-) continuous availability of the product – Since the obligation to indemnify for defects is not mandatory law, the PSS contract can specify and modulate this obligation to ensure the continuous availability of the product. This can be either truly continuous availability, or availability for a specified amount of time, for example by reserving for planned or unplanned outages.[2217] Nevertheless, there is some caution for the PSS supplier when formulating such near-continuous availability clauses. Indeed, since this obligation is generally considered an essential obligation of the PSS contract, a limitation to an unreasonably low availability of the product could amount to a "disguised" exemption clause.[2218] Exemption clauses are subject to strict validity limits, including the fact that they may not exempt the debtor of liability for non-performance of one or more essential obligations of the contract, thereby devoiding the PSS contract of its purpose.[2219] It is therefore advisable that the availability specified in the PSS contract remains close to a (near) continuous availability and that ((un)planned) interruptions

---

2214 Art. 3.3, (1) Terms and Conditions Swapfiets.

2215 Art. 6.2 Terms and Conditions Fairphone Easy.

2216 C. Borucki, H. Slachmuylders, B. Keirsbilck, D. Gruyaert and E. Terryn, *Model clauses for Product-as-a-Service (PaaS) contracts*, CE Center. Circular Economy Policy Research Center, 2022–23, 56.

2217 H. Slachmuylders, "Movable Servitization. Contractual Liability in the B2C Relationship" in B. Keirsbilck, E. Terryn, J. Eyckmans, S. Rousseau and D. Voinot (eds.), *Servitization and circular economy: economic and legal challenges*, Antwerp, Intersentia, 2023, (135) 150; A. Van Vaerenbergh and F. Leyman, "'Product als dienst'-overeenkomsten, een stap in de richting van de circulaire economie", *MER* 2019, (20) 26. See for an example Art. 7 of Agoria's Standard Agreement for Efficiency as a Service.

2218 **Belgium**: S. Stijns, *Verbintenissenrecht*, Boek 1, Bruges, Die Keure, 2022, 214–215. **The Netherlands**: R.H.C. Jongeneel, "Aansprakelijkheidsbeperking" in B. Wessels and R.H.C. Jongeneel (eds.), *Algemene voorwaarden*, Deventer, Wolters Kluwer, 2017, (385) 386.

2219 See *supra* no. 312.

are minimised as much as possible, unless a lower availability is common and expected within a certain industry or for a certain business model.[2220]

490. Remedying failure to guarantee (near-) continuous availability – In the event of a failure to guarantee the (near-) continuous availability of the product, the PSS supplier must remedy the defect. Here, the PSS contract can also modulate or further specify this obligation. For example, it may provide in the event of unavailability of the product or other impairment of its functioning, the PSS supplier must make all reasonable efforts to restore access to the product as soon as possible. Alternatively, the contract may provide a specified period of time for the PSS supplier to remedy the defect. Here, a distinction may also be made between a maximum time to respond, i.e. the maximum time for the PSS supplier to confirm the receipt of the complaint and provide an indication of a timeframe for remedying the defect, or a maximum time to resolve the defect (e.g. within 24 or 48 hours).[2221] Depending on the wording of the clause, this obligation will be qualified as an obligation of result or an obligation of means.[2222]

491. Defects *sensu lato*: PSS supplier's own act and certain acts of third parties – Besides the obligation to indemnify the PSS user from material defects (defects *sensu strictu*), a lack of conformity of the rented product can also arise from an act by the PSS supplier itself or by third parties (defects *sensu lato*). Under certain circumstances, these acts will also trigger the PSS supplier's liability.

492. Obligation to indemnify for one's own acts – The PSS supplier's obligation to indemnify for its own acts means that, during the term of the PSS contract, the PSS supplier may not commit any legal or material act that could, either directly or indirectly, interfere with the use or enjoyment of the rented product.[2223] This obligation applies equally to the PSS supplier's auxiliaries such as subcontractors providing certain additional (digital) services to the

2220 C. Borucki, H. Slachmuylders, B. Keirsbilck, D. Gruyaert and E. Terryn, *Model clauses for Product-as-a-Service (PaaS) contracts*, CE Center. Circular Economy Policy Research Center, 2022–23, 56.

2221 H. Slachmuylders, "Movable Servitization. Contractual Liability in the B2C Relationship" in B. Keirsbilck, E. Terryn, J. Eyckmans, S. Rousseau and D. Voinot (eds.), *Servitization and circular economy: economic and legal challenges*, Antwerp, Intersentia, 2023, (135) 150.

2222 See *supra* no. 276.

2223 **Belgium**: S. Marysse, "Rechten en verbintenissen van de verhuurder" in M. Dambre, B. Hubeau and S. Stijns (eds.), *Handboek algemeen huurrecht*, Bruges, Die Keure, 2015, (415) 451. See for an application: Ct. Tournai (BE) 9 September 2003, *JLMB* 2005, 782. **The Netherlands**: H.J. Rossel and A.H.T. Heisterkamp, *Mr. C. Assers Handleiding tot de beoefening van het Nederlands Burgerlijk Recht. 7. Bijzondere overeenkomsten. Deel II. Huur*, Deventer, Wolters Kluwer, 2021, no. 30 and no. 27. This situation is also covered by the obligation to leave the property at the PSS user's disposal (Art. 7:203 DCC).

product.[2224] This obligation entails, *inter alia*, that the PSS supplier may not change (the configuration of) the product, unless otherwise stipulated in the PSS contract.[2225] Another aspect of this obligation implies that the PSS supplier is not allowed to materially disturb the quiet enjoyment, for example by conducting unreasonably frequent visits to ascertain the state of maintenance of the product.[2226] However, often the very purpose of the PSS contract is to carry out periodic inspection and maintenance in order to extend the life of the product and "unburden" the consumer. As the obligation to indemnify for one's own acts is not mandatory law, it is to some extent possible[2227] and necessary to work out a reasonable periodic maintenance schedule in the PSS contract so that the PSS user is not unnecessarily disturbed in his quiet enjoyment. In addition, making the product unusable (remotely or otherwise), for example in case the monthly fees are not paid, also violates the PSS supplier's obligation to indemnify the PSS user for its own acts.[2228]

493. Obligation to indemnify for acts of third parties – A third sub-obligation of the obligation to ensure the quiet rental enjoyment of the product (defects *sensu lato*), is the PSS supplier's obligation to indemnify for certain acts of third parties. This obligation only relates to legal defects (BE: *rechtsstoornissen, troubles de droit*; NL: *bewering van recht*) and not to factual defects (*feitelijke stoornissen, troubles de fait*).[2229] This means that the PSS supplier must indemnify

2224 Y. Merchiers, *Le bail en général*, Brussels, Larcier, 2015, 184–185, no. 189.

2225 Art. 1723 old BCC. See also *supra* no. 435 on replacing the product with a different one.

2226 **Belgium**: S. Marysse, "Rechten en verbintenissen van de verhuurder" in M. Dambre, B. Hubeau and S. Stijns (eds.), *Handboek algemeen huurrecht*, Bruges, Die Keure, 2015, (415) 456–457; J. Vankerckhove, P. Coeckelberghs, A. Devreux, J.-M. Letier, B. Louveaux, B. Vandeputte and M. Vlies, *Le louage de choses 1: Les baux en général*, Brussels, Larcier, 2000, 448, no. 622. **The Netherlands**: H.J. Rossel and A.H.T. Heisterkamp, *Mr. C. Assers Handleiding tot de beoefening van het Nederlands Burgerlijk Recht. 7. Bijzondere overeenkomsten. Deel II. Huur*, Deventer, Wolters Kluwer, 2021, no. 30.

2227 However, the indemnity for own defects cannot be waived entirely. See: H. De Page, *Traité élémentaire de droit civil belge*, IV, Brussels, Bruylant, 1972, 631, no. 614. Accordingly, a clause stating that the PSS supplier can check the status of the rented product at any time will disturb the PSS user's quiet rental enjoyment. See e.g. J.P. St. Gilles Brussels (BE) 8 December 1980, *T.Vred.* 1982, 162.

2228 **Belgium**: Compare with Marysse, who argues that making the rented property uninhabitable under the pretext of non-payment of the rent violates the lessor's obligation to indemnify for his own acts. S. Marysse, "Rechten en verbintenissen van de verhuurder" in M. Dambre, B. Hubeau and S. Stijns (eds.), *Handboek algemeen huurrecht*, Bruges, Die Keure, 2015, (415) 458, no. 107. However, see for the application of the enac by the PSS supplier *supra* no. 299. **The Netherlands**: See e.g. Hof Arnhem-Leeuwarden (NL) 07 August 2018, ECLI:NL:GHARL:2018:7133, *WR* 2019/9, case note J.A. Tuinman and Hof 's-Hertogenbosch (NL) 11 April 2017, ECLI:NL:GHSHE:2017:1578, *NJF* 2017/496 (Rent arrears do not justify obstructing access to the rented property (by changing the locks) if the rental agreement has not (yet) been legally terminated). H.J. Rossel and A.H.T. Heisterkamp, *Mr. C. Assers Handleiding tot de beoefening van het Nederlands Burgerlijk Recht. 7. Bijzondere overeenkomsten. Deel II. Huur*, Deventer, Wolters Kluwer, 2021, no. 27.

2229 **Belgium**: M. Dambre, *Bijzondere overeenkomsten: de essentie*, Bruges, Die Keure, 2022, 211. **The Netherlands**: e.g. H.J. Rossel and A.H.T. Heisterkamp, *Mr. C. Assers Handleiding tot de*

the PSS user for the rights that third parties would claim to have over the rented product.[2230] Under Dutch law, the additional rule applies that rights claimed by a third party (i.e. legal defects) without an actual factual defect does not trigger the indemnification obligation of the PSS supplier.[2231] Examples of acts of third parties that will trigger the PSS supplier's responsibility to indemnify the PSS user include the situation where a third party claims to have a right of use over the product (e.g. another rental contract) or that he owns the rented product. The remedies open to the PSS user for legal defects differ from the remedies for other defects. In case of legal defects, the PSS user should notify the PSS supplier of this legal defect, upon which the PSS supplier should intervene to defend the PSS user's interests against the third party.[2232] However, these situations will be rare in case of PSS contracts. In contrast, the PSS supplier must not assume responsibility for third parties who interfere with the enjoyment of the product but do not assert a right to it (i.e. factual defects).[2233] Examples of these factual defects caused by third parties are damage caused by vandalism, theft of the product, or government measures that prohibit the use of the product.[2234] As these examples illustrate, these factual defects will occur more frequently than legal defects, and are thus borne by the PSS user, who will have to bring a claim against the third party to stop the factual defect.

494. No provision on correct installation of rented product – Contrary to the consumer sales rules, the rules on the rental contract for movables do not contain an explicit provision dealing with the incorrect installation of the product.[2235] In case of conformity problems due to incorrect

beoefening van het Nederlands Burgerlijk Recht. 7. Bijzondere overeenkomsten. Deel II. Huur, Deventer, Wolters Kluwer, 2021, no. 36–38.

2230 **Belgium**: Art. 1726 and 1727 old BCC. V. Sagaert, B. Tilleman and A.-L. Verbeke, *Vermogensrecht in kort bestek*, Antwerp, Intersentia, 2022, 270, no. 718.

2231 **The Netherlands**: Art. 7:204(3) DCC. H.J. Rossel and A.H.T. Heisterkamp, *Mr. C. Assers Handleiding tot de beoefening van het Nederlands Burgerlijk Recht. 7. Bijzondere overeenkomsten. Deel II. Huur*, Deventer, Wolters Kluwer, 2021, no. 36 and no. 38; A.M. Kloosterman, "Art. 204 – Burgerlijk Wetboek Boek 7. Gebrek zaak bij huur" in *Sdu Commentaar Huurrecht*, 9 August 2022, para. 5.2; A.M. Kloosterman, "De verplichtingen van de verhuurder" in A.M. Kloosterman, H.J. Rossel and M.H. Rozeboom (eds.), *Hoofdlijnen in het huurrecht. Met vragen en antwoorden*, Deventer, Wolters Kluwer, 2020, (39) 48.

2232 **Belgium**: Art. 1726 *in fine* old BCC *juncto* Art. 1727 old BCC. S. Marysse, "Rechten en verbintenissen van de verhuurder" in M. Dambre, B. Hubeau and S. Stijns (eds.), *Handboek algemeen huurrecht*, Bruges, Die Keure, 2015, (415) 465–466. **The Netherlands**: Art. 7:211 DCC. See also: H.J. Rossel and A.H.T. Heisterkamp, *Mr. C. Assers Handleiding tot de beoefening van het Nederlands Burgerlijk Recht. 7. Bijzondere overeenkomsten. Deel II. Huur*, Deventer, Wolters Kluwer, 2021, no. 59.

2233 **Belgium**: Art. 1725 old BCC. **The Netherlands**: Art. 7:204(3) DCC.

2234 **Belgium**: S. Marysse, "Rechten en verbintenissen van de verhuurder" in M. Dambre, B. Hubeau and S. Stijns (eds.), *Handboek algemeen huurrecht*, Bruges, Die Keure, 2015, (415) 463–464. **The Netherlands**: H.J. Rossel and A.H.T. Heisterkamp, *Mr. C. Assers Handleiding tot de beoefening van het Nederlands Burgerlijk Recht. 7. Bijzondere overeenkomsten. Deel II. Huur*, Deventer, Wolters Kluwer, 2021, no. 37.

2235 Compare with Art. 8 SGD, Art. 1649*ter*, §8 old BCC and Art. 7:18a(1) DCC. See *supra* no. 465.

installation, the rules regarding the contract for services (Belgium) and the contract for works (the Netherlands) will therefore have to be considered.[2236] However, incorrect installation will also result in the PSS user not being able to make useful use of the product. This is also acknowledged in the DCFR, where a provision is included dealing with the conformity of incorrectly installed products in consumer rental contracts similar to that of the consumer sales contract.[2237]

495. Conformity of digital content and digital services part of the use-oriented PSS contract – If the rented product includes digital content or digital services (as will be the case with connected "smart" products), conformity of these digital elements must also be assessed in light of the DCD's conformity requirements.[2238] Similar to the SGD, this Directive contains detailed provisions on the subjective and objective conformity requirements for digital content and digital services.[2239]

496. Digital content and digital services: subjective conformity requirements – The subjective conformity requirements result directly from the contractual relationship between the PSS supplier and the PSS user. Thus, the description, quantity and quality, functionality, compatibility, interoperability and other features of the digital content or digital service must be in accordance with the contract; the digital content or digital service must be fit for the particular purpose required by the PSS user (if this has been communicated to and accepted by the PSS supplier); and the accessories, (installation) instructions, customer assistance and updates must be supplied as provided for in the contract.[2240]

497. Digital content and digital services: objective conformity requirements – The objective conformity requirements are indirectly part of the contract because the PSS user can reasonably expect them to be. For example, the digital content or digital service must be fit for the purposes for which digital content or digital services of this type would normally be used; the digital content or digital service must possess the quantity, quality and performance features (e.g. functionality, compatibility, accessibility, continuity and security) normal for digital content or digital services of the same type; it

---

2236 See *infra* no. 706–707.

2237 Art. IV.B. – 3:105 DCFR.

2238 See *supra* no. 410. See also for an application of the Belgian implementation of the DCD on a washing machine as a service contract: H. Slachmuylders, "Belgian draft law for digital content and digital services – relevance for Product as a Service contracts", *CCM Blog* 10 January 2022, https://law.kuleuven.be/ccm/blog/?p=286.

2239 EU: Art. 7 and 8 DCD. **Belgium**: Art. 1701/5, 1701/6 and 1701/7 old BCC. **The Netherlands**: Art. 50ae-50af DCC.

2240 EU: Art. 7 DCD. **Belgium**: Art. 1701/5 old BCC. **The Netherlands**: Art. 50ae(1) DCC.

must be supplied along with accessories and instructions which the PSS user may reasonably expect to receive; and the digital content or digital service must comply with any trial version or preview made available by the PSS supplier before the conclusion of the contract.[2241] The PSS supplier must also ensure that the PSS user is informed of and supplied with updates (including security updates) that are necessary to keep the digital service in conformity.[2242]

498. Possibility to deviate from objective conformity requirements in the PSS contract – Similar to the rules under the SGD, the PSS supplier may deviate from these objective conformity requirements in the PSS contract.[2243] Just like under the SGD, this requires that, at the time of conclusion of the contract, the consumer was particularly informed that a particular characteristic of the digital content or digital service (e.g. the availability of future updates) was deviating from the objective conformity requirements *and* the PSS user expressly and separately accepted that deviation when concluding the contract.[2244]

4.3.2.3. Liability for non-conformity and remedies

499. Liability for non-conformity – Similar to product-oriented PSS, the PSS supplier will incur liability if the rented product is not in conformity with the PSS contract. As we have seen, the consumer sales rules lay down a detailed regime listing subjective and objective conformity criteria, whereas the rules for the rental contract for movables set out these objective and subjective conformity requirements in more general terms. However, despite this difference in wording, there does not seem to be a substantial difference between the concept of conformity under the consumer sales contract and conformity under the rental contract for movables.[2245] If the PSS user can prove that the product does not meet the criteria agreed in the contract or does not correspond to what the PSS user is entitled to expect, the PSS supplier will be liable. Nevertheless, a key difference lies in the mandatory nature of the conformity requirements under consumer sales law[2246, 2247] compared to the non-mandatory nature of

2241 EU: Art. 8(1) DCD. **Belgium**: Art. 1701/6, §1 old BCC. **The Netherlands: Art.** Art. 50ae(2) DCC.

2242 EU: Art. 8(2) DCD. **Belgium**: Art. 1701/6, §2 old BCC. **The Netherlands**: Art. 50ae(4) DCC.

2243 Compare with *supra* no. 464.

2244 EU: Art. 8(5) DCD. **Belgium**: Art. 1701/6, §4 old BCC. **The Netherlands**: Art. 50ae(6) DCC.

2245 See in this sense also M.B.M. Loos, "Servitization, consumentenhuur en consumentenkoop", *WPNR* 2022/7396, (944) 945.

2246 EU: Art. 21 SGD. **Belgium**: art. 1649*octies* old BCC. See also Art. VI.83, 14° BCEL (blacklisting clauses that waive or restrict the provisions on the legal guarantee). **The Netherlands**: Art. 7:6(1) DCC.

2247 Yet this should be nuanced in light of the possibility for the PSS supplier to deviate from objective conformity requirements under certain circumstances (Art. 7.3 SGD). See *supra* no. 464.

conformity under the rules for the rental contract for movables with consumers. In this sense, PSS users are better protected in product-oriented PSS than in use-oriented PSS.

500. No strict liability period, PSS supplier is liable for defects present at the start of and arising during the PSS contract – Another difference between product-oriented and use-oriented PSS is the period in which the PSS supplier will be liable. For consumer sales contracts, according to the SGD and its Belgian implementing provisions, the legal guarantee period is 2 years, while under Dutch law a lifespan guarantee applies depending on the expected lifetime of the product.[2248] Under the rental contract for movables, there is no similar legal guarantee period, but the PSS supplier is liable for defects that exist at the start of the PSS contract and those that arise during the PSS contract.

501. No presumption period – Under both the rules on consumer sales and the rules on rental contracts for movables, the PSS user must prove the lack of conformity of the product. In the case of a consumer sales contract, as mentioned above, the PSS user benefits here from a presumption period in which any defect that manifests itself within this period is presumed to have already existed at the time of delivery.[2249] In contrast, such a presumption period is lacking in the rules of the rental contract for movables. In fact, the PSS user is even (rebuttably) presumed to be liable for any damages or losses to the product that occurred during the PSS contract.[2250, 2251] However, this does not apply if no rental inventory was drawn up at the beginning of the contract, as in that case the PSS user is presumed to have received the product in the condition it is in at the end of the contract.[2252] The PSS supplier must then prove that the damage occurred during the PSS contract.[2253] Additionally, the PSS user will also not be liable for damage to the product that is caused by normal wear and tear.[2254] So the rules of the rental contract for movables have a different angle:

2248 See *supra* no. 466–468.

2249 See *supra* no. 469.

2250 **Belgium**: Art. 1732 old BCC. Nevertheless, the PSS user can prove that the damage or losses are not due to his fault. It is therefore a rebuttable presumption. **The Netherlands**: Art. 7:218(1) and (2) DCC. See also Art. 7:218(3) which states that, unless a rental inventory was drawn up (cf. Art. 7:224(2) DCC), the PSS user-lessee is also presumed to have to have received the product in undamaged condition.

2251 See *supra* no. 436.

2252 **Belgium**: Art. 1731, §1 old BCC. **The Netherlands**: Art. 7:224(2) DCC.

2253 **Belgium**: T. Vandromme, "Artikel 1731 oud BW – Staat gehuurde goed op einde huurovereenkomst" in *Focus op bijzondere overeenkomsten*, Mechelen, Wolters Kluwer, 2022, (182) 183. **The Netherlands**: H.J. Rossel and A.H.T. Heisterkamp, *Mr. C. Assers Handleiding tot de beoefening van het Nederlands Burgerlijk Recht. 7. Bijzondere overeenkomsten. Deel II. Huur*, Deventer, Wolters Kluwer, 2021, no. 97.

2254 **Belgium**: Art. 1731, §2 old BCC. **The Netherlands**: Art. 7:224(2) DCC.

they make clear when the PSS user is not liable against the PSS supplier, while the sales contract rules make clear to what extent the seller is liable.[2255] Another key difference between consumer sales law and the rental rules is the mandatory nature of the presumption period in consumer sales law, while Article 1731 old BCC and Article 7:224(2) DCC are not mandatory law.[2256]

502. Belgian law: general contract law remedies in case of non-conformity – The Belgian rules of the rental contract do not have a separate set of remedies in case of non-conformity of the product. This means that if the PSS user can prove the lack of conformity of the product, he has access to the remedies of general contract law.[2257, 2258] In the first place, the PSS user can temporarily suspend his obligations under the PSS contract (*exceptio non adimpleti contractus*, "enac") in order to induce the PSS supplier to remedy the defect.[2259] A second option is to pursue performance in kind, where the defect is repaired, either by the PSS supplier itself or at its expense by the PSS user or a third party.[2260] Furthermore, the PSS user can opt for a price reduction to compensate for the reduction in use,[2261] or claim compensation for damages for all damages suffered by the PSS user.[2262] As a final resort, the PSS user can opt for the termination of the contract, provided the defect is sufficiently serious.[2263] The termination can be combined with an additional compensation for damages.[2264] Contrary to the system of consumer sales law, these remedies are not mandatory law, so the PSS contract can deviate from them, modulate them, or even (partially) exclude some of these remedies. Yet the control mechanism of unfair terms must also be taken into account here, which can render manifestly unbalanced clauses null and void.[2265]

503. Dutch law: both specific remedies and general contract law in case of non-conformity – The Dutch rental contract rules do contain some specific provisions on the remedies open to the PSS user if he can prove that there is a defect in the product. In addition to these specific remedies, the PSS user also

2255 M.B.M. Loos, "Servitization, consumentenhuur en consumentenkoop", *WPNR* 2022/7396, (944) 945.

2256 **Belgium**: T. Vandromme, "Artikel 1731 oud BW – Staat gehuurde goed op einde huurovereenkomst" in *Focus op bijzondere overeenkomsten*, Mechelen, Wolters Kluwer, 2022, (182) 183. **The Netherlands**: M.B.M. Loos, "Servitization, consumentenhuur en consumentenkoop", *WPNR* 2022/7396, (944) 945.

2257 M. Dambre, *Bijzondere overeenkomsten: de essentie*, Bruges, Die Keure, 2022, 217.

2258 For a discussion of these remedies, see *supra* section 2.6.6.

2259 Art. 5.98 and 5.239 BCC.

2260 Art. 5.234 BCC.

2261 Art. 5.97 BCC.

2262 Art. 5.237 BCC.

2263 Art. 5.91 BCC.

2264 See e.g. J.P. St. Gilles Brussels (BE) 19 October 1989, *T.Vred.* 1992, 131.

2265 See e.g. Art. VI.83, 31° BCEL and the general test of Art. I.8, 22° BCEL.

has the general contract law provisions in Book 6 DCC[2266] at its disposal.[2267] This includes the right for the PSS supplier to suspend his obligations ("enac") under the PSS contract.[2268, 2269] The remedies from the rental contract rules do largely parallel those of Dutch general contract law[2270] and will be discussed in the following paragraphs.

504. Right to repair the defect (performance in kind) – In the first place, the rules of the rental contract state that the PSS user may in principle expect the PSS supplier to remedy the defect by repairing the product (i.e. performance in kind).[2271] This obligation arises when the PSS user has reported[2272] the defect and indicated that he wants the defect remedied.[2273] However, this right to performance in kind is subject to some important limitations. As mentioned above and unless otherwise stipulated in the PSS contract, the PSS supplier is not liable for minor repairs and defects caused by the PSS user.[2274] More importantly, the PSS user has no right to repair if this would be impossible or would require expenditure that cannot be expected of the PSS supplier under the given circumstances.[2275] In addition, contrary to consumer sales law,[2276] the rules of the rental contract do not include a right to replacement of the product, not even for movables.[2277]

2266 See *supra* section 2.6.6.

2267 Art. 7:205 DCC. See on the relationship of the specific provisions with the general contract law provisions: A.M. Kloosterman, "Art. 205 – Burgerlijk Wetboek Boek 7. Schakelbepaling" in *Sdu Commentaar Huurrecht*, 10 August 2022, para. 1 and 2. See also: H.J. Rossel and A.H.T. Heisterkamp, *Mr. C. Assers Handleiding tot de beoefening van het Nederlands Burgerlijk Recht. 7. Bijzondere overeenkomsten. Deel II. Huur*, Deventer, Wolters Kluwer, 2021, no. 39.

2268 Art. 6:52–6:57 DCC and Art. 6:262 DCC. See also C.H. Sieburgh, *Mr. C. Assers Handleiding tot de beoefening van het Nederlands Burgerlijk Recht. 6. Verbintenissenrecht. Deel I. De verbintenis in het algemeen, eerste gedeelte*, Deventer, Wolters Kluwer, 2020, no. 270–286.

2269 Explanatory Memorandum, *Parliamentary Papers II* 1997/98, 26089, no. 3, 15.

2270 Compare with the right to performance (Art. 3:296 DCC), termination (Art. 6:265 *et seq.* DCC) and compensation for damages (Art. 6:74 DCC). See: A.M. Kloosterman, "Art. 205 – Burgerlijk Wetboek Boek 7. Schakelbepaling" in *Sdu Commentaar Huurrecht*, 10 August 2022, para. 2–4 for an analysis of the similarities and differences between the rental contract rules and general contract law.

2271 Art. 7:206(1) DCC.

2272 See Art. 7:222 DCC which requires the PSS user to report this defect without delay. Failing to do so, the PSS user will be obliged to compensate the PSS supplier for the damage caused by the negligence.

2273 H.J. Rossel and A.H.T. Heisterkamp, *Mr. C. Assers Handleiding tot de beoefening van het Nederlands Burgerlijk Recht. 7. Bijzondere overeenkomsten. Deel II. Huur*, Deventer, Wolters Kluwer, 2021, no. 40.

2274 Art. 706(2) DCC.

2275 M.B.M. Loos, "Servitization, consumentenhuur en consumentenkoop", *WPNR* 2022/7396, (944) 946. See for some examples regarding the application of this exception: Explanatory Memorandum, *Parliamentary Papers II* 1997/98, 26089, no. 3, 16 and Explanatory Memorandum, *Parliamentary Papers II* 1999/00, 26089, no. 6, 9.

2276 Compare with Art. 13.2 SGD and Art. 7:21(1) *sub* c. DCC.

2277 M.B.M. Loos, "Servitization, consumentenhuur en consumentenkoop", *WPNR* 2022/7396, (944) 946.

505. Repair by PSS user in case of default PSS supplier – If the PSS supplier fails to remedy the defect although it was obliged to do so, the PSS user may do so himself and recover the (reasonable) costs incurred for this from the PSS supplier, if necessary, by offsetting them against the rental price.[2278] This provision goes beyond the performance remedy of general contract law, as the PSS user does not have to seek a judicial authorisation.[2279] It is required though that the PSS supplier is in default (*in verzuim*) of remedying the defect.[2280] This basically means that the PSS user will generally have to issue a notice of default in which the PSS supplier is given a deadline.[2281] If the PSS supplier does not remedy the defect within this period, the PSS user can repair the product himself. This provision is (semi-)mandatory law and can thus not be deviated from in the PSS contract to the detriment of the consumer.[2282]

506. Right to price reduction in case of defect – The second remedy open to the PSS user is the right to proportionate price reduction until the defect is remedied.[2283] The rationale behind this remedy is that a defect reduces the PSS user's rental enjoyment.[2284] This reduction in enjoyment is compensated by a reduction of the rental fee.[2285] It also applies if the PSS supplier is not obliged to repair the defect (e.g. because it is impossible or would be disproportionate), in which case the PSS user is entitled to a permanent price reduction.[2286] The PSS user is entitled to such a price reduction either from the day he notified the PSS supplier of the defect, or the day the PSS supplier had sufficient knowledge of the defect to take action, until the day the defect is remedied.[2287] Unlike the

---

2278 Art. 7:206(3), first sentence DCC.

2279 Compare with Art. 3:299 DCC. A.M. Kloosterman, "Art. 205 – Burgerlijk Wetboek Boek 7. Schakelbepaling" in *Sdu Commentaar Huurrecht*, 10 August 2022, para. 2 (under the title "*Zelf verhelpen*"). Nevertheless, obtaining such an authorisation can be useful, especially for costly repairs where the PSS user is not sure they will be borne by the PSS supplier. See: Explanatory Memorandum, *Parliamentary Papers II* 1999/00, 26089, no. 6, 10. See also: A.W. Jongbloed, "Huur" in H.N. Schelhaas and A.J. Verheij (eds.), *Bijzondere overeenkomsten in Studiereeks Burgerlijk Recht*, Deventer, Wolters Kluwer, 2023, (159) 171, no. 175.

2280 Art. 6:81 DCC.

2281 Art. 6:82 DCC.

2282 Art. 7:206(3), second sentence DCC.

2283 Art. 7:207(1) DCC. This is a *lex specialis* of the rule of partial termination of Art. 6:270 DCC.

2284 A.W. Jongbloed, "Huur" in H.N. Schelhaas and A.J. Verheij (eds.), *Bijzondere overeenkomsten in Studiereeks Burgerlijk Recht*, Deventer, Wolters Kluwer, 2023, (159) 171, no. 176; A.M. Kloosterman, "De verplichtingen van de verhuurder" in A.M. Kloosterman, H.J. Rossel and M.H. Rozeboom (eds.), *Hoofdlijnen in het huurrecht. Met vragen en antwoorden*, Deventer, Wolters Kluwer, 2020, (39) 51.

2285 H.J. Rossel and A.H.T. Heisterkamp, *Mr. C. Assers Handleiding tot de beoefening van het Nederlands Burgerlijk Recht. 7. Bijzondere overeenkomsten. Deel II. Huur*, Deventer, Wolters Kluwer, 2021, no. 48.

2286 Explanatory Memorandum, *Parliamentary Papers II* 1997/98, 26089, no. 3, 13.

2287 H.J. Rossel and A.H.T. Heisterkamp, *Mr. C. Assers Handleiding tot de beoefening van het Nederlands Burgerlijk Recht. 7. Bijzondere overeenkomsten. Deel II. Huur*, Deventer, Wolters Kluwer, 2021, no. 48.

remedy of repair, it is not required that the PSS supplier is in default.[2288, 2289] It goes without saying that this remedy does not exist for defects that are to be borne by the PSS user, such as minor repairs (unless otherwise provided in the PSS contract) or defects for which the PSS user is liable to the PSS supplier.[2290]

507. Compensation for damages caused by the defect – In addition to the right to repair the defect and price reduction, the PSS user can also claim compensation for damages caused by a defect in the product.[2291] The PSS supplier will be obliged to pay compensation for damages if either the defect was present at the start of the PSS contract and the PSS supplier knew or should have known about it or informed the PSS user that the defect was not present, or the defect arose after the contract was entered into and is imputable[2292] to him.[2293] This remedy applies only to damages arising from the defect itself. If the PSS supplier does not remedy the defect (in a timely manner), the PSS user will have to rely on the provisions of general contract law[2294] for compensation of (consequential) damages.[2295]

508. Specific remedies of the rental contract are (semi-)mandatory law for defects the PSS supplier knew or should have known – The PSS contract can in principle contractually limit the right to repair the defect, as well as the right to price reduction and compensation for damages.[2296] However, this

2288 Art. 6:81–6:82 DCC.

2289 A.M. Kloosterman, "Art. 205 – Burgerlijk Wetboek Boek 7. Schakelbepaling" in *Sdu Commentaar Huurrecht*, 10 August 2022, para. 3 (under the title *"Is verzuim of toerekenbaarheid vereist?"*); H.J. Rossel and A.H.T. Heisterkamp, *Mr. C. Assers Handleiding tot de beoefening van het Nederlands Burgerlijk Recht. 7. Bijzondere overeenkomsten. Deel II. Huur*, Deventer, Wolters Kluwer, 2021, no. 49; A.M. Kloosterman, "De verplichtingen van de verhuurder" in A.M. Kloosterman, H.J. Rossel and M.H. Rozeboom (eds.), *Hoofdlijnen in het huurrecht. Met vragen en antwoorden*, Deventer, Wolters Kluwer, 2020, (39) 52.

2290 Art. 7:207(2) DCC.

2291 A.W. Jongbloed, "Huur" in H.N. Schelhaas and A.J. Verheij (eds.), *Bijzondere overeenkomsten in Studiereeks Burgerlijk Recht*, Deventer, Wolters Kluwer, 2023, (159) 171–172, no. 177.

2292 Compare with Art. 6:74 DCC.

2293 Art. 7:208 DCC. A.M. Kloosterman, "De verplichtingen van de verhuurder" in A.M. Kloosterman, H.J. Rossel and M.H. Rozeboom (eds.), *Hoofdlijnen in het huurrecht. Met vragen en antwoorden*, Deventer, Wolters Kluwer, 2020, (39) 53–54.

2294 Art. 6:74 and 6:75 DCC.

2295 H.J. Rossel and A.H.T. Heisterkamp, *Mr. C. Assers Handleiding tot de beoefening van het Nederlands Burgerlijk Recht. 7. Bijzondere overeenkomsten. Deel II. Huur*, Deventer, Wolters Kluwer, 2021, no. 55; A.W. Jongbloed, "Huur" in H.N. Schelhaas and A.J. Verheij (eds.), *Bijzondere overeenkomsten in Studiereeks Burgerlijk Recht*, Deventer, Wolters Kluwer, 2023, (159) 171–172, no. 177; A.M. Kloosterman, "De verplichtingen van de verhuurder" in A.M. Kloosterman, H.J. Rossel and M.H. Rozeboom (eds.), *Hoofdlijnen in het huurrecht. Met vragen en antwoorden*, Deventer, Wolters Kluwer, 2020, (39) 54. See also: Explanatory Memorandum, *Parliamentary Papers II* 1997/98, 26089, no. 3, 19.

2296 H.J. Rossel and A.H.T. Heisterkamp, *Mr. C. Assers Handleiding tot de beoefening van het Nederlands Burgerlijk Recht. 7. Bijzondere overeenkomsten. Deel II. Huur*, Deventer, Wolters Kluwer, 2021, no. 43.

cannot be done to the detriment of the consumer insofar as it concerns defects that existed at the time of entering into the PSS contract and were or should have been known to the PSS supplier at the time.[2297] So in this particular case, these remedies are (semi-)mandatory law in favour of the PSS user.[2298] According to the explanatory memorandum, professional lessors (i.e. PSS suppliers) can even be reasonably expected to investigate whether the rented product is suitable for the use that the lessee (i.e. the PSS user, especially if they are a consumer) wants to make of it.[2299] The point of this provision it thus to avoid that the PSS supplier cannot invoke the specific remedies for defects that the PSS supplier knew or should have known and the PSS user did not have to expect because he did not know them.[2300]

509. Influence of (semi-)mandatory nature specific remedies on non-mandatory nature of concept of defect – As mentioned above, the concept of defect[2301] is not mandatory law, so parties can contractually define what characteristics of the product should be considered a defect in their contractual relationship.[2302] Yet, it is argued in legal doctrine that the freedom to contractually define the concept of defect should also be limited in these circumstances where the PSS supplier knew or should have known the defect at the start of the PSS contract.[2303] In other words, the PSS supplier cannot circumvent this (semi-) mandatory provision by defining the concept of defect very narrowly in general terms. This does of course not apply to the situation where there is a specific defect known to both parties and accepted by the PSS user.[2304]

510. Termination in case of a defect that renders use of the product completely impossible – Since a defect constitutes a non-performance on the part of the PSS supplier,[2305] the PSS user has – also in view of Article 7:205

2297 Art. 7:209 DCC.

2298 A.W. Jongbloed, "Huur" in H.N. Schelhaas and A.J. Verheij (eds.), *Bijzondere overeenkomsten in Studiereeks Burgerlijk Recht*, Deventer, Wolters Kluwer, 2023, (159) 172, no. 178.

2299 Explanatory Memorandum, *Parliamentary Papers II* 1997/98, 26089, no. 3, 20.

2300 Explanatory Memorandum, *Parliamentary Papers II* 1999/00, 26089, no. 6, 14. Compare also with HR (NL) 3 September 2010, ECLI:NL:HR:2010:BM3980, (*KPN/Tamminga*), *NJ* 2010/474, para. 4.2.

2301 Art. 7:204 DCC.

2302 See *supra* no. 478.

2303 H.J. Rossel and A.H.T. Heisterkamp, *Mr. C. Assers Handleiding tot de beoefening van het Nederlands Burgerlijk Recht. 7. Bijzondere overeenkomsten. Deel II. Huur*, Deventer, Wolters Kluwer, 2021, no. 44. Contra: Opinion AG T. Huydecoper, 7 May 2010, in HR 3 September 2010, (KPN/Tamminga), ECLI:NL:PHR:2010:BM3980, para. 40–45.

2304 H.J. Rossel and A.H.T. Heisterkamp, *Mr. C. Assers Handleiding tot de beoefening van het Nederlands Burgerlijk Recht. 7. Bijzondere overeenkomsten. Deel II. Huur*, Deventer, Wolters Kluwer, 2021, no. 44.

2305 See in this sense e.g. HR (NL) 23 February 2018, ECLI:NL:HR:2018:283, *WR* 2018/121, para. 3.3.3.

DCC – in principle the right to terminate the PSS contract based on the rules of general contract law.[2306] This requires that the non-performance is sufficiently serious to justify the termination (i.e. a fundamental non-performance).[2307] The right to terminate the contract even applies if the non-performance is not imputable to the PSS supplier.[2308] In addition to this general contract law remedy, a final specific remedy allows either party, i.e. also the PSS supplier, to terminate the PSS contract extrajudicially in the situation where a defect that the PSS supplier is not obliged to remedy[2309] renders the use of the product completely impossible.[2310] This remedy is mainly to the advantage of the PSS supplier, as the PSS user can already invoke the right of termination under general contract law for a defect which makes the use of the product impossible and which the PSS supplier is not obliged to repair (as there is a fundamental non-performance in this case).[2311]

511. DCD: LIABILITY FOR LACK OF CONFORMITY OF DIGITAL CONTENT OR DIGITAL SERVICES PART OF THE USE-ORIENTED PSS CONTRACT – If digital content or digital services are part of the use-oriented PSS contract, the rules of the DCD and its national implementation apply. Under these rules, the PSS supplier will be liable for any lack of conformity that exists at the time of delivery of the digital content or digital services.[2312] As regards the time limits, Belgian and Dutch law take a slightly different approach.[2313] Under Belgian law, if the PSS contract features a single act of supply or a series of individual acts of supply of the digital content or digital services, the guarantee period shall be two years from the time of supply.[2314] If, on the other hand, the PSS contract provides for a continuous supply over a period of time, which will be the majority of the PSS contracts, the guarantee period is equal to the duration of the contract.[2315] In both cases, the consumer's action for non-conformity is subject to a limitation period of one year from when he has discovered the lack of conformity.[2316]

2306 Art. 6:265(1) DCC.

2307 C.H. Sieburgh, *Mr. C. Assers Handleiding tot de beoefening van het Nederlands Burgerlijk Recht. 6. Verbintenissenrecht. Deel III. Algemeen overeenkomstenrecht*, Deventer, Wolters Kluwer, 2022, no. 684.

2308 H.J. Rossel and A.H.T. Heisterkamp, *Mr. C. Assers Handleiding tot de beoefening van het Nederlands Burgerlijk Recht. 7. Bijzondere overeenkomsten. Deel II. Huur*, Deventer, Wolters Kluwer, 2021, no. 57.

2309 In the sense of Art. 7:206(1) DCC.

2310 Art. 7:210 DCC.

2311 H.J. Rossel and A.H.T. Heisterkamp, *Mr. C. Assers Handleiding tot de beoefening van het Nederlands Burgerlijk Recht. 7. Bijzondere overeenkomsten. Deel II. Huur*, Deventer, Wolters Kluwer, 2021, no. 57.

2312 EU: Art. 11(1) DCD. **Belgium**: Art. 1701/8 old BCC. **The Netherlands**: Art. 50 ag(1) DCC.

2313 See Art. 11(2) and 11(3) DCD, which allow Member States to introduce guarantee periods and/or limitation periods.

2314 Art. 1701/8, §2 old BCC.

2315 Art. 1701/8, §3 old BCC.

2316 Art. 1701/8, §2, (4) old BCC and Art. 1701/8, §3, (4) old BCC.

Dutch law only contains a limitation period. Indeed, the consumer's action for non-conformity prescribes two years after the delivery, unless the consumer did not know or should not have known of the defect, taking into account at least the price or digital representation of value and the reasonable expectations regarding the duration for which he can use the digital content or digital service.[2317] Thus, both for contracts featuring a single act of supply or a series of individual acts of supply and contracts providing for a continuous supply over a period of time, the delivery of the digital content or digital services is used as the starting point of the two-year limitation period.[2318] For continuously supplied digital content or digital service, this means that the PSS supplier remains liable for a lack of conformity that becomes apparent two years after the last delivery, unless the consumer did not know or should not have known of the defect, in which case the time limit starts even later.[2319]

512. DCD: REMEDIES FOR LACK OF CONFORMITY OF DIGITAL CONTENT OR DIGITAL SERVICES PART OF THE USE-ORIENTED PSS CONTRACT – Three remedies are available to the PSS user in case of a lack of conformity of any digital content or digital service that is part of the use-oriented PSS contract. According to the DCD and its national implementation, the PSS user will be entitled to have the digital content or digital service brought into conformity, to receive a proportionate price reduction, or to terminate the contract.[2320] There is a hierarchy between these remedies: first, an attempt should be made to bring the goods into conformity (i.e. performance in kind). Only afterwards is the consumer entitled to a proportionate price reduction or the termination of the contract.[2321] When bringing the digital service into conformity with the contract, this must be done free of charge, within a reasonable time and without any significant inconvenience to the consumer.[2322] The remedies of proportional price reduction and termination of the contract are available for the PSS user in four cases: a) the PSS supplier did not bring the digital content or digital service in conformity with the PSS contract (either because this is impossible or disproportionate or for another reason connected to the PSS supplier); b) despite the attempt to make the digital service in conformity with the contract, there appears to be a lack of conformity; c) the seriousness of the lack of conformity justifies immediate price reduction or termination; and d) the trader has

2317 Art. 50 ag(2) DCC.

2318 Art. 50 ag(2) DCC. See also: Explanatory Memorandum, *Parliamentary Papers II* 2020–21, 35734, no. 3, 51.

2319 Art. 7:50ag(2) DCC; Explanatory Memorandum, *Parliamentary Papers II* 2020–21, 35734, no. 3, 51.

2320 EU: Art. 14(1) DCD. **Belgium**: Art. 1701/10 old BCC. **The Netherlands**: Art. 50 ai(1) DCC.

2321 EU: Art. 14(2) DCD. **Belgium**: Art. 1701/12, §1 and Art. 1701/11, §1 old BCC. **The Netherlands**: Art. 50ai(2) DCC.

2322 EU: Art. 14(3) DCD. **Belgium**: Art. 1701/11, §2 old BCC. **The Netherlands**: Art. 50ai(3) DCC.

explicitly or implicitly declared that he would not bring the digital service into conformity.[2323]

4.3.3. RESULT-ORIENTED PSS: NO HARMONISED RULES

4.3.3.1. Difficulties to assess quality and conformity of services

513. DIFFICULTIES TO ASSESS QUALITY AND CONFORMITY OF SERVICES – Compared to the sales contract and the rental contract, assessing the quality and conformity of the performance is more difficult for service contracts. This is due to several reasons.[2324] As mentioned above, the extremely varied and heterogeneous nature of services makes it difficult to establish uniform rules for service contracts.[2325] It is challenging to establish a uniform quality standard for services due to the immaterial nature of the main object of the performance and the fact that performance cannot be assessed against the value or physical characteristics of a product.[2326] Moreover, due to a knowledge gap between the service provider and the service recipient, it is often not straightforward for the service recipient to verify whether the service was performed correctly and in conformity with the contract.[2327] A final reason can be found in the fact that services often require a certain level of input from the customer of the service, for

---

2323 EU: Art. 14(4) DCD. **Belgium**: Art. 1701/12, §1 old BCC. **The Netherlands**: Art. 50ai(4) DCC.

2324 See on some of the distinguishing characteristics of services: C. WENDEHORST, "Das Vertragsrecht der Dienstleistungen im deutschen und künftigen europäischen Recht", *Archiv für die civilistische Praxis* 2006, (205) 226–230.

2325 See *supra* no. 40. Compare also with A. DE FRANCESCHI, "Ensuring Circularity in Service Contracts" in B. KEIRSBILCK, E. TERRYN, J. EYCKMANS, S. ROUSSEAU and D. VOINOT (eds.), *Servitization and circular economy: economic and legal challenges*, Antwerp, Intersentia, 2023, (167) 170; V. MAK and E. TERRYN, "Circular Economy and Consumer Protection: The Consumer as a Citizen and the Limits of Empowerment Through Consumer Law", *Journal of Consumer Policy* 2020, vol. 43, (227) 241; F. ZOLL, "From a Product-Based Economy to Services? – Legal Aspects of an Economy in Transition" in B. KEIRSBILCK and E. TERRYN (eds.), *Consumer Protection in a Circular Economy*, Antwerp, Intersentia, 2019, (149) 153 and T. HEREMANS, *Professional services in the EU internal market: Quality regulation and self-regulation*, Oxford, Hart Publishing, 2012, 233–234; F. ZOLL, "Das Dienstleistungsrecht im Vorschlag für ein Gemeinsames Europäisches Kaufrecht" in H. SCHULTE-NÖLKE, F. ZOLL, N. JANSEN and R. SCHULZE (eds.), *Der Entwurf für ein optimales Europäisches Kaufrecht*, Munich, Sellier, 2012, (279) 287; C. JANSEN, "Principles of European Law on Service Contracts: Background, Genesis, and Drafting Method" in R. ZIMMERMAN (ed.), *Service Contracts*, Tübingen, Mohr Siebeck, 2010, (43) 48–49.

2326 V. MAK and E. TERRYN, "Circular Economy and Consumer Protection: The Consumer as a Citizen and the Limits of Empowerment Through Consumer Law", *Journal of Consumer Policy* 2020, vol. 43, (227) 241; F. ZOLL, "From a Product-Based Economy to Services? – Legal Aspects of an Economy in Transition" in B. KEIRSBILCK and E. TERRYN (eds.), *Consumer Protection in a Circular Economy*, Antwerp, Intersentia, 2019, (149) 153.

2327 F. ZOLL, "From a Product-Based Economy to Services? – Legal Aspects of an Economy in Transition" in B. KEIRSBILCK and E. TERRYN (eds.), *Consumer Protection in a Circular Economy*, Antwerp, Intersentia, 2019, (149) 153.

example by providing information, instructions, etc.[2328] These reasons explain why, so far, not much progress has been made in terms of EU harmonisation of service contracts.

514. Difficulties to assess quality and conformity of services in result oriented PSS – Result-oriented PSS perfectly illustrate these difficulties to judge the quality of the service. After all, result-oriented PSS offers greatly vary between one another and are generally complex bundles of services. Their conformity is no longer linked to a specific product, but to an immaterial contractually defined result.[2329] The PSS supplier is free to decide which products are necessary to guarantee this contractually stipulated result. At the same time, the PSS user will often lack the tools or the technical knowledge to assess the conformity of the service with the contract. This is especially the case if technical and complex output specifications are mentioned in the contract. Furthermore, the PSS supplier often depends to some extent on the behaviour and input of the PSS user to execute the service correctly. For example, if he does not treat the products made available with the necessary care or according to the given instructions, this can cause interruptions in the provided service.

4.3.3.2. National rules for conformity for service contracts and result-oriented PSS

515. Lack of harmonisation regarding conformity for service contracts – A harmonised legal framework on the concept of conformity and remedies for non-conformity in service contracts and result-oriented PSS is thus currently lacking at the EU level. Therefore, national contract law again provides the framework to determine whether the service provided is in conformity with the PSS contract. As established above, result-oriented PSS under Belgian and Dutch law are generally governed by the rules of the contract for services. Both under Belgian and Dutch law, the principal obligation of the contract for services requires the PSS supplier to perform the service and, in doing so, to take the care of a good service provider.[2330] The Belgian rules of the contract for services do not contain an explicit provision on the obligation to perform the contractually

---

2328 C. Wendehorst, "Das Vertragsrecht der Dienstleistungen im deutschen und künftigen europäischen Recht", *Archiv für die civilistische Praxis* 2006, (205) 229.

2329 V. Mak and E. Terryn, "Circular Economy and Consumer Protection: The Consumer as a Citizen and the Limits of Empowerment Through Consumer Law", *Journal of Consumer Policy* 2020, vol. 43, (227) 241.

2330 **Belgium**: V. Sagaert, B. Tilleman and A.-L. Verbeke, *Vermogensrecht in kort bestek*, Antwerp, Intersentia, 2022, 437, no. 1087; B. Kohl, *Contrat d'entreprise*, Brussels, Bruylant, 2016, 270; W. Goossens, *Aanneming van werk: het gemeenrechtelijk dienstencontract*, Bruges, Die Keure, 2003, 695. **The Netherlands**: Art. 7:401 DCC; T.F.E. Tjong Tjin Tai, *Asser 7-IV Bijzondere Overeenkomsten - Opdracht, incl. de geneeskundige behandelingsovereenkomst en de reisovereenkomst*, Deventer, Wolters Kluwer, 2022, no. 93; J.J. Dammingh,

agreed service (it is, by contrast, included in the rules of the mandate contract[2331]), but this obligation naturally applies to all (service) contracts.[2332] The Dutch rules of the contract for services, on the other hand, explicitly confirm this obligation as a *lex specialis* from the rule of general contract law that the debtor must exercise the care of a good debtor in the performance of his obligations.[2333]

516. Conformity presupposes performance of the service in accordance with the PSS contract, the instructions given by the PSS user and the standards of good workmanship – The obligation to perform the service in conformity with the contract is materialised in three ways. It entails that (i) the PSS supplier must perform the service according to what the parties have expressly agreed in the PSS contract; (ii) where applicable, the PSS supplier must follow the instructions given by the PSS user[2334]; and (iii) the performed service must conform with the so-called "standards of good workmanship" (BE: *regels van de kunst, règles de l'art*[2335]).[2336] So, also in result-oriented PSS, conformity has a subjective and an objective component.

"Dienstverlening: de overeenkomst van opdracht" in E.H. Hondius and V. Mak (eds.), *Handboek Consumentenrecht*, Vijfde druk, Zutphen, Paris, 2020, (267) 273.

2331 See Art. 1991(1) old BCC.

2332 W. Goossens, *Aanneming van werk: het gemeenrechtelijk dienstencontract*, Bruges, Die Keure, 2003, 695.

2333 See Art. 6:27 DCC. According to some authors, Art 7:401 BW is a needless *lex specialis* of the general contractual norm. See: T.F.E. Tjong Tjin Tai, *Asser 7-IV Bijzondere Overeenkomsten – Opdracht, incl. de geneeskundige behandelingsovereenkomst en de reisovereenkomst*, Deventer, Wolters Kluwer, 2022, no. 93 and the references cited there.

2334 In **the Netherlands**, this is explicitly confirmed in Art. 7:402(1) DCC, which requires the PSS supplier to comply with timely and responsible instructions regarding the execution of the service. See: J.J. Dammingh, "Dienstverlening: de overeenkomst van opdracht" in E.H. Hondius and V. Mak (eds.), *Handboek Consumentenrecht*, Vijfde druk, Zutphen, Paris, 2020, (267) 279. In **Belgium**, the (old) BCC does not contain an explicit provision in this regard, but the possibility for the client to give instructions to the service provider is also generally accepted. See e.g. P.-A. Foriers, "Le contrat de prestation de services: obligations des parties et responsabilité contractuelle" in F. Glansdorff and P.-A. Foriers (eds.), *Les contrats de service*, Brussels, Jeune Barreau de Bruxelles, 1994, (121) 131, no. 11. See also: B. Kohl, *Contrat d'entreprise*, Brussels, Bruylant, 2016, 271; W. Goossens, *Aanneming van werk: het gemeenrechtelijk dienstencontract*, Bruges, Die Keure, 2003, 701, both with reference to Cass. (BE) 16 January 1962, *Pas.* 1962, I, 571 (*"Attendu que le louage d'ouvrage [n'exclut pas la possibilité] d'instructions générales à observer, d'un contrôle exercé sur le locateur"*).

2335 In **the Netherlands**, there is not really a similar term. Nevertheless, the rules and practices accepted or prevailing in the relevant industry also play a role in shaping the PSS supplier's obligation to take the care of a good service provider (Art. 7:401 DCC). See: T.F.E. Tjong Tjin Tai, *Asser 7-IV Bijzondere Overeenkomsten – Opdracht, incl. de geneeskundige behandelingsovereenkomst en de reisovereenkomst*, Deventer, Wolters Kluwer, 2022, no. 97 and no. 87.

2336 **Belgium**: V. Sagaert, B. Tilleman and A.-L. Verbeke, *Vermogensrecht in kort bestek*, Antwerp, Intersentia, 2022, 437, no. 1087. **The Netherlands**: T.F.E. Tjong Tjin Tai, *Asser 7-IV Bijzondere Overeenkomsten – Opdracht, incl. de geneeskundige behandelingsovereenkomst en de reisovereenkomst*, Deventer, Wolters Kluwer, 2022, no. 97.

The subjective component concerns the description of the service in the PSS contract, and the concrete output specifications and promised continuity of the service.[2337] The objective component is fleshed out by the "standards of good workmanship" that the PSS user can expect, even if the PSS contract is silent in this respect. This means that the PSS supplier must perform the service as a good PSS supplier from the same industry or sector and placed in the same circumstances would perform it.[2338]

517. Obligation of result versus obligation of means – The PSS supplier's obligation to perform the service can be qualified as either an obligation of result or an obligation of means.[2339] This depends on the concrete circumstances, such as the wording of the PSS contract and the agreements between the parties, but also on the person of the PSS supplier and whether the outcome of the service is subject to chance (i.e. aleatory nature of the service).[2340, 2341] Whether an obligation classifies as an obligation of result or obligation of means is thus a question of interpreting the result-oriented PSS contract.[2342] The outcome of this classification exercise is not insignificant, as it has important consequences on determining a potential breach of contract as well as on the burden of proof for the PSS user.[2343] Given the specific characteristics of result-oriented PSS (i.e. providing a contractually promised solution instead of the ownership of a product) the obligations of the PSS supplier will often be obligations of result.[2344]

2337 See *infra* no. 518–519.

2338 **Belgium**: B. Tilleman, S. De Rey, N. Debruyne, T. Gladinez, N. Van Damme and F. Van den Abeele, "Overzicht van rechtspraak bijzondere overeenkomsten aanneming (2007–2021)", *TPR* 2022, (365) 491, no. 97. **The Netherlands**: T.F.E. Tjong Tjin Tai, *Asser 7-IV Bijzondere Overeenkomsten – Opdracht, incl. de geneeskundige behandelingsovereenkomst en de reisovereenkomst*, Deventer, Wolters Kluwer, 2022, no. 94; T.L. Wildenbeest, "Art. 401 t/m 404, 412 – Burgerlijk Wetboek Boek 7" in *Sdu Commentaar Vermogensrecht*, 18 February 2022, para. 1.

2339 See on this distinction *supra* no. 271.

2340 **Belgium**: See e.g. B. Kohl, *Contrat d'entreprise*, Brussels, Bruylant, 2016, 280–281, no. 119; L. Van Valckenborgh, "De kwalificatie van een verbintenis als resultaats- of middelenverbintenis", *TBBR* 2011, (222) 222–231. **The Netherlands**: Under the Dutch rules of the contract for services, the obligation to perform the service is generally classified only as an obligation of means. Nevertheless, obligations of result can also exist here, depending on the concrete circumstances. See: T.F.E. Tjong Tjin Tai, *Asser 7-IV Bijzondere Overeenkomsten – Opdracht, incl. de geneeskundige behandelingsovereenkomst en de reisovereenkomst*, Deventer, Wolters Kluwer, 2022, no. 85 and T.F.E. Tjong Tjin Tai, *Zorgplichten en zorgethiek*, Kluwer, Deventer, 2006, 172. See also J.D.A. Den Tonkelaar, *Resultaatsverbintenissen en inspanningsverbintenissen*, Zwolle, Tjeenk Willink, 1982, 64 *et seq.*

2341 See more extensively on the criteria for distinguishing between an obligation of result and an obligation of means *supra* no. 275–278.

2342 **Belgium**: Cass. (BE) 5 December 2002, *Arr.Cass.* 2002, 2662, *JT* 2003, 228, *TBBR* 2004, 203, case note W. Goossens, *RW* 2005–06, 420, case note A. Van Oevelen. **The Netherlands**: HR (NL) 14 April 2006, ECLI:NL:HR:2006:AU6521, *NJ* 2006/259.

2343 See *supra* no. 271.

2344 H. Slachmuylders, "Movable Servitization. Contractual Liability in the B2C Relationship" in B. Keirsbilck, E. Terryn, J. Eyckmans, S. Rousseau and D. Voinot (eds.), *Servitization*

518. Performance agreed in the PSS contract: output specifications – The agreed performance in the PSS contract constitutes a starting point for assessing the conformity of the service. As mentioned above, result-oriented PSS contracts generally do not refer to individual products, but to more immaterial concepts (e.g. "light", "indoor climate", "heating", etc.) and the desired result to be achieved.[2345] These immaterial concepts are usually further specified in the PSS contract in the form of so-called output specifications, i.e. the requirements in terms of functionality, appearance, quality, durability, etc.[2346] For example, a "light as a service" contract may specify a minimum number of lighting hours at a minimum wattage or brightness level, a maximum number of lamps that may be defective at a time, a maximum electricity usage, etc. For an "ink as a service" contract, one can think of a minimum number of pages per month, quality of printed pages, energy efficiency of the printer, etc. Yet another example is a "ventilation-as-a-service" contract, where output specifications can relate to the room temperature, the amount of CO2 in the air, the energy usage, etc.

> Terms and Conditions HP Instant Ink – Art. 6(a) Selection of a Service Plan. "Selection of a Service Plan. When You create Your Service Account You will select one of the offered Service plans (each a "Service Plan") described in the "how it works", "THE PLANS", and "FREQUENTLY ASKED QUESTIONS" sections found at www.hpinstantink.com ("Service Description Terms"). Each Service Plan entitles You to print the specified number of pages ("Service Plan Pages") during each one (1) month period ("Month Period") for a designated fee ("Service Plan Fee"). Additional pages printed will be charged in blocks of available pages as described in Your Service Plan ("Additional Sets"). [...]"

> Terms and Conditions HP Instant Ink – Art. 6(b) Printed Page. "a "Printed Page" is a page upon which any amount of printing is performed by your printer. Printing on both sides of the same sheet of paper counts as two (2) pages. A page is the type and size of media referenced in your printer's specifications."

These output specifications are often described in the definitions part of the PSS contract. They act as anchor points by defining the minimum characteristics of the service to be provided. Depending on their content and wording, they serve as an important indication whether a particular obligation is an obligation of result or an obligation of means. It is therefore recommended for the PSS supplier

and circular economy: economic and legal challenges, Antwerp, Intersentia, 2023, (135) 158; A. De Boeck, "De toenemende "verdiensting": verbintenisrechtelijke vraagstukken bij de kringloopeconomie", *TBBR* 2020, (14) 16.

2345 H. Slachmuylders, "Movable Servitization. Contractual Liability in the B2C Relationship" in B. Keirsbilck, E. Terryn, J. Eyckmans, S. Rousseau and D. Voinot (eds.), *Servitization and circular economy: economic and legal challenges*, Antwerp, Intersentia, 2023, (135) 150.

2346 A. Van Vaerenbergh and F. Leyman, "'Product als dienst'-overeenkomsten, een stap in de richting van de circulaire economie", *MER* 2019, (20) 26.

to pay sufficient attention to the formulation of these output specifications when drafting the PSS contract.[2347]

519. PERFORMANCE AGREED IN THE PSS CONTRACT: AVAILABILITY OF THE SERVICE – Besides the output specifications, the conformity of the service will also be assessed against the continuity of the service agreed in the PSS contract (i.e. the availability of the PSS).[2348] The contracting parties can agree on a continuous continuity of the service (24/7, 365 days a year) but may also stipulate a clause in the contract addressing planned or unplanned interruptions.[2349] Still, as the obligation to ensure the availability of the service is an essential obligation, a clause stipulating an unreasonably low availability of the service has the risk of being deemed a "disguised" exemption clause, requiring it to meet the strict validity requirements for exemption clauses.[2350] In particular, a clause exempting the PSS supplier from any of the essential obligations of the PSS contract will be invalid as such an exemption would devoid the PSS contract of its purpose.[2351] Examples of clauses on the availability of the service can be found in the terms and conditions of *Villo* and *Dott*:

> TERMS AND CONDITIONS VILLO – Art. 5.4 "The service is accessible within the limit of bicycles available at each station throughout the year, 7 days a week without interruption, except in case of force majeure or issuance by the competent authorities of a full or partial, temporary or permanent restriction on bicycle traffic."

> TERMS AND CONDITIONS DOTT[2352] – "Our Services may not be available 24/7. There may be circumstances where our Services are interrupted, delayed or unavailable, including due to maintenance, upgrades, urgent repairs. We also reserve the right to

2347 For an example of such a contractual clause, see *infra* no. 608.

2348 H. SLACHMUYLDERS, "Movable Servitization. Contractual Liability in the B2C Relationship" in B. KEIRSBILCK, E. TERRYN, J. EYCKMANS, S. ROUSSEAU and D. VOINOT (eds.), *Servitization and circular economy: economic and legal challenges*, Antwerp, Intersentia, 2023, (135) 150.

2349 H. SLACHMUYLDERS, "Économie de la fonctionnalité – Le contrat de service: défis juridiques et solutions contractuelles", *Revue Juridique de l'Environnement* 2022, vol. 47, afl. 1, (111) 119; A. VAN VAERENBERGH and F. LEYMAN, "'Product als dienst'-overeenkomsten, een stap in de richting van de circulaire economie", *MER* 2019, (20) 26.

2350 See *supra* no. 312.

2351 **Belgium**: Art. 5.89, §1(4) BCC; V. SAGAERT, *Beginselen van verbintenissenrecht. De contractuele en quasi-contractuele verbintenissen*, Leuven, LeA Uitgevers, 2023, 136; S. STIJNS, *Verbintenissenrecht*, Boek 1, Bruges, Die Keure, 2022, 214; P. WÉRY, *Droit des obligations. Volume 1. Theorie générale du contrat*, Brussels, Larcier, 2021, 784–785, no. 768. **The Netherlands**: T.F.E. TJONG TJIN TAI, *Asser 7-IV Bijzondere Overeenkomsten – Opdracht, incl. de geneeskundige behandelingsovereenkomst en de reisovereenkomst*, Deventer, Wolters Kluwer, 2022, no. 98; C.H. SIEBURGH, *Mr. C. Assers Handleiding tot de beoefening van het Nederlands Burgerlijk Recht. 6. Verbintenissenrecht. Deel I. De verbintenis in het algemeen, eerste gedeelte*, Deventer, Wolters Kluwer, 2020, no. 364.

2352 Depending on the angle you look at Dott with (right of use over specific free-floating e-scooter rather than micro-mobility service as a whole), its business model arguably resembles more that of a use-oriented PSS. Compare also with Art. 3 Terms and Conditions Dott, which qualifies every ride as an individual rental contract for the specific Vehicle. Nevertheless, this suspend the Services in whole or in part when this is necessary for the purposes of our legitimate interests. You can identify which Vehicles are available at any time via our App or via Third Party Platforms. The number of vehicles is limited and Vehicle availability is never guaranteed."

The contractual wording and agreements of the parties on the continuity of the service is again a key element for the qualification of the PSS supplier's obligation as an obligation of result or an obligation of means.[2353] As described above, this qualification has important consequences for the contractual liability of the provider.[2354] For example, qualifying the provision of "light as a service" as an obligation of result will have the effect that the provider will be liable in the event of interruption unless he can prove *force majeure*.[2355] Similarly, the PSS contract can specify that a certain obligation constitutes an obligation of means, for example by providing that it is sufficient for the provider to make reasonable efforts to ensure the continuity of the service.[2356, 2357]

520. Assistance in case of unavailability of the service – The continuity of the service is closely linked to the availability of assistance services in case of defects, interruptions or other circumstances resulting in the unavailability of the service.[2358] Hence, result-oriented PSS contracts will generally also include a contractual arrangement obligating the PSS supplier to reinstate the availability of the service in case of defects or other interruptions. This can take various forms where the wording used will again affect the qualification of the obligation as an obligation of result or an obligation of means. For example, a clause requiring the PSS supplier to take all reasonable efforts to resolve the problem as soon as possible will take the form of an obligation of means. Strict (fixed) deadlines, on the other hand, are more likely to indicate an obligation of result. For instance, the PSS contract may define a maximum "time to respond" (i.e. the time in which the PSS supplier must acknowledge receipt of the problem

particular clause is also interesting from the perspective of result-oriented PSS, as it defines the availability of the micro-mobility service as a whole.

2353 See *supra* no. 271 and no. 517.

2354 **Belgium**: S. Stijns, *Verbintenissenrecht*, Boek 1, Bruges, Die Keure, 2022, 10–12; P. Van Ommeslaghe, *Droit des obligations, I*, Brussels, Bruylant, 2010, 39–40. **The Netherlands**: C.H. Sieburgh, *Mr. C. Assers Handleiding tot de beoefening van het Nederlands Burgerlijk Recht. 6. Verbintenissenrecht. Deel I. De verbintenis in het algemeen, eerste gedeelte*, Deventer, Wolters Kluwer, 2020, no. 192, 337 and 370.

2355 See by analogy: Antwerp (BE) 22 November 2004, *RW* 2007–2008, 1079, where it was assumed that the supply of Internet access qualified as an obligation of result. Consequently, the supplier is liable in the event of interruption, except for proof of *force majeure*.

2356 B. Keirsbilck, E. Terryn and E. Van Gool, "Consumentenbescherming bij servitisation en product-dienst systemen (PDS)", *TPR* 2019, (817) 870–871.

2357 See for model clauses on the availability of the service *infra* no. 610.

2358 H. Slachmuylders, "Movable Servitization. Contractual Liability in the B2C Relationship" in B. Keirsbilck, E. Terryn, J. Eyckmans, S. Rousseau and D. Voinot (eds.), *Servitization and circular economy: economic and legal challenges*, Antwerp, Intersentia, 2023, (135) 150.

and give an indication of the expected downtime) and/or a maximum "time to solution" (i.e. the time in which the PSS supplier must resolve the problem).[2359]

521. Output specifications, service availability and assistance are often specified in service level agreement ("SLA") – The output specifications, availability of the service and time periods for assistance in case of service unavailability are often specified in a service level agreement ("SLA"). An SLA can be defined as a reciprocal agreement between a customer and a service provider, in which the parties agree on several things: (i) a delineation of the services that the service provider will provide, (ii) in which the services will be assessed according to specific measurable realistic and time-bound criteria, the *service levels*, (iii) which will be regularly reported, and (iv) in which compliance with the service levels will be evaluated, (v) non-compliance will be negatively sanctioned and exceeding these service levels can in some cases be positively rewarded.[2360]

522. SLA as an instrument to measure and evaluate whether PSS supplier complies with obligations – An SLA thus allows to measure and evaluate whether the result-oriented PSS was performed correctly. This may include further specifying which interruptions are considered downtime (e.g. planned interruptions do not count towards service unavailability, while unplanned interruptions do). If certain output specifications are not met, if unavailability of the service is greater than allowed in the SLA, or if the assistance services take longer than contractually agreed, the SLA may set out a penalty for the PSS supplier (e.g. in the form of indemnity clause or by granting a reduction for future instalments of the monthly fee). An example can be found in the terms and conditions for a "heat pump as-a-service" model offered by "*Klimaatgarant*",[2361] a Dutch HVAC company that strives to develop energy neutral homes. *Klimaatgarant* guarantees in these terms and conditions that the system including the ventilation system does not use any electricity at net. This means that the electricity generated by the system will be higher or equal to the electricity used by the heat pump system and the ventilation system.[2362] The contract contains a price reduction clause[2363] if this guarantee is not met:

2359 See for proposed model clauses *infra* no. 613.

2360 **Belgium**: M. Taeymans and E. Jacobs, *IT-contracten*, Mechelen, Kluwer, 2020, 171. See for a similar definition K. De Vulder and K. Scheerlinck, "De bijzondere sanctionering van de contractuele wanprestatie in service level agreements" in K. Swinnen and M. Muylle (eds.), *De contractuele fout*, Bruges, Die Keure, 2019, (65) 66–67. **The Netherlands**: P. Wit and C.E. Drion, "De Service Level Agreement: een bijzondere overeenkomst?", *Contracteren* 2005/2, (32) 33.

2361 https://www.klimaatgarant.nl.

2362 See Art. 6.2 Terms and Conditions Klimaatgarant (unpublished, the terms and conditions are available with the author).

2363 The purpose of a price reduction clause is to grant a price reduction for breach of contract that consists in the fact that a lower quantity or quality of service has been provided. Thus, a

Terms and Conditions Klimaatgarant – Art. 6.2.7 "Specifically, the guarantee means that at the end of the first five years after the commencement of the Contract and further at each end of a five-year period thereafter, the System's netted consumption of electricity, calculated from the delivery of the home to the first User, will be determined after adjustment and settlement in accordance with Articles 6.2.1. to 6.2.5. If the adjusted consumption exceeds X kWh per year, Klimaatgarant shall provide a compensation to User for the 'additional' electricity consumed, to the extent it has not already been compensated for an earlier period. The compensation per kWh is equal to the most recent kWh rate paid by User including VAT and environmental tax."

523. Standards of good workmanship as objective conformity requirement – In addition to the performance explicitly agreed in the PSS contract, a more objective component of conformity must also be taken into account, namely the performance of the service in accordance with the "standards of good workmanship". Several elements are relevant in assessing the standards of good workmanship applicable to a result-oriented PSS contract. First, any (sector specific) legal and regulatory standards governing the service to be provided are of course considered. For example, legal safety standards for ventilation systems can be relevant in assessing whether a ventilation-as-a-service system is installed and operated properly. Second, the standards of good workmanship also relate to the materials and products used in the performance of the service. Thus, the PSS supplier will have to use materials that are free of defects, suitable for the intended use and in line with contractual requirements. In particular, with a view to fostering the circular economy, the use of sustainable and environmentally friendly materials can be considered. Third, the nature of the service and the stipulated price are important.[2364] Fourth, the increasing prevalence of and interest in standardisation and certification for services also influences the standards of good workmanship.[2365]

price reduction clause does not aim to set a fixed amount in damages for breach of contract (and must therefore be distinguished from an indemnity clause), but merely stipulates a compensation mechanism for an overpayment. See: I. Claeys and T. Tanghe, *Nieuw Algemeen Contractenrecht*, Antwerp, Intersentia, 2023, 973. Although price reduction clauses are not always easily distinguished from indemnity clauses, the difference is important as the latter can be mitigated by the court (compare with Art. 5.88, §2 BCC).

2364 **Belgium**: A. Van Oevelen, *Overeenkomsten. 2: Bijzondere overeenkomsten: E. Aanneming van werk, lastgeving, in Beginselen van Belgisch Privaatrecht*, Mechelen, Wolters Kluwer, 2017, 157, no. 131. **The Netherlands**: T.F.E. Tjong Tjin Tai, *Asser 7-IV Bijzondere Overeenkomsten – Opdracht, incl. de geneeskundige behandelingsovereenkomst en de reisovereenkomst*, Deventer, Wolters Kluwer, 2022, no. 97 and 98; J.J. Dammingh, "Dienstverlening: de overeenkomst van opdracht" in E.H. Hondius and V. Mak (eds.), *Handboek Consumentenrecht*, Vijfde druk, Zutphen, Paris, 2020, (267) 275.

2365 See: CEN and CENELEC, "CEN and CENELEC Joint Response to the European Commission Standardization Strategy Roadmap", 6 August 2021, available at https://www.cencenelec.eu/media/Policy%20Opinions/2021-08-06_cen-clc_response_ec_standardizarion_strategy_roadmap.pdf, 14, with explicit reference to servitisation. Standardisation is also on the agenda

524. Relevance of standardisation for determination of standards of good workmanship – Standards are technical specifications for a product or service, adopted by a recognised standardisation body.[2366, 2367] Their use is voluntary, unless compliance with these standards is mandated by a legal, regulatory or contractual provision.[2368] Non-compliance with these standards can be taken into account when assessing the non-conformity of the service with the standards of good workmanship and may lead to breach of contract on the part of the PSS supplier, even if there is no contractual reference to them.[2369] However, compliance with these technical standards does not necessarily mean that the PSS supplier is in the clear. In some circumstances the courts can impose a stricter standard on the PSS supplier and decide that a certain performance, although it is in conformity with a technical standard, is not in conformity with the standards of good workmanship and thus constitutes a breach of the PSS contract.[2370]

525. Conformity of digital content and digital services part of the result-oriented PSS contract – If result-oriented PSS includes digital content or digital services (as will be the case with connected "smart" products), conformity of these digital elements must also be assessed in light of the DCD's conformity requirements. These conformity requirements have already been discussed above in the section on conformity of use-oriented PSS and apply similarly to result-oriented PSS.[2371]

---

of the European Commission. See: EC, *An EU Strategy on Standardisation. Setting global standards in support of a resilient, green and digital EU single market*, 2.2.2022, COM(2022) 31 final, 3.

2366 See for example the European Committee for Standardization (CEN) (https://www.cencenelec.eu/about-cen/), the International Organization for Standardization (ISO) (https://www.iso.org/home.html), the Belgian Bureau voor Normalisatie/Bureau de Normalisation (NBN) (https://www.nbn.be), and the Royal Netherlands Standardisation Institute (NEN) (https://www.nen.nl/en/).

2367 See Art. 2(1) Regulation (EU) No 1025/2012 of the European Parliament and of the Council of 25 October 2012 on European standardisation, *OJ L* 316, 14.11.2012, 12–33 ('European standardisation regulation'). For **Belgium**, see also Art. VIII.1(1) BCEL.

2368 Art. 2 European standardisation regulation; Art. VIII.1(2) BCEL.

2369 **Belgium**: B. Kohl, *Contrat d'entreprise*, Brussels, Bruylant, 2016, 276; M. Dambre, *Bijzondere overeenkomsten: de essentie*, Bruges, Die Keure, 2022, 387–389. Under Belgian law, non-compliance with a standard gives rise to a (rebuttable) presumption that the work is not in compliance with the standards of good workmanship. See for applications e.g. Brussels (BE) 3 May 1995, *Res Jur.Imm.* 1995, 265 (sound insulation standard) and Brussels (BE) 9 February 1994, *RGAR* 1996, no. 12.657 (standard for permanent ventilation of a bathroom). **The Netherlands**: T.F.E. Tjong Tjin Tai, *Asser 7-IV Bijzondere Overeenkomsten – Opdracht, incl. de geneeskundige behandelingsovereenkomst en de reisovereenkomst*, Deventer, Wolters Kluwer, 2022, no. 87.

2370 **Belgium**: B. Kohl, *Contrat d'entreprise*, Brussels, Bruylant, 2016, 276–277. See also: M. Dambre, *Bijzondere overeenkomsten: de essentie*, Bruges, Die Keure, 2022, 389. **The Netherlands**: T.F.E. Tjong Tjin Tai, *Asser 7-IV Bijzondere Overeenkomsten – Opdracht, incl. de geneeskundige behandelingsovereenkomst en de reisovereenkomst*, Deventer, Wolters Kluwer, 2022, no. 97.

2371 See *supra* no. 495–498.

4.3.3.3. *Liability and remedies for non-conformity of the service provided*

526. Liability for non-conformity under Belgian law: distinction before and after acceptance of the performed service – For establishing the liability of the PSS supplier under Belgian law, a distinction must be made between the period before and after the acceptance of the completed performance of the service.[2372] The acceptance is a unilateral act (*eenzijdige rechtshandeling, acte juridique unilateral*) by which the client acknowledges that the service has been completed and is carried out in conformity with the contract, which at the same time releases the service provider from liability for non-conforming performance.[2373] The notion of acceptance is by no means limited to service contracts relating to (immovable) material services, and therefore applies to any service contract.[2374] There is, however, a difference in the degree of formalism that comes with the acceptance. For result-oriented PSS, this acceptance will generally not be very formalistic or explicit (unlike, for example, construction contracts for immovable goods). In fact, it will rather amount to a negative act, namely the absence of protest or reservation.[2375]

Before the acceptance of the performed service, the PSS supplier is liable for any late or non-conforming performance according to the general rules on contractual liability. After the acceptance, the situation is slightly different. Indeed, the acceptance by the PSS user has the effect of releasing the PSS supplier from liability for non-conforming performance and/or (visible) defects in the performance of the service.[2376] This means that after the acceptance, the PSS user can in principle only claim liability for hidden defects resulting from the performed service.[2377] The idea is that since the PSS user could not discover these

---

2372 B. Kohl, *Contrat d'entreprise*, Brussels, Bruylant, 2016, 459, no. 185.

2373 B. Tilleman, S. De Rey, N. Debruyne, T. Gladinez, N. Van Damme and F. Van den Abeele, "Overzicht van rechtspraak bijzondere overeenkomsten aanneming (2007–2021)", *TPR* 2022, (365) 459, no. 82; B. Kohl, *Contrat d'entreprise*, Brussels, Bruylant, 2016, 404–405, no. 164.

2374 W. Goossens, *Aanneming van werk: het gemeenrechtelijk dienstencontract*, Bruges, Die Keure, 2003, 944.

2375 W. Goossens, Aanneming van werk: het gemeenrechtelijk dienstencontract, Bruges, Die Keure, 2003, 944. See also for examples of a tacit acceptance: B. Tilleman, S. De Rey, N. Debruyne, T. Gladinez, N. Van Damme and F. Van den Abeele, "Overzicht van rechtspraak bijzondere overeenkomsten aanneming (2007–2021)", *TPR* 2022, (365) 459–460, no. 83.

2376 B. Tilleman, S. De Rey, N. Debruyne, T. Gladinez, N. Van Damme and F. Van den Abeele, "Overzicht van rechtspraak bijzondere overeenkomsten aanneming (2007–2021)", *TPR* 2022, (365) 461, no. 86; W. Goossens, Aanneming van werk: het gemeenrechtelijk dienstencontract, Bruges, Die Keure, 2003, 946.

2377 Cass. (BE) 25 October 1985, *Arr.Cass.* 1985–86, 270, *Pas.* 1986, I, 226, *JT* 1986, 438, *T.Aann.* 1986, 204, case note J. Embrechts; B. Tilleman, S. De Rey, N. Debruyne, T. Gladinez, N. Van Damme and F. Van den Abeele, "Overzicht van rechtspraak bijzondere overeenkomsten aanneming (2007–2021)", *TPR* 2022, (365) 461, no. 86; See for an analysis and overview of the requirements: A. Van Oevelen, "Kwaliteitsstandaarden bij de verkoop van goederen en de

defects due to their hidden nature at the time of service delivery, the acceptance does not cover them.[2378] This liability for hidden defects is also subject to the "ordinary" contractual liability rules of general contract law, with a ten-year limitation period from the acceptance (guarantee period).[2379] In addition, there is also a procedural period that is different from the guarantee period. This is the period within which the client must file a claim against the service provider, which is generally assumed to be within a reasonable time after he became aware (or should have become aware) of the defect.[2380]

527. LIABILITY FOR NON-CONFORMITY UNDER DUTCH LAW – The Dutch contract for services rules do not have the same concept of acceptance with the corresponding legal consequences as under the Belgian contract for services and under the Dutch contract for works.[2381] This means that the PSS supplier is liable for shortcomings in the performance of the PSS contract under the "ordinary" rules of general contract law, in particular those on breach of contract.[2382] However, the PSS user must take timely action against the PSS supplier in case of non-performance or incorrect performance of the service.[2383] This follows from the duty to complain[2384] (*klachtplicht*) stemming from the general law of obligations on the one hand and the general limitation rules[2385] on the other.

levering van diensten" in I. CLAEYS, W. DELVA and R. STEENNOT (eds.), *Aansprakelijkheid, veiligheid en kwaliteit*, Ghent, Kluwer, 2015, (1) 57–60.

2378 A. VAN OEVELEN, "Kwaliteitsstandaarden bij de verkoop van goederen en de levering van diensten" in I. CLAEYS, W. DELVA and R. STEENNOT (eds.), *Aansprakelijkheid, veiligheid en kwaliteit*, Ghent, Kluwer, 2015, (1) 58.

2379 Art. 5.82 *et seq.* and Art. 2262*bis*, §1 old BCC. B. TILLEMAN, S. DE REY, N. DEBRUYNE, T. GLADINEZ, N. VAN DAMME and F. VAN DEN ABEELE, "Overzicht van rechtspraak bijzondere overeenkomsten aanneming (2007–2021)", *TPR* 2022, (365) 461, no. 86.

2380 See B. TILLEMAN, S. DE REY, N. DEBRUYNE, T. GLADINEZ, N. VAN DAMME and F. VAN DEN ABEELE, "Overzicht van rechtspraak bijzondere overeenkomsten aanneming (2007–2021)", *TPR* 2022, (365) 570–573, no. 159–160 and the references of case law cited there.

2381 Compare with Art. 7:758 DCC. For a discussion of the concept of acceptance under the Dutch rules of the contract for works in the context of the obligation to install the product, see *infra* no. 705–706.

2382 See Art. 6:74 DCC (regarding the non-performance of a contractual obligation) and Art. 7:401 DCC (regarding the failure to perform the service as a good service provider). See: T.F.E. TJONG TJIN TAI, *Asser 7-IV Bijzondere Overeenkomsten – Opdracht, incl. de geneeskundige behandelingsovereenkomst en de reisovereenkomst*, Deventer, Wolters Kluwer, 2022, no. 191 and no. 197. For a discussion of the liability for breach of contract, see: C.H. SIEBURGH, *Mr. C. Assers Handleiding tot de beoefening van het Nederlands Burgerlijk Recht. 6. Verbintenissenrecht. Deel I. De verbintenis in het algemeen, eerste gedeelte*, Deventer, Wolters Kluwer, 2020, no. 332 *et seq.*

2383 T.F.E. TJONG TJIN TAI, *Asser 7-IV Bijzondere Overeenkomsten – Opdracht, incl. de geneeskundige behandelingsovereenkomst en de reisovereenkomst*, Deventer, Wolters Kluwer, 2022, no. 214a.

2384 Art. 6:89 DCC. See for an application: HR (NL) 11 June 2010, ECLI:NL:HR:2010:BL8297, *NJ* 2010/331.

2385 Art. 3:306 DCC *et seq.* The general limitation period is 20 years (Art. 3:306 DCC). However, in the majority of cases there will be a shorter limitation period of 5 years, e.g. in legal actions

The duty to complain entails that the PSS user can no longer claim contractual liability if he has not complained to the PSS supplier within due time after he discovered or should reasonably have discovered the non-conformity.[2386] As a result, if the PSS user does not take action within a reasonable time after discovering the non-conformity of the service, this will result in forfeiture of rights (*verval van recht*).

528. General contract law remedies in case of non-conformity of service provided – Both the Belgian and Dutch rules of the contract for services do not contain specific rules on remedies available in case of non-conformity of the service provided. This means that for shortcomings in the performance of the service, the PSS supplier is liable under the ordinary rules of general contract law.[2387] As discussed above,[2388] the PSS user can first claim specific performance of the obligation, possibly with additional compensation for late performance of the obligation.[2389] For example, the PSS user may demand performance from the PSS supplier if the service is unavailable, or if a product used for the performance of the service is defective and is not repaired or repaired late. Generally, performance must be carried out by the PSS supplier itself, but the PSS user may also ask the court to authorise him to perform the obligation himself, or have it performed by a third party at the PSS supplier's

for the performance of obligations under contracts to give or do (Art. 3:307 DCC), in legal actions to pay damages (Art. 3:310 DCC) or legal actions for the termination of a contract due to non-performance (Art. 3:311 DCC). See: C.H. Sieburgh, *Mr. C. Assers Handleiding tot de beoefening van het Nederlands Burgerlijk Recht. 6. Verbintenissenrecht. Deel II. De verbintenis in het algemeen, tweede gedeelte*, Deventer, Wolters Kluwer, 2021, no. 378 and 397 *et seq*. See also: M.W.E. Koopmann, "Verjaring van rechtsvorderingen wegens tekortkomingen" in D.F.H. Stein, V. Tweehuysen and S.E. Bartels (eds.), *Verjaring. Onderneming en Recht, nr. 120*, Deventer, Wolters Kluwer, 2020, (23) 24.

2386 Art. 6:89 DCC. HR (NL) 8 February 2013, ECLI:NL:HR:2013:BY4600, (*Van de Steeg/ Rabobank*), *NJ* 2014/497, case note J. Hijma.

2387 **Belgium**: B. Kohl, *Contrat d'entreprise*, Brussels, Bruylant, 2016, 459, no. 185; C. Marr, "Le contrat d'entreprise hors construction et la protection des consommateurs" in P. De Page, B. Sindic and C. Marr (eds.), *Récyclage en droit: Droit des contrats*, Liège, Anthemis, 2007, (145) 171–173. See also: M. Dambre, *Bijzondere overeenkomsten: de essentie*, Bruges, Die Keure, 2022, 393–395. **The Netherlands**: T.F.E. Tjong Tjin Tai, *Asser 7-IV Bijzondere Overeenkomsten - Opdracht, incl. de geneeskundige behandelingsovereenkomst en de reisovereenkomst*, Deventer, Wolters Kluwer, 2022, no. 191 and 197.

2388 See *supra* no. 299 and H. Slachmuylders, "Movable Servitization. Contractual Liability in the B2C Relationship" in B. Keirsbilck, E. Terryn, J. Eyckmans, S. Rousseau and D. Voinot (eds.), *Servitization and circular economy: economic and legal challenges*, Antwerp, Intersentia, 2023, (135) 159–160. See also for **Belgium**: B. Kohl, *Contrat d'entreprise*, Brussels, Bruylant, 2016, 462–541 and C. Marr, "Le contrat d'entreprise hors construction et la protection des consommateurs" in P. De Page, B. Sindic and C. Marr (eds.), *Récyclage en droit: Droit des contrats*, Liège, Anthemis, 2007, (145) 173–195. For **the Netherlands**: G.T. de Jong, H.B. Krans and M.H. Wissink, *Verbintenissenrecht algemeen (Studiereeks Burgerlijk Recht, deel 4)*, Deventer, Wolters Kluwer, 2018, 107–108.

2389 **Belgium**: Art. 5.84 and Art. 5.234–5.236 BCC. **The Netherlands**: Art. 3:296(1) DCC.

expense.[2390] Under Belgian law, provided certain requirements are met, the PSS user does not have to await judicial authorisation and can opt for an extrajudicial replacement.[2391] A second possibility for the PSS user is to claim damages instead of performance.[2392] Third, the PSS user may also choose to terminate the contract, possibly with additional damages.[2393] This does however require a fundamental non-performance.[2394] If the non-performance is not sufficiently serious to justify the termination of the PSS contract, the fourth option for the PSS user is the right to a proportionate price reduction.[2395] Alternatively, the PSS user can also temporarily suspend his obligations under the PSS contract (*exceptio non adimpleti contractus*, "enac") in order to induce to PSS supplier to perform the service according to the PSS contract.[2396]

529. Remedies are not mandatory law – These remedies are not mandatory law, so the PSS contract can deviate from them, modulate them, or even (partially) exclude some of these remedies. For example, the PSS contract may limit the possibility to request authorisation for the performance of the obligation by the PSS user or a third party, may contractually regulate the conditions for suspension or termination of the PSS contract, and may include express termination clauses or indemnity clauses.[2397] The PSS supplier's freedom is not unlimited, however, as the control mechanism of unfair terms already discussed above allows PSS users to combat clauses in the PSS contract that restrict their the legal rights in a significantly imbalanced way.[2398]

530. DCD: liability for lack of conformity of digital content or digital services part of the result-oriented PSS contract – If digital content or digital services are part of the result-oriented PSS contract, the PSS supplier will be liable for any lack of conformity that exists at their time of delivery.[2399] The time limits and remedies for this liability for lack of conformity were already discussed above, under the section on conformity in use-oriented PSS.[2400]

2390 **Belgium**: Art. 5.85 and 5.235 BCC. **The Netherlands**: Art. 3:299 DCC.

2391 **Belgium**: Art. 5.85(3) BCC.

2392 **Belgium**: Art. 5.86 and 5.237–5.238 BCC. **The Netherlands**: Art. 6:74(1) DCC.

2393 **Belgium**: Art. 5.90–5.96 BCC. **The Netherlands**: Art. 6:265–6:277 DCC.

2394 **Belgium**: Art. 5.90 BCC. **The Netherlands**: Art. 6:265(1) DCC.

2395 **Belgium**: Art. 5.97 BCC. **The Netherlands**: Art. 6:265 and 6:270 DCC.

2396 **Belgium**: Art. 5.98 and 5.239 BCC. **The Netherlands**: Art. 6:52–6:57 and Art. 6:262–6:264 DCC.

2397 H. Slachmuylders, "Movable Servitization. Contractual Liability in the B2C Relationship" in B. Keirsbilck, E. Terryn, J. Eyckmans, S. Rousseau and D. Voinot (eds.), *Servitization and circular economy: economic and legal challenges*, Antwerp, Intersentia, 2023, (135) 160.

2398 This is discussed more in depth *supra* in section 2.6.6.

2399 EU: Art. 11.1 DCD. **Belgium**: Art. 1701/8 old BCC. **The Netherlands**: Art. 50 ag(1) DCC.

2400 See *supra* no. 511 and no. 512.

4.4. LEGISLATIVE INTERVENTION NEEDED?

4.4.1. EVALUATION OF CURRENT LEGAL FRAMEWORK

4.4.1.1. Use-oriented PSS

531. Rules of the rental contract already provide to a certain extent a useful legal framework for use-oriented PSS – The rules of the rental contract already provide to a certain extent a useful legal framework for the PSS supplier's obligation to provide the product in use-oriented PSS. After all, both Belgian law and Dutch law contain rules on making the rented product available and have a legal framework in place regarding the conformity of the product both at the start of the rental contract and during the rental contract. Yet there are shortcomings to these legal rules, especially when viewed in the context of the emerging trend of servitisation.

532. Shortcomings in terms of legal certainty: conformity rules are formulated in general terms and not well adapted to movables – In the first place, the Belgian rules on making the product available and on conformity of the product are formulated in very general terms and are not well adapted to movable goods. As explained above, this is mainly because the Belgian general rental contract rules still date back to the Napoleonic era and do not contain specific rules for movables, as the rental of movables was relatively rare at that time.[2401] This lacuna is solved by applying the rules of the rental contract for immovables by analogy to rental contracts for movables (unless they are incompatible), but it is not always crystal clear how these general provisions on delivery in good state of repair and ensuring the quiet rental enjoyment (i.e. conformity) must be applied to the rental of movables. As a result, this analogical application does not foster legal certainty for the PSS user. Even though the Dutch Civil Code is more recent than the old BCC, there is also little to no specific attention to the rental of movable goods. The rental contract for movables is subjected to the same general provisions on making the product available and remedying defects. Also here, applying the general provisions on defects of the rented product to movable goods sometimes requires some creativity. An evaluation in terms of legal certainty of both legal systems therefore shows that a more detailed conformity regime for movables – comparable to the concept of conformity in consumer sales contracts – would foster legal certainty for consumers (considering) engaging in use-oriented PSS contracts.

533. Shortcomings in terms of coherence & consistency and fair balance between rights and obligations: comparison with consumer

2401 See *supra* no. 387.

SALES RULES – These shortcomings become even more apparent when looking at the evaluation criteria of coherence & consistency and the need for a fair balance between the rights and obligations of the parties. It follows from the analysis above that the professional (PSS) supplier of movable products (either in the capacity of seller or lessor) must provide products that are in conformity with the (PSS) contract. Under the consumer sales rules, this concept of conformity is elaborated in great detail in both subjective and objective conformity criteria.[2402] For the rental contract for movables, on the other hand, these conformity requirements are described much more summarily. From a coherence and consistency perspective, it is therefore difficult to see why consumers' rights concerning the conformity of the product are regulated more comprehensively and more detailed if they gain access to a movable product by buying it, than if they merely wish to obtain its use and enjoyment under a product-as-a-service contract.

Evaluating the conformity regime of the rental contract for movables from the perspective of the fair balance criterion yields the same results. The focus of the consumer sales rules is on the situations where the seller is liable to the consumer. After all, the provisions of the consumer sales contract assume that the seller is liable to the consumer for any lack of conformity of the product that existed at the time of delivery.[2403] If this lack of conformity arises within 1 year of delivery (the so-called presumption period), it is even presumed that this lack of conformity already existed at the time of delivery.[2404] This of course significantly strengthens the consumer's evidentiary position.

The rental contract rules, on the other hand, have as their starting point that the consumer-lessee is liable to the lessor for any damage to the product that occurred during the term of the contract.[2405] The rental contract rules then provide some rules on when the consumer-lessee is not liable to the lessor. First, the burden of proof shifts if no rental inventory was drawn up at the beginning of the contract.[2406] In this case, the lessee-consumer is presumed to have received the product in the condition it is in at the end of the contract, and the lessor must prove that the damage originated during the rental contract. Second, the lessee-consumer is not liable for damages due to normal wear and tear. The burden of proof is on the lessee.[2407] Finally, the lessee-consumer is not liable for defects, in which case the lessor is obligated to remedy them.[2408] However, this is not the case for minor defects, which remain in principle the responsibility of

2402 See *supra* no. 450 *et seq.*

2403 See *supra* no. 466.

2404 See *supra* no. 469.

2405 See *supra* no. 436.

2406 *Ibid.*

2407 M. DAMBRE, "Rechten en verbintenissen van de huurder" in M. DAMBRE, B. HUBEAU and S. STIJNS (eds.), *Handboek algemeen huurrecht*, Bruges, Die Keure, 2015, (513) 583–584.

2408 See *supra* no. 482.

the lessee (unless otherwise agreed in the contract).[2409] This difference in legal position between a consumer-buyer and a consumer-lessee who is confronted with minor defects is also difficult to explain. While this distinction may be understandable for the rental of immovable goods, it does not make sense for the rental of movable (consumer) goods.[2410]

534. Evaluation in terms of sustainability – Finally, there are also arguments based on the evaluative criterion of sustainability. When evaluating the current regime on making the product available and conformity of the product in terms of sustainability, two things stand out.

First, regarding the obligation to make the product available under Belgian law, the scope of the special (mandatory) risk regime of Article 20 CRD is extended to *all* contracts (therefore including use-oriented PSS contracts) where a business dispatches goods to a consumer.[2411] This protection against loss or damage to products during the shipping process is obviously beneficial from a consumer protection perspective for the PSS user-lessee concluding a PSS contract remotely.[2412] However, in legal doctrine, it was already pointed out that the fact that the risk only transfers when the consumer (or the person he designated) takes physical possession of the product can result in more failed deliveries as carriers rarely leave these goods on the doorstep or with a neighbour because of the risks associated with unattended delivered products.[2413] These failed deliveries then require a second delivery attempt, resulting in additional environmental impact.[2414] Several strategies can be used to reduce failed deliveries, such as consumer information with more specific delivery times (e.g. track & trace), smart mailboxes at the consumer's home where carriers can safely deposit packages and the use of (manned or automated) parcel pick up points.[2415]

2409 See *supra* no. 485.

2410 See in the same sense: M.B.M. Loos, "Servitization, consumentenhuur en consumentenkoop", *WPNR* 2022/7396, (944) 946.

2411 See *supra* no. 438.

2412 G. Howells, C. Twigg-Flesner and T. Wilhelmsson, *Rethinking EU Consumer Law*, Abingdon, Routledge, 2018, 178–179.

2413 See E. Terryn and E. Van Gool, "The Role of European Consumer Regulation in Shaping the Environmental Impact of E-Commerce", *EuCML* 2021, vol. 10, afl. 3, (89) 93 and E. Terryn and E. Van Gool, "Kunnen we e-commerce vergroenen door het consumentencontractenrecht te herzien?", *Tijdschrift voor Consumentenrecht en handelspraktijken* 2021, vol. 1, (15) 19 with reference to A. McKinnon and D. Tallam, "Unattended delivery to the home: an assessment of the security implications", *International Journal of Retail & Distribution Management* 2003, vol. 31 issue 1, (30) 30–35 (where risks were identified such as theft by a passer-by, damage due to bad weather conditions, animals or third parties, the risk of fraud due to wrongful denial of receipt, etc.).

2414 E. Terryn and E. Van Gool, "The Role of European Consumer Regulation in Shaping the Environmental Impact of E-Commerce", *EuCML* 2021, vol. 10, afl. 3, (89) 93 with references.

2415 See for a more in-depth discussion with examples: E. Terryn and E. Van Gool, "The Role of European Consumer Regulation in Shaping the Environmental Impact of E-Commerce", *EuCML* 2021, vol. 10, afl. 3, (89) 93–94 and E. Terryn and E. Van Gool, "Kunnen we

However, as this issue is not exclusive to (use-oriented) PSS contracts but also applies to sales contracts, these will not be discussed in depth.[2416]

More importantly for use-oriented PSS, a few arguments for a stronger legal conformity regime can be identified when considering the legal conformity regime for the rental contract for movables in terms of sustainability. In this regard, the fact that minor defects are the responsibility of the PSS user-lessee stands out the most. Placing the burden of minor repairs on the PSS user-lessee may discourage them from investing in sustainable and durable repair practices. Indeed, there is a risk that lessees will opt for cheap and quick fixes that prioritise immediate cost savings rather than long-term sustainability. Even if consumers were willing to perform sustainable repairs, repairing movable goods such as bicycles, household appliances and consumer electronics requires specific knowledge and materials/parts that are not always available to consumers. This is also the reason why many PSS suppliers explicitly prohibit the PSS user from repairing the product himself.[2417] From the other side of the market, PSS suppliers-lessors who are relieved of repair responsibilities for minor defects may also be discouraged to offer sustainable and durable products as part of their PSS offers, as they do not have to perform the minor repairs anyway. Placing responsibility for minor defects on the PSS supplier has a possible drawback though, as it can create situations of moral hazard where the PSS user may not handle the product with due care because he is not responsible for minor repairs. However, the lessor is not responsible for defects caused by the lessee's fault,[2418] which provides a safeguard so the PSS supplier will not be responsible for minor defects resulting from abuse of the product by the PSS user.

Additionally, there are some general arguments for more detailed conformity requirements for the rental of movables. Strengthening legal obligations for PSS suppliers-lessors to remedy defects may encourage them to provide better-maintained and longer-lasting products. This is particularly true for sales contracts,[2419] but certainly plays a role for rental contracts as well.[2420]

---

e-commerce vergroenen door het consumentencontractenrecht te herzien?", *Tijdschrift voor Consumentenrecht en handelspraktijken* 2021, vol. 1, (15) 19–20.

2416 For an overview of legal solutions, see: E. Terryn and E. Van Gool, "The Role of European Consumer Regulation in Shaping the Environmental Impact of E-Commerce", *EuCML* 2021, vol. 10, afl. 3, (89) 94 and E. Terryn and E. Van Gool, "Kunnen we e-commerce vergroenen door het consumentencontractenrecht te herzien?", *Tijdschrift voor Consumentenrecht en handelspraktijken* 2021, vol. 1, (15) 20–21.

2417 See *infra* no. 739.

2418 See *supra* no. 484.

2419 E. Van Gool and A. Michel, "The New Consumer Sales Directive 2019/771 and Sustainable Consumption", *EuCML* 2021, vol. 10, afl. 4, (136) 141; F. Gomez, "Economic Analysis of the Directive" in C.M. Bianca and S. Grundmann (eds.), *EU sales directive: commentary*, Antwerp, Intersentia, 2002, 57–59.

2420 See e.g. the above-mentioned example of Swapfiets (fn. 178). Swapfiets pushes its suppliers to provide more durable parts for their bikes (such as flexible mudguards that do not break when something strikes them instead of the traditional hard plastic mudguards). As

Incentives to offer more durable products as part of use-oriented PSS can contribute to resource conservation by reducing the frequency of replacements and minimising the overall demand for new products. Moreover, stronger legal obligations to remedy defects has the result of empowering consumers.[2421] Indeed, when PSS suppliers-lessors have strong obligations to address defects promptly this enhances legal certainty and provides consumers with greater assurance, trust and confidence in their choice for a use-oriented PSS. This can encourage consumers to choose servitised business models over purchasing products, as they are certain their rights are protected. This in turn can lead to more sustainable consumption behaviour being adopted by consumers. A possible downside of more extensive conformity requirements is of course that these may lead to higher prices. However, the question is whether this is not balanced by the fact that consumers should not fear costs for minor repairs, and are likely willing to pay extra for convenience, reassurance, and their contribution to a more sustainable economy and society.[2422]

535. Legal framework for use-oriented PSS needs modernisation and improvement – These shortcomings make it necessary to modernise and improve the legal framework of use-oriented PSS.[2423] The ideal opportunity to do this now presents itself in Belgium. As part of the reform of the Belgian Civil Code,[2424] a modernisation exercise is under way that should lead to a new Book 7 on special contracts.[2425] In my view, this is an excellent opportunity to rethink the rules on rental contracts for movables and service contracts so that consumers engaging in (use-oriented) PSS contracts can benefit from a

Swapfiets gets a fee per flat tyre, this provides an incentive for this supplier to also supply sustainable products. See: P. Lalkens, "De zoektocht naar de volledig recycleerbare fiets", *FD* 26 February 2023, https://fd.nl/bedrijfsleven/1468479/de-zoektocht-naar-de-volledig-recyclebare-fiets.

2421 The same rationale was also behind the adoption of EU conformity rules for sales contracts, see: recital 5 CSD and G. Howells, C. Twigg-Flesner and T. Wilhelmsson, *Rethinking EU Consumer Law*, Abingdon, Routledge, 2018, 168.

2422 However, it is important to note that there is often a mismatch between consumer's publicly declared willingness to buy sustainable products or engage in environmentally friendly business models and their actual (unsustainable) behaviour (the so-called value-action gap). See e.g. A. Kollmuss and J. Agyeman, "Mind the Gap: why do people act environmentally and what are the barriers to pro-environmental behavior", *Environ. Educ. Res.* 2002, vol. 8 issue 3, (239) 240.

2423 See also: H. Slachmuylders, "Movable Servitization. Contractual Liability in the B2C Relationship" in B. Keirsbilck, E. Terryn, J. Eyckmans, S. Rousseau and D. Voinot (eds.), *Servitization and circular economy: economic and legal challenges*, Antwerp, Intersentia, 2023, (135) 144.

2424 https://justitie.belgium.be/nl/bwcc.

2425 See: Ministerial Decree of 15 June 2021 establishing Commissions for the reform of contract law and the law of limitation, *BS* 2 July 2021. Bernard Tilleman and Paul-Alain Foriers are the chairs of the Commission for the reform of contract law. This led to the draft law of 16 April 2024 inserting Book 7 "special contracts" into the Civil Code. See: Explanatory Memorandum, *Parliamentary Papers* Chamber of Representatives 2023–24, no. 55–3973/001.

modern legal framework.[2426] In the Netherlands too, there are voices calling for reforming the rules of the rental contract for movables to address, not only, but also the legal challenges caused by growing trend of servitisation.[2427]

4.4.1.2. Result-oriented PSS

536. CONTRACT FOR SERVICES: INCOMPLETE AND OUTDATED LEGAL FRAMEWORK FOR RESULT-ORIENTED PSS – As already mentioned above,[2428] the Belgian contract for services serves as one of the prime examples of regulatory obsolescence.[2429] Indeed, despite its very broad scope, applying to both material and intellectual performances,[2430] and the fact that it is the most widely used special contract together with the sales contract,[2431] the old BCC devotes only 13 provisions to it, which remained unchanged since 1804.[2432] They mainly relate to the occurrence of a risk[2433] and the client's right to unilaterally terminate the contract,[2434] and do not even include a definition of the contract for services.[2435] This incomplete character of the rules of the contract for services can be explained by the fact that it was impossible in 1804 to envisage the technical advances and the surge of the services industry which would characterise the 20th century.[2436] Still, even more than the rental contract for movables, the

---

2426 See: S. De Rey, "Naar een boek 'bijzondere overeenkomsten' in het Nieuw Burgerlijk Wetboek? Enkele perspectieven" in S. De Rey, N. Van Damme and T. Gladinez (eds.), *Grenzen voorbij. Liber discipulorum Bernard Tilleman*, Antwerp, Intersentia, 2020, (361) 369 referring to the fact that the limited legal framework on the rental contract for movables is no longer tenable in the light of contemporary practice.

2427 M.B.M. Loos, "Servitization, consumentenhuur en consumentenkoop", *WPNR* 2022/7396, (944) 947.

2428 See *supra* no. 376.

2429 B. Kohl, "Le contrat d'entreprise: proposition de réforme du Code civil" in R. Jafferali, P. Foriers and E. Van Den Haute (eds.), *Entre tradition et pragmatisme. Liber amicorum Paul Alain Foriers*, Volume 1, Brussels, Larcier, 2021, (481) 484.

2430 Cass. (BE) 13 October 1910, *JCB* 1911, 26.

2431 C. Marr, "Le contrat d'entreprise hors construction et la protection des consommateurs" in P. De Page, B. Sindic and C. Marr (eds.), *Récyclage en droit: Droit des contrats*, Liège, Anthemis, 2007, (145) 155.

2432 Art. 1787–1799 old BCC. In addition, see Art. 2270 old BCC (ten-year limitation period for defects affecting major works) and Art. 20, 12° and Art. 27, 5°of the Belgian Mortgage Act (both establishing preferential rights, either for the subcontractor or for contractors and architects). See also: F. Glansdorff, "Les contrats de service: notion et qualifications" in F. Glansdorff and P.-A. Foriers (eds.), *Les contrats de service*, Brussels, Jeune barreau de Bruxelles, 1994, (1) 9.

2433 Art. 1788–1792 old BCC.

2434 Art. 1794 old BCC.

2435 C. Marr, "Le contrat d'entreprise hors construction et la protection des consommateurs" in P. De Page, B. Sindic and C. Marr (eds.), *Récyclage en droit: Droit des contrats*, Liège, Anthemis, 2007, (145) 171.

2436 B. Kohl, "Le contrat d'entreprise: proposition de réforme du Code civil" in R. Jafferali, P. Foriers and E. Van Den Haute (eds.), *Entre tradition et pragmatisme. Liber amicorum Paul Alain Foriers*, Volume 1, Brussels, Larcier, 2021, (481) 485.

rules on the contract for services as they are set out in the old BCC are totally outdated, do not reflect developments in case law, and not well adapted to new developments in practice, result-oriented PSS in particular. Dating from 1992, the Dutch rules on the contract for services are more recent and provide to some extent a more complete legal framework for service contracts. However, also these rules remain rather general and therefore provide only little concrete guidance for as-a-service contracts in practice.[2437] Still, they can – together with the DCFR – provide an important source of inspiration for a future reform of the Belgian rules on the contract for services.[2438]

4.4.1.3. Three possible solutions

537. Three possible solutions – This book sets out and evaluates three possible solutions for the outdated and/or incomplete legal framework for use-oriented and result-oriented PSS. These solutions vary in terms of how ambitious/easily achievable they are. First, a proposal for **modernised national rules** on conformity for the Belgian rental contract (for movables) and the Belgian contract for services is made (option 1). Regarding the latter, standardisation of services will also receive attention, as this allows to consider the specific characteristics of (result-oriented) PSS, while still having general rules for all service contracts. Second, the option of an **EU directive** on the quality and conformity of (bundles of) services is explored (option 2). This is certainly the most ambitious option, but – provided there is enough political will – could provide (use-oriented and result-oriented) PSS with a specific and detailed regulatory framework. Third, the **use of balanced standard contracts and model clauses** is considered (option 3). This solution can be considered the "low-hanging fruit" since it requires, in principle, no legislative intervention. Therefore, it is discussed in section 4.5. Of course, choosing one option should not necessarily rule out the others. It is perfectly possible that an "and-and" approach in the end will yield the best results.

538. Modernisation by means of national law reform or EU directive? – The question arises what form a modern legal framework for PSS contracts should take. There are roughly two possibilities here, namely a national contract law reform (option 1) or an EU directive which harmonises service contracts (option 2).

2437 See in this sense: S. van Gulijk, "De juridische kwalificatie van verdienstelijking in de gebouwde omgeving", *WPNR* 2021, vol. 7326, (409) 414.

2438 Compare also with B. Kohl, "Le contrat d'entreprise: proposition de réforme du Code civil" in R. Jafferali, P. Foriers and E. Van Den Haute (eds.), *Entre tradition et pragmatisme. Liber amicorum Paul Alain Foriers*, Volume 1, Brussels, Larcier, 2021, (481) 485–486, where inspiration is taken from Dutch law, French law, the DCFR and the Law of Quebec for giving some pointers for a reform of the old BCC rules on the contract for services.

As regards to option 1, Loos argues that it is not necessary nor useful to wait for EU legislation on servitisation.[2439] After all, he claims, the EU legislator is mostly focused on the sale of goods and digital content and digital services, and on the development of digital markets. As use-oriented PSS relate to the use of movables, a national contract law reform of the rental contract for movables would be better suited to deal with these issues.[2440] This is certainly a compelling argument. After all, the rental contract (for movables) already provides to some extent a useful (yet outdated) framework for use-oriented PSS. Deciding on an EU legal framework for the rental contract for movables would be an ambitious and difficult task, where there is also a significant risk of creating inconsistencies with the national rental contract rules for immovables. Therefore, national reparations to the current outdated legal framework could potentially provide a better solution for regulating use-oriented PSS contracts. Regarding result-oriented PSS, the same argument could be made. Indeed, in the area of service contract law, it has already been proved difficult in the past to find common ground between the EU Member States.[2441] As a result, it might be even more difficult to decide on an EU legal framework for service contracts than for rental contracts.

Option 2 would be to harmonise (use-oriented and result-oriented) PSS contracts by means of a (minimum or maximum harmonisation) EU directive. So far, the legislative initiatives of the European Commission were focused on making the traditional linear framework more sustainable (e.g. by means of eco-design requirements, promoting sustainable remedies in consumer sales, by adopting waste law rules, etc.).[2442] This is of course the right course of action and should continue in the future. However, so far, there is significantly less legislative attention for alternatives for the traditional linear business models based on the sale of goods. Indeed, while business models based on servitisation are occasionally mentioned,[2443] the legislative actions and proposals of the European Commission have so far been limited to establishing and supporting

---

2439 M.B.M. Loos, "Servitization, consumentenhuur en consumentenkoop", *WPNR* 2022/7396, (944) 947.

2440 M.B.M. Loos, "Servitization, consumentenhuur en consumentenkoop", *WPNR* 2022/7396, (944) 947.

2441 Compare with EC, *Proposal for a Council Directive on the liability of suppliers of services*, 18.1.1991, COM(90) 482 final which was ultimately shut down by the Commission due to fierce opposition by the Member States.

2442 Compare with *supra* no. 4. See for an extensive overview and evaluation, including policy suggestions of how different legal instruments can make the traditional legal framework more sustainable throughout the design and production stage, the marketing and pre-contractual stage, the use stage and the waste stage: A. Michel, *Premature Obsolescence: In Search of an Improved Legal Framework*, Cambridge, Intersentia, 2023, 672 p.

2443 J. Hojnik, "Servitization, IoT and Circular Economy. Need for Regulatory Intervention at EU Level? " in B. Keirsbilck, E. Terryn, J. Eyckmans, S. Rousseau and D. Voinot (eds.), *Servitization and circular economy: economic and legal challenges*, Antwerp, Intersentia, 2023, (33) 62.

stakeholder platforms[2444] including a Circular Business Hub[2445] for identifying drivers and barriers for servitised circular business models. In my view, the ideal EU approach would also entail complementary efforts that promote both buying sustainable and durable goods and buying less goods as a result of a shift to a society where using and accessing products becomes more important than acquiring their ownership.

In this book, the modernisation of national contract law (option 1) (alongside with option 3, the use of standard contracts and model clauses[2446]) is put forward as the preferred solution.[2447] The DCFR, which already contains rules on the rental contract for movables, and the SGD and the DCD can act as a source of inspiration for these modernisation works and will therefore be considered for making legislative proposals. Additionally, the new Belgian draft law of 16 April 2024 inserting Book 7 "special contracts" into the Civil Code was also considered.[2448] The proposed provisions that are be introduced below were drafted with the Belgian legal system in mind. However, this does not mean that they cannot provide inspiration for a possible Dutch reform of rental contract law, or even for a specific EU directive on servitised contracts.

The focus on a national contract law reform, however, does not mean that the question of EU harmonisation (option 2) is completely neglected. Indeed, this section will also explore the option of adopting an EU directive on the quality and conformity of (bundles of) services and/or PSS contracts.[2449] This could, provided there is sufficient political will, lead to a broader harmonisation of private law, providing a robust legal framework for service contracts and/or PSS across the different EU Member States. So far, however, this does not seem to be on the EU Commission's agenda.

4.4.2. MODERNISATION OF NATIONAL CONTRACT LAW

4.4.2.1. Use-oriented PSS: modernisation of rental contract law

539. Reading guide and plan of action – This section will put forward proposed provisions on two obligations of the lessor. The first set of proposed

2444 E.g. the European Circular Economy Stakeholder Platform. See: https://circulareconomy.europa.eu/platform/.

2445 See: EC, *Communication on making sustainable products the norm*, 30.3.2022, COM(2022) 140 final, 11 and EC, *Proposal for a Regulation of the European Parliament and of the Council establishing a framework for setting ecodesign requirements for sustainable products and repealing Directive 2009/125/EC*, 30.3.2022, COM(2022) 142 final 10, 100, 103.

2446 See *infra* section 4.5.

2447 See section 4.4.2.

2448 Explanatory Memorandum, *Parliamentary Papers* Chamber of Representatives 2023–24, no. 55–3973/001.

2449 See *infra* section 4.4.3.

provisions relate to the obligation to make available a rented good that is in conformity with the contract. The second set of proposed provisions deals with the obligation to indemnify for the lessor's own acts and for acts of third parties. These obligations are also addressed in the draft law of 16 April 2024 inserting Book 7 "special contracts" into the Civil Code ("the Draft Law").[2450] In addition, the Draft Law provides for a third obligation for the lessor, namely to compensate the lessee for fit-out or alteration works, if applicable.[2451] However, given the nature and content of (movable) PSS contracts, this obligation is less relevant for this book and is therefore not explicitly discussed.

For the numbering of the proposed provisions, it was opted to take the same approach as the Draft Law, namely a numbering system consisting of three numbers.[2452] The first number refers to the book (i.e. Book 7), the second to the title (2 for the sales contract, 3 for the rental contract, 4 for the contract for services) and the third to the article number itself. Since this book limits itself to proposing provisions and not a complete legislative framework (unlike the Draft Law), the numbering used in this book will be structured as X1, X2, X3, etc. to indicate that this numbering is not set in stone and that the proposed provisions can be implemented in a broader modernised legal framework.

A. Obligation to deliver the rented good in conformity with the contract

540. Obligation to deliver the rented good in conformity with the contract – Proposed provision #1 provides a general overview of the obligation to deliver the rented good in conformity with the contract and would therefore replace Article 1719 old BCC. It is in line with Article 7.3.4 of the Draft Law. It specifies that this obligation both includes the delivery of the rented good and the conformity of the rented good throughout the entire duration of the contract (including the maintenance and repair necessary for this purpose). The obligation to deliver the rented good in conformity with the contract, as well as the provisions dealing with its sub-obligation, apply in both B2B and B2C relationships and to both the rental contract for movables and the rental contract for immovables (except for any deviating provisions in the rules applicable to "special" rental contracts such as the rental contract for residential property).

2450 See proposed Art. 7.3.3., 1° and 3° BCC, Explanatory Memorandum, *Parliamentary Papers* Chamber of Representatives 2023–24, no. 55-3973/001, 212.

2451 Proposed Art. 7.3.3, 2° BCC, Explanatory Memorandum, *Parliamentary Papers* Chamber of Representatives 2023–24, no. 55-3973/001, 212.

2452 Compare with Explanatory Memorandum, *Parliamentary Papers* Chamber of Representatives 2023–24, no. 55-3973/001, 7.

Proposed Provision #1

Art. 7.3.X1. Delivery in conformity with the rental contract

§1. The obligation to deliver the rented good in conformity with the contract includes:

1° the delivery of the rented good;

2° the conformity of the rented good throughout the duration of the rental contract, including the maintenance and repairs necessary for this purpose.

§2. The obligation to deliver the rented good in conformity with the contract also applies to the accessories of the rented good.

§3. In a rental contract for a consumer good where the lessor is a business and the lessee is a consumer where the lessor dispatches the goods to the consumer, the risk of loss of or damage to the good shall pass to the consumer upon delivery of the good.

Notwithstanding the first paragraph, where the consumer good is handed over to a carrier with whom the consumer himself has concluded a contract of carriage and who has not been proposed by the lessor, the risk shall pass upon delivery to the carrier.

This paragraph is mandatory law in favour of the consumer.

541. Delivery obligation – The obligation to deliver the rented good in conformity with the contract comprises two sub-obligations, namely a delivery obligation and a conformity obligation. Proposed provision #2 deals with the delivery obligation. Its content is very similar to Article 7.3.5 of the Draft Law, albeit that a non-exhaustive list of examples of the material, symbolic or intellectual handing over of the good is given.

542. The manner in which the rented good is delivered – The delivery obligation in the first place means that the rented good must be made available to the lessee. The first paragraph of proposed provision #2 therefore specifies how the rented good can be delivered. This can either be the material handing over of the good (for example, the delivery of a rented washing machine), but can also happen in a more symbolic way, for instance by unlocking a free-floating e-scooter through an app.

543. Time and place of delivery – Paragraph 2 of proposed provision #2 deals with the place where the good must be made available in the absence of

any contractual arrangements. This proposed paragraph refers to the existing rules of Belgian general contract law on the time and place of the performance, namely Art. 5.203 BCC.[2453] According to this provision, the content of the rental contract will determine the time and place of delivery. In the absence of contractual arrangements, it states that the rented good must be delivered as soon as the obligation is due (generally the start of the rental contract) and at the place where the good is located at the time of conclusion of the rental contract. This reflects the current legal framework and also fits well with contractual practice.

544. Transfer of risk in B2C rental contracts for consumer goods where the good is dispatched to the consumer – In the Draft Law, it was proposed to integrate the content of Article VI.44 BCEL (which implements Article 20 CRD) in the provision on transfer of risk of the sales contract rules to improve the accessibility of this provision.[2454] However, as the scope of Article VI.44 BCEL extends beyond consumer sales contracts,[2455] its integration into the BCC does not lead to its abolition. Instead, proposed Article 7.2.19 §3 BCC is a repetition of the principles of Article VI.44 BCEL in order to paint the complete picture of the risk regime for sales contracts without changing the provision in the BCEL.

The Draft Law does not contain a similar provision to proposed Article 7.2.19, §3 BCC for the rental contract rules (nor the rules on the contract for services). Nevertheless, the same argument could be made here, namely that the accessibility of this provision requires that the rules on the risk are in the same place as the rules on the delivery of the rented good. This is why §3 of proposed provision #1 integrates the principles of Article VI.44 BCEL into the rules of the rental contract.

545. Delivery also implies granting the use and enjoyment of the rented good – Besides making the rented good available (through material or symbolic or intellectual handing-over), the delivery obligation also implies granting the use and enjoyment of the rented good. This component of the delivery obligation is reflected in paragraph 3 of proposed provision #2 and confirms the continuous nature of the delivery obligation for the rental contract (as opposed to the delivery obligation for the sales contract).[2456]

2453 The same approach is also used under Dutch law (Art. 6:41 DCC). See *supra* fn. 1913.

2454 See proposed Art. 7.2.19, §3 BCC; Explanatory Memorandum, *Parliamentary Papers* Chamber of Representatives 2023–24, no. 55–3973/001, 25 and 37.

2455 Under Belgian law, its scope was extended to all contracts with consumers (including unnamed contracts), see *supra* no. 438.

2456 Compare with Explanatory Memorandum, *Parliamentary Papers* Chamber of Representatives 2023–24, no. 55–3973/001, 68.

> **Proposed Provision #2**
>
> **Art. 7.3.X2. Delivery of the rented good**
>
> **§1. The rented good is delivered through the material, symbolic or intellectual handing over of the good. It takes place, inter alia, through the delivery of documents, keys or codes that allow taking possession of the good.**
>
> **§2. The lessor must deliver the rented good at the time and place determined in accordance with Art. 5.203.**
>
> **§3. The delivery implies granting the use and enjoyment of the rented good during the duration of the contract.**

546. Obligation to deliver the accessories of the rented good – The obligation to deliver the rented product also extends to the accessories of this good. This is explicitly confirmed in proposed provision #3.

> **Proposed Provision #3**
>
> **Art. 7.3.X3. Delivery of accessories of the rented good**
>
> **The rented good must be delivered along with any accessories, including packaging, and installation instructions or other instructions, as stipulated by the rental contract and as the lessee may reasonably expect.**

547. Remedies for failure to deliver the rented good – Proposed provision #4 refers to the general contract law remedies set out in Article 5.83 BCC. It is not necessary nor desirable to have different remedies for a failure to deliver the rented good.

> **Proposed Provision #4**
>
> **Art. 7.3.X4. Remedies for failure to make the rented good available**
>
> **In case of a failure to deliver the rented good, the lessee has access to the remedies mentioned in Art. 5.83.**

548. Conformity obligation – Proposed provision #5 deals with the conformity component of the lessor's obligation to deliver the rented good in conformity with the rental contract. Here, the terminology "conformity" was explicitly chosen instead of the current phrasing "ensuring the quiet rental

enjoyment". This achieves more alignment of the rental contract rules with the consumer sales rules,[2457] which enhances legal certainty for consumers and ensures coherence and consistency of (consumer) contract law. Indeed, having consistent principles and terminology across different types of (consumer) contracts, in this case the concept of "conformity", ensures that the rights and obligations of the parties become clearer and more defined, regardless of the contractual qualification of the contract. This makes it easier for parties involved to understand their rights and responsibilities, making the (consumer) contract law framework more robust.

549. Reference to two different sets of conformity requirements – The second paragraph of proposed provision #5 refers to two sets of conformity requirements, which are further operationalised in proposed provision #6, #7 and #8. This mirrors the approach of the SGD and the DCD.[2458] In this way, the provision on the obligation to make available a good that is in conformity with the contract can remain concise, yet complete. In the Draft Law, the notions of objective conformity and subjective conformity are not retained in the context of conformity for consumer sales contracts.[2459] The reasoning behind this would be that these concepts do not have their origin in in Belgian law and that a proper implementation would require these concepts to be converted to Belgian terminology.[2460] In my view, however, transposing these concepts does have added value. After all, these concepts are already well established in legal doctrine on Belgian (consumer) contract law, and this ensures consistency and coherence with EU law. Additionally, although the criteria in the two sets of conformity requirements are indeed exemplative (as highlighted in the Explanatory Memorandum of the Draft Law),[2461] they are still a useful point of reference when assessing the conformity of a good with the contract.

550. Conformity throughout the duration of the rental contract – The lessor's conformity obligation applies both at the time of delivery and

---

[2457] See in the same sense: V. Ulfbeck, "Circularity in Servitization. Managing the Need for Product Change in Contract and Product Liability Law" in B. Keirsbilck, E. Terryn, J. Eyckmans, S. Rousseau and D. Voinot (eds.), *Servitization and circular economy: economic and legal challenges*, Antwerp, Intersentia, 2023, (93) 96 with reference to the UK rules on vehicle leasing contracts. See: https://bvrla.co.uk/static/uploaded/7b6a57ed-6aeb-4b45-bf985aca01f13437.pdf. However, she rightly points out that the current remedies of consumer sales law (where replacement can be chosen over repair) do not work for product-as-a-service contracts. See also contra: T. Hartlief, "Koop als gids voor het contractenrecht?", *NJB* 2019/2493, (3007) 3007 where it is argued that the sales contract should no longer be the guide for contract law, but that we need a paradigm shift to a (digital) service contract law.

[2458] Compare with Art. 5 SGD and Art. 6 DCD.

[2459] Explanatory Memorandum, *Parliamentary Papers* Chamber of Representatives 2023–24, no. 55-3973/001, 51–52.

[2460] *Ibid.*

[2461] Explanatory Memorandum, *Parliamentary Papers* Chamber of Representatives 2023–24, no. 55-3973/001, 52.

throughout the duration of the rental contract.[2462] This is why paragraph 3 of proposed provision #5 also contains the obligation for the lessor to carry out the maintenance of the rented good and necessary repairs. This paragraph would replace the obligation to ensure the quiet rental enjoyment,[2463] more specifically the sub-obligation to deliver the rented property in a good state of repair and to do all necessary repairs during the rental period, as well as its sub-obligation to indemnify for defects.[2464] This maintenance and repair obligation is subject to an exception though. Indeed, according to the second sub-paragraph of this paragraph, the lessor is not responsible for the maintenance and repair that are the lessee's responsibility under proposed provision #9 (minor maintenance and repairs borne by the lessee).[2465]

551. Liability for any lack of conformity, even if the lessor did not know or should not have known about its existence – Paragraph 4 of proposed provision #5 stipulates that the lessor is liable for any lack of conformity, even for those he did not know about or should not have known about. This is already the case under the current Belgian rental contract rules and is also retained in the Draft Law.[2466]

Proposed Provision #5

Art. 7.3.X5. Conformity with the rental contract

§1. The lessor must deliver a rented good that is in conformity with the rental contract.

§2. In order to conform with the rental contract, the rented good shall meet what the contract stipulates (subjective conformity) and what the lessee can reasonably expect (objective conformity).

§3. The lessor must ensure that, throughout the duration of the rental contract, the rented good remains in conformity with the rental contract. To this end, the lessor shall carry out the maintenance and necessary repairs.

Nothing in this article affects the lessee's obligations under Art. 7.3.X9.

§4. The lessor is liable for any lack of conformity, even if he did not know or should not have known about its existence.

2462 Compare with Explanatory Memorandum, *Parliamentary Papers* Chamber of Representatives 2023–24, no. 55-3973/001, 69.

2463 Art. 1719, 3° old BCC.

2464 See Art. 1720 and 1721 old BCC. The other two sub-obligations of the obligation to ensure the quiet rental enjoyment, namely Art. 1723 old BCC (obligation to indemnify for lessor's own acts) and Art. 1725–1727 old BCC (obligation to indemnify for certain acts of third parties), will be discussed *infra* in section 4.4.2.1B.

2465 See *infra* no. 556 and 557.

2466 Compare with Art. 1721(1), *in fine* old BCC and proposed Art. 7.3.6, §3 BCC, Explanatory Memorandum, *Parliamentary Papers* Chamber of Representatives 2023–24, no. 55-3973/001, 213.

552. SUBJECTIVE CONFORMITY REQUIREMENTS – The first set of conformity requirements relates to subjective conformity requirements, i.e. requirements that arise directly from the contractual relationship between the lessee and the lessor. These are set out in proposed provision #6, which is based on Article 6 SGD and Article 7 DCD (both on subjective requirements for conformity), as well as Article IV.B. – 3:102(2) DCFR and Article IV.B. – 3:103(a) DCFR (which cover both rental contracts for movables and immovables). These criteria should be interpreted for use-oriented PSS involving movable goods in the same way as for consumer sales of movable goods.

Proposed Provision #6

Art. 7.3.X6. Subjective conformity requirements

In order to conform with the rental contract, the rented goods shall, where applicable:

1° be of the description, type, quantity, quality, and possess the functionality, compatibility, interoperability and other features, as required by the rental contract;

2° be fit for any particular purpose for which the lessee requires them and which the lessee made known to the lessor at the latest at the time of the conclusion of the rental contract, and in respect of which the lessor has given acceptance.

553. OBJECTIVE CONFORMITY REQUIREMENTS – The second set of conformity requirements concerns the objective conformity requirements and can be found in the first paragraph of proposed provision #7. These criteria relate to what the lessee can reasonably expect when renting a (movable) good. Sources of inspiration for this proposed provision were Art. 7 SGD and Art. 8 DCD (objective requirements for conformity), as well as Art. IV. B. – 3:103 DCFR (Fitness for purpose, qualities, packaging, etc.). Also here, these criteria can be interpreted in the same way for rental contracts (for movable goods) as for consumer sales contracts and contracts for digital content or digital services.

554. DEVIATION FROM OBJECTIVE CONFORMITY REQUIREMENTS IN THE RENTAL CONTRACT – Just like consumer sales rules, rental contracts sometimes require more flexibility in terms of conformity requirements.[2467] For instance, when renting used or refurbished goods, certain conformity requirements may not be fully met. To allow for this flexibility, paragraph 2 of proposed provision #7 allows for deviation in the rental contract from these objective conformity requirements. The proposed paragraph opts for a double transparency and

[2467] Compare with *supra* no. 464.

acceptance requirement for this deviation similar to the consumer sales and digital content and digital services rules. First, the lessee must be specifically informed that a particular characteristic of the product deviates from the objective conformity requirements. Second, he must expressly and separately accept this deviation, for example by means of a separate consent form, by ticking a box, or pressing a button.

Proposed Provision #7

Art. 7.3.X7. Objective conformity requirements

§1. In addition to complying with any subjective conformity requirements, the rented goods shall:

1° Be of the quantity and possess the qualities and other features, including in relation to durability, functionality, compatibility and security normal for goods of the same type as the lessee may reasonably expect given the nature of the rented goods and taking into account any public statement within the meaning of Art. 7.3.X8.

2° be fit for the purposes for which goods of the same description would normally be used.

§2. There shall be no lack of conformity within the meaning of paragraph 1 if, at the time of conclusion of the rental contract, the lessee was specifically informed that a particular characteristic of the rented good was deviating from the objective requirements for conformity laid down in paragraph 1 and the lessee expressly and separately accepted that deviation when concluding the rental contract.

555. Objective conformity of the rented good is also assessed taking into account public statements – Proposed provision #8 elaborates on the role of public statements made by or on behalf of the lessor, or other persons in previous links of the chain of transactions. After all, proposed provision #7 (objective conformity requirements) stipulates that these public statements are also taken into account when assessing the reasonable expectations of the lessee regarding the quality, quantity, and other features of the rented good. A similar provision applies to the consumer sales contract and the digital content and digital services rules,[2468] ensuring that the concept of conformity is applied as uniformly as possible, regardless of contractual qualification. The question arises whether this might not go too far in the case of a rental contract where the good is rented by a non-professional lessor. Yet, several arguments exist for applying

[2468] Art. 7(1), (d), *in fine* SGD *juncto* Art. 7(2) SGD and Art. 8(1)(d), *in fine* DCD *juncto* Art. 8(2) DCD.

this provision to rental contracts with non-professional lessors as well. First, advertisements and public statements by producers of rented goods will play an important role in creating the lessee's expectations of the normal characteristics of the rented goods, also if the lessor is not a business. Second, the fact that the lessor is bound by public statements can be dealt with in a flexible way, for example by interpreting §2, 1° of proposed provision #8 (lessor is not and could not have been aware of the statement) broadly. Third, objective conformity requirements can be deviated from in the rental contract (see §2 of proposed provision #7), so any public statements on the quality, quantity of other features of the product which the lessor is unable to guarantee can be excluded. Finally, as a similar conformity provision applies to the sales contract, the lessor can in turn sue his seller or his lessor for non-conformity of the good he rents out.[2469]

> **Proposed Provision #8**
>
> **Art. 7.3.X8. Public statements**
>
> **§1. The conformity of the rented good is also assessed taking into account, inter alia, any public statement made by or on behalf of the lessor, or other persons in previous links of the chain of transactions, particularly in advertising or on labelling.**
>
> **§2. The lessor shall not be bound by public statements:**
>
> **1° of which he was not, and could not reasonably have been, aware;**
>
> **2° of which he proves that, by the time of conclusion of the contract, they had been corrected in the same way as, or in a way comparable to how, they had been made;**
>
> **3° of which he proves that they could not have influenced the decision to enter into the rental contract.**

556. Minor maintenance and repairs borne by the lessee – As mentioned above, the lessor's obligation to ensure the conformity of the good throughout the duration of the contract, particularly by carrying out the necessary maintenance and repairs (proposed provision #5, §3) is subject to an exception.[2470] Indeed, according to the second sentence of proposed provision #5, §3, the lessor is not responsible for the maintenance and repair that are the lessee's responsibility under proposed provision #9. This is similar to the approach of the Draft Law.[2471]

2469 Compare also with the right of redress, *infra* no. 568.

2470 See *supra* no. 550.

2471 Compare with proposed Art. 7.3.6, §2 BCC *juncto* proposed Art. 7.3.22–7.3.23. BCC.

Paragraph 1 of proposed provision #9 places the responsibility for cleaning the good and minor maintenance on the lessee. These obligations are very much linked to the lessee's obligation to use the good as a prudent and reasonable lessee.[2472] For example, in the context of PSS, one can think of lubricating a bicycle chain, cleaning the filter of a washing machine, washing a bicycle, inflating tyres, removing dust in the charging port of a smartphone, etc. By devoting an explicit paragraph to cleaning and minor maintenance, the distinction from the actual "repairs" borne by the lessee becomes clearer.

Paragraph 2 of proposed provision #9 deals with the repairs borne by the lessee. Two categories can be distinguished. First, §2, 1° lists the so-called "minor repairs", as is also the case in Article 1754 old BCC. There are some good reasons why the responsibility for minor repairs is placed with the lessee, at least in rental contracts for immovable goods.[2473] After all, these are defects that result from the normal use of the rented good and involve relatively little costs.[2474] Moreover, it is not always feasible nor desirable for the lessor to visit the lessee on site for every minor defect. Article 1754 old BCC refers to local custom for determining which repairs constitute "minor repairs" and uses a (dated) list of examples, all of which relate to immovable goods.[2475] Second, §2, 2° refers to repairs resulting from improper use of the rented good or lack of maintenance on the part of the lessee. In other words, the lessor will not be responsible for repairs if the lack of conformity was caused by the fault of the lessee. This makes sense, as making the lessor liable for defects caused by the fault of the lessee would give rise to a high risk of moral hazard, which is unacceptable both from a fair balance and sustainability perspective.

The exception for repairs only due to normal wear and tear or *force majeure* reiterates the existing rule of Article 1755 old BCC and is also in line with the Draft Law.[2476]

557. B2C RENTAL CONTRACTS FOR MOVABLES: MINOR REPAIRS BORNE BY THE LESSOR – Up until this point, proposed provision #9 is mainly a re-codification of current law and follows the approach of the Draft Law. However, §3 of proposed provision #9 deviates from this approach for B2C rental contracts for consumer goods.

Unlike Art. 1754 old BCC and proposed Article 7.3.23(1), 1° BCC, which place the responsibility for minor repairs on the lessee, §3 of proposed provision

2472 See *infra* section 7.3.1.2. Compare also with Explanatory Memorandum, *Parliamentary Papers* Chamber of Representatives 2023–24, no. 55-3973/001, 77.

2473 See in the same sense: M.B.M. Loos, "Servitization, consumentenhuur en consumentenkoop", *WPNR* 2022/7396, (944) 946.

2474 H.J. Rossel and A.H.T. Heisterkamp, *Mr. C. Assers Handleiding tot de beoefening van het Nederlands Burgerlijk Recht. 7. Bijzondere overeenkomsten. Deel II. Huur*, Deventer, Wolters Kluwer, 2021, no. 108.

2475 Compare also with proposed Art. 7.3.22(2) and 7.3.23(2) BCC, which allow for adopting a list in a Royal Decree.

2476 Compare with proposed Art. 7.3.23 BCC.

#9 provides for an exception in B2C rental contracts for movables. Thus, the lessor will be responsible for minor repairs in the case of a rental contract for a consumer good where the lessor is a business, and the lessee is a consumer. This is motivated by the observation that the difference in legal position between the consumer-buyer and the consumer-lessee is difficult to justify for movable consumer goods.[2477] After all, if the consumer buys a good, the seller will be liable for minor defects, while under the current rental contract rules, the consumer who only wishes to rent that same good will be responsible for minor defects. In addition, the lessor is in most cases better placed to repair these minor defects, both in terms of motivation and incentives and in terms of having the knowledge and materials needed to carry out durable and quality repairs.[2478] Finally, this fits nicely with the situation in practice, as many use-oriented PSS contracts deviate from the obligation of the PSS user-lessee to perform minor repairs.[2479]

The scope of this proposed exception is limited in multiple ways. *Ratione personae* it only applies to B2C rental contracts, i.e. rental contracts where the lessor is a business, and the lessee is a consumer. *Ratione materiae*, the exception only applies to "consumer goods". The concept of "consumer good" (*consumptiegoed, bien de consummation*) has the same meaning as under the consumer sales rules, namely any movable tangible good, except (a) domestic animals; and (b) water, gas and electricity not made ready for sale in a limited volume or a set quantity.[2480] The exception also only applies to "minor repairs" (§2, 1°). Repairs resulting from improper use of the rented good or lack of maintenance on the part of the lessee (§2, 2°) remain the lessee's responsibility. This is logical, since deciding otherwise would give rise to an unacceptable risk of moral hazard.

The second sub-paragraph of §3 provides for a possible deviation of the rule that the lessor is responsible for minor defects in B2C rental contracts for movables to give more flexibility to the contracting parties. Deviating from this rule may be useful, for example, for long-term rental contracts for movables, such as in the case of a leased vehicle. The requirements for deviating from this responsibility for minor defects are similar to the requirements for deviating from the objective conformity requirements in consumer sales contracts.[2481] Thus, the consumer-lessee must be specifically informed that he will be responsible for minor repairs and the consumer has expressly and separately accepted that deviation when concluding the rental contract. As established above, a mere clause in the general terms and conditions does not suffice in

[2477] See *supra* no. 533.
[2478] See *supra* no. 534.
[2479] See *infra* no. 735.
[2480] See Art. 2(5)(a) SGD; Art. 1649*bis*, §1, 4° old BCC and proposed Art. 7.2.38, 1° BCC.
[2481] See *supra* no. 464. Compare with Art. 7(5) SGD; Art. 1649*ter*, §7 old BCC and proposed Art. 7.2.42, §3, 2°, (2) BCC.

this regard.[2482] Instead, this acceptance can be derived from explicitly clicking or ticking a box during the (online) order process or from a separate consent form.[2483]

> Proposed Provision #9
>
> **Art. 7.3.X9. Minor maintenance and repairs borne by the lessee**
>
> **§1. The lessee regularly cleans the good and does minor maintenance like a reasonable and prudent person.**
>
> **§2. Except for repairs only due to aging, normal wear and tear and *force majeure*, the lessee is responsible for:**
>
> **1° minor repairs; and**
>
> **2° repairs resulting from improper use of the rented good or lack of maintenance on the part of the lessee.**
>
> **§3. In derogation from §2, 1°, the lessor shall be responsible for minor repairs in the case of a rental contract for a consumer good where the lessor is a business and the lessee is a consumer.**
>
> **The business can only deviate from its responsibility for minor repairs if, at the time of the conclusion of the rental contract, the consumer was specifically informed that he is responsible for minor repairs and the consumer expressly and separately accepted that deviation when concluding the rental contract.**

558. Incorrect installation in the case of rental contracts for movables – This research also proposes that, similar to the consumer sales contract rules, a provision should also be adopted for rental contracts for consumer goods where the lessor is a business and the lessee a consumer establishing a lack of conformity if the rented good is incorrectly installed. This proposed provision (numbered Art. 7.3.X10) will be discussed *infra* in the section on installation of the product.[2484]

559. Notification period and limitation period – With regard to the notification period (proposed provision #10) and the limitation period (proposed provision #11), the approach of the Draft Law is convincing and can be followed.[2485] Thus, according to §1 of proposed provision #10, the lessee

2482 See *supra* no. 464 and the references cited there.
2483 *Ibid.*
2484 See *infra* section 6.2.5.1A.
2485 Compare with proposed Art. 7.3.7. and 7.3.8. BCC.

must notify the lessor of any lack of conformity from the moment he discovered or should have discovered it. §2 of proposed provision #10 constitutes an application of the obligation to limit damages and is in line with Article 7:222 DCC. Contrary to the sales contract, a breach of the duty to notify the lessor of any lack of conformity does not lead to a forfeiture of the right to repair, but only to a forfeiture of compensation for damages for loss of rental enjoyment.[2486]

Proposed Provision #10

Art. 7.3.X11. Notification period

§1. The lessee shall notify the lessor of the lack of conformity within a reasonable time from the moment he discovered or should have discovered it. The reasonable time shall be assessed on the basis of all relevant circumstances and, in particular, the nature of the good, the nature of the lack of conformity, the capacity of the parties and customs.

§2. If the lessee fails to give notice of the existence of the lack of conformity within a reasonable time and unless he renounces with full knowledge of the facts, he retains his rights to have the property brought into conformity by the lessor for the future but loses the right to invoke the sanctions relating to the loss of use and enjoyment suffered. He is also obliged to repair the damage caused by his negligence.

With regard to the limitation period, there is no specific limitation period *de lege lata* for the obligation to indemnify for defects. As a result, the ten-year period of general contract law applies.[2487] In practice, however, the issue of prescription only comes into play after the extinction of the rental contract, since the conformity obligation is a continuous obligation throughout the duration of the rental contract. Therefore, §1 of proposed provision #11 takes the extinction of the rental contract as a starting point. As the action cannot be prescribe during the term of the rental contract, a shorter prescription period of two years – which is in line with other limitation periods of the Draft Law – is appropriate.[2488] Paragraph 2 of proposed provision #11 provides for an exception though. If the lessee does not bring a claim against the lessor within two years after the notification, he loses the right to claim damages for the loss of use and enjoyment suffered.

2486 See: Explanatory Memorandum, *Parliamentary Papers* Chamber of Representatives 2023–24, no. 55–3973/001, 69.

2487 Art. 2262*bis*, §1, (1) old BCC.

2488 Compare also with Explanatory Memorandum, *Parliamentary Papers* Chamber of Representatives 2023–24, no. 55–3973/001, 70.

Proposed Provision #11

Art. 7.3.X12. Limitation period

§1. The action for a lack of conformity prescribes after two years from the extinction of the rental contract.

§2. However, the action based on the loss of use and enjoyment suffered as a result of a lack of conformity prescribes two years from the time the lessee made the notification.

§3. The period is suspended during negotiations between the parties and the judicial or extrajudicial contradictory expert examination.

560. (Semi-)mandatory conformity rules in consumer rental contracts – The current Belgian rules on conformity in rental contracts (for movables) are not mandatory law.[2489] As already mentioned higher, this offers only limited consumer protection. To increase consumer protection for use-oriented PSS (but also other rental contracts for movables), proposed provision #12 sets out limits on derogation from the conformity rights in B2C rental contracts for consumer goods (i.e. movables). Additionally, this also has the advantage of furthering sustainability, as stronger conformity rules can provide incentives for the lessor-PSS supplier to offer more quality and durable products for rent.[2490] The proposed provision is partly inspired by Dutch law[2491] as well as the DCFR[2492] and is also consistent with the consumer sales rules and the rules on digital content and digital services.[2493] To consistently fit within the Belgian legal system, the sanction of being deemed unwritten (*voor niet-geschreven gehouden, réputée non écrite*), which is also used in Book 5 BCC, was chosen for any contractual terms concluded before the lack of conformity was brought to the attention of the lessor and which, to the detriment of the consumer, restrict or deviate from the legal rights of the consumer concerning the conformity of the rented consumer good. The proposed provision finally explicitly confirms that the parties may agree to contractual terms that go beyond the protection of the conformity rules.

2489 See *supra* no. 487.
2490 See *supra* no. 534.
2491 See Art. 7:209 DCC. However, this applies only to defects that the lessor knew or should have known about.
2492 Compare with Art. IV. B. – 1:103 DCFR (limits on derogation from conformity rights in a consumer contract for lease).
2493 Compare with Art. 21 SGD and Art. 22 DCD.

Proposed Provision #12

Art. 7.3.X13. Limits on derogation from conformity rights in rental contracts with consumers

In the case of a rental contract for a consumer good where the lessor is a business and the lessee is a consumer, any contractual term or agreement concluded with the lessor prior to notifying the lessor of a lack which, to the detriment of the consumer, excludes, derogates from or varies the effect of the consumer's rights under this section is deemed unwritten.

561. Unfair terms: blacklisting terms derogating from the obligation to ensure the conformity of the rented good – In order to be consistent, the mandatory nature of the conformity rights in rental contracts with consumers should also be added to the Belgian unfair terms blacklist, as is now already the case with the consumer sales rules and the rules on the supply of digital content and digital services.[2494] This would result in proposed amendment #4.

Proposed Amendment #4

Art. VI.83

In contracts concluded between a business and a consumer, are unlawful in any case, the terms and conditions, or combinations of terms and conditions which have the object or effect of:

[...]

14° exclude or restrict the legal guarantee for hidden defects, provided by articles 1641 to 1649 of the old Civil Code, [**the conformity rights in rental contracts for consumer goods where the lessor is a business and the lessee is a consumer provided by Art. 7.3.X1. to Art. 7.3.X20. of the Civil Code**], or the legal obligation to deliver a good, digital content or digital service that is in conformity with the contract, provided by articles 1649*bis* to 1649*nonies* and 1701/1 to 1701/19 of the old Civil Code;

562. Remedies for lack of conformity: transplanting consumer sales remedies does not work for rental contracts – When considering what remedies must be available for a lack of conformity in a rental contracts for movables, transplanting the remedies of the current consumer sales rules does not really work, at least not for use-oriented PSS with a circular economy

[2494] Art. VI.83, 14° BCEL.

context in mind.[2495] After all, these rules make it possible for the consumer to choose replacement over repair,[2496] and it is unclear[2497] (at least under the current rules[2498]) whether replacement with remanufactured, repaired or second-hand goods is possible. Indeed, so far, several courts have already held that the consumer has the right of replacement with a new product instead of a refurbished one.[2499] It is therefore necessary to consider which remedies are most fitting for the rental contract (for movables).

563. Right to have the defect remedied: repair – In the rental contract, the remedy of repair (inherently a sustainable remedy) plays an important role. Indeed, the Dutch rental contract rules and the DCFR have as their starting

---

[2495] V. Ulfbeck, "Circularity in Servitization. Managing the Need for Product Change in Contract and Product Liability Law" in B. Keirsbilck, E. Terryn, J. Eyckmans, S. Rousseau and D. Voinot (eds.), *Servitization and circular economy: economic and legal challenges*, Antwerp, Intersentia, 2023, (93) 96.

[2496] The Proposal for the Right to Repair Directive proposed to change this. See: Art. 12 of EC, *Proposal for a Directive of the European Parliament and of the Council on common rules promoting the repair of goods and amending Regulation (EU) 2017/2394, Directives (EU) 2019/771 and (EU) 2020/1828*, 22.3.2023, COM(2023) 155 final, where an amendment to Art. 13(2) of the SGD was proposed which stated that if the costs for replacement are equal to or greater than the costs for repair, the seller must repair the goods in order to bring those goods in conformity. This amendment thus aimed to limit consumer choice between the primary remedies and elevates repair as the primary remedy, provided the costs for replacement are equal to or greater than the costs for repair. However, this amendment did not make it into the final directive and instead measures to incentivise consumers to opt for repair were adopted. See *supra* no. 471. As a result, also in the future, consumers will still be able to choose replacement over repair.

[2497] See: E. Van Gool and A. Michel, "The New Consumer Sales Directive 2019/771 and Sustainable Consumption", *EuCML* 2021, vol. 10, afl. 4, (136) 145–146 and V. Mak and E. Lujinovic, "Towards a Circular Economy in EU Consumer Markets – Legal Possibilities and Legal Challenges and the Dutch Example", *EuCML* 2019, (4) 9.

[2498] Art. 16(4) of the Right to Repair Directive provides more clarity on this issue, by amending Art. 14(1) SGD so that "*the seller may provide, upon the explicit request by the consumer, a refurbished good to fulfil his obligation to replace the good*" (own emphasis). While this is a step in the right direction, it is regrettable that the consumer may still decide that he wants replacement by a new good. See further on this *infra* no. 728.

[2499] Ct. Amsterdam (NL) 18 April 2017, ECLI:NL:RBAMS:2017:2519, (*Apple Retail Netherlands*), *AR* 2017/2104; Ct. Amsterdam (NL) 8 July 2016, ECLI:NL:RBAMS:2016:4197, (*Apple Retail Netherlands*), *TvC* 2017, 183, case note V. Mak; Ct. Glostrup (DK) 9 December 2016, Case number BS 10E-3689/2014 (all three deciding that Apple must provide the consumer with a new product and not a refurbished one to replace a defective product). See: V. Mak and E. Terryn, "Circular Economy and Consumer Protection: The Consumer as a Citizen and the Limits of Empowerment Through Consumer Law", *Journal of Consumer Policy* 2020, vol. 43, (227) 236. Contra: Supreme Court Norway (NO) 17 February 2006, *Rt* 2006, s 179 as cited by E. Maitre-Ekern and C. Dalhammar, "A Scandinavian Perspective on the Role of Consumers in the Circular Economy" in B. Keirsbilck and E. Terryn (eds.), *Consumer protection in a circular economy*, Antwerp, Intersentia, 2019, (201) 215 (The Norwegian Supreme Court ruled that the seller can refuse to replace boots whose heels are broken six weeks after purchase and repair them instead as replacing them would involve unreasonable costs. In its reasoning, it also highlighted that repair is the more sustainable remedy).

point that the lessee has a right to have the defect remedied.[2500] The Belgian rental contract rules do not contain specific provisions on the remedies for defects but as these are governed by general contract law, specific performance (performance in kind) is also the starting point here. Generally, this right to have the defect remedied is fulfilled by repairing the rented product or having it repaired by a third party. However, the remedy to have the defect remedied by repairing does not only benefit the lessee. It is often also to the lessor's advantage to bring the rented good back into conformity so that the rental contract can continue. This "right to cure" of the lessor, explicitly confirmed in the DCFR for example, is therefore the mirror image of the lessee's right to have the defect remedied.[2501] In addition, repair is also reflected in the lessee's right to remedy the defect himself or have it done by a third party at the lessor's expense if the lessor fails to remedy the defect.[2502] Under Dutch law, this right is even mandatory law.

564. Rent reduction – Besides repair, rent reduction is a second fundamental remedy for the rental contract. Thus, the lessee may be authorised to reduce the rent for the period in which the value of the lessor's performance is reduced due to a lack of conformity in the rented product, provided he has notified this lack of conformity to the lessor.[2503] This remedy allows the lessee to be compensated for the reduced rental enjoyment. Moreover, rent reduction can also be a sustainable remedy, for example in the case of non-repairable goods that are still usable (think of a smartphone with a scratched backside or furniture with a stain).[2504] After all, this allows the rented good to remain in useful use rather than having to be replaced or the contract to be terminated altogether.[2505]

565. Damages and termination – If the lessee-PSS user suffers damages on grounds other than the reduction in rental enjoyment, he may also seek (additional) damages to be fully compensated. This can for instance be the case if the non-conforming product causes damages to the home or personal belongings of the lessee-PSS user. Finally, if the lack of conformity is sufficiently serious (for example because the lessee-PSS user has lost confidence in the lessor-PSS supplier), the lessee can claim termination of the rental contract, possibly with additional damages. This has the effect of returning the rented good to the lessor-PSS supplier. Fortunately, termination does not necessarily mean that the

---

2500 **The Netherlands**: Art. 7:206(1) DCC. **DCFR**: Art. IV. B. – 4:101 DCFR.

2501 See Art. IV. B. – 4:101(2) DCFR.

2502 Art. 7:206(3) DCC.

2503 **The Netherlands**: Art. 7:207(1) DCC. **DCFR**: Art. IV. B. – 4:102(1) DCFR.

2504 See: C.M.D.S. Pavillon, "Is ons stelsel van remedies future-proof? Remedies in het kooprecht en de overgang naar een circulaire economie", *WPNR* 2023, vol. 7399, (97) 104.

2505 Compare also with: K. Kryla-Cudna, "Sales contracts and the circular economy", *ERPL* 2020, vol. 28, afl. 6, (1207) 1210 (in the context of the sales contract).

good can no longer be used. If the rented good is not completely defective or can be repaired, it can still be offered to another lessee. As a result, also termination need not necessarily be an unsustainable remedy.

566. Current Belgian general contract law remedies are "fit for purpose" – The analysis above shows that repair (as a form of specific performance, either by the lessor or by the lessee or a third party), rent reduction, damages and termination are the desirable remedies for the rental contract. As these remedies (including the case law of the Belgian Court of Cassation on the subject) were recently (re)codified in Book 5 the "new" BCC, it does not seem necessary to come up with a separate set of remedies for non-conformity in the rental contract. Therefore, proposed provision #13 stipulates that the general contract law remedies of the BCC also apply in case of a lack of conformity of the rented good. As already mentioned, this has the advantage that the same rules on remedies apply to all (consumer) contracts as much as possible, with only a few special rules in the case of e.g. the sales contract.[2506] This is also consistent with the approach of the Draft Law and the current remedies of the rental contract.[2507]

Proposed Provision #13

Art. 7.3.X14. Remedies for lack of conformity

In case of a lack of conformity, the lessee has access to the remedies mentioned in Art. 5.83.

567. Increased consumer protection by making remedies mandatory law in rental contracts with consumers – To protect consumer interests, proposed provision #11 elevates the rules on remedies mentioned in Art. 5.83 BCC to the status of mandatory law in B2C rental contracts for movables. Consequently, the rental contract cannot exclude the general contract law remedies, nor derogate from them or vary their effects. This reinforces consumer rights in a similar fashion to the consumer sales contract and ensures that

[2506] See in this sense also: H. Slachmuylders, "Movable Servitization. Contractual Liability in the B2C Relationship" in B. Keirsbilck, E. Terryn, J. Eyckmans, S. Rousseau and D. Voinot (eds.), *Servitization and circular economy: economic and legal challenges*, Antwerp, Intersentia, 2023, (135) 165–166; B. Keirsbilck and E. Terryn, "Duurzaamheid en consumentenrecht" in A. Van Hoe and G. Croisant (eds.), *Droit et durabilité / Recht en duurzaamheid*, Antwerp, Intersentia, 2022, (433) 489 and M.E. Storme, "Remedies bij digitale inhoud en diensten" in E. Terryn and I. Claeys (eds.), *Nieuw recht inzake koop & digitale inhoud en diensten*, Antwerp, Intersentia, 2020, (233) 259.

[2507] Compare with proposed Art. 7.3.15. BCC; Explanatory Memorandum, Parliamentary Papers Chamber of Representatives 2023–24, no. 55-3973/001, 73.

consumers are not unfairly disadvantaged by the rental contract/PSS contract and have access to these essential remedies in case of a lack of conformity of the rented product.

Proposed Provision #14

Art. 7.3.X15. Limits on derogation from rules on remedies in rental contracts with consumers

In the case of a rental contract for a consumer good where the lessor is a business and the lessee is a consumer, the parties may not, to the detriment of the consumer, exclude the application of the rules on remedies in Art. 5.83 BCC, or derogate from or vary their effects.

568. PROTECTING PSS SUPPLIERS-LESSORS THROUGH A RIGHT OF REDRESS – The fact that lessors of movable goods or PSS suppliers are liable for non-conforming rented goods in contracts with consumers can lead to situations where they are unfairly burdened because the lack of conformity was beyond their control. For example, this lack of conformity could be imputable to a manufacturer who sold the product to the lessor-PSS supplier, or even to another PSS supplier offering part of the product itself as a service through a lease, rental or service contract.[2508] Proposed provision #15 therefore contains a right of redress, similar to the consumer sales rules and the rules on digital content and digital services,[2509] which allows the lessor-PSS supplier the ability to pursue remedies against the person or persons liable within the chain of commercial transactions.[2510] It also adds that the manufacturer or other lessor higher in the chain of transactions cannot invoke exemption clauses excluding or limiting this contractual liability.[2511] This provision thus protects the interests of the (small) lessor-PSS supplier against the consequences of a lack of conformity of the rented product which is caused by an act or omission of another person in the transaction chain.

2508 See the above-mentioned Swapfiets example mentioned in fn. 178 and fn. 2420.

2509 Compare with **EU**: Art. 18 SGD and Art. 20 DCD. **Belgium**: Art. 1649*sexiessexies* old BCC and Art. 1701/16 old BCC. **The Netherlands**: Art. 7:25 DCC and Art. 7:50am DCC.

2510 See on the right of redress for **Belgium** e.g. B. KEIRSBILCK, "Verhaalsrechten", *DCCR* 2022, issue 2–3, (103) 103–132 (including a short comparative law section where Dutch law is discussed). See for **the Netherlands**: T.J.K. VAN SANTEN, *Artikel 7:25 BW: een analyse van zijn oorsprong, strekking en reikwijdte, (R&P nr. CA23)*, Deventer, Wolters Kluwer, 2021, 390 p.

2511 This is in line with Art. 1649*sexies* old BCC and Art. 1701/16 old BCC.

Proposed Provision #15

Art. 7.3X16. Right of redress

In the case of a rental contract for a consumer good where the lessor is a business and the lessee is a consumer, where the lessor is liable to the lessee because of a lack of conformity which is imputable to a person in a previous link of the chain of transactions, the lessor shall be entitled to pursue remedies against that person on the basis of his contractual liability concerning the rented good without any contractual clause having the effect of excluding or limiting this liability being enforceable against him.

B. Obligation to indemnify the lessee for own acts and acts of third parties

569. Obligation to indemnify the lessee for the lessor's own acts and acts of third parties – Proposed provision #16 deals with the lessor's obligation to indemnify the lessee for the lessor's own acts and acts of third parties. We already find this in both Belgian and Dutch law, namely the Belgian obligation to ensure the quiet rental enjoyment during the rental contract, which includes the obligation to indemnify for the lessor's own acts, and the Dutch obligation to leave the rented good at the disposal of the lessee.[2512] Additionally, this also encompasses the obligation to indemnify the lessee for legal defects, i.e. legal claims of third parties which prevent or are otherwise likely to interfere with the lessee's use in accordance with the contract.[2513] It was opted not to deviate from the current regime but rather to simplify it. Paragraph 1 of proposed provision #16 in that confirms the obligation of the lessor to indemnify for both his own acts and the acts of third parties. In paragraph 2, it is specified that the lessor's obligation to indemnify for his own acts applies to factual defects (i.e. any impairment of the use or enjoyment of the rented good resulting from an act of the lessor) as well as legal defects. Paragraph 3 of proposed provision #16 deals with the obligation to indemnify for acts of third parties. Here, it is specified that this obligation only relates to actual legal claims (i.e. not factual defects) by third parties on the rented good before or after the conclusion of the rental contract, even if the lessor had no knowledge or could not have had knowledge of them. However, this obligation does not apply to any legal defects that the lessor has expressly communicated to the lessee before the conclusion of the rental contract. This proposed provision is in line with the Draft Law.[2514]

2512 **Belgium**: Art. 1719, 3° old BCC and Art. 1723 old BCC. **The Netherlands**: Art. 7:203 DCC.

2513 **Belgium**: Art. 1725–1727 old BCC. **The Netherlands**: Art. 7:204(3) DCC.

2514 Compare with proposed Art. 7.3.11. BCC; Explanatory Memorandum, *Parliamentary Papers* Chamber of Representatives 2023–24, no. 55-3973/001, 214–215.

Proposed Provision #16

Art. 7.3.X17. Obligation to indemnify for own acts and acts of third parties

§1. The lessor must indemnify the lessee for his own acts and acts of third parties.

§2. The obligation to indemnify for own acts concerns, throughout the duration of the rental contract:

1° any impairment of the use or enjoyment of the rented good resulting from an act of the lessor; and

2° any legal claim on the rented good by the lessor.

§3. The obligation to indemnify for acts of third parties concerns, throughout the duration of the rental contract, only actual legal claims on the rented good by third parties, regardless of whether they originate before or after the conclusion of the rental contract.

This obligation to indemnify applies even to acts of third parties of which the lessor had no knowledge or could not have had knowledge.

However, this obligation to indemnify does not apply to the specific impairments that the lessor has expressly communicated to the lessee before the conclusion of the rental contract.

570. Acts of third parties: lessee's obligation to notify and lessor's obligation to intervene in court – Proposed provision #17 also recodifies the existing situation for legal defects caused by third parties.[2515] If the lessee is confronted with a legal defect invoked by a third party, he must notify the lessor (§1). After all, a legal defect also interferes with the rights and interests of the lessor. If no notification is given, the lessee will be responsible for any damages caused by his negligence.[2516] Additionally, the indemnity obligation ceases to exist if the lessee did not notify the lessor and is condemned by a judgment of last instance, if the lessor can prove that there were sufficient grounds to dismiss the claim.[2517] If the third party brings an action in court against the lessee, §2 of proposed provision #17 requires the lessor to intervene in the proceedings, in

2515 Compare with Art. 1727 old BCC.

2516 Compare also with Art. 7:222 DCC.

2517 See: Cass. (BE) 29 October 1981, *Pas.* 1982, I., 304. This solution is an analogous application of Art. 1640 old BCC. S. Marysse, "Rechten en verbintenissen van de verhuurder" in M. Dambre, B. Hubeau and S. Stijns (eds.), *Handboek algemeen huurrecht*, Bruges, Die Keure, 2015, (415) 465, no. 132.

order to defend the interests of the lessee. This proposed provision is also in line with the Draft Law.[2518]

Proposed Provision #17

Art. 7.3.X18. Lessee's obligation to notify and lessor's intervention in the proceedings

§1. If a lessee faces a legal claim from a third party, the lessee must notify the lessor without any delay, failing which he shall be obligated to compensate the lessor for the damage caused by the negligence. If the lessee fails to notify the lessor of the legal defect, the obligation to indemnify ceases if the lessee has been condemned by a judgment of last instance or judgment against which no further appeal is admissible, if the lessor proves that there were sufficient grounds to dismiss the claim.

§2. If a third party brings a legal claim against the lessee that affects or otherwise interferes with the lessee's right to use the rented good in accordance with the contract, the lessor shall be obliged, after notification thereof by the lessee, to intervene in the proceedings in order to defend the interests of the lessee.

571. LIMITS ON EXEMPTION FROM OBLIGATION TO INDEMNIFY FOR OWN ACTS OR ACTS OF THIRD PARTIES – The obligation to indemnify for the lessor's own acts and acts of third parties is not mandatory law so parties can flesh out their own legal regime. However, some limits must be placed on the lessor's contractual freedom so that the contract is not completely eroded. Therefore, in line with proposed Article 7.3.14. of the Draft Law, paragraph 1 of proposed provision #18 prohibits contractual terms that completely or partially exclude the lessor's obligation to indemnify for his own acts. Additionally, §2 provides that the lessor cannot limit or exclude his obligation to indemnify for acts of third parties for legal defects he knew or should have known about.

Proposed Provision #18

Art. 7.3.X19. Limits on exemption from obligation to indemnify for own acts or acts of third parties

§1. A contractual term that partially or completely exempts the lessor from its obligation to indemnify for its own acts shall be deemed unwritten.

§2. The obligation of indemnity for acts of third parties may be excluded or limited unless the lessor knew or should have known about the risk of third parties invoking any right or reasonably based claim.

2518 Compare with proposed Art. 7.3.13. BCC.

572. Remedies – In case the lessor fails to indemnify for his own acts or legal defects caused by third parties, proposed provision #19 specifies that the lessee has recourse to the remedies of general contract law. For failures to indemnify for the acts of third parties, however, chances are quite significant that specific performance (performance in kind) will not be possible. In this case, the lessee will have recourse to the sanction of termination, possibly with damages or, alternatively, a proportionate reduction of the price.[2519] The same approach is also taken in the Draft Law.[2520]

Proposed Provision #19

Art. 7.3.X20. Remedies in case of failure to indemnify for own acts or acts of third parties

In case of a failure to indemnify for one's own acts or the acts of third parties, the lessee has access to the remedies mentioned in Art. 5.83.

4.4.2.2. Modernisation of (Belgian) contract law on services, including the role of standardisation of services

573. Modernisation of Belgian services contract law – Besides picking the low-hanging fruit through the development of standard contracts,[2521] various authors rightly agree that the Belgian national legal framework of conformity for service contracts should also be modernised and improved.[2522] However, as already established above, the heterogenic nature of services makes this no easy task.[2523] Broadly speaking, two approaches to modernising the Belgian legal framework on service-based contracts are possible. The first one is providing very specific detailed rules for every different type of service. However, this seems like an impossible task, first because there are an enormous number of different services, and second because the development of legal rules is slow, which in turn risks making the legal framework obsolete again in a short period

---

2519 Compare also with Art. 1726 old BCC.

2520 Compare with proposed Art. 7.3.15. BCC.

2521 See *infra* section 4.5.

2522 See e.g. B. Kohl, "Le contrat d'entreprise: proposition de réforme du Code civil" in R. Jafferali, P. Foriers and E. Van Den Haute (eds.), *Entre tradition et pragmatisme. Liber amicorum Paul Alain Foriers*, Volume 1, Brussels, Larcier, 2021, (481) 484–485 and 525–526; S. De Rey, "Naar een boek 'bijzondere overeenkomsten' in het Nieuw Burgerlijk Wetboek? Enkele perspectieven" in S. De Rey, N. Van Damme and T. Gladinez (eds.), *Grenzen voorbij. Liber discipulorum Bernard Tilleman*, Antwerp, Intersentia, 2020, (361) 364–365 and 367–369; B. Keirsbilck and E. Terryn, "Duurzaamheid en consumentenrecht" in A. Van Hoe and G. Croisant (eds.), *Droit et durabilité / Recht en duurzaamheid*, Antwerp, Intersentia, 2022, (433) 489.

2523 See *supra* no. 40, no. 65 and no. 513.

of time.[2524] This risk applies especially to (result-oriented) PSS, as the market for these contracts is still in full development.

The second way to regulate service contracts at the national level is by drafting general legal rules. This option seems preferable for a few reasons. First, general rules, if well-drafted, can be applied to all service contracts, regardless of their specific nature. This results in consistency and simplicity and avoids qualification issues within the broad category of service contracts. Additionally, general legal rules are more flexible and adaptable to changes in the market and emerging service industries. Consequently, these rules are more future proof, allowing to address new challenges and technologies without the need for extensive amendments to various regulations. Finally, modernising the rules on service contracts by drafting general legal rules fits within the spirit of the "new" BCC, namely opting for a (re)codification of current law (including recent evolutions in case law and legal doctrine) rather than a complete revolution. The Dutch rules of the contract for services (*opdracht*) as well as the provisions on services in the DCFR can serve as a source of inspiration here, as these contain general legal provisions applicable to a wide range of service contracts.

A. Performance and delivery of the service in conformity with the contract

574. Concept of conformity as cornerstone for general rules for services – A first important part of the modernised rules for service contracts should be an explicit obligation to perform the promised service in conformity with the contract.[2525] This means that the service provider must perform the service according to the contractual provisions and, where applicable, according to the (reasonable) instructions of the client. Additionally, the service provider must perform the service according to the rules of good workmanship, which means acting as a professional, reasonable, and diligent service provider in the same circumstances.[2526] The concept of conformity is thus at the core of these proposed rules on services contracts in the (Belgian) Civil Code. It follows a similar approach of subjective (what is stipulated in the contract) and objective (what the client can reasonably expect) requirements to assess the conformity with the contract, as we also find in the (consumer) sales contract and the proposed rules for the rental contract for movables set out above. These general principles for assessing the conformity of services are translated into paragraph 1 and 2 of proposed provision #21.[2527]

2524 F. Zoll, "From a Product-Based Economy to Services? – Legal Aspects of an Economy in Transition" in B. Keirsbilck and E. Terryn (eds.), *Consumer Protection in a Circular Economy*, Antwerp, Intersentia, 2019, (149) 156.

2525 See in the same sense: B. Kohl, "Le contrat d'entreprise: proposition de réforme du Code civil" in R. Jafferali, P. Foriers and E. Van Den Haute (eds.), *Entre tradition et pragmatisme. Liber amicorum Paul Alain Foriers*, Volume 1, Brussels, Larcier, 2021, (481) 492.

2526 Compare with: Cass. (BE) 25 October 1974, *Pas.* I, 1974, 241.

2527 See *infra* p. 455.

575. STANDARDISATION OF SERVICES AS AN ADDITIONAL INSTRUMENT TO ASSESS AND OPERATIONALISE THE CONFORMITY OF SERVICES – These general conformity principles, in particular the concept of the rules of good workmanship, can be further operationalised by service standards.[2528] This has the advantage that standardisation can deal more flexibly with the diversity of services-oriented contracts and PSS than seems possible with a traditional hard law approach.[2529] Contrary to product-related standards,[2530] service standards are more of a legal nature than technical, as they also determine the legal relationship between parties of services, for example with regard to the making of the contract, the content of the contract, the performance of the contract and remedies under the contract.[2531] As such, they largely resemble standard terms and conditions.[2532] Service standards may relate to specific sectors (e.g. standards on financial services[2533] or tourism services[2534]), or they can deal with horizontal issues, i.e. issues applicable across different service sectors[2535] (e.g. dispute resolution[2536] or complaints handling[2537]).[2538]

2528 See in this sense: A. De Franceschi, "Ensuring Circularity in Service Contracts" in B. Keirsbilck, E. Terryn, J. Eyckmans, S. Rousseau and D. Voinot (eds.), *Servitization and circular economy: economic and legal challenges*, Antwerp, Intersentia, 2023, (167) 172; V. Mak and E. Terryn, "Circular Economy and Consumer Protection: The Consumer as a Citizen and the Limits of Empowerment Through Consumer Law", *Journal of Consumer Policy* 2020, vol. 43, (227) 242; F. Zoll, "From a Product-Based Economy to Services? – Legal Aspects of an Economy in Transition" in B. Keirsbilck and E. Terryn (eds.), *Consumer Protection in a Circular Economy*, Antwerp, Intersentia, 2019, (149) 156.

2529 F. Zoll, "From a Product-Based Economy to Services? – Legal Aspects of an Economy in Transition" in B. Keirsbilck and E. Terryn (eds.), *Consumer Protection in a Circular Economy*, Antwerp, Intersentia, 2019, (149) 156.

2530 E.g. standards containing technical specifications for twist drills (ISO 5419:1982), light bulb sockets (IEC 60238:2016) or standardised formats of stationery (ISO 618:1974).

2531 H.-W. Micklitz, *Services Standards: Defining the Core Consumer Elements and their Minimum Requirements*, Study commissioned by ANEC, the European Consumer Voice in Standardisation, Brussels, 2007, 21.

2532 C. Busch, "DIN-Normen für Dienstleistungen – Das Europäische Normungskomitee produziert Musterverträge", *Neue Juristische Wochenschrift* 2010, (3061) 3061.

2533 See e.g. ISO 20022.

2534 See e.g. ISO 18513:2021 on Tourism services, Hotels and other types of tourism accommodation.

2535 See for a very general service standard: EN 17371–2:2022 on Services contracts – Guidance for the design, content and structure of contracts. This document, however, is not applicable to B2C service contracts or for works contracts. See on the genesis of this standard also: C. Busch, "Towards a "New Approach" for the Platform Ecosystem: A European Standard for Fairness in Platform-to-Business Relations", *EuCML* 2017, (227) 228 and P. Delimatsis, "Standardisation in services – European ambitions and sectoral realities", *European Law Review* 2016, (513) 531.

2536 See ISO 10003:2018 on Quality management, Customer satisfaction, Guidelines for dispute resolution external to organizations.

2537 See ISO 10002:2018 on Quality management, Customer satisfaction, Guidelines for complaints handling in organizations.

2538 P. Delimatsis, "Standardisation in services – European ambitions and sectoral realities", *European Law Review* 2016, (513) 516.

These service standards can guide consumers and service providers (for example through consumer information) and possibly play an additional role in assessing the non-performance and conformity of (result-oriented) PSS.[2539, 2540] They can either act as a subjective element for conformity (if the PSS contract specifically states that the service will comply with standard X) or as an objective element for conformity (for example, if these service standards become a measure for the rules of good workmanship).[2541] In the second sub-paragraph of §2, 2° of proposed provision #21, this link between the concept of conformity and service standards is explicitly confirmed.[2542]

576. Weaknesses to using standardisation for assessing conformity of result-oriented PSS – Standardisation alone, however, cannot fully address the gap in consumer protection resulting from the lack of a comprehensive EU framework and the limited national contract law rules for services.[2543] A first reason is that the use of standards is generally voluntary, so PSS suppliers can choose whether they adopt or adhere to certain standards.[2544] As a result, voluntary standards will never provide the same level of consumer protection as mandatory legal rules. This should however be nuanced, as the use of standards can be (directly or indirectly) made

2539 A. De Franceschi, "Ensuring Circularity in Service Contracts" in B. Keirsbilck, E. Terryn, J. Eyckmans, S. Rousseau and D. Voinot (eds.), *Servitization and circular economy: economic and legal challenges*, Antwerp, Intersentia, 2023, (167) 172;; F. Zoll, "From a Product-Based Economy to Services? – Legal Aspects of an Economy in Transition" in B. Keirsbilck and E. Terryn (eds.), *Consumer Protection in a Circular Economy*, Antwerp, Intersentia, 2019, (149) 156. See also: C. Busch, "Towards a "New Approach" for the Platform Ecosystem: A European Standard for Fairness in Platform-to-Business Relations", *EuCML* 2017, (227) 228 and C. Busch, "Towards a "New Approach" in European Consumer Law: Standardisation and Co-Regulation in the Digital Single Market", *EuCML* 2016, (197) 198, both mentioning specific instances where compliance with a standard can involve a presumption of conformity with the corresponding directive (e.g. for health and safety requirements).

2540 Some courts already take recourse to technical standards to assess contractual liability. See *supra* no. 524.

2541 F. Zoll, "From a Product-Based Economy to Services? – Legal Aspects of an Economy in Transition" in B. Keirsbilck and E. Terryn (eds.), *Consumer Protection in a Circular Economy*, Antwerp, Intersentia, 2019, (149) 156; C. Busch, "DIN-Normen für Dienstleistungen – Das Europäische Normungskomitee produziert Musterverträge", *Neue Juristische Wochenschrift* 2010, (3061) 3064 and 3066.

2542 See *infra* p. 455.

2543 V. Mak and E. Terryn, "Circular Economy and Consumer Protection: The Consumer as a Citizen and the Limits of Empowerment Through Consumer Law", *Journal of Consumer Policy* 2020, vol. 43, (227) 242.

2544 V. Mak and E. Terryn, "Circular Economy and Consumer Protection: The Consumer as a Citizen and the Limits of Empowerment Through Consumer Law", *Journal of Consumer Policy* 2020, vol. 43, (227) 242.

mandatory for certain services by special legal provisions,[2545] or become inescapable through the reality of the market.[2546]

A second reason is that if mandatory rules exist at the national or EU level, standards cannot deviate from them, even if this would bring more consumer protection or sustainability benefits.[2547] This weakness, however, must also be nuanced, as only little mandatory rules exist for result-oriented PSS, so there is quite some room for standardisation.

A third possible weakness relates to the legitimacy of standards. While standards have an indirect legitimacy stemming from the merit of the expert groups developing the standards, they remain drawn up by standardisation bodies and not by public (elected) authorities. This process is not always transparent, nor are consumer organisations always consulted and involved.[2548] As a result, consumer protection is not necessarily guaranteed through the development of service standards.[2549] In this sense, MICKLITZ rightly argues that sufficient involvement of consumer representatives in standardisation, for example by means of a right to participate, a right to access to the relevant documents and sufficient funding, is needed and should be legally guaranteed.[2550]

A final weakness of using technical standards to assess the conformity of PSS is that they are not published in official legal gazettes (unlike laws and other legal rules) but are protected by copyright laws and must be purchased from a standardisation organisation.[2551] Consequently, PSS users do not have as easy access to these standards as would be the case if the conformity of the service was regulated by hard law. As this lack of transparency makes it harder

---

[2545] V. HATZOPOULOS, *Regulating Services in the European Union*, Oxford, Oxford University Press, 2012, 277–278: *"[Standards] are non-binding, unless introduced into some text of hard law, such as a Directive."*

[2546] F. ZOLL, "From a Product-Based Economy to Services? – Legal Aspects of an Economy in Transition" in B. KEIRSBILCK and E. TERRYN (eds.), *Consumer Protection in a Circular Economy*, Antwerp, Intersentia, 2019, (149) 156.

[2547] V. MAK and E. TERRYN, "Circular Economy and Consumer Protection: The Consumer as a Citizen and the Limits of Empowerment Through Consumer Law", *Journal of Consumer Policy* 2020, vol. 43, (227) 242.

[2548] H.-W. MICKLITZ, *Services Standards: Defining the Core Consumer Elements and their Minimum Requirements*, Study commissioned by ANEC, the European Consumer Voice in Standardisation, Brussels, 2007, 53.

[2549] V. MAK and E. TERRYN, "Circular Economy and Consumer Protection: The Consumer as a Citizen and the Limits of Empowerment Through Consumer Law", *Journal of Consumer Policy* 2020, vol. 43, (227) 242.

[2550] H.-W. MICKLITZ, *Services Standards: Defining the Core Consumer Elements and their Minimum Requirements*, Study commissioned by ANEC, the European Consumer Voice in Standardisation, Brussels, 2007, 209. See in the same sense: V. MAK and E. TERRYN, "Circular Economy and Consumer Protection: The Consumer as a Citizen and the Limits of Empowerment Through Consumer Law", *Journal of Consumer Policy* 2020, vol. 43, (227) 242.

[2551] C. BUSCH, "DIN-Normen für Dienstleistungen – Das Europäische Normungskomitee produziert Musterverträge", *Neue Juristische Wochenschrift* 2010, (3061) 3062.

for the PSS user to assess whether the performed service is in conformity with the PSS contract, this obviously does not benefit the legal certainty of the PSS user. For long, this seemed like the weakness that was the hardest to overcome. While a potential (but partial) solution could be to have a well-functioning monitoring and compliance mechanism so conformity assessment bodies or public authorities can assess the compliance of service providers with standards, this still does not grant access to these standards to consumers and PSS users. However, this weakness seems resolved following a very recent case of the CJEU.

577. Solution in CJEU case law: harmonised standards are EU law that must be accessible to the public – The lack of transparency of technical standards was at the centre of a very recent CJEU case. In *Public.Resource.Org*[2552] the CJEU had to address whether technical standards developed by standardisation bodies and referred to in EU regulations, directives or EU law in general should be considered "EU law" that must be accessible to the public. The facts where the following: Public.Resource.Org. Inc. and Right to Know CLG, both non-profit organisations whose focus is to make the law freely accessible to all citizens, made a request to the Commission for access to four harmonised standards under the Public Access to Documents Regulation.[2553] This was refused by the Commission, claiming inter alia that the harmonised technical standards were protected by copyright held by the standardisation body in question.

Public.Resource.Org. Inc. and Right to Know CLG appealed this decision to the General Court, essentially arguing (i) that the requested harmonised standards formed part of "EU law" and therefore should be freely accessible without charge, meaning that no exception to the right of access could apply to them (in other words, that those standards could not be protected by copyright); and (ii) that granting citizens of the EU access to EU law is an overriding public interest, within the meaning of the Public Access to Documents Regulation, that justifies access to the requested technical standards. Both arguments, however, were dismissed by the General Court.[2554]

The decision of the General Court was appealed to the CJEU, where the Grand Chamber only addressed the second claim without dealing with the issue of copyright. It referred to Article 2(1)-(2) and 4(2) of the Public Access

2552 CJEU, Judgment of 5 March 2024, C-588/21 P, *Public.Resource.Org and Right to Know v Commission and Others*, ECLI:EU:C:2024:201. See for an analysis of this judgment: B. Lundqvist, "Right to access harmonised standards: Public.Resource.Org and Right to Know v Commission and Others, C-588/21 P", 20 March 2024, available at https://eulawlive.com/op-ed-right-to-access-harmonised-standards-public-resource-org-and-right-to-know-v-commission-and-others-c-588–21-p-by-bjorn-lundqvist/.

2553 Regulation (EC) No 1049/2001 of the European Parliament and of the Council of 30 May 2001 regarding public access to European Parliament, Council and Commission documents, *OJ L* 145, 31/05/2001, 43–48.

2554 General Court (Fifth Chamber), 14 July 2021, T-185/19, *Public.Resource.Org and Right to Know v Commission*, ECLI:EU:T:2021:445.

to Documents Regulation which grant a right of access to documents of the Parliament, Council and Commission, which are to refuse access to a document if disclosure would undermine the protection of commercial interests of a natural or legal person, including intellectual property, unless there is an overriding public interest in disclosure.[2555] The CJEU ruled that there is indeed an overriding public interest justifying the disclosure of the requested harmonised standards.[2556] For establishing this, the CJEU relied on Article 2 TEU, which provides that the EU is based on the principle of the rule of law, which requires free access to EU law for all natural or legal persons of the EU, and that individuals must be able to ascertain unequivocally what their rights and obligations are.[2557] That free access must, according to the CJEU, in particular enable any person whom legislation seeks to protect to verify that the persons to whom the rules laid down by that law are addressed actually comply with those rules.[2558] It also held that the requested harmonised standards do form part of EU law, and therefore the right of access to these documents is ensured under the first sub-paragraph of Article 15(3) TFEU and Article 42 of the Charter, which is implemented in the Public Access to Documents Regulation.[2559]

578. Opportunities for PSS and service contracts resulting from this CJEU case law – According the CJEU, access must thus be granted to harmonised technical standards that are used in (and constitute) EU law, albeit without mentioning whether the standardisation bodies can still claim copyright. This could pave the way for a business model for standardisation of services where the Commission (or national legislator) pays the (royalty) fees or the fees for the preparatory work conducted by the standardisation body, with the right for the Commission (or national legislator) to make the harmonised standard available to the public.[2560] This way, standards for PSS business models can effectively be used for assessing the conformity of the service with the PSS contract.

579. Policy recommendation #2: encourage developing and adopting service standards for PSS – Although the EU Regulation 2012/1025 on European Standardisation[2561] also applies to services and no longer just to goods

---

2555 CJEU, Judgment of 5 March 2024, C-588/21 P, *Public.Resource.Org and Right to Know v Commission and Others*, ECLI:EU:C:2024:201, para. 67 and 68.

2556 *Ibid.*, para. 85.

2557 *Ibid.*, para. 81, with reference to CJEU, Judgment of 22 February 2022, C-160/20, *Stichting Rookpreventie Jeugd and Others*, ECLI:EU:C:2022:101, para. 41.

2558 *Ibid.*, para. 81.

2559 *Ibid.*, para. 80 and 84.

2560 B. Lundqvist, "Right to access harmonised standards: Public.Resource.Org and Right to Know v Commission and Others, C-588/21 P", 20 March 2024, available at https://eulawlive.com/op-ed-right-to-access-harmonised-standards-public-resource-org-and-right-to-know-v-commission-and-others-c-588–21-p-by-bjorn-lundqvist/.

2561 Regulation (EU) No 1025/2012 of the European Parliament and of the Council of 25 October 2012 on European standardisation, *OJ* L 316, 14.11.2012, 12–33.

since 2012,[2562] the use of standards for services is still in its infancy compared to goods.[2563] Although there are already initiatives at the national level to develop circular economy standards,[2564] specific standards for (result-oriented) PSS are so far still lacking. As a result, sector-specific standards should be developed (at EU or national level) with minimum rules for the quality of services, and more specifically PSS. In my view, the absolute preference should be on harmonised European standards, as differences between national service standards (just like product standards) can create barriers to trade and thus hinder the European single market for services.[2565] This leads to policy recommendation #2, proposing to adopt measures that encourage the European Committee for Standardisation (CEN) and National Standardisation Bodies (either in a supportive role or on their own if no action is taken at the EU level) to develop standards for (result-oriented) PSS and other product-as-a-service contracts. Additionally, measures should be taken to increase the uptake of service standards by PSS suppliers, to give publicity to these service standards and PSS suppliers who adopt them, and to enable conformity assessment bodies or other public authorities to assess the compliance with these standards.

These policy recommendations do not require legislative change. After all, Article 26 of the Services Directive, under the title "quality of services", already gives a mandate to the European Commission and Member States to advocate standardisation of services for enhancing the quality of services.[2566] This includes measures encouraging promotion and external assessment of the quality of services by, amongst others, consumer organisations.[2567]

2562 See: https://ec.europa.eu/growth/single-market/services/service-standards_en.

2563 P. Delimatsis, "Standardisation in services – European ambitions and sectoral realities", *European Law Review* 2016, (513) 523–524 and 533; H. Schepel, *The Constitution of Private Governance: Product Standards in the Regulation of Integrating Markets*, Oxford, Hart Publishing, 2005, 460 p. See, however, amongst many others, the following examples of standards for services: EN ISO 17100:2015 (Requirements for translation services); EN 15838:2009 (Customer contact centres); EN 14804:2005 (Language study tour providers); EN 15017:2015 (Funeral Services); EN 12522:1998 (Furniture removal for private individuals).

2564 See e.g. British Standard 8001; http://ecostandard.org/news_events/first-standard-on-circular-economy/. See for a discussion of this standard: S. Pauliuk, "Critical appraisal of the circular economy standard BS 8001:2017 and a dashboard of quantitative system indicators for its implementation in organizations", *Resources, Conservation and Recycling* 2018, vol. 129, 81–92.

2565 C. Busch, "DIN-Normen für Dienstleistungen – Das Europäische Normungskomitee produziert Musterverträge", *Neue Juristische Wochenschrift* 2010, (3061) 3062.

2566 See on this provision: European Commission, Directorate-General for Internal market, Industry, Entrepreneurship and SMEs, *Handbook on the implementation of the Services Directive*, Luxemburg, Publications Office of the European Union, 2022, 87–88; C. Barnard, "Unravelling the Services Directive", *CML Rev.* 2008, vol. 45, (323) 378–379 and H.-W. Micklitz, *Services Standards: Defining the Core Consumer Elements and their Minimum Requirements*, Study commissioned by ANEC, the European Consumer Voice in Standardisation, Brussels, 2007, 65 *et seq.*

2567 See Art. 26(3) and (4) SD.

Policy Recommendation #2

- **Consider adopting measures that encourage CEN (the European Committee for Standardisation) and NSBs (National Standardisation Bodies) to develop standards for product-as-a-service contracts/(result-oriented) PSS, in collaboration with industry stakeholders and consumer organisations. These standards should cover areas such as service quality, safety, data protection, customer support, and environmental sustainability.**
- **Consider providing incentives for service providers/PSS suppliers to adopt these service standards voluntarily. This could include tax benefits, grants, or preferential access to government contracts for businesses that meet the required standards.**
- **Consider setting up a system to recognise and publicise service providers/PSS suppliers that demonstrate exemplary adherence to these service standards.**
- **Consider launching public awareness campaigns to educate consumers about the benefits of standardised services/PSS. This could encourage consumers to engage in business models that adhere to recognised standards, thereby creating market demand for standardised services/PSS.**
- **Consider establishing a monitoring and compliance mechanism to ensure that service providers/PSS suppliers stating that they adhere to certain standards effectively meet these standards.**
- **Consider working together with standardisation bodies in order to develop standards for the conformity of (product-as-a) service contracts, which can be referred to in EU or national legislation and made publicly available following the payment of the (royalty) fees by the EU or Member States.**

580. HIGHER STANDARD OF SKILL AND CARE – In some circumstances, the person of the service supplier is relevant for assessing the conformity of the service. This is for example the case with a famous and highly specialised service provider who professes that he uses a high level of skill and care in the performance of the service. In this situation, it is not unreasonable to set the bar higher for the service provider, as the last sub-paragraph of §2, 2° of proposed provision #21 aims to do. This sub-paragraph is also in line with the Dutch approach of interpreting the care of a good service provider[2568] (Art. 7:401 DCC) and draws inspiration from Article IV. C. – 2:105(2) of the DCFR.

[2568] T.F.E. TJONG TJIN TAI, *Asser 7-IV Bijzondere Overeenkomsten – Opdracht, incl. de geneeskundige behandelingsovereenkomst en de reisovereenkomst*, Deventer, Wolters Kluwer, 2022, no. 97.

581. LACK OF CONFORMITY ANTERIOR TO DELIVERY DUE TO IMPUTABLE NON-PERFORMANCE – Paragraph 3 of proposed provision #21 provides that the service provider is liable for any lack of conformity that exists (even if it has not yet become apparent) at the time of delivery. As such, this paragraph reflects the concept that the lack of conformity must be anterior to the delivery and that the service provider will not be liable for any lack of conformity that originates after the delivery. In addition, the service provider will only be liable if the lack of conformity is due to an imputable non-performance. This was also already the case under the current rules of the contract for services.

> Proposed Provision #21
>
> Art. 7.4.X1. Performance of the service in conformity with the contract
>
> §1. The service provider must perform the service in conformity with the contract.
>
> §2. In order for the service to be in conformity with the contract:
>
> 1° it shall meet what the contract stipulates (subjective conformity); and
>
> 2° what the client may reasonably expect (objective conformity).
>
> The client's reasonable expectations are determined by law, custom, good faith, the nature of the service, the capacity of the service provider and the rules of good workmanship. The rules of good workmanship refers to the skill and care of a professional, reasonable and diligent service provider in the same circumstances.
>
> The rules of good workmanship shall also be interpreted with due regard to standards developed by national or international standardisation bodies which were adopted or purported to be adopted by the service provider.
>
> If the service provider professes a higher standard of skill and care, the service provider must exercise that skill and care.
>
> §3. The service provider is liable for any lack of conformity that exists at the time of delivery, even if this lack of conformity does not become apparent until later, insofar as this lack of conformity is due to an imputable non-performance by the service provider.

Proposed provision #21 is very similar to the Draft Law, namely proposed Article 7.4.15 BCC. The main difference lies in the description of the subjective conformity requirements, i.e. what the client may reasonably expect. In the Draft Law, it is clarified that the reasonable expectations of the client are determined by the law, custom, good faith, the nature of the service, the capacity of the service provider and the circumstances of the case. In proposed provision #21, explicit reference is also made to the rules of good workmanship, with specific attention and reference to technical (service) standards. This of course fits well with policy recommendation #2, which encourages the legislator and policy makers to promote and make use of the possibility to operationalise the concept of conformity with technical standards. The explicit confirmation of the service provider's public statements on his (higher) standard of skill and care as a subjective conformity criterion is also not found in the Draft Law. Nevertheless, content-wise both approaches essentially cover the same ideas and concepts, as the explanatory memorandum also states that the rules of good workmanship and public statements are relevant to assess conformity of the performed service with the contract.

582. Instructions by the client – The conformity of the service is also assessed in light of the instructions and directions of the client (i.e. the PSS user).[2569] Under Dutch law and the DCFR, the obligation of the service provider (i.e. the PSS supplier) to follow the instructions and directions of the client is explicitly confirmed, provided these instructions and directions are timely and reasonable.[2570] Under Belgian law, the same principle applies, although the old BCC lacks a provision on this topic.[2571] Paragraph 1 of proposed provision #22 therefore proposes to codify this principle into the Belgian rules on the contract for services. However, it is appropriate to make this provision only of default law, so that the PSS contract can derogate from this power of instruction. This is mainly relevant for standardised "package services" (as will often be the case with PSS). For a specific example where it may be useful to exclude the possibility of the PSS supplier to provide instructions to the PSS supplier, reference can be made to a ventilation-as-a-service contract. These contracts often include output specifications on the desired temperature of the PSS user's rooms, which is achieved, amongst other things, by an automatic shading system that activates when the sun shines on the windows. If the PSS user overrides the automatic activation (for example, via the ventilation system app), this may result in the output specifications not being met.[2572]

2569 See *supra* no. 516.

2570 **The Netherlands**: Art. 7:204(1) DCC. **DCFR**: Art. IV. C. – 2:107 DCFR. Compare also with Art. 1:109 PELSC.

2571 See *supra* fn. 2334 and the references there.

2572 Example discussed during the workshop "Data-driven servitization in creating healthy spaces", 9 September 2020, Ghent within the framework of the Renson chair (see: https://www.kuleuven.be/fundraising/chairs/institutes-cross-group/renson-chair-for-data-driven-servitization-in-creating-healthy-spaces).

583. Duty to warn – It is evidently important that the client's instructions and directions are reasonable and do not result in compromising the desired result of the service. If this would be the case, Dutch law and the DCFR contain a contractual obligation for the service provider to warn the client of these issues.[2573] The same principle also applies under Belgian law despite there being no explicit provision in the old BCC.[2574] Under certain circumstances (e.g. a violation of a provision of criminal law or if the act would violate applicable professional rules[2575]), this can even lead to a duty to refuse to follow the client's instructions.[2576] The question arises as to what the consequences are if the client ignores these warnings or insists on following the instructions. According to the DCFR, the service provider shall not be liable if he followed the client's instructions, provided he duly warned the client of the associated risks.[2577] Also under Belgian and Dutch law, this will generally result in the service provider not being liable.[2578] Moreover, the DCC even explicitly allows the service provider to terminate the contract on compelling grounds if the client continues to insist on following these instructions despite the warning or refusal of the service provider.[2579] Paragraph 2 and 3 of proposed provision #22 combine these two solutions for service providers that are confronted with instructions by the client that are unreasonable or may compromise the agreed result.

2573 **The Netherlands**: T.F.E. Tjong Tjin Tai, *Asser 7-IV Bijzondere Overeenkomsten - Opdracht, incl. de geneeskundige behandelingsovereenkomst en de reisovereenkomst*, Deventer, Wolters Kluwer, 2022, no. 104. **DCFR**: Art. IV. C. – 2:107(2) DCFR *juncto* Art. IV. C. – 2:108 DCFR.

2574 **Belgium**: B. Tilleman, S. De Rey, N. Debruyne, T. Gladinez, N. Van Damme and F. Van den Abeele, "Overzicht van rechtspraak bijzondere overeenkomsten aanneming (2007–2021)", *TPR* 2022, (365) 491, no. 96; W. Goossens, *Aanneming van werk: het gemeenrechtelijk dienstencontract*, Bruges, Die Keure, 2003, 797, no. 883; B. Kohl, *Contrat d'entreprise*, Brussels, Bruylant, 2016, 271 and 340.

2575 Compare with B. Wessels, "Algemene bepalingen inzake de overeenkomst van opdracht" in C. Van Dam and B. Wessels (eds.), *Opdracht en dienstverlening*, Zwolle, Tjeenk Willink, 1994, (1) 20.

2576 **Belgium**: W. Goossens, *Aanneming van werk: het gemeenrechtelijk dienstencontract*, Bruges, Die Keure, 2003, 705 and 797. **The Netherlands**: C.J. Van Zeben, W.H.M. Reehuis and E.E. Slob, *Parlementaire Geschiedenis van het Nieuwe Burgerlijk Wetboek. Invoering Boeken 3, 5 en 6: Boek 7: Bijzondere overeenkomsten titels 1, 7, 9 en 14*, Deventer, Kluwer, 1991, 324; T.F.E. Tjong Tjin Tai, *Asser 7-IV Bijzondere Overeenkomsten – Opdracht, incl. de geneeskundige behandelingsovereenkomst en de reisovereenkomst*, Deventer, Wolters Kluwer, 2022, no. 105–107.

2577 Art. IV. C. – 2:107(2) *juncto* Art. IV. C. – 2:108 DCFR.

2578 **Belgium**: see B. Kohl, *Contrat d'entreprise*, Brussels, Bruylant, 2016, 342 and the case law cited there. See also W. Goossens, *Aanneming van werk: het gemeenrechtelijk dienstencontract*, Bruges, Die Keure, 2003, 806 and the examples mentioned. **The Netherlands**: T.F.E. Tjong Tjin Tai, *Zorgplichten en zorgethiek*, Kluwer, Deventer, 2006, 196–197. See for examples (in the financial sector): HR (NL) 14 July 2006, ECLI:NL:HR:2006:AC3202, *RvdW* 2006, 745; HR (NL) 23 June 2006, ECLI:NL:PHR:2006:AV9439, *RvdW* 2006, 657 and (for attorneys): HR (NL) 2 February 2007, ECLI:NL:HR:2007:AZ4564 (*Juresta*), *NJ* 2007/92; HR (NL) 8 September 2000, ECLI:NL:PHR:2000:AA7040, (*A./Timmers*), *NJ* 2000/614.

2579 Art. 7:402(2) DCC. See also: C.J.H. Brunner, "De opdracht (Ontwerp boek 7, titel 7)", *WPNR* 1974, vol. 5285, (783) 786.

Proposed Provision #22

Art. 7.4.X2. Instructions of the client

§1. The service provider must follow all timely and reasonable instructions of the client regarding the performance of the agreed service.

§2. The service provider shall not be liable for the non-performance of the obligation to perform the service in conformity with the contract (Art. 7.4.X1.) resulting from following the client's instructions, provided that the client was duly warned by the service provider of the risks that following these instructions:

1° may not achieve the agreed or intended result;

2° may harm other interests of the client; or

3° may be more expensive or take longer than agreed in the contract.

§3. The service provider who is reasonably unwilling to perform the service according to the instructions of the client may terminate the contract.

In the Draft Law, the link between the instructions of the client and the concept of conformity of the performed service is not explicitly made in the legal text of proposed Article 7.4.15 BCC. The importance of the client's instructions for the concept of conformity is only mentioned in the explanatory memorandum.[2580] Still, this does not mean that the instructions and directions of the client are entirely absent in the Draft Law. Indeed, these principles are found in the cooperation obligation laid down in proposed Article 7.4.5 BCC (which is also referenced in the section of the explanatory memorandum discussing proposed Article 7.4.15 BCC). In my view, however, it is appropriate to make an explicit reference in the rules regarding conformity to the client's instructions, preferably by means of an explicit provision (cf. proposed provision #22) or at least by means of a cross-reference.

584. Burden of proof that lack of conformity is due to imputable non-performance – Paragraph 1 of proposed provision #23 places the burden of proof that the lack of conformity is anterior to the delivery and due to an imputable non-performance on the client. Paragraph 2 continues by stating that this is assessed in accordance with the general law of obligations, namely Article 5.225 and Article 5.72 BCC. It also explicitly mentions that the obligation to perform the service can either be an obligation of result or an obligation of

[2580] Explanatory Memorandum, *Parliamentary Papers* Chamber of Representatives 2023–24, no. 55-3973/001, 129–130.

means. As these terms are already defined in the general law of obligations, it was opted to only make reference to the provisions in Book 5 BCC instead of defining these terms once more.[2581]

> **Proposed Provision #23**
>
> **Art. 7.4.X3. Proof of lack of conformity**
>
> **§1. The client bears the burden of proof that the lack of conformity existed at the time of delivery and is due to an imputable non-performance.**
>
> **§2. Whether the lack of conformity is due to an imputable non-performance is assessed in accordance with Art. 5.225 and Art. 5.72, in particular in view of the question whether the obligation to perform the service in conformity with the contract is an obligation of result or an obligation of means.**

The principles behind proposed provision #23 are the same as proposed Article 7.4.16 of the Draft Law. The main (textual) difference lies in the fact that proposed provision #23 explicitly references the qualification of the obligation to perform the service as either an obligation of result or an obligation of means. In my view, this does provide added value, especially given the importance of the qualification of the obligation for the liability of the service provider.

585. Liability period – Proposed provision #24 deals with the liability period in which the service provider can be held liable for a lack of conformity. In essence, it concerns the time period in which the client can prove that the lack of conformity is due to an imputable non-performance by the service provider. The acceptance (and not the delivery) of the service is taken as the starting point, since the client can still refuse the acceptance of the service after the delivery in case the performed service contains a lack of conformity.[2582] This proposed provision does not really innovate, since the same ten-year period already applies under current law.[2583] The Draft Law (proposed Article 7.4.17 BCC) has retained these principles as well.

> **Proposed Provision #24**
>
> **Art. 7.4.X4. Liability period**
>
> **The service provider is only liable for any lack of conformity that becomes apparent within ten years after the acceptance of the completed service (Art. 7.4.X8).**

2581 See Art. 5.72 BCC.
2582 See *infra* no. 590.
2583 Compare with Art. 2262*bis* old BCC.

586. Notification period – The proposed provision on the notification period (#25), namely the requirement to give notice within a reasonable time, is aligned with the proposed notification period for the rental contract,[2584] as well as the proposed provisions in the Draft Law concerning the notification period for sales contracts and contracts for services (proposed Articles 7.2.33 and 7.4.18 BCC). Similar to the Draft Law, the proposed provision specifies that the notification must be given *"at the earliest at the time of delivery."* This makes sense, since for visible defects, notification of the lack of conformity within a reasonable time implies that the notification happens immediately, namely at the time of acceptance (or refusal) of the service. For hidden defects, proposed provision #25 (just like proposed Article 7.4.18 BCC of the Draft Law) changes the principle under current law that it is not sufficient that the client notifies the service provider of a hidden defects, but that he must instead bring a claim in court against the service provider within this reasonable time. This approach is more equitable as clients are often unaware of this rule and often try to seek an amicable solution with the service provider first before filing a claim in court. This may lead to a situation where they are then to laid to file a claim in court (especially if the service provider tries to abuse this principle by stalling the negotiations).[2585] Moreover, this way, the rules of the contract for services are in line with the proposed rules for the notification obligation for the sales contract contained in the Draft Law (proposed Article 7.2.33 BCC).[2586]

Proposed Provision #25

Art. 7.4.X5. Notification period

§1. The client shall notify the service provider of the lack of conformity within a reasonable time from the moment he discovered or should have discovered it, and at the earliest at the time of delivery.

The reasonable time shall be assessed on the basis of all relevant circumstances and, in particular, the nature of the service, the nature of the lack of conformity, the capacity of the parties and customs.

§2. If the client fails to give notice of the existence of the lack of conformity within the reasonable time, he loses the right to hold the service provider liable for this lack of conformity.

2584 See *supra* no. 559.

2585 Explanatory Memorandum, *Parliamentary Papers* Chamber of Representatives 2023–24, no. 55-3973/001, 132.

2586 *Ibid.*

587. Remedies for lack of conformity of the service – The question arises as to the remedies available to the client/PSS user in case of a lack of conformity of the performed service. Just like with the rental contract, it does not seem necessary to deviate from the general contract law remedies.[2587] Therefore, proposed provision #26 confirms that the client has access to the remedies mentioned in Article 5.83 of the BCC. The reading together of proposed provision #26 (remedies for lack of conformity) with proposed provision #21, §3 result in the client having access to these remedies both for lack of conformity prior to acceptance (visible defects) and for any lack of conformity that the client should not reasonably have discovered at the time of acceptance (hidden defects).

Proposed Provision #26

Art. 7.4.X6. Remedies for lack of conformity

In case of a lack of conformity of the performed service, the client has access to the remedies mentioned in Art. 5.83.

588. Delivery of the service – When the service is fully performed, the service provider must deliver its results to the client. If goods are produced as part of the service, this happens through the material, symbolic or intellectual hand-over of the good. These principles are laid down in proposed provision #27, which is based on proposed Article 7.4.20 BCC of the Draft Law.

Proposed Provision #27

Art. 7.4.X7. Delivery of the service

The delivery implies the completion of the service and, where applicable, the material, symbolic or intellectual hand-over of the good resulting from the service.

589. Time and place of delivery – The obligation to perform and deliver the service in conformity with the contract should also be accompanied with an explicit provision of the period in which the service must be performed and delivered. In the first place, the parties can freely agree the period in which the service must be fully performed. By lack of an explicit contractual arrangement,

[2587] See in this sense (for the situation before the acceptance of the performed service) B. Kohl, "Le contrat d'entreprise: proposition de réforme du Code civil" in R. Jafferali, P. Foriers and E. Van Den Haute (eds.), *Entre tradition et pragmatisme. Liber amicorum Paul Alain Foriers*, Volume 1, Brussels, Larcier, 2021, (481) 505.

the service must be provided within a reasonable period.[2588] These principles are laid down in the first two paragraphs of proposed provision #28. The third paragraph of proposed provision #28 deals with the place of the delivery and refers to the principles of general contract law. This approach is consistent with the Draft Law.[2589]

Proposed Provision #28

Art. 7.4.X7. Time and place of delivery

§1. The service provider must deliver the service within the period agreed by the parties.

§2. If no period is agreed in the service contract, the service shall be delivered within a reasonable period, taken into account the nature of the service and the circumstances under which it must be performed.

§3. The place of delivery is determined in accordance with Art. 5.203.

590. Acceptance of the performed service – Because the acceptance of the performed service has such important consequences,[2590] the modernised Belgian rules on the contract for services should also include a provision on this concept. As already mentioned above, an assessment and acceptance of the delivered performance by the client takes place in all service contracts, and it is therefore not limited to material (immovable) services. However, the form in which the acceptance takes place often differs. For intellectual services or services relating to movable goods, such as PSS, the acceptance often happens tacitly, for example by paying the price without reservations. For more important services, such as building contracts for immovable goods, the acceptance is most often (but not necessarily) explicitly formalised in an official report (*proces verbaal, procès verbal*).

Proposed provision #29 deals with the acceptance and its consequences. This provision was largely inspired by the Dutch rules of the contract for works, namely Article 7:758 DCC. Additionally, it was influenced by proposed Articles 7.4.9, 7.4.24 and 7.4.25 BCC of the Draft Law, which deal with the acceptance of the service, transfer of ownership and transfer of risk respectively.

2588 B. Kohl, "Le contrat d'entreprise: proposition de réforme du Code civil" in R. Jafferali, P. Foriers and E. Van Den Haute (eds.), *Entre tradition et pragmatisme. Liber amicorum Paul Alain Foriers*, Volume 1, Brussels, Larcier, 2021, (481) 492.

2589 Compare with proposed Art. 7.4.21 BCC.

2590 See *supra* no. 526: The acceptance releases the service provider from liability for non-conforming performance and at the same time transfers the risk from the service provider to the client (Art. 1788 old BCC).

The first paragraph of proposed provision #29 sets out the obligation of the client to inspect and accept the performed service within a reasonable time after the delivery. The acceptance may either be explicit or tacit. If the client does not accept or refuse the delivered service within a reasonable time, the client is deemed to have tacitly accepted it. If the service is not delivered on time or not in conformity with the contract, the client must refuse to accept it, or accept it with one or more reservations, as appropriate. Following the acceptance, the service provider will be released from liability for any lack of conformity which the client should reasonably have discovered (in other words, visible defects). On the other hand, the service provider remains liable for hidden defects after the acceptance of the work or service.

The first difference with the Draft Law lies in the fact that under proposed provision #29, the service provider does not have to accept the service at the place and time of delivery (unlike the Draft Law), but within a reasonable time after delivery. After all, especially in the case of PSS, it is perfectly possible that the service is delivered continuously. The requirement that the client must accept the performed service at the time and place of delivery would require the client to refuse acceptance of the service immediately when a lack of conformity arises during the performance of the continuously performed service. In many cases, however, a lack of conformity will not always become noticeable immediately, so a reasonable time is more appropriate. This is also the approach of the Dutch rules of the contract for works. The second difference with the Draft Law is the fact that the presumption of tacit acceptance if the client does not accept or refuse within a reasonable time is not included in the Draft Law. Instead, according to the explanatory memorandum of the Draft Law, in the absence of an acceptance by the client, the service provider may seek a judgment containing such (explicit) acceptance.[2591] In my view, it is not unreasonable to have a presumption of tacit acceptance to protect the interests of the service provider against clients who take too long to accept (or refuse) the service in order to escape their obligation to pay the price.

591. Handing-over and transfer of risk – The second paragraph of proposed provision #29 deals with the handing-over of a good resulting from the service, where applicable. It confirms the principle that the handing-over should happen at the time and place of delivery. This is in line with proposed Article 7.4.9 BCC. In addition, similar to proposed Article 7.4.25 BCC of the Draft Law, this paragraph provides that the risk is transferred following the acceptance of the service. This is also a (re-)codification of the current rules of the contract for services.[2592]

2591 See Explanatory Memorandum, *Parliamentary Papers* Chamber of Representatives 2023–24, no. 55–3973/001, 122.

2592 Compare with Art. 1788 old BCC.

Proposed Provision #29

Art. 7.4.X8. Acceptance of the service

§1. The client shall inspect and accept the performed service within a reasonable time after the delivery of the service.

The acceptance may be explicit or tacit. If the client does not accept or refuse the delivered service within a reasonable time, the client is deemed to have tacitly accepted it.

If the service is not delivered on time or not in conformity with the contract, the client shall refuse to accept it, or accept it with one or more reservations, as appropriate.

The acceptance of the service without reservation releases the service provider from liability for late performance or any lack of conformity that the client should reasonably have discovered at the time of acceptance.

§2. If the service implies the handing-over of a good resulting from the service, the client takes receipt of it at the place and time of acceptance. From this moment on, the good is at the client's risk.

§3. Where the service aims at manufacturing or constructing a good, the acceptance of the performed service by the client leads to the transfer of ownership of the good.

Nevertheless, the ownership of materials supplied by the service provider is transferred to the client as they are incorporated into a good over which the client has a right of ownership or a right of use in rem.

592. Transfer of ownership – The third paragraph of proposed provision #29 deals with the transfer of ownership if the service aims at manufacturing or constructing a good. It codifies the current rules on the contract for services and is fully aligned with proposed Article 7.4.24 BCC of the Draft Law.

B. Obligation to indemnify the client for own acts and acts of third parties

593. Obligation to indemnify the client for the service provider's own acts and acts of third parties – Proposed provision #30, which follows the approach of the Draft Law,[2593] is based on proposed provision #16. Thus, the principles applying to the service provider's obligation to indemnify

[2593] Compare with proposed Art. 7.4.26 BCC.

the client for his own acts and acts of third parties are largely the same as those under the rental contract (and can also be aligned with the rules of the sales contract).[2594] The main differences are the following. First, §1 requires that the acts be imputable to the service provider. This is logical since, contrary to the sales contract and the rental contract, the obligation to indemnify is either an obligation of means or an obligation of result and not an obligation of guarantee. Second, only legal claims on the good by third parties that originate before the transfer of ownership are covered by this obligation. This is explained by the fact that the acceptance of the performed service entails the transfer of ownership from the service provider to the client, which eliminates the risk of impairment of the good by legal claims of third parties due to a fault of the service provider. Paragraph 4 of proposed provision #30 clarifies that Articles 7.3.X18 (intervention in legal proceedings by the service provider), 7.3.X19 (exemption clauses) and 7.3.X20 (remedies) apply mutatis mutandis.

Proposed Provision #30

Art. 7.4.X9. Obligation to indemnify for own acts and acts of third parties

§1. The service provider must indemnify the client for his own acts and acts of third parties that impair the result of the service, provided these acts are imputable to him.

§2. The obligation to indemnify for own acts concerns, regardless of the date:

1° any impairment of the use or enjoyment of the good resulting from an act of the lessor; and

2° any legal claim on the good by the lessor.

§3. The obligation to indemnify for acts of third parties only concerns actual legal claims on the good by third parties, that originate before the transfer of ownership of the good.

This obligation to indemnify applies even to acts of third parties of which the service provider had no knowledge or could not have had knowledge.

However, this obligation to indemnify does not apply to the specific impairments that the lessor has expressly communicated to the client before the conclusion of the contract.

§4. Articles 7.3.X18 till 7.3.X20 shall apply mutatis mutandis.

[2594] Compare with *supra* no. 491–493.

4.4.3. TOWARDS AN EU DIRECTIVE ON THE QUALITY AND CONFORMITY OF (BUNDLES OF) SERVICES?

594. Towards EU harmonisation for service contracts and/or PSS? – Besides developing and promoting balanced standard contracts for PSS and modernising the national legal framework for the rental contract (for movables) and the contract for services (potentially complemented with standardisation of services), there is a third – more ambitious – option to be explored. This option involves the adoption of an EU directive on the quality and conformity of (bundles of) services and/or PSS contracts, as already proposed by several authors in legal doctrine.[2595] Regulating service contracts and/or PSS at EU level could, provided there is sufficient political will, lead to a broader harmonisation of private law, providing a robust legal framework for service contracts and/or PSS across the different EU Member States. So far, however, a more general reform of EU service contract law and harmonisation efforts for as-a-service contracts does not seem to be on the EU Commission's agenda. Nevertheless, this section explores some questions and concerns should the Commission decide to move forward with this idea.

595. Subject matter of the directive: general rules for all services or specific to PSS? – The first question to consider is the subject matter of the directive. There are roughly two possibilities. Either it applies to *all* service contracts (subject to some exceptions) (option 2a), or it takes a more *specific* approach, applying to "packages" or "bundles" of services, to capture the concept of as-a-service business models and PSS (option 2b).

596. Option 2a. General directive on conformity and quality of (almost) all service contracts – The first possible approach is developing a harmonised general legal framework for (almost) all service contracts (option 2a). For this legal framework, the DCD can act as a source of inspiration, essentially extending the consumer protection for services in the digital environment to the analogic environment.[2596] After all, this directive was innovative in that it did not focus on a strict distinction between different typologies of contracts,

---

[2595] See e.g. A. De Franceschi, "Ensuring Circularity in Service Contracts" in B. Keirsbilck, E. Terryn, J. Eyckmans, S. Rousseau and D. Voinot (eds.), *Servitization and circular economy: economic and legal challenges*, Antwerp, Intersentia, 2023, (167) 170–171; V. Mak and E. Terryn, "Circular Economy and Consumer Protection: The Consumer as a Citizen and the Limits of Empowerment Through Consumer Law", *Journal of Consumer Policy* 2020, vol. 43, (227) 241–242; F. Zoll, "From a Product-Based Economy to Services? – Legal Aspects of an Economy in Transition" in B. Keirsbilck and E. Terryn (eds.), *Consumer Protection in a Circular Economy*, Antwerp, Intersentia, 2019, (149) 154.

[2596] A. De Franceschi, "Ensuring Circularity in Service Contracts" in B. Keirsbilck, E. Terryn, J. Eyckmans, S. Rousseau and D. Voinot (eds.), *Servitization and circular economy: economic and legal challenges*, Antwerp, Intersentia, 2023, (167) 171.

but on the contrary used general and overarching notions of non-performance applicable to a wide spectrum of different contracts.[2597] Additionally or alternatively, the general rules in the DCFR on service contracts can also be considered for drafting these general rules. In essence, this would boil down to also introducing the EU concept of conformity for services contracts. However, due to the above-mentioned heterogeneity of services, developing general rules for (almost) all services in the analogic environment will not be an easy task. Additionally, two other downsides to this approach can be identified. Most likely, there will have to be significant exceptions from the scope of the directive (e.g. financial services, healthcare services, transport services, rental contracts,[2598] etc.).[2599] Moreover, due to the large scope of the directive, there is a risk that the provisions on conformity and quality of the service will have to remain quite broad and vague. This would still leave a need for interpretation through case law, contractual provisions, standardisation of services, etc. Still, adopting a harmonised concept of conformity for (almost) all service contracts would be a significant step forward from the status quo.

597. Option 2b. Specific directive for "packages" or "bundles" of services – Option 2b consists in the adoption of a more specific directive for PSS. This way, the heterogeneity of services is addressed one directive (and one type of services) at a time. In order to avoid terminological difficulties caused to the plethora of descriptions and the often-complex nature of servitised business models (e.g. PSS, product-as-a-service, access-based consumption, etc.), it is necessary to use neutral legal concepts for defining the scope of this directive. This can be done, for example, by referring to a "package" or "bundle" of services relating to the use of a product or to a specific functional result. Inspiration for this provision on the scope of the directive can be found in the Package Travel Directive,[2600] which applies to "packages" of two or more travel services.[2601]

2597 See in this sense: F. Zoll, "From a Product-Based Economy to Services? – Legal Aspects of an Economy in Transition" in B. Keirsbilck and E. Terryn (eds.), *Consumer Protection in a Circular Economy*, Antwerp, Intersentia, 2019, (149) 154 and A. De Franceschi, "Ensuring Circularity in Service Contracts" in B. Keirsbilck, E. Terryn, J. Eyckmans, S. Rousseau and D. Voinot (eds.), *Servitization and circular economy: economic and legal challenges*, Antwerp, Intersentia, 2023, (167) 171.

2598 Potentially, a distinction here could be made between rental contracts for immovables and rental contracts for movables. It seems like especially the former category would benefit from a national contract law approach, but arguably rental contracts for movables are also better regulated at the national level. See *supra* no. 538.

2599 Compare also with Art. 2(2) SD, excluding various activities from the scope of the Services Directive.

2600 Directive (EU) 2015/2302 of the European Parliament and of the Council of 25 November 2015 on package travel and linked travel arrangements, amending Regulation (EC) No 2006/2004 and Directive 2011/83/EU of the European Parliament and of the Council and repealing Council Directive 90/314/EEC, *OJ L* 326, 11.12.2015, 1–33.

2601 See Art. 2(1) *juncto* Art. 3(2) Package Travel Directive.

598. Content of the directive: expanding the rules of the DCD (where possible) to the analogic environment? – The next question that arises is as to what content the directive should have. Also here, there are roughly two options. A first option is to stick purely to rules regarding conformity and quality and the remedies for non-conformity, in a similar way to the DCD. This option seems particularly useful if the chosen solution is adopting a general directive for all service contracts (option 2a), as these concepts apply more or less across the board to all services regardless of their heterogeneity.

599. Content of the directive: fully-fledged system of rules for "packages" or "bundles" of services? – A second option consists in adopting a fully-fledged system of rules for "package services" or "bundles of services", similar to the Package Travel Directive.[2602] Indeed, this maximum harmonisation[2603] directive contains rules in the various stages of the package travel contract, including rules on precontractual information and requirements regarding the content of the contract[2604]; rules on changes to the contract[2605]; rules on the performance of the contract, including remedies for non-performance and assistance obligations[2606]; and rules protecting the traveller from insolvency of the organiser.[2607] This approach seems most useful for a specific directive on PSS (option 2b), setting out rules regarding precontractual information and content of the PSS contract (including the characteristics of the service, output specifications and the way the price is calculated), performance and non-performance of the service (including remedies), and rules regarding changes to the service or the terms of the PSS contract. Additionally, the adoption of rules in this directive that provide safeguards for the PSS user in case of insolvency of the PSS supplier can also be considered. These safeguards may include a right of first refusal for the product, but also rules on refunds of payments made by the PSS user as the promised services are not performed, or even the possibility of continuing (part of) the PSS contract with a third party/another PSS supplier.

600. Minimum or maximum harmonisation? – A third question concerns the level of harmonisation of the directive. As is well known, EU law

[2602] Compare with F. Zoll, "From a Product-Based Economy to Services? – Legal Aspects of an Economy in Transition" in B. Keirsbilck and E. Terryn (eds.), *Consumer Protection in a Circular Economy*, Antwerp, Intersentia, 2019, (149) 154.

[2603] See Art. 4 Package Travel Directive.

[2604] Art. 5–7 Package Travel Directive.

[2605] See Art. 9 Package Travel Directive (transfer of the package travel contract to another traveller), Art. 10 Package Travel Directive (changes to the price) and Art. 11 Package Travel Directive (changes of other contract terms). Additionally, Art. 12 Package Travel Directive provides rules regarding the termination of the package travel contract and a right of withdrawal before the start of the package.

[2606] See Art. 13–16 Package Travel Directive.

[2607] Art. 17–18 Package Travel Directive.

distinguishes between minimum and maximum (or full) harmonisation.[2608] Minimum harmonisation directives set a minimum threshold that national implementing provisions must meet. However, national implementing provisions may go further, for example by adopting or maintaining national legislation that provides a higher level of consumer protection (also called "gold-plating").[2609] With maximum harmonisation, on the other hand, there is no more room for divergent national provisions within the scope of the harmonised rules. Deviating from the EU rules is only possible if the maximum harmonisation directive itself provides for exceptions or based on the "escape hatches" of Article 114(4) and (5) TFEU.[2610]

601. (Criticised) arguments in favour of maximum harmonisation – In the field of European consumer law, maximum harmonisation has been the preferred and prevailing harmonisation technique to achieve a "high level of consumer protection" since the start of the 21st century.[2611] The big proponents of maximum harmonisation are mainly businesses and the European Commission. The arguments in favour of maximum harmonisation can be summarised as follows.[2612] First, within the harmonised area, businesses face less divergent national legal rules, which would facilitate cross-border trade and reduce transaction costs. For consumers, the consequence of maximum harmonisation is that only one set of rules applies in the EU, which is said to increase consumer confidence in cross-border trade, contributing in turn to the realisation of the internal market. Finally, maximum harmonisation would lead to more legal certainty, which benefits both consumers and business.[2613] However, with regard

2608 R. Schulze, F. Zoll and J. Watson, *European Contract Law*, Baden-Baden, Nomos München, Oxford, Hart Publishing, 2021, 14–15.

2609 See H.-W. Micklitz, N. Reich and S. Weatherill, "EU Treaty Revision and Consumer Policy", *Journal of Consumer Policy* 2004, vol. 27, (367) 385–386 pointing out that the minimum harmonisation nature of EU consumer law initially appeased the Member States by ensuring that there was still room for national policy goals and more stringent consumer protection.

2610 E. Terryn and E.V. Irambona, *Duurzame consumptie en maximum harmonisatie: water en vuur?*, Available at SSRN: https://ssrn.com/abstract=4376907, 2023, 10; H.-W. Micklitz, "Squaring the Circle? Reconciling Consumer Law and the Circular Economy", *EuCML* 2019, vol. 6, (229) 234. See also: C.M.D.S. Pavillon, "Herijking van consumentencontractenrecht: duurzaamheid als nieuw ijkpunt?" in C.M.D.S. Pavillon and W.H. van Boom (eds.), *Preadviezen Vereniging voor Burgerlijk Recht: Privaatrechtelijke bescherming herijkt*, Zutphen, Paris, 2021, (11) 54.

2611 EC, *Consumer Policy Strategy 2002–2006*, 7.5.2002, COM(2002) 208 final, point 3.1.2. See also: EC, *Green paper on the Review of the Consumer Acquis*, 8.2.2007, COM(2006) 744 final 6–7 and 10–11.

2612 See for these arguments e.g. EC, *Green paper on the Review of the Consumer Acquis*, 8.2.2007, COM(2006) 744 final, as cited and summarised by E. Terryn and E.V. Irambona, *Duurzame consumptie en maximum harmonisatie: water en vuur?*, Available at SSRN: https://ssrn.com/abstract=4376907, 2023, 11.

2613 E. Terryn and E.V. Irambona, *Duurzame consumptie en maximum harmonisatie: water en vuur?*, Available at SSRN: https://ssrn.com/abstract=4376907, 2023, 11.

to consumer contract law and commercial practices law, these arguments have already been extensively criticised in legal doctrine.[2614] For instance, scholars point to the lack of convincing empirical evidence that maximum harmonisation is necessary to encourage consumers to engage in cross-border trade.[2615] Additionally, they question the reduction of transaction costs as harmonisation evidently also entails transaction costs.[2616] Furthermore, they point out that as long as there is no fully harmonised European private law,[2617] businesses still have to take into account different rules of national private law when drafting contracts, even with maximum harmonisation.[2618] This was recently illustrated by the 27 EU-wide national reports presented at a conference in Ferrara on "Harmonising Digital Contract Law, The Impact of the EU Directives 2019/770 and 2019/771 and the Regulation of Digital Platforms" organised by ALBERTO DE FRANCESCHI and REINER SCHULZE.[2619] The conference showed that despite the maximum harmonisation nature, the different national approaches to implementing these directives vary widely, resulting in an increasingly complex

2614 See e.g. E. TERRYN and E.V. IRAMBONA, *Duurzame consumptie en maximum harmonisatie: water en vuur?*, Available at SSRN: https://ssrn.com/abstract=4376907, 2023, 11–12; E. TERRYN, *Bedenktijden in het consumentenrecht*, Antwerp, Intersentia, 2008, 68–80; M. FAURE, "Towards a maximum harmonization of consumer contract law?!?", *Maastricht Journal of European and Comparative Law* 2008, vol. 15 issue 4, (433) 433–445; R. VAN DEN BERGH, "The Uneasy Case for Harmonising Consumer Law" in K. HEINE and W. KERBER (eds.), *Zentralität und Dezentralität von Regulierung in Europa*, Stuttgard, Lucius & Lucius, 2007, (184) 184–206; T. WILHELMSSON, "The Abuse of the Confident Consumer as a Justification for EC Consumer Law", *Journal of Consumer Policy* 2004, vol. 27 issue 3, (317) 317–377.

2615 See e.g. E. TERRYN, *Bedenktijden in het consumentenrecht*, Antwerp, Intersentia, 2008, 69–70 and the studies and references cited there.

2616 See e.g. M. FAURE, "Towards a maximum harmonization of consumer contract law?!?", *Maastricht Journal of European and Comparative Law* 2008, vol. 15, afl. 4, (433) 439–341.

2617 Attempts for moving towards a more comprehensive harmonisation of European private law have so far proved unsuccessful. See for example the withdrawn proposal on a Common European Sales Law ('CESL'): EC, *Proposal for a Regulation of the European Parliament and of the Council on a Common European Sales Law*, 11.10.2011, COM(2011) 635 final and the Commission's 2008 proposal for the CRD aiming to combine the Doorstep Sales Directive 85/377/EEC, the Distance Selling Directive 97/7/EC, The Unfair Contract Terms Directive 93/13/EEC and the Consumer Sales Directive 1999/44/EC into one directive EC, *Proposal for a Directive of the European Parliament and of the Council on consumer rights*, 8.10.2008, COM(2008) 614, final, which was met with much resistance from Member States and legal scholars. See: H.-W. MICKLITZ and N. REICH, "Crónica de una muerte anunciada: the Commission Proposal for a 'Directive on Consumer Rights'", *CML Rev.* 2009, vol. 46, (471) 471–519; P. ROTT and E. TERRYN, "The Proposal for a Directive on Consumer Rights: No Single Set of Rules", *ZEUP* 2009, vol. 3, (456) 456–488. This ultimately led to a much-reduced version of the proposal being adopted, replacing only the Doorstep Selling Directive and Distance Selling Directive, and leaving the Unfair Contract Terms Directive and Consumer Sales Directive unchanged.

2618 E. TERRYN and E.V. IRAMBONA, *Duurzame consumptie en maximum harmonisatie: water en vuur?*, Available at SSRN: https://ssrn.com/abstract=4376907, 2023, 11.

2619 See for the published national reports: A. DE FRANCESCHI and R. SCHULZE (eds.), *Harmonizing Digital Contract Law. The Impact of EU Directives 2019/770 and 2019/771 and the Regulation of Online Platforms*, Beck, Hart, Nomos, 2023, 608 p.

and sometimes even fragmented national law, where rules in national civil codes can at times be more favourable to consumers.[2620]

602. Arguments in favour of minimum harmonisation – Despite the prevailing use of maximum harmonisation for consumer contract law directives since the turn of the century, there are still arguments pro minimum harmonisation. For example, minimum harmonisation allows taking into account differences in national expectations and/or different needs of consumers.[2621] This is certainly relevant for PSS, as the range and uptake of B2C as-a-service business models is not yet the same in every EU Member State. Additionally, minimum harmonisation avoids the risk that Member States and their administrations are reduced to "implementation bodies" that merely copy and paste the EU provisions into national law without any critical thinking.[2622] Especially in the area of service contract law, where finding common ground between Member States has already proved difficult in the past,[2623] minimum harmonisation can ensure that minimum rules can be set at EU level while leaving room for national approaches and accents. Furthermore, minimum harmonisation allows for gold-plating EU law, not only from the point of view of consumer protection, but also in terms of sustainability. Therefore, as convincingly argued by Terryn & Irambona, it can facilitate much-needed national experiments regarding environmental sustainability, which can also inspire[2624] the European legislator.[2625]

603. Alternative: regulatory sandboxes? – Besides minimum harmonisation, there exists another solution for facilitating national experimentation for promoting environmental sustainability in consumer law. Indeed, as argued by Terryn & Irambona and Micklitz et al., the practice of setting up "regulatory sandboxes" may create opportunities for national experiments without the risk of fragmenting the internal market associated

---

2620 H.-W. Micklitz, "The Full Harmonization Dream", *EuCML* 2022, vol. 11 issue 4, (117) 117–121.

2621 E. Terryn and E.V. Irambona, *Duurzame consumptie en maximum harmonisatie: water en vuur?*, Available at SSRN: https://ssrn.com/abstract=4376907, 2023, 12.

2622 H.-W. Micklitz, "The Full Harmonization Dream", *EuCML* 2022, vol. 11, afl. 4, (117) 120.

2623 Compare with EC, *Proposal for a Council Directive on the liability of suppliers of services*, 18.1.1991, COM(90) 482 final which was ultimately shut down by the Commission due to fierce opposition by the Member States.

2624 See Recital 46 EC, *Proposal for a Regulation of the European Parliament and of the Council establishing a framework for setting ecodesign requirements for sustainable products and repealing Directive 2009/125/EC*, 30.3.2022, COM(2022) 142 final, referring to recent national initiatives such as those in France and Germany that aim to avoid the destruction of unsold consumer products.

2625 E. Terryn and E.V. Irambona, *Duurzame consumptie en maximum harmonisatie: water en vuur?*, Available at SSRN: https://ssrn.com/abstract=4376907, 2023, 13.

with leaving maximum harmonisation completely behind.[2626] Regulatory sandboxes are temporary experimental legal frameworks that allow innovative products and services to be safely tested in a real-life environment controlled by a regulator or competent authority, without a risk of compromising the legal system as a whole.[2627] This can, for example, be done by waiving or modifying regulatory or implementation requirements, or by providing bespoke guidance and certainty about the application of certain rules to specific situations.[2628] So far, regulatory sandboxes have already been used at the national level in diverse sectors such as the financial services sector, energy sector and transport sector.[2629] Moreover, following the conclusions of the Council of the European Union on the benefits of regulatory sandboxes,[2630] the European Commission introduced a provision on regulatory sandboxes in the proposal for a Regulation on Artificial Intelligence ("the AI Act").[2631]

604. Regulatory sandboxes within consumer (service) (contract) law? – Also within the field of consumer (service) (contract) law, one might consider using or allowing national regulatory sandboxes to pursue sustainability goals. After all, promoting sustainable consumption also requires innovative legal solutions and business models, including PSS. A prerequisite for regulatory sandboxes, however, is that the results and effects of these national experiments

2626 E. Terryn and E.V. Irambona, *Duurzame consumptie en maximum harmonisatie: water en vuur?*, Available at SSRN: https://ssrn.com/abstract=4376907, 2023, 17–20; H.-W. Micklitz, V. Mehnert, L. Specht-Riemenscheider, C. Liedtke and P. Kenning, *Recht auf Reparatur. Veröffentlichungen des Sachverständigenrats für Verbraucherfragen*, Berlin, Sachverständigenrat für Verbraucherfragen, 2022, 58.

2627 S. Ranchordas, "Experimental lawmaking in the EU: Regulatory Sandboxes", *University of Groningen Faculty of Law Research Paper* No. 12/2021, 22 October 2021, Available at SSRN: https://ssrn.com/abstract=3963810, (1) 1–2; T. Madiega and A.L. Van De Pol, *Artificial intelligence act and regulatory sandboxes*, https://www.europarl.europa.eu/RegData/etudes/BRIE/2022/733544/EPRS_BRI(2022)733544_EN.pdf, European Parliamentary Research Service, PE 733.544 – June 2022, 2; Council of the European Union, *Council Conclusions on Regulatory sandboxes and experimentation clauses as tools for an innovation-friendly, future-proof and resilient regulatory framework that masters disruptive challenges in the digital age*, 16 November 2020, https://data.consilium.europa.eu/doc/document/ST-13026-2020-INIT/en/pdf.

2628 S. Ranchordas, "Experimental lawmaking in the EU: Regulatory Sandboxes", *University of Groningen Faculty of Law Research Paper* No. 12/2021, 22 October 2021, Available at SSRN: https://ssrn.com/abstract=3963810, (1) 1.

2629 See for a discussion of some examples: E. Terryn and E.V. Irambona, *Duurzame consumptie en maximum harmonisatie: water en vuur?*, Available at SSRN: https://ssrn.com/abstract=4376907, 2023, 18.

2630 Council of the European Union, *Council Conclusions on Regulatory sandboxes and experimentation clauses as tools for an innovation-friendly, future-proof and resilient regulatory framework that masters disruptive challenges in the digital age*, 16 November 2020, https://data.consilium.europa.eu/doc/document/ST-13026-2020-INIT/en/pdf.

2631 See Art. 53 EC, *Proposal for a Regulation of the European Parliament and of the Council laying down harmonised rules on Artificial Intelligence (Artificial Intelligence Act) and amening certain legislative acts*, 21.4.2021, COM(2021) 206 final.

are thoroughly monitored at EU level, both to avoid the risk of fragmentation of the internal market and so that these experiments can in turn lead to successful experiments being given a European legal framework.[2632]

Policy Recommendation #3

- **Consider further harmonisation of rules on service contracts by means of an EU directive. This could either take the form of further extending the principles from the DCD to the analogue environment (i.e. broader scope), or by adopting a specific directive for "packages" or "bundles" of services relating to the use of a product or to a specific functional result (i.e. more specific scope). The Package Travel Directive can serve as a source of inspiration for the latter solution.**
- **Consider leaving enough room for Member States to have their own national approaches and accents for rules on service contracts. This can either be done by using a minimum harmonisation technique for this directive, by setting up "regulatory sandboxes" that allow for national experiments, or by providing sufficient exceptions to the maximum harmonisation nature of the directive that allow to go further, also in terms of guaranteeing the environmental sustainability of service contracts and PSS.**

4.5. MODEL CLAUSES ON AVAILABILITY OF THE PRODUCT/SERVICE

605. Model clauses on availability of the product/service – This section sets out model clauses dealing with the obligation to make the product available and to ensure the conformity of the product/service with the PSS contract. Although some of these clauses are specifically drafted for use-oriented PSS or result-oriented PSS respectively, they can often be used for both types of PSS contracts (sometimes provided minor modifications are made). After all, the obligation to make the product/service available will often boil down to the same principles in both use-oriented and result-oriented PSS, namely providing the product/service and ensuring its enjoyment and availability.

606. Model clauses on making the product available – In use-oriented PSS, the obligation to make the product/service available means the PSS supplier will have to deliver the rented product to the PSS user. The first model clause sets out the general right of the PSS user to use the product. Here, the product can be

[2632] E. Terryn and E.V. Irambona, *Duurzame consumptie en maximum harmonisatie: water en vuur?*, Available at SSRN: https://ssrn.com/abstract=4376907, 2023, 19.

described and identified so the PSS user knows which product he can expect.[2633] The second model clause stipulates the PSS supplier's delivery obligation, including the modalities for delivery (place and time). The third model clause confirms the fact that the rented product should be in a good state of repair, suitable for its ordinary use or the PSS user's intended use. As such, this model clause contains the obligation for the PSS supplier to deliver a product that is in conformity with the contract. The fourth model clause deals with the PSS user's obligation to report any defects of the delivered product within a reasonable amount of time.

Model clause #16: obligation to make the product available

- **For the duration of the contract, [the PSS user] will have the use of [description of the product].**
- **[The PSS supplier] makes the product available to [the PSS user] [within specified reasonable period of time after conclusion of the contract/on a specified date] at [location of delivery (e.g. the house of the PSS user)].[2634]**
- **[The PSS supplier] ensures that the product is [in a good condition/in a good state of repair], suitable for [its ordinary use/the use intended by the PSS user].[2635]**
- **[The PSS user] reports any defects of the product within [reasonable period of time] to [the PSS supplier].[2636]**

607. Model clause on providing the service – This clause contains the obligation for the PSS supplier in a result-oriented PSS contract to provide the service. It explicitly refers to the output specifications, which can be defined elsewhere in the contract.[2637] Additionally, this model clause clarifies that part of the obligation to provide the service is making the product(s) required for the performance of the service available to the PSS user. These products may either be explicitly listed in (an annex to) the contract or left to the discretion of the PSS supplier. The modalities of the delivery (time and place) may also be included.

2633 See *supra* no. 433 for examples of how this description can be included in the PSS contract.

2634 Model clause based partly on: C. Borucki, H. Slachmuylders, B. Keirsbilck, D. Gruyaert and E. Terryn, *Model clauses for Product-as-a-Service (PaaS) contracts*, CE Center. Circular Economy Policy Research Center, 2022–23, 45.

2635 *Ibid.*

2636 *Ibid.*

2637 See for model clauses on output specifications *infra* no. 608.

Model clause #17: obligation to provide the service

- **[The PSS supplier] shall provide the service in accordance with the terms of this contract, ensuring full compliance with the output specifications defined in [Art. X/Annex X]. To this end, [the PSS supplier] makes available to [the PSS user] the product(s) required for the performance of the service [as set out in the Art. Y/Annex Y] [within specified reasonable period of time after conclusion of the contract/on a specified date] at [location of delivery (e.g. the house of the PSS user)]. [The PSS user] has the product(s) at his disposal and may use it/ them [without limit/only for a specified number of uses, volumes or used/ for a specified number of uses, volumes or users and against payment of an extra fee if this specified number is exceeded] during the duration of the contract.**

608. Model clauses on output specifications – In result-oriented PSS contracts, the agreed performance in the PSS contract constitutes a starting point for assessing the conformity of the service. As mentioned above, output specifications can act as anchor points for assessing the conformity in result-oriented PSS as they define the minimum characteristic of the service to be provided.[2638] The following model clauses provide examples of contractual terms defining output specifications.

Model clause #18: definition of "output"[2639]

- **"Output" (e.g. light, air quality, hours of engine power, printed pages, etc.): [identification of the output specifications].**

- **(Example 1: "Output (light)": Light means the radiation of energy by a LED light source with a minimum level of brightness of 800 lm, a warm temperature colour of 2700 k and an energy efficiency of at least 100 lm/w.)**

- **(Example 2: "Output (printed pages)": The Service Plan allows the user 150 printed pages for one (1) month. A "printed page" is a page on which any amount of printing is done by the printer. Printing on both sides of the same sheet of paper counts as two (2) pages. Printed pages are A4 size, with a resolution of 600 x 600 dpi for black text on plain paper and 2400 x 1200 dpi for colour prints using photo paper. The minimum capacity of the printer is 12 ppm[2640] for black ink and 10 ppm for coloured ink.)**

2638 See *supra* no. 518.

2639 Model clauses based partly on: C. Borucki, H. Slachmuylders, B. Keirsbilck, D. Gruyaert and E. Terryn, *Model clauses for Product-as-a-Service (PaaS) contracts*, CE Center. Circular Economy Policy Research Center, 2022–23, 3.

2640 Ppm = 'pages per minute'.

609. Model clause on availability of the product/quiet rental enjoyment – This clause translates the obligation of the lessor to ensure the quiet rental enjoyment of the rented good to the context of a use-oriented PSS contract. This way, it obliges the PSS supplier to ensure the continuous availability of the product to the PSS user.

Model clause #19: availability of the product[2641]

- **[The PSS supplier] ensures [the PSS user's] quiet rental enjoyment of the product throughout the duration of the contract.**

610. Model clauses on availability of the service – In result-oriented PSS contracts (but often also in use-oriented PSS), the conformity of the service will be assessed in light of the promised continuity and availability of the service. Therefore, contracts for (result-oriented) PSS need to include a model clause on the availability of the service. As mentioned above,[2642] depending on the wording of the contractual terms, these obligations will be qualified as an obligation of means or an obligation of result. Examples of model clauses for both types of obligations are set out below.

Model clause #20: availability of the service (obligation of means)[2643]

- **[The PSS supplier] uses [all reasonable/best efforts] to ensure a continuous availability of the [product/service].**

Model clause #21: availability of the service (obligation of result)[2644]

- **[The PSS supplier] guarantees a continuous availability of the [product/service], except in cases of *force majeure*.**
- **[The PSS supplier] guarantees the availability of the [product/service] for [95%] of the time.**

2641 Model clause based on: C. Borucki, H. Slachmuylders, B. Keirsbilck, D. Gruyaert and E. Terryn, *Model clauses for Product-as-a-Service (PaaS) contracts*, CE Center. Circular Economy Policy Research Center, 2022–23, 45.

2642 See *supra* no. 519.

2643 Model clause based partly on: C. Borucki, H. Slachmuylders, B. Keirsbilck, D. Gruyaert and E. Terryn, *Model clauses for Product-as-a-Service (PaaS) contracts*, CE Center. Circular Economy Policy Research Center, 2022–23, 45.

2644 Model clauses based partly on: C. Borucki, H. Slachmuylders, B. Keirsbilck, D. Gruyaert and E. Terryn, *Model clauses for Product-as-a-Service (PaaS) contracts*, CE Center. Circular Economy Policy Research Center, 2022–23, 45.

611. Model clauses on planned interruptions – In addition to model clauses on the availability of the service, model clauses on planned and unplanned interruptions also serve a crucial purpose, both in result-oriented and use-oriented PSS contracts. After all, these interruptions will influence the effective availability of the product/service. Planned interruptions are often required due to maintenance, upgrades, or other pre-arranged activities necessary for the proper functioning of the product or service. As these interruptions are foreseeable, it is not unreasonable to require the PSS supplier to make all reasonable efforts to minimise the impact of these interruptions and to warn the PSS user in advance of these planned interruptions within a reasonable time. Planned interruptions may affect the output specifications of the result-oriented PSS. Therefore, the clause should also outline how such events will be factored into the evaluation and measurement of the promised performance. These can either fully count towards the output specifications outlined in the PSS contract or the SLA, or they can be excluded (potentially provided the total time of these unplanned interruptions remains under a maximum amount of time).

Model clause #22: planned interruptions

- [The PSS supplier] may need to perform planned maintenance, upgrades or other necessary activities that could result in interruptions to the service. [The PSS supplier] shall make reasonable efforts to minimise the impact of planned interruptions and provide written notice to the User of any planned interruptions at least [48 hours, one week, etc.] in advance. The notice shall include the date, time, and expected duration of the planned interruption, as well as any alternative arrangements or workarounds, if applicable.

- Planned interruptions shall be limited to a maximum of [4 hours, 24 hours, etc.] per occurrence.

- [The PSS supplier] shall adhere to the agreed-upon output specifications and Service Level Agreement (SLA) regarding availability of the service. Planned interruptions shall be counted towards downtime or unavailability and may trigger the compensation or remedies outlined in the SLA, if applicable.

- Planned interruptions shall not be counted towards downtime or unavailability, and any impact on the output specifications shall be excluded during these periods.

- Planned interruptions shall not be counted towards downtime or unavailability, and any impact on the output specifications shall be excluded during these periods, provided that the total duration of all planned interruption does not exceed [24 hours] per [week, month, year].

612. Model clauses on unplanned interruptions – Contrary to planned interruptions, unplanned interruptions are generally unforeseeable. If an unplanned interruption occurs, it is important to ensure that the service is restored as soon as possible. Additionally, it is opportune for the PSS supplier to provide a diagnosis of the problem to the PSS user as soon as possible, as well as an expected timeline for resolution. The first model clause below addresses all these issues. The next question that arises is as to what consequences there are for unplanned interruptions in terms of contractual liability of the PSS supplier. Generally, unplanned interruption will count towards downtime and unavailability and may give rise to damages and/or compensation. Therefore, the second model clause confirms that unplanned interruptions shall be counted towards downtime or unavailability and may trigger the contractual liability of the PSS supplier.

Model clause #23: unplanned interruptions

- **Unforeseen events or circumstances may lead to unplanned interruptions in the service. [The PSS supplier] shall make reasonable efforts to promptly resolve any unplanned interruptions and restore the service to its normal operation. [The PSS supplier] shall notify the User of any unplanned interruptions as soon as possible, detailing the nature of the interruption and the expected timeline for resolution.**
- **[The PSS supplier] shall adhere to the agreed-upon output specifications and Service Level Agreement (SLA) regarding availability of the service. Unplanned interruptions shall be counted towards downtime or unavailability and may trigger the compensation or remedies outlined in the SLA, if applicable.**

613. Model clauses on assistance in case of unavailability – The PSS contract should also include clauses on assistance in case of unplanned interruptions or any other availability of the service. Generally, the PSS user has the right that the interruption is resolved as soon as possible. Depending on the wording of the clause, the obligation of the PSS supplier to provide customer assistance in case of unavailability will be qualified as an obligation of result or obligation of means. Examples for both types of obligations are set out below.

Model clause #24: assistance in case of unavailability (obligation of result)

- **In the event of unavailability of the service or any other disruption in its functioning, [The PSS supplier] restores access to the service within [48 hours].[2645]**

[2645] Model clause based on: C. Borucki, H. Slachmuylders, B. Keirsbilck, D. Gruyaert and E. Terryn, *Model clauses for Product-as-a-Service (PaaS) contracts*, CE Center. Circular Economy Policy Research Center, 2022–23, 46.

- **[The PSS supplier] will respond to any reported service unavailability within [24 hours] of receiving a notification from the User. Upon receiving a notification of service unavailability, [the PSS supplier] shall resolve the issue and restore the service to its normal functioning within [48 hours].**

Model clause #25: assistance in case of unavailability (obligation of means)

- **In the event of unavailability of the service or any other disruption in its functioning, the [PSS supplier] uses [all reasonable efforts/best efforts] to restore access to the service as soon as possible.**[2646]

- **[The PSS supplier] makes [reasonable efforts] to respond to any reported service unavailability within [24 hours] of receiving a notification from the User. The response time may vary depending on the severity and complexity of the issue. Upon receiving a notification of service unavailability, [the PSS supplier] shall make [reasonable efforts] to resolve the issue and restore the service to its normal functioning within [48 hours]. The time to solution may vary depending on the nature of the problem, the availability of necessary resources (e.g. spare parts), and any third-party involvement required for solving the problem.**

4.6. CONCLUSION

614. Ensuring the availability of the product/service: conclusion – This chapter dealt with the main obligation of the PSS supplier, namely the obligation to ensure the availability of the product and or service. Two sub-obligations of this main obligation can be distinguished. First, the PSS supplier must make the product/service available, which generally implies a delivery obligation. Depending on how the PSS contract is qualified, the way the risk is transferred also differs. This obligation to deliver the product/service and the corresponding risk regime was discussed in section 4.2. Second, the product and/or service must be in conformity with the PSS contract. The questions regarding conformity requirements, liability for non-conformity and available remedies were discussed in section 4.3. Section 4.4 evaluated the current regulatory framework and made some normative recommendations, while also taking into account the draft law of 16 April 2024 inserting Book 7 "special contracts" into the Civil Code. Finally, section 4.5 listed some model clauses dealing with the obligation to ensure the availability of the product/service.

[2646] Model clause based on: C. Borucki, H. Slachmuylders, B. Keirsbilck, D. Gruyaert and E. Terryn, *Model clauses for Product-as-a-Service (PaaS) contracts*, CE Center. Circular Economy Policy Research Center, 2022–23, 46.

615. Conclusion on delivery of the product/service and transfer of risk – The first section of this chapter dealt with the **delivery of the product/service and the transfer or risk.**[2647]

In **product-oriented PSS**, the PSS user becomes the owner of the product that is the object of the PSS contract. As a result, the contract qualifies as a sales contract. Under both Belgian and Dutch law, the delivery is one of the main obligations of the PSS supplier-seller, implying that the sold product (and its accessories) must be transferred to the PSS user-buyer so that he can take control and possession over it. The concrete modalities of delivery (e.g. place and time) are generally regulated in the PSS contract. In the absence of contractual regulations, both Belgian law and Dutch law contain default rules on the modalities of the delivery. Moreover, the CRD provides that, unless the parties have agreed otherwise, the PSS supplier-seller must deliver the product without undue delay and in any case within 30 days from the conclusion of the contract.

As regards the question of transfer of risk, there is an essential difference between Belgian and Dutch law. Under Belgian law, both the transfer of ownership and the transfer of risk happen *solo consensu*, namely when the parties agree on the product and the price. Under Dutch law, on the other hand, the delivery determines the transfer of risk. However, in the case where the product is shipped to the consumer, the CRD provides that the risk of loss or damage to the product is only transferred when the PSS user-buyer (or someone he designates other than the carrier) takes physical possession of the product.

In **use-oriented PSS**, the PSS user no longer becomes the owner of the product but instead receives a right of use. This means that in most cases, the contract qualifies as a rental contract for movables. Both under Belgian and Dutch law, the PSS supplier-lessor will be obliged to deliver the product (and its accessories) to the PSS user-lessee, which can either be done by physically handing over the product, or by delivering the product symbolically or intellectually. The modalities of the delivery (e.g. place and time) are generally set out in the PSS contract. In the (rare) absence of contractual regulations, both Belgian and Dutch general contract law must be consulted for some rules of thumb. In any case, the Belgian blacklist prohibits the PSS supplier to unilaterally determine or change the delivery period. Similarly, the Dutch grey list contains a presumption that clauses providing for an unusually long or long or inadequately defined period for performance (i.e. delivery) are unreasonably onerous. The question was also discussed as to the validity of clauses stipulating that the PSS supplier may replace the product with a similar product if the PSS supplier deems it necessary. Both under Belgian law and Dutch law, such clauses may conflict with the unfair terms rules, especially in case of a (sharp) degradation of the new product's functionalities and specifications compared to the initial product.

2647 See *supra* section 4.2.

As regards the question of transfer of risk, both the Belgian and Dutch rental contract rules provide that damages to the product or losses thereof shall be borne by the PSS user, unless he can prove that they were caused by no fault of his own. Additionally, under Belgian law, the special (mandatory) risk regime arising from Article 20 CRD was implemented in the BCEL and extended to *all* contracts where a business sends goods to a consumer. As such, it also applies to rental contracts. The risk regime of the rental contract for movables is in principle not mandatory law. However, under Belgian law – and arguably also under Dutch law – contractual clauses imposing the risk for loss or damage to the product on the PSS user-consumer in case of *force majeure*, as is for example the case when the product is stolen and the PSS user has taken all necessary and reasonable precautions to avoid this, will be regarded unfair. This also includes clauses stipulating that the PSS user must pay a deductible if the product is stolen. A potential solution could be to require the PSS user to take out insurance.

In **result-oriented PSS**, as the object of the contract is a complex and integrated service, the contract no longer takes the form of a rental contract but a contract for services. In a contract for services, providing the service takes precedence and the product is made available to facilitate this provision of the service. In many cases, the product will be located with the PSS user (and therefore delivered to his premises). As such, the contract for services may be accompanied by an accessory deposit contract (where the PSS user is the depositary), including a contractual provision granting the PSS user a right of use over the product.

As regards the question of transfer of risk, the contract for services does not have as its object the transfer of ownership of the product. As a result, the PSS supplier – as owner – will bear the risk for loss or theft of the products for providing the service. Nevertheless, if the product has been destroyed or lost due to a fault by the PSS user, the latter will of course be contractually liable. If the contract for services is accompanied by an accessory deposit contract, the PSS user has a duty of care and an obligation to return the product. The duty of care is an obligation of means, requiring the PSS user to take the necessary precautions against loss or depreciation. The return obligation is an obligation of result, where the existence of *force majeure* in case the PSS user cannot return the product will be assessed in light of his duty of care. Just like under the rental contract for movables, the risk regime is not mandatory law. However, the risk of *force majeure* cannot be imposed on the PSS user-consumer, regardless of whether this is done explicitly or implicitly.

616. Conclusion on conformity of the product/service with the PSS contract – The second section of this chapter dealt with the **conformity of the product/service with the PSS contract.**[2648]

2648 See *supra* section 4.3.

In **product-oriented PSS**, the rules on (non-)conformity are fully harmonised by the SGD, which makes a distinction between subjective and objective conformity requirements. Subjective conformity requirements relate to what the contracting parties have stipulated in their contract, including precontractual discussions. Objective conformity requirements, on the other hand, are indirectly part of the contract because the consumer can reasonably expect them to be. Both sets of conformity should be seen side by side and complement each other without any hierarchical distinction. Since incorrect installation of the purchased product can also render it unusable for its intended purpose, the SGD also explicitly provides that any non-conformity arising from the incorrect installation of the product shall be regarded as a non-conformity of the product itself, provided: (i) the installation forms part of the contract and was carried out by the PSS supplier (or under its responsibility); or (ii) the installation was done by the PSS user and the incorrect installation is due to shortcomings in the installation instructions provided by the PSS supplier.

The PSS supplier is liable for any lack of conformity that exists at the time of delivery of the product during the guarantee period. Under the SGD and Belgian law, this guarantee period is two years from the delivery. Under Dutch law, on the other hand, an "open system" based on the expected lifetime of the product applies. To help consumers prove that a lack of conformity already existed at the time of delivery, the SGD provides for a (rebuttable) presumption period in which the anteriority of the lack of conformity is presumed. Under the SGD, this presumption period is one year, although Member States may introduce a longer period, as is the case under Belgian law (but not under Dutch law). If the product shows a lack of conformity, the PSS user-buyer has access to a number of remedies, characterised by a certain hierarchy (the so-called hierarchy of remedies). Repair and replacement are the primary remedies, while price reduction and termination are the secondary remedies. Almost all provisions of the SGD on (liability and remedies for) non-conformity (except for the objective conformity requirements) are mandatory law, so the contracting parties are not allowed to deviate from them in the product-oriented PSS contract.

In **use-oriented PSS**, there are no harmonised rules regarding (non-)conformity. As a result, it is a matter of national law (in particular, the rules of the rental contract) whether the delivered product "as-a-service" is in conformity with the PSS contract. Under both the Belgian and the Dutch rental contract rules, the conformity of the rented product is assessed both at the start and during the rental contract. Similar to the sales contract, the concept of conformity falls into two (types of) conformity requirements, namely subjective conformity (what the rental contract stipulates) and objective conformity (what the lessee may reasonably expect). At the start of the rental contract, the rented product must be in a good state of repair to be in conformity with the contract. During the rental contract, the PSS user-lessor must indemnify the PSS user-lessee for defects of the rented good (under Belgian law, this is known as the obligation to ensure the quiet rental enjoyment). This includes both material defects, as well as the PSS supplier-lessor's own acts and acts of third parties that impair the PSS user-lessee's use and enjoyment of the rented product. There are limits to the PSS supplier-lessor's obligation to indemnify for defects though. Both under Belgian and Dutch law, the PSS supplier-lessor will not be liable for (material) defects caused by the fault of the PSS user-consumer, as well as for minor (material) defects. However, as the concept of conformity is not mandatory law under both the Belgian and Dutch rental contract rules, deviating from these rules in the PSS contract is generally allowed. This means that the PSS contract may limit or expand the scope of the concept defect. For example, many PSS contracts stipulate that the PSS supplier-lessor is also responsible for remedying minor defects, to truly "unburden" the PSS user-lessee.

Similar to product-oriented PSS, the PSS supplier will incur liability if the rented product is not in conformity with the use-oriented PSS contract. Unlike the consumer sales rules, there is no similar legal guarantee period of two years. Instead, the PSS supplier is liable for defects that exist at the start of the PSS contract and those that arise during the PSS contract. As with the consumer sales contract, the PSS user must prove the non-conformity of the rented product. However, for rental contracts, the PSS user does not benefit from a presumption period. In fact, the PSS user is even (rebuttably) presumed to be liable for any damages or losses to the product that occurred during the PSS contract. He can escape this by proving that the damages existed before the start of the rental contract or that they are due to normal wear and tear. This burden of proof shifts if no rental inventory was drawn up at the start of the contract. Then, the PSS supplier must prove that the damage occurred during the PSS contract. These rules are not mandatory law so the parties can deviate from them in the PSS contract. As to the remedies for lack of conformity, the Belgian rental contract rules do not have a separate set of remedies in case of non-conformity of the rented product. This means that if the PSS user can prove the lack of conformity of the product, he has access to the remedies of general contract law. These remedies are not mandatory law. Under Dutch law, the PSS user has access to the specific remedies of the rental contract (repair, rent reduction, compensation for damages) as well as the remedies arising from general contract law. Contrary to Belgian law, these remedies are mandatory law in contracts with consumers for defects the PSS supplier knew or should have known.

If digital content or digital services are part of the use-oriented PSS contract, the rules of the DCD and its national implementation apply. Under these rules, the PSS supplier will be liable for any lack of conformity that exists at the time of delivery of the digital content or digital services. As regards the time limits, there are some differences between Belgian and Dutch law. Under Belgian law, the guarantee period for a use-oriented PSS contract featuring a single act of supply or a series of individual acts of supply of the digital content or digital services, the guarantee period shall be two years from the time of supply. If, on the other hand, the use-oriented PSS contract provides for a continuous supply of digital services or digital content, which will be the majority of the cases, the guarantee period is equal to the duration of the contract. Additionally, in both cases, the consumer's action for non-conformity is subject to a limitation period of one year from when he has discovered the lack of conformity. Under Dutch law, the consumer's action for non-conformity prescribes two years after the (in the case of contracts for continuous supply, last) delivery, unless the consumer did not know or should not have known of the defect, taking into account at least the price or digital representation of value and the reasonable expectations regarding the duration for which he can use the digital content or digital service. There are three (mandatory) remedies available to the PSS user in case of a lack of conformity of any digital content or digital service that is part of the PSS contract, namely having the digital content or digital service brought in conformity (i.e. performance in kind), proportionate price reduction or the termination of the contract. There is a hierarchy between these remedies. First, an attempt should be made to bring the digital content or service into conformity; only afterwards is the consumer entitled to proportionate price reduction or termination.

For **result-oriented PSS**, a harmonised legal framework on the concept of conformity and remedies for non-conformity is currently lacking at the EU level as well. Therefore, national contract law again provides the framework to determine whether the service provided is in conformity with the PSS contract. Under both the Belgian and Dutch contract for services, the obligation to perform the service in conformity with the contract entails that (i) the PSS supplier must perform the service according to what the parties have expressly agreed in the PSS contract (subjective conformity); (ii) where applicable, the PSS supplier must follow the instructions given by the PSS user; and (iii) the performed service must conform with what the client may reasonably expect, the so-called, "standards of good workmanship" (objective conformity). This obligation may either be an obligation of result or an obligation of means, depending on the specific circumstances of the case. In this sense, the contractual definition of the output specifications as well as the promised continuity of the service will play an important role in determining the nature of the obligation and by extension the conformity of the performed service. Additionally, technical standards adopted by a standardisation body may also be considered when assessing the conformity of the service.

As regards the question of liability for non-conformity, Belgian law makes a distinction between the period before and after the acceptance of the service. Before the acceptance of the service, the PSS supplier is liable for any late or non-conforming performance according to the general rules of contractual liability. After the acceptance, the PSS supplier is released from liability for non-conforming performance and/or (visible) defects and the PSS user will only be able to claim liability for hidden defects. Dutch law, on the other hand, does not have this strict distinction, but the PSS supplier will be liable for shortcomings in the performance of the service under the "ordinary" rules of general contract law. Both the Belgian and the Dutch rules of the contract for services do not contain specific rules on remedies available in case on non-conformity of the provided service. This means that the PSS user has access to the remedies of general contract law. These remedies are not mandatory law, so the PSS contract can deviate from them, modulate them, or even (partially) exclude (some of) them.

If digital content or digital services are part of the use-oriented PSS contract, the same rules on (liability for) non-conformity of the DCD and its national implementation, as discussed in the context of use-oriented PSS, apply.

617. CONCLUSION ON THE NECESSITY OF LEGISLATIVE INTERVENTIONS – The third section of this chapter has evaluated **the current regulatory framework** and has made some **normative recommendations**, taking into account the draft law of 16 April 2024 inserting Book 7 "special contracts" into the Civil Code.[2649]

The **current rental contract rules** already provide to a certain extent a useful legal framework for the PSS supplier's obligation to provide the product/service in use-oriented PSS. After all, both Belgian and Dutch law contain rules on making the rented product available and have a legal framework in place regarding the conformity of the product both at the start of the rental contract and during the rental contract. However, there are shortcomings to these legal rules, especially when considering the emerging trend of servitisation. In the first place, the conformity rules of the rental contract are formulated in general terms and not well adapted to movable goods. A more detailed conformity regime for the rental of movables – comparable to the concept of conformity in consumer sales contracts – would foster legal certainty for consumers. Second, when comparing the consumer sales rules with the rental contract for movables, it is clear that while the concept of conformity is roughly the same under both types of contracts, the conformity rules of the consumer sales contract are set out in much greater detail than the rental contract rules. From a coherence and consistency perspective, it is difficult to see why consumer's rights concerning the conformity of the product are regulated more comprehensively and more detailed if they gain access to a movable product by buying it, than if they merely wish to obtain its use and enjoyment under a rental contract/product-as-a-service contract. Additionally, the difference in legal position between a consumer-buyer and a consumer-lessee confronted with a lack of conformity is difficult to explain. Under the consumer sales contract rules, the starting point is

[2649] See *supra* section 4.4.

that the seller will be liable for any lack of conformity that existed at the time of delivery. The rental contract rules, on the other hand, have as their starting point that the consumer-lessee is liable to the lessor for any damage that occurred during the term of the contract. The rental contract rules then set out rules when the consumer-lessee is not liable to the lessor, for instance when no rental inventory was drawn up at the beginning of the contract, if the damage is due to normal wear and tear, of if the non-conformity qualifies as a defect for which the lessor is responsible. However, in principle, and contrary to the sales contract, minor defects remain the responsibility of the lessee (unless otherwise agreed in the contract). Finally, there are also strong arguments from a sustainability perspective for a stronger legal conformity regime for rental contracts for movables. Indeed, strengthening legal obligations for PSS suppliers-lessors to remedy defects may encourage them to provide better-maintained and longer-lasting products.

The **current rules of the contract for services**, at least under Belgian law, serve as one of the prime examples of regulatory obsolescence. Indeed, despite its very broad scope and the fact that it is the most widely used special contract together with the sales contract, the old BCC only devotes 13 (mostly non-mandatory) provisions to it, which remained unchanged since 1804. The current rules on the contract for services as they are set out in the old BCC are outdated, do not reflect developments in case law, and are not well adapted to new developments in practice, in particular (result-oriented) PSS. The Dutch rules on the contract for services, dating from 1992, are more recent and to some extent provide a more complete legal framework for service contracts. However, also these rules remain rather general and provide only little concrete guidance for as-a-service contracts in practice.

This chapter has proposed three possible solutions for the outdated and/or incomplete legal framework for use-oriented and result-oriented PSS. First, a proposal for **modernised national rules on conformity** for the Belgian rental contract (for movables) and the Belgian contract services was made (option 1). This option was chosen as the preferred solution.

For the rental contract, two sets of provisions were proposed, namely on the obligation to deliver the good in conformity with the contract and on the obligation to indemnify for the lessor's own acts and for acts of third parties. In developing these proposed provisions, an attempt was made to (re)codify the existing framework (including legal doctrine and case law) as much as possible, while also aligning it as much as possible with the rules on conformity in consumer sales contracts. In particular, the rules on (subjective and objective) conformity of rented goods at the start of the contract and during the contract were largely inspired on those of the consumer sales contract. Additionally, for B2C rental contracts for consumer goods (i.e. movables), it was proposed to deviate from the current rule that the lessee is responsible for minor defects.

Thus, it was proposed that the lessor should be liable for minor defects, unless they are due to improper use or lack of maintenance by the lessee, or if at the time of the conclusion of the contract, the consumer was specifically informed of this deviation, which he separately and expressly accepted. Moreover, it was proposed to elevate the conformity rules (and the rules on remedies for non-conformity) of the B2C rental contract for consumer goods to (semi-)mandatory law to ensure additional consumer protection and to align the rules with the consumer sales contract.

For the contract for services as well, an attempt was made to (re)codify the existing framework (including legal doctrine and case law) for conformity of services and align it with the rules of the (consumer) sales contract. Thus, two sets of provisions were proposed, namely on the performance and delivery of the service in conformity with the contract and on the obligation of the service provider to indemnify for his own acts and acts of third parties. In particular, there was specific attention to the role standardisation of services may play to assess the conformity of (result-oriented) PSS and service contracts in general.

Second, the option of an **EU directive** on the quality and conformity of (bundles of) services was explored (option 2). This is the more ambitious option, but – provided there is enough political will – could provide (use-oriented and result-oriented) PSS with a specific and detailed regulatory framework. Two possible approaches were highlighted. The first possible approach is developing a harmonised general legal framework for (almost) all service contracts (option 2a). For this legal framework, the DCD can act as a source of inspiration, essentially extending the consumer protection for services in the digital environment to the analogic environment. Additionally or alternatively, the rules of the DCFR can also be considered for drafting these general rules. The second option would be to adopt a more specific directive for PSS, by referring to a "package" or "bundle" of services related to the use of a product or a specific functional result (option 2b). Inspiration for such a directive can be found in the Package Travel Directive, which applies to "packages" of two or more travel services. Regardless of which approach is taken, to leave enough room for the Member States to have their own national approaches and accents for rules on service contracts, it was proposed to either use a minimum harmonisation technique for this directive, to set up "regulatory sandboxes" that allow for national experiments, or by providing sufficient exceptions to the nature of maximum harmonisation. So far, however, a more general reform of EU service contract law and harmonisation efforts for as-a-service contracts does not seem to be on the EU Commission's Agenda.

Third, **the use of balanced standard contracts and model clauses** was proposed (option 3). This solution can be considered the "low-hanging fruit" since it requires, in principle, no legislative intervention. The model clauses on the availability of the product/service were set out in the fourth section of this chapter.

618. Conclusion on model clauses for PSS supplier's obligation to ensure availability – The final section of this chapter has provided some **model clauses on the PSS supplier's obligation to ensure the availability of the product/service** for both use-oriented and result-oriented PSS.[2650]

Besides general clauses on the obligation to make the product or service available, these model clauses deal with output specifications, the availability of the product and/or service, planned and unplanned interruptions, and assistance in case of unavailability of the product and/or service. They include both examples of obligations of means and obligations of result.

[2650] See *supra* section 4.5.

5. PAYMENT OF THE PRICE

"Price is what you pay.
Value is what you get."
- Warren Buffet[2651]

5.1. INTRODUCTION

619. Main obligation of PSS user is paying the price – The main obligation of the PSS user is the obligation to pay the price stipulated in the PSS contract.[2652] This obligation is discussed in section 5.2 for the three main types of PSS. First, the legal framework of the obligation to pay the price is discussed. This includes the legal basis of the obligation to pay the price and the rules on the modalities of the payment. Second, this section looks at the different components of the price (e.g. periodical fee, pay-per-use fee, mandatory insurance fee, start-up cost, etc.) that may be included in the PSS contract. Third, the PSS supplier's transparency requirements regarding the price of the PSS are explored. Fourth, this section deals with the remedies in case of non-payment by the PSS user. In section 5.3, this chapter looks at price change clauses. These are clauses included in the PSS contract that allow the PSS supplier to increase the price, which are often used to hedge against changed circumstances. It discusses the limits to price change clauses and evaluates some examples of price change clauses found in the analysed PSS contracts. Additionally, clauses allowing to change the other terms of the PSS contract are also discussed in this section. Finally, section 5.4 addresses set off, which is a mode of extinguishment of obligations where the obligation of the PSS user to pay the price is "compensated" with a claim the PSS user has on the PSS supplier. In this section, the validity of and limits to set off clauses are also discussed.

2651 W.E. Buffett, *Berkshire Hathaway Inc 2008 Shareholder Letter*, www.berkshirehathaway.com/letters/2008ltr.pdf, 27 February 2009, 5.

2652 H. Slachmuylders, "Économie de la fonctionnalité – Le contrat de service: défis juridiques et solutions contractuelles", *Revue Juridique de l'Environnement* 2022, vol. 47, afl. 1, (111) 119.

5.2. OBLIGATION OF THE PSS USER TO PAY THE PRICE

5.2.1. LEGAL FRAMEWORK OF OBLIGATION TO PAY THE PRICE

620. Obligation to pay the price as essential characteristic of the PSS contract and main obligation for the PSS user – For each of the three main types of PSS, the obligation to pay the price constitutes an essential element of the PSS contract and the main obligation of the PSS user. As a result, contractual clauses on the price of the PSS will be regarded as "core terms" within the meaning of the UCTD and thus be exempt from the unfairness test (unless they are not transparent).[2653] This section discusses the legal basis of the PSS user's payment obligation.

621. Product-oriented PSS: paying the purchase price – As the PSS user becomes the owner of the product that is the object of a product-oriented PSS contract, the rules of the sales contract apply.[2654] Both the Belgian and Dutch sales contract rules explicitly conform that the buyer's main obligation is to pay the price.[2655] This also already follows from the definition of the sales contract.[2656]

622. Purchase price must be determined or determinable – The purchase price in product-oriented PSS must be determined or at least determinable.[2657] In most cases, the price to be paid is mentioned in the PSS offer or stated in the PSS contract, and thus explicitly determined. Alternatively, the price of a sales contract can also be determinable,[2658] e.g. if it can be determined based on (a series of) objective calculations, without an element of

2653 See *supra* no. 146.

2654 See *supra* no. 371.

2655 **Belgium**: Art. 1650 old BCC; V. Sagaert, B. Tilleman and A.-L. Verbeke, *Vermogensrecht in kort bestek*, Antwerp, Intersentia, 2022, 210; M. Dambre, *Bijzondere overeenkomsten: de essentie*, Bruges, Die Keure, 2022, 108. **The Netherlands**: Art. 7:26(1) DCC; P. Klik, *Koop en Consumentenkoop*, Deventer, Wolters Kluwer, 2022, 235; J. Hijma, *Mr. C. Assers Handleiding tot de beoefening van het Nederlands Burgerlijk Recht. 7. Bijzondere overeenkomsten. Deel I. Koop en ruil*, Deventer, Kluwer, 2019, no. 723.

2656 **Belgium**: See Art. 1582 old BCC, which defines the sales contract as *"a contract whereby one party undertakes to deliver a good and the other party undertakes to pay a price for it"* (own emphasis). See for a similar definition in **The Netherlands**: Art. 7:1 DCC: *"Sale is the agreement under which one party engages himself to give a good and the other party to pay a price for it"* (own emphasis).

2657 **Belgium**: See Art. 1591 old BCC. **The Netherlands**: J. Hijma, *Mr. C. Assers Handleiding tot de beoefening van het Nederlands Burgerlijk Recht. 7. Bijzondere overeenkomsten. Deel I. Koop en ruil*, Deventer, Kluwer, 2019, no. 393.

2658 **Belgium**: See Art. 5.49 BCC.

appreciation by the PSS supplier or user.[2659] Traditional examples are a market price, day price, and so on, but for product-oriented PSS, one can also imagine the price of the product being determined by a catalogue, depending on the specific characteristics of the product. Under both Belgian and Dutch law, letting a third party determine the price is also possible,[2660] but this option is not really used for (product-oriented) PSS. The question arises whether the price may also be determined unilaterally by the PSS supplier. While this is possible under the Belgian general law of obligations (e.g. in service contracts such as the contract for services or mandate), this is not the case for the sales contract.[2661] Moreover, in B2C relationships, the Belgian blacklist of unfair terms also explicitly prohibits the unilateral determination of the price by the PSS supplier at the time of delivery.[2662] In contrast, the unilateral determination of the price by one of the parties is valid under Dutch law,[2663] although it is subject to the requirements of reasonableness and fairness.[2664] However, in sales contracts with consumers, the buyer can terminate the contract if the seller increases the purchase price after the conclusion of the contract, unless it has been stipulated that delivery will take place more than three months after the sale.[2665]

623. Use-oriented PSS: paying the rental price – For use-oriented PSS, the qualification as a rental contract for movables implies that the main obligation of the PSS user is to pay the rental price at the agreed times.[2666] The rental price is agreed upon by both parties in the PSS contract and generally stays the same throughout the duration of the contract (potentially subject to indexation, see *infra*). Alternatively, the parties may agree to progressively increase or decrease the rent as the PSS contract continues.[2667] For example, with use-oriented PSS, it is an option to stipulate a discounted rental price if

---

2659 **Belgium**: V. Sagaert, B. Tilleman and A.-L. Verbeke, *Vermogensrecht in kort bestek*, Antwerp, Intersentia, 2022, 115–116. **The Netherlands**: J. Hijma, *Mr. C. Assers Handleiding tot de beoefening van het Nederlands Burgerlijk Recht. 7. Bijzondere overeenkomsten. Deel I. Koop en ruil*, Deventer, Kluwer, 2019, no. 393.

2660 **Belgium**: See Art. 1592 old BCC. **The Netherlands**: See Art. 1501(2) old DCC. This provision, however, did not make its return in the "new" DCC as it was deemed redundant. See: C.J. Van Zeben, J.W. Du Pon, W.H.M. Reehuis and E.E. Slob, *Parlementaire Geschiedenis van het Nieuwe Burgerlijk Wetboek. Invoering Boeken 3, 5 en 6: Boek 6: Algemeen gedeelte van het verbintenissenrecht*, Deventer, Kluwer, 1990, 54. Under current Dutch law, this situation is covered by the rules of the settlement agreement (*vaststellingsovereenkomst*). See Art. 7:900(2) DCC.

2661 P. Brulez, *Koop en aanneming: faux amis?*, Antwerp, Intersentia, 2015, 213–237.

2662 Art. VI.83, 2° and 3° BCEL.

2663 J. Hijma, *Mr. C. Assers Handleiding tot de beoefening van het Nederlands Burgerlijk Recht. 7. Bijzondere overeenkomsten. Deel I. Koop en ruil*, Deventer, Kluwer, 2019, no. 395.

2664 See Art. 7:904(1) *juncto* Art. 7:906(2) DCC.

2665 Art. 7:35 DCC. Compare also with Art. 6:236, *sub* i. DCC.

2666 **Belgium**: Art. 1728(2) old BCC. **The Netherlands**: Art. 7:212 DCC.

2667 M. Dambre, "Rechten en verbintenissen van de huurder" in M. Dambre, B. Hubeau and S. Stijns (eds.), *Handboek algemeen huurrecht*, Bruges, Die Keure, 2015, (513) 521.

the PSS user rents for multiple years without asking for a replacement of the product (e.g. reduced rental price for smartphone or bicycle as of the third year it is in the possession of the PSS user). An example can be found in the terms and conditions of *Fairphone Easy*.

> TERMS AND CONDITIONS FAIRPHONE EASY – Art. 7.2 "Every year in which You remain a user of Fairphone Easy and maintain the device in line with the conditions of these Terms, the monthly fee is reduced by two (2) euros. After three (3) years of remaining a user of Fairphone Easy, We will give you a bonus of a four (4) euro reduction."

Such a clause benefits both the PSS supplier and the PSS user as well as the environment. After all, it means lower costs and more revenue reliability for the PSS supplier, the PSS user pays a lower price if he uses the same product for longer, and fewer raw materials are consumed if the product does not need to be replaced. As with the sales contract, the rental price is an essential element of the rental contract,[2668] which must be determined or at least determinable.[2669] The fact that the rental price may also be determinable, means that a pay-per-use rental price is also among the possibilities.[2670]

624. PRODUCT- AND USE-ORIENTED PSS: PAYING THE PRICE OF ADDITIONAL SERVICES – Besides the purchase price or the rental price, the PSS user must also pay the price of the additional services added to the PSS. In case of additional services related to the delivery of the product (most notably installation), the absorption theory will generally be used so the rules of the sales or rental contract on payment of the price also govern the payment obligation of these additional services.[2671] Where the additional services are less integrated with the delivery of the product, the cumulation theory is often better fitting. In this case, the payment obligation of the PSS user for these additional services is governed under Belgian law by the rules of the contract for services[2672] and, under Dutch law (depending on the qualification of the additional services[2673]) by the contract

2668 See the definition of the rental contract. **Belgium**: Art. 1709 old BCC: "*Rental of goods is a contract whereby one party undertakes to let the other have the enjoyment of a good for a certain time, and at a certain price, which the latter undertakes to pay.*" (Own emphasis). **The Netherlands**: Art. 7:201(1) DCC: "*The rental contract is the contract whereby one party, the lessor, undertakes to provide the other party, the lessee, with the use of a good or part thereof and the lessee undertakes to provide a counter performance.*" (Own emphasis).

2669 Cass. (BE) 20 May 1994, *Arr.Cass.* 1994, 507, *Pas.* 1994, I, 492, *RW* 1995–96, 600, *T.Vred.* 1996, 57, case note K. CREYF.

2670 B. KEIRSBILCK, E. TERRYN and E. VAN GOOL, "Consumentenbescherming bij servitisation en product-dienst systemen (PDS)", *TPR* 2019, (817) 835.

2671 See *supra* no. 380 and 407.

2672 See Art. 1710 old BCC: "*Hire of work is a contract in which one party undertakes to perform something for another, in return for payment of a price negotiated between them.*" (Own emphasis).

2673 See *supra* no. 377.

for services or the contract for works.[2674] Contrary to the sales contract, these contracts do not necessarily require a determined price at the time of conclusion of the contract. In certain cases, the service provider will be able to unilaterally and *a posteriori* set a reasonable price for the services provided.[2675] Nevertheless, with PSS there will generally be a fixed price for these additional services, or at least a pay-per-use formula so that the PSS user should not expect any surprises when getting his monthly bill.

625. Result-oriented PSS: paying the price of the service – Both under Belgian law and Dutch law, result-oriented PSS are qualified as a contract for services. Under Belgian law, payment of the price is an essential obligation of the contract for services.[2676] In general, there are three systems to determine the price in a contract for services.[2677] Thus, the price of a contract for services can either be undetermined (*onbepaalde prijs, prix laissé à la discrétion de l'entrepreneur*), determined (or fixed) (*vaste prijs, prix ferme/forfait absolu*), or calculated by means of a price schedule (*op bestek, à bordereau de prix*). In case of an undetermined price, the price is not agreed in advance but is set afterwards by the service provider, according to the size of the work and the prices of materials and working hours. This is therefore a form of party decision[2678] (*partijbeslissing, décision de partie*), which is subject to the limits of the principle of reasonableness and fairness and the prohibition of abuse of law.[2679] In result-oriented PSS contracts with consumers, however, this is not an option as businesses offering services to consumers must indicate their price in writing, legibly, prominently and unambiguously.[2680] Result-oriented PSS will therefore either be offered at a fixed price or by means of a price list. With a fixed or determined price, the PSS supplier commits to provide the service at a predetermined unchangeable price. This means that the PSS user will pay the same price each month (or each 3 months, each year, etc.) for the agreed service, regardless of whether the products made available need to be repaired or replaced, more energy is consumed, or energy prices skyrocket. With result-

---

2674 See Art. 7:405 DCC (for the contract for services) & Art. 7:750, Art. 7:752, Art. 7:753 and 7:755 DCC (for the contract for works).

2675 **Belgium**: B. Kohl, *Contrat d'entreprise*, Brussels, Bruylant, 2016, 191–192 and 220–226. **The Netherlands**: See for the contract for services: T.F.E. Tjong Tjin Tai, *Asser 7-IV Bijzondere Overeenkomsten – Opdracht, incl. de geneeskundige behandelingsovereenkomst en de reisovereenkomst*, Deventer, Wolters Kluwer, 2022, no. 132. See for the contract for works: M.A.M.C. Van den Berg and S. van Gulijk, *Mr. C. Assers Handleiding tot de beoefening van het Nederlands Burgerlijk Recht. 7. Bijzondere overeenkomsten. Deel VI. Aanneming van werk*, Deventer, Wolters Kluwer, 2022, no. 129.

2676 See Art. 1710 old BCC. If a service is provided free of charge, this is no contract for services but an unnamed contract. See *supra* no. 368, under (iii).

2677 B. Kohl, *Contrat d'entreprise*, Brussels, Bruylant, 2016, 192 *et seq.*

2678 Art. 5.70 BCC.

2679 V. Sagaert, B. Tilleman and A.-L. Verbeke, *Vermogensrecht in kort bestek*, Antwerp, Intersentia, 2022, 444.

2680 Art. VI.3, §2 BCEL.

oriented PSS using a price schedule, the price of the service is calculated every time a certain period (e.g. every month, every year) has passed. This means that the price the PSS user will pay depends on the output of the service he receives. This system of price determination is therefore mostly used in pay-per-use result-oriented PSS contracts. Besides these three systems, there is also an intermediate system to determine the price of a contract for services, namely a relative fixed price (*betrekkelijk vaste prijs, forfait relatif*).[2681] This combines the system of a fixed price with a price schedule for any additional work required by the client. This is the case, for example, when the PSS user pays a fixed monthly fee for a maximum output set in the PSS contract (e.g. 300 light-hours per month, 500 pages per month, etc.). If the PSS user exceeds this contractually defined output, a relative fixed prices allows for charging an additional fee based on a price schedule.[2682]

Unlike Belgian law, a counter performance is not among the essential elements of the Dutch contract for services. This means that, unlike a sales contract, a contract for services may or may not be concluded against payment of a price.[2683] However, if the contract was entered into by the service provider in the course of his profession or business, the client will have to pay a price.[2684] The amount and method of calculating the price is generally stipulated in the contract. If a price is due but the amount has not been determined in the contract, the DCC provides that the client must pay the price calculated in the customary way or, failing that, a reasonable price.[2685] In practice, the result-oriented PSS contract will always include a price as agreed by the parties. Given the freedom of contract, the parties have various options to contractually define the price of the service. They can use hourly, daily or monthly rates, fixed amounts for specific services or combinations such as a fixed amount for a certain level of service with an additional rate for any additional services that are not included in the package.[2686] As a result, the parties have the same options for stipulating the price of the result-oriented PSS under Dutch law than under Belgian law.

626. TIMING OF THE PAYMENT – The timing of the payment is generally set out in the PSS contract. Most of the analysed PSS contracts stipulate that the monthly fee is due in advance of each month. As for the exact date of the payments, there

---

2681 M. DAMBRE, *Bijzondere overeenkomsten: de essentie*, Bruges, Die Keure, 2022, 385.

2682 See *infra* no. 635.

2683 T.F.E. TJONG TJIN TAI, *Asser 7-IV Bijzondere Overeenkomsten – Opdracht, incl. de geneeskundige behandelingsovereenkomst en de reisovereenkomst*, Deventer, Wolters Kluwer, 2022, no. 126.

2684 Art. 7:405(1) DCC.

2685 Art. 7:405(2) DCC.

2686 T.F.E. TJONG TJIN TAI, *Asser 7-IV Bijzondere Overeenkomsten – Opdracht, incl. de geneeskundige behandelingsovereenkomst en de reisovereenkomst*, Deventer, Wolters Kluwer, 2022, no. 132.

are broadly two options. A first option is that the contract starts on the first day of the month the contract was entered into, with a pro rata discount for the days when the PSS user was unable to use the product. Thereafter, the monthly fee will be charged each time prior to the month. Examples of this approach can be found, amongst others, in the terms and conditions of *Blue Movement*, *Papillon* and *Bundles*. This option has the advantage for the PSS supplier that the billing cycles of all its contracts are the same and for the PSS user that it is clear to which month the monthly payments relate. If a pay-per-use fee supplements the monthly fee, as is the case with *Bundles*, a logical approach is to calculate this fee at the end of the month and include it on the next invoice.

> Terms and conditions Blue Movement – Art. 5.1 "The one-off amount is due at the time of entering into the Contract and must be paid at that time." Art. 5.2 "The Monthly Fee is due from the first day of the month in which the Contract was entered into. The Lessee receives a pro rata discount for the first month for the days he did not have access to the Product. This will be deducted from the Monthly Fee at the first collection." Art. 5.3 "Thereafter, the Monthly Fee will be debited each time immediately prior to the next month."

> Terms and conditions Papillon – Art. 3 "The monthly rent of the Product, including VAT, is shown in Annex 1 under the column 'rent incl. VAT'. If a Product is delivered in the course of the month, the monthly rent of that Product is taken into account pro rata for calculation of the rent. The rental price is payable in advance in the hands of the lessor no later than the tenth day of the preceding month, by transfer to the account of the lessor with number [bank account] or by direct debit."

> Terms and conditions Bundles – Art. 4.1 "Customer pays the Monthly Fee to Bundles each time prior to the month for which the Monthly Charge is paid." Art. 4.2 "The Monthly Fee is calculated from the first day of the month in which the Contract is concluded. For the first month, Customer receives a pro-rata discount for the days that Customer did not have access to the Product." Art. 4.3 "In addition to the Monthly Fee, the Customer will pay Bundles an additional usage fee based on the use of the Product. If applicable, this usage fee is specified in the Contract and is calculated monthly in arrears and included on the next invoice to the Customer."

A second option is that the billing cycle of the PSS contract starts on the day of the month on which the PSS user has activated his subscription. For example, if the contract was concluded 15 September, the PSS user's payment method will be debited each month on the 15th. An example of this option can be found in the terms and conditions of *Fairphone Easy*. This has the advantage that no pro rata discount must be given for the first month. On the other hand, this will result in the PSS supplier having different billing cycles for all its customers.

> Terms and conditions Fairphone Easy – Art. 9.1 "[...] The payments will be due in advance of each month on the day which You have activated your Subscription.

Payments must be immediately payable via automatic collection. The payment date cannot be amended."

Exceptionally, the PSS contract provides that the monthly fee is due after the month to which it relates. For example, the terms and conditions of *HP Instant Ink* stipulate that the PSS user's payment option will be charged for the monthly fee and, where applicable, the pay-per-use fee for additional pages printed one month after the first use of the service. The advantages of this approach are that the PSS supplier must only issue one invoice for every monthly period and both the monthly fee and pay-per-use fee relate to the correct month. This also provides transparency to the PSS user about its usage of the service and the associated costs. On the other hand, a potential downside for the PSS supplier is that he cannot suspend the performance of the service if the PSS user fails to pay his monthly fee.

TERMS AND CONDITIONS HP INSTANT INK – Art. 7, a., 2. "Your monthly billing cycle ('Billing Cycle') for the Service will begin on the date of First Use [...]." Art. 7, a., 3. "Beginning one month after Your First Use, Your Payment Method will be charged on a Monthly Period [...] basis for (i) the amount of Your Service Plan Fee, and (ii) any charges for additional pages over and above your Service Plan ('Overage Fees'), [...] plus taxes. For example, if Your First Use is on January 1st, Your Payment Method will be charged on or after February 1st for Your Monthly Fee for January; if Your First Use is on February 1st, Your Payment Method will be charged on or after March 1st for Your Monthly Fee for February."

If no time of payment was specified in the PSS contract, the default rules applicable to the PSS contract in question should be considered. For example, for product-oriented PSS, the default sales rules stipulate that the price is due upon delivery of the good.[2687] In contrast, for use-oriented PSS, the default rules of the rental contract do not specify a specific time when payment is due. Consequently, the common intent of the parties should be identified, or if this is impossible, what is customary or reasonable and fair.[2688] Generally, it can be assumed that the rental price must be paid before or at the start of each rental period. For PSS contracts that are qualified as a contract for services (in particular result-oriented PSS or short-term use-oriented PSS on a pay-per-use basis), the price is only due after the services have been provided.[2689] Since PSS contracts constitute

---

2687 **Belgium**: Art. 1651 old BCC. **The Netherlands**: Art. 7:26(2) DCC.

2688 **Belgium**: M. DAMBRE, "Rechten en verbintenissen van de huurder" in M. DAMBRE, B. HUBEAU and S. STIJNS (eds.), *Handboek algemeen huurrecht*, Bruges, Die Keure, 2015, (513) 523. **The Netherlands**: Explanatory Memorandum, *Parliamentary Papers II* 1997/98, 26089, no. 3, 23; H.J. ROSSEL and A.H.T. HEISTERKAMP, *Mr. C. Assers Handleiding tot de beoefening van het Nederlands Burgerlijk Recht. 7. Bijzondere overeenkomsten. Deel II. Huur*, Deventer, Wolters Kluwer, 2021, no. 65.

2689 **Belgium**: B. KOHL, *Contrat d'entreprise*, Brussels, Bruylant, 2016, 431, no. 176. **The Netherlands**: T.F.E. TJONG TJIN TAI, *Asser 7-IV Bijzondere Overeenkomsten – Opdracht,*

continuous service contracts (contrary to, e.g. a construction contract where, as a general rule, the payments become due when the work is completed) the service provider will bill periodically for the provided services.[2690] This can either be by means of a monthly invoice for the services provided (e.g. the monthly fee and any pay-per-use fees) or after each individual transaction (e.g. after each pay-per-use ride on a free-floating e-scooter).

627. Payment method: cash (chartal money), deposits (scriptural money) or electronic money?[2691] – Besides the timing of the payment, the question arises of how the payment should be made. Under Belgian law, it is traditionally held in case law and legal doctrine that the creditor of a sum of money is entitled to be paid with cash (i.e. banknotes or coins), except if a legal or contractual provision allows or even prescribes another means of payment (e.g. scriptural money or electronic money).[2692] However, with the emergence and increasing acceptance of scriptural and electronic payment methods,[2693] such as bank transfers, debit cards (e.g. Bancontact), credit cards (e.g. Visa, Mastercard, American Express), Internet payment systems (e.g. PayPal[2694]) and mobile payments (e.g. scanning a QR code, SMS, Payconic,[2695] a "Tikkie",[2696] etc.), this seems to be an outdated proposition in need of modernisation.[2697] In any case, there are now numerous legal exceptions to the classic principle of payment with chartal money, making electronic payments the rule rather than

incl. de geneeskundige behandelingsovereenkomst en de reisovereenkomst, Deventer, Wolters Kluwer, 2022, no. 129.

2690 T.F.E. Tjong Tjin Tai, *Asser 7-IV Bijzondere Overeenkomsten – Opdracht, incl. de geneeskundige behandelingsovereenkomst en de reisovereenkomst*, Deventer, Wolters Kluwer, 2022, no. 129.

2691 In legal doctrine, three types of money are generally distinguished. Chartal money or cash (*chartaal geld, monnaie fiduciaire*) are banknotes and coins usually issued by, or at least under the authority of, the government. Scriptural money or deposits (*giraal geld, monnaie scripturale*) are immediately available in an account at a financial institution. Electronic money or e-money (*elektronisch geld, monnaie électronique*) is a monetary value on an electronic medium that constitutes a claim against the issuing institution. See e.g. S. Loosveld, *Geld, geldschulden en deviezen. Belgisch, Europees en internationaal perspectief*, Brussels, Larcier, 2007, 5–6.

2692 See T. Vansweevelt and B. Weyts, "Nakoming van verbintenissen of betaling" in T. Vansweevelt and B. Weyts (eds.), *Handboek Verbintenissenrecht (tweede editie)*, Brussels, Intersentia, 2023, (897) 924, no. 1161 and the references cited there.

2693 See for a legal analysis: R. Steennot, "Girale en elektronische betaaltechnieken" in *Handels- en economisch recht, Deel 1, Ondernemingsrecht, Volume B in Beginselen van Belgisch Privaatrecht*, Mechelen, Kluwer, 2011, (1867) 1867–1895.

2694 www.paypal.com.

2695 www.payconiq.be/en.

2696 www.tikkie.me.

2697 See in this sense e.g. T. Vansweevelt and B. Weyts, "Nakoming van verbintenissen of betaling" in T. Vansweevelt and B. Weyts (eds.), *Handboek Verbintenissenrecht (tweede editie)*, Brussels, Intersentia, 2023, (897) 924; S. Loosveld, *Geld, geldschulden en deviezen. Belgisch, Europees en internationaal perspectief*, Brussels, Larcier, 2007, 279; G. Schrans and R. Steennot, *Algemeen deel van het financieel recht*, Antwerp, Intersentia, 2003, 20–22.

the exception.[2698] For example, in Belgium, businesses must since 1 July 2022 *also* offer an electronic means of payment when the payment in euro is made in the simultaneous presence of the consumer and the business[2699] and the anti-money laundering rules prohibit cash payments of more than 3000 euros regardless of the total amount of the transaction, e.g. from a consumer to a trader or service provider, except for transactions between consumers.[2700] Under Dutch law, on the other hand, the possibility to pay with scriptural money is explicitly confirmed in the DCC. Article 6:114(1) DCC explicitly provides that if the creditor has a bank account suitable for scriptural money payments in the country where payment must or may be made, then the debtor may pay his debt by transferring the indebted amount to that bank account, unless the creditor has validly excluded a payment to that account.[2701]

When analysing the selected PSS contracts, it is clear that payment by electronic means (i.e. with scriptural or electronic money) has become the norm. Most PSS suppliers require the PSS user to pay via direct debit (e.g. SEPA mandate) or credit card. There are several reasons for this. First, most PSS contracts are concluded online, making cash transactions more difficult than electronic payments. The PSS supplier and PSS user will generally only be in each other's physical presence a limited number of times (if at all). These include the moment of installation and/or delivery, and moments of (scheduled) maintenance or repair. These limited occasions do not suffice to ensure the regular payment of the periodical fee. Second, direct debit or credit card payments ensure that the PSS supplier receives the periodic fee every month, as the payment takes place automatically without the PSS user having to take the initiative. This reduces the risk of unpaid invoices and associated costs. Finally, electronic payments have many other advantages: they are fast, transparent, enable better control, facilitate proof, etc.

> Terms and conditions Blue Movement – Art. 5.4 "Payment is made by direct debit or other means of payment (as stated in the ordering process or the Website), executed by BSH or by a third party designated by BSH. The Lessee is obliged to ensure sufficient balance on his bank account."

2698 See for an overview T. Vansweevelt and B. Weyts, "Nakoming van verbintenissen of betaling" in T. Vansweevelt and B. Weyts (eds.), *Handboek Verbintenissenrecht (tweede editie)*, Brussels, Intersentia, 2023, (897) 925, no. 1162.

2699 Art. VI.7/4 BCEL. See further on this provision: Z. Vanhoyland, "Commentaar bij artikel VI.7/4 WER" in *OHRA. Artikelsgewijze commentaar Handels- en economisch recht*, afl. 100, Mechelen, Wolters Kluwer, 2023, (69) 69–86; E. Callens, R. Steennot and N. Rogge, "Meer mogelijkheden tot bevrijdend betalen zonder cash", *Bank. Fin.R.* 2022, (211) 211–221 and Z. Vanhoyland, "Verplichte terbeschikkingstelling elektronisch betaalmiddel in b2c-verhouding", *DCCR* 2022, (81) 81–90.

2700 Art. 67, §2 Act of 18 September 2017 on the prevention of money laundering and terrorist financing and on restricting the use of cash, *BS* 6 October 2017.

2701 Art. 6:114(1) DCC. See for a discussion: G.T. de Jong, H.B. Krans and M.H. Wissink, *Verbintenissenrecht algemeen (Studiereeks Burgerlijk Recht, deel 4)*, Deventer, Wolters Kluwer, 2022, 86–87, no. 105 and no. 106.

Terms and conditions Fairphone *Easy* – Art. 9.1 "When concluding an As-a-Service Agreement and taking out a Subscription, You must be the holder of a Dutch bank account under which direct debit deductions are possible. You are obliged to authorise a direct debit mandate to have all related costs debited from the bank account number You have provided. [...]."

Terms and conditions Swapfiets – Art. 10.1 "The Renter is obliged the authorise a direct debit payment, as applicable, for the monthly subscription costs and any other applicable charges at the end of the Subscription."

Terms and conditions Villo – Art. 3.3(3) "The customer can choose between two payment methods: the SEPA mandate or the bank card authorising the [PSS supplier] to collect the amounts due."

628. Refusal by the PSS user to pay via direct debit? – Most PSS suppliers thus require the PSS user to pay the price via direct debit. The question arises whether the PSS user can refuse to pay for the service by direct debit. Under Belgian law, clauses that have the object or effect of increasing the price announced for a product because the consumer refuses to pay via direct debit are blacklisted.[2702] However, this blacklist provision only offers limited protection. It does not prohibit businesses from offering discounts to consumers who are prepared to pay by direct debit.[2703] In addition, as the examples of the blacklist must be interpreted strictly, this provision also does not prohibit clauses that make the use of direct debit payments mandatory.[2704] This means that businesses can still encourage or even require consumers to pay via direct debit, as long as they do not charge the "cost" of a direct debit refusal to the consumer if this was not included in the announced price.[2705] An obligation to pay via direct debit will, in my view, also not be unfair based on the general unfairness test[2706] given the interests of businesses and the advantages of direct debit payments already mentioned above.[2707] Under Dutch law, the blacklist and grey list do not contain a similar provision. In addition, also here, these terms will, in my view, not be unreasonably onerous within the meaning of the general test.[2708] As a result, if the PSS supplier stipulates

2702 See Art. VI.83, 32° BCEL. Compare also with Art. VI.83, 33° BCEL, which contains a similar prohibition to increase the announced price if the consumer refuses to receive his invoices by electronic mail.

2703 R. Steennot, "Commentaar bij art. VI.83, 32° WER" in *Handels- en economisch recht. Commentaar met overzicht van rechtspraak en rechtsleer*, Mechelen, Kluwer, Loose-leaf, 2017, (605) 605–606.

2704 See e.g. G. Straetmans and R. Steennot, *Handboek consumentenbescherming en marktpraktijken*, Antwerp, Intersentia, 2023, 368, no. 391.

2705 P. Cambie, *Onrechtmatige bedingen*, Ghent, Larcier, 2009, 340.

2706 Art. I.8, 22° BCEL.

2707 See *supra* no. 627.

2708 Art. 6:233, *sub* a. DCC.

in its general terms and conditions that the use of direct debit payments is mandatory, in practice the PSS user will have little choice but to accept this, as the alternative is not to enter into the PSS contract.

629. Digital content and digital services: possibility to pay with personal data – If digital content and digital services are added to the PSS contract, payment for these services is not only possible in money, but also in the form of personal data. This possibility was explicitly recognised by the DCD, elevating personal data as an effective means of a counter-performance.[2709] This was done so the DCD would also apply to seemingly "free" contracts where service providers collect personal data to create value, which is of course a laudable cause.[2710] However, this approach has been criticised in legal doctrine, mainly because the commercialisation of personal data is at odds with the protection of personal data, which constitutes a fundamental right, and because of concerns regarding the compatibility with the GDPR.[2711] As questions of data protection law are excluded from the scope of this book, this is not further addressed. Still, from a perspective of contract law, one burning question remains. Given that the DCD explicitly refers to and asserts priority of the GDPR rules,[2712] what happens if the consumer withdraws his consent for data processing under Article 7(3) GDPR?[2713] This issue remains unresolved at the EU level and is therefore left to the Member States.[2714]

2709 See Art. 3(1) DCD (except where the data are solely used for technical or regulatory purposes). See also recitals 24 and 25 DCD. For implementation in **Belgium**, see Art. 1701/2, §2 old BCC. For **the Netherlands**, see: Art. 7:50ab(1), *sub* b. DCC.

2710 See in this sense also J. Morais Carvalho, "Sale of Goods and Supply of Digital Content and Digital Services – Overview of Directives 2019/770 and 2019/771", *EuCML* 2019, (194) 197.

2711 See e.g. J. Vanherpe, "White Smoke, but Smoke Nonetheless: Some (Burning) Questions Regarding the Directives on Sale of Goods and Supply of Digital Content", *ERPL* 2020, (251) 256–257; L. Drechsler, "Data As Counter-Performance: A New Way Forward Or A Step Back For The Fundamental Right Of Data Protection?", *Datenschutz & LegalTech/ Data Protection & LegalTech* 2018, (35) 35–43; H. Schulte-Nölke, "Personal data is not a counter-performance! Plea for a data driven rethinking of contract and consumer law", *TvC* 2018, (74) 74–76. See also: European Data Protection Supervisor, *Opinion 4/2017 on the Proposal for a Directive on certain aspects concerning contracts for the supply of digital content*, 14 March 2017, 3 and 7. However, see: M. Narciso, "'Gratuitous' Digital Content Contracts in EU Consumer Law", *EuCML* 2017, (198) 198–206.

2712 See Art. 3(8) DCD. See: D. Staudenmayer, "The Directives on Digital Contracts: First Steps Towards the Private Law of the Digital Economy", *ERPL* 2020, vol. 28, afl. 2, (219) 234, section 2.1.3.1.

2713 D. Staudenmayer, "The Directives on Digital Contracts: First Steps Towards the Private Law of the Digital Economy", *ERPL* 2020, vol. 28, afl. 2, (219) 227–228.

2714 See recitals 39 and 40 DCD. See also: K. Sein and G. Spindler, "The new Directive on Contracts for the Supply of Digital Content and Digital Services – Scope of Application and Trader's Obligation to Supply – Part 1", *ERCL* 2019, (265) 264–265.

Also at the national level, questions remain regarding the consequences of the withdrawal of consent.[2715] Dutch law in this sense explicitly contains a provision stating that the consumer's withdrawal of consent results in the fact that he is no longer bound by the contract provided he does not (also) pay a price for it.[2716] The withdrawal of consent by the consumer therefore implies a unilateral termination of the digital content or digital services contract that is part of the PSS.[2717] According to the explanatory memorandum, the consumer is in this case not obliged to return any performance received, as this would undermine the protection offered to the consumer by the GDPR.[2718] The consumer also cannot be held liable for breach of contract in this case, but at the same time, the PSS supplier cannot be expected to continue fulfilling its obligations and has the right to block the consumer's access to the digital content or service.[2719] In Belgium, on the other hand, the legislator has so far not addressed this issue. The question therefore arises whether the withdrawal of consent should be seen as a breach of contract, where the remedies for breach of contract (specific performance, termination, damages) can be invoked against the consumer. In my view, although this is the most logical answer from a strict contract law perspective, it would negate the protection intended by the GDPR.[2720] Therefore, the Belgian legislator should consider adopting a solution for this issue, where the Dutch provision can potentially serve as a useful inspiration.

Policy Recommendation #4

- **Consider adopting a provision dealing with the contractual consequences of the withdrawal of consent under Article 7(3) GDPR in contracts for the supply of digital content or digital services where payment is done in the form of providing personal data. Article 7:50ab(5) DCC can serve as an example, allowing the consumer to withdraw his consent without any obligation to return the performance received and without incurring contractual liability, while the supplier is not obliged to continue performing its obligations under the contract.**

2715 See on this: C. Langhanke and M. Schmidt-Kessel, "Consumer Data as Consideration", *EuCML* 2015, (218) 222.

2716 Art. 7:50ab(5) DCC.

2717 M.B.M. Loos, "The Netherlands" in A. De Franceschi and R. Schulze (eds.), *Harmonizing Digital Contract Law. The Impact of EU Directives 2019/770 and 2019/771 and the Regulation of Online Platforms*, Beck, Hart, Nomos, 2023, 521, with reference to Explanatory Memorandum, *Parliamentary Papers II*, 2020/21, 35 734, no. 3, 11. Compare also with V. Mak and G.-J. Zwenne, *Onderzoek over betalen met persoonsgegevens en consumentenbescherming*, University of Leiden, Commissioned by Ministerie van Economische Zaken en Klimaat (EZK), November 2021, 18.

2718 Explanatory Memorandum, *Parliamentary Papers II*, 2020/21, 35 734, no. 3, 12.

2719 Explanatory Memorandum, *Parliamentary Papers II*, 2020/21, 35 734, no. 3, 12.

2720 Compare also with Recital 42 GDPR: "*[...] Consent should not be regarded as freely given if the data subject has no genuine or free choice or is unable to refuse or withdraw consent without detriment.*" ".

5.2.2. PRICE COMPONENTS: A DEEP DIVE INTO COMMERCIAL REALITY

630. PRICING STRATEGY OF THE SUPPLIER AND CONTRACTUAL ARRANGEMENTS ON THE PRICE OF THE PSS – The amount and composition of this price depends on the pricing strategy of the PSS supplier, which is reflected in the PSS contract. After all, it is important for businesses to consider their pricing strategy to recover the purchase of the product and the investments made. A possible factor in this pricing strategy is whether the supplier can reuse the products at the end of the contract with another user or whether the products can be used in another way (remanufacturing, refurbishing, etc.). In almost all cases, the PSS contract will require the PSS user to pay a periodic fee for the services provided. Other PSS offers are offered on a pay-per-use basis. In addition, it is certainly possible that the PSS contract stipulates a start-up fee. Furthermore, in the event of premature termination of the contract, the PSS contract may also stipulate that the PSS user pays an early termination fee to recover the investment costs incurred.[2721] Finally, some PSS offers include an option to purchase the product at the end of the PSS contract.

631. PERIODICAL FEE – Almost all PSS offers on the market stipulate a periodic fee in exchange for the service. This price can be set in different ways. Often different packages are offered, ranging from a "basic" package to a "premium" package. Depending on the amount of the monthly fee, the PSS user will be able to enjoy better products, more functionality, and/or more additional services. For example, in the Netherlands, *Swapfiets* offers a choice between 4 bikes, ranging from an "original" model starting from € 19,90 per month to a fully electric "power 7" model that will set you back € 79,90 per month.[2722] Some PSS suppliers have a cheaper offer for students or young people or offer a discounted family subscription. For example, in Brussels, students pay € 19,90 instead of € 21,90 per month for a flexible (i.e. monthly cancellable) Swapfiets Deluxe 7.[2723] Moreover, the periodic fee often becomes lower the longer the PSS user engages himself. For example, with *Blue Movement's* "Serie 4" washing machine you can choose between a minimum term of 1+ year (from € 14.99 per month) or 6+ years (from € 11.99 per month).[2724] As illustrated below, *Fairphone Easy* has a similar pricing strategy where the base service fee is cheaper for longer minimum term contracts. The longer the duration of the contract, the cheaper the monthly fee

2721 A. VAN VAERENBERGH and F. LEYMAN, "'Product als dienst'-overeenkomsten, een stap in de richting van de circulaire economie", *MER* 2019, (20) 26–27.

2722 See: https://swapfiets.nl/en-NL/bikes.

2723 See: https://swapfiets.be/en-BE/brussels/deluxe-7/configure.

2724 www.bluemovement.com/nl-nl/abonnementen/wasmachines/WAN28277NL.

becomes. Thus, although flexibility is seen as one of the biggest advantages of PSS contracts, PSS users also pay the price for increased flexibility.

TERMS AND CONDITIONS LIVE LIGHT – Art. 8.2 "The Tenant owes Live Light a Usage Fee for the use of the Goods. The amount of the monthly Usage Fee, which is paid in advance by direct debit each time, is specified in the order confirmation."

TERMS AND CONDITIONS PAPILLON – Art. 3 "The monthly rent of the Product, including VAT, is shown in Annex 1 under the column "rent incl. VAT." [...]."

TERMS AND CONDITIONS DRESSR – Art. 4 (Dressr subscription), (3) "We may offer a variety of membership plans, including free trials, discounted pricing for limited times or special third-party promotional plans that may have different or additional terms disclosed to you at or before sign-up. [...]."

TERMS AND CONDITIONS FAIRPHONE EASY – Art. 9.2 "You agree to pay the following: a) the base service fee depending on the Subscription [...]."

Subscription period	**Base service fee**
Minimum three (3) months	Twenty-nine (29) euros incl. VAT
Minimum thirty-six (36) months	Twenty-four (24) euros incl. VAT
Minimum sixty (60) months	Nineteen (19) euros incl. VAT

632. PSS OFFERS BASED ON A LEASING OR HIRE PURCHASE MODEL: PRICE DEPENDS ON NEW VALUE OF THE PRODUCT – In the case of PSS offers based on a leasing or hire purchase model, the price will often depend on the new value of the product. With *Mudjeans'* Lease a Jeans, for example, the retail price of the jeans is divided over 12 months. After paying the total price of the jeans, you can choose to keep the jeans (and acquire the ownership) or trade them in for another model.[2725] Also with *Live Light*, the monthly fee of the "furniture as a service" is calculated based on the retail price. The PSS user can then later choose if he wants to swap, return, or buy the furniture, without ever paying more than the retail price.[2726]

633. NEW VERSUS REFURBISHED PRODUCTS – Another possible factor that may influence the periodic fee is whether the product provided as a service is new or refurbished. For example, *Blue Movement* allows consumers to choose between new and refurbished household appliances.[2727] If consumers choose the

2725 https://mudjeans.nl/pages/lease-a-jeans-old.
2726 www.live-light.com/how-it-works.
2727 E.g. Blue Movement's "Serie 4" washing machine as a service has two pricing options: "new" starting at € 12,99 per month and "refurbished" starting at € 11,99 per month. See: www.bluemovement.com/nl-nl/abonnementen/wasmachines.

refurbished option, they pay a lower amount per month. This can of course be encouraged from a sustainability perspective. After all, it makes it possible for the PSS supplier to repair and reintroduce household appliances to the market, thus extending their lifespan.

634. Model clauses on periodical fee – The following model clauses offer examples of clauses on the PSS user's obligation to pay the periodic fee. The first example is most suited for use-oriented PSS, as it refers to a recurrent (rental) fee for the use of the product. The second example is aimed at result-oriented PSS, as it refers to a service fee, which covers the costs of the performance of the service by the PSS supplier.

Model clause #25: periodical fee[2728]

- **[The PSS user] is charged a fixed, recurrent (rental) fee [of specified amount/as shown in Annex X] for the use of the product that is due [specified frequency (e.g. monthly, quarterly, annually)].**
- **[The PSS user] is charged a [specified frequency (e.g. monthly, quarterly, annually)] service fee, which covers all costs of the performance of the service by [the PSS supplier] under this contract.**

635. Pay-per-use fee – A second frequently used pricing strategy is PSS contracts based on a pay-per-use fee. The well-known "free floating" e-scooters in big cities are a common example of this.[2729] For example, if a PSS user wishes to use one of the scooters offered by *Dott,* the price will consist of an unlock fee (e.g. € 1 to unlock the scooter), supplemented by use fees which are calculated based on the duration of the use of the scooter (e.g. € 0,20 per minute).

> Terms and conditions Dott – Art. 5 (Fees, charges and payment) "*The fees for the use of our Vehicles are charged on a pay per use basis. Each time you wish to use a Vehicle you may be charged an unlock fee in addition to use fees which are calculated based on the duration of your use of the Vehicle.* The fees are disclosed in your User Account or by the Third Party Platform before you unlock a Vehicle [...]. The fees are calculated from the moment the Vehicle is unlocked until the moment the Vehicle is locked via your User Account or by the Third Party Platform. The fees will be rounded up to the nearest unit of time based on the applicable billing model (i.e. per second, per minute or per hour). Both the applicable unlock fee and the applicable

2728 Model clauses based partly on C. Borucki, H. Slachmuylders, B. Keirsbilck, D. Gruyaert and E. Terryn, *Model clauses for Product-as-a-Service (PaaS) contracts*, CE Center. Circular Economy Policy Research Center, 2022–23, 47.

2729 See e.g. Lime (www.li.me/en-us/home); Bird (www.bird.co/); and Dott (https://ridedott.com/nl).

billing model and fees charged can be viewed in the App or Third Party Platform prior to riding. All fees are non-refundable and inclusive of VAT [...]." (Own emphasis).

636. Pay-per-use fee supplementing periodic fee – Pay-per-use fees are also often used to supplement the periodic fee depending on the use of the product by the PSS user. *Bundles*, for example, has different pricing plans depending on how many washes are run and *HP Instant Ink* also provides a pay-per-use fee when more pages are printed than included in the PSS user's subscription.

Terms and conditions Bundles – Art. 4.3 "*In addition to the Monthly Fee, the Customer will pay Bundles an additional usage fee based on the use of the Product.* If applicable, this usage fee is specified in the Contract and is calculated monthly in arrears and included on the next invoice to the Customer." (Own emphasis).

Terms and conditions HP Instant ink – Art. 7, a., 5. "*Unless otherwise separately specified, for each month that You print more than the number of Your Service Plan Pages plus any applicable Rollover Pages, Your Payment Method will be charged for the Overage fee associated with those additional pages, plus additional taxes.* For example, for ink, if Your Service Plan entitles You to print fifty (50) pages for a Service Plan Fee of € 1.99 and thereafter to pay € 1.00 for each multiple of ten (10) pages, and if You print a total of sixty-six (66) pages in a Month Period where you had no Rollover Pages available, then Your Payment Method would be charged the Monthly Fee of € 1.99 plus € 2.00 in Overage Fees, for a total of € 3.99, including Taxes." (Own emphasis).

637. Model clauses on pay-per-use fee – The following model clauses provides examples of pay-per-use clauses. According to the first model clause, the PSS supplier may set a price on a "pay-per-use", "pay-per-volume" or "pay-per-user" basis. Here, a distinction in pricing may also be made between a price for a for an initial number of uses, volumes or users, and a (discounted) price for (a larger amount of) subsequent uses, volumes or users. The second model clause provides an example of a pricing structure where the PSS user pays on a pay-per-use basis for the excess use that exceeds his subscription. Finally, the third model clause serves as an example where the price of the PSS is determinable and depends on a pricing schedule added to the PSS contract, for example in an annex.

Model clause #26: pay-per-use fee[2730]

- **[The PSS user] is charged for the use-of the product on a [pay-per-use/pay-per-volume/pay-per-user] basis. The price per [use/specified volume (e.g. 1000 kg of laundry washed)/specified number of users] is [specified amount] [for the first [specified amount/specified volume/specified number] of [uses/volume/users] and [specified amount] for all subsequent [specified amount/specified volume/specified number] of [uses/volume/users]].**
- **If [the PSS user] exceeds the allowed number of [uses/volume/users], [the PSS user] pays an extra fee of [specified amount] per additional [use/volume/user].**
- **The pricing for [the use of the product by the PSS user/the service provided by the PSS supplier] under this contract is set forth in the pricing schedule [in Annex X].**

638. Pay-per-use fee and time out of internet connection – Pay-per-use fees are often calculated based on usage data collected through the use of the internet. This is why PSS suppliers often require the PSS user to keep the product connected to the internet. Some PSS contracts include a clause which states that in the event of internet failure (even if due to *force majeure*, for example a fault by the Internet Service Provider ("ISP")) of the product, a fixed usage fee will be charged. An example can be found in the terms and conditions of *Bundles*, where in case of missing information due to a non-working internet connection, a fixed number of fifteen washes will be charged. As was already established above, such a clause will not pass the unfair terms test.[2731] After all, the result of this clause would be that the risk of *force majeure* would be borne by the consumer, which is not permitted under Belgian law and arguably also not under Dutch law.[2732] Additionally, even if there is no *force majeure* and the PSS user is in breach of contract, this clause could also be considered an excessive indemnity clause. Indeed, according to Article VI.83, 24° BCEL, are unfair: clauses that, in the event of non-performance or delay in performance of the consumer's obligations, set compensation amounts that are clearly disproportionate to the harm that may be suffered by the business. Under Dutch law, excessive indemnity clauses are not on the grey- or blacklist, but they can be challenged when they are unreasonably onerous within the meaning of Article 6:233, *sub* a. DCC. In this specific example, a fixed charge of fifteen washing cycles, regardless

[2730] Model clauses based partly on C. Borucki, H. Slachmuylders, B. Keirsbilck, D. Gruyaert and E. Terryn, *Model clauses for Product-as-a-Service (PaaS) contracts*, CE Center. Circular Economy Policy Research Center, 2022–23, 46–47.

[2731] See *supra* no. 291 and no. 440.

[2732] **Belgium**: B. Keirsbilck, E. Terryn and E. Van Gool, "Consumentenbescherming bij servitisation en product-dienst systemen (PDS)", *TPR* 2019, (817) 873–874. **The Netherlands**: see M.B.M. Loos, *Algemene voorwaarden*, The Hague, Boom juridisch, 2018, 313, no. 345a who argues that these terms can fall within the scope of paragraph 1, point (e) of the indicative list of the UCTD Annex (which, in turn, also affect Dutch law).

of the duration of the internet failure (i.e. even in case of a short interruption), does indeed seem excessive. A better alternative can be found in the terms and conditions of *HP Instant Ink*. According to these terms, the cartridges of the smart printer will be disabled if the device is not connected to the internet and the PSS user will therefore not be able to print until the internet connection is restored. The PSS user will still have to pay the monthly fee, but no additional fixed costs will be charged.

> TERMS AND CONDITIONS BUNDLES – Art. 4.4 "Bundles' usage measurement data is leading in determining the usage fee. If data is missing due to a non-working internet connection, this is at the risk of the Customer and Bundles will determine the number of wash cycles in all reasonableness and based on experience, with a minimum of 15 wash cycles per month."

> TERMS AND CONDITIONS HP INSTANT INK – Art. 5, c. "Your Printer Needs to be Connected to the Internet. In order to be able to use the Service in an uninterrupted manner, You agree to maintain connectivity of Your Printer to the Internet and to not remove or disable any remote monitoring software or functionality on Your printer; [...] If Your printer is not connected to the Internet, then the Subscription Cartridges (as defined in section d. below) will be disabled and You will not be able to use them to print; however, You will continue to be charged for the Service as described in Section 7 'Paying for Your Service'. In order to reactivate disabled cartridges, You will need to reconnect Your printer to the Internet and keep it connected. [...]."

639. MODEL CLAUSE ON TIME-OUT OF INTERNET CONNECTION – The following model clause can be used as a fair example of a clause on time-outs of the product's connection with the internet. It confirms the obligation for the PSS user to keep the product connected to the internet to facilitate monitoring the use of the product. Additionally, it also contains a prohibition to tamper with the monitoring software or to purposely disconnect the product. If the product is nevertheless disconnected, instead of charging a minimum usage fee (which would be unfair if the interruption is caused by *force majeure*), it provides that the product will be disabled, and the service will be suspended until internet connection is restored. The suspension of the service (which can be seen as an application of the *enac*) does not affect the PSS user's payment obligation under the contract.

Model clause #27: time-out of internet connection

- **The product must always remain connected to the internet to facilitate monitoring the use of the product. [The PSS user] may not remove or disable any remote monitoring software or disconnect the product from the internet. If the product is not connected to the internet, the product will be automatically disabled, rendering it inoperable. [The PSS user] will not be able to use the product until connection with the internet is restored. The suspension of the service due to lack of internet connectivity does not affect [the PSS user's] obligation to pay the price as stipulated in the contract.**

640. Start-up or one-off fee – Some PSS suppliers, such as *Swapfiets* and *Blue Movement*, charge a one-time start-up fee or one-off fee when the PSS user enters into the PSS contract.[2733] This start-up fee usually aims to cover the costs associated with processing orders, managing logistics (e.g. checking whether the product meets all the conformity requirements, delivery and installation of the product, etc.) and other expenses linked with concluding a new PSS contract (e.g. conducting a credit check of the consumer). Additionally, charging a start-up fee can also provide financial security for PSS suppliers, who may need to cover certain upfront costs, such as financing the product, insurance, maintenance, etc. Contrary to a deposit,[2734] this start-up fee will not be returned to the PSS user at the end of the contract.

> Terms and conditions Swapfiets – Art. 6.1 "The term of the Subscription ("Subscription Period") is agreed upon in the order process. To the extent agreed in the Order Process, Swapfiets may charge Renter with a one-time fee."

> Terms and conditions Blue Movement – Art. 4.1 "On conclusion of the Contract, the Renter shall owe BSH a One-Off Amount. This One-Off Amount is stated in the ordering process on the Website and in the confirmation email sent by BSH to the Tenant after the conclusion of the Agreement. This One-Off Amount will not be returned to Tenant."

A start-up fee can also be used to prevent PSS users from abusing their flexibility to cancel the PSS contract on a monthly basis, or to cover the costs associated with on and off subscriptions. Consider a flexible *Swapfiets* contract, for example. If the PSS user can terminate the contract every month, he might be tempted to cancel the contract before leaving on a three-week holiday and then conclude a new contract after returning. This, of course, entails significant costs for the PSS supplier. He must ensure that the product can be inspected and/or collected, has administrative costs to close the file, and then faces administrative and logistical costs again to make the product available again after the PSS user's break from the PSS contract. In the terms and conditions of *Swapfiets*, a solution for this problem was implemented. According to these terms, if a new contract is concluded within three months of an earlier contract, a start-up cost of € 30 is applicable. This seems fair, as it allows *Swapfiets* to recover the incurred administrative and logistic costs.

> Terms and conditions Swapfiets – Art. 6.9 "If the Renter wishes to enter another Subscription within three months of the End Date, a start-up cost of EUR 30 is applicable."

[2733] Additionally, until recently, Mudjeans used a start-up fee for its "Lease a Jeans" formula. Consumers paid a one-off membership fee of € 20, after which they could lease a pair of jeans for € 7.5 per month. Currently, however, only a periodic fee of € 9.95 per month is charged. See: https://mudjeans.eu/pages/lease-a-jeans.

[2734] See *infra* no. 642.

641. MODEL CLAUSE ON START-UP OR ONE-OFF FEE – The model clause below allows the PSS supplier to charge a one-time start-up fee. The PSS contract may further specify that (unlike a deposit) this start-up fee is non-refundable.

Model clause #28: start-up fee

- **[The PSS supplier] charges an initial one-time start-up fee of [specified amount]. [This fee is non-refundable].**

642. DEPOSIT – PSS suppliers also often require the PSS user to pay a deposit. The main idea of requiring a deposit is mitigating the risk of moral hazard. Indeed, the deposit acts as a form of insurance for the PSS supplier against potential damages, misuse, or non-compliance with the terms of service. At the same time, the deposit serves as an incentive for the PSS user to use the product or the service responsibly. If the PSS user knows that he can get his deposit back upon complying with the terms and conditions and keeping the product in a good state of repair, he will be encouraged to treat the product more carefully. Finally, the deposit can provide security for non-payment of the monthly fee and other costs by the PSS user or ensure that the PSS user returns the product at the end of the contract. Contrary to the one-off or start-up fee, the deposit will generally be returned to the PSS user at the end of the contract, provided all the conditions are met.

> Terms and conditions Bundles – Art. 4.5 "Client shall pay to Bundles a deposit as specified in the Contract. After termination of the Contract, Bundles will return the deposit to Client within 14 days, provided that all conditions have been met."

> Terms and conditions Fairphone Easy – 4.6 "Fairphone requires payment of the Subscription and a one-time fee of ninety (90) euros as a deposit upon Your order. The deposit will be returned to You within 14 days after you have returned the device to Us upon termination. The deposit will be returned to the same account unless You tell us otherwise. Should You fail to update Your bank account details in a timely manner, this may lead to delays in receiving your deposit. Fairphone reserves the right to deduct an amount of the deposit to resolve any outstanding payments."

643. MODEL CLAUSE ON DEPOSIT – The following model clause provides that the PSS user must pay a deposit to protect the PSS supplier against potential damages, misuse, losses or other non-compliance with the terms and conditions of the PSS contract. This model clauses also stipulates the conditions and timing for reimbursement of the deposit to the PSS user. Finally, it allows the PSS supplier to deduct an amount of the deposit to resolve any outstanding payments or to compensate for any damages to the product or other damages caused by non-compliance with the terms of the PSS contract.

Model clause #29: deposit

- **[The PSS user] shall pay a deposit of [specified amount]. The deposit will be reimbursed to [the PSS user] within [reasonable amount of time (e.g, 14 days)] after [the product is returned upon termination/the product is collected upon termination/the service has been fully performed]. [The PSS supplier] reserves the right to deduct an amount of the deposit to resolve any outstanding payments or to compensate for any damages to the product or any other damages caused by non-compliance with the terms of this contract.**

644. (MANDATORY) INSURANCE FEES – PSS suppliers can also require the PSS user to pay an insurance fee for insuring the product. As already discussed above, contractually requiring the PSS user to take out insurance is a strategy to mitigate the risk of loss and damages to the product.[2735] There are two possible approaches: either the PSS supplier leaves the PSS user free in his choice of insurance company, and the PSS user himself is responsible to purchase insurance and pay the premium to the insurer, or the PSS supplier arranges the insurance with an insurance company of his choice and charges the insurance premium to the PSS user. Of course, this insurance premium can also be implicitly contained in the monthly fee without a need to include a contractual clause to this effect.

645. MODEL CLAUSES ON (MANDATORY) INSURANCE FEES – The following model clauses deal with these two possible approaches. The first one provides an example of a clause where the PSS user must choose an insurance company and is responsible for paying the insurance premiums. The second model clause states that the PSS supplier takes out the insurance for the product and the insurance premiums are included in the periodic fee.

Model clause #30: insurance fee

- **[The PSS user] shall select an insurance company of their choice to obtain and maintain insurance coverage during the entire period of use, as a measure to mitigate the risk of loss, damage, or theft of the product. [The PSS user] shall be solely responsible for paying the insurance fees, and ensuring that the policy remains active for the duration of the contract. Proof of insurance must be provided to the PSS supplier upon request.**

- **[The PSS supplier] shall obtain and maintain insurance coverage for the product through an insurance company of their choice. [The PSS user] shall be responsible to pay the insurance fees, which is included in the periodic fee for the use of the product.**

2735 See also *supra* no. 443.

646. Purchase option – A final element of the PSS supplier's pricing strategy is whether, when and at what price the PSS user can potentially buy the product. As discussed above under section dealing with the similarities and differences between PSS contracts and leasing contracts, there are several options.[2736] In most cases, the PSS user will not have a purchase option, as the possibility of transferring ownership of the product is contrary to the purpose and idea behind servitisation and circular business models such as PSS.[2737] In some cases, the PSS user will have a purchase option for the product, which can take multiple forms. First, the PSS user may have the option to purchase the product at the end of the PSS contract, either at a contractually specified residual value or at the market price. Alternatively, the PSS user may have the option to purchase the product at any time during the contract at the market price of the product at that specific time. Finally, the PSS user may even have a purchase obligation, although this would constitute a financial leasing contract and no longer a PSS in the strict sense of the word.

5.2.3. TRANSPARENCY REGARDING THE PRICE OF THE PSS

647. Difficulty to compare prices of different PSS offers – The combination of different pricing components (periodic fees, discount for long-term contracts, start-up fees, pay-per-use fees, insurance fees, etc.) can make it difficult for an average consumer to compare the prices of different PSS offers (by the same or by different PSS suppliers).[2738] For example, for consumers who want to use a product for a longer period of time, it may be more advantageous to pay a higher start-up cost but lower monthly fee than no start-up cost and a higher monthly fee, while for consumers who want more flexibility, the opposite may be true. There is also a risk that various additional (pay-per-use) fees on top of the periodic fee will still burden consumers with unexpected costs, which is precisely what servitisation and PSS are said to avoid. On top of the different pricing structures, the services offered by PSS suppliers itself are not easily compared. For instance, the products offered "as a service" may differ from one another, for example in terms of energy consumption, functionalities, different models, etc. In addition, not all PSS offers include the same additional services, whose value is already difficult to determine and compare in the first place. Moreover, consumers may be offered joined offers, ancillary products or services, product modifications or updates, which will also influence the final price. Finally, the

2736 See *supra* section 3.4.3.

2737 Compare, however, with *supra* no. 399.

2738 See in the same sense e.g. H. Beale, "From sales to servitisation" in S. Grundmann and Y.M. Atamer (eds.), *European sales law. Challenges in the 21st century*, Cambridge, Intersentia, 2023, (47) 68–70.

option to purchase the product (and at what price – residual value or market value) may also be relevant for consumers in determining whether a particular PSS offer represents a "good deal", depending on their needs. The question arises whether the pre-contractual information requirements and transparency requirements from the EU consumer acquis and its national implementation provide sufficient consumer protection against this risk of difficulties in price comparisons of different PSS offers.

648. Pre-contractual information requirements and the price of the PSS – As already touched upon above, several pre-contractual information obligations to which PSS suppliers are subject relate to the price of the service.[2739] First, the provisions of the SD require that PSS suppliers must make information available to the PSS user about the price of the service, where a price is pre-determined for a given type of service.[2740] Where the price is not-pre-determined by the PSS supplier for a given type of service, the price of the service or, if an exact price cannot be given, the method for calculating the price so that it can be checked, or a sufficiently detailed estimate, must be given upon the PSS user's request.[2741] Second, the general information requirements of the CRD state require that before the consumer is bound by a (non-distance or off-premises) PSS contract, the PSS supplier must (actively) provide the consumer with information in a clear and comprehensible matter on the total price[2742] of the services, or where the nature of the services is such that the price cannot reasonably be calculated in advance, the manner in which the price is to be calculated, as well as, where applicable, all additional freight, delivery or postal charges or, where those charges cannot reasonably be calculated in advance, the fact that such additional charges may be payable.[2743] This information may be provided in the general terms and conditions.[2744] In case of a distance or off-premises PSS contract, the same information requirements regarding the total price apply, with additional rules in the case of a contract of indeterminate duration or a contract containing a subscription, which will be the case for PSS contracts.[2745] Then, the total price must also include the total costs per billing period. Where such contracts are charged at a fixed rate, the total price shall also mean the total monthly costs. Where the total costs cannot be reasonably

---

2739 See *supra* no. 87–88.

2740 EU: Art. 22(1)(i) SD. **Belgium**: Art. III.74, 12° BCEL. **The Netherlands**: Art. 6:230b(9) DCC.

2741 EU: Art. 22(3)(a) SD. **Belgium**: Art. III.76, 1° BCEL. **The Netherlands**: Art. 6:230d(1) DCC.

2742 See also Art. VI.4 BCEL, which states that the total price to be paid by the consumer must include value-added tax, all other taxes and the cost of all services which the consumer is obliged to pay in addition.

2743 EU: Art. 5(1)(c) CRD. **Belgium**: Art. VI.2, 3° BCEL. **The Netherlands**: Art. 6:230l *sub* c. DCC.

2744 CJEU, Judgment of 24 February 2022, C-536/20, *Tiketa*, ECLI:EU:C:2022:112, para. 46.

2745 EU: Art. 6(1)(e) CRD. **Belgium**: Art. VI.46, 5° BCEL. **The Netherlands**: Art. 6:230m(1), *sub* e. DCC.

calculated in advance, the manner in which the price is to be calculated shall be provided.[2746]

From these pre-contractual information requirements, which apply cumulatively, we can deduce that the periodical (monthly) fee and any start-up fee, installation or other one-off fee should be properly disclosed to the consumer before the PSS contract is concluded. This includes VAT and other taxes, and any costs for additional services which the PSS user is obliged to pay in addition, such as mandatory insurance fees. For PSS contracts with pay-per-use components, it is also important that the manner in which this pay-per-use is calculated is properly disclosed before the consumer concludes the PSS contract.

649. Burden of proof and consequences of non-compliance with information requirements regarding the price of the PSS – As already mentioned above,[2747] for the information requirements of the SD and distance and off-premises contracts, the burden of proof that the information requirements are complied with is explicitly placed on the PSS supplier.[2748] For the general information requirements of the CRD, however, this is not the case. This would mean that, in the absence of special rules, the PSS user would bear the burden of proof that he did not receive the information on the price of the PSS (*actori incumbit probatio*).[2749] However, Steennot and Straetmans argue that placing the burden of proof on the consumer would make it very difficult for him to assert his rights under the CRD and this would therefore be contrary to the principle of effectiveness.[2750] While there is indeed already EU case law hinting in this direction, the CJEU has not yet ruled in the specific context of Article 5 CRD.[2751]

As for the legal consequences of giving false or incomplete information about the price of the PSS, this may in the first place constitute a misleading

2746 *Ibid.*

2747 See *supra* no. 87–88.

2748 **Belgium**: See Art. III.78 BCEL and Art. VI.62 and VI.63 BCEL. **The Netherlands**: Art. 6:230n(4) DCC.

2749 **Belgium**: See in this sense e.g. A. De Boeck, "General information obligations in Belgian (and French) law of obligations versus article 2 of Book VI 'Market practices and consumer protection' in the Belgian Economic Law Code", *REDC* 2013, (399) 404. See for an example: Antwerp (BE) 18 June 2019, *Limb.Rechtsl.* 2020, 22. **The Netherlands**: M.Y. Schaub, "De informatieplichten van de Dienstenrichtlijn (art. 6:230a-f BW)", *TvC* 2014, (21), para. 3.2.

2750 G. Straetmans and R. Steennot, *Handboek consumentenbescherming en marktpraktijken*, Antwerp, Intersentia, 2023, 96–97.

2751 See CJEU, Judgment of 18 December 2014, C-449/13, *Consumer Finance*, ECLI:EU:C:2014:2464 (where the CJEU placed the burden of proof in relation to the information requirements of the CCD 1 on the creditor by relying on the effectiveness principle) and CJEU, Judgment of 10 June 2021, Joined cases C-776/19-C-1982/19, *BNP Paribas Personal Finance*, ECLI:EU:C:2021:470 (where the CJEU considered that effective consumer protection cannot be ensured if the consumer has to prove a negative fact, i.e.i.e. prove that the company did not provide him with all the required information necessary to comply with the transparency requirement.).

omission[2752] or a misleading action within the meaning of the UCPD.[2753] Under Belgian law, the penalties for unfair commercial practices towards consumers may be severe. If a certain practice of providing incomplete or false information is considered misleading, the court may (but is not obliged to) rule that the PSS supplier must refund the amounts paid by the consumer, without returning the product already delivered.[2754] In the context of PSS contracts, it seems to me that this provision should be interpreted to mean that the services already performed do not have to be returned or reimbursed, but the products that are part of the as-a-service contract do have to be returned to the PSS supplier-owner. Under Dutch law, a contract concluded as a result of an unfair commercial practice is voidable.[2755] In addition to these specific remedies, the PSS user-consumer may also invoke the sanctions of general contract law, such as the possibility of claiming (extra)contractual liability, or the nullity of the contract if the conditions of one of the vices of consent are met.[2756]

650. UCTD TRANSPARENCY TEST AND THE PRICE OF THE PSS – As discussed above, the transparency requirements of the UCTD apply to all types of (not-individually negotiated[2757]) contract terms, thus including "core terms".[2758] Thus, contractual clauses on the price of the PSS are also subject to the transparency test of the UCTD and its national implementation.[2759] The UCTD transparency test requires that the PSS user must be given a reasonable opportunity to examine the contractual clauses on the price of the PSS and, even more importantly, that they must be in plain intelligible language, i.e. that they are formally and grammatically intelligible and that the average consumer can evaluate their economic consequences.[2760] For example, a price determination based on a very complicated calculation, with complex parameters, could potentially be considered untransparent. This will mainly be a concern for result-oriented PSS, such as ventilation as a service, heating as a service or light as a service, where consumers generally have less knowledge about the complex services offered. For

2752 E.g. if not all elements of the price are mentioned. See for examples: Pres. Comm. Mons (sum. proc.) (BE) 9 March 2012, *Jaarboek Marktpraktijken* 2012, 181 and J.P. Oudenaarde (BE) 7 December 2020, *T.Vred.* 2021, 555, case note. R. STEENNOT.

2753 EU: Art. 6 UCPD (misleading actions) and Art. 7 UCPD (misleading omissions). **Belgium**: Art. VI.97 BCEL (misleading actions) and Art. VI.99 BCEL (misleading omissions). **The Netherlands**: Art. 6:193c DCC (misleading actions) and Art. 6:193d DCC (misleading omissions).

2754 Art. VI.38(2) BCEL. See for an application: J.P. Charleroi (BE) 1 February 2017, *T.Vred.* 2017, 510, case note H. JACQUEMIN.

2755 Art. 6:193j(3) DCC.

2756 See *supra* no. 92.

2757 Except for under **Belgian law**, where *all* terms in B2C contracts (even if individually negotiated) are subjected to the control regime of unfair terms.

2758 See *supra* no. 155.

2759 See Art. 5 and (2) UCTD. **Belgium**: Art. VI.37, §1 WER. **The Netherlands**: Art. 6:238(2) DCC.

2760 See e.g. CJEU, Judgment of 30 April 2014, C-26/13, *Kásler*, ECLI:EU:C:2014:282, para. 71–75. See more in-depth *supra* no. 156 and 157.

use-oriented PSS with a pay-per-use component that is relatively straightforward (e.g. number of washes, number of minutes per ride on an e-scooter, etc.), this will be less of a concern. The UCTD transparency test is without prejudice to the specific pre-contractual and contractual information requirements regarding the price of the PSS. In fact, these information requirements are also taken into account for the transparency test under the UCTD, on a case-by-case basis, and in light of their scope and purpose.[2761]

651. Consequences of untransparent terms on the price of the PSS – As already mentioned above, the national courts are under the obligation to *ex officio* assess the unfairness – and therefore also the transparency – of terms that fall within the scope of the UCTD.[2762] If a contractual term on the price of the PSS is considered untransparent, the UCTD provides that it should not be binding on the PSS user-consumer.[2763] Under Belgian law, this means that the term is prohibited and null and void, while under Dutch law, the term is voidable.[2764] Since terms on the price of the PSS relate to the essential elements of the PSS contract, the nullity on the terms means that the PSS contract cannot continue to exist.[2765]

652. Evaluation: EU consumer acquis provides remedies for untransparent pricing but challenges remain – The (pre-)contractual information requirements of the EU consumer acquis and the transparency requirement of the UCTD thus require the PSS supplier to properly inform the (prospective) PSS user of how the price of the PSS is calculated. In addition, even if the PSS user was informed of how the price of the PSS is determined, too complicated price calculations with complex parameters that are not intelligible for the average consumer could be considered untransparent and therefore rendered null and void. As a result, the EU consumer acquis already contains multiple provisions protecting the PSS user-consumer against false, misleading, or unclear clauses on the price of the PSS (including any terms containing hidden costs). However, also here, one of the biggest flaws of information obligations should be reiterated, namely that consumers do not sufficiently read and/or understand the information made available.[2766] Consequently, even if the PSS supplier provides all the necessary information, it is not guaranteed that the PSS user-consumer gets the "best deal" for his specific needs. In addition, for service contracts in general and servitised business models in particular,

---

2761 EC, *Guidance on the interpretation of Council Directive 93/13/EEC on unfair terms in consumer contracts*, 27.9.2019, 2019/C 323/04 28.

2762 See *supra* no. 151.

2763 See Art. 5 *juncto* Art. 6(1) UCTD.

2764 **Belgium**: Art. VI.37, §1 *juncto* Art. VI.84, §1 BCEL. **The Netherlands**: Art. 6:238(2) *juncto* Art. 6:233 DCC.

2765 Compare with *supra* no. 177.

2766 See *supra* no. 116.

it is very difficult to have an objective comparison mechanism. After all, the products and additional services are rather variable between different PSS offers and their value is hard to compare based on pre-contractual information alone. This means that challenges will remain when comparing different PSS offers, and that introducing additional information requirements does not constitute a real solution. In my view, a better solution relates to the role of consumer organisations. After all, they are in a good position to inform the consumer, for example, by making useful comparisons between different PSS offers or between opting for a PSS contract and buying the product.

5.2.4. REMEDIES IN CASE OF NON-PAYMENT OF THE PRICE

653. General contract law remedies if PSS user does not pay the price (on time) – If the PSS user does not pay the price of the PSS (on time), the PSS supplier has access to the general contract law remedies.[2767] In the first place, this means that the PSS supplier can invoke the *exception non adimpleti contractus* (enac) to suspend the performance of its obligations until the PSS user pays the price of the service. Second, the PSS supplier can opt for the remedy of performance, which will amount to claiming the overdue periodical fees through real execution or a debt collection agency. Third, if there is a fundamental non-performance (i.e. the non-performance is sufficiently serious, for example when multiple payments are missed), the PSS supplier can choose to terminate the PSS contract. Finally, the PSS supplier can claim damages (exclusively or in combination with the remedies mentioned earlier), for example through contractual or statutory negligence interest or an indemnity clause.

654. Negligence interest as sanction for late payment of the price – If the PSS user is late in fulfilling his obligation to pay the price of the PSS, he will have to pay damages for delay.[2768] This takes the form of negligence interest (*nalatigheidsinterest, intérêts de retard*).[2769]

2767 See *supra* section 2.6.6.

2768 **Belgium**: S. Stijns, *Verbintenissenrecht*, Boek 2, Bruges, Die Keure, 2009, 104, no. 148. **The Netherlands**: Art. 6:85 DCC; G.T. de Jong, H.B. Krans and M.H. Wissink, *Verbintenissenrecht algemeen (Studiereeks Burgerlijk Recht, deel 4)*, Deventer, Wolters Kluwer, 2022, 191, no. 197.

2769 Under Belgian law, a distinction is made between moratory interest (*moratoire interesten, intérêts moratoires*) and compensatory interest (*compensatoire interesten, intérêts compensatoires*), both defined in Art. 5.206(2) and (3) BCC respectively. Moratory interest relates to monetary debts (*geldschulden, obligation de somme*), i.e.i.e. a sum of money that is numerically determined or can be determined according to legally or contractually defined means of calculation. Compensatory interest relates to value debts (*waardeschulden, obligation de valeur*), i.e.i.e. compensation for damages whose amount is not numerically determined by law or by contract, nor can it be determined according to a predetermined basis of calculation and is therefore (usually) only determined by a court. The obligation

655. Requirement for negligence interest: PSS user must be in default – Both under Belgian and Dutch law, negligence interests as compensation for late performance of the obligation to pay the price of the PSS are only due when the PSS user is in default. This means that negligence interest is due from the day of the notice of default, unless the PSS contract or the law[2770] provides that the PSS user is in default by operation of law.[2771]

656. Statutory or contractual interest rate – In principle, the damages for delay in the performance of the obligation to pay the price of the PSS are fixed at a flat rate, namely the statutory interest rate.[2772] The Belgian statutory interest rate for 2024 is 5.75% per year and the Dutch statutory interest rate for 2024 is 7% per year.[2773] The PSS supplier does not have to prove the existence and amount of these damages.[2774] At the same time, neither the PSS supplier nor the PSS user can prove that the real amount of damages is higher, respectively lower than the statutory rate.[2775] However, under Belgian law, there is an exception to this principle. In case of an intentional fault of the debtor, the damages may exceed the interest at the statutory rate, provided the creditor can prove the amount of the actual damages.[2776] The statutory interest rate is only default law, so the PSS contract can stipulate a different contractual interest rate.[2777] The analysis of the real-life PSS contracts shows that in practice, PSS suppliers often confirm the fact that the PSS user will owe the statutory interest if payment is not made on time. This is for instance the case in the terms and conditions of

to pay the price of the PSS is a monetary debt, so the Belgian rules on moratory interest (Art. 5.240 BCC) apply. See more in-depth on this distinction: I. Samoy, S. Stijns and S. Jansen, "Dommages et intérêts compensatoires et moratoires (Rapport belge)" in B. Dubuisson and P. Jourdain (eds.), *Le dommage et sa réparation dans la responsabilité contractuelle et extracontractuelle*, Brussels, Bruylant, 2015, (145) 145–213.

2770 Especially under Dutch law, the DCC contains quite a few exceptions on the requirement of a prior notice of default, with Art. 6:83, *sub* a. DCC (no requirement of a notice of default if a time limit has expired without the obligation being fulfilled) being the most important.

2771 **Belgium**: Art. 5.240(3) BCC. **The Netherlands**: Art. 6:85 and 6:119(1) DCC.

2772 **Belgium**: Art. 5.240(1) BCC. **The Netherlands**: Art. 6:119(1) DCC.

2773 **Belgium**: See Art. 2, §1 Act 5 May 1865 on interest-bearing loans, *BS* 15 August 1865: *"Every calendar year, the legal interest rate in both civil and commercial matters is determined as follows: the average of the 1-year EURIBOR interest rate during the month of December of the previous year is rounded up to the higher quarter percent; the interest rate thus obtained is increased by 2 percent."* **The Netherlands**: Art. 6:120(1) DCC; www.rijksoverheid.nl/onderwerpen/schulden/vraag-en-antwoord/hoogte-wettelijke-rente.

2774 **Belgium**: Art. 5.240(2) DCC.

2775 **Belgium**: Explanatory Memorandum, *Parliamentary Papers* Kamer 2020–21, no. 55–1806/1, 275; I. Claeys and T. Tanghe, *Nieuw Algemeen Contractenrecht*, Antwerp, Intersentia, 2023, 727. **The Netherlands**: F.H.J. Mijnssen, *Verbintenissen tot betaling van een geldsom (Mon. BW nr. B39)*, Deventer, Wolters Kluwer, 2017, 44, no. 20.1; G.T. de Jong, H.B. Krans and M.H. Wissink, *Verbintenissenrecht algemeen (Studiereeks Burgerlijk Recht, deel 4)*, Deventer, Wolters Kluwer, 2022, 89, no. 109.

2776 Art. 5.240(4) BCC; Explanatory Memorandum, *Parliamentary Papers* Kamer 2020–21, no. 55–1806/1, 275.

2777 **Belgium**: Art. 5.240(1), *in fine* BCC. **The Netherlands**: Art. 6:119(3) DCC.

Blue Movement and *Dressr* (cited below), but also in the terms and conditions of *Bundles* and *Swapfiets*. Other PSS suppliers, such as *Fairphone Easy* and *Repeat/ Gerrard Street*, do not explicitly mention any statutory or contractual interest but refer to administrative and extrajudicial costs associated with collection, which will be borne by the PSS user in case of non-payment. An example of a contractual interest rate can be found in the terms and conditions of *Live Light*, where it is stipulated that the PSS user shall be required to pay 1% interest per month if a payment term is exceeded.

> Terms and conditions Blue Movement – Art. 5.7 "If payment is not made on time, the User shall be in breach of its obligations under the Contract and shall be in default by operation of law. BSH will then request the User to still fulfil his payment obligation within 14 days, whereby it will be notified that if payment is still not made within 14 days, *the User will owe the statutory interest* and BSH will claim compensation for the extrajudicial collection costs (being a maximum of: 15% on outstanding amounts up to € 2500; 10% on the next € 2500 and 5% on the next € 5000 with a minimum of € 40). [...]" (own emphasis).

> Terms and conditions Dressr – Art. 12 (Past due accounts and collections) "Should You not pay within the term set for payment, Dressr shall be released from all obligations vis-à-vis You and may, on its own initiative, cancel all services. *Every late payment shall, after a first notice of default by email, give rise to the charging of interest on arrears at the legal rate.*" (own emphasis).

> Terms and conditions Live Light – Art. 8.3 "If a payment term is exceeded, the Tenant will be in default by operation of law and, without any notice of default required, *shall be required to pay 1% interest per month, to be calculated from the due date.* [...]" (own emphasis).

657. Limits to (excessive) contractual interest rates – Clauses in the PSS contract stipulating a contractual interest rate are essentially a specific type of indemnity clauses.[2778] After all, they determine liquidated damages (using an interest rate) for a particular breach of contract (i.e. a delay in payment) for a particular type of obligation (i.e. monetary debts). This means that if these contractual interest terms are excessive, they can be challenged using the unfair contract terms rules regarding indemnity clauses.

Under Belgian law, book XIX of the BCEL fiercely limits the possibility to charge extra fees to consumers in case of late payment.[2779] If the PSS user has not paid the price by the agreed due date, the PSS supplier must in the first place send a free payment reminder, either by post or electronically.[2780] This free payment reminder must at least mention: (i) the balance due; (ii) the amount that will be

[2778] See on indemnity clauses *supra* no. 304.

[2779] See for an in-depth discussion of book XIX BCEL: G. Straetmans and R. Steennot, *Handboek consumentenbescherming en marktpraktijken*, Antwerp, Intersentia, 2023, 483–492.

[2780] Art. XIX.2, §1 *juncto* Art. XIX.2, §2, (1) BCEL.

due under the indemnity clause; (iii) the details of the business; (iv) a description of the occurrence and due date of the debt; and (v) the term of payment.[2781] In the case of contracts for regular delivery of goods and services, as will be the case with PSS, the business must only send the reminders for non-payment three times a year free of charge.[2782] From the fourth late payment in a year, the PSS supplier may charge reminder fees, which may not exceed € 7,50 plus postage.[2783] After this first payment reminder, the consumer must be given another fourteen-day payment period, which starts on the third working day after the reminder is sent, or the day after if it was sent if the PSS supplier has sent the reminder electronically.[2784] The burden of proof lies with the PSS supplier and these rules are mandatory law.[2785]

The PSS supplier may only charge interest on arrears to the extent expressly provided for in advance in the terms and conditions of the PSS contract and after expiry of the additional fourteen-day period. However, if the PSS supplier is a small or medium-sized enterprise ("SME"),[2786] it may stipulate that the interest on arrears already starts to run on the day after the first payment reminder is sent.[2787] The interest on arrears that may be charged is also subject to a ceiling, namely no more than the reference interest rate[2788] (currently 3,75%) plus 8%, as meant in Article 5, §2 of the Belgian Act of 2 August 2002 on combating late payments in commercial transactions, and this on the amount still to be paid.[2789] In the case of a lump-sum indemnity clause, other caps apply.[2790]

In addition to these specific provisions, the Belgian blacklist also contains two provisions dealing with indemnity clauses. First, Article VI.83, 17° BCEL requires that indemnity clauses must be reciprocal and equivalent.[2791] This blacklisted item also applies to contractual terms fixing a higher interest rate for late payment than the rate applicable under general contract law (the statutory interest rate).[2792, 2793] Second, Article VI.83, 24° BCEL prohibits

2781 Art. XIX.2, §3 BCEL.
2782 Art. XIX.2, §2, (2) BCEL.
2783 *Ibid.*
2784 Art. XIX.2, §1 BCEL.
2785 Art. XIX.2, §5 and §6 BCEL.
2786 Within the meaning of Art. 1:24, §1 of the Belgian Companies and Associations Code.
2787 Art. XIX.2, §4 BCEL.
2788 This is the interest rate used by the European Central Bank for basic refinancing operations.
2789 Art. XIX.4, 1° BCEL.
2790 See *infra* no. 659.
2791 See also *supra* no. 304.
2792 R. Steennot, "Commentaar bij art. VI.83, 17° WER" in *Handels- en economisch recht. Commentaar met overzicht van rechtspraak en rechtsleer*, Mechelen, Kluwer, loose-leaf, 2017, (489) 497, no. 3. See for examples,. Ghent (BE) 26 October 2012, *Jaarboek Marktpraktijken* 2012, 286, case note. P. Cambie, *TGR* 2014, 46; Ghent (BE) 4 January 2012, *NjW* 2012, 73, case note R. Steennot; Ghent (BE) 20 December 2010, *Jaarboek Marktpraktijken* 2010, 182, case note P. Cambie.
2793 In contrast, clauses that merely confirm the situation of general contract law, namely that the consumer owes moratory interest at the statutory rate, do not have to meet the requirements

excessive indemnity clauses, i.e. clauses where the compensation for late or non-performance is clearly disproportionate to the disadvantage the PSS supplier may suffer.[2794] Nevertheless, it seems rather unlikely that the Belgian courts will consider contractual interest rates that comply with book XIX BCEL unfair.[2795]

Under Dutch law, excessive contractual interest rates in the general terms and conditions of the PSS supplier may be combated using the general test (unreasonably onerous terms) of Article 6:233, *sub* a DCC, as these terms are not included in the Dutch blacklist or grey list.[2796] In addition, they can also be tested against the open norm of reasonableness and fairness laid down in Article 6:248(2) DCC.[2797] Under both Belgian and Dutch law, it seems that the statutory interest rate will be leading in determining whether there is effectively an excessive contractual interest rate. In addition, the actual loss suffered by the PSS supplier may also be taken into account (e.g. the interest rate of a credit taken out by the PSS supplier to bridge the late or non-payment of the periodical fee). If a contractual interest rate is indeed excessive, the national courts will have to set aside the term. As the CJEU clarified in *Asbeek Brusse*,[2798] the possibility under national general contract law to mitigate excessive indemnity clauses to a reasonable amount[2799] may not be applied in contracts with consumers.[2800]

The following model clause can be used in order to comply with both the Belgian and Dutch provisions on (contractual) interest on arrears.

Model clause #31: Interest on arrears

- **In the event of late payment, [the PSS user] shall pay interest on the outstanding overdue amount at a rate of [specified reasonable rate, under Belgian law capped at reference interest rate (currently 3,75%) plus 8%, as meant in Article 5, §2 of the Belgian Act of 2 August 2002 on combating late payments in commercial transactions] per [specified adverb of frequency], calculated from [B2C: the fifteenth calendar day after the third business day following the first notice of default; B2C (SME): the calendar day following the first notice of default].**[2801]

of reciprocity and equivalence. See e.g. Mons (BE) 19 January 2011, *Jaarboek Marktpraktijken* 2011, 220.

2794 See also *supra* no. 304.

2795 See in this sense also: G. Straetmans and R. Steennot, *Handboek consumentenbescherming en marktpraktijken*, Antwerp, Intersentia, 2023, 388.

2796 G.T. de Jong, H.B. Krans and M.H. Wissink, *Verbintenissenrecht algemeen (Studiereeks Burgerlijk Recht, deel 4)*, Deventer, Wolters Kluwer, 2022, 210, no. 216.

2797 HR (NL) 17 December 2004, ECLI:NL:HR:2004:AR4151, *NJ* 2005/271.

2798 CJEU, Judgment of 30 May 2013, C-488/11, *Asbeek Brusse*, ECLI:EU:C:2013:341, para. 54–60.

2799 **Belgium**: Art. 5.88 BCC. **The Netherlands**: Art. 6:92 DCC.

2800 See also *supra* no. 178.

2801 Model clause partly based on C. Borucki, H. Slachmuylders, B. Keirsbilck, D. Gruyaert and E. Terryn, *Model clauses for Product-as-a-Service (PaaS) contracts*, CE Center. Circular Economy Policy Research Center, 2022–23, 48.

658. COMPOUND INTEREST (ANATOCISM) – Under Belgian law, there is a principal prohibition on compound interest (also called "anatocism"), i.e. the incorporation of accrued interest into the capital.[2802] Traditionally it was held that this provision is of public order,[2803] but according to the Explanatory Memorandum of the new BCC it is "only" mandatory law.[2804] According to this provision, capitalisation is only allowed for interest that has been due for more than one year. In addition, the creditor and the debtor must have entered into a special contract to this effect, or the creditor must have given the debtor written notice.[2805] Under Dutch law, on the other hand – and unlike the situation under the old DCC – establishes that compound interest is the general rule. Thus, at the end of each year, the amount on which statutory interest is calculated is increased by the unpaid interest due over that year.[2806]

659. INDEMNITY CLAUSES IN ADDITION TO NEGLIGENCE INTEREST – In addition to interest clauses (either clauses confirming the statutory interest rate or clauses setting a contractual interest rate), the PSS contract may also contain additional indemnity clauses. In principle, these can be claimed cumulatively, provided they do not relate to the same damages.[2807] For example, the interest clause may relate to the late payment (i.e. compensation for the delay), while the indemnity clauses may relate to the legal costs or collection costs the PSS supplier must make to seek payment.[2808] The terms and conditions of *Blue Movement* provide a good example of the combination of an interest clause for the delay in payment and an indemnity clause for the extrajudicial collection costs. Additionally, the terms and conditions of *Dressr* provide another example, albeit less explicitly.

> TERMS AND CONDITIONS BLUE MOVEMENT – Art. 5.7 "If payment is not made on time, the User shall be in breach of its obligations under the Contract and shall be in default by operation of law. BSH will then request the User to still fulfil his payment obligation within 14 days, whereby it will be notified that if payment is still not made within 14 days, *the User will owe the statutory interest and BSH will claim compensation for the extrajudicial collection costs (being a maximum of: 15% on outstanding amounts up to € 2500; 10% on the next € 2500 and 5% on the next € 5000 with a minimum of € 40)*. […]" (own emphasis).[2809]

2802 Art. 5.207 BCC.
2803 See e.g. R. KRUITHOF, H. BOCKEN, F. DE LY and B. DE TEMMERMAN, "Verbintenissenrecht (1981–1992). Overzicht van rechtspraak", *TPR* 1994, (171) 659.
2804 Explanatory Memorandum, *Parliamentary Papers* Kamer, 2020–21, no. 55–1806/001, 249.
2805 Art. 5.207 BCC.
2806 Art. 6:119(2) DCC.
2807 See in this sense: I. CLAEYS and T. TANGHE, *Nieuw Algemeen Contractenrecht*, Antwerp, Intersentia, 2023, 751.
2808 See for an application: Liège (BE) 9 January 2003, *JLMB* 1507.
2809 Compare also with Art. 5.5 Terms and Conditions Bundles.

> TERMS AND CONDITIONS DRESSR – Art. 12 (Past due accounts and collections) "[...] Every late payment shall, after a first notice of default by email, give rise to the charging of interest on arrears at the legal rate. *You will also have to pay a fixed penalty of 10%*, calculated on the remaining total amount due in principal, with a maximum of 1.250 EUR" (own emphasis).

However, there are limits to the combination of indemnity clauses and (contractual) interest clauses. Under Belgian law, besides caps on contractual interest rates, Book XIX provides for caps on indemnity clauses for late payments.[2810] Thus, a late payment fee may not exceed: (i) 20 euros, if the balance due is less than or equal to 150 euros; (ii) 30 euros plus 10% of the amount due on the tranche between 150.01 and 500 euros if the balance due is between 150.01 and 500 euros; and (iii) 65 euros plus 5% of the amount due on the tranche above 500.01 euros with a maximum of 2,000 euros if the balance due is above 500 euros.[2811] Additionally, under both Belgian and Dutch law, the damages (including interest) the PSS user must pay if he does not pay the monthly fee (on time) cannot be excessive. According to the CJEU in *Radlinger and Radlingerová*, in assessing whether an indemnity clause is unfair, the cumulative effect of all relevant clauses of the contract in question must be taken into account by the national court.[2812]

In this sense, the indemnity clause for non-payment in the terms and conditions of *Live Light* will most likely be unfair, at least under Belgian law. After all, the contractual interest rate of 1% per month translates into an interest rate of 12.683% per year, which exceeds the reference interest rate (currently 3,75%) plus 8%, as meant in Article 5, §2 of the Belgian Act of 2 August 2002. Moreover, this term stipulates an additional flat fee of 15% of the *annual* usage fee (i.e. not limited to the overdue fees) *and* reimbursement of legal costs, which surpasses the cap of Article XIX.4, 2° BCEL. Also under Dutch law, the combination of all these components seems disproportionate with the damage *Live Light* is suffering because of the late payment. As a result, the clause will most likely be considered unfair.

> TERMS AND CONDITIONS LIVE LIGHT – Art. 8.3 "If a payment term is exceeded, the Tenant will be in default by operation of law and, without any notice of default required, shall be required to pay 1% interest per month, to be calculated from the due date. *Live Light is also entitled to flat-rate compensation of 15% of the annual Usage Fee, with a minimum of 250 euros, plus the reimbursement of legal costs.*" (own emphasis)

2810 Compare with *supra* no. 657.

2811 Art. XIX.4, 2° BCEL.

2812 CJEU, Judgment of 21 April 2016, C-377/14, *Radlinger and Radlingerová*, ECLI:EU:C:2016:283, para. 101.

The following model clause can be used in order to comply with both the Belgian and Dutch provisions on late payment fees.

Model clause #32: late payment fee

- **In the event of late payment, [the PSS user] shall pay a late payment fee of [specified reasonable amount, under Belgian law capped in accordance with Art. XIX.4, 2° BCEL] per [specified adverb of frequency], calculated from [B2C: the fifteenth calendar day after the third business day following the first notice of default; B2C (SME): the calendar day following the first notice of default].[2813]**

660. Failure of direct debit or credit card payment – As discussed above, PSS suppliers often contractually require the PSS user to pay via direct debit or via credit card.[2814] Several analysed PSS contracts anticipate the situations where automatic payments fail (e.g. because of insufficient funds), where the SEPA direct debit mandate is revoked or where payments are reversed by the PSS user. If the automatic payments fail, most PSS suppliers usually give the PSS user another attempt to complete the payment, either by retrying at a later time, or by offering the PSS user the possibility to pay using a different means of payment, for example a payment link. In case the PSS user remains in default, the PSS supplier's next step will generally be to hand the claim over to a debt collection agency or bringing the claim before the court. In addition, other remedies can also be invoked, such as the enac (e.g. by remotely locking the device) or termination of the PSS contract. The terms and conditions of *Fairphone Easy* and *Swapphone* cited below provide an example of this. Moreover, the terms and conditions of *Swapphone* also contain an indemnity clause in case the PSS user reverses an amount or blocks *Swapphone's* account by revoking the SEPA mandate. In my view, this clause is not excessive, as it fixes the fine at a reasonable amount of € 25, with the right to claim additional damages.

> Terms and conditions Fairphone Easy – Art. 9.3 "If a payment fails due to insufficient funds, a retry of the same payment will be scheduled two (2) days from the moment the first transaction failed. This process will be executed a maximum of three (3) times following the initial transaction attempt. Please note that following the third attempt, You will be in default of payment and Fairphone may engage a debt collection agency as per clause 9.4." Art. 9.4 "Repeated failure of debit payments will result in Fairphone engaging a debt collection agency. All administrative and extrajudicial costs associated with collection will be payable by You. Fairphone may also suspend the device remotely."

[2813] Model clause partly based on C. Borucki, H. Slachmuylders, B. Keirsbilck, D. Gruyaert and E. Terryn, *Model clauses for Product-as-a-Service (PaaS) contracts*, CE Center. Circular Economy Policy Research Center, 2022–23, 48.

[2814] See *supra* no. 627–628.

> Terms and conditions Swapphone – Art. 9.1 "When entering into a Rental contract, the Lessee is obliged to also provide a direct debit authorisation for the monthly rent and any other fees/fines due. […] The Lessee must be in possession of a SEPA bank account number. *He is not allowed to reverse the amount and/or block the account. If the Lessee reverses an amount and/or blocks Swapphone's account, the Lessee shall forfeit an immediately due and payable fine to Swapphone in the amount of € 25* (in words: twenty-five euros) without prejudice to Swapphone's right to claim (additional) damages as well as the right to lock the smartphone through a lost mode." Art. 9.2 "when the rent and/or other fees/fines cannot be collected for whatever reason (e.g. reversal, insufficient balance, etc.), the Lessee will be given the opportunity to pay by means of a payment link. This link will remain valid for five (5) days." Art. 9.3 "*If the Lessee has not yet paid via the payment link referred to in paragraph 2 of this article, the claim will be handed over to [Collection Agency] for collection.* [The Collection Agency] will grant the Lessee a period of fourteen (14) days to still fulfil the payment obligations. If payment is not made within this 14-day period, the Lessee will owe statutory interest on the outstanding amount and Swapphone is entitled to charge the (extrajudicial) collection costs in accordance with the law. In this case, Swapphone is also entitled to immediately terminate or dissolve the Rental Contract […] and is also entitled to (remotely) lock the Smartphone by means of a lost mode." (Own emphasis).

5.3. PRICE CHANGES

5.3.1. PRICE CHANGES DURING LONG-TERM PSS CONTRACTS

661. Increasing the periodic fee during the course of the PSS contract? – PSS contracts are generally characterised by the fact that a long-term relationship is established between the PSS supplier and the PSS user. During this long-term relationship, circumstances can change, potentially affecting the pricing strategy of the PSS supplier. The question therefore arises whether the PSS supplier can pass on price increases resulting from circumstances such as changed legislation, rising material costs and wages, changed market conditions, etc. This question is especially relevant given the rise in inflation, which began in mid-2021 and was caused by pandemic-related economic disruption, supply chain issues, fiscal and monetary stimulus measures by governments and central banks in response to lockdowns, and the impact of the Russian invasion of Ukraine on global oil and natural gas prices. There are two possible ways the periodic fee can be increased during the PSS contract. Either this can be the result of price indexation, or this can be due to a (unilateral) price change clause.

662. Price indexation – Price indexation refers to the practice of periodically adjusting prices in the PSS contract in accordance with changes in a contractually specified price index (e.g. the consumer price index (sometimes abbreviated as "CPI")). The purpose of price indexation is to maintain the real value of payments and transactions over time in the face of inflation (or, exceptionally, deflation). For use-oriented PSS, the rules of the rental contract stipulate, as a starting point, that the base rental price remains the same over the course of the PSS contract. However, the parties are free to include a price indexation clause in their contract. Such a clause has as its effect that the base rental price fluctuates according to a certain benchmark, such as the exchange rate of a foreign currency, the price of a particular commodity or consumer prices.[2815] Contrary to the rules for the rental contract for immovable goods,[2816] the Belgian and Dutch rental contract rules contain no provisions on price indexation clauses for the rental of movables. The parties are therefore free to determine what applies in their contractual relationship (subject to the limits discussed further). For result-oriented PSS, neither the Belgian nor the Dutch rules of the contract for services contain special provisions on the indexation of the price of the service. Consequently, the principle of freedom of contract applies and the parties can include a price indexation clause in the PSS contract to periodically adjust the monthly fee (within certain limits, see *infra*).

663. Price change clauses – A second way the periodical fee can be increased during the term of the PSS contract is through a price change clause. With a price change clause, the PSS supplier reserves the right to (unilaterally) change the price of the service for the future, regardless of any indexation formula. Examples of price change clauses can, among others, be found in the terms and conditions of *Blue Movement* and *Swapfiets*. Since price change clauses allow the PSS supplier to unilaterally modify one of the essential elements of the PSS contract (i.e. the price of the service), they are subjected especially in contracts with consumers, to certain limits and validity requirements.

> Terms and conditions Blue Movement – Art. 4.4 "BSH is entitled to pass on price increases resulting from legislation to the Renter. However, BSH will not increase the Monthly Fee within three months of concluding the agreement."

> Terms and conditions Swapfiets – Art. 13.1 "Swapfiets reserves the right to change the costs of a Subscription. Changes will be communicated to the Renter via e-mail at least one month before the effective date. The Renter will not be permitted to terminate the Subscription due to a price change, unless the change takes place within three months of the conclusion of the Subscription and the Renter is a consumer."

2815 S. Marysse, "Rechten en verbintenissen van de verhuurder" in M. Dambre, B. Hubeau and S. Stijns (eds.), *Handboek algemeen huurrecht*, Bruges, Die Keure, 2015, (415) 532.

2816 **Belgium**: See Art. 1728*bis* old BCC and Art. 34 Flemish Decree of 9 November 2018 concerning provisions on the rental of residential property or parts thereof, *BS* 7 December 2018. **The Netherlands**: Art. 7:248 and 7:251 DCC (for rental of residential property).

5.3.2. LIMITS TO PRICE CHANGE CLAUSES

664. Belgian law: limits to price change clauses based on elements that depend solely on the will of the PSS supplier – Two provisions on the Belgian blacklist deal with the (im)possibility for the PSS supplier to unilaterally increase the price based on elements that depend solely on its will, i.e. discretionary price change clauses.[2817] A distinction is made between open-ended PSS contracts and fixed-term PSS contracts.[2818]

For open-ended contracts, terms allowing the supplier to unilaterally increase the price based on elements that depend solely on its will are allowed, but only if the PSS user is given the right to terminate the contract without costs or damages within a reasonable period of time before the new price comes into effect.[2819] In the case of a PSS contract, a period of one month seems to be a reasonable period of time.[2820]

For fixed-term contracts, there is a strict prohibition for such terms, even if the consumer can terminate the contract.[2821] So, the distinction between open-ended and fixed-term PSS contracts is quite essential.[2822] The question arises whether a price change clause in a PSS contract of open-ended duration, but which cannot be terminated before a certain period (e.g. the first year),[2823] should be assessed under the rules for open-ended contracts or fixed-term contracts. On this question, Belgian case law has already ruled that the fact that the contract cannot be terminated during an initial 12-month period does not make it a fixed-term contract.[2824]

2817 Art. VI.83, 2° and Art. VI.83, 3° BCEL.

2818 R. Steennot, "Commentaar bij art. VI.83, 2° WER" in *Handels- en economisch recht. Commentaar met overzicht van rechtspraak en rechtsleer*, Mechelen, Kluwer, loose-leaf, 2017, (387) 390.

2819 Art. VI.83, 2° BCEL.

2820 Compare with R. Steennot, "Commentaar bij art. VI.83, 2° WER" in *Handels- en economisch recht. Commentaar met overzicht van rechtspraak en rechtsleer*, Mechelen, Kluwer, loose-leaf, 2017, (387) 393.

2821 Art. VI.83, 3° BCEL. F. Bogaert and B. Van Baeveghem, "Contractuele aspecten van de Wet Marktpraktijken" in I. Claeys, R. Steennot and M. Tison (eds.), *Economisch Recht: Ondernemingen, concurrenten en consumenten. Postuniversitaire Cyclus Willy Delva 2010–2011*, Mechelen, Kluwer, 2011, (1) 34.

2822 R. Steennot, "Commentaar bij art. VI.83, 3° WER" in *Handels- en economisch recht. Commentaar met overzicht van rechtspraak en rechtsleer*, Mechelen, Kluwer, loose-leaf, 2017, (401) 403.

2823 See e.g. Art. 2.1 Terms and Conditions Repeat/Gerrard Street: *"The headphones are rented for a minimum of one period (one month or one year depending on the subscription) and the Subscription has an open-ended duration. The notice period is one month. Cancellation should be done via 'My Account' on the Repeat/Gerrard Street website before the start of the next period"* (own emphasis).

2824 See: Brussels (BE) 25 June 2014, *Jaarboek Marktpraktijken* 2014, 272, case note M. De Man; Comm. Liège (BE) 25 June 2013, *NjW* 2014, 608, case note R. Steennot (at first instance) and Liège (BE) 9 October 2014, *NjW* 2014, 459, case note R. Steennot (on appeal).

665. Belgian law: "objective" price change clauses are allowed – Price change clauses are therefore allowed, provided that objective criteria[2825] (i.e. not solely depending on the will of the PSS supplier) are stipulated in the contract.[2826] These could include commodity and wage prices, the inflation rate, interest rates, etc.[2827] The presence of one objective element is sufficient not to fall under Article VI.83, 2° and 3° BCEL (depend *solely* on the will of the PSS supplier).[2828] An example can be found in the terms and conditions of *Cambio*, which reserves the right to adjust kilometre rates in the event of a changing fuel price or sharply rising electricity price.

> Terms and conditions Cambio – Art. 8.1 "Cambio reserves the right to adjust kilometre rates with immediate effect in the event of a changing fuel price or sharply increasing electricity price in accordance with the conditions in the price list applicable at the time."

666. Belgian law: price indexation clauses are also allowed – There is an exception to the principle that discretionary price change clauses in fixed-terms PSS contracts and discretionary price change clauses without termination option in open-ended contracts are prohibited.[2829] Indeed, under Belgian law, price indexation clauses are permitted for both open-ended and fixed-term contracts, provided they are not illegal and the manner in which prices are adjusted is explicitly described in the contract.[2830] This provision resembles the Annex of the UCTD, which also provides in an exception for price indexation

---

However, critical of this case law: P. Cambie, "Hoe wordt de consument beschermd tegen prijsstijgingen?", *DCCR* 2023, issue 139, (3) 11.

2825 According to the case law of the CJEU, these should also be in plain intelligible language. See: CJEU, Judgment of 26 April 2012, C-472/10, *Invitel*, ECLI:EU:C:2012:242, para. 31.

2826 F. Bogaert and B. Van Baeveghem, "Contractuele aspecten van de Wet Marktpraktijken" in I. Claeys, R. Steennot and M. Tison (eds.), *Economisch Recht: Ondernemingen, concurrenten en consumenten. Postuniversitaire Cyclus Willy Delva 2010–2011*, Mechelen, Kluwer, 2011, (1) 33.

2827 P. Cambie, *Onrechtmatige bedingen*, Ghent, Larcier, 2009, 226; I. Demuynck, *De inhoudelijke controle van onrechtmatige bedingen*, Thesis submitted to obtain the degree of Doctor of Laws, University of Ghent, 2000, 520.

2828 I. Demuynck, *De inhoudelijke controle van onrechtmatige bedingen*, Thesis submitted to obtain the degree of Doctor of Laws, University of Ghent, 2000, 520.

2829 R. Steennot, "Commentaar bij art. VI.83, 3° WER" in *Handels- en economisch recht. Commentaar met overzicht van rechtspraak en rechtsleer*, Mechelen, Kluwer, loose-leaf, 2017, (401) 405; P. Cambie, *Onrechtmatige bedingen*, Ghent, Larcier, 2009, 226 and 231; I. Demuynck, *De inhoudelijke controle van onrechtmatige bedingen*, Thesis submitted to obtain the degree of Doctor of Laws, University of Ghent, 2000, 526.

2830 Art. VI.83, 2°, *sub* a) BCEL (for open-ended contracts) *juncto* Art. VI.83, 3°, second sentence BCEL (which states that the exception of Art. VI.83, 2°, *sub* a) BCEL also applies to fixed-term contracts). In addition, financial services providers may reserve the right to change the interest rate to be paid by or to the consumer unilaterally, without any notice in case of valid reason, provided that the financial services provider is obliged to notify the consumer of the change as soon as possible and the consumer is free to terminate the contract without delay. See Art. VI.83, 2°, *sub* b) BCEL *juncto* Art. VI.83, 3°, second sentence BCEL.

clauses, provided that the method by which the prices vary is explicitly described.[2831]

667. "Provided that they are not illegal": Article 57 Programme Act of 30 March 1976 on economic recovery measures – Price indexation clauses are thus allowed under Belgian law, "*provided that they are not illegal*"."[2832] The legality of price indexation clauses depends, amongst others, on the criteria laid down in the *Act of 30 March 1976 on economic recovery measures.*[2833] This is an old programme act that mainly introduced temporary measures to combat the energy crisis and skyrocketing inflation rates in the 1970s. Pursuant to this Act, any formula for indexing industrial and/or commercial prices, tariffs and parameters of price fluctuation formulas in function of the consumer price index, or any other index, is prohibited in principle. Any clause or application contrary to this prohibition is void by operation of law.[2834] Price indexation clauses are permitted provided that they are only applicable up to an amount not exceeding 80% of the final price, and the revision is made by reference to parameters representing real costs (e.g. wages, energy, building materials, etc.). Moreover, each parameter may only be applicable to that part of the price corresponding to the costs it represents.[2835] These rules do not apply to rental fees, salaries, wages, benefits, social contributions, fees of liberal professionals, sectors for which an exemption is provided by the minister and contracts with a foreign element (except where the services were performed in Belgium and the contract was concluded by persons residing in Belgium).[2836]

668. Evaluation: distinction between rental contracts and contracts for services gives rise to legal uncertainty – Given the

---

2831 Para. 2, point (d) UCTD Annex.

2832 A. Van Oevelen, "Overmachts- en herzieningsbedingen in het gemene recht en in overeenkomsten met consumenten" in S. Stijns and K. Vanderschot (eds.), *Contractuele clausules rond de (niet-)uitvoering en beëindiging van contracten*, Antwerp, Intersentia, 2006, (267) 281.

2833 Act of 30 March 1976 on economic recovery measures, *BS* 1 April 1976 (*Wet van 30 maart 1976 betreffende de economische herstelmaatregelen, Loi du 30 mars 1976 relative aux mesures de redressement économique*). See: J. Schraeyen, E. Enkels, S. Van den Broeke and T. De Clerck, *Algemene voorwaarden*, 2012, Ghent, Larcier, 2012, 88–91 for a more in-depth discussion, including a model clause with a compliant price formula. See also: J. Vansevenant and O. Vanden Berghe, "Prijsherzieningsclausules in relaties tussen private ondernemingen: een stand van zaken na 45 jaar beperkende wetgeving", *TBH* 2023, (353) 353–375 for a critical analysis of this 45-year-old act in light of the recent surge of inflation.

2834 Art. 57, §1 Act of 30 March 1976 on economic recovery measures.

2835 Art. 57, §2 Act of 30 March 1976 on economic recovery measures. See also: Cass. (BE) 13 September 2001, *Arr.Cass.* 2001, 1439, *Pas.* 2001, 1387, *TBP* 2003, 209, case note Van Haegenborgh (If the value of a parameter in a price indexation clause deviate significantly from the actual share of costs that the parameter represents in the price determined by the agreement, the price indexation clause is null and void).

2836 Art. 57, §3 and §6 Act of 30 March 1976 on economic recovery measures.

exclusion of rental fees from the scope of the Act of 30 March on economic recovery measures, the contractual qualification of the PSS contract is very important for the permissibility of price indexation clauses.[2837] The rationale behind this exclusion is that a (mandatory) provision already exists in the BCC for the indexation of rental fees, namely Article 1728*bis* old BCC.[2838] Therefore, if (part of) the PSS contract qualifies as a rental contract, the (complicated) formula of the Act of 30 March 1976 will not apply. If, on the other hand, the PSS contract qualifies as a service contract, these rules will have to be taken into account. In my view, this difference unnecessarily complicates the application of price indexation clauses for PSS contracts, especially as PSS contracts often include both elements of the rental contract and elements of a services contract. This of course does not enhance legal certainty for companies seeking to offer PSS contracts and consumers considering entering into PSS contracts. Additionally, this is exacerbated by the fact that Article 1728*bis* old BCC only applies to rental contracts for immovables and thus does not apply to movable PSS contracts.[2839] Thus, the rationale that there is a special regime for rental contracts to justify the difference between rental fees and service fees is flawed. Additionally, the question is whether the regime of the Act of 30 March 1976 is really necessary as price indexation clauses are not prohibited by the BCEL (and the UCTD Annex).[2840] Furthermore, the statutory formula for price change clauses which are allowed under the Act of 30 March 1976 is needlessly complex[2841] and the question even arises whether an average consumer is able to foresee the economic consequences arising from such a clause (cf. the concept of transparency in *Invitel*[2842]). It therefore seems that the *raison d'être* of this provision, which was introduced to combat a crisis of more than 45 years ago and is hidden in an old programme act, as part of Belgian contract law should be thoroughly re-evaluated.[2843]

2837 See *supra* no. 352 *et seq.*

2838 J. Schraeyen, E. Enkels, S. Van den Broeke and T. De Clerck, *Algemene voorwaarden*, 2012, Ghent, Larcier, 2012, 90. See for a discussion of this provision: M. Dambre, *Bijzondere overeenkomsten: de essentie*, Bruges, Die Keure, 2022, 222–223; Y. Merchiers, *Le bail en général*, Brussels, Larcier, 2015, 151–152, no. 111.

2839 C. Marr, "Le contrat de location mobilière: quelle réglementation appliquer face au mutisme du Code Civil?", *TBBR* 2008, (217) 218, no. 5; Y. Merchiers, *Le bail en général*, Brussels, Larcier, 2015, 356, no. 608.

2840 See in the same sense: P. Cambie, "Hoe wordt de consument beschermd tegen prijsstijgingen?", *DCCR* 2023, afl. 139, (3) 14; I. Demuynck, *De inhoudelijke controle van onrechtmatige bedingen*, Thesis submitted to obtain the degree of Doctor of Laws, University of Ghent, 2000, 527.

2841 See *infra* no. 678 for a model clause complying with the statutory formula of Art. 57 Act of 30 March 1976.

2842 CJEU, Judgment of 26 April 2012, C-472/10, *Invitel*, ECLI:EU:C:2012:242, para. 28.

2843 In the same sense: J. Vansevenant and O. Vanden Berghe, "Prijsherzieningsclausules in relaties tussen private ondernemingen: een stand van zaken na 45 jaar beperkende wetgeving", *TBH* 2023, (353) 375.

669. Solution: repealing Article 57 Act of 30 March 1976 and introducing a new (uniform) regime for price indexation clauses in the BCC – The benefits and legal basis of Article 57 of the Act of 30 March 1976 thus merit a thorough re-evaluation. In my view, it would be better to repeal the provision and clarify the role of price indexation clauses in Book 7 of the "new" BCC. Preferably, this new regime for price indexation clauses does not distinguish between rental contracts (for movables) and contracts for services, as this may create legal uncertainty – especially in mixed contracts such as PSS contracts with both a use and a service component. In my view, the basic rule should be that a contract will not be indexed unless the parties explicitly include an indexation clause in their contract. Since the CJEU has already held that traders can have a legitimate interest in changing the prices and rates of their services, and that a price change using an objective consumer price index does not raise any concerns,[2844] it does not seem necessary to impose special limits or requirements for indexation clauses in contracts with consumers. After all, the transparency requirement of the UCTD also remains applicable, allowing to combat incomprehensible or complex price indexation terms that would result in the average consumer not being able to foresee the economic consequences of the contract.[2845] If the legislator would nevertheless still consider it appropriate to adopt additional consumer protection measures, a possible solution would be to adopt a (mandatory) provision similar to Article 1728*bis* old BCC so that indexation is done only once per year and according to a (less complex) statutory formula.

Policy Recommendation #5

- **Consider repealing Article 57 Act of 30 March 1976 on economic recovery measures.**
- **Consider leaving price indexation clauses to the contractual freedom of the parties, or – if legislative intervention is still deemed necessary – consider introducing a new (uniform) regime for price indexation clauses in Book 7 of the "new" BCC where inspiration can be drawn from Article 1728*bis* old BCC.**

670. Dutch law: no price increases within the first three months of the conclusion of the contract – Dutch law blacklists clauses allowing the supplier to increase the price set out in the contract within the first three months of the conclusion of the contract unless the PSS user can in that case

2844 See CJEU, Judgment of 26 November 2015, C-326/14, *Verein für Konsumenteninformation/A1 Telekom Austria AG*, ECLI:EU:C:2015:782 12.

2845 CJEU, Judgment of 21 March 2013, C-92/11, *RWE Vertrieb AG*, ECLI:EU:C:2013:180, para. 49; CJEU, Judgment of 26 April 2012, C-472/10, *Invitel*, ECLI:EU:C:2012:242, para. 28.

terminate the contract.[2846] The Dutch blacklist thus leaves a lot more room to include (discretionary) price change clauses in the PSS contract compared to Belgian law.[2847] The only restriction is that for three months after the conclusion of the contract, the PSS user must be able to terminate the contract. Belgian law, on the other hand, completely prohibits discretionary price change clauses in fixed-term contracts or, in open-ended contracts, requires that the consumer can terminate the contract at any time during the contract in the event of a price change if the new price is based on elements solely dependent on the will of the PSS supplier.

671. Dutch law: no explicit exception for price indexation clauses – Contrary to the UCTD Annex and the BCEL, the Dutch blacklist and grey list do not contain an explicit exception for price indexation clauses. Of course, the exception in the UCTD Annex is also taken into account when assessing the (un)fairness of a price change clause under Dutch law. In practice, Dutch PSS contracts sometimes include a price indexation clause based on an objective consumption price index,[2848] often the inflation index of the Dutch Central Bureau of Statistics[2849] ("Dutch CBS").[2850]

672. General unfairness test with particular relevance for two terms listed in the UCTD Annex – The Belgian and Dutch blacklists are not the whole story. Price change clauses can also be combated using the general unfairness test.[2851] For this, the "indicative and non-exhaustive list of terms which may be regarded as unfair"[2852] laid down in the UCTD Annex is highly important.[2853] Two points of the indicative list are relevant in particular. First, Paragraph 1, point (j) of the UCTD Annex states that may be unfair, terms with the object or effect of: *"enabling the seller or supplier to alter the terms of the contract unilaterally without a valid reason which is specified in the contract"*." This also includes terms allowing for price changes.[2854] Second, Paragraph 1, point (l) of the UCTD Annex mentions terms with the object or effect of *"allowing the supplier to increase his price without giving the consumer the*

2846 Art. 6:236, *sub* i. DCC. M.B.M. Loos, *Algemene voorwaarden*, The Hague, Boom juridisch, 2018, 263.

2847 Of course, Paragraph 1, point (l) UCTD Annex is still relevant also under Dutch law, as this provision is relevant for assessing terms under the general unfairness test.

2848 This was confirmed by the European Court of Justice in CJEU, Judgment of 26 November 2015, C-326/14, *Verein für Konsumenteninformation/A1 Telekom Austria AG*, ECLI:EU:C:2015:782, para. 26–27.

2849 See: http://cbs.nl.

2850 See *infra* no. 677.

2851 EU: Art. 3(1) UCTD. **Belgium**: Art. I.8, 22° BCEL. **The Netherlands**: Art. 6:233, *sub* a. DCC.

2852 Art. 3(3) UCTD.

2853 CJEU, Judgment of 26 April 2012, C-472/10, *Invitel*, ECLI:EU:C:2012:242, para. 26.

2854 This can be derived from the fact that Paragraph 2, point (b) of the UCTD Annex (exception for financial services) is an exception to Paragraph 1, point (j) UCTD Annex.

corresponding right to cancel the contract if the final price is too high in relation to the price agreed when the contract was concluded."

5.3.3. EXAMPLES OF PRICE-CHANGE CLAUSES

673. CLAUSES ALLOWING PRICE INCREASES RESULTING FROM CHANGES IN THE LEGAL FRAMEWORK – A first example of price change clauses can be found in the terms and conditions of *Blue Movement.* According to this clause, the PSS supplier is entitled to pass on price increases resulting from legislation to the PSS user. Additionally, it is added that the PSS supplier will not increase prices within the first three months of concluding the PSS contract.

> TERMS AND CONDITIONS BLUE MOVEMENT – Art. 4.4 "BSH is entitled to pass on price increases resulting from legislation to the Renter. However, BSH will not increase the Monthly Fee within three months of concluding the agreement."

Such clauses are permissible under Belgian law, even in fixed-term PSS contracts. After all, "objective" price change clauses, i.e. price change clauses that do not depend solely on the will of the PSS supplier, do not fall under Article VI.83, 2° and 3° BCEL.[2855] If price changes are the result of new legislation, these clauses are of course not covered by these provisions, as changes in legislation are not dependent on the will of the PSS supplier. Of course, this requires that the price increase is indeed due to the change in legislation (e.g. additional taxes or other charges). Also under Dutch law, these clauses are allowed. The Dutch blacklist only contains a prohibition of terms that allow the PSS supplier to increase the price within the first three months of the contract unless the consumer can in that case terminate the contract.[2856] This means that if the PSS supplier increases the price because of new legislation after at least three months have passed, as is the case with this clause, it does not fall within the scope of the blacklisted term. However, there is still one potential exception to the permissibility of these clauses. If the new price is too high in comparison with the original price of the PSS contract, the court may consider that the term is unfair based on the indicative list of the UCTD and/or the general unfairness test.[2857]

674. CLAUSES ALLOWING TO CHANGE PRICING STRUCTURE AFTER A CERTAIN MINIMUM PERIOD – A second example of price change clauses are terms allowing the PSS user to change the pricing structure after a certain minimum period, with a termination option for the PSS user. This is for instance the case in the terms and conditions of *Grover.* This contract allows the PSS supplier to change

---

[2855] See *supra* no. 665.

[2856] See *supra* no. 670.

[2857] Paragraph 1, point (l) UCTD Annex. See *supra* no. 672.

the use fees for the period after the end of the minimum contract term. The PSS user will be informed six weeks before the change and he can cancel the contract up to two weeks before the price change takes effect.

> TERMS AND CONDITIONS GROVER – Art. 9.2 "*Grover has the right to change the use fees for the period after the end of the minimum contract term.* Grover will inform You of the change at the latest six weeks before the change takes effect. *If You do not agree with the change, You can cancel the contract* up to two weeks before the price change takes effect. If no notice of the termination is given, Your agreement will be assumed. Grover will inform separately of the possibility of termination and the observation of the deadline." (own emphasis).

Under Belgian law, the first question that arises is whether it is a fixed-term or open-ended PSS contract. As mentioned above, there are examples in Belgian case law stating that contracts with a certain minimum duration, followed by an open-ended contract, should not be considered fixed-term contracts but open-ended contracts.[2858] As a result, the fairness of this clause should be assessed against the rules applicable to open-ended contracts.[2859] In this case, it is indeed a discretionary price change clause, i.e. the price increase depends solely on the will of the PSS supplier, and thus it falls under the scope of the blacklisted provision. However, as the PSS user has a reasonable time to decide to cancel the PSS contract (up to two weeks before the price change takes effect), it will not be unfair under the Belgian blacklist.[2860] Under Dutch law, this clause is also allowed. Even if the minimum term would be less than three months, the PSS user still has a termination possibility before the new price takes effect.[2861]

675. CLAUSES ALLOWING TO CHANGE PRICING STRUCTURE AT ANY TIME, WITH TERMINATION OPTION – A third category of price change clauses allow the PSS supplier to change the subscription pricing at any time. For example, the terms and conditions of *Dressr* state that the PSS supplier reserves the right to change subscription pricing at any time, but if they do, they will give the PSS user written notice of such change first. If the PSS user does not agree with the new pricing, he can cancel the subscription without penalty and can continue to use the services through the end of the period for which he paid at the previous pricing.

> TERMS AND CONDITIONS DRESSR – Art. 4 (Dressr subscription), under 6 "Our subscription will automatically renew at the then-current prices for the same length of time as your original membership term. *Our pricing and applicable taxes and fees*

2858 Brussels (BE) 25 June 2014, *Jaarboek Marktpraktijken* 2014, 272, case note M. DE MAN; Comm. Liège (BE) 25 June 2013, *NjW* 2014, 608, case note R. STEENNOT (at first instance) and Liège (BE) 9 October 2014, *NjW* 2014, 459, case note R. STEENNOT (on appeal).

2859 Art. VI.83, 2° BCEL.

2860 See *supra* no. 664.

2861 See *supra* no. 670.

> *may change over time, so the pricing from one subscription term to the next may be different. We reserve the right to change subscription pricing at any time, but if we do, we will give you written notice of such change first. If you do not agree with the new pricing, you can cancel your subscription without penalty* and can continue using the Services through the end of the period for which you have paid at the previous pricing." Art. 14 (Changes to and termination of subscription), first sentence "Dressr reserves the right to alter or change any and all aspects of the site or subscription at any time, including the subscription fee." (Own emphasis)

According to this clause, the price of the service may change from one subscription term to the next. *Dressr* offers two types of fixed-term contracts, namely 1-month contracts and 3-month contracts,[2862] which are automatically renewed for the same term as the original contract. A contract renewal has the effect that the "old" PSS contract is extinguished, and a "new" PSS contract is subsequently entered into with the same content as the original contract.[2863] As a result, this clause does not fall within the scope of the Belgian blacklisted terms on price change clauses. After all, this is not an open-ended contract, but a succession of fixed-term contracts. Additionally, the price change does not take place *during* the fixed-term contract, but only *after* the fixed-term contract, namely when the renewed contract enters into force. Although this clause therefore does not fall within the scope of the two blacklisted terms on price changes, Belgian law does provide some consumer protection elsewhere. Indeed, Article VI.91 BCEL provides rules for tacit renewal clauses of B2C fixed-term service contracts or contracts having as their object both goods and services.[2864] On the one hand, the PSS supplier has an information obligation regarding the tacit renewal.[2865] On the other, the PSS user-consumer can, after the tacit renewal of a fixed-term contract, terminate the contract at any time without compensation, respecting the notice period stipulated in the contract, which may not exceed two months.[2866] In this case, *Dressr* did not comply with the information requirements, as the clause is not on the first page of the terms and conditions and is not placed in bold and in a frame separate from the text. Additionally, no information is given on the termination possibility of Article VI.91, §2 BCEL nor on the deadline by which the PSS user-consumer can object to the tacit renewal. Although Article VI.91 BCEL does not contain a specific civil sanction in case of non-compliance with this provision, the clause can of

[2862] See: https://dressr.be/memberships/#startyourmembership.

[2863] See Art. 5.78(3) BCC.

[2864] See also *supra* no. 328.

[2865] See Art. VI.91, §1 BCEL: The clause should be placed in bold letters and in a frame separate from the text, on the front of the first page and must state the consequences of the tacit renewal, including the termination possibility laid down in Art. VI.91, §2 BCEL, as well as the deadline by which the consumer can object to the tacit renewal of the contract and the way in which he notifies this objection.

[2866] Art. VI.91, §2 BCEL.

course be tested against the general standard and/or the transparency obligation of the rules on unfair contract terms, which may render the renewed contract null and void.[2867]

Under Dutch law, as the PSS user has the possibility to cancel the subscription without penalty, this clause does not fall under the scope of Article 6:236, *sub* i. DCC. In addition, this clause also does not fall under Article 6:236, *sub* j. DCC. This blacklisted term prohibits clauses of tacit renewal for regular delivery of goods or provision of services unless the consumer has the option to terminate the continued contract at any time with not more than one month's notice.[2868] The termination possibility offered by *Dressr* thus "saves" the clause from being regarded as unreasonably onerous under the Dutch blacklist. For the same reason, this clause is also unlikely to be considered unfair under the general test read together with the UCTD Annex.

676. Clauses allowing to change pricing structure at any time, without termination option – As a second example of terms allowing to change the price structure at any time, the terms and conditions of *Swapfiets* provide that the PSS supplier has the right to change the costs of the subscription, which will be communicated to the PSS user at least one month before the price change takes effect. However, in this case, the PSS user does *not* have the right to terminate the contract, unless the price change takes place within three months of the conclusion of the contract.

> Terms and conditions Swapfiets – Art. 13.1 "Swapfiets reserves the right to change the costs of a Subscription. Changes will be communicated to the Renter via e-mail at least one month before the effective date. The Renter will not be permitted to terminate the Subscription due to a price change, unless the change takes place within three months of the conclusion of the Subscription and the Renter is a consumer."

Under Belgian law, such a term is not permitted. Indeed, if the PSS contract constitutes a fixed-term contract, discretionary price change clauses during the contract term are forbidden *per se*.[2869] If the PSS contract constitutes an open-ended contract, discretionary price change clauses are only allowed if the PSS user-consumer can terminate the contract free of charge in case of a price increase.[2870] In this case, the PSS user cannot terminate the contract, unless the

---

2867 R. Steennot and E. Terryn, "Commentaar bij artikel VI.91 WER" in *Handels- en economisch recht. Commentaar met overzicht van rechtspraak en rechtsleer*, Mechelen, Kluwer, Loose-leaf, 2022, (29) 38, no. 13.

2868 See on the limits on tacit renewal clauses under Dutch law: R.H.C. Jongeneel, "De zwarte lijst" in B. Wessels and R.H.C. Jongeneel (eds.), *Algemene voorwaarden*, Deventer, Wolters Kluwer, 2017, (253) 277–284.

2869 See *supra* no. 664.

2870 *Ibid.*

change takes place in the first three months of the contract. As a result, even if the contract with *Swapfiets* were to be an open-ended contract (which it generally is not), it is therefore contrary to the Belgian blacklist. Under Dutch law, on the other hand, this clause does not fall under the scope of the blacklisted term, as the PSS user can terminate the subscription if the price change takes place within three months of the conclusion of the contract.[2871] However, if the price change is significant compared to the original price, there still is a strong possibility that this clause could be considered unreasonably onerous based on the general unfairness test combined with Paragraph 1, point (l) of the UCTD Annex, as the PSS user-consumer has no termination option.[2872]

677. Price indexation clauses – Apart from price change clauses, various PSS contracts, especially in the Netherlands, also contain price indexation clauses. For example, the general terms and conditions of *Blue Movement* state that the PSS supplier has the right to annually adjust the monthly fee based on the inflation index of the Dutch Central Bureau of Statistics[2873] ("Dutch CBS"). The competing PSS offer *Bundles* has a similar clause in its contract entitling the PSS supplier to annually index the monthly fee based on the consumer price index of the Dutch CBS.

> Terms and conditions Blue Movement – Art. 4.5 "BSH is entitled to adjust the Monthly Amount annually on the basis of the inflation index of the Central Bureau of Statistics."

> Terms and conditions Bundles – Art. 4.6 "Unless stated otherwise, the prices mentioned in the Agreement and these general terms and conditions include VAT. *Bundles is entitled to index the Monthly Fee annually on the basis of the consumer price index* as made available by the CBS (www.cbs.nl)." (Own emphasis).

As discussed above, these price indexation clauses are allowed under the UCTD Annex and do not violate the Dutch blacklist and grey list.[2874] Belgian law also allows price indexation clauses provided they are not illegal and the manner in which prices are adjusted is explicitly described in the contract.[2875] Here, the legality of these clauses depends particularly on whether the contract is qualified as a rental contract or a contract for services. Indeed, as Article 57 of the Act of 30 March 1976 on economic recovery measures does not apply to rental contracts, a qualification of the PSS contract as a rental contract for movables will mean that price indexation according to the consumer price index is

---

2871 See *supra* no. 670.
2872 See *supra* no. 672.
2873 See: http://cbs.nl.
2874 See *supra* no. 666 and 671.
2875 See *supra* no. 666.

allowed. This is true even though Article 1728*bis* old BCC, whose existence is said to be the rationale behind the exclusion from the scope of Article 57 Act of 30 March 1976, does not apply to the rental contract for movables. In contrast, a qualification of the PSS contract as a contract for services means that Article 57 of the Act of 30 March 1976 on economic recovery measures does apply, and that price indexation based on the consumer price index will be forbidden, except if the price indexation clause complies with the (complicated) formula laid down in this provision. As already argued above, this distinction does not make sense and may give rise to legal uncertainty.[2876] In my view, it would therefore be better to repeal Article 57 of the Act of 30 March 1976 and have a uniform regime for price indexation clauses in rental contracts for movables and contracts for services.[2877] As the contracts of *Blue Movement* and *Bundles* will as a general rule qualify as a rental contract for movables, these price indexation clauses will be valid, also under Belgian law. However, this is not necessarily the case for all use-oriented PSS (and certainty not result-oriented PSS), as they may in some circumstances also be qualified as contracts for services.[2878]

678. Solution: price change clauses that pass the test of both Belgian and Dutch unfair contract terms rules – In this section, the limits to including price changes in the PSS contract were discussed. These limits are necessary to protect the interests of consumers, who, after all, should not face unexpected (and exorbitant) price changes. Still, PSS suppliers can have a legitimate interest in including price change clauses in their PSS contracts given the long-term nature of these contracts and the risk of changing circumstances during the contract. This was also already recognised by the CJEU with regard to electronic communication services.[2879] Therefore, a potential solution would be to include a price change clause in the PSS contract that balances the interests of the PSS supplier and the PSS user.

To comply with both the Dutch and the Belgian unfair terms rules, the following principles must be taken into account: (i) discretionary price change clauses (i.e. price changes that depend solely on the will of the PSS supplier) may not be included in fixed-term contracts. In the event of renewal (tacit or otherwise) of the fixed-term contract, on the other hand, the PSS supplier may change the price of the service. However, in the case of the tacit renewal of a fixed-term contract, the PSS user also must have a termination option; (ii) in open-ended contracts, discretionary price change clauses are allowed, but the consumer must have a termination option free of charge; and (iii) the PSS supplier may not increase the price in the first three months of the contract,

2876 See *supra* no. 668.
2877 See *supra* no. 669.
2878 See *supra* section 3.4.2.
2879 CJEU, Judgment of 26 November 2015, C-326/14, *Verein für Konsumenteninformation/A1 Telekom Austria AG*, ECLI:EU:C:2015:782.

unless the PSS user has a termination option without penalty; and (iv) price indexation clauses based on the consumer price index (or any other index) can under current Belgian law only be included in PSS contracts that qualify as rental contracts. Under Dutch law, there are no limits to price indexation clauses. This translates into the model clauses set out hereafter.

Additionally, under Belgian law, Article VI.91 BCEL also protects the PSS user-consumer from price changes resulting from the tacit renewal of the PSS contract (i.e. the situation where a clause in the PSS contract provides for tacit renewal of the contract but reserves the right to increase the price for these subsequent contracts).[2880] A model clause complying with the principles set out in Article VI.91 BCEL was already set out above (model clause #12).[2881]

Model clause #33: price change clause in fixed-term contracts

- **The contract will be for a fixed term as outlined in the order confirmation. During the term of this fixed-term contract, [the PSS supplier] may not unilaterally change the price of the service.**

- **Unless [You/the PSS user] object to the tacit renewal of the contract [by email/ by contacting our customer service/through your online account] at the latest [2 days] before the end of the contract, the contract will be automatically renewed for the same length as the original contract term.[2882] Upon renewal of the contract, the PSS supplier reserves the right to adjust the price of the service. However, if the price of the service is increased, [the PSS supplier] will give [You/ the PSS user] written notice of this change before the renewal of the contract and [You/the PSS user] will have the possibility to terminate the contract without penalty. After the tacit renewal of the contract, [You/the PSS user] may terminate the contract at any time without penalty, subject to a notice period of [max. two months].**

- **[The PSS supplier] reserves the right to change the price of the service due to [objective reason, e.g. (tax) legislation].[2883] In case the price chance occurs within the first three months of the contract, the PSS user will have the option to terminate the contract without penalty.[2884]**

2880 See *supra* no. 675.

2881 See *supra* no. 341.

2882 Under Belgian law, this tacit renewal clause should be placed in bold letters and in a frame separate from the text, on the front of the first page of the contract. See Art. VI.91 BCEL.

2883 If the price change is due to an objective reason, it is no longer a discretionary price change clause and Art. VI.83, 2° and 3° BCEL do no longer apply.

2884 Under Dutch law, also objective price change clauses are subject to the conditions that the consumer must be able to terminate the contract without penalty if the price is increased in the first three months of the contract.

Model clause #34: price change clause in open-ended contracts

- [The PSS supplier] reserves the right to unilaterally change the price of the service, subject to providing [You/the PSS user] with advance notice of [a reasonable period, e.g. one month]. In the event of a price change, [You/the PSS user] shall have the right to terminate the contract without penalty within [a reasonable period, e.g. one week] before the new price comes into effect.
- [The PSS supplier] reserves the right to change the price of the service due to [objective reason, e.g. (tax) legislation]. However, if the price chance occurs within the first three months of the contract, the PSS user will have the option to terminate the contract without penalty.

Model clause #35: price indexation clauses (both fixed-term and open-ended contracts)

- [The PSS supplier] is entitled to index the Monthly Fee annually on the basis of [the consumer price index] as made available by [Statbel (www.statbel.fgov.be)/ the CBS (www.cbs.nl)].[2885]
- [The PSS supplier] is entitled to index the Monthly fee [annually/every three months][2886] based on the following formula[2887]:

$$\rho = \rho_0 \times (a \times \frac{W_1}{W_0} + b \times \frac{M_1}{M_0} + \dots + z)$$ [2888]

Where:

- W_1 = Wage cost in a given year (year of indexation), based on [reference wages Agoria]
- W_0 = Original wage cost (base year), based on [reference wages Agoria]

2885 For PSS contracts governed under Dutch law or (use-oriented) PSS contracts that qualify as rental contracts.

2886 In theory the price indexation can take place at any time, but often only periodic adjustments are provided for. As a rule, there is no minimum period between indexation, unlike indexation in rental contracts (Art. 1728*bis* old BCC).

2887 For PSS contracts governed under Belgian law that are not qualified as rental contracts but contracts for services.

2888 Formula based on: J. Vansevenant and O. Vanden Berghe, "Prijsherzieningsclausules in relaties tussen private ondernemingen: een stand van zaken na 45 jaar beperkende wetgeving", *TBH* 2023, (353) 359, no. 21 and J. Schraeyen, E. Enkels, S. Van den Broeke and T. De Clerck, *Algemene voorwaarden*, 2012, Ghent, Larcier, 2012, 90–91.

- **M_1 = Cost of materials in a given year (year of indexation), based on [reference cost of materials Agoria]**
- **M_0 = Original cost of materials (base year), based on [reference cost of materials Agoria]**

Comments[2889]:

- **$a + b + \ldots + z = 1$**
- **$a + b + \ldots$ = maximum 0,8**
- **z = minimum 0,2**

5.3.4. CLAUSES TO UNILATERALLY CHANGE OTHER TERMS OF THE PSS CONTRACT

679. CLAUSES ALLOWING THE PSS SUPPLIER TO UNILATERALLY CHANGE OTHER ELEMENTS OF THE PSS CONTRACT – Besides price change clauses, various analysed PSS contracts also include clauses allowing the PSS supplier to unilaterally modify other elements of the contract. To protect consumers, these modification clauses are subject to certain limits. Depending on the object of the modification, i.e. the contract terms, the key characteristics of the product/ service, or the delivery or performance period, different limits and conditions of validity apply.

680. CLAUSES ALLOWING TO CHANGE THE TERMS OF THE PSS CONTRACT – A first type of modification clauses constitute clauses that allow the PSS supplier to unilaterally modify the terms of the PSS contract. Examples of unilateral modification clauses can, among others, be found in the terms and conditions of *Blue Movement*, *Fairphone Easy*, *Swapfiets*, and *Dressr.*

> TERMS AND CONDITIONS BLUE MOVEMENT – Art. 16.1 "BSH is entitled to modify these General Terms and Conditions unilaterally. BSH shall communicate any material modification to the General Terms and Conditions to the User at least one month before they take effect. If the User does not wish to agree to such a change, the User has the right to terminate the Contract until the new conditions come into force. If the User does not terminate the Contract, it will continue under the new conditions."

[2889] The larger z, the less the new price may differ from the original price. The larger the factors a, b, …, the more these factors weigh on the new price.

Terms and conditions Fairphone Easy – Art. 11.3 "We reserve the right, at our sole discretion, to change, modify, add, amend and remove any part of these Terms and Conditions from time to time. We will notify You of these changes with our communication platforms. However, it is your own responsibility to check the changes made."

Terms and conditions Swapfiets – Art. 13.2 "Changes to the Terms and Conditions will be made known at least one month before becoming applicable, by a notification on www.swapfiets.be and via an e-mail to the Renter."

Terms and conditions Dressr – Art. 4 (Dressr subscription) under (4) "Dressr reserves the right to modify, terminate or otherwise amend any subscription membership plans, provided the User will have 14 days' prior written notice before and is entitled to a full refund of fees already paid if he prefers to cancel his subscription rather than continue under any modified or amended terms."

681. Belgian law: distinction between open-ended and fixed-term contracts – Under Belgian law, clauses allowing to change the terms to the detriment of the consumer are subject to the same two points on the Belgian blacklist as price change clauses, namely Article VI.83, 2° BCEL (for open-ended PSS contracts) and Article VI.83, 3° BCEL (for fixed-term PSS contracts). As with price change clauses, the PSS supplier has more contractual freedom in open-ended PSS contracts than in fixed-term PSS contracts. Thus, the PSS supplier can reserve the right to change the contract terms based on elements that depend solely on its will, provided that the PSS user-consumer is notified in advance of these changes and that he has a reasonable period of time to terminate the contract without penalty before the changes come into effect.[2890] For fixed-term PSS contracts, the Belgian blacklist is more stringent. Here, the PSS supplier is in principle prohibited from reserving the right to change the contract terms to the detriment of the consumer based on elements that depend solely on its will.[2891] In contrast, "objective" modification clauses, i.e. clauses that allow the PSS supplier to change to terms of the contract according to elements that do not depend solely on its will, are not covered by these two blacklisted items and therefore allowed in both fixed-term and open-ended PSS contracts (of course subject to the general unfairness test).[2892] This could include, for example, legislation that imposes certain recycling or end-of-life obligations on the PSS supplier that differ from the original circular guarantees the PSS supplier included in the PSS contract. Alternatively, case law ruling that a certain clause is unfair in (PSS) contracts with consumers, could also be considered an objective reason to change that term of the contract. An example of such an "objective" modification clause can be found in the terms and conditions of *HP Instant*

[2890] Art. VI.83, 2° BCEL.
[2891] Art. VI.83, 3° BCEL.
[2892] Compare also with *supra* no. 665.

Ink, where changes in technology and changes in regulatory requirements or legislative changes are mentioned as reasons for HP to change the terms of the contract.

> Terms and conditions HP Instant Ink – Art. 3 "HP may modify this Agreement or any part, version, or feature of the service [...] at any time to: *a. reflect changes in HP technology/other systems; b. reflect changes in regulatory requirements, legislative changes or ombudsman decisions*; c. implement new service offerings, promotions or programs being made available; implement minor adjustments and improvements. These changes will not affect Your use of the service; e. reflect changes in HP's costs; and f. any other reason. [...]" (Own emphasis).

682. No limits on modification clauses in Dutch unfair terms lists, but relevance of UCTD Annex – The Dutch lists of unfair terms do not impose limits on modification clauses regarding the terms of the contract. However, the indicative list of the UCTD (in the Netherlands also called the "blue list") must also be taken into account.[2893] Indeed, Paragraph 1, point (j) of the UCTD Annex mentions terms which have the object or effect of *"enabling the seller or supplier to alter the terms of the contract unilaterally without a valid reason which is specified in the contract"* as terms which may be regarded as unfair. However, the scope of point (j) is somewhat narrowed down by Paragraph 2, point (b), second subparagraph UCTD Annex, which adds that in open-ended contracts, unilateral modification clauses where the seller or supplier is required to inform the consumer with reasonable notice of the modifications and that the consumer is free to terminate the contract are not covered. As a result, PSS suppliers have more contractual freedom to include modification clauses in open-ended contracts than in fixed-term contracts. Thus, according to point (j), the unfairness of a modification clause lies in the absence of a valid reason for modification stated in the PSS contract. Valid reasons can again include new legislation or case law, but potentially also changed market conditions, provided these are sufficiently identified in the PSS contract.[2894] The inclusion of a reason for modification or other restrictions on the power to modify the terms of the contract may prevent arbitrariness and the national court will therefore be more likely to find that the modification clause passes the unfairness test. On the other hand, clauses with a (too) broad or even unlimited modification power, where only a limited modification power is appropriate, will fail the general unfairness test.[2895] Another element in considering the fairness of a modification clause is

---

2893 See: R.H.C. Jongeneel, "De blauwe lijst" in B. Wessels and R.H.C. Jongeneel (eds.), *Algemene voorwaarden*, Deventer, Wolters Kluwer, 2017, (355) 378.

2894 Compare with M.B.M. Loos, *Algemene voorwaarden*, The Hague, Boom juridisch, 2018, no. 363.

2895 Compare with R.H.C. Jongeneel, "De blauwe lijst" in B. Wessels and R.H.C. Jongeneel (eds.), *Algemene voorwaarden*, Deventer, Wolters Kluwer, 2017, (355) 378–379.

whether the PSS user has the right to terminate the PSS contract after the PSS supplier has notified him of the new terms. If the PSS user can indeed terminate the PSS contract and has the freedom to switch to another PSS supplier, courts will be more likely to decide that the clause is not unfair. In this sense, this right to terminate the PSS contract cannot be purely formal but the consumer must have an actual opportunity to exercise this right.[2896, 2897]

683. Solution: modification clauses that pass the test of both Belgian and Dutch unfair contract terms rules – As with price change clauses, a balance must be struck between consumer protection interests on the one hand (i.e. not being faced with detrimental or unexpected contractual terms during the term of the contract) and the interests of PSS suppliers on the other.[2898] Indeed, during long-term PSS contracts, the latter may face changing circumstances (e.g. new legislation, case law, changing market conditions, development of new business models, etc.) that render it necessary to change the terms of the service. Therefore, a potential solution would be to include a modification clause in the PSS contract that balances the interests of both the PSS supplier and the PSS user. Taking into account the Belgian, Dutch and EU unfair terms rules, this translates into the following model clauses:

Model clause #36: modification clause in open-ended contracts

- **[The PSS supplier] reserves the right to unilaterally modify the terms of the service, subject to providing [You/the PSS user] with advance notice of [a reasonable period, e.g. one month]. In the event of a modification of the terms, [You/the PSS user] shall have the right to terminate the contract without penalty within [a reasonable period, e.g. one week] before the new terms come into effect.**

Model clause #37: "objective" modification clause in fixed-term and open-ended contracts

- **[The PSS supplier] reserves the right to change the terms of the service due to [objective reason, e.g. new legislation].**

2896 Compare with CJEU, Judgment of 21 March 2013, C-92/11, *RWE Vertrieb AG*, ECLI:EU:C:2013:180, para. 54.

2897 E.g. there will be no "actual" opportunity to terminate the contract if the PSS supplier has a monopoly or if the PSS user was not informed of the change in due time. Additionally, it is conceivable that terminating the PSS contract would entail disproportionate costs for the consumer, as could be the case with expensive dismantling costs for products installed in the consumer's home (e.g. a heat pump).

2898 Compare with *supra* no. 678.

684. Clauses allowing to unilaterally change the essential characteristics of the service – A second type of modification clauses are clauses allowing to change the essential characteristics of the product/service. Examples of these clauses have already been discussed above, namely clauses allowing the PSS supplier to replace the product with a similar/different product.[2899] Under Belgian law, these clauses are blacklisted, provided the characteristics of the service are indeed *essential*.[2900] The essential nature of the characteristics of the service must be assessed on a case-by-case basis (based on the foreseeable use of the product or service), unless the PSS user specifically informed the PSS supplier of the use he want to make of the product/service and this was accepted by the PSS supplier.[2901] As already discussed above, under Dutch law, these clauses may fall under the grey list.[2902] Indeed, are presumed unreasonably onerous: clauses that give the PSS supplier the ability to provide a performance that differs substantially from the promised performance, unless the PSS user is authorised to terminate the contract in that case.[2903]

685. Clauses allowing to unilaterally change the delivery or performance period – A third type of modification clauses allows the PSS supplier to unilaterally change the delivery or performance period. These clauses were also already discussed above.[2904] Under Belgian law, these terms are blacklisted.[2905] Under Dutch law, these clauses may fall under the scope of the grey list. Indeed, are presumed unreasonably onerous: clauses giving the PSS supplier an unusually long or inadequately defined period for performance (i.e. delivery).[2906]

5.4. SET OFF AND SET OFF CLAUSES

5.4.1. SET OFF

686. Set off: concept – Besides paying the periodical fee, the PSS user may also fulfil his obligation to pay the price of the PSS by invoking set off. Set off (BE: *schuldvergelijking, compensation*; NL: *verrekening*) is a mode of extinguishment of obligations. It occurs when reciprocal obligations are extinguished to the

2899 See *supra* no. 435.
2900 Art. VI.83, 4° BCEL.
2901 Compare with *supra* no. 435. See also: G. Straetmans and R. Steennot, *Handboek consumentenbescherming en marktpraktijken*, Antwerp, Intersentia, 2023, 373.
2902 See *supra* no. 435.
2903 Art. 6:237, *sub* c. DCC.
2904 See *supra* no. 431.
2905 Art. VI.83, 5° BCEL.
2906 Art. 6:237, *sub* e. DCC.

extent of the smaller amount or quantity.[2907] In other words, if the PSS supplier and the PSS user have reciprocal claims against each other, and if the conditions for set off are met,[2908] then at least one claim and one debt will be "compensated" to the extent of the smaller amount. Thus, if the PSS supplier owes any amounts to the PSS user, this can be compensated with the monthly fee if the conditions of set off are met. Under Belgian law, this set off occurs by operation of law, i.e. automatically without any declaration being required and even without the knowledge of the debtors.[2909] Under Dutch law, on the other hand, a declaration is required.[2910]

687. Clauses restricting or limiting set off – The rules relating to set off are in principle not mandatory, so parties can deviate from them.[2911] This can, for example, take the form of a set off clause stating that recourse to set off by one or both parties is impossible. However, in contracts with consumers, set off clauses are subject to limits.

2907 **Belgium**: Art. 5.254(1) BCC. Cass. (BE) 5 January 2016, *RW* 2017–18, 107, case note X.; Cass. (BE) 2 October 2014, AR C.13.0284.F, *Arr.Cass.* 2014, 2045, *Pas.* 2014, 2041, *JLMB* 2016, 830, *RW* 2015–16, 1101; Cass. (BE) 17 December 2010, AR C.10.0146.N, *Arr.Cass.* 2010, 3054, *Pas.* 2010, 3269, *RW* 2011–12, 181, case note R. Houben. See also: R. Houben, "De wederkerigheidsvoorwaarde voor schuldvergelijking op het snijvlak van verbintenissen- en zakenrecht", *TPR* 2011, (75) 75–122. **The Netherlands**: Art. 6:127 DCC. See also: B.A. Schuijling, *Verrekening, Monografieën BW nr. B40*, Deventer, Wolters Kluwer, 2019, 118 p.

2908 **Belgium**: According to Art. 5.255(2) BCC, *statutory* set-off requires that: (i) two reciprocal claims exist; (ii) the claims exist between the same persons (i.e.i.e. the PSS user and PSS supplier); (iii) both claims have money as their object (or a fungible good of the same kind); (iv) the obligations exist and are certain; and (v) the obligations are due and payable. According to Art. 5.254(3) BCC, besides statutory set off (*wettelijke schuldvergelijking, compensation légale*), there are also contractual set off (*conventionele schuldvergelijking, compensation conventionelle*) and judicial set off (*gerechtelijke schuldvergelijking, compensation judiciaire*). See e.g. R. Steennot, "Schuldvergelijking" in *Comm.Bijz.Ov.*, Mechelen, Kluwer, loose-leaf, 2012, (195) no. 1–35; R. Houben, *Schuldvergelijking*, Antwerp, Intersentia, 2010, 618 p. **The Netherlands**: According to Art. 6:217(2) DCC, set off requires that (i) the parties involved (i.e.i.e. the PSS supplier and PSS user) are reciprocally each other's creditor and debtor; (ii) the debtor has a performance due that corresponds to its debt; (iii) the debtor is authorised to pay its debt; and (iv) the debtor is authorised to enforce the payment of its claim. See also: B.A. Schuijling, *Verrekening, Monografieën BW nr. B40*, Deventer, Wolters Kluwer, 2019, 7.

2909 Art. 5.255(1) BCC; S. Stijns and S. De Rey, "Het nieuwe verbintenissenrecht in Boek 5 BW – Deel II", *RW* 2022–23, (963) 992, no. 109.

2910 Art. 6:217(1) DCC.

2911 **Belgium**: J. Stuyck and B. Keirsbilck, *Handels- en economisch recht. 2: Mededingingsrecht. A: Handelspraktijken en contracten met consumenten in Beginselen van Belgisch Privaatrecht*, Mechelen, Kluwer, 2024, 829–830; R. Steennot, "Commentaar bij art. VI.83, 16° WER" in *Handels- en economisch recht. Commentaar met overzicht van rechtspraak en rechtsleer*, Mechelen, Kluwer, loose-leaf, 2017, (485) 487; J. Schraeyen, E. Enkels, S. Van den Broeke and T. De Clerck, *Algemene voorwaarden*, 2012, Ghent, Larcier, 2012, 92. **The Netherlands**: HR (NL) 21 November 1969, ECLI:NL:HR:1969:AC4971, (*Hansen/Van der Meer*), *NJ* 1970/179; B.A. Schuijling and V.G. Koolen, "Contractuele verrekening", *Tijdschrift Overeenkomst in de Rechtspraktijk* 2020, (4) 4; B.A. Schuijling, *Verrekening, Monografieën BW nr. B40*, Deventer, Wolters Kluwer, 2019, 71.

5.4.2. LIMITS TO SET OFF CLAUSES

688. Belgian law: clauses depriving the consumer of the right to set off are unfair – Belgian law aims to avoid set off clauses that are to the detriment of the consumer by including clauses that deprive the consumer of the right to invoke set off on the blacklist.[2912] Consequently, the PSS user may defend himself from a claim for payment by the PSS supplier by invoking set off, provided that the requirements for set off are met, which in practice often means that he must have a similar claim (in money or a fungible good of the same kind) against the PSS supplier. However, this requirement will often not be met, meaning that the consumer can still not rely on set off.[2913] Indeed, the obligations of the PSS supplier mostly constitute obligations to do or not do something (to deliver the product, to maintain or repair the product, to replace the product, etc.) and not obligations to pay (although they do exist, for example: repayment of the deposit or advance, repayment of any repair costs incurred by the PSS user, etc.). Even if the obligation of the PSS supplier constitutes an obligation to pay, it will often not be possible to invoke set off because the obligation is not certain and/or due and payable, for example because the PSS supplier disputes it.[2914]

689. Dutch law: set off clauses presumed unreasonably onerous – Under Dutch law, clauses which exclude or limit the consumer's right to set off, or which grant the PSS supplier a more far-reaching right to set off than the law grants him, are included on the grey list and are therefore presumed to be unreasonably onerous.[2915] Consequently, unless the PSS supplier can prove that the set off clause is not unreasonably onerous in that specific case,[2916] the clause is

---

2912 Art. VI.83, 16° BCEL. R. Steennot, "Commentaar bij art. VI.83, 16° WER" in *Handels- en economisch recht. Commentaar met overzicht van rechtspraak en rechtsleer*, Mechelen, Kluwer, loose-leaf, 2017, (485) 487; P. Cambie, *Onrechtmatige bedingen*, Ghent, Larcier, 2009, 257.

2913 See I. Demuynck, *De inhoudelijke controle van onrechtmatige bedingen*, Thesis submitted to obtain the degree of Doctor of Laws, University of Ghent, 2000, 496–497. See also: J. Stuyck and B. Keirsbilck, *Handels- en economisch recht. 2: Mededingingsrecht. A: Handelspraktijken en contracten met consumenten in Beginselen van Belgisch Privaatrecht*, Mechelen, Kluwer, 2024, 830; Art. VI.83, 16° BCEL. R. Steennot, "Commentaar bij art. VI.83, 16° WER" in *Handels- en economisch recht. Commentaar met overzicht van rechtspraak en rechtsleer*, Mechelen, Kluwer, loose-leaf, 2017, (485) 487; M. Flamée, "De onrechtmatige bedingen" in P. De Vroede (ed.), *Handelspraktijken. Het nieuwe in de wet van 14 juli 1991 betreffende de handelspraktijken en de voorlichting en bescherming van de consument*, Bruges, Die Keure, 1995, (93) 102.

2914 R. Steennot, "Schuldvergelijking" in *Comm.Bijz.Ov.*, Mechelen, Kluwer, loose-leaf, 2012, (195) 200. See also: Liège (BE) 4 December 1997, *TBBR* 1998, 369; Mons (BE) 21 June 1988, *Pas.* 1989, II, 239.

2915 Art. 6:237, *sub* g. DCC.

2916 Not unreasonably onerous, according to Jongeneel, is the clause prohibiting set off if the user of the general terms and conditions has a legitimate interest in doing so, such as the user of general terms and conditions which has a "somewhat extensive and complicated

voidable by the PSS user.[2917] In addition, reliance on the clause could potentially also be contrary to the standards of reasonableness and fairness.[2918] Finally, the limitation or exclusion of set off also appears on the UCTD's indicative grey list. Indeed, paragraph 1, point (b) of this list concerns a clause that has the object or effect of "*inappropriately excluding or limiting the legal rights of the consumer vis-à-vis the seller or supplier [...] including the option of offsetting a debt owed to the seller or supplier against any claim which the consumer may have against him*"."[2919]

690. Examples of unfair set of clauses – The terms and conditions of *Live Light* include an unfair set off clause. According to these terms, the PSS user is not entitled to set off amount it owes *Live Light* against amounts it claims. *Live Light* on the other hand is always entitled to set off amounts it owes the PSS user against amounts it claims.

> Terms and conditions Live Light – Art. 8.4 "The Tenant is not entitled to set off amounts it owes Live Light against amounts it claims. Live Light is always entitled to set off amounts it owes the Tenant against amounts it claims."

As it excludes set off by the PSS user, this clause clearly falls under the description of the Belgian blacklist and is therefore prohibited and will be null and void.[2920] Also under Dutch law, this clause falls within the ambit of the grey list of terms that are presumed to be unreasonably onerous.[2921] Indeed, this clause excludes the consumer's right to set off while also giving Live Light a far-reaching right to set off its debts against the PSS user against the amounts it claims. Therefore, if the PSS supplier cannot present specific and legitimate circumstances to invalidate the presumption that the clause is unreasonably onerous, it will also

---

administration." PSS suppliers, in my view, do not fall under this exception. See: R.H.C. Jongeneel, "De grijze lijst" in B. Wessels and R.H.C. Jongeneel (eds.), *Algemene voorwaarden*, Deventer, Wolters Kluwer, 2017, (311) 324.

2917 B.A. Schuijling, *Verrekening, Monografieën BW nr. B40*, Deventer, Wolters Kluwer, 2019, 73–74, no. 60. For an example, see: District Ct. Zaandam (NL) 3 May 2001, *TvC* 2002, 138. In this case, no circumstances were presented to invalidate the presumption that the clause was unreasonably onerous.

2918 Art. 6:248(2) DCC. See HR (NL) 16 January 1987, ECLI:NL:PHR:1987:AG5509, (*Hooijen/THB*), *NJ* 1987/553, case note W.C.L. van der Grinten. The PSS user can choose whether he relies on the restrictive effect of reasonableness and fairness or the voidability of unreasonably onerous clauses. See: HR (NL) 14 June 2002, ECLI:NL:PHR:2002:AE0659, (*Bramer/Hofman Beheer*), *NJ* 2003/112, case note J. Hijma. The fact that the clause is not unreasonably onerous does not *ipso facto* mean that the clause is also not contrary to the principles of reasonableness and fairness. See: HR (NL) 23 February 2001, ECLI:NL:HR:2001:AB0220, (*Montoya en Cloudstorm/ABN Amro*), *NJ* 2001/277.

2919 Paragraph 1, point (b) UCTD Annex.

2920 Art. VI.83, 16° *juncto* Art. VI.84 BCEL. See also Art. 14.2 Terms and Conditions Live Light, which provides that the applicable law to the contract is Belgian law.

2921 Art. 6:237, *sub* g. DCC.

under Dutch law be unfair and thus voidable. This presumption seems difficult to rebut in this case. Even if this clause did not fall under the Belgian blacklist or Dutch grey list, it would most likely still be considered unfair under the general test, as it clearly creates an imbalance between the rights and obligations of the company and the consumer.

Similarly, *Bundles* also has an unfair set off clause in its contract. The terms stipulate that the PSS user may under no circumstances set off (alleged) claims on *Bundles* against debts to *Bundles*.

> TERMS AND CONDITIONS BUNDLES – Art. 5.3 "[…] Client may under no circumstances set off (alleged) claims on Bundles against debts to Bundles."

To the extent that the statutory requirements for set off are met, i.e. the claims of the PSS user are not mere alleged claims, this clause will be null and void under Belgian law and voidable under Dutch law.

691. EXAMPLE OF A FAIR SET OFF CLAUSE – The terms and conditions of *Grover* also contain a set off clause, but in this case, it passes the test of the various lists of unfair terms. These terms and conditions state that PSS users can only set off claims that are uncontested by *Grover* or claims against *Grover* that have been established as final and absolute against *Grover's* payment claim.

> TERMS AND CONDITIONS GROVER – Art. 10.4 "*Customers may only set-off claims that are uncontested by Grover or claims against Grover that have been established as final and absolute against Grover's payment claim.* The Customer may exercise a right of withholding only if its counterclaim is based on the same contractual relationship." (own emphasis).

The reason this clause stands the test is because it reflects the general rules on set off under both Belgian and Dutch law. Indeed, Belgian law also has as requirements for set off that the claims of the PSS user exist, are certain, and are due and payable.[2922] Similarly, Dutch law requires that the debtor is authorised to pay its debt and the debtor is authorised to enforce the payment of its claim for set off, which is not the case if the claims are contested or not final and absolute.[2923]

5.4.3. MODEL SET OFF CLAUSE

692. MODEL SET OFF CLAUSE – In my view, the current rules and requirements for set off strike a fair balance between the rights and obligations of both the PSS

[2922] Art. 5.255(2) BCC. See *supra* fn. 2908.

[2923] Art. 6:217(2) DCC. See *supra* fn. 2908.

supplier and the PSS user. If PSS suppliers wish to include a set off clause in their PSS contract anyway (although not strictly necessary), the clause used by *Grover* mentioned above can act as an inspiration. This translates into the following model clause:

Model clause #38 – set off

- **[The PSS user] may only set off payment claims that are uncontested by [the PSS supplier] or payment claims against [the PSS supplier] that have been established as final and absolute against [the PSS supplier's] payment claim.**

5.5. CONCLUSION

693. Payment of the price: conclusion – This chapter dealt with the main obligation of the PSS user, namely paying the price stipulated in the PSS contract. First, the legal framework of this obligation was discussed in section 5.2. To begin, this section addressed the legal basis of this obligation and the (default) rules on modalities of payment for the three main types of PSS contracts. Next, the discussion focused on the various pricing components found in the analysed components and possible contractual arrangements of the price. Thus, real-life contractual clauses on the periodical fee, pay-per-use fee, mandatory insurance fee, start-up cost, etc. were analysed and good practices were identified to draft model clauses on the price of the PSS for both use-oriented and result-oriented PSS. In addition, this section looked at transparency requirements and pre-contractual information requirements related to the price of the PSS. Following that, the remedies for non-payment of the price were discussed. Second, section 5.3 dealt with price change clause and other clauses allowing to change the terms of the PSS contract. Third, section 5.4 addressed set off, including the validity of and limits to set off clauses.

694. Conclusion on the legal framework of the obligation of the PSS user to pay the price – The first section of this chapter dealt with the **obligation of the PSS user to pay the price.**[2924]

For each of the three main types of PSS, the obligation to pay the price constitutes an essential element of the PSS contract and is the main obligation of the PSS user. Indeed, the sales contract rules, the rental contract rules, and the rules of the contract for services all provide that the PSS user-consumer must pay the price. Generally (especially in contracts with consumers[2925]), this price must be determined or at least determinable. Determined means that the price is

[2924] See *supra* section 5.2.

[2925] See under Belgian law: Art. VI.3, §2 BCEL.

explicitly stated in the PSS contract, while a determinable price is found through (a series of) objective calculations without an element of appreciation by the PSS supplier. The latter may for example be the case if the PSS contract includes a price schedule for certain (pay-per-use) services. As to the modalities of the PSS contract, the timing of the payment, as well as the payment method are generally set out in the PSS contract. When analysing the selected PSS contracts, it is clear that payment by electronic means has become the norm. Most PSS suppliers require the PSS user to pay via direct debit (e.g. a SEPA mandate) or a credit card. Both under Belgian and Dutch law, such requirements are generally not regarded unfair. The only exception are clauses that have the object or effect of increasing the announced price for a product because the consumer refuses to pay via direct debit, which are blacklisted under Belgian law. However, clauses giving a reduction if the PSS user pays via direct debit or clauses making the direct debit method mandatory do not fall under the scope of this blacklisted provision. As regards digital content and digital services that are added to the PSS contract, the DCD introduced the option to pay in the form of personal data, elevating this as an effective means of counter-performance. Nevertheless, this approach has been subject to significant criticism in legal doctrine and may give rise to practical issues, especially if the PSS user withdraws his consent for data processing as allowed under the GDPR. Taking Dutch law as an example, this research has urged the Belgian legislator to adopt a provision on the consequences of the withdrawal of consent for contract for the supply of digital content or digital services where the price is (only) paid with personal data.

The amount and composition of the price of the PSS depends on the pricing strategy of the PSS supplier, which is reflected in the contractual arrangements in the PSS contract. In almost all cases, the PSS contract requires the PSS user to pay a periodical fee. Depending on the amount of the periodical fee, the PSS user will be able to enjoy better products, more functionality, and/or more additional services. The periodical fee may also vary depending on the duration of the PSS contract (with longer-term contracts often being cheaper). Additionally, the fact that the products offered "as-a-service" are refurbished rather than new may affect the price as well. The pricing of PSS contracts often includes a pay-per-use component. Either the entire service is priced on a pay-per-use model (as is the case with free-floating e-scooters), or the periodical fee is supplemented by a pay-per-use fee (as may be the case for a certain amount of washes with a smart washing machine, or pages printed with a smart printer). Often, these pay-per-use fees are based on the monitoring of usage data of the product, which requires constant internet connection. Some of the PSS contracts analysed therefore stipulate indemnity clauses if the internet connection of the product would be interrupted (charging a fixed amount of uses in case of loss of internet connection). In many cases, the validity of these clauses is questionable. Therefore, it is in this situation better to include a clause that allows (remotely) disabling the product if the internet connection is interrupted. Besides the periodical fee and/or pay-per-use fee, the PSS contract may stipulate a (non-refundable) start-up fee. This fee usually aims to cover the costs associated with processing orders, managing logistics and other expenses linked with concluding a new PSS contract (e.g. delivery, installation, credit-checks of the consumer, etc.) This start-up fee should not be confused with a deposit, which protects the PSS user against the issue of moral hazard and will be refunded at the end of the PSS contract. Other potential components of the price may be a (mandatory) insurance fee and/or a purchase option at the end of the PSS contract. Throughout this section, best practices of real-life contracts were analysed, and good practices were identified to draft model clauses on the price of the PSS for both use-oriented and result-oriented PSS.

The combination of all the different pricing components (in combination with the main characteristics of the product/service) can make it difficult for an average consumer to compare the prices of different PSS offers. Transparency requirements and pre-contractual information requirements may help for the consumer to make informed decisions. Throughout this section, various (pre-) contractual information requirements were discussed, among others those found in the SD, the CRD and the UCTD. Generally, the burden of proof that these information requirements have been met lies with the PSS supplier. Nevertheless, one of the biggest flaws of information requirements also apply here, namely that consumers do not sufficiently read and/or understand the information made available. Consequently, even if the PSS supplier provides all the necessary information, it is not guaranteed that the PSS user-consumer gets the "best deal" for his specific needs. Here, consumer organisations could play an important role, for example, by making comparisons between different PSS offers (and between PSS offers and buying the product outright) in their communications to consumers.

If the PSS user-consumer does not pay the price of the PSS (on time), the PSS supplier has access to the general contract law remedies. While the remedy of performance in kind, the *enac* and the remedy of termination apply in the same way as with other obligations, the remedy of compensation for damages takes a slightly different form in the case of non-payment of the price of PSS. Indeed, if the PSS user is in default of paying the price, negligence interests will be charged as a compensation for late performance of this obligation. In principle, the damages for delay in the performance of the obligation to pay the price of the PSS are fixed at a flat rate, namely the statutory interest rate. However, this statutory interest rate is only default law, so the PSS contract may stipulate a different contractual interest rate. These clauses stipulating a contractual interest rate are qualified as a specific type of indemnity clauses. As such, they are subject to the same limits to "normal" indemnity clauses. Thus, under Belgian law, they must be reciprocal and may not be excessive. Under Dutch law, excessive statutory interest clauses are not black- or grey listed but are combatable under the general test or the principles of reasonableness and fairness. Under Both Belgian and

Dutch law, the statutory interest rate will play an important role to determine the unreasonable nature of the statutory interest rate. Additionally, under Belgian law, Book XIX[2926] of the BCEL (on debts of the consumer) contains specific caps on the interests that may be charged in case of late payment by the PSS user. If in addition to interest clauses, the PSS contract also contains other indemnity clauses, these can be claimed cumulatively, provided they do not relate to the same damages. However, also here, these indemnity clauses may not be excessive (which is assessed together with the damages due to the interest clauses).

695. Conclusion on price changes and changes to other terms of the PSS contract – The second section of this chapter dealt with **price changes and changes to other terms of the PSS contract.**[2927] It analyses the applicable legal rules, discusses and evaluates some clauses found in the PSS contracts analysed dealing with these topics, and formulates model clauses that comply with both the Belgian and Dutch (consumer protection) rules.

PSS contracts often involve long-term relationships between the PSS supplier and the PSS user. During this long-term relationship, circumstances can change (e.g. changed legislation, rising material costs and wages, etc.), potentially affecting the pricing strategy of the PSS supplier. The periodical fee of the PSS may change in two ways. First, **price indexation** allows to periodically adjust the price in the PSS contract in accordance with changes in a contractually specified index (e.g. the consumer prices index). For use-oriented PSS, the rules of the rental contract for movables[2928] stipulate, as a starting point, that the base rental fee remains the same over the course of the PSS contract. However, the parties are in principle free to include a price indexation clause in their contract. For result-oriented PSS (or use-oriented PSS qualifying as a contract for services), neither the Belgian nor the Dutch rules of the contract for services contain special provisions on the indexation of the price of the service. Consequently, the price will only be adjusted if the parties have included a price indexation clause in the PSS contract. Second, **price change clauses** give the PSS supplier the right to (unilaterally) change the price of the service for the future, regardless of any indexation formula. However, since price change clauses allow the PSS supplier to unilaterally change one of the essential elements of the PSS contract, they are subjected to certain limits and validity requirements, especially in contracts with consumers.

Under Belgian law, two provisions on the blacklist deal with the (im) possibility for the PSS supplier to include **"discretionary" price change clauses**, i.e. clauses allowing the PSS supplier to unilaterally increase the price based on elements that depend *solely* on its will. For open-ended PSS contracts, such closes

2926 See Art. XIX.4 BCEL.

2927 See *supra* section 5.3.

2928 Contrary to the rental contract rules for immovables, see: Art. 1728*bis* old BCC and Art. 7:248 and 7:251 DCC.

are allowed, but only if the PSS user is given the right to terminate the contract without costs or damages within a reasonable period of time before the new price comes into effect. In the case of PSS contracts, a period of one month seems to be a reasonable amount of time. For fixed-term PSS contracts, there is a strict prohibition for such terms, even if the PSS user-consumer can terminate the PSS contract. On the other hand, "objective" price change clauses (i.e. price change clauses based on objective criteria and not solely on the will of the PSS suppler) are allowed in both fixed-term and open-ended PSS contracts. Under Dutch law, clauses that allow the supplier to increase the price set out in the contract within the first three months of the contract are blacklisted and therefore prohibited, unless the PSS user can in that case terminate the PSS contract. As such, Dutch law leaves more room to include (discretionary) price change clauses in PSS contracts compared to Belgian law.

As regards **price indexation clauses**, the Belgian blacklist explicitly states that price indexation clauses are allowed, *"provided they are not illegal"*." The legality of price indexation clauses depends, amongst others, on the provisions of the *Act of 30 March 1976 on economic recovery measures*. This Act, which introduced temporary measures to combat the energy crisis and skyrocketing inflation in the 1970s, provides as a general rule that price indexation clauses are prohibited, unless they comply with a specific (and complicated) formula. The scope of this prohibition is limited though, as it does not apply to rental fees. As such, the contractual qualification of the PSS contract is very important for the permissibility of price indexation clauses. If (part of) the PSS contract qualifies as a rental contract (as will often be the case for use-oriented PSS), the (complicated) requirements for price indexation clauses do not apply. In other cases, for example with result-oriented PSS that qualify as a contract for services, price indexation clauses will have to comply with this complex formula. In this book, it is argued that the provision included in Article 57 of the Act of 30 March 1976 merits a thorough re-evaluation. It proposed to repeal Article 57 of the Act of 30 March 1976 and clarify the role of price indexation clauses in the BCC, in particular in Book 7 on special contracts. Preferably, this new regime for price indexation clauses does not contain significant differences between the rules applicable to the rental contract (for movables) and the services contract. It could take as the basic rule that the price of a (consumer) contract will not be indexed unless the parties explicitly include such as clause in their contract. Since the CJEU has already held that using an objective consumer price index to change the price in principle does not raise any concerns, it does not seem necessary to impose further special limits or requirements to price indexation clauses. Nevertheless, if the legislator would want to provide more consumer protection, this could be done by adopting a (mandatory) provision similar to Article 1728*bis* old BCC so that indexation is done only once per year and according to a (less complex) statutory formula.

The Dutch blacklist and grey list do not mention price indexation clauses as an exception to the rules for price change clauses. However, the exception in the UCTD Annex is of course also taken into account when assessing the (un)fairness of a price change clause and a price indexation clause under Dutch law. Contrary to Belgian law, Dutch law has no similar prohibition on price indexation clauses as found in Article 57 of the Act of 30 March 1976. Therefore, in practice, many Dutch PSS contracts contain price indexation clauses based on an objective consumption price index, often the inflation index of the Dutch Central Bureau of Statistics.

Besides price change clauses, various analysed PSS contracts also contain **modification clauses** allowing the PSS supplier to unilaterally modify other elements of the contracts. The Belgian blacklist contains a similar protection mechanism as price change clauses for clauses allowing to change the contract terms to the detriment of the consumer. Thus, in open-ended PSS contracts, the PSS supplier can reserve the right to change the contract terms based on elements that depend solely on its will, provided that the PSS user-consumer is notified in advance of these changes and that he has a reasonable period of time to terminate the contract without penalty before the changes come into effect. In fixed-term PSS contracts, on the other hand, clauses that give the PSS supplier the right to change the contract terms to the detriment of the consumer based on elements that depend solely on its will are prohibited in any case, even if the PSS user-consumer has the right to terminate the contract. As with price change clauses, these blacklisted items only apply to "discretionary" clauses. "Objective" modification clauses (i.e. not depending solely on the will of the PSS supplier), on the other hand, are not covered by the blacklist and therefore allowed in both fixed-term and open-ended PSS contracts (provided they are not unfair on the basis of another provision such as the general unfairness test). Under Dutch law, there is no similar prohibition on the Dutch blacklist or grey list. Nevertheless, the indicative list of the UCTD, which mentions terms *"enabling the seller or supplier to alter the terms of the contract unilaterally without a valid reason which is specified in the contract"* as terms which may be regarded as unfair, must also be taken into account. This item is subject to an exception, namely open-ended contracts where the consumer is informed with reasonable notice of the modifications and where he is free to subsequently terminate the contract. Thus, also under Dutch law, PSS suppliers have more freedom to include modification clauses in open-ended PSS contracts than in fixed-term PSS contracts.

696. Conclusion on set off and set off clauses – The third section of this chapter dealt with an alternative way for the PSS user to fulfil his obligation to pay the price, namely by invoking **set off**.[2929]

[2929] See *supra* section 5.4.

Set off is a mode of extinguishment of obligations where reciprocal obligations are extinguished to the extent of the small amount or quantity. In other words, if the PSS supplier and the PSS user have reciprocal claims against each other and the conditions for set off are met, then at least one claim and one debt will be "compensated" to the extent of the smaller amount. The rules on set off are in principle not mandatory law, both in Belgium and in the Netherlands. However, both legal systems contain some limits on set off clauses. Under Belgian law, clauses that deprive the consumer of the right to invoke set off are blacklisted. Under Dutch law, clauses excluding or limiting the consumer's right to set off or that grant the PSS supplier a more far-reaching right to set off than the law, are included on the Dutch grey list and therefore presumed to be unreasonably onerous. According to this research, the current rules and requirements for set off strike a fair balance between the rights and obligations of both the PSS supplier and the PSS user. Therefore, it did not propose normative solutions on set off but only drafted a model clause that can be used by PSS suppliers wishing to include a set off clause in the PSS contract.

6. ADDITIONAL SERVICES

"After-sales service is more important than assistance before sales. It is through such service that one gets permanent customers."
– Kōnosuke Matsushita[2930]

6.1. INTRODUCTION

697. ADDITIONAL SERVICES AND SPECIFIC OBLIGATIONS OF THE PSS SUPPLIER – Besides the general obligation to ensure the availability of the product/service, the PSS supplier often also offers additional services. This chapter first deals with the obligation to install the product (section 6.2). Then, it discusses the obligation to maintain and repair or replace the product (section 6.3). Third, it looks at the obligation to supply updates for connected "smart" products (section 6.4). Finally, this chapter looks at ways to include innovation obligations in the PSS contract (section 6.5).

6.2. INSTALLATION OF THE PRODUCT

698. OBLIGATION OF THE PSS SUPPLIER TO INSTALL THE PRODUCT – Very often, the PSS contract will include an obligation for the PSS supplier to install the product, especially for larger products such as home appliances, kitchens, HVAC equipment, etc.[2931] The term "installation" should be understood broadly, and includes putting together parts provided to the PSS user, mounting the product on other objects including any necessary adjustments (such as connecting a rented washing machine to the water supply and water discharge) as well as the replacement of parts.[2932] Several issues are relevant here. First, the question arises as to when the product is properly installed, and the consequences of

2930 Kōnosuke Matsushita (松下 幸之助) was a Japanese industrialist who founded Panasonic, one of the largest Japanese consumer electronics companies.

2931 See e.g. Art. 5.1 Terms and Conditions Live Light, Art. 6 Terms and Conditions Blue Movement, and Art. 7.1 Terms and Conditions Bundles.

2932 Compare with C. VON BAR, E. CLIVE, H. SCHULTE-NÖLKE, H. BEALE, J. HERRE, J. HUET, M. STORME, S. SWANN, P. VARUL, A. VENEZIANO and F. ZOLL (eds.), *Principles, Definitions and Model Rules of European Private Law. Draft Common Frame of Reference (DCFR)*, www.law.kuleuven.be/personal/mstorme/european-private-law_en.pdf, 2009, 1531.

incorrect installation. Second, it is advisable to make proper arrangements in the PSS contract about the timing and location of the installation (including what requirements the location must meet to be suitable for installation of the product). Here, the price of the installation must also be considered. This may either be included in the monthly fee or consist of a separate installation fee.[2933]

6.2.1. PRODUCT-ORIENTED PSS: INSTALLATION AS CONFORMITY REQUIREMENT

699. CONSUMER SALES RULES ALSO APPLY TO INSTALLATION IN PRODUCT-ORIENTED PSS – When determining whether the product supplied as part of the product-oriented PSS is correctly installed, the first question arises as to which rules apply (i.e. a question of qualification). According to the recitals of the SGD, the installation of the product could be covered by the consumer sales rules if the installation forms part of the sales contract and has to be carried out by the seller and or under the seller's responsibility.[2934] Where a contract includes elements of both sales of goods and provision of services, the recital leaves it to national law to determine whether the whole contract can be classified as a sales contract within the meaning of this directive.[2935] As already mentioned earlier,[2936] under Belgian law, the absorption theory is most often used,[2937] which results in the consumer sales rules being applicable if the service is ancillary to the sale.[2938] This will most often be the case if the PSS supplier (or a third party designated by the PSS supplier) installs the product at the premises of the PSS user.[2939] Dutch law applies the cumulation theory resulting in the application of the sales contract rules to the sales component and the rules of the contract for works to the installation component.[2940] However, if the PSS user with whom

---

2933 Compare also with *supra* no. 631 and 639.

2934 Recital 17 SGD.

2935 *Ibid.*

2936 See *supra* no. 380 for Belgian law and no. 382 for Dutch law.

2937 Art. 5.67(2) BCC.

2938 B. TILLEMAN and F. VAN DEN ABEELE, *Bijzondere overeenkomsten – A. Koop – Deel 2 Gevolgen van de koop*, Mechelen, Kluwer, 2022, 742–743; B. TILLEMAN, S. DE REY, N. DEBRUYNE, T. GLADINEZ, N. VAN DAMME and F. VAN DEN ABEELE, "Overzicht van rechtspraak bijzondere overeenkomsten aanneming (2007–2021)", *TPR* 2022, (365) 381–382, no. 10. However, see: CJEU, 7 September 2017, C-247/16, *Schottelius*, ECLI:EU:C:2017:638, para. 44–46 where the CJEU ruled that the consumer sales rules do not apply to the sale of filtration system featuring a pump as part of a broader services contract for the renovation of a pool. In this case, the sale was only ancillary to the contract for works (*accessorium sequitur principale*).

2939 See for an application: Antwerp (BE) 30 June 2020, *TBBR* 2022, 175 (incorrect installation of a consumer good that is part of the contract is considered a lack of conformity of the good when the installation is part of the sale. Such is the case for the improper installation of a cooktop when a kitchen is sold and installed).

2940 J. HIJMA, *Mr. C. Assers Handleiding tot de beoefening van het Nederlands Burgerlijk Recht. 7. Bijzondere overeenkomsten. Deel I. Koop en ruil*, Deventer, Kluwer, 2019, no. 21.

the product is installed is a consumer, the contract is *also* considered a sales contract, which means the sales rules and the rules of the contract for works apply simultaneously. In case of conflicting provisions, the consumer sales rules take precedence.[2941]

700. Correct installation as conformity requirement – As already discussed above,[2942] the consumer sales rules provide that where the installation as part of product-oriented PSS (e.g. the installation of a smart kitchen, a smart ventilation system, etc.) was carried out by the PSS supplier or under his responsibility, an incorrect installation results in a lack of conformity of the product.[2943] The same applies to situations where the installation was done by the PSS user (or someone he designated[2944]) and the incorrect installation was due to shortcomings in the installation instructions.[2945] The consumer sales rules thus give the PSS user access to the same extensive (mandatory) arsenal of remedies for a defective installation than a defect in the product itself. A special feature of Dutch law is that the PSS user-consumer has two options in the event of a defective installation of the product: he can argue that the defective installation is tantamount to a lack of conformity of the product itself, but he can also invoke the rules of the contract for works to have the defective installation remedied.[2946]

6.2.2. USE-ORIENTED PSS: CONFORMITY OF THE RENTED GOOD OR ADDITIONAL SERVICE?

701. What rules apply to installation in use-oriented PSS? – In use-oriented PSS, installation of the product is an additional service that comes on top of providing a right of use over the product. Depending on which qualification theory is applied, the applicable rules are different.

702. Absorption theory: installation assessed against rental contract (conformity) rules – A first option would be to consider the obligation to install the product as an "accessory" to the obligation to make the

2941 Art. 7:5(4) DCC. M.A.M.C. Van den Berg and S. van Gulijk, *Mr. C. Assers Handleiding tot de beoefening van het Nederlands Burgerlijk Recht. 7. Bijzondere overeenkomsten. Deel VI. Aanneming van werk*, Deventer, Wolters Kluwer, 2022, no. 35.

2942 See *supra* no. 465.

2943 EU: Art. 8(a) SGD. See also recital 34. **Belgium**: Art. 1649*ter*, §8, 1° old BCC. **The Netherlands**: Art. 7:18(1)a DCC.

2944 Recital 34 SGD clarifies that this does not necessarily have to be the consumer himself, the installation can also be carried out by a friend or professional hired by the consumer.

2945 EU: Art. 8(b) SGD. **Belgium**: Art. 1649*ter*, §8, 2° old BCC. **The Netherlands**: Art. 7:18(1)a DCC.

2946 Explanatory Memorandum, *Parliamentary Papers II* 2000/1, 27809, no. 3, 20.

product available to the PSS user. This approach thus applies the absorption theory where the service component is absorbed by the rental contract for movables.[2947] An eventual incorrect installation would then be assessed and remedied under the rules regarding defects, which were already discussed above.[2948]

703. Cumulation theory: installation assessed against rules of the contract for services/contract for works – Another possibility to look at this, is that the service component is sufficiently distinct from the rental component, in which case it is preferable to apply the cumulation theory to the use-oriented PSS.[2949] This is especially conceivable in situations where the installation does not coincide with the delivery of the product but is carried out later (e.g. during repairs or improvements to the product). In this case, the installation will be covered by the Belgian rules of the contract for services and the Dutch rules of the contract for works.

704. Performance of the installation in conformity with the contract and standards of good workmanship – Under the Belgian rules on the contract for services and the Dutch rules of the contract for works, the PSS supplier must perform the work – i.e. the installation – in conformity with the contract and according to the standards of good workmanship.[2950-2951] Generally, this will be an obligation of result,[2952] unless the PSS contract explicitly or implicitly states otherwise, or the involvement of the PSS user is so great that an obligation of means is more appropriate.[2953-2954]

705. Acceptance and reception of the completed work after fully performed installation – After the installation has been carried out, the PSS

2947 See on the absorption theory in use-oriented PSS *supra* no. 407.

2948 **Belgium**: Art. 1719, 1° and 3°, Art. 1720 and Art. 1721 old BCC. **The Netherlands**: Art. 7:203–7:204 DCC and Art 7:206–7:208 DCC. See *supra* no. 474 *et seq.*

2949 See on the cumulation theory in use-oriented PSS *supra* no. 408.

2950 **Belgium**: B. Tilleman, S. De Rey, N. Debruyne, T. Gladinez, N. Van Damme and F. Van den Abeele, "Overzicht van rechtspraak bijzondere overeenkomsten aanneming (2007–2021)", *TPR* 2022, (365) 491, no. 97; V. Sagaert, B. Tilleman and A.-L. Verbeke, *Vermogensrecht in kort bestek*, Antwerp, Intersentia, 2022, 437, no. 1087. Compare also with *supra* no. 516. **The Netherlands**: The obligation to perform the work is derived from Art. 7:750(1) DCC. M.A.M.C. Van den Berg and S. van Gulijk, *Mr. C. Assers Handleiding tot de beoefening van het Nederlands Burgerlijk Recht. 7. Bijzondere overeenkomsten. Deel VI. Aanneming van werk*, Deventer, Wolters Kluwer, 2022, no. 79.

2951 See also *supra* no. 516.

2952 Compare also with Art. IV. C. – 2:106 DCFR.

2953 **Belgium**: B. Kohl, *Contrat d'entreprise*, Brussels, Bruylant, 2016, 280–282, no. 119. **The Netherlands**: M.A.M.C. Van den Berg and S. van Gulijk, *Mr. C. Assers Handleiding tot de beoefening van het Nederlands Burgerlijk Recht. 7. Bijzondere overeenkomsten. Deel VI. Aanneming van werk*, Deventer, Wolters Kluwer, 2022, no. 79–80.

2954 See for the distinction between obligations of result and obligations of means also *supra* no. 271–279.

supplier must *hand over* the completed work (i.e. the installed product), which effectively means that the installed product is made available to the PSS user and comes under his control.[2955] The PSS user must in turn review and *accept* the installation, resulting in the reception of the completed work (*oplevering, réception*).[2956] As already touched upon above,[2957] the acceptance is a unilateral act by which the PSS user acknowledges that the installation has been completed and is carried out in conformity with the PSS contract.[2958] As this installation obligation generally relates to a relatively simple performance, this review and acceptance will not be very formalistic or explicit (unlike, for example, construction contracts for immovable goods). In fact, it will rather amount to a negative act, namely the absence of protest or reservation.[2959]

706. LIABILITY FOR DEFECTIVE INSTALLATION AFTER ACCEPTANCE OF THE COMPLETED INSTALLATION: ONLY HIDDEN DEFECTS – As regards the liability for

---

2955 **Belgium**: W. GOOSSENS, Aanneming van werk: het gemeenrechtelijk dienstencontract, Bruges, Die Keure, 2003, 726. **The Netherlands**: Explanatory Memorandum, *Parliamentary Papers II* 1992/93, 23095, no. 3, 17; M.A.B. CHAO-DUIVIS, "Aanneming van werk" in H.N. SCHELHAAS and A.J. VERHEIJ (eds.), *Bijzondere overeenkomsten in Studiereeks Burgerlijk Recht*, Deventer, Kluwer, 2021, (445) 458, no. 382; M.A.M.C. VAN DEN BERG and S. VAN GULIJK, *Mr. C. Assers Handleiding tot de beoefening van het Nederlands Burgerlijk Recht. 7. Bijzondere overeenkomsten. Deel VI. Aanneming van werk*, Deventer, Wolters Kluwer, 2022, no. 114; C.E.C. JANSEN, *Aanneming van werk, Monografieën BW nr. 84*, Deventer, Kluwer, 2013, no. 30.

2956 **Belgium**: B. TILLEMAN, S. DE REY, N. DEBRUYNE, T. GLADINEZ, N. VAN DAMME and F. VAN DEN ABEELE, "Overzicht van rechtspraak bijzondere overeenkomsten aanneming (2007–2021)", *TPR* 2022, (365) 459, no. 82; B. KOHL, *Contrat d'entreprise*, Brussels, Bruylant, 2016, 404–405, no. 164. **The Netherlands**: Art. 7:758(1), second sentence DCC; M.A.M.C. VAN DEN BERG and S. VAN GULIJK, *Mr. C. Assers Handleiding tot de beoefening van het Nederlands Burgerlijk Recht. 7. Bijzondere overeenkomsten. Deel VI. Aanneming van werk*, Deventer, Wolters Kluwer, 2022, no. 115; C.E.C. JANSEN, *Aanneming van werk, Monografieën BW nr. 84*, Deventer, Kluwer, 2013, no. 31 and 66.

2957 See *supra* no. 526.

2958 **Belgium**: B. TILLEMAN, S. DE REY, N. DEBRUYNE, T. GLADINEZ, N. VAN DAMME and F. VAN DEN ABEELE, "Overzicht van rechtspraak bijzondere overeenkomsten aanneming (2007–2021)", *TPR* 2022, (365) 459, no. 82; B. KOHL, *Contrat d'entreprise*, Brussels, Bruylant, 2016, 404–405, no. 164. **The Netherlands**: Art. 7:758(1), second sentence DCC; M.A.M.C. VAN DEN BERG and S. VAN GULIJK, *Mr. C. Assers Handleiding tot de beoefening van het Nederlands Burgerlijk Recht. 7. Bijzondere overeenkomsten. Deel VI. Aanneming van werk*, Deventer, Wolters Kluwer, 2022, no. 115; C.E.C. JANSEN, *Aanneming van werk, Monografieën BW nr. 84*, Deventer, Kluwer, 2013, no. 31 and 66.

2959 **Belgium**: W. GOOSSENS, Aanneming van werk: het gemeenrechtelijk dienstencontract, Bruges, Die Keure, 2003, 944. See also for examples of a tacit acceptance: B. TILLEMAN, S. DE REY, N. DEBRUYNE, T. GLADINEZ, N. VAN DAMME and F. VAN DEN ABEELE, "Overzicht van rechtspraak bijzondere overeenkomsten aanneming (2007–2021)", *TPR* 2022, (365) 459–460, no. 83. **The Netherlands**: On tacit acceptance under Dutch law, see: Art. 7:758(1) first sentence DCC. See for an example e.g. Amsterdam (NL) 4 October 2016, ECLI:NL:GHAMS:2016:4026, *rechtspraak.nl*. According to Explanatory Memorandum, *Parliamentary Papers II* 1992/93, 23095, no. 3, 28, if the work is easy to review, the period after which the acceptance is tacit can be short or even non-existent. See in this sense: Hof 's-Hertogenbosch (NL) 13 October 2020, ECLI:NL:GHSHE:2020:3163.

a defective installation, a distinction must again be made between the period before and after the acceptance of the completed installation.[2960-2961] Before the acceptance of the completed work, the PSS supplier is liable for any late or non-conforming installation according to the general rules on contractual liability. After the acceptance, the situation is different. Indeed, under the rules of the contract for services/contract for works, the acceptance by the PSS user has the effect of releasing the PSS supplier from liability for non-conforming performance and/or (visible) defects in the performance of the installation.[2962] This means that after the acceptance, the PSS user can in principle only claim liability for hidden defects resulting from the installation.[2963] Under Belgian law, the liability for hidden defects is subject to the "ordinary" (non-mandatory) contractual liability rules of general contract law, subject to a ten-year limitation period.[2964] The Dutch rules for the contract for works, on the other hand, contain specific provisions on liability for (hidden) defects, including a specific double limitation period.[2965] This liability regime is based on the premise that, on the one hand, the PSS supplier should in principle be given the opportunity to remove the defects in the installation itself[2966] and, on the other, that the PSS user has the right to demand that the PSS supplier removes the defects within a reasonable time.[2967] However, if performance in kind would be disproportional or impossible, compensation for damages is also possible.[2968] If the PSS supplier

2960 B. Kohl, *Contrat d'entreprise*, Brussels, Bruylant, 2016, 459, no. 185.

2961 See also *supra* no. 526.

2962 **Belgium**: B. Tilleman, S. De Rey, N. Debruyne, T. Gladinez, N. Van Damme and F. Van den Abeele, "Overzicht van rechtspraak bijzondere overeenkomsten aanneming (2007–2021)", *TPR* 2022, (365) 461, no. 86; W. Goossens, Aanneming van werk: het gemeenrechtelijk dienstencontract, Bruges, Die Keure, 2003, 946. **The Netherlands**: Art. 7:758(3) DCC. M.A.M.C. Van den Berg and S. van Gulijk, *Mr. C. Assers Handleiding tot de beoefening van het Nederlands Burgerlijk Recht. 7. Bijzondere overeenkomsten. Deel VI. Aanneming van werk*, Deventer, Wolters Kluwer, 2022, no. 119.

2963 **Belgium**: Cass. (BE) 25 October 1985, *Arr.Cass.* 1985–86, 270, *Pas.* 1986, I, 226, *JT* 1986, 438, *T.Aann.* 1986, 204, case note J. Embrechts; B. Tilleman, S. De Rey, N. Debruyne, T. Gladinez, N. Van Damme and F. Van den Abeele, "Overzicht van rechtspraak bijzondere overeenkomsten aanneming (2007–2021)", *TPR* 2022, (365) 461, no. 86; See for an analysis and overview of the requirements: A. Van Oevelen, "Kwaliteitsstandaarden bij de verkoop van goederen en de levering van diensten" in I. Claeys, W. Delva and R. Steennot (eds.), *Aansprakelijkheid, veiligheid en kwaliteit*, Ghent, Kluwer, 2015, (1) 57–60. **The Netherlands**: See Art. 7:758(3) *juncto* Art. 7:759 DCC.

2964 Art. 5.82 *et seq.* and Art. 2262*bis*, §1 old BCC. B. Tilleman, S. De Rey, N. Debruyne, T. Gladinez, N. Van Damme and F. Van den Abeele, "Overzicht van rechtspraak bijzondere overeenkomsten aanneming (2007–2021)", *TPR* 2022, (365) 461, no. 86. See also *supra* no. 526.

2965 See Art. 7:761 DCC. First, this is a two-year period from the time the PSS user protested about a defect. Second, it involves a 10-year period from the time of reception of the completed work. See for a discussion: M.A.M.C. Van den Berg and S. van Gulijk, *Mr. C. Assers Handleiding tot de beoefening van het Nederlands Burgerlijk Recht. 7. Bijzondere overeenkomsten. Deel VI. Aanneming van werk*, Deventer, Wolters Kluwer, 2022, no. 122.

2966 Art. 7:759(1) DCC.

2967 Art. 7:759(2) DCC.

2968 HR (NL) 5 January 2001, ECLI:NL:HR:2001:AA9311, (*Multi Vastgoed/Nethou*), *NJ* 2001/79. See also: M.A.B. Chao-Duivis, "Aanneming van werk" in H.N. Schelhaas and A.J.

knew about the hidden defects in the installation and concealed them, its liability cannot be limited nor subjected to a shorter limitation period.[2969]

707. NUANCE: LIABILITY FOR DEFECTIVE INSTALLATION AFTER ACCEPTANCE AND OBLIGATION TO ENSURE (NEAR-)CONTINUOUS AVAILABILITY OF THE SERVICE – However, the distinction between the liability for a defective installation before and after the acceptance of the completed work must be nuanced. Indeed, the fact that the PSS user can only claim liability for hidden defects after acceptance of the installation does not really work for (use-oriented) PSS contracts.[2970] After all, there continues to exist a relationship between the PSS user and the PSS supplier, even after the acceptance and reception of the completed installation. If the installation is faulty, this will have an impact on the PSS supplier's obligation to ensure the (near-)continuous availability of the service.[2971] As a failure to ensure the (near-)continuous availability of the service constitutes a defect, the PSS user will in this case be able to invoke the remedies for non-conformity of the rental contract for movables.

6.2.3. RESULT-ORIENTED PSS: INSTALLATION PART OF COMPLEX SERVICE CONTRACT

708. RESULT-ORIENTED PSS: INSTALLATION AS PART OF COMPLEX SERVICE CONTRACT – In result-oriented PSS, the PSS supplier undertakes to achieve a specific result or outcome for the PSS user as specified in a rather complex service contract. Generally, the PSS supplier has a large degree of autonomy in deciding on how to achieve this result. It often requires installing or implementing products, (software)systems, or other solutions. Consequently, this installation component will also be a part of this larger complex service contract.

709. BELGIAN LAW: WHOLE RESULT-ORIENTED PSS CONTRACT COVERED BY CONTRACT FOR SERVICES, INCLUDING INSTALLATION COMPONENT – Under Belgian law, result-oriented PSS are generally covered by the rules of the contract for services.[2972] As part of the broader services contract, the installation

VERHEIJ (eds.), *Bijzondere overeenkomsten in Studiereeks Burgerlijk Recht*, Deventer, Kluwer, 2021, (445) no. 383. See for an application: Ct. Rotterdam (NL) 5 December 2007, ECLI:NL:RBROT:2007:BC1207, *RCR* 2008, 29.

2969 Art. 7:762 DCC. This provision is mandatory law. See: Explanatory Memorandum, *Parliamentary Papers II* 1992/93, 23095, no. 3, 15.

2970 In the same sense, see: S. VAN GULIJK, "De juridische kwalificatie van verdienstelijking in de gebouwde omgeving", *WPNR* 2021, vol. 7326, (409) 414 who argues that the transient nature of the contract for works, which comes to an end with the acceptance and reception of the work is not really suitable for "as-a-service" business models.

2971 See *supra* no. 488.

2972 See *supra* no. 414.

component will also be covered by these rules. Again, this means that the PSS supplier must perform the installation in accordance with the rules of good workmanship, the provisions of the contract, and, where applicable, the instructions of the PSS user.[2973] In practice, as these rules are non-mandatory, the contractual provisions will play the most important role in assessing the conformity of the installation with the PSS contract (also in view of determining whether the installation obligation is one of means or one of result). If the installation is faulty or otherwise not in conformity with the contract, the PSS user has recourse to the remedies of general contract law.[2974]

710. Dutch law: installation component covered by contract for works or absorption by contract for services? – The question what rules apply under Dutch law to the installation component in result-oriented PSS is harder to answer. After all, Dutch law makes a distinction between the contract for services (*opdracht*) and the contract for works (*aanneming van werk*).[2975] Strictly speaking, the installation component would be covered by the rules of the contract for works as it aims at "*the construction and delivery of a tangible good.*"[2976-2977] However, as also argued by van Gulijk, the transient nature of the contract for works, which comes to an end with the acceptance and reception of the work, does not really work in the context of "as-a-service" business models.[2978] Additionally, the installation component is not the main object of the result-oriented PSS contract, as it is merely an instrument in achieving the contractually agreed result. This means that a faulty installation will lead to a non-performance of the main obligation to provide the service. In my view, it is therefore better to consider the larger result-oriented PSS contract as aiming at "*activities other than the construction of a tangible good.*" Applying the absorption theory, the rules of the contract for services should then also be applied to the installation component. However, these rules are again very general and do not provide concrete guidelines for installation. Consequently, here too, the contractual provisions (in particular those concerning the result to be achieved), and the general standard that the PSS supplier must perform the service as a good service provider, will govern the PSS user's rights concerning the installation.[2979]

2973 Compare with *supra* no. 519.

2974 Compare with *supra* no. 528. For an in-depth discussion of these remedies, see *supra* section 2.6.6.

2975 See *supra* no. 377.

2976 Art. 7:750 DCC.

2977 For the applicable rules, see the application of the contract for works to the installation component in use-oriented PSS *supra* no. 703–707.

2978 S. van Gulijk, "De juridische kwalificatie van verdienstelijking in de gebouwde omgeving", *WPNR* 2021, vol. 7326, (409) 414.

2979 See *supra* no. 515 and 516.

6.2.4. CONTRACTUAL ARRANGEMENTS ON INSTALLATION

711. Contractual agreements on place and time of the installation – As mentioned, it is advisable to have proper contractual arrangements regarding the timing and location of product installation (including the requirements that the location must meet to be suitable for product installation), and/or the price of the installation. As there is no significant difference between product-oriented PSS, use-oriented PSS and result-oriented PSS (and no/limited mandatory rules), these issues will be discussed together for the three types of PSS.

712. Location of the installation – The product must be installed at the location intended by the consumer. This will mostly be the address he gave up during the conclusion of the contract, either online or in a physical store of the PSS supplier. Alternatively, the PSS contract may stipulate that the PSS supplier will contact the PSS user to agree on a place and time when the product is ready for delivery and installation.

> Terms and conditions Live Light – Art. 5.1 "Live Light is responsible for arranging the transport and installation of the Goods at the Tenant and the specified address."

713. Requirements for the location where the product will be installed – The PSS contract may also include the requirements the location must meet for the PSS supplier to be able to successfully install the product. This may include being spacious enough to fit the dimensions of the product (including allowing sufficient airflow); the location having a level surface capable of supporting the weight of the product; the availability of a socket, electrical outlet, water supply and water drainage, etc. within 2 meters of the intended position of the product; the fact that the room is well ventilated, and so on. By informing the PSS user of these requirements in the PSS contract, the PSS supplier can reasonably place the responsibility for the suitability of the location on the PSS user.

> Terms and conditions Live Light – Art. 5.4 "The dimensions and data specified in the quote must be checked by the Tenant. The Tenant is responsible for assessing the suitability of the location in which the Goods will be installed."

> Terms and conditions Papillon – Art. 4.2 "The Product will be installed on site to the extent that the actual situation allows it in a safe manner (on the ground floor up to a maximum of the second floor without lift, higher floors with lift to the extent that the product and its packaging fit in the lift and the use of the lift for such transport is allowed according to the applicable regulations, if applicable to the product: socket, water supply and drainage is provided, etc.)[...]."

For PSS that require a more complex installation (which will often especially be the case with result-oriented PSS), the PSS contract may also stipulate a right for the PSS supplier to perform a site survey to check the suitability of the location before installing the product.

> Terms and conditions Saman Group – Art. 7.1 "The installation of the heat pump system will be provided by or on behalf of Saman Group. Saman Group reserves the right to determine the types of materials used for the components of the Heat Pump System. [...] Installation of the Heat Pump System will not take place until the Premises meet the standards and requirements set by Saman Group."

714. What if the location is not suited for the PSS? – The PSS contract may also include a clause on the consequences if the location is not suited for the PSS. If reasonable modifications are necessary to make the location suitable, it is not unreasonable to ask the PSS user to bear these costs. If, however, reasonable modifications are not possible or if the PSS user wishes not to bear these costs, the PSS contract can also include a clause on the consequences for the PSS contract. For example, it is possible to stipulate that in this case, all obligations are extinguished for the future[2980] or that both parties can terminate the contract.

For example, the terms and conditions of *Saman Group* provide that if the installation is not possible, the PSS supplier will inform the PSS user of the additional work or costs that are required. Both parties can then terminate the PSS contract within seven days. In this case, *Saman Group* bears the costs of the work preparation. Another alternative used by one of the PSS contracts analysed is including an indemnity clause stipulating a fee for damages incurred by PSS supplier because of a failed installation and/or unsuccessful site survey imputable to the PSS user. For instance, the contract used by *Live Light* provides that if the product cannot be installed (on the agreed date) because of the PSS user, *Live Light* may retain the delivery costs and charge reasonable costs for a new installation. This includes the situation where the PSS user miscalculated the available space for the product. However, it is important to keep in mind that non-reciprocal indemnity clauses are not permitted in contracts with consumers under Belgian law.[2981] This means that for this clause to be valid, there must be a similar clause that establishes compensation for a failed installation imputable to the PSS supplier.

2980 On the consumer side, this can take the form of an early termination clause. On the side of the PSS supplier, this clause can be seen as a suspensive condition (*opschortende voorwaarde, condition suspensive*). See in this sense, including model clauses: C. Borucki, H. Slachmuylders, B. Keirsbilck, D. Gruyaert and E. Terryn, *Model clauses for Product-as-a-Service (PaaS) contracts*, CE Center. Circular Economy Policy Research Center, 2022–23, 60.

2981 Art. VI.83, 17° BCEL. See also *supra* no. 305. Under Dutch law, the grey list and blacklist do not contain a similar provision. Still, in some cases these terms can also be challenged based on Art. 6:233, *sub* a. DCC.

TERMS AND CONDITIONS SAMAN GROUP – Art. 5.1 "Based on the Rental Contract, Saman Group will provide the work preparation. This can be done either on site or remotely. If it is determined by Saman Group from the work preparation that the installation of the Heat Pump System is not possible or additional work and/or costs are required, Saman Group will notify the Lessee in writing. Both parties then have the right to terminate the Rental Contract within seven (7) calendar days after the day on which the work preparation took place, free of charge and with immediate effect. Saman Group shall in this case bear the costs of the work preparation."

TERMS AND CONDITIONS LIVE LIGHT – Art. 5.8 "If the goods cannot be installed or cannot be installed on the agreed date for any reason attributable to the Tenant (a delay in the delivery of a home or business space, a miscalculation of the available space or access to the location, etc.), the delivery costs paid by the Tenant to Live Light will remain acquired for Live Light. Live Light may charge reasonable costs to the Tenant for a delivery on a newly agreed date."

715. TIME OF THE INSTALLATION – Generally, the time when the installation takes place is the same as the time of the delivery of the product.[2982] The PSS contract will generally include a clause on how the parties are to agree upon a time and date for installation.

TERMS AND CONDITIONS BLUE MOVEMENT – Art. 6.1 "After concluding the Contract, BSH or BSH's logistics partner will contact the User to make an appointment for delivery and installation of the Product."

TERMS AND CONDITIONS LIVE LIGHT – Art. 5.5 "The installation of the Goods will be scheduled during normal working hours and under normal working conditions. [...]"

716. RESCHEDULING THE INSTALLATION – It is also useful to include a clause in the PSS contract dealing with the situation where the PSS use r or the PSS supplier must reschedule the appointment for installation. For example, the PSS contract may include a right to reschedule the appointment once, at the latest seven days before the installation will take place. This is for instance the case in the PSS contract used by *Saman Group*. If PSS user cancels the installation at a later date, it is not unreasonable for the PSS supplier to charge for this. Nevertheless, it should also be pointed out here that, at least under Belgian law, indemnity clauses should be reciprocal.[2983] This means that, for such an indemnity clause to be valid, the PSS contract must also contain an indemnity clause in case the PSS supplier reschedules the installation appointment last minute.

TERMS AND CONDITIONS SAMAN GROUP – Art. 7.2 "Lessee may reschedule the appointment for installation once up to seven (7) calendar days before the day on

---

2982 See *supra* no. 431.
2983 Art. VI.83, 17° BCEL, compare with *supra* no. 714.

which installation is scheduled without any charge. Thereafter, the applicable costs incurred will be charged by Saman Group to Lessee."

717. PRICE OF THE INSTALLATION – There are different options regarding the price of the installation. Often, the installation will be free of charge, which means that the installation is included in the monthly fees paid by the PSS user. Alternatively, it is possible that the PSS contract explicitly stipulates an installation or delivery fee to cover the costs of the installation. A middle way consists in the PSS supplier offering free installation, unless additional costs must be incurred (e.g. renting a removal lift because the product has to be taken to a high floor without an elevator). The PSS contracts analysed show that the latter option is the most common in practice. In any case, it does not seem unreasonable to charge a delivery/installation fee nor recover the additional cost of hiring moving/installation equipment from the PSS user.

TERMS AND CONDITIONS BLUE MOVEMENT – Art. 6.2 "If no lift is available, BSH delivers the Product up to the fourth floor as standard." Art. 6.3 "If and to the extent that: (i) the delivery of the Product requires large equipment (e.g. a removal lift or crane); (ii) the Product has to be delivered to a floor higher than the floor without a lift; and/or (iii) there are other particularities affecting the delivery that should reasonably be known to the User, the User is obliged to inform BSH of this in due time. In such a case, the additional costs of delivery shall be borne by the User. If BSH cannot deliver the Product because the User has not informed it of such special circumstances in due time, BSH is entitled to retain the One-off Fee."

TERMS AND CONDITIONS BUNDLES – Art 6.2 "Delivery and installation is free of charge, unless a removal lift, crane, boat or all-terrain vehicle is required for delivery and/or installation. User is obliged and undertakes vis-à-vis Bundles to communicate to Bundles in good time all (additional) information required for the Contract, including information relating to matters that affect the (costs of and) work on installation. Additional costs for installation shall be determined in mutual agreement and shall be for User's expense."

TERMS AND CONDITIONS LIVE LIGHT – Art. 8.1 "Unless otherwise agreed, the delivery costs and the Rent for the first month must be paid immediately upon conclusion of the Rental agreement." Art. 5.5 "[…] The Tenant must inform Live Light if a ladder lift has to be used for the installation. Any additional costs for this are for the account of the Tenant."

6.2.5. LEGISLATIVE INTERVENTION NEEDED?

718. THREE POSSIBLE SOLUTIONS – In line with the evaluation and possible solutions set out above for the PSS supplier's obligation to make the product/service available,[2984] this section proposes three possible solutions for the PSS

2984 See *supra* section 4.4.1.

supplier's obligation to install the product. First, a proposal for **modernisation of national rental contract law** (option 1) is made. Second, the option of including an installation obligation in an **EU directive** (option 2) is explored. Third, the **use of balanced standard contracts and model clauses** (option 3) is considered in section 6.2.6.

6.2.5.1. Modernisation of national contract law

A. Use-oriented PSS: installation as conformity requirement

719. Installation as a conformity requirement for the rental contract – As already mentioned above, this research proposes that, similar to the consumer sales rules, a provision should be adopted for B2C rental contracts for consumer goods which establishes a lack of conformity if the rented good is incorrectly installed.[2985]

Thus, the purpose of proposed provision #31 is to explicitly extend the rules of the B2C rental contract on lack of conformity to the situation where the installation is part of the rental contract and is carried out incorrectly by either the lessor or the lessee according to the lessor's instructions. This follows the approach in the DCFR[2986] and also mirrors the provisions in the SGD and its national implementation providing that incorrect installation also gives rise to a lack of conformity of the product.[2987] This has the advantage that there is no need to discuss whether the installation obligation is absorbed by the rental contract or constitutes an "accessory" obligation of which the non-performance can give rise to different consequences than the remedies available under the rental contract.[2988]

720. Criticism: installation as separate conformity requirement not necessary? – Some authors have already questioned – in the context of the consumer sales contract – the usefulness of including a separate conformity requirement for incorrect installation.[2989] The idea is that when a consumer orders a good and contractually agrees with the seller that it should be installed,

---

2985 See *supra* no. 558.

2986 Art. IV. B. – 3:105 DCFR.

2987 EU: Art. 8 SGD. **Belgium**: Art. 1649*ter*, §8 old BCC. **The Netherlands**: Art. 7:18a DCC. See *supra* no. 465.

2988 C. Von Bar, E. Clive, H. Schulte-Nölke, H. Beale, J. Herre, J. Huet, M. Storme, S. Swann, P. Varul, A. Veneziano and F. Zoll (eds.), *Principles, Definitions and Model Rules of European Private Law. Draft Common Frame of Reference (DCFR)*, www.law.kuleuven.be/personal/mstorme/european-private-law_en.pdf, 2009, 1531.

2989 S. Martens, "Art. 18:203 (5)" in N. Jansen and R. Zimmermann, *Commentaries on European Contract Laws*, Oxford, Oxford University Press, 2018, 2013; B. Tilleman and F. Van den Abeele, *Bijzondere overeenkomsten – A. Koop – Deel 2 Gevolgen van de koop*, Mechelen, Kluwer, 2022, 812, no. 739.

that good is not in conformity with the contract if it does not work after installation. From the consumer's point of view, it does not matter whether the good itself was already defective before the installation or only because of the installation.[2990]

Nevertheless, in terms of consistency and coherence, it makes sense to have the same rules under the (B2C) rental contract for movables as for the consumer sales contract. Moreover, such a provision promotes legal certainty as it is declarative of the fact that the concept of conformity must be interpreted broadly and requires the assessment of the rental contract as a whole.

Proposed Provision #31

Art. 7.3.X10. Incorrect installation of the rented goods

In the case of a rental contract for a consumer good where the lessor is a business and the lessee is a consumer, where the rented goods are incorrectly installed, any lack of conformity resulting from the incorrect installation shall be regarded as lack of conformity of the rented goods if:

1° the installation forms part of the rental contract and was carried out by the lessor or under the lessor's responsibility;

2° the installation, intended to be carried out by the lessee, was done by the lessee and the incorrect installation was due to shortcomings in the installation instructions provided by the lessor.

B. Result-oriented PSS: installation in conformity with the contract

721. Installation covered by the obligation to perform the service in conformity with the contract – For result-oriented PSS, it does not seem necessary to have a specific provision on the PSS supplier's obligation to install the product. After all, these contracts in their entirety qualify as a contract for services. As such, the conformity of the installation will also be assessed against the proposed provisions for performance of the service in conformity with the contract, which were already discussed above.[2991]

6.2.5.2. Installation obligation as part of EU directive?

722. Installation as part of EU directive? – The PSS supplier's obligation to install the product may also be regulated at the EU level, by means of an EU

2990 *Ibid.*

2991 See *supra* section 4.4.2.2A.

directive (option 2).[2992] If option 2a is chosen (a general directive on conformity and quality of (almost) all service contracts), no specific explanation is needed. In that case, the installation is a service like any other that should be tested against the same uniform conformity rules. If option 2b is chosen (a specific directive for "packages" or "bundles" of services) there is potentially a more explicit role for the PSS supplier's obligation to install the product. First, it would make sense to mention the additional installation service in the provision on the scope of the "package services"/"bundles of services" directive. Thus, "installation" can be one of the examples of additional services that result in there being a "package" or "bundle" of two or more services. Second, option 2b would allow to include specific rules for the various stages of the "package services" contract into the EU directive. This way, minimum requirements for the installation could be included in the directive, for example on the modalities of the installation (e.g. timing of the installation) and on the conformity requirements of the installation (e.g. installation in accordance with standards of good workmanship, industry standards, manufacturer guidelines, etc.). Moreover, specific rules on the remedies for failure to comply with these provisions may also be included.

6.2.6. MODEL CLAUSES ON THE INSTALLATION OF THE PRODUCT

723. Model clauses on installation of the product – Besides legislative intervention at the national or EU level, the third option is again the use of balanced (model) contractual clauses to lay down the rights and obligations of the parties. The following model clauses can both be used for use-oriented and result-oriented PSS contracts. The first two model clauses concern the modalities of the installation (e.g. the time and place of the installation). Here, a specific time period in which the PSS supplier must install the product upon conclusion of the PSS contract may explicitly be stipulated in the PSS contract. The third model clause covers the conformity of the installation. Thus, it refers to the standards of good workmanship, as well as industry standards, manufacturer guidelines and any applicable regulations or laws. The fourth, fifth and sixth model clauses deal with the necessary access the PSS supplier needs to carry out the installation. They stipulate that the PSS user should provide access to the premises and equipment as reasonably required for carrying out the installation and make sure that the premises and equipment are ready. They also place an obligation on the PSS supplier to use the premises and equipment of the PSS user in function of the installation, in an efficient manner and with due care and attention (also in view of the instructions from the PSS user). Finally, the last

---

[2992] The different options for regulating service contracts at the EU level were already discussed *supra* in section 4.4.3.

model clause deals with testing the installed product(s) upon completion of the installation. This model clause largely parallels the rules on acceptance of the performed service and provides that the PSS user has the right to participate in the testing process. If the product does not function as required or desired, it stipulates an obligation for the PSS supplier to remedy any identified deficiencies to ensure that the product(s) meet the agreed performance criteria.

Model clause #39 – installation of the product(s)

- **[The PSS supplier] installs the product(s) needed for providing the Service and delivering the Output in accordance with this contract at the place and location intended by [the PSS user].**
- **The installation of the product(s) will take place within [20 working days] of the conclusion of the contract. The installation time and date will be determined by mutual agreement between [the PSS supplier] and [the PSS user].**
- **The installation shall be conducted in accordance with the standards of good workmanship, including industry standards, manufacturer guidelines and any applicable regulations or laws.**
- **[The PSS user] shall provide [the PSS supplier] with access to the premises and equipment of [the PSS user] as [the PSS supplier] reasonably required for carrying out the installation.**
- **[The PSS user] shall be responsible for ensuring that the premises and equipment are ready and comply with the specifications outlined by [the PSS supplier].**
- **[The PSS supplier] shall use the premises and equipment of [the PSS user] in function of the installation, in an efficient manner, with due care and attention, including any specific and appropriate instructions from [the PSS user].**
- **Upon completion of the installation, [the PSS supplier] shall test whether the product(s) are correctly installed and fully functional in the presence of [the PSS user], who has the right to participate in the testing process. [The PSS supplier] shall promptly remedy any identified deficiencies to ensure that the product(s) meet the agreed performance criteria.**

6.3. MAINTENANCE, REPAIR AND REPLACEMENT

724. Maintenance, repair and replacement – Besides the obligation to install the product, PSS contracts generally entail that the PSS supplier is responsible for the maintenance, repair and replacement of the product made available as part of the service.[2993] In this way, the PSS supplier guarantees that the PSS user will be "taken care of" and that he can make uninterrupted use of the service. This section deals with these obligations for the three types of PSS contracts. It discusses the respective legal bases and modalities of these obligations. Finally, it is considered whether legislative intervention is needed, and model clauses on these obligations are proposed that can be used in use-oriented and result-oriented PSS contracts.

6.3.1. PRODUCT-ORIENTED PSS

725. Sales contract rules do not contain rules on maintenance of the product: maintenance as additional service – In product-oriented PSS contracts, the obligation of the PSS supplier to maintain the product is not derived from the (consumer) sales rules but generally arises from the fact that maintenance is added to the contract as an additional service. As a result, there is a mixed contract with both elements of the (consumer) sales contract and a service contract. Since this combination does not involve "the supply of goods to be manufactured or produced", but a sales contract with purely ancillary service contract, it is fitting to apply the cumulation theory.[2994] As a result, the Belgian rules of the contract for services (*aanneming, contrat d'entreprise*) and the Dutch rules of the contract for works (*aanneming van werk*) will apply to these additional maintenance services.[2995] This means, amongst others, that the maintenance services will have to be performed in conformity with the terms of the contract and in accordance with the standards of good workmanship.[2996] In addition, in the absence of a clause to the contrary, specific rules on the PSS user's right to unilaterally terminate the maintenance contract (provided he compensates the PSS supplier) also apply.[2997] In practice, the content of the maintenance services (i.e. what the PSS user can expect), the frequency of the

2993 H. Slachmuylders, "Movable Servitization. Contractual Liability in the B2C Relationship" in B. Keirsbilck, E. Terryn, J. Eyckmans, S. Rousseau and D. Voinot (eds.), *Servitization and circular economy: economic and legal challenges*, Antwerp, Intersentia, 2023, (135) 150; H. Slachmuylders, "Économie de la fonctionnalité – Le contrat de service: défis juridiques et solutions contractuelles", *Revue Juridique de l'Environnement* 2022, vol. 47, afl. 1, (111) 119.

2994 Compare with CJEU, 7 September 2017, C-247/16, *Schottelius*, ECLI:EU:C:2017:638, para. 44–45. See also *supra* no. 380.

2995 See *supra* no. 375 (for Belgium) and no. 377 (for the Netherlands).

2996 **Belgium**: B. Tilleman, S. De Rey, N. Debruyne, T. Gladinez, N. Van Damme and F. Van den Abeele, "Overzicht van rechtspraak bijzondere overeenkomsten aanneming (2007–2021)", *TPR* 2022, (365) 491, no. 97; V. Sagaert, B. Tilleman and A.-L. Verbeke, *Vermogensrecht in kort bestek*, Antwerp, Intersentia, 2022, 437, no. 1087. **The Netherlands**: The obligation to perform the work is derived from Art. 7:750(1) DCC. M.A.M.C. Van den Berg and S. van Gulijk, *Mr. C. Assers Handleiding tot de beoefening van het Nederlands Burgerlijk Recht. 7. Bijzondere overeenkomsten. Deel VI. Aanneming van werk*, Deventer, Wolters Kluwer, 2022, no. 79.

2997 **Belgium**: Art. 1794 old BCC. **The Netherlands**: Art. 7:764 DCC.

maintenance services, and the termination options of the contract will be fully regulated in the PSS contract/additional maintenance contract.

726. Repair as remedy for non-conformity or as additional service – The PSS supplier's obligation to repair the product in product-oriented PSS can have two legal bases. First, the PSS user may be entitled to repair of the product as a (primary) remedy for a lack of conformity of the product.[2998] If the PSS user-buyer opts for repair of the non-conforming product, the PSS supplier-seller must carry out the repairs free of charge, within a reasonable period of time from the moment he was informed by the PSS user-buyer of the lack of conformity, and without any significant inconvenience to the PSS user-buyer.[2999] The new Right to Repair Directive will add to these requirements that during repair, the seller may provide the consumer free of charge with a replacement good, including a refurbished good, on loan.[3000] Additionally, to promote repair as the more sustainable remedy for non-conformity, it amends Article 10 SGD to provide for an extension of the liability period by twelve months if the buyer opts for the remedy of repair to bring the goods into conformity.[3001] Second, for repairs that fall outside the scope of the legal guarantee, the PSS supplier's obligation to repair may also arise from an additional repair contract. In this case, just like product-oriented PSS with additional maintenance services, the cumulation theory should be applied so the repair services are covered by the rules of the Belgian contract for services and the Dutch contract for works.[3002] Also here, these rules are rather general (and generally only default law) so most of the content of the repair services (including the maximum duration of the repairs, the termination options, whether a replacement good is made available during the time of repair, etc.) will be set out in the PSS contract/additional repair contract.

727. Repair as additional service: incentives of the new Right to Repair Directive – Thus, if the defect of the product falls outside the scope of the legal guarantee of the SGD, the consumer can only have its product repaired if the PSS supplier-seller offers an additional repair service. The new Right to Repair Directive aims to promote repair and incentivise consumers to choose repair, also in those situations where the legal guarantee does not apply.[3003]

2998 EU: Art. 13(2) SGD. **Belgium**: Art. 1649*quinquies*, §2 *juncto* Art. 1649*quinquies*, §3 old BCC. **The Netherlands**: Art. 7:21(1) *juncto* Art. 7:21(2) DCC. See also *supra* no. 471.

2999 EU: Art. 14(1) SGD. **Belgium**: Art. 1649*quinquies*, §3 old BCC. **The Netherlands**: 7:21(3) DCC. See also *supra* no. 471.

3000 Art. 16(4) Right to Repair Directive, which will amend Art. 14(1) SGD. See also Recital 42 Right to Repair Directive.

3001 See Art. 16(2)(a) Right to Repair Directive. See also *supra* no. 467.

3002 Compare with *supra* no. 725.

3003 See Recital 16 Right to Repair Directive.

First, it introduces a (voluntary) European repair information form, which repairers can offer to consumers.[3004] This form contains information like repair conditions, time needed to finish the repair, prices, the availability of temporary replacement products, etc.[3005] It must be provided free of charge, although the consumer may be charged to pay the necessary costs of the diagnostic service.[3006] If the repairer provides this form to the consumer, the conditions set out in the form will be binding on the former for 30 days, unless the consumer and repairer agree to extend this period.[3007]

Second, the Right to Repair Directive envisages to develop a European online repair platform where consumers may find the different repair services at EU level but also cross borders and in each Member State.[3008]

Third, it places on manufacturers[3009, 3010] an obligation to repair upon the consumer's request for goods for which EU legal acts lay down repairability requirements (e.g. washing machines, dishwashers, refrigerators, vacuum cleaners).[3011] This repair shall either be carried out free of charge or for a reasonable price and must be carried out within a reasonable period of time.[3012] The obligation to repair does not apply where repair is factually or legally impossible.[3013] Manufacturers may not refuse to repair these goods for the sole reason that a previous repair has been performed by other repairers or other persons.[3014] Consumers may seek repair from any repairer from their choice.[3015] Linked with this obligation to repair, manufacturers must provide information on their website regarding spare parts for the goods for which EU legal acts lay down repairability requirements, must make them available to all parties in the repair sector at a reasonable price and are prohibited from using practices that prevent the use of second-hand or 3D printed spare parts by independent repairers.[3016]

3004 Art. 4(1) Right to Repair Directive.

3005 Art. 4(4) Right to Repair Directive.

3006 See Art. 4(2) and (3) and Recital 12 Right to Repair Directive.

3007 Art. 4(5) Right to Repair Directive.

3008 Art. 7 Right to Repair Directive.

3009 As defined in Art. 2(43) Ecodesign Directive.

3010 Where the manufacturer is established outside the EU, its authorised representative in the EU shall perform this obligation. Where there is no authorised representative, the importer shall perform this obligation. Where there is no importer, the distributor shall perform this obligation. The manufacturer, authorised representative, importer and distributor may sub-contract repair in order to fulfil their obligation to repair. See Art. 5(2) and Art. 5(1) Right to Repair Directive.

3011 Art. 5(1) Right to Repair Directive.

3012 Art. 5(2) right to Repair Directive.

3013 Art. 5(1) Right to Repair Directive. See also Recital 24 Right to Repair Directive.

3014 Art. 5(7) Right to Repair Directive.

3015 Art. 5(8) right to Repair Directive.

3016 Art. 5(5)-(6) Right to Repair Directive.

728. Replacement as remedy for non-conformity – In product-oriented PSS, the replacement of the product is also a primary remedy for a lack of conformity of the product.[3017] As with the remedy of repair, the PSS supplier-seller must carry out the replacement free of charge, within a reasonable period of time from the moment he was informed by the PSS user-buyer of the lack of conformity, and without any significant inconvenience to the PSS user-buyer.[3018] As already discussed above, under the SGD, there was some uncertainty regarding the question whether the seller may replace non-conforming goods by a refurbished good.[3019] In this regard, various national courts ruled that the consumer is entitled to replacement by a new product and not a refurbished one.[3020] This uncertainty was addressed by the new Right to Repair Directive. According to this directive, the seller may provide, upon the explicit request by the consumer a refurbished good to fulfil his obligation to replace the good.[3021] While it is a step in the right direction that the possibility of replacement by a refurbished good is explicitly recognised, it is regrettable that the PSS supplier-seller is only able to do so "*upon the explicit request by the consumer.*" It can be expected that, in practice, consumers will still prefer new rather than refurbished goods, so there is a risk that this provision will remain rather ineffectual.

729. Replacement by buying a new (or refurbished/second-hand) product – Besides replacement as remedy for non-conformity, the PSS supplier-seller has no obligation to replace the product in a product-oriented PSS contract. This means that if the conditions for liability for non-conformity are not met, the only alternative for the PSS user-buyer to replace the product is purchasing a new (or refurbished/second-hand) one.

6.3.2. USE-ORIENTED PSS

730. Maintenance of the product: responsibility of the PSS supplier-lessor – Since use-oriented PSS are qualified as rental contracts, the maintenance obligation of the PSS supplier has a different legal basis than in product-oriented PSS. Indeed, in the absence of a contractual provision to the contrary, one of the obligations of the lessor is to maintain the good in such condition that it is suitable for the use for which it has

3017 EU: Art. 13(2) SGD. **Belgium**: Art. 1649*quinquies*, §2 *juncto* Art. 1649*quinquies*, §3 old BCC. **The Netherlands**: Art. 7:21(1) *juncto* Art. 7:21(2) DCC. See also *supra* no. 471.

3018 EU: Art. 14(1) SGD. **Belgium**: Art. 1649*quinquies*, §3 old BCC. **The Netherlands**: 7:21(3) DCC. See also *supra* no. 471.

3019 See *supra* no. 563.

3020 See *supra* no. 563 and the case law cited there.

3021 Art. 16(4) Right to Repair Directive, which amends 14(1) SGD. See also Recital 42 Right to Repair Directive.

been rented.[3022] As a result, the PSS supplier is bound to this maintenance obligation from the nature of the use-oriented PSS contract as rental contract itself, without the need for any contractual clause.[3023] Unlike the PSS supplier-lessor's obligation to repair,[3024] the obligation to maintain does not (yet) require damage to the rented product.[3025] This means that the PSS supplier is required to maintain the product (e.g. washing machine, bicycle, Cambio car, ventilation system, etc.) so that the PSS user can continue to enjoy the agreed use. There are three main options for arranging maintenance. First, maintenance can be carried out when the PSS user notifies the supplier of a defect. Second, the PSS contract may contain a scheduled maintenance plan. Finally, in the case of "smart" connected products, preventive maintenance may be carried out based on the user data collected by the sensors of the product.

731. Duty of the PSS user to notify the PSS supplier of need for maintenance – To ensure that the PSS supplier-lessor knows when it should fulfil its maintenance obligation, the PSS user-lessee has a duty to notify it of any degradations, malfunctions or other damages as part of his obligation to treat the product as a prudent and reasonable person.[3026, 3027] The PSS contract may further specify the time period in which the PSS user must notify the PSS supplier. For example, the terms and conditions of *Blue Movement* state that the PSS user must notify the PSS supplier within 5 calendar days after discovering a malfunction or defect.[3028] If the PSS user does not inform the PSS supplier of the

---

3022 **Belgium**: Art. 1719, 2° old BCC. S. Marysse, "Rechten en verbintenissen van de verhuurder" in M. Dambre, B. Hubeau and S. Stijns (eds.), *Handboek algemeen huurrecht*, Bruges, Die Keure, 2015, (415) 435, no. 47oef haha; C. Marr, "Le contrat de location de biens meubles" in *Guide juridique de l'entreprise. Traité théorique et pratique*, Book 39, Waterloo, Kluwer, 2007, 27, no. 350. **The Netherlands**: This follows from Art. 7:204(2) DCC, which states that there is a defect if the good does not give the lessee the enjoyment he is entitled to expect from a "well-maintained" good of the kind covered by the contract. See: Explanatory Memorandum, *Parliamentary Papers II* 2001/02, 26089, no. 162, 13; Explanatory Memorandum, *Parliamentary Papers II* 1999/00, 26089, no. 6, 12 and Explanatory Memorandum, *Parliamentary Papers II* 2000/01, 26932, no. 5, 9; H.J. Rossel and A.H.T. Heisterkamp, *Mr. C. Assers Handleiding tot de beoefening van het Nederlands Burgerlijk Recht. 7. Bijzondere overeenkomsten. Deel II. Huur*, Deventer, Wolters Kluwer, 2021, no. 41.

3023 S. Marysse, "Rechten en verbintenissen van de verhuurder" in M. Dambre, B. Hubeau and S. Stijns (eds.), *Handboek algemeen huurrecht*, Bruges, Die Keure, 2015, (415) 435.

3024 See *infra* no. 734.

3025 J. Vankerckhove, P. Coeckelberghs, A. Devreux, J.-M. Letier, B. Louveaux, B. Vandeputte and M. Vlies, *Le louage de choses 1: Les baux en général*, Brussels, Larcier, 2000, 428, no. 588.

3026 See *infra* section 7.3.1.2.

3027 S. Marysse, "Rechten en verbintenissen van de verhuurder" in M. Dambre, B. Hubeau and S. Stijns (eds.), *Handboek algemeen huurrecht*, Bruges, Die Keure, 2015, (415) 437, no. 51; C. Marr, "Le contrat de location de biens meubles" in *Guide juridique de l'entreprise. Traité théorique et pratique*, Book 39, Waterloo, Kluwer, 2007, 27, no. 360.

3028 Art. 9.1 Terms and Conditions Blue Movement. Compare also with Art. 10.3 Terms and Conditions Bundles, which also stipulates a term of 5 calendar days.

need for maintenance (in due time), this may result in his contractual liability for damage to the product caused by late maintenance.[3029] Once the PSS user has notified the PSS supplier, he has the right to a prompt intervention.[3030] This time period in which the PSS supplier must comply with its obligation to maintain after a notification by the PSS user may in turn also be further specified in the PSS contract. For instance, the terms and conditions of *Repeat/Gerrard Street* state that it aims to deliver the replacement part within 92 hours.[3031] For *Blue Movement*, interventions must be performed within five calendar days.[3032]

732. MAINTENANCE BASED ON A SCHEDULED MAINTENANCE PLAN – In addition to unplanned maintenance based on the PSS user's notifications, the PSS contract may also set out a scheduled maintenance plan with planned maintenance moments. Scheduled maintenance has various benefits. Indeed, scheduled maintenance helps identify potential issues with the product before they become critical problems or defects. This may improve reliability of the product and reduce unexpected downtime for the PSS user, which may lead to improved customer satisfaction. Additionally, scheduled maintenance may extend the product's lifespan by helping to identify and address wear and tear in a timely manner. This may also result in cost savings for the PSS supplier by avoiding costly repairs and replacements of the product.

733. PREVENTIVE MAINTENANCE BASED ON USER DATA – A third possibility for planning maintenance activities is by using user data for preventive maintenance. Indeed, the fact that more and more "smart" products are offered through PSS contracts also offers enormous advantages for maintenance and repair. The sensors in these products make it possible to carry out preventive maintenance. This enables intervention to be carried out at the right time, also potentially extending the products' lifespan. Yet there are also challenges involved. After all, the access to and use of user data is critical to conduct preventive maintenance. This must be carefully balanced with privacy and data protection considerations and compliance with, for example, the GDPR.

734. REPAIR OF THE PRODUCT: NECESSARY REPAIRS ARE RESPONSIBILITY OF THE PSS SUPPLIER-LESSOR – The rules of the rental contract require the PSS supplier-lessor to perform all necessary repairs to the product during the term of the PSS contract, except for the ("minor") repairs that are at the expense of

3029 T. PAPART, "Droits et obligations du bailleur – L'entretien, les réparations et les autres obligations du bailleur"" in G. BENOIT, I. DURANT, P.-A. FORIERS, M. VANWIJCK-ALEXANDRE and P. WÉRY (eds.), *Le droit commun du bail*, Bruges, Die Keure, 2006, (133) 135, no. 57.

3030 T. PAPART, "Droits et obligations du bailleur – L'entretien, les réparations et les autres obligations du bailleur" in G. BENOIT, I. DURANT, P.-A. FORIERS, M. VANWIJCK-ALEXANDRE and P. WÉRY (eds.), *Le droit commun du bail*, Bruges, Die Keure, 2006, (133) 140, no. 74.

3031 Art. 5.1 Terms and Conditions Repeat/Gerrard Street.

3032 Art. 9.2 Terms and Conditions Blue Movement.

the PSS user-lessee.[3033, 3034] The term "necessary repairs" is to be interpreted broadly. It includes all repairs without which the normal use of the product would be hampered, or the PSS user would suffer loss of rental enjoyment or other damage.[3035] As with the PSS supplier's maintenance obligation, this repair obligation arises from the qualification as a rental contract and does not require a specific contractual obligation. Unlike the PSS supplier-lessors' maintenance obligation, the repair obligation of the PSS supplier-lessor requires that damages or defects have occurred to the product.[3036] The cause of these damages or defects is not relevant. Therefore, the PSS supplier will have to perform the necessary repairs caused by the normal use of the product, its age or *force majeure*.[3037] However, the PSS supplier will not be responsible for the repairs of damages or defects caused by the fault of the PSS user (or the persons for whom he is responsible).[3038-3039] As with the PSS supplier's maintenance obligation, the PSS user has a duty to notify the PSS supplier of any damages or defects that require repair.[3040] This duty to notify (e.g. the time period in which notification must be made) may be further specified in the PSS contract. If the PSS user does not notify the PSS supplier (in due time), he risks being contractually liable for the additional damages caused by this late notification.

735. Minor repairs: in principle responsibility of the PSS user-lessee but often contractually assigned to the PSS supplier – According to the Belgian and Dutch rental contract rules, the PSS supplier-lessor will in principle not be responsible for the repairs that are at the expense of the PSS user-lessee.[3041] These include the so-called "minor repairs", i.e. repairs of fairly

3033 See *infra* no. 735.

3034 **Belgium**: Art. 1720 old BCC. S. Marysse, "Rechten en verbintenissen van de verhuurder" in M. Dambre, B. Hubeau and S. Stijns (eds.), *Handboek algemeen huurrecht*, Bruges, Die Keure, 2015, (415) 440, no. 58. **The Netherlands**: Art. 7:206 DCC. H.J. Rossel and A.H.T. Heisterkamp, *Mr. C. Assers Handleiding tot de beoefening van het Nederlands Burgerlijk Recht. 7. Bijzondere overeenkomsten. Deel II. Huur*, Deventer, Wolters Kluwer, 2021, no. 40.

3035 T. Papart, "Droits et obligations du bailleur – L'entretien, les réparations et les autres obligations du bailleur"" in G. Benoit, I. Durant, P.-A. Foriers, M. Vanwijck-Alexandre and P. Wéry (eds.), *Le droit commun du bail*, Bruges, Die Keure, 2006, (133) 137, no. 66.

3036 S. Marysse, "Rechten en verbintenissen van de verhuurder" in M. Dambre, B. Hubeau and S. Stijns (eds.), *Handboek algemeen huurrecht*, Bruges, Die Keure, 2015, (415) 438, no. 52.

3037 S. Marysse, "Rechten en verbintenissen van de verhuurder" in M. Dambre, B. Hubeau and S. Stijns (eds.), *Handboek algemeen huurrecht*, Bruges, Die Keure, 2015, (415) 438, no. 53.

3038 **Belgium**: Art. 1732 and 1735 old BCC. **The Netherlands**: Art. 7:206(2) DCC.

3039 See also *infra* no. 737.

3040 **Belgium**: S. Marysse, "Rechten en verbintenissen van de verhuurder" in M. Dambre, B. Hubeau and S. Stijns (eds.), *Handboek algemeen huurrecht*, Bruges, Die Keure, 2015, (415) 438–439, no. 54. **The Netherlands**: This follows from the phrase *"at the request of the lessee"* in Art. 7:206(1) DCC. See: H.J. Rossel and A.H.T. Heisterkamp, *Mr. C. Assers Handleiding tot de beoefening van het Nederlands Burgerlijk Recht. 7. Bijzondere overeenkomsten. Deel II. Huur*, Deventer, Wolters Kluwer, 2021, no. 40.

3041 **Belgium**: Art. 1754 old BCC *juncto* Art. 1720(2) *in fine* old BCC. M. Dambre, "Rechten en verbintenissen van de huurder" in M. Dambre, B. Hubeau and S. Stijns (eds.),

insignificant damage or costs thar are assumed to be due to the normal use of the product by the PSS user-lessee.[3042] In certain circumstances, however, the PSS user-lessee will not be responsible for minor repairs. In Belgium, the PSS user is not responsible for minor repairs caused by aging or *force majeure*.[3043] In the Netherlands, the PSS user does not have to carry out minor repairs caused by aging or normal use,[3044] but he is responsible for minor repairs due to *force majeure*.[3045] However, as the PSS user-lessee's obligation to carry out minor repairs is only default law, the PSS contract may deviate from this by stating that the PSS supplier is also responsible for minor defects and repairs or that he is responsible for "all" repairs. In practice, most (use-oriented) PSS contracts do indeed contain such a clause to truly "unburden" the PSS user.[3046] This is the case, for example, in the terms of conditions of *Swapfiets*, where it is stated that the PSS user is entitled to free repair of defects caused by wear and tear and normal use of the bike (e.g. a flat tire, a broken (chain) guard, a torn saddle and broken lighting).[3047]

736. METHODS FOR ORGANISING REPAIR – There are different possible methods for organising the repair of the product. First, the traditional option is for the PSS supplier to send a technician or repairer to the PSS user's premises who will inspect the product, and repair or replace it if necessary. This approach is most appropriate for products that are not easily transportable, such as a ventilation system or large household appliances. For example, the terms and conditions of *Bundles* state that maintenance and repairs are generally carried out at the PSS user's premises.[3048] An obvious downside of this method is that it may take a while before a technician or repairer is available to repair the product can be repaired. Additionally, some defects or products may require more lengthy

---

Handboek algemeen huurrecht, Bruges, Die Keure, 2015, (513) 562; Y. MERCHIERS, *Le bail en général*, Brussels, Larcier, 2015, 215–216, no. 263. **The Netherlands**: Art. 7:217 DCC *juncto* Art. 7:204(2) and 7:206(2) DCC. H.J. ROSSEL and A.H.T. HEISTERKAMP, *Mr. C. Assers Handleiding tot de beoefening van het Nederlands Burgerlijk Recht. 7. Bijzondere overeenkomsten. Deel II. Huur*, Deventer, Wolters Kluwer, 2021, no. 108; J.K. SIX-HUMMEL, *Groene Serie Huurrecht, art. 7:217 BW*, Deventer, Kluwer, loose-leaf, 2012, para. 21.

3042 **Belgium**: M. DAMBRE, "Rechten en verbintenissen van de huurder" in M. DAMBRE, B. HUBEAU and S. STIJNS (eds.), *Handboek algemeen huurrecht*, Bruges, Die Keure, 2015, (513) 562, no. 139. **The Netherlands**: H.J. ROSSEL and A.H.T. HEISTERKAMP, *Mr. C. Assers Handleiding tot de beoefening van het Nederlands Burgerlijk Recht. 7. Bijzondere overeenkomsten. Deel II. Huur*, Deventer, Wolters Kluwer, 2021, no. 42 and 108.

3043 Art. 1755 old BCC. M. DAMBRE, "Rechten en verbintenissen van de huurder" in M. DAMBRE, B. HUBEAU and S. STIJNS (eds.), *Handboek algemeen huurrecht*, Bruges, Die Keure, 2015, (513) 563.

3044 Art. 7:224(2) DCC.

3045 Explanatory Memorandum, *Parliamentary Papers II* 1997/98, 26089, no. 3, 27; J.K. SIX-HUMMEL, *Groene Serie Huurrecht, art. 7:217 BW*, Deventer, Kluwer, loose-leaf, 2012, para. 21.

3046 V. MAK, "Consumentenbescherming bij servitisation", *TPR* 2019, (779) 794–795, no. 16.

3047 Art. 3.3 Terms and Conditions Swapfiets.

3048 Art. 10.4 Terms and conditions Bundles. Compare also with Art. 9.4 Terms and Conditions Blue Movement.

repairs. This may result in longer downtime for the PSS user and may potentially affect the achievement of the output specifications by the PSS supplier.[3049] This is why other business models allow the defective product to be immediately exchanged for a working one. *Swapfiets*, for example, allows you to "swap" the rented bicycle if it is defect. Upon making an appointment, the PSS user will receive a new bicycle immediately (i.e. within 48 hours) and *Swapfiets* will repair the other bicycle, which will be made available to the next user at a later stage.[3050] This has the advantage that the PSS user is confronted with as little downtime as possible and (almost) always has access to a functional product. "Swapping" the product is also useful for PSS contracts involving smaller products, such as consumer electronics. Indeed, with these products, it will be easier to send them to the PSS supplier via parcel shipping instead of making a physical appointment. The PSS supplier can then immediately send a replacement product to the PSS user and repair, refurbish or otherwise repurpose the defective product. *Fairphone Easy* and *Swapphone* are examples of PSS suppliers using this method for arranging repairs.[3051] In yet some other cases, it is beneficial to allow and enable PSS users to carry out repairs themselves. For example, the *Fairphone-as-a-Service* project states as a unique selling point of a modular smartphone that many repairs can be easily performed by the PSS user itself using modules from a reserve pool. While the PSS user is allowed to do the repairs himself, *Fairphone* remains responsible for the handling costs for repairs and replacements.[3052]

737. Avoiding moral hazard: limits to (free) maintenance and repair in case of misuse, intentional damage or damage exceeding normal wear and tear – Offering unconditional free maintenance and repair makes the PSS supplier vulnerable to abuse. For example, PSS users may use the product carelessly or even intentionally break the product to get a new one (another example of the moral hazard problem).[3053] In this sense, the rental contract rules provide that the lessor is not responsible for repairing the damage or defects that are caused by the fault of the lessee, his sub-lessees or the persons he allows to use the good.[3054] To avoid these forms of moral hazard, PSS suppliers also often

3049 Compare with *supra* no. 518 *et seq.*

3050 Art. 5.1 Terms and Conditions Swapfiets.

3051 See Art. 6.1 Terms and Conditions Fairphone Easy and Art. 6 Terms and Conditions Swapphone.

3052 Circle Economy, "The Circular Phone, Legal, operational and financial solutions to unlock the potential of the 'Fairphone-as-a-service' model", 31 December 2017, available at www.circle-economy.com/resources/the-circular-phone 8.

3053 See on customer misbehaviour in service contracts and renting contracts e.g. T. Schaefers, K. Wittkowski, S. Benoit and R. Ferraro, "Contagious Effects of Customer Misbehavior in Access-Based Services", *Journal of Service Research* 2015, vol. 19, afl. 1, (3) 3–21 and J.F. Durgee and G.C. O'Connor, "An exploration into renting as consumption behavior", *Psychology & Marketing* 1995, vol. 12, afl. 2, (89) 89–104.

3054 **Belgium**: Art. 1732 and 1735 old BCC. **The Netherlands**: Art. 7:206(2), Art. 7:218(1) and Art. 7:219 DCC.

include contractual exceptions to these maintenance and repair obligations in the PSS contract, for example in case of misuse, intentional damage or damage that exceeds normal wear and tear.[3055] If the PSS user indeed misuses or intentionally damages the product, the PSS supplier can then recover the cost of repair or maintenance from the PSS user or even terminate the PSS contract (with or without additional compensation for damages).

> Terms and conditions Swapfiets – Art. 8.3 "In case of damage or/and wear and tear to the bicycle other than what is to be expected by normal use, at the discretion of Swapfiets, Swapfiets reserves the right to recover the costs from the Renter."

> Terms and conditions Blue Movement – Art. 9.3 "Costs of repairs shall in principle be borne by BSH. If there is negligent or improper use of the Appliance by the Lessee (in other words, the Lessee has not behaved as a good lessee and/or otherwise acted contrary to his obligations under Article 9), the costs including call-out, repair, replacement or damage shall be borne by the Lessee."

> Terms and conditions Live Light – Art. 9.2 "The Tenant is liable to Live Light for all damage to the Goods and/or the total or partial destruction of the Goods by whatever cause, regardless of whether it is personally responsible for the damage, loss or theft or making the Goods unusable or worthless."

738. Limited number of exceptional repairs for damage exceeding normal wear and tear – Some PSS suppliers do not go so far as to impose liability on the PSS user for all damage exceeding normal wear and tear. Instead, they provide in the PSS contract that he PSS user is entitled to a limited number of exceptional repairs, the costs of which are borne by the PSS supplier. The PSS contract may further specify which exceptional repairs of which defects are covered by this right. For example, the terms and conditions of *Fairphone Easy* stipulate that the PSS user is allowed to replace his screen or battery once per year. Anything beyond this yearly allowance is subject to additional charges.[3056]

> Terms and conditions Fairphone Easy – Art. 6.2 "You may swap Your device in case the following applied: […] Your screen is damaged. You will be able to replace Your screen once a year. Please note anything beyond this yearly allowance will be subject to additional charges; Your battery is damaged. You will be able to replace Your battery once a year. Please note anything beyond this yearly allowance will be subject to additional charges."

3055 See e.g. Art. 8.3 Terms and Conditions Swapfiets; Art. 9.3 Terms and Conditions Blue Movement; Art. 9.2 Terms and Conditions Live Light, and Art. 10.2 and 10.4 Terms and Conditions Bundles.

3056 Art. 6.2 Terms and Conditions Fairphone Easy.

739. Maintenance and repairs by the PSS user or a third party? – The question arises whether the PSS user may perform the maintenance and repair of the product himself or engage a third party to carry out the repairs. In practice, we see that most of the selected PSS contracts explicitly prohibit PSS users from carrying out repairs on the products themselves or hiring a third party to do so.[3057] This makes sense. After all, PSS suppliers are best placed to carry out these repairs in a sustainable and qualitative manner.[3058] In addition, this also ensures that the PSS user is "taken care of" and does not have to fear unexpected costs. The question arises whether the PSS user may also not remedy the situation himself if the PSS supplier is in default of his obligation to maintain or repair. Under the Belgian rental contract rules, the lessee is in principle not allowed to carry out repairs himself or hire a third party to do so (and recover the associated costs) that are the responsibility of the lessor without the lessor's or the court's consent.[3059] There are however exceptions to this rule, namely if the conditions for *negotiorum gestio*[3060] (*zaakwaarneming, gestion d'affaire*) or extrajudicial replacement[3061] are met. The Belgian rules on extrajudicial replacement are, however, only default law, so parties can validly deviate from them in the PSS contract.[3062] In contrast, the Dutch rental contract rules explicitly confirm that if the lessor is in default of maintaining or repairing the product, the lessee may do so himself and recover the costs incurred (provided they were reasonable) from the lessor by setting them off against the rental price.[3063] As this provision is (semi-) mandatory law, it cannot be deviated from to the detriment of the lessee.[3064] Consequently, under Dutch law, PSS suppliers have fewer options to completely prohibit maintenance or repair by the PSS user or a third party than under Belgian law.

3057 See e.g. Art. 10.3 Terms and Conditions Bundles; Art. 9. 2 Terms and Conditions Blue Movement; Art. 6.11 Terms and Conditions Swapphone.

3058 See in this sense Art. 5.4 Terms and Conditions Fairphone Easy: "*To allow for both the device and its components to be re-used with multiple consumers and limit e-waste, ensure circularity and preserve the life of the device for as long as possible, You are prohibited from the following: [...] engaging a third party to repair the device; engaging in self repair unless advised by Fairphone.*"

3059 E. Van den Haute, *Traité des contrats spéciaux*, Brussels, Larcier, 2024, 617, no. 582; S. Marysse, "Rechten en verbintenissen van de verhuurder" in M. Dambre, B. Hubeau and S. Stijns (eds.), *Handboek algemeen huurrecht*, Bruges, Die Keure, 2015, (415) 439. See for an application: Liège (BE) 23 January 1980, *JL* 1982, 1.

3060 See Art. 5.128–5.132 BCC.

3061 Art. 5.85(3) BCC. This requires urgency or other exceptional circumstances, a notice of default granting a final grace period, taking appropriate measures to establish the non-performance and a written notification of the extrajudicial replacement.

3062 Subject to Art. VI.83, 30° BCEL, which prohibits clauses that unduly restrict the consumer's legal rights in the event of non-performance. However, it can be argued that it is not unfair to exclude the right of (extrajudicial) replacement of the debtor, as the core of this remedy (i.e. the right to performance of the maintenance and repair obligation) remains intact.

3063 Art. 7:206(3) DCC.

3064 Art. 7:206(3) *in fine* DCC.

740. Replacement of the product: no right to replacement under rental contract rules unless contractually granted by the PSS contract – The Belgian and Dutch rental contract rules in principle do not contain a right for the PSS user to claim a replacement of the product in case of a defect. Indeed, under the Belgian rental contract rules, if the good is destroyed or lost during the term of the rental contract, the contract shall be automatically terminated.[3065] Under Dutch law, if the good has a defect that the lessor is not required to remedy (namely because this is impossible or would require unreasonable expenses from the lessor),[3066] and this defect makes the rental enjoyment completely impossible, both parties can terminate the contract.[3067] This can be explained by the fact that the rules of the rental contract are mostly focused on the rental of immovable goods, where the lessor can in most cases not be expected to replace the destroyed rented immovable good with a new immovable good. However, as already discussed above, in the context of the rental of movables, and PSS contracts in particular, the contracting parties will generally want to continue the contract because the destroyed rented good can (easily) be replaced.[3068] As a result, PSS contracts in practice often contain a contractual right to replacement of the product in case of defects or destruction of the product.

6.3.3. RESULT-ORIENTED PSS

741. Maintenance, repair and replacement as part of complex service contract: governed by rules regarding conformity of the service and contractual arrangements – In result-oriented PSS, maintenance, repair and replacement obligations are all part of the complex and integrated service contract. As a result, the rules of the contract for services apply. Both the Belgian and Dutch rules on the contract for services do not provide specific provisions for maintenance, repair and replacement obligations. Instead, these obligations (including a potential prohibition for the PSS user to repair or replace the product himself or engage a third party to do so) are governed by the rules on the conformity of the service with the contract and the contractual arrangements by the parties.[3069] Additionally, service standards relating to maintenance and repair may also be relevant for assessing the conformity of the maintenance and repair services with the result-oriented PSS contract.[3070] In practice, the contractual arrangements on the rights and obligations of the parties regarding maintenance, repair and replacement of the product in result-oriented PSS contracts will largely resemble those of use-oriented PSS discussed in the previous section.

3065 Art. 1722 old BCC discussed *supra* no. 439.

3066 See Art. 7:206(1) DCC.

3067 Art. 7:210 DCC *juncto* Art. 6:267 DCC. See *supra* no. 439.

3068 See *supra* no. 439.

3069 See on conformity of the service in result-oriented PSS *supra* section 4.3.3.

3070 See *supra* no. 524 and *infra* no. 743.

6.3.4. LEGISLATIVE INTERVENTION NEEDED?

742. THREE POSSIBLE SOLUTIONS – In line with the evaluation and legislative proposals already discussed above,[3071] the same three solutions can be considered for the PSS supplier's obligations to maintain and repair the product. As a reminder, these include (i) the **modernisation of national contract law** (option 1), (ii) including maintenance and repair in an **EU directive** (option 2), and (iii) the **use of balanced standard contracts and model clauses** (option 3). The first two options are discussed in this section. The model clauses on maintenance, repair and replacement are set out in section 6.3.5.

743. ADDITIONAL SOLUTION: STANDARDISATION OF REPAIR SERVICES – Besides these three solutions, standardisation of services could also play a role in the context of the PSS supplier's obligation to repair the product.[3072] As also cited by the Right to Repair Directive (although in a different context), a (voluntary) (European) quality standard for repair services could also prove useful to assess the conformity and quality of repair services.[3073] The content of this service standard could include, for example, the time to complete repair, the availability of temporary replacement goods, quality assurances such as a commercial guarantee on repair, and the availability of additional services such as removal, installation and transportation offered by repairers.[3074] (European) repair standards could boost consumer trust in repair services and allow better assessment of the conformity of repair services with the PSS contract.

6.3.4.1. Modernisation of national contract law

A. Use-oriented PSS: modernising rental contract rules on maintenance and repair

744. MAINTENANCE AND REPAIR COVERED BY THE RULES ON CONFORMITY THROUGHOUT THE RENTAL CONTRACT – A proposed provision on the lessor's obligation to maintain the rented good and carry out the necessary repairs was already set out above, in proposed provision #5.[3075] Indeed, these obligations were included in the lessor's conformity obligation throughout the duration of the rented contract, which proposes to replace the current provision on the lessor's obligation to ensure the quiet rental enjoyment. This proposed provision provides for an exception though, namely maintenance and repairs that are the responsibility of the lessee.

3071 Compare with *supra* section 4.4.1.3 and 6.2.5.
3072 See on standardisation of services also *supra* no. 575–579.
3073 Compare with Recital 38 of the Right to Repair Directive.
3074 *Ibid.*
3075 See *supra* no. 550.

745. Maintenance and repairs that are the responsibility of the lessee – According to proposed provision #9, also already set out above, minor maintenance and minor repairs, as well as repairs resulting from improper use or lack of maintenance, are the responsibility of the lessee.[3076] As such, it re-codifies the current rules of the Belgian rental contract. However, this research proposed a deviation from the current rental contract rules on minor repairs and the proposed provision in the Draft Law.[3077] Indeed, in B2C rental contracts for consumer goods (i.e. movable tangible goods), it is proposed to make the lessor responsible for minor repairs.[3078] The rationale behind this proposal is to better align the legal position of the consumer-lessee who acquires the use of a consumer good by renting it with the legal position of the consumer-buyer who acquires the ownership of the same good.[3079] As already explained above, the scope of this exception is limited in multiple ways (only B2C, only consumer goods, not applicable to minor maintenance or repairs due to improper use or lack of maintenance) and can be deviated from by the contractual parties, provided the consumer was specifically informed that he is responsible for minor repairs and the consumer expressly and separately accepted this deviation when concluding the rental contract.[3080]

B. Result-oriented PSS: conformity rules also cover maintenance and repair

746. No specific provision on maintenance and repair necessary for contract for services – It is not necessary to include a specific provision on maintenance and repair in the rules of the contract for services. After all, the conformity of repair and maintenance are also covered by the general rules on conformity of the contract for services, of which the proposed provisions were discussed above.[3081]

6.3.4.2. Maintenance and repair as part of EU directive?

747. Maintenance and repair as part of EU directive? – As with the installation obligation, the PSS supplier's obligations to maintain and repair the product may also be regulated at the EU level by means of an EU directive (option 2).[3082] Again, if a general directive on conformity and quality of (almost) all service contracts is chosen (option 2a), no specific explanation is needed since

3076 See *supra* no. 556 *et seq.*
3077 Compare with Art. 1754 old BCC and proposed Art. 7.3.23(1), 1° BCC.
3078 See *supra* no. 557.
3079 *Ibid.*
3080 *Ibid.*
3081 See *supra* section 4.4.2.2.
3082 Compare with *supra* section 6.2.5.2 and see for an overview of the different options for regulation at the EU level *supra* section 4.4.3.

maintenance and repair will be subject to the same uniform conformity rules as other services. If a specific directive for "packages" or "bundles" of services is chosen (option 2b), the maintenance and repair services may be included in the provision on the scope of the "package services"/"bundles of services" directive. Additionally, more substantive rules on maintenance and repair may be included in a specific section of the directive. These substantive rules could for example cover the timing of repair and maintenance, notice requirements for the PSS user, the need or possibility for a replacement product during reparations, conformity of the maintenance and repair services and remedies for lack of conformity, etc.

6.3.5. MODEL CLAUSES ON MAINTENANCE, REPAIR AND REPLACEMENT

748. Model clauses on general maintenance obligation of the PSS supplier – The obligation to maintain the product is one of the essential obligations in a use-oriented and result-oriented PSS contract. Indeed, it ensures that the product's lifetime is extended, benefiting both the PSS supplier (who has fewer costs related to product replacement), the PSS user (who experiences less downtime of the product/service) and the environment (which benefits from products having the longest possible lifetime). The following model clauses contain a general obligation to maintain the product. They provide that the PSS supplier shall perform the maintenance and bear the associated costs (unless those caused by issues and defects exceeding normal wear and tear) so that the product remains operational, functional and available in accordance with the output specifications set out elsewhere in the PSS contract.[3083] They also define what is to be understood under normal wear and tear. Additionally, specific maintenance activities may also be enumerated in the contract.

Model clause #40 – General maintenance obligation

- **[The PSS supplier] shall perform maintenance for the products supplied under this contract to ensure that the products remain operational, functional and available to [the PSS user] in accordance with the output specifications outlined in [reference to the specific Article or Annex of the PSS contract]. [The PSS supplier] bears the costs of all maintenance necessary because of normal wear and tear. [The PSS user] is liable for all maintenance costs resulting from issues or defects exceeding normal wear and tear.**

[3083] See on output specifications *supra* no. 607.

- **For the purposes of this clause, issues or defects caused by normal wear and tear are [specified examples (e.g. limescale build up on the heating element of the washing machine, worn or flat tire, etc.)]].**
- **The maintenance services include [specific maintenance activities (e.g. regular inspections, testing, adjustments, repairs or replacements, software updates and support systems)].**

749. Model clause on responsive maintenance – A first way of practically organising the maintenance of the product is through responsive maintenance. This model clause requires the PSS user to notify the PSS supplier of any defects, malfunctions or other damage.[3084] The PSS contract may specify a reasonable period within which the PSS user must make this notification. Then, this model clause stipulates that after the notification by the PSS user, the PSS supplier must promptly respond and intervene to resolve the defect, malfunction or other issue. Again, the PSS contract may stipulate a reasonable timeframe within which this intervention must take place.

Model clause #41 – Responsive maintenance

- **In the event of a defect, malfunction or other damages to the product, [the PSS user] shall notify [the PSS supplier] of the issue within [specified reasonable timeframe (e.g. 48 hours, 5 calendar days)]. [The PSS supplier] shall respond and intervene promptly, and in no event later than [specified reasonable timeframe (e.g. 48 hours, 5 calendar days)] after receiving such notification.**

750. Model clause on scheduled maintenance – A second way of practically organising the maintenance of the product is through scheduled maintenance. The following model clause provides an example of the different ways a PSS contract can include a maintenance schedule. This clause can either be included in the PSS contract itself, or in an annex to the PSS contract. First, the PSS contract may outline a specified frequency for the maintenance services (e.g. monthly, quarterly, annually). Second, a determinable event may be chosen, such as the start or end of the heating season, after the PSS user has cycled 1000 km with the (e-)bicycle, or after 100 000 pages were printed. Finally, the PSS contract may also include a specified maintenance schedule with the exact dates the maintenance of the product will take place.

[3084] Compare also with the duty to notify the PSS supplier-lessor as part of the obligation to treat the product as a prudent and reasonable person discussed *infra* no. 837.

Model clause #42 – Scheduled maintenance

- [The PSS supplier] shall perform scheduled maintenance on the product at regular intervals. This scheduled maintenance is performed [specified frequency (e.g. monthly, quarterly, annually)/every specified day of the month/quarter (e.g. every first Friday)/every determinable event (e.g. every start/end of the heating season, after 1000 km, after printing 100 000 pages, etc.)/in accordance with a specified maintenance schedule containing exact dates (which can be set out in an annex to the PSS contract)].

751. Model clauses on preventive maintenance (including selected clauses on data protection) – A third way of practically organising the maintenance of the product is through preventive maintenance based on user data collected by the (sensors of the) product or digital services used in the performance of the service. This way, the product (or digital service) itself will indicate when maintenance is needed. The main advantage of this method is that maintenance is carried out "right on time" based on the actual use of the product, i.e. not unnecessarily early but also before defects have occurred. The first model clause sets out an example of how preventive maintenance based on user data can be contractually implemented in the PSS contract.

The use of user data collected by the product or digital service for the purpose of preventive maintenance may in some cases be at odds with principles of data protection law. Indeed, some data collected by the PSS supplier may give an insight into the PSS user's private life. For instance, in "heating as-a-service" or "ventilation as-a-service" contracts, the personal data collected by the system may allow to determine when a person is home[3085] or how many people are in a certain room at a certain moment in time.[3086] While this can offer benefits in terms of efficiency and optimisation when the heating or ventilation system needs to be active, it can also give the PSS supplier an insight into an intimate part of the PSS user's private life.

To mitigate these data protection risks, the second model clause confirms the legal obligation for the PSS supplier to at all times comply with the General Data Protection Regulation ("GDPR") and all applicable data protection laws. To ensure compliance with these legal instruments, it is appropriate to include clauses in the PSS contract on – amongst others – the purpose of data processing, the lawful basis for data processing (e.g. the data subject's explicit consent[3087]) and the measures taken to ensure that the PSS user's personal data are adequately secured. Since questions of data protection law fall outside of the

3085 Which may be relevant to create a personal "heating profile" or "ventilation profile".

3086 This can be derived, for example, from the data collected by CO2 sensors implemented in a ventilation-as-a-service system.

3087 See Art. 6(1)(a) GDPR. Other lawful bases are also possible, for example when the processing is necessary for the performance of the PSS contract (Art. 6(1)(b) GDPR).

scope of this book,[3088] the third, fourth, fifth and sixth model clauses are non-exhaustive examples. Actual compliance with the GDPR or other data protection laws might require additional clauses.

Model clause #43 – Preventive maintenance based on user data

- **[The PSS supplier] shall perform preventive maintenance on the product at regular intervals. These intervals are determined based on the analysis of user data collected by [the product/sensors of the product/the digital service]. Whenever the system indicates the need for maintenance, [the PSS supplier] will contact [the PSS user] to negotiate in good faith an exact date and time for the maintenance of the product.**

- **When analysing user data for the purpose of preventive maintenance, [the PSS supplier] shall at all times comply with the General Data Protection Regulation ("GDPR") and any applicable data protection laws.**

- **In particular, [the PSS supplier] shall only process personal data for preventive maintenance purposes and shall not disclose or transfer personal data to third parties without the express consent of [the PSS user], unless required to do so by law.**[3089]

- **[The PSS user's] personal data are retained are retained for [x] months / years [as long as necessary to fulfil the purposes for which they are collected]. After this period, the data are securely deleted, unless the retention of the data is required by law.**[3090]

- **Before signing the contract, [the PSS user] consents to the processing of personal data for the following purposes by placing a checkmark in the designated checkbox**[3091]**:**
  [by means of example:
  O performing the contractual obligations (e.g. predictive maintenance)[3092]**;**
  O measuring app activity;

[3088] See *supra* no. 70.

[3089] Model clause based on C. Borucki, H. Slachmuylders, B. Keirsbilck, D. Gruyaert and E. Terryn, *Model clauses for Product-as-a-Service (PaaS) contracts*, CE Center. Circular Economy Policy Research Center, 2022–23, 62.

[3090] Model clause based on C. Borucki, H. Slachmuylders, B. Keirsbilck, D. Gruyaert and E. Terryn, *Model clauses for Product-as-a-Service (PaaS) contracts*, CE Center. Circular Economy Policy Research Center, 2022–23, 62.

[3091] These checkboxes may not be pre-ticked. See e.g. CJEU, Judgment of 11 November 2020, C-61/19, *Orange Romania*, ECLI:EU:C:2020:901, para. 37; CJEU, Judgment of 1 October 2019, C-673/17, *Planet49*, ECLI:EU:C:2019:801, para. 55 and 57.

[3092] This clause specifically deals with the possibility of using consent as a basis for data collection. Other lawful bases are also possible. For example, consent is not necessary if processing the data is necessary for the performance of contractual obligations (Art. 6(1)(b) GDPR).

> **O producing app statistics;**
> **O improving services;**
> **O generating a custom user profile;**
> **O ...][3093]**
>
> - **[The PSS supplier] maintains appropriate technical and organisational measures to ensure a level of security appropriate to the risk involved in the processing of [the PSS user's] personal data and to protect personal data against accidental or unlawful destruction, loss, alteration, unauthorised disclosure or access.[3094]**

752. MODEL CLAUSES ON REPAIR OF THE PRODUCT – The following clauses outline the PSS supplier's obligation to repair the product. First of all, the first model clause provides that the PSS supplier shall carry out *all* repairs during the contract. In PSS contracts qualifying as a contract for services, this clause defines the service to be provided by the PSS supplier, as there are no default rules in this regard. In PSS contracts qualifying as a rental contract, this clause deviates from Articles 1754 old BCC and Article 7:217 DCC, which provide that the lessee is responsible for minor repairs.[3095] Additionally, in line with the obligation to treat the product with the care of a reasonable and prudent person,[3096] this clause stipulates that the PSS supplier shall (only) bear the costs of the repairs resulting from inherent hardware issues or damages or defects caused by normal wear and tear. The PSS user will be liable for all repair costs resulting from damages or defects that are not covered by these instances. This way, the risk of moral hazard is combated. The second model clause can be used to further specify the concept of damages or defects resulting from normal wear and tear. This both has advantages for the PSS supplier (who will be able to prove that certain repair costs should be covered by the PSS user) and the PSS user (who has legal certainty as to what repair costs are covered by the PSS contract).

3093 Model clause based on C. BORUCKI, H. SLACHMUYLDERS, B. KEIRSBILCK, D. GRUYAERT and E. TERRYN, *Model clauses for Product-as-a-Service (PaaS) contracts*, CE Center. Circular Economy Policy Research Center, 2022–23, 62.

3094 Model clause based on C. BORUCKI, H. SLACHMUYLDERS, B. KEIRSBILCK, D. GRUYAERT and E. TERRYN, *Model clauses for Product-as-a-Service (PaaS) contracts*, CE Center. Circular Economy Policy Research Center, 2022–23, 63.

3095 See *supra* no. 735.

3096 See *infra* no. 828.

Model clause #44 – Repair of the product

- **[The PSS supplier] shall carry out all repairs to the product during the contract. [The PSS supplier] shall bear the costs of the repairs resulting from inherent hardware issues and damages or defects resulting from normal wear and tear of the product. [The PSS user] is liable for all repair costs resulting from damages or defects exceeding normal wear and tear.**
- **For the purposes of this clause, damages or defects resulting from normal wear and tear are [specified examples (e.g. limescale build up on the heating element of the washing machine, worn or flat tire, etc.)]].**

753. Model clauses on methods for organising repair – The following model clauses set out the methods used by the PSS supplier for organising the repair of the product. As discussed above, there are different methods to do so.[3097] For larger products, built-in products or products that are not easily transportable, it is most appropriate to stipulate that repair will be carried out at the PSS user's premises. On the other hand, for smaller products (e.g. consumer electronics), it will generally be easier to perform the repairs at the premises of the PSS supplier. In this case, the PSS user can either make a physical appointment to bring the product to a sales or service point of the PSS supplier or send the product by parcel shipment to the PSS supplier. A third common option for organising the repair of the product is by allowing the PSS user to "swap" the product if it is damaged or defect. This way, upon making an appointment at a sales or service point or contacting the PSS supplier online, the PSS user will receive a new product "immediately" (e.g. within 24 or 48 hours). This has the advantage that the PSS user is confronted with as little downtime as possible and (almost) always has access to a functional product. The PSS user will then have to return the defect or damaged product to the PSS supplier, either during the appointment or by parcel shipping, so the PSS supplier can repair, refurbish or remanufacture the defective product in order to make it available to a next PSS user at a later stage.

Model clause #45 – Methods for organising the repair of the product

- **The repair of large, built-in or otherwise not easily transported products is carried out at [the PSS user's] premises. [The PSS supplier] shall, upon notification from [the PSS user] and subsequent confirmation of the need for repair, dispatch a qualified technician to the [PSS user's] premises to perform the necessary repairs. [The PSS supplier] shall [use all reasonable efforts to] ensure that the technician**

3097 See *supra* no. 736.

- arrives within a timeframe agreed upon at the timeframe agreed upon at the time of [the PSS user's] notification. All repairs shall be conducted in a manner that minimises disruption to [the PSS user] and to ensure that the product is returned to its proper functioning state as promptly as possible.

- The repair of small, sufficiently portable or otherwise easily transportable products is carried out at [the PSS supplier's] premises. [The PSS user] shall have the option to either: (i) deliver the product to a designated sales or service point operated by [the PSS supplier]; or (ii) send the product to [the PSS supplier] via a parcel shipping method approved by [the PSS supplier]. The shipping costs shall be borne by [the PSS supplier/the PSS user]. All repairs shall be conducted in a timely manner and [the PSS supplier] shall communicate with [the PSS user] regarding the status of the repair and the expected return date of the product.

- If the product requires repair, [the PSS user] is entitled to "swap" the product. "Swapping" means that upon presenting a defective product at a designated sales or service point operated by [the PSS supplier] or sending it to [the PSS supplier] via an approved parcel shipping method, [the PSS user] shall be entitled to receive an equivalent replacement product within [specified timeframe (e.g. 24, 48 hours)]. [The PSS supplier] will then repair, refurbish or remanufacture the original product and, once functional, reintroduce it into the system for use by another user. [The PSS supplier] ensures that replacement products are of similar or better functionality and quality.

754. Model clauses on limits to (free) maintenance and repair – To avoid moral hazard, PSS suppliers may include a clause in the PSS contract stating that they will not be responsible for maintenance or repair for damages or defects caused by misuse or neglect of the product, nor for intentional damage or damage exceeding normal wear and tear. In most cases, PSS suppliers will still repair or maintain the product itself in these cases (as the PSS user will often be less suited to carry out the repairs or maintenance) and then recover the costs incurred from the PSS user. As mentioned above, PSS suppliers will sometimes grant a number of free "exceptional repairs" to the PSS user as an additional service, competitive advantage or commercial gesture.[3098] The second model clause can be used as an example of such a contractual provision. It may set out the number of exceptional repairs and the time period in which the PSS user may benefit from these exceptional repairs. To increase transparency, PSS suppliers may further specify which exceptional repairs are covered by this obligation.

[3098] See *supra* no. 738.

Model clause #46 – Limits to maintenance and repair

- **[The PSS supplier] shall not be responsible for maintenance or repair of any damage or defects resulting from misuse, neglect, intentional damage and damage beyond normal wear and tear. [The PSS user] is liable for all costs incurred by [the PSS supplier] as a result of these damages or defects.**
- **By way of derogating from the previous clause, [the PSS user] is granted [specified number] of exceptional repair[s] beyond normal wear and tear per [specified time period]. Any exceptional repair beyond this [periodical] allowance will be subject to additional charges.**
- **For the purpose of this clause, "exceptional repairs" are [specified repairs (e.g. a cracked screen, a broken battery, etc.)].**

755. Model clauses on repair by the PSS user or a third party – The following model clauses deal with the issue of repair by the PSS user or a third party. The first model clause prohibits the PSS user to attempt to repair the product himself, as well as having a third party attempt to repair the product. As such, this clause excludes the extrajudicial replacement of the debtor (i.e. the PSS supplier) as a contractual remedy for the obligation to remedy defects.[3099] This clause is allowed under Belgian law, as the rules on remedies for breach of contract are default law. Moreover, the essence of the remedy (namely the right to performance of the obligation to repair) remains intact, so it does not inappropriately limit or exclude the legal rights of the PSS user.[3100]

Under Dutch law, however, the rental contract rules allow the PSS user to remedy defects himself if the PSS supplier remains in default. In this case, the PSS user may recover the (reasonable) costs incurred, if desired by deducting them from the rental price.[3101] As this provision is mandatory law,[3102] excluding the remedy of extrajudicial replacement of the debtor will not be allowed in PSS contracts that qualify as a rental contrat under Dutch law. As a result, the first model clause will not be valid under Dutch law. Therefore, the second model clause, which is valid under both Belgian and Dutch law, provides an alternative where the PSS user is prohibited from carrying out repairs to the product himself (or engage a third party to do so), unless the PSS supplier is in default or in case of emergency situations (where the conditions for *negotiorum gestio* will be met).[3103]

3099 See *supra* no. 301.
3100 Compare with Art. VI.83, 30° BCEL.
3101 Art. 7:206(3) DCC.
3102 Art. 7:206(3), *in fine* DCC.
3103 See *supra* no. 739.

In yet some other cases, it is beneficial to allow and enable PSS users to carry out repairs themselves. This is especially the case with modular products which are designed to be easily repairable by the PSS user himself. The third model clause provides the contractual framework for allowing self-repair in the PSS contract. It states that the PSS supplier shall provide the modules necessary to repair the product, either at the PSS user's request, or from a designated reserve pool. The latter is useful, for example, in the case of wearable or consumable parts, such as ink cartridges for a printer or a filter in a ventilation system. In B2B sectors, a reserve pool may also be appropriate where a large number of products (e.g. smartphones for employees) or essential products or installations for the company are provided and repairs must be performed quickly.

Model clause #47 – Repair by the PSS user or a third party[3104]

- **[The PSS user] shall not attempt to repair or modify the product himself, nor have a third party attempt to repair or modify the product. [[The PSS user] shall be liable for any damage or costs caused by an unauthorised repair or modification attempt].**

- **[The PSS user] may only attempt to repair the product, or have a third party attempt to repair the product if [the PSS supplier] has not responded to the notification of the issues or defects by the [PSS user] within [specified reasonable period of time (e.g. after 48 hours)/if there is an emergency situation (i.e. specified emergency situations (e.g. flooding of the PSS user's home caused by the washing machine, malfunctioning of the ventilation or heating system during extremely hot or cold days, etc.)]. [[The PSS user] shall be liable for any damage or costs caused by an unauthorised repair attempt].**

- **[The PSS user] is allowed to self-repair the modular products provided under this contract using modules provided by [the PSS supplier] [at [the PSS user's] request/from a designated reserve pool]. [The PSS user] shall carry out self-repairs in accordance with [the PSS supplier's] instructions and guidelines. Upon completion of the self-repair, the defective modules must be returned to [the PSS supplier] via parcel shipment. [The PSS supplier] is responsible for all handling costs associated with the delivery and return of modules, including but not limited to shipping, logistics, inventory management and proper disposal of defective modules. [The PSS supplier] remains liable for the performance and quality of the provided modules and the overall functionality of the product post-repair, notwithstanding [the PSS user's] involvement in the repair process.**

3104 Model clauses based on C. Borucki, H. Slachmuylders, B. Keirsbilck, D. Gruyaert and E. Terryn, *Model clauses for Product-as-a-Service (PaaS) contracts*, CE Center. Circular Economy Policy Research Center, 2022–23, 53–54.

6.4. UPDATES

756. Obligation to supply updates – PSS contracts often relate to "smart" connected products. These "smart" products contain digital elements and additional digital services, such as remote control through an app, the possibility (for both the PSS user and the PSS supplier) to monitor the use of the product, predictive maintenance, etc. If the product which is the object of the PSS contract contains digital elements or is supplemented with additional digital services, the PSS supplier generally will have an obligation to supply updates. These updates may extend the functionalities of the "smart" products, adapt them to technical developments, protect them against new security threats or have other purposes,[3105] such as adapting the digital service to comply with market standards, technical norms or any legal developments (in terms of data protection law for example).[3106] Thus, they may concern the operating system of the product, support for mobile apps, security updates, etc.

757. Reading guide – Updates are an important element for assessing the conformity of the "smart" product with the PSS contract. This is also recognised in both the SGD (applicable to product-oriented PSS relating to "goods with digital elements") and the DCD (applicable to use-oriented and result-oriented PSS with "digital services"), where updates are considered both subjective and objective conformity requirements.[3107] This section first discusses the obligation of the PSS supplier to supply updates. This is done by analysing the legal framework of the PSS supplier's update obligation and considering to what extent the PSS contracts analysed include clauses on this update obligation. Second, this section addresses the question of whether and to what extent the PSS user is obliged to install the updates. Finally, an evaluation of the current legal framework is made and possible solutions in the form of model clauses for the PSS supplier's obligation to supply updates are proposed.

6.4.1. OBLIGATION OF THE PSS SUPPLIER TO SUPPLY UPDATES

6.4.1. Updates as conformity requirement

758. Updates as subjective conformity requirement – Updates are explicitly mentioned as a subjective conformity requirement in both the SGD

3105 Compare with Recital 28 SGD.

3106 H. Jacquemin, "La conformité des biens, des contenus numériques et des services numériques, l'articulation des délais et la modification des éléments numériques", *DCCR* 2022, issue 135–136, (25) 39–40.

3107 See also *supra* no. 455 and 497.

and the DCD.[3108] For the SGD, the reason for this is that goods sold increasingly contain digital elements. As for the DCD, this logically stems from the very nature of digital content and digital services themselves, and the fact that these are constantly evolving.[3109] Except for the updates that are necessary to maintain the conformity of the good with digital elements or the digital service part of the PSS contract (i.e. that are part of the objective conformity requirements), the parties are in principle free to determine which updates the PSS supplier must provide (and for what time). If the updates are not supplied as stipulated in the PSS contract (both in terms of frequency, quality, and the period of time in which the PSS supplier must supply updates), this constitutes a lack of conformity for which the PSS supplier will be liable (even if this lack of conformity could not have been present at the time of delivery).

759. Updates as objective conformity requirement – Besides the explicit mention of updates as a subjective conformity requirement, it was also deemed necessary to include rules on updates in the context of the objective conformity criteria, both for goods with digital elements and for digital content and digital services. Thus, the seller or supplier must, both under the SGD and DCD, ensure that the consumer is informed of and supplied with updates, including security updates, that are necessary to keep those goods or digital content or digital services in conformity.[3110] In other words, the PSS supplier must supply updates which ensure that the "smart" product or digital service part of the PSS remains fit for its normal use and continues to provide the quality the PSS user can reasonably expect. This could, for example, include security updates or updates to correct "bugs" in the software.[3111] In contrast, updates that are not necessary to keep the goods or digital services in conformity, such as newer versions with new functionalities, do not fall under the scope of the objective conformity requirements.[3112] As a result, the PSS supplier must only supply these updates if this was explicitly agreed in the PSS contract (in other words, this is an issue of subjective conformity).[3113]

760. Period during which PSS supplier must supply updates – Both the SGD and the DCD also stipulate the period during which the PSS supplier

---

3108 EU: Art. 6(d) SGD and Art. 7(d) DCD. **Belgium**: Art. 1649*ter*, §2, 4° old BCC and Art. 1701/5, 4° old BCC. **The Netherlands**: Art. 7:18(1), *sub* d. DCC and Art. 7:50ae(1), *sub* d. DCC.

3109 See Recital 44 DCD.

3110 EU: Art. 7(3) SGD and Art. 8(2) DCD. See also Recital 30 SGD and Recital 47 DCD. **Belgium**: Art. 1649*ter*, §5 old BCC and Art. 1701/6, §2 old BCC. **The Netherlands**: Art. 7:18(4) DCC and Art. 7:50ae(4) DCC.

3111 H. Jacquemin, "La conformité des biens, des contenus numériques et des services numériques, l'articulation des délais et la modification des éléments numériques", *DCCR* 2022, afl. 135–136, (25) 39–40.

3112 See Recital 30 SGD.

3113 See *supra* no. 758.

must provide the updates necessary to keep the goods with digital elements or digital content or digital services in conformity (i.e. objective conformity). A distinction is made depending on whether the contract provides for (i) a single supply of digital content or digital services or (ii) the continuous supply of digital content or digital services over a certain period of time. In the case of a single act of supply (or several individual acts), the PSS supplier must provide updates within the period which the consumer can reasonably expect given the type and purpose of the digital content or digital service and taking into account the circumstances and nature of the contract.[3114] In the case of continuous supply of the digital content or digital services, the PSS supplier must provide updates for the entire period during which it has contractually undertaken to provide the digital content or digital service.[3115] In the case of product-oriented PSS relating goods with digital elements, this period may not be less than two years.[3116]

761. Information requirements and blacklisted practices regarding updates – The Directive on Empowering Consumers for the Green Transition introduces specific information requirements in the CRD and adds a few unfair practices regarding updates to the annex of the UCPD regarding updates in contracts for goods with digital elements, for digital content and for digital services. As for the information requirements, it adds that traders must provide the consumer with information on the minimum period, whether expressed as a period of time or by reference to a date, during which the producer or the provider provides software updates.[3117] As regards the blacklist of the UCPD, it adds withholding information from the consumer about the fact that a software update will negatively impact the functioning of goods with digital elements or the use of digital content or digital services; and presenting a software update as necessary when it only enhances functionality features.[3118]

762. Single act of supply *versus* continuous supply of digital content and digital services – Thus, to determine the period for which the PSS supplier should provide updates, the distinction between a single act of supply and continuous supply of digital content and digital services has important consequences. Nevertheless, neither the SGD and DCD nor their national implementation contain definitions of these concepts. However, a link can

[3114] EU: Art. 7(3)(a) SGD and Art. 8(2)(a) DCD. **Belgium**: Art. 1649*ter*, §5, 1° old BCC and Art. 1701/6, §2, 1° old BCC. **The Netherlands**: Art. 7:18(4) DCC and Art. 7:50ae(4) DCC.

[3115] EU: Art. 7(3)(b) SGD and Art. 8(2)(b) DCD. **Belgium**: Art. 1649*ter*, §5, 2° *juncto* Art. 1649*quater*, §1, (1) old BCC and Art. 1701/6, §2, 2° old BCC.

[3116] EU: Art. 7(3)(b) SGD *juncto* Art. 10(2) SGD. **Belgium**: Art. Art. 1649*ter*, §5, 2° *juncto* Art. 1649*quater*, §1, (2) old BCC.

[3117] Art. 2(2)(b) Directive on Empowering Consumers for the Green Transition which amends Art. 5(1) CRD by inserting point (ed) and Art. 2(3)(c) Directive on Empowering Consumers for the Green Transition which amends Art. 6(1) CRD by inserting point (lc).

[3118] See the amendments to Annex I of the UCPD, by inserting point 23d. and 23e.

be made with the well-known distinction between contracts of immediate performance and contracts of continuous performance. The former contracts are performed "at once" (a typical example is a sales contract), while the latter are those whose performance is spread continuously over time (e.g. a rental contract).[3119] The difference between the two methods of supply can be further explained through a number of examples, with a specific focus on the three types of PSS.

For use-oriented or result-oriented PSS containing digital content or digital services, the rules of the DCD are relevant. First, the digital content or digital services can be provided through a single act of supply (or a series of individual acts of supply). The recitals of the DCD give as an example the case where consumers download an e-book and store it on their personal device.[3120] Similarly, the supply can consist of a series of such individual acts, for instance where consumers receive a link to download a new e-book every week.[3121] The distinctive element of a single act of supply is that consumers thereafter have the possibility to access and use the digital content or digital service indefinitely.[3122] If we apply these principles to PSS contracts, one may consider a use-oriented PSS contract for a smartphone, which comes preloaded with simple apps (e.g. a calculator app) or specific music albums or ebooks. Second, the digital content or digital services may be supplied in a continuous manner during a certain (fixed or indefinite) period of time (e.g. a subscription of one year). The recitals of the DCD provide as examples a two-year cloud storage contract, an indefinite social media platform membership, web-streaming of video clips, and (fixed-term or indeterminate contracts for) anti-virus software or digital games that are updated periodically or when new features become available.[3123] The distinctive element of a continuous supply is therefore the fact that the digital content or digital service is available or accessible to consumers only for the fixed duration of the contract or for as long as the indefinite contract is in force.[3124] In the context of use-oriented and result-oriented PSS, this continuous mode of supply will be the most commonly used. Indeed, the additional digital services that supplement the use component of the product will often be based on subscriptions that have the same duration as the PSS contract itself. For example, use-oriented or result-oriented PSS may be supplemented by an app providing continuous support for monitoring including an online environment where the data can be consulted, such as in the case of *Bundles* (see the term cited below). If the subscription is terminated, the PSS user loses access to these additional digital services.

3119 P. Wéry, *Droit des obligations. Volume 1. Theorie générale du contrat*, Brussels, Larcier, 2021, 113, no. 75.
3120 Recital 56 DCD.
3121 *Ibid.*
3122 *Ibid.*
3123 Recital 57 DCD.
3124 *Ibid.*

Terms and conditions Bundles – Art. 9 "The Customer will receive from Bundles, if reasonably possible, at least once a month via the Wash-App, which is in any case accessible via an internet browser, an overview based on the usage data of the Bundles Buddy containing at least data on the usage of the Subscription and an approximation of the consumption costs of the Appliance."

For product-oriented PSS that relate to goods with digital elements, the rules of the SGD are relevant. Also here, the digital content or digital services integrated or interconnected with the good may be provided through a single act of supply or in a continuous manner. An example of the former may include a "smart" fridge, which comes preloaded with images for the screensaver or background or simple apps such as a notes app. For the digital content or digital services that are continuously supplied, one may consider a smartwatch with a running app with a subscription-based training programme or a "smart" fridge or coffee maker with a subscription-based app that allows you to monitor the contents of the fridge or bean reserve of the coffee maker and order groceries or coffee online when these appliances are running low on stock.

763. Possibility to deviate from objective conformity requirements regarding updates – As already discussed above, the PSS supplier can under certain circumstances deviate from the objective conformity requirements, including the obligation to supply updates.[3125] This requires that, at the time of concluding the PSS contract, the PSS user was specifically informed that no updates to the digital content or digital service would be supplied *and* that the PSS user expressly and separately (e.g. by expressly ticking a box during the online order process) accepted this deviation from the objective conformity rules regarding updates.[3126]

764. Obligation to supply updates lies on the PSS supplier, even if updates are in practice provided by third party – It is notable that the obligation to provide updates (and the associated liability) rests on the seller or supplier, when in practice updates often have to be provided by a third party (e.g. the manufacturer of the product or a software developer). For example, if the manufacturer of a smartphone does not supply the necessary updates, the PSS user can sue the PSS supplier for lack of conformity. This is less of a factor in PSS offerings characterised by a high degree of disintermediation (and where the PSS supplier and manufacturer are therefore the same entity) but is certainty something to take in mind in PSS where the PSS supplier offers products of a separate manufacturer (e.g. *Swapphone* which offers subscriptions for Apple iPhone or Samsung Galaxy smartphones). Of course, in turn, the PSS supplier

[3125] See *supra* no. 464 and 498.

[3126] EU: Art. 8(5) DCD. **Belgium**: Art. 1701/6, §4 old BCC. **The Netherlands**: Art. 50ae(6) DCC.

can then exercise its right of redress to hold the manufacturer liable for not providing the necessary updates.[3127]

6.4.1.2. Contractual arrangements on the PSS supplier's update obligation

765. PSS CONTRACTS ANALYSED DO NOT CONTAIN CLAUSES ON UPDATES – Somewhat surprisingly, none of the PSS contracts analysed contain clauses on the frequency, timing, quality or even availability of updates. While this is of course logical for PSS contracts that do not include connected products such as *Swapfiets* and the clothing libraries *Lena* and *Dressr*, a clause on the update obligation of the PSS supplier would not be out of place in PSS contracts that do relate to connected products, such as *Swapphone*, *Grover* and *Fairphone Easy*. In the case of the first two PSS offers, this is still somewhat understandable, as these PSS suppliers depend on their suppliers-manufacturers (e.g. Apple, Samsung, other manufacturers of consumer electronics) to provide the updates.[3128] However, in the case of the latter, *Fairphone* is both the manufacturer and the PSS supplier. Consequently, in this case one might expect a clause regarding updates to be included, especially since *Fairphone's* mission is to produce, sell and offer smartphones that last as long as possible.[3129] In this sense, an explicit update obligation for new features and versions could help counter the problem of "psychological obsolescence" of smartphones.[3130] As another example, *Bundles*, while including a clause in the contract on the Wash-App and its functionality and accessibility,[3131] does not mention anything about the availability, frequency and timing of any updates supplied for this app. This means that in the case of the real-life PSS contracts analysed, only the objective conformity requirement on updates (i.e. informing of and supplying the PSS user with updates that are necessary to keep the goods or digital content or digital services in conformity) will be relevant for considering the conformity of the digital elements of the PSS contract.

766. PSS CONTRACTS ANALYSED DO NOT DEVIATE FROM OBJECTIVE CONFORMITY REQUIREMENTS – The fact that no explicit clauses on updates are included in the PSS contracts analysed therefore means that PSS users will not

---

3127 EU: Art. 18 SGD and Art. 20 DCD. **Belgium**: Art. 1649*sexiessexies* old BCC and Art. 1701/16 old BCC. **The Netherlands**: Art. 7:25 DCC and Art. 7:50am DCC.

3128 Compare with *supra* no. 764 where it was already mentioned that it is notable that the update obligation lies on the seller or supplier, while updates will generally be provided by the manufacturer.

3129 See https://shop.fairphone.com/about-us.

3130 Psychological obsolescence relates to instances where products are no longer attractive or satisfying in the eyes of consumers even though they are still functioning, which eventually leads to the purchase of a new product. See more in-depth on this concept: A. MICHEL, *Premature Obsolescence: In Search of an Improved Legal Framework*, Cambridge, Intersentia, 2023, 84–87 and the references cited there.

3131 See Art. 9 Terms and Conditions Bundles.

have a legal right to updates regarding new versions or functionalities when they engage in these contracts. As mentioned above, this could bring a risk of "psychological obsolescence" if a certain product is not regularly updated with new features. However, at the same time, the PSS contracts analysed also do not deviate from the objective conformity requirements. As a result, the PSS user-consumer will still have access to the updates necessary to keep the product in conformity, which is of course the most important part for ensuring that the products last as long as possible.

767. (B2B) TEMPLATE CONTRACTS ANALYSED ALSO DO NOT CONTAIN CLAUSES ON UPDATES – Also the (B2B) template contracts of *Agoria* and *Fairphone as a Service* do not contain any explicit clauses on updates. However, this should be nuanced to a certain extent, as the paper explaining the business model of *Fairphone's* circular service contract template mentions both hardware maintenance and updates and software maintenance and updates.[3132] Here, it is stated that security updates will be performed once a month to implement the latest security patches and stability fixes. The PSS user is responsible for allowing these.[3133] In addition, it is mentioned that Fairphone may decide to upgrade the operating system of the smartphones when necessary, balancing both costs and utility for customers.[3134] While these updates thus are part of the circular business model, this is however not reflected in the contract itself.

768. NO UPDATE OBLIGATION IN THE PSS CONTRACT DOES NOT MEAN THAT NO UPDATES WILL BE SUPPLIED – The fact that PSS users do not have a contractually determined legal right to updates regarding new versions or functionalities when they engage in the analysed PSS contracts does not necessarily mean that no such updates will be provided. After all, an update obligation may also be included in the contract between the manufacturer and the PSS supplier, which of course also benefits the PSS user. In addition, there may be other motives for making updates available to the PSS user. For example, the manufacturer may also provide updates with new functionalities on its own initiative (without a legal obligation) to remain competitive in the market, or to build a reputation as having durable products with advanced and cutting-edge software. An example may illustrate this. Generally, Apple smartphones are updated at a faster pace and for a much longer time than their Android counterparts. This is seen as a competitive advantage by many smartphone enthusiasts.[3135] As a result, the PSS

[3132] CIRCLE ECONOMY, "The Circular Phone, Legal, operational and financial solutions to unlock the potential of the 'Fairphone-as-a-service' model", 31 December 2017, available at www.circle-economy.com/resources/the-circular-phone, 8–9.

[3133] *Ibid.*

[3134] *Ibid.*

[3135] See e.g. J. HILDENBRAND, "With iOS 14, Apple once again crushes Android makers on software support", Android Central, 22 June 2020, available at www.androidcentral.com/apple-once-again-crushes-android-makers-update-support.

contract's silence on updates should not necessarily be seen as negative, provided that in practice updates that prolong the expected lifetime of the product are indeed supplied.

6.4.2. OBLIGATION OF THE PSS USER TO INSTALL UPDATES

769. Installing the updates supplied – Installing the supplied software updates is thus important for the conformity of the additional digital services and connected "smart" products that are part of the PSS contract. In the case of additional digital services provided online or in the form of SaaS ("Software as a Service"), updates generally take place automatically, without any action being required on the part of the PSS user-consumer. In contrast, for apps or software installed on a device, the PSS user-consumer must in principle authorise and install the updates (or configure the system settings so that all updates are automatically authorised and installed). The question arises whether the PSS user has an obligation to install these updates.

770. No explicit legal obligation for the PSS user to install the updates – Neither the SGD and the DCD nor their national implementing provisions stipulate an explicit obligation for the PSS user-consumer to install the updates supplied.[3136] Nevertheless, if the PSS user fails to install the updates within a reasonable time, he will no longer be able to hold the PSS supplier liable for any lack of conformity resulting *solely* from the lack of the relevant update.[3137] Two cumulative conditions must be met for this exception to the PSS supplier's liability for non-conformity to apply. First, the PSS supplier must have informed the PSS user-consumer about the availability of the update(s) and the consequences of a failure to installing it, and the failure to install or incorrect installation of the update may not be due to shortcomings in the installation instructions provided to the PSS user-consumer.[3138]

771. Contractually including an obligation to install the updates – Although there is thus no legal obligation on the PSS user-consumer to install the updates supplied by the PSS supplier, it is, however, to the latter's advantage that the updates, especially security updates, are indeed installed. This is because the PSS supplier retains ownership of the product, and the security risks associated with not updating the product can affect its lifetime or trigger a need for repairs

---

3136 Compare also with Recital 30 SGD and Recital 47 DCD, which state that the consumer should remain free to choose whether to install the updates provided.

3137 EU: Art. 7(4) SGD and Art. 8(3) DCD. **Belgium**: Art. 1649*ter*, §6 old BCC and Art. 1701/6, §3 old BCC. **The Netherlands**: Art. 7:18(5) DCC and Art. 7:50ae(5) DCC.

3138 *Ibid.*

that would not otherwise have been necessary. The PSS supplier may therefore stipulate in the PSS contract that the PSS user-consumer must timely update the "smart" products, apps or software used in the performance of the contract or that he must enable automatic updates.[3139] In my view, this is not contrary to (or at least should not be contrary to) the SGD and DCD. After all, the freedom to choose whether to install the updates provided, as stated in Recital 30 SGD and Recital 47 DCD, refers to the situation where the consumer is the owner of the good with digital elements or the recipient of the digital service (often on his own device). As such, only he has something to lose in not installing these (security) updates. In the case of use-oriented and result-oriented PSS, on the other hand, it is the PSS supplier who bears the risk of damage to the product if no (security) updates are installed. Thus, in this case, this update obligation can be regarded as a concretisation of the duty to take care of the product, which in my view justifies a contractual restriction on the consumer's right to choose to update or not.

6.4.3. LEGISLATIVE INTERVENTION NEEDED?

772. Updates as a necessary element of a modernised EU consumer law – There is no doubt that explicitly including updates as objective and subjective conformity criteria in the SGD and the DCD was a necessary step for the modernisation of EU consumer law in our increasingly digitalised society. The question now arises whether the rules on updates are fit for purpose, or whether legislative intervention is still needed. In terms of the evaluation criteria of legal certainty and consistency and coherence, no specific problems seem to arise. The evaluation criteria of sustainability and fair balance, on the other hand, deserve some more analysis.

773. Evaluation in terms of sustainability: updates as conformity requirement may combat "premature obsolescence" – When evaluating the update obligation of the SGD and DCD from the perspective of (environmental) sustainability, it is clear that adding updates as both a subjective and objective conformity requirement is certainly a step in the right direction. Indeed, these conformity criteria have great potential to combat "premature obsolescence" of consumer electronics (particularly "smart", connected products), which have a significant impact on sustainable development in terms of resource extraction, labour conditions and e-waste.[3140] The additional

---

[3139] H. Slachmuylders, "iPhone as a Service? Some thoughts on Apple's rumoured hardware subscription service", *CCM Blog* 4 April 2022, https://law.kuleuven.be/ccm/blog/?p=321.

[3140] E. Van Gool and A. Michel, "The New Consumer Sales Directive 2019/771 and Sustainable Consumption", *EuCML* 2021, vol. 10, afl. 4, (136) 139, with reference to V. Rizos, J. Bryhn, M. Alessi, A. Campmas and A. Zarra, *Identifying the Impact of the Circular Economy on the*

information requirements and blacklisted unfair practices regarding updates introduced by the Directive on Empowering Consumers for the Green Transition also contribute to this.[3141]

However, the SGD and DCD only require the PSS supplier to supply updates necessary to keep the product or digital service in conformity, including security updates. The PSS supplier is not obliged to supply updates regarding new versions or new features unless this was contractually agreed (in which case these contractually agreed updates constitute a subjective conformity requirement). In the context of the circular economy, new versions or features of the product or digital service may play an important role in making the product last for a longer time, especially in terms of avoiding "psychological obsolescence". For PSS suppliers that aim to offer a truly sustainable PSS, providing regular updates can therefore be an important selling point. The question then arises whether there should be a legal obligation to offer new versions or new features as well. In my view, this question should be answered in the negative as it would have too great an impact on freedom of enterprise. At the same time, the market reality and the principle of freedom of contract provide – in my view – sufficient incentives for providing updates with new versions and new features.[3142]

774. Evaluation in terms of fair balance of rights and liabilities: PSS supplier should not be "left" with liability for lack of updates that is beyond its control – The fact that the obligation to supply the updates lies on the PSS supplier, while these are generally developed by a third party,[3143] may lead to the risk that the PSS supplier is held liable for a lack of updates that is beyond its control. This could potentially lead to a situation where this update obligation places an unreasonably high burden on the PSS supplier. However, one might say the same thing about the liability for any "traditional" lack of conformity of consumer goods (i.e. a lack of conformity not due to a lack of updates). Indeed, it is often not the seller but the manufacturer who is responsible for problems that make the goods not fit for the use the consumer may reasonably expect, such as manufacturing defects, problems regarding the quality of the good, etc. At the same time, the seller (or in this case, PSS supplier) is, contrary to the manufacturer, still the most approachable point of contact for consumers who are confronted with a lack of conformity of the product. Traditionally, this is solved by giving the seller a right of redress against his contracting party higher up the supply chain, so that he is not "stuck" with the liability for a lack

Fast-Moving Consumer Goods (FMCG) industry: Opportunities and challenges for businesses, workers and consumers – mobile phones as an example, European Economic and Social Committee, 2019, 10–20 and 37–48.

3141 See *supra* no. 761.

3142 See *supra* no. 768.

3143 See *supra* no. 764.

of conformity of the product which is not due to his fault.[3144] Also in the case of updates, the fact that the PSS supplier is responsible for supplying updates therefore does not necessarily need to be a problem, as long as the PSS supplier has an adequate right of redress allowing to bring a claim against its contracting party (i.e. the manufacturer or a distributor who can in turn bring a claim against the manufacturer) for the lack of updates. Here, however, problems sometimes arise in practice, notably due to the lack of parallelism under Belgian law between the common sales rules and consumer sales rules, and the lack of a parallel B2B regime for conformity of digital content and digital services.[3145] Also under Dutch law, there is a no complete parallelism between the consumer sales rules and the general sales rules, and between the rules for digital content and digital services and general contract law, which again could complicate the exercise of a right of redress.[3146] As a result, streamlining the concept of non-conformity and the available remedies for a lack of conformity for all sales contracts and other named contracts, as was already proposed above, is also necessary for ensuring that the PSS supplier has indeed an adequate right of redress allowing to bring a claim against its contracting party.[3147]

775. Conclusion: no legislative intervention to SGD and DCD needed, national law should provide for adequate right of redress – In view of this assessment, the new rules of the SGD and DCD regarding updates are fit for purpose and not in need of any legislative review. However, to avoid that the PSS supplier is "left" with the liability for a lack of updates that is beyond its control, it is important that the PSS supplier has an adequate right of redress against the third party responsible for these updates (e.g. the manufacturer of the product or a software developer). This is essentially a matter of national law as both regimes provide that the PSS supplier has a right of redress, but not (explicitly) which remedies and deadlines apply: a recourse must be made to the general law of obligations. In the first place, streamlining the concept of non-conformity and remedies for non-conformity is an essential step for ensuring the presence of an adequate right of redress. Additionally, strengthening the seller or supplier's

3144 See for an analysis of the right of redress under EU law, Belgian law and Dutch law: B. Keirsbilck, "Verhaalsrechten", *DCCR* 2022, afl. 2–3, (103) 103–132.

3145 See: B. Keirsbilck, "Verhaalsrechten", *DCCR* 2022, afl. 2–3, (103) 118–127. Thus, the notion of "non-conformity" in the consumer sales rules is considerably broader than the notion of "hidden defect" of common sales law, there is a lack of parallelism between the remedies available, and the time limits within which the claim must be brought differ between the two regimes. For digital content and digital services, there is no parallel B2B regime, so the PSS supplier will have to exercise its right of redress based on general contract law and the specific rules on remedies for non-conformity of the underlying contract (sales contract, rental contract, contract for services, etc.).

3146 See: T.J.K. Van Santen, "Het recht van verhaal van de eindverkoper: in Duitsland, Nederland en de toekomst", *Contracteren* 2018, issue 3, (97) 102–103.

3147 See *supra* section 4.4.2.

right of redress itself would also help protect the PSS supplier against liability for lack of updates beyond its control. For example, in Belgium, it was already proposed (but not retained) to further expand Article 1649*sexiessexies* old BCC so that if a seller were to be held liable for a lack of conformity by a consumer, he would be able to recover all the costs incurred from the producer or any other intermediary in the contractual chain, unless the lack of conformity was due to the seller himself. The proposal also included a mandatory payment term of one month.[3148] This is of course just one proposal; alternatives are certainly possible.

Policy Recommendation #6

- **At the national level, consider streamlining the concept of conformity and the remedies for non-conformity across all (B2C and B2B) named contracts (sales contract, rental contract, contract for services, etc.) so the PSS supplier is not "trapped" in a situation where it is liable for a lack of updates beyond its control, but it cannot hold its contractual party liable due to the lack of parallelism between the B2C and B2B rules in terms of the conformity concepts, remedies and time limits.**
- **Consider strengthening the right of redress, either at the EU level or at the national level, so that the PSS supplier that is confronted with liability for lack of updates beyond its control has an adequate recourse against the producer or other intermediary in the contractual chain who is responsible for supplying updates.**

6.4.4. MODEL CLAUSES ON THE OBLIGATION TO SUPPLY UPDATES

776. Model clauses on the PSS supplier's obligation to supply updates – Given the importance of updates both as objective and subjective element for the conformity of the PSS, it is appropriate for PSS suppliers to include clauses in the PSS contract on the nature, frequency and timeliness of updates and the term for which these updates will be provided.[3149] The first model clause relates to the PSS supplier's "objective" update obligation (i.e. updates as an objective conformity requirement). It confirms the PSS supplier's legal obligation to inform and supply the PSS user with updates, including security updates, necessary to keep the product/service in conformity. As most PSS contracts will provide for

[3148] See the proposed Articles VI.91/12-VI.91/14 BCEL draft law on the protection of consumers in the sale of consumer goods (tabled by Ms Leen Dierick), 5 November 2019, *Parliamentary Papers* Chamber of Representatives, DOC 55, 0693/001, as cited by B. Keirsbilck, "Verhaalsrechten", *DCCR* 2022, afl. 2–3, (103) 125.

[3149] H. Slachmuylders, "iPhone as a Service? Some thoughts on Apple's rumoured hardware subscription service", *CCM Blog* 4 April 2022, https://law.kuleuven.be/ccm/blog/?p=321.

a continuous supply of digital content or digital services, this obligation applies during the entire term of the contract. The second model clause can be used to include a "subjective" update obligation in the PSS contract (i.e. contractually agreed updates not necessary for keeping the product/service in conformity). This update obligation relates to updates regarding regular new versions or new features of the product/service. The PSS supplier can choose to supply these updates for the entire term of the PSS contract or for a specified timeframe, e.g. for four years after the conclusion of the contract. Moreover, the PSS supplier can also choose the frequency of these updates (e.g. annually or every six months). The third, fourth and fifth model clauses provide additional content to the update obligations. This includes an obligation to provide information and documentation on the updates, ensuring that the new versions or features are compatible and interoperable and a commitment that the PSS supplier will provide technical support and assistance if necessary.

Model clause #48 – Obligation to supply updates (continuous supply of digital content/services)

- **During the term of the contract, [the PSS supplier] shall promptly inform [the PSS user] of any updates, including security updates, deemed necessary to keep the product/service in conformity. These updates shall be supplied to [the PSS user] within a reasonable time after development so as to mitigate or remedy potential (security) risks or non-conformities in a timely manner.**

- **[During the term of the contract/for (four) years after the conclusion of the contract], [the PSS supplier] agrees to inform and supply [the PSS user] with [annual] software updates. Each [annual] software update shall contain new versions or new features of the product/service, which may enhance the functionality, performance, energy efficiency or usability of the product/service. The [annual] updates shall be delivered to [the PSS user] no later than [specify date or timeframe].**

- **[The PSS supplier] shall provide comprehensive documentation and information detailing the nature, scope, and impact of the updates, as well as installation instructions, facilitating [the PSS user's] understanding and integration of the updates.**

- **[The PSS supplier] shall ensure that the new versions or new features included in the updates are compatible and interoperable with existing systems, applications, or environments utilised by [the PSS user.]**

- **[The PSS supplier] shall offer technical support and assistance to [the PSS user] during the integration, implementation, or troubleshooting of the new versions or features, as necessary.**

777. Evaluation in terms of fair balance and sustainability: PSS supplier has legitimate interest in PSS user installing security and conformity updates – When considering the evaluative criterion of a fair balance between the rights of the PSS supplier and the rights of the PSS user, the PSS supplier has a legitimate interest in the PSS user installing updates relating to the security or conformity of the product/service. After all, he retains the ownership of the product and will incur additional costs if the product breaks down due to a failure of the PSS user to install the updates supplied. Moreover, security threats due to not updating the product may place the PSS supplier's servers and potentially even (personal) data of other PSS users at risk. The PSS user, on the other hand, experiences only little downsides of being obliged to install the updates. Unless the updates significantly reduce the performance and useful lifespan of the product, the main downside for the PSS user is the fact that he generally cannot use the product while the updates are being implemented. This can be solved by scheduling the updates during periods where the impact is minimal (e.g. at night). In my view, the interests of the PSS supplier clearly outweigh the potential downsides of the PSS user in this regard. Additionally, there are also arguments from a sustainability perspective. After all, if the security and conformity updates are promptly installed and implemented, this can lead to a longer lifetime of the product. As a result, it would, in my view, not be unfair to include a clause in the PSS contract containing an obligation for the PSS user to install the security or conformity updates supplied by the PSS supplier within a reasonable time.

778. Potential solution: update obligation for the PSS user – A potential solution consists therefore in including a clause in the PSS contract stipulating that the PSS user-consumer must timely install security and conformity updates for the "smart" products, apps or software used in the performance of the contract. The first three model clauses provide examples on how to include such obligation in the PSS contract. It is key that the PSS user has a reasonable amount of time for complying with his update obligation. Potentially, a distinction can be made between "critical" updates, which should be installed as soon as possible and "non-critical" updates, which can be installed during scheduled maintenance windows (e.g. during the night) or other periods of minimal impact. Of course, this also requires that the PSS supplier provides information of the critical or non-critical nature of the update in question. The fourth model clause provides an example of a clause requiring the PSS user to enable automatic updates. This ensures that the last security and conformity updates are always installed, without placing a burden on the PSS user-consumer to authorise and install them.

Model clause #49 – Obligation to install updates pertaining to security or conformity of the product/service

- [The PSS user] shall install any updates, including security updates, deemed necessary to keep the product/service in conformity within [a reasonable amount of time].
- [The PSS user] shall promptly install [critical] conformity or security updates provided by [the PSS supplier] upon receipt.
- [The PSS user] shall make reasonable efforts to install [non-critical] conformity or security updates during scheduled maintenance windows or periods of minimal operational impact, as outlined in the Annex to this contract.
- [The PSS user] shall enable automatic updates for the product/service, to ensure the timely delivery and installation of essential security patches and conformity updates.
- [The PSS user] shall comply with any installation instructions, guidelines or recommendations provided by [the PSS supplier] to ensure the proper implementation and integration of conformity or security updates.

The last two model clauses on the update obligation of the PSS user deal with the consequences of a failure of the PSS user to install the security or conformity updates. Thus, it is confirmed that the PSS user will not be able to claim liability for any lack of conformity caused by a failure to install the relevant security or conformity updates, unless this lack of conformity is otherwise caused by the PSS supplier's negligence or breach of contract. Additionally, a clause can be included that the PSS user is liable for any damages to the product caused by the failure to install the updates. As already mentioned above, in my view, this does not go against the right to choose whether or not to update included in the recitals of the SGD and DCD as it is a concretisation of the duty to take care of the product.[3150] For this indemnity clause to apply, however, the PSS supplier will have to prove that the damages are indeed caused by the PSS user's failure to install the updates and it will have to prove the amount of these damages.

Model clause #50 – Consequences of a failure to install security or conformity updates

- If [the PSS user] fails to install, within a reasonable time, the updates pertaining to the security or conformity of the product/service, [the PSS supplier] will not be liable for any lack of conformity (e.g. performance degradation, disruptions in the service, other adverse effects) directly resulting from this failure to install the relevant security or conformity updates, unless such lack of conformity is attributable to [the PSS supplier's] negligence or breach of contract.

[3150] See *supra* no. 771.

- **[The PSS user] will be liable for any damages [to the product/in any other way incurred by [the PSS supplier]] due to the failure of timely installing security or conformity updates, unless these damages are attributable to [the PSS supplier's] negligence or breach of contract.**

779. Updates pertaining to new versions or new features: no obligation to install but right to choose – For updates containing new versions or new features that do not aim to patch security or conformity issues, an obligation for the PSS user to install the updates is not necessary in my view. In contrast, a right for the PSS user to choose whether to install the updates is more appropriate. This also reflects the idea of the SGD and DCD, where it is acknowledged in the recitals that the consumer can in principle choose to install the updates supplied.[3151] The first model clause gives an example of how such a right to choose can be implemented in the PSS contract. The second model clause then deals with the consequences of a refusal of the PSS user to install optional updates containing new versions or new features. In this case, the PSS user acknowledges that he may miss out on certain functionalities, for which the PSS supplier will not be liable.

Model clause #51 – right to choose to install updates pertaining to new versions or new features

- **[The PSS user] has the right to choose whether to install updates containing new features or new versions, which do not pertain to the security or conformity of the product/service.**
- **[The PSS user] acknowledges that opting out of installing updates containing new features or new versions may limit their access to certain functionalities, improvements or innovations introduced by [the PSS supplier]. [The PSS supplier] will not be liable for any lack of functionalities, improvements or innovations that are due to not installing the optional updates.**

6.5. INNOVATION

6.5.1. INNOVATION OBLIGATIONS

780. Innovation obligations – In the light of the transition toward a more circular economy, it is essential to consider technological innovation in PSS contracts.[3152] After all, technologic and scientific advances are ever in motion

[3151] Recital 30 SGD and Recital 47 DCD. See also *supra* no. 770.

[3152] H. Slachmuylders, "Movable Servitization. Contractual Liability in the B2C Relationship" in B. Keirsbilck, E. Terryn, J. Eyckmans, S. Rousseau and D. Voinot (eds.), *Servitization*

and can enable a more sustainable, economical or more efficient use of the product/service (even during the lifetime of the product).[3153] While the legal framework for PSS contracts does not explicitly require PSS suppliers to innovate during the contract period, parties can include such innovation obligations in their PSS contracts themselves.[3154] These contractual innovation obligations can drive sustainable practices, enhance customer satisfaction, and contribute to the overall success of the PSS business model. This section discusses some examples of how such an innovation obligation can be included in the PSS contract.

781. General innovation obligation – A first option is to include a general obligation to innovate in the PSS contract. An example of such a clause can be found in the optional clauses of *Agoria's* Efficiency-as-a-Service ("EaaS") template contract (Art. 6.1, cited below). Generally, the PSS supplier will want to formulate such a general innovation obligation as an obligation of means, as innovative breakthroughs are not a given. This is also reflected in *Agoria's* EaaS template contract, by using the phrase "*shall strive to enhance and otherwise develop in a proactive manner*" (own emphasis). Note, however, that an overly broad obligation "*to innovate*", "*to make the product better*" or "*to enhance and otherwise develop the services*" is most likely not sufficiently determinable to be enforceable.[3155] As a result, if the parties want to include innovation obligations that are not just a "paper tiger", they should consider including more specific innovation obligations with specified targets (e.g. in terms of performance or sustainability) in their PSS contract.[3156]

> Template contract Agoria Efficiency-as-a-Service (optional clauses) – Art. 6.1 "The Service Provider shall have an ongoing obligation to develop its business, service concepts, methods and processes and shall strive to enhance and otherwise develop in a proactive manner the Services and Service Level Requirements provided to Client, especially in terms of technological development and to maintain their competitiveness in terms of both quality and price in the market."

---

and circular economy: economic and legal challenges, Antwerp, Intersentia, 2023, (135) 151–152; H. Slachmuylders, "Économie de la fonctionnalité – Le contrat de service: défis juridiques et solutions contractuelles", *Revue Juridique de l'Environnement* 2022, vol. 47, afl. 1, (111) 120.

3153 A. Van Vaerenbergh and F. Leyman, "'Product als dienst'-overeenkomsten, een stap in de richting van de circulaire economie", *MER* 2019, (20) 27; Circle Economy, "The Circular Phone, Legal, operational and financial solutions to unlock the potential of the 'Fairphone-as-a-service' model", 31 December 2017, available at www.circle-economy.com/resources/the-circular-phone, 24.

3154 C. Borucki, H. Slachmuylders, B. Keirsbilck, D. Gruyaert and E. Terryn, *Model clauses for Product-as-a-Service (PaaS) contracts*, CE Center. Circular Economy Policy Research Center, 2022–23, 33.

3155 C. Borucki, H. Slachmuylders, B. Keirsbilck, D. Gruyaert and E. Terryn, *Model clauses for Product-as-a-Service (PaaS) contracts*, CE Center. Circular Economy Policy Research Center, 2022–23, 64.

3156 See *infra* no. 783.

782. Obligation to stay up to date and informed of latest technological developments – A general innovation obligation can go hand in hand with an obligation for the PSS supplier to stay up to date with recent developments, trends and technological innovations related to the products and services offered. Potentially, this can also include an obligation to inform the PSS user about these new developments. The optional clauses of *Agoria's* EaaS contract also contain an example of such a clause:

> Template contract Agoria Efficiency-as-a-Service (optional clauses) – Art. 6.2 "The Service Provider shall inform Client on a yearly basis of all improvements, trends and innovations of which it becomes aware in relation to new technology, business rules, processes and management, operational and costs improvements related to the Services and which may support Client' strategy, competitive and/or financial position or customer service to Client' customers or their experience thereof."

783. Specific innovation obligations – As mentioned above, an overly broad obligation to innovate will most likely not be sufficiently determinable to be enforceable.[3157] If the parties therefore want to include a "hard" obligation to innovate, this must be done through sufficiently specific (and measurable) characteristics, for example relating to performance, energy efficiency or sustainability (e.g. percentage of CO2 reductions, percentage of recycled or repurposed materials or products, etc.). For example, the parties can agree that the heat pump or ventilation system installed in the PSS user's house is to use 10% less energy within five years after the conclusion of the PSS contract. This can then for example be achieved by optimising the times at which the system activates using a digital user profile generated on the basis of the actual use by the PSS user.[3158] Depending on their formulation, these specific innovation obligations will be qualified as an obligation of result or an obligation of means. Failure to comply with the obligation to innovate that is qualified as an obligation of result can then be sanctioned using an indemnity clause on the side of the PSS supplier, which can be taken into account in the assessment of whether the indemnity clause is reciprocal (which is required under Belgian law).[3159]

784. Replacing the product to comply with innovation obligation? – Sometimes innovation can (only) be pursued or achieved by replacing the product with a newer version. In that case, the innovation obligation may conflict with the limits to the possibility to unilaterally change the essential

---

3157 See *supra* no. 781.

3158 C. Borucki, H. Slachmuylders, B. Keirsbilck, D. Gruyaert and E. Terryn, *Model clauses for Product-as-a-Service (PaaS) contracts*, CE Center. Circular Economy Policy Research Center, 2022–23, 64.

3159 Art. VI.83, 17° BCEL. See *supra* no. 304.

characteristics of the product/service.[3160] However, as the notion of innovation implies that the consumer is in a better position after the change of the product, these limits should not pose many difficulties. To protect the PSS user from unilateral changes to the characteristics of the product/service without a valid reason, a clause may also be included stating that the replacement of the product by a new version presented as "innovative" can only be done if the new version is demonstrably better than the previous product (e.g. in terms of the energy efficiency rating based on an independent verification or recognised energy label).[3161]

785. Too extensive innovation obligations are not always desirable or achievable – The previous paragraphs have dealt with examples on how an obligation to innovation can be included in the PSS contract. However, too extensive innovation duties are not always desirable or achievable. Think, for example, of sectors characterised by very rapid technological development, such as the smartphone industry. If the PSS contract would require the PSS supplier to provide state-of-the-art or latest generation devices, this would mean that the smartphone would have to be replaced every time new hardware becomes available.[3162-3163] This would be detrimental from both a financial and a circular economy point of view if the outdated smartphones are not refurbished or otherwise reused.[3164] At the same time, it is important to consider the entire life cycle[3165] of products before replacing them with a more (energy-)efficient version. This does not only include the use phase of the products, but also the manufacturing, transport and waste phases. If

---

3160 **Belgium**: Art. VI.83, 4° BCEL. **The Netherlands**: Art. 6:237, *sub* c. DCC. See on these limits to replacing the product, *supra* no. 435.

3161 C. Borucki, H. Slachmuylders, B. Keirsbilck, D. Gruyaert and E. Terryn, *Model clauses for Product-as-a-Service (PaaS) contracts*, CE Center. Circular Economy Policy Research Center, 2022–23, 66.

3162 Circle Economy, "The Circular Phone, Legal, operational and financial solutions to unlock the potential of the 'Fairphone-as-a-service' model", 31 December 2017, available at www.circle-economy.com/resources/the-circular-phone, 8.

3163 Compare also with Apple's *iPhone Upgrade Program* (available in the United States). This business model is an instalment sales contract where the price of the smartphone is spread over 24 monthly payments with 0% interest. The sale is "bundled" with a subscription on Apple Care+. As such, the profit behind this business model is made by the iPhone sales and the bundled maintenance and repair subscriptions. The consumer has the possibility to trade in his iPhone (i.e. to "upgrade") once he has made 12 monthly payments. See: www.apple.com/shop/iphone/iphone-upgrade-program.

3164 H. Slachmuylders, "iPhone as a Service? Some thoughts on Apple's rumoured hardware subscription service", *CCM Blog* 4 April 2022, https://law.kuleuven.be/ccm/blog/?p=321.

3165 See for a definition of "life cycle": Art. 2(13) EC, *Proposal for a Directive of the European Parliament and of the Council on substantiation and communication of explicit environmental claims (Green Claims Directive)*, 22.3.2023, COM(2023) 166 final: "*'Life cycle' means the consecutive and interlinked stages of a product's life, consisting of raw material acquisition or generation from natural resources, pre-processing, manufacturing, storage, distribution, installation, use, maintenance, repair, upgrading, refurbishment as well as re-use and end-of-life.*"

products are replaced too often, the resources and energy required to produce and dispose of the old products may outweigh the benefits of the improvements, thus leading to a net increase in negative environmental impacts despite the improved efficiency of the new product.[3166]

786. Finding a compromise between innovation, circularity and cost-effectiveness: products of *"the generally accepted technological level"* – A possible alternative to replacing the product every time a new version becomes available in sectors characterised by rapid technological developments is requiring that the PSS supplier provides hardware that meets *"the generally accepted technological level."* For example, the Fairphone-as-a-Service Circular Service Contract Template contains the following clause relating to the provision of hardware:

> Template contract Fairphone-as-a-service – "The functionality and usability of the Product(s) shall be at least equal to what is generally accepted to be the functionality and usability of products of the type of the Product(s) in the market taking into account the circular objectives that are being pursued with this Contract by the Service provider."[3167]

This *"generally accepted technology"* clause, combined with the fact that the Fairphone-as-a-Service template contract allows the use of refurbished models, enables the PSS supplier to provide services considering both functionality and circularity at a reasonable price. One could go even further, by including a clause that products are only replaced when it is certain that the replacement of the product will have a net positive gain. In other words, the environmental impact of the production of the replacement product(s) and the discarding of the old product(s) must be offset by the environmental gains of the new version. This way, products are not replaced unnecessarily.

787. Innovation obligations are still relatively niche and more common in B2B contracts – So far, explicit innovation obligations are still relatively niche and more likely to be found in B2B contracts than in B2C contracts. In fact, none of the B2C PSS contracts analysed contain an explicit innovation obligation. Nevertheless, also in B2C contracts, PSS suppliers will generally attach importance to innovation to maximise efficiency and minimise costs (e.g. less energy consumption or fewer repairs). This often goes hand in

---

3166 C. Borucki, H. Slachmuylders, B. Keirsbilck, D. Gruyaert and E. Terryn, *Model clauses for Product-as-a-Service (PaaS) contracts*, CE Center. Circular Economy Policy Research Center, 2022–23, 66.

3167 See Circle Economy, "The Circular Phone, Legal, operational and financial solutions to unlock the potential of the 'Fairphone-as-a-service' model", 31 December 2017, available at www.circle-economy.com/resources/the-circular-phone, Annex A, part 2.

hand with a commitment to a more sustainable business model. For example, the company *Swapfiets* pushes its suppliers to provide more durable parts for their bikes (such as flexible mudguards that do not break when something strikes them instead of the traditional hard plastic mudguards).[3168] Additionally, it is developing a new frame for e-bikes on which electric motors from different manufacturers can be mounted. If a manufacturer no longer supplies a motor, another motor can still be installed, extending the economic life of the frame.[3169] Thus, although innovation clauses have not explicitly found their way into B2C PSS contracts so far, innovation also plays an important role in B2C relations, given the market reality and economic benefits of providing an advanced, innovative and durable product.

6.5.2. LEGISLATIVE INTERVENTION NEEDED?

788. No legislative intervention needed – The current legal framework for PSS contracts (or any other service contracts for that matter) does not impose an explicit innovation obligation on the PSS supplier/service provider. This does not seem necessary either; imposing such an obligation would, in my view, go too much against the principle of contractual freedom and the freedom of enterprise. If the parties want to implement an innovation obligation in their contractual relationship, they have the tools to do so, for example by means of the model clauses set out in the next section.

6.5.3. MODEL CLAUSES ON THE OBLIGATION TO INNOVATE

789. Model clauses on the obligation to innovate – In the context of the circular economy, it may be desirable to include such innovation clauses into the PSS contract. This is primarily the case for B2B contracts, but innovation clauses can certainly also play a role in B2C PSS contracts. The following model clauses can act as a source of inspiration for PSS suppliers wishing to include an innovation obligation or commitment into their PSS contracts.

790. Model clauses on general innovation obligation – The first model clause is an example of a general innovation obligation. As already set out above, it makes sense to formulate this clause as an obligation of means, as innovative breakthroughs are not guaranteed.[3170]

[3168] P. Lalkens, "De zoektocht naar de volledig recycleerbare fiets", *FD* 26 February 2023, available at https://fd.nl/bedrijfsleven/1468479/de-zoektocht-naar-de-volledig-recyclebare-fiets.

[3169] *Ibid.*

[3170] See *supra* no. 781.

Model clause #52 – general innovation obligation[3171]

- [The PSS supplier] uses all [reasonable/best] efforts to develop and implement new technologies, service concepts, processes or methods that will enhance and develop [the product and associated services or service level requirements (this can further be specified using specific characteristics such as the product's performance, sustainability, recyclability, energy efficiency, life expectancy, etc.)].
- [The PSS supplier] monitors all technological and market trends, developments and improvements and evaluates whether they can be incorporated into the performance of the obligations under this contract. This evaluation shall take into account the impact of these innovations, improvements and market trends in terms of [objectives to be pursued by the innovation obligation (e.g. performance, quality, sustainability, economic efficiency, price, etc.)].

791. MODEL CLAUSES ON SPECIFIC INNOVATION OBLIGATIONS – If the parties want to include more "hard" innovation obligations, they can include specific innovation obligations, specifying the specific features and timeframe in which the product/service is to be improved. Depending on their formulation, these obligations may qualify as an obligation of result or an obligation of means.[3172]

Model clause #53 – specific innovation obligation (obligation of result)

- Within [specified timeframe], the product shall achieve [an absolute improvement of a certain characteristic (e.g. minimum energy efficiency rating)/a relative improvement of a certain characteristic (e.g. percentage of energy savings)].[3173]

Model clause #54 – specific innovation obligation (obligation of means)

- [The PSS supplier] uses all [reasonable/best] efforts to ensure that the product achieves an absolute improvement of a certain characteristic (e.g. minimum energy efficiency rating)/a relative improvement of a certain characteristic (e.g. percentage of energy savings)] within [specified timeframe].[3174]

3171 Model clauses based on C. BORUCKI, H. SLACHMUYLDERS, B. KEIRSBILCK, D. GRUYAERT and E. TERRYN, *Model clauses for Product-as-a-Service (PaaS) contracts*, CE Center. Circular Economy Policy Research Center, 2022–23, 64 and Art. 6.1 and Art. 6.2 Template Contract Agoria Efficiency-as-a-Service (optional clauses).

3172 See *supra* no. 783.

3173 Model clause based on C. BORUCKI, H. SLACHMUYLDERS, B. KEIRSBILCK, D. GRUYAERT and E. TERRYN, *Model clauses for Product-as-a-Service (PaaS) contracts*, CE Center. Circular Economy Policy Research Center, 2022–23, 64.

3174 Model clause based on C. BORUCKI, H. SLACHMUYLDERS, B. KEIRSBILCK, D. GRUYAERT and E. TERRYN, *Model clauses for Product-as-a-Service (PaaS) contracts*, CE Center. Circular Economy Policy Research Center, 2022–23, 64.

792. Indemnity clause in case of non-compliance with innovation obligation – In the case of an innovation obligation that is formulated as an obligation of result, the parties may include an indemnity clause in case the promised innovation or improvements are not achieved. This has the advantage that the PSS user does not need to prove the damages caused by the failure of the PSS supplier to comply with its obligation to innovate. Moreover, the presence of an indemnity clause on the part of the PSS supplier is relevant in the assessment of whether other indemnity clauses in the PSS contract on the part of the PSS user are reciprocal.[3175]

Model clause #55 – indemnity clause if promised innovation or improvements have not been achieved

- **If [the PSS supplier] fails to fulfil the innovation obligation set out above, [the PSS user] is entitled to damages to the amount of [specified amount (e.g. a fixed sum of damages/a dynamic sum of damages; the latter can be useful if the PSS contract contains an obligation to save energy, in which case the parties can agree that the PSS supplier will reimburse the PSS user for the excess amount of energy used (e.g. € X/kWh)].**[3176]

793. Clauses on replacing the product by a new improved version – In some cases, the PSS supplier will only be able to comply with its obligation to innovate if it is entitled to replace the initially delivered product(s) with a new and improved version. The following model clauses give the PSS supplier this right. To protect the interests of the PSS user-consumer, and to avoid that the clause is considered unfair (e.g. because of the limits to clauses allowing to change the essential characteristics of the product[3177]) the first two model clauses make the replacement of the product(s) by a new version dependent of i) the PSS user-consumer's acceptance of the proposed replacement; and ii) the fact that the new version is demonstrably better than the initial product (which may depend, for example, of an independent verification of a certification body). Alternatively, a third model clause provides that the initially delivered product may only be replaced if the improvements by the new version outweigh the negative environmental impacts of the new product over its entire life cycle (i.e. not only the use stage but also the manufacturing, transport and disposal phase). Thus, it is avoided that the product is replaced too frequently under the pretext of innovation. Such a clause is of course beneficial from a sustainability perspective. However, this also requires a certain awareness and sense of responsibility from the side of the PSS users-consumers. Indeed, if they always want to have the latest and

[3175] See *supra* no. 783.

[3176] Model clause based on C. Borucki, H. Slachmuylders, B. Keirsbilck, D. Gruyaert and E. Terryn, *Model clauses for Product-as-a-Service (PaaS) contracts*, CE Center. Circular Economy Policy Research Center, 2022–23, 64 and Art. 6.2.7 Terms and Conditions Klimaatgarant, cited and discussed *supra* no. 522.

[3177] See *supra* no. 435.

most innovative model, the effect of this clause towards environmental sustainability will be limited. Alternatively, a "generally accepted technology" clause as drafted in the fourth model clause below can allow the PSS supplier to decide when to upgrade the initially delivered product (i.e. when its functionality and usability is no longer equal to the generally accepted technology), while also taking into account sustainability and circularity objectives.[3178]

Model clause #56 – replacing the product with a new innovative product

- **To comply with the obligation to innovate, [the PSS supplier] may replace the initially delivered product(s) with a new and improved version. [The PSS supplier] is to notify [the PSS user] of any proposed replacement, including information on the characteristics of the proposed new version. Following the [PSS user's] acceptance of the proposed replacement, the [PSS supplier] and [PSS user] will negotiate in good faith to reach an agreement on a date and time for the replacement of the product(s).[3179]**

- **[The PSS supplier] may only replace the initially delivered product(s) with a new or improved version if the new version is achieving [a demonstrable specified improvement (e.g. a higher energy efficiency rating)] when compared to the initial product(s)[, as verified by an independent third-party certification body].[3180]**

- **The initially delivered product(s) may only be replaced with a new or improved version if the environmental impacts of the production of the new version and the disposal of the initially delivered product(s) are offset by the improvements of the new version within [specified period of time][, as verified by an independent third-party certification body]. [The PSS user] may refuse the proposed replacement if the anticipated benefits do not justify the environmental impacts associated with the replacement.[3181]**

- **To comply with the obligation to innovate, [the PSS supplier] may replace the initially delivered product(s) with a new and improved version. Taking into account the circular objectives that are being pursued with this contract, the [specific characteristics (e.g. functionality, usability, energy efficiency, etc.)] of the product shall be equal to what is generally accepted to be the functionality and usability of products of the same type in the market.[3182]**

3178 See *supra* no. 786.

3179 Model clause based on C. Borucki, H. Slachmuylders, B. Keirsbilck, D. Gruyaert and E. Terryn, *Model clauses for Product-as-a-Service (PaaS) contracts*, CE Center. Circular Economy Policy Research Center, 2022–23, 65.

3180 Model clause partly based on C. Borucki, H. Slachmuylders, B. Keirsbilck, D. Gruyaert and E. Terryn, *Model clauses for Product-as-a-Service (PaaS) contracts*, CE Center. Circular Economy Policy Research Center, 2022–23, 65.

3181 Model clause based on C. Borucki, H. Slachmuylders, B. Keirsbilck, D. Gruyaert and E. Terryn, *Model clauses for Product-as-a-Service (PaaS) contracts*, CE Center. Circular Economy Policy Research Center, 2022–23, 65.

3182 Model clause inspired by the Template Contract Fairphone-as-a-Service. See: Circle Economy, "The Circular Phone, Legal, operational and financial solutions to unlock the

794. Costs associated with replacing the product with a new improved version – The PSS contract may also specify who must bear the costs of replacing the product(s) with the new innovative version. Either this can be included in the service offered by the PSS supplier, or the PSS user is to bear the additional costs of being able to "upgrade" the products used in the performance of the service. A real-life example can be found in the terms and conditions of *Fairphone Easy*.[3183]

> Terms and conditions Fairphone Easy – Art. 4.9 "During the Subscription period, You may upgrade Your Fairphone device ('Upgrade'), if a new device is launched. Please note that an Upgrade will be subject to an additional premium."

If the PSS user bears the cost of upgrading the product(s) used in the performance of the service, it is appropriate to include a right for the PSS user to refuse the proposed replacement because the envisaged benefits and improvements do not justify these costs.

Model clause #57 – costs of replacing the product with a new innovative product

- **The costs of replacing the product(s) following the [PSS supplier's] obligation to innovate are borne by [the PSS supplier/the PSS user]. These costs include [specific cost items (e.g. installation, setup, surcharge of the more expensive product(s), etc.)] and are fixed at [reasonable amount].[3184]**
- **[The PSS user] has the right to refuse the proposed replacement if the envisaged benefits and improvements do not justify the costs associated with the replacement. In this case, [the PSS supplier] has fulfilled its obligation to innovate.[3185]**

6.6. CONCLUSION

795. Additional services: conclusion – This chapter dealt with the additional services the PSS supplier generally offers in addition to the obligation to ensure the availability of the product/service. First, the obligation to install the

potential of the 'Fairphone-as-a-service' model", 31 December 2017, available at www.circle-economy.com/resources/the-circular-phone, Annex A, part 2.

3183 Compare also with Apple's *iPhone Upgrade Program* mentioned *supra* fn. 3160.

3184 Model clause partly based on C. Borucki, H. Slachmuylders, B. Keirsbilck, D. Gruyaert and E. Terryn, *Model clauses for Product-as-a-Service (PaaS) contracts*, CE Center. Circular Economy Policy Research Center, 2022–23, 66.

3185 Model clause based on C. Borucki, H. Slachmuylders, B. Keirsbilck, D. Gruyaert and E. Terryn, *Model clauses for Product-as-a-Service (PaaS) contracts*, CE Center. Circular Economy Policy Research Center, 2022–23, 66.

product was discussed in section 6.2. This additional service will often be present in PSS contracts for larger products, such as home appliances, kitchens, HVAC equipment, etc. Second, section 6.3 analysed the obligation to maintain and repair or replace the product. In this way, the PSS supplier guarantees that the PSS user will be "taken care of" and that he can make uninterrupted use of the service. Third, section 6.4 looked at the obligation to supply updates for connected "smart" products. Finally, this chapter considered how innovation obligations may be included in the PSS contract, which was described in section 6.5.

796. Conclusion on obligation to install the product – The first section of this chapter dealt with the **installation of the product.**[3186] The term "installation" should be understood broadly and includes putting together parts provided to the PSS user, mounting the product on other objects including any necessary adjustments (such as connecting a rented washing machine to the water supply and water discharge) as well as the replacement of parts. This section discussed two issues in particular. First, the conformity of the installation and the consequences of incorrect installation was discussed. Second, possible contractual arrangements (e.g. timing, location, price) of the installation obligation in the PSS contract were explored. Finally, this section proposed some normative solutions and outlined some model clauses on the obligation to install the product.

In the context of **product-oriented PSS**, the consumer sales rules provide that where the installation was carried out by the PSS supplier-seller or under his responsibility, an incorrect installation results in a lack of conformity of the product. The same applies to situations where the installation was done by the PSS user (or someone he designated) and the incorrect installation was caused by shortcomings in the installation instructions. The consumer sales rules thus give the PSS user access to the same extensive arsenal of remedies for a defective installation than a defect in the product itself. A special feature of Dutch law is that the PSS user-consumer may choose between the remedies of the consumer sales contract and the remedies of the contract for works as both sets of rules apply simultaneously due to the cumulation theory (whereby the consumer sales rules take precedence in case of conflict). In contrast, under Belgian law, the absorption theory is used if the installation is ancillary to the sale, making (only) the consumer sales rules applicable to the entire contract.

In **use-oriented PSS contracts**, the installation of the product is an additional service that comes on top of providing a right of use over the product. Depending on which qualification theory is used, the applicable conformity rules are different. A first option is to apply the absorption theory, which results in the service component being absorbed by the rental contract for movables. An eventual incorrect installation would then be assessed and remedied under

[3186] See *supra* section 6.2.

the rules regarding defects. Alternatively, if the service component is sufficiently distinct from the rental component, it is preferable to apply the cumulation theory. In this case, the installation will be covered by the conformity rules of the Belgian contract for services (*aanneming, contrat d'entreprise*) and the Dutch contract for works (*aanneming*).

In **result-oriented PSS**, the installation component is part of a larger complex service contract. Under Belgian law, the conformity of the installation must therefore be assessed under the rules of the contract for services. Under Dutch law, the question what rules apply to the installation component is harder to answer given the distinction between the Dutch contract for services (*opdracht*) and the contract for works (*aanneming van werk*). Strictly speaking, the installation component would be covered by the rules of the contract for works as it aims at "*the construction and delivery of a tangible good.*" However, the transient nature of the contract for works, which comes to an end with the acceptance and reception of the work, does not really work in the context of "as-a-service" business models. Additionally, the installation component is not the main object of the result-oriented PSS contract, as it is merely an instrument in achieving the contractually agreed result. Therefore, it was argued to consider the larger result-oriented PSS contract as aiming at "*activities other than the construction of a tangible good.*" Applying the absorption theory, the rules of the contract for services (*opdracht*) should then also be applied to the installation component.

De lege ferenda, **three possible solutions** for the PSS supplier's obligation to install the product were discussed. First, in the context of a **modernisation of national contract law**, it was proposed to adopt a provision for B2C rental contracts for consumer goods similar to the consumer sales rules which established a lack of conformity if the rented good is incorrectly installed. This avoids the discussion whether the installation obligation is absorbed by the rental contract or constitutes an "accessory" obligation of which the non-performance can give rise to different consequences than the remedies available under the rental contract. For result-oriented PSS, on the other hand, it was not deemed necessary to have a specific provision on the PSS supplier's obligation to install the product. After all, these contracts in their entirety qualify as a contract for services under Belgian law, and therefore the (proposed) conformity requirements of the contract for services (which were discussed above in chapter 4) will also apply to the installation. Second, the PSS supplier's obligation to install the product may also be regulated at the EU level, by means of an **EU directive.** If the approach of a general directive on conformity and quality of (almost) all service contracts is chosen, the installation is a service like any other that should be tested against the same uniform conformity rules. By contrast, if a specific directive for "packages" or "bundles" of services is chosen, installation services may take a more central place, both in terms of the scope of the specific directive and its substantive provisions. Third, this book has proposed **model**

clauses for the PSS supplier's obligation to install the product, which were in part inspired by clauses from the analysed PSS contracts.

797. Conclusion on obligation to maintain, repair and/or replace the product – The second section of this chapter dealt with the PSS supplier's **obligation to maintain, repair and/or replace** the product in the three main types of PSS contracts.[3187] It discussed the respective legal bases and modalities of these obligations, proposed legislative solutions and outlined model clauses for use-oriented and result-oriented PSS.

In the context of **product-oriented PSS**, the PSS supplier's **obligation to maintain** the product is not derived from the (consumer) sales rules but generally arises from the fact that maintenance is added to the contract as an additional service. As a result, there is a mixed contract with both the elements of the (consumer) sales contract and a service contract. Since this combination does not involve "the supply of goods to be manufactured or produced", but a sales contract with a purely ancillary service contract, it is fitting to apply the cumulation theory. Thus, the conformity of these additional maintenance services will be assessed against the rules of the Belgian contract for services (*aanneming, contrat d'entreprise*) and the Dutch contract for works (*aanneming van werk*). The PSS supplier's **obligation to repair** may have two legal bases. The PSS user-buyer may either be entitled to free repair of the product as a (primary) remedy for non-conformity of the product, or, for repairs that fall outside the scope of the legal guarantee, the repair obligation may arise from an additional repair contract. In the latter case, applying the cumulation theory will result in the rules of the Belgian contract for services and the Dutch contract for works being applicable to the repair services. The new Right to Repair Directive provides incentives to promote repair and incentivise consumers to choose repair also in cases where the legal guarantee does not apply, for example by introducing a (voluntary) European repair information form, developing a European online repair platform and imposing on manufacturers an obligation to repair upon the consumer's request for goods for which EU legal acts lay down repairability requirements. **Replacement** (free of charge and without significant inconvenience for the consumer) is also a primary remedy for a lack of conformity in product-oriented PSS. The new Right to Repair Directive addressed an uncertainty under the SGD as to whether the replacement may be carried out by means of a refurbished product, by stating that this is allowed "*upon the explicit request by the consumer.*" From a sustainability point of view, it is regrettable that the consent of the consumer is required for this option. As consumers often prefer new rather than refurbished goods, there is a risk that this provision will remain ineffective. Apart from replacement as a remedy for non-conformity, the PSS supplier will generally not have an obligation to replace

[3187] See *supra* section 6.3.

the product. This means that in that case the only alternative for the PSS user-buyer will be to purchase a new (or refurbished/second-hand) one.

In **use-oriented PSS**, one of the obligations of the PSS supplier-lessor is to **maintain the product** in such condition that it is suitable for the use for which it has been rented. As a result, the PSS supplier is bound to this maintenance obligation from the nature of the use-oriented PSS contract as a rental contract itself, without the need for a contractual clause. Generally, maintenance will be carried out when the PSS user-lessee notifies the PSS supplier of a defect. Alternatively, the PSS contract may contain a scheduled maintenance plan, or preventive maintenance may be carried out based on user data collected by "smart" products. The rules of the rental contract also require the PSS supplier lessor to **perform all necessary repairs** to the product during the term of the PSS contract, except for the repairs that are at the expense of the PSS user-lessee. The term "necessary repairs" is to be interpreted broadly. It includes all repairs without which the normal use of the product would be hampered, or the PSS user would suffer loss of rental enjoyment or other damage. It is not relevant whether they are necessary because of normal use, age, or *force majeure*. However, the PSS supplier will not be responsible for repairs of damages or defects caused by the fault of the PSS user. Moreover, the PSS supplier-lessor is in principle[3188] not responsible for repairs that are at the expense of the PSS user-lessee, which are the so-called "minor repairs" (and minor maintenance). In practice, however, most PSS contracts contractually place the responsibility for these minor repairs on the PSS supplier. As to **replacement**, the Belgian and Dutch rental contract rules in principle do not contain a right for the PSS user-lessee to claim a replacement of the product in case of a defect. Under Belgian law, if the good is destroyed or lost during the term of the rental contract, the contract is automatically terminated. Under Dutch law, both parties can in this case terminate the contract. Nevertheless, in the context of rental for movables and (use-oriented) PSS, the contracting parties will generally want to continue the contract because the rented good can easily be replaced. This can be solved by including a contractual right to replacement in the use-oriented PSS contract.

In **result-oriented PSS**, maintenance, repair and replacement obligations are all part of the complex and integrated service contract. As a result, the rules of the contract for services (potentially supplemented by service standards related to maintenance and repair), and the parties' contractual arrangements will shape these obligations.

De lege ferenda, three possible solutions were again proposed, building on the solutions and proposed provisions already set out above. As a reminder, these include (i) the **modernisation of national contract law** (i.e. repair and

[3188] Under Belgian law, the PSS user-lessee will not be responsible for minor repairs necessary because of aging of the product or *force majeure*. Under Dutch law, the PSS user-lessee does not have to carry out minor repairs caused by aging or normal use, but he is responsible for minor repairs caused by *force majeure*.

maintenance as part of the conformity rules set out in chapter 4), (ii) including maintenance and repair in an **EU directive** (especially in the context of a specific directive for "packages" or "bundles" of services (option 2b)), and (iii) the **use of balanced standard contracts and model clauses** (inspired also by clauses found in the analysed PSS contracts). Besides these three solutions, **standardisation of services** was also put forward. Indeed, a (voluntary) (European) quality standard for repair services could boost consumer trust and prove useful to assess the conformity and quality of repair services. The content of this service standard could include, for example, the time to complete repair, the availability of temporary replacement goods, quality assurances such as a commercial guarantee on repair, and the availability of additional services such as removal, installation and transportation offered by repairers.

798. Conclusion on obligation to supply updates – The third section of this chapter dealt with the PSS supplier's **obligation to supply updates** and the PSS user's obligation to **install** these **updates.**[3189] These obligations are relevant in PSS contracts relating to "smart" connected products that contain digital elements and additional digital services, such as remote control through an app, the possibility (for both the PSS user and the PSS supplier) to monitor the use of the product, predictive maintenance, etc. Updates may extend the functionalities of these "smart" products, adapt them to technical developments, protect them against new security threats or have other purposes, such as adapting the digital service to comply with market standards, technical norms or any legal developments (in terms of data protection law for example). As such, they may concern the operating system of the product, support for mobile apps, security updates, etc.

The **PSS supplier's obligation to supply updates** is found in both the SGD (applicable to product-oriented PSS relating to "goods with digital elements") and the DCD (applicable to use-oriented and result-oriented PSS with "digital services"). Indeed, updates are an important element for assessing the conformity of the "smart" product with the PSS contract, as the availability of updates is both a subjective and objective conformity requirement.[3190] As regards subjective conformity, the PSS supplier must supply updates as stipulated in the PSS contract. For complying with the objective conformity requirements, the PSS supplier must supply updates that ensure that the "smart" product or digital service part of the PSS remains fit for its normal use and continues to provide the quality the PSS user can reasonably expect. This could, for example, include security updates or updates to correct "bugs" in the software. In contrast, updates that are not necessary to keep the "smart" product or digital service part of the PSS in conformity (e.g. newer versions with new functionalities) are not

3189 See *supra* section 6.4.

3190 See also *supra* no. 455 and 497.

covered by the objective conformity requirements. As a result, the PSS supplier must only supply these updates if this was explicitly agreed in the PSS contract (subjective conformity).

Somewhat surprisingly, none of the analysed PSS contracts contained any **clauses on the frequency, timing, quality or even availability of updates** regarding non-essential updates such as new versions or new functionalities. While this is logical for PSS relating to non-connected products (e.g. *Swapfiets*, *Live Light*, *Lena*, *Dressr*), a clause on the update obligation would not be out of place in PSS contracts that do relate to connected products, such as *Swapphone*, *Grover* and *Fairphone Easy*. However, the fact that no update clauses are included in the analysed PSS contracts, does not mean that no such updates will be provided. Indeed, PSS users may benefit from any update obligation that is included in the contract between the manufacturer and PSS supplier. Additionally, the manufacturer may also provide updates with new functionalities on its own initiative (without an explicit legal obligation). The PSS contract's silence on updates should thus not necessarily be construed to mean that there will be no updates on new functionalities at all. Nevertheless, to encourage PSS suppliers to include clauses regarding updates in their PSS contracts, model clauses on the obligation to supply updates were drafted and set out in this section.

Since installing updates is important for the conformity of the "smart" products and the additional digital services, the question arises as to whether there is an **obligation for the PSS user to install the updates**. Neither the SGD and the DCD nor their national implementation stipulate an explicit obligation for the PSS user-consumer to stipulate the updates supplied. Nevertheless, if the PSS user fails to install the updates within a reasonable time, he will no longer be able to hold the PSS supplier liable for any lack of conformity resulting *solely* from the lack of the relevant update. Additionally, a contractual obligation to install the updates (or to enable automatic updates) may be included in the PSS contract.

As regards the question whether **legislative intervention** is needed, this book concluded that the new rules of the SGD and DCD regarding updates are fit for purpose and not in need of any legislative review. However, to avoid that the PSS supplier is "left" with the liability for a lack of updates that is beyond its control, national contract law should grant the PSS supplier an adequate right of address against the third party responsible for these updates (e.g. the manufacturer of the product or a software developer). Therefore, it was recommended to consider streamlining the concept of conformity and the remedy for non-conformity across all (B2C and B2B) named contracts so the PSS supplier is not "trapped" in a situation where it is liable for a lack of updates beyond its control, but it cannot hold its contractual party liable due to the lack of parallelism between the B2B and B2C rules in terms of the conformity concepts, remedies and time limits. Additionally, it was also recommended to strengthen the right of redress altogether, either at the EU level or national level.

799. Conclusion on innovation obligations – The fourth section of this chapter dealt with possible **innovation obligations** that could be included in the PSS contract.[3191] Technological innovation in PSS contracts may further the transition towards a more circular economy, for example by enabling a more sustainable, economical or more efficient use of the product/service. While the legal framework for PSS contracts does not explicitly require PSS suppliers to innovate during the contract period, parties can include such innovation obligations into their PSS contract themselves.

Contractual innovation obligations may take various forms. A first option is to include a general innovation obligation into the PSS contract. Such clauses will generally be formulated rather broadly as innovative breakthroughs are not a given, resulting in them being qualified as an obligation of means. A general innovation obligation may be accompanied with an obligation to stay up to date and informed of the latest technological developments. Alternatively, including specific innovation obligations into the PSS contracts allows to place a "hard" obligation to innovate on the PSS supplier. This requires sufficiently specific (and measurable) characteristics, for example relating to performance, energy efficiency or sustainability. Finally, an innovation obligation may entail an obligation to replace the product with a newer version. However, too extensive innovation duties are not always desirable or achievable (both from a cost-perspective and a sustainability perspective). A compromise between innovation, circularity and cost-effectiveness could therefore be reached by including a clause in the PSS contract that the PSS supplier must provide "*products of the generally accepted technological level.*" Regardless of all these options, it is important to note that explicit innovation obligations are still relatively niche and more likely to be found in B2B contracts. None of the analysed PSS contracts contained an explicit innovation obligation. However, this does not mean that PSS supplier in B2C markets do not attach importance to innovation to maximise efficiency and minimise costs (e.g. less energy consumption and fewer repairs). In fact, many PSS suppliers are continuously innovating, even without an explicit legal obligation to do so.

As regards the question whether **legislative intervention** is needed, this book posits that is not necessary to include an explicit innovation obligation in the legal framework for PSS contracts. Imposing such an obligation would disproportionally restrict the principle of contractual freedom and the freedom of enterprise. If the parties want to implement an innovation obligation in their contractual relationship, they have the tools to do so, for example by means of the model clauses set out in this section.

[3191] See *supra* section 6.5.

7. OWNERSHIP, MORAL HAZARD, AND END OF THE CONTRACT/ END-OF-LIFE OF THE PRODUCT

"Is consumer law as it was developed
in the consumer society the problem?
Is 'irresponsible' behaviour of consumers the problem?
Is the consumer the problem?
Are we the problem?"
– Hans-W. Micklitz[3192]

7.1. INTRODUCTION

800. Ownership, moral hazard, and end-of-life of the product – An essential characteristic of use-oriented and result-oriented PSS (and contrary to product-oriented PSS where ownership is still transferred) is that the PSS supplier wishes to retain the ownership of the product. The first section of this chapter (section 7.2) therefore deals with the question of how the PSS supplier can protect its right of ownership of the product. The second section of this chapter (section 7.3) discusses moral hazard, i.e. the risk that PSS user will treat the product less carefully then if he were the owner of the product. Here, particular attention is given to how this risk can be (contractually) mitigated. Finally, the third section (section 7.4) deals with the end-of-life stage of the product. Here, the responsibilities of the PSS supplier regarding collection, repurposing, and/or disposal of the product in use-oriented and result-oriented PSS are discussed compared to the responsibilities of the PSS supplier in product-oriented PSS. Additionally, this section also analyses how circular guarantees can be incorporated into the PSS contract.

7.2. OWNERSHIP OF THE PRODUCT

801. Ownership takes a back seat in a circular and servitised economy – In a circular and servitised economy, particularly in use-oriented

[3192] H.-W. Micklitz, "Squaring the Circle? Reconciling Consumer Law and the Circular Economy", *EuCML* 2019, vol. 6, (229) 230.

and result-oriented PSS, rights of use and service contracts are more important than transferring the ownership of the product.[3193] In fact, in these business models, the PSS supplier will want to avoid that the ownership of the product is transferred to the PSS user. This section deals with the property law aspects of movable servitisation and PSS contracts, more specifically the question how the PSS supplier can protect its right of ownership of the product. As this book mainly focuses on the contractual aspects of servitisation and PSS, it does not intend to provide a comprehensive analysis of all property law challenges associated with servitisation and PSS.[3194] Nevertheless, the question of ownership is too important not to address. Therefore, this chapter will briefly touch upon the main property law challenges for the PSS supplier and focus on the (contractual) solutions it can employ to protect its right of ownership of the product.

7.2.1. ACCESSION AS PROBLEM FOR SERVITISATION AND PSS CONTRACTS

802. Immovable accession of incorporated products – In use-oriented and result-oriented PSS, the PSS user is granted a right of use while the PSS supplier retains the ownership of the product. In some cases, however, the products used in the performance of the contract will be incorporated in an immovable good (by nature) owned by the PSS user.[3195] For example, a heat pump or ventilation system will generally be installed in the PSS user's home,

---

3193 V. Sagaert and K. De Schepper, "Property Law and Circular Economy" in B. Keirsbilck, E. Terryn, J. Eyckmans, S. Rousseau and D. Voinot (eds.), *Servitization and circular economy: economic and legal challenges*, Antwerp, Intersentia, 2023, (181) 181.

3194 See on the property law challenges of the circular economy the research project of Kato De Schepper (www.law.kuleuven.be/goederenrecht/leden/00147729) on "The unitary principle in property law: an enemy to the circular economy?" (*"Het eenheidsbeginsel in het goederenrecht: een vijand voor de circulaire economie?"*). See also for **Belgium** e.g. V. Sagaert and K. De Schepper, "Property Law and Circular Economy" in B. Keirsbilck, E. Terryn, J. Eyckmans, S. Rousseau and D. Voinot (eds.), *Servitization and circular economy: economic and legal challenges*, Antwerp, Intersentia, 2023, (181) 181–209; V. Sagaert, "De zakenrechtelijke motoren van een circulaire vastgoedeconomie: een SWOT-analyse", *TPR* 2021, (1543) 1543–1558; B. Verheye, "Toekomst van de circulaire vastgoedeconomie", *TPR* 2019, (107) 107–196. For **the Netherlands**, see the research project by Ellen Maathuis at the Radboud University Nijmegen (www.ru.nl/personen/maathuis-e). See also e.g. E.C.A. Vermeulen, *Circulair bouwen: knelpunten en oplossingen in het goederenrecht: van eigendom naar product-as-a-service*, Nijmegen, Ars Aequi Libri, 2020, 110 p.; R. Koolhoven, "Gebouwen en hun bestanddelen in een meer circulair goederenrecht" in C.W. Backes, M.N. Boeve, R. Koolhoven and D.J. Versteeg (eds.), *Circulair bouwen. Preadviezen voor de vereniging van bouwrecht 46*, Den Haag, Stichting Instituut voor Bouwrecht, 2018, (6) 6–54; M.A.B. Chao-Duivis, "Privaatrechtelijke aspecten van de circulaire economie in het bijzonder circulair bouwen (Deel I)", *TBR* 2017/139, (915) 915–921; M.A.B. Chao-Duivis, "Privaatrechtelijke aspecten van de circulaire economie in het bijzonder circulair bouwen (Deel II)", *TBR* 2017/154, (1032) 1032–1041.

3195 **Belgium**: See Art. 3.47 BCC: *"Immovable goods are immovable by their nature, by incorporation or by purpose."* **The Netherlands**: Art. 3:3 DCC.

in a way it cannot easily be separated from that building.[3196] In this case, the product has become immovable by incorporation.[3197] As a result of the principle of accession (*natrekking, accession*), the owner of the immovable good – i.e. the PSS user's home – will also become the owner of the inherent components of that good – i.e. the heat pump or ventilation system.[3198] However, this situation entails risks for the PSS supplier, especially if the PSS user becomes insolvent.[3199] If the products are incorporated in the PSS user's home, there is a risk that the PSS user becomes the owner of the product, which will therefore end up in the PSS user's estate, even if the parties did not intend to transfer the ownership.[3200]

7.2.2. SOLUTIONS FOR AVOIDING ACCESSION

803. Avoiding accession and safeguarding the PSS supplier's ownership right – The principle of accession thus threatens the position of the PSS supplier and is at odds with the idea behind circular and servitised business models, where the parties want to prevent the transfer of ownership.[3201] As a result, the PSS supplier must search for ways to counteract the operation of

3196 Under Belgian law, a good can also become immovable by incorporation even if it can be separated without breaking and damaging the good of the inherent component itself. Indeed, a good is also deemed to be immovable when it is "*permanently and customarily attached or fixed to the property.*" See: Cass. (BE) 15 September 1988, *Arr.Cass.* 1988–89, 60, *RW* 1988–89, 879, *TBBR* 1990, 211, case note J. Kokelenberg, *AFT* 1989, 78, case note F. Laurent. See for an in-depth discussion: V. Sagaert, *Goederenrecht*, Mechelen, Wolters Kluwer, 2021, no. 211 *et seq.*

3197 **Belgium**: See Art. 3.47(2) BCC: "*Immovable by incorporation are buildings and plantations that, because they are incorporated in goods immovable by their nature, are an inherent component thereof*" *juncto* Art. 3.8, §2 BCC: "*An inherent component of a good is an essential element of that good that cannot be separated from it without affecting the material or functional substance of that good.*" **The Netherlands**: In Dutch legal doctrine, there is an ongoing discussion about the relationship between Art. 5:3 DCC (the unity principle, *eenheidsbeginsel*) and Art. 3:4 DCC (component formation, *bestanddeelvorming*) on the one hand and Art. 3:3 DCC (incorporation criterion for immovables) and Art. 5:20 (immovable accession) on the other hand. See for an overview of the discussion e.g. H.W. Heyman and S.E. Bartels, *Vastgoedtransacties: Koop*, Deventer, Kluwer, 2021, 49–53 and 54 *et seq.* See also: P.J. Van der Plank, *Natrekking door onroerende zaken*, Deventer, Wolters Kluwer, 2016, 279 p.

3198 **Belgium**: Art. 3.55 BCC. **The Netherlands**: Art. 5:20 DCC.

3199 V. Sagaert and K. De Schepper, "Property Law and Circular Economy" in B. Keirsbilck, E. Terryn, J. Eyckmans, S. Rousseau and D. Voinot (eds.), *Servitization and circular economy: economic and legal challenges*, Antwerp, Intersentia, 2023, (181) 185, no. 6.

3200 *Ibid.*

3201 **Belgium**: D. Gruyaert, "Privaat en publiek goederenrecht en duurzaamheid" in A. Van Hoe and G. Croisant (eds.), *Droit et durabilité / Recht en duurzaamheid*, Antwerp, Intersentia, 2022, (495) 525, no. 35; B. Verheye, "Toekomst van de circulaire vastgoedeconomie", *TPR* 2019, (107) 160, no. 33. **The Netherlands**: R. Koolhoven, "Gebouwen en hun bestanddelen in een meer circulair goederenrecht" in C.W. Backes, M.N. Boeve, R. Koolhoven and D.J. Versteeg (eds.), *Circulair bouwen. Preadviezen voor de vereniging van bouwrecht 46*, Den Haag, Stichting Instituut voor Bouwrecht, 2018, (6) 18; M.A.B. Chao-Duivis, "Privaatrechtelijke aspecten van de circulaire economie in het bijzonder circulair bouwen

immovable accession to protect its right of ownership of the product. However, contrary to contract law where many of the provisions are only default law, the rules on accession are part of mandatory property law so parties are not free to contractually derogate from these provisions.[3202] Nevertheless, there are some legal exceptions to the principle of accession on which the parties can rely, namely the building right (also called right of *superficies*), the retention of title, and the accessory building right/accessory right of *superficies*.[3203]

7.2.2.1. Building right/right of superficies

804. BUILDING RIGHT/RIGHT OF *SUPERFICIES* – A first exception to the principle of accession is the creation of a building right (*opstalrecht, droit de superficie*), also called a right of *superficies*.[3204] The creation of a building right entails that the right holder who has built a construction upon the land or building of a third party (i.e. the PSS supplier who has installed the product in the PSS user's home) remains the owner of that construction, even if it is incorporated into the other party's land or building. Under Belgian law, the maximum duration of a building right is since 1 September 2021 extended to 99 years and can in some circumstances even be perpetual.[3205] Under Dutch law, the parties are free to determine the duration of the building right and can therefore also decide to make the right perpetual.[3206] Since this maximum duration exceeds the average lifetime of the products offered as part of a PSS (e.g. a ventilation system, heat pump, etc.), a building right therefore opens up interesting opportunities to avoid accession.[3207]

(Deel II)", *TBR* 2017/154, (1032) 1036–1037; V. MAK, "Van ownership naar access. Is toegang de nieuwe eigendom?", *Ars Aequi* 2018, (664) 668.

3202 V. SAGAERT and K. DE SCHEPPER, "Property Law and Circular Economy" in B. KEIRSBILCK, E. TERRYN, J. EYCKMANS, S. ROUSSEAU and D. VOINOT (eds.), *Servitization and circular economy: economic and legal challenges*, Antwerp, Intersentia, 2023, (181) 193, no. 14 with reference to S. VAN ERP and B. AKKERMANS (eds.), *Ius Commune Casebooks for the Common Law of Europe. Cases Materials & Text on Property Law*, Oxford, Hart, 2012, 65–75.

3203 V. SAGAERT and K. DE SCHEPPER, "Property Law and Circular Economy" in B. KEIRSBILCK, E. TERRYN, J. EYCKMANS, S. ROUSSEAU and D. VOINOT (eds.), *Servitization and circular economy: economic and legal challenges*, Antwerp, Intersentia, 2023, (181) 193–194.

3204 **Belgium**: Art. 3.177 BCC. **The Netherlands** Art. 5:101(1) DCC.

3205 Art. 3.180 BCC.

3206 Art. 5:104(2) *juncto* Art. 5:86 DCC. However, in two cases, a perpetual building right may be terminated earlier, namely (i) in case of judicial termination or amendment after 25 years after its creation at the request of the owner or the holder of the building right (Art. 5:104(2) *juncto* Art. 5.97 DCC); and (ii) the building owner's right to terminate the agreement, unless contractually excluded (Art. 5:104(2) *juncto* Art. 5:87–5:88 DCC). See W.H.M. REEHUIS, A.H.T. HEISTERKAMP, G.E. VAN MAANEN and G.T. DE JONG, *Pitlo, Het Nederlands burgerlijk recht, deel 3, Goederenrecht*, Deventer, Wolters Kluwer, 2021, 555–556, no. 676–677.

3207 V. SAGAERT, "De zakenrechtelijke motoren van een circulaire vastgoedeconomie: een SWOT-analyse", *TPR* 2021, (1543) 1546, no. 5.

805. Limitations and downsides of creating a building right – Although the creation of a building right offers interesting opportunities, it is subject to an important limitation, namely the unity principle (*eenheidsbeginsel, principe d'unité*). According to this principle, a right *in rem* (in this case a building right) can only have a sufficiently independent construction as its object, and not an inherent component of another good.[3208] Consequently, a building right cannot be granted for mere improvements and repairs to a certain good.[3209] Both Belgian and Dutch case law and legal doctrine is very casuistic on this issue. Typical examples of constructions that are considered not sufficiently independent are PVC windows,[3210] wall coverings, floors, roofing, doors, roller shutters, fitted kitchens and bathrooms.[3211] This means that the unity principle can put a brake on circular and servitised business models, at least for products/materials that are not sufficiently independent.[3212, 3213] As a result, voices have been raised in legal doctrine to adopt a flexible approach to the unity principle.[3214] However, at present, it is far from certain that this modern (minority) view will be followed in case law.[3215]

3208 **Belgium**: Art. 3.8, §2 BCC; V. Sagaert, *Goederenrecht*, Mechelen, Wolters Kluwer, 2021, no. 1106. **The Netherlands**: S.E. Bartels, A.I.M. van Mierlo and H.D. Ploeger, *Mr. C. Assers Handleiding tot de beoefening van het Nederlands Burgerlijk Recht. 3. Vermogensrecht algemeen. Deel IV. Algemeen goederenrecht*, Deventer, Wolters Kluwer, 2021, no. 65 *et seq.*

3209 V. Sagaert, *Goederenrecht*, Mechelen, Wolters Kluwer, 2021, no. 1106.

3210 Brussels (BE) 27 February 2001, *RW* 2001–02, 844.

3211 **Belgium**: V. Sagaert and K. De Schepper, "Property Law and Circular Economy" in B. Keirsbilck, E. Terryn, J. Eyckmans, S. Rousseau and D. Voinot (eds.), *Servitization and circular economy: economic and legal challenges*, Antwerp, Intersentia, 2023, (181) 196–197; V. Sagaert, "De zakenrechtelijke motoren van een circulaire vastgoedeconomie: een SWOT-analyse", *TPR* 2021, (1543) 1548, no. 8. **The Netherlands**: E.C.M. Wolfert, "Bestanddeel of zaak? Over het onderscheid en de samenhang tussen de artikelen 3:4 en 5:20 NBW", *WPNR* 2003/5625, (279) 280; H.D. Ploeger, *Horizontale splitsing van eigendom*, Deventer, Wolters Kluwer, 1997, 218.

3212 See for an analysis of different products/parts of a building that can be offered as part of a PSS and whether they are sufficiently independent: D. Gruyaert, V. Sagaert, E. Terryn and B. Verheye, *Het concept "PaaS" in vastgoedprojecten – aandachtspunten goederenrechtelijk*, 2023, 3–4, available at https://circulair-parkgebouw.be/media/PaaS-goederenrechtelijk.pdf. Generally, products such as a heat pump, solar boiler, etc. will be sufficiently independent. For ventilation equipment, it will depend on the specific circumstances (i.e.i.e. the degree of incorporation).

3213 See e.g. B. Verheye, "Toekomst van de circulaire vastgoedeconomie", *TPR* 2019, (107) 158–166; T. Hartlief, "Het huis van de toekomst", *Nederlands Juristenblad* 2019, (1429) 1429; B. Akkermans, "Duurzaam goederenrecht: naar een herrijking van ons goederenrechtelijk stelsel?", *TPR* 2018, (1437) 1451, no. 21.

3214 See e.g. B. Verheye, "Toekomst van de circulaire vastgoedeconomie", *TPR* 2019, (107) 107–196; H. Mes, H.D. Ploeger and B.A.M. Janssen, "Eigendom van onroerende zaken, met name natrekking (titels 1 en 3). Flexibele eigendomsverhoudingen in het vastgoedrecht" in L.C.A. Verstappen (ed.), *Boek 5 BW van de toekomst: over vernieuwingen in het zakenrecht*, Den Haag, Sdu Juridische Uitgevers, 2016, (145) 158–166.

3215 D. Gruyaert, V. Sagaert, E. Terryn and B. Verheye, *Het concept "PaaS" in vastgoedprojecten – aandachtspunten goederenrechtelijk*, 2023, 3, available at https://circulair-parkgebouw.be/media/PaaS-goederenrechtelijk.pdf.

The unity principle is not the only limitation for using a building right in the context of PSS contracts. Indeed, for being enforceable against third parties, a building right requires an authentic deed which is registered in the land registers.[3216] This will not always be economically viable, as registering will in practice often be costly and time-consuming.[3217] Nevertheless, a non-published building right is not enforceable against the creditors of the PSS user, therefore providing only limited protection. Moreover, explaining the need for establishing a building right to the prospective PSS user will not always be an easy task, as at first sight most PSS contracts constitute an essentially movable transaction in the eyes of the PSS user.[3218]

806. Example of the creation of a building right in practice: Klimaatgarant – Despite these limitations and downsides, there are real-life business models that make use of a building right to protect the PSS supplier's right of ownership. For example, the terms and conditions of *Klimaatgarant* explicitly state that a building right shall be established for the benefit of the PSS supplier, which shall be included in the deed of delivery.[3219] This is also confirmed in the recitals of the contract, where it is stated that *Klimaatgarant* owns the installation, and a building right has been or will be established for its benefit.[3220]

> Terms and conditions Klimaatgarant – Art. 1.3 "The System is and shall remain the property of KG. For this purpose, a building right shall be established for the benefit of KG which shall be included in the deed of delivery. The user acknowledges that the System does not become part of the house by being installed in and/or on the house, nor does it become the property of the owner of the house by accession."

7.2.2.2. Retention of title

807. Retention of title for use-oriented and result-oriented PSS? – The question arises whether there are alternative ways of avoiding accession in PSS contracts. Under Belgian law, the possibility of using the legal device of the retention of title (*eigendomsvoorbehoud, réserve de propriété*) has been examined in legal doctrine. In more traditional contracts, such as the sales contract (and therefore also product-oriented PSS), the retention of title allows the seller

3216 V. Sagaert and K. De Schepper, "Property Law and Circular Economy" in B. Keirsbilck, E. Terryn, J. Eyckmans, S. Rousseau and D. Voinot (eds.), *Servitization and circular economy: economic and legal challenges*, Antwerp, Intersentia, 2023, (181) 197.

3217 *Ibid.*

3218 *Ibid.*

3219 See Art. 1.3 Terms and Conditions Klimaatgarant (unpublished, the terms and conditions are available with the author).

3220 See Recital B Terms and Conditions Klimaatgarant (unpublished, the terms and conditions are available with the author).

to retain the ownership of the product sold until the buyer has fully paid the purchase price or until other contractually stipulated conditions have been met.[3221] In use-oriented and result-oriented PSS contracts, on the other hand, the goal is not to retain the ownership "until", but to avoid the transfer of ownership altogether. Some authors in legal doctrine argue that a retention of title clause is not useful in PSS contracts as there is no sale and therefore no intention to transfer the ownership.[3222] A contrary point of view is convincingly defended by SAGAERT and DE SCHEPPER, who argue that the retention of title is indeed useful in the context of use-oriented and result-oriented PSS contracts.[3223]

Their argument starts from the observation that the retention of title was recently reformed by the Belgian Pledge Act,[3224] which entered into force on 1 January 2018. Under the new regime, the retention of title can survive incorporation and therefore prevent accession from taking place, provided the retention of title is registered in the pledge register.[3225] Contrary to the building right, there is no authentic deed required for this registration and the costs are rather limited.[3226] In addition, the reform also put an end to prior legal uncertainty regarding mixed contracts that included both a sales and services component by confirming that a contracting party can exercise a retention of title "*regardless of the legal nature of the contract in which it is included.*"[3227] As a result, a retention of title clause is also valid and enforceable in service contracts that also involve the supply of goods, even if the service component is dominant.[3228]

The main question is then whether the retention of title can be used in contracts that do not have the finality to transfer ownership, such as use-oriented and result-oriented PSS. According to SAGAERT and DE SCHEPPER, there are three arguments why this question should be answered in the affirmative. First, they argue that from a coherence perspective, it would be illogical that the PSS

3221 See on the retention of title e.g. A. APERS and D. GRUYAERT, "Eigendomsvoorbehoud en onroerende incorporatie volgende de nieuwe Pandwet: welk nieuws onder de zon?", *TPR* 2015, (83) 83–124.

3222 A. VAN VAERENBERGH and F. LEYMAN, "'Product als dienst'-overeenkomsten, een stap in de richting van de circulaire economie", *MER* 2019, (20) 30, no. 40–41.

3223 See V. SAGAERT and K. DE SCHEPPER, "Property Law and Circular Economy" in B. KEIRSBILCK, E. TERRYN, J. EYCKMANS, S. ROUSSEAU and D. VOINOT (eds.), *Servitization and circular economy: economic and legal challenges*, Antwerp, Intersentia, 2023, (181) 198–206 and V. SAGAERT, "De zakenrechtelijke motoren van een circulaire vastgoedeconomie: een SWOT-analyse", *TPR* 2021, (1543) 1549–1554.

3224 The costs of registration vary depending on the value of the goods. See: Act of 11 July 2013 amending the Civil Code as regards collateral security over movable property and repealing various provisions on the subject, *BS* 2 August 2013.

3225 Art. 71 Belgian Pledge Act.

3226 See Royal Decree of 14 September 2017 implementing the articles of title XVII of book III of the Civil Code concerning the use of the National Pledge Register, *BS* 26 September 2017.

3227 Art. 69(3) Belgian Pledge Act.

3228 Explanatory Memorandum, *Parliamentary Papers* Chamber of Representatives 2012–13, no. 2463/009, 2.

supplier would be able to retain ownership by means of a contractual clause in a contract that has a finality to transfer ownership (i.e. sales contracts), while it would not be able to do so in a contract where it is the common intent of the parties that no ownership is transferred (i.e. use contracts).[3229] Second, they refer to the general formulation of Article 69(3) of the Belgian Pledge Act which states that the retention of title is valid and enforceable, regardless of the nature of the contract. Consequently, the retention of title may not only cover the claim arising from a service contract but also allow this security to be granted in respect of a use contract.[3230] Third, they argue that for the transparency in relation to third parties, all necessary guarantees are present in terms of publicity. Indeed, as long as the retention of title is registered in the pledge register, it makes no difference whether the underlying claim arises from a sales contract, service contract or use contract.[3231] As a result, Article 71 of the Belgian Pledge Act can indeed prevent the accession from taking place in use-oriented and result-oriented PSS contract, provided the retention of title has been registered in the pledge register.

808. Registered retention of title gives the PSS supplier a very strong position – Under Belgian law, if the retention of title is registered in the pledge register, this gives the PSS supplier a very strong position. Indeed, even after incorporation, the retention of title takes priority over all other security rights, including mortgage, as soon as it is registered, regardless of the time at which publicity was given to a concurring property right (the so-called "super priority").[3232]

809. Subsidiary pledge as additional safety net – If the parties to the PSS contract have included a retention of title clause in the PSS contract and the nature of the product/service entails that there is a risk of incorporation (and therefore accession), the parties can also include a clause that encumbers the product with a pledge (*pand*, *gage*). This pledge acts as a safety net if, for whatever reason, the retention of title would remain without effect.[3233] It is up to

---

3229 V. Sagaert and K. De Schepper, "Property Law and Circular Economy" in B. Keirsbilck, E. Terryn, J. Eyckmans, S. Rousseau and D. Voinot (eds.), *Servitization and circular economy: economic and legal challenges*, Antwerp, Intersentia, 2023, (181) 202.

3230 V. Sagaert and K. De Schepper, "Property Law and Circular Economy" in B. Keirsbilck, E. Terryn, J. Eyckmans, S. Rousseau and D. Voinot (eds.), *Servitization and circular economy: economic and legal challenges*, Antwerp, Intersentia, 2023, (181) 203.

3231 *Ibid.*

3232 Art. 58(2) Belgian Pledge Act; A. Apers and D. Gruyaert, "Eigendomsvoorbehoud en onroerende incorporatie volgende de nieuwe Pandwet: welk nieuws onder de zon?", *TPR* 2015, (83) 101–104, no. 13.

3233 V. Sagaert and K. De Schepper, "Property Law and Circular Economy" in B. Keirsbilck, E. Terryn, J. Eyckmans, S. Rousseau and D. Voinot (eds.), *Servitization and circular economy: economic and legal challenges*, Antwerp, Intersentia, 2023, (181) 204, no. 25.

the parties to decide whether the costs of registration are worth this additional protection.[3234]

810. DUTCH LAW: RETENTION OF TITLE DOES NOT PROVIDE SOLUTION FOR USE-ORIENTED AND RESULT-ORIENTED PSS – Under Dutch law, the legal device of the retention of title does not provide a solution for use-oriented and result-oriented PSS. First, contrary to Belgian law, the retention of title extinguishes if the good becomes an inherent component of another good.[3235] As a result, the good cannot survive the incorporation and accession will take place. Additionally, the scope of the retention of title is limited to the purchase price and the accessories.[3236] As a result, under Dutch law, other solutions (such as the creation of a building right) will have to be employed by the PSS supplier to protect its right of ownership of the product.

811. EXAMPLES OF RETENTION OF TITLE CLAUSES IN PRACTICE – Most PSS contracts explicitly contain a clause confirming the ownership situation of the product. These clauses generally state that the PSS supplier will remain the owner of the product for the entire duration of the PSS contract. Additionally, they generally also contain a prohibition to dispose of, sell, give in use to third parties or create or grant any security right (e.g. a pledge) for the benefit of third parties. The terms and conditions of *Blue Movement*, *Fairphone Easy*, *Swapfiets* and *Live Light* provide good examples of such clauses.

> TERMS AND CONDITIONS BLUE MOVEMENT – Art. 10.1 "BSH remains the owner of the Product at all times. The Lessee is not permitted to dispose of, sell, give the Product to third parties for use, or establish any security (such as but not limited to a pledge) on the product."

> TERMS AND CONDITIONS FAIRPHONE EASY – "Your As-a-Service Agreement provides You with the right to use Your device for the duration of Your Subscription. The device remains property of Fairphone for the entire duration of the As-a-Service Agreement. You have no right, interest nor claim over the device except as an End-User, nor can you pledge the device to third parties."

> TERMS AND CONDITIONS SWAPFIETS – Art. 4.4 "The Bicycle will at all times remain the property of Swapfiets. The Renter is not allowed to create or grant any security right or other right in respect of the Bicycle for a third party's benefit."

3234 The registration costs range from € 20 to € 500, depending on the value of the secured asset. See: Art. 14 Royal Decree implementing the articles of Title XVII of Book III of the Civil Code, concerning the use of the National Pledge Register, *BS* 26 September 2017.

3235 S.E. BARTELS, A.I.M. VAN MIERLO and H.D. PLOEGER, *Mr. C. Assers Handleiding tot de beoefening van het Nederlands Burgerlijk Recht. 3. Vermogensrecht algemeen. Deel IV. Algemeen goederenrecht*, Deventer, Wolters Kluwer, 2021, no. 66d.

3236 Art. 3:92(2) DCC.

> Terms and conditions Live Light – Art. 4.1 "The Goods remain the property of Live Light at all times. The Goods are only provided by Live Light to the Tenant for rental purposes." 4.2 "The Tenant must refrain from any behaviour that could infringe Live Light's property rights. The tenant may not dispose of, pledge or otherwise encumber them for the benefit of third parties."

The terms and conditions of *Lena* explicitly use the words "retention of title". What is interesting about these terms and conditions, is that the retention of title clause is formulated in a way that the PSS supplier retains the ownership until the PSS user (in the words of the clause: "*Lessee/Buyer*") has paid the total sale price of the items. Indeed, PSS users of this clothing library have the option to buy the clothes they rent as part of the service. As such, this clause largely resembles "traditional" retention of title clauses where the ownership is retained "until" instead of avoiding transfer of ownership altoghether.[3237] Indeed, in this case, the nature of the PSS contract can change from a rental contract to a sales contract if the PSS user decides to exercise the purchase option for the clothes. If this purchase option is exercised, the ownership of the product (i.e. the clothing item) is transferred to the PSS user-buyer.

> Terms and conditions Lena Library – Art. 6 (Retention of Title). Art. 6.1 "The items delivered by LENA remain the property of LENA until the time of payment of the total sale price by the Lessee/Buyer." Art. 6.2 "As long as the delivered items are the property of LENA, it is not allowed to modify them in any way."

The clauses discussed above all have in common that the risk of incorporation of the product is relatively low or even non-existent (Live Light's furniture-as-a-service is perhaps an exception, although incorporation will also in this case be rather rare). In the case of Saman Group, on the other hand, incorporation (and therefore accession) of the heat pump is very much a risk to consider. Here, the terms and conditions also confirm that the heat pump system shall remain the property of the PSS supplier during the rental period, and that the PSS user is prohibited from establishing or allowing any security right on the product. Additionally, it is stated that the heat pump system will not become part of the building of the PSS user. While this retention of title clause provides a useful protection against incorporation and accession of the heat pump, no reference is made to a registration of the retention of title in the pledge register. For the retention of title clause to be enforceable against third parties, this registration will however be necessary.[3238]

> Terms and conditions Saman Group – Art. 6.2 "During the rental period as stipulated in the Rental Contract, the Lessee and Saman Group agree that the Heat

[3237] Compare with *supra* no. 807.

[3238] See *supra* no. 807–808.

Pump System shall remain the property of Saman Group and the Heat Pump System shall not become part of the Dwelling. The Lessee is not allowed to dispose of, (sub) rent, or deposit the Heat Pump System or parts thereof. The Lessee is also prohibited from establishing or allowing any security or limited right to be established thereon." Art. 6.3 "The Lessee only becomes the owner of the Heat Pump System after taking over the Heat Pump System on the basis of conditions set out in Article 12. During the term of the Rental Contract, the Lessee expressly declares not to own the Heat Pump System." Art. 6.4 "If, due to amended legislation, the Heat Pump System becomes or may become the property of the owner of the Dwelling, the Lessee must fully cooperate with Saman Group in order to amend the Rental Contract."

7.2.2.3. Accessory building right/right of superficies

812. ACCESSORY BUILDING RIGHT/RIGHT OF *SUPERFICIES* – In addition to building right and a (registered) retention of title clause, there is a third option to consider if the parties want to avoid incorporation and accession of the product, namely an accessory building right (*accessoir opstalrecht, superficie-conséquence*).[3239] An accessory building right, also called accessory right of *superficies*, is a building right resulting from a personal, property or administrative right of use which a third party acquires over someone's immovable property (e.g. accessory to a rental contract, ground lease, or concession).[3240] It follows the legal regime of the main right and its duration is also the same as this main right.[3241] Under Belgian law, accessory building rights are automatically granted for any structure built under a right of use that contains an authorisation to build.[3242] Under Dutch law, on the other hand, the creation of the accessory building right does not happen automatically but requires an explicit contractual agreement by the parties.[3243]

813. ACCESSORY BUILDING RIGHTS IN PSS CONTRACTS – So how can accessory building rights be used to avoid immovable accession in PSS contracts? This requires a careful drafting of the PSS contract. For example, the clause on ownership in the PSS contract could be drafted so that during the term of the PSS contract, the PSS supplier obtains a (free or inexpensive) right of use (e.g.

3239 V. SAGAERT and K. DE SCHEPPER, "Property Law and Circular Economy" in B. KEIRSBILCK, E. TERRYN, J. EYCKMANS, S. ROUSSEAU and D. VOINOT (eds.), *Servitization and circular economy: economic and legal challenges*, Antwerp, Intersentia, 2023, (181) 206–207.

3240 *Ibid.*

3241 **Belgium**: Art. 3.182 BCC; Cass. (BE) 9 February 1956, *Arr.Cass.* 1956, 470. **The Netherlands**: Art. 5:101(2) DCC; W.H.M. REEHUIS, A.H.T. HEISTERKAMP, G.E. VAN MAANEN and G.T. DE JONG, *Pitlo, Het Nederlands burgerlijk recht, deel 3, Goederenrecht*, Deventer, Wolters Kluwer, 2021, 550, no. 668.

3242 See e.g. N. BERNARD, "Droits d'emphytéose et de superficie" in N. BERNARD (ed.), *Le droit des biens réformé*, Brussels, Larcier, 2021, (235) 289; S. BOULY, *Onroerende natrekking en horizontale eigendomssplitsingen*, Antwerp, Intersentia, 2015, 319, no. 268.

3243 See e.g. T.E. BOOMS, "De oorsprong der soorten en het afhankelijke opstalrecht", *WPNR* 2015/7075, (757) 763.

a loan or inexpensive rental contract) of (part of) the PSS user's immovable property to place the product (of which he retains the ownership), and which he then in turn rents to the PSS user.[3244] To make things more specific, the PSS supplier could conclude a loan contract with the PSS user granting the former a free right of use of parts of the PSS user's home. Based on this free use contract, the PSS supplier can then install the product, for example a heat pump, on the PSS user's premises while retaining the ownership (this can even be combined with a retention of title clause[3245]). Then, the PSS supplier rents that heat pump to the PSS user, who has a right of use during the term of the PSS contract. The PSS supplier's right of ownership then arises from the accessory building right, which follows from the use contract (under Belgian law, automatically; under Dutch law, if contractually agreed).

814. Limitations to accessory building rights – Also in the case of accessory building rights there are however limitations, mainly because accessory building rights are also subject to the unitary principle.[3246] This means that also in the case of an accessory building right, the product must be sufficiently independent.[3247, 3248]

7.2.3. OTHER RISKS OF LOSS OF OWNERSHIP

815. Most products offered in the PSS contracts analysed remain movable (no accession), yet other risks of loss of ownership – In most of the PSS contracts analysed, the risk of accession of the product is rather low. Indeed, in the case of smartphones, bicycles, clothes, but also washing machines and furniture, these products are generally not incorporated in or joined with the PSS user's home. As a result, they remain movable and no immovable accession takes place.[3249] Nevertheless, the PSS supplier still risks losing the ownership of the product in some cases, particularly because it loses the physical possession of the product. First, there is the risk that the PSS user will pretend that he owns the product anyway and sell it, either separately or as part of his property (e.g. sale of a house including contents such as furniture and washing

---

3244 V. Sagaert and K. De Schepper, "Property Law and Circular Economy" in B. Keirsbilck, E. Terryn, J. Eyckmans, S. Rousseau and D. Voinot (eds.), *Servitization and circular economy: economic and legal challenges*, Antwerp, Intersentia, 2023, (181) 207.

3245 V. Sagaert, "De zakenrechtelijke motoren van een circulaire vastgoedeconomie: een SWOT-analyse", *TPR* 2021, (1543) 1555, no. 18.

3246 V. Sagaert, *Goederenrecht*, Mechelen, Wolters Kluwer, 2021, no. 1093.

3247 See *supra* no. 805.

3248 V. Sagaert and K. De Schepper, "Property Law and Circular Economy" in B. Keirsbilck, E. Terryn, J. Eyckmans, S. Rousseau and D. Voinot (eds.), *Servitization and circular economy: economic and legal challenges*, Antwerp, Intersentia, 2023, (181) 207–208.

3249 B. Verheye, "Toekomst van de circulaire vastgoedeconomie", *TPR* 2019, (107) 181, no. 48.

machine). Second, there is the risk of insolvency of the PSS user, where there is a risk that third-party creditors may seize the product.

816. First risk: PSS user sells the product – A first risk entails that the PSS user sells or otherwise disposes of the product, even though this is against the nature of the PSS contract (as rental contract/contract for services) and is often also explicitly prohibited in the terms and conditions of the PSS contract.[3250] In other words, the PSS supplier faces the risk that the PSS user sells the product to a third party, who assumes that the PSS user owns the product and thus has power of disposition.

Under Belgian law, this situation is governed by Article 3.28 BCC,[3251] which provides a special rule of acquisitive prescription (*verkrijgende verjaring, prescription acquisitive*) protecting the third-party acquirer of a movable good against the lack of power of disposition of his legal predecessor, provided that certain requirements are met.[3252] For this special protection rule to apply, this requires: (i) the possessor has acquired the movable good for consideration; (ii) the possessor is acting in good faith; good faith is however presumed[3253]; and (iii) the possession must be undisturbed and unambiguous; this is also presumed.[3254, 3255] If these requirements are met, the third party acquirer of the movable good (i.e. the third party who bought the product of the PSS user) is considered the owner, either immediately – if the true owner (i.e. PSS supplier) has voluntarily placed the good in the detention of the seller (i.e. PSS user) – or, if the true owner (i.e. PSS supplier) involuntarily lost the detention of the product, in the absence of revindication within three years of the loss of possession.[3256] In the case of PSS contracts, the first situation will always apply.[3257]

Under Dutch law, a similar solution to this situation applies. Indeed, Article 3:86(1) DCC protects the third-party acquirer a of movable good (that is not a register good) against the lack of power of disposition of the seller (i.e. the PSS user) if (i) there was a valid delivery; (ii) the third-party acquirer has a valid title; (iii) the third-party acquirer is acting in good faith; and (iv) the transaction was for consideration.[3258] In addition, the third-party acquirer, if requested to

---

3250 See the real-life clauses already discussed *supra* no. 811.

3251 Formerly Art. 2279 old BCC.

3252 See V. Sagaert, *Goederenrecht*, Mechelen, Wolters Kluwer, 2021, 1089, no. 1229 *et seq.*

3253 See Art. 3.22 BCC.

3254 See Art. 3.21 BCC.

3255 Art. 3.28, §1 BCC. See for an in-depth discussion of these requirements: V. Sagaert, *Goederenrecht*, Mechelen, Wolters Kluwer, 2021, 1093–1099, no. 1234–1244.

3256 Art. 3.28, §1 BCC. See for a discussion: V. Sagaert, *Goederenrecht*, Mechelen, Wolters Kluwer, 2021, 1100–1104, no. 1246–1251.

3257 B. Verheye, "Toekomst van de circulaire vastgoedeconomie", *TPR* 2019, (107) 182–183, no. 51.

3258 See on this protection regime for the third-party acquirer of movable goods that are not register goods: H.J. Snijders and E.B. Rank-Berenschot, *Goederenrecht (Studiereeks Burgerlijk Recht)*, Deventer, Wolters Kluwer, 2022, no. 365 *et seq.* and S.E. Bartels, A.I.M. van Mierlo and H.D. Ploeger, *Mr. C. Assers Handleiding tot de beoefening van het*

do so within three years of its acquisition, must give to the original owner of the movable good (i.e. PSS supplier) information necessary to find its legal predecessor (i.e. the PSS user).[3259]

817. PRACTICAL SOLUTION: ENSURING THAT THE THIRD-PARTY ACQUIRER IS NOT CONSIDERED TO BE ACTING IN GOOD FAITH BY PUBLICITY OF OWNERSHIP SITUATION – Under both Belgian and Dutch law, the PSS supplier is thus at risk of losing the ownership of the product to a good faith third-party acquirer. In this case, the PSS supplier will only be left with a contractual claim against the PSS user for restitution based on the PSS contract, instead of the much more advantageous right of ownership (which is a right *in rem*). Nevertheless, the PSS supplier (or other owner of the product such as a leasing company) can mitigate this risk by a relatively simple and practical solution, namely by affixing to the product in a durable and visible way a label or nameplate indicating the ownership situation of the product (e.g. "*property of [PSS supplier] and rented/ provided as-a-service to [PSS user]*").[3260] This will ensure that the third-party acquirer cannot be in good faith, as he will be aware that the PSS user is not the owner and is therefore lacking power of disposition. A real-life example of this practical solution can be found in the terms and conditions of *Swapfiets*, where it is stated that the bicycle may contain advertisements (which is in practice the logo of *Swapfiets*).[3261]

> TERMS AND CONDITIONS SWAPFIETS – Art. 3.6 "The Bicycle may contain advertisements. If the advertisement has been damaged or completely removed from the Bicycle, the Renter should notify Swapfiets immediately."

An example that this solution works in practice can be found in Dutch case law on the crime or receiving stolen goods (*heling*), where it was already ruled that a "Swapfiets" is a recognisable rental bike with a distinctive blue front wheel and the designation of the name "Swapfiets" on the frame. As a result, according to the court, the accused in this case must have reasonably expected that the bicycle was obtained by crime.[3262]

Nederlands Burgerlijk Recht. 3. Vermogensrecht algemeen. Deel IV. Algemeen goederenrecht, Deventer, Wolters Kluwer, 2021, no. 400 *et seq.*

3259 B. VERHEYE, "Toekomst van de circulaire vastgoedeconomie", *TPR* 2019, (107) 184–185, no. 52.

3260 H. SLACHMUYLDERS, B. KEIRSBILCK, E. TERRYN and E. VAN GOOL, "Duurzaam ondernemen en het recht: circulaire bedrijfsmodellen – juridische knelpunten" in *De rol van de bedrijfsjurist in de duurzame ontwikkeling van de onderneming / Le rôle du juriste d'entreprise dans le développement durable: Jaarboek Dag van de bedrijfsjurist 2020/Annuaire Journée du juriste d'entreprise 2020*, Brussels, Larcier, 2021, (7) 33–34, no. 37; B. VERHEYE, "Toekomst van de circulaire vastgoedeconomie", *TPR* 2019, (107) 183.

3261 Compare also with Art. 4.10 Terms and Conditions Swapphone, which contains a similar clause.

3262 Amsterdam (NL) 26 January 2022, ECLI:NL:GHAMS:2022:204, *Rechtspraak.nl*.

818. SECOND RISK: INSOLVENCY OF PSS USER – A second risk relates to the risk of insolvency of the PSS user. Can the PSS supplier revindicate the movable goods from the estate even though the other creditors of the PSS user assume in good faith that these goods belong to the insolvent PSS user? Under Belgian law, the ownership right of the PSS supplier indeed means that it can revindicate the product from the concurrent creditors of the insolvent PSS user.[3263] The concurrent creditors cannot invoke Article 3.28 BCC.[3264] Also under Dutch law, the PSS supplier's right of ownership will allow revindicating the product, without the concurrent creditors being able to assert a right to it.[3265] As a result, the PSS supplier that is confronted with the insolvency of its PSS user should generally not be too concerned that it will lose the non-incorporated product in the insolvency proceedings.[3266] Optionally, to facilitate the revindication, the PSS contract may also stipulate that the PSS user must disclose the ownership situation of the product to the bankruptcy trustee or any other person claiming the surrender of the product. An example of this can be found in the terms and conditions of *Swapphone* and *Live Light*.

> TERMS AND CONDITIONS SWAPPHONE – Art. 5.5 "The Lessee is obliged to immediately notify the person claiming the surrender of the Smartphone or a part thereof, the bankruptcy trustee, the administrator, the seizing bailiff, the lienholder or unspecified third parties of the existence of Swapphone's ownership right and to inform Swapphone within 24 hours in this regard."

> TERMS AND CONDITIONS LIVE LIGHT – Art. 4.3 "The Tenant will immediately notify Live Light in writing if the Goods are seized or any other claim is made on (any part of) them. If the Tenant is aware that the Goods might be seized, it must notify Live Light thereof. If (any part of) the Goods (is) are seized or if the Tenant is subject to (provisional) suspension of payments or bankruptcy, it must immediately notify the bailiff, administrator or receiver executing the seizure about Live Light's property rights."

7.2.4. LEGISLATIVE INTERVENTION NEEDED?

819. SUGGESTIONS FOR PROPERTY LAW REFORMS FALL OUTSIDE THE SCOPE OF THIS BOOK, YET RECENT BELGIAN REFORMS ALREADY PROVIDE SOLUTIONS FACILITATING SERVITISATION AND CIRCULAR BUSINESS MODELS – This brief overview of some of the property law challenges faced by the PSS supplier

3263 Art. XX.194 BCEL. See also Art. XX.196 BCEL, which confirms this principle regarding the depositor of a movable good to an insolvent depositary.

3264 See on Art. 2279–2280 old BCC (now Art. 3.28 BCC): B. VERHEYE, "Toekomst van de circulaire vastgoedeconomie", *TPR* 2019, (107) 185–186, no. 53, and the references cited there.

3265 H.J. SNIJDERS and E.B. RANK-BERENSCHOT, *Goederenrecht (Studiereeks Burgerlijk Recht)*, Deventer, Wolters Kluwer, 2022, 52, no. 68.

3266 B. VERHEYE, "Toekomst van de circulaire vastgoedeconomie", *TPR* 2019, (107) 185–186, no. 53.

demonstrates that property law is not necessarily the greatest facilitator of servitisation and circular business models. At the same time, however, recent developments and reforms in Belgian property law have introduced several tools and solutions allowing to further the idea of servitisation and circularity, in addition to practical solutions that the PSS supplier can employ to protect its ownership right of the product. Indeed, more than under Dutch law, the parties have the possibility to avoid incorporation (and thus accession) of the product, for instance by using a building right, a registered retention of title clause and/or an accessory building right. To complement the contract law analysis of servitised business models and PSS contracts, these solutions were briefly discussed in this chapter, as the issue of ownership is too important not to address. However, the main focus and scope of this book do not allow to make suggestions for property law reforms. Therefore, this is left to further research,[3267] and the book will further focus on the contractual clauses that can be used in the PSS contract to allow the PSS supplier to retain the ownership of the product.

7.2.5. MODEL CLAUSES ON OWNERSHIP OF THE PRODUCT

820. Model clauses on retention of title – The following clauses deal with the PSS supplier's retention of title. The first model clause is a general model clause that can be used for all (use-oriented and result-oriented) PSS contracts, regardless of whether the product is incorporated in the PSS user's immovable property or not. It confirms that the product and all of its parts and accessories remain the property of the PSS supplier or other legal entity (such as a leasing company) and no ownership or other legal title is transferred to the PSS user. The second model clause confirms that the PSS user is not allowed to dispose of, (sub)rent or deposit the product and its parts and accessories, nor establishing a security right or limited right on the product. Model clause three and four deal with the issue of incorporation of the product. The third model clause stipulates that the product remains property of the PSS supplier and shall not become part of the PSS user's immovable property. This clause is mainly useful in PSS contracts where incorporation is not necessary, but also not inconceivable (e.g. washing machines or furniture that can be built in or fixed in place). The fourth model clause is useful for products that are generally incorporated in the PSS user's immovable property, such as a heat pump or ventilation system. It confirms that no accession shall take place as a result of this incorporation.

3267 See, for Belgian property law, for example the research project of Kato De Schepper on "The unitary principle in property law: an enemy to the circular economy?" ("*Het eenheidsbeginsel in het goederenrecht: een vijand voor de circulaire economie?*"). For Dutch property law, see the research project by Ellen Maathuis at the Radboud University Nijmegen.

Model clause #58 – retention of title

- **The product and all of its parts and accessories[, such as instruction manuals, batteries, keys, etc.] remain the property of [the PSS supplier/other identified legal entity (e.g. leasing company if the PSS supplier is not the owner of the product)] and no ownership or other legal title to the product will be transferred to [the PSS user].[3268]**
- **[The PSS user] is not allowed to dispose of, (sub)rent, or deposit the product and all of its parts or accessories. [The PSS user] is also prohibited from establishing or allowing to establish any security or limited right on the product.**
- **During the term of the contract, [the PSS user] and [PSS supplier] agree that the product shall remain the property of [the PSS Supplier/other identified legal entity (e.g. leasing company if the PSS supplier is not the owner of the product)] and that the product shall not become part of the [PSS user's] immovable property.**
- **No accession shall take place if the product is incorporated in the immovable good of [the PSS user] or installed above, on, or below the land of [the PSS user]. The product and all of its parts and accessories remain the property of [the PSS supplier/other identified legal entity (e.g. leasing company if the PSS supplier is not the owner of the product)].[3269]**

Finally, the last model clause on the retention of title deals with the registration of the retention of title in the pledge register. This registration gives publicity to the retention of title and constitutes a requirement for the enforceability of this retention of title clause against third parties. If there is a risk of incorporation of the product, this is necessary to safeguard the ownership right of the PSS supplier. The parties to the PSS contract can define in their PSS contract who is responsible for this registration and who bears the costs of registration.

Model clause #59 – registration of the retention of title in the pledge register

- **[The PSS supplier/PSS user] registers the retention of title in the pledge register at the General Administration of Patrimonial Documentation. The costs of this registration are borne by [the PSS supplier/the PSS user].[3270]**

3268 Model clause based on C. Borucki, H. Slachmuylders, B. Keirsbilck, D. Gruyaert and E. Terryn, *Model clauses for Product-as-a-Service (PaaS) contracts*, CE Center. Circular Economy Policy Research Center, 2022–23, 68.

3269 Model clause based on C. Borucki, H. Slachmuylders, B. Keirsbilck, D. Gruyaert and E. Terryn, *Model clauses for Product-as-a-Service (PaaS) contracts*, CE Center. Circular Economy Policy Research Center, 2022–23, 69.

3270 Model clause based on C. Borucki, H. Slachmuylders, B. Keirsbilck, D. Gruyaert and E. Terryn, *Model clauses for Product-as-a-Service (PaaS) contracts*, CE Center. Circular Economy Policy Research Center, 2022–23, 68.

821. Model clause on subsidiary pledge – If the parties have included a retention of title clause in the PSS contract and the nature of the service entails that there is a risk of incorporation (e.g. in the case of a heat pump or ventilation system), the parties can also choose to include a clause that encumbers the product with a (subsidiary) pledge as additional protection.[3271] The following model clause can be used to this end, provided the parties decide the costs of the registration of the pledge is worth the additional protection.

Model clause #60 – subsidiary pledge

- **To the extent that the retention of title clause stipulated in Art. [XXX] is without effect, the product is encumbered with a pledge. This pledge is registered in the pledge register at the General Administration of Patrimonial Documentation by [the PSS supplier/PSS user]. [The PSS supplier/PSS user] bears the costs of this registration.**[3272]

822. Model clause on accessory building right – For products that are incorporated in the PSS user's home, an accessory building right is one of the possible solutions to avoid immovable accession.[3273] An example of how such an accessory building right may be formulated in the PSS contract can be found in model clause #61.

Model clause #61 – accessory building right

- **[The PSS supplier] and [the PSS user] agree that [the PSS supplier] receives a right of use on the parts of the immovable property of the [PSS user] where the product is [installed/placed/incorporated]. To this end, [a loan contract/a rental contract for the price of €XXX] is concluded between [the PSS supplier] and [the PSS user]. Pursuant to the accessory building right to this [loan contract/rental contract], the [PSS supplier] shall, during the term of the contract, retain the ownership of the product [installed/incorporated/placed] in the PSS user's immovable property.**

In a second step, the product is then made available to the PSS user based on a rental contract or contract for services. Model clauses on the PSS supplier's obligation to make the product available were already set out above.[3274]

3271 See *supra* no. 809.

3272 Model clause based on C. Borucki, H. Slachmuylders, B. Keirsbilck, D. Gruyaert and E. Terryn, *Model clauses for Product-as-a-Service (PaaS) contracts*, CE Center. Circular Economy Policy Research Center, 2022–23, 69. See also: V. Sagaert and K. De Schepper, "Property Law and Circular Economy" in B. Keirsbilck, E. Terryn, J. Eyckmans, S. Rousseau and D. Voinot (eds.), *Servitization and circular economy: economic and legal challenges*, Antwerp, Intersentia, 2023, (181) 204, no. 25.

3273 See *supra* no. 812–813.

3274 See *supra* section 4.5.

823. Model clause on applying label/publicity on the product – To protect the product against acquisitive prescription by a good faith third-party acquirer, the parties can agree in the PSS contract that the PSS supplier has the right to affix a name tag or label to give publicity to the ownership status of the product. Such a clause may be formulated as set out hereinafter.

> **Model clause #62 – publicity of ownership situation**
>
> - **[The PSS supplier] has the right to apply [(e.g. a label, name tag, publicity, advertisements, etc.)] on the product that informs its reader that the product is the property of [the PSS supplier/ other identified legal entity (e.g. leasing company if the PSS supplier is not the owner of the product]. This [label/name tag/etc.] does not affect the functionality of the product. [The PSS user] is not allowed to remove, deface or alter the [label/name tag/etc.)]. If the [label/name tag/etc.] has been damaged or completely removed from the product, [the PSS user] shall notify [the PSS supplier] immediately.**[3275]

824. Model clause on compensation for loss of ownership – The parties may also include a compensation clause in the PSS contract for the situation where, despite the protective measures (e.g. registered retention of title clause, accessory building right, publicity on the ownership of the product, etc.), the PSS supplier still loses the right to revindicate the product or is unable to exercise this right effectively. To avoid that the risk of *force majeure* is placed on the PSS user,[3276] the following model clause limits this compensation obligation to situations where the right to revindicate the product is caused by imputable behaviour of the PSS user. As it may be considered an indemnity clause, it is advisable to also include a reciprocal indemnity clause to the benefit of the consumer.[3277]

> **Model clause #63 – compensation for loss of ownership**
>
> - **If [the PSS supplier] loses the right to revindicate the product or is unable to exercise this right effectively because of the imputable behaviour of [the PSS user], [the PSS user] is liable to pay compensation for the loss of ownership equal to the value of the product at the time of loss of the right to revindicate.**[3278]

3275 Model clause based on C. Borucki, H. Slachmuylders, B. Keirsbilck, D. Gruyaert and E. Terryn, *Model clauses for Product-as-a-Service (PaaS) contracts*, CE Center. Circular Economy Policy Research Center, 2022–23, 71 and Art. 3.6 Terms and Conditions Swapfiets, discussed *supra* no. 817.

3276 Compare with *supra* no. 291 and 440.

3277 See *supra* no. 304.

3278 Model clause based on C. Borucki, H. Slachmuylders, B. Keirsbilck, D. Gruyaert and E. Terryn, *Model clauses for Product-as-a-Service (PaaS) contracts*, CE Center. Circular Economy Policy Research Center, 2022–23, 70.

7.3. MORAL HAZARD

825. Risk of moral hazard and solutions to mitigate this risk – As was already explained above,[3279] PSS contracts come with a risk of moral hazard.[3280] This is the risk that PSS users may behave less diligently and treat the product less carefully because they do not own it.[3281] Or, in other words: "*don't be gentle, it's a rental.*"[3282] This may result in increased wear and tear, decreased product lifespan and potential conflicts between the PSS supplier and the PSS user regarding liability for damages. Additionally, this risk of moral hazard may lead to rebound effects of PSS,[3283] causing PSS to have a limited or even negative effect on environmental sustainability.[3284] This section discusses various solutions PSS suppliers can use to mitigate the risk of moral hazard.[3285] First, PSS suppliers can include an obligation to take care of the product in the PSS contract (section 7.3.1). Second, the possibility to impose limits to moving the product to ensure its safety is discussed (section 7.3.2). Finally, this section looks at incentives and "bonusses" the PSS supplier may offer to PSS users if they make proper use of the product (section 7.3.3).

7.3.1. OBLIGATION OF THE PSS USER TO TAKE CARE OF THE PRODUCT

826. Obligation to take care of the product – A first solution to limit the risk of moral hazard is to include a provision in the PSS contract that

3279 See *supra* no. 31.

3280 H. Gebauer, C. Saul and S. Joncourt, "Use-oriented product service systems in the early industry life cycle", *Ekonomiaz* 2016, vol. 89, (194) 212 and 218.

3281 See on customer misbehaviour in service contracts and renting contracts: T. Schaefers, K. Wittkowski, S. Benoit and R. Ferraro, "Contagious Effects of Customer Misbehavior in Access-Based Services", *Journal of Service Research* 2015, vol. 19, afl. 1, (3) 3–21 and J.F. Durgee and G.C. O'Connor, "An exploration into renting as consumption behavior", *Psychology & Marketing* 1995, vol. 12, afl. 2, (89) 89–104.

3282 Phrase often used in internet memes or in urban slang. See: www.urbandictionary.com/define.php?term=Don%27t%20be%20gentle%2C%20It%27s%20a%20rental.

3283 European Environment Agency, *EAA Report 2017/6 Circular by Design – Products in the Circular Economy*, Luxembourg, EU Publications Office, 2017, 18–19; European Environment Agency, *EAA Report 2016/2 Circular by design – Products in the circular economy*, Luxembourg, EU Publications Office, 2016, 15–16. H. Herring and R. Roy, "Technological innovation, energy efficient design, and the rebound effect", *Technovation* 2007, vol. 27, afl. 4, (194) 194; E.G. Hertwich, "Consumption and the rebound effect: An industrial ecology perspective", *J. Ind. Ecol.* 2005, vol. 9, afl. 1–2, (85) 85; B. Jansen, M. Van Lieshout, M. Scheppers and R. Servaes, *Producten worden diensten: een duurzame waardepropositie voor Vlaanderen*, Mechelen, OVAM, 2010, 108. See for a study of the "rebound effects" of car-sharing in Flanders also: D.A. Chapman, J. Eyckmans and K. Van Acker, "Does Car-Sharing Reduce Car-Use? An Impact Evaluation of Car-Sharing in Flanders, Belgium", *Sustainability* 2020, vol. 12, afl. 19, 8155.

3284 See *supra* no. 36.

3285 Moreover, solutions to reduce the risk of moral hazard have already been touched upon a few times above in the context of other obligations. See, for example, no. 400, 738, § and 755.

obligates the PSS user to use the product with due care. This section will first discuss this obligation for the three main types of PSS contracts, by looking at the applicable legal framework and by analysing real-life PSS contracts. Then, it will examine whether legislative intervention on the obligation to take care of the product is needed. Finally, it sets out model clauses which can be used in to include an obligation to take care of the product in prospective PSS contracts.

7.3.1.1. Product-oriented PSS: no explicit obligation to take care of the product

827. PSS USER-BUYER IS OWNER OF THE PRODUCT: IN PRINCIPLE NO OBLIGATION TO TAKE CARE OF THE PRODUCT – For product-oriented PSS, the obligation to take care of the product does at first sight not really come into play, as the PSS user-buyer is the owner of the product. This means that the consequences of the PSS user-buyer's failure to treat the product with due care will in principle only be borne by the PSS user-buyer himself. For this reason, the (consumer) sales rules do not contain a specific legal obligation to take care of the purchased good. Nevertheless, the duty to take care of the product is not entirely absent in product-oriented PSS contracts. Indeed, in the first place, the PSS user-buyer will not be able to invoke the PSS supplier-seller's liability for lack of conformity of the product if the damage to the product was caused by the fault of the PSS user-buyer.[3286] Additionally, the maintenance component of the product-oriented PSS contract may contain limits on the free maintenance or repair of the product if the defects were caused by the careless use of the product by the PSS user-buyer.[3287] As a result, while the (consumer) sales rules contain no legal obligation to take care of the product in product-oriented PSS, in practice the PSS user-buyer will have every interest in taking good care of the product. This is either because he will otherwise bear the costs of repairing the damage or replacing the product, or because a contractual obligation in the product-oriented PSS contract requires a certain standard of care to benefit from the additional services.

7.3.1.2. Use-oriented PSS: obligation to take care of the product as a prudent and reasonable person/good lessee

828. QUALIFICATION AS A RENTAL CONTRACT IMPLIES OBLIGATION FOR THE PSS USER TO TAKE CARE OF THE PRODUCT AS A PRUDENT AND REASONABLE PERSON/GOOD LESSEE – For use-oriented PSS qualifying as a rental contract, the second main obligation of the PSS user, besides paying the price, is to take

---

3286 Indeed, this conflicts with the requirement that the lack of conformity must exists at the time of delivery of the product. See *supra* no. 466.

3287 See *supra* no. 737.

care of the rented product as a prudent and reasonable person/a good lessee.[3288] Thus, unlike the sales contract, the legal rules governing rental contracts do contain an explicit (but non-mandatory) obligation to take care of the rented good. the legal rules governing rental contracts do contain an explicit obligation This is based on the idea that the lessee must return the good, to which he only has a temporary right, to the lessor at the end of the rental contract.[3289] Given the wording of this obligation, it is clear that it qualifies as an obligation of means.[3290] Nevertheless, this obligation can be enhanced by using a more stringent criterion or formulation in the PSS contract.

829. Making the abstract criterion more concrete – The abstract criterion of the prudent and reasonable person/good lessee can be further developed and clarified in the PSS contract to make it more concrete.[3291] For example, the PSS supplier may refer to the user manual or provide information sheets explaining the correct use of the product (and requiring that the consumer reads and signs the user manual or information sheets). For example, the *Papillon* project uses a "washing machine proof of use" (*"Gebruiksbewijs wasmachine"*) document, which provides clear and transparent instructions on maintenance, daily use, tips for low-cost use and information on what to do in the event of problems. This document must be signed by the consumer at the start of the contract.

3288 **Belgium**: Art. 1728, 1° old BCC. This provision uses the term "good family father" (*goede huisvader/bon père de famille*, derived from the Latin term *bonus pater familias*). **The Netherlands**: Art. 7:213 DCC, where it is stated that the lessee must behave as a "good lessee".

3289 M. Dambre, "Rechten en verbintenissen van de huurder" in M. Dambre, B. Hubeau and S. Stijns (eds.), *Handboek algemeen huurrecht*, Bruges, Die Keure, 2015, (513) 559–560, no. 134 and 136.

3290 M. Dambre, "Rechten en verbintenissen van de huurder" in M. Dambre, B. Hubeau and S. Stijns (eds.), *Handboek algemeen huurrecht*, Bruges, Die Keure, 2015, (513) 560, no. 135.

3291 H. Slachmuylders, "Movable Servitization. Contractual Liability in the B2C Relationship" in B. Keirsbilck, E. Terryn, J. Eyckmans, S. Rousseau and D. Voinot (eds.), *Servitization and circular economy: economic and legal challenges*, Antwerp, Intersentia, 2023, (135) 153; H. Slachmuylders, "Économie de la fonctionnalité – Le contrat de service: défis juridiques et solutions contractuelles", *Revue Juridique de l'Environnement* 2022, vol. 47, afl. 1, (111) 119.

Figure 10. Information sheet used by the *Papillon* project

WAT DOEN BIJ PROBLEMEN

- Kijk eerst en vooral even in de gebruiksaanwijzing onder het hoofdstuk "Storingen en hoe deze te verhelpen"
- Bij aanduiding van een foutcode "E:...", raadpleeg eerst uw gebruiksaanwijzing voor u een technieker belt.
- BIJ VRAGEN CONTACTEER DE BOSCH CARE LINE 02/475.71.09 met vermelding van de gegevens op de sticker aan de binnenzijde van de deur:

Papillon project

Service

☎: 02 475 71 09

SAMENLEVINGSOPBOUW West-Vlaanderen BOSCH

Ik verklaar hierbij kennis te hebben genomen van de inhoud van dit document en de aanwijzingen daarin opgenomen te zullen respecteren.

Naam: (Handtekening)

Datum:

SAMENLEVINGSOPBOUW West-Vlaanderen BOSCH

Papillon project

GEBRUIKSBEWIJS WASMACHINE
WAN28261FG

VOOR GEBRUIK

- Allereerst, neem de gebruiksaanwijzing bij de hand en lees deze van het begin tot het einde. Bewaar deze gebruiksaanwijzig zorgvuldig.
- Voor de eerste ingebruikname: vergewis u dat de plaatsing correct gebeurd is, d.w.z. stabiliteit van het toestel, elektriciteit, watertoevoer en -afvoer . De aansluitkabel mag niet worden geknikt, gekneld of gewijzigd en mag niet in contact komen met hittebronnen. De transportbeveiligingen moeten verwijderd zijn.
- Plaats het toestel niet in een ruimte waar het kan vriezen.
- Een nieuw toestel dient voor het eerste gebruik gereinigd te worden. Kies hiervoor de wascyclus "Katoen aan 90°C" zonder wasgoed in de trommel. Giet 1 liter water in compartiment II van de wasmiddellade en voeg wat wasmiddel toe. Beperk de hoeveelheid wasmiddel om schuimvorming te voorkomen. Na deze wascyclus is uw toestel gereed voor huishoudelijk gebruik.

KEUZE VAN HET WASMIDDEL

- Er zijn ontzettend veel producten op de markt ! Als algemene regel kunnen we stellen dat poeders aanbevolen zijn voor wassen aan hogere temperaturen en dat vloeibare wasmiddelen het best zijn voor wassen aan lagere temperaturen.
- Correct doseren is heel belangrijk !!! Hou bij het doseren rekening met o.a. het gekozen programma, de temperatuur, de belading, de vuiltegraad, de hardheid van het leidingwater ..... EN de instructies van de wasmiddelfabrikant op de verpakking van hun producten.
- De wasmiddellade bestaat uit 3 compartimenten:
  I = te vullen bij voorwas
  II = hoofdwas
  ❀ = wasverzachter (max.niet overschrijden)

SAMENLEVINGSOPBOUW West-Vlaanderen BOSCH

DAGELIJKS GEBRUIK

Voorbereiden van het wasgoed

- Controleer de inhoud van vb. broekzakken , zorg ervoor dat er geen metalen voorwerpen (vb.paperclips) in het wasgoed blijven. Was fijn textiel (vb. panties, beugel-bh's) in een waszakje.
- Verwijder gordijnhaken. Sluit ritsen. Knoop knopen van overtrekken dicht.

Sorteren van wasgoed

- Sorteer uw was volgens de instructies en specificaties op de textiel-labels.
- Kies in functie hiervan het programma en de temperatuur.
- Overschrijd de maximale beladingscapaciteit niet. Te veel wasgoed heeft een negatieve invloed op het wasresultaat.
- Was textiel van verschillende grootte door elkaar. Stukken wasgoed van verschillende groottes verdelen zich beter tijdens het droogzwieren. Afzonderlijke stukken wasgoed kunnen leiden tot een onevenwichtige belading. (waardoor er eventueel niet gedroogzwierd wordt).

Programma kiezen

- U kan de standaardinstellingen gebruiken of deze wijzigen. Raadpleeg de wastabel in de gebruikshandleiding en of programmakaart.
- Eventueel kan u nog voor extra programma-instellingen opteren (vb. Speed / Eco – Extra water / Anti-kreuk ......).
- Met de optie "Eco" wast u energiezuinig (de wastijd wordt wel automatisch verlengd).

SAMENLEVINGSOPBOUW West-Vlaanderen BOSCH

TIPS VOOR GOEDKOOP GEBRUIK

- Steek niet te veel in de wasmachine - respecteer de maximumkilo's (7 kg voor witte was – 2 k g voor fijne was).
- Zorg ervoor dat er geen metalen voorwerpen -zoals munten, haarspeldjes- in het wasgoed blijven (tip: controleer ook broekzakken).
- Sluit alle ritsen en knopen.
- Verwijder gordijnhaken.
- Was fijn textiel (= panty's, beugel-bh's) in een waszakje.
- Gebruik de juiste dosis wasmiddel (poeder/vloeibaar) rekening houdend met: hoeveelheid en soort wasgoed, vuiltegraad, waterhardheid van het leidingwater en de aanbevelingen op de verpakking van de wasmiddelen.
- Als je dag- en nachttarief hebt: probeer je wasmachine zoveel mogelijk te laten starten tijdens het nachttarief ('s avonds en op zaterdag en zondag, geen feestdagen). Gebruik hiervoor de starttijduitstelling.
- Gebruik het programma met de pijl voor witte/bonte was: dit is het zuinigste programma (ook al duurt dit programma wat langer dan andere mogelijke programma's).

TIPS VOOR ONDERHOUD

- Uw wasmachine onderhouden is een kwestie van regelmatig nazicht en gebruik zoals een "goede huisvader". Deur en korven evenals de flexibele elementen dienen steeds met zorg te worden geopend, uitgetrokken of verplaatst te worden.
- Laat na gebruik van de wasmachine de wasmiddellade en de vuldeur open.
- Houd het toestel netjes:
  - ✔ Reinig regelmatig met een vochtig doek de rubberen deurdichting
  - ✔ Spoel regelmatig de wasmiddellade schoon
- Laat om de 2-3 maanden de wasmachine draaien aan 90°C ZONDER wasgoed. Gebruik geen bleekmiddelen.
- Controleer regelmatig de pomp (een achtergebleven muntstukje, knoop ....zouden de afvoerpomp kunnen verstoppen).
- Ontkalken is enkel nodig indien men niet de juiste hoeveelheid wasmiddel gebruikt.

SAMENLEVINGSOPBOUW West-Vlaanderen BOSCH

SAMENLEVINGSOPBOUW West-Vlaanderen BOSCH

These instructions for correct use the product or the service can provide guidance to determine whether a PSS user has not acted as a prudent and reasonable person in fulfilling his obligations under the PSS contract.

830. Additional use of information sheets and user manuals: information about sustainable use of the product – In the light of the transition to a circular economy, these information sheets and user manuals may also have an additional use. Indeed, they can also be used to inform the PSS user on how to use the product or service in the most sustainable and economical way. Optionally, apps could also be used to allow consumers to keep track of their consumption and usage and thus help them make the greenest and most sustainable choice. However, when relying on usage data to influence the behaviour of the consumer, possible disadvantages for the consumer should also be considered. For example, the consumer's right to privacy must be sufficiently guaranteed and he must be protected from undue influence.[3292] At the very least, consumers must be made aware that sustainability objectives are taken into account when their behaviour is being steered.

831. Taking necessary precautions against theft or loss of the product – The care of a prudent and reasonable person also implies that the PSS user must take the necessary precautions against theft, especially if the product is used outdoors (as is the case with bicycles or other micro-mobility products). To this end, the PSS contract may require that the PSS user must lock the product and must be able to present the key to the lock if the product is stolen despite these preventive anti-theft measures. An example of such a clause can be found in the terms and conditions of *Swapfiets* and *Villo.*

> Terms and conditions Swapfiets – Art. 7.3 "In order to prevent incidents such as loss, theft and damage, the Bicycle must always be double locked with the provided ring lock and chain lock. Where possible, the Bicycle must be secured to an object using the chain lock. In addition, when connected to the Bicycle, the battery must always be secured with the provided lock." Art. 7.2 "If the Customer does not, or not in good time, report a loss or theft of the Bicycle, or if the Customer cannot hand over the Bicycle key to Swapfiets, the Customer will owe the compensation established in Table 1."

> Terms and conditions Villo – Art. 7.3 "The user watches over the bicycle he has taken and undertakes to do everything possible to prevent its disappearance,

[3292] See in this sense: B.B. Duivenvoorde, "Datagedreven marketing en de toekomst van het consumentenrecht: tijd voor een nieuwe beschermingsgedachte?", *TvC* 2021, (203) 202–203, with reference to N. Helberger, O. Lynskey, H.-W. Micklitz, P. Rott, M. Sax and J. Strycharz, *EU Consumer Protection 2.0. Structural asymmetries in digital consumer markets*, Brussels, BEUC, 2021, 207 p. See also: V. Mak, "Gedachten bij een gepersonaliseerd consumentenrecht", *TvC* 2018, (274) 274–276.

including the obligation to systematically lock the anti-theft system as soon as he interrupts the use of the bicycle in order to secure it."

832. Using the accessories provided by the PSS supplier – Another way in which the abstract criterion of the prudent and reasonable person can be made more concrete is by stipulating in the contract that the PSS user must use the product with the accessories provided by the PSS supplier. For example, the terms and conditions of *Fairphone Easy* and *Swapphone* require the PSS user to use the smartphone with a protective case and a screen protector to avoid damage to the product.

Terms and conditions Fairphone Easy – Art. 4.7 "To prevent damage, You are required to use the back cover protector and the standard screen protector during the term of the As-a-Service Agreement on Your Fairphone device."

Terms and conditions Swapphone – Art. 4.8 "To prevent damage(s) to the Smartphone, it comes with a protection case and Nano screen protector. Lessee is obliged to have and keep the protection case and Nano screen protection on the Smartphone for the duration of the Rental Contract. If the protection case and/or Nano screen is broken or damaged so that the Smartphone is not or no longer sufficiently protected, Lessee is obliged to replace the protection case or Nano screen at his own expense. If damage occurs to the Smartphone during the Rental Contract, which damage could not occur if the protection case and Nano screen protection were (carefully) used, the full repair costs will be for the Lessee's account, in which case these costs will be at most equal to the device values as mentioned in Table 1."

833. Obligation to use the rented product in accordance with its purpose – Besides the obligation to take the care of a prudent and reasonable person/good lessee, the rental contract rules also require the PSS user to use the rented product in accordance with its purpose (*bestemming, destination*).[3293] In the context of the rental of movables, this means that the PSS user must only use the product as contractually agreed. This may for example mean for personal use and not for commercial purposes, see for example the terms and conditions of *Blue Movement* and *Swapfiets* cited below. *Cambio* has even more limitations on the authorised use of the vehicles. Additionally, it means that the PSS user may not alter or change the appearance and composition of the product.[3294]

Terms and conditions Blue Movement – Art. 8.2 "The lessee may only use the Product for (its own) private use and not, without prior consent of BSH, for any business of commercial use."

3293 **Belgium**: Art. 1728, 1° old BCC. **The Netherlands**: Art. 7:214 DCC.

3294 **Belgium**: M. Dambre, "Rechten en verbintenissen van de huurder" in M. Dambre, B. Hubeau and S. Stijns (eds.), *Handboek algemeen huurrecht*, Bruges, Die Keure, 2015, (513) 567–568, no. 156–157. **The Netherlands**: H.J. Rossel and A.H.T. Heisterkamp, *Mr. C. Assers Handleiding tot de beoefening van het Nederlands Burgerlijk Recht. 7. Bijzondere overeenkomsten. Deel II. Huur*, Deventer, Wolters Kluwer, 2021, no. 80.

Terms and conditions Swapfiets – Art. 4.2 "The Bicycle is intended only for personal use by the Renter. The Renter is not allowed to use the Bicycle as an entrepreneur (i.e. using the Bicycle for e.g. the professional delivery of goods is prohibited). [...]."

Terms and conditions Cambio – Art. 3 "It is forbidden to use the vehicles in violation of the applicable insurance conditions. In particular, the vehicles may not be used to participate in motor racing events or to transport highly flammable, toxic or other dangerous substances. Also prohibited is [...] the use of a vehicle to teach a person how to drive unless in a car category specifically provided for that purpose; the use of the vehicle to carry out unlawful acts (even if they are only punishable under the law of the place of the act) and any other use outside the contractually authorised uses. Finally, it is also not allowed to smoke, vape or take animals in a Cambio vehicle, unless in a closed carry basket provided for that purpose.

834. Subletting the product is in principle allowed, unless contractually prohibited – Linked to the issue of using the product in accordance with its purpose, the question arises whether the PSS user may sublet the product or give it in use to a third party. Under both Belgian and Dutch law, this is possible if not prohibited by the PSS contract.[3295] In practice, many PSS contracts, however, contain a contractual prohibition to sublet the product and/or allow third parties to make use of it. For example, the terms and conditions of *Blue Movement* and *Swapphone* explicitly prohibit subletting the product and giving it in use to third parties. The terms and conditions of *Bundles*, on the other hand, prohibit subletting the product but allow third parties to use the product for non-commercial purposes if the PSS user supervises them.

Terms and conditions Blue Movement – Art. 8.4 "The Lessee is not allowed to sublet the Product, give it in use to third parties, [...]."

Terms and conditions Swapphone – Art. 5.3 "[...] The Smartphone is for the personal use of the Lessee only. The Lessee is prohibited from renting out [...] or in any way giving it in use to third parties [...]."

Terms and conditions Bundles – Art. 8.4 "The PSS user is not allowed to sublet the product [...]." Art. 8.3 "The PSS user has the right to allow third parties to use the Product for non-commercial purposes. The PSS user must then, however, supervise the care with which third parties handle the Product and the PSS user remains liable for any damage caused by careless or improper use by third parties."

835. Examples of contract terms on the obligation to take care of the product and use the product in accordance with its purpose – When analysing the terms and conditions used in practice, PSS suppliers are clearly aware of the need to include an obligation to take care of the product and to use

[3295] **Belgium:** Art. 1717(1) old BCC. **The Netherlands:** Art. 7:221 DCC.

the product in accordance with its purpose. Although the wording and content of these clauses differs across PSS offerings (see the various examples cited below), all the PSS contracts analysed contain similar obligations. Indeed, these clauses generally start by confirming the (abstract) obligation for the PSS user to act as a good lessee and/or to take good care of the product. Then, this abstract obligation is made more concrete, for example by referring to the user manual and/or the instructions given by the PSS supplier and/or the manufacturer. Additionally, legal rules can also be relevant in assessing whether the PSS user behaved as a reasonable and careful person. For example, the terms and conditions of *Villo* explicitly refer to the road traffic regulations and *Swapphone* also refers to applicable laws and regulations.[3296] Yet another way to shape this obligation is to stipulate that the PSS user must take appropriate measures to prevent loss and damages. Besides the general and abstract obligation to treat the product as a reasonable and careful person/good lessee, most of these clauses also state that the product must be used for the purpose for which it is intended. This is then often further operationalised by stating that the product may only be used for personal use or that the PSS user may not make any chances to the product.

> Terms and conditions Blue Movement – Art. 8.1 "The Lessee is obliged to behave as a good Lessee, i.e. the Lessee must take good care of the Product. This means that the Lessee will at least keep the Product in good condition and will use and maintain the Product in accordance with the (additional) instructions and manuals given by BSH and that the Lessee will not use the Product in a way that the Lessee knows or should reasonably know is inappropriate. The Lessee shall secure the Product against damage and/or theft, shall not make any changes to it and shall limit any damage as much as possible. The Lessee shall not remove any codes or seals."

> Terms and conditions Swapphone – Art. 5.1 "The Lessee is obliged to use the Smartphone carefully, skilfully, diligently and in accordance with applicable laws and regulations and instructions of Swapphone and/or the manufacturer for the purpose for which it is intended. The Lessee shall not use the Smartphone in violation with the above."

> Terms and conditions Live Light – Art. 5.12 "The User must act with due diligence and use the Goods carefully. The User must in any case: a) use the Goods for the purpose for which they are intended, b) keep the Goods in the same condition as when they were put into use, c) take appropriate measures to prevent and limit damage, loss and theft, and d) make no changes to the goods."

> Terms and conditions Lena Library – Art. 3.1 "The Lessee should manage and look after the rented good as a good Lessee." Art. 3.2 "The Lessee shall comply with the washing instructions."

3296 Compare also with Art. 3 Terms and Conditions Cambio cited *supra* no. 833, where reference is made to the fact that the PSS user may not use the vehicle for any unlawful acts.

TERMS AND CONDITIONS SWAPFIETS – Art. 4.1 "The Renter makes normal use and takes due care of the Bicycle, in accordance with the instructions given by Swapfiets." Art. 4.7 "The Renter may not make any changes to the Bicycle that cannot be removed without damaging the Bicycle and is not permitted to manipulate in any way the electronics and/or software of the Bicycle." Art. 7.3 "In order to prevent incidents such as loss, theft or damage, the Bicycle must always be double locked with the provided ring lock and chain lock. When possible, the Bicycle must be secured to an object using the chain lock. In addition, when connected to the Bicycle, the battery must always be secured with the provided lock."

TERMS AND CONDITIONS VILLO – Art. 7.2 "The customer agrees to use the bicycle for personal use, as a prudent, careful and informed person, in accordance with the purpose for which it is designed, and in compliance with the current general terms and conditions and the road traffic regulations."

836. PSS SUPPLIER MAY CHECK WHETHER THE PSS USER COMPLIES WITH THE OBLIGATION TO TAKE CARE OF THE PRODUCT DURING MAINTENANCE OR REPAIR INTERVENTIONS – The obligation to maintain, repair and/or replace the product is relevant in the assessment of whether the PSS user complies with the obligation to take care of the product and use the product in accordance with its purpose. Indeed, whenever a visit or intervention by the PSS supplier takes place, the PSS supplier will be able to control whether the PSS user complies with this obligation. If the PSS user is in breach with the obligation to take care of the product, the PSS supplier may invoke the general contract law remedies, namely suspending its obligations ("enac"), performance of the obligation, termination of the PSS contract (if the breach is sufficiently serious) and/or compensation for damages. Moreover, as already discussed above,[3297] the PSS user's obligation to take care of the product may be linked with the PSS supplier's obligation to maintain and/or repair the product. Indeed, the PSS contract may contain contractual exceptions to free maintenance and repair by the PSS supplier if the PSS user misuses or abuses the product, if he does not comply with the standard of care of a reasonable and careful person, and/or if he does not use the product in accordance with its purpose. An example of this possibility of the PSS supplier to check whether the PSS user complies with the obligation to take care of the product can be found in the terms and conditions of *Swapfiets*. Here, it is stated that the PSS supplier has the right to check the condition of the bicycle, and that the PSS user must cooperate with any necessary servicing or maintenance.

TERMS AND CONDITIONS SWAPFIETS – Art. 8.2 "Swapfiets reserves the right to check the condition of the Bicycle. Customer shall cooperate with any necessary servicing or maintenance, on demand by Swapfiets."

[3297] See *supra* no. 737.

837. Duty to warn/notify and damage control – The obligation to treat the product as a prudent and reasonable person also means that the PSS user has a duty to warn/notify.[3298] This duty to warn/notify entails that the PSS user must inform the PSS supplier of any defects and necessary repairs.[3299] After all, as holder of the product, the PSS user is best placed to monitor the condition of the product and whether repairs are needed. Various PSS contracts, including those of *Saman Group, Swapfiets* and *Blue Movement* confirm this duty to (timely) warn the PSS supplier in the terms and conditions (often also stating a specific term in which this notification of any defects must be done). In addition to informing the PSS supplier of any defects or necessary repairs, the obligation to treat the product as a prudent and reasonable person also entails that the PSS user must take reasonable measures to prevent any damage from deteriorating.

> Terms and conditions Saman Group – Art. 8.4 "The Lessee shall use the Heat Pump System in accordance with its purpose and check its correct operation on a weekly basis and report malfunctions, faults and/or defects to Saman Group within 1 working day."
>
> Terms and conditions Swapfiets – Art. 8.1 "The Renter must report damage to the Bicycle caused by vandalism to Swapfiets within 24 hours."
>
> Terms and conditions Blue Movement – Art. 9.1 "The Lessee shall report any malfunction, defect, fault, theft and/or damage to the Product to BSH if reasonably possible within 5 calendar days after he discovers it or should reasonably have discovered it. The Lessee is liable for damage to the Product and other damage caused by late reporting."[3300]

7.3.1.3. Result-oriented PSS: obligation of the client to cooperate and duty of care accessory deposit contract

838. Obligation to take the care of a good client: duty to cooperate – In result-oriented PSS, the focus is no longer on the specific product, but on the service offered by the PSS supplier. Therefore, the Belgian and Dutch rules on the contract for services do not contain an (explicit) obligation to take care of the product, but rather an obligation to take the care of a good client.[3301] This

---

3298 **Belgium**: M. Dambre, "Rechten en verbintenissen van de huurder" in M. Dambre, B. Hubeau and S. Stijns (eds.), *Handboek algemeen huurrecht*, Bruges, Die Keure, 2015, (513) 564, no. 147. **The Netherlands**: Art. 7:222 DCC; H.J. Rossel and A.H.T. Heisterkamp, *Mr. C. Assers Handleiding tot de beoefening van het Nederlands Burgerlijk Recht. 7. Bijzondere overeenkomsten. Deel II. Huur*, Deventer, Wolters Kluwer, 2021, no. 110.

3299 See also *supra* no. 479, no. 731 and no. 735.

3300 Compare also with Art. 10.3 Terms and Conditions Bundles, which contains a similarly formulated clause.

3301 **Belgium**: W. Goossens, *Aanneming van werk: het gemeenrechtelijk dienstencontract*, Bruges, Die Keure, 2003, 906, no. 979 *et seq.* **The Netherlands**: T.F.E. Tjong Tjin Tai, *Asser 7-IV*

obligation stems from the principle of good faith (under Belgian law) and the requirements of reasonableness and fairness (under Dutch law) and generally entails that the PSS user has an information duty and a duty to cooperate.[3302] In my view, it can also be inferred from this obligation that the PSS user has a duty of care towards the products made available, which are the property of the PSS supplier-service provider. Since the obligation to take the care of a good client is not mandatory law, it can be contractually regulated and further specified, as is the case, for example, in the terms and conditions of *HP Instant Ink*. These terms and conditions stipulate that the PSS user may not misuse the service or otherwise participate in any illegal activities. Similarly, the (B2B) template contract of *Agoria Efficiency-as-a-Service* also contains an obligation for the client to take all due care and attention.

> Terms and conditions HP Instant Ink – Art. 4, sub e) "By using the Service, you hereby declare that: […] e) *You will not misuse the service or otherwise participate in any illegal activity in connection with the service.* You agree that you, and not HP, are responsible for anything printed on your printer while using the service." (own emphasis).

> Template contract Agoria EaaS – Art. 3.1.2.1 "The Client will use the Service Provider equipment for the sole purpose of receiving and/or using the Services, and *will use the Service Provider Equipment in an efficient manner and using all due care and attention.*" Art. 3.1.2.2. "If the Client notices a defect in (a part of) the Service Provider Equipment, *the Client will inform* the Service Provider thereof within the term outlined in Schedule 2, while *taking all reasonable measures to prevent any deterioration of the damage*. Following the receipt of such notification, the Service Provider will carry out the necessary steps in accordance with Schedule 2, so as to ensure that the Service Level Requirements are met at all times" (own emphasis).

839. Accessory deposit contract as part of result-oriented PSS involves duty of care and restitution obligation – As was already discussed above, result-oriented PSS where the product made available is located with the PSS user are often accompanied by an accessory deposit contract, including a contractual provision granting the PSS user a right to use the product.[3303] If the result-oriented PSS contract contains an accessory deposit contract, the PSS user has a duty of care and an obligation to return

---

Bijzondere Overeenkomsten – Opdracht, incl. de geneeskundige behandelingsovereenkomst en de reisovereenkomst, Deventer, Wolters Kluwer, 2022, no. 125.

3302 **Belgium**: W. Goossens, *Aanneming van werk: het gemeenrechtelijk dienstencontract*, Bruges, Die Keure, 2003, 909 and 914 *et seq*. **The Netherlands**: T.F.E. Tjong Tjin Tai, *Asser 7-IV Bijzondere Overeenkomsten – Opdracht, incl. de geneeskundige behandelingsovereenkomst en de reisovereenkomst*, Deventer, Wolters Kluwer, 2022, no. 125.

3303 See *supra* no. 445 and the references cited there.

the product.[3304] The duty of care is an obligation of means where, since the deposit component of the PSS contract is done in the interest of the PSS user, the conduct of the PSS user is tested against the benchmark of a prudent and reasonable person in the same case.[3305] This means that the PSS user must take the necessary precautions against loss or depreciation, either due to an act of a third party (e.g. theft) or external circumstances (e.g. fire or water damage). The obligation to return the product, on the other hand, is an obligation of result.[3306] This means that the PSS user will be liable if he cannot return the product, unless he can prove *force majeure*.[3307] The existence of *force majeure* is assessed in the light of the PSS user's duty of care, in particular whether the PSS user has taken all necessary and reasonable measures to take care of the product.[3308]

840. Obligation to take the care of a good client and duty of care of accessory deposit contract have similar content as duty of care rental contract – When comparing the obligation to take the care of a good client and the duty of care stemming from the accessory deposit contract part of the result-oriented PSS, it is clear that, in essence, the content of the PSS user's obligations regarding the product(s) made available in result-oriented PSS do not really differ from those in use-oriented PSS. Indeed, the PSS user will have an obligation to take care of the product as a prudent and reasonable person, have an obligation to notify the PSS supplier of any defects, and an obligation take all necessary precautions for avoiding that any damage to the product deteriorates. At the end of the contract term, the PSS user will have to return the product in good condition to the PSS supplier. As with use-oriented PSS, PSS suppliers do well to confirm and further specify these obligations in the PSS contract.

3304 **Belgium**: Art. 1915 old BCC; V. Sagaert, B. Tilleman and A.-L. Verbeke, *Vermogensrecht in kort bestek*, Antwerp, Intersentia, 2022, 488–489. **The Netherlands**: Art. 7:600 DCC; A.J. Verheij, "Bewaarneming" in H.N. Schelhaas and A.J. Verheij (eds.), *Bijzondere overeenkomsten in Studiereeks Burgerlijk Recht*, Deventer, Wolters Kluwer, 2023, (417) 422, no. 370; A.C. van Schaick, *Asser 7-VIII Bewaarneming, borgtocht, vaststellingsovereenkomst, bruikleen, altijddurende rente, spel en weddenschap*, Deventer, Wolters Kluwer, 2018, no. 1.

3305 **Belgium**: Art. 1928 old BCC (*culpa levis in abstracto*). Compare with the lower standard of Art. 1927 old BCC which requires the depositary to take care of the goods in the same way as he does for his own goods (*culpa levis in concreto*). **The Netherlands**: Art. 7:602 DCC. N.E. Groeneveld-Tijssens, *Bewaarneming, Mon. BW B73*, Deventer, Wolters Kluwer, 2020, 11, no. 10–11; A.C. van Schaick, *Asser 7-VIII Bewaarneming, borgtocht, vaststellingsovereenkomst, bruikleen, altijddurende rente, spel en weddenschap*, Deventer, Wolters Kluwer, 2018, no. 9–10.

3306 **Belgium**: E.g. Ghent (BE) 27 February 2004, *TWVR* 2004, 197 and Brussels (BE) 4 January 2000, *RGAR* 2001, 13.398. **The Netherlands**: A.J. Verheij, "Bewaarneming" in H.N. Schelhaas and A.J. Verheij (eds.), *Bijzondere overeenkomsten in Studiereeks Burgerlijk Recht*, Deventer, Wolters Kluwer, 2023, (417) 430, no. 376.

3307 **Belgium**: Art. 1929 old BCC. **The Netherlands**: Art. 6:75 DCC. A.J. Verheij, "Bewaarneming" in H.N. Schelhaas and A.J. Verheij (eds.), *Bijzondere overeenkomsten in Studiereeks Burgerlijk Recht*, Deventer, Wolters Kluwer, 2023, (417) 430, no. 376; N.E. Groeneveld-Tijssens, *Bewaarneming, Mon. BW B73*, Deventer, Wolters Kluwer, 2020, 29–30, no. 25.

3308 Cass. (BE) 7 March 2008, *Arr.Cass.* 2008, 651, *Pas.* 2008, 627, *RW* 2011–12, 583.

In practice, there will often not be much difference between the provisions on this obligation found in use-oriented PSS contracts and those found in result-oriented PSS contracts.

7.3.2. CONTRACTUAL LIMITS TO MOVING THE PRODUCT

841. CONTRACTUAL LIMITS OR REQUIREMENTS TO MOVING OR RELOCATING THE PRODUCT – Some PSS contracts contractually limit the PSS user's freedom to move or relocate the product, which can be seen as a contractual specification of the obligation to take care of the product. The idea behind these clauses is that moving or relocating the product entails a risk of damage to the product. This may lead to unforeseen technical issues and support challenges and diminish the quality of the service. Moreover, difficulties can arise regarding the revindication and recovery of the product at the end of the PSS contract if the product was moved or relocated without the PSS supplier's knowledge. To this end, terms in the PSS contract often subject moving or relocating the rented washing machine, coffee maker or other product to prior authorisation or even completely prohibit this. For example, the terms and conditions of *Bundles* provide that the PSS supplier should always be contacted before moving the product. Upon notification, the PSS supplier provides the PSS user with relocation instructions. Alternatively, the PSS user can also request the PSS supplier to perform the relocation of the product against the payment of a relocation fee. In addition to *Bundles*, prior authorisation requirements can also be found in the PSS contracts of *Live Light* and *Papillon*.

> TERMS AND CONDITIONS BUNDLES – Art. 6.6 "If the User wishes to move the Appliance (indoors or outdoors), Bundles should always be contacted. Bundles shall provide the User with relocation instructions. The User shall be liable for any damage arising from such relocation. Bundles can also carry out the relocation for the User and in that case, upon payment of the Relocation Fee, shall (arrange for) the relocation, if reasonably possible, within 5 working days."

> TERMS AND CONDITIONS LIVE LIGHT – Art. 5.11 "The Goods may only be relocated after Live Light gives written consent."

> TERMS AND CONDITIONS PAPILLON – Art. 5.1 "The Appliance is intended only for the use specified in the user manual. The User further undertakes to use the Appliance only for domestic use and *not to move the Appliance, unless otherwise agreed by VZW and BSH.*" (Own emphasis).

Blue Movement, on the other hand, does not require the PSS user to ask for prior authorisation to move or relocate the product. Indeed, according to the terms and conditions of Blue Movement, contacting the PSS supplier is optional (this follows from the wording "*User may contact BSH*" (own emphasis)). If the PSS user however does contact BSH (i.e. the PSS supplier), it will arrange for the relocation of the product free of charge (maximum once per year and provided the PSS user does not terminate the contract within six months of the relocation). If, on the other hand, the PSS user does not contact the PSS supplier, he will be liable for any associated costs and damage caused by this relocation.[3309] As a result, contacting the PSS supplier is the most advantageous option for the PSS user, as the relocation is arranged for him and he bears no risk of liability.

> Terms and conditions Blue Movement – Art. 6.9 "If User moves the Large Domestic Appliance to an address other than the delivery address, User may contact BSH and BSH will arrange for the relocation of the Appliance free of charge if requested, unless User cancels the Contract within six months of relocation. In that case, BSH will charge User a relocation fee of € 150. User can make use of this relocation arrangement maximum once per 12 calendar months."

842. Limits to the locations where the product can be moved – In some cases, moving or relocating the product is limited to one Member State or the locations where the PSS supplier offers its services. Examples of this practice can be found in the terms and conditions of *Blue Movement* and *Live Light*. This makes sense and will therefore, in my view, not be considered unfair by the national courts. The reason is that cross-border transport of the product (especially outside the PSS supplier's operating area) may lead to revindication issues or different national legal rules on the revindication procedure being applicable (with which the PSS supplier will not always be familiar or knowledgeable).

> Terms and conditions Blue Movement – Art. 6.11 "Movement of the Large Domestic Appliance may only take place within the Netherlands."

> Terms and conditions Live Light – Art. 5.11 "The goods may never be moved to a location outside Live Light's service area."

843. (Un)fairness of clauses limiting the PSS user's freedom to move or relocate the product – The question arises whether these clauses limiting the PSS user's freedom to move or relocate the product can be validly used in contracts with consumers. As these terms are not included in any of the Belgian or Dutch blacklists or grey lists, the (un)fairness of these terms must be assessed using the general unfairness test. As explained above, the assessment under the general test starts from the rules that would apply under national default law.[3310] In principle, the Belgian and Dutch rules for the rental contract do not

---

3309 See *infra* no. 844.

3310 See *supra* no. 162. CJEU, Judgment of 14 March 2013, C-415/11, *Mohamed Aziz*, ECLI:EU:C:2013:164.

stand in the way of moving or relocating the product insofar as this is consistent with a prudent and careful use and corresponds to the purpose of the rented product.[3311] Similarly, the Belgian and Dutch rules of the contract for services do not contain any rules on this issue. However, these rules are not mandatory law, so the contractual parties can deviate from them. Considering the legitimate interests of the PSS supplier, namely to maintain the value of the product as possible and facilitate any revindication, it would seem that a prior authorisation to move the product would generally not create a significant imbalance in the parties' rights and obligations to the detriment of the PSS user.[3312] On the other hand, a total ban on moving or relocating the product implies a more far-reaching restriction of the PSS user's rights. After all, the starting point of the rental contract rules is that the PSS user-lessee is free to move the product. As a result, a balancing act will be required taking into account the risk of damage to the product (and revindication issues) and the PSS user's interests. Other clauses of the contract will also be relevant for this balancing exercise, including the sanction for breach of the relocation ban and the question whether the consumer can freely terminate the contract if he moves to a new home.

844. Liability of PSS user for damage caused by (unauthorised) relocation of the product – In line with limits or restrictions to moving the product, PSS contract often explicitly stipulate that the PSS user-consumer is liable for any damage caused by the (unauthorised) relocation. This is, for example, the case in the terms and conditions of *Blue Movement* and *Bundles*. In essence, these clauses cited below confirm the general law of obligations, namely the fact that the PSS supplier can claim compensation for damages if the PSS user does not comply with his obligations and this causes damage to the product or causes additional costs to the PSS supplier. On the other hand, if the clause in the PSS contract contains a fixed amount of compensation to be paid in case of an unauthorised relocation, it is an indemnity clause. In that case, the validity requirements for indemnity clauses must be met, namely that they must not be excessive and, under Belgian law, must be reciprocal.[3313]

> Terms and conditions Blue Movement – Art. 6.10 "If the User moves the Large Domestic Appliance to an address other than the delivery address without the knowledge of BSH, the User shall be liable for associated costs and any damage arising from such relocation."

[3311] **Belgium**: Art. 1728, 1° old BCC; M. Dambre, *Bijzondere overeenkomsten: de essentie*, Bruges, Die Keure, 2022, 227. **The Netherlands**: Art. 7:213 and Art. 7:214 DCC; H.J. Rossel and A.H.T. Heisterkamp, *Mr. C. Assers Handleiding tot de beoefening van het Nederlands Burgerlijk Recht. 7. Bijzondere overeenkomsten. Deel II. Huur*, Deventer, Wolters Kluwer, 2021, no. 71 and 80.

[3312] See in the same sense: B. Keirsbilck, E. Terryn and E. Van Gool, "Consumentenbescherming bij servitisation en product-dienst systemen (PDS)", *TPR* 2019, (817) 850–851.

[3313] See *supra* no. 304.

TERMS AND CONDITIONS BUNDLES – Art. 6.6 "[...] The User shall be liable for any damage arising from such relocation [...]."

7.3.3. INCENTIVES FOR PROPER USE OF THE PRODUCT

845. HOW TO ENFORCE THE OBLIGATION TO TAKE CARE OF THE PRODUCT? – Most PSS contracts thus contain an obligation to take care of the product, which can be further contractually specified depending on the specific business model. The question then arises how this obligation can be enforced. Of course, as always, the general contract law remedies are available to the PSS supplier if the PSS user fails to take due care of the product.[3314] However, this is merely an *ex-post* solution, which is only available when it is actually too late and the product has already been misused or damaged. Consequently, alternative *ex-ante* solutions are needed to encourage the PSS user to take care of the product. This can roughly take two forms: either by means of a deposit, which is a negative protection against moral hazard, or by means of incentives which positively reward the PSS user if he takes good care of the product.

846. DEPOSIT AS (NEGATIVE) PROTECTION AGAINST MORAL HAZARD – As discussed above in the context of the PSS user's obligation to pay the price,[3315] PSS users are often required to pay a deposit, which may be withheld in the event of damage to the product, failure to return the product, or otherwise failing to comply with the terms of the PSS contract. A deposit may not only be required in use-oriented PSS (which qualify as rental contracts) but may also be required in result-oriented PSS contracts where a product is provided to the PSS user-consumer. A deposit can mitigate the risk of moral hazard in a few ways. First, it acts as a form of insurance for the PSS supplier against potential damages, misuse, or non-compliance with the terms of the service. If the PSS supplier does suffer damage due to incorrect or careless use of the product, a deposit makes it easier to recover the costs from the PSS user. Second, the deposit acts as an incentive for the PSS user to use the product or the service responsibly. If the PSS user knows that he can get his deposit back upon complying with the terms and conditions, keeping the product in a good state of repair and returning it to the PSS supplier at the end of the contract, he will be encouraged to treat the product more carefully. In other words, the requirement to pay a deposit causes the PSS user to have "skin in the game". Examples of PSS suppliers requiring the PSS user to pay a deposit are *Bundles* and *Fairphone Easy*.

3314 See *supra* section 2.6.

3315 See *supra* no. 642.

> Terms and conditions Bundles – Art. 4.5 "Client shall pay to Bundles a deposit as specified in the Contract. After termination of the Contract, Bundles will return the deposit to Client within 14 days, provided that all conditions have been met."

> Terms and conditions Fairphone Easy – 4.6 "Fairphone requires payment of the Subscription and a one-time fee of ninety (90) euros as a deposit upon Your order. The deposit will be returned to You within 14 days after you have returned the device to Us upon termination. The deposit will be returned to the same account unless You tell us otherwise. Should You fail to update Your bank account details in a timely manner, this may lead to delays in receiving your deposit. Fairphone reserves the right to deduct an amount of the deposit to resolve any outstanding payments."

847. Including incentives in the PSS contract to positively reward PSS users who treat their product with due care – A second solution for mitigating the risk of moral hazard is including incentives in the PSS contract to positively reward PSS users who treat their product with due care. This may take the form of "bonusses", such as a discount on the next invoice, loyalty points, or a free extension of the maintenance contract.[3316] Other types of incentives or even gifts are also possible. Offering positive incentives may lead to a mutually beneficial relationship where the interests of the PSS supplier, the PSS user and the environment are all aligned. Indeed, the PSS supplier will be confronted with less repair and/or replacements costs, the PSS user gets a reduction or other advantages if he treats the product with due care and the environment is benefitted by the fact that resources must be used to repair or replace the product.

848. Example of positive incentives: Fairphone Easy – The terms and conditions of *Fairphone Easy* contain a good example of clauses providing incentives for the PSS user to take good care of the product. Every year the PSS user keeps his Fairphone smartphone damages free, he receives a discount of 2 euro per month. After 3 years, a bonus discount of 4 euro per month is granted. Of course, it is important that the PSS user is aware of these incentives so that he can take them into account in his behaviour. The PSS supplier of *Fairphone Easy* has thought of this too: these incentives are also explicitly marketed on its website, so also PSS users who do not read the terms and conditions are aware of them (see Figure 11).

> Terms and Conditions Fairphone Easy – Art. 7.2 "Every year in which You remain a user of Fairphone Easy and maintain the device in line with the condition of these Terms, the monthly fee is reduced by two (2) euros. After three (3) years of remaining a user of Fairphone Easy, We will give you a bonus of a four (4) euro reduction."

[3316] C. Borucki, H. Slachmuylders, B. Keirsbilck, D. Gruyaert and E. Terryn, *Model clauses for Product-as-a-Service (PaaS) contracts*, CE Center. Circular Economy Policy Research Center, 2022–23, 54.

Figure 11. Fairphone Easy website highlighting the incentives for proper use of the product[3317]

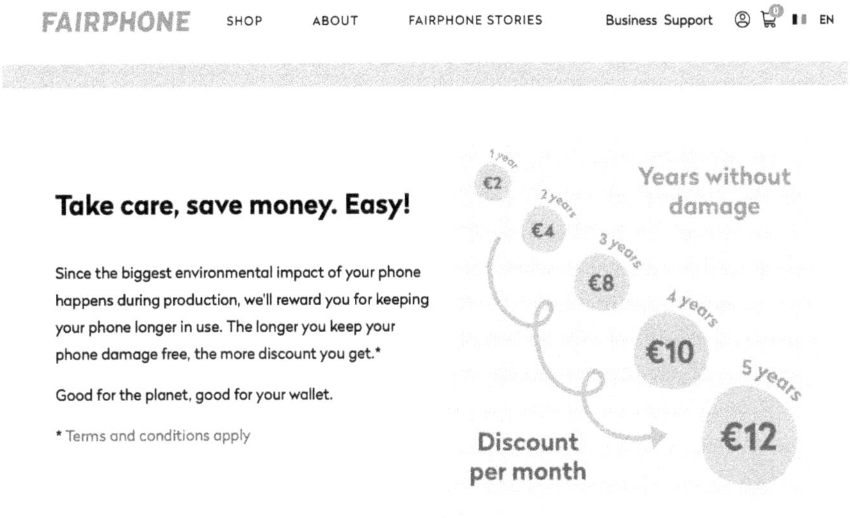

7.3.4. LEGISLATIVE INTERVENTION NEEDED?

849. THREE POSSIBLE SOLUTIONS – Consistent with the legislative proposals discussed above, three solutions can be explored to reduce the risk of moral hazard. These are: (i) the **modernisation of national contract law** (option 1), (ii) incorporating rules to mitigate moral hazard in an **EU directive** (option 2), and (iii) the **use of balanced standard contracts and model clauses** (option 3).[3318] The first two options are examined in this section. The model clauses that can be used to mitigate moral hazard are set out in section 7.3.5.

7.3.4.1. Modernisation of national contract law

A. Use-oriented PSS

850. RENTAL CONTRACT RULES ON OBLIGATION TO TAKE CARE OF THE PRODUCT CONTAIN THE RIGHT PRINCIPLES, BUT ROOM FOR MODERNISATION – When evaluating the rules of the rental contract in the context of the obligation to take care of the product, it is clear that the principles of Article 1728, 1° old BCC are still fit for purpose. Indeed, this provision contains an abstract criterion according to which the PSS user must use the rented good as a "good family

3317 Screenshot taken from: https://shop.fairphone.com/fairphone-easy?ci=BE.
3318 Compare with *supra* section 4.4.1.3, section 6.2.5 and section 6.3.4.

father" (*goede huisvader/bon père de famille*, derived from the Latin term *bonus pater familias*). Its content still holds up today, but the wording should best be changed so that the old-fashioned and non-inclusive language "good family father" is replaced by a more appropriate alternative, namely that of the "prudent and reasonable person" (*voorzichtig en redelijk persoon, personne prudente et raisonnable*). This would have the additional advantage that the wording of the rental contract rules is aligned with the general standard of care found in the general law of obligations, which makes sense from a coherence and consistency perspective.[3319] This translates into the first paragraph of proposed provision #32. Apart from this legal-technical detail, the current rules do provide a clear and balanced framework, while also leaving sufficient contractual freedom to contractually shape this abstract criterion (e.g. through user manuals, instructions, information on correct use of the product and/or by referring to legislation such as the road traffic regulations). Consequently, no substantive changes should be made in this regard. The Draft Law re-codifies this obligation in a similar way as well.[3320]

851. Two sub-obligations of obligation to use the rented good as a prudent and reasonable person – The second paragraph of proposed provision #32 outlines two sub-obligations of the obligation to use the rented good as a prudent and reasonable person. These include (i) respecting the purpose of the rented good and (ii) notifying the lessor of any damage for which the obligation to repair lies with the lessor. This does not constitute a substantive change to the rules of the rental contract, but rather a (re)codification of the principles that also applied under Article 1728, 1° old BCC.[3321, 3322] The Draft Law also requires the lessee to respect the purpose of the rented good, while the duty to notify is not (explicitly) mentioned.[3323]

3319 Compare with Art. 5.72 BCC.

3320 See proposed Art. 7.3.21, §1 BCC.

3321 Compare with *supra* no. 833 (on the obligation to use the product in accordance with its purpose) and *supra* no. 837 (on the lessee's duty to warn/notify the lessor of any damage to the rented good).

3322 In legal doctrine on the old BCC, the use of the rented good as a prudent and reasonable person and the use of the good in accordance with its purpose are regarded as two distinct obligations. The idea is that a use according to the agreed purpose does not necessarily imply a use as a prudent and reasonable person. See e.g. M. Dambre, "Rechten en verbintenissen van de huurder" in M. Dambre, B. Hubeau and S. Stijns (eds.), *Handboek algemeen huurrecht*, Bruges, Die Keure, 2015, (513) 559; Y. Merchiers, *Le bail en général*, Brussels, Larcier, 2015, no. 253. However, the reverse can be argued in my view: if the lessee does not use the rented good according to its purpose, he will also not use the good as a prudent and reasonable person. Hence why reference is already made to the use of the rented good in accordance with its purpose in the context of the obligation to use the rented good as a prudent and reasonable person. In any case, proposed provision #33 also separately addresses the obligation to use the rented good in accordance with its purpose.

3323 See proposed Art. 7.3.21, §1 BCC.

This of course does not mean that the duty to notify is absent under the Draft Law, since it falls under the scope of using the rented good as a prudent and reasonable person (which is included).

> **Proposed provision #32**
>
> **Art. 7.3.X21. Obligation to use the rented good as a prudent and reasonable person**
>
> **§1 The lessee uses the rented good as a prudent and reasonable person.**
>
> **§2 The obligation under §1 includes, but is not limited to:**
>
> **1° using the rented good in accordance with its intended purpose; and**
>
> **2° promptly notifying the lessor of any damage that falls under the lessor's responsibility to repair.**

852. Obligation to use the rented good in accordance with its purpose – The obligation of the lessee to use the rented good in accordance with its purpose laid down in Article 1728, 1° old BCC is also still fit for purpose. It is a sufficiently general provision, which can be further fleshed out in the PSS contract. As a result, this provision may be retained in a modernised special contract law. Paragraph 1 of proposed provision #33 sets out this obligation and adds that the lessee is not allowed to change the purpose of the rented good without the prior consent of the lessor. This confirms the rule that already applies under the old BCC but is not explicitly set out in Article 1728, 1° old BCC. Paragraph 2 of proposed provision #33 deals with the fact that the lessee is not allowed to make changes to the rented good without the prior consent of the lessor. This too already applies under the old BCC but has not been included in the legal text of Article 1728, 1° old BCC. Consequently, this too is a mere codification exercise. An exception is provided for changes made by the lessee that are in accordance with the purpose of the rented good which can be removed without any damage at the end of the rental contract. In the case of immovable goods, this could include, for example, furnishing works or painting work that can be undone at the end of the contract. For movable goods, this could include installing accessories on a bicycle, putting a screen protector on a smartphone, etc. Finally, this paragraph states that the fact that the changes can be removed is not enough; the lessee also has an obligation to effectively undo these changes at the end of the contract. This proposed provision was largely inspired by the Draft Law, namely by proposed Article 7.3.21, §1, (2) and Article 7.3.21, §2 BCC.

Proposed provision #33

Art. 7.3.X22. Obligation to use the rented good in accordance with its purpose

§1 The lessee uses the rented good in accordance with its purpose. The lessee may not alter the purpose without the prior consent of the lessor.

§2 The lessee may not make any alterations to the rented good without the prior consent of the lessor. However, the lessee may make temporary changes that are consistent with the good's purpose and can be removed without causing damage at the end of the rental term. The lessee is required to restore the good to its original condition by undoing such changes upon termination of the rental contract.

853. Contractual limits to moving the rented good and incentives for correct use: no need for legislative intervention – Currently, the old BCC does not contain any provisions on contractual limits on moving the rented good, nor on incentives to positively reward the lessee if he uses the good as a prudent and reasonable person. Indeed, the current premise of the rental contract rules is that the lessee may move the good at his own discretion (as long as it is in accordance with the purpose of the good and in line with the obligation to use the product as a prudent and reasonable person).[3324] Additionally, the lessee's failure to use the product as a prudent and reasonable person is only negatively sanctioned by means of the general contract law remedies but not positively rewarded. In my view, it is also unnecessary to have any legal provisions on contractual limits on moving the rented good or incentives for correct use. After all, the principle of freedom of contract allows the parties to flesh out their own contractual regime on a case-by-case basis, tailored to the specific business model in question. As for contractual clauses that impose (too) far-reaching restrictions to the lessee's freedom to move or relocate the rented good, the general test of the UCTD and its national implementing provisions is, in my view, sufficiently equipped to make a balancing exercise between the rights and obligations of the PSS user and the PSS supplier and, if necessary, to set aside manifestly unbalanced clauses.

B. Result-oriented PSS

854. Taking the care of a good client: duty to cooperate – Besides the obligation to pay the price, the contract for services also entails other obligations for the client, most notably the obligation to take the care of a good client. Paragraph 1 of proposed provision #34 translates this into a general obligation

[3324] See *supra* no. 843.

for the client to cooperate with the service provider. For this, inspiration is taken, amongst others, from Article IV.C. – 2:103 DCFR.[3325] Paragraph 2 of proposed provision #34 then lists four "sub-obligations" of the client's obligation to cooperate with the service provider. First, the client must enable the service provider to perform the obligations under the contract. This is a rather broad obligation which can entail, for example, making available the premises, the materials or the goods necessary for the performance of the obligations under the service contract and/or obtaining the necessary permits or licences.[3326] This obligation also implies that the customer may not obstruct the service provider in the performance of its obligations under the contract. In the context of PSS contract, this may also mean that the PSS user must treat the products made available "as-a-service" with due care, as careless use by the PSS user will result in the PSS supplier-service provider having difficulties with performing its obligations under the service contract. Second, the client must take all reasonable measures to ensure the safety of the service provider.[3327] This "sub-obligation" is mainly relevant in the context of service contracts regarding (immovable) construction works but can also be applied to other service contracts. In the context of PSS contracts, it could even be broadly interpreted to mean that the PSS user must also take reasonable measures to keep safe the goods owned by the PSS supplier used in the performance of the service. Third, an information obligation is stipulated.[3328] This information obligation also includes a duty to warn or notify the service provider of any (impending) defects in the performance of the service. In the context of PSS contracts, defects of the product will also fall under the scope of this obligation. Finally, proposed provision #34 includes the obligation of the client to, where applicable, coordinate the work of the different service providers involved in the performance of the service.[3329] The Draft Law contains a duty to cooperate as well, which mainly focuses on the information the service provider and client must provide to each other and the instructions the client must give to the service provider.[3330] As such, the content of proposed provision #34 is broader, as it also contains the safety obligation, a coordination obligation[3331] and a general obligation to enable the service prover to perform the service.

3325 See also Art. 1:104 PELSC.

3326 See e.g. B. Kohl, *Contrat d'entreprise*, Brussels, Bruylant, 2016, 380–396; W. Goossens, *Aanneming van werk: het gemeenrechtelijk dienstencontract*, Bruges, Die Keure, 2003, 915–922.

3327 Compare with B. Kohl, *Contrat d'entreprise*, Brussels, Bruylant, 2016, 398–401; W. Goossens, *Aanneming van werk: het gemeenrechtelijk dienstencontract*, Bruges, Die Keure, 2003, 922–926.

3328 See e.g. W. Goossens, *Aanneming van werk: het gemeenrechtelijk dienstencontract*, Bruges, Die Keure, 2003, 926–929.

3329 See B. Kohl, *Contrat d'entreprise*, Brussels, Bruylant, 2016, 396–398; W. Goossens, *Aanneming van werk: het gemeenrechtelijk dienstencontract*, Bruges, Die Keure, 2003, 929–932.

3330 See proposed Art. 7.4.5 BCC.

3331 This is included in the Draft Law in proposed Art. 7.4.10 BCC.

Proposed provision #34

Art. 7.4.X10. Obligation to cooperate

§1 The client has the obligation to cooperate with the service provider.

§2 The obligation to cooperate implies in particular:

1° The client to enable the service provider to perform the obligations under the contract;

2° The client to take all reasonable measures ensure the safety of the service provider;

3° The client to provide the service provider with any information that may reasonably be considered necessary to enable the service provider to perform the obligations under the contract;

4° Where applicable, the client to coordinate the work of the different service providers involved in the performance of the service, each of which is linked to the client by a separate contract.

855. (ACCESSORY) DEPOSIT CONTRACT: DEFINITION – Besides the client's obligation to cooperate, (re)codifying the duty of care of the (accessory) deposit contract is the most appropriate way to regulate the PSS user's obligation to take care of the product in result-oriented PSS. In Draft Law, it was opined that the deposit contract should no longer be regarded as a separate named contract, but as a *specialis* of the contract for services.[3332] This makes sense, as it has the advantage that the general rules of the contract for services can also be applied to the deposit contract (e.g. the rules on performance of the service in conformity with the contract), requiring only a few specific provisions on the deposit of goods. In my view, it is useful to add to the definition of the deposit contract[3333] that the deposit of goods can either be the main object of the contract (i.e. an "independent" deposit contract) or accessory to another contract. This confirms the existing case law and legal doctrine on this issue.

The downside of considering the accessory deposit contract as a *specialis* of the contract for services, however, is that in cases where the client of a contract for services is the depository (such as the PSS user in result-oriented PSS), he is at the same time client (under the main service contract) and service provider (under the accessory deposit contract). This may result in confusing terminology issues. Indeed, in the traditional examples of an accessory deposit contract, the client is the depositor, and the service provider is the depositary (think of a

3332 Explanatory Memorandum, *Parliamentary Papers* Kamer, 2020–21, no. 55-1806/001, 95.
3333 See proposed Art. 7.4.2(2) BCC.

garage who repairs and keeps the car of a client). In the case of result-oriented PSS, it is the other way around, resulting in a terminological asymmetry. Nevertheless, this is only a terminological issue and will in practice most likely not give rise to any problems.

> **Proposed provision #35**
>
> **Art. 7.4.X11. Deposit contract**
>
> **§1 The deposit contract is a contract for services that has as its object the keeping of a good by the service provider. In this case, the service provider is referred to as the depositary and the client as depositor.**
>
> **§2 The deposit of goods can either be the main object of the contract or accessory to another contract.**

856. (ACCESSORY) DEPOSIT CONTRACT: RIGHT OF USE FOR THE DEPOSITARY – In the context of result-oriented PSS, it is paramount that the PSS user has a right of use under the accessory deposit contract. Still, for the rules on the deposit contract, the main starting point should still be that the depositary may not use the deposited good. Proposed provision #36 sets out three exceptions to this general rule, namely (i) if the depositor authorises him to do so; (ii) if this use is necessary for the performance of the contact; and (iii) if the use of the good is necessary to keep it in good condition. In this sense, proposed provision #36 was inspired by the Draft Law, namely by proposed Article 7.4.23 BCC. In the case of result-oriented PSS, the PSS user's right of use will generally fall under 1° and/or 2°. Indeed, the PSS supplier will generally grant an explicit right to use the deposited product to the PSS user in the PSS contract. If such a provision is absent, it is clear that the use of the deposited good by the PSS user is necessary for the performance of the PSS contract.

> **Proposed provision #36**
>
> **Art. 7.4.X12. Use of the deposited good**
>
> **The depositary may not use the deposited good, except:**
>
> **1° the depositor authorises him to do so;**
>
> **2° the use of the good is necessary for the performance of the contract;**
>
> **3° the use of the good is necessary to keep it in good condition.**

857. (ACCESSORY) DEPOSIT CONTRACT: DUTY OF CARE – The following proposed provision sets out the main obligation of the depositary, which is to keep the entrusted good. This is an obligation of means. To this end, the second paragraph of this proposed provision states that the depositary must exercise the care of a prudent and reasonable person. This way, the duty of care of the (accessory) deposit contract is aligned with the duty of care under a rental contract. The Draft Law does not contain a similar obligation, but instead it is covered by the general obligation to perform the service in conformity with the contract.[3334] Nevertheless, given the special finality of the deposit contract, it is useful – in my view – to specify the standard of care the depositary needs to uphold.

Proposed provision #37

Art. 7.4.X13. Obligation to keep the deposited good

§1 The depositary keeps the good entrusted to him by the depositor.

§2 In keeping the good, the depositary shall exercise the care of a prudent and reasonable person.

7.3.4.2. Mitigating the risk of moral hazard in an EU directive?

858. MITIGATING MORAL HAZARD AS PART OF EU DIRECTIVE? – If EU harmonisation for contracts for ("bundles" or "packages" of) services is chosen by the EU legislator, this directive should also take into account the risk of moral hazard and how this risk can be countered. In case of option 2a (a general directive on conformity and quality of (almost) all service contracts), the most logical way to do this is by including a general obligation for the client to take the care of a good client/a duty to cooperate. For this, inspiration can be drawn from the DCFR[3335] and proposed provision #34 set out above.[3336] If option 2b is chosen (a specific directive for "packages" or "bundles" of services) a more tailor-made approach is possible. This directive could then include a general obligation to take care of the product that is the object of the service contract, but also more specific obligations, such as an obligation to take reasonable measures against theft and loss, an obligation to use the product in line with the instructions of the service provider, rules on the required deposit, etc. For the content of these specific provisions, inspiration can be drawn from the model clauses set out below.

3334 See proposed Art. 7.4.15 BCC.
3335 See Art. VI.C. – 2:103 DCFR.
3336 See *supra* no. 612.

7.3.5. MODEL CLAUSES ON MITIGATING MORAL HAZARD

7.3.5.1. Model clauses on the obligation to take care of the product

859. Model clause on a general duty of care – A first model clause that the PSS supplier could include in the PSS contract to mitigate the risk of moral hazard is a general duty of care. Model clause #64 uses the general abstract criterion of the prudent and reasonable person or that of a good lessee. This general criterion can be further elaborated, namely that this means that the PSS user must take good care of the product, only use the product in accordance with its purpose or that he must use it in a safe and proper manner. Additionally, even though a prudent and reasonable person does not intentionally damage a product, it could also be useful to explicitly include this in the PSS contract to further minimise the risk of moral hazard.

Model clause #64 – General duty of care

- **[The PSS user] must use the product [as a prudent and reasonable person/as a good lessee]. This means that [the PSS user] is obligated to take good care of the product and only use the product in accordance with [its purpose/its intended use] and in a [safe and proper] manner. [[The PSS user] does not intentionally damage the product].**

860. Model clause making the general duty of care more concrete – To make the general duty of care more concrete, the PSS supplier can include a clause further detailing how a prudent and reasonable person would take care of the product. One way of doing this, is by referring to the instruction manual of the product or the instructions supplied by the PSS supplier itself or by the manufacturer of the product. Legal regulations, such as road traffic regulations, can also be used to colour in the general duty of care. To ensure that the PSS supplier can prove that the PSS user was aware of the contents of this user manual or instructions, it is appropriate to add these as an annex to the PSS contract and/or have the PSS user sign a copy of them.

Model clause #65 – Obligation to use the product in accordance with user manual/instructions of the PSS supplier

- **[The PSS user] must use the product in accordance with [the instruction manual/ instructions of the [PSS supplier/manufacturer]/legal regulations] [that are annexed to this contract] [and signed by [the PSS user]].**

861. Model clause requiring the PSS user to use to product with its supplied accessories – In some cases, damage to the product can be prevented by using the accessories it is supplied with by the PSS supplier. A typical example is the use of a screen protector or protective case for a smartphone. Model clause #66 therefore adds details to the general duty of care by stipulating that the PSS user must use the accessories provided by the PSS supplier.

Model clause #66 – Obligation to use the product with its accessories[3337]

- **[The PSS user] must use the product together with all accessories provided by [the PSS supplier]. These accessories are [specified accessories (e.g. screen protector, protective case, bicycle lock for bicycles, etc.)].**

862. Model clause requiring the PSS user to take reasonable precautions against theft and loss – A specific instance of an obligation to use the product with its supplied accessories is the obligation to secure the product (e.g. a bicycle or e-scooter) with the supplied locks to avoid theft or loss of the product or its accessories. The question arises as to the consequences if the product is stolen or lost despite these reasonable precautions. As was already discussed above, various PSS contracts state that in case of theft or loss of the product, the PSS user owes a deductible.[3338] However, in the situation where the PSS user did indeed take all reasonable precautions, these clauses may in essence result in the risk of *force majeure* being placed on the PSS user, which is not allowed in contracts with consumers, at least under Belgian law.[3339] Therefore, model clause #67 states that in case of theft of loss of the product, the PSS user must indeed pay a reasonable amount as compensation for damages, unless he can prove that he took all reasonable precautions to avoid the theft or the loss of the product. The PSS contract may than further elaborate on how the PSS user can prove that he took these reasonable precautions, for example if he can present the key to the bicycle or prove that he locked the premises where the product was located. This way, the interests of the PSS supplier and the PSS user are adequately balanced, while also mitigating the risk of moral hazard, which in turn also furthers sustainability interests.

3337 Model clause based on C. Borucki, H. Slachmuylders, B. Keirsbilck, D. Gruyaert and E. Terryn, *Model clauses for Product-as-a-Service (PaaS) contracts*, CE Center. Circular Economy Policy Research Center, 2022–23, 51.

3338 See *supra* no. 442.

3339 See Art. VI.83, 12° BCEL and Paragraph 1, point (e) of the UCTD Annex, discussed *supra* no. 443.

Model clause #67 – Obligation to take reasonable precautions against theft and loss[3340]

- **[The PSS user] secures the product and all of its accessories[, such as batteries, keys, etc.] against theft [with the locks provided by [the PSS supplier]]. If the product or any of its accessories are stolen or otherwise lost, [the PSS user] reports this theft or loss to [the PSS supplier] within [specified reasonable time period (e.g. 24 hours, 48 hours)]. [An employee of [the PSS supplier] will assist [the PSS user] in reporting the theft or loss to the police]. [In case of theft or loss of the product, [the PSS user] is to pay [reasonable amount] to the [PSS supplier], unless he can prove that he took all reasonable precautions to avoid the theft or loss]. [[The PSS user] will be deemed to have taken all necessary precautions if [specified action (e.g. he can present the key of the bicycle, he locked the premises where the product was located, etc.)].**

863. Model clause on sanctions for fraudulent declaration of theft – The PSS contract may also stipulate an indemnity clause in case the PSS user committed fraud and there is no actual theft. This can also be combined with a termination clause stating that this constitutes a sufficiently serious breach of contract, which allows the PSS supplier to immediately terminate the contract.[3341] These clauses can be formulated in a way that these remedies can be invoked if the police find that the PSS user has falsely reported the product as stolen or if PSS supplier has a "reasonable suspicion" that the PSS user has made a false declaration. The first option is obviously the more objective way to formulate these clauses, while the latter option will make it easier for the PSS supplier to effectively invoke these remedies. In any case, the PSS user will be able to challenge the application of the indemnity clause or termination clause in court. This means that the court may assess *a posteriori* whether the PSS supplier's "reasonable suspicions" were justified and the PSS supplier was right to claim compensation for damages or the termination of the contract.[3342]

3340 Model clause partly based on C. Borucki, H. Slachmuylders, B. Keirsbilck, D. Gruyaert and E. Terryn, *Model clauses for Product-as-a-Service (PaaS) contracts*, CE Center. Circular Economy Policy Research Center, 2022–23, 51–52.

3341 See on termination clauses *supra* no. 322.

3342 See C. Borucki, H. Slachmuylders, B. Keirsbilck, D. Gruyaert and E. Terryn, *Model clauses for Product-as-a-Service (PaaS) contracts*, CE Center. Circular Economy Policy Research Center, 2022–23, 52.

Model clause #68 – Sanctions for fraudulent declaration of theft[3343]

- [If the police find/if [the PSS supplier] has a reasonable suspicion] that [the PSS user] falsely reported the product as stolen, the [the PSS user] is to pay [reasonable amount] to [the PSS supplier]. [This compensation for damages is without prejudice to the right to terminate the contract [without notice], as this act in bad faith constitutes a sufficiently serious breach of contract by [the PSS user]].

864. Model clause on prohibited use of the product – The general duty of care can also be further defined by prohibiting certain uses of the product. For example, the PSS contract may prohibit the PSS user to use an e-scooter on unpaved roads or a *Cambio* vehicle in motor racing events. Moreover, the PSS contract may require the PSS user to only use proprietary laundry detergent for the washing machine or prohibit third-party ink cartridges for a printer.

Model clause #69 – Prohibited use of the product

- [The PSS user] may not use the product [specified circumstances (e.g. outdoors, on unpaved roads, during extreme weather, with non-proprietary laundry detergent, with third-party ink cartridges, in motor racing events, to transport highly flammable, toxic or other dangerous substances, etc.)].[3344]

865. Model clause allowing only private (no business or commercial) use – As part of the obligation to use the product in accordance with its purpose, the PSS contract may stipulate that the PSS user may only use the product for (its own) private use and not for any business or commercial use (see model clause #70). This is particularly relevant in the context of *Swapfiets* bicycles or micro-mobility PSS offers, as the vehicles offered as part of these business models are often used to professionally deliver meals or other goods. Of course, such a business or commercial use may lead to a more intensive use of the product, which in turn may affect the lifespan of the product.

Model clause #70 – Obligation to only use the product for private use

- [The PSS user] may only use the product for (its own) private use and not, without prior consent of [the PSS supplier], for any business or commercial use.

[3343] Model clauses partly based on C. Borucki, H. Slachmuylders, B. Keirsbilck, D. Gruyaert and E. Terryn, *Model clauses for Product-as-a-Service (PaaS) contracts*, CE Center. Circular Economy Policy Research Center, 2022–23, 52.

[3344] Model clause based on C. Borucki, H. Slachmuylders, B. Keirsbilck, D. Gruyaert and E. Terryn, *Model clauses for Product-as-a-Service (PaaS) contracts*, CE Center. Circular Economy Policy Research Center, 2022–23, 51.

- **The product is exclusively for the use of [the PSS user] [and any person in his household]. [The PSS user] will not share access to the product with any other person who is not authorised to use the product.**

866. Model clause on allowing third parties to use the product (for non-commercial use) – Alternatively, the PSS contract may provide that third parties may use the product for non-commercial purposes, provided that the PSS user supervises the care with which they treat the product and that he remains liable for any damage caused by these third parties.

Model clause #71 – Use of the product by third parties

- **[The PSS user] has the right to allow third parties to use the product for non-commercial purposes. [The PSS user] is to supervise the due care with which these third parties handle the product and is liable for any damage resulting from improper use.**

867. Model clause on the obligation to notify the PSS supplier of any defects – The PSS contract may place an obligation on the PSS user to conduct reasonable checks to verify that the product remains in a good and safe condition throughout the duration of the PSS contract and, if necessary, report any issues or defects to the PSS supplier within a reasonable time. Clauses imposing such an obligation on the PSS user may, for example, define what is meant by "reasonable checks" and also specify within which period of time the PSS user must notify these defects to the PSS supplier. Additionally, the PSS contract may require the PSS user to refrain from using the product if any issues or defects arise to prevent further deterioration of the damage. Of course, this results in the product/service being unavailable to the PSS user. It is advisable that the consequences of this unavailability are set out elsewhere in the PSS contract.[3345]

Model clause #72 – Obligation to check the condition of the product and notify defects

- **[The PSS user] is obligated to conduct reasonable checks to verify that the product remains in a good and safe condition throughout the contract. [Reasonable checks include specified actions (e.g. checking for loose screws, checking for proper functioning of lights, checking for appropriate battery level, etc.)]. If the [PSS user] notices that the product no longer functions properly, [the PSS user] reports any issues or defects with the product to [the PSS supplier]**

[3345] See for model clauses on the unavailability of the product *supra* no. 611–613.

[immediately/within specified reasonable period of time (e.g. 48 hours)]. [The PSS user] refrains from using the product until [the PSS supplier] authorises the use. [The PSS user] is liable for any damage resulting from using the product in the meantime. [The PSS supplier] undertakes to repair the product in accordance with the terms of this contract.

7.3.5.2. Model clauses on limits to moving the product

868. Model clauses on limits to moving the product – As discussed above, when stipulating limits on moving the product in the PSS contract, an outright ban on moving the product will probably be considered disproportionate.[3346] After all, the starting point of the rental contract rules is that the PSS user-lessee may freely move the product. Requiring the prior authorisation of the PSS supplier, on the other hand, will most likely be considered a balanced clause. Therefore, if PSS suppliers want to include a balanced clause on limits to move or relocate the product, the following model clauses can act as a source of inspiration. The first model clause contains a duty to notify the PSS supplier of any relocation of the product. Upon this notice, the PSS supplier will then give relocation instructions. Alternatively, this model clause sets out the possibility to rely on the PSS supplier for relocating the product. This can either be free of charge or against the payment of a (reasonable) relocation fee. The second model clause states that the PSS user may only move or relocate the product if he obtains the prior authorisation of the PSS supplier. To make the clause more predictable and balanced, it is confirmed that this authorisation will always be given if certain requirements are met. The model clause further provides that the PSS supplier must respond to the PSS user's request within a reasonable amount of time, otherwise the PSS user may assume the tacit approval of the request.

Model clause #73 – Limits on moving the product

- **If [the PSS user] wishes to move the product (indoors or outdoors), he must contact [the PSS supplier]. [The PSS supplier] shall supply [the PSS user] with relocation instructions. If requested by [the PSS user], [the PSS supplier] arranges for the relocation of the product within [reasonable time (e.g. 5 working days)]. This relocation service is offered [against payment of a relocation fee of €XXX/free of charge[, unless [the PSS user] cancels the contract within specified period (e.g. 6 months) in which case a relocation fee of €XXX will be charged]. [[The PSS user] can make use of this relocation arrangement maximum once per specified period (e.g. 12 calendar months).]**

[3346] See *supra* no. 843.

- **[The PSS user] may not move or relocate the product without written consent of [the PSS supplier]. This consent shall always be given provided that [requirements (e.g. the new location is suited for the product, the new location is not outside the PSS supplier's service area, etc.)]. [The PSS supplier] answers the request within [reasonable amount of time (e.g. certain amount of business days]. If [the PSS supplier] fails to respond timely, [the PSS user] may assume that the request has been tacitly approved.**

869. Model clause on prohibition to move or relocate the product outside the PSS supplier's service area – The third model clause provides an example of clauses that prohibit the PSS user from moving the product outside the PSS supplier's service area. This clause is useful for avoiding issues with the revindication of the product. Additionally, it avoids situations where the PSS supplier must sue the PSS users in jurisdictions where it does not normally operate.

Model clause #74 – Prohibited relocation of the product

- **The product may never be moved to a location outside [the PSS supplier's] service area.**

870. Model clause on liability for damage or costs caused by unauthorised relocation – A last model clause on limits to moving the product deals with the liability for damages or costs caused by unauthorised relocations or relocations that were not performed by the PSS supplier. This model clause just confirms that the PSS user will be liable for any damages caused by these behaviours. Alternatively, the PSS supplier may include an indemnity clause, provided the requirements of validity of indemnity clauses are met.[3347]

Model clause #75 – Liability for damage or costs caused by unauthorised relocation

- **[The PSS user] shall be liable for any damage or costs arising from [an unauthorised relocation/relocation not performed by the PSS supplier].**

7.3.5.3. Model clauses on incentives for proper use of the product

871. Model clauses on incentives for proper use of the product – To mitigate the risk of moral hazard in a positive way, the PSS contract may include clauses incentivising the PSS user to take due care of the product. The following

[3347] See *supra* no. 304.

two model clauses deal with incentives in the form of "bonusses" for proper use of the product over a certain amount of time. This can either be done by giving a discount to the PSS user on the future monthly fee, or by granting "loyalty points" which can be used in the web shop of the PSS supplier or to extend the PSS contract free of charge.

> **Model clause #76 – Incentives for proper use of the product**
>
> - **[The PSS user] receives a discount of [specified amount (e.g. 5%, 2 euros, etc.)] on the monthly fee for [specified timeframe (e.g. every year)] in which [the PSS user] remains a user of the service and uses and maintains the product [in line with the conditions of these terms/as a prudent and reasonable person/in accordance with the instruction manual/for its ordinary purpose and in a safe and proper manner]. Proper use is presumed if [specified circumstances (e.g. if the product has not required any repairs beyond routine maintenance, if the (un)scheduled maintenance did not exceed a certain amount of time, etc.)].**
> - **[The PSS user] receives a [specified amount] of loyalty points for [specified timeframe (e.g. every year, every month)] in which [the PSS user] remains a user of the service and uses and maintains the product [in line with the conditions of these terms/as a prudent and reasonable person/in accordance with the instruction manual/for its ordinary purpose and in a safe and proper manner]. Proper use is presumed if [specified circumstances (e.g. if the product has not required any repairs beyond routine maintenance, if the (un)scheduled maintenance did not exceed a certain amount of time, etc.)]. Loyalty points can be used [in the web shop of [the PSS supplier]/to extend the contract by a free [specified amount of time (e.g. month)]].**

7.4. END OF THE CONTRACT AND END-OF-LIFE

872. End of the PSS contract and end-of-life of the product – From the point of view of the circular economy, it is a good idea to consider what happens to the products at the end of the PSS contract or at the end of their useful economic life. In most cases, the PSS user will have to return the products and the PSS supplier will undertake to take them back or have them taken back by a third party.[3348] In other cases, however, this may not always be feasible or affordable because the products cannot be taken back easily or have a relatively low residual value. Examples are ventilation systems installed in the PSS user's home. In that case, it may be stipulated that the PSS user becomes the owner

[3348] See e.g. Art. 13.1 Terms and Conditions Bundles, Art. 6.7 Terms and Conditions Swapfiets, Art. 12.4 Terms and Conditions Blue Movement, and Art. 7.2 Terms and Conditions Live Light.

of the products after the agreement has been concluded when all periodic fees have been paid or in the event of payment of an early termination fee.[3349] This section discusses the obligations that come into play at the end of the contract. First, the PSS user's obligation to return the product (section 7.4.1) is analysed. Second, the mirror obligation, namely the PSS supplier's obligation to take back the product (section 7.4.2) is addressed. Third, circular guarantees are discussed, namely clauses that stipulate that the product should be taken back in line with sustainability and circularity practices and goals (section 7.4.3). Fourth, this section evaluates and considers whether solutions are needed *de lege ferenda* with regard to these obligations in the form of legislative interventions (section 7.4.4). Finally, the last section sets out model clauses for the PSS user's obligation to return the product, the PSS supplier's obligation to take back the product and circular guarantees (section 7.4.5).

7.4.1. OBLIGATION OF THE PSS USER TO RETURN THE PRODUCT

7.4.1.1. Product-oriented PSS: no obligation to return the product

873. Ownership of the product implies absence of return obligation – In product-oriented PSS, the PSS user-buyer acquires the ownership of the product. This means that he is not under the obligation to return the product to the PSS supplier-seller. However, as discussed below, in some cases, the PSS supplier-seller does have an obligation to take back the product despite the absence of a restitution obligation for the PSS user.[3350] In this case, the decision whether the PSS user wants to return the product to the PSS supplier-seller is left to their discretion.

7.4.1.2. Use-oriented PSS: restitution obligation

874. Qualification as rental contract implies restitution obligation – Contrary to product-oriented PSS, the PSS user of a use-oriented PSS does not acquire the ownership of the product but only a right of use. As a result, the rules of the rental contract generally apply.[3351] Both under Belgian and Dutch law, a qualification as a rental contract implies that the PSS user has a restitution obligation at the end of the PSS contract.[3352] This restitution obligation implies

3349 See on the consequences of such a transfer of ownership at the end of the contract *supra* section 3.4.3.

3350 See *infra* section 7.4.2.1.

3351 See *supra* section 3.4.

3352 **Belgium**: This follows from the definition of the rental contract (Art. 1709 old BCC) and Art. 1731, §2 old BCC. See also: R. Timmermans, *Inleiding tot het Vlaams*

that the PSS user-lessee must return the product to the PSS supplier-lessor and that he must compensate the PSS supplier-lessor for the damage to the rented product, also called the rental damage.[3353]

875. CONTRACTUAL CLAUSES ON THE MODALITIES OF THE RESTITUTION OBLIGATION – Several PSS contracts confirm the legal obligation to return the rented product upon termination of the PSS contract and stipulate the modalities of this return. For larger products such as household appliances, the contract often states that the PSS supplier will collect the product at the PSS user's premises, on a time and date specified by the PSS supplier. This is for example the case with *Bundles*, *Papillon* and *Blue Movement* (for larger appliances). If the product is not available for pickup at the agreed time, or if the PSS user is not home for the collection appointment, it is not unreasonable to charge a collection cost to the PSS user. For smaller products, on the other hand, the PSS user will generally receive return instructions to return the product himself, for example via (registered) post delivery service. Examples of such clauses can be found in the terms and conditions of *Blue Movement* (for smaller appliances), *Gerrard Street/Repeat*, *Swapphone* and *Fairphone Easy*. In the case of pay-per-use PSS contracts, the PSS user can comply with his obligation to return the product by ending the ride in an app, or by returning the product to a (charging) station or parking spot. In the case of free-floating e-scooters, such as *Lime* and *Dott*, this is done by ending the ride on the app which locks the e-scooter and taking a picture to prove that there is no damage to the e-scooter and that it is parked at a legal (e-scooter) parking space.[3354] In the case of *Villo* and *Cambio*, the PSS user can return the product by parking the bicycle or car in one of the PSS supplier's bicycle stations or parking spots, which then registers the end of the ride in the PSS supplier's app or system.[3355]

> TERMS AND CONDITIONS BUNDLES – Art. 13.1 "Upon termination of the Contract, the property of Bundles, being *the Appliance and, where relevant, the Bundles Buddy shall be collected from the User's address on a date and time to be specified by Bundles* and User shall return the Appliance 'as a whole' to Bundles in complete original and clean condition, including associated documents and accessories." (Own emphasis).

Woninghuurdecreet, Mechelen, Wolters Kluwer, 2018, 198; T. VANDROMME, "Commentaar bij art. 1731 oud BW" in *Bijzondere overeenkomsten. Artikelsgewijze commentaar met overzicht van rechtspraak en rechtsleer*, Mechelen, Wolters Kluwer, loose-leaf, 2021, (145) 148, no. 4. **The Netherlands**: Art. 7:224(1) DCC. J.K. SIX-HUMMEL, *Groene Serie Huurrecht, art. 7:224 BW*, Deventer, Kluwer, loose-leaf, 2012, note 21; H.J. ROSSEL and A.H.T. HEISTERKAMP, *Mr. C. Assers Handleiding tot de beoefening van het Nederlands Burgerlijk Recht. 7. Bijzondere overeenkomsten. Deel II. Huur*, Deventer, Wolters Kluwer, 2021, 121, no. 129.

3353 M. DAMBRE, "Rechten en verbintenissen van de huurder" in M. DAMBRE, B. HUBEAU and S. STIJNS (eds.), *Handboek algemeen huurrecht*, Bruges, Die Keure, 2015, (513) 580, no. 192.

3354 See Art. 7.2 (Treat Our Products Like They Were Your Own – Damage) Terms and Conditions Lime and Art. 3.2 (Starting and ending a ride) Terms and Conditions Dott.

3355 Art. 3.5 Terms and Conditions Villo and Art. 13.1 Terms and Conditions Cambio.

Terms and conditions Papillon – Art. 8.2 "The Lessee undertakes to return the Appliance to the VZW at the end of the Rental Period. As far as possible prior to the termination of the Contract, *the date for collection of the Appliance will be mutually agreed between the Lessee and the Lessor.* If the Appliance cannot be collected on this date, the cost for collection shall be borne by the Lessee."

Terms and conditions Blue Movement – Art. 11.4 "After termination by BSH or the Lessee, BSH will contact the Lessee by phone to make a *collection appointment for a Large Domestic Appliance or for instructions on how to return a Small Domestic Appliance.* [...]." (Own emphasis).

Terms and conditions Gerrard Street/Repeat – Art. 9.2 "You can cancel your subscription at any time by returning the headphones using the return form. [...]"

Terms and conditions Fairphone Easy – Art. 7.6 "[...] *You are obliged to return the device back to Us within one week following the receipt of the Return Merchandise Authorisation* (RMA). To return the device, you must contact Customer Support as soon as possible prior to initiating a return to obtain an RMO. *Follow the instructions sent by email to correctly label and sufficiently pack the device and drop it off at the nearest return point in order to return it to Us.* The package must include the shipping label and other information that may be communicated as necessary for the return. [...]" (Own emphasis).

876. Restitution obligation is obligation of result – The lessee's restitution obligation is, at least under Belgian law, considered an obligation of result.[3356] Consequently, the PSS user will be contractually liable if he cannot (fully) fulfil his obligation to return the product by the date and time specified in het PSS contract, or in the absence of a contractual provision, no later than the end of the PSS contract. He can, however, escape this contractual liability by proving *force majeure*.[3357] Additionally, and this is specific to the rental contract, he can prove that the damages were not caused by his fault, for example

3356 **Belgium**: See: Cass. (BE) 16 November 1944, *Pas.* 1945, I, 34; Cass. (BE) 20 June 1940, *Pas.* 1940, I, 170; M. Dambre, "Rechten en verbintenissen van de huurder" in M. Dambre, B. Hubeau and S. Stijns (eds.), *Handboek algemeen huurrecht*, Bruges, Die Keure, 2015, (513) 582–583; Y. Merchiers, *Le bail en général*, Brussels, Larcier, 2015, 219, no. 272. See also: T. Vandromme, "Artikel 1732 oud BW – Aansprakelijkheid huurder voor beschadigingen aan gehuurde goed" in *Focus op bijzondere overeenkomsten*, Mechelen, Wolters Kluwer, 2022, (183) 184. **The Netherlands**: It can be assumed that this is also the case under Dutch law. Consequently, the PSS user will be liable in the event of the impossibility of returning the product unless he can prove that this is not imputable to him, i.e.i.e. if this is not due to his fault, nor for his risk under the law, juridical act or generally accepted principles (Art. 6:75 DCC).

3357 **Belgium**: Art. 5.226 BCC. **The Netherlands**: Art. 6:75 DCC. See for applications: HR (NL) 1 November 2013, ECLI:NL:HR:2013:1080, *RvdW* 2013/1315 (Theft of rented sound equipment, not imputable breach of contract); HR (NL) 24 October 1997, ECLI:NL:HR:1997:ZC2469, (*Spruijt/Tichelaar*), *NJ* 1998/69 (stolen rental car without fault of renter, not imputable breach of contract). Whether a defence based on *force majeure* will be successful depends on the specific circumstances. For more examples see the lower case law

by showing that he used the product as a reasonable and careful person and/or that the damages are due to the age of the product.[3358] As such, the restitution obligation is in line with the obligation to treat the product as a reasonable and careful person (*bonus pater familias*).[3359]

877. CONDITION OF THE PRODUCT UPON RETURN AT THE END OF THE USE-ORIENTED PSS CONTRACT – The PSS user must return the product in the condition in which he received it, except for wear and tear due to normal use.[3360] This means he will be liable for any damages to the product or losses thereof incurred during the PSS contract, unless he can prove that they were caused by no fault of his own.[3361] To determine any damages to the product, a comparison must be made between the condition of the product at the start of the PSS contract and the condition of the product when it is returned.[3362] This is done on the basis of a circumstantial rental inventory (*plaatsbeschrijving, état de lieux*) in which the product is described in detail, possibly with photographs.[3363] In practice, some PSS suppliers indeed require the PSS user to sign a form at the time of delivery where the condition of the product is described, which can be used as a circumstantial rental inventory.[3364] In the absence of a circumstantial rental inventory, there is a rebuttable presumption that the PSS user received the product in the same condition as the condition of the product at the end of the PSS contract.[3365] This means that if such a circumstantial rental inventory is lacking, the PSS supplier must prove that the damage was caused during the PSS contract, and that it is not due to normal wear and tear.[3366]

---

cited in J.K. SIX-HUMMEL, *Groene Serie Huurrecht, art. 7:224 BW*, Deventer, Kluwer, loose-leaf, 2012, note 21.

3358 **Belgium**: DAMBRE refers to the obligation of Art. 1732 old BCC as a "weakened" obligation of result. See: M. DAMBRE, "Rechten en verbintenissen van de huurder" in M. DAMBRE, B. HUBEAU and S. STIJNS (eds.), *Handboek algemeen huurrecht*, Bruges, Die Keure, 2015, (513) 582, no. 201. **The Netherlands**: Art. 7:244(2) DCC. H.J. ROSSEL and A.H.T. HEISTERKAMP, *Mr. C. Assers Handleiding tot de beoefening van het Nederlands Burgerlijk Recht. 7. Bijzondere overeenkomsten. Deel II. Huur*, Deventer, Wolters Kluwer, 2021, 124, no. 133. See also: Opinion AG G.R.B. VAN PEURSEM, 28 October 2016, in HR 16 December 2016, ECLI:NL:PHR:2016:1074, para. 2.1–2.12.

3359 Art. 1728 old BCC.

3360 **Belgium**: M. DAMBRE, *Bijzondere overeenkomsten: de essentie*, Bruges, Die Keure, 2022, 232. **The Netherlands**: J.K. SIX-HUMMEL, *Groene Serie Huurrecht, art. 7:224 BW*, Deventer, Kluwer, loose-leaf, 2012, note 21.

3361 **Belgium**: Art. 1732 old BCC. See also specifically for fire damage: Art. 1733 old BCC. **The Netherlands**: Art. 7:224(2) DCC.

3362 Cass. (BE) 3 June 2004, *Arr.Cass.* 2004, 982; T. VANDROMME, "Commentaar bij art. 1731 oud BW" in *Bijzondere overeenkomsten. Artikelsgewijze commentaar met overzicht van rechtspraak en rechtsleer*, Mechelen, Wolters Kluwer, loose-leaf, 2021, (145) 154, no. 10.

3363 See also *supra* no. 437.

3364 See e.g. Art. 4.3 Terms and Conditions Papillon, discussed *supra* no. 478.

3365 **Belgium**: Art. 1731, §1 old BCC. **The Netherlands**: Art. 7:224(2), last sentence DCC and Art. 7:218(2) DCC.

3366 M.B.M. LOOS, "Servitization, consumentenhuur en consumentenkoop", *WPNR* 2022/7396, (944) 945.

878. CONTRACTUAL CLAUSES ON THE CONDITION OF THE PRODUCT AT THE END OF THE CONTRACT – The condition of the product upon its return at the end of the contract is also addressed in the PSS contracts analysed. For example, some of these clauses, such as the clause found in the terms and conditions of *Bundles*, specify that the PSS user must return the equipment in its entirety to the PSS supplier, in complete original and clean condition, including its accessories.[3367] Other clauses, such as in the case of *Fairphone Easy*, also state that the PSS user must return the product in the condition it was made available and that the PSS user will be liable for returning a damaged product, but that this excludes normal wear and tear or damages covered by the Fairphone Warranty.[3368] It is also an option to further define in the PSS contract what is seen as normal wear and tear. For example, the terms and conditions of *Swapphone* state that normal wear and tear includes light signs of use on the smartphone, not being noticeable (deep) scratches.[3369] Similarly, the terms and conditions of *Blue Movement* require the product to be returned in "*clean and original condition*", which is defined as an Appliance that has no stains, nasty odours, caked-on grease or food residues, nor any damage or breakages.[3370]

> TERMS AND CONDITIONS BUNDLES – Art. 13.1 "[...] User shall return the Appliance 'as a whole' to Bundles in complete original and clean condition, including associated documents and accessories."
>
> TERMS AND CONDITIONS FAIRPHONE EASY – Art. 7.7 "When You return the device back to Fairphone, ensure that the device is returned [...] in the same conditions as it was made available to You [...]. You may incur an additional surcharge where the device is returned to Us in a damaged condition. This excludes normal wear and tear or damages covered by the Fairphone Warranty."
>
> TERMS AND CONDITIONS SWAPPHONE – Art. 12.1 "At the end of the Rental Contract or in case of termination or dissolution of the Rental Contract [...], the Lessee is obliged to return the Smartphone to Swapphone in the same condition as it was made available to the Lessee at the start of the Rental Contract, except for normal wear and tear. Normal wear and tear is understood to include light signs of use of the Smartphone, not being noticeable (deep) scratches."
>
> TERMS AND CONDITIONS BLUE MOVEMENT – Art. 12.6 "If the Appliance is not in complete, original or clean condition, including the documents and accessories belonging to the Appliance, BSH shall be entitled to recover from the User the costs it has to incur to repair or replace the Appliance and/or associated documents and

---

3367 Art. 13.1 Terms and Conditions Bundles.
3368 Art. 7.7 Terms and Conditions Fairphone Easy. Compare also with Art. 8.3 Terms and Conditions Papillon.
3369 Art. 12.1 Terms and Conditions Swapphone.
3370 Art. 12.6 Terms and Conditions Blue Movement.

accessories, as well as the lost profit. 'Clean condition' means, inter alia, an Appliance that has no stains, bad odours, caked-on grease or food residues. 'Original condition' means, inter alia, an Appliance without damage or breakages."

879. Specific conditions for smartphones: deactivate Find my iPhone and/or remove passwords, user accounts and personal data – For smartphones, PSS contracts often add an additional, specific requirement for the return conditions of the product. Indeed, PSS contracts relating to smartphones, such as *Swapphone*, *Fairphone Easy* and *Grover*, require the PSS user to deactivate the "Find my iPhone" application and/or disable or remove any security passwords, user accounts and personal data. This is necessary to enable the PSS supplier to make the smartphone available again, as a locked or password-protected smartphone cannot be (re-)used by other PSS users.

> Terms and conditions Swapphone – Art. 7.13 "[...] When returning the Smartphone, *the Find my iPhone application and/or Google account must be disabled by the Lessee.* If this application is not disabled, the Smartphone is no longer (re) usable for Swapphone. [...]" (Own emphasis).

> Terms and conditions Fairphone Easy – Art. 7.7 "[...] When You return the device back to Fairphone; *ensure the device is returned in line with clause 6.4 of these Terms*, in the same condition as it was made available to You and operating with the same OS. [...]." Art. 6.4 "In case of a swap, You are responsible for making a separate back-up of any material stored (including personal data) on the device, *to delete any personal data, to disable any security passwords*, remove any removable accessories on the device and any removable memory storage and SIM cards. [...]" (Own emphasis).

> Terms and conditions Grover – "You are obligated to return the Rental Item to Grover, including all equipment directly upon the end of the contract. You shall return the Rental Item in the condition it was in when You received it – apart from the normal signs of use – *in particular, You shall remove the password protection, linking of the Rental Item to a personal account or other lock that prevents or hinders the use of the Rental Item by third parties.*" (Own emphasis).

880. Impossibility to return the product because of theft or loss – The question arises as to the consequences if the PSS user cannot return the product at the end of the contract because it is stolen or otherwise lost. Various PSS contracts state that in this case, the PSS user is liable for the replacement value of the product or that he must pay a deductible/compensation for damages.[3371] However, notwithstanding these clauses, the answer to this question is more complex and depends on whether the theft or loss of the

[3371] See e.g. Art. 9.5 Terms and Conditions Blue Movement; Art. 10.8 Terms and Conditions Bundles; Art. 7.1 Terms and Conditions Papillon; Art. 6.1 Terms and Conditions Repeat/ Gerrard Street; Art. 4.2 Terms and Conditions Lena; Art. 9.3 Terms and Conditions Live

product constitutes *force majeure*. Indeed, as was already discussed above,[3372] under the Belgian rental contract rules, the PSS contract shall be automatically terminated if the product is destroyed or lost during the term of the PSS contract due to unforeseen circumstances or *force majeure*.[3373] In this case, the PSS user will not be obliged to pay damages and is released from his obligation to return the product.[3374] Also under Dutch law, the PSS user-lessee who cannot return the product because it is stolen or lost may try to invoke *force majeure*.[3375] Whether this defence will succeed depends heavily on the circumstances of the specific case.[3376] If the court accepts that the theft or loss is due to *force majeure*, the PSS user will be released from his obligation to return the product and will not have to pay compensation for damages.[3377] In the context of PSS contracts, one could argue that the PSS user-lessee will indeed be able to invoke *force majeure* if he has taken all reasonable precautions to avoid theft or loss of the product (such as double-locking a bicycle to a fixed object).[3378] As was already discussed above,[3379] clauses that place the risk of *force majeure* on the PSS user-consumer are not allowed under Belgian law, and arguably also under Dutch law.[3380] As a result, any clauses in the PSS contract that require the PSS user to pay compensation for theft of the product even if he has taken all reasonable precautions can, in my view, be set aside using the unfair contract terms control mechanism.

881. Remedies for failure to return the product at the end of the contract – The question arises as to the consequences of a failure of the PSS user to comply with his restitution obligation. In other words, what if the PSS user does not return the product but keeps using it even after the end of the PSS contract? Two hypotheses are conceivable. In a first hypothesis, the PSS user keeps paying the monthly fee and the PSS supplier does not object to

---

Light; Art. 7.1 Terms and Conditions Swapfiets (deductible instead of replacement value); and Art. 8.5 Terms and Conditions Swapphone (deductible instead of replacement value).

3372 See *supra* no. 439.

3373 Art. 1722 old BCC. See for an application: Ct. Nivelles (BE) 30 October 2003, *Res Jur.Imm.* 2004, 7 (destruction of rented sanding machines. According to Art. 1722 old BCC, the lessee is released from his obligation to pay the rental fee of the destroyed sanding machines as well as from his obligation to return the goods (Art. 1732 old BCC)).

3374 *Ibid.*

3375 Art. 6:75 DCC.

3376 H.J. Rossel and A.H.T. Heisterkamp, *Mr. C. Assers Handleiding tot de beoefening van het Nederlands Burgerlijk Recht. 7. Bijzondere overeenkomsten. Deel II. Huur*, Deventer, Wolters Kluwer, 2021, no. 131.

3377 See for an analysis of examples in case law: J.K. Six-Hummel, *Groene Serie Huurrecht, art. 7:224 BW*, Deventer, Kluwer, loose-leaf, 2012, note 21.

3378 C. Marr, "Le contrat de location de biens meubles" in *Guide juridique de l'entreprise. Traité théorique et pratique*, Book 39, Waterloo, Kluwer, 2007, 45, no. 730.

3379 See *supra* no. 442.

3380 **Belgium**: Art. VI.83, 12° BCEL. **The Netherlands**: See: M.B.M. Loos, *Algemene voorwaarden*, The Hague, Boom juridisch, 2018, 313, no. 345a, with reference to Paragraph 1, point (e) of the UCTD Annex.

the continued use of the product. In this case, the PSS contract will be tacitly renewed.[3381] To avoid any uncertainty as to the possibility and terms of the tacitly renewed rental contract, it is a good idea to include a clause in the PSS contract confirming the possibility of tacit renewal and stipulating under what conditions this will happen (especially with regard to the duration of the renewed contract). For example, the terms and conditions of *Grover* state that "*if [the PSS user] continue[s] the use of the Rental Item after the end of the contract, the rental will be extended for one further month, respectively, unless Grover objects thereto.*"[3382] In a second hypothesis, the PSS supplier does object to the continued use of the product, in which case it can claim performance of the PSS user's restitution obligation or revindicate the product, potentially with additional damages. Additionally, the Dutch Civil Code also explicitly states that in this case, the PSS supplier may claim compensation equal to the monthly fee for the time in which the PSS user keeps the product in his possession, without prejudice to its right to claim additional damages.[3383]

882. Remedies for rental damage: compensation for damages – If the comparison of the condition of the product at the end of the contract with the circumstantial rental inventory shows that there is rental damage that is not due to normal wear and tear and/or due to *force majeure*, the PSS supplier is entitled to compensation for damages.[3384] The right to compensation only exists when the product is returned and therefore not during the duration of the PSS contract (even in the case of an interim control by the PSS supplier or an interim rental inventory[3385]).[3386] The amount of compensation corresponds to

---

3381 **Belgium**: C. Marr, "Le contrat de location de biens meubles" in *Guide juridique de l'entreprise. Traité théorique et pratique*, Book 39, Waterloo, Kluwer, 2007, 22, no. 220. However, as regards the terms and effects of the tacit renewal, particularly as regards the term of the renewed rental contract, it is generally assumed that Art. 1738–1740 old BCC do not apply, at least in a strict sense, to the rental of movables. See: Y. Merchiers, *Le bail en général*, Brussels, Larcier, 2015, no. 618. **The Netherlands**: Art. 7:230 DCC; H.J. Rossel and A.H.T. Heisterkamp, *Mr. C. Assers Handleiding tot de beoefening van het Nederlands Burgerlijk Recht. 7. Bijzondere overeenkomsten. Deel II. Huur*, Deventer, Wolters Kluwer, 2021, no. 168.

3382 Art. 5.6 Terms and Conditions Grover.

3383 See Art. 7:225 DCC; H.J. Rossel and A.H.T. Heisterkamp, *Mr. C. Assers Handleiding tot de beoefening van het Nederlands Burgerlijk Recht. 7. Bijzondere overeenkomsten. Deel II. Huur*, Deventer, Wolters Kluwer, 2021, no. 132.

3384 **Belgium**: M. Dambre, "Rechten en verbintenissen van de huurder" in M. Dambre, B. Hubeau and S. Stijns (eds.), *Handboek algemeen huurrecht*, Bruges, Die Keure, 2015, (513) 602–604, no. 247–250. **The Netherlands**: H.J. Rossel and A.H.T. Heisterkamp, *Mr. C. Assers Handleiding tot de beoefening van het Nederlands Burgerlijk Recht. 7. Bijzondere overeenkomsten. Deel II. Huur*, Deventer, Wolters Kluwer, 2021, no. 136.

3385 Of course, if the product must be replaced or "swapped" and the damage is due to careless use by the PSS user, it is not unreasonable to charge a compensation for damages. Compare with Art. 8.3 Terms and Conditions Swapfiets.

3386 **Belgium**: Cass. (BE) 25 February 2005, *Arr.Cass.* 2005, 481; V. Sagaert, B. Tilleman and A.-L. Verbeke, *Vermogensrecht in kort bestek*, Antwerp, Intersentia, 2022, 275, no. 732.

the demonstrable costs to repair or replace the product.[3387] Additionally, under Dutch law, under Dutch law, the PSS supplier can also claim damages equal to the rental price if the PSS user returns the product late.[3388] To ensure that the PSS supplier is indeed compensated for rental damage after the PSS user has returned the product, the former may reserve in the PSS contract to set off any repair or replacement costs against the deposit.[3389]

7.4.1.3. Result-oriented PSS: restitution obligation

883. Contract for services: in principle no restitution obligation – The fact that result-oriented PSS are generally qualified as a contract for services and not as a rental contract has, at first sight, important consequences in terms of the existence of a restitution obligation.[3390] In principle, a qualification as a contract for services implies that the product remains under the service provider's responsibility who retains mastery over the good.[3391] This also means that, unlike under the rental contract, the client will generally not have an obligation to return the good.

884. Accessory deposit contract: duty of care and restitution obligation – It is, however, clear that the situation is slightly different in the case of a result-oriented PSS contract. Indeed, in these contracts, the product will generally be located with the PSS user who is granted a contractual right of use of the product.[3392] In this case, the contract for services will be accompanied by an accessory deposit contract (including a contractual provision granting the PSS user a right of use over the product).[3393] Under this accessory deposit contract, the PSS user has a duty of care and an obligation to return the product.[3394]

The Netherlands: H.J. Rossel and A.H.T. Heisterkamp, *Mr. C. Assers Handleiding tot de beoefening van het Nederlands Burgerlijk Recht. 7. Bijzondere overeenkomsten. Deel II. Huur*, Deventer, Wolters Kluwer, 2021, no. 136.

3387 *Ibid.*

3388 Art. 7:225 DCC. See *supra* no. 881.

3389 See Art. 13.2 Terms and Conditions Bundles: "*If the Appliance is no longer present or is not in complete, original and clean condition, Bundles shall be entitled to recover the costs it has to incur to repair or replace the Appliance from User and/or set them off against the deposit.*" See on set off and set off clauses also *supra* section 5.4.

3390 See on the importance of the distinction: W. Goossens, *Aanneming van werk: het gemeenrechtelijk dienstencontract*, Bruges, Die Keure, 2003, 119–120, no. 136.

3391 B. Keirsbilck, E. Terryn and E. Van Gool, "Consumentenbescherming bij servitisation en product-dienst systemen (PDS)", *TPR* 2019, (817) 851, no. 34; W. Goossens, *Aanneming van werk: het gemeenrechtelijk dienstencontract*, Bruges, Die Keure, 2003, 119–120, no. 136.

3392 See *supra* no. 446.

3393 *Ibid.*

3394 **Belgium**: Art. 1915 old BCC; V. Sagaert, B. Tilleman and A.-L. Verbeke, *Vermogensrecht in kort bestek*, Antwerp, Intersentia, 2022, 488–489. **The Netherlands**: Art. 7:600 DCC; A.J. Verheij, "Bewaarneming" in H.N. Schelhaas and A.J. Verheij (eds.), *Bijzondere overeenkomsten in Studiereeks Burgerlijk Recht*, Deventer, Wolters Kluwer, 2023, (417) 422,

The duty of care is an obligation of means where, as the deposit component of the PSS contract is done in the interest of the PSS user, the conduct of the PSS user is tested against the benchmark of a prudent and reasonable person in the same case.[3395] This means that the PSS user must take the necessary precautions against loss or depreciation, either due to an act of a third party (e.g. theft) or external circumstances (e.g. fire or water damage). The obligation to return the product, on the other hand, is an obligation of result.[3396] This means that the PSS user will be liable if he cannot return the product, unless he can prove *force majeure*.[3397] At least under Belgian law, the existence of *force majeure* is also assessed in the light of the PSS user's duty of care, in particular whether the PSS user has taken all necessary and reasonable precautions for avoiding the loss of the product.[3398, 3399] Since these rules contain rather abstract standards, it is appropriate to further specify and define the content of the duty of care in the PSS contract to make this obligation more concrete, similar to how this would be done in use-oriented PSS.[3400] Indeed, as these rules are not mandatory law, the contracting parties have considerable freedom to contractually regulate this duty of care and restitution obligation in the PSS contract. Nevertheless, it should be noted that the prohibition on placing the risk of *force majeure* on the PSS user-consumer also applies to result-oriented PSS.[3401] Consequently, clauses that charge the PSS user a compensation or deductible in case of theft of the product where the PSS user took all necessary precautions will also be regarded unfair in result-oriented PSS contracts.

885. Restitution obligation in result-oriented PSS strongly resembles restitution obligation in use-oriented PSS – If we compare result-oriented PSS containing an accessory deposit contract with use-oriented PSS, the restitution

no. 370; A.C. van Schaick, *Asser 7-VIII Bewaarneming, borgtocht, vaststellingsovereenkomst, bruikleen, altijddurende rente, spel en weddenschap*, Deventer, Wolters Kluwer, 2018, no. 1.

3395 **Belgium**: Art. 1928 old BCC (*culpa levis in abstracto*). Compare with the lower standard of Art. 1927 old BCC which requires the depositary to take care of the goods in the same way as he does for his own goods (*culpa levis in concreto*). **The Netherlands**: Art. 7:602 DCC. N.E. Groeneveld-Tijssens, *Bewaarneming, Mon. BW B73*, Deventer, Wolters Kluwer, 2020, 11, no. 10–11; A.C. van Schaick, *Asser 7-VIII Bewaarneming, borgtocht, vaststellingsovereenkomst, bruikleen, altijddurende rente, spel en weddenschap*, Deventer, Wolters Kluwer, 2018, no. 9–10.

3396 **Belgium**: E.g. Ghent (BE) 27 February 2004, *TWVR* 2004, 197 and Brussels (BE) 4 January 2000, *RGAR* 2001, 13.398. **The Netherlands**: Art. 7:605(4) DCC; A.J. Verheij, "Bewaarneming" in H.N. Schelhaas and A.J. Verheij (eds.), *Bijzondere overeenkomsten in Studiereeks Burgerlijk Recht*, Deventer, Wolters Kluwer, 2023, (417) 442, no. 372.

3397 **Belgium**: Art. 1929 old BCC. **The Netherlands**: Art. 6:75 DCC. A.J. Verheij, "Bewaarneming" in H.N. Schelhaas and A.J. Verheij (eds.), *Bijzondere overeenkomsten in Studiereeks Burgerlijk Recht*, Deventer, Wolters Kluwer, 2023, (417) 442, no. 372; N.E. Groeneveld-Tijssens, *Bewaarneming, Mon. BW B73*, Deventer, Wolters Kluwer, 2020, 29–30, no. 25.

3398 Cass. (BE) 7 March 2008, *Arr.Cass.* 2008, 651, *Pas.* 2008, 627, *RW* 2011–12, 583.

3399 Compare also with *supra* no. 880.

3400 Compare with *supra* no. 876.

3401 See *supra* no. 442 and no. 880.

obligations in both types of PSS strongly resemble each other. Indeed, just like with a qualification as a rental contract, the PSS user will have an obligation to take care of the product, which is assessed in the light of the general standard of care of the prudent and reasonable person. This abstract criterion can be made more concrete in the PSS contract, for example by specifying the precautions the PSS user must take to avoid theft or loss of the product. Additionally, under both types of PSS, the PSS user has an obligation to return the product at the end of the contract, which is an obligation of result also assessed in the light of the PSS user's duty of care. This means that the PSS user will be liable if he cannot return the product unless he can prove *force majeure* (where the precautions taken by the PSS user to avoid theft or loss are also taken into account).

886. Condition of the product upon return at the end of the result-oriented PSS contract – The question arises as to the condition of the product upon return at the end of the result-oriented PSS contract. Although the restitution obligations in use-oriented and result-oriented PSS contracts strongly resemble each other, there are some differences. First, under the Belgian rules of the deposit contract, the PSS user-depositary must return the product only in the condition it is in at the time of return.[3402] Any damage it has suffered through no fault of the PSS user-depositary shall be borne by the PSS supplier-depositor.[3403] This means that, in the absence of a contractual clause to the contrary, the PSS supplier will have to prove that the PSS user breached its duty of care which caused damage to the product. This differs from the Belgian rules of the rental contract where the PSS user-lessee must return the product in the same condition as it was at the start of the contract (except for normal wear and tear).[3404] Under Dutch law, on the other hand, in the absence of a contractual clause to the contrary, the PSS user-depositary must return the product in the condition he received it.[3405] Unlike the Dutch rental contract rules, no exception is made for normal wear and tear.[3406] Thus, if the product is damaged (including normal wear and tear), the PSS user will be liable unless he can prove this is due to *force majeure*, which is assessed in light of his duty of care. Second, contrary to the rental contract, the rules of the (accessory) deposit contract do not require a circumstantial (rental) inventory. This also means that there is also no rebuttable presumption that the PSS user received the product in the same condition as the condition of the product at the end of the PSS contract if such circumstantial (rental) inventory is lacking.[3407] Nevertheless, even if an inventory of the product is not required, it is a good idea to let the PSS user sign

3402 Art. 1933 old BCC.
3403 *Ibid.*
3404 Art. 1732 old BCC.
3405 Art. 7:605(4) DCC.
3406 Art. 7:224(2) DCC.
3407 Compare with **Belgium**: Art. 1731, §1 old BCC and **The Netherlands**: Art. 7:224(2) DCC.

a form indicating the description of the product at the start of the contract. After all, without this form, it will be difficult for the PSS supplier to prove that the damage to the product is the fault of the PSS user.

7.4.2. OBLIGATION OF THE PSS SUPPLIER TO TAKE BACK THE PRODUCT

7.4.2.1. Product-oriented PSS

887. SALES CONTRACT RULES DO NOT CONTAIN AN OBLIGATION FOR THE PSS SUPPLIER TO TAKE BACK THE PRODUCT – In principle, the (consumer) sales rules in the Belgian and Dutch Civil Codes do not contain an obligation for the seller of a product to take back the product at the end of its useful economic life. This is because traditional sales contracts generally entail a one-off transaction where the contractual relationship ends with the delivery of the purchased good.[3408] Since the consumer becomes the owner of the product, he does not have to return it to the PSS supplier-seller after a certain period of time (unlike a rental contract or contract for services). However, this does not mean that the PSS supplier-seller will never have an obligation to take back the product. This may either result from a contractual obligation in the PSS contract where the PSS supplier undertakes to take back and repurpose the product if the PSS user does no longer need it, or from a statutory obligation arising from (EU or national) waste law.

888. TAKE BACK AND REPURPOSE/RECYCLE SERVICE AS AFTER-SALES SERVICE – Product-oriented PSS contracts may include a (contractual) take back obligation as an after-sales service. The PSS supplier-seller then undertakes to repurpose or recycle the product. The collection of the product can take various forms: either the consumer can bring his products to a physical store or collection point, or the PSS supplier can pick them up at the consumer's home. As a real-life example, Ikea offers a return and recycle service for old mattresses, couches and electronic devices.[3409] For mattresses and electronic devices, this return service is offered free of charge. For couches, the consumer pays 29 euro.

889. TAKE BACK OBLIGATION ARISING FROM (EU OR NATIONAL) WASTE LAW – In a variety of cases, the take back obligation will not (only) arise from the PSS contract itself, but (also) from a statutory legal obligation found in EU or national waste law.[3410] Current EU waste law consists of general rules, such as the Waste

---

3408 See *supra* no. 12.

3409 See: www.ikea.com/be/nl/customer-service/services/removal/.

3410 Although a thorough analysis of EU and national waste law falls outside the scope of this research, it is appropriate to briefly mention these requirements in the context of the PSS supplier's obligation to take back the product. See more in-depth on the role of waste law in

Framework Directive[3411] ("WFD"), and more sector-specific rules, including the Waste Electrical and Electronic Equipment Directive[3412] ("WEEE Directive"), the Batteries Directive[3413] and the Directive on end-of-life vehicles[3414] ("ELV Directive").[3415] These legal instruments contain, amongst others, targets on collection and recycling activities and promote repair, reuse and recycling.[3416] Additionally, they contain minimum requirements for extended producer responsibility schemes. The EU Member States generally have a wide margin of discretion to implement these EU rules, and in various cases, these Member States have adopted additional national initiatives.[3417]

890. Take back obligation as part of extended producer responsibility – In the context of the PSS supplier's obligation to take back the product, extended producer responsibility ("EPR") is very relevant.[3418] This concept is established in the WFD and makes the producer[3419] of a product responsible for the financial and/or organisational aspects in the product's end-of-life and waste stage.[3420] The WFD lays the foundations for EPR and enables Member States to establish EPR schemes.[3421] Indeed, according the WFD, Member States may take national legislative or non-legislative measures to oblige producers to accept returned products and the waste that remains after those products have been used, as well as the subsequent management of the waste and the financial responsibility for such activities.[3422] This may also include the obligation to

the end-of-life stage of consumer products: A. Michel, *Premature Obsolescence: In Search of an Improved Legal Framework*, Cambridge, Intersentia, 2023, 593–640.

3411 Directive 2008/98/EC of the European Parliament and of the Council of 19 November 2008 on waste and repealing certain Directives, *OJ L* 312, 22.11.2008, 3–30.

3412 Directive 2012/19/EU of the European Parliament and of the Council of 4 July 2012 on waste electrical and electronic equipment (WEEE) (recast), *OJ L* 197, 24.7.2°12, 38–71.

3413 Directive 2006/66/EC of the European Parliament and of the Council of 6 September 2006 on batteries and accumulators and waste batteries and accumulators and repealing Directive 91/157/EEC, *OJ L* 266, 29.9.2006, 1–14.

3414 Directive 2000/53/EC of the European Parliament and of the Council of 18 September 2000 on end-of-life vehicles, *OJ L* 269, 21.10.2000, 34–43.

3415 A. Michel, *Premature Obsolescence: In Search of an Improved Legal Framework*, Cambridge, Intersentia, 2023, 593–594, no. 907.

3416 *Ibid.*

3417 *Ibid.*

3418 See more in-depth on extended producer responsibility: A. Michel, *Premature Obsolescence: In Search of an Improved Legal Framework*, Cambridge, Intersentia, 2023, 621, no. 943 *et seq.*

3419 This is broadly defined in Art. 8(1) WFD as *"any natural or legal person who professionally develops, manufactures, processes, treats, sells or imports products."*

3420 See Art. 8 *juncto* Art. 3(21) WFD. EPR is further implemented in sectoral directives: See Art. 12 WEEE Directive, Art. 16 Batteries Directive, Art. 5 ELV Directive. See also Art. 7 of European Parliament and Council Directive 94/62/EC of 20 December 1994 on packaging and packaging waste, *OJ L* 365, 31.12.1994, 10–23.

3421 A. Michel, *Premature Obsolescence: In Search of an Improved Legal Framework*, Cambridge, Intersentia, 2023, 622, no. 944.

3422 Art. 8(2), second subpara. WFD.

provide publicly available information as to the extent to which the product is re-usable and recyclable.[3423] The WEEE, Batteries and ELV Directives make EPR mandatory in the EU. Additionally, Member States may also introduce mandatory or voluntary EPR schemes for other types of waste streams.[3424]

A specific take back obligation for (product-oriented) PSS contracts relating to electrical and electronic equipment, such as washing machines, coffee makers, smartphones, and other consumer electronics, can be found in the WEEE Directive. This directive requires that end-users can return the WEEE free of charge in collection facilities that are available and accessible, with no obligation to buy an EEE product of an equivalent type.[3425] PSS suppliers that qualify as producers within the context of EU waste law can meet their EPR obligations either individually or by means of a collective compliance mechanism (i.e. by becoming a member of a so-called producer responsibility organisation ("PRO")).[3426] For example, in Belgium, *Recupel* acts as the PRO for electrical and electronic equipment, as well as lamps.[3427] Its Dutch counterparts are *Wecycle* and *WEEE Nederland*.[3428]

7.4.2.2. Use-oriented PSS

891. Obligation to accept the returned product at the end of the PSS contract – The PSS supplier's obligation to accept the returned product at the end of the PSS contract is the mirror obligation of the PSS user's obligation to return the product. Indeed, without the cooperation of the PSS supplier, the PSS user will not be able to fulfil its obligation, and the former will be in creditor's default. Unlike the PSS user's obligation to return the good, the obligation to accept the returned good is not explicitly written down in the rental contract rules of the old BCC or the DCC. Thus, by lack of a default legal framework on this obligation, the contractual arrangements between the parties to the PSS contract will largely shape this obligation.

892. Contractual arrangements on the obligation to accept the returned product – Like the PSS user's obligation to return the product, the obligation to accept the returned product can take various forms.[3429] For large products such as large household appliances, the PSS contract will generally provide that the PSS supplier will make an appointment with the PSS user to

3423 *Ibid.*

3424 A. Michel, *Premature Obsolescence: In Search of an Improved Legal Framework*, Cambridge, Intersentia, 2023, 622, no. 945.

3425 See Art. 5 WEEE Directive.

3426 A. Michel, *Premature Obsolescence: In Search of an Improved Legal Framework*, Cambridge, Intersentia, 2023, 623, no. 947.

3427 See: www.recupel.be/en/about-recupel/legislation-authorities.

3428 See wecycle.nl and www.weee.nl.

3429 Compare with *supra* no. 875.

collect the product at the latter's home.[3430] This may be combined with a check-up of the goods for any rental damage on the spot when they are returned, as is the case with *Live Light*.[3431] Alternatively, mostly for smaller products, the PSS supplier may give return instructions to the PSS user. Generally, these instructions will give guidance on how the PSS user can the return the product through parcel shipping and/or provide a shipping label. Once the PSS supplier has received the product, he is obligated to process this return. In this regard, the terms and conditions of *Fairphone Easy* provide that *Fairphone* will send an email confirmation upon the successful return of the device.[3432] In still other cases, especially with pay-per-use PSS, the obligation to accept the returned product does not happen physically at the PSS user's or PSS supplier's premises, nor by returning the product via parcel shipping, but through a (charging) station and/or app. In the case of free-floating e-scooters, such as *Lime* and *Dott*, this is done by ending the ride on the app which locks the e-scooter and taking a picture to prove that there is no damage to the e-scooter and that it is parked at a legal (e-scooter) parking space.[3433] In the case of *Villo* and *Cambio*, the acceptance of the returned product happens when the PSS user parks the bicycle or car in one of the PSS supplier's bicycle stations or parking spots, which then registers the end of the ride in the PSS supplier's app or system.[3434]

893. Bearing the costs of the return? – Whether the PSS supplier bears the costs associated with the return of the product is up to the contractual agreements in the PSS contract. In some cases, the PSS supplier will indeed undertake to bear the costs of the collection of the product or the shipping costs. This is for example the case with *Blue Movement* and *Dressr*.[3435] However, this is not necessarily the case in all analysed PSS contracts. For example, the terms and conditions of *Swapphone* provide that the PSS user bears the cost for returning the smartphone.[3436] This is also the case in the terms and conditions of *Repeat/Gerrard Street*, where it is also stipulated that the PSS user is responsible for the costs of the return shipment.[3437]

894. Trade-in schemes for products other than those offered as part of the PSS – Some PSS suppliers offer a trade-in scheme where they accept and

---

3430 See e.g. Art. 11.4 and 12.4 Terms and Conditions Blue Movement and Art. 13.1 Terms and Conditions Bundles.

3431 See Art. 7.3 Terms and Conditions Live Light.

3432 See Art. 7.8 Terms and Conditions Fairphone Easy.

3433 See Art. 7.2 (Treat Our Products Like They Were Your Own – Damage) Terms and Conditions Lime and Art. 3.2 (Starting and ending a ride) Terms and Conditions Dott.

3434 Art. 3.5 Terms and Conditions Villo and Art. 13.1 Terms and Conditions Cambio.

3435 See Art. 12.8 Terms and Conditions Blue Movement and Art. 11 (returns) Terms and Conditions Dressr.

3436 Art. 7.9 Terms and Conditions Swapphone.

3437 Art. 4.5–4.6 *juncto* Art. 4.3 Terms and Conditions Repeat/Gerrard Street.

collect the PSS user's old product at the time of delivery of the PSS and undertake to repurpose or recycle it. For example, the terms and conditions of *Bundles* stipulate that *Bundles* will collect the PSS user-consumer's old washing machine if he so wishes.[3438] In return for his old product, the PSS user sometimes even gets a reduction on the subscription price of the PSS. This is for example the case with *Swapfiets*, which offers a trade-in scheme for old bicycles.[3439] In some cases, these trade-in schemes are offered voluntarily by the PSS supplier, while in other cases they are offered to fulfil the waste law obligations of the PSS supplier-producer already discussed above.[3440]

895. Contractual (circular) guarantees for sustainable repurposing after taking back the product – From the point of view of the circular economy, merely accepting the returned product at the end of the PSS contact is of course not enough. In order for the PSS to be truly sustainable, the PSS supplier must offer so-called circular guarantees where the PSS supplier undertakes to repurpose the returned product(s) in a sustainable way. These circular guarantees will be discussed further below.[3441]

7.4.2.3. Result-oriented PSS

896. Obligation to accept the returned product as mirror obligation of the PSS user's restitution obligation under accessory deposit contract – As discussed above, result-oriented PSS that contain an accessory deposit contract also entail a restitution obligation for the PSS user comparable to the restitution obligation in a rental contract.[3442] Also in case of result-oriented PSS, the mirror obligation of this restitution obligation is the PSS supplier's obligation to accept the returned product at the end of the PSS contract. Both in the Belgian and Dutch deposit contract rules, this obligation is not explicitly mentioned. As a result, the content and modalities of this obligation will depend on the contractual arrangements in the PSS contract, similar to those in use-oriented PSS.[3443]

897. Obligation to accept returned product and repurpose/recycling as part of the complex service contract – Another way to look at the PSS supplier's obligation to accept and/or repurpose (including recycling) the returned product at the end of the contract in result-oriented PSS is by considering this obligation as a part of the complex integrated service contract. This means that the performance of this obligation by the PSS supplier will be

3438 Art. 6.7 Terms and Conditions Bundles.
3439 Art. 11.1 Terms and Conditions Swapfiets.
3440 See *supra* no. 889 and 890.
3441 See *infra* section 7.4.3.
3442 See *supra* no. 884.
3443 Compare with *supra* no. 892.

assessed in the light of the conformity requirements for the contract for services, namely the obligation to perform the service in conformity with the contract and according to the rules of good workmanship.[3444]

898. WASTE LAW AND CIRCULAR GUARANTEES – Also in the case of result-oriented PSS, the PSS supplier may qualify as a "producer" within the meaning of EU or national waste law.[3445] In this case, the PSS supplier will have to comply with the obligations arising from these waste law rules, in particular the obligations regarding extended producer responsibility.[3446] Additionally, also in result-oriented PSS, the PSS contract may include circular guarantees that place a contractual obligation on the PSS supplier to repurpose the product in a sustainable manner.[3447]

7.4.3. CIRCULAR GUARANTEES

899. CIRCULAR GUARANTEES: RE-USING RETURNED PRODUCTS IN A SUSTAINABLE WAY – In the previous sections, the PSS user's obligation to return the product and the PSS supplier's obligation to take back the product were discussed. However, an obligation to take back the product does not necessarily guarantee that the PSS supplier will re-use the product in a sustainable way, for example through re-use, refurbishing, re-manufacturing, upcycling, etc. Therefore, from the point of view of the circular economy, it is a good idea to include in the PSS contract a clause in which the supplier undertakes to repurpose the returned product in a high quality and circular manner itself or to use a third party for this purpose.[3448] For the purpose of this book, such clauses are referred to as "circular guarantees".

900. OTHER CIRCULAR GUARANTEES: CONTRACTUALISING CIRCULAR ECONOMY AND (ENVIRONMENTAL) SUSTAINABILITY VALUES INTO THE PSS CONTRACT – Besides circular guarantees on re-using or repurposing the returned products in a sustainable way, circular guarantees can also be used to also include other circular economy and (environmental) sustainability values in the PSS contract, such as circular design, the use of responsibly extracted resources and good labour conditions. Indeed, these clauses contractualise certain values which the

---

3444 See *supra* section 4.3.3.2.
3445 See *supra* no. 490.
3446 *Ibid.*
3447 See *infra* section 7.4.3.
3448 C.M.D.S. PAVILLON, "Herijking van consumentencontractenrecht: duurzaamheid als nieuw ijkpunt?" in C.M.D.S. PAVILLON and W.H. VAN BOOM (eds.), *Preadviezen Vereniging voor Burgerlijk Recht: Privaatrechtelijke bescherming herijkt*, Zutphen, Paris, 2021, (11) 75; A. VAN VAERENBERGH and F. LEYMAN, "'Product als dienst'-overeenkomsten, een stap in de richting van de circulaire economie", *MER* 2019, (20) 27.

contractual parties undertake to respect as contractual obligations.[3449] In this way, certain economic, environmental, and sometimes even social values are not only "behind" the contract or present in the marketing of the PSS supplier, but explicitly mentioned and operationalised in the PSS contract. These circular guarantees or contractual sustainability clauses can either be included in the general terms and conditions of the PSS supplier, the special conditions of the PSS contract (where applicable), or by making reference to another document such as the CSR principles included in the PSS supplier's corporate codes of conduct,[3450] internal policies, and global, European or domestic initiatives concerning circular economy, climate change mitigation or other sustainability objectives.[3451]

901. Monitoring compliance with circular guarantees and sustainability clauses – If the PSS supplier includes a circular guarantee or sustainability clause in the PSS contract, it is important that these guarantees and the corresponding obligations are effectively complied with. Assessing whether the PSS supplier is compliant with the circular guarantees will not always be an easy task, especially for consumers, as non-compliance will often not be verifiable just from the appearance and qualities of the product itself. Various solutions can be used to ensure that the PSS user-consumer can control whether the PSS supplier has complied with its circular guarantees. First, the PSS supplier may conduct a self-assessment of its activities and supply chain (including internal reports or audits). This has the advantages that it is cost-effective, timely and more flexible. Potential downsides are the increased risk of biased audits, a lack of transparency, conflicts of interests and overall credibility concerns. Second, the PSS supplier may allow monitoring or audits by an independent third party (either announced or unannounced). This has the advantage that external audits are generally more objective, more transparent and seen as more credible. Potential disadvantages include the fact that these external audits are costly, more complex and may entail confidentiality concerns. Third, a combination of both internal and external audits and monitoring may be chosen. Regardless of which monitoring scheme is chosen, it is advisable to describe the assessment criteria, monitoring methods and procedures and reporting practices in the PSS contract in order to ensure maximum transparency.

[3449] C. Poncibò, "The Contractualisation of Environmental Sustainability", *ERCL* 2016, vol. 12, afl. 4, (335) 344.

[3450] For examples of such documents of PSS suppliers (particularly with regard to sustainability), see e.g. https://sustainability.swapfiets.com/?_gl=1*1b2a3tf* (Swapfiets); www.li.me/nl-be/why/sustainability (Lime); https://dressr.be/about-us/#sustainability (Dressr); www.bluemovement.com/nl-en/about-us (Blue Movement), etc.

[3451] However, this may raise issues regarding the incorporation of the principles in this document into the PSS contract, in other words, whether the referenced document becomes a valid part of the PSS contract. For this, reference can be made to *supra* section 2.3.2.1.

902. Assessing and enforcing compliance with circular guarantees by consumer or environmental organisations? – Despite the contractual possibilities to include circular guarantees and sustainability clauses and their associated monitoring and audit schemes in the PSS contract, it is not easy for an individual PSS user-consumer to assess compliance with these obligations. After all, an average PSS user-consumer will generally not have the time or knowledge to understand the lengthy and often technical documents resulting from such an audit. Additionally, even if the PSS user-consumer were to understand that the PSS supplier did not comply with its circularity obligations, it is far from certain that he will have the resources or priorities to initiate legal proceedings to enforce these circular guarantees. Here, there is a potential role for consumer or environmental organisations, which may be better placed to assess circular guarantees, and take legal action if necessary. These organisations seem increasingly concerned with issues of misleading environmental claims, as can be illustrated, for example, by the recent case brought by the "Foundation for the Promotion of the Fossil-free Movement"[3452] before the Court of Amsterdam, which found the Dutch airline KLM guilty of practices of "climate washing".[3453]

903. Contractual remedies for non-compliance with circular guarantees or sustainability clauses – The question arises as to the remedies available to the PSS user in case of non-compliance with the circular guarantees or sustainability clauses included in the PSS contract. First of all, the distinction between circular guarantees as an obligation of result and obligation of means will play an important role. Indeed, if the circular guarantee is formulated as an obligation of means (e.g. "*the PSS supplier takes all reasonable efforts to…*"), the PSS user-consumer will have a much harder time proving that the impossibility to meet the circularity or sustainability targets in the PSS contract constitute a breach of contract. In the case of an obligation of result, on the other hand (e.g. "*the PSS supplier ensures…*"), the mere fact that the circular targets were not met is enough to establish the existence of a breach of contract. The PSS supplier can then only escape liability if he proves *force majeure*. If there is indeed a breach of contract, the PSS user-consumer will have access to the remedies of general contract law and/or the specific remedies outlined in the PSS contract.[3454] For example, the remedy of performance can consist in the PSS supplier being ordered to take adequate measures to address the shortfall in meeting the circular targets. Additionally, the PSS supplier may be liable for damages, either in combination with the remedy of performance or by means of substitute damages. To alleviate the burden of proof for the PSS user-

3452 Stichting ter Bevordering van de Fossielvrij-Beweging, see: https://gofossilfree.org/nl/wiezijnwij/.

3453 See Ct. Amsterdam (NL) 20 March 2024, ECLI:NL:RBAMS:2024:1512, *rechtspraak.nl*.

3454 See *supra* section 2.6.6.

consumer, the PSS contract may contain an indemnity clause.[3455] Finally, the PSS user-consumer may claim the termination of the PSS contract if the breach of the circular guarantee constitutes a fundamental breach of contract. This will depend on the formulation and the agreements of the parties, as circular guarantees and sustainability clauses can either be qualified as an essential (or fundamental) or non-essential (non-fundamental) contractual obligation. Only in the former case will the PSS user-consumer be entitled to terminate the contract. If the circular guarantee is considered non-essential, the PSS user-consumer will only be entitled to claim performance, price reduction and/or damages.

7.4.4. LEGISLATIVE INTERVENTION NEEDED?

904. Three possible solutions – Again, three possible solutions may be adopted to tackle the challenges in the end of contract/product end-of-life stage. These include: (i) the **modernisation of national contract law** (option 1), (ii) incorporating rules on end of contract/end-of-life of the product in an **EU directive** (option 2), and (iii) the **use of balanced standard contracts and model clauses** (option 3).[3456] The first two options are examined in this section. The model clauses relating to the end of contract/product end-of-life stage are set out in section 7.4.5.

7.4.4.1. Modernisation of national contract law

A. Use-oriented PSS

905. Obligation of the PSS user to return the rented good – When evaluating the current provisions of the PSS user's obligation to return the rented good, the current principles of the rental contract rules are still fit for purpose. Therefore, proposed provision #38 largely repeats these principles and reformulates them into a modernised and concise provision. It thereby largely follows the approach of proposed Article 7.3.25 of the Draft Law. The first paragraph confirms the obligation of the lessee to return the rented good to the lessor in the same condition in which he received it, except for the damage caused by age, normal wear and tear or *force majeure*. The second paragraph stipulates that the lessee is liable for any damages caused to the rented good during the rental contract, including fire damages, unless he can prove that they were not caused by his fault. Finally, the third paragraph confirms that the lessee is liable for any damages caused by sub-lessees or third parties that use the rented good with the lessee's permission.

[3455] See for an example clause *infra* no. 920.

[3456] Compare with *supra* section 4.4.1.3, section 6.2.5, section 6.3.4 and section 7.3.4.

This proposed provision strikes a balance between the rights and obligations of the lessor and the lessee, as the lessee will not be liable for damages due to normal wear and tear and *force majeure*, while the lessor can claim compensation for any damages to the rented good that are due to the fault of the lessor. The fact that the lessee is responsible for damages during the rental contract is important from a sustainability perspective, as it can mitigate the risk of moral hazard and provide an incentive for the lessee to use the good with due care. Finally, this provision still leaves enough room for contractual freedom, for example for the parties to contractually define what is considered as "*normal wear and tear.*"

Proposed provision #38

Art. 7.3.X23. Obligation to return the rented good

§1 At the end of the rental period, the lessee must return the rented good to the lessor in the same condition in which he received it subject to the damages resulting from age, normal wear and tear and *force majeure.*

§2 The lessee is liable for damages to the rented good that occurred during the rental period, including damage caused by fire, unless he proves that they arose through no fault of his own.

§3 The lessee is liable for damages to the rented good caused by sub-lessees or through the actions of those who use the rented good with the lessee's consent.

906. Proof of the condition in which the rented good was received – The provisions of the rental contract on the proof of the condition in which the rented good was received are also still fit for purpose. Indeed, by requiring that a detailed initial description of the rented good is drawn up at the start of the rental contract, both the lessor and the lessee are protected.[3457] The lessor can use this detailed initial description to prove that certain damages present at the end of the rental contract constitute rental damage, as they were caused by the fault of the lessee. At the same time, an initial description enables the lessee to prove that certain damages were already present and therefore not due to his fault. If, on the other hand, no initial rental description is drawn up, it is appropriate to shift the burden of proof in order to protect the lessee. This is balanced, as the lessor can still provide proof that the rented good was in a different condition at the start of the rental contract than it is in at the time of the extinguishment of the rental contract by all legal means.[3458] Therefore, proposed provision #39 repeats and recodifies the principles of Article 1731 old BCC, largely following

3457 Compare with Art. 1731, §2 old BCC.
3458 Compare with Art. 1731, §1 old BCC.

the approach of proposed Article 7.3.26 of the Draft Law. The only difference with the old BCC is that the order of the two provisions is changed. In my view, this order is better and more logical because this way the default situation (i.e. a detailed initial description was drawn up) is handled first, and the exception situation (i.e. no detailed initial description was drawn up) is mentioned second.

Proposed provision #39

Art. 7.3.X24. Proof of the condition in which the rented good was received

§1 If a detailed initial description of the rented good has been drawn up, the lessee is deemed to have received the rented good in the condition indicated in the initial description, except for that which has been destroyed or damaged due to age or *force majeure*.

§2 If no detailed initial description of the rented good has been drawn up, the lessee is deemed to have received the rented good in the condition it is in at the time of extinguishment of the rental contract, subject to proof to the contrary by all legal means.

907. Obligation of the PSS supplier on return of the goods – The current Belgian (and also Dutch) rental contract rules do not contain an explicit obligation for the PSS supplier-lessor to take back the returned goods. Such an obligation is also not included in the Draft Law. Proposed provision #40 therefore aims to introduce an explicit obligation for the lessor to take all measures to enable the lessee to perform his obligation to return the rented good and to accept the rented good as required by the contract. For the first two points of this proposed obligation, inspiration was drawn from Article IV. B. – 3:106 DCFR. These general obligations on taking back the rented good can then be further defined in the PSS contract. For example, the "*measures reasonably expected to enable the lessee to return the good*", may be further contractually defined as picking up the good, or providing the lessee with a shipping label.[3459] The general obligation to "*accept the return as required by the contract*" may be further fleshed out in the PSS contract by defining the time period the lessor has to process the return of the product.[3460] The third point of proposed provision #40 is only relevant for the rental of movable goods. It makes a link with circular guarantees in the PSS contract and/or the applicable environmental regulations (such as those found in EU or national waste law).

[3459] See the model clauses *supra* no. 915.
[3460] *Ibid.*

Proposed provision #40

Art. 7.3.X25. Obligations on taking back the rented good

The lessor must:

1° take all measures that can reasonably be expected in order to enable the lessee to perform its obligation to return the rented good;

2° accept the return of the rented good as required by the contract; and

3° where applicable, ensure that the returned movable good is re-used, remanufactured or recycled in a sustainable manner as provided in the rental contract or applicable environmental regulations.

B. Result-oriented PSS

908. (Accessory) deposit contract: PSS user's obligation to return the deposited good – Also in the case of a result-oriented PSS containing an accessory deposit contract, the PSS user has an obligation to return the good. In this regard, proposed provision #41 states that the depositary (i.e. the PSS user) must return the deposited goods in the same condition in which he received them, subject to the damages due to age and normal use of the good, provided the depositary is allowed to use the good. This provision is a quasi-literal translation of the client's obligation to return the kept goods of proposed article 7.4.27, §2 BCC. This way, the PSS user's obligation to return the product in a result-oriented PSS contract is also aligned with the same obligation in a use-oriented PSS (which is qualified as a rental contract). Additionally, the depositary's obligation to return the goods will of course also extinguish if the goods have been lost due to *force majeure* (unless he was in default).[3461] The existence of *force majeure* must be assessed in light of the depositary's duty of care, which was set out above.[3462] Also this is aligned with the rules of the rental contract.

Proposed provision #41

Art. 7.4.X14. Obligation to return the deposited goods

The depositary shall return the deposited goods in the same condition in which he received them, subject to the damages due to age and normal use of the good, if the latter is allowed.

3461 See Art. 5.226(2) BCC.

3462 See *supra* no. 857.

909. (Accessory) deposit contract: PSS supplier's obligation to accept the returned deposited good – The mirror obligation of the PSS user-depositary's obligation to return the product is again the PSS supplier-depositor's obligation to accept the returned product. In my view, however, it is not necessary to include an explicit provision to this extent. The reason for this, as already mentioned higher, is that the deposit contract in the new BCC will most likely be a *specialis* contract of the general contract for services. In this regard, the depositor's obligation to accept the returned deposited good will be covered by proposed provision #34, namely the client's duty to cooperate.[3463] In particular, this will fall under the scope of §2, 1° of this proposed provision, namely the fact that the client must enable the "service provider" (i.e. the PSS user- depositary) to perform the obligations (i.e. returning the product) under the contract.

7.4.4.2. End of the contract and end-of life as part of an EU directive?

910. End of the contract and end-of-life as part of an EU directive? – The question arises how rules on end of contract/end-of-life of the product could be incorporated in an EU directive (option 2). In case of a general directive on conformity and quality of (almost) all service contracts (option 2a), this would most likely take the form of rules on an (accessory) deposit contract that is part of the service contract. The directive could then stipulate provisions on a duty of care and a restitution obligation similar to the ones proposed above in the context of a national law reform. If a specific directive for "packages" or "bundles" of services (option 2b) is chosen, the directive could include general obligations to return and take back the product, which could be further operationalised in more specific provisions. These could for example elaborate on the condition of the returned product and the modalities of how the return takes place. Additionally, a specific section on circular guarantees and sustainability clauses, where applicable, as well as their enforceability could also receive a place in the directive. For the content of all these specific provisions, inspiration can be drawn from the model clauses set out below.

7.4.5. MODEL CLAUSES ON THE END OF THE CONTRACT AND PRODUCT END-OF-LIFE

7.4.5.1. Model clauses on the obligation to return the product

911. Model clauses on the PSS user's obligation to return the product – The following model clauses can be used to shape the PSS user's obligation to return the product at the end of the PSS contract. The first model clause is

[3463] See *supra* no. 854.

particularly suited for larger products, as this requires the PSS user and the PSS supplier to agree on a date and time for collection of the product. The second model clause is suited for smaller products, which can be returned through parcel shipping. The last model clause can be used for pay-per-use PSS, such as free-floating e-scooters.

Model clause #77 – Obligation to return the product

- **Upon termination of the contract, [the PSS user] undertakes to return the product and its accessories to [the PSS supplier]. To this end, [the PSS supplier] will contact [the PSS user] to agree on a date and time for collection of the product [at the PSS user's address]. [If the product cannot be collected on this date, the costs for collection shall be borne by [the PSS user]].**

- **Upon termination of the contract, [the PSS user] undertakes to return the product and its accessories to [the PSS supplier]. To this end, [the PSS user] shall follow the return instructions [sent by email] [by the PSS supplier] to correctly label and adequately pack the product and drop it off at a return point. [The package must include the shipping label provided by the PSS supplier and other information that may be communicated as necessary for the return.]**

- **[The PSS user] can end [the ride] [at one of the (charging) stations/reserved parking spaces/through the app]. [The PSS user] must ensure that he [has parked/deposited/locked] [the vehicle (e.g. car, e-scooter, etc.)] in a proper manner.**

912. Model clause on costs of the return and whether a shipping label is provided by the PSS supplier – It is appropriate to include in the PSS contract who bears the costs of the return and whether the PSS supplier will provide a shipping label or whether the PSS user must ship the product himself. The first situation is preferable, as the PSS supplier will generally be able to negotiate better prices with carriers and is better placed to organise the logistics of the return. In addition, this "unburdens" the PSS user-consumer when returning the product, as he would otherwise have to go through additional administration or pay additional shipping fees.

Model clause #78 – Costs of the return

- **[The PSS supplier/the PSS user] bears the costs of the return. [The PSS user] [must use the shipping label provided by the PSS supplier/must ship the product himself via a carrier of his choice].**

913. Model clauses on the condition of the returned product – The following model clauses deal with the condition of the returned product. The first clause confirms and operationalises the PSS user's obligation to return the product in the same condition as it was made available at the start of the contract, except for normal wear and tear. Here, it is appropriate to further specify what is considered normal wear and tear under the PSS contract. The second model clause stipulates that if the PSS user does not comply with his obligation to return the product in a complete, original, or clean condition, the PSS supplier is entitled to recover the repair or replacement costs. To increase legal certainty for PSS users and to avoid that they are confronted with unexpected costs, these (reasonable) repair and replacement costs may be listed in an annex to the PSS contract. If these repair or replacement costs are unreasonably high, they may be combated based on the unfair contract terms rules on indemnity clauses.[3464]

Model clause #79 – Condition of the returned product

- **At the end of the contract or in case of early termination of the contract, [the PSS user] is obliged to return the product [and all associated documents and accessories] to [the PSS supplier] in the same condition as it was made available at the start of the contract, except for normal wear and tear. "Normal wear and tear" means, amongst others, [specified characteristics (e.g. no noticeable deep scratches, no cracks, etc.)].**

- **If the product is not in complete, original or clean condition [including the associated documents and accessories], [the PSS supplier] is entitled to recover the costs it has to incur to repair or replace the product and/or associated documents and accessories.**

- **A list of repair and replacement costs is set out in [Annex A] to this contract.**

7.4.5.2. Model clauses on the obligation to take back the product

914. MODEL CLAUSE ON THE PSS SUPPLIER'S OBLIGATION TO TAKE BACK THE PRODUCT – The following model clause is a general clause outlining the obligation of the PSS supplier to take back the product returned by the PSS user. From a circular economy perspective, it is advisable to include an obligation for the PSS supplier to process and repurpose the product in accordance with applicable circular economy principles. These circular economy principles can then be outlined further in the contract, for example by means of a circular guarantee.[3465]

3464 See *supra* no. 304.

3465 See for model clauses for circular guarantees *infra* no. 916 *et seq.*

> **Model clause #80 – Obligation to take back the product**
>
> - [The PSS supplier] takes back all products and accessories provided under this contract [at the end of their useful economic life and/or at the end of the contract] [, except in the case where [the PSS user] decides to exercise the purchase option provided for in Art. X of this contract]. [The PSS supplier] ensures that all products taken back are handled, processed and repurposed in accordance with applicable circular economy principles [as further outlined in Art. X of this contract].

915. MODEL CLAUSES ON MODALITIES OF THE OBLIGATION TO TAKE BACK THE PRODUCT – The following model clauses outline the procedure the PSS supplier will follow to take back the product. They are the mirror clauses of the PSS user's obligation to return the product at the end of the PSS contract.[3466] The first clause is useful for larger products, which have to be collected by the PSS supplier or a logistics partner of the PSS supplier. The second model clause can be used for smaller products that are returned through parcel shipping. Finally, the last clause requires the PSS supplier to set up a system (either with a physical (charging) station or through an app) which allows the PSS user to end the pay-per-use service.

> **Model clause #81 – Modalities of obligation to take back the product**
>
> - At the end of the contract, [the PSS supplier] will contact [the PSS user] to agree on a date and time for collection of the product [at the PSS user's address]. [The PSS supplier/the PSS supplier's logistics partner] will check the product for damage at the time of collection, in the presence of [the PSS user] or a person authorised by him. A return slip with information about the return of the product and any visible damage will be drawn up by [The PSS supplier/the PSS supplier's logistics partner] and must be signed by [the PSS user].
>
> - At the end of the contract, [the PSS supplier] will provide [the PSS user] with return instructions[, including a shipping label] [by email]. After receiving the returned product, [the PSS supplier] shall process and confirm the return [by email] within [specified time period (e.g. 5 working days)].
>
> - [The PSS supplier] shall provide [(charging) stations/reserved parking spaces/an app] where the [PSS user] can end [the ride]. After [the PSS user] [has parked/deposited/locked] [the vehicle (e.g. car, e-scooter, etc.)], [the PSS supplier] confirms the end of the ride and the costs of the ride [by email].

[3466] Compare with *supra* no. 911.

7.4.5.3. *Model clauses for circular guarantees*

916. Model clauses on the re-use of the product – The following model clauses place an obligation on the PSS supplier to re-use the product(s) used in the performance of the service. There are different options here. First, the PSS contract may state that the PSS supplier must use the individual, specified product used by the PSS user. Alternatively, the clause on the re-use of the product may be more general by setting out a more general obligation for the PSS supplier to re-use a certain percentage of all products at the end of all contracts and/or end of useful lifespan. Depending on the formulation of the clause, these obligations will be qualified as an obligation of result or an obligation of means.

Model clause #82 – Re-use of the product[3467]

- **[The PSS supplier] [re-uses/takes all reasonable efforts to reuse] the individual product used by [the PSS user].**
- **[The PSS supplier] [re-uses/takes all reasonable efforts to reuse] [specification of circularity goal, relating to all products (e.g. 50% of all products taken back].**

917. Model clauses on repurposing the product in a circular manner – Besides clauses on the re-use of the product, the PSS contract may also contain broader clauses on repurposing the product in a circular manner. The first model clause contains a general obligation to repurpose the product in a circular manner. This is then further operationalised in the second and third model clause. The second clause outlines the other circular strategies the PSS must use if re-use of the product is not (reasonably) possible. The third model clause states that recycling the product is an *ultimum remedium*, which may only be relied on when all the other circular alternatives are not reasonably feasible.

Model clause #83 – Repurposing the product in a circular manner

- **If the product is returned to [the PSS supplier] for whatever reason (e.g. (early) termination of the contract, replacement of the product, etc.), [the PSS supplier] [takes all reasonable efforts to/is required to] repurpose the product in a circular manner.**[3468]

3467 Model clauses based on C. Borucki, H. Slachmuylders, B. Keirsbilck, D. Gruyaert and E. Terryn, *Model clauses for Product-as-a-Service (PaaS) contracts*, CE Center. Circular Economy Policy Research Center, 2022–23, 67.

3468 Model clause based on C. Borucki, H. Slachmuylders, B. Keirsbilck, D. Gruyaert and E. Terryn, *Model clauses for Product-as-a-Service (PaaS) contracts*, CE Center. Circular Economy Policy Research Center, 2022–23, 67.

- **For the purpose of this contract, repurposing the product in a circular manner means prioritising the re-use of the product in its entirety, with minimal disassembly or processing. Where this is not [reasonably] possible, [the PSS supplier] uses other circular alternatives to re-use, such as refurbishing, reconditioning, remanufacturing or otherwise repurposing.**

- **If none of the circular alternatives to re-use are [reasonably] feasible, [the PSS supplier] recycles the product in an environmentally responsible manner [in accordance with a specified recycling scheme/in accordance with specified recycling instructions].**[3469]

918. Other circular guarantees – As mentioned above, circular guarantees can also be used to also include other circular economy and (environmental) sustainability values in the PSS contract, such as circular design, the use of responsibly extracted resources and good labour conditions.[3470] The first model clause entails a general circular guarantee to minimise waste and maximise the lifespan of the products used in the performance of the service. The second model clause deals with circular design. The third model clause contains an obligation to only source materials and resources from responsibly managed and certified sources. For this, reference can be made to specific standards such as the Responsible Minerals Initiative (RMI) for minerals.[3471] Finally, the last model clause deals with social aspect of sustainability, by requiring that all products and services provided under the PSS contract adhere with internationally recognised labour standards.

Model clause #84 – Circular guarantees

- **[The PSS supplier] [takes all reasonable efforts] to minimise waste and maximise the lifespan of the products used in the performance of the service in order to maximise resource efficiency.**[3472]

- **[The PSS supplier] shall [ensure/take all reasonable efforts] that all products provided under this contract are designed with circularity principles in mind, aiming for longevity, repairability, potential for remanufacturing, and recyclability. For this aim, relevant design considerations are [prioritising the use of renewable materials and minimisation of waste throughout the entire product lifecycle].**

3469 Model clause based on C. Borucki, H. Slachmuylders, B. Keirsbilck, D. Gruyaert and E. Terryn, *Model clauses for Product-as-a-Service (PaaS) contracts*, CE Center. Circular Economy Policy Research Center, 2022–23, 67.

3470 See *supra* no. 900.

3471 See www.responsiblemineralsinitiative.org.

3472 Model clause based on C. Borucki, H. Slachmuylders, B. Keirsbilck, D. Gruyaert and E. Terryn, *Model clauses for Product-as-a-Service (PaaS) contracts*, CE Center. Circular Economy Policy Research Center, 2022–23, 66.

- **[The PSS supplier] [commits/takes all reasonable efforts] to only source materials and resources used for the products and services offered under this contract from responsibly managed and certified sources. This includes adherence to standards such as [specified standards (e.g. the Responsible Minerals Initiative (RMI))]. [The PSS supplier] shall provide transparency regarding the origin of materials and resources and ensure that suppliers further down the supply chain also adhere to these standards.**

- **[The PSS supplier] warrants that all products and services provided under this contract are produced in compliance with internationally recognised labour standards, including but limited to fair wages, safe working conditions, and the prohibition of child labour and forced labour. [The PSS supplier] shall ensure that suppliers further down the supply chain also adhere to these standards.**

919. MODEL CLAUSES ON VERIFIABILITY, MONITORING AND AUDITS OF COMPLIANCE WITH THE CIRCULAR GUARANTEES – To make the circular guarantee effective, and to avoid "greenwashing", it is appropriate that there is a control mechanism that ensures whether the PSS supplier has indeed met the promised circular economy and sustainability objectives set out in the PSS contract. This requires transparency and accountability. One way to achieve this, is by setting up a monitoring or auditing system that is independent of the PSS supplier. The following model clauses provide a framework for such a monitoring or auditing scheme by an independent third party. The first clause places an obligation on the PSS supplier to keep records of its efforts for furthering circularity and sustainability and make these records available to the independent auditor. The second clause contains an obligation to allow and facilitate the audits, as well as an obligation to cooperate with the auditors. Additionally, it specifies the timeframes and methods for these audits. The third and fourth clause address how the findings of the independent audits will be presented and communicated. Here, it can also be clarified how the PSS supplier will work with and communicate the results of the independent audits and, if there are shortcomings in meeting the circularity and sustainability targets, a requirement to consider in the report how these shortcomings will be remedied in the future.

Model clause #85 – Verifiability and monitoring of circular guarantees[3473]

- **[The PSS supplier] keeps records of its efforts for furthering circular economy and sustainability objectives and makes them available for auditing or reporting purposes.**

[3473] Model clauses based on C. BORUCKI, H. SLACHMUYLDERS, B. KEIRSBILCK, D. GRUYAERT and E. TERRYN, *Model clauses for Product-as-a-Service (PaaS) contracts*, CE Center. Circular Economy Policy Research Center, 2022–23, 67–68.

- [The PSS supplier] agrees to allow external audits of its compliance with the circular guarantees set out in this contract by [specified independent third party]. These audits take place [specified interval (e.g. quarterly, annually)]. They are conducted using [specified methods and standards]. [The PSS supplier] cooperates fully with the auditor and provides all necessary information and access to facilities.
- The auditor provides [the PSS supplier] with a written report of its findings[, including any recommendations for improvement,] within [specified time period (e.g. 30 days after completion of the audit)].
- [The PSS supplier] publishes a report on its efforts for achieving the specified circular economy and sustainability objectives [specified interval (e.g. annually, quarterly, etc.)]. If certain specified circularity and sustainability objectives were not met during the audited timeframe, the report includes a plan to address the shortcomings in the future.

920. Indemnity clause in case of non-fulfilment of circularity guarantees – To avoid that the circularity guarantees in the PSS contract remain a "paper tiger", it can be useful to include an indemnity clause in case of non-fulfilment of the circular objectives. This clause alleviates the burden of proof for the PSS user, who would otherwise have to rely on the remedy of compensation for damages of general contract law, which requires proof that the PSS user indeed suffered damages.[3474] This will not always be straightforward in the case of a failure to fulfil the circular guarantee, as the harm to the PSS user will be mostly "indirect". One may think of emotional distress, climate damage *sensu lato* (which is often prospective and cannot always be easily individualised), but also the loss of a chance to contract with a PSS supplier offering truly sustainable PSS business models, etc. With an indemnity clause, on the other hand, the contracting parties avoid any discussions in this regard by making clear that, for them, a failure to fulfil a circular guarantee outlined in the PSS contract does indeed result in a right to compensation for damages for the PSS user.

Model clause #86 – Indemnity clause for non-fulfilment of circularity guarantees

- In the event that [the PSS supplier] fails to meet the circularity guarantees as outlined in this contract, [the PSS supplier] shall be liable to pay damages of [reasonable amount] to [the PSS user/an NGO furthering circularity objectives (in the name of the PSS user)] as a compensation for such failure.

[3474] See *supra* no. 299.

921. Essential/non-essential nature of circular guarantees – The following model clauses can be used to define in the PSS contract whether the circular guarantees constitute an essential obligation, a breach of which entitles the PSS user to terminate the contract.[3475] Given the far-reaching consequences of a termination of the PSS contract, it is conceivable that PSS suppliers will generally qualify the circular guarantees as non-essential obligations.

> **Model clause #87 – Essential/non-essential nature of circular guarantees**
>
> - **The parties acknowledge and agree that the circular guarantees outline in this contract are considered essential obligations. A material breach of these circular guarantees will constitute a fundamental breach of contract, in which case [the PSS user] shall have the right to terminate the contract [with immediate effect] [upon written notice to the PSS supplier/upon a judicial decision].**
> - **The parties acknowledge and agree that the circular guarantees outlined in this contract are considered non-essential obligations. In the event of a breach of these circular guarantees, the PSS user shall not be entitled to terminate the contract.**

7.5. CONCLUSION

922. Ownership, moral hazard, and end of contract/end-of-life of the product: conclusion – This chapter dealt with the consequences and implications of the essential characteristic of use-oriented and result-oriented PSS, namely that the PSS supplier retains the ownership of the product. First, section 7.2 analysed how the PSS supplier can protect its right of ownership of the product against accession and acquisitive prescription. Second, section 7.3 discussed the risk of moral hazard, as well as ways to (contractually) mitigate this risk. Third, the PSS supplier's obligations regarding collection, repurposing, and/or disposal of the product in the end of contract/end-of-life stage of use-oriented and result-oriented PSS contracts were examined in section 7.4. Here, it was also considered how circular guarantees can be incorporated into the PSS contract.

923. Conclusion on ownership of the product – The first section of this chapter started from the observation that **ownership takes a back seat in a circular and servitised economy.**[3476] Indeed, in use-oriented and result-oriented PSS, rights of use and service contracts are more important than transferring

[3475] See *supra* no. 903.
[3476] See *supra* section 7.2.

the ownership of the product. In fact, the PSS supplier will want to avoid that ownership of the product is transferred to the PSS user. If the product is incorporated or installed into an immovable good, the biggest "enemy" of the PSS supplier is the principle of accession. According to this principle, the owner of an immovable good (e.g. the PSS user's home) will also become the owner of the inherent components of that good (e.g. the heat pump or ventilation system installed in the PSS user's home). However, even if the product is not incorporated into the PSS user's home, the PSS supplier still risks losing the ownership of the product since it loses the physical possession of the product. This follows from the rule of acquisitive prescription, which protects the third-party acquirer of a movable good against the lack of power of disposition of his legal predecessor, and the risk that the PSS user becomes insolvent.

A few legal solutions can be used to **avoid immovable accession** of the product. A first exception to the principle of accession is the creation of a **building right** (also called a right of *superficies*). A building right entails that the right holder who has built a construction on the land or building of a third party (i.e. the PSS supplier who has installed the product in the PSS user's home) remains the owner of that construction, even if it is incorporated into the other party's (i.e. the PSS user) immovable good. However, due to the unity principle, this solution can only be used for product/materials that are sufficiently independent from the immovable good and are not considered an inherent component of it. Additionally, for being enforceable against third parties, a building right requires an authentic deed which is registered in the land registers, which will not always be economically viable as registering will in practice be costly and time-consuming. A second solution could be to including a **retention of title clause** in the PSS contract. Under Belgian law (contrary to Dutch law), the retention of title can survive incorporation and therefore prevent accession from taking place, provided the retention of title clause is registered in the pledge register. While there is no unanimity in legal doctrine regarding the question whether the retention of title can be used in contracts that do not have the finality to transfer ownership (such as use-oriented and result-oriented PSS), there are strong legal arguments in favour of answering this question in the affirmative. Additionally, the product may also be encumbered with a **subsidiary pledge** which acts as a safety net if, for whatever reason, the retention of title would remain without effect. It is up to the parties to decide whether the costs of registration are worth the additional protection. A third possible solution to avoid incorporation and accession is an **accessory building right**. This is a building right resulting from a personal, property or administrative right of use which a third party acquires over someone's immovable property (e.g. accessory to a rental contract, ground lease or concession). To give a concrete example, the PSS supplier could conclude a loan contract with the PSS user granting the former a free right of use of parts of the PSS user's home. Based on this free use contract, the PSS supplier can then install the product, for example a heat pump, on the PSS user's premises while retaining the ownership. Then, the PSS supplier rents that heat pump to the PSS user, who has a right of use during the term of the PSS contract. The PSS supplier's right of ownership then arises from the accessory building right, which follows from the use contract.

The PSS supplier will also want to protect itself from **other risks of loss of ownership** associated with losing physical possession of the movable product. A first risk entails that the PSS user sells or otherwise disposes of the product. Under both Belgian and Dutch law, the **acquisitive prescription** principle protects a third-party buyer of a movable good against the lack of power of disposition of his seller if certain requirements are met. One of these requirements is that the third-party acquirer must be acting in good faith. The PSS supplier can therefore mitigate this risk by affixing to the product in a durable and visible way a label or nameplate indicating the ownership situation of the product. This will ensure that the third-party acquirer cannot be in good faith, as he will be aware that the PSS user is not the owner and therefore is lacking power of disposition. A second risk relates to the **risk of the PSS user's insolvency**. Can the PSS supplier revindicate the movable goods from the estate even though the other creditors assume in good faith that these goods belong to the insolvent PSS user? Both under Belgian and Dutch law, the PSS supplier's right of ownership will allow revindicating the product, without the concurrent creditors being able to assert a right to it. As a result, the PSS supplier confronted with an insolvent PSS user should generally not be too concerned of losing the non-incorporated product in insolvency proceedings. To facilitate the revindication, the PSS contract may include an obligation for the insolvent PSS user to disclose the ownership situation of the product to the bankruptcy trustee.

Since the main focus and scope of this book is limited to contractual issues of PSS contracts, no legislative recommendations have been made for property law reform. This is left to further research. Instead, this book focused on the **contractual clauses** that can be used in the PSS contract to allow the PSS supplier to retain the ownership of the product.

924. Conclusion on moral hazard – The second section of this chapter discussed the **risk of moral hazard and the solutions to mitigate this risk.**[3477] Moral hazard means that PSS users may behave less diligently and treat the product less carefully because they do not own it. This may result in increased wear and tear, decreased product lifespan and potential conflicts between the PSS supplier and the PSS user regarding liability for damages. Additionally, moral hazard may lead to rebound effects of PSS, causing PSS to have a limited or even negative effect on environmental sustainability.

A first solution to mitigate the risk of moral hazard is to include an **obligation to take care of the product** in the PSS contract. In **product-oriented PSS**, this

[3477] See *supra* section 7.3.

does not really come into play, as the PSS user-buyer is the owner of the product. This means that if he fails to treat the product with due care, (only) he will bear the consequences. Nevertheless, the way the consumer takes care of the product is not entirely irrelevant in product-oriented PSS, as the PSS user-buyer will not be able to invoke the PSS supplier-seller's liability for lack of conformity of the product if the damage to the product was caused by the PSS user-buyer's fault. In **use-oriented PSS**, the rules of the rental contract provide that the PSS user-lessee must take care of the rented product as a prudent and reasonable person/good lessee. This is an abstract criterium that can be further operationalised in the PSS contract, for example by referring to the user manual or providing information sheets explaining the correct use of the product. Additionally, the PSS contract may provide that the PSS user must use the product with the accessories provided by the PSS supplier (e.g. protective smartphone case, bicycle lock, etc.). In **result-oriented PSS**, since the focus is on the service rather than the use of the product, the rules of the contract for services do not contain an (explicit) obligation to take care of the product. Instead, the duty to take care of the product can be inferred from the PSS user's obligation to take the care of a good client and the duty to cooperate. Of course, the content of these obligations may also be defined in the result-oriented PSS contract. If the result-oriented PSS contract contains an accessory deposit contract, the PSS user has a duty of care and an obligation to return the product, which are interpreted in a similar way as the obligation to take the care of a prudent and reasonable person/good lessee in the rental contract.

Some PSS contracts contractually limit the PSS user's freedom to move or relocate the product to avoid damage to and loss of the product. These **limits to moving the product** can be seen as a contractual specification of the obligation to take care of the product. Most often, these limits include a requirement to notify the PSS supplier that the product will be moved and/or a requirement to request prior authorisation before moving the product. Some PSS suppliers also offer (free or paid) relocation services. On the question of the validity of these clauses, it seems that, in general, a requirement of prior authorisation to move the product would not create a significant imbalance in the parties' rights and obligations to the detriment of the PSS user-consumer. On the other hand, a total ban on moving or locating the product implies a more far-reaching restriction of the PSS user's rights. As a result, a balancing exercise will be necessary that takes into account the risk of damage to the product (and potential revindication issues) on the one hand, and the interests of the PSS user on the other.

A third solution for avoiding the risk of moral hazard is the practice where the PSS supplier offers **incentives and "bonusses"** to the PSS user if he makes proper use of the product. This can roughly take two forms: either by means of a deposit, which is a negative protection against moral hazard, or by means of incentives that positively reward the PSS user if he takes good care of the product. PSS users are often required to pay a **deposit**, which may be withheld in the event of damage to the product, failure to return the product, or otherwise failing to comply with the terms of the PSS contract. As such, the deposit acts as an incentive for the PSS user to use the product or the service responsibly, as he knows that he can get his deposit back upon complying with the terms and conditions, keeping the product in a good state of repair and timely returning it to the PSS supplier. Alternatively, the PSS supplier may **positively reward** PSS users who treat their product with due care by offering "bonusses" such as a discount on the next invoice, loyalty points, or a free extension of the maintenance contract. This may lead to a mutually beneficial relationship where the interests of the PSS supplier, the PSS user and the environment are all aligned.

When considering **normative solutions**, three possible solutions can again be envisaged. These include (i) a modernisation of national contract law; (ii) an EU directive; and (iii) balanced model clauses and standard contracts.

With regard to modernisation of national contract law for use-oriented PSS, the **principles of the rental contract on the duty to take care of the product are still fit for purpose.** Indeed, the abstract criterion that the PSS user must use the rented good as a "good family father", including the possibility to contractually make this criterion more concrete, still holds today. However, a reformulation so that the old-fashioned and non-inclusive language is replaced by a more appropriate and modern alternative, namely the "reasonable and careful person", is most welcome. Additionally, this would have the advantage that the rental contract rules are terminologically aligned with book 5 of the BCC. The other aspects of this obligation can also be (re)codified without much change. As regards the question whether statutory legal provisions on **limits to moving the rented good and incentives for correct use** of the good are necessary, it seems that this question should be answered in the negative. After all, the principle of freedom of contract allows the parties to flesh out their own contractual regime on a case-by-case basis, tailored to the specific business model in question. For clauses that impose too far-reaching restrictions on the PSS user-lessee's freedom to move or relocate the product, they can be combated using the general test of the UCTD and its implementing provisions.

In terms of modernising national contract law for result-oriented PSS, the **obligation to take the care of a good client** could be (re)codified as a general obligation to cooperate with the service provider. Taking inspiration from the DCFR, this obligation could fall apart into four "sub-obligations", namely (i) enabling the service provider to perform the contract; (ii) ensuring the safety of the service provider; (iii) providing any necessary information; and (iv) coordinate the work of different service providers. The first two sub-obligations are particularly relevant to result-oriented PSS, as they could imply an obligation of the client to take the necessary care of the product(s) made available as part of the contract. Additionally, (re)codifying rules of the (accessory) deposit contract, in particular the duty of care of the PSS user-depositary as well as his right of use of the product, may also provide a solid legal framework for the PSS user's obligation to take care of the product in result-oriented PSS.

If the EU legislator would opt for **EU harmonisation**, the new directive should also take into account the risk of moral hazard and how this risk can be countered. This could either be done by including a general obligation for the client to take the care of a good client/a duty to cooperate in a general directive on conformity of services (option 2a) or by including more specific obligations (such as taking reasonable measures against theft and loss, using the product in line with the instructions of the service provider, rules on the required deposit, etc) in a more specific directive for "packages" or "bundles" of services (option 2b).

925. Conclusion on end of the contract/product end-of-life – The third section of this chapter dealt with the question **what happens to the products at the end of the PSS contract or at the end of their useful economic life.**[3478] Thus, it discussed the PSS user's obligation to return the product, the PSS supplier's mirror obligation to take back the product, and the possibility to include circular guarantees in the PSS contract. It also proposed some normative solutions in the form of proposals for legislative intervention and model clauses.

Contrary to product-oriented PSS, **the PSS user has an obligation to return the product** in use-oriented and result-oriented PSS. This follows from the fact that the PSS user does not acquire the ownership of the product but only a right of use. For **use-oriented PSS**, the Belgian and Dutch rental contract rules provide that the PSS user-lessee must return the product to the PSS supplier-lessor and compensate the latter for the damage to the rented product. This restitution obligation is qualified as an obligation of result which is also assessed in light of the PSS user's duty to take care of the product. The PSS user must return the product in the condition in which he received it, except for wear and tear due to normal use. This means he will be liable for any damages to the product or losses thereof, unless he can prove that they were caused by no fault of his own. The damages are determined by comparing the condition of the product when it is returned with the condition at the start of the PSS contract, laid down in a circumstantial rental inventory. In the absence of a circumstantial rental inventory, there is a presumption that the PSS user received the product in the same condition it is in at the end of the PSS contract. This means that if such a circumstantial rental inventory is lacking, the PSS supplier must prove that the damage was caused during the rental contract, and that it is not due to normal wear and tear.

In **result-oriented PSS**, the contract for services will generally be accompanied by an accessory deposit contract (including a contractual provision granting the PSS user a right of use over the product). Under this accessory deposit contract, the PSS user has a duty of care and an obligation to return

3478 See *supra* section 7.4.

the product, which are assessed in a similar way as the PSS user's duty of care and restitution obligation under the rental contract. However, the condition in which the product must be returned differs from the rental contract. Under the Belgian rules of the deposit contract, the PSS user-depositary must return the product only in the condition it is in at the time of return. Any damage it has suffered through no fault of the PSS user-depositary shall be borne by the PSS supplier-depositor. This means that, in the absence of a contractual clause to the contrary, the PSS supplier will have to prove that the PSS user breached its duty of care which caused damage to the product. Under Dutch law, on the other hand, in the absence of a contractual clause to the contrary, the PSS user-depositary must return the product in the condition he received it. Thus, if the product is damaged (including normal wear and tear), the PSS user will be liable unless he can prove this is due to *force majeure*, which is assessed in light of his duty of care. Second, contrary to the Belgian and Dutch rental contract rules, the (accessory) deposit contract does not require a circumstantial (rental) inventory. This also means that there is also no rebuttable presumption that the PSS user received the product in the same condition as the condition of the product at the end of the PSS contract if such circumstantial (rental) inventory is lacking. Nevertheless, even if an inventory of the product is not required, it is a good idea to let the PSS user sign a form indicating the description of the product at the start of the contract. After all, without this form, it will be difficult for the PSS supplier to prove that the damage to the product is the fault of the PSS user.

The PSS supplier's obligation to take back the product also takes different forms depending on the type of PSS. For **product-oriented PSS**, the Belgian and Dutch (consumer) sales rules in principle do not contain an obligation for the seller to take back the product at the end of its useful life. However, this does not mean that the PSS supplier-seller will never have such an obligation. This may either result from a contractual obligation in the PSS contract (taking back the product and repurposing/recycling it as an additional service) or from a statutory obligation arising from (EU or national) waste law. In **use-oriented PSS** and **result oriented PSS**, on the other hand, the PSS supplier does have an obligation to take back the product, which is the mirror obligation of the PSS user's responsibility to return the product. Indeed, without the cooperation of the PSS supplier, the PSS user will not be able to fulfil its restitution obligation under the rental contract or (accessory) deposit contract and the former will be in creditor's default. Unlike the PSS user's obligation to return the good, the obligation to accept the returned good is not explicitly written down in the old BCC or the DCC. Thus, as a result of a default legal framework, the contractual obligations in the PSS contract will largely shape this take back obligation.

From the point of view of the circular economy, it is a good idea to include **circular guarantees** in the PSS contract. After all, an obligation to take back the product does not necessarily guarantee that the PSS supplier will repurpose the product in a sustainable way, for example through re-use, refurbishing, re-manufacturing, upcycling, etc. Thus, this section provided examples of ways how the PSS supplier may contractualise circular economy and (environmental) sustainability values into the PSS contract, for example by undertaking to repurpose the returned product in a high quality and circular manner, as well as how such clauses may be enforced.

De lege ferenda, this chapter again proposed three possible solutions. First, proposals were made for the **modernisation of national contract law** (option 1). For use-oriented PSS, two provisions for the rental contract were proposed, namely on the lessee's obligation to return the rented good and the lessor's obligation to take back the rented good. For result-oriented PSS, a provision was drafted for the obligation of the PSS user-depositary to return the deposited goods in an (accessory) deposit contract. It was not deemed necessary to draft a mirror provision for the PSS supplier-depositor to accept the returned product, as this will be covered by proposed provision #34 (the client's duty to cooperate). Second, it was considered how rules on end of contract/end-of-life of the product could be incorporated in an **EU directive** (option 2). Either more general provisions on the duty of care and restitution obligation of the (accessory) deposit contract may be included in a general directive on conformity of services, or more specific provisions tailored to PSS may be included in a specific directive for "packages" or "bundles" of services. Finally, the potential of **using balanced standard contracts and model clauses** (option 3) was highlighted, both for the PSS user's obligation to return the product and the PSS supplier's obligation to take back the product, as well as in terms of circular guarantees and sustainability clauses.

8. GENERAL CONCLUSION AND POLICY RECOMMENDATIONS

"The circular economy gives us opportunity
to build a system that can run in the long term,
and the time is right for it to reach scale"
– Ken Webster[3479]

926. SERVITISATION, CIRCULAR BUSINESS MODELS AND PSS CONTRACTS – This book[3480] focused on the "servitisation" of the economy – a shift from buying products to using "products-as-service" – which is said to have a huge potential towards a more circular economy in the movable consumer products and services sector. The idea is that, since service suppliers retain ownership of the products offered "as-a-service", it is in their best interest to ensure they last a long time. This can be done by offering high-quality and durable products that can easily be taken back, repaired, refurbished and/or recycled at the end of their useful life. The umbrella term used throughout this book is "product-service systems" ("PSS"), meaning a "*marketable set of products and services, capable of jointly fulfilling a user's need.*"

927. ONE CENTRAL RESEARCH QUESTION… – Although the trend of servitisation has huge potential, also in economic terms, consumers often feel uncertain and hesitant to engage in new circular business models and PSS contracts. This may be explained by behavioural barriers and the lack of a clear regulatory framework. Moreover, the sustainability of PSS is not necessarily a given. Studies have shown that in some cases PSS even have a negative effect on sustainability due to careless use of a product by those who are not the owner ("moral hazard") or due to an increase in "unnecessary" consumption of PSS that are cheaper than purchasing the product outright (so-called "rebound effects"). The aim of this research was to describe and evaluate the legal

[3479] Ken Webster is a director of the International Society for Circular Economy (is4ce.org). From 2010 – end 2018 he was Head of Innovation for the Ellen MacArthur Foundation, a circular economy pioneer organisation.

[3480] This book is the result of a doctoral research project that was funded as part of C2 Project C24M/19/003. The C2 project has also led to the publication of the book B. KEIRSBILCK, E. TERRYN, J. EYCKMANS, S. ROUSSEAU, D. VOINOT (eds.), "Servitization and circular economy: economic and legal challenges", Antwerp, Intersentia, 2023, 217 p.

framework of PSS contracts and propose legal solutions in order to promote balanced and truly sustainable PSS contracts. This translated into the following central research question: "*How are PSS contracts currently regulated under EU and national consumer contract law (Belgium, The Netherlands) and, if necessary, how could the current regulatory framework be improved?*"

928. ...TACKLED IN FOUR BUILDING BLOCKS – The answer to this central research question was built up from four building blocks. *First*, this research developed a conceptual framework that offers a grip throughout the rest of this research. *Second*, it brought together and described the relevant EU rules as well as the national contract laws applicable to PSS contracts. *Third*, it evaluated the current regulatory framework based on the evaluative criteria of legal certainty, consistency and coherence, fair balance and sustainability in order to identify its strengths and weaknesses. *Fourth*, legal solutions were proposed to tackle the identified weaknesses and to promote balanced, truly sustainable PSS contracts. Instead of tackling these last three building blocks in separate parts, it was opted to take an integrated approach. Thus, the chapters of this book are structured around the different components of the PSS contract and the distinct phases of the contractual timeline rather than having three separate chapters for description, evaluation and normative aspects. This conclusion revisits these building blocks as the structure for the conclusions in order to align with the four sub-research questions of this book.

929. CONCEPTUAL FRAMEWORK: THREE MAIN TYPES OF PSS – The conceptual framework of this research was derived from the most widely accepted and reported categorisation of PSS, which distinguishes between three main types of PSS based on the object of the contract and the shift in ownership. Nevertheless, its importance should not be exaggerated, as PSS often exhibit characteristics of more than one type and there is often no clear-cut borderline.

(i) **Product-oriented PSS**, consist of a traditional sale of a product on top of which (after-sales) services (maintenance, repair, etc.) are added. These business models therefore still entail a transfer of ownership.

(ii) **Use-oriented PSS** entail a right of use for the user of a specific product against payment of a one-off or periodical fee. In these contracts, the service provider retains the ownership and responsibility for the product during its entire life cycle. Some use-oriented PSS are limited to a mere right of use against payment, but others are also combined with additional services. Examples include contracts whereby household appliances (e.g. "*Bundles*", "*Blue Movement*"), bicycles (e.g. "*Swapfiets*") or furniture ("*Live Light*") are made available to consumers.

(iii) **Result-oriented PSS** do not relate to one or more specific products but a specific functional result. To fulfil this specific need, the producer is given the freedom to achieve this result in the most efficient way. In return, the customer pays a service fee for a certain quality or continuity that is guaranteed by a performance contract. the price for this service can be calculated both on a "pay-per-use" basis or a subscription basis. A good example is Philips's *"light-as-a-service"* model.

The focus of this book – and especially its normative recommendations – was on business models that do not entail a transfer of ownership (use-oriented and result-oriented PSS). Nevertheless, product-oriented PSS were also discussed to make useful comparisons.

930. Limited EU regulatory framework for service contracts and PSS – The current legal framework has only limited EU harmonisation for service contracts and PSS. Contrary to the legal framework of (consumer) sales contracts, which is based on the SGD, there is not a general set of rules for (conformity of) service contracts. However, this does not mean that there is a complete lack of regulation at the EU level. Several EU directives apply to and have an impact on PSS contracts. For example, the SD, CRD and the E-commerce Directive contain (pre-contractual) information requirements for service providers, the UCPD prohibits unfair commercial practices by the service provider, and the CRD grants a right of withdrawal to the consumer. The UCTD plays perhaps the most important role. After all, this directive makes it possible to set limits to the contractual freedom of service providers and to challenge unfair terms in service contracts. Nevertheless, the UCTD only offers a negative protection mechanism, which allows the annulment of unbalanced clauses, but does not guarantee a minimum of rights and remedies for PSS consumers. Regarding digital content and digital services added to a PSS contract, the DCD contains conformity rules that offer significant consumer protection. However, the DCD only applies to those parts of the contract that contain the digital content or the digital services. Other services remain subject to national contract law on service contracts.

931. Limited national regulatory framework for service contracts and PSS – Given the lack of an extensive legal framework at the EU level, the rules applicable to PSS contracts are mostly found at the national level and in the PSS contract itself. Indeed, the rights and obligations of the parties find their origin in general contract law, the rules of special contract law (in particular the rules for the rental contract for movables and the contract for services) and the general terms and conditions of PSS contracts. However, also at the national level, there is only limited protection for consumers engaging in (use-oriented and result-oriented) PSS contracts. Contrary to the mandatory legal regime of the consumer sales contract, the legal regimes of the rental contract for movables and the contract for services lack an extensive (mandatory) legal framework on the conformity of the product/service.

932. Obligations of the parties to the PSS contract – In this book, the EU legal framework, national general contract law (BE, NL), the national law on special contracts (BE, NL) and the content of the general terms and conditions of 20 real-life PSS contracts were all considered together to discuss the obligations of the PSS user and PSS supplier. This was done throughout 6 chapters (Chapter 2–7), each dealing with a separate aspect of PSS contracts.

933. PSS under general contract law – Chapter 2 delved into the basic principles of national general contract law and their application to PSS contracts. These rules apply to all types of PSS, regardless of their contractual qualification. It started with the formation of PSS contracts, discussing their validity requirements, the process of offer and acceptance, pre-contractual information requirements and the conclusion of the contract through representation. It then explored the frequent use of standard contracts and general terms, addressing their enforceability and (un)fairness through an analysis of the national requirements for incorporation of general terms and conditions and the unfairness test of the UCTD and its national implementation. The chapter also examined the right of withdrawal for PSS users, highlighting the differences between PSS contracts that qualify as sales contracts (product-oriented PSS) and those that qualify as service contracts within the meaning of the CRD (use-oriented and result-oriented PSS). This was followed by a discussion on the interpretation of PSS contracts, with emphasis on sustainability and circular economy goals. Further, Chapter 2 addressed liability for breach of contract, covering the qualification of obligations as obligations of means, result or guarantee, *force majeure*, and remedies for breach of contract. Finally, it reviewed the rules on the duration of PSS contracts, comparing fixed-term and open-ended PSS contracts and the possibility of early termination or contract extension/renewal.

934. Contractual qualification of the three main types of PSS – The book continued in Chapter 3 with the contractual qualification of the three main types of PSS. The results of this chapter are exclusively descriptive, and as such no normative recommendations were made. Nevertheless, these findings are very relevant for businesses as the result of this qualification exercise determines the national default rules applicable to the PSS contract (provided that the PSS contract does not deviate from them). The fact that product-oriented PSS still entail the transfer of ownership of a product generally leads to their qualification as a sales contract under Belgian and Dutch law. Use-oriented and result-oriented PSS contracts, on the other hand, no longer involve a transfer of ownership. Instead, they provide the PSS user with a right of use over a product supplemented with additional services, or a complex and integrated service. In most cases, these contracts will be qualified as a rental contract for movables and/or a contract for services. Where the PSS user receives a right of use of a product against payment of a fee – as with many use-oriented PSS – the contract will in principle be qualified as a rental contract. Additional services, such as maintenance and repair, a take-back obligation for recycling, etc., will generally be governed by the rules of the contract for services (or in the Netherlands, the contract for works). The qualification becomes more complex where the PSS contract covers both the use of a product and the provision of a service. In this case, the qualification theories for mixed contracts (absorption, cumulation, "*sui generis*") should be used to determine the applicable rules. Where the PSS user enters into an integrated service contract guaranteeing a specific functional result – as is the case for result-oriented PSS – the contract will be qualified as a contract for services because there is no longer a right of use of a specific product. Where the use-oriented or result-oriented PSS contract is supplemented by digital services (e.g. apps allowing to monitor the use of the product), these digital services will be governed by the rules of the DCD, while the other aspects of the PSS contract remain subject to the rules of the rental contract and/or the contract for services.

935. OBLIGATION OF THE PSS SUPPLIER TO ENSURE THE AVAILABILITY OF THE PRODUCT/SERVICE – The main obligation of the PSS supplier, namely the obligation to ensure the availability of the product and/or service was analysed in Chapter 4. This is the most extensive chapter of the book, and its findings also play a significant role in other chapters, most notably in Chapter 6 on additional services. The obligation to ensure the availability of the product/service breaks down into two sub aspects.

(i) First, the PSS supplier must make the product and/or the service available to the PSS user. This implies a **delivery obligation**. The concrete modalities of delivery (e.g. place and time) are generally regulated in the PSS contract. In the absence of contractual regulations, both Belgian law and Dutch law contain default rules on the modalities of the delivery.

(ii) **Second, the product/service must be in conformity with the PSS contract.** For product-oriented PSS, the rules on (non-)conformity are fully harmonised by the SGD, which makes a distinction between subjective and objective conformity requirements. Subjective conformity requirements relate to what the contracting parties have stipulated in their contract, including precontractual discussions. Objective conformity requirements, on the other hand, are indirectly part of the contract because the consumer can reasonably expect them to be. The PSS supplier is liable for any lack of conformity that exists at the time of delivery of the product during the guarantee period, with a (rebuttable) presumption period in which the anteriority of the lack of conformity is presumed. If the product shows a lack of conformity, the PSS user-buyer has access to a number of remedies, characterised by the so-called hierarchy of remedies. Repair and replacement are the primary remedies, while price reduction and termination are the secondary remedies.

In use-oriented PSS, there are no harmonised rules regarding (non-) conformity. As a result, it is a matter of national law (in particular, the rules of the rental contract) whether the delivered product "as-a-service" is in conformity with the PSS contract. Similar to the sales contract, the concept of conformity falls into two (types of) conformity requirements, namely subjective conformity (what the rental contract stipulates) and objective conformity (what the lessee may reasonably expect). At the start of the rental contract, the rented product must be in a good state of repair to be in conformity with the contract. During the rental contract, the PSS user-lessor must indemnify the PSS user-lessee for defects of the rented good. There are limits to the PSS supplier-lessor's obligation to indemnify for defects. Both under Belgian and Dutch law, the PSS supplier-lessor will not be liable for defects caused by the fault of the PSS user-lessee, as well as for minor defects. Unlike for the consumer sales rules, the concept of conformity is not mandatory law under both the Belgian and Dutch rental contract rules. This means that the PSS contract may limit or expand the scope of the concept defect, for example, by stipulating that the PSS supplier-lessor is also responsible for remedying minor defects.

Similar to product-oriented PSS, the PSS supplier will incur liability if the rented product is not in conformity with the use-oriented PSS contract. Unlike the consumer sales rules, there is no similar legal guarantee period of two years. Instead, the PSS supplier is liable for defects that exist at the start of the PSS contract and those that arise during the PSS contract. As with the consumer sales contract, the PSS user must prove the non-conformity of the rented product. However, for rental contracts, the PSS user does not benefit from a presumption period. In fact, the PSS user is even (rebuttably) presumed to be liable for any damages or losses to the product that occurred during the PSS contract. He can escape liability by proving that the damages existed before the start of the rental contract or that they are due to normal wear and tear. These rules are not mandatory law so the parties can deviate from them in the PSS contract. As to the remedies for lack of conformity, the Belgian rental contract rules do not have a separate set of remedies in case of non-conformity of the rented product. This means that if the PSS user can prove the lack of conformity of the product, he has access to the remedies of general contract law. These remedies are not mandatory law. Under Dutch law, the PSS user has access to the specific remedies of the rental contract (repair, rent reduction, compensation for damages) as well as the remedies arising from general contract law. Contrary to Belgian law, these remedies are mandatory law in contracts with consumers for defects the PSS supplier knew or should have known.

For result-oriented PSS, a harmonised legal framework on the concept of conformity and remedies for non-conformity is also lacking at the EU level. Therefore, national contract law again provides the framework to determine whether the service provided is in conformity with the PSS contract. Under both the Belgian and Dutch rules of the contract for services, the obligation to perform the service in conformity with the contract entails that (i) the PSS supplier must perform the service according to what the parties have expressly agreed in the PSS contract (subjective conformity); (ii) where applicable, the PSS supplier must follow the instructions given by the PSS user; and (iii) the service must conform with what the client may reasonably expect, the so-called, "standards of good workmanship" (objective conformity). This obligation may either be an obligation of result or an obligation of means, depending on the specific circumstances of the case. In this sense, the contractual definition of the output specifications as well as the promised continuity of the service will play an important role in determining the nature of the obligation and by extension the conformity of the performed service. Additionally, technical standards adopted by a standardisation body may also be considered when assessing the conformity of the service.

As regards the question of liability for non-conformity, Belgian law distinguishes between the period before and after the acceptance of the service. Before the acceptance of the service, the PSS supplier is liable for any late or non-conforming performance according to the general rules of contractual liability. After the acceptance, the PSS supplier is released from liability for non-conforming performance and/or (visible) defects and the PSS user will only be able to claim liability for hidden defects. Dutch law, on the other hand, does not have this strict distinction, but the PSS supplier will be liable for shortcomings in the performance of the service under the "ordinary" rules of general contract law. Both the Belgian and the Dutch rules of the contract for services do not contain specific rules on remedies available in case of non-conformity of the provided service. This means that the PSS user has access to the remedies of general contract law, which are not mandatory law, so the PSS contract can deviate from them, modulate them, or even (partially) exclude (some of) them.

If digital content or digital services are part of use-oriented or result-oriented PSS, they are subject to the DCD and its national implementation. Under these rules, the PSS supplier will be liable for any lack of conformity that exists at the time of delivery of the digital content or digital services during the guarantee period. There are three (mandatory) remedies available to the PSS user in case of a lack of conformity of any digital content or digital service that is part of the PSS contract, namely having the digital content or digital service brought in conformity (i.e. performance in kind), proportionate price reduction or the termination of the contract. There is a hierarchy between these remedies. First, an attempt should be made to bring the digital content or service into conformity; only afterwards is the consumer entitled to proportionate price reduction or termination.

936. Obligation of the PSS user to pay the price of the PSS – The main obligation of the PSS user, namely paying the price of the PSS, was discussed in Chapter 5. The obligation to pay the price can take different forms and may have different components (e.g. periodical fees, pay-per-use fees, start-up costs, mandatory insurance fees, etc.). As to the modalities of the PSS contract, the timing of the payment, as well as the payment method are generally set out in the PSS contract. Payment by electronic means has become the norm. Most PSS suppliers require the PSS user to pay via direct debit (e.g. a SEPA mandate) or a credit card. The combination of all the different pricing components (in combination with the main characteristics of the product/service) can make it difficult for an average consumer to compare the prices of different PSS offers. Transparency requirements and pre-contractual information requirements (e.g. those found in the SD, the CRD and the UCTD) may help the consumer to make informed decisions. Nevertheless, one of the biggest flaws of information requirements apply here, namely that consumers do not sufficiently read and/or understand the information made available. If the PSS user-consumer does not pay the price of the PSS (on time), the PSS supplier has access to the general contract law remedies, with the remedy of negligence interests as a specific form of compensation for damages. Moreover, this chapter dealt with the practice, validity and limits of price change clauses and other modification clauses. Thus, this section described the concept of price change clauses and modification clauses in long-term PSS contracts and has set out the limits to the freedom of the parties to include such clauses in their contract. The last section of this chapter dealt with set off clauses (i.e. clauses dealing with the mode of extinguishment where reciprocal obligations are extinguished to the extent of the smaller amount or quantity). It discussed the concept of set off and set off clauses, as well as the limits to these clauses.

937. Additional services – Chapter 6 dealt with the additional services often offered by the PSS supplier in addition to its obligation to make the product/service available. These include the PSS supplier's installation obligation, the obligation to maintain and repair or replace the product, the PSS supplier's obligation to supply updates and the PSS user's obligation to install the supplied updates. Additionally, it is also possible to include innovation obligations into the PSS contract. In some cases, national contract law sets out a default legal framework for these additional services (e.g. the rules on maintenance and repair in the rental contract). The rules on updates find their origin in the harmonised legal framework of the SGD and DCD. In other cases, however, these additional services are fully left to the contractual arrangements in the PSS contract. In any case, the concept of conformity (with both objective and subjective conformity requirements) as discussed in Chapter 4 will be relevant for many of these additional services.

938. Ownership, moral hazard and end of contract/end-of-life of the product – Chapter 7 discussed the consequences arising from the fact that consumers do no longer own the products they use within the framework of use-oriented or result-oriented PSS contracts. It started by setting out solutions for the PSS supplier to protect its right of ownership against accession, such as establishing an (accessory) building right or a pledge and/or including a retention of title clause in the PSS contract. Other risks of loss of ownership (and possible solutions to these risks) were also analysed, such as the risk of acquisitive prescription of the movable product (which can be combated by placing a non-removable name tag on the product). It continued with the risk of moral hazard and how to combat this in the PSS contract. The main solution is the PSS user's obligation to take care of the product. Additionally, contractual limits to moving the product can be included. This can either be a prohibition to move the product without express consent of the PSS supplier, or a prohibition to cross borders with the product. Finally, incentives for proper use of the product may be included in the PSS contract, such as rewards if no maintenance, repair or replacement of the product is needed within a certain period of time. Finally, it examined the legal issues related to the end of the PSS contract and end-of-life stage of the product. This includes the obligation of the PSS user to return the product and its mirror obligation, namely the PSS supplier's obligation to take back the product. Additionally, circular guarantees, i.e. clauses placing an obligation on the PSS supplier to repurpose the product in a sustainable way, were also considered.

939. Evaluation of the current legal framework – The current regulatory framework was evaluated based on four evaluative criteria, namely legal certainty, coherence and consistency, fair balance and sustainability. Instead of opting for a separate evaluative chapter, this was done in an integrated manner in the chapters discussed above. The following conclusions may be deducted from the evaluative analysis.

940. Rental contract rules already provide to a certain extent a useful legal framework for use-oriented PSS – The rules of the rental contract already provide to a certain extent a useful legal framework for use-oriented PSS. After all, the provisions of the rental contract provide default rules on the conformity of the rented product and on the basic obligations of the parties. Yet there are shortcomings to these legal rules in the context of servitisation for movables. In the first place, the rental contract rules are formulated in very general terms and are not well adapted to movable goods. Under Belgian law, the rules of the rental contract for immovables are applied by analogy, but it is not always clear how the general provisions on delivery in good state of repair and ensuring the quiet rental enjoyment (i.e. conformity) must be applied to the rental of movables. As a result, this analogical application does not foster legal certainty for the PSS user. Second, from a coherence and consistency perspective, as well as from a fair balance perspective, it is difficult to see why consumers' rights (for example on conformity) are regulated more comprehensively and more detailed if they gain access to a movable product by buying it, than if they merely wish to obtain its use and enjoyment under a product-as-a-service contract. Finally, there are also arguments based on the evaluative criterion of sustainability. The current rule that the PSS user-lessee is responsible for minor repairs is less suited for B2C rental contracts for movables, as it may lead them to opt for quick, unsustainable fixes, while discouraging PSS suppliers-lessors from offering durable products. Moreover, strengthening legal obligations for PSS suppliers-lessor to remedy defects in general could lead to better-maintained products, increased consumer confidence, and more sustainable consumption patterns. The potential additional costs associated with a stronger conformity regime for the rental contract (for movables) could in turn be justified by the added convenience and environmental benefits.

941. Rules on contract for services are incomplete and outdated for result-oriented PSS – The current Belgian rules on the contract for services serves as one of the prime examples of regulatory obsolescence. Despite its very broad scope, applying to both material and intellectual performances, and the fact that it is the most widely used special contract together with the sales contract, the old BCC devotes only 13 provisions to it, which remained unchanged since 1804. They mainly relate to the occurrence of a risk and the client's right to unilaterally terminate the contract, and do not even include a definition of the contract for services. Even more than the rental contract for movables, the rules on the contract for services in the old BCC are totally outdated, do not reflect developments in case law, and are not well adapted to new developments in practice, result-oriented PSS in particular. Dating from 1992, the Dutch rules on the contract for services are more recent and provide to a considerable extent a more complete legal framework for service contracts.

However, these rules remain rather general as well and therefore provide only little concrete guidance for product-as-a-service contracts in practice.

942. LEGAL FRAMEWORK FOR USE-ORIENTED AND RESULT-ORIENTED PSS NEEDS MODERNISATION AND IMPROVEMENT – These shortcomings make it necessary to modernise and improve the legal framework of rental contracts for movables and contracts for services. The ideal opportunity to do this now presents itself in Belgium. As part of the reform of the Belgian Civil Code, a modernisation exercise is under way that should lead to a new Book 7 on special contracts. Although servitisation was not as such taken into account as a factor in drafting the proposed rules of Book 7, my analysis has shown that the proposed rules are by and large fit for product-as-a-service contracts, with a few minor and one major correction.

943. THREE POSSIBLE NORMATIVE SOLUTIONS – This research proposes three possible solutions for the outdated and/or incomplete legal framework for use-oriented and result-oriented PSS. These solutions vary in terms of how ambitious/easily achievable they are. First, it proposes **modernised national rules** on conformity for the Belgian rental contract (for movables) and the Belgian contract for services (option 1). Regarding the latter, standardisation of services also receives attention, as this allows to consider the specific characteristics of (result-oriented) PSS, while still having general rules for all service contracts. Second, this research explores the option of an **EU directive** on the quality and conformity of (bundles of) services (option 2). This is certainly the most ambitious option, but – provided there is enough political will – could provide (use-oriented and result-oriented) PSS with a specific and detailed regulatory framework. Third, it considers the **use of balanced standard contracts and model clauses** (option 3). This solution can be considered the "low-hanging fruit" since it requires, in principle, no legislative intervention. Of course, choosing one option should not necessarily rule out the others. It is perfectly possible that a cumulative approach in the end will yield the best results.

944. LEGISLATIVE CHANGES AT THE NATIONAL LEVEL – First, building on the descriptive and evaluative conclusions following from the first three research questions, this research proposes a **new regulatory framework at the national level (Belgium) for rental contracts (for movables) and contracts for services** (option 1). This new framework was developed to balance the interests of service suppliers and consumers, while also considering (environmental) sustainability interests. The main principles of this new regulatory framework can be summarised as follows. First, it aims to minimise qualification problems as much as possible through internal homogenisation, for example by adopting a uniform notion of (non-)conformity for all (consumer) contracts, inspired by the provisions of EU sales law and the DCFR. Second, it aims to boost legal certainty

and consumer protection by proposing more appropriate and modern default rules on the main obligation of the service provider/PSS supplier (i.e. performing the service and making the product available), as well as remedies for breach of contract. Also here, inspiration is drawn from EU sales law and the DCFR. Third, the potential role of standardisation of services (both at the national level and the EU level) is highlighted as a tool to operationalise the default rules containing the abstract notions of (non-)conformity and (non-)performance. The proposed national legal framework was developed throughout the five years of the PhD research underlying this book. Upon publication of the Draft Law of 16 April 2024 inserting Book 7 "special contracts" into the Civil Code during the end-phase of this research, these proposals were further finetuned and cross-checked with the published Draft Law.

945. Legislative changes and policy recommendations at the EU level – The research also has set out **proposals for legislative changes and policy recommendations at the EU level.** First and foremost, the EU legislator was urged to consider harmonising (use-oriented and result-oriented) PSS contracts by means of an EU directive (option 2). This could either take the form of a general directive on conformity of services (i.e. broader scope – option 2a), or by adopting a specific directive for "packages" or "bundles" of services relating to the use of a product or to a specific functional result (i.e. more specific scope – option 2b). For the first solution, inspiration can be drawn from the SGD and DCD, for example by further extending the principles from the DCD to the offline environment. For the second solution, the Package Travel Directive can serve as a source of inspiration. This directive contains rules in the various stages of the package travel contract, including rules on precontractual information and requirements regarding the content of the contract; rules on changes to the contract; rules on the performance of the contract, including remedies for non-performance and assistance obligations; and rules protecting the traveller from insolvency of the organiser. Thus, a similar approach could be taken for PSS by adopting a fully-fledged system of rules for "package services" or "bundles of services". As to the question whether the directive should be minimum or maximum harmonisation, it was proposed to leave enough room for Member States to have their own national approaches and accents for rules on service contracts. This can either be done by using a minimum harmonisation technique for this directive, by setting up "regulatory sandboxes" that allow for national experiments, or by providing sufficient exceptions to the maximum harmonisation nature of the directive that allow to go further, also in terms of guaranteeing the environmental sustainability of service contracts and PSS. Additionally, this research has also proposed concrete legislative changes to address ambiguities regarding the distinction between the notions "contracts for services", "contracts in respect of goods" and "sales contracts" in the context of the consequences of exercising the right of withdrawal.

The proposed policy recommendations at the EU level include, among others, (i) adopting measures encouraging European standardisation organisations to develop service standards for PSS contracts, as well as providing incentives for PSS suppliers to adopt these service standards; (ii) setting up labelling schemes (e.g. similar to energy labelling schemes) with harmonised quality criteria (e.g. in terms of fairness, sustainability, etc.) for PSS standard contracts; (iii) taking measures to facilitate the development and adoption of standard contracts for PSS; and (iv) conduct further research on streamlining the unfair terms list of the UCTD, for example by replacing the indicative and non-exhaustive list of the Annex to the UCTD with a uniform blacklist and/or grey list at the EU level by making use of a (corrected) maximum harmonisation technique. The content of this blacklist and/or grey list can be determined by a comparative law analysis at the national level, as well as using the DCFR and/or CESL as a starting point. Additionally, some room could be left to the Member States to include additional unfair terms to the blacklist and/or grey list taking into account local legal developments and contractual practices. If adopted, the existing EU consumer acquis should be aligned with these proposed legislative changes and policy recommendations, for example by including additional unfair practices on the UCPD blacklist.

946. Model clauses for PSS contracts – Third, **model clauses for PSS contracts** were set out with the aim of promoting the adoption of (truly sustainable) PSS business models (option 3).[3481] These model clauses contribute to the adoption of PSS business models on three fronts. On the business side, businesses often face increased transaction costs if they wish to offer product-as-a-service contracts due to the need to draft more complex contracts. By using these model clauses, businesses save more time, effort and resources than when they would create customised clauses from scratch. On the consumer side, these model clauses were drafted with the aim of protecting the interests of consumers, which are usually the weaker party to these contracts. These model clauses are compliant with mandatory rules regarding business-to-consumer relationships, both under EU, Belgian and Dutch law. This does not only benefit consumers, as non-compliance with these mandatory rules can have far-reaching consequences for businesses, such as partial nullity of the unfair clause in question without the possibility to rely on national default rules. As regards sustainability, these model clauses also take into account the sustainability and circularity challenges and opportunities for PSS, for example by including clauses that combat the risk of moral hazard, clauses and recitals dealing with contractual interpretation

[3481] See also the research report for the *Steunpunt Circulaire Economie* which translates the findings of this book and associated doctoral research into model clauses that can be freely used by businesses: C. Borucki, H. Slachmuylders, B. Keirsbilck, D. Gruyaert and E. Terryn, *Model clauses for Product-as-a-Service (PaaS) contracts*, CE Center. Circular Economy Policy Research Center, 2022–23, 95 p.

and environmental sustainability, and clauses containing explicit circular guarantees. These model clauses can act as the low-hanging fruit to create an adequate legal regime for PSS contracts. A potential next step for the (EU or national) legislator could be to endorse similar model clauses or standard contracts in order to create a "presumption of fairness" if PSS suppliers use these terms and conditions for their PSS contracts.

947. Preferred solution(s) identified by this research – In this book, the modernisation of national contract law (option 1) (alongside with option 3, the use of standard contracts and model clauses) was put forward as the preferred solution. The focus on a national contract law reform, however, does not mean that the question of EU harmonisation (option 2) should be completely neglected. Indeed, an EU directive on the quality and conformity of (bundles of) services and/or PSS contracts could lead to a broader harmonisation of private law, and consequently facilitate the use of PSS throughout the EU, both on the supply and the demand side. So far, however, this does not seem to be on the agenda of the European Commission, the European Parliament or EU Member States.

948. Final thoughts: desirability of (promoting) PSS contracts? – On a more fundamental level, one could ask the question whether it is truly desirable to promote PSS business models. While the idea of PSS business models (service providers retaining the ownership of the product and thus having an incentive to make it last as long as possible) certainly is promising, there are three main problems that arise. First, not all PSS are truly sustainable, with some even having a negative impact on (environmental) sustainability. Second, consumers are *de lege lata* less adequately protected under the rules of the rental contract for movables or the rules of the contract for services than under a (consumer) sales contract. Finally, engaging in PSS business models is still often more expensive for consumers than if they were to buy the same product.

This research aimed to (at least partly) solve the first two problems, namely by proposing legal solutions to ensure consumer protection in circular PSS business models, while also taking into account and promoting (environmental) sustainability interests. The last issue seems harder to address. PSS suppliers often justify the higher price of PSS by stating that the additional services and their associated "peace of mind" for the consumer (i.e. because they will not be confronted with unexpected costs) also come at a cost. This argument certainly has some merit. Nevertheless, it seems to me that, for the time being, PSS business models – at least in B2C markets – are more likely to represent a niche in the market (think students, expats or young professionals who prefer flexibility and a "hassle-free" lifestyle) than a mainstream solution for all consumer products. Perhaps this will change as the (B2C) market for PSS business models develops further, with increased competition among PSS suppliers and PSS business models leading to lower prices for consumers. In that sense, the question also arises whether, in the era of the throwaway society where low-quality consumer products are dumped on the EU market, economic incentives (e.g. making less sustainable products more expensive, or subsidising sustainable business models or products) might be needed to encourage consumers to adopt sustainable consumption patterns (including circular business models such as PSS). Of course, this will require a thorough evaluation of our society and economic model, in which the (economic, social and philosophical) role of ownership and property will have to be critically examined.

In any case, the trend of servitisation and offering business models such as product-as-a-service contracts and (circular) PSS is here to stay. It will therefore come down to adequately protecting consumers and ensuring the sustainability of these business models as much as possible, in every stage of the product/service lifecycle. With this book, I hope to have contributed (at least in part) to realising these goals in order to move ever closer to a more circular economy.

ANNEX A
ANALYSED TERMS AND CONDITIONS

1. Blue Movement (2 January 2023)

T&Cs Blue Movement

2. Bundles (1 December 2016)

T&Cs Bundles

3. Papillon (2018)

T&Cs Papillon

Papillon infosheet

4. Fairphone Easy

T&Cs Fairphone Easy

5. Swapphone (September 2020)

T&Cs Swapphone

6. Grover (1 April 2022)

T&Cs Grover

7. Gerrard Street/Repeat (1 March 2019)

T&Cs Gerrard Street

8. Mudjeans

T&Cs Mudjeans

9. Dressr (15 July 2021)

T&Cs Dressr

10. Lena fashion library

T&Cs Lena

11. Live Light (2020)

T&Cs live light

12. Saman heat pumps (May 2022)

T&Cs Saman heat pump

13. HP Instant Ink (December 2020)

T&Cs HP Instant Ink

14. Swapfiets (Version 3.1 July 2020)

T&Cs Swapfiets

15. Villo (2021)

T&Cs Villo

16. Cambio (1 October 2022)

T&Cs Cambio

17. Lime (January 2023)

T&Cs Lime

18. Dott (19 April 2022)

T&Cs Dott

19. Agoria "efficiency-as-a-Service" template agreement

Agoria EaaS Template

Agoria optional T&Cs

20. Circular Economy Circular service contract template

Fairphone template

ANNEX B
LIST OF STAKEHOLDERS C2 PROJECT

1. European Commission
2. OVAM (Flemish environmental authority)
3. KBC Group (banking)
4. BSH (Businesses offering home appliances "as-a-service")
5. Agoria (Business organisation of technology-driven companies)
6. IBJ (Professional organisation of in-house legal counsel)
7. UNIZO (Trade organisation)
8. COMEOS (Trade organisation)
9. BEUC (European consumer organisation)
10. Test-Aankoop (Belgian consumer organisation)
11. Peerby (Sharing and renting platform)
12. Aliloca (Business helping rental services grow)
13. Vlaanderen Circulair (Flemish policy maker circular economy)
14. Möbius (Consultancy company involved in circular economy projects)
15. Op wielekes (Business model for renting children's bicycles)
16. Decathlon (Project We Play Circular: sport as a service)
17. Renson (Business active in the HVAC sector)
18. European Patent Office
19. ETAP (Business offering "light-as-a-service")
20. Daikin (Business active in the HVAC sector)
21. P2S (Consultancy company involved in servitisation projects)
22. VOKA (Employers' organisation)
23. POM West Flanders (Policy maker)
24. Tillup (Business active in the logistics sector)
25. Mediamarkt Saturn retail group (Business active in the retail sector (consumer electronics))
26. Pollet Water Group (Business active in the water sector)
27. Ariadne Innovation (Digital platform for a more sustainable textiles & fashion industry)

CONSUMER COMPETITION MARKET SERIES

The books in the CONSUMER COMPETITION MARKET SERIES bundle the results of research activities of the CONSUMER COMPETITION MARKET (CCM) institute of the KU Leuven, co-directed by Wouter Devroe, Bert Keirsbilck and Evelyne Terryn.

The series focuses on the legal infrastructure of the internal market of the European Union in the broadest sense. Like CCM itself, the series deals in an integrated way with consumer law, B2B and B2C commercial practices law, sectoral market regulation, the four freedoms (free movement of persons, goods, services and capital) and competition (including EU and national antitrust law, EU merger control and EU state aid law).

Published titles within the Series:

1. Bert Keirsbilck and Evelyne Terryn, *Consumer Protection in a Circular Economy*
   ISBN 978-1-78068-657-8

2. Wouter Devroe, Bert Keirsbilck and Evelyne Terryn, *Nieuw economisch recht in b2b-relaties. Mededinging, misbruik van economische afhankelijkheid, onrechtmatige bedingen en oneerlijke handelspraktijken*
   ISBN 978-9-40001-104-5

3. Bert Keirsbilck and Evelyne Terryn, *Unfair Trading Practices In The Food Supply Chain. Implications of directive (EU) 2019/633*
   ISBN 978-1-78068-980-7

4. Bert Keirsbilck, Evelyne Terryn, Johan Eyckmans, Sandra Rousseau and Denis Voinot, *Servitization and circular economy: economic and legal challenges*
   ISBN 978-1-83970-263-1

5. Elisa Paredis, Bert Keirsbilck, Evelyne Terryn en Tom Verdonk, *Unfair Trading Practices in the Agricultural and Food Supply Chain. Implementation of Directive (EU) 2019/663 in the EU-2*
   ISBN 978-9-400-01803-7

www.ingramcontent.com/pod-product-compliance
Ingram Content Group UK Ltd.
Pitfield, Milton Keynes, MK11 3LW, UK
UKHW052044051026
8980IPUK00043BA/917

9 781839 704918